37 YEARS NEET

Physics

Chapterwise-Topicwise
Solutions (2024-1988)

Sunny Kumar
Dr. Preeti Kumari

arihant
SUCCESS AND NOTHING LESS

arihant
SUCCESS AND NOTHING LESS

ARIHANT PRAKASHAN (Series), MEERUT

Administrative & Production Offices

Regd. Office

'Ramchhaya' 4577/15, Agarwal Road, Darya Ganj, New Delhi -110002
Tele: 011- 47630600, 43518550

Head Office

Kalindi, TP Nagar, Meerut (UP) - 250002
Tel: 0121-7156203, 7156204

Sales & Support Offices

Agra, Ahmedabad, Bengaluru, Bareilly, Chennai, Delhi, Guwahati, Hyderabad, Jaipur, Jhansi, Kolkata, Lucknow, Nagpur & Pune.

PRICE ₹365.00

PO No : TXT-XX-XXXXXXX-X-XX

Published by Arihant Publications (India) Ltd.

For further information about the books published by Arihant, log on to www.arihantbooks.com or e-mail at info@arihantbooks.com

Follow us on

Preface

Whenever a student decides to prepare for any examination his/her first and foremost curiosity is to know about the type of questions that are expected in the exam. This becomes more important in the context of competitive entrance examinations where there is neck-to-neck competition.

We feel great pleasure in presenting before you this book containing Error Free Chapterwise Topicwise Solutions of CBSE AIPMT/NEET Physics Questions from the years 1988 to 2024.

Special features of this edition are:

- Questions are tagged with NCERT references which will help in differentiating important concepts of NCERT from the rest.
- Key ideas, Concept Enhancer and Alternate solutions are added to detailed explanations to boost learning.

We hope this chapterwise solved papers would be highly beneficial to the students. After going through this book, the students would be able to have the complete idea of the questions being asked in NEET.

It has been our efforts to provide correct solutions to the best of our knowledge and opinion. We would be grateful if any discrepancies or mistakes in the questions or answers are brought to our notice so that these could be rectified in subsequent editions.

Publisher

Contents

Class 11

Class 12

Syllabus

UNIT 1 Physics & Measurement

Units of measurements, System of Units, SI Units, fundamental and derived units, **least count**, significant figures, Errors in measurements, Dimensions of Physics quantities, dimensional analysis and its applications.

UNIT 2 Kinematics

The frame of reference, motion in a straight line, Position- time graph, speed and velocity; Uniform and non-uniform motion, average speed and instantaneous velocity. **Uniformly** accelerated motion, velocity-time, position-time graph, relations for uniformly accelerated motion, Scalars and Vectors. Vector addition and subtraction, scalar and vector products. Unit Vector, Resolution of a Vector, Relative Velocity. Motion in a plane, Projectile Motion. Uniform Circular Motion.

UNIT 3 Laws of Motion

Force and inertia, Newton's First law of motion: Momentum, Newton's Second law of motion, Impulses: Newton's third law of motion. Law of conservation of linear momentum and its applications. Equilibrium of concurrent forces. Static and Kinetic friction, laws of friction, rolling friction. Dynamics of uniform circular motion: centripetal force and its applications: vehicle on a level circular road. vehicle on a banked road.

UNIT 4 Work, Energy and Power

Work done by a constant force and a variable force; kinetic and potential energies. work-energy theorem, power.

The potential energy of spring conservation of mechanical energy. conservative and non-conservative forces; motion in a vertical circle: Elastic and inelastic collisions in one and two dimensions.

UNIT 5 Rotational Motion

Centre of the mass of a two-particles system, Centre of the mass of a rigid body: Basic concepts of rotational motion; moment of a force; torque, angular momentum, conservation of angular momentum and its applications;

The moment of inertia, the radius of gyration, values of moments of inertia for simple geometrical objects, parallel and perpendicular axes theorems. and their applications. Equilibrium of rigid bodies. rigid body rotation and equations of rotational motion, comparison of linear and rotational motions.

UNIT 6 Gravitation

The universal law of gravitation. Acceleration due to gravity and its variation with altitude and depth. Kepler's law of planetary motion. Gravitational potential energy; gravitational potential.

Escape velocity, Motion of a satellite, orbital velocity, Time period and energy of satellite.

UNIT 7 Properties of Solids and Liquids

Elastic behaviour, Stress-strain relationship, Hooke's law, Young's modulus, bulk modulus, modulus of rigidity. Pressure due to a fluid column; Pascal's law and its applications. Effect of gravity on fluid pressure. 'Viscosity, Stokes' law, terminal velocity, streamline, and turbulent flow.critical velocity, Bemoulli's principle and its applications. Surface energy and surface tension, angle of contact, excess of pressure across a curved surface, application of surface tension - drops, bubbles, and capillary rise. Heat, temperature, thermal expansion; specific heat capacity, calorimetry; change of state, latent heat. Heat transfer-conduction, convection and radiation.

UNIT 8 Thermodynamics

Thermal equilibrium, zeroth law of thermodynamics, the concept of temperature. Heat, work, and internal energy. The first law of thermodynamics, isothermal and adiabatic processes.

The second law of thermodynamics: reversible and irreversible processes.

UNIT 9 Kinetic Theory of Gases

Equation of state of a perfect gas, work done on compressing a gas, Kinetic theory of gases - assumptions, the concept of pressure. Kinetic interpretation of temperature: **RMS speed of gas molecules:** Degrees of freedom. Law of equipartition of energy and applications to specific heat capacities of gases; Mean free path. **Avogadro's number.**

UNIT 10 Oscillations and Waves

Oscillations and periodic motion - time period, frequency, displacement as a function of time.

Periodic functions, Simple Harmonic Motion (SHM) and its equation; phase: oscillations of a spring -restoring force and force constant: energy in SHM - Kinetic and potential energies; Simple pendulum - derivation of expression for its time period:

Wave motion, Longitudinal and transverse waves, speed of travelling wave. Displacement relation for a progressive wave. Principle of superposition of waves, reflection of waves. Standing waves in strings and organ pipes, fundamental mode and harmonics. Beats.

UNIT 11 Electrostatics

Conservation of charge. Coulomb's law forces between two point charges, forces between multiple charges: superposition principle and continuous charge distribution. Electric field: Electric field due to a point charge, Electric field lines. Electric dipole, Electric field due to a dipole. Torque on a dipole in a uniform electric field.

Electric flux, Gauss's law and its applications to find field due to infinitely long uniformly charged straight wire, uniformly charged infinite plane sheet and uniformly charged thin spherical shell. Electric potential and its calculation for a point charge, electric dipole and system of charges; potential difference, Equipotential surfaces, Electrical potential energy of a system of two point charges and of electric dipole in an electrostatic field.

Conductors and insulators, Dielectrics and electric polarization, capacitors and capacitances, the combination of capacitors in series and parallel, capacitance of a parallel plate capacitor with and without dielectric medium between the plates. Energy stored in a capacitor.

UNIT 12 Current Electricity

Electric current, Drift velocity, mobility and their relation with electric current. Ohm,s law, Electrical resistance, V-I characteristics of Ohmic and non-ohmic conductors. Electrical energy and power, Electrical resistivity and conductivity. Series and parallel combinations of resistors; Temperature dependence of resistance.

Internal resistance, potential difference and emf of a cell, a combination of cells in series and parallel. Kirchhoff's laws and their applications. Wheatstone bridge, Metre Bridge.

UNIT 13 Magnetic Effects of Current and Magnetism

Biot - Savart law and its application to current carrying circular loop. Ampere's law and its applications to infinitely long current carrying straight wire and solenoid. Force on a moving charge in uniform magnetic and electric fields.

Force on a current-carrying conductor in a uniform magnetic field. The force between two parallel currents carrying conductors-definition of ampere. Torque experienced by a current loop in a uniform magnetic field: Moving coil galvanometer, its sensitivity and conversion to ammeter and voltmeter.

Current loop as a magnetic dipole and its magnetic dipole moment. Bar magnet as an equivalent solenoid. magnetic field lines; Magnetic field due to a magnetic dipole (bar magnet) along its axis and perpendicular to its axis. Torque on a magnetic dipole in a uniform magnetic field. Para, dia and ferromagnetic substances with examples, Effect of temperature on magnetic properties.

UNIT 14 Electromagnetic Induction and Alternating Currents

Electromagnetic induction: Faraday's law, Induced emf and current: Lenz's law, Eddy currents, Self and mutual inductance. Alternating currents, peak and RMS value of alternating current/voltage : reactance and impedance: LCR series circuit, resonance : power in AC circuits, wattless current, AC generator and transformer.

UNIT 15 Electromagnetic Waves

Displacement current, Electromagnetic waves and their characteristics, Transverse nature of electromagnetic waves, Electromagnetic spectrum (radio waves, microwaves, infrared, visible, ultraviolet. X-rays. Gamma rays), Applications of e.m. waves.

UNIT 16 Optics

Reflection of light, spherical mirrors, mirror formula. Refraction of light at plane and spherical surfaces, thin lens formula and lens maker formula. Total internal reflection and its applications.

Magnification, power of a lens, Combination of thin lenses in contact, Refraction of light through a prism. Microscope and astronomical telescope (reflecting and refracting) and their magnifying powers.

Wave optics: wavefront and Huygens' principle, Laws of reflection and refraction using Huygens principle, Interference, Young's double-slit experiment and expression for fringe width, coherent sources, and sustained interference of light. Diffraction due to a single slit, width of central maximum.. Polarization, plane-polarized light: Brewster's law, uses of plane-polarized light and Polaroid.

UNIT 17 Dual Nature of Matter and Radiation

Dual nature of radiation. Photoelectric effect. Hertz and Lenard's observations; Einstein's photoelectric equation: particle nature of light. Matter waves-wave nature of particle, de-Broglie relation.

UNIT 18 Atoms and Nuclei

Alpha-particle scattering experiment; Rutherford's model of atom; Bohr model, energy levels, hydrogen spectrum. Composition and size of nucleus, atomic masses, mass-energy relation, mass defect; binding energy per nucleon and its variation with mass number, nuclear fission, and fusion.

UNIT 19 Electronic Devices

Semiconductors; semiconductor diode: I-V characteristics in forward and reverse bias; diode as a rectifier; I-V characteristics of LED. the photodiode, solar cell, and Zener diode; Zener diode as a voltage regulator. Logic gates (OR, AND, NOT, NAND and NOR).

UNIT 20 Experimental Skills

Familiarity with the basic approach and observations of the experiments and activities:

1. Varnier calipers-its use to measure the internal and external diameter and depth of a vessel.
2. Screw gauge-its use to determine thickness/diameter of thin sheet/wire.
3. Simple pendulum-dissipation of energy by plotting a graph between the square of amplitude and time.
4. Metre Scale - the mass of a given object by the principle of moments.
5. Young's modulus of elasticity of the material of a metallic wire.
6. Surface tension of water by capillary rise and effect of detergents,
7. Co-efficient of viscosity of a given viscous liquid by measuring terminal velocity of a given spherical body.
8. Speed of sound in air at room temperature using a resonance tube.
9. Specific heat capacity of a given (i) solid and (ii) liquid by method of mixtures.
10. The resistivity of the material of a given wire using a metre bridge.
11. The resistance of a given wire using Ohm's law.
12. Resistance and figure of merit of a galvanometer by half deflection method.
13. The focal length of;
    (i) Convex mirror
    (ii) Concave mirror and
    (iii) Convex lens, using the parallax method.
14. The plot of the angle of deviation vs angle of incidence for a triangular prism.
15. Refractive index of a glass slab using a travelling microscope.
16. Characteristic curves of a p-n junction diode in forward and reverse bias.
17. Characteristic curves of a Zener diode and finding reverse break down voltage.
18. Identification of Diode, LED,. Resistor. A capacitor from a mixed collection of such items.

C-01

NEET Chapterwise
Topicwise Physics

In NEET 2024, 2 questions were visible from this chapter. In past 5 years, 3 questions from topic-1, 6 questions from topic-2 and 5 questions from topic-3 were asked.

For detailed analysis scan QR code

UNITS AND MEASUREMENTS

Topic 1 Physical Quantities and Their Units

01 The quantities which have the same dimensions as those of solid angle are ***[NCERT (New) Pg. 2, NEET 2024]***

(a) strain and angle (b) stress and angle
(c) strain and arc (d) angular speed and stress

02 Plane angle and solid angle have ***[NCERT (New) Pg. 2, NEET 2022]***

(a) dimensions but no units
(b) no units and no dimensions
(c) Both units and dimensions
(d) units but no dimensions

03 The angle of 1 (minute of arc) in radian is nearly equal to ***[NCERT (New) Pg. 2, NEET (Oct.) 2020]***

(a) 2.91×10^{-4} rad (b) 4.85×10^{-4} rad
(c) 4.80×10^{-6} rad (d) 1.75×10^{-2} rad

04 The unit of thermal conductivity is ***[NCERT (New) Pg. 7, NEET (National) 2019]***

(a) $\text{J m}^{-1}\ \text{K}^{-1}$ (b) W m K^{-1}
(c) $\text{W m}^{-1}\ \text{K}^{-1}$ (d) J m K^{-1}

05 The damping force on an oscillator is directly proportional to the velocity. The units of the constant of proportionality are ***[NCERT (New) Pg. 7, AIPMT 2012]***

(a) kg m s^{-1} (b) kg m s^{-2}
(c) kg s^{-1} (d) kg s

06 The density of a material in CGS system of units is $4\ \text{g cm}^{-3}$. In a system of units in which unit of length is 10 cm and unit of mass is 100 g, the value of density of material will be ***[AIPMT 2011]***

(a) 0.04 (b) 0.4
(c) 40 (d) 400

07 The unit of permittivity of free space, ε_0 is ***[NCERT (New) Pg. 3, AIPMT 2004]***

(a) Coulomb/Newton-Metre
(b) Newton - Metre^2 / Coulomb^2
(c) Coulomb^2 / Newton -Metre^2
(d) Coulomb^2 / (Newton - Metre)^2

08 The value of Planck's constant in SI unit is ***[NCERT (New) Pg. 3, AIPMT 2002]***

(a) 6.63×10^{-31} J-s (b) 6.63×10^{-30} kg - m / s
(c) 6.63×10^{-32} kg - m^2 (d) 6.63×10^{-34} J - s

09 The unit of Stefan-Boltzmann's constant is ***[NCERT (New) Pg. 3, AIPMT 2002]***

(a) $\text{W/m}^2\text{K}^4$ (b) W/m^2 (c) W/m^2 K (d) $\text{W/m}^2\ \text{K}^2$

10 In a particular system, the unit of length, mass and time are chosen to be 10 cm, 10 g and 0.1 s respectively. The unit of force in this system will be equivalent to ***[AIPMT 1994]***

(a) 0.1 N (b) 1 N (c) 10 N (d) 100 N

11 If $x = at + bt^2$, where x is the distance travelled by the body in kilometre while t is the time in second, then the unit of b is ***[AIPMT 1989]***

(a) km/s (b) km - s (c) km / s^2 (d) km - s^2

Topic 2 Dimensional Analysis and its Applications

01 A force defined by $F = \alpha t^2 + \beta t$ acts on a particle at a given time t. The factor which is dimensionless, if α and β are constants, is ***[NCERT (New) Pg. 7, NEET 2024]***

(a) $\frac{\beta t}{\alpha}$ (b) $\frac{\alpha t}{\beta}$ (c) $\alpha\beta t$ (d) $\frac{\alpha\beta}{t}$

02 The dimensions $[\text{MLT}^{-2}\text{A}^{-2}]$ belong to the ***[NCERT (New) Pg. 7, NEET 2022]***

(a) magnetic flux (b) self inductance
(c) magnetic permeability (d) electric permittivity

03 Match List I with List II. ***[NCERT (New) Pg. 7, NEET 2022]***

List I	List II
(A) Gravitational constant (G)	(i) $[\text{L}^2\text{T}^{-2}]$
(B) Gravitational potential energy	(ii) $[\text{M}^{-1}\text{L}^3\text{T}^{-2}]$
(C) Gravitational potential	(iii) $[\text{LT}^{-2}]$
(D) Gravitational intensity	(iv) $[\text{ML}^2\text{T}^{-2}]$

Choose the correct answer from the options given below
(a) A-(ii) B-(iv), C-(i) D-(iii)
(b) A-(ii), B-(iv), C-(iii) D-(i)
(c) A-(iv), B-(ii) C-(i), D-(iii)
(d) A-(ii), B-(i), C-(iv), D-(iii)

04 If force F, acceleration a and time t are chosen as the fundamental physical quantities. Find the dimensions of energy. *[NCERT (New) Pg. 7, NEET 2021]*
(a) [Fat] (b) [Fat^2]
(c) [Fat^{-1}] (d) [$Fa^{-1}t$]

05 If E and G respectively denote energy and gravitational constant then E/G has the dimensions of *[NCERT (New) Pg. 7, NEET 2021]*
(a) [$M^2L^{-1}T^0$] (b) [$ML^{-1}T^{-1}$]
(c) [ML^0T^0] (d) [$M^2L^{-2}T^{-1}$]

06 Dimensions of stress are *[NCERT (New) Pg. 7, NEET (Sep.) 2020]*
(a) [ML^2T^{-2}] (b) [ML^0T^{-2}]
(c) [$ML^{-1}T^{-2}$] (d) [MLT^{-2}]

07 A physical quantity of the dimensions of length that can be formed out of c, G and $\frac{e^2}{4\pi\varepsilon_0}$ is [c is velocity of light, G is universal constant of gravitation and e is charge] *[NCERT (New) Pg. 9, NEET 2017]*
(a) $\frac{1}{c^2}\left[G\frac{e^2}{4\pi\varepsilon_0}\right]^{1/2}$ (b) $c^2\left[G\frac{e^2}{4\pi\varepsilon_0}\right]^{1/2}$
(c) $\frac{1}{c^2}\left[\frac{e^2}{G\,4\pi\varepsilon_0}\right]^{1/2}$ (d) $\frac{1}{c}G\frac{e^2}{4\pi\varepsilon_0}$

08 Planck's constant h, speed of light in vacuum c and Newton's gravitational constant G are three fundamental constant. Which of the following combinations of these has the dimension of length? *[NCERT (New) Pg. 9, NEET-II 2016]*
(a) $\frac{\sqrt{hG}}{c^{3/2}}$ (b) $\frac{\sqrt{hG}}{c^{5/2}}$ (c) $\sqrt{\frac{hc}{G}}$ (d) $\sqrt{\frac{Gc}{h^{3/2}}}$

09 If energy E, velocity v and time t are chosen as the fundamental quantities, the dimensional formula of surface tension will be *[AIPMT 2015]*
(a) [$Ev^{-2}t^{-1}$] (b) [$Ev^{-1}t^{-2}$]
(c) [$Ev^{-2}t^{-2}$] (d) [$E^{-2}v^{-1}t^{-3}$]

10 If dimensions of critical velocity v_c of a liquid flowing through a tube are expressed as [$\eta^x\rho^y r^z$], where η, ρ and r are the coefficient of viscosity of liquid, density of liquid and radius of the tube respectively, then the values of x, y and z are given by *[NCERT (New) Pg. 9, AIPMT 2015]*
(a) 1, −1, −1 (b) −1, −1, 1
(c) −1, −1, −1 (d) 1, 1, 1

11 If force F, velocity v and time T are taken as fundamental units, then the dimensions of mass are *[NCERT (New) Pg. 9, AIPMT 2014]*
(a) [FvT^{-1}] (b) [FvT^{-2}]
(c) [$Fv^{-1}T^{-1}$] (d) [$Fv^{-1}T$]

12 The pair of quantities having same dimensions is *[NCERT (New) Pg. 7, NEET 2013]*
(a) impulse and surface tension
(b) angular momentum and work
(c) work and torque
(d) Young's modulus and energy

13 The dimensions of $(\mu_0\varepsilon_0)^{-1/2}$ are *[NCERT (New) Pg. 7, AIPMT 2012]*
(a) [$L^{1/2}T^{-1/2}$] (b) [$L^{-1}T$]
(c) [LT^{-1}] (d) [$L^{1/2}T^{1/2}$]

14 The dimensions of $\frac{1}{2}\varepsilon_0E^2$, where ε_0 is permittivity of free space and E is electric field, are *[AIPMT 2010]*
(a) [ML^2T^{-2}] (b) [$ML^{-1}T^{-2}$]
(c) [ML^2T^{-1}] (d) [MLT^{-1}]

15 If the dimensions of a physical quantity are given by [$M^aL^bT^c$], then the physical quantity will be *[NCERT (New) Pg. 9, AIPMT 2009]*
(a) pressure if $a = 1, b = -1, c = -2$
(b) velocity if $a = 1, b = 0, c = -1$
(c) acceleration if $a = 1, b = 1, c = -2$
(d) force if $a = 0, b = -1, c = -2$

16 Which two of the following five physical parameters have the same dimensions? *[NCERT (New) Pg. 7-8, AIPMT 2008]*
(i) Energy density (ii) Refractive index
(iii) Dielectric constant (iv) Young's modulus
(v) Magnetic field
(a) (ii) and (iv) (b) (iii) and (v)
(c) (i) and (iv) (d) (i) and (v)

17 Dimensions of resistance in an electrical circuit, in terms of dimension of mass M, length L, time T and current I, would be *[AIPMT 2007]*
(a) [$ML^2T^{-3}I^{-1}$] (b) [ML^2T^{-2}]
(c) [$ML^2T^{-1}I^{-1}$] (d) [$ML^2T^{-3}I^{-2}$]

18 The velocity v of a particle at time t is given by $v = at + \frac{b}{t+c}$, where a, b and c are constants. The dimensions of a, b and c are respectively *[NCERT (New) Pg. 8, AIPMT 2006]*
(a) [LT^{-2}], [L] and [T] (b) [L^2], [T] and [LT^2]
(c) [LT^2], [LT] and [L] (d) [L], [LT] and [T^2]

19 The ratio of the dimensions of Planck's constant and that of the moment of inertia is the dimension of *[AIPMT 2005]*
(a) frequency (b) velocity
(c) angular momentum (d) time

20 The dimensions of universal gravitational constant are *[AIPMT 2004, 1992]*
(a) $[M^{-1}L^3T^{-2}]$ (b) $[ML^2T^{-1}]$
(c) $[M^{-2}L^3T^{-2}]$ (d) $[M^{-2}L^2T^{-1}]$

21 Planck's constant has the dimensions of *[NCERT (New) Pg. 7, AIPMT 2001]*
(a) linear momentum (b) angular momentum
(c) energy (d) power

22 A pair of physical quantities having same dimensional formula is *[AIPMT 2000]*
(a) force and torque
(b) work and energy
(c) force and impulse
(d) linear momentum and angular momentum

23 The dimensional formula for magnetic flux is *[NCERT (New) Pg. 7, AIPMT 1999]*
(a) $[ML^2T^{-2}A^{-1}]$ (b) $[ML^3T^{-2}A^{-2}]$
(c) $[M^0L^{-2}T^2A^{-2}]$ (d) $[ML^2T^{-1}A^2]$

24 The force F on a sphere of radius r moving in a medium with velocity v is given by $F = 6\pi\eta rv$. The dimensions of η are *[NCERT (New) Pg. 8, AIPMT 1997]*
(a) $[ML^{-3}]$ (b) $[MLT^{-2}]$
(c) $[MT^{-1}]$ (d) $[ML^{-1}T^{-1}]$

25 Which of the following will have the dimensions of time ? *[AIPMT 1996]*
(a) LC (b) R/L
(c) L/R (d) C/L

26 An equation is given as $\left(p+\frac{a}{V^2}\right)=b\frac{\theta}{V}$, where p = pressure, V = volume and θ = absolute temperature. If a and b are constants, then dimensions of a will be *[AIPMT 1996]*
(a) $[ML^5T^{-2}]$ (b) $[M^{-1}L^5T^2]$
(c) $[ML^{-5}T^{-1}]$ (d) $[ML^5T]$

27 Which of the following is a dimensional constant ? *[NCERT (New) Pg. 7, AIPMT 1995]*
(a) Refractive index (b) Poisson's ratio
(c) Relative density (d) Gravitational constant

28 Turpentine oil is flowing through a tube of length l and radius r. The pressure difference between the two ends of the tube is p. The viscosity of oil is given by

$$\eta=\frac{p(r^2-x^2)}{4vl}$$

where, v is the velocity of oil at distance x from the axis of the tube. The dimensions of η are *[AIPMT 1993]*
(a) $[M^0L^0T^0]$ (b) $[MLT^{-1}]$
(c) $[ML^2T^{-2}]$ (d) $[ML^{-1}T^{-1}]$

29 The time dependence of physical quantity p is given by $p = p_0 \exp(-\alpha t^2)$, where α is a constant and t is the time. The constant α *[NCERT (New) Pg. 8, AIPMT 1992]*
(a) is dimensionless (b) has dimensions $[T^{-2}]$
(c) has dimensions $[T^2]$ (d) has dimensions of p

30 If p represents radiation pressure, c represents speed of light and S represents radiation energy striking unit area per sec. The non-zero integers x, y, z such that $p^xS^yc^z$ is dimensionless are *[NCERT (New) Pg. 9, AIPMT 1992]*
(a) $x=1, y=1, z=1$ (b) $x=-1, y=1, z=1$
(c) $x=1, y=-1, z=1$ (d) $x=1, y=1, z=-1$

31 The dimensional formula for permeability of free space, μ_0 is *[AIPMT 1991]*
(a) $[MLT^{-2}A^{-2}]$ (b) $[ML^{-1}T^2A^{-2}]$
(c) $[ML^{-1}T^{-2}A^2]$ (d) $[MLT^{-2}A^{-1}]$

32 The frequency of vibration f of a mass m suspended from a spring of spring constant k is given by a relation of the type $f = Cm^xk^y$, where C is a dimensionless constant. The values of x and y are *[NCERT (New) Pg. 9, AIPMT 1990]*
(a) $x=\frac{1}{2}, y=\frac{1}{2}$ (b) $x=-\frac{1}{2}, y=-\frac{1}{2}$
(c) $x=\frac{1}{2}, y=-\frac{1}{2}$ (d) $x=-\frac{1}{2}, y=\frac{1}{2}$

33 According to Newton, the viscous force acting between liquid layers of area A and velocity gradient $\frac{\Delta v}{\Delta z}$ is given by $F=-\eta A\frac{dv}{dz}$, where η is constant called coefficient of viscosity. The dimensional formula of η is *[AIPMT 1990]*
(a) $[ML^{-2}T^{-2}]$ (b) $[M^0L^0T^0]$
(c) $[ML^2T^{-2}]$ (d) $[ML^{-1}T^{-1}]$

34 The dimensional formula of pressure is *[NCERT (New) Pg. 7, AIPMT 1990]*
(a) $[MLT^{-2}]$ (b) $[ML^{-1}T^2]$
(c) $[ML^{-1}T^{-2}]$ (d) $[MLT^{-2}]$

35 The dimensional formula of torque is *[NCERT (New) Pg. 7, AIPMT 1989]*
(a) $[ML^2T^{-2}]$ (b) $[MLT^{-2}]$
(c) $[ML^{-1}T^{-2}]$ (d) $[ML^{-2}T^{-2}]$

36 Dimensional formula of self-inductance is *[AIPMT 1989]*
(a) $[MLT^{-2}A^{-2}]$ (b) $[ML^2T^{-1}A^{-2}]$
(c) $[ML^2T^{-2}A^{-2}]$ (d) $[ML^2T^{-2}A^{-1}]$

37 From the following quantities, which one has dimensions different from the remaining three ? *[NCERT (New) Pg. 7, AIPMT 1989]*
(a) Energy per unit volume
(b) Force per unit area
(c) Product of voltage and charge per unit volume
(d) Angular momentum

38 The dimensional formula for angular momentum is *[AIPMT 1988]*

(a) $[M^0L^2T^{-2}]$ (b) $[ML^2T^{-1}]$
(c) $[MLT^{-1}]$ (d) $[ML^2T^{-2}]$

39 If C and R denote capacitance and resistance, respectively, then the dimensional formula of CR is *[NCERT (New) Pg. 7, AIPMT 1988]*

(a) $[M^0L^0T]$
(b) $[M^0L^0T^0]$
(c) $[M^0L^0T^{-1}]$
(d) Not expressible in terms of [MLT]

Topic 3 Accuracy, Precision of Measuring Instruments Significant Figures and Error in Measurements

01 The errors in the measurement which arise due to unpredictable fluctuations in temperature and voltage supply are *[NEET 2023]*

(a) personal errors (b) least count errors
(c) random errors (d) instrumental errors

02 A metal wire has mass (0.4 ± 0.002) g, radius (0.3 ± 0.001) mm and length (5 ± 0.02) cm. The maximum possible percentage error in the measurement of density will nearly be *[NEET 2023]*

(a) 1.3% (b) 1.6% (c) 1.4% (d) 1.2%

03 The area of a rectangular field (in m^2) of length 55.3m and breadth 25m after rounding off the value for correct significant digits is *[NCERT (New) Pg. 5, NEET 2022]*

(a) 1382 (b) 1382.5
(c) 14×10^2 (d) 138×10^1

04 Time intervals measured by a clock give the following readings 1.25 s, 1.24 s, 1.27 s, 1.21 s and 1.28 s. What is the percentage relative error of the observations ? *[NCERT (Old) Pg. 24, NEET (Oct.) 2020]*

(a) 2% (b) 4%
(c) 16% (d) 1.6%

05 Taking into account of the significant figures, what is the value of 9.99 m − 0.0099 m ? *[NCERT (New) Pg. 5, NEET (Sep.) 2020]*

(a) 9.98 m (b) 9.980 m
(c) 9.9 m (d) 9.9801 m

06 In an experiment, the percentage of error occurred in the measurement of physical quantities A, B, C and D are 1%, 2%, 3% and 4% respectively. Then the maximum percentage of error in the measurement X, where $X = \frac{A^2 B^{1/2}}{C^{1/3} D^3}$, will be *[NCERT (Old) Pg. 27, NEET 2019]*

(a) 10% (b) (3/13)%
(c) 16% (d) −10%

07 In an experiment, four quantities a, b, c and d are measured with percentage error 1%, 2%, 3% and 4% respectively. Quantity P is calculated $P = \frac{a^3 b^2}{cd}$%. Error in P is *[NCERT (Old) Pg. 27, NEET 2013]*

(a) 14% (b) 10%
(c) 7% (d) 4%

08 A student measures the distance traversed in free fall of a body, initially at rest, in a given time. He uses this data to estimate g, the acceleration due to gravity. If the maximum percentage errors in measurement of the distance and the time are e_1 and e_2 respectively, the percentage error in the estimation of g is *[NCERT (Old) Pg. 26, AIPMT 2010]*

(a) $e_2 - e_1$ (b) $e_1 + 2e_2$
(c) $e_1 + e_2$ (d) $e_1 - 2e_2$

09 If the error in the measurement of radius of a sphere is 2%, then the error in the determination of volume of the sphere will be *[NCERT (Old) Pg. 27, AIPMT 2008]*

(a) 4% (b) 6%
(c) 8% (d) 2%

10 The density of a cube is measured by measuring its mass and length of its sides. If the maximum error in the measurement of mass and length are 4% and 3% respectively, the maximum error in the measurement of density will be *[AIPMT 1996]*

(a) 7% (b) 9%
(c) 12% (d) 13%

11 The percentage errors in the measurement of mass and speed are 2% and 3% respectively. The error in kinetic energy obtained by measuring mass and speed, will be *[NCERT (Old) Pg. 27, AIPMT 1995]*

(a) 12% (b) 10%
(c) 8% (d) 2%

12 A certain body weighs 22.42 g and has a measured volume of 4.7 cc. The possible error in the measurement of mass and volume are 0.01 g and 0.1 cc. Then, maximum error in the density will be *[AIPMT 1991]*

(a) 22% (b) 2%
(c) 0.2% (d) 0.02%

Key Index

Topic 1

1 (a)	2 (d)	3 (a)	4 (c)	5 (c)	6 (c)	7 (c)	8 (d)	9 (a)	10 (a)
11 (c)									

Topic 2

1 (b)	2 (c)	3 (a)	4 (b)	5 (a)	6 (c)	7 (a)	8 (a)	9 (c)	10 (a)
11 (d)	12 (c)	13 (c)	14 (b)	15 (a)	16 (c)	17 (d)	18 (a)	19 (a)	20 (a)
21 (b)	22 (b)	23 (a)	24 (d)	25 (c)	26 (a)	27 (d)	28 (d)	29 (b)	30 (c)
31 (a)	32 (d)	33 (d)	34 (c)	35 (a)	36 (c)	37 (d)	38 (b)	39 (a)	

Topic 3

1 (c)	2 (b)	3 (c)	4 (d)	5 (a)	6 (c)	7 (a)	8 (b)	9 (b)	10 (d)
11 (c)	12 (b)								

Detailed **Explanations**

Topic 1

01. *(a)* Strain and angle are dimensionless quantities as solid angle.
Arc has dimension of length.
Stress has dimension of pressure.

02. *(d)* Plane angle is measured in radian whereas solid angle is measured in steradian.
Therefore, plane angle and solid angle have units but no dimensions.

03. *(a)* 1 minute $= \frac{1}{60}$ degree

$$= \frac{1}{60} \times \frac{\pi}{180} = 2.91 \times 10^{-4} \text{ rad}$$

04. *(c)* The rate of heat flow through a conductor of length L and area of cross-section A is given by

$$\frac{dQ}{dt} = KA\frac{\Delta T}{L} \text{ J/s or watt}$$

where, K = coefficient of thermal conductivity and

ΔT = change in temperature

$$\Rightarrow \quad K = \frac{L}{A\,\Delta T}\frac{dQ}{dt}$$

$$\therefore \text{Unit of } K = \frac{\text{Metre}}{(\text{Metre})^2 \times \text{Kelvin}} \times \text{Watt} = \text{Wm}^{-1}\ \text{K}^{-1}$$

05. *(c)* Damping force is given as

$$F \propto v \quad \text{or} \quad F = kv$$

where, k is the constant of proportionality,

$$\therefore\ k = \frac{F}{v} = \frac{\text{N}}{\text{ms}^{-1}} = \frac{\text{kg ms}^{-2}}{\text{ms}^{-1}} = \text{kg s}^{-1}$$

06. *(c)*

key idea

If n_1 and n_2 are magnitudes of physical quantities and u_1 and u_2 are their respective units. Then, $n_1u_1 = n_2u_2$

In CGS system, density is given as $\rho = 4\,\text{g cm}^{-3}$

In CGS system; unit of length = 1 cm
Unit of mass = 1 g

In another system of units, the unit of mass is given as 100 g and unit of length is 10 cm. So from $n_1u_1 = n_2u_2$, we have density,

$$\rho = \frac{4\left(\frac{100\text{ g}}{100}\right)}{\left(\frac{10}{10}\text{cm}\right)^3} = \frac{\frac{4}{100}}{\left(\frac{1}{10}\right)^3} \times \frac{100\text{ g}}{(10\text{ cm})^3}$$

$$= \frac{4}{100} \times (10)^3 \times \frac{100\text{ g}}{10^3\text{ cm}^3} = 40 \text{ unit}$$

07. *(c)* According to Coulomb's law, the electrostatic force

$$F = \frac{1}{4\pi\varepsilon_0} \times \frac{q_1q_2}{r^2}$$

and ε_0 = permittivity of free space

$$\Rightarrow \quad \varepsilon_0 = \frac{1}{4\pi} \times \frac{q_1q_2}{r^2F}$$

Substituting the units for q, r and F, we obtain unit of ε_0

$$= \frac{\text{Coulomb} \times \text{Coulomb}}{\text{Newton - (Metre)}^2} = \frac{(\text{Coulomb})^2}{\text{Newton - (Metre)}^2}$$

08. *(d)* The value of Planck's constant is 6.63×10^{-34} and J-s is unit of the Planck's constant.

09. *(a)* Energy radiated by body at absolute temperature T having surface area A per second it given by

$$\frac{E}{t} = \sigma AT^4$$

where, σ is Stefan-Boltzmann's constant.

i.e. $\sigma = \frac{E/t}{AT^4} = \frac{\text{W}}{\text{m}^2\text{K}^4}$

10. *(a)* Force $F = [\text{MLT}^{-2}]$

$$= (10\text{ g})\ (10\text{ cm})\ (0.1\text{ s})^{-2}$$

Changing these units into MKS system

$$F = (10^{-2}\text{ kg})\ (10^{-1}\text{ m})\ (10^{-1}\text{s})^{-2}$$

$$= 10^{-1}\text{ N} = 0.1\text{N} = 10^{-1}\text{ N} = 0.1\text{ N}$$

11. *(c)* As $x = at + bt^2$

According to the concept of dimensional analysis and principle of homogeneity.

$\therefore$ Unit of x = unit of bt^2

$\therefore$ Unit of $b = \dfrac{\text{unit of } x}{\text{unit of } t^2} = \text{km}/\text{s}^2$

Topic 2

01. *(b)* Given, $F = \alpha t^2 + \beta t$

We know that dimensions on the both sides will be the same, i.e.,

$$[F] = [\alpha t^2] = [\beta t]$$

$\Rightarrow [\alpha][T^2] = [ML^1T^{-2}]$

$\Rightarrow \alpha = [M^1L^1T^{-4}]$

and $[\beta][T] = [M^1LT^{-2}]$

$\Rightarrow \beta = [M^1L^1T^{-3}]$

(a) $\dfrac{[\beta t]}{[\alpha]} = \dfrac{[M^1L^1T^{-2}]}{[M^1L^1T^{-4}]} = [T^2]$

(b) $\dfrac{[\alpha t]}{[\beta]} = \dfrac{[M^1L^1T^{-4}][T]}{[M^1L^1T^{-3}]} = [M^0L^0T^0]$

02. *(c)*

key idea

Students are advised to remember dimensional formulae of commonly used constants such as $G, \epsilon_0, \mu_0, R, h$ etc.

As we know that, magnetic flux

$\phi_B = B.A$

Thus, dimension of magnetic flux

$= [ML^2T^{-2}A^{-1}]$

Dimension of self induction,

$L = [ML^2T^{-2}A^{-2}]$

Dimension of magnetic permeability,

$\mu_0 = [MLT^{-2}A^{-2}]$

Dimension of electrical permitivity

$\varepsilon = [M^{-1}L^{-3}T^4A^2]$

So, the correct option is (c).

03. *(a)* From Newton's law of gravitation we know that,

$$F = \frac{Gm_1m_2}{r^2}$$

where symbols have their usual meaning.

i.e., $G = \dfrac{Fr^2}{m_1m_2} = \dfrac{[MLT^{-2}L^2]}{[M^2]}$

$= [M^{-1}L^3T^{-2}]$

Dimension formula of gravitational potential energy, $U = [ML^2T^{-2}]$

Gravitational potential is given by

$= \dfrac{\text{Gravitational potential energy}}{\text{Mass}}$

$= \dfrac{U}{M} = \dfrac{[ML^2T^{-2}]}{[M]} = [L^2T^{-2}]$

Gravitational intensity is also called acceleration due to gravity i.e. g

Thus, dimension formula of g is $[LT^{-2}]$.

04. *(b)* Energy depends on force, acceleration and time as,

$$[E] = [F]^a[a]^b[t]^c$$

$\Rightarrow [ML^2T^{-2}] = [MLT^{-2}]^a[LT^{-2}]^b[T]^c$

$\Rightarrow [ML^2T^{-2}] = [M]^a[L]^{a+b}[T]^{-2a-2b+c}$

Comparing the powers of M, L and T on both sides, we get

$a = 1, a + b = 2$

and $-2a - 2b + c = -2$

$\Rightarrow 1 + b = 2 \Rightarrow b = 1,$

$\Rightarrow -2(1) - 2(1) + c = -2 \Rightarrow c = 2$

The dimensions of the energy are $[F^1a^1t^2]$.

> **• Concept Enhancer**
>
> According to principle of homogeneity, the dimensions of a physical quantity must be correct, if the terms occuring on both sides of the equations are same. This principle is used to determine dimension of an unknown quantity or derive a physical quantity in terms of other quantities.

05. *(a)* The dimensions of energy

$[E] = [F]\cdot[d]$

$\Rightarrow [E] = [MLT^{-2}][L] = [ML^2T^{-2}]$

As we know that, the expression of gravitational force,

$$F = \frac{GM_1M_2}{r^2} \Rightarrow G = \frac{Fr^2}{M_1M_2}$$

$\therefore [G] = \dfrac{[F][r^2]}{[M_1][M_2]}$

$\Rightarrow [G] = \dfrac{[MLT^{-2}][L]^2}{[M][M]} = [M^{-1}L^3T^{-2}]$

The dimensions of

$\dfrac{E}{G} = \dfrac{[ML^2T^{-2}]}{[M^{-1}L^3T^{-2}]}$

$\Rightarrow \left[\dfrac{E}{G}\right] = [M^2L^{-1}T^0]$

06. *(c)* Stress $= \dfrac{\text{Force}}{\text{Area}}$

$\therefore$ Dimensions of stress $= \dfrac{[MLT^{-2}]}{[L^2]}$

$= [ML^{-1}T^{-2}]$

07. *(a)* As force, $F = \dfrac{e^2}{4\pi\varepsilon_0 r^2}$

$\Rightarrow \dfrac{e^2}{4\pi\varepsilon_0} = r^2\cdot F$

Putting dimensions of r and F, we get,

$\Rightarrow \left[\dfrac{e^2}{4\pi\varepsilon_0}\right] = [ML^3T^{-2}]$ ...(i)

Also, force, $F = \dfrac{Gm^2}{r^2}$

$\Rightarrow [G] = \dfrac{[MLT^{-2}][L^2]}{[M^2]}$

$\Rightarrow [G] = [M^{-1}L^3T^{-2}]$ ...(ii)

and $\left[\dfrac{1}{c^2}\right] = \dfrac{1}{[L^2T^{-2}]}$

$= [L^{-2}T^2]$ ...(iii)

Now, checking optionwise,

$= \dfrac{1}{c^2}\left(\dfrac{Ge^2}{4\pi\varepsilon_0}\right)^{1/2}$

$= [L^{-2}T^2][L^6T^{-4}]^{1/2} = [L]$

08. *(a)* Given, Planck's constant $= h$

Speed of light in vacuum $= c$

Newton's gravitational constant $= G$

According to question, the length can be written as

$l \propto h^a c^b G^c$

or $l = k h^a c^b G^c$

Writing dimensions of physical quantity on both sides,

$[M^0L^1T^0] = [ML^2T^{-1}]^a[LT^{-1}]^b[M^{-1}L^3T^{-2}]^c$

Applying the principle of homogeneity, we get

$a - c = 0$ ... (i)

$2a + b + 3c = 1$ ... (ii)

$-a - b - 2c = 0$ ... (iii)

Solving the Eq. (i), (ii) and (iii), we get

$a = c = \dfrac{1}{2}, \; b = \dfrac{-3}{2}$

Thus, we get, $l = k\dfrac{\sqrt{hG}}{c^{3/2}}$

where, k is a dimensionless constant.

09. *(c)* We know that

Surface tension $(S) = \dfrac{\text{Force }(F)}{\text{Length }(L)}$

So, $[S] = \dfrac{[MLT^{-2}]}{[L]} = [ML^0T^{-2}]$

Energy (E) = Force $\times$ Displacement

$\Rightarrow [E] = [ML^2T^{-2}]$

Velocity $(v) = \dfrac{\text{Displacement}}{\text{Time}}$

$\Rightarrow [v] = [LT^{-1}]$

As, $S \propto E^a v^b t^c$

From the principle of homogeneity,

[LHS] = [RHS]

$\Rightarrow [ML^0T^{-2}] = [ML^2T^{-2}]^a [LT^{-1}]^b [T]^c$

$\Rightarrow [ML^0T^{-2}] = [M^aL^{2a+b}T^{-2a-b+c}]$

Equating the power on both sides, we get

$a = 1, 2a + b = 0, b = -2$

$\Rightarrow -2a - b + c = -2$

$\Rightarrow c = (2a + b) - 2 = 0 - 2 = -2$

So, $[S] = [Ev^{-2}t^{-2}]$

10. *(a)*

key idea

Use the principle of homogeneity of dimensions i.e., a physical equation will be dimensionally correct, if the dimensions of all the terms occuring on both sides of the equation are same.

Critical velocity of liquid flowing through a tube are expressed as

$v_c \propto \eta^x \rho^y r^z$

Coefficient of viscosity of liquid,

$\eta = [ML^{-1}T^{-1}]$

Density of liquid, $\rho = [ML^{-3}]$

Radius of a tube $r = [L]$

Critical velocity of liquid

$v_c = [M^0L^1T^{-1}]$

$\Rightarrow [M^0L^1T^{-1}] = [ML^{-1}T^{-1}]^x [ML^{-3}]^y [L]^z$

$[M^0L^1T^{-1}] = [M^{x+y}L^{-x-3y+z}T^{-x}]$

Comparing exponents of M, L and T, we get

$x + y = 0, -x - 3y + z = 1, -x = -1$

$\Rightarrow z = -1, x = 1, y = -1$

11. *(d)* We know that,

$F = ma$

$\Rightarrow F = \frac{mv}{t} \Rightarrow m = \frac{Ft}{v}$

$[M] = \frac{[F][T]}{[v]} = [Fv^{-1}T]$

12. *(c)* As we know that impulse

= Force × Time

∴ Dimension of impulse

$= [MLT^{-2}][T] = [MLT^{-1}]$

Surface tension $= \frac{\text{Force}}{\text{Length}}$

Dimension formula of surface tension

$= \frac{[MLT^{-2}]}{[L]} = [ML^0T^{-2}]$

Angular momentum = Moment of inertia × Angular velocity

Dimension formula of angular momentum $= [ML^2][T^{-1}]$

$= [ML^2T^{-1}]$

Work = Force × Distance

Dimension formula of work

$= [MLT^{-2}] \times [L] = [ML^2T^{-2}]$

Dimension formula of work = (Energy)

$= [ML^2T^{-2}]$

Torque = Force × Perpendicular distance

Dimensional formula of torque

$= [MLT^{-2}] \times [L]$

$= [ML^2T^{-2}]$

Young's modulus of elasticity

$= \frac{\text{Force/ area}}{\text{Change in length / Original length}}$

Dimensional formula of Young's modulus $= \frac{[MLT^{-2}]/[L^2]}{[L]/[L]}$

$= [ML^{-1}T^{-2}]$

Hence, among the given options work and torque have the same dimensions $[ML^2T^{-2}]$.

Alternate Solution

Since both work and torque are expressed as force multiplied by distance, therefore both quantities will have same dimensions.

13. *(c)* $(\mu_0\varepsilon_0)^{-1/2}$ is the expression for velocity of light.

As $c = \frac{1}{\sqrt{\mu_0\varepsilon_0}}$

So, dimension of $c = [LT^{-1}]$

14. *(b)* As we know that,

Dimension of $\varepsilon_0 = [M^{-1}L^{-3}T^4A^2]$

Dimension of $E = [MLT^{-3}A^{-1}]$

So, dimension of

$\frac{1}{2}\varepsilon_0 E^2 = [M^{-1}L^{-3}T^4A^2] \times [MLT^{-3}A^{-1}]^2$

$= [ML^{-1}T^{-2}]$

15. *(a)* (i) Dimensions of velocity

$= [M^0L^1T^{-1}]$

Here, $a = 0, b = 1, c = -1$

(ii) Dimensions of acceleration

$= [M^0L^1T^{-2}]$

Here, $a = 0, b = 1, c = -2$

(iii) Dimensions of force $= [M^1L^1T^{-2}]$

Here, $a = 1, b = 1, T = -2$

(iv) Dimensions of pressure

$= [M^1L^{-1}T^{-2}]$

∴ Here, $a = 1, b = -1, c = -2$

∴ The physical quantity is pressure.

16. *(c)* Energy density $= \frac{\text{Energy}}{\text{Volume}} \Rightarrow u = \frac{E}{V}$

Dimensions of $u = \frac{\text{Dimensions of } E}{\text{Dimensions of } V}$

$= \frac{[ML^2T^{-2}]}{[L^3]}$

$= [ML^{-1}T^{-2}]$

Refractive index is a dimensionless quantity. Dielectric constant is a dimensionless quantity.

Young's modulus

$= \frac{\text{Longitudinal stress}}{\text{Longitudinal strain}} = \frac{F/A}{\Delta l/l}$

$= [ML^{-1}T^{-2}]$

Magnetic field

$= \frac{\text{Force}}{\text{Charge} \times \text{Velocity}}$

$= \frac{F}{qv} = \frac{[MLT^{-2}]}{[AT][LT^{-1}]}$

$= [MT^{-2}A^{-1}]$

17. *(d)* According to Ohm's law, $V \propto I$

and $V = IR$

Resistance, $R = \frac{\text{Potential difference}}{\text{Current}}$

$= \frac{V}{i} = \frac{W}{qi}$

(∵ Potential difference is equal to the work done per unit charge)

So, dimensions of R

$= \frac{\text{Dimensions of work}}{\text{Dimensions of charge} \times \text{Dimensions of current}}$

$= \frac{[ML^2T^{-2}]}{[IT][I]} = [ML^2T^{-3}I^{-2}]$

18. *(a)* The given expression is,

$v = at + \frac{b}{t + c}$

From principle of homogeneity

$[a][t] = [v]$

$[a] = \frac{[v]}{[t]} = \frac{[LT^{-1}]}{[T]} = [LT^{-2}]$

Similarly, $[c] = [t] = [\text{T}]$

Further, $\dfrac{[b]}{[t+c]} = [v]$

or $[b] = [v][t+c]$

or $[b] = [\text{LT}^{-1}][\text{T}] = [\text{L}]$

19. *(a)* Planck's constant

$$h = \frac{E}{f} = \frac{[\text{ML}^2\text{T}^{-2}]}{[\text{T}^{-1}]} = [\text{ML}^2\text{T}^{-1}]$$

Moment of inertia

$$I = M \times R^2$$
$$I = [\text{ML}^2]$$

from options,

Frequency $= [\text{T}^{-1}]$

Velocity $= [\text{LT}^{-1}]$

Angular momentum = moment of inertia × angular velocity

$$= I \times \omega = [\text{ML}^2] \times [\text{T}^{-1}]$$
$$L = [\text{ML}^2\text{T}^{-1}]$$

Ratio of $h/I = \dfrac{[\text{ML}^2\text{T}^{-1}]}{[\text{ML}^2]} = [\text{T}^{-1}]$

which is dimensionally same as frequency.

> ***Alternate Solution***
>
> $$\frac{\text{Planck constant } (h)}{\text{Moment of inertia } (I)} = \frac{E/\nu}{I} = \frac{E \times T}{I}$$
> $$= \frac{(\text{kg-m}^2/\text{s}^2)\ \text{s}}{(\text{kg-m}^2)} = \frac{1}{s} = \frac{1}{\text{time}} = \text{frequency}$$
>
> Thus, dimensions of $\frac{h}{I}$ is same as that of frequency.

20. *(a)* From Newton's law of gravitation,

$$F = \frac{GM_1M_2}{r^2}$$
$$G = \frac{F \cdot r^2}{M_1M_2} = \frac{[\text{MLT}^{-2}][\text{L}^2]}{[\text{M}][\text{M}]}$$
$$G = [\text{M}^{-1}\text{L}^3\text{T}^{-2}]$$

21. *(b)* Planck's constant

$$h = \frac{E}{f} = [\text{ML}^2\text{T}^{-1}]$$

Linear momentum $= mv$

$$= [\text{M}][\text{LT}^{-1}] = [\text{MLT}^{-1}]$$

Angular momentum $= I \times \omega$

$$= [\text{ML}^2][\text{T}^{-1}] = [\text{ML}^2\text{T}^{-1}]$$

Energy $= F \times d = [\text{MLT}^{-2}][\text{L}]$

$$= [\text{ML}^2\text{T}^{-2}]$$

Power $= F \times v = [\text{MLT}^{-2}][\text{LT}^{-1}]$

$$= [\text{ML}^2\text{T}^{-3}]$$

22. *(b)* Force = Mass × Acceleration

or $F = ma$

$$= [\text{M}][\text{LT}^{-2}] = [\text{MLT}^{-2}]$$

Torque = Moment of inertia × Angular acceleration

or $\tau = I \times \alpha$

$$= [\text{ML}^2][\text{T}^{-2}] = [\text{ML}^2\text{T}^{-2}]$$

(b) Work = Force × Displacement

or $W = F \times d$

$$= [\text{MLT}^{-2}][\text{L}]$$
$$= [\text{ML}^2\text{T}^{-2}]$$

Energy $= \dfrac{1}{2} \times \text{Mass} \times (\text{Velocity})^2$

or $K = \dfrac{1}{2}mv^2 = [\text{M}][\text{LT}^{-1}]^2$

$$= [\text{ML}^2\text{T}^{-2}]$$

(c) Force as discussed above

$$[F] = [\text{MLT}^{-2}]$$

Impulse = Force × Time-interval

$\therefore$ $[I] = [\text{MLT}^{-2}][\text{T}] = [\text{MLT}^{-1}]$

(d) Linear momentum

Mass × Velocity

or $p = mv$

$\therefore$ $[p] = [\text{M}][\text{LT}^{-1}]$

$$= [\text{MLT}^{-1}]$$

Angular momentum = Moment of inertia × Angular velocity

or $[L] = [I] \times [\omega]$

$\therefore$ $[L] = [\text{ML}^2][\text{T}^{-1}]$

$$= [\text{ML}^2\text{T}^{-1}]$$

Hence, we observe that option (b) is correct.

> ***Alternate Solution***
>
> Work done = Force × Displacement, which gives energy spent/received.
>
> Thus, work and energy have same dimensions.

23. *(a)* Mathematically, magnetic flux

$$\phi = BA \quad \ldots\text{(i)}$$

but magnetic force

$$F = Bil \quad \text{or} \quad B = \frac{F}{il}$$

Putting the value of B in Eq. (i), we have $\phi = \dfrac{F}{il}A$

Thus, dimensions of

$$\phi = \frac{[\text{MLT}^{-2}][\text{L}^2]}{[\text{AL}]}$$
$$= [\text{ML}^2\text{T}^{-2}\text{A}^{-1}]$$

24. *(d)* Viscous force on a sphere of radius r is

$$F = 6\pi\eta rv \Rightarrow \eta = \frac{F}{6\pi rv}$$
$$[\eta] = \frac{[F]}{[r][v]} = \frac{[\text{MLT}^{-2}]}{[\text{L}][\text{LT}^{-1}]} = [\text{ML}^{-1}\text{T}^{-1}]$$

25. *(c)* L/R is time constant of R-L circuit so, dimensions of L/R is same as that of time.

Alternative

$$\frac{\text{Dimensions of } L}{\text{Dimensions of } R} = \frac{[\text{ML}^2\text{T}^{-2}\text{A}^{-2}]}{[\text{ML}^2\text{T}^{-3}\text{A}^{-2}]}$$
$$= [\text{T}]$$

> • Concept **Enhancer**
>
> $RC, \frac{R}{L}$ and $\sqrt{LC}$ have dimensions of time.

26. *(a)*

key idea

A physical quantity having same dimensional formula can be subtracted or added to itself.

From principle of homogeneity of dimensions.

Dimensions of p = Dimensions of $\dfrac{a}{V^2}$

$$p = \frac{a}{V^2} \Rightarrow a = pV^2$$
$$= [\text{ML}^{-1}\text{T}^{-2}][\text{L}^3]^2 = [\text{ML}^5\text{T}^{-2}]$$

27. *(d)* A quantity which has dimensions and also has a constant value is called dimensional constant.

Here, gravitational constant G is a dimensional constant.

28. *(d)*

key idea

Students are advised to remember dimensional formulae of coefficients such as η (viscosity) σ (Stefan's constant), R_∞ (Rydberg constant), Boltzmann's constant (k_B).

Pressure, $p = \dfrac{\text{Force}}{\text{Area}} = \dfrac{[\text{MLT}^{-2}]}{[\text{L}^2]}$

$$= [\text{ML}^{-1}\text{T}^{-2}]$$

Velocity, $v = [\text{LT}^{-1}]$

From principle of homogeneity, the dimensions of r^2 and x^2 are same.

So, the dimensions of viscosity,

$$\eta = \frac{[\text{ML}^{-1}\text{T}^{-2}][\text{L}^2]}{[\text{LT}^{-1}][\text{L}]} = [\text{ML}^{-1}\text{T}^{-1}]$$

29. (b) $p = p_0 \exp(-\alpha t^2)$

As powers of exponential quantity is dimensionless, so αt^2 is dimensionless.

or αt^2 = dimensionless = $[M^0L^0T^0]$

$\therefore \quad \alpha = \frac{1}{t^2} = \frac{1}{[T^2]} = [T^{-2}]$

30. (c) Radiation pressure,

$$p = [ML^{-1}T^{-2}]$$

Velocity of light, $c = [LT^{-1}]$

Energy striking unit area per second

$$S = \frac{[ML^2T^{-2}]}{[L^2T]} = [MT^{-3}]$$

Now, $p^x S^y c^z$ is dimensionless.

$\therefore \quad [M^0L^0T^0] = p^x S^y c^z$

or $[M^0L^0T^0] = [M^1L^{-1}T^{-2}]^x [M^1T^{-3}]^y [L^1T^{-1}]^z$

or $[M^0L^0T^0]$

$= [M]^{x+y}[L]^{-x+z}[T]^{-2x-3y-z}$

From principle of homogeneity of dimensions

$x + y = 0 \quad \ldots(i)$

$-x + z = 0 \quad \ldots(ii)$

$-2x - 3y - z = 0 \quad \ldots(iii)$

Solving Eqs. (i), (ii) and (iii), we get

$x = 1, \quad y = -1, \quad z = 1$

31. (a) From Biot-Savart law,

$$dB = \frac{\mu_0}{4\pi}\frac{Idl\sin\theta}{r^2}$$

Idl = current element

r = displacement vector

$$\mu_0 = \frac{4\pi r^2(dB)}{Idl\sin\theta} = \frac{[L^2][MT^{-2}A^{-1}]}{[A][L]}$$

$= [MLT^{-2}A^{-2}]$

32. (d) As $f = Cm^x k^y$

$\therefore$ (Dimension of f) = C (dimension of $m)^x \times$ (dimensions of $k)^y$

$[T^{-1}] = C\,[M]^x [MT^{-2}]^y \quad \ldots(i)$

$\left(\text{where, } k = \frac{\text{force}}{\text{length}}\right)$

Applying the principle of homogeneity of dimensions, we get

$x + y = 0, \; -2y = -1$ or $y = \frac{1}{2}$

$\therefore \quad x = -\frac{1}{2}$

33. (d) As $F = -\eta A\frac{dv}{dz} \Rightarrow \eta = -\frac{F}{A\left(\frac{dv}{dz}\right)}$

As $\quad F = [MLT^{-2}],\; A = [L^2]$

$dv = [LT^{-1}],\; dz = [L]$

$\therefore \quad \eta = \frac{[MLT^{-2}][L]}{[L^2][LT^{-1}]}$

$= [ML^{-1}T^{-1}]$

34. (c) Pressure $= \frac{\text{Force}}{\text{Area}} = \frac{F}{A} = \frac{[MLT^{-2}]}{[L^2]}$

$= [ML^{-1}T^{-2}]$

35. (a) Torque $\tau = \mathbf{r} \times \mathbf{F}$

Dimensions of τ = dimension of $\mathbf{r}$ $\times$ dimension of $\mathbf{F}$

$= [L][MLT^{-2}] = [ML^2T^{-2}]$

36. (c) As we know that emf induced in the inductors is given by

$$e = L\frac{di}{dt} \Rightarrow L = \frac{edt}{di} = \frac{W}{q}\cdot\frac{dt}{di}$$

$$= \frac{[ML^2T^{-2}][T]}{[AT][A]} = [ML^2T^{-2}A^{-2}]$$

37. (d) Dimensions of energy per unit volume

$$= \frac{\text{Dimensions of energy}}{\text{Dimensions of volume}}$$

$$= \frac{[ML^2T^{-2}]}{[L^3]} = [ML^{-1}T^{-2}]$$

Dimensions of force per unit area

$$= \frac{\text{Dimensions of force}}{\text{Dimensions of area}}$$

$$= \frac{[MLT^{-2}]}{[L^2]} = [ML^{-1}T^{-2}]$$

Voltage $\times$ Charge/ Volume

$$= \frac{\left(\frac{W}{q}\right)\times(it)}{l^3}$$

$$= \frac{(W)}{(l^3)} = \frac{[ML^2T^{-2}]}{[L^3]}$$

$= [ML^{-1}T^{-2}]$

Angular momentum

$= (r)(p) = (r)(mv)$

$= [L][M][LT^{-1}]$

$= [ML^2T^{-1}]$

38. (b) Angular momentum,

$L = \mathbf{r} \times \mathbf{p} = r \times mv$

$\therefore$ Dimensional formula for angular momentum

$= [L][M][LT^{-1}]$

$= [ML^2T^{-1}]$

39. (a) Dimensional formula of CR is given by

$$\because \quad C = \frac{q}{V} = \frac{q}{\left(\frac{W}{q}\right)} = \frac{q^2}{W}$$

$$= \frac{(it)^2}{F\cdot x} = \frac{[AT]^2}{[ML^2T^{-2}]}$$

$= [M^{-1}L^{-2}T^4A^2]$

and $R = \frac{V}{i} = \frac{W}{qi} = \frac{F\cdot x}{i^2 t} = \frac{[ML^2T^{-2}]}{[AT][A]}$

$= [ML^2T^{-3}A^{-2}]$

$\therefore$ Dimensional formula of CR

$= [M^{-1}L^{-2}T^4A^2]\;[ML^2T^{-3}A^{-2}]$

$= [M^0L^0T]$

Topic 3

01. (c) Random errors can arise due to random and unpredictable fluctuations in temperature and voltage supply.

02. (b) Given, $M = (0.4 \pm 0.002)$ g

$R = (0.3 \pm 0.001)$ mm

$L = (5 \pm 0.02)$ cm

$\therefore$ Density of the wire, $\rho = \frac{M}{\pi r^2 L}$

$\therefore$ Maximum percentage error in the measurement of density of wire.

$$\frac{\Delta\rho}{\rho}\times 100 = \frac{\Delta M}{M}\times 100 + 2\times\frac{\Delta r}{r}\times 100 + \frac{\Delta L}{L}\times 100$$

$$= \frac{0.002}{0.4}\times 100 + 2\times\frac{0.001}{0.3}\times 100 + \frac{0.02}{5}\times 100$$

$= 0.5 + 0.67 + 0.4 = 1.57\% \approx 1.6\%$

03. (c) Area = Length $\times$ Breadth

$= 55.3 \times 25 = 1382.5$

$= 13.825 \times 10^2 = 13.83 \times 10^2$

Now, length has 3 significant figures and breadth has 2 significant figures. In multiplication answer must have minimum significant figure.

So, $\quad 13.8 \times 10^2 = 14 \times 10^2$

• Concept Enhancer

A significant figure is rounding off a number. It follows the following laws

(i) All the non-zero digits are always significant.

(ii) Any zero between two significant digits are taken as significant.

(iii) The trailing zero(s) in the number with a decimal part are significant figures.

04. (d) Mean time interval

$$\overline{T} = \frac{1.25 + 1.24 + 1.27 + 1.21 + 1.28}{5}$$

$$\Rightarrow \quad = \frac{6.25}{5} = 1.25 \text{ s}$$

Mean absolute error,

$$\Delta\overline{T} = \frac{|\Delta T_1| + |\Delta T_2| + |\Delta T_3| + |\Delta T_4| + |\Delta T_5|}{5}$$

$$\Rightarrow \quad = \frac{|1.25 - 1.25| + |1.25 - 1.24| + |1.25 - 1.27| + |1.25 - 1.21| + |1.25 - 1.28|}{5}$$

$$\Rightarrow \frac{0 + 0.01 + 0.02 + 0.04 + 0.03}{5} = \frac{0.1}{5} = 0.02\text{s}$$

∴ Percentage relative error

$$= \frac{\Delta\overline{T}}{\overline{T}} \times 100$$

$$= \frac{0.02}{1.25} \times 100 = 1.6\%$$

05. (a) The difference between 9.99 m and 0.0099 m is

$$= 9.99 - 0.0099 = 9.9801 \text{ m}$$

Taking significant figures into account, as both the values has two significant figures after decimal.

So, their difference will also have two significant figures after decimal, i.e. 9.98 m.

06. (c)

key idea

We can solve by comparing, $A = \frac{x^m y^n}{z^p}$

Percentage error in A is given by

$$\left(\frac{\Delta A}{A} \times 100\%\right) = m\frac{\Delta x}{x} \times 100\% + n\frac{\Delta y}{y} \times 100\% + p\frac{\Delta z}{z} \times 100\%$$

Given, error in measurement of $A = 1\%$

Error in measurement of $B = 2\%$

Error in measurement of $C = 3\%$

Error in measurement of $D = 4\%$

Given, $X = \frac{A^2 B^{\frac{1}{2}}}{C^{\frac{1}{3}} D^3}$

Maximum percentage error in

$$X = \left(\frac{\Delta X}{X}\right) \times 100\%$$

$$= \left(2\frac{\Delta A}{A} + \frac{1}{2}\frac{\Delta B}{B} + \frac{1}{3}\frac{\Delta C}{C} + 3\frac{\Delta D}{D}\right) \times 100\%$$

$$= \left(2 \times 1 + \frac{1}{2} \times 2 + \frac{1}{3} \times 3 + 3 \times 4\right) \times 100\%$$

$$= 16\%$$

07. (a) As given, $P = \frac{a^3 b^2}{cd}$

$$\therefore \quad \frac{\Delta P}{P} \times 100 = \left(\frac{3\Delta a}{a} + \frac{2\Delta b}{b} + \frac{\Delta c}{c} + \frac{\Delta d}{d}\right) \times 100$$

$$= 3\frac{\Delta a}{a} \times 100 + 2\frac{\Delta b}{b} \times 100 + \frac{\Delta c}{c} \times 100 + \frac{\Delta d}{d} \times 100$$

$$= (3 \times 1 + 2 \times 2 + 3 + 4)\%$$

$$= (3 + 4 + 3 + 4)\% = 14\%$$

08. (b) Distance travelled during free is given by

$$h = \frac{1}{2}gt^2 \quad (\because u = 0 \text{ in free fall})$$

$$\Rightarrow \quad g = \frac{2h}{t^2} \quad \text{...(i)}$$

Percentage error in measurement of distance $= e_1$

Percentage error in measurement of time $= e_2$

Now taking logrithm of Eq. (i), we get

$$\ln g = \ln h - 2\ln t \quad \text{... (ii)}$$

Differentiating the Eq. (ii), we get

$$\frac{dg'}{g'} = \frac{dh}{h} - \frac{2dt}{t}$$

For maximum permissible error,

$$\left(\frac{dg}{g} \times 100\%\right)_{\max} = \left(\frac{dh}{h} \times 100\%\right) + 2\left(\frac{dt}{t} \times 100\%\right)$$

Putting values of the percentage error in measurement of distance and time we get

$$\left(\frac{dg}{g} \times 100\%\right) = e_1 + 2e_2$$

• **Concept Enhancer**

$\ln\frac{x}{y} = \ln x - \ln y$

$\ln xy = \ln x + \ln y$ and $\ln x^2 = 2\ln x$

Do not get confused with the positive sign taken for maximum error in time while calculating the maximum error in g. We always take the absolute (i.e. + ve) value of errors for all independent variables (h, t) while calculating.

09. (b) Volume of a sphere,

$$V = \frac{4}{3}\pi r^3$$

$$\therefore \quad \frac{\Delta V}{V} \times 100 = \frac{3 \times \Delta r}{r} \times 100$$

Here, $\frac{\Delta r}{r} \times 100 = 2\%$

$$\therefore \quad \frac{\Delta V}{V} \times 100 = 3 \times 2\% = 6\%$$

10. (d) As density of a cube,

$$\rho = \frac{m}{V} = \frac{m}{l^3}$$

$$\therefore \quad \frac{\Delta\rho}{\rho} \times 100 = \pm\left(\frac{\Delta m}{m} + 3\frac{\Delta l}{l}\right) \times 100\%$$

$$= \pm(4 + 3 \times 3)\% = \pm 13\%$$

11. (c) Kinetic energy, $K = \frac{1}{2}mv^2$

$$\therefore \quad \frac{\Delta K}{K} \times 100 = \frac{\Delta m}{m} \times 100 + 2 \times \frac{\Delta v}{v} \times 100$$

Here, $\frac{\Delta m}{m} \times 100 = 2\%$

$$\Rightarrow \quad \frac{\Delta v}{v} \times 100 = 3\%$$

$$\therefore \quad \frac{\Delta K}{K} \times 100 = 2\% + 2 \times 3\% = 8\%$$

12. (b) Density $= \frac{\text{Mass}}{\text{Volume}}$

$$\rho = m/V$$

$$\therefore \quad \frac{\Delta\rho}{\rho} = \frac{\Delta m}{m} + \frac{\Delta V}{V}$$

Here, $\Delta m = 0.01$ g, $m = 22.42$ g

$\Delta V = 0.1$ cc

$V = 4.7$ cc

$$\therefore \quad \frac{\Delta\rho}{\rho} = \left(\frac{0.01}{22.42} + \frac{0.1}{4.7}\right) \times 100 = 2\%$$

In NEET 2024, 1 question were visible from this chapter. In past 5 years, 1 question from topic-1, 7 questions from topic-2 and 2 questions from topic-3 were asked.
For detailed analysis scan QR code

MOTION IN A STRAIGHT LINE

Topic 1 Terms Related to Motion

01 A vehicle travels half the distance with speed v and the remaining distance with speed $2v$. Its average speed is *[NCERT (Old) Pg. 42, NEET 2023]*
(a) $\frac{2v}{3}$ (b) $\frac{4v}{3}$ (c) $\frac{3v}{4}$ (d) $\frac{v}{3}$

02 A person travelling in a straight line moves with a constant velocity v_1 for certain distance x and with a constant velocity v_2 for next equal distance. The average velocity v is given by the relation *[NCERT (Old) Pg. 42, NEET (Odisha) 2019]*
(a) $\frac{1}{v}=\frac{1}{v_1}+\frac{1}{v_2}$ (b) $\frac{2}{v}=\frac{1}{v_1}+\frac{1}{v_2}$
(c) $\frac{v}{2}=\frac{v_1+v_2}{2}$ (d) $v=\sqrt{v_1 v_2}$

03 Preeti reached the metro station and found that the escalator was not working. She walked up the stationary escalator in time t_1. On other days, if she remains stationary on the moving escalator, then the escalator takes her up in time t_2. The time taken by her to walk up on the moving escalator will be *[NCERT (Old) Pg. 52, NEET 2017]*
(a) $\frac{t_1+t_2}{2}$ (b) $\frac{t_1 t_2}{t_2-t_1}$ (c) $\frac{t_1 t_2}{t_2+t_1}$ (d) t_1-t_2

04 If the velocity of a particle is $v = At + Bt^2$, where A and B are constants, then the distance travelled by it between 1 s and 2 s is *[NCERT (Old) Pg. 43, NEET 2016]*
(a) $3A+7B$ (b) $\frac{3}{2}A+\frac{7}{3}B$
(c) $\frac{A}{2}+\frac{B}{3}$ (d) $\frac{3}{2}A+4B3$

05 Two cars P and Q start from a point at the same time in a straight line and their positions are represented by $x_P(t)=at+bt^2$ and $x_Q(t)=ft-t^2$. At what time do the cars have the same velocity ? *[NEET 2016]*
(a) $\frac{a-f}{1+b}$ (b) $\frac{a+f}{2(b-1)}$
(c) $\frac{a+f}{2(1+b)}$ (d) $\frac{f-a}{2(1+b)}$

06 A particle of unit mass undergoes one-dimensional motion such that its velocity varies according to $v(x)=\beta x^{-2n}$ where, β and n are constants and x is the position of the particle. The acceleration of the particle as a function of x, is given by *[NCERT (New) Pg. 15, AIPMT 2015]*
(a) $-2n\beta^2 x^{-2n-1}$ (b) $-2n\beta^2 x^{-4n-1}$
(c) $-2\beta^2 x^{-2n+1}$ (d) $-2n\beta^2 e^{-4n+1}$

07 The displacement x (in metre) of a particle of mass m (in kg) moving in one dimension under the action of a force, is related to time t (in s) by $t=\sqrt{x}+3$. The displacement of the particle when its velocity is zero, will be *[NCERT (New) Pg. 14, NEET 2013]*
(a) 4 m (b) 0 m (zero) (c) 6 m (d) 2 m

08 The motion of a particle along a straight line is described by equation $x=8+12t-t^3$ where, x is in metre and t in second. The retardation of the particle when its velocity becomes zero, is *[AIPMT 2012]*
(a) 24 ms^{-2} (b) zero
(c) 6 ms^{-2} (d) 12 ms^{-2}

09 A particle covers half of its total distance with speed v_1 and the rest half distance with speed v_2. Its average speed during the complete journey is *[AIPMT 2011]*
(a) $\frac{v_1+v_2}{2}$ (b) $\frac{v_1 v_2}{v_1+v_2}$
(c) $\frac{2v_1 v_2}{v_1+v_2}$ (d) $\frac{v_1^2 v_2^2}{v_1^2+v_2^2}$

10 A body is moving with velocity 30 m/s towards East. After 10 s, its velocity becomes 40 m/s towards North. The average acceleration of the body is *[NCERT (New) Pg. 16, AIPMT 2011]*

(a) 7 m/s^2 (b) $\sqrt{7} \text{ m/s}^2$
(c) 5 m/s^2 (d) 1 m/s^2

11 A particle moves a distance x in time t. According to the equation $x = (t+5)^{-1}$. The acceleration of particle is proportional to *[NCERT (New) Pg. 15, AIPMT 2010]*

(a) $(v)^{3/2}$ (b) $(x)^2$
(c) $(x)^{-2}$ (d) $(v)^{2/3}$

12 A particle moving along X-axis has acceleration f, at time t, given by $f = f_0\left(1-\frac{t}{T}\right)$, where f_0 and T are constants. The particle at $t = 0$ has zero velocity. In the time interval between $t = 0$ and the instant when $f = 0$, the particle's velocity v_x is *[AIPMT 2007]*

(a) f_0T (b) $\frac{1}{2}f_0T^2$
(c) f_0T^2 (d) $\frac{1}{2}f_0T$

13 A car moves from X to Y with a uniform speed v_u and returns to X with a uniform speed v_d. The average speed for this round trip is *[AIPMT 2007]*

(a) $\frac{2v_dv_u}{v_d+v_u}$ (b) $\sqrt{v_uv_d}$ (c) $\frac{v_dv_u}{v_d+v_u}$ (d) $\frac{v_u+v_d}{2}$

14 The position x of a particle w.r.t. time t along x-axis is given by $x = 9t^2 - t^3$, where x is in metre and t in second. What will be the position of this particle when it achieves maximum speed along the $+x$ direction? *[NCERT (New) Pg. 15, AIPMT 2007]*

(a) 32 m (b) 54 m
(c) 81 m (d) 24 m

15 A particle moves along a straight line OX. At a time t (in second), the distance x (in metre) of the particle from O is given by $x = 40 + 12t - t^3$.
How long would the particle travel before coming to rest? *[AIPMT 2006]*

(a) 24 m (b) 40 m (c) 56 m (d) 16 m

16 A car runs at a constant speed on a circular track of radius 100 m, taking 62.8 s for every circular lap. The average velocity and average speed for each circular lap, respectively is *[AIPMT 2006]*

(a) 10 m/s, 0 (b) 0, 0
(c) 0, 10 m/s (d) 10 m/s, 10 m/s

17 The displacement x of a particle varies with time t as $x = ae^{-\alpha t} + be^{\beta t}$, where a, b, α and β are positive constants. The velocity of the particle will *[NCERT (New) Pg. 15, AIPMT 2005]*

(a) decrease with time (b) be independent of α and β
(c) drop to zero when $\alpha = \beta$ (d) increase with time

18 A particle moves along a straight line such that its displacement at any time t is given by $s = 3t^3 + 7t^2 + 14t + 5$. The acceleration of the particle at $t = 1$ s is *[AIPMT 2000]*

(a) 18 m/s^2 (b) 32 m/s^2
(c) 29 m/s^2 (d) 24 m/s^2

19 The position x of a particle varies with time t, as $x = at^2 - bt^3$. The acceleration of the particle will be zero at time t equals to *[NCERT (New) Pg. 15, AIPMT 1997]*

(a) zero (b) $\frac{a}{3b}$
(c) $\frac{2a}{3b}$ (d) $\frac{a}{b}$

20 The acceleration of a particle is increasing linearly with time t as bt. The particle starts from origin with an initial velocity v_0. The distance travelled by the particle in time t will be *[NCERT (New) Pg. 18, AIPMT 1995]*

(a) $v_0t + \frac{1}{3}bt^2$ (b) $v_0t + \frac{1}{2}bt^2$
(c) $v_0t + \frac{1}{6}bt^3$ (d) $v_0t + \frac{1}{3}bt^3$

21 A car accelerates from rest at a constant rate α for some time, after which it decelerates at a constant rate β and comes to rest. If the total time elapsed is t, then the maximum velocity acquired by the car is *[NCERT (New) Pg. 18, AIPMT 1994]*

(a) $\left(\frac{\alpha^2+\beta^2}{\alpha\beta}\right)t$ (b) $\left(\frac{\alpha^2-\beta^2}{\alpha\beta}\right)t$
(c) $\frac{(\alpha+\beta)t}{\alpha\beta}$ (d) $\left(\frac{\alpha\beta t}{\alpha+\beta}\right)$

22 A particle moves along a straight line such that its displacement at any time t is given by $s = (t^3 - 6t^2 + 3t + 4)$ m
The velocity when the acceleration is zero, is *[AIPMT 1994]*

(a) 3 ms^{-1} (b) -12 ms^{-1}
(c) 42 ms^{-1} (d) -9 ms^{-1}

23 A bus travelling the first one-third distance at a speed of 10 km/h, the next one-third at 20 km/h and the last one-third at 60 km/h. The average speed of the bus is *[NCERT (Old) Pg. 42, AIPMT 1991]*

(a) 9 km/h (b) 16 km/h
(c) 18 km/h (d) 48 km/h

24 A car moves a distance of 200 m. It covers the first-half of the distance at speed 40 km/h and the second-half of distance at speed v km/h. The average speed is 48 km/h. Find the value of v. *[NCERT (Old) Pg. 42, AIPMT 1991]*

(a) 56 km/h (b) 60 km/h
(c) 50 km/h (d) 48 km/h

25 A car covers the first-half of the distance between two places at 40 km/h and other half at 60 km/h. The average speed of the car is *[NCERT (Old) Pg. 42, AIPMT 1990]*

(a) 40 km/h (b) 48 km/h
(c) 50 km/h (d) 60 km/h

Topic 2 Kinematics Equations of Uniformly and Non-uniformly Accelerated Motion

01 A bullet from a gun is fired on a rectangular wooden block with velocity u. When bullet travels 24 cm through the block along its length horizontally, velocity of bullet becomes $u/3$. Then it further penetrates into the block in the same direction before coming to rest exactly at the other end of the block. The total length of the block is *[NCERT (Old) Pg. 48, NEET 2023]*

(a) 24 cm (b) 28 cm (c) 30 cm (d) 27 cm

02 A horizontal bridge is built across a river. A student standing on the bridge throws a small ball vertically upwards with a velocity 4 m s^{-1}. The ball strikes the water surface after 4 s. The height of bridge above water surface is (Take, $g = 10$ m s^{-2}). *[NEET 2023]*

(a) 60 m (b) 64 m (c) 68 m (d) 56 m

03 The ratio of the distances travelled by a freely falling body in the 1st, 2nd, 3rd and 4th second *[NCERT (New) Pg. 20, NEET 2022]*

(a) 1 : 4 : 9 : 16 (b) 1 : 3 : 5 : 7
(c) 1 : 1 : 1 : 1 (d) 1 : 2 : 3 : 4

04 A car starts from rest and accelerates at 5 m/s^2. At $t = 4$ s, a ball is dropped out of a window by a person sitting in the car. What is the velocity and acceleration of the ball at $t = 6$ s ? (Take, $g = 10$ m/s^2) *[NCERT (New) Pg. 17, NEET 2021]*

(a) 20 m/s, 5 m/s^2 (b) 20 m/s, 0
(c) $20\sqrt{2}$ m/s, 0 (d) $20\sqrt{2}$ m/s, 10 m/s^2

05 A small block slides down on a smooth inclined plane, starting from rest at time $t = 0$. Let s_n be the distance travelled by the block in the interval $t = n - 1$ to $t = n$. Then, the ratio $\frac{s_n}{s_{n+1}}$ is *[NEET 2021]*

(a) $\frac{2n-1}{2n}$ (b) $\frac{2n-1}{2n+1}$ (c) $\frac{2n+1}{2n-1}$ (d) $\frac{2n}{2n-1}$

06 A person sitting in the ground floor of a building notices through the window of height 1.5 m, a ball dropped from the roof of the building crosses the window in 0.1 s. What is the velocity of the ball when it is at the topmost point of the window ? ($g = 10$ m/s^2) *[NCERT (New) Pg. 20, NEET (Oct.) 2020]*

(a) 15.5 m/s (b) 14.5 m/s (c) 4.5 m/s (d) 20 m/s

07 A ball is thrown vertically downward with a velocity of 20 m/s from the top of a tower. It hits the ground after some time with a velocity of 80 m/s. The height of the tower is ($g = 10$ m/s^2) *[NEET (Sep.) 2020]*

(a) 340 m (b) 320 m (c) 300 m (d) 360 m

08 A person standing on the floor of an elevator drops a coin. The coin reaches the floor in time t_1 if the elevator is at rest and in time t_2 if the elevator is moving uniformly. Then which of the following option is correct ? *[NCERT (Old) Pg. 52, NEET (Odisha) 2019]*

(a) $t_1 < t_2$ or $t_1 > t_2$ depending upon whether the lift is going up or down
(b) $t_1 < t_2$ (c) $t_1 > t_2$ (d) $t_1 = t_2$

09 A toy car with charge q moves on a frictionless horizontal plane surface under the influence of a uniform electric field **E**. Due to the force q**E**, its velocity increases from 0 to 6 m/s in one second duration. At that instant, the direction of the field is reversed. The car continues to move for two more seconds under the influence of this field. The average velocity and the average speed of the toy car between 0 to 3 s are respectively *[NEET 2018]*

(a) 1 m/s, 3.5 m/s (b) 1 m/s, 3 m/s
(c) 2 m/s, 4 m/s (d) 1.5 m/s, 3 m/s

10 A stone falls freely under gravity. It covers distances h_1, h_2 and h_3 in the first 5s, the next 5s and the next 5s respectively. The relation between h_1, h_2 and h_3 is *[NCERT (New) Pg. 19, NEET 2013]*

(a) $h_1 = 2h_2 = 3h_3$ (b) $h_1 = \frac{h_2}{3} = \frac{h_3}{5}$
(c) $h_2 = 3h_1$ and $h_3 = 3h_2$ (d) $h_1 = h_2 = h_3$

11 A boy standing at the top of a tower of 20 m height drops a stone. Assuming, $g = 10$ ms^{-2}, the velocity with which it hits the ground is *[NCERT (New) Pg. 19, AIPMT 2011]*

(a) 20 m/s (b) 40 m/s (c) 5 m/s (d) 10 m/s

12 A ball is dropped from a high rise platform at $t = 0$ starting from rest. After 6 s, another ball is thrown downwards from the same platform with a speed v. The two balls meet at $t = 18$ s. What is the value of v ? (Take, $g = 10$ ms^{-2}) *[AIPMT 2010]*

(a) 75 ms^{-1} (b) 55 ms^{-1} (c) 40 ms^{-1} (d) 60 ms^{-1}

13 A particle starts its motion from rest under the action of a constant force. If the distance covered in first 10 s is s_1 and that covered in the first 20 s is s_2, then *[NCERT (Old) Pg. 42, AIPMT 2009]*

(a) $s_2 = 2s_1$ (b) $s_2 = 3s_1$
(c) $s_2 = 4s_1$ (d) $s_2 = s_1$

14 A particle moves in a straight line with a constant acceleration. It changes its velocity from 10 ms^{-1} to 20 ms^{-1} while passing through a distance 135 m in t s. The value of t is *[AIPMT 2008]*

(a) 10 (b) 1.8 (c) 12 (d) 9

15 The distance travelled by a particle starting from rest and moving with an acceleration $4/3 ms^{-2}$ in the third-second is *[NCERT (New) Pg. 18, AIPMT 2008]*
(a) 6 m (b) 4 m (c) $\frac{10}{3}$ m (d) $\frac{19}{3}$ m

16 Two bodies A (of mass 1 kg) and B (of mass 3 kg) are dropped from heights of 16 m and 25 m, respectively. The ratio of the time taken by them to reach the ground is *[AIPMT 2006]*
(a) –5/4 (b) 12/5 (c) 5/12 (d) 4/5

17 A man throws balls with the same speed vertically upwards one after the other at an interval of 2 s. What should be the speed of the throw so that more than two balls are in the sky at any time ? (Take, $g = 9.8 m/s^2$) *[AIPMT 2003]*
(a) Any speed less than 19.6 m/s
(b) Only with speed 19.6 m/s
(c) More than 19.6 m/s
(d) At least 9.8 m/s

18 If a ball is thrown vertically upwards with speed u, the distance covered during the last t s of its ascent is *[NCERT (New) Pg. 19, AIPMT 2003]*
(a) $ut - \frac{1}{2}gt^2$ (b) $(u + gt)t$ (c) ut (d) $\frac{1}{2}gt^2$

19 A stone is thrown vertically upwards. When stone is at a height half of its maximum height, its speed is 10 m/s, then the maximum height attained by the stone is ($g = 10 m/s^2$) *[AIPMT 2001]*
(a) 8 m (b) 10 m (c) 15 m (d) 20 m

20 If a car at rest, accelerates uniformly to a speed of 144 km/h in 20s, it covers a distance of *[NCERT (New) Pg. 18, AIPMT 1997]*
(a) 2880 m (b) 1440 m (c) 400 m (d) 20 m

21 If a ball is thrown vertically upwards with a velocity of 40 m/s, then velocity of the ball after 2s will be ($g = 10 m/s^2$) *[AIPMT 1996]*
(a) 15 m/s (b) 20 m/s (c) 25 m/s (d) 28 m/s

22 A body dropped from a height h with initial velocity zero, strikes the ground with a velocity 3 m/s. Another body of same mass dropped from the same height h with an initial velocity of 4 m/s. The final velocity of second mass, with which it strikes the ground is *[NCERT (New) Pg. 18, AIPMT 1996]*
(a) 5 m/s (b) 12 m/s (c) 3 m/s (d) 4 m/s

23 Three different objects of masses m_1, m_2 and m_3 are allowed to fall from rest and from the same point O along three different frictionless paths. The speeds of the three objects on reaching the ground will be in the ratio of *[AIPMT 1995]*
(a) $m_1 : m_2 : m_3$ (b) $m_1 : 2m_2 : 3m_3$
(c) 1:1:1 (d) $\frac{1}{m_1} : \frac{1}{m_2} : \frac{1}{m_3}$

24 The water drops fall at regular intervals from a tap 5 m above the ground. The third drop is leaving the tap at an instant when the first drop touches the ground. How far above the ground is the second drop at that instant ? (Take, $g = 10 m/s^2$) *[NCERT (New) Pg. 19, AIPMT 1995]*
(a) 1.25 m (b) 2.50 m
(c) 3.75 m (d) 5.00 m

25 A body is thrown vertically upwards from the ground. It reaches a maximum height of 20 m in 5 s. After what time it will reach the ground from its maximum height position ? *[NCERT (New) Pg. 19, AIPMT 1995]*
(a) 2.5 s (b) 5 s
(c) 10 s (d) 25 s

26 A stone released with zero velocity from the top of a tower, reaches the ground in 4 s. The height of the tower is ($g = 10 m/s^2$) *[NCERT (New) Pg. 19, AIPMT 1995]*
(a) 20 m (b) 40 m
(c) 80 m (d) 160 m

27 The velocity of train increases uniformly from 20 km/h to 60 km/h in 4 h. The distance travelled by the train during this period is *[AIPMT 1994]*
(a) 160 km (b) 180 km
(c) 100 km (d) 120 km

28 A body starts from rest. what is the ratio of the distance travelled by the body during the 4th and 3rd second ? *[NCERT (New) Pg. 18, AIPMT 1993]*
(a) $\frac{7}{5}$ (b) $\frac{5}{7}$
(c) $\frac{7}{3}$ (d) $\frac{3}{7}$

29 A body dropped from top of a tower fall through 40 m during the last two seconds of its fall. The height of tower is ($g = 10 m/s^2$) *[AIPMT 1991]*
(a) 60 m (b) 45 m
(c) 80 m (d) 50 m

30 What will be the ratio of the distance moved by a freely falling body from rest in 4th and 5th second of journey ? *[NCERT (New) Pg. 18, AIPMT 1989]*
(a) 4 : 5 (b) 7 : 9
(c) 16 : 25 (d) 1 : 1

31 A car is moving along a straight road with a uniform acceleration. It passes through two points P and Q separated by a distance with velocity 30 km/h and 40 km/h, respectively. The velocity of the car midway between P and Q is *[AIPMT 1988]*
(a) 33.3 km/h
(b) $20\sqrt{2}$ km/h
(c) $25\sqrt{2}$ km/h
(d) 035 km/h

Topic 3 Graphs Related to Motion

01 The velocity v-time t plot of the motion of a body is shown below. ***[NEET 2024]***

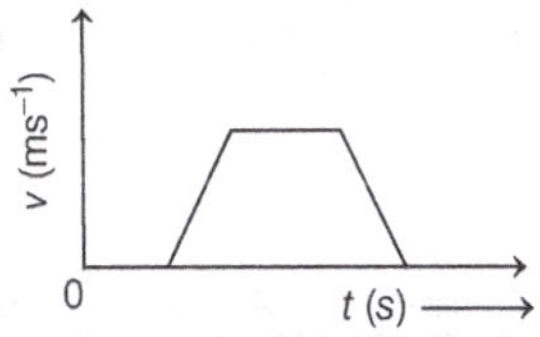

The acceleration a-time t graph that best suits this motion is

(a) 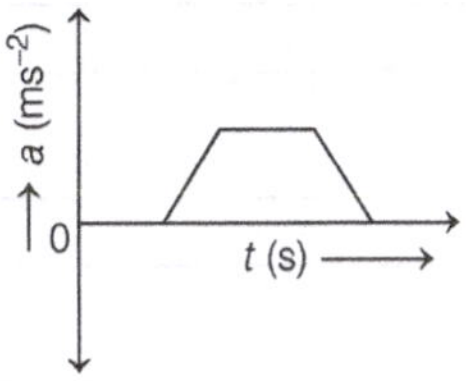
(b) 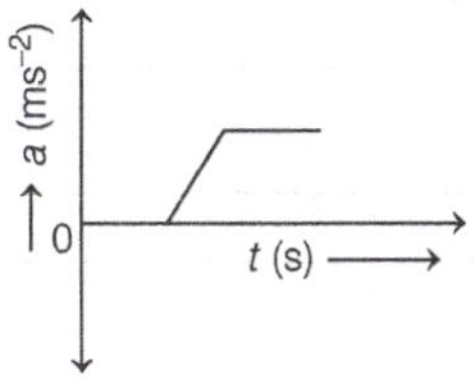
(c) 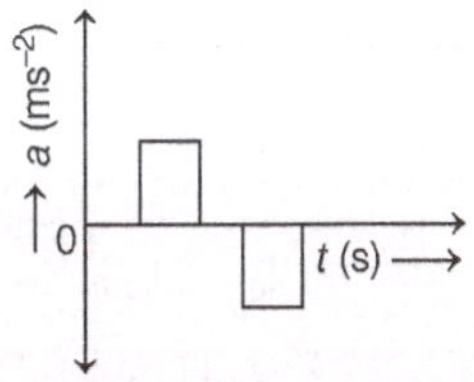
(d) 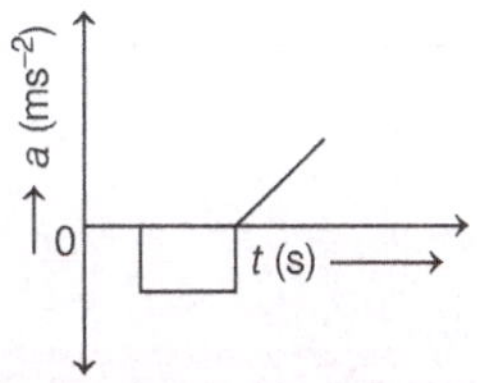

02 The displacement-time graph of two moving particles make angles of 30° and 45° with the X-axis as shown in the figure. The ratio of their respective velocity is ***[NCERT (New) Pg. 14, NEET 2022]***

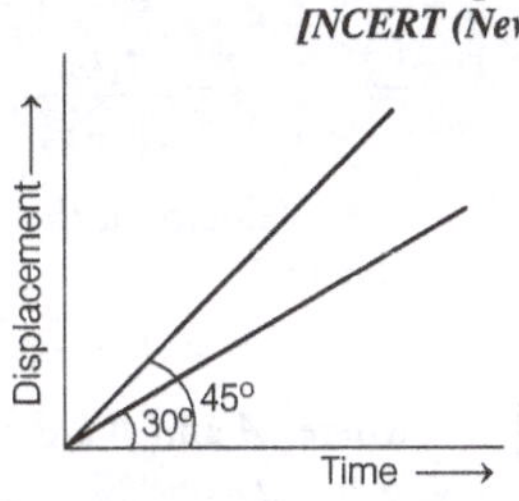

(a) 1 : 1 (b) 1 : 2 (c) $1:\sqrt{3}$ (d) $\sqrt{3}:1$

03 A particle shows distance-time curve as given in this figure. The maximum instantaneous velocity of the particle is around the point ***[NCERT (New) Pg. 14, AIPMT 2008]***

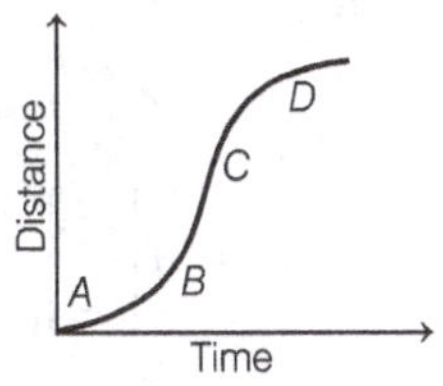

(a) B (b) C
(c) D (d) A

04 The displacement-time graph of moving particle is shown below.

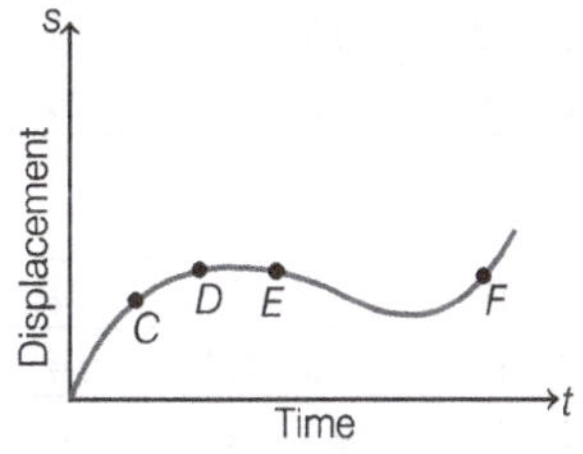

The instantaneous velocity of the particle is negative at the point ***[NCERT (New) Pg. 14, AIPMT 1994]***

(a) D (b) F
(c) C (d) E

05 Which of the following curves does not represent motion in one dimension? ***[AIPMT 1992]***

(a) 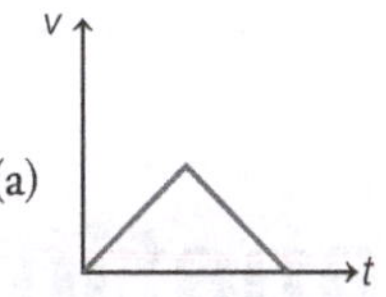
(b) 
(c) 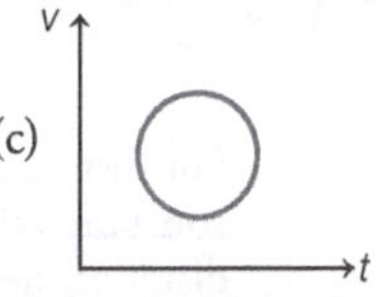
(d) 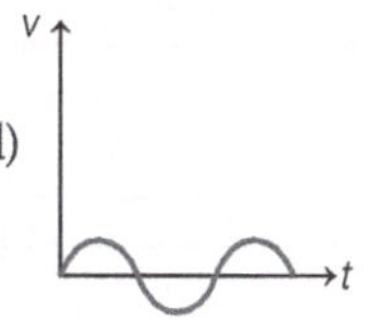

Topic 4 Relative Motion in One Dimension

01 A bus is moving with a speed of 10 ms^{-1} on a straight road. A scooterist wishes to overtake the bus in 100 s. If the bus is at a distance of 1 km from the scooterist, with what speed should the scooterist chase the bus? ***[NCERT (Old) Pg. 51, AIPMT 2009]***

(a) 20 ms^{-1} (b) 40 ms^{-1}
(c) 25 ms^{-1} (d) 10 ms^{-1}

02 A train of 150 m length is going towards North direction at a speed of 10 m/s. A parrot flies at the speed of 5 m/s towards South direction parallel to the railways track. The time taken by the parrot to cross the train is ***[NCERT (Old) Pg. 51, AIPMT 1992]***

(a) 12 s (b) 8 s
(c) 15 s (d) 10 s

• Key **Index**

Topic 1

1 (b)	2 (b)	3 (c)	4 (b)	5 (d)	6 (b)	7 (b)	8 (d)	9 (c)	10 (c)
11 (a)	12 (d)	13 (a)	14 (b)	15 (c)	16 (c)	17 (d)	18 (b)	19 (b)	20 (c)
21 (d)	22 (d)	23 (c)	24 (b)	25 (b)					

Topic 2

1 (d)	2 (b)	3 (b)	4 (d)	5 (b)	6 (b)	7 (c)	8 (d)	9 (b)	10 (b)
11 (a)	12 (a)	13 (c)	14 (d)	15 (c)	16 (d)	17 (c)	18 (d)	19 (b)	20 (c)
21 (b)	22 (a)	23 (c)	24 (c)	25 (b)	26 (c)	27 (a)	28 (a)	29 (b)	30 (b)
31 (c)									

Topic 3

1 (c)	2 (c)	3 (b)	4 (d)	5 (c)

Topic 4

1 (a)	2 (d)

Detailed **Explanations**

01. *(b)*

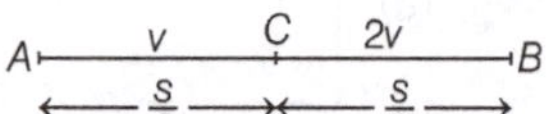

Time taken by vehicle to cover first half,

$$t_1 = \frac{s/2}{v} = \frac{s}{2v}$$

Time taken by vehicle to cover second half,

$$t_2 = \frac{s/2}{2v} = \frac{s}{4v}$$

∴ Average speed,

$$v_{avg} = \frac{\text{total distance covered}}{\text{total time taken}}$$

$$= \frac{\frac{s}{2} + \frac{s}{2}}{t_1 + t_2} = \frac{s}{\frac{s}{2v} + \frac{s}{4v}} = \frac{4v}{3}$$

02. *(b)*

key idea

To find average velocity, identify time intervals in which velocities are covered accordingly. Divide the discrete section of distances (s_1, s_2, s_3 ....) w.r.t corresponding (v_1, v_2, v_3 .....) velocity.
Average velocity,

$$v_{avg} = \frac{\text{Total distance (s)}}{\frac{s_1}{v_1} + \frac{s_2}{v_2} + \frac{s_3}{v_3} .....}$$

For distance x, the person moves with constant velocity v_1 and for another x distance, he moves with constant velocity of v_2, then

Total distance travelled,

$$d = x + x = 2x$$

Total time-taken,

$$t = t_1 + t_2$$

$$= \frac{x}{v_1} + \frac{x}{v_2} \quad \left[\because t = \frac{\text{Distance}}{\text{Velocity}}\right]$$

The average velocity,

$$v_{avg} = \frac{\text{total distance}}{\text{total time}} = \frac{d}{t}$$

$$v = \frac{2x}{\frac{x}{v_1} + \frac{x}{v_2}} = \frac{2}{\frac{1}{v_1} + \frac{1}{v_2}} \quad [\because v_{avg} = v]$$

$$\Rightarrow \frac{1}{v_1} + \frac{1}{v_2} = \frac{2}{v}$$

03. *(c)* Speed of walking $= \frac{h}{t_1} = v_1$

Speed of escalator $= \frac{h}{t_2} = v_2$

Time taken when she walks over running escalator,

$$t = \frac{h}{v_1 + v_2}$$

$$\Rightarrow \frac{1}{t} = \frac{v_1}{h} + \frac{v_2}{h} = \frac{1}{t_1} + \frac{1}{t_2}$$

$$\Rightarrow t = \frac{t_1 t_2}{t_1 + t_2}$$

04. *(b)* Velocity of the particle is given as

$$v = At + Bt^2$$

where, A and B are constants.

$$\Rightarrow \frac{dx}{dt} = At + Bt^2 \quad \left[\because v = \frac{dx}{dt}\right]$$

$$\Rightarrow dx = (At + Bt^2)\, dt$$

Integrating both sides, we get

$$\int_{x_1}^{x_2} dx = \int_1^2 (At + Bt^2)\, dt$$

$$= A\int_1^2 t\, dt + B\int_1^2 t^2 dt$$

$$= A\left[\frac{t^2}{2}\right]_1^2 + B\left[\frac{t^3}{3}\right]_1^2$$

$$= \frac{A}{2}(2^2 - 1^2) + \frac{B}{3}(2^3 - 1^3)$$

∴ Distance travelled between 1s and 2s is

$$\Delta x = \frac{A}{2} \times (3) + \frac{B}{3}(7) = \frac{3A}{2} + \frac{7B}{3}$$

05. *(d)* Velocity of each car is given by

$$v_P = \frac{dx_p(t)}{dt} = a + 2bt$$

and $v_Q = \dfrac{dx_Q(t)}{dt} = f - 2t$

It is given that $v_P = v_Q$

$\Rightarrow \quad a + 2bt = f - 2t$

$\Rightarrow \quad t = \dfrac{f-a}{2(b+1)}$

06. *(b)* Given, $v = \beta x^{-2n}$

$$a = \frac{dv}{dt} = \frac{dx}{dt}\cdot\frac{dv}{dx}$$

$\Rightarrow \quad a = v\dfrac{dv}{dx} = (\beta x^{-2n})(-2n\beta x^{-2n-1})$

$\Rightarrow \quad a = -2n\beta^2 x^{-4n-1}$

07. *(b)* Given, $t = \sqrt{x} + 3$

or $\quad \sqrt{x} = t - 3$

Squaring both sides, we get

$$x = (t-3)^2$$

Velocity, $v = \dfrac{dx}{dt} = \dfrac{d}{dt}(t-3)^2 = 2(t-3)$

The displacement of the particle when velocity is zero can be found, by finding the value of t at $v = 0$.

i.e., $2(t-3) = 0 \Rightarrow t = 3$ s

Thus, displacement, $x = (t-3)^2$

$$x = (3-3)^2 \quad (\because t = 3 \text{ at } v = 0)$$

$\Rightarrow \quad x = 0$ m

08. *(d)* Given, $x = 8 + 12t - t^3$

We know, $v = \dfrac{dx}{dt} = 12 - 3t^2$

and acceleration, $a = \dfrac{dv}{dt} = -6t$

At $t = 2$ s

$v = 0$ and $a = -6 \times 2$

$a = -12$ m/s^2

So, retardation of the particle $= 12$ m/s^2

• **Concept Enhancer**

If time dependent displacement equation is given, then double differentiation of displacement with respect to time gives acceleration and single differentiation with respect to time gives velocity of the body.

09. *(c)* Let s be the total distance and t_1 and t_2 be the time taken for first half and second half distance.

$\Rightarrow t_1 = \dfrac{s}{2v_1}$ and $t_2 = \dfrac{s}{2v_2}$

Average speed, $v_{avg} = \dfrac{\text{Total distance}}{\text{Total time}}$

$$= \frac{s}{t_1 + t_2} = \frac{s}{\dfrac{s}{2v_1} + \dfrac{s}{2v_2}} = \frac{2v_1v_2}{v_1 + v_2}$$

10. *(c)* Given,

$v_i = 30\hat{\mathbf{i}}$

and $v_f = 40\hat{\mathbf{j}}$

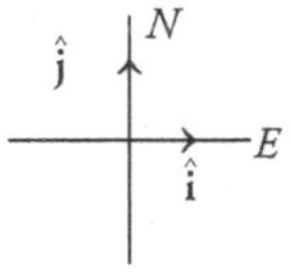

Average acceleration,

$$a = \frac{\text{Change in velocity}}{\text{Total time}}$$

$$a = \frac{|\mathbf{v}_f - \mathbf{v}_i|}{\Delta t} = \frac{|40\hat{\mathbf{j}} - 30\hat{\mathbf{i}}|}{10}$$

$$= \frac{\sqrt{30^2 + 40^2}}{10}$$

$$= \frac{\sqrt{900 + 1600}}{10} = 5 \text{ ms}^{-2}$$

11. *(a)* Given, distance

$$x = (t+5)^{-1} \quad \ldots\text{(i)}$$

Differentiating Eq. (i) w.r.t. t, we get

$$\frac{dx}{dt} = (v) = \frac{-1}{(t+5)^2} \quad \ldots\text{(ii)}$$

Again, differentiating Eq. (ii) w.r.t. t, we get

$$\frac{d^2x}{dt^2} = a = \frac{2}{(t+5)^3} \quad \ldots\text{(iii)}$$

Comparing Eqs. (ii) and (iii), we get

$$a \propto (v)^{3/2}$$

12. *(d)* Acceleration,

$$f = f_0\left(1 - \frac{t}{T}\right)$$

or $\quad f = \dfrac{dv}{dt} = f_0\left(1 - \dfrac{t}{T}\right) \quad \left[\because f = \dfrac{dv}{dt}\right]$

or $\quad dv = f_0\left(1 - \dfrac{t}{T}\right)dt \quad \ldots\text{(i)}$

Integrating Eq. (i) on both sides,

$$\int dv = \int f_0\left(1 - \frac{t}{T}\right)dt$$

$\therefore \quad v = f_0 t - \dfrac{f_0}{T}\cdot\dfrac{t^2}{2} + c \quad \ldots\text{(ii)}$

where, c is constant of integration.

Now, when $t = 0$, $v = 0$.

So, from Eq. (ii), we get $c = 0$

$\therefore \quad v = f_0 t - \dfrac{f_0}{T}\cdot\dfrac{t^2}{2} \quad \ldots\text{(iii)}$

As, $\quad f = f_0\left(1 - \dfrac{t}{T}\right)$

When, $f = 0$,

$$0 = f_0\left(1 - \frac{t}{T}\right)$$

As, $\quad f_0 \neq 0$, so, $1 - \dfrac{t}{T} = 0$

$\therefore \quad t = T$

Substituting, $t = T$ in Eq. (iii), we get

$$v_x = f_0T - \frac{f_0}{T}\cdot\frac{T^2}{2}$$

$$= f_0T - \frac{f_0T}{2} = \frac{1}{2}f_0T$$

13. *(a)* Average speed

$$= \frac{\text{Total distance travelled}}{\text{Time taken}}$$

Let t_1 and t_2 be times taken by the car to go from X to Y and then from Y to X respectively.

Then, $t_1 + t_2 = \dfrac{XY}{v_u} + \dfrac{XY}{v_d}$

$$= XY\left(\frac{v_u + v_d}{v_uv_d}\right)$$

Total distance travelled

$$= XY + XY = 2\,XY$$

Therefore, average speed of the car for this round trip is

$$v_{avg} = \frac{2\,XY}{XY\left(\dfrac{v_u + v_d}{v_uv_d}\right)}$$

or $\quad v_{avg} = \dfrac{2\,v_uv_d}{v_u + v_d}$

14. *(b)* Given, the position x of a particle w.r.t. time t along X-axis

$$x = 9t^2 - t^3 \quad \ldots\text{(i)}$$

Differentiating Eq. (i), w.r.t. time, we get speed, i.e.

$$v = \frac{dx}{dt} = \frac{d}{dt}(9t^2 - t^3)$$

or $\quad v = 18t - 3t^2 \quad \ldots\text{(ii)}$

Again differentiating Eq. (ii), with respect to time, we get acceleration, i.e.

$$a = \frac{dv}{dt} = \frac{d}{dt}(18t - 3t^2)$$

or $\quad a = 18 - 6t \quad \ldots\text{(iii)}$

Now, when speed of particle is maximum, its acceleration becomes zero, i.e.

$$a = 0$$

i.e., $18 - 6t = 0$ or $t = 3$ s

Putting in Eq. (i), we obtain position of particle at that time

$$x = 9(3)^2 - (3)^3 = 9(9) - 27$$

$$= 81 - 27 = 54 \text{ m}$$

15. *(c)* Distance travelled by the particle is

$$x = 40 + 12t - t^3$$

We know that, velocity is the rate of change of distance i.e. $v = \frac{dx}{dt}$.

$$\therefore \quad v = \frac{d}{dt}(40 + 12t - t^3)$$

$$= 0 + 12 - 3t^2$$

but final velocity, $v = 0$

$$\therefore \quad 12 - 3t^2 = 0$$

or $$t^2 = \frac{12}{3} = 4$$

or $$t = 2\text{ s}$$

Hence, distance travelled by the particle before coming to rest is given by

$$x = 40 + 12(2) - (2)^3$$
$$= 40 + 24 - 8$$
$$= 64 - 8 = 56\text{ m}$$

• Concept Enhancer

First differentiating x (displacement equation), we get velocity of the body, since body comes to rest so velocity becomes zero. Now, by putting the value of time t in displacement equation, we get the distance travelled by the body when it comes to rest.

16. *(c)* Given, radius, $r = 100$ m

Time taken for one circular lap,

$$t = 62.8\text{ s}$$

Distance travelled in one lap, $d = 2\pi r$

$$\therefore \text{ Average speed} = \frac{\text{Distance}}{\text{Time}} = \frac{2\pi r}{t}$$

$$= 2 \times \frac{22}{7} \times \frac{100}{62.8} = 10\text{ ms}^{-1}$$

Since, after every circular lap, the car comes back to starting point. Therefore, displacement, $d = 0$

$$\therefore \text{ Average velocity} = \frac{\text{Displacement}}{\text{Time}} = 0$$

17. *(d)* Given, $x = ae^{-\alpha t} + be^{\beta t}$

Velocity, $v = \frac{dx}{dt} = -a\alpha e^{-\alpha t} + b\beta e^{\beta t}$

$\therefore \quad \frac{dv}{dt} = a\alpha^2 e^{-\alpha t} + b\beta^2 e^{\beta t}$ is always > 0

$\therefore$ v is increasing function of t.

As a result, velocity goes on increasing with time.

18. *(b)* The displacement of a particle along a straight line is

$$s = 3t^3 + 7t^2 + 14t + 5$$

$$v = \frac{ds}{dt} = \frac{d}{dt}(3t^3 + 7t^2 + 14t + 5)$$

$$= \frac{d}{dt}(3t^3) + \frac{d}{dt}(7t^2) + \frac{d}{dt}(14t) + \frac{d}{dt}(5)$$

$$v = 3\frac{d}{dt}(t^3) + 7\frac{d}{dt}(t^2) + 14\frac{d}{dt}(t) + 0$$

(as differentiation of a constant is zero)

Now use $\frac{d}{dt}(x^n) = nx^{n-1}$

So, $v = 3(3)t^{3-1} + 7(2)(t^{2-1}) + 14(t^{1-1})$

$$\Rightarrow \quad v = 9t^2 + 14t + 14 \qquad (\because t^0 = 1)$$

$$a = \frac{dv}{dt} = \frac{d}{dt}(9t^2 + 14t + 14)$$

$$= 18t + 14 + 0 = 18t + 14$$

At $t = 1$ s,

$$a = 18(1) + 14 = 18 + 14 = 32\text{ m/s}^2$$

19. *(b)* Acceleration,

$$a = \frac{dv}{dt} = \frac{d^2x}{dt^2},$$

Velocity, $v = \frac{dx}{dt}$.

The given equation is

$$x = at^2 - bt^3$$

Velocity, $v = \frac{dx}{dt} = 2at - 3bt^2$

Acceleration, $a = \frac{dv}{dt} = 2a - 6bt$

but $\quad a = 0 \qquad$ (given)

$\therefore \quad 2a - 6bt = 0$

or $\quad 6bt = 2a$

or $\quad t = \frac{2a}{6b} = \frac{a}{3b}$

20. *(c)* According to question, acceleration $\propto bt$

i.e., $$\frac{d^2x}{dt^2} \propto bt \qquad \text{...(i)}$$

Integrating both sides, we get

$$\int \frac{d^2x}{dt^2} = \int bt$$

$$\Rightarrow \quad \frac{dx}{dt} = \frac{bt^2}{2} + C \qquad \text{...(ii)}$$

Since, the body starts from origin at initial velocity v_0

We have, $t = 0$, $v = \frac{dx}{dt} = v_0$

$\Rightarrow \quad v_0 = C$

Thus Eq. (ii) becomes,

$$\frac{dx}{dt} = \frac{bt^2}{2} + v_0$$

$$dx = \frac{bt^2}{2}dt + v_0 dt$$

Integrating both sides, we get

$$\int dx = \int \frac{bt^2}{2}dt + \int v_0 dt$$

$$x = \frac{bt^3}{6} + v_0 t + c$$

At $t = 0$, $x = 0$

Therefore, $c = 0$

$$\Rightarrow \quad x = \frac{bt^3}{6} + v_0 t$$

21. *(d)* This situation is plotted on v-t graph. In v-t graph, OA represents the accelerated part and AB represents the decelerated part.

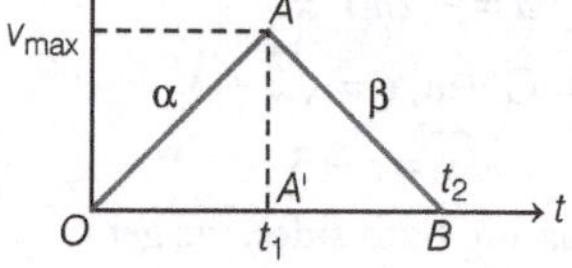

Let t_1 and t_2 be the times for part OA and AB, respectively.

At point A, velocity is maximum and let it be v_{max}.

$\therefore \quad v_{max} = \alpha t_1 = \beta t_2$

But $\quad t = t_1 + t_2 = \frac{v_{max}}{\alpha} + \frac{v_{max}}{\beta}$

$$= v_{max}\left(\frac{1}{\alpha} + \frac{1}{\beta}\right)$$

$$= v_{max}\left(\frac{\alpha + \beta}{\alpha\beta}\right)$$

or $$v_{max} = t\left(\frac{\alpha\beta}{\alpha + \beta}\right)$$

Alternate Solution

This problem can also be solved by checking the dimensions on both sides. On checking the dimensions, we note that the dimensions of option (d) match with that of velocity.

22. *(d)* Given, $s = t^3 - 6t^2 + 3t + 4$

$\therefore$ Velocity, $v = \frac{ds}{dt} = 3t^2 - 12t + 3$ ...(i)

Acceleration a is given by

$$a = \frac{dv}{dt}$$

$$\therefore \quad a = 6t - 12 \qquad \text{...(ii)}$$

For $a = 0$, we have $0 = 6t - 12$

or $\quad t = 2$ s

Hence, at $t = 2$ s the velocity will be

$$v = 3 \times 2^2 - 12 \times 2 + 3$$
$$= -9\text{ ms}^{-1}$$

23. *(c)*

key idea

Average speed can be calculated as the total distance travelled divided by the total time taken.

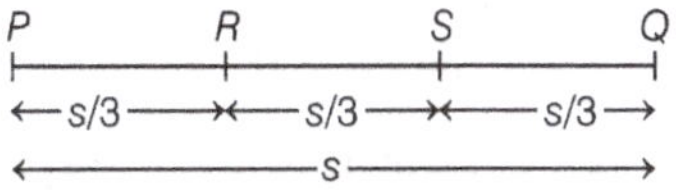

Average speed, $v_{avg} = \dfrac{s}{\text{Total time}}$

Let s be the total distance and t_1, t_2, t_3 be times taken in covering distances 1st one-third, 2nd one-third and remaining one-third respectively.

$\therefore \quad t_1 = \dfrac{(s/3)}{10}, t_2 = \dfrac{(s/3)}{20}$ and $t_3 = \dfrac{(s/3)}{60}$

$\therefore$ Average speed

$$= \frac{\text{Total distance}}{\text{Total time}}$$

$$= \frac{s}{t_1 + t_2 + t_3}$$

$$= \frac{s}{\dfrac{(s/3)}{10} + \dfrac{(s/3)}{20} + \dfrac{(s/3)}{60}}$$

$$= \frac{s}{(s/18)} = 18 \text{ km/h}$$

24. *(b)* Average speed $= \dfrac{\text{Total distance}}{\text{Total time}}$

Let t_1, t_2 be time taken during first-half and second-half respectively.

So, $t_1 = \dfrac{0.1\text{h}}{40}$ and $t_2 = \dfrac{0.1}{v}$

So, according to average speed formula

$$48 = \frac{0.2}{\dfrac{0.1}{40} + \dfrac{0.1}{v}} = \frac{0.2}{\dfrac{1}{400} + \dfrac{1}{10v}}$$

$$\Rightarrow 48 = \frac{80v}{v + 40} \Rightarrow v = 60 \text{ km/h}$$

25. *(b)* Time taken by car to travel first-half length,

$$t_1 = \frac{\left(\dfrac{d}{2}\right)}{40} = \frac{d}{80}$$

Time taken by car to travel second-half length,

$$t_2 = \frac{\left(\dfrac{d}{2}\right)}{60} = \frac{d}{120}$$

$\therefore$ Total time $= t_1 + t_2 = \dfrac{d}{80} + \dfrac{d}{120}$

$$= d\left(\frac{1}{80} + \frac{1}{120}\right) = \frac{d}{48}$$

$\therefore$ Average speed $= \dfrac{d}{t_1 + t_2} = \dfrac{d}{\left(\dfrac{d}{48}\right)}$

$$= 48 \text{ km/h}$$

Alternate Solution

$$v_{avg} = \frac{2v_1v_2}{v_1 + v_2} = \frac{2 \times 40 \times 60}{40 + 60} = 48 \text{ km/h}$$

Topic 2

01. *(d)* The given situation is shown below.

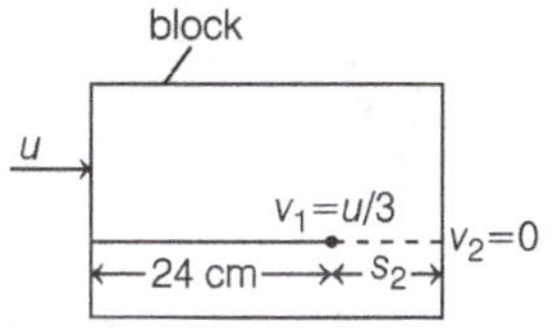

$$s_1 = 24 \text{ cm}$$

Using, $v^2 = u^2 - 2as$

$$\Rightarrow \quad v_1^2 = u^2 - 2as_1$$

$$\Rightarrow \quad \left(\frac{u}{3}\right)^2 = u^2 - 2a \times 0.24$$

$$\Rightarrow \quad 0.48a = \frac{8}{9}u^2$$

$$\Rightarrow \quad a = \frac{8u^2}{9 \times 0.48} = \frac{u^2}{0.54}$$

According to second condition,

$$0 = v_1^2 - 2as_2$$

$$\Rightarrow \quad 0 = \left(\frac{u}{3}\right)^2 - 2 \times \frac{u^2}{0.54} \times s_2$$

$$\Rightarrow \quad \frac{u^2}{9} = \frac{2u^2}{0.54}s_2$$

$$\Rightarrow \quad s_2 = \frac{0.54}{9 \times 2} = 0.03 \text{ m} = 3 \text{ cm}$$

$\therefore$ Total length of the block $= s_1 + s_2$
$= 24 + 3 = 27$ cm

02. *(b)* Maximum height attain by the ball, $h' = \dfrac{v^2}{2g} = \dfrac{4^2}{2 \times 10} = 0.8$ m

Time of flight from bridge to bridge

$$t_1 = \frac{2v}{g} = \frac{2 \times 4}{10} = 0.8 \text{ s}$$

Total time of flight is given as 4 s. Time taken by the ball to reach at the surface of water from highest point,

$$t_2 = 4 - \frac{t_1}{2} = 4 - \frac{0.8}{2} = 3.6 \text{ s}$$

$$\therefore \quad h = 0 \times t_2 + \frac{1}{2}gt_2^2$$

$$h = \frac{1}{2} \times 10 \times (3.6)^2 = 64.8 \text{ m}$$

$\therefore$ Now, height of bridge above water surface

$$H = h - h'$$
$$= 64.8 - 0.8 = 64 \text{ m}$$

03. *(b)*

key idea

You can use the equation of motion for tth second for a freely falling body, which given by

$s_t = u + \dfrac{1}{2}g(2t - 1)$.

Distance travelled by freely falling body in nth second

$$s_n = u + \frac{1}{2}g(2n - 1)$$

$$= 0 + \frac{1}{2}g(2n - 1)$$

$$s_n = \frac{1}{2}g(2n - 1)$$

Distance travelled by body in first second $(n = 1 \text{ s})$

$$s_1 = \frac{1}{2}g(2 \times 1 - 1) = \frac{g}{2}$$

Distance travelled by body in 2nd second $(n = 2 \text{ s})$

$$s_2 = \frac{1}{2}g(2 \times 2 - 1) = \frac{3g}{2}$$

Distance travelled by body in 3rd second $(n = 3 \text{ s})$

$$s_3 = \frac{1}{2}g\,(2 \times 3 - 1) = \frac{5g}{2}$$

Distance travelled by body in 4th second $(n = 4 \text{ s})$

$$s_4 = \frac{1}{2}g(2 \times 4 - 1) = \frac{7g}{2}$$

$$\therefore \; s_1 : s_2 : s_3 : s_4 = \frac{g}{2} : \frac{3g}{2} : \frac{5g}{2} : \frac{7g}{2}$$
$$= 1 : 3 : 5 : 7$$

04. *(d)* Given,

The acceleration of a car, $a = 5 \text{ m/s}^2$

At $\quad t = 4$ s, $v = u + at$

$\Rightarrow \quad v = 0 + (5)4 \Rightarrow v = 20$ m/s

At $t = 4$ s, the ball is dropped out of a window by a person sitting in the car. The velocity of the ball in the x-direction,

$v_x = 20$ m/s (due to the car)

Therefore, in the y-direction,

$a_y = g = 10 \text{ m/s}^2$

$\therefore \quad v_y = u + a_y t \Rightarrow v_y = 0 + 10 \times 2$

$\Rightarrow \quad v_y = 20$ m/s

The net velocity at t = 6s,

$$v = \sqrt{v_x^2 + v_y^2}$$

$$\Rightarrow \quad v = \sqrt{(20)^2 + (20)^2}$$

$$\Rightarrow \quad v = 20\sqrt{2} \text{ m/s}$$

Thus, the velocity of the ball at t = 6 s is $20\sqrt{2}$ m/s.

and there is no acceleration in the x-direction, $\quad a_x = 0 \text{ ms}^{-2}$

In y-direction, $a_y = 10 \text{ ms}^{-2}$

Now, we shall determine the net acceleration at t = 6 s, $a = \sqrt{a_x^2 + a_y^2}$

$$\Rightarrow \quad a = \sqrt{(0) + (10)^2} = 10 \text{ ms}^{-2}$$

05. *(b)*

key idea

You can find distance travelled by the block for the n th second using following formula :

$$s_n = u + \frac{a}{2}(2n - 1)$$

where, u is the initial velocity and a is the acceleration.

Distance covered in nth seconds,

$$s_n = u + \frac{a}{2}(2n - 1)$$

$$\Rightarrow \quad s_n = 0 + \frac{a}{2}(2n - 1)$$

$$\Rightarrow \quad s_n = \frac{a}{2}(2n - 1) \qquad \text{...(i)}$$

Distance cover in $(n+1)$th seconds,

$$s_{n+1} = u + \frac{a}{2}[2(n+1) - 1]$$

$$\Rightarrow s_{n+1} = 0 + \frac{a}{2}(2n + 2 - 1)$$

$$\Rightarrow s_{n+1} = \frac{a}{2}(2n + 1) \qquad \text{...(ii)}$$

On dividing Eq. (i) by Eq. (ii), we get

$$\frac{s_n}{s_{n+1}} = \frac{\frac{a}{2}(2n-1)}{\frac{a}{2}(2n+1)} = \frac{(2n-1)}{(2n+1)}$$

06. *(b)* According to question, time taken by the ball to cross the window,

t = 0.1s and h = 1.5 m

If u be the velocity at the top most point of the window, $h = ut + \frac{1}{2}gt^2$

$$\Rightarrow \quad 1.5 = u \times 0.1 + \frac{1}{2} \times 10 \times (0.1)^2$$

$$= 14.5 \text{ m/s}$$

07. *(c)* Given, u = 20 m/s, v = 80 m/s and h = ?

From kinematic equation of motion,

$$v^2 = u^2 + 2gh$$

$$\Rightarrow \quad h = \frac{v^2 - u^2}{2g} = \frac{(80)^2 - (20)^2}{2 \times 10}$$

$$(\because \text{ given, } g = 10 \text{ m/s}^2)$$

$$= 300 \text{ m}$$

08. *(d)* Let h be the height through which the coin is dropped. Then, according to the equation of motion,

$$h = ut + \frac{1}{2}gt^2$$

$$\Rightarrow \quad t = \sqrt{\frac{2h}{g}} \qquad [\because u = 0]$$

$$\Rightarrow \quad t \propto \frac{1}{\sqrt{g}}$$

As the elevator is moving uniformly i.e. its velocity is constant, so the acceleration is zero.

$\therefore$ Relative acceleration of the lift when it is either moving upward or downward is given as, $g' = g \pm a = g \pm 0 = g$

Hence, the time for the coin to reach the floor will remain same i.e. $t_1 = t_2$.

09. *(b)* According to the question,

For the time duration $0 < t < 1$s, the velocity increases from 0 to 6 ms^{-1}

As the direction of field has been reversed for, $1 < t < 2$s : the velocity firstly decreases from 6 ms^{-1} to 0.

Then, for $2 < t < 3$s; as the field strength is same; the magnitude of acceleration would be same, but velocity increases from 0 to − 6 ms^{-1}.

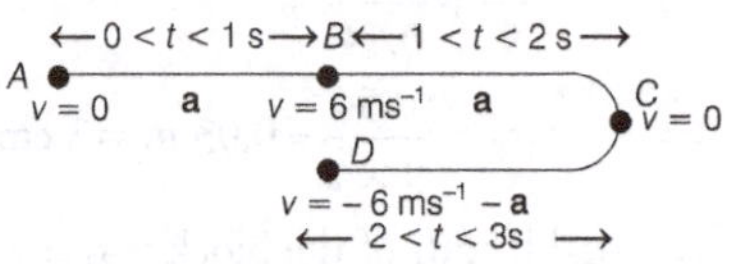

Acceleration of the car

$$|a| = \left|\frac{v - u}{t}\right| = \frac{6 - 0}{1} = 6 \text{ ms}^{-2}$$

The displacement of the particle is given as

$$s = ut + \frac{1}{2}at^2$$

For $t = 0$ to $t = 1$s,

$$u = 0, a = +6 \text{ m/s}^2$$

$$\Rightarrow \quad s_1 = 0 + \frac{1}{2} \times 6 \times (1)^2 = 3 \text{ m}$$

For $t = 1$s to $t = 2$s,

$$u = 6 \text{ ms}^{-1}, a = -6 \text{ ms}^{-2}$$

$$\Rightarrow \quad s_2 = 6 \times 1 - \frac{1}{2} \times 6 \times (1)^2$$

$$= 6 - 3 = 3 \text{ m}$$

For $t = 2$s to $t = 3$s,

$$u = 0, a = -6 \text{ ms}^{-2}$$

$$\Rightarrow \quad s_3 = 0 - \frac{1}{2} \times 6 \times (1)^2 = -3 \text{ m}$$

$\therefore$ Net displacement, $s = s_1 + s_2 + s_3$

$$= 3 \text{ m} + 3 \text{ m} - 3 \text{ m} = 3 \text{ m}$$

Hence, average velocity

$$= \frac{\text{Net displacement}}{\text{Total time}}$$

$$= \frac{3}{3} = 1 \text{ m s}^{-1}$$

Total distance travelled, d = 9 m

$$\text{Hence, average speed} = \frac{\text{Total distance}}{\text{Total time}}$$

$$= \frac{9}{3} = 3 \text{ m s}^{-1}$$

Alternate Solution

Given condition can be represented through graph also as shown below.

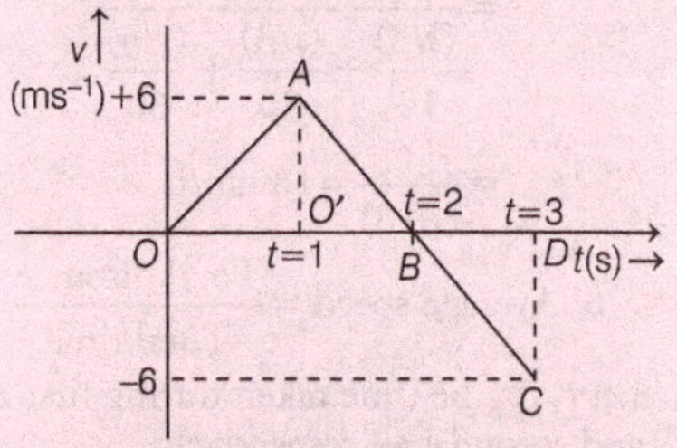

$\therefore$ Displacement in three seconds

= Area under the graph

= Area of $\Delta OAO'$ + Area of $\Delta AO'B$ − Area of ΔBCD

$$= \frac{1}{2} \times 1 \times 6 + \frac{1}{2} \times 1 \times 6 - \frac{1}{2} \times 6 \times 1 = 3 \text{ m}$$

$\therefore$ Average velocity $= \frac{3}{3} = 1 \text{ ms}^{-1}$.

Total distance travelled, d = 9 m

$\therefore$ Average speed $= \frac{9}{3} = 3 \text{ ms}^{-1}$

10. *(b)* For free fall from a height, $u = 0$

$\therefore$ Distance covered by stone in first 5 s,

$$h_1 = 0 + \frac{1}{2}g(5)^2 = \frac{25}{2}g \qquad \text{...(i)}$$

$\therefore$ Distance covered in first 10 s,

$$s_2 = 0 + \frac{1}{2}g(10)^2 = \frac{100}{2}g$$

$\therefore$ Distance covered in second 5 s

$$h_2 = s_2 - h_1$$

$$= \frac{100}{2}g - \frac{25}{2}g = \frac{75}{2}g \qquad \text{...(ii)}$$

Distance covered in first 15 s,

$$s_3 = 0 + \frac{1}{2} g (15)^2$$

$$= \frac{225}{2} g$$

$\therefore$ Distance covered in last 5 s,

$$h_3 = s_3 - s_2 = \frac{225}{2} g - \frac{100}{2} g$$

$$= \frac{125}{2} g \quad \text{...(iii)}$$

From Eqs. (i), (ii) and (iii), we get

$$h_1 : h_2 : h_3 = \frac{25}{2} g : \frac{75}{2} g : \frac{125}{2} g$$

$$= 1 : 3 : 5$$

$$\Rightarrow \quad h_1 = \frac{h_2}{3} = \frac{h_3}{5}$$

11. *(a)* Given, $g = 10 \text{ m/s}^2$

and $h = 20$ m

We have $v = \sqrt{2gh} = \sqrt{2 \times 10 \times 20}$

$$= \sqrt{400}$$

$$= 20 \text{ m/s}$$

12. *(a)* For first ball, $u = 0$

$$\therefore \quad s_1 = \frac{1}{2} g t_1^2 = \frac{1}{2} \times g (18)^2$$

For second ball, initial velocity $= v$

$$\therefore \quad s_2 = v t_2 + \frac{1}{2} g t_2^2$$

$$t_2 = 18 - 6 = 12 \text{ s}$$

$$\Rightarrow \quad s_2 = v \times 12 + \frac{1}{2} g (12)^2$$

Here, $s_1 = s_2$

$$\frac{1}{2} g (18)^2 = 12v + \frac{1}{2} g (12)^2$$

On solving, we get

$$\Rightarrow \quad v = 75 \text{ ms}^{-1}$$

13. *(c)* Since, the body starts from rest

$$u = 0$$

$$\therefore \quad s = \frac{1}{2} a t^2$$

Now, $s_1 = \frac{1}{2} a (10)^2 \quad \text{...(i)}$

and $s_2 = \frac{1}{2} a (20)^2 \quad \text{...(ii)}$

Dividing Eq. (i) and Eq. (ii), we get

$$\frac{s_1}{s_2} = \frac{(10)^2}{(20)^2} = s_2 = 4 s_1$$

14. *(d)* Using $v^2 - u^2 = 2as$

$$(20)^2 - (10)^2 = 2 \times a \times 135$$

$$\Rightarrow \quad a = \frac{300}{270} = \frac{10}{9}$$

Now, using $v - u = at$

$$20 - 10 = \frac{10}{9} \times t$$

$$\Rightarrow \quad t = 9 \text{ s}$$

15. *(c)* Distance travelled in nth second is given by

$$s_n = u + \frac{1}{2} a (2n - 1)$$

Here, $u = 0$, $a = \frac{4}{3}$

$$\therefore \quad s_3 = 0 + \frac{1}{2} \times \frac{4}{3} \times (6 - 1) = \frac{10}{3} \text{ m}$$

16. *(d)* From second equation of motion

$$h = ut + \frac{1}{2} g t^2$$

or $h = 0 + \frac{1}{2} g t^2$

$$\therefore \quad \frac{h_1}{h_2} = \left(\frac{t_1}{t_2}\right)^2$$

Given, $h_1 = 16$ m, $h_2 = 25$ m

$$\therefore \quad \frac{t_1}{t_2} = \sqrt{\frac{h_1}{h_2}}$$

$$= \sqrt{\frac{16}{25}} = \frac{4}{5}$$

17. *(c)* At maximum height, final speed is zero i.e, $v = 0$

So, $u = gt$ or $t = \frac{u}{g}$

In 2 s, $u = 2 \times 9.8 = 19.6$ m/s

If man throws the ball with velocity of 19.6 m/s, then after 2 s, it will reach the maximum height. When he throws 2nd ball, 1st is at top. When he throws third ball, 1st will come to ground and 2nd will be at the top.

Therefore, only 2 balls are in air. If he wants to keep more than 2 balls in air, he should throw the ball with a speed greater than 19.6 m/s.

18. *(d)* Let the ball takes T second to reach maximum height H.

$$v = u - gT$$

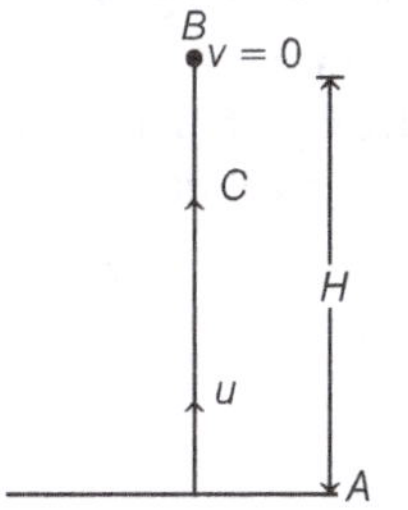

put $v = 0$ (at height H)

$$\therefore \quad u = gT \text{ or } T = \frac{u}{g} \quad \text{...(i)}$$

Velocity attained by the ball in $(T - t)$ s is,

$$v' = u - g(T - t) = u - gT + gt$$

$$= u - g\frac{u}{g} + gt = u - u + gt$$

$$v' = gt \quad \text{...(ii)}$$

Hence, distance travelled in last t sec of its ascent

$$CB = v't - \frac{1}{2} g t^2 = (gt)t - \frac{1}{2} g t^2$$

$$= g t^2 - \frac{1}{2} g t^2 \quad \text{[From Eq. (ii)]}$$

$$= \frac{1}{2} g t^2$$

19. *(b)* Let u be the initial velocity and H be the maximum height attained.

At height $h = \frac{H}{2}$, we have

$$v = v_1 = 10 \text{ m/s}$$

From third equation of motion,

$$v_1^2 = u^2 - 2gh$$

(Negative sign indicates that velocity and acceleration are in opposite direction)

or $(10)^2 = u^2 - 2g\frac{H}{2} \quad \text{...(i)}$

At height H,

$$v_2 = 0$$

$$v_2^2 = u^2 - 2gH$$

or $0 = u^2 - 2gH \quad \text{...(ii)}$

Subtract Eq. (ii) from Eq. (i), we get

$$(10)^2 = 2g\frac{H}{2}$$

or $H = \frac{(10)^2}{g}$

or $H = \frac{(10)^2}{10} = 10$ m

Alternate Solution

Maximum height attained by the stone,

$$H = \frac{u^2}{2g}$$

When, $H = \frac{H}{2}, u = 10 \text{ m/s}$

$$\frac{H}{2} = \frac{(10)^2}{2g} \quad \text{or } H = \frac{100}{10} = 10 \text{ m}$$

20. *(c)* $a = \frac{v - u}{t} = \frac{40 - 0}{20} = 2 \text{ m/s}^2$

$\therefore$ Distance covered,

$$s = ut + \frac{1}{2} a t^2$$

$$= 0 + \frac{1}{2} \times 2 \times (20)^2 = 400 \text{ m}$$

• Concept Enhancer

First of all, find acceleration from the given values and then using the equation of motion calculate the distance travelled.

21. *(b)*

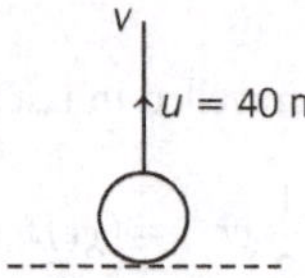

Here, initial velocity of ball, $u = 40$ m/s

Acceleration of ball, $a = -g$ m/s^2

$= -10$ m/s^2

Time = 2 s

From first equation of motion,

$v = u + at = 40 - 10 \times 2$

$\Rightarrow \quad v = 20$ m/s

22. *(a)*

key idea

To solve this question, you should familiar with kinematic equations for uniformly accelerated motion.

Given, initial velocity of first body,

$u_1 = 0$

Final velocity of first body, $v_1 = 3$ m/s

initial velocity of second body,

$u_2 = 4$ m/s

Height, $h = \frac{v_1^2}{2g} = \frac{(3)^2}{2 \times 9.8} = 0.46$ m

Thus, the required velocity of the second body, $v_2 = \sqrt{u_2^2 + 2gh}$

$= \sqrt{(4)^2 + 2 \times 9.8 \times 0.46}$

$= 5$ m/s

23. *(c)* When an object falls freely under gravity, then its speed depends only on its height of fall and is independent of the mass of the object.

As all objects are falling through the same height, therefore their speeds on reaching the ground will be in the ratio of 1 : 1 : 1.

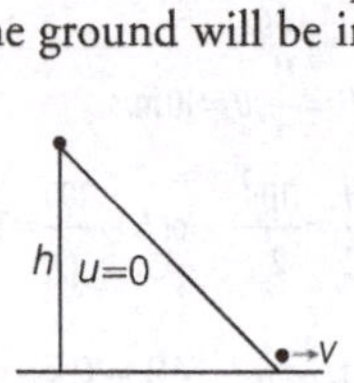

Alternate Solution

The vertical displacement for all the three is same and paths are frictionless. So, by conservation of mechanical energy,

$\frac{1}{2} mv^2 = mgl \Rightarrow v = \sqrt{2gl}$

So, $v_1 : v_2 : v_3 = 1 : 1 : 1$

24. *(c)* Let t be the time interval of two drops. For third drop to fall

$$5 = \frac{1}{2} g (2t)^2 \qquad [\text{As } u = 0]$$

or $$\frac{1}{2} gt^2 = \frac{5}{4} \qquad \ldots\text{(i)}$$

Let x be the distance through which second drop falls for time t, then

$$x = \frac{1}{2} gt^2 = \frac{5}{4} \text{ m} \quad [\text{from Eq. (i)}]$$

Thus, height of second drop from ground

$$= \left(5 - \frac{5}{4}\right) \text{m} = \left(\frac{15}{4}\right) \text{m}$$

$= 3.75$ m

25. *(b)* Time taken by the body to reach the ground from some height is the same as taken to reach that height. Hence, time to reach the ground from its maximum height is 5 s.

26. *(c)* Initial velocity of stone, $u = 0$

Time to reach at ground, $t = 4$ s

Acceleration, $a = +g = 10$ m /s^2

(As motion of body is along the acceleration due to gravity.)

$\therefore$ Height of tower,

$$h = ut + \frac{1}{2} gt^2$$

$$= (0 \times 4) + \frac{1}{2} \times 10 \times 4^2 = 80 \text{ m}$$

27. *(a)*

key idea

First find acceleration from 1st equation of motion, then put the value of a in 2nd equation of motion to find distance s.

Given, initial velocity, $u = 20$ km/h

Final velocity, $v = 60$ km/h

Time taken, $t = 4$ h

From 1st Eq. of motion, we have

$v = u + at$

$\Rightarrow 60 - 20 = a \times 4$

$$\frac{40}{4} = a \Rightarrow a = 10 \text{ km/h}^2$$

Therefore, distance travelled in 4h will be

$$s = ut + \frac{1}{2} at^2$$

$$= 20 \times 4 + \frac{1}{2} \times 10 \times (4)^2$$

$$= 80 + 16 \times 5 = 160 \text{ km}$$

28. *(a)* Distance travelled by the body in nth second is given by

$$s_n = u + \frac{a}{2}(2n - 1)$$

Here, $u = 0$

$\therefore$ For 4th second, $s_4 = \frac{a}{2}(2 \times 4 - 1)$

and For 3rd second, $s_3 = \frac{a}{2}(2 \times 3 - 1)$

Hence, $\frac{s_4}{s_3} = \frac{(2 \times 4 - 1)}{(2 \times 3 - 1)} = \frac{7}{5}$

29. *(b)*

key idea

The distance travelled nth second is given by $s_n = u + \frac{a}{2}(2n - 1)$.

Use this equation to find the distance travelled in n th and $(n - 1)$ th second. According to question, $40 = s_n + s_{n-1}$

Solve this equation to find t and then find height of the tower.

Total distance travelled in last 2 s of fall is

$$s = s_t + s_{(t-1)}$$

$$= \left[0 + \frac{g}{2}(2t - 1)\right] + \left[0 + \frac{g}{2}(2(t-1) - 1)\right]$$

$$= \frac{g}{2}(2t - 1) + \frac{g}{2}(2t - 3)$$

$$= \frac{g}{2}(4t - 4) = \frac{10}{2} \times 4(t - 1)$$

or $40 = 20(t - 1)$

or $t = 2 + 1 = 3$ s

Distance travelled in t s is

$$s = ut + \frac{1}{2} at^2$$

$$= 0 + \frac{1}{2} \times 10 \times 3^2 = 45 \text{ m}$$

30. *(b)* As distance travelled in nth second is given by

$$s_n = u + \frac{1}{2} g (2n - 1)$$

∴ For 4 th second,

$$s_4 = \frac{1}{2} \times 9.8\,(2 \times 4 - 1)$$
$$= 4.9 \times 7 \text{ m}$$

and for 5th second,

$$s_5 = \frac{1}{2} \times 9.8\,(2 \times 5 - 1)$$
$$= 4.9 \times 9 \text{ m}$$

$$\therefore \quad \frac{s_4}{s_5} = \frac{7}{9}$$

31. *(c)* If a is the acceleration of the car, then

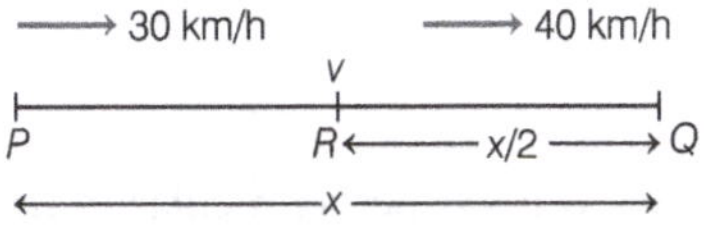

For part PQ, $40^2 - 30^2 = 2ax$

or $$a = \frac{350}{x} \quad \text{...(i)}$$

For part RQ, $$40^2 - v^2 = \frac{2ax}{2} \quad \text{...(ii)}$$

Putting value of a from Eq. (i) in Eq. (ii), we have

$$40^2 - v^2 = 2\left(\frac{350}{x}\right)\frac{x}{2}$$

or $40^2 - v^2 = 350$ or $v^2 = 1250$

$$\Rightarrow \quad v = 25\sqrt{2} \text{ km/h}$$

Topic 3

01. *(c)* We know that

$$a = \frac{dv}{dt}$$

For v = constant, $a = 0$

Thus, for v-t graph when v is positive and linearly increasing a will be positive constant and if v is decreasing linearly a will be negative constant.

Hence, option (c) is correct.

02. *(c)* We know that, slope of displacement-time graph for a moving object gives velocity of moving object.

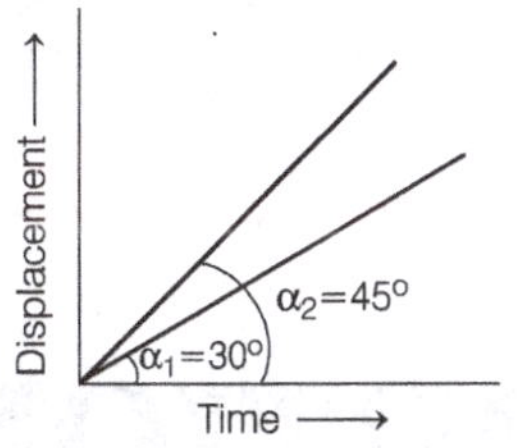

$$v_1 = \tan\alpha_1 = \tan 30° = \frac{1}{\sqrt{3}}$$

and $$v_2 = \tan\alpha_2 = \tan 45° = 1$$

$$\therefore \quad \frac{v_1}{v_2} = \frac{1/\sqrt{3}}{1} = \frac{1}{\sqrt{3}}$$

$$\therefore \quad v_1 : v_2 = 1 : \sqrt{3}$$

> **Concept Enhancer**
>
> The slope of a displacement-time graph is equal to velocity i.e., $\tan\theta = v$. Therefore, the graph with highest slope will have highest velocity.

03. *(b)* Maximum velocity point means, the point at which $\frac{dx}{dt}$ i.e. the slope of the graph is maximum.

At point C, slope is maximum.

> **Concept Enhancer**
>
> Displacement-time graph for an object at rest is a straight line with zero slope.
> Displacement-time graph for an object having uniform motion is a straight line with non-zero slope.
> Displacement-time graph for an object with uniform acceleration is a parabola.

04. *(d)* Instantaneous velocity is the slope of displacement-time graph. At point E, the slope is negative, so instantaneous velocity of the particle is negative.

05. *(c)* In option (c), particle have two velocities at a particular instant of time, which is impossible.

Topic 4

01. *(a)* Let v be the relative velocity of scooter S w.r.t. bus B, then

$$v = v_S - v_B$$

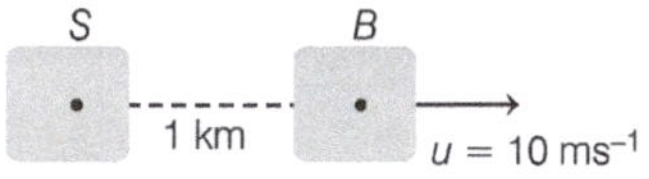

$$\therefore \quad v_S = v + v_B \quad \text{...(i)}$$

Relative velocity = Displacement / Time

$$= \frac{1000}{100} = 10 \text{ ms}^{-1}$$

Now, substituting the value of v in Eq. (i), we get

$$v_S = 10 + 10$$
$$= 20 \text{ ms}^{-1}$$

02. *(d)* Let v_A be the velocity of train, v_B be the velocity of parrot. Velocity of A w.r.t. B is given by $v_{AB} = v_A - v_B$.

Relative velocity of the parrot w.r.t. the train

$$= |(-5) - 10| \text{ ms}^{-1}$$
$$= 15 \text{ ms}^{-1}$$

Time taken by the parrot to cross the train

$$= \frac{150}{15} = 10 \text{ s}$$

C-03

NEET Chapterwise Topicwise Physics

In NEET 2024, 1 question were visible from this chapter. In past 5 years, 2 questions from topic-2 and 3 questions from topic-4 were asked.
For detailed analysis scan QR code

MOTION IN A PLANE

Topic 1 Vectors

01 If the magnitude of sum of two vectors is equal to the magnitude of difference of the two vectors, the angle between these vectors is *[NCERT (New) Pg. 34, NEET 2016, AIPMT 1991]*

(a) 90° (b) 45°
(c) 180° (d) 0°

02 Six vectors **a** to **f** have the magnitudes and directions indicated in the figure. Which of the following statements is true? *[NCERT (New) Pg. 30, AIPMT 2010]*

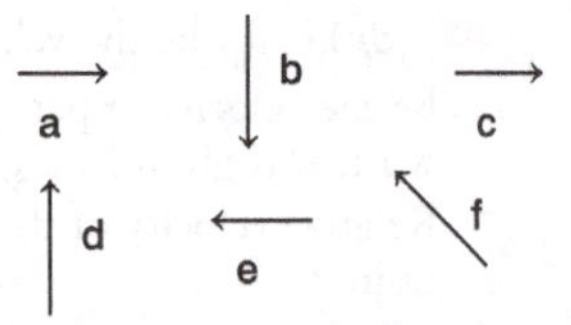

(a) **b** + **c** = **f** (b) **d** + **c** = **f**
(c) **d** + **e** = **f** (d) **b** + **e** = **f**

03 **A** and **B** are two vectors and θ is the angle between them. If $|\mathbf{A}\times\mathbf{B}| = \sqrt{3}\,(\mathbf{A}\cdot\mathbf{B})$, then the value of θ is *[AIPMT 2007]*

(a) 60° (b) 45° (c) 30° (d) 90°

04 The vectors **A** and **B** are such that $|\mathbf{A}+\mathbf{B}| = |\mathbf{A}-\mathbf{B}|$. The angle between the two vectors is *[AIPMT 2006, 1996, 1991]*

(a) 45° (b) 90° (c) 60° (d) 5°

05 If a vector $2\hat{i} + 3\hat{j} + 8\hat{k}$ is perpendicular to the vector $4\hat{j} - 4\hat{i} + \alpha\hat{k}$, then the value of α is *[AIPMT 2005]*

(a) −1 (b) 1/2 (c) −1/2 (d) 1

06 If $|\mathbf{A}\times\mathbf{B}| = \sqrt{3}\,\mathbf{A}\cdot\mathbf{B}$, then the value of $|\mathbf{A}+\mathbf{B}|$ is *[AIPMT 2004]*

(a) $(A^2 + B^2 + AB)^{1/2}$ (b) $\left(A^2 + B^2 + \frac{AB}{\sqrt{3}}\right)^{1/2}$
(c) $A + B$ (d) $(A^2 + B^2 + \sqrt{3}\,AB)^{1/2}$

07 The vector sum of two forces is perpendicular to their vector differences. In that case, the forces *[AIPMT 2003]*

(a) are not equal to each other in magnitude
(b) cannot be predicted
(c) are equal to each other
(d) are equal to each other in magnitude

08 If a unit vector is represented by $0.5\hat{i} + 0.8\hat{j} + c\hat{k}$, then the value of c is *[NCERT (New) Pg. 30, AIPMT 1999]*

(a) 1 (b) $\sqrt{0.11}$ (c) $\sqrt{0.01}$ (d) 0.39

09 Which of the following is not a vector quantity? *[AIPMT 1995]*

(a) Speed (b) Velocity
(c) Torque (d) Displacement

10 The resultant of $\mathbf{A}\times 0$ will be equal to *[AIPMT 1992]*

(a) zero (b) A
(c) zero vector (d) unit vector

11 The angle between **A** and **B** is θ. The value of the triple product $\mathbf{A}\cdot(\mathbf{B}\times\mathbf{A})$ is *[AIPMT 1989]*

(a) A^2B (b) zero
(c) $A^2B\sin\theta$ (d) $A^2B\cos\theta$

Topic 2 Motion in a Plane and Projectile Motion

01 A bullet is fired from a gun at the speed of 280 m s^{-1} in the direction 30° above the horizontal. The maximum height attained by the bullet is ($g = 9.8$ m s^{-2}, sin 30° = 0.5) *[NCERT (New) Pg. 39, NEET 2023]*

(a) 2000 m (b) 1000 m (c) 3000 m (d) 2800 m

02 A car starts from rest and accelerates at 5 m/s^2. At $t = 4$ s, a ball is dropped out of a window by a person sitting in the car. What is the velocity and acceleration of the ball at $t = 6$ s? (Take, $g = 10$ m/s^2) *[NEET 2021]*

(a) $20\sqrt{2}$ m/s, 10 m/s^2 (b) 20 m/s, 5 m/s^2
(c) 20 m/s, 0 (d) $20\sqrt{2}$ m/s, 0

03 Two bullets are fired horizontally and simultaneously towards each other from roof tops of two buildings 100 m apart and of same height of 200 m with the same velocity of 25 m/s. When and where will the two bullets collides. ($g = 10$ m/s^2) *[NEET (Odisha) 2019]*
(a) After 2s at a height 180 m
(b) After 2s at a height of 20 m
(c) After 4s at a height of 120 m
(d) They will not collide

04 When an object is shot from the bottom of a long smooth inclined plane kept at an angle 60° with horizontal, it can travel a distance x_1 along the plane. But when the inclination is decreased to 30° and the same object is shot with the same velocity, it can travel x_2 distance. Then, $x_1 : x_2$ will be *[NCERT (New) Pg. 39, NEET (National) 2019]*
(a) $\sqrt{2}:1$ (b) $1:\sqrt{3}$
(c) $1:2\sqrt{3}$ (d) $1:\sqrt{2}$

05 The x and y coordinates of the particle at any time are $x = 5t - 2t^2$ and $y = 10t$ respectively, where x and y are in metres and t is in second. The acceleration of the particle at $t = 2$ s is *[NEET 2017]*
(a) 0 (b) 5 m/s^2
(c) −4 m/s^2 (d) −8 m/s^2

06 A particle moves so that its position vector is given by $\mathbf{r} = \cos\omega t\,\hat{x} + \sin\omega t\,\hat{y}$ where, ω is a constant. Which of the following is true? *[NCERT (New) Pg. 42, NEET 2016]*
(a) Velocity and acceleration both are perpendicular to **r**.
(b) Velocity and acceleration both are parallel to **r**.
(c) Velocity is perpendicular to **r** and acceleration is directed towards the origin.
(d) Velocity is perpendicular to **r** and acceleration is directed away from the origin.

07 The position vector of a particle **R** as a function of time is given by
$$\mathbf{R} = 4\sin(2\pi t)\,\hat{i} + 4\cos(2\pi t)\,\hat{j}$$
where R is in metre, t is in seconds and $\hat{i}$ and $\hat{j}$ denote unit vectors along x and y-directions, respectively. Which one of the following statements is wrong for the motion of particle? *[AIPMT 2015]*
(a) Acceleration is along − **R**.
(b) Magnitude of acceleration vector is $\frac{v^2}{R}$, where v is the velocity of particle.
(c) Magnitude of the velocity of particle is 8 m/s.
(d) Path of the particle is a circle of radius 4 m.

08 A projectile is fired from the surface of the earth with a velocity of 5 ms^{-1} at angle θ with the horizontal. Another projectile fired from another planet with a velocity of 3 ms^{-1} at the same angle follows a trajectory which is identical with the trajectory of the projectile fired from the earth. The value of the acceleration due to gravity on the planet is (in ms^{-2}) is (given, $g = 9.8$ ms $^{-2}$) *[AIPMT 2014]*
(a) 3.5 (b) 5.9
(c) 16.3 (d) 110.8

09 A particle is moving such that its position co-ordinates (x, y) are (2m, 3m) at time $t = 0$, (6m, 7m) at time $t = 2$ s and (13m, 14m) at time $t = 5$ s. Average velocity vector ($\mathbf{v}_{av}$) from $t = 0$ to $t = 5$ s is *[NCERT (New) Pg. 35, AIPMT 2014]*
(a) $\frac{1}{5}(13\hat{i} + 14\hat{j})$ (b) $\frac{7}{3}(\hat{i} + \hat{j})$
(c) $2(\hat{i} + \hat{j})$ (d) $\frac{11}{5}(\hat{i} + \hat{j})$

10 The velocity of a projectile at the initial point A is $(2\hat{i} + 3\hat{j})$ m/s. Its velocity (in m/s) at point B is *[NEET 2013]*

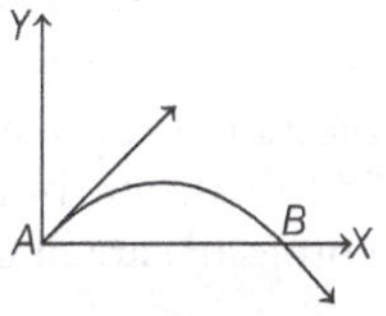

(a) $-2\hat{i} - 3\hat{j}$ (b) $-2\hat{i} + 3\hat{j}$
(c) $2\hat{i} - 3\hat{j}$ (d) $2\hat{i} + 3\hat{j}$

11 The horizontal range and the maximum height of a projectile are equal. The angle of projection of the projectile is *[NCERT (New) Pg. 39, AIPMT 2012]*
(a) $\theta = \tan^{-1}\left(\frac{1}{4}\right)$ (b) $\theta = \tan^{-1}(4)$
(c) $\theta = \tan^{-1}(2)$ (d) $\theta = 45°$

12 A particle has initial velocity $(2\hat{i} + 3\hat{j})$ and acceleration $(0.3\hat{i} + 0.2\hat{j})$. The magnitude of velocity after 10 s will be *[AIPMT 2012]*
(a) $9\sqrt{2}$ units (b) $5\sqrt{2}$ units
(c) 5 units (d) 9 units

13 A missile is fired for maximum range with an initial velocity of 20 m/s. If $g = 10$ m / s^2, the range of the missile is *[NCERT (New) Pg. 39, AIPMT 2011]*
(a) 50 m (b) 60 m
(c) 20 m (d) 40 m

14 A body is moving with velocity 30 m/s towards East. After 10 s its velocity becomes 40 m/s towards North. The average acceleration of the body is *[AIPMT 2011]*
(a) 1 m/s^2 (b) 7 m/s^2
(c) $\sqrt{7}$ m/s^2 (d) 5 m/s^2

15 The speed of a projectile at its maximum height is half of its initial speed. The angle of projection is *[NCERT (New) Pg. 39, AIPMT 2010]*
(a) 60° (b) 15°
(c) 30° (d) 45°

16 A particle moves in XY-plane according to rule $x = a\sin\omega t$ and $y = a\cos\omega t$. The particle follows *[AIPMT 2010]*
(a) an elliptical path
(b) a circular path
(c) a parabolic path
(d) a straight line path inclined equally to X and Y-axes

17 A particle has initial velocity $(3\hat{i} + 4\hat{j})$ and has acceleration $(0.4\,\hat{i} + 0.3\,\hat{j})$. Its speed after 10 s is *[AIPMT 2010]*
(a) 7 unit (b) $7\sqrt{2}$ unit
(c) 8.5 unit (d) 10 unit

18 A particle starting from the origin (0, 0) moves in a straight line in the (x, y) plane. Its coordinates at a later time are $(\sqrt{3}, 3)$. The path of the particle makes with the X-axis an angle of *[NCERT (New) Pg. 32, AIPMT 2007]*
(a) 30° (c) 45° (c) 60° (d) 0°

19 For angles of projection of a projectile at angles $(45° - \theta)$ and $(45° + \theta)$, the horizontal ranges described by the projectile are in the ratio of *[AIPMT 2006]*
(a) 1 : 1 (b) 2 : 3 (c) 1 : 2 (d) 2 : 1

20 A particle moves in a plane with constant acceleration in a direction different from the initial velocity. The path of the particle is *[AIPMT 2005]*
(a) an ellipse (b) a parabola
(c) an arc of a circle (d) a straight line

21 A man is slipping on a frictionless inclined plane and a bag falls down from the same height. Then, the velocity of both is related as (v_m = velocity of man and v_B = velocity of bag) *[AIPMT 2000]*
(a) $v_B > v_m$ (b) $v_B < v_m$
(c) $v_B = v_m$ (d) v_B and v_m can't be related

22 Two particles are projected with same initial velocities at an angle 30° and 60° with the horizontal. Then, *[NCERT (New) Pg. 39, AIPMT 2000]*
(a) their heights will be equal
(b) their ranges will be equal
(c) their time of flights will be equal
(d) their ranges will be different

23 Two particles A and B are connected by a rigid rod AB. The rod slides along perpendicular rails as shown here. The velocity of A to the right is 10m/s. What is the velocity of B when angle $\alpha = 60°$? *[AIPMT 1998]*

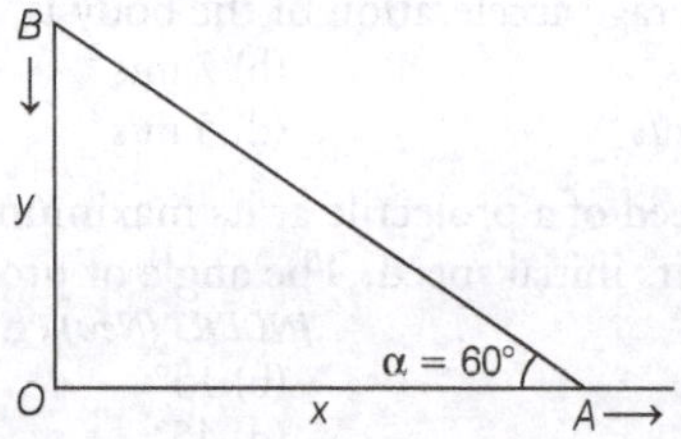

(a) 9.8 m/s (b) 10 m/s
(c) 5.8 m/s (d) 17.3 m/s

24 If a body A of mass M is thrown with velocity v at an angle of 30° to the horizontal and another body B of the same mass is thrown with the same speed at an angle of 60° to the horizontal, the ratio of horizontal range of A to B will be *[AIPMT 1992]*
(a) 1 : 3 (b) 1 : 1 (c) $1:\sqrt{3}$ (d) $\sqrt{3}:1$

Topic 3 Relative Velocity in Two Dimensions

01 The speed of a swimmer in still water is 20 m/s. The speed of river water is 10 m/s and is flowing due East. If he is standing on the South bank and wishes to cross the river along the shortest path, then the angle at which he should make his strokes w.r.t. North is given by *[NCERT (Old) Pg. 76, NEET (National) 2019]*
(a) 0° (b) 60° West
(c) 45° West (d) 30° West

02 A ship A is moving Westwards with a speed of 10 km h^{-1} and a ship B 100 km South of A, is moving Northwards with a speed of 10 km h^{-1}. The time after which the distance between them becomes shortest is *[NCERT (New) Pg. 36, AIPMT 2015]*
(a) 0 h (b) 5 h (c) $5\sqrt{2}$ h (d) $10\sqrt{2}$ h

03 Two boys are standing at the ends A and B of a ground where $AB = a$. The boy at B starts running in a direction perpendicular to AB with velocity v_1. The boy at A starts running simultaneously with velocity v and catches the other in a time t, where t is *[NCERT (Old) Pg. 76, AIPMT 2005]*
(a) $\dfrac{a}{\sqrt{v^2 + v_1^2}}$ (b) $\dfrac{a}{v + v_1}$ (c) $\dfrac{a}{v - v_1}$ (d) $\sqrt{\dfrac{a^2}{v^2 - v_1^2}}$

04 The width of river is 1 km. The velocity of boat is 5 km/h. The boat covered the width of river in shortest time 15 min. Then the velocity of river stream is *[AIPMT 2000, 1998]*
(a) 3 km/h (b) 4 km/h
(c) $\sqrt{29}$ km/h (d) $\sqrt{41}$ km/h

05 A person swims in a river aiming to reach exactly opposite point on the bank of a river. His speed of swimming is 0.5 m/s at an angle 120° with the direction of flow of water. The speed of water in stream is *[NCERT (Old) Pg. 76, AIPMT 1999]*
(a) 1.0 m/s (b) 0.5 m/s
(c) 0.25 m/s (d) 0.43 m/s

06 The speed of a boat is 5 km/h in still water. It crosses a river of width 1.0 km along the shortest possible path in 15 min. The velocity of the river water is (in km/h) *[AIPMT 1998]*
(a) 5 (b) 1 (c) 3 (d) 4

Topic 4 Uniform Circular Motion

01 A particle moving with uniform speed in a circular path maintains *[NCERT (New) Pg. 40, NEET 2024]*
(a) constant velocity
(b) constant acceleration
(c) constant velocity but varying acceleration
(d) varying velocity and varying acceleration

02 The angular acceleration of a body, moving along the circumference of a circle, is *[NEET 2023]*
(a) along the radius towards the centre
(b) along the tangent to its position
(c) along the axis of rotation
(d) along the radius, away from centre

03 A particle moving in a circle of radius R with a uniform speed takes a time T to complete one revolution. If this particle were projected with the same speed at an angle θ to the horizontal, the maximum height attained by it equals $4R$. The angle of projection θ is then given by *[NCERT (New) Pg. 42, NEET 2021]*
(a) $\theta = \cos^{-1}\left(\frac{gT^2}{\pi^2 R}\right)^{1/2}$
(b) $\theta = \cos^{-1}\left(\frac{\pi^2 R}{gT^2}\right)^{1/2}$
(c) $\theta = \sin^{-1}\left(\frac{\pi^2 R}{gT^2}\right)^{1/2}$
(d) $\theta = \sin^{-1}\left(\frac{2gT^2}{\pi^2 R}\right)^{1/2}$

04 Two particles A and B are moving in uniform circular motion in concentric circles of radii r_A and r_B with speed v_A and v_B respectively. Their time period of rotation is the same. The ratio of angular speed of A to that of B will be *[NEET 2019]*
(a) 1 : 1 (b) $r_A : r_B$ (c) $v_A : v_B$ (d) $r_B : r_A$

05 In the given figure, $a = 15$ m/s^2 represents the total acceleration of a particle moving in the clockwise direction in a circle of radius $R = 2.5$ m at a given instant of time. The speed of the particle is *[NCERT (New) Pg. 42, NEET 2016]*

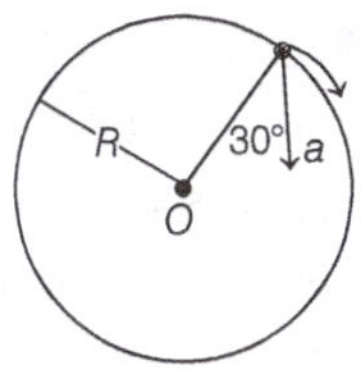

(a) 4.5 m/s (b) 5.0 m/s
(c) 5.7 m/s (d) 6.2 m/s

06 A particle moves in a circle of radius 5 cm with constant speed and time period 0.2π s. The acceleration of the particle is *[AIPMT 2011]*
(a) 25 m/s^2 (b) 36 m/s^2
(c) 5 m/s^2 (d) 15 m/s^2

07 A car runs at a constant speed on a circular track of radius 100 m, taking 62.8 s for every circular lap. The average velocity and average speed for each circular lap, respectively is *[AIPMT 2006]*
(a) 0, 0 (b) 0, 10 m/s
(c) 10 m/s, 10 m/s (d) 10 m/s, 0

08 A stone tied to the end of a string of 1 m long is whirled in a horizontal circle with a constant speed. If the stone makes 22 revolutions in 44 s, what is the magnitude and direction of acceleration of the stone ? *[NCERT (New) Pg. 42, AIPMT 2005]*
(a) $\frac{\pi^2}{4}$ ms^{-2} and direction along the radius towards the centre
(b) π^2 ms^{-2} and direction along the radius away from centre
(c) π^2 ms^{-2} and direction along the radius towards the centre
(d) π^2 ms^{-2} and direction along the tangent to the circle

09 The circular motion of a particle with constant speed is *[AIPMT 2005]*
(a) simple harmonic but not periodic
(b) periodic and simple harmonic
(c) neither periodic nor simple harmonic
(d) periodic but not simple harmonic

10 A particle of mass M is revolving along a circle of radius R and another particle of mass m is revolving in a circle of radius r. If time periods of both particles are same, then the ratio of their angular velocities is *[NCERT (New) Pg. 42, AIPMT 2001]*
(a) 1 (b) $\frac{R}{r}$
(c) $\frac{r}{R}$ (d) $\sqrt{\frac{R}{r}}$

11 What is the linear velocity, if angular velocity vector $\omega = 3\hat{i} - 4\hat{j} + \hat{k}$ and position vector $\mathbf{r} = 5\hat{i} - 6\hat{j} + 6\hat{k}$? *[NCERT (New) Pg. 42, AIPMT 1999]*
(a) $6\hat{i} + 2\hat{j} - 3\hat{k}$ (b) $-18\hat{i} - 13\hat{j} + 2\hat{k}$
(c) $18\hat{i} + 13\hat{j} - 2\hat{k}$ (d) $6\hat{i} - 2\hat{j} + 8\hat{k}$

12 A body is whirled in a horizontal circle of radius 20 cm. It has an angular velocity of 10 rad/s. What is its linear velocity at any point on circular path ? *[AIPMT 1996]*
(a) $\sqrt{2}$ m/s (b) 2 m/s
(c) 10 m/s (d) 20 m/s

Key Index

Topic 1

1 (a)	2 (c)	3 (a)	4 (b)	5 (c)	6 (a)	7 (d)	8 (b)	9 (a)	10 (c)
11 (b)									

Topic 2

1 (b)	2 (a)	3 (a)	4 (b)	5 (c)	6 (c)	7 (c)	8 (a)	9 (d)	10 (c)
11 (b)	12 (b)	13 (d)	14 (d)	15 (a)	16 (b)	17 (b)	18 (c)	19 (a)	20 (b)
21 (c)	22 (b)	23 (d)	24 (b)						

Topic 3

1 (d)	2 (b)	3 (d)	4 (a)	5 (c)	6 (c)

Topic 4

1 (d)	2 (c)	3 (d)	4 (a)	5 (c)	6 (c)	7 (b)	8 (c)	9 (d)	10 (a)
11 (b)	12 (b)								

Detailed **Explanations**

Topic 1

01. *(a)* $|\mathbf{P}+\mathbf{Q}| = |\mathbf{P}-\mathbf{Q}|$

Let angle between **P** and **Q** is ϕ.

$\therefore \quad P^2+Q^2+2PQ\cos\phi$

$= P^2+Q^2-2PQ\cos\phi$

$\Rightarrow \quad 4PQ\cos\phi = 0$

$\Rightarrow \quad \cos\phi = 0 \quad [\because P, Q \neq 0]$

$\Rightarrow \quad \phi = \frac{\pi}{2} = 90°$

> • Concept **Enhancer**
>
> If two vector **A** and **B** are such that $\mathbf{A} \neq \mathbf{B}$ and if $|\mathbf{A}+\mathbf{B}| = |\mathbf{A}-\mathbf{B}|$ then $\cos\theta = 0$, and if $|\mathbf{A}+\mathbf{B}| = |\mathbf{A}|+|\mathbf{B}|$ then $\cos\theta = 1$

02. *(c)* From the triangle law of vector addition,

$\therefore \quad \mathbf{d}+\mathbf{e}=\mathbf{f}$

03. *(a)* Given, $|\mathbf{A}\times\mathbf{B}| = \sqrt{3}(\mathbf{A}\cdot\mathbf{B})$

$\Rightarrow \quad AB\sin\theta = \sqrt{3}\,AB\cos\theta$

$\Rightarrow \quad \tan\theta = \sqrt{3}$

$\therefore \quad \theta = 60°$

04. *(b)* Given,

$|\mathbf{A}+\mathbf{B}| = |\mathbf{A}-\mathbf{B}|$

$\Rightarrow \quad |\mathbf{A}+\mathbf{B}|^2 = |\mathbf{A}-\mathbf{B}|^2$

$\Rightarrow |\mathbf{A}|^2+|\mathbf{B}|^2+2\mathbf{A}.\mathbf{B}$

$= |\mathbf{A}|^2+|\mathbf{B}|^2-2\mathbf{A}\mathbf{B}$

$\Rightarrow \quad 4\mathbf{A}\cdot\mathbf{B} = 0$

$\Rightarrow |\mathbf{A}||\mathbf{B}|\cos\theta = 0$

$\Rightarrow \quad \cos\theta = 0$

or $\quad \theta = \frac{\pi}{2} = 90°$

05. *(c)* Let, $\mathbf{a} = 2\hat{i}+3\hat{j}+8\hat{k}$

$\mathbf{b} = 4\hat{j}-4\hat{i}+\alpha\hat{k}$

$= -4\hat{i}+4\hat{j}+\alpha\hat{k}$

According to the question,

$\mathbf{a}\perp\mathbf{b}$

$\Rightarrow \quad \mathbf{a}\cdot\mathbf{b} = 0$

$\Rightarrow (2\hat{i}+3\hat{j}+8\hat{k})\cdot(-4\hat{i}+4\hat{j}+\alpha\hat{k}) = 0$

$\Rightarrow -8+12+8\alpha = 0$

$\Rightarrow \quad 8\alpha = -4$

$\therefore \quad \alpha = -\frac{4}{8} = -\frac{1}{2}$

06. *(a)* Given, $|\mathbf{A}\times\mathbf{B}| = \sqrt{3}\,\mathbf{A}\cdot\mathbf{B}$

$\Rightarrow \quad AB\sin\theta = \sqrt{3}\,AB\cos\theta$

or $\quad \tan\theta = \sqrt{3}$

$\therefore \quad \theta = 60°$

$\therefore |\mathbf{A}+\mathbf{B}| = \sqrt{A^2+B^2+2AB\cos 60°}$

$= \sqrt{A^2+B^2+2AB\times\frac{1}{2}}$

$= (A^2+B^2+AB)^{1/2}$

07. *(d)* $\mathbf{F}_1 = \mathbf{A}+\mathbf{B}$ ...(i)

$\mathbf{F}_2 = \mathbf{A}-\mathbf{B}$

Since, $\quad \mathbf{F}_1\cdot\mathbf{F}_2 = 0$

or $\quad (\mathbf{A}+\mathbf{B})\cdot(\mathbf{A}-\mathbf{B}) = 0$

or $A^2-\mathbf{A}\cdot\mathbf{B}+\mathbf{B}\cdot\mathbf{A}-B^2 = 0$

or $\quad A^2 = B^2$ or $|\mathbf{A}| = |\mathbf{B}|$

08. *(b)* $\therefore \quad |\hat{n}| = |0.5\hat{i}+0.8\hat{j}+c\hat{k}| = 1$

or $\quad \sqrt{(0.5)^2+(0.8)^2+c^2} = 1$

or $0.25+0.64+c^2 = 1$

or $\quad 0.89+c^2 = 1$

or $c^2 = 1-0.89 = 0.11$

$\Rightarrow c = \sqrt{0.11}$

09. *(a)* Speed is a scalar quantity. It gives no idea about the direction of motion of the object. Velocity, torque and displacement are vector quantities, as these have both magnitude and direction.

> • Concept **Enhancer**
>
> Torque is a vector quantity. It is a cross product of two vectors.
> i.e. $\tau = \mathbf{r} \times \mathbf{F}$

10. *(c)* From the properties of vector product, the cross product of any vector with zero is a null vector or zero vector.

11. *(b)* In scalar triple product of vectors, the positions of dot and cross can be interchanged, i.e.

$$\mathbf{A} \cdot (\mathbf{B} \times \mathbf{A}) = (\mathbf{A} \times \mathbf{B}) \cdot \mathbf{A} = (\mathbf{A} \times \mathbf{A}) \cdot \mathbf{B}$$

But $\mathbf{A} \times \mathbf{A} = 0$

$\therefore \mathbf{A} \cdot (\mathbf{B} \times \mathbf{A}) = 0$

> ***Alternate Solution***
>
> $\mathbf{A} \cdot (\mathbf{B} \times \mathbf{A})$
>
> Let $\mathbf{B} \times \mathbf{A} = \mathbf{C}$
>
> The direction of $\mathbf{C}$ is $\perp$ $\mathbf{A}$ and $\mathbf{B}$ from the cross product formula.
>
> So, $\mathbf{A} \cdot \mathbf{C} = 0$
>
> Since, $\mathbf{A}$ and $\mathbf{C}$ are $\perp$ to each other
>
> $\Rightarrow \mathbf{A} \cdot (\mathbf{B} \times \mathbf{A}) = 0$

Topic 2

01. *(b)* Given, $u = 280 \text{ ms}^{-1}, \theta = 30°$

$\therefore$ Maximum height attained by the bullet.

$$H_{max} = \frac{u^2 \sin^2 \theta}{2g} = \frac{(280)^2 \sin^2 30°}{2 \times 9.8}$$

$$= \frac{(280)^2 \times (0.5)^2}{2 \times 9.8} = 1000 \text{ m}$$

02. *(a)* Given,

Initial velocity, $u = 0$ m/s

Acceleration, $a = 5 \text{ m/s}^2$

Velocity at $t = 4$ s, $v = u + at$

$v = 5 \times 4 = 20$ m/s

At this time a ball is dropped out of a window by a person sitting in the car. The velocity of ball after $t = 6$ s is given by

Vertical velocity of ball,

$$v_y = u_{ball} + a(\Delta t)$$
$$= 0 + 10 \times (6 - 4) = 20 \text{ ms}^{-1}$$

Horizontal velocity of ball,

$$v_x = 20 \text{ ms}^{-1}$$

So, magnitude of velocity of ball

$$v_{net} = \sqrt{v_x^2 + v_y^2}$$
$$= 20\sqrt{2} \text{ m/s}$$

Acceleration of the ball will be equal to gravitational acceleration g.

i.e. 10 m/s^2

03. *(a)*

> **key idea**
>
> Since both bullets are fixed from the same height, find their relative speed and obtain the horizontal distance where the bullet will collide. Using this distance the time taken for bullet to collide can be calculated. During this time interval, find the vertical distance.

The situation can be shown as below

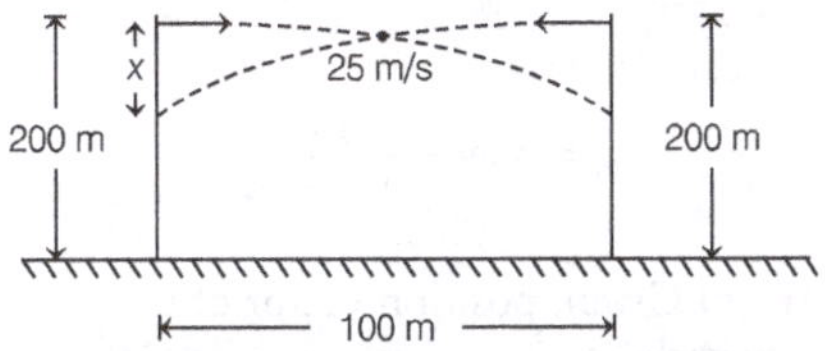

where, x be the vertical distance travelled from the top of the building and t be the time at which they collide.

As two bullets are fired toward each other, So, their relative velocity will be

$$v_{rel} = 25 - (-25) = 50 \text{ ms}^{-1}$$

Then, time $t = \dfrac{d}{v_{rel}} = \dfrac{100}{50} = 2$ s

The distance or height at which they collide is

$$x = ut + \frac{1}{2}at^2$$

$\because \quad u = 0$

$\therefore \quad x = -\dfrac{1}{2}gt^2 \quad [\because u = 0 \text{ and } a = -g]$

$\Rightarrow \quad x = -\dfrac{1}{2} \times 10(2)^2 = -20$ m

The negative sign shows that the bullets will collide 20 m below the top of tower i.e. at a height of $(200 - 20) = 180$ m from the ground after 2 s.

04. *(b)* The motion of object shot in two cases can be depicted as below.

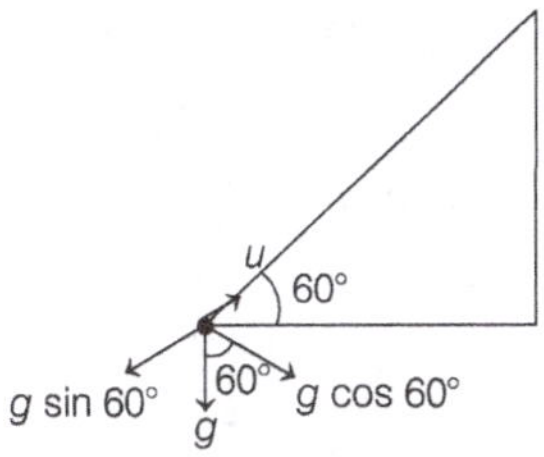

Case I

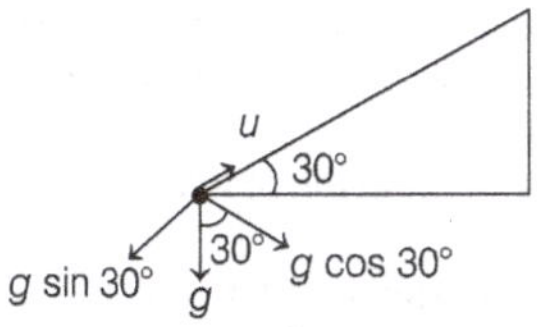

Case II

Using third equation of motion,

$$v^2 = u^2 - 2gh \quad (\because a = -g) \quad \ldots(i)$$

As the object stops finally, so

$v = 0$

For inclined motion,

$g = g \sin \theta$ and $h = x$

Substituting these values in Eq. (i), we get

$\Rightarrow \quad u^2 = 2g \sin \theta \, x$

$\Rightarrow \quad x = \dfrac{u^2}{2g \sin \theta}$

For case I, $\quad x_1 = \dfrac{u^2}{2g \sin 60°}$

For case II, $x_2 = \dfrac{u^2}{2g \sin 30°}$

$\Rightarrow \quad \dfrac{x_1}{x_2} = \dfrac{u^2}{2g \sin 60°} \times \dfrac{2g \sin 30°}{u^2}$

$= \dfrac{1}{2} \times \dfrac{2}{\sqrt{3}} = \dfrac{1}{\sqrt{3}}$ or $1 : \sqrt{3}$

05. *(c)* Given, $x = 5t - 2t^2$

Velocity of the particle,

$$v_x = \frac{dx}{dt} = \frac{d}{dt}(5t - 2t^2) = 5 - 4t$$

Acceleration, $a_x = \dfrac{d}{dt} v_x = -4 \text{ ms}^{-2}$

Also, $\quad y = 10t$

Velocity, $\quad v_y = \dfrac{dy}{dt} = 10$

$\therefore$ Acceleration $a_y = \dfrac{dv_y}{dt} = 0$

$\therefore$ Net acceleration of the particle,

$$\mathbf{a}_{net} = a_x \hat{\mathbf{i}} + a_y \hat{\mathbf{j}} = (-4 \text{ ms}^{-2})\hat{\mathbf{i}}$$

or $\quad \mathbf{a}_{net} = -4\,\hat{\mathbf{i}} \text{ ms}^{-2}$

$\Rightarrow \quad \mathbf{a}_{net} = -4 \text{ ms}^{-2}$

06. *(c)* Given, position vector

$\mathbf{r} = (\cos \omega t \, \hat{\mathbf{x}} + \sin \omega t \, \hat{\mathbf{y}})$ m

Velocity is given by $\mathbf{v} = \dfrac{d\mathbf{r}}{dt}$

$\Rightarrow \mathbf{v} = -\omega \sin \omega t \hat{\mathbf{x}} + \omega \cos \omega t \hat{\mathbf{y}}$ m/s

Acceleration is given by $\mathbf{a} = \dfrac{d\mathbf{v}}{dt}$

$\Rightarrow \mathbf{a} = -\omega^2 \cos \omega t \hat{\mathbf{x}} - \omega^2 \sin \omega t \hat{\mathbf{y}} \text{ m/s}^2$

If the dot product of two vectors is zero, that means the vectors are perpendicular to each other.

$\mathbf{v} \cdot \mathbf{r} = -\omega \sin \omega t \cos \omega t + \omega \sin \omega t \cos \omega t = 0$

$\therefore$ **v** is perpendicular to **r**.

$\mathbf{a} \cdot \mathbf{r} = -\omega^2 \cos^2 \omega t - \omega^2 \sin^2 \omega t$

$= -\omega^2 (\cos^2 \omega t + \sin^2 \omega t) = -\omega^2$

$\therefore$ **a** is anti-parallel to **r** or it indicates that acceleration is directed towards the origin.

• Concept **Enhancer**

Two vectors are perpendicular if their dot product is zero i.e. $\mathbf{A} \cdot \mathbf{B} = 0$

and parallel, if their dot product is 1.

i.e. $\mathbf{A} \cdot \mathbf{B} = 1$

and antiparallel, if their dot product is −1

i.e. $\mathbf{A} \cdot \mathbf{B} = -1$

07. (c) (i) The position vector of a particle R as a function of time is given by

$$\mathbf{R} = 4 \sin (2\pi t)\,\hat{i} + 4 \cos (2\pi t)\,\hat{j}$$

X-axis component, $x = 4 \sin 2\pi t$ ...(i)

Y-axis component,

$$y = 4 \cos 2\pi t \quad \text{...(ii)}$$

Squaring and adding both equations, we get

$$x^2 + y^2 = 4^2 [\sin^2 (2\pi t) + \cos^2 (2\pi t)]$$

i.e. $x^2 + y^2 = 4^2$ i.e. equation of circle and radius is 4 m.

(ii) Acceleration vector, $\mathbf{a} = \dfrac{v^2}{R}(-\hat{\mathbf{R}})$,

while v is velocity of a particle.

(iii) Magnitude of acceleration vector,

$$a = \frac{v^2}{R}$$

(iv) As, we have

$$v_x = \frac{dx}{dt} = +4 (\cos 2\pi t)\, 2\pi$$

and $v_y = \dfrac{dy}{dt} = -4 (\sin 2\pi t)\, 2\pi$

Net resultant velocity,

$$v = \sqrt{v_x^2 + v_y^2}$$

$$= \sqrt{(8\pi)^2 (\cos^2 2\pi t + \sin^2 2\pi t)}$$

$$v = 8\pi$$

$[\because \cos^2 2\pi t + \sin^2 2\pi t = 1]$

So, option (c) is incorrect.

08. (a) The trajectory of a projectile projected at angle θ with the horizontal direction from ground is given by

$$y = x \tan \theta - \frac{gx^2}{2u^2 \cos^2 \theta}$$

For equal trajectories for same angle of projection,

$$\frac{g}{u^2} = \text{constant} \Rightarrow \frac{9.8}{5^2} = \frac{g'}{3^2}$$

$$g' = \frac{9.8 \times 9}{25} = 3.5 \text{ ms}^{-2}$$

• Concept **Enhancer**

When a particle is thrown obliquely near the earth's surface, it moves along a curved path under constant acceleration. This type of motion of particle is called projectile motion.

Maximum height It is the highest distance that a body can reach during its projectile motion.

$$H = \frac{u^2 \sin^2 \theta}{2g}$$

Equation of trajectory,

$$y = x \tan \theta - \frac{gx^2}{2u^2 \cos^2 \theta}$$

09. (d) Given, position vector of the particle at

$t = 0$, $\mathbf{r}_1 = (2\hat{i} + 3\hat{j})$

and $t = 5$ s, $\mathbf{r}_2 = (13\hat{i} + 14\hat{j})$

Average velocity vector

$$\mathbf{v}_{avg} = \frac{\text{Net displacement}}{\text{Time taken}} = \frac{\mathbf{r}_2 - \mathbf{r}_1}{5}$$

$$= \frac{(13 - 2)\hat{i} + (14 - 3)\hat{j}}{5}$$

$$= \frac{11\hat{i} + 11\hat{j}}{5} = \frac{11}{5}(\hat{i} + \hat{j})$$

10. (c)

key idea

As we know that during entire projectile motion only velocity of y-component changes, whereas velocity of x-component remains constant. Use this to solve the problem.

From the figure, the x-component remains unchanged, while the y-component is reversed. Thus, the velocity at point B is $(2\hat{i} - 3\hat{j})$ ms^{-1}.

11. (b) According to question,

$$R = H$$

$$\Rightarrow \quad \frac{u^2 \sin 2\theta}{g} = \frac{u^2 \sin^2 \theta}{2g}$$

$$\frac{u^2 (2 \sin \theta \cos \theta)}{g} = \frac{u^2 \sin^2 \theta}{2g}$$

$$\Rightarrow \quad 2 \cos \theta = \frac{\sin \theta}{2}$$

$$\Rightarrow \quad \tan \theta = 4 \Rightarrow \theta = \tan^{-1}(4)$$

12. (b) Given, initial velocity,

$$\mathbf{u} = (2\hat{i} + 3\hat{j})$$

Acceleration, $a = (0.3\hat{i} + 0.2\hat{j})$

time, $t = 10$ s

final velocity, $\mathbf{v} = u + at$

$$= (2\hat{i} + 3\hat{j}) + (0.3\hat{i} + 0.2\hat{j}) \times 10$$

$$= (2\hat{i} + 3\hat{j}) + (3\hat{i} + 2\hat{j}) = (5\hat{i} + 5\hat{j})$$

$$|\mathbf{v}| = \sqrt{(5)^2 + (5)^2} = 5\sqrt{2} \text{ units}$$

13. (d) For maximum range,

$$\theta = 45°$$

So, $R_{max} = \dfrac{u^2 \sin(2 \times 45)}{g} = \dfrac{u^2}{g}$

Given, $u = 20$ ms^{-1} and $g = 10$ ms^{-2}

$$R_{max} = \frac{(20)^2}{10} = \frac{400}{10} = 40 \text{ m}$$

14. (d) Given, initial velocity of body, $u = 30$ m/s towards east.

Final velocity, $v = 40$ m/s towards north

Let $u = 30(+\hat{i})$ and $v = 40(\hat{j})$

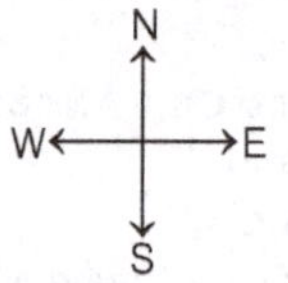

From 1st, equation of motion, we get

$\mathbf{v} = \mathbf{u} + \mathbf{a}t$

$$40\hat{j} = +30\hat{i} + \mathbf{a}(10) \quad (\because \text{Time} = 10 \text{ s})$$

$$\Rightarrow 40\hat{j} - 30\hat{i} = 10\,\mathbf{a} \Rightarrow \mathbf{a} = 4\hat{j} - 3\hat{i}$$

$$|\mathbf{a}| = \sqrt{4^2 + 3^2} = 5 \text{ ms}^{-2}$$

15. (a) At highest point, vertical component of velocity is zero. Horizontal component of velocity ($u \cos\theta$) remains same as the acceleration in horizontal direction is zero.

$\therefore \quad v_x = u \cos\theta$

Given, $u \cos\theta = \dfrac{u}{2}$

$$\Rightarrow \quad \cos\theta = \frac{1}{2} \Rightarrow \theta = 60°$$

16. (b) Given, $x = a \sin \omega t$

$$y = a \cos \omega t$$

Thus,

$$x^2 + y^2 = a^2 \sin^2 \omega t + a^2 \cos^2 \omega t$$

$$= a^2 (\sin^2 \omega t + \cos^2 \omega t)$$

$$\Rightarrow x^2 + y^2 = a^2$$

Which is an equation of circle with origin at (0, 0) and radius a.

17. (b) Given, initial velocity, $u = 3\hat{i} + 4\hat{j}$

Final velocity, $v = ?$

Acceleration, $a = (0.4\,\hat{i} + 0.3\hat{j})$

Time, $t = 10$ s

From first equation of motion,

$$v = u + at$$

$$v = 3\hat{i} + 4\hat{j} + 10(0.4\hat{i} + 0.3\hat{j})$$

$$v = 7\hat{i} + 7\hat{j}$$

$$\Rightarrow |v| = 7\sqrt{2}$$

18. *(c)* The given situation is shown below

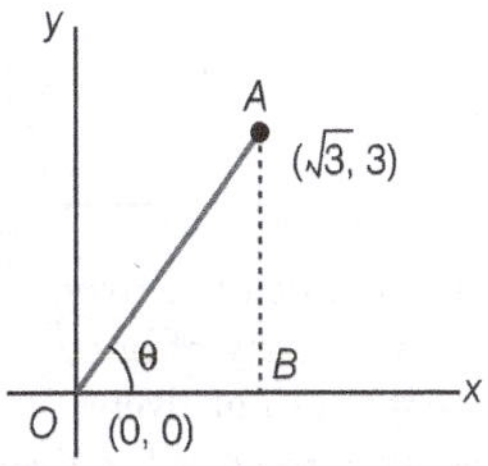

$\tan\theta$ = slope of line OA

= path of the particle 1 making angle θ

$$\tan\theta = \frac{3-0}{\sqrt{3}-0} = \sqrt{3}$$

$$\theta = 60°$$

19. *(a)* We know that, horizontal ranges for complementary angles of projection will be same.

The projectiles are projected at angles $(45° - \theta)$ and $(45° + \theta)$ which are complementary to each other i.e. two angles add up to give 90°. Hence, horizontal ranges will be equal. Thus, the required ratio is 1 : 1.

Alternate Solution

Horizontal range of projectile, $R = \frac{u^2 \sin 2\alpha}{g}$

For $\alpha = (45° - \theta)$, $R_1 = \frac{u^2 \sin 2(45° - \theta)}{g}$

$$= \frac{u^2 \sin(90° - 2\theta)}{g} = \frac{u^2 \cos 2\theta}{g}$$

For $\alpha = (45° + \theta)$,

$$R_2 = \frac{u^2 \sin 2(45° + \theta)}{g}$$

$$= \frac{u^2 \sin(90° + 2\theta)}{g} = \frac{u^2 \cos 2\theta}{g}$$

Hence, $\frac{R_1}{R_2} = \frac{1}{1}$ or $R_1 : R_2 = 1 : 1$

20. *(b)*

key idea

The given condition is of a projectile motion. Since, the projectile motion follows a parabolic trajectory, the given particle must also form a parabolic path.

When a particle moves in a plane with constant acceleration in a different direction from initial velocity, it moves in a parabolic path.

Let the velocity be v and acceleration be **a**, angle between them be θ. ($\theta < 90°$).

Component of velocity in direction of a is $v\cos\theta$ and in direction perpendicular to **a** is $v\sin\theta$.

From equation of motion, we get,

$$y = v\cos\theta t + \frac{1}{2}at^2 \quad \ldots(i)$$

In direction perpendicular to acceleration,

$$x = v\sin\theta t$$

$$\Rightarrow t = \frac{x}{v\sin\theta} \quad \ldots(ii)$$

Substituting (ii) in Eq. (i) we get

$$y = v\cos\theta \frac{x}{v\sin\theta} + \frac{1}{2}a\left(\frac{x^2}{v^2\sin^2\theta}\right)$$

$$\Rightarrow y = \frac{x}{\cot\theta} + \frac{a}{2}\frac{x^2}{v^2\sin^2\theta}$$

This is a form of parabola

$$y = Ax^2 + Bx$$

21. *(c)* The given situation is shown below.

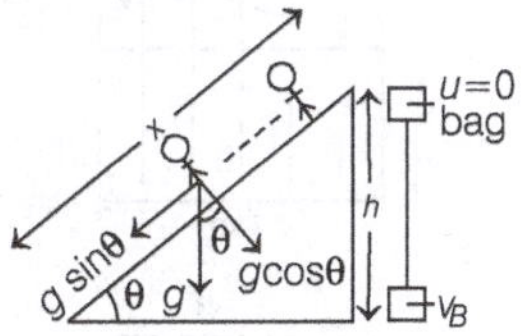

If v_B be the velocity of bag when it reaches at the ground, then

$$v_B^2 = 0 + 2gh \Rightarrow v_B = \sqrt{2gh} \quad \ldots(i)$$

If v_m be the velocity of man when it reaches at ground, then

$$v_m^2 = 0 + 2g\sin\theta \cdot x = 2g \times \frac{h}{x} \cdot x$$

$$\Rightarrow v_m^2 = 2gh$$

$$\Rightarrow v_m = \sqrt{2gh} \quad \ldots(ii)$$

From Eqs. (i) and (ii), we get

$$v_B = v_m$$

22. *(b)* (a) Maximum height in case of projectile is given by

$$H = \frac{u^2\sin^2\theta}{2g} \Rightarrow \frac{H_1}{H_2} = \frac{\sin^2\theta_1}{\sin^2\theta_2}$$

$$= \frac{\sin^2 30°}{\sin^2 60°} = \frac{\left(\frac{1}{2}\right)^2}{\left(\frac{\sqrt{3}}{2}\right)^2} = \frac{1}{3}$$

(b) Range $R = \frac{u^2 \sin 2\theta}{g}$

$$\Rightarrow \frac{R_1}{R_2} = \frac{\sin(2 \times 30°)}{\sin(2 \times 60°)}$$

$$= \frac{\sin 60°}{\sin 120°} = \frac{\frac{\sqrt{3}}{2}}{\frac{\sqrt{3}}{2}} = 1$$

$$\Rightarrow R_1 = R_2$$

(c) Time of flight

$$T = \frac{2u\sin\theta}{g} \Rightarrow \frac{T_1}{T_2} = \frac{\sin\theta_1}{\sin\theta_2}$$

$$= \frac{\sin 30°}{\sin 60°} = \frac{1/2}{\sqrt{3}/2} = \frac{1}{\sqrt{3}}$$

Alternate Solution

In this problem, it is given that two particles are projected at angles 30° and 60° which are complementary angles. We know that horizontal range will be same for complementary angles. Hence, their ranges will be equal.

23. *(d)* $\therefore v_x = \frac{dx}{dt}$ and $v_y = \frac{dy}{dt}$

From figure, given in question

$$\tan\alpha = \frac{y}{x}$$

$$\Rightarrow y = x\tan\alpha \quad \ldots(i)$$

Differentiating Eq. (i), w.r.t. t, we get

$$\frac{dy}{dt} = \frac{dx}{dt}\tan\alpha$$

$$\Rightarrow v_y = v_x \tan\alpha$$

Here, $v_x = 10$ m/s, $\alpha = 60°$

$\therefore v_y = 10\tan 60° = 10\sqrt{3} = 17.3$ m/s

24. *(b)* Given, mass of A and B are the same M and thrown with same velocity v.

The angle of projection of $A = 30°$.

The angle of projection of $B = 60°$

$\therefore$ Horizontal range of A,

$$R_A = \frac{v^2\sin(2 \times 30°)}{g} = \frac{v^2 \sin 60°}{g}$$

Horizontal range of B,

$$R_B = \frac{v^2\sin(2 \times 60°)}{g}$$

$$= \frac{v^2 \sin 120°}{g}$$

$\therefore$ Ratio of horizontal range,

$$\frac{R_A}{R_B} = \frac{\sin 60°}{\sin 120°} = \frac{0.866}{0.866} = 1 : 1$$

Topic 3

01. (d) Given, speed of river, $v_R = 10$ m/s

Speed of swimmer in still water,
$v_{SN} = 20$ m/s.

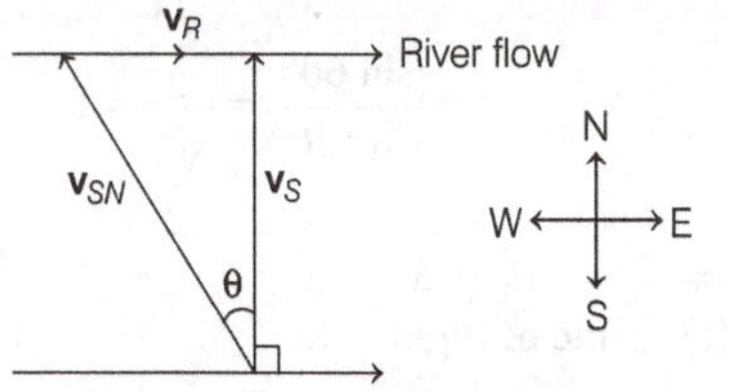

For the shortest path to cross the river, he should swim at an angle $(90° + \theta)$ with the stream flow. From the figure above, according to figure.

$$\mathbf{v}_S = \mathbf{v}_{SN} + \mathbf{v}_R$$

So, angle θ is given by

$$\sin\theta = \left|\frac{\mathbf{v}_R}{\mathbf{v}_{SN}}\right| = \frac{10}{20} = \frac{1}{2}$$

$$\Rightarrow \quad \theta = 30°$$

As the river is flowing in East direction, so he should swim towards West.

02. (b) It is clear from the diagram that the shortest distance between the ship A and B is PQ.

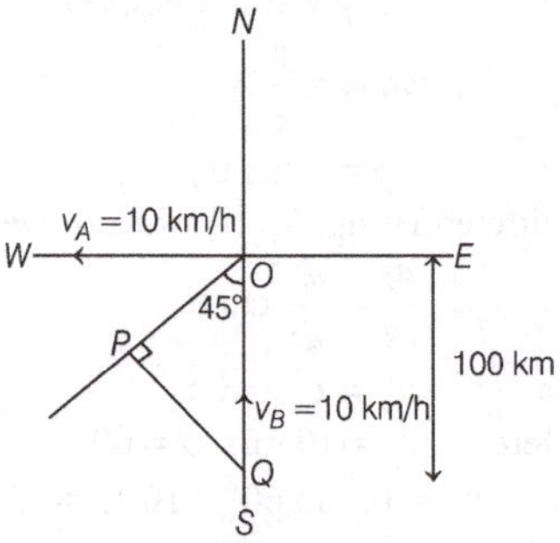

Here, $\sin 45° = \dfrac{PQ}{OQ}$

$$\Rightarrow \quad PQ = 100 \times \frac{1}{\sqrt{2}} = 50\sqrt{2} \text{ km}$$

Also, $v_{AB} = \sqrt{v_A^2 + v_B^2} = \sqrt{10^2 + 10^2}$

$$= 10\sqrt{2} \text{ km/h}$$

So, time taken for them to reach shortest path is

$$t = \frac{PQ}{v_{AB}} = \frac{50\sqrt{2}}{10\sqrt{2}} = 5 \text{ h}$$

03. (d) Given, $AB = a$

When B starts running perpendicular to AB with velocity v_1 and A also start moving with velocity v. Thus, A will catch B at point C in time t.

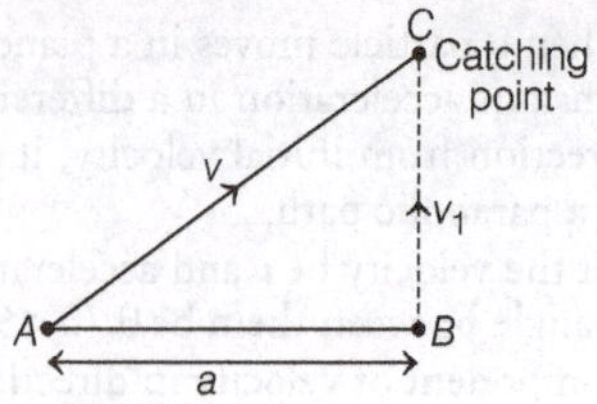

From the figure,

$$(vt)^2 = (v_1 t)^2 + (a)^2$$

$$\Rightarrow \quad t^2 = \frac{a^2}{v^2 - v_1^2}$$

$$\Rightarrow \quad t = \sqrt{\frac{a^2}{v^2 - v_1^2}} = \frac{a}{\sqrt{v^2 - v_1^2}}$$

04. (a) Given, width of river, $d = 1$ km

Velocity of boat, $v_b = 5$ km/h

The boat covered the width of river in time $t = 15$ min $= \dfrac{1}{4}$ h

Speed in the direction of shortest path

$$= \frac{\text{shortest path}}{\text{time}}$$

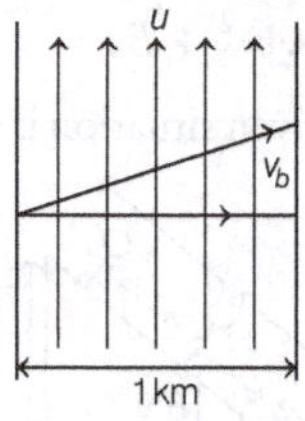

$$\Rightarrow \quad t = \frac{d}{\sqrt{v_b^2 - u^2}}$$

$$\Rightarrow \quad \frac{1}{4} = \frac{1}{\sqrt{5^2 - u^2}} = \frac{1}{\sqrt{25 - u^2}}$$

$$\Rightarrow \quad \frac{1}{16} = \frac{1}{25 - u^2}$$

$$\Rightarrow \quad 25 - u^2 = 16 \Rightarrow u^2 = 9$$

$$\Rightarrow \quad u = 3 \text{ km/h}$$

Hence, the speed of the river is equal to 3 km/h.

05. (c) Let u be the speed of stream and v be the speed of person started from A. He wants to reach at point B directed opposite to A.

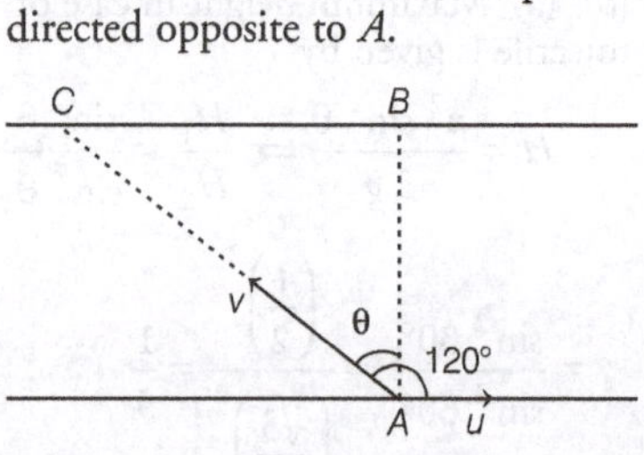

As given, v makes an angle of 120° with direction of flow u, the resultant of v and u is along AB.

From figure $u = v\sin\theta = v\sin 30°$

$$\therefore \quad u = \frac{v}{2} = \frac{0.5}{2} \quad (\because v = 0.5 \text{ m/s})$$

$$= 0.25 \text{ m/s}$$

06. (c)

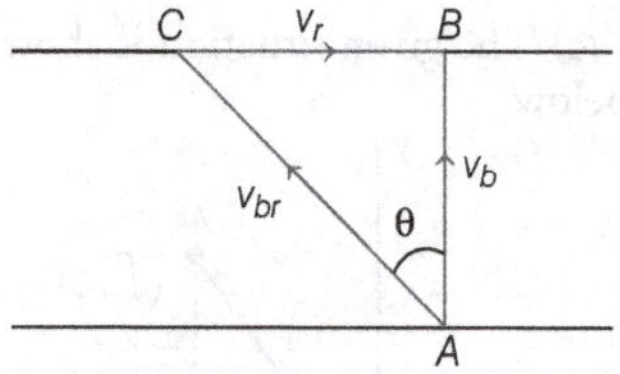

Let v_r = velocity of river

v_{br} = velocity of boat in still water

and w = width of river

Time taken to cross the river

$$= 15 \text{ min} = \frac{15}{60} \text{ h} = \frac{1}{4} \text{ h}$$

Shortest path is taken when v_b is along AB. In this case,

$$\mathbf{v}_{br}^2 = \mathbf{v}_r^2 + \mathbf{v}_b^2$$

Now, $t = \dfrac{w}{v_b} = \dfrac{w}{\sqrt{v_{br}^2 - v_r^2}}$

$$\therefore \quad \frac{1}{4} = \frac{1}{\sqrt{5^2 - v_r^2}}$$

$$\Rightarrow \quad 5^2 - \mathbf{v}_r^2 = 16 \Rightarrow \mathbf{v}_r^2 = 25 - 16 = 9$$

$$\therefore \quad \mathbf{v}_r = \sqrt{9} = 3 \text{ km/h}$$

Alternate Solution

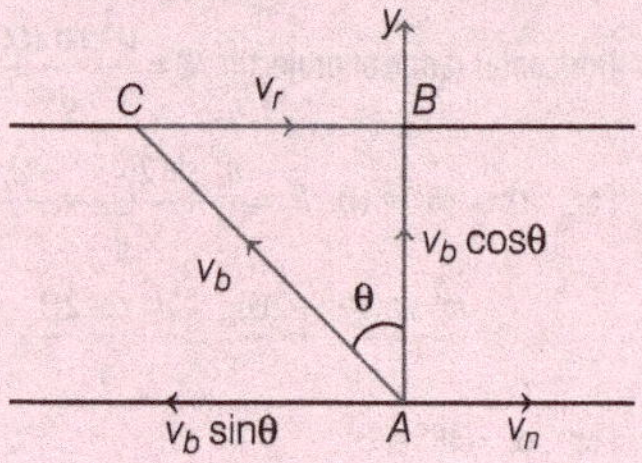

$$t = \frac{15}{60} = \frac{1}{4} \text{ h}$$

$\Rightarrow$ Time taken by the boat to cross the river,

$$t = \frac{y}{v_b \cos\theta}$$

$$\Rightarrow \quad \frac{1}{4} = \frac{1}{5\cos\theta} \Rightarrow \cos\theta = \frac{4}{5}$$

So, $\sin\theta = \sqrt{1 - \cos^2\theta} = \sqrt{1 - \left(\frac{4}{5}\right)^2} = \frac{3}{5}$

For the boat to reach at B

$$v_b \sin\theta = v_r \Rightarrow 5 \times \frac{3}{5} = v_r$$

$$\Rightarrow \quad v_r = 3 \text{ km/h}$$

Topic 4

01. *(d)* In uniform circular motion, direction of motion changes continuously. Circular motion is an accelerated motion. So, uniform circular motion have varying velocity and varying acceleration.

02. *(c)* The direction of angular acceleration of a body moving along the circumference of the circular path is perpendicular to the plane in which rotation takes place i.e. along the axis of rotation.

03. *(d)* Maximum height attained it is given as

$$H_{max} = \frac{u^2 \sin^2 \theta}{2g} \quad \ldots(i)$$

$$H_{max} = 4R \quad \text{(given)}$$

Also, we know that, speed of the particle in circular path,

$$u = \frac{2\pi R}{T}$$

Substituting the values in the Eq. (i), we get

$$4R = \frac{\left(\frac{2\pi R}{T}\right)^2 \sin^2 \theta}{2g}$$

$$\Rightarrow \quad \sin \theta = \left(\frac{2gT^2}{\pi^2 R}\right)^{1/2}$$

$$\theta = \sin^{-1}\left(\frac{2gT^2}{\pi^2 R}\right)^{1/2}$$

04. *(a)* Given, two particle are rotating in circles of radii r_A and r_B.

Time taken for particle A to revolve one revolution, $t_A = \frac{2\pi r_A}{v_A}$

Time taken for particle B to revolve one revolution

$$t_B = \frac{2\pi r_B}{v_B}$$

Since, $t_A = t_B \Rightarrow \frac{2\pi r_A}{v_A} = \frac{2\pi r_B}{v_B}$

or $\frac{v_A}{r_A} = \frac{v_B}{r_B} \Rightarrow \omega_A = \omega_B$

Hence, the ratio of their angular speed will be 1:1.

• Concept Enhancer

Angular velocity is defined as the rate at which the object is rotated about an axis and it is written as

$$\omega = \frac{2\pi}{T} \Rightarrow \text{Thus for } \frac{\omega_A}{\omega_B} = \frac{\frac{2\pi}{T_A}}{\frac{2\pi}{T_B}} = \frac{T_B}{T_A}$$

05. *(c)* Centripetal acceleration of a particle moving on a circular path is given by

$$a_c = \frac{v^2}{R}$$

In the given figure,

$$a_c = a\cos 30° = 15\cos 30° \text{ m/s}^2$$

$$\Rightarrow \frac{v^2}{R} = 15\cos 30°$$

$$\Rightarrow v^2 = R \times 15 \times \frac{\sqrt{3}}{2} = 2.5 \times 15 \times \frac{\sqrt{3}}{2}$$

$$\therefore \quad v = 5.7 \text{ m/s}$$

06. *(c)* Given, $r = 5 \text{ cm} = 5 \times 10^{-2}$ m

$$T = 0.2\,\pi \text{s}$$

We know that acceleration is given by

$$a = r\omega^2 = \frac{4\pi^2}{T^2} r$$

$$= \frac{4 \times \pi^2 \times 5 \times 10^{-2}}{(0.2\,\pi)^2} = 5 \text{ m/s}^2$$

07. *(b)* Given, displacement = 0 (for circular motion in one turn)

distance = $2\pi r$ (for each rotation)

Hence, average velocity

$$= \frac{\text{Displacement}}{\text{Time-interval}} = \frac{0}{t} = 0$$

$$\text{Average speed} = \frac{\text{Distance}}{\text{Time - interval}}$$

$$= \frac{2\pi r}{t} = \frac{2 \times 3.14 \times 100}{62.8}$$

$$= 10 \text{ ms}^{-1}$$

08. *(c)* Since, speed is constant throughout the motion, so, it is a uniform circular motion. Therefore, its radial acceleration is given by

$$a_r = r\omega^2$$

$$= r\left(\frac{2\pi n}{t}\right)^2 = r \times \frac{4\pi^2 n^2}{t^2}$$

$$= \frac{1 \times 4 \times \pi^2 \times (22)^2}{(44)^2}$$

$$= \pi^2 \text{ m/s}^2$$

09. *(d)* In a circular motion, particle repeats its motion after equal intervals of time. So, particle moving on a circular path is periodic but not simple harmonic as it does not execute to and fro motion about a fixed point.

10. *(a)* Angular velocity of particle is given by

$$\omega = \frac{2\pi}{T}$$

or $\quad \omega \propto \frac{1}{T}$

[T = time period of the particle]

It simply implies that ω does not depend on mass of the body and radius of the circle.

$$\therefore \quad \frac{\omega_1}{\omega_2} = \frac{T_2}{T_1}$$

but given time period is same, i.e.

$$T_1 = T_2$$

Hence, $\quad \frac{\omega_1}{\omega_2} = \frac{1}{1}$

11. *(b)* The relation between linear velocity **v**, angular velocity ω and position vector **r** is given by

$$\mathbf{v} = \omega \times \mathbf{r}$$

$$= (3\hat{i} - 4\hat{j} + \hat{k}) \times (5\hat{i} - 6\hat{j} + 6\hat{k})$$

$$= \begin{vmatrix} \hat{i} & \hat{j} & \hat{k} \\ 3 & -4 & 1 \\ 5 & -6 & 6 \end{vmatrix}$$

$$= \hat{i}\begin{vmatrix} -4 & 1 \\ -6 & 6 \end{vmatrix} - \hat{j}\begin{vmatrix} 3 & 1 \\ 5 & 6 \end{vmatrix} + \hat{k}\begin{vmatrix} 3 & -4 \\ 5 & -6 \end{vmatrix}$$

$$= (-24 + 6)\,\hat{i} - (18 - 5)\,\hat{j} + (-18 + 20)\,\hat{k}$$

$$= -18\hat{i} - 13\hat{j} + 2\hat{k}$$

Alternate Solution

$$\mathbf{v} = \omega \times \mathbf{r}$$

$$= (3\hat{i} - 4\hat{j} + \hat{k}) \times (5\hat{i} - 6\hat{j} + 6\hat{k})$$

$$= (3 \times 5)(\hat{i} \times \hat{i}) + [3 \times (-6)](\hat{i} \times \hat{j}) + (3 \times 6)(\hat{i} \times \hat{k}) + (-4 \times 5)(\hat{j} \times \hat{i}) + (-4 \times -6)(\hat{j} \times \hat{j}) + (-4 \times 6)(\hat{j} \times \hat{k}) + (1 \times 5)(\hat{k} \times \hat{i}) + (1 \times -6)(\hat{k} \times \hat{j}) + (1 \times 6)(\hat{k} \times \hat{k})$$

Use $\hat{i} \times \hat{j} = -\hat{j} \times \hat{i} = \hat{k}$

$\hat{j} \times \hat{k} = -\hat{k} \times \hat{j} = \hat{i}$

and $\hat{k} \times \hat{i} = -\hat{i} \times \hat{k} = \hat{j}$

Thus, $\mathbf{v} = 0 + (-18)(\hat{k}) + (18)(-\hat{j}) + (-20)(-\hat{k}) + 0 + (-24)(\hat{i}) + (5)(\hat{j}) + (-6)(-\hat{i}) + 0$

$$= -18\hat{k} - 18\hat{j} + 20\hat{k} - 24\hat{i} + 5\hat{j} + 6\hat{i}$$

$$= -18\hat{i} - 13\hat{j} + 2\hat{k}$$

12. *(b)* Linear speed

= radius × angular speed

or $\quad v = r\omega$

Here, $\quad r = 20 \text{ cm} = 0.20$ m

$\omega = 10$ rad / s

$\therefore \quad v = 0.20 \times 10$

$\Rightarrow \quad v = 2$ m / s

C-04

NEET Chapterwise
Topicwise Physics

In NEET 2024, 2 questions were visible from this chapter. In past 5 years, 2 questions from topic-1, 1 question from topic-2, 2 questions from topic-3 and 3 questions from topic-4 and 1 question from topic-5 were asked.

For detailed analysis scan QR code

LAWS OF MOTION

Topic 1 Newton's Laws of Motion

01 A horizontal force 10 N is applied to a block A as shown in figure. The mass of blocks A and B are 2 kg and 3 kg respectively. The blocks slide over a frictionless surface. The force exerted by block A on block B is *[NEET 2024]*

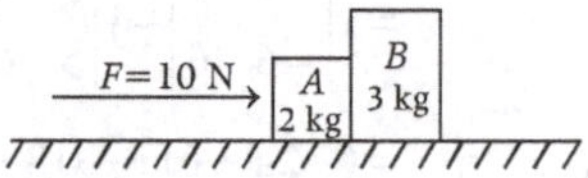

(a) zero (b) 4 N (c) 6 N (d) 10 N

02 A truck is stationary and has a bob suspended by a light string, in a frame attached to the truck. The truck, suddenly moves to the right with an acceleration of a. The pendulum will tilt *[NCERT (New) Pg. 53, NEET (Odisha) 2020]*

(a) to the left and the angle of inclination of the pendulum with the vertical is $\sin^{-1}\left(\frac{g}{a}\right)$

(b) to the left and angle of inclination of the pendulum with the vertical is $\tan^{-1}\left(\frac{a}{g}\right)$

(c) to the left and angle of inclination of the pendulum with the vertical is $\sin^{-1}\left(\frac{a}{g}\right)$

(d) to the left and angle of inclination of the pendulum with the vertical is $\tan^{-1}\left(\frac{g}{a}\right)$

03 A particle moving with velocity $\mathbf{v}$ is acted by three forces shown by the vector triangle PQR. The velocity of the particle will *[NEET (National) 2019]*

(a) decrease
(b) remain constant
(c) change according to the smallest force QR
(d) increase

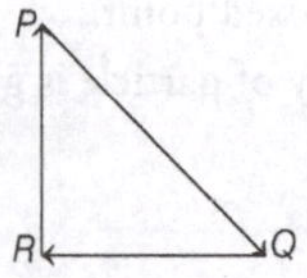

04 A balloon with mass m is descending down with an acceleration a (where, $a < g$). How much mass should be removed from it so that it starts moving up with an acceleration a? *NCERT (New) Pg. 53, AIPMT 2014]*

(a) $\frac{2ma}{g+a}$ (b) $\frac{2ma}{g-a}$

(c) $\frac{ma}{g+a}$ (d) $\frac{ma}{g-a}$

05 A body, under the action of a force $\mathbf{F} = 6\hat{\mathbf{i}} - 8\hat{\mathbf{j}} + 10\hat{\mathbf{k}}$, acquires an acceleration of 1 ms^{-2}. The mass of this body must be *[NCERT (New) Pg. 53, AIPMT 2009]*

(a) $2\sqrt{10}$ kg (b) 10 kg
(c) 20 kg (d) $10\sqrt{2}$ kg

06 A block of mass m is placed on a smooth wedge of inclination θ. The whole system is accelerated horizontally, so that the block does not slip on the wedge. The force exerted by the wedge on the block (g is acceleration due to gravity) will be *[AIPMT 2004]*

(a) $mg\cos\theta$ (b) $mg\sin\theta$ (c) mg (d) $\frac{mg\sin\theta}{\cos\theta}$

07 An object of mass 3 kg is at rest. If a force $\mathbf{F} = (6t^2\hat{\mathbf{i}} + 4t\hat{\mathbf{j}})$ N is applied on the object, then the velocity of the object at $t = 3$ s is *[AIPMT 2002]*

(a) $18\hat{\mathbf{i}} + 3\hat{\mathbf{j}}$ (b) $18\hat{\mathbf{i}} + 6\hat{\mathbf{j}}$
(c) $3\hat{\mathbf{i}} + 18\hat{\mathbf{j}}$ (d) $18\hat{\mathbf{i}} + 4\hat{\mathbf{j}}$

08 A player takes 0.1 s in catching a ball of mass 150 g moving with velocity of 20 m/s. The force imparted by the ball on the hands of the player is *[NCERT (New) Pg. 54, AIPMT 2001]*

(a) 0.3 N (b) 3 N
(c) 30 N (d) 300 N

09 The force on a rocket moving with a velocity 300 m/s is 210 N. The rate of combustion of fuel of rocket is *[NCERT (New) Pg. 54, AIPMT 1999]*

(a) 0.7 kg/s (b) 1.4 kg/s
(c) 0.07 kg/s (d) 10.7 kg/s

10 A 5000 kg rocket is set for vertical firing. The exhaust speed is 800 ms^{-1}. To give an initial upward acceleration of 20 m/s^2, the amount of gas ejected per second to supply the needed thrust will be ($g = 10\ ms^{-2}$) **[AIPMT 1998]**

(a) 127.5 kg s^{-1} (b) 187.5 kg s^{-1}
(c) 185.5 kg s^{-1} (d) 137.5 kg s^{-1}

11 A 10 N force is applied on a body produces an acceleration of 1 m/s^2. The mass of the body is **[AIPMT 1996]**

(a) 5 kg (b) 10 kg
(c) 15 kg (d) 20 kg

12 If the force on a rocket moving with a velocity of 300 m/s is 345 N, then the rate of combustion of the fuel is **[NCERT (New) Pg. 54, AIPMT 1995]**

(a) 0.55 kg/s (b) 0.75 kg/s
(c) 1.15 kg/s (d) 2.25 kg/s

13 A satellite in a force free space sweeps stationary interplanetary dust at a rate $\left(\frac{dM}{dt}\right) = \alpha v$. The acceleration of satellite is **[AIPMT 1994]**

(a) $-\frac{2\alpha v^2}{M}$ (b) $-\frac{\alpha v^2}{M}$
(c) $-\frac{\alpha v^2}{2M}$ (d) $-\alpha v^2$

14 Physical independence of force is a consequence of **[NCERT (New) Pg. 51, AIPMT 1991]**

(a) third law of motion (b) second law of motion
(c) first law of motion (d) All of these

15 A 600 kg rocket is set for a vertical firing. If the exhaust speed is 1000 ms^{-1}, the mass of the gas ejected per second to supply the thrust needed to overcome the weight of rocket is **[NCERT (New) Pg. 54, AIPMT 1990]**

(a) 117.6 kg s^{-1} (b) 58.6 kg s^{-1}
(c) 6 kg s^{-1} (d) 76.4 kg s^{-1}

Topic 2 Impulse and Conservation of Momentum

01 A ball of mass 0.15 kg is dropped from a height 10 m, strikes the ground and rebounds to the same height. The magnitude of impulse imparted to the ball is nearly ($g = 10\ m/s^2$) **[NEET 2021]**

(a) 0 (b) 4.2 kg-m/s
(c) 2.1 kg-m/s (d) 1.4 kg-m/s

02 An object flying in air with velocity $(20\hat{i} + 25\hat{j} - 12\hat{k})$ suddenly breaks in two pieces whose masses are in the ratio 1 : 5. The smaller mass flies off with a velocity $(100\hat{i} + 35\hat{j} + 8\hat{k})$. The velocity of the larger piece will be **[NCERT (New) Pg. 58, Odisha NEET 2019]**

(a) $4\hat{i} + 23\hat{j} - 16\hat{k}$ (b) $-100\hat{i} - 35\hat{j} - 8\hat{k}$
(c) $20\hat{i} + 15\hat{j} - 80\hat{k}$ (d) $-20\hat{i} - 15\hat{j} - 80\hat{k}$

03 A rigid ball of mass m strikes a rigid wall at 60° and gets reflected without loss of speed as shown in the figure. The value of impulse imparted by the wall on the ball will be **[NEET 2016]**

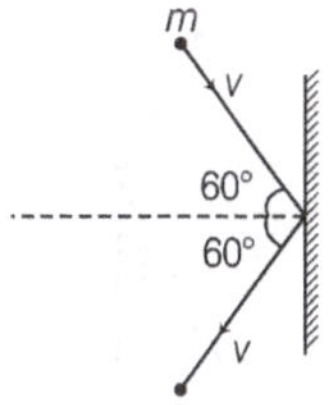

(a) mv (b) $2mv$
(c) $mv/2$ (d) $mv/3$

04 A bullet of mass 10 g moving horizontal with a velocity of 400 m/s strikes a wood block of mass 2 kg which is suspended by light inextensible string of length 5 m. As result, the centre of gravity of the block found to rise a vertical distance of 10 cm. The speed of the bullet after it emerges of horizontally from the block will be **[NCERT (New) Pg. 57, NEET 2016]**

(a) 100 m/s (b) 80 m/s
(c) 120 m/s (d) 160 m/s

05 An explosion breaks a rock into three parts in a horizontal plane. Two of them go off at right angles to each other. The first part of mass 1 kg moves with a speed of 12 ms^{-1} and the second part of mass 2 kg moves with 8 ms^{-1} speed. If the third part flies off with 4 ms^{-1} speed, then its mass is **[NEET 2013]**

(a) 3 kg (b) 5 kg
(c) 7 kg (d) 17 kg

06 A body of mass M hits normally a rigid wall with velocity v and bounces back with the same velocity. The impulse experienced by the body is **[AIPMT 2011]**

(a) Mv (b) 1.5 Mv
(c) 2 Mv (d) zero

07 A man of 50 kg mass is standing in a gravity free space at a height of 10 m above the floor. He throws a stone of 0.5 kg mass downwards with a speed 2 ms^{-1}. When the stone reaches the floor, the distance of the man above the floor will be **[AIPMT 2010]**

(a) 9.9 m (b) 10.1 m
(c) 10 m (d) 20 m

08 An explosion blows a rock into three parts. Two parts go off at right angles to each other. These two are, 1 kg first part moving with a velocity of 12 ms^{-1} and 2 kg second part moving with a velocity of 8 ms^{-1}. If the third part flies off with a velocity of 4 ms^{-1}, its mass would be **[NCERT (New) Pg. 85, AIPMT 2009]**

(a) 5 kg (b) 7 kg
(c) 17 kg (d) 3 kg

09 A 0.5 kg ball moving with a speed of 12 m/s strikes a hard wall at an angle of 30° with the wall. It is reflected with the same speed and at the same angle. If the ball is in contact with the wall for 0.25 s, the average force acting on the wall is *[NCERT (New) Pg. 57, AIPMT 2006]*

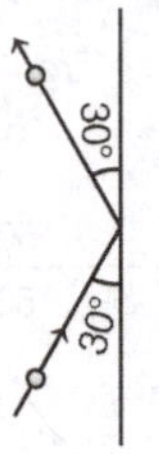

(a) 48 N (b) 24 N (c) 12 N (d) 96 N

10 If a cricketer catches a ball of mass 150 g moving with a velocity of 20 m/s, then he experiences a force of (time taken to complete the catch is 0.1 s) *[NCERT (New) Pg. 58, AIPMT 2001]*

(a) 300 N (b) 30 N (c) 3 N (d) 0.3 N

11 A particle of mass 1 kg is thrown vertically upwards with speed 100 m/s. After 5 s, it explodes into two parts. One part of mass 400 g comes back with speed 25 m/s, what is the speed of other part just after explosion? *[AIPMT 2000]*

(a) 100 m/s upwards (b) 600 m/s upwards
(c) 100 m/s downwards (d) 300 m/s upwards

12 A bullet is fired from a gun. The force on the bullet is given by

$$F = 600 - 2 \times 10^5\, t$$

where, F is in Newton and t in second. The force on the bullet becomes zero as soon as it leaves the barrel. What is the average impulse imparted to the bullet ? *[NCERT (New) Pg. 58, AIPMT 1998]*

(a) 8 N-s (b) Zero (c) 0.9 N-s (d) 1.8 N-s

13 A man fires a bullet of mass 200 g at a speed of 5 m/s. The gun is of one kg mass. By what velocity the gun rebounds backward ? *[AIPMT 1996]*

(a) 1 m/s (b) 0.01 m/s (c) 0.1 m/s (d) 10 m/s

14 A particle of mass m is moving with a uniform velocity v_1. It is given an impulse such that its velocity becomes v_2. The impulse is equal to *[AIPMT 1990]*

(a) $m[|v_2| - |v_1|]$ (b) $\frac{1}{2}m(v_2^2 - v_1^2)$
(c) $m(v_1 + v_2)$ (d) $m(v_2 - v_1)$

15 A body of mass 5 kg explodes at rest into three fragments with masses in the ratio 1 : 1 : 3. The fragments with equal masses fly in mutually perpendicular directions with speed of 21 m/s. The velocity of heaviest fragment in m/s will be *[NCERT (New) Pg. 85, AIPMT 1989]*

(a) $3\sqrt{2}$ (b) $7\sqrt{2}$ (c) $\sqrt{2}$ (d) $5\sqrt{2}$

Topic 3 Equilibrium of a Particle and Common Forces in Mechanics

01 A small block slides down on a smooth inclined plane, starting from rest at time $t = 0$. Let s_n be the distance travelled by the block in the interval $t = n - 1$ to $t = n$. Then, the ratio $\frac{s_n}{s_{n+1}}$ is *[NCERT (New) Pg. 58, NEET 2021]*

(a) $\frac{2n}{2n-1}$ (b) $\frac{2n-1}{2n}$ (c) $\frac{2n-1}{2n+1}$ (d) $\frac{2n+1}{2n-1}$

02 Two bodies of mass 4 kg and 6 kg are tied to the ends of a massless string. The string passes over a pulley which is frictionless (see figure). The acceleration of the system in terms of acceleration due to gravity g is *[NEET (Sep.) 2020]*

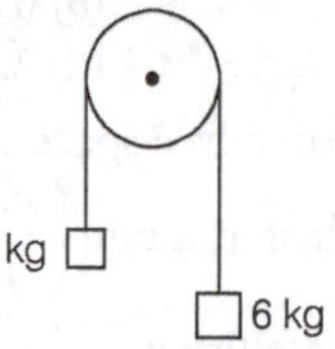

(a) $g/2$ (b) $g/5$ (c) $g/10$ (d) g

03 A block of mass m is placed on a smooth inclined wedge ABC of inclination θ as shown in the figure. The wedge is given an acceleration a towards the right. The relation between a and θ for the block to remain stationary on the wedge is *[NCERT (New) Pg. 58, NEET 2018]*

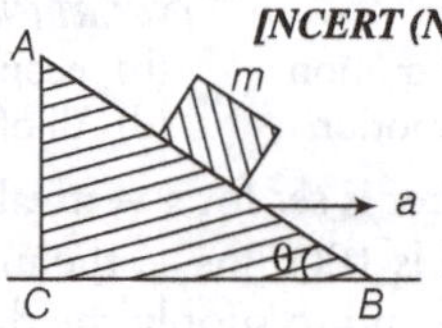

(a) $a = g\cos\theta$ (b) $a = \frac{g}{\sin\theta}$
(c) $a = \frac{g}{\operatorname{cosec}\theta}$ (d) $a = g\tan\theta$

04 Two blocks A and B of masses $3m$ and m, respectively are connected by a massless and inextensible string. The whole system is suspended by a massless spring as shown in figure. The magnitudes of acceleration of A and B immediately after the string is cut, are respectively *[NEET 2017]*

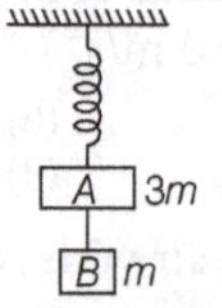

(a) $g, \frac{g}{3}$ (b) $\frac{g}{3}, g$
(c) g, g (d) $\frac{g}{3}, \frac{g}{3}$

05 Three blocks A, B and C of masses 4 kg, 2 kg and 1 kg respectively, are in contact on a frictionless surface, as shown. If a force of 14 N is applied on the 4 kg block, then the contact force between A and B is *[NCERT (New) Pg. 58, AIPMT 2015]*

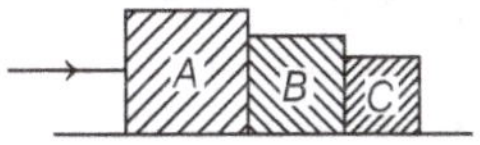

(a) 2 N (b) 6 N (c) 8 N (d) 18 N

06 Three blocks with masses m, $2m$ and $3m$ are connected by strings, as shown in the figure. After an upward force F is applied on block m, the masses move upward at constant speed v. What is the net force on the block of mass $2m$? (g is the acceleration due to gravity). *[NEET 2013]*

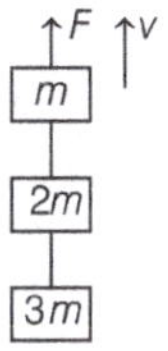

(a) Zero (b) 2 mg
(c) 3 mg (d) 6 mg

07 A person of mass 60 kg is inside a lift of mass 940 kg and presses the button on control panel. The lift starts moving upwards with an acceleration 1.0 m/s^2. If $g = 10$ m / s^2, the tension in the supporting cable is *[NCERT (New) Pg. 59, AIPMT 2011]*
(a) 9680 N (b) 11000 N
(c) 1200 N (d) 8600 N

08 The mass of a lift is 2000 kg. When the tension in the supporting cable is 28000 N, then its acceleration is *[AIPMT 2009]*
(a) 30 ms^{-2} downwards
(b) 4 ms^{-2} upwards
(c) 4 ms^{-2} downwards
(d) 14 ms^{-2} upwards

09 A man weighs 80 kg. He stands on a weighing scale in a lift which is moving upwards with a uniform acceleration of 5 m / s^2. What would be the reading on the scale ? (Take, $g = 10$ m / s^2) *[AIPMT 2003]*
(a) 800 N (b) 1200 N
(c) Zero (d) 400 N

10 A monkey of mass 20 kg is holding a vertical rope. The rope will not break, when a mass of 25 kg is suspended from it but will break, if the mass exceeds 25 kg. What is the maximum acceleration with which the monkey can climb up along the rope ? (Take $g = 10$ m / s^2) *[AIPMT 2003]*
(a) 25 m/s^2 (b) 2.5 m/s^2
(c) 5 m/s^2 (d) 10 m/s^2

11 A lift of mass 1000 kg is moving upwards with an acceleration of 1 m/s^2. The tension developed in the string, which is connected to lift is ($g = 9.8$ m/s^2) *[NCERT (New) Pg. 58, AIPMT 2002]*
(a) 9800 N (b) 10800 N
(c) 11000 N (d) 10000 N

12 Two masses $M_1 = 5$ kg, $M_2 = 10$ kg are connected at the ends of an inextensible string passing over a frictionless pulley as shown. When masses are released, then acceleration of masses will be *[NCERT (New) Pg. 58, AIPMT 2000]*

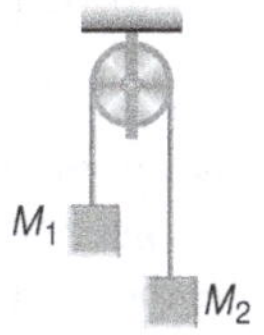

(a) g (b) $\frac{g}{2}$
(c) $\frac{g}{3}$ (d) $\frac{g}{4}$

13 A mass of 1 kg is suspended by a thread. It is
1. lifted up with an acceleration 4.9 m/s^2,
2. lowered with an acceleration 4.9 m/s^2.
The ratio of the tensions is *[AIPMT 1998]*
(a) 3 : 1 (b) 1 : 3
(c) 1 : 2 (d) 2 : 1

Topic 4 Friction

01 A football player is moving southward and suddenly turns eastward with the same speed to avoid an opponent. The force that acts on the player while turning is *[NCERT (New) Pg. 60, NEET 2023]*
(a) along northward (b) along north-east
(c) along south-west (d) along eastward

02 Calculate the maximum acceleration of a moving car so that a body lying on the floor of the car remains stationary. The coefficient of static friction between the body and the floor is 0.15 ($g = 10$ m s^{-2}). *[NCERT (New) Pg. 61, NEET 2023]*
(a) 150 m s^{-2} (b) 1.5 m s^{-2}
(c) 50 m s^{-2} (d) 1.2 m s^{-2}

03 Calculate the acceleration of the block and trolly system shown in the figure. The coefficient of kinetic friction between the trolly and the surface is 0.05. ($g = 10$ m/s^2, mass of the string is negligible and no other friction exists). *[NEET (Oct.) 2020]*

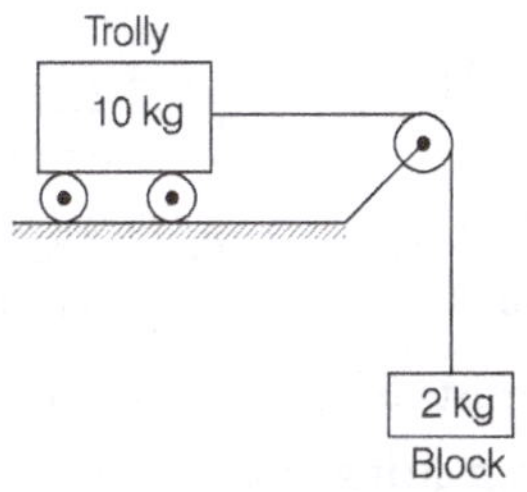

(a) 1.25 m/s^2 (b) 1.50 m/s^2
(c) 1.66 m/s^2 (d) 1.00 m/s^2

04 A body of mass m is kept on a rough horizontal surface (coefficient of friction $= \mu$). Horizontal force is applied on the body but it does not move. The resultant of normal reaction and the frictional force acting on the object is given F, where F is *[NEET (Odisha) 2019]*

(a) $|F| = mg + \mu\, mg$ (b) $|F| = \mu mg$

(c) $|F| \leq mg\sqrt{1+\mu^2}$ (d) $|F| = mg$

05 Which one of the following statements is incorrect ? *[NCERT (New) Pg. 61, NEET 2018]*

(a) Frictional force opposes the relative motion

(b) Limiting value of static friction is directly proportional to normal reaction

(c) Rolling friction is smaller than sliding friction

(d) Coefficient of sliding friction has dimensions of length

06 A plank with a box on it at one end is gradually raised about the other end. As the angle of inclination with the horizontal reaches 30°, the box starts to slip and slides 4.0 m down the plank in 4.0 s. The coefficients of static and kinetic friction between the box and the plank will be, respectively *[AIPMT 2015]*

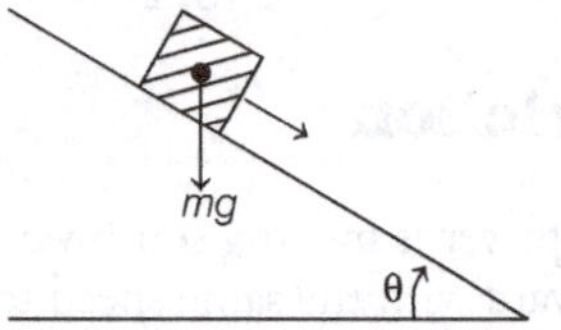

(a) 0.6 and 0.6 (b) 0.6 and 0.5

(c) 0.5 and 0.6 (d) 0.4 and 0.3

07 A block A of mass m_1 rests on a horizontal table. A light string connected to it passes over a frictionless pulley at the edge of table and from its other end another block B of mass m_2 is suspended. The coefficient of kinetic friction between the block and the table is μ_k. When the block A is sliding on the table, the tension in the string is *[NCERT (New) Pg. 61, AIPMT 2015]*

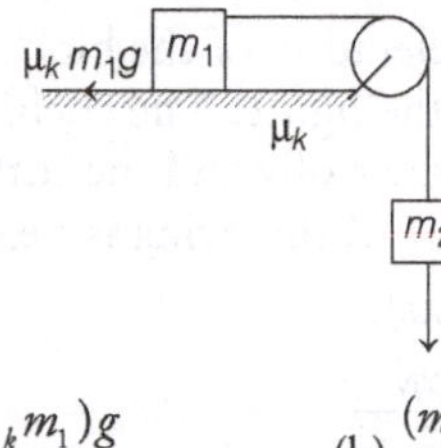

(a) $\dfrac{(m_2 + \mu_k m_1)g}{(m_1 + m_2)}$ (b) $\dfrac{(m_2 - \mu_k m_1)g}{(m_1 + m_2)}$

(c) $\dfrac{m_1 m_2 (1 + \mu_k)g}{(m_1 + m_2)}$ (d) $\dfrac{m_1 m_2 (1 - \mu_k)g}{(m_1 + m_2)}$

08 A system consists of three masses m_1, m_2 and m_3 connected by a string passing over a pulley P. The mass m_1 hangs freely and m_2 and m_3 are on a rough horizontal table (the coefficient of friction $= \mu$). The pulley is frictionless and of negligible mass. The downward acceleration of mass m_1 is (Assume, $m_1 = m_2 = m_3 = m$) *[NCERT (New) Pg. 61, AIPMT 2014]*

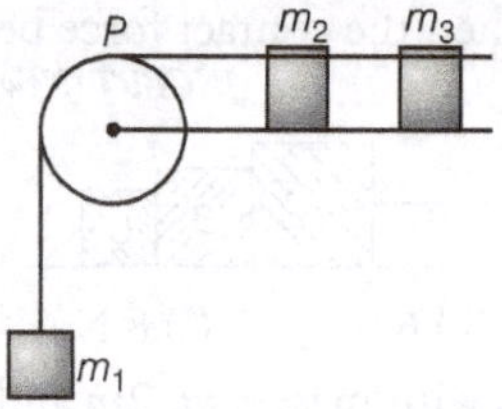

(a) $\dfrac{g(1 - g\mu)}{9}$ (b) $\dfrac{2g\mu}{3}$

(c) $\dfrac{g(1 - 2\mu)}{3}$ (d) $\dfrac{g(1 - 2\mu)}{2}$

09 A block of mass m is in contact with the cart C as shown in the figure.

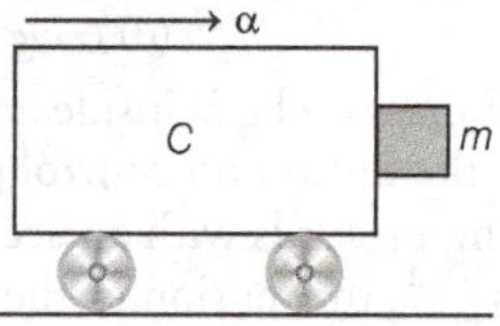

The coefficient of static friction between the block and the cart is μ. The acceleration α of the cart that will prevent the block from falling satisfies *[AIPMT 2010]*

(a) $\alpha > \dfrac{mg}{\mu}$ (b) $\alpha > \dfrac{g}{\mu m}$

(c) $\alpha \geq \dfrac{g}{\mu}$ (d) $\alpha < \dfrac{g}{\mu}$

10 A block B is pushed momentarily along a horizontal surface with an initial velocity v. If μ is the coefficient of sliding friction between block B and the surface, block B will come to rest after a time *[NCERT (New) Pg. 61, AIPMT 2007]*

(a) $\dfrac{v}{g\mu}$ (b) $\dfrac{g\mu}{v}$ (c) $\dfrac{g}{v}$ (d) $\dfrac{v}{g}$

11 The coefficient of static friction, μ_s, between block A of mass 2 kg and the table as shown in the figure, is 0.2. What would be the maximum mass value of block B, so that the two blocks do not move ? The string and the pulley are assumed to be smooth and massless ($g = 10\ \text{m/s}^2$) *[AIPMT 2004]*

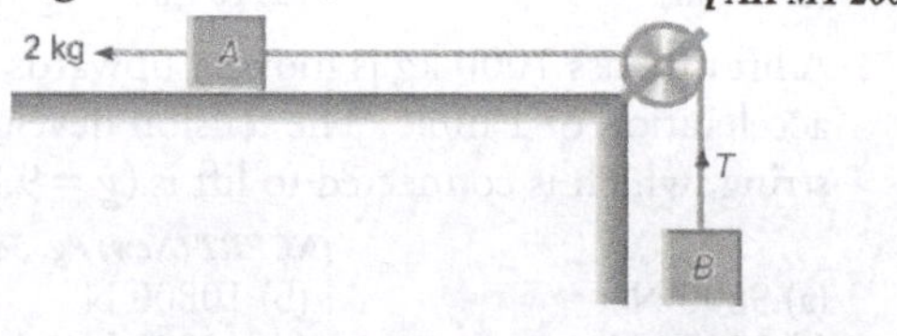

(a) 2.0 kg (b) 4.0 kg (c) 0.2 kg (d) 0.4 kg

12 A block of mass 10 kg is placed on a rough horizontal surface having coefficient of friction $\mu = 0.5$. If a horizontal force of 100 N is applied on it, then the acceleration of the block will be (Take, $g = 10\ m/s^2$)

[NCERT (New) Pg. 61, AIPMT 2002]

(a) $15\ m/s^2$ (b) $10\ m/s^2$
(c) $5\ m/s^2$ (d) $0.5\ m/s^2$

13 A block has been placed on an inclined plane with the slope angle θ, block slides down the plane at constant speed. The coefficient of kinetic friction is equal to *[NCERT (New) Pg. 61, AIPMT 1993]*

(a) $\sin\theta$ (b) $\cos\theta$
(c) g (d) $\tan\theta$

14 Consider, a car moving along a straight horizontal road with a speed of 72 km/h. If the coefficient of static friction between the tyres and the road is 0.5, the shortest distance in which the car can be stopped is (Take, $g = 10\ m/s^2$) *[AIPMT 1992]*

(a) 30 m (b) 40 m
(c) 72 m (d) 20 m

15 A heavy uniform chain lies on horizontal table top. If the coefficient of friction between the chain and the table surface is 0.25, then the maximum percentage of the length of the chain that can hang over one edge of the table is *[AIPMT 1991]*

(a) 20% (b) 25%
(c) 35% (d) 15%

16 Starting from rest, a body slides down a 45° inclined plane in twice the time it takes to slide down the same distance in the absence of friction. The coefficient of friction between the body and the inclined plane is *[AIPMT 1988]*

(a) 0.80 (b) 0.75 (c) 0.25 (d) 0.33

Topic 5 Dynamics of Circular Motion

01 A wheel of a bullock cart is rolling on a level road as shown in the figure below. If its linear speed is v in the direction shown, which one of the following options is correct (P and Q are any highest and lowest points on the wheel, respectively)?

[NCERT (New) Pg. 121, NEET 2024]

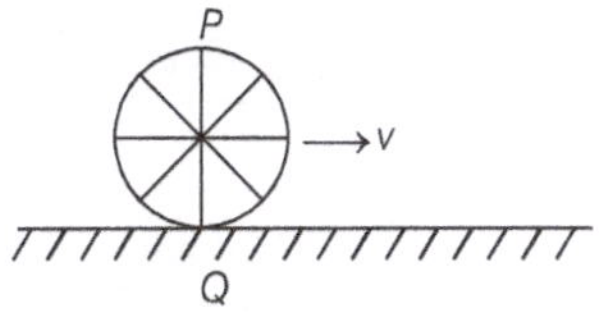

(a) Point P moves slower than point Q
(b) Point P moves faster than point Q
(c) Both the points P and Q move with equal speed
(d) Point P has zero speed

02 Two particles A and B are moving in uniform circular motion in concentric circles of radii r_A and r_B with speed v_A and v_B, respectively. Their time period of rotation is the same. The ratio of angular speed of A to that of B will be

[NCERT (New) Pg. 63, NEET (National) 2019]

(a) $v_A : v_B$ (b) $r_B : r_A$
(c) $1:1$ (d) $r_A : r_B$

03 A block of mass 10 kg is in contact against the inner wall of a hollow cylindrical drum of radius 1 m. The coefficient of friction between the block and the inner wall of the cylinder is 0.1. The minimum angular velocity needed for the cylinder to keep the block stationary when the cylinder is vertical and rotating about its axis, will be ($g = 10\ m/s^2$)

[NCERT (New) Pg. 63, NEET (National) 2019]

(a) $\frac{10}{2\pi}$ rad/s (b) 10 rad/s
(c) 10π rad/s (d) $\sqrt{10}$ rad/s

04 One end of the string of length l is connected to a particle of mass m and the other end is connected to a small peg on a smooth horizontal table. If the particle moves in circle with speed v, the net force on the particle (directed towards center) will be (T represents the tension in the string) *[NEET 2017]*

(a) T (b) $T + \frac{mv^2}{l}$
(c) $T - \frac{mv^2}{l}$ (d) zero

05 A car is negotiating a curved road of radius R. The road is banked at angle θ. The coefficient of friction between the tyres of the car and the road is μ_s. The maximum safe velocity on this road is

[NCERT (New) Pg. 64, NEET 2016]

(a) $\sqrt{gR\left(\frac{\mu_s + \tan\theta}{1-\mu_s\tan\theta}\right)}$ (b) $\sqrt{\frac{g}{R}\left(\frac{\mu_s + \tan\theta}{1-\mu_s\tan\theta}\right)}$

(c) $\sqrt{\frac{g}{R^2}\left(\frac{\mu_s + \tan\theta}{1-\mu_s\tan\theta}\right)}$ (d) $\sqrt{gR^2\left(\frac{\mu_s + \tan\theta}{1-\mu_s\tan\theta}\right)}$

06 A car of mass m is moving on a level circular track of radius R. If μ_s represents the static friction between the road and tyres of the car, the maximum speed of the car in circular motion is given by *[AIPMT 2012]*

(a) $\sqrt{\mu_s mRg}$ (b) $\sqrt{\frac{Rg}{\mu_s}}$ (c) $\frac{mRg}{\mu_s}$ (d) $\sqrt{\mu_s Rg}$

07 A car of mass 1000 kg negotiates a banked curve of radius 90 m on a frictionless road. If the banking angle is 45°, the speed of the car is *[AIPMT 2012]*

(a) $20\ ms^{-1}$ (b) $30\ ms^{-1}$
(c) $5\ ms^{-1}$ (d) $10\ ms^{-1}$

08 A gramophone record is revolving with an angular velocity ω. A coin is placed at a distance r from the centre of the record. The static coefficient of friction is μ. The coin will revolve with the record if *[NCERT (New) Pg. 64, AIPMT 2010]*

(a) $r = \mu g \omega^2$ (b) $r < \frac{\omega^2}{\mu g}$ (c) $r \leq \frac{\mu g}{\omega^2}$ (d) $r \geq \frac{\mu g}{\omega^2}$

09 A 500 kg car takes a round turn of radius 50 m with a velocity of 36 km/h. The centripetal force is *[AIPMT 1999]*

(a) 250 N (b) 750 N (c) 1000 N (d) 1200 N

10 A ball of mass 0.25 kg attached to the end of a string of length 1.96 m is moving in a horizontal circle. The string will break if the tension is more than 25 N. What is the maximum speed with which the ball can be moved ? *[NCERT (New) Pg. 64, AIPMT 1998]*

(a) 14 m/s (b) 3 m/s
(c) 3.92 m/s (d) 5 m/s

11 When milk is churned, cream gets separated due to *[NCERT (New) Pg. 64, AIPMT 1991]*

(a) centripetal force (b) centrifugal force
(c) frictional force (d) gravitational force

• Key **Index**

Topic 1

1 (c)	2 (b)	3 (b)	4 (a)	5 (d)	6 (*)	7 (b)	8 (c)	9 (a)	10 (b)
11 (b)	12 (c)	13 (b)	14 (c)	15 (c)					

Topic 2

1 (b)	2 (a)	3 (a)	4 (c)	5 (b)	6 (c)	7 (b)	8 (a)	9 (b)	10 (b)
11 (a)	12 (c)	13 (a)	14 (d)	15 (b)					

Topic 3

1 (c)	2 (b)	3 (d)	4 (b)	5 (b)	6 (a)	7 (b)	8 (b)	9 (b)	10 (b)
11 (b)	12 (c)	13 (a)							

Topic 4

1 (b)	2 (b)	3 (a)	4 (c)	5 (d)	6 (b)	7 (c)	8 (c)	9 (c)	10 (a)
11 (d)	12 (c)	13 (d)	14 (b)	15 (a)	16 (b)				

Topic 5

1 (b)	2 (c)	3 (b)	4 (a)	5 (a)	6 (d)	7 (b)	8 (c)	9 (c)	10 (a)
11 (b)									

Detailed Explanations

Topic 1

01. *(c)* Net force on A and $B = 10$ N

Acceleration of both A and $B = \dfrac{F}{m}$

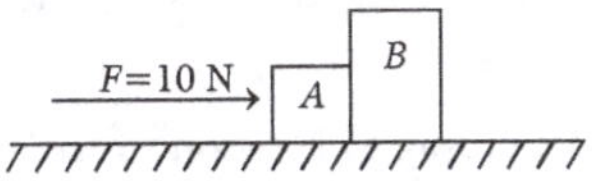

$$a = \frac{10}{5} = 2 \text{ ms}^{-2}$$

For block A

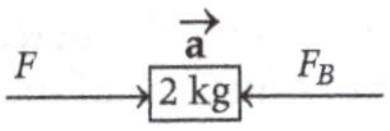

F_B = Force exerted by block B on A

$$F - F_B = 2 \times a$$

$$\Rightarrow \quad 10 - F_B = 2 \times 2 \Rightarrow F_B = 6 \text{ N}$$

For block B

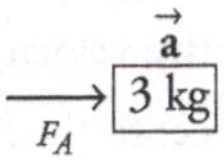

Force exerted by A on B

$$F_A = 3a = 3 \times 2 = 6 \text{ N}$$

02. *(b)* As the truck move to the right, so the bob will move to the left due to inertia of rest with acceleration a.

Thus, the given situation can be drawn as

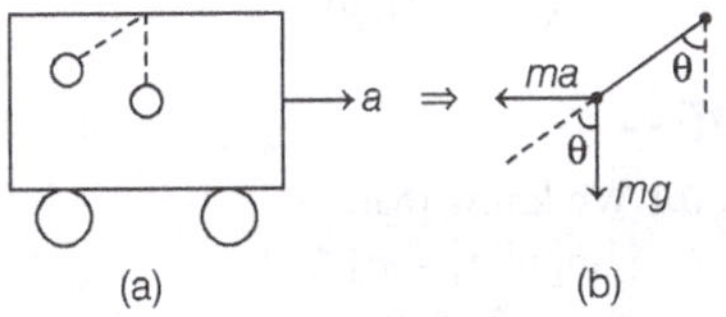

From the above diagram (b) as the string moves by an angle of θ with the vertical then the tangent angle is

$$\tan\theta = \frac{ma}{mg} \Rightarrow \theta = \tan^{-1}\left(\frac{a}{g}\right)$$

• Concept Enhancer

When a bob is suspended from the ceiling of a moving truck with acceleration **a**, there will be a pseudo force (due to inertia) acting on it in the opposite direction of the motion of truck as seen by an observer inside the truck.

In this situation, angle of inclination of pendulum with the vertical is given by

$$\tan\theta = \left(\frac{\text{acceleration of vehicle}}{g}\right)$$

03. *(b)* As the three forces are represented by three sides of a triangle taken in order, then they will be in equilibrium.

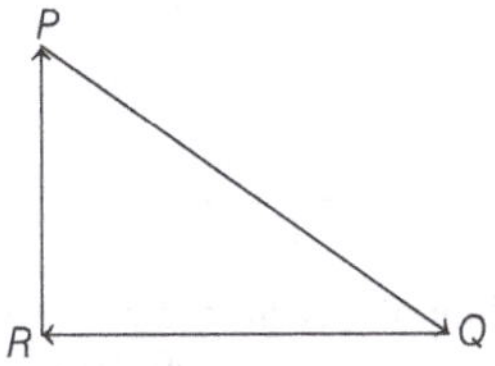

$$\Rightarrow \mathbf{F}_{\text{net}} = \mathbf{F}_{PQ} + \mathbf{F}_{QR} + \mathbf{F}_{RP} = 0$$

$$\mathbf{F}_{\text{net}} = m \times \mathbf{a} = m\frac{d\mathbf{v}}{dt} = 0$$

$$\Rightarrow \quad \frac{d\mathbf{v}}{dt} = 0 \text{ or } \mathbf{v} = \text{constant}$$

So, the velocity of particle remain constant.

04. *(a)* When, the balloon is descending down with acceleration a

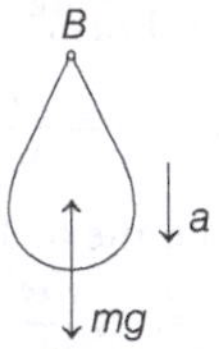

So, from free body diagram

$$mg - B = m \times a \qquad \ldots\text{(i)}$$

[B = Buoyant force]

Here, we should assume that while removing same mass, the volume of balloon and hence,buoyant force will not change.

Let the new mass of the balloon be m'.

So, mass removed $(m - m')$

So, $\quad B - m'g = m' \times a \qquad \ldots\text{(ii)}$

Adding Eqs. (i) and (ii),

$$mg - m'g = ma + m'a$$

$$(mg - ma) = m'(g + a)$$

$$\Rightarrow \quad m(g - a) = m'(g + a)$$

$$m' = \frac{m(g - a)}{g + a}$$

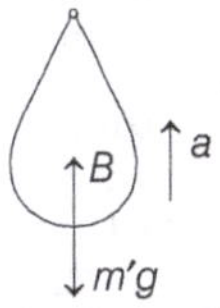

So, mass removed $= m - m'$

$$= m\left[1 - \frac{(g - a)}{(g + a)}\right]$$

$$= m\left[\frac{(g + a) - (g - a)}{(g + a)}\right]$$

$$= m\left[\frac{g + a - g + a}{g + a}\right]$$

$$\Rightarrow \quad \Delta m = \frac{2ma}{g + a}$$

05. *(d)* Here, $\mathbf{F} = 6\hat{\mathbf{i}} - 8\hat{\mathbf{j}} + 10\hat{\mathbf{k}}$

$$|F| = \sqrt{36 + 64 + 100}$$

$$= 10\sqrt{2} \text{ N}$$

$$\therefore \quad m = \frac{F}{a} = \frac{10\sqrt{2}}{1} \qquad [\because F = ma]$$

$$= 10\sqrt{2} \text{ kg}$$

06. *(*)* Let an acceleration to the wedge be given towards left, then the block (being in non-inertial frame) has a pseudo acceleration to the right because of which the block is not slipping

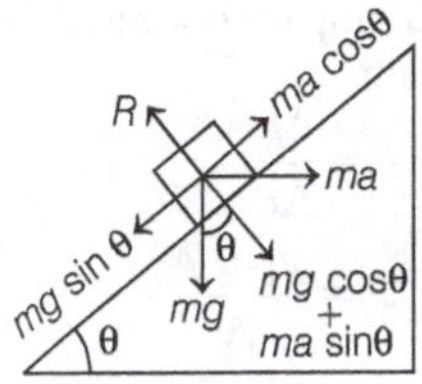

$$\therefore \quad mg\sin\theta = ma\cos\theta$$

$$\Rightarrow \quad a = \frac{g\sin\theta}{\cos\theta}$$

Force exerted by the wedge on the block,

$$R = mg\cos\theta + ma\sin\theta$$

$$= mg\cos\theta + m\left(\frac{g\sin\theta}{\cos\theta}\right)\cdot\sin\theta$$

$$= \frac{mg}{\cos\theta}(\cos^2\theta + \sin^2\theta) = \frac{mg}{\cos\theta}$$

07. *(b)*

key idea

From force, acceleration is determined by the relation $\mathbf{a} = \dfrac{\mathbf{F}}{m}$, which is also written as $\mathbf{a} = \dfrac{dv}{dt}$. On integrating, we get velocity.

According to Newton's second law,

i.e. $\quad \mathbf{F} = \dfrac{dp}{dt}$

or $$F = m\frac{dv}{dt} \quad \ldots(i)$$

Given, $m = 3$ kg, $t = 3$ s

$$F = (6t^2\hat{i} + 4t\hat{j})\,N$$

Substituting these values in Eq. (i), we get

$$(6t^2\hat{i} + 4t\hat{j}) = 3\frac{dv}{dt}$$

or $$dv = \frac{1}{3}(6t^2\hat{i} + 4t\hat{j})\,dt$$

Now, taking integration of both sides, we get

$$\int dv = \int_0^t \frac{1}{3}(6t^2\hat{i} + 4t\hat{j})\,dt$$

$$v = \frac{1}{3}\int_0^t (6t^2\hat{i} + 4t\hat{j})\,dt$$

but $t = 3$ s (given)

$\therefore$ $$v = \frac{1}{3}\int_0^3 (6t^2\hat{i} + 4t\hat{j})\,dt$$

or $$v = \frac{1}{3}\left[\frac{6t^3}{3}\hat{i} + \frac{4t^2}{2}\hat{j}\right]_0^3$$

$$= 18\hat{i} + 6\hat{j}$$

08. *(c)* Force imparted = rate of change of momentum

$$F = \frac{\Delta p}{\Delta t}$$

or $$F = \frac{p_1 - p_2}{\Delta t}$$

or $$F = \frac{m(v_1 - v_2)}{\Delta t}$$

Here, mass of body

$$m = 150\text{ g} = 0.150\text{ kg},$$

$$v_1 = 20\text{ m/s},$$

$$v_2 = 0$$

Time taken,

$$\Delta t = 0.1\text{ s}$$

$\therefore$ $$F = \frac{0.150 \times (20 - 0)}{0.1} = 30\text{ N}$$

09. *(a)* Thrust on the rocket

$$F_t = v_r\left(-\frac{dm}{dt}\right) \text{ (upwards)}$$

Rate of combustion of fuel

$$-\frac{dm}{dt} = \frac{F_t}{v_r}$$

Given, $F_t = 210$ N

$v_r = 300$ m/s

$\therefore$ $$-\frac{dm}{dt} = \frac{210}{300} = 0.7\text{ kg/s}$$

10. *(b)* Thrust on the rocket

$$F_t = v_r\left(-\frac{dm}{dt}\right) \text{ (upwards)}$$

Weight of the rocket

$$w = mg \text{ (downwards)}$$

Net force on the rocket

$$F_{net} = F_t - w$$

$\Rightarrow$ $$ma = v_r\left(\frac{-dm}{dt}\right) - mg$$

$\Rightarrow$ $$\left(\frac{-dm}{dt}\right) = \frac{m(g+a)}{v_r}$$

$\therefore$ Rate of gas ejected per second

$$= \frac{5000\,(10 + 20)}{800}$$

$$= \frac{5000 \times 30}{800}$$

$$= 187.5\text{ kg s}^{-1}$$

11. *(b)* As we know,

Force, $F = ma$

Here, $F = 10$ N

$a = 1\text{ m/s}^2$

$\therefore$ $$m = \frac{F}{a} = \frac{10}{1} = 10\text{ kg}$$

12. *(c)* Thrust on the rocket,

$$F = -u\frac{dm}{dt}$$

The negative sign indicates that thrust on the rocket is in a direction opposite to the direction of escaping gases.

Here, velocity of the rocket

$$u = 300\text{ m/s}$$

and force $F = 345$ N

$\therefore$ Rate of combustion of fuel

$$-\left(\frac{dm}{dt}\right) = \frac{F}{u} = \frac{345}{300}$$

$$= 1.15\text{ kg/s}$$

13. *(b)* Thrust on the satellite is the force with which the satellite moves upwards in space. It is given by

$$F = -u\frac{dM}{dt}$$

Here, initial velocity

$u = v$, rate of change of mass

$$\frac{dM}{dt} = \alpha v$$

As we know that,

$$F = -v\frac{dM}{dt} = -v(\alpha v) = -\alpha v^2$$

$$\text{Acceleration} = \frac{F}{M} = -\frac{\alpha v^2}{M}$$

> **• Concept Enhancer**
>
> When there is no external force on a rocket
>
> Then, $F = m\frac{dv}{dt} + v\frac{dm}{dt}$
>
> where F is thrust due to both decreasing mass and increasing velocity.
>
> When the velocity is maintained (i.e. kept constant) the force is given by $F = -\frac{vdm}{dt}$
>
> where negative sign indicates the mass is decreasing.

14. *(c)* According to Newton's first law of motion, a body continues to be in a state of rest or of uniform motion, unless it is acted upon by an external force to change the state. Hence, Newton's first law of motion is related to physical independence of force.

15. *(c)* Thrust on the rocket,

$$F = -u\frac{dm}{dt}$$

where, u is relative velocity of exhaust gases with respect to the rocket. $\frac{dm}{dt}$ is rate of combustion of fuel at that instant.

$\therefore$ $$F = -u\frac{dm}{dt} = mg$$

$\Rightarrow$ $$-\frac{dm}{dt} = \frac{mg}{u}$$

Here, $m = 600$ kg, $u = 1000\text{ ms}^{-1}$

$\therefore$ $$-\frac{dm}{dt} = \frac{600 \times 10}{1000} = 6\text{ kg s}^{-1}$$

Topic 2

01. *(b)* We know that,

$$|\text{Impulse}| = m|\Delta v|$$

where, $\Delta v = v_2 - v_1$

Here, v_2 is velocity with which is rebound

v_1 is velocity just before striking to the ground.

For case (1), ball dropped from the 10 m height and strikes to the ground. Now, the velocity of the ball just before striking to the ground is

$$v_1 = -\sqrt{2gh}$$

$\Rightarrow$ $$v_1 = -\sqrt{2(10)(10)}$$

$\Rightarrow$ $$v_1 = -10\sqrt{2}\text{ m/s}$$

For case (2), ball rebounds to the same height. The velocity with which the ball rebounds

$$v_2 = \sqrt{2gh}$$

$\Rightarrow \qquad v_2 = \sqrt{2(10)(10)} = 10\sqrt{2}$ m/s

Now, magnitude of the impulse imparted to the ball,

$$|\text{Impulse}| = m\,|\Delta v|$$
$$= 0.15\,|10\sqrt{2} - (-10\sqrt{2})|$$
$$= 0.15\,|2 \times 10\sqrt{2}|$$
$$= 4.2 \text{ kg m / s}$$

Alternate Solution

Impulse = change in linear moment = $\Delta \mathbf{p}$

Velocity of ball dropped from height h, is given by $v = \sqrt{2gh}$

$\therefore\ \mathbf{I} = 0.15 \times \sqrt{2gh}\,(\hat{\mathbf{j}}) - 0.15 \times \sqrt{2gh}\,(-\hat{\mathbf{j}})$

$= 2[0.15 \times \sqrt{2gh}]\,\hat{\mathbf{j}} = 0.3 \times \sqrt{2gh}\,\hat{\mathbf{j}}$

$= 0.3 \times \sqrt{2 \times 10 \times 10}\,\hat{\mathbf{j}}$

$= 3\sqrt{2}\,\hat{\mathbf{j}} = 4.2\,\hat{\mathbf{j}}$

$\Rightarrow$ Magnitude of impulse = 4.2 kg m/s

02. *(a)* The given question can be shown diagramatically here,

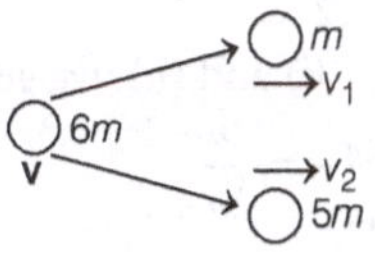

From the conservation of linear momentum, we have

$6mv = mv_1 + 5mv_2$

Given, $v = 20\hat{i} + 25\hat{j} - 12\hat{k}$,

$v_1 = 100\hat{i} + 35\hat{j} + 8\hat{k}$

Thus, $6(20\hat{i} + 25\hat{j} - 12\hat{k})$

$= 100\hat{i} + 35\hat{j} + 8\hat{k} + 5v_2$

$\Rightarrow 5v_2 = 20\hat{i} + 115\hat{j} - 80\hat{k}$

$\Rightarrow \quad v_2 = 4\hat{i} + 23\hat{j} - 16\hat{k}$

03. *(a)* As we know that, impulse is imparted due to change in perpendicular components of momentum of ball.

$$J = \Delta p = mv_f - mv_i$$
$$= mv\cos 60° - (-mv\cos 60°)$$
$$= 2mv\cos 60° = 2mv \times \frac{1}{2} = mv$$

04. *(c)* According to the law of conservation of momentum,

$$p_i = p_f$$

$\Rightarrow (0.01) \times 400 + 0 = 2\,v + (0.01)v'$ ...(i)

Also velocity v of the block just after the collision is

$v = \sqrt{2gh} = \sqrt{2 \times 10 \times 0.1} = \sqrt{2}$ ...(ii)

$\Rightarrow$ From Eqs. (i) and (ii), we have

$v' \approx 120$ m/s

05. *(b)* According to question,

We have, $\mathbf{p}_1 + \mathbf{p}_2 + \mathbf{p}_3 = 0 \quad [\because p = mv]$

$\therefore\ 1 \times 12\hat{\mathbf{i}} + 2 \times 8\hat{\mathbf{j}} + \mathbf{p}_3 = 0$

$\Rightarrow \qquad 12\hat{\mathbf{i}} + 16\hat{\mathbf{j}} + \mathbf{p}_3 = 0$

$\Rightarrow \qquad \mathbf{p}_3 = -(12\hat{\mathbf{i}} + 16\hat{\mathbf{j}})$

$\therefore \qquad \mathbf{p}_3 = \sqrt{(12)^2 + (16)^2}$

$= \sqrt{144 + 256} = 20$ kg-m/s

Now, $\quad p_3 = m_3 v_3$

$\Rightarrow \qquad m_3 = \dfrac{p_3}{v_3} = \dfrac{20}{4} = 5$ kg

06. *(c)* Impulse $= Mv - (-Mv) = 2\,Mv$ (which is change in linear momentum)

07. *(b)* For the given situation,

$$mr = \text{constant}$$
$$m_1 r_1 = m_2 r_2$$
$$\Rightarrow \quad r_2 = \frac{m_1 r_1}{m_2}$$
$$= \frac{0.5 \times 10}{50}$$
$$= 0.1 \text{ m}$$

So, distance travelled by the man will be

$10 + 0.1 = 10.1$ m

Alternate Solution

Apply conservation of angular momentum, we get $M_{man}v - M_{stone}\,v_{stone} = 0$

or $\quad 50v - 0.5 \times 2 = 0 \Rightarrow v = 0.02$ m/s

Time taken by stone to reach ground,

$t = \dfrac{10}{2} = 5$ s

Distance travelled by man is 5 s,

$d = v \times t = 0.02 \times 5 = 0.1$ m

(in upward direction)

Thus distance of man above the floor,

$h = 10 + 0.1 = 10.1$ m

08. *(a)* Momentum of first part

$= 1 \times 12 = 12$ kg ms^{-1}

Momentum of the second part

$= 2 \times 8 = 16$ kg ms^{-1}

$\therefore$ Resultant momentum

$= \sqrt{(12)^2 + (16)^2}$

$= 20$ kg ms^{-1}

The third part should also have the same momentum.

Let the mass of the third part be M, then

$4 \times M = 20$, $M = 5$ kg

Alternate Solution

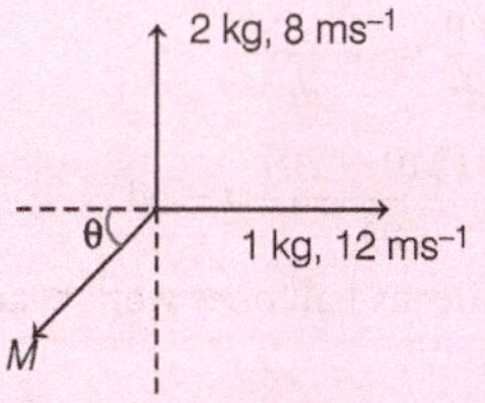

$Mv\cos\theta = 12$ ...(i)

$Mv\sin\theta = 16$ ...(ii)

Dividing Eqs. (ii) and (i), we get

$\tan\theta = \dfrac{16}{12} = \dfrac{4}{3}$

$M = \dfrac{12 \times 5}{4 \times 3} = \dfrac{60}{12} = 5$ kg

09. *(b)* The given situation is shown below.

$$|\mathbf{OA}| = |\mathbf{OB}| = v$$

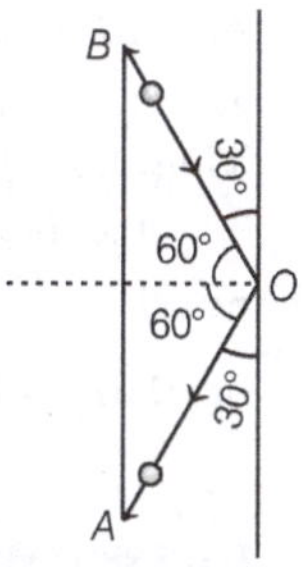

As the magnitudes of **OA** and **OB** are equal, the components of **OA** and **OB** along the wall are equal and in the same direction, while those perpendicular to the wall are equal and opposite. Thus, the change in momentum is only due to the change in direction of the perpendicular components.

Hence,

$$\Delta p = OB\sin 30° - (-OA\sin 30°)$$
$$= 2\,mv\sin 30°$$

Its time rate will appear in the form of average force acting on the wall.

$\therefore \qquad F \times t = 2mv\sin 30° \quad$ or

$$F = \frac{2mv\sin 30°}{t}$$

Given, $m = 0.5$ kg, $v = 12$ m / s,

$t = 0.25$ s

$\theta = 30°$

Hence, $F = \dfrac{2 \times 0.5 \times 12\sin 30°}{0.25}$

$= 24$ N

10. *(b)* Given, mass of ball, $m = 150$ g

$= 0.15$ kg

Initial velocity of ball,

$u = 20$ m/s

Final velocity of ball,

$v = 0$ m/s

Force experienced by the cricketer

$$F = \frac{dp}{dt} = \frac{m(v-u)}{dt}$$

$$= \frac{0.15(0-20)}{0.1} = -30\ N$$

– ve sign means ball does work against the cricketer.

11. *(a)* According to 1st equation of motion, velocity of particle after 5 s

$$v = u - gt$$

$$v = 100 - 10 \times 5$$

$$= 100 - 50 = 50\ m/s\ \text{(upwards)}$$

Applying conservation of linear momentum gives

$$Mv = m_1v_1 + m_2v_2 \quad \ldots(i)$$

Taking upward direction positive, the velocity v_1 will be negative.

$\therefore \quad v_1 = -25$ m/s, $v = 50$ m/s

Also, $M = 1$ kg, $m_1 = 400$ g = 0.4 kg

and $m_2 = (M - m_1) = 1 - 0.4 = 0.6$ kg

Thus, Eq. (i) becomes,

$$1 \times 50 = 0.4 \times (-25) + 0.6\,v_2$$

or $\quad 50 = -10 + 0.6v_2$

or $0.6v_2 = 60$ or $v_2 = \frac{60}{0.6} = 100$ m/s

12. *(c)*

key idea

To calculate impulse, first of all calculate the time during which force becomes zero.

Then apply $I = \int_0^t F dt$

Given, $F = 600 - 2 \times 10^5\, t$

When, bullet leaves the barrel, the force on the bullet becomes zero.

So, $600 - 2 \times 10^5\, t = 0$

$$\Rightarrow \quad t = \frac{600}{2 \times 10^5} = 3 \times 10^{-3}\ s$$

Then, average impulse imparted to the bullet

$$I = \int_0^t F dt$$

$$= \int_0^{3 \times 10^{-3}} (600 - 2 \times 10^5\, t)\, dt$$

$$= \left[600\,t - \frac{2 \times 10^5\, t^2}{2}\right]_0^{3 \times 10^{-3}}$$

$$= 600 \times 3 \times 10^{-3} - 10^5 \times (3 \times 10^{-3})^2$$

$$= 1.8 - 0.9 = 0.9\ \text{N-s}$$

Alternate Solution

As obtained in previous method, the time taken by bullet when it leaves the barrel

$$t = 3 \times 10^{-3}\ s$$

Let F_1 and F_2 denote the forces at the time of firing of bullets i.e. at $t = 0$ and at the time of leaving the bullet i.e.

at $\quad t = 3 \times 10^{-3}$ s.

$$F_1 = 600 - 2 \times 10^5 \times 0 = 600\ N$$

$$F_2 = 600 - 2 \times 10^5 \times 3 \times 10^{-3} = 0$$

Mean value of force

$$F = \frac{1}{2}(F_1 + F_2) = \frac{600+0}{2} = 300\ N$$

Thus, impulse $= F \times t = 300 \times 3 \times 10^{-3} = 0.9$ N-s

13. *(a)* Given, mass of bullet,

$$m_b = 200\ g = 0.2\ kg$$

Velocity of bullet,

$$v_b = 5\ m/s$$

Mass of gun, $m_g = 1$ kg

According to conforvation of linear momentum, censer velocity of the gun is,

$$v = \frac{m_b v_b}{m_g}$$

$$= \frac{0.2 \times 5}{1} = 1\ m/s$$

14. *(d)* Impulse of a force, which is the product of average force during impact and the time for which the impact lasts, is measured by the total change in linear momentum produced during the impact.

Here, $\mathbf{p}_1 = mv_1$, $\mathbf{p}_2 = mv_2$

Impulse, $I = mv_2 - mv_1 = m(v_2 - v_1)$

• Concept **Enhancer**

Impulse of a force can be calculated as the product of large force applied to the small time to which force act.

$\Rightarrow$ Impulse $= p_2 - p_1$

15. *(b)* Momentum of first fragment,

$$p_1 = m \times 21 = 21m$$

Similarly, $p_2 = 21m$

Resultant momentum,

$$p = \sqrt{p_1^2 + p_2^2}$$

$$= \sqrt{(21m)^2 + (21m)^2}$$

$$= 21m\sqrt{2}$$

but according to given situation,

$$3mv = 21m\sqrt{2}$$

$$\Rightarrow \quad v = 7\sqrt{2}\ m/s$$

Topic 3

01. *(c)* Let θ be the inclination.

By equation of uniformly accelerated motion, distance travelled by object during *n* th second is given by

$$s_n = u + \frac{a}{2}(2n-1)$$

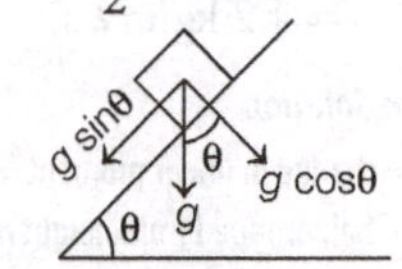

$$\Rightarrow s_n = 0 + \frac{g \sin\theta}{2}(2n-1)$$

$$s_n = \frac{g \sin\theta}{2}(2n-1) \quad \ldots(i)$$

Distance travelled during $(n+1)$th second.

$$s_{n+1} = 0 + \frac{g \sin\theta}{2}[2(n+1) - 1]$$

$$= \frac{g \sin\theta}{2}(2n+1) \quad \ldots(ii)$$

Using Eqs. (i) and (ii), we get

$$\frac{s_n}{s_{n+1}} = \frac{2n-1}{2n+1}$$

02. *(b)* Given, $m_1 = 4$ kg, $m_2 = 6$ kg

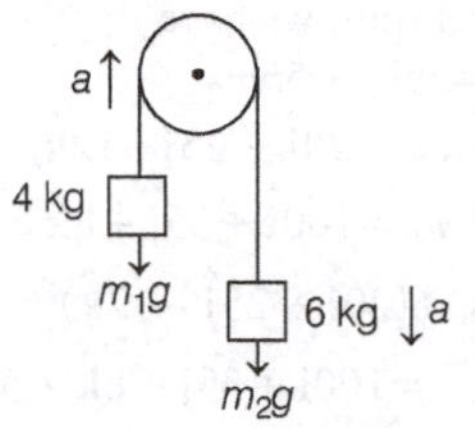

From the above free body diagram, the relation for acceleration of the given system can be given as

$$a = \left(\frac{m_2 - m_1}{m_1 + m_2}\right) \cdot g = \left(\frac{6-4}{4+6}\right) \times g = \frac{g}{5}$$

03. *(d)*

key idea

Draw free body diagram and apply pseudo force in non-inertial frame (wedge).

According to the question, the FBD of the given condition will be

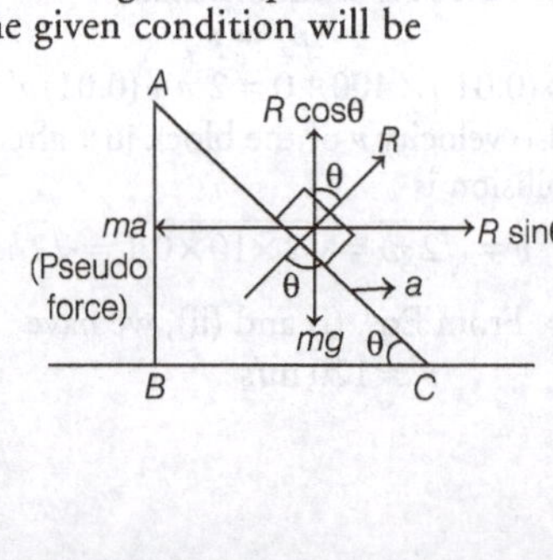

Since, the wedge is accelerating towards right with a, thus a pseudo force acts in the left direction in order to keep the block stationary. As, the system is in equilibrium.

$\therefore \quad \Sigma F_x = 0 \text{ or } \Sigma F_y = 0$

$\Rightarrow \quad R \sin\theta = ma$

or $\quad mg \sin\theta = ma \quad \ldots$(i)

Similarly, $\quad R\cos\theta = mg$

or $\quad mg\cos\theta = mg \quad \ldots$(ii)

Dividing Eq. (i) by Eq (ii), we get

$$\frac{mg\sin\theta}{mg\cos\theta} = \frac{ma}{mg} \Rightarrow \tan\theta = \frac{a}{g}$$

or $\quad a = g\tan\theta$

04. *(b)* Initially system, is in equilibrium with a total weight of $4mg$ over spring.

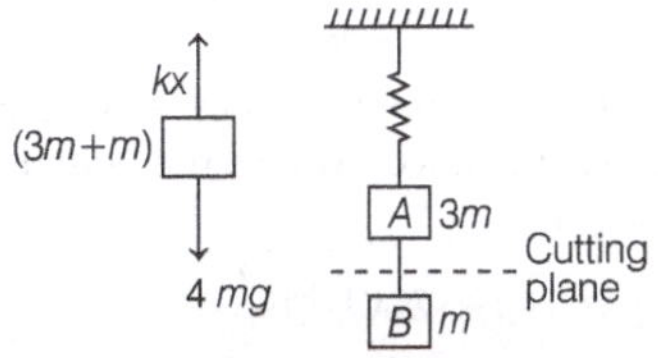

$\therefore \quad kx = 4mg$

When string is cut at the location as shown.

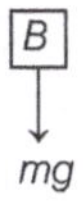

So,force on mass, $B = mg$

$\therefore$ Acceleration of mass, $B = g$

For mass A, free body diagram is

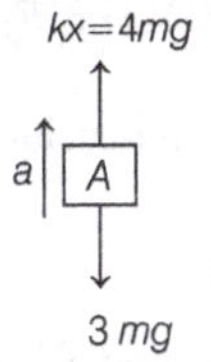

If a = acceleration of block of mass A, then

$$F_{net} = 4mg - 3mg$$

$\Rightarrow \quad 3m \cdot a_A = mg$ or $a_A = \dfrac{g}{3}$

So, accelerations for blocks A and B are

$$a_A = \frac{g}{3} \text{ and } a_B = g$$

05. *(b)* Given, $m_A = 4$ kg

$m_B = 2$ kg and $m_C = 1$ kg

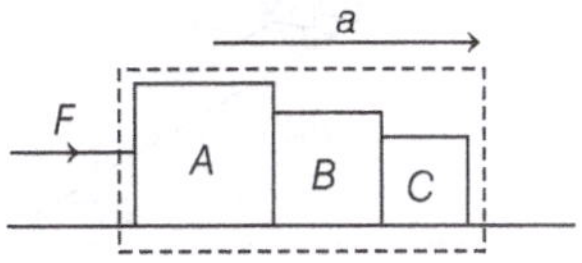

So, total mass $(M) = 4 + 2 + 1 = 7$ kg

Now, $F = Ma \Rightarrow 14 = 7a \Rightarrow a = 2\text{ m/s}^2$

FBD of block A,

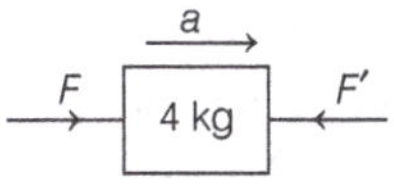

$F - F' = 4a$

$\Rightarrow F' = 14 - 4 \times 2 \Rightarrow F' = 6$ N

06. *(a)* Since, all the blocks are moving with constant velocity and we know that, if velocity is constant, acceleration of the body becomes zero. Hence, the net force on all the blocks will be zero.

07. *(b)* Total mass, m

= Mass of lift + Mass of person

$= 940 + 60 = 1000$ kg

So, from the free body diagram

$$T - mg = ma$$

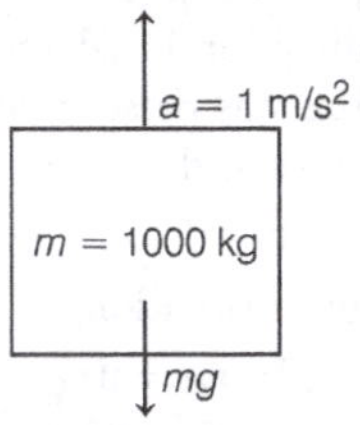

Hence, $T - 1000 \times 10 = 1000 \times 1$

$T = 11000$ N

08. *(b)* Here, lift is accelerating upward at the rate of a.

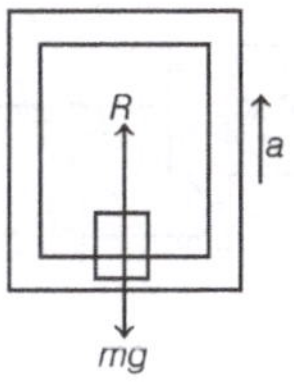

Hence, equation of motion is written as

$$R - mg = ma$$

$28000 - 20000 = 2000a$

$[\because g = 10\text{ ms}^{-2}]$

$\Rightarrow \quad a = \dfrac{8000}{2000} = 4\text{ ms}^{-2}$ (upwards)

09. *(b)* Mass of man, $M = 80$ kg

Acceleration of lift, $a = 5\text{ m/s}^2$

When, lift is moving upwards, the reading of weighing scale will be equal to R.

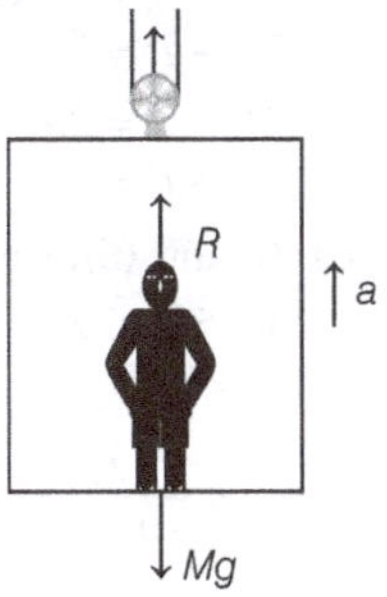

The equation of motion gives

$R - Mg = Ma$ or

$R = Mg + Ma = M(g + a)$

$\therefore \quad R = 80(10 + 5) = 80 \times 15 = 1200$ N

10. *(b)* Maximum bearable tension in the rope

$$T = 25 \times 10 = 250\text{ N}$$

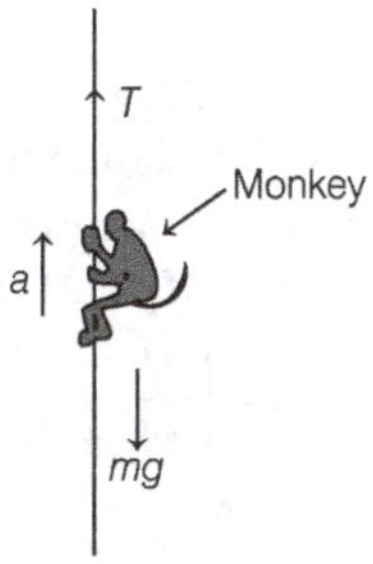

From the figure, $T - mg = ma$

or acceleration, $a = \dfrac{T - mg}{m}$

Given, mass $m = 20$ kg, $g = 10\text{ m/s}^2$,

Taking, $T = 250$ N

Hence, $\quad a = \dfrac{250 - 20 \times 10}{20} = \dfrac{50}{20}$

$= 2.5\text{ m/s}^2$

11. *(b)* When, lift move upwards with some acceleration, then according to free body diagram of the lift

$T - mg = ma$

or $\quad T = m(g + a)$

Given, $m = 1000$ kg, $a = 1\text{ m/s}^2$,

$g = 9.8\text{ m/s}^2$

Thus, $T = 1000(9.8 + 1)$

$= 1000 \times 10.8$

$= 10800$ N

12. *(c)*

key idea

In the case of masses hanging from a pulley by a string, the tension in whole string is same, say equal to T.

The FBD of the given situation is shown below.

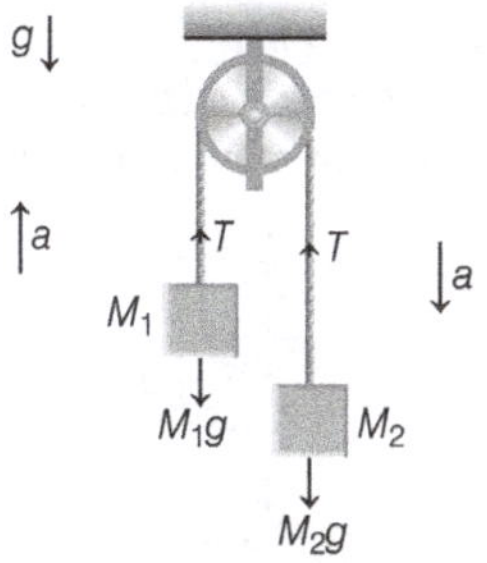

As $M_2 > M_1$, so mass M_2 moves down and mass M_1 moves up with the same acceleration a (say). The arrangement of the motion is represented in the figure.

According to free body diagram of mass M_2, is

$$M_2 g - T = M_2 a \quad \ldots(i)$$

According to free body diagram of mass M_1, is

$$T - M_1 g = M_1 a \quad \ldots(ii)$$

Adding Eqs. (i) and (ii), we get

$$(M_2 g - T) + (T - M_1 g) = (M_1 + M_2)a$$

$$(M_2 - M_1)g = (M_1 + M_2)a$$

$$\Rightarrow \quad a = \left(\frac{M_2 - M_1}{M_1 + M_2}\right) g$$

Given, $M_1 = 5$ kg,

$M_2 = 10$ kg

Hence, $a = \left(\frac{10-5}{5+10}\right) g = \frac{5}{15} g = \frac{g}{3}$ m/s^2.

Alternate Solution

Acceleration, $a = \frac{(F_{net})\text{ system}}{\text{Net mass}}$

$= \frac{(10-5)\times g}{5+10} = \frac{g}{3}$ m/s^2

Note In a mass-pulley system, the tension in the string is always towards the pulley.

13. *(a)* (i) When, mass is lifted upwards with an acceleration a, then according to free body diagram

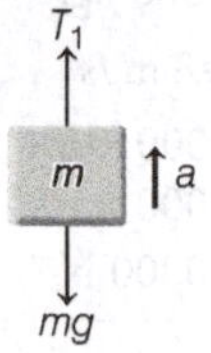

$$T_1 - mg = ma$$

$$\Rightarrow \quad T_1 = mg + ma$$

$$T_1 = m(g + a)$$

Substituting the values, we obtain

$\therefore \quad T_1 = (1)(9.8 + 4.9) = 14.7$ N

(ii) When, mass is lowered downwards with an acceleration a, then

$$mg - T_2 = ma$$

$$\Rightarrow T_2 = mg - ma = m(g - a)$$

Substituting the values, we have

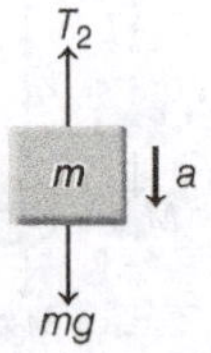

$$T_2 = (1)(9.8 - 4.9) = 4.9 \text{ N}$$

Then, ratio of tensions

$$\frac{T_1}{T_2} = \frac{14.7}{4.9} = \frac{3}{1}$$

$$\Rightarrow \quad T_1 : T_2 = 3:1$$

Topic 4

01. *(b)* Friction force always works against the motion of the football player. Here, football player is moving in the southward, so friction will act in northword. From the Newton's law of motion, force is in the direction of change in momentum. Since, the football player is just trying to move in the east direction in which no initial momentum was present, so force will be in north-east direction.

02. *(b)* Given, $\mu = 0.15$

For the given situation,

$$F = ma = \mu mg$$

$$\Rightarrow \quad a = \mu g = 0.15 \times 10$$

$$= 1.5 \text{ ms}^{-2}$$

03. *(a)* The given situation is shown in the following diagram.

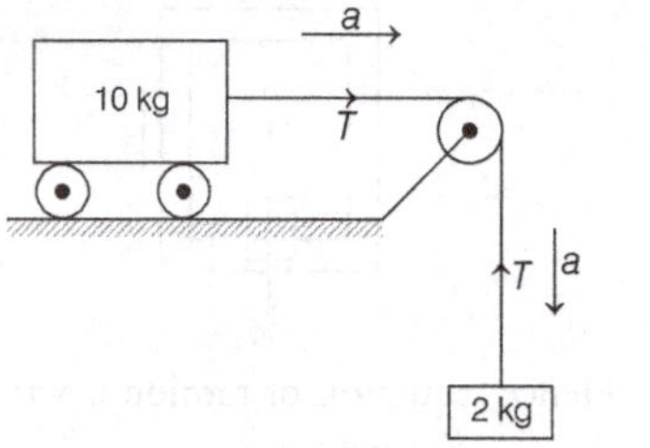

If a be the acceleration of the system then, equation of motion of 10 kg trolly,

$$T - \mu R = 10a$$

$$\Rightarrow \quad T - 0.05 \times 10g = 10a$$

$$[\because \mu = 0.05, R = 10g]$$

$$\Rightarrow T - 0.05 \times 10 \times 10 = 10a$$

$$\Rightarrow \quad T - 5 = 10a \quad \ldots(i)$$

Equation of motion of 2 kg block,

$$2g - T = 2a$$

$$2 \times 10 - T = 2a$$

$$20 - T = 2a \quad \ldots(ii)$$

Adding Eqs. (i) and (ii), we have

$$20 - 5 = 12a$$

$$\Rightarrow \quad 15 = 12a$$

$$\Rightarrow \quad a = \frac{15}{12} = \frac{5}{4} = 1.25 \text{ ms}^{-2}$$

04. *(c)* The situation can be drawn as

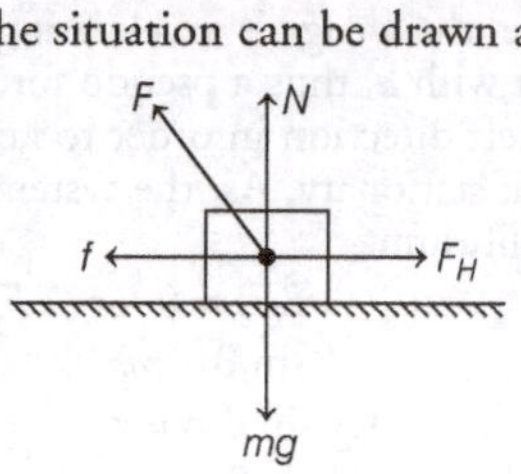

The frictional force,

$$f = \mu N = \mu mg$$

$$[\because N = mg]$$

From free body diagram (FBD), the resultant force is

$$|\mathbf{F}| = \sqrt{N^2 + f^2}$$

$$= \sqrt{(mg)^2 + (\mu mg)^2}$$

$$= mg\sqrt{1 + \mu^2}$$

This is the minimum force required to move the object. But as the body is not moving

$$\therefore \quad |\mathbf{F}| \leq mg\sqrt{1 + \mu^2}$$

05. *(d)* The coefficient of sliding is given as

$$\mu_S = \frac{N}{F_{sliding}}$$

where, N is the normal reaction and $F_{sliding}$ is the sliding force. As, the dimensions of N and $F_{sliding}$ are same.

Thus, μ_S is a dimensionless quantity.

06. *(b)*

key idea

Whenever a body is subjected to slope down with friction μ, on an inclined plane, the acceleration is given by

$a = g(\sin\theta - \mu\cos\theta)$

Given a plank with a box on its one end is gradually raised about the end having angle of inclination is 30°, the box starts to slip and slides down 4 m the plank in 4 s as shown in figure.

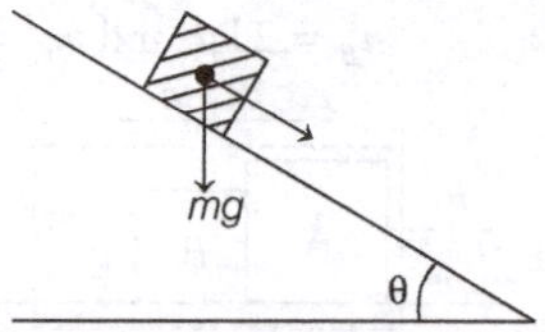

The coefficient of static friction,

$$\mu_s = \tan 30° = \frac{1}{\sqrt{3}} = 0.6$$

So, distance covered by a box,

$$s = ut + \frac{1}{2}at^2$$

Here, $u = 0$

and $a = g(\sin\theta - \mu\cos\theta)$

$$\therefore \quad 4 = \frac{1}{2}g(\sin 30^\circ - \mu_k \cos 30^\circ)(4)^2$$

$$\Rightarrow \quad 0.5 = 10 \times \frac{1}{2} - \mu_k \times 10 \times \frac{\sqrt{3}}{2}$$

$$\Rightarrow \quad 5\sqrt{3}\,\mu_k = 4.5$$

$$\Rightarrow \quad \mu_k = 0.51 \simeq 0.5$$

07. *(c)* FBD of block *A*,

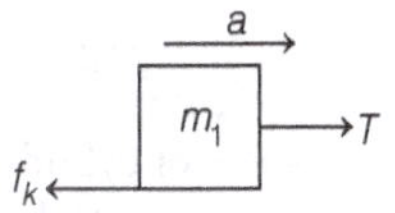

$$T - m_1 a = f_k \quad \ldots(i)$$

FBD of block *B*,

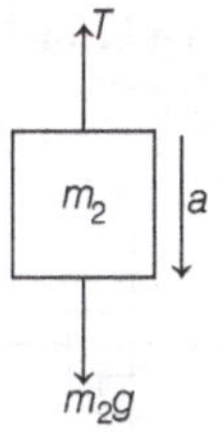

$$m_2 g - T = m_2 a \quad \ldots(ii)$$

Adding Eqs. (i) and (ii), we get

$$m_2 g - m_1 a = m_2 a + f_k$$

$$\Rightarrow m_2 g - m_1 a = m_2 a + \mu_k m_1 g$$

$$\Rightarrow \quad a = \frac{(m_2 - \mu_k m_1)g}{m_1 + m_2}$$

From Eq. (ii),

$$T = m_2(g - a)$$

$$= m_2\left[1 - \frac{(m_2 - \mu_k m_1)}{m_1 + m_2}\right]g$$

$$T = \frac{m_1 m_2(1 + \mu_k)}{m_1 + m_2}g$$

Alternate Solution

$$\text{Acceleration }(a) = \frac{\text{Net Force}}{\text{Mass}} = \frac{m_2 g - \mu_k m_1 g}{m_1 + m_2}$$

For equilibrium condition,

$$m_2 g - T = m_2(a)$$

$$\Rightarrow m_2 g - T = m_2 \frac{(m_2 g - \mu_k m_1 g)}{m_1 + m_2}$$

$$\Rightarrow \quad T = \frac{m_1 m_2(1 + \mu_k)}{m_1 + m_2}g$$

08. *(c)* First of all consider the forces on the blocks

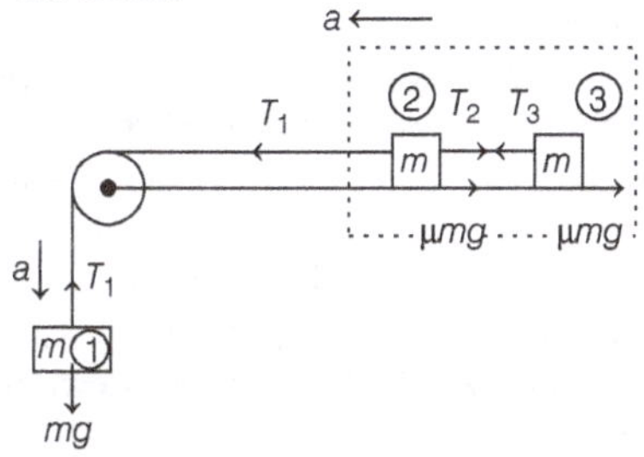

For the Ist block, $[\because m_1 = m_2 = m_3]$

$$mg - T_1 = m \times a \quad \ldots(i)$$

Let us consider 2nd and 3rd block as a system.

So, $T_1 - 2\mu mg = 2m \times a \quad \ldots(ii)$

Addiing Eqs. (i) and (ii)

$$mg(1 - 2\mu) = 3m \times a$$

$$\Rightarrow \quad a = \frac{g}{3}(1 - 2\mu)$$

09. *(c)* When, a cart moves with some acceleration towards right, then a pseudo force $(m\alpha)$ acts on block towards left. This force $(m\alpha)$ is action force by a block on cart

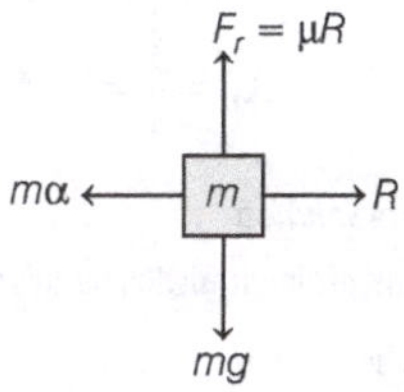

Now, block will remain static w.r.t. cart, if frictional force

$$\mu R \ge mg$$

$$\Rightarrow \quad \mu\, m\alpha \ge mg \quad [\text{as } R = m\alpha]$$

$$\Rightarrow \quad \alpha \ge \frac{g}{\mu}$$

10. *(a)* Block *B* will come to rest, if force applied to it will vanish due to frictional force acting between block *B* and surface, i.e. frictional force = force applied

i.e. $\mu mg = ma$

or $\mu mg = m\left(\frac{v}{t}\right)$ or $t = \frac{v}{\mu g}$

11. *(d)* Let the mass of the block *B* be *M*.

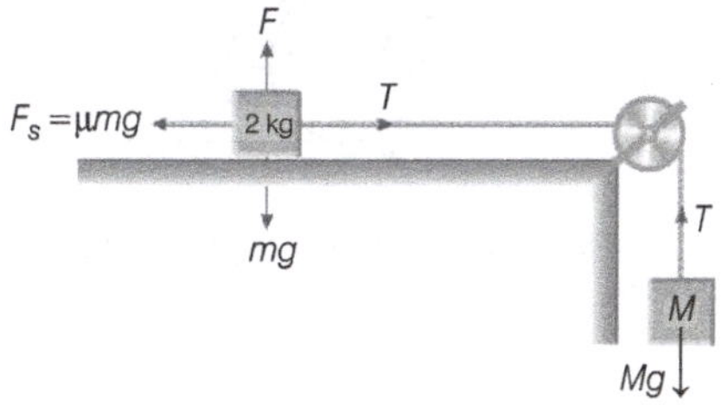

In equilibrium,

$$T - Mg = 0$$

$$\Rightarrow \quad T = Mg \quad \ldots(i)$$

If blocks do not move, then

$$T = f_s$$

where, f_s = frictional force

$$= \mu_s R = \mu_s mg$$

$$\therefore \quad T = \mu_s mg \quad \ldots(ii)$$

Thus, from Eqs. (i) and (ii), we have

$$Mg = \mu_s mg$$

or $M = \mu_s m$

Given, $\mu_s = 0.2$, $m = 2$ kg

$$\therefore \quad M = 0.2 \times 2 = 0.4 \text{ kg}$$

12. *(c)* Free body diagram of block is

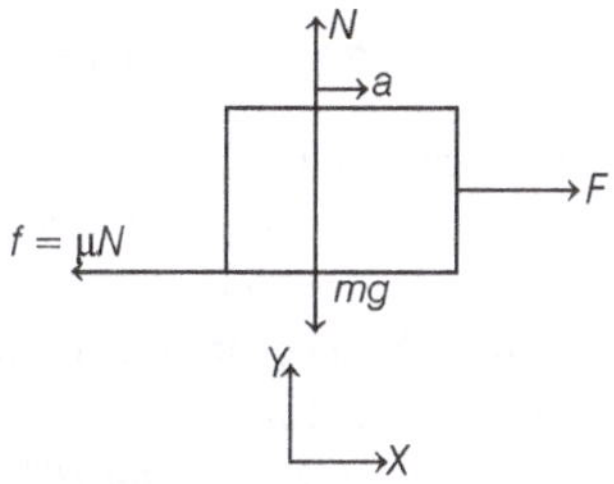

From Newton's second law along *X*-axis

$$\Sigma F_x = ma$$

i.e. $F - f = ma$

or $F - \mu mg = ma$

$$\text{or} \quad a = \frac{F - \mu mg}{m}$$

Given, $F = 100$ N,

$\mu = 0.5$, $m = 10$ kg

$g = 10 \text{ m/s}^2$

Substituting, the values in the above relation for acceleration of block,

$$a = \frac{(100) - (0.5)(10)(10)}{(10)}$$

$$= 5 \text{ m/s}^2$$

13. *(d)*

key idea

Coefficient of kinetic friction between any two surface in contact is equal to the tangent of the angle of inclination between them.

The given situation is shown below

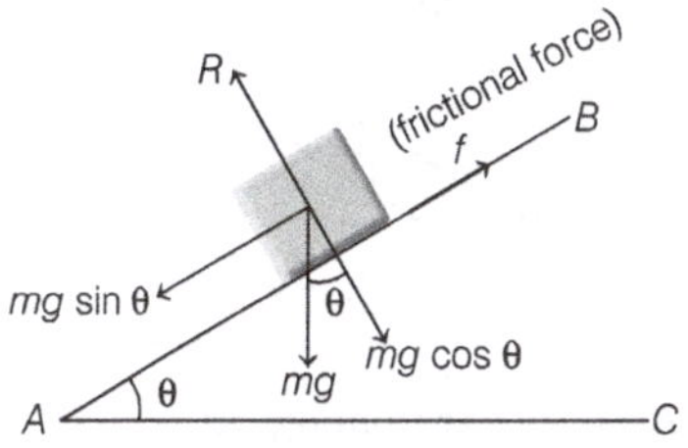

AB is an inclined plane such that a body placed on it just begins to slide down

$$\angle BAC = \theta = \text{angle of repose}$$

In equilibrium,

$$f = mg \sin\theta \text{ and } R = mg \cos\theta$$

$$\therefore \quad \frac{f}{R} = \frac{mg \sin\theta}{mg \cos\theta} = \tan\theta$$

i.e. $\quad \mu = \tan\theta$

14. *(b)* When, static friction is present, then acceleration of body is given by

$$a = -\mu g$$

Here, initial velocity

$$u = 72 \text{ km h}^{-1}$$

$$= 72 \times \frac{5}{18} = 20 \text{ m/s}$$

Final velocity $v = 0$

$$\therefore \quad a = -\mu g = -0.5 \times 10$$

$$= -5 \text{ m/s}^2$$

Now, from third equation of motion,

i.e. $\quad v^2 = u^2 + 2as$

$$s = \frac{v^2 - u^2}{2a} = \frac{0 - (20)^2}{2 \times (-5)} = 40 \text{ m}$$

15. *(a)* The force of friction should balance the weight of chain hanging. If M is the mass of whole chain of length L and x is the length of chain hanging to balance, then

$$\mu \frac{M}{L}(L - x) g = \frac{M}{L} xg$$

or $\quad \mu (L - x) = x$

or $\quad x = \dfrac{\mu L}{\mu + 1} = \dfrac{0.25 L}{1.25} \quad (\text{As, } \mu = 0.25)$

$$\therefore \quad x = \frac{L}{5}$$

or $\quad \dfrac{x}{L} = \dfrac{1}{5} = \dfrac{1}{5} \times 100 = 20\%$

16. *(b)* When, a plane is inclined to the horizontal at an angle θ, which is greater than the angle of repose, the body placed on the inclined plane slides down with an acceleration a.

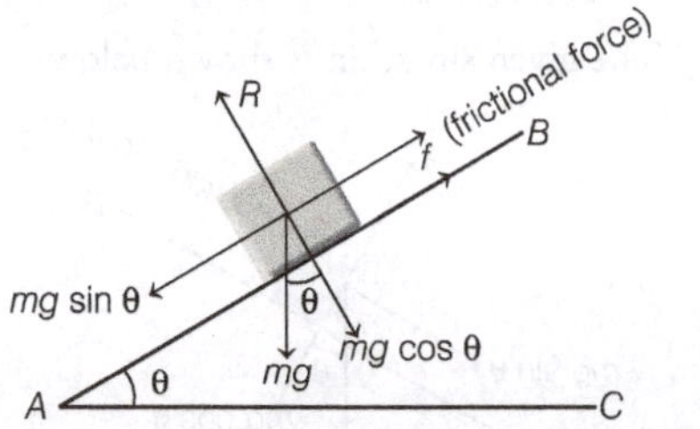

As, it is clear from figure

$$R = mg \cos\theta \quad \text{...(i)}$$

Net force on the body down the inclined plane which means it is sliding downwards

$$F = mg \sin\theta - f \quad \text{...(ii)}$$

i.e. $\quad F = ma = mg \sin\theta - \mu R$

$$(\because f = \mu R)$$

$$\therefore \quad ma = mg \sin\theta - \mu\, mg \cos\theta$$

$$= mg (\sin\theta - \mu \cos\theta)$$

Hence, $a = g (\sin\theta - \mu \cos\theta)$

$\therefore$ Time taken by body to slide down the plane

$$t_1 = \sqrt{\frac{2s}{a}} = \sqrt{\frac{2s}{g(\sin\theta - \mu\cos\theta)}}$$

When friction is absent, then time taken to slide down the plane

$$t_2 = \sqrt{\frac{2s}{g \sin\theta}}$$

$$\because \quad t_1 = 2t_2 \quad \text{(given)}$$

$$\therefore \quad t_1^2 = 4t_2^2$$

or $\quad \dfrac{2s}{g(\sin\theta - \mu\cos\theta)} = \dfrac{2s \times 4}{g \sin\theta}$

or $\quad \sin\theta = 4 \sin\theta - 4\mu \cos\theta$

or $\quad \mu = \dfrac{3}{4} \tan\theta = \dfrac{3}{4} \tan 45°$

$$\therefore \quad \mu = \frac{3}{4} = 0.75$$

Alternate Solution

Coefficient of kinetic friction for this special case can also be given by, $\mu = \tan\theta\left(1 - \frac{1}{n^2}\right)$

Where n = the multiplicity factor by which the block sides down without friction.

Thus, $\mu = \tan 45°\left(1 - \frac{1}{2^2}\right)$

$$= 1 - \frac{1}{4} = \frac{3}{4} = 0.75$$

Topic 5

01. *(b)* In rolling motion, wheel is rolling with velocity v. All the points move with different velocity as shown

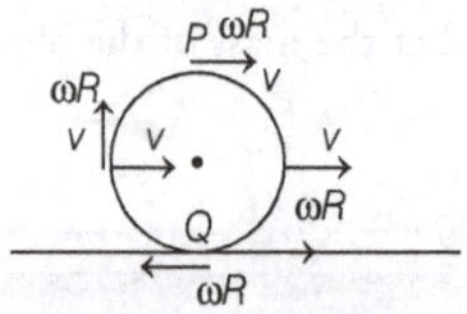

Thus, the velocity of P is greater than velocity at Q.

02. *(c)* The angular speed of a particle in a uniform circular motion is given by

$$\omega = \frac{\text{angle of circle}}{\text{Time}}$$

$\omega = \dfrac{2\pi}{T}$, where T is the time period of rotation

For particle A, $\omega_A = \dfrac{2\pi}{T_A}$

For particle B, $\omega_B = \dfrac{2\pi}{T_B}$

$$\therefore \quad \frac{\omega_A}{\omega_B} = \frac{2\pi}{T_A} \times \frac{T_B}{2\pi} = \frac{T_B}{T_A} = \frac{1}{1} \text{ or } 1:1$$

$$[\because T_A = T_B \text{ (given)}]$$

03. *(b)* Given, mass of cylinder

$$m = 10 \text{ kg}$$

radius of cylinder, $r = 1$ m

coefficient of friction, $\mu = 0.1$.

The given situation can be as shown in the figure given below.

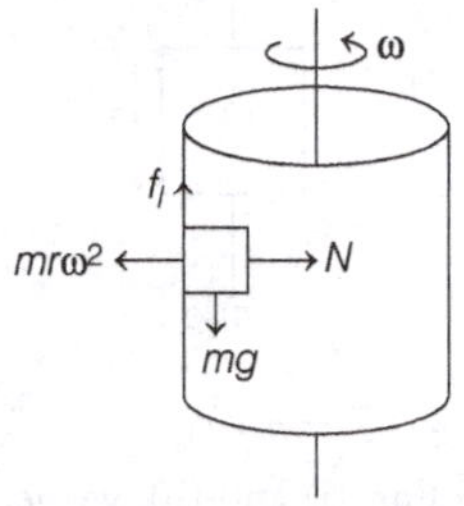

From the above figure, it can be concluded that the block will be stationary when the limiting friction f_l is equal to or greater than the downward force or weight of block, i.e.

$$f_l \geq mg \quad \text{...(i)}$$

Also, the magnitude of limiting friction between two bodies is directly proportional to the normal reaction N between them, i.e.

$$f_l \propto N \text{ or } f_l = \mu N \quad \text{...(ii)}$$

From Eqs. (i) and (ii), we get

$$\mu N \geq mg \text{ or } \mu(mr\omega^2) \geq mg$$

$$[\because N = mr\omega^2]$$

$$\Rightarrow \quad \omega \geq \sqrt{\frac{g}{r\mu}}$$

Thus, the minimum angular velocity is

$$\omega_{\min} = \sqrt{\frac{g}{r\mu}}$$

$$= \sqrt{\frac{10}{1 \times 0.1}} = 10 \text{ rad/s}$$

• Concept Enhancer

The centrifugal force is the internal force in all the objects when we look at the object in a rotating frame of reference and it is written as

$$F=\frac{mv^2}{r}$$

and angular velocity is defined as the ratio of the velocity of a moving object to the radius of that object and is written as;

$$\omega=\frac{v}{r}$$

04. *(a)* Consider the string of length l connected to a particle as shown in the figure.

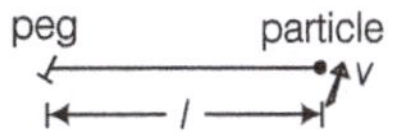

Speed of the particle is v. As the particle is in uniform circular motion, net force on the particle must be equal to centripetal force which is provided by the tension T.

$\therefore$ Net force = Centripetal force

$$\Rightarrow \quad \frac{mv^2}{l}=T$$

05. *(a)* Given, situation can be drawn as shown in figure below.

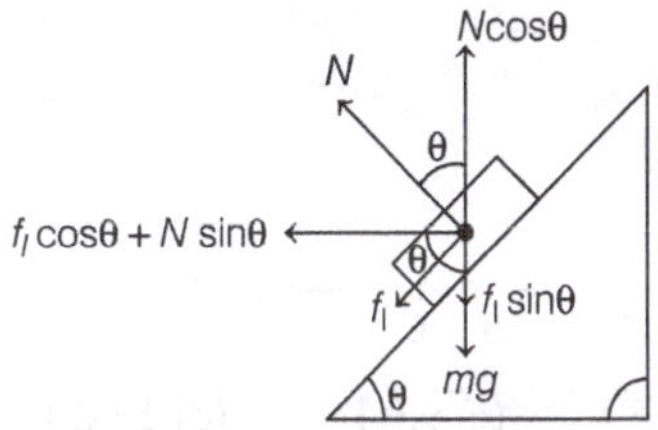

Considering the case of vertical equilibrium

$$N\cos\theta = mg + f_l\sin\theta$$

$$\Rightarrow \quad mg = N\cos\theta - f_l\sin\theta \ldots\text{(i)}$$

Considering the case of horizontal equilibrium,

$$N\sin\theta + f_l\cos\theta = \frac{mv^2}{R} \quad \ldots\text{(ii)}$$

Dividing Eq. (ii) by Eq. (i), then

$$\frac{v^2}{Rg}=\frac{\sin\theta+\mu_s\cos\theta}{\cos\theta-\mu_s\sin\theta}$$

$$\left[\frac{f_l}{N}=\mu_s\right]$$

$$\Rightarrow \quad v=\sqrt{Rg\left(\frac{\sin\theta+\mu_s\cos\theta}{\cos\theta-\mu_s\sin\theta}\right)}$$

$$\Rightarrow \quad v=\sqrt{Rg\left(\frac{\tan\theta+\mu_s}{1-\mu_s\tan\theta}\right)}$$

• Concept Enhancer

When a vehicle goes round a curved road, it requires some centripetal force. While rounding the curve, the wheels of the vehicle have a tendency to leave the curved path and regain its original path i.e. straight line. Now the force of friction b/w wheels and the roads opposes this tendency. This force of friction acts forwards the centre of the circular track and provides the necessary centripetal force.

06. *(d)* For maximum speed of car in a circular track,

$$\mu_s mg \geq \frac{mv^2}{R}$$

$$\Rightarrow \quad v \leq \sqrt{\mu_s Rg}$$

$$\therefore \quad v_{\max}=\sqrt{\mu_s Rg}$$

07. *(b)* The angle of banking,

$$\tan\theta=\frac{v^2}{rg}$$

Given, $\theta=45°$

Radius of banked curve road

$$r=90\text{ m and } g=10\text{ m/s}^2$$

$$\Rightarrow \tan 45°=\frac{v^2}{90\times 10}$$

$$v=\sqrt{90\times 10\times \tan 45°}$$

$$=\sqrt{90\times 10\times 1}=30\text{ m/s}$$

08. *(c)* When the disc spins, the frictional force between the gramophone record and coin is μmg.

The coin will revolve with record, if

$$f_{\text{frictional}} \geq F_{\text{centripetal}}$$

i.e. $\quad \mu mg \geq m\omega^2 r$

$$\frac{\mu g}{r}\geq \omega^2$$

$$\Rightarrow \quad r\leq \frac{\mu g}{\omega^2}$$

09. *(c)* Given, mass of the car,

$$m=500\text{ kg}$$

Radius of turn,

$$r=50\text{ m}$$

Velocity, $v=36$ km/h

$$=36\times\frac{5}{18}=10\text{ m/s}$$

Centripetal force,

$$F_c=\frac{mv^2}{r}$$

$$=\frac{500\times(10)^2}{50}=1000\text{ N}$$

10. *(a)* For a ball to move in horizontal circle, the ball should satisfy the condition

Tension in the string

= Centripetal force

$$\Rightarrow \quad T_{\max}=\frac{Mv_{\max}^2}{R}$$

$$\Rightarrow v_{\max}=\sqrt{\frac{T_{\max}\cdot R}{M}} \quad \ldots\text{(i)}$$

Making substitution, we obtain

$$v_{\max}=\sqrt{\frac{25\times 1.96}{0.25}}$$

$$=\sqrt{196}=14\text{ m / s}$$

11. *(b)* Centrifugation is a process which involves the use of the centrifugal force for the sedimentation of heterogeneous mixtures with a centrifuge for churning milk to separate cream from it.

C-05

NEET Chapterwise Topicwise Physics

In NEET 2024, 3 questions was visible from this chapter. In past 5 years, 3 question from topic-2, 0 question from topic-3, 4 questions from topic-4, 1 question from topic-5 and 1 question from topic-6 were asked.

WORK, ENERGY AND POWER

Topic 1 Work

01 A force $F = 20 + 10y$ acts on a particle in y-direction, where F is in Newton and y in metre. Work done by this force to move the particle from $y = 0$ to $y = 1$ m is *[NCERT (New) Pg. 75, NEET (National) 2019]*

(a) 5 J (b) 25 J (c) 20 J (d) 30 J

02 A particle moves from a point $(-2\hat{i} + 5\hat{j})$ to $(4\hat{j} + 3\hat{k})$ when a force of $(4\hat{i} + 3\hat{j})$ N is applied. How much work has been done by the force? *[NEET 2016]*

(a) 8 J (b) 11 J (c) 5 J (d) 2 J

03 A uniform force of $(3\hat{i} + \hat{j})$ N acts on a particle of mass 2 kg. Hence, the particle is displaced from position $(2\hat{i} + \hat{k})$ m to position $(4\hat{i} + 3\hat{j} - \hat{k})$ m. The work done by the force on the particle is *[NEET 2013]*

(a) 9 J (b) 6 J (c) 13 J (d) 15 J

04 Force F on a particle moving in a straight line varries with distance d as shown in the figure. The work done on the particle during its displacement of 12 m is *[NCERT (New) Pg. 76, AIPMT 2011]*

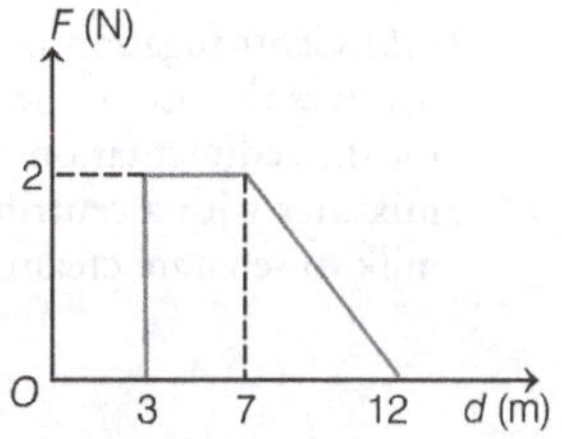

(a) 21 J (b) 26 J (c) 13 J (d) 18 J

05 A body of mass 3 kg is under a constant force, which causes a displacement s in metre in it, given by the relation $s = \frac{1}{3}t^2$, where t is in second. Work done by the force in 2 s is *[NCERT (New) Pg. 74, AIPMT 2006]*

(a) $\frac{5}{19}$ J (b) $\frac{3}{8}$ J

(c) $\frac{8}{3}$ J (d) $\frac{19}{5}$ J

06 A force F acting on an object varies with distance x as shown here. The force is in newton and x is in metre. The work done by the force in moving the object from $x = 0$ to $x = 6$ m is *[NCERT (New) Pg. 76, AIPMT 2005]*

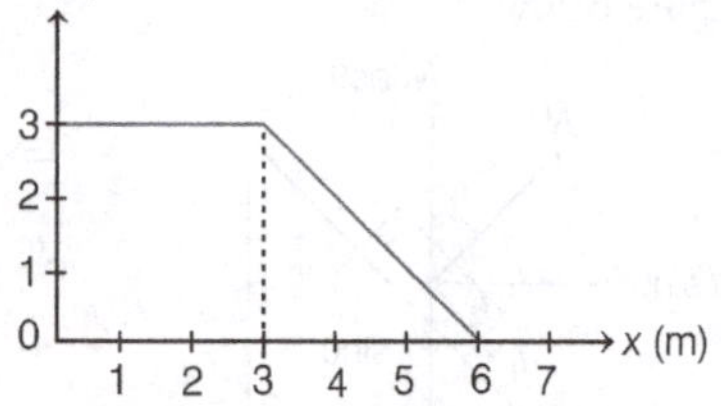

(a) 4.5 J (b) 13.5 J (c) 9.0 J (d) 18.0 J

07 A force acts on a 3 g particle in such a way that the position of the particle as a function of time is given by $x = 3t - 4t^2 + t^3$, where x is in metre and t is in second. The work done during the first 4 s is *[NCERT (New) Pg. 75, AIPMT 1998]*

(a) 490 mJ (b) 450 mJ (c) 240 mJ (d) 530 mJ

08 A body moves a distance of 10 m along a straight line under the action of a 5 N force. If the work done is 25 J, then angle between the force and direction of motion of the body is *[NCERT (New) Pg. 74, AIPMT 1997]*

(a) 60° (b) 75° (c) 30° (d) 45°

09 A body, constrained to move in y-direction, is subjected to a force given by $F = (-2\hat{i} + 15\hat{j} + 6\hat{k})$ N. The work done by this force in moving the body through a distance of $10\hat{j}$ m along Y-axis, is *[AIPMT 1994]*

(a) 150 J (b) 20 J (c) 190 J (d) 160 J

Topic 2 Kinetic and Potential Energy

01 The potential energy of a long spring when stretched by 2 cm is U. If the spring is stretched by 8 cm, potential energy stored in it will be *[NEET 2023]*
(a) $4U$ (b) $8U$
(c) $16U$ (d) $2U$

02 A particle is released from height S from the surface of the Earth. At a certain height its kinetic energy is three times its potential energy. The height from the surface of Earth and the speed of the particle at that instant are, respectively *[NCERT (New) Pg. 74, NEET 2021]*
(a) $\frac{S}{4}, \frac{3gS}{2}$ (b) $\frac{S}{4}, \frac{\sqrt{3gS}}{2}$
(c) $\frac{S}{2}, \frac{\sqrt{3gS}}{2}$ (d) $\frac{S}{4}, \sqrt{\frac{3gS}{2}}$

03 The energy required to break one bond in DNA is 10^{-20} J. This value (in eV) is nearly *[NEET (Sep.) 2020]*
(a) 0.6 (b) 0.06
(c) 0.006 (d) 6

04 A particle of mass 10 g moves along a circle of radius 6.4 cm with a constant tangential acceleration. What is the magnitude of this acceleration, if the kinetic energy of the particle becomes equal to 8×10^{-4} J by the end of the second revolution after the beginning of the motion? *[NEET 2016]*
(a) 0.15 m/s^2 (b) 0.18 m/s^2
(c) 0.2 m/s^2 (d) 0.1 m/s^2

05 Two similar springs P and Q have spring constants K_P and K_Q, such that $K_P > K_Q$. They are stretched, first by the same amount (case *a*), then by the same force (case *b*). The work done by the springs W_P and W_Q are related as, in case (*a*) and case (*b*), respectively *[NCERT (New) Pg. 80, AIPMT 2015]*
(a) $W_P = W_Q, W_P > W_Q$ (b) $W_P = W_Q, W_P = W_Q$
(c) $W_P > W_Q, W_Q > W_P$ (d) $W_P < W_Q, W_Q < W_P$

06 A body of mass $4m$ is lying in XY-plane at rest. It suddenly explodes into three pieces. Two pieces each of mass m move perpendicular to each other with equal speeds v. The total kinetic energy generated due to explosion is *[NCERT (New) Pg. 85, AIPMT 2014]*
(a) mv^2 (b) $\frac{3}{2}mv^2$
(c) $2mv^2$ (d) $4mv^2$

07 A particle with total energy E is moving in a potential energy region $U(x)$. Motion of the particle is restricted to the region when *[NEET 2013]*
(a) $U(x) < E$ (b) $U(x) = 0$
(c) $U(x) \le E$ (d) $U(x) > E$

08 The potential energy of a particle in a force field is $U = \frac{A}{r^2} - \frac{B}{r}$, where A and B are positive constants and r is the distance of particle from the centre of the field. For stable equilibrium, the distance of the particle is *[AIPMT 2012]*
(a) $B/2A$ (b) $2A/B$
(c) A/B (d) B/A

09 A particle of mass m_1 is moving with a velocity v_1 and another particle of mass m_2 is moving with a velocity v_2. Both of them have the same momentum, but their different kinetic energies are E_1 and E_2 respectively. If $m_1 > m_2$, then *[NCERT (New) Pg. 74, AIPMT 2004]*
(a) $E_1 < E_2$ (b) $\frac{E_1}{E_2} = \frac{m_1}{m_2}$ (c) $E_1 > E_2$ (d) $E_1 = E_2$

10 A ball of mass 2 kg and another of mass 4 kg are dropped together from a 60 ft tall building. After, a fall of 30 ft each towards earth, their respective kinetic energies will be in the ratio of *[AIPMT 2004]*
(a) $\sqrt{2}:1$ (b) 1 : 4 (c) 1 : 2 (d) $1:\sqrt{2}$

11 When a long spring is stretched by 2 cm, its potential energy is U. If the spring is stretched by 10 cm, the potential energy stored in it will be *[NCERT (New) Pg. 77, AIPMT 2003]*
(a) $U/5$ (b) $5U$ (c) $10U$ (d) $25U$

12 A stationary particle explodes into two particles of masses m_1 and m_2, which move in opposite directions with velocities v_1 and v_2. The ratio of their kinetic energies E_1/E_2 is *[NCERT (New) Pg. 84, AIPMT 2003]*
(a) 1 (b) $\frac{m_1 v_2}{m_2 v_1}$ (c) $\frac{m_2}{m_1}$ (d) $\frac{m_1}{m_2}$

13 If kinetic energy of a body is increased by 300%, then percentage change in momentum will be *[AIPMT 2002]*
(a) 100% (b) 150% (c) 265% (d) 73.2%

14 A stone is thrown at an angle of 45° to the horizontal with kinetic energy K. The kinetic energy at the highest point is *[AIPMT 2001]*
(a) $\frac{K}{2}$ (b) $\frac{K}{\sqrt{2}}$ (c) K (d) zero

15 Two springs A and B having spring constant k_A and k_B $(k_A = 2k_B)$ are stretched by applying force of equal magnitude. If energy stored in spring A is E_A then energy stored in B will be *[AIPMT 2001]*
(a) $2E_A$ (b) $E_A/4$ (c) $E_A/2$ (d) $4E_A$

16 Two bodies of masses m and $4m$ are moving with equal kinetic energies. The ratio of their linear momenta is *[NCERT (New) Pg. 74, AIPMT 1998, 1997, 1989]*
(a) 1 : 2 (b) 1 : 4 (c) 4 : 1 (d) 1 : 1

17 Two bodies with kinetic energies in the ratio 4 : 1 are moving with equal linear momentum. The ratio of their masses is *[AIPMT 1999]*

(a) 1 : 2 (b) 1 : 1
(c) 4 : 1 (d) 1 : 4

18 A particle is projected making an angle of 45° with horizontal having kinetic energy K. The kinetic energy at highest point will be *[AIPMT 2001, 1997]*

(a) $\frac{K}{\sqrt{2}}$ (b) $\frac{K}{2}$
(c) $2K$ (d) K

19 The potential energy between two atoms, in a molecule, is given by $U(x) = \frac{a}{x^{12}} - \frac{b}{x^6}$ where a and b are positive constants and x is the distance between the atoms. The atom is in stable equilibrium, when *[NCERT (New) Pg. 78, AIPMT 1995]*

(a) $x = \left(\frac{2a}{b}\right)^{1/6}$
(b) $x = \left(\frac{11a}{5b}\right)^{1/6}$
(c) $x = 0$
(d) $x = \left(\frac{a}{2b}\right)^{1/6}$

20 If the momentum of a body is increased by 50%, then the percentage increase in its kinetic energy is *[AIPMT 1995]*

(a) 50% (b) 100%
(c) 125% (d) 200%

21 The KE acquired by a mass m in travelling a certain distance d, starting from rest, under the action of a constant force is directly proportional to *[AIPMT 1994]*

(a) m (b) $\sqrt{m}$
(c) $\frac{1}{\sqrt{m}}$ (d) Independent of m

22 Two masses 1 g and 9 g are moving with equal kinetic energies. The ratio of the magnitudes of their respective linear momenta is *[AIPMT 1993]*

(a) 1:9 (b) 9:1
(c) 1:3 (d) 3:1

23 Force acting on a particle moving in a straight line varies with velocity of the particle as $F = \frac{k}{v}$, here k is constant. The work done by this force in time t is *[NCERT (New) Pg. 74, AIPMT 1993]*

(a) $\frac{k}{v^2} \cdot t$ (b) $2kt$
(c) kt (d) $\frac{2kt}{v^2}$

Topic 3 Work Energy Theorem and Conservation of Energy

01 An object of mass 500 g, initially at rest acted upon by a variable force whose x component varies with x in the manner shown. The velocities of the object a point $x = 8$ m and $x = 12$ m, would be the respective values of (nearly) *[NCERT (New) Pg. 76, NEET (Odisha) 2019]*

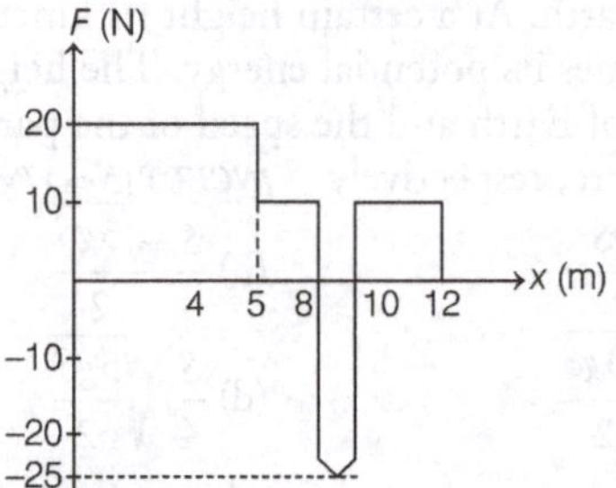

(a) 18 m/s and 24.4 m/s (b) 23 m/s and 24.4 m/s
(c) 23 m/s and 20.6 m/s (d) 18 m/s and 20.6 m/s

02 Consider a drop of rain water having mass 1 g falling from a height of 1 km. It hits the ground with a speed of 50 m/s. Take g constant with a value of 10 m/s^2. The work done by the (i) gravitational force and the (ii) resistive force of air is *[NCERT (New) Pg. 73, NEET 2017]*

(a) (i) −10 J, (ii) − 8.25 J
(b) (i) 1.25 J, (ii) − 8.25 J
(c) (i) 100 J, (ii) 8.75 J
(d) (i) 10 J, (ii) − 8.75 J

03 A block of mass 10 kg, moving in x-direction with a constant speed of 10 ms^{-1}, is subjected to a retarding force $F = 0.1\,x$ J/m during its travel from $x = 20$ m to 30 m. Its final KE will be *[NCERT (New) Pg. 73, AIPMT 2015]*

(a) 475 J (b) 450 J
(c) 275 J (d) 250 J

04 A ball is thrown vertically downwards from a height of 20 m with an initial velocity v_0. It collides with the ground, loses 50% of its energy in collision and rebounds to the same height. The initial velocity v_0 is (Take, $g = 10$ ms^{-2}) *[AIPMT 2015]*

(a) 14 ms^{-1} (b) 20 ms^{-1}
(c) 28 ms^{-1} (d) 10 ms^{-1}

05 The potential energy of a system increases, if work is done *[AIPMT 2011]*

(a) by the system against a conservative force
(b) by the system against a non-conservative force
(c) upon the system by a conservative force
(d) upon the system by a non-conservative force

06 A force of 250 N is requried to lift a 75 kg mass through a pulley system. In order to lift the mass through 3 m, the rope has to be pulled through 12m. The efficiency of system is *[AIPMT 2011]*
(a) 50% (b) 75% (c) 33% (d) 90%

07 A body of mass 1 kg is thrown upwards with a velocity 20 ms^{-1}. It momentarily comes to rest after attaining a height of 18 m.
How much energy is lost due to air friction? (Take, $g = 10\ ms^{-2}$) *[NCERT (New) Pg. 74, AIPMT 2009]*
(a) 20 J (b) 30 J (c) 40 J (d) 10 J

08 A block of mass M is attached to the lower end of a vertical spring. The spring is hung from a ceiling and has force constant value k. The mass is released from rest with the spring initially unstretched. The maximum extension produced in the length of the spring will be *[NCERT (New) Pg. 78, AIPMT 2009]*
(a) Mg/k (b) $2\ Mg/k$ (c) $4\ Mg/k$ (d) $Mg/2k$

09 A shell of mass 200 g is ejected from a gun of mass 4 kg by an explosion that generates 1.05 kJ of energy. The initial velocity of the shell is *[AIPMT 2008]*
(a) 100 ms^{-1} (b) 80 ms^{-1}
(c) 40 ms^{-1} (d) 120 ms^{-1}

10 A vertical spring with force constant k is fixed on a table. A ball of mass m at a height h above the free upper end of the spring falls vertically on the spring so that the spring is compressed by a distance d. The net work done in the process is *[AIPMT 2007]*
(a) $mg(h+d) - \frac{1}{2}kd^2$ (b) $mg(h-d) - \frac{1}{2}kd^2$
(c) $mg(h-d) + \frac{1}{2}kd^2$ (d) $mg(h+d) + \frac{1}{2}kd^2$

11 300 J of work is done in sliding a 2 kg block up an inclined plane of height 10 m. Taking $g = 10\ m/s^2$, work done against friction is *[AIPMT 2006]*
(a) 200 J (b) 100 J
(c) zero (d) 1000 J

12 A mass of 0.5 kg moving with a speed of 1.5 m/s on a horizontal smooth surface, collides with a nearly weightless spring of force constant $k = 50$ N/m. The maximum compression of the spring would be *[AIPMT 2004]*

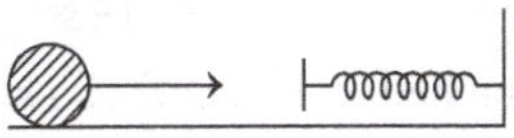

(a) 0.15 m (b) 0.12 m
(c) 1.5 m (d) 0.5 m

13 A child is swinging a swing. Minimum and maximum heights of swing from the earth's surface are 0.75 m and 2 m, respectively. The maximum velocity of this swing is *[AIPMT 2001]*
(a) 5 m/s (b) 10 m/s
(c) 15 m/s (d) 20 m/s

14 A rubber ball is dropped from a height of 5 m on a planet where the acceleration due to gravity is not known. On bouncing it rises to 1.8 m. The ball loses its velocity on bouncing by a factor of *[AIPMT 1998]*
(a) 16/25 (b) 2/5 (c) 3/5 (d) 9/25

15 A bullet of mass 10 g leaves a rifle at an initial velocity of 1000 m/s and strikes the earth at the same level with a velocity of 500 m/s. The work done in joule to overcome the resistance of air will be *[NCERT (New) Pg. 74, AIPMT 1989]*
(a) 375 (b) 3750 (c) 5000 (d) 500

Topic 4 Power

01 Two heaters A and B have power rating of 1 kW and 2 kW, respectively. Those two are first connected in series and then in parallel to a fixed power source. The ratio of power outputs for these two cases is *[NCERT (New) Pg. 83, NEET 2024]*
(a) 1 : 1 (b) 2 : 9 (c) 1 : 2 (d) 2 : 3

02 At any instant of time t, the displacement of any particle is given by $2t - 1$ (SI unit) under the influence of force of 5 N. The value of instantaneous power is (in SI unit) *[NCERT (New) Pg. 83, NEET 2024]*
(a) 10 (b) 5 (c) 7 (d) 6

03 An electric lift with a maximum load of 2000 kg (lift + passengers) is moving up with a constant speed of 1.5 m/s. The frictional force opposing the motion is 3000 N. The minimum power delivered by the motor to the lift in watts is ($g = 10\ m/s^{-2}$) *[NCERT (New) Pg. 83, NEET 2022]*
(a) 23000 (b) 20000 (c) 34500 (d) 23500

04 Water falls from a height of 60 m at the rate of 15 kg/s to operate a turbine. The losses due to frictional force are 10% of the input energy. How much power is generated by the turbine? ($g = 10\ m/s^2$) *[NEET 2021]*
(a) 10.2 kW (b) 8.1 kW (c) 12.3 kW (d) 7.0 kW

05 A body of mass 1 kg begins to move under the action of a time dependent force $\mathbf{F} = (2t\,\hat{i} + 3t^2\,\hat{j})$ N, where $\hat{i}$ and $\hat{j}$ are unit vectors along X and Y axes. What power will be developed by the force at the time (t)? *[NCERT (New) Pg. 74, NEET 2016]*
(a) $(2t^2 + 4t^4)$ W (b) $(2t^3 + 3t^4)$ W
(c) $(2t^3 + 3t^5)$ W (d) $(2t + 3t^3)$ W

06 A particle of mass m is driven by a machine that delivers a constant power k watts. If the particle starts from rest, the force on the particle at time t is *[AIPMT 2015]*
(a) $\sqrt{\frac{mk}{2}}\, t^{-1/2}$ (b) $\sqrt{mk}\, t^{-1/2}$ (c) $\sqrt{2mk}\, t^{-1/2}$ (d) $\frac{1}{2}\sqrt{mk}\, t^{-1/2}$

07 The heart of a man pumps 5 L of blood through the arteries per minute at a pressure of 150 mm of mercury. If the density of mercury be 13.6×10^3 kg / m^3 and $g = 10$ m / s^2, then the power of heart in watt is **[AIPMT 2015]**
(a) 1.70 (b) 2.35 (c) 3.0 (d) 1.50

08 One coolie takes 1 minute to raise a suitcase through a height of 2 m but the second coolie takes 30 s to raise the same suitcase to the same height. The powers of two coolies are in the ratio **[NEET 2013]**
(a) 1 : 3 (b) 2 : 1 (c) 3 : 1 (d) 1 : 2

09 A car of mass m starts from rest and accelerates so that the instantaneous power delivered to the car has a constant magnitude P_0. The instantaneous velocity of this car is proportional to **[NCERT (New) Pg. 83, AIPMT 2012]**
(a) $t^2 P_0$ (b) $t^{1/2}$ (c) $t^{-1/2}$ (d) $\frac{t}{\sqrt{m}}$

10 A body projected vertically from the earth reaches a height equal to earth's radius before returning to the earth. The power exerted by the gravitational force is greatest **[NCERT (New) Pg. 83, AIPMT 2011]**
(a) at the highest position of the body
(b) at the instant just before the body hits the earth
(c) it remains constant all through
(d) at the instant just after the body is projected

11 An engine pumps water through a hose pipe. Water passes through the pipe and leaves it with a velocity of 2 ms^{-1}. The mass per unit length of water in the pipe is 100 kg m^{-1}. What is the power of the engine ? **[AIPMT 2010]**
(a) 400 W (b) 200 W
(c) 100 W (d) 800 W

12 A particle of mass M, starting from rest, undergoes uniform acceleration. If the speed acquired in time t is v, the power delivered to the particle is **[AIPMT 2010]**
(a) $\frac{Mv^2}{t}$ (b) $\frac{1}{2}\frac{Mv^2}{t^2}$ (c) $\frac{Mv^2}{t^2}$ (d) $\frac{1}{2}\frac{Mv^2}{t}$

13 An engine pumps water continuously through a hose. Water leaves the hose with a velocity v and m is the mass per unit length of the water jet. What is the rate at which kinetic energy is imparted to water ? **[NCERT (New) Pg. 83, AIPMT 2009]**
(a) $\frac{1}{2}mv^3$ (b) mv^3 (c) $\frac{1}{2}mv^2$ (d) $\frac{1}{2}m^2v^2$

14 Water falls from a height of 60 m at the rate of 15 kg/s to operate a turbine. The losses due to frictional forces are 10% of energy. How much power is generated by the turbine ? (Take, $g = 10$ m / s^2) **[AIPMT 2008]**
(a) 8.1 kW (b) 10.2 kW
(c) 12.3 kW (d) 7.0 kW

15 If $\mathbf{F} = (60\hat{i} + 15\hat{j} - 3\hat{k})$ N and $\mathbf{v} = (2\hat{i} - 4\hat{j} + 5\hat{k})$ m/s, then instantaneous power is **[AIPMT 2000]**
(a) 195 W (b) 45 W (c) 75 W (d) 100 W

16 How much water a pump of 2 kW can raise in one minute to a height of 10 m ? (Take, $g = 10$ m / s^2) **[AIPMT 1990]**
(a) 1000 L (b) 1200 L (c) 100 L (d) 2000 L

Topic 5 Motion in Vertical Circle

01 A point mass m is moved in a vertical circle of radius r with the help of a string. The velocity of the mass is $\sqrt{7gr}$ at the lowest point. The tension in the string at the lowest point is **[NEET (Oct.) 2020]**
(a) $6mg$ (b) $7mg$ (c) $8mg$ (d) $1mg$

02 A mass m is attached to a thin wire and whirled in a vertical circle. The wire is most likely to break when **[NEET (National) 2019]**
(a) the wire is horizontal
(b) the mass is at the lowest point
(c) inclined at an angle of 60° from vertical
(d) the mass is at the highest point

03 A body initially at rest and sliding along a frictionless track from a height h (as shown in the figure) just completes a vertical circle of diameter $AB = D$. The height h is equal to **[NEET 2018]**

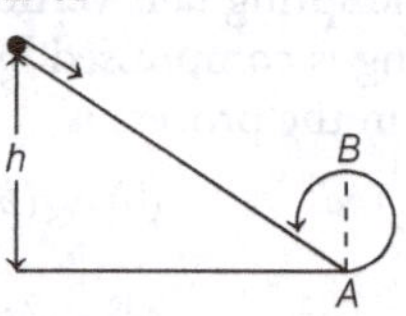

(a) $\frac{7}{5}D$ (b) D (c) $\frac{3}{2}D$ (d) $\frac{5}{4}D$

04 A stone is tied to a string of length l and is whirled in a vertical circle with the other end of the string as the centre. At a certain instant of time, the stone is at its lowest position and has a speed u. The magnitude of the change in velocity as it reaches a position where the string is horizontal (g being acceleration due to gravity) is **[AIPMT 2004]**
(a) $\sqrt{2(u^2 - gl)}$ (b) $\sqrt{u^2 - gl}$
(c) $u - \sqrt{u^2 - 2gl}$ (d) $\sqrt{2gl}$

05 A stone is attached to one end of a string and rotated in a vertical circle. If string breaks at the position of maximum tension, it will break at **[AIPMT 2000]**

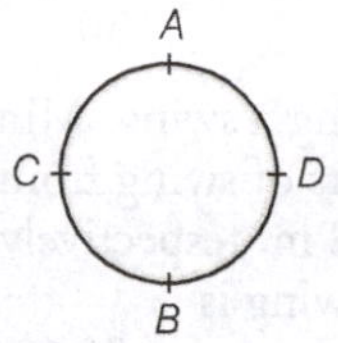

(a) A (b) B (c) C (d) D

06 As shown in the figure, a mass is performing vertical circular motion. The average velocity of the particle is increased, then at which point will the string break? *[AIPMT 2000]*

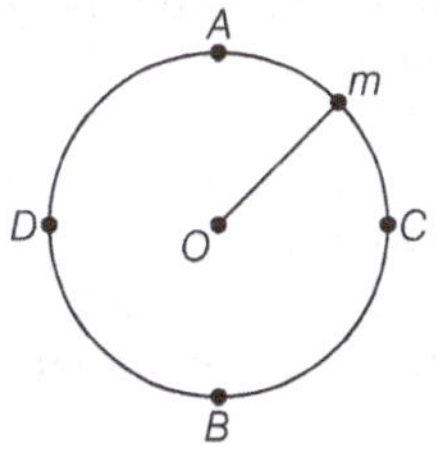

(a) A (b) B (c) C (d) D

Topic 6 Collision

01 Two bodies A and B of same mass undergo completely inelastic one dimensional collision. The body A moves with velocity v_1 while body B is at rest before collision. The velocity of the system after collision is v_2. The ratio is *[NCERT (New) Pg. 84, NEET 2024]*
(a) 1 : 2 (b) 2 : 1 (c) 4 : 1 (d) 1 : 4

02 An object flying in air with velocity $(20\hat{i}+25\hat{j}-12\hat{k})$ suddenly breaks in two pieces whose masses are in the ratio 1:5. The smaller mass flies off with a velocity $(100\hat{i}+35\hat{j}+8\hat{k})$. The velocity of the larger piece will be *[NCERT (New) Pg. 84, NEET (Odisha) 2019]*
(a) $4\hat{i}+23\hat{j}-16\hat{k}$ (b) $-100\hat{i}-35\hat{j}-8\hat{k}$
(c) $20\hat{i}+15\hat{j}-80\hat{k}$ (d) $-20\hat{i}-15\hat{j}-80\hat{k}$

03 A particle of mass 5 m at rest suddenly breaks on its own into three fragments. Two fragments of mass m each move along mutually perpendicular direction with each speed v. The energy released during the process is *[NCERT (New) Pg. 85, NEET (Odisha) 2019]*
(a) $\frac{3}{5}mv^2$ (b) $\frac{5}{3}mv^2$ (c) $\frac{3}{2}mv^2$ (d) $\frac{4}{3}mv^2$

04 Body A of mass $4m$ moving with speed u collides with another body B of mass $2m$, at rest. The collision is head on and elastic in nature. After the collision the fraction of energy lost by the colliding body A is *[NEET (National) 2019]*
(a) $\frac{8}{9}$ (b) $\frac{4}{9}$
(c) $\frac{5}{9}$ (d) $\frac{1}{9}$

05 A moving block having mass m, collides with another stationary block having mass $4m$. The lighter block comes to rest after collision. When the initial velocity of the lighter block is v, then the value of coefficient of restitution e will be *[NEET 2018]*
(a) 0.8 (b) 0.25 (c) 0.5 (d) 0.4

06 Two identical balls A and B having velocities of 0.5 m/s and -0.3 m/s respectively collide elastically in one dimension. The velocities of B and A after the collision respectively will be *[NCERT (New) Pg. 84, NEET 2016]*
(a) -0.5 m/s and 0.3 m/s (b) 0.5 m/s and -0.3 m/s
(c) -0.3 m/s and 0.5 m/s (d) 0.3 m/s and 0.5 m/s

07 A bullet of mass 10 g moving horizontally with a velocity of 400 m/s strikes a wooden block of mass 2 kg which is suspended by light inextensible string of length 5 m. As a result, the centre of gravity of the block is found to rise a vertical distance of 10 cm. The speed of the bullet after it emerges out horizontally from the block will be *[NCERT (New) Pg. 84, AIPMT 2016]*
(a) 100 m s^{-1} (b) 80 m s^{-1} (c) 120 m s^{-1} (d) 160 m s^{-1}

08 Two particles of masses m_1, m_2 move with initial velocities u_1 and u_2. On collision, one of the particles get excited to higher level, after absorbing energy ε. If final velocities of particles be v_1 and v_2, then we must have *[AIPMT 2015]*
(a) $m_1^2 u_1 + m_2^2 u_2 - \varepsilon = m_1^2 v_1 + m_2^2 v_2$
(b) $\frac{1}{2}m_1 u_1^2 + \frac{1}{2}m_2 u_2^2 = \frac{1}{2}m_1 v_1^2 + \frac{1}{2}m_2 v_2^2 - \varepsilon$
(c) $\frac{1}{2}m_1 u_1^2 + \frac{1}{2}m_2 u_2^2 - \varepsilon = \frac{1}{2}m_1 v_1^2 + \frac{1}{2}m_2 v_2^2$
(d) $\frac{1}{2}m_1^2 u_1^2 + \frac{1}{2}m_2^2 u_2^2 + \varepsilon = \frac{1}{2}m_1^2 v_1^2 + \frac{1}{2}m_2^2 v_2^2$

09 Two particles A and B, move with constant velocities $\mathbf{v}_1$ and $\mathbf{v}_2$. At the initial moment their position vectors are $\mathbf{r}_1$ and $\mathbf{r}_2$, respectively. The condition for particles A and B for their collision is *[NCERT (New) Pg. 84, AIPMT 2015]*
(a) $\mathbf{r}_1 \times \mathbf{v}_1 = \mathbf{r}_2 \times \mathbf{v}_2$ (b) $\mathbf{r}_1 - \mathbf{r}_2 = \mathbf{v}_1 - \mathbf{v}_2$
(c) $\frac{\mathbf{r}_1 - \mathbf{r}_2}{|\mathbf{r}_1 - \mathbf{r}_2|} = \frac{\mathbf{v}_2 - \mathbf{v}_1}{|\mathbf{v}_2 - \mathbf{v}_1|}$ (d) $\mathbf{r}_1 \cdot \mathbf{v}_1 = \mathbf{r}_2 \cdot \mathbf{v}_2$

10 On a frictionless surface, a block of mass M moving at speed v collides elastically with another block of same mass M which is initially at rest. After collision the first block moves at an angle θ to its initial direction and has a speed $v/3$. The second block's speed after the collision is *[AIPMT 2015]*
(a) $2\sqrt{2}/3\,v$ (b) $3/4\,v$ (c) $3/\sqrt{2}\,v$ (d) $\sqrt{3}/2\,v$

11 Two spheres A and B of masses m_1 and m_2 respectively collide. A is at rest initially and B is moving with velocity v along X-axis. After collision B has a velocity $v/2$ in a direction perpendicular to the original direction. The mass A moves after collision in the direction *[AIPMT 2012]*
(a) same as that of B (b) opposite to that of B
(c) $\theta = \tan^{-1}\left(\frac{1}{2}\right)$ to the X-axis
(d) $\theta = \tan^{-1}\left(-\frac{1}{2}\right)$ to the X-axis

12 A mass m moving horizontally (along the X-axis) with velocity v collides and sticks to a mass of $3m$ moving vertically upward (along the Y-axis) with velocity $2v$. The final velocity of the combination is *[NCERT (New) Pg. 85, AIPMT 2011]*

(a) $\frac{3}{2}v\hat{i}+\frac{1}{4}v\hat{j}$ (b) $\frac{1}{4}v\hat{i}+\frac{3}{2}v\hat{j}$
(c) $\frac{1}{3}v\hat{i}+\frac{2}{3}v\hat{j}$ (d) $\frac{2}{3}v\hat{i}+\frac{1}{3}v\hat{j}$

13 A ball moving with velocity 2 ms^{-1} collides head on with another stationary ball of double the mass. If the coefficient of restitution is 0.5, then their velocities (in ms^{-1}) after collision will be *[AIPMT 2010]*

(a) 0,1 (b) 1, 1
(c) 1, 0.5 (d) 0, 2

14 A bomb of mass 30 kg at rest explodes into two pieces of masses 18 kg and 12 kg. The velocity of 18 kg mass is 6 ms^{-1}. The kinetic energy of the other mass is *[AIPMT 2005]*

(a) 256 J (b) 486 J
(c) 524 J (d) 324 J

15 Two equal masses m_1 and m_2 moving along the same straight line with velocities + 3 m/s and − 5 m/s respectively collide elastically. Their velocities after the collision will be respectively *[AIPMT 1998]*

(a) + 4 m/s for both (b) − 3 m/s and + 5 m/s
(c) − 4 m/s and + 4 m/s (d) − 5 m/s and + 3 m/s

16 A metal ball of mass 2 kg moving with a velocity of 36 km/h has a head on collision with a stationary ball of mass 3 kg. If after the collision, the two balls move together, the loss in kinetic energy due to collision is *[AIPMT 1997]*

(a) 140 J (b) 100 J (c) 60 J (d) 40 J

17 A body of mass m moving with velocity 3 km / h collides with a body of mass 2 m at rest. Now, the coalesced mass starts to move with a velocity *[NCERT (New) Pg. 84, AIPMT 1996]*

(a) 1 km/h (b) 2 km/h
(c) 3 km/h (d) 4 km/h

18 The coefficient of restitution e for a perfectly elastic collision is *[NCERT (New) Pg. 84, AIPMT 1988]*

(a) 1 (b) zero
(c) infinite (d) − 1

• Key **Index**

Topic 1

1 (b)	2 (c)	3 (a)	4 (c)	5 (c)	6 (b)	7 (d)	8 (a)	9 (a)

Topic 2

1 (c)	2 (d)	3 (b)	4 (d)	5 (c)	6 (b)	7 (a)	8 (b)	9 (a)	10 (c)
11 (d)	12 (c)	13 (a)	14 (a)	15 (a)	16 (a)	17 (d)	18 (b)	19 (a)	20 (c)
21 (d)	22 (c)	23 (c)							

Topic 3

1 (c)	2 (d)	3 (a)	4 (b)	5 (a)	6 (b)	7 (a)	8 (b)	9 (a)	10 (a)
11 (b)	12 (a)	13 (a)	14 (b)	15 (b)					

Topic 4

1 (b)	2 (a)	3 (c)	4 (b)	5 (c)	6 (a)	7 (a)	8 (d)	9 (b)	10 (b)
11 (d)	12 (d)	13 (a)	14 (a)	15 (b)	16 (b)				

Topic 5

1 (c)	2 (b)	3 (d)	4 (a)	5 (b)	6 (b)

Topic 6

1 (b)	2 (a)	3 (d)	4 (a)	5 (b)	6 (b)	7 (c)	8 (c)	9 (c)	10 (a)
11 (d)	12 (b)	13 (a)	14 (b)	15 (d)	16 (c)	17 (a)	18 (a)		

Detailed **Explanations**

Topic 1

01. *(b)*

key idea

Work done, $W = \int_{y_1}^{y_2}$ Force × (distance element)

$\int_{y_1}^{y_2} F.dy$

Work done by a force F, which is variable in nature in moving a particle from y_1 to y_2 is given by

$$W = \int_{y_1}^{y_2} F \cdot dy \quad \text{... (i)}$$

Here, force, $F = 20 + 10y$, $y_1 = 0$
and $y_2 = 1\text{ m}$
Substituting the given values in Eq. (i), we get

$$\Rightarrow W = \int_0^1 (20 + 10y)dy = \left[20y + \frac{10y^2}{2}\right]_0^1$$
$$= 20(1-0) + 5(1-0)^2 = 25\text{ J}$$

02. *(c)* Position vectors of the particles are

$\mathbf{r}_1 = -2\hat{i} + 5\hat{j}$ and $\mathbf{r}_2 = 4\hat{j} + 3\hat{k}$

∴ Displacement of the particle,

$$\Delta\mathbf{s} = \mathbf{r}_2 - \mathbf{r}_1 = 4\hat{j} + 3\hat{k} - (-2\hat{i} + 5\hat{j})$$
$$= 2\hat{i} - \hat{j} + 3\hat{k}$$

Force on the particle, $\mathbf{F} = (4\hat{i} + 3\hat{j})$ N

∴ Work done, $W = \mathbf{F} \cdot \Delta\mathbf{s}$
$$= (4\hat{i} + 3\hat{j}) \cdot (2\hat{i} - \hat{j} + 3\hat{k})$$
$$= 8 - 3 = 5\text{ J}$$

03. *(a)* Given, force $F = 3(\hat{i} + \hat{j})$ N

$\mathbf{r}_1 = (2\hat{i} + \hat{k})$ m

and $\mathbf{r}_2 = (4\hat{i} + 3\hat{j} - \hat{k})$ m

∴ $\mathbf{s} = \mathbf{r}_2 - \mathbf{r}_1 = (4\hat{i} + 3\hat{j} - \hat{k}) - (2\hat{i} + \hat{k})$
$= (2\hat{i} + 3\hat{j} - 2\hat{k})$ m

∴ $W = \mathbf{F} \cdot \mathbf{s} = (3\hat{i} + \hat{j}) \cdot (2\hat{i} + 3\hat{j} - 2\hat{k})$
$= 6 + 3 + 0 = 6 + 3 = 9$ J

04. *(c)* Work done = Area under (F-d) graph

$$W = 2 \times (7-3) + \frac{1}{2} \times 2 \times (12-7)$$
$$= 8 + \frac{1}{2} \times 10 = 8 + 5 = 13\text{ J}$$

• Concept Enhancer

Work done is equal to area under the curve in *F-d* graph.

05. *(c)*

key idea

Work done = Force × Displacement

$W = ma \times s$ ... (i)

Find acceleration from displacement and put it into Eq. (i).

Work done by the force
= force × displacement

or $W = F \times s$ ...(i)

$F = ma$ ...(ii)

Hence, from Eqs. (i) and (ii), we get

$$W = mas = m\left(\frac{d^2s}{dt^2}\right)s \quad \left(\because a = \frac{d^2s}{dt^2}\right) \quad \text{...(iii)}$$

Now, we have, $s = \frac{1}{3}t^2$

$$\therefore \quad \frac{d^2s}{dt^2} = \frac{d}{dt}\left[\frac{d}{dt}\left(\frac{1}{3}t^2\right)\right]$$
$$= \frac{d}{dt} \times \left(\frac{2}{3}t\right) = \frac{2}{3}$$

Hence, Eq. (iii) becomes

$$W = \frac{2}{3}ms = \frac{2}{3}m \times \frac{1}{3}t^2 = \frac{2}{9}mt^2$$

We have, $m = 3$ kg, $t = 2$ s

$$\therefore \quad W = \frac{2}{9} \times 3 \times (2)^2 = \frac{8}{3}\text{ J}$$

06. *(b)* W = Area of square + area of triangle

$$= 3 \times 3 + \frac{1}{2} \times 3 \times 3$$
$$= 9 + 4.5 = 13.5\text{ J}$$

07. *(d)* Given, mass of particle,

$m = 3\text{ g} = 3 \times 10^{-3}$ kg

Position of particle, $x = 3t - 4t^2 + t^3$

Time, $t = 4$ s

We know that,

$$v = \frac{dx}{dt} = 3 - 8t + 3t^2 \quad \text{...(i)}$$

and
$$a = \frac{dv}{dt} = 0 - 8 + 6t \quad \text{...(ii)}$$

Now, work done, $dW = Fdx$

$dW = (ma)\,dx$

$dW = (0.003)(-8 + 6t)(3 - 8t + 3t^2)dt$
$= (0.003)(18t^3 - 72t^2 + 82t - 24)dt$

Integrating both sides

$$\int dW = \int (0.003)(18t^3 - 72t^2 + 82t - 24)dt$$

$$\Rightarrow W = (0.003)\int_0^4 (18t^3 - 72t^2 + 82t - 24)dt$$

$\Rightarrow W = 0.003 \times 176 = 0.528\text{ J} = 0.530\text{ J}$
≈ 530 mJ

08. *(a)*

key idea

Work done = $F \cdot s \cos\theta$

$\Rightarrow \cos\theta = \frac{W}{Fs} \Rightarrow \theta = \cos^{-1}\left(\frac{W}{Fs}\right)$

Given, distance $s = 10$ m
Force, $F = 5$ N
Work done, $W = 25$ J
Work done, $W = Fs\cos\theta$

∴ $25 = 5 \times 10\cos\theta = 50\cos\theta$

or $\cos\theta = \frac{25}{50} = 0.5$ or $\theta = 60°$

09. *(a)* Given force,

$\mathbf{F} = (-2\hat{i} + 15\hat{j} + 6\hat{k})$ N

displacement, $\mathbf{s} = 10\hat{j}$

Work done,

$W = \mathbf{F} \cdot \mathbf{s} = (-2\hat{i} + 15\hat{j} + 6\hat{k}) \cdot (10\hat{j})$
$= 150$ J

Topic 2

01. *(c)* Given, when $x_1 = 2$ cm

Then, $U_1 = U \Rightarrow \frac{1}{2}kx_1^2 = U$

$$\Rightarrow \quad k = \frac{2U}{x_1^2} \quad \text{...(i)}$$

When $x_2 = 8$ cm, then $U = \frac{1}{2}kx_2^2$

$$= \frac{1}{2} \times \frac{2U}{x_1^2} \times x_2^2 \quad \text{[From Eq. (i)]}$$

$$= U \cdot \left(\frac{x_2}{x_1}\right)^2 = U\left(\frac{8}{2}\right)^2 = 16U$$

02. *(d)*

key idea

At any instant of time, Total energy = KE + PE

Kinetic energy $= \frac{1}{2}mv^2$

and potential energy $= mgx$ (x is height from the surface of earth).

Kinetic energy

$= 3$ (potential energy)

$\Rightarrow$ $KE = 3mgx$

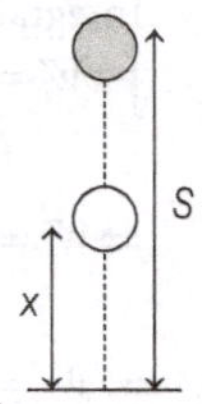

At height S, total energy,

$TE = PE + KE$

$TE = mgS + 0 = mgS$

At height x, total energy,

$TE = PE + KE = mgx + 3mgx$

$mgS = 4mgx$

$\Rightarrow \quad x = \frac{S}{4} \quad \ldots(i)$

Now, we shall determine the speed of the particle at this height.

As, $KE = 3 \times mgx$

$KE = 3 \times mg\frac{S}{4}$ [from Eq. (i)]

$\frac{1}{2}mv^2 = \frac{3}{4}mgS$

$\Rightarrow \quad v = \sqrt{\frac{3}{2}gS}$

03. *(b)* Given, $E = 10^{-20}$ J

In terms of eV, we get

$$E = \frac{10^{-20}}{1.6 \times 10^{-19}} \text{ eV} = 0.06 \text{ eV}$$

04. *(d)* Given, $m = 0.01$ kg

$r = 6.4$ cm $= 6.4 \times 10^{-2}$ m

$\because \quad KE = 8 \times 10^{-4}$ J

$\therefore \quad \frac{1}{2}mv^2 = 8 \times 10^{-4}$ J

$\Rightarrow v^2 = \frac{16 \times 10^{-4}}{0.01} = 16 \times 10^{-2} \quad \ldots(i)$

As it is given that KE of particle is equal to 8×10^{-4} J by the end of second revolution after the beginning of motion of particle. It means, its initial velocity (u) is 0 m/s at this moment.

$\because$ By Newton's 3rd equation of motion,

$v^2 = u^2 + 2a_t s$

$\Rightarrow v^2 = 2a_t s$ or $v^2 = 2a_t(4\pi r)$

($\because$ particle covers 2 revolutions)

$\Rightarrow a_t = \frac{v^2}{8\pi r} = \frac{16 \times 10^{-2}}{8 \times 3.14 \times 6.4 \times 10^{-2}}$

($\because$ from Eq. (i), $v^2 = 16 \times 10^{-2}$)

$\therefore \quad a_t = 0.1$ m/s^2

Alternate Solution

Using work energy theorem;

Work done by the force = Change in KE

$\Rightarrow W_{tangential} + W_{centripetal} = K_f - k_i$

$\Rightarrow a_f = \frac{k_f}{4\pi rm} = \frac{8 \times 10^{-4}}{4 \times \frac{22}{7} \times 6.4 \times 10^{-2} \times 10^{-2}}$

$= 0.099 \approx 0.1$ m/s^2

05. *(c)* Given, $K_P > K_Q$

In case (a), the elongation is same

i.e. $\quad x_1 = x_2 = x$

So, $\quad W_P = \frac{1}{2}K_P x^2$

and $\quad W_Q = \frac{1}{2}K_Q x^2$

$\therefore \quad \frac{W_P}{W_Q} = \frac{K_P}{K_Q} > 1$

In case (b), the spring force is same

i.e. $\quad F_1 = F_2 = F$

So, $\quad x_1 = \frac{F}{K_P}, x_2 = \frac{F}{K_Q}$

$\therefore \quad W_P = \frac{1}{2}K_P x_1^2$

$= \frac{1}{2}K_P \frac{F^2}{K_P^2} = \frac{1}{2}\frac{F^2}{K_P}$

and $\quad W_Q = \frac{1}{2}K_Q x_2^2 = \frac{1}{2}K_Q \cdot \frac{F^2}{K_Q^2}$

$= \frac{1}{2}\frac{F^2}{K_Q}$

$\therefore \quad \frac{W_P}{W_Q} = \frac{K_Q}{K_P} < 1 = W_P < W_Q$

06. *(b)* Given,

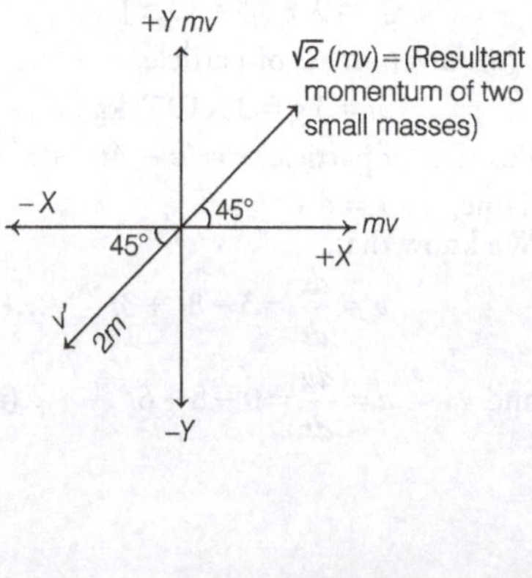

According to question, the third part of mass $2m$ will move as shown in the figure, because the total momentum of the system after explosion must remain zero. Let the velocity of third part be v'.

From the conservation of momentum

$\sqrt{2}(mv) = (2m) \times v'$

$\Rightarrow \quad v' = \frac{v}{\sqrt{2}}$

So, total kinetic energy generated by the explosion

$= \frac{1}{2}mv^2 + \frac{1}{2}mv^2 + \frac{1}{2}(2m)v'^2$

$= mv^2 + m \times \left(\frac{v}{\sqrt{2}}\right)^2$

$= mv^2 + \frac{mv^2}{2} = \frac{3}{2}mv^2$

07. *(a)* We know that,

Total energy

$=$ Potential energy $+$ Kinetic energy

$E = U(x) + KE(x)$

or $E - U(x) = KE(x)$

If the particle is moving, kinetic energy must be positive or $KE(x) > 0$

then $E - U(x) = KE(x) > 0$

$\Rightarrow \quad E > U(x)$ or $U(x) < E$

08. *(b)* Given, the potential energy of a particle in a force field,

$$U = \frac{A}{r^2} - \frac{B}{r}$$

For stable equilibrium,

$F = -\frac{dU}{dr} = 0$

$= -\frac{dU}{dr} = 2Ar^{-3} - Br^{-2}$

$0 = \frac{2A}{r^3} - \frac{B}{r^2} \quad \left(\text{As } \frac{-dU}{dr} = 0\right)$

or $\quad \frac{2A}{r} = B$

The distance of particle from the centre of the field

$$r = \frac{2A}{B}$$

Concept Enhancer

When potential energy of a particle in force field is function of distance r, then

Its stable equilibrium is given by $F = \frac{-dU}{dr} = 0$

09. *(a)* Kinetic energy is given by

$$E = \frac{p^2}{2m} \text{ or } p = \sqrt{2mE}$$

Therefore, $\frac{p_1}{p_2} = \sqrt{\frac{m_1 E_1}{m_2 E_2}}$

but it is given that, $p_1 = p_2$

$\therefore \quad m_1 E_1 = m_2 E_2$ or $\frac{E_1}{E_2} = \frac{m_2}{m_1}$ ...(i)

Now, $m_1 > m_2$ or $\frac{m_1}{m_2} > 1$ ...(ii)

Thus, from Eqs. (i) and (ii), we get

$$\frac{E_1}{E_2} < 1 \text{ or } E_1 < E_2$$

10. *(c)* Given, $v_1 = v_2 = v$ at a 30 ft height from falling point.

$$m_1 = 2 \text{ kg}, m_2 = 4 \text{ kg}$$

Thus, $\frac{K_1}{K_2} = \frac{\frac{1}{2} m_1 v^2}{\frac{1}{2} m_2 v^2} = \frac{m_1}{m_2} = \frac{2}{4} = \frac{1}{2}$

> **• Concept Enhancer**
> Velocity of freely falling body does not depend on its mass. It depends on the height from which it has been dropped.

11. *(d)* Given, when spring is stretched by 2 cm, potential energy is U.

i.e. $U = \frac{1}{2} kx^2 = \frac{1}{2} k(2)^2 = \frac{1}{2} k \times 4$

Again when spring is stretched by 10 cm, Potential energy,

$$U' = \frac{1}{2} kx^2 = \frac{1}{2} k(10)^2 = \frac{1}{2} k \times 100$$

Therefore, $\frac{U'}{U} = \frac{\frac{1}{2} k \times 100}{\frac{1}{2} k \times 4} = 25$

$\Rightarrow \quad U' = 25U$

12. *(c)* From conservation of linear momentum,

Initial momentum p_{initial} = Find momentum p_{final}

$$0 = m_1 v_1 - m_2 v_2$$

or $\quad m_1 v_1 = m_2 v_2$

or $\quad \frac{v_1}{v_2} = \frac{m_2}{m_1}$ ...(i)

Thus, ratio of kinetic energies,

$$\frac{K_1}{K_2} = \frac{\frac{1}{2} m_1 v_1^2}{\frac{1}{2} m_2 v_2^2} = \frac{m_1}{m_2} \times \left(\frac{m_2}{m_1}\right)^2 = \frac{m_2}{m_1}$$

13. *(a)* Kinetic energy

$$K = \frac{1}{2m}(p^2) \text{ or } p = \sqrt{2mK}$$

If kinetic energy of a body is increased by 300%, let its momentum becomes p'.

New kinetic energy

$$K' = K + \frac{300}{100} K = 4K$$

Therefore, momentum is given by

$$p' = \sqrt{2m \times 4K} = 2\sqrt{2mK} = 2p$$

Hence, percentage change (increase) in momentum

$$\frac{\Delta p}{p} \times 100 = \frac{p' - p}{p} \times 100$$

$$= \left(\frac{p'}{p} - 1\right) \times 100$$

$$= \left(\frac{2p}{p} - 1\right) \times 100 = 100\%$$

14. *(a)* At the highest point

$$v_x = u \cos\theta$$

$$v_y = 0$$

$$K_H = \frac{1}{2} mv_x^2$$

or $\quad K_H = \frac{1}{2} mu^2 \cos^2\theta$ ...(i)

Initial kinetic energy is

$$K = \frac{1}{2} mu^2 \quad \text{...(ii)}$$

From Eqs. (i) and (ii), we get

$$K_H = K \cos^2\theta = K \cos^2 45°$$

$$= K \times \left(\frac{1}{\sqrt{2}}\right)^2 = \frac{K}{2}$$

15. *(a)* Given, spring constant of spring $A = k_A$

Spring constant of spring $B = k_B$

Also, $\quad k_A = 2k_B$

Given, $\quad F_1 = F_2$

i.e. $\quad k_A x_A = k_B x_B$

$$2k_B x_A = k_B x_B$$

$\Rightarrow \quad 2x_A = x_B$

Now energy stored in spring A

$$= \frac{1}{2} k_A x_A^2 = E_A$$

energy stored in spring B

$$= \frac{1}{2} k_B x_B^2 = \frac{1}{2} \frac{k_A}{2} (2x_A)^2$$

$$= \frac{1}{4} k_A 4x_A^2$$

$\Rightarrow \quad k_A x_A^2 = E_B$

Therefore, $\frac{E_A}{E_B} = \frac{\frac{1}{2} k_A x_A^2}{k_A x_A^2} \Rightarrow \frac{1}{2}$

$$2E_A = E_B$$

> **• Concept Enhancer**
> The energy associated with the state of compression or extension of an elastic spring is called potential energy of spring. Potential energy of stretched or compressed spring, $E = \frac{1}{2} kx^2$.

16. *(a)* Given, masses of two bodies are m and $4m$ respectively,

Given, that $\text{KE}_1 = \text{KE}_2$

$$\frac{1}{2} m_1 v_1^2 = \frac{1}{2} m_2 v_2^2$$

$\Rightarrow \quad m(v_1^2) = (4m)v_2^2$

$\Rightarrow \quad v_1^2 = 4v_2^2 \Rightarrow v_1 = 2v_2$

Now momenta,

$$p_1 = m_1 v_1 = m(2v_2)$$

and $\quad p_2 = m_2 v_2 = 4m(v_2)$

Thus, $\frac{p_1}{p_2} = \frac{m(2v_2)}{4mv_2} = \frac{1}{2}$

> ***Alternate Solution***
>
> $\text{KE} = \frac{p^2}{2m}$
>
> Since KE for both bodies is equal.
>
> Therefore, $\frac{p_1^2}{2m_1} = \frac{p_2^2}{2m_2}$
>
> $\Rightarrow \quad \frac{p_1^2}{2m} = \frac{p_2^2}{8m} \Rightarrow \frac{p_1^2}{p_2^2} = \frac{1}{4}$
>
> $\Rightarrow \quad \frac{p_1}{p_2} = \frac{1}{2}$

17. *(d)* As we know that, relation between kinetic energy and momentum is given by

$$\text{KE} = \frac{p^2}{2m}$$

If $p_1 = p_2$ for two bodies

So, $\quad \text{KE} \propto \frac{1}{m_1}$

Therefore, ratio of two masses is given by

$$\frac{m_1}{m_2} = \frac{\text{KE}_2}{\text{KE}_1} = \frac{1}{4} \quad \left[\because \frac{\text{KE}_1}{\text{KE}_2} = \frac{4}{1}\right]$$

18. *(b)* Given,

Kinetic energy of the particle = K

$$= \frac{1}{2} mv^2$$

Angle of projection, $\theta = 45°$

Velocity of the particle at the highest point, $v_1 = v\cos\theta = v \cos 45° = \frac{v}{\sqrt{2}}$

Therefore, kinetic energy of the particle

$$= \frac{1}{2}m\left(\frac{v}{\sqrt{2}}\right)^2 = \frac{1}{4}mv^2 = \frac{K}{2}$$

> • Concept **Enhancer**
>
> At highest point the vertical component of velocity is zero and horizontal component of velocity is given by $v_H = v\cos\theta$

19. *(a)* The potential energy between two atoms in a molecule is given by

$$U(x) = \frac{a}{x^{12}} - \frac{b}{x^6}$$

The atom is in stable equilibrium. Therefore, condition for stable equilibrium

$$F = \frac{-dU(x)}{dx} = 0$$

$$\Rightarrow \quad -\frac{d}{dx}\left[\frac{a}{x^{12}} - \frac{b}{x^6}\right] = 0$$

$$\Rightarrow \quad 12ax^{-13} - 6bx^{-7} = 0$$

or $\frac{12a}{x^{13}} = \frac{6b}{x^7} \Rightarrow \frac{2a}{b} = x^6$

$$\Rightarrow \quad x = \left(\frac{2a}{b}\right)^{\frac{1}{6}}$$

20. *(c)* Let p_1 be the initial momentum and p_2 be the final momentum

So, $p_2 = \frac{150}{100}p_1$

i.e. $mv_2 = \frac{15}{10}mv_1 \qquad \left(\begin{array}{l} p_1 = mv_1 \\ p_2 = mv_2 \end{array}\right)$

or $\frac{v_2}{v_1} = \frac{15}{10}$

Now, $\frac{E_2}{E_1} = \frac{\frac{1}{2}mv_2^2}{\frac{1}{2}mv_1^2}$

$$= \left(\frac{v_2}{v_1}\right)^2 = \left(\frac{15}{10}\right)^2 = \frac{225}{100}$$

Clearly, $E_2 > E_1$

So, percentage increase in KE

$$= \frac{(E_2 - E_1)}{E_1} \times 100 = \left(\frac{225}{100} - 1\right) \times 100$$

$= 125\%$

21. *(d)* Kinetic energy acquired by the body

$$\text{KE} = \frac{1}{2}mv^2$$

If body starts from rest, then final velocity achieved by body in displacement d is

$$v^2 = 0 + 2ad = 2ad$$

but $a = \frac{F}{m}$

$\therefore \quad v^2 = 2\left(\frac{F}{m}\right)d$

Hence, $\text{KE} = \frac{1}{2}m \times 2\left(\frac{F}{m}\right)d = Fd$

or KE acquired = Work done $= F \times d$ = constant

So, KE acquired is independent of mass m.

22. *(c)* Given, $\text{KE}_1 = \text{KE}_2$

$$\frac{1}{2}m_1v_1^2 = \frac{1}{2}m_2v_2^2$$

or $\frac{v_2^2}{v_1^2} = \frac{m_1}{m_2}$ or $\frac{v_2}{v_1} = \sqrt{\frac{m_1}{m_2}}$

As, $p_2 = m_2v_2$ and $p_1 = m_1v_1$

$$\therefore \quad \frac{p_2}{p_1} = \frac{m_2v_2}{m_1v_1} = \frac{m_2}{m_1}\sqrt{\frac{m_1}{m_2}} = \sqrt{\frac{m_2^2m_1}{m_1^2m_2}}$$

$$\frac{p_2}{p_1} = \sqrt{\frac{m_2}{m_1}} \text{ or } \frac{p_1}{p_2} = \sqrt{\frac{m_1}{m_2}}$$

Here, $m_1 = 1\text{ g}, m_2 = 9\text{ g}$

$$\therefore \quad \frac{p_1}{p_2} = \sqrt{\frac{1}{9}} = \frac{1}{3}$$

23. *(c)* Given force, $F = \frac{k}{v}$

$$\therefore \quad m\frac{dv}{dt} = \frac{k}{v} \Rightarrow vdv = \frac{k}{m}dt$$

$$\Rightarrow \int v\,dv = \int \frac{k}{m}dt \Rightarrow \frac{v^2}{2} = \frac{k}{m}t$$

$$\Rightarrow \frac{1}{2}mv^2 = kt \Rightarrow W = \frac{1}{2}mv^2 = kt$$

Topic 3

01. *(c)* From work-energy theorem,

$$W = \Delta\text{KE} \qquad \ldots\text{(i)}$$

$\therefore$ At $x = 8$ m,

W = Area $ABDO$ + Area $CEFD$
$= 20 \times 5 + 10 \times 3 = 130$ J

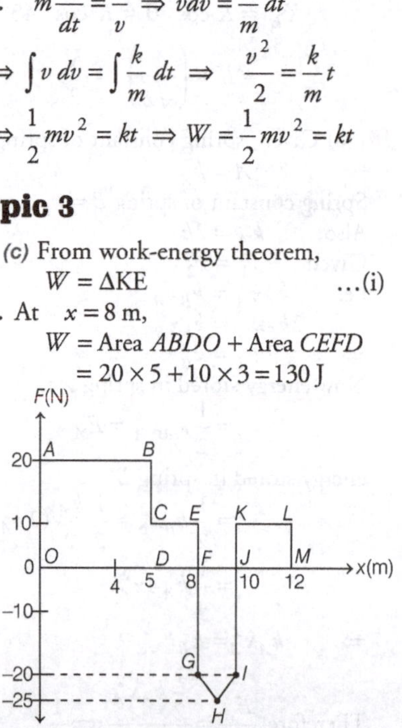

Using Eq. (i)

$$\Rightarrow \quad 130 = \frac{1}{2}mv^2 = \frac{1}{2} \times \frac{500}{1000}v^2$$

$$\Rightarrow \quad v = 2\sqrt{130} = 22.8 \approx 23 \text{ m/s}$$

At $x = 12$ m

W = Area $ABDO$ + Area $CEFD$ + Area $FGHIJ$ + Area $KLMJ$

$$W = 20 \times 5 + 10 \times 3 + (-20 \times 2) + \left(\frac{1}{2} \times -5 \times 2\right)$$

$+ 10 \times 2$ [∵ Area $FGHIJ$ = Area $FGIJ$ + Area GHI]

$= 100 + 30 - 40 - 5 + 20 = 105$ J

Using Eq. (i)

$$\therefore \quad 105 = \frac{1}{2} \times \frac{1}{2} \times v^2$$

$$\Rightarrow \quad v = 2\sqrt{105} \simeq 20.6 \text{ ms}^{-1}$$

02. *(d)* By work-energy theorem, we have change in KE = work done by all of the forces.

Work done by gravitational force,

$$W_{\text{gravity}} = mgh$$

$$= 10^{-3} \times 10 \times 1 \times 10^3 = 10 \text{ J}$$

Now, from work-energy theorem, we have

$$\Delta K = W_{\text{gravity}} + W_{\text{air resistance}}$$

$$\Rightarrow \quad \frac{1}{2} \times mv^2 = mgh + W_{\text{air resistance}}$$

$$\Rightarrow W_{\text{air resistance}} = \frac{1}{2}mv^2 - mgh$$

$$= 10^{-3}\left(\frac{1}{2} \times 50 \times 50 - 10 \times 10^3\right)$$

$= -8.75$ J

03. *(a)* From work-energy theorem,

Work done = Change in KE

$\Rightarrow \quad W = K_f - K_i$

$\Rightarrow \quad K_f = W + K_i$

$$= \int_{x_1}^{x_2} Fx\,dx + \frac{1}{2}mv^2$$

$$= \int_{20}^{30} -0.1\,x\,dx + \frac{1}{2} \times 10 \times 10^2$$

$$= -0.1\left[\frac{x^2}{2}\right]_{20}^{30} + 500$$

$$= -0.05\,[30^2 - 20^2] + 500$$

$$= -0.05\,[900 - 400] + 500$$

$$\Rightarrow \quad K_f = -25 + 500 = 475 \text{ J}$$

04. *(b)* Suppose a ball rebounds with speed v,

$$v = \sqrt{2gh} = \sqrt{2 \times 10 \times 20}$$

$= 20$ m/s

Energy of a ball just after rebound,

$$E = \frac{1}{2}mv^2 = 200\text{ m}$$

As, 50% of energy loses in collision means just before collision energy is 400 m.
According to law of conservation of energy, we have

$$\frac{1}{2}mv_0^2 + mgh = 400\text{ m}$$

$$\Rightarrow \quad \frac{1}{2}mv_0^2 + m \times 10 \times 20 = 400\text{ m}$$

$$\Rightarrow \quad v_0 = 20\text{ m/s}$$

05. *(a)* The potential energy of a system increases, if work is done by the system against a conservative force.

$$-\Delta U = W_{\text{conservative force}}$$

> **• Concept Enhancer**
>
> Work done due to conservative force in a loop is always zero.
>
> Work done due to conservative force is only depending on the initial and final position. e.g., gravity, spring force.

06. *(b)* Efficiency of the system,

$$= \frac{\text{output work}}{\text{input work}} = \frac{mgh}{F \cdot s}$$

$$= \frac{75g \times 3}{250 \times 12} = 0.75 = 75\%$$

07. *(a)* Therefore, loss of energy

$$= \text{KE} - \text{PE} = \frac{1}{2}mv^2 - mgh$$

$$= \frac{1}{2} \times 1 \times 400 - 1 \times 10 \times 18$$

$$= 200 - 180 = 20\text{ J}$$

> **• Concept Enhancer**
>
> Apply conservation of energy.
>
> Initially body possesses only kinetic energy and after attaining a height, the kinetic energy is zero.

08. *(b)* Let x be the extension in the spring.
Applying conservation of energy

$$Mg\,x - \frac{1}{2}k\,x^2 = 0 - 0$$

$$\Rightarrow \quad x = \frac{2\,Mg}{k}$$

09. *(a)* Let the velocity of shell be v and that of gun be v'.
Then, according to conservation of linear momentum.

$$4v' + 0.2\,v = 0 \quad \ldots\text{(i)}$$

Using conservation of energy

$$\frac{1}{2} \times 4 \times v'^2 + \frac{1}{2} \times 0.2 \times v^2 = 1050 \quad \ldots\text{(ii)}$$

$$\Rightarrow \quad v = 100\text{ m/s}$$

10. *(a)* Work done by gravitational force

$$= mg\,(h + d)$$

Work done on spring $= 0.5\,kd^2$

Total work done on the ball

$$= W_g + W_{\text{by spring}}$$

$$= mg\,(h + d) - 0.5\,kd^2$$

$$= mg(h + d) - \frac{1}{2}kd^2$$

11. *(b)* Net work done in sliding a body up to a height h on inclined plane
= Work done against gravitational force
+ Work done against frictional force

$$\Rightarrow \quad W = W_g + W_f \quad \ldots\text{(i)}$$

but $W = 300\text{ J}$

$$W_g = mgh$$

$$= 2 \times 10 \times 10 = 200\text{ J}$$

Putting in Eq. (i), we get

$$300 = 200 + W_f$$

$$\Rightarrow \quad W_f = 300 - 200 = 100\text{ J}$$

12. *(a)*

> **key idea**
>
> When a moving particle collides, it imparts its energy to the colliding body. In this case when the mass collides with light spring and its KE is stored as potential energy in the spring.
>
> Therefore, $\frac{1}{2}mv^2 = \frac{1}{2}kx^2$

Given, speed of moving mass,

$$v = 1.5\text{ m/s}$$

Spring constant, $k = 50\text{ N/m}$
Mass, $m = 0.5\text{ kg}$
The kinetic energy of the moving mass will be converted into potential energy in the spring when the spring is at maximum compression x.

$$\therefore \quad \frac{1}{2}mv^2 = \frac{1}{2}kx_0^2$$

$$\Rightarrow \quad x_0 = v\sqrt{\frac{m}{k}} = \sqrt{\frac{0.5}{50}} \times 1.5 = 0.15\text{ m}$$

13. *(a)* From energy conservation

$$\frac{1}{2}mv_{\max}^2 = mg(H_2 - H_1)$$

Here, H_1 = minimum height of swing from the earth's surface
$= 0.75$ m

H_2 = maximum height of swing from earth's surface = 2 m

$$\therefore \quad \frac{1}{2}mv_{\max}^2 = mg(2 - 0.75)$$

$$\text{or} \quad v_{\max} = \sqrt{2 \times 10 \times 1.25}$$

$$= \sqrt{25} = 5\text{ m/s}$$

14. *(b)* Potential energy = Kinetic energy

$$\text{i.e.} \quad mgh = \frac{1}{2}mv^2$$

$$\Rightarrow \quad v = \sqrt{2\,gh}$$

If h_1 and h_2 are the initial and final heights, then

$$v_1 = \sqrt{2\,gh_1}$$

$$v_2 = \sqrt{2\,gh_2}$$

Loss in velocity

$$\Delta v = v_1 - v_2 = \sqrt{2\,gh_1} - \sqrt{2\,gh_2}$$

$\therefore$ Fractional loss in velocity

$$= \frac{\Delta v}{v_1} = \frac{\sqrt{2\,gh_1} - \sqrt{2\,gh_2}}{\sqrt{2\,gh_1}} = 1 - \sqrt{\frac{h_2}{h_1}}$$

Substituting the values, we have

$$\therefore \quad \frac{\Delta v}{v_1} = 1 - \sqrt{\frac{1.8}{5}} = 1 - \sqrt{0.36} = 1 - 0.6$$

$$= 0.4 = \frac{2}{5}$$

15. *(b)*

> **key idea**
>
> When a bullet is fired, it is slowed down due to air resistance faced by the bullet. The bullet does work against the air resistance and its kinetic energy is lost. Due to this the velocity of the bullet decreases.

According to work-energy theorem, work done by a force in displacing a body measures the change in kinetic energy of the body or work done by a force is equal to change in KE of the body.

$$\text{or} \quad W = \Delta E$$

$$= \text{final KE} - \text{initial KE}$$

$$= \frac{1}{2}mv^2 - \frac{1}{2}mu^2$$

$$\frac{1}{2}m(v^2 - u^2)$$

Given, $v = 1000\text{ m/s}$,

$$m = 10 = 0.01\text{ kg}$$

$$u = 500\text{ m/s}$$

Putting the values of m, u, v

$$\therefore \quad W = \frac{1}{2} \times 0.01\,[(1000)^2 - (500)^2]$$

$$= 3750\text{ J}$$

Topic 4

01. *(b)* Given,

$P_1 = 1\text{ kW}$

$P_2 = 2\text{ kW}$

$$P_{series} = \frac{P_1 P_2}{P_1 + P_2} \text{ and } P_{parallel} = P_1 + P_2$$

According to question,

$$\frac{P_{series}}{P_{parallel}} = \frac{\frac{1 \times 2}{1+2}}{1 \times 2} = \frac{2}{3 \times 3} = \frac{2}{9}$$

02. *(a)* Given,

$x = 2t - 1$ unit

Force, $F = 5\text{ N}$

Instantaneous power, $P = F \cdot v$

Thus, $P = F\dfrac{dx}{dt}$

$$= 5 \times \frac{d(2t-1)}{dt}$$

$$= 5 \times 2 = 10 \text{ unit}$$

03. *(c)* Given, velocity,

$v = 1.5\text{ m/s}$

Mass of lift and passenger,

$m = 2000\text{ kg}$

Frictional force on lift = 3000 N

Here, we are given that the velocity is constant therefore for the constant velocity, acceleration is zero.

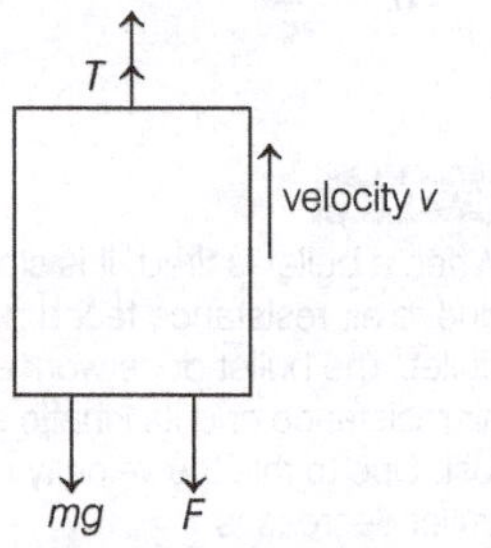

Tension, $T = mg + F$

$= 2000 \times 10 + 3000$

$= 23000\text{ N}$

Power, $P = T.v$

$= 23000 \times 1.5$

$= 34500\text{ W}$

• Concept Enhancer

The power can also be written as $P = F \cdot v$ or $P = T \cdot v$

Where both F and T represent force and tension, respectively and v represent velocity.

04. *(b)* Given, the rate of flow of the water,

$$\frac{m}{t} = 15\text{ kg/s}$$

The height of the water fall,

$h = 60\text{ m}$

The power used in the turbine

$= (100 - 10)\ \% = 90\%$

We know that, power generated by the turbine = change in potential energy

$$= 0.90\frac{mgh}{t}$$

$= 0.90 \times 15 \times 10 \times 60$

$= 8100\text{ W} = 8.1\text{ kW}$

05. *(c)* Given,

$m = 1\text{ g}$

$\mathbf{F} = (2t\hat{\mathbf{i}} + 3t^2\hat{\mathbf{j}})\text{ N}$

$\because \quad \mathbf{F} = m\mathbf{a} \Rightarrow \mathbf{a} = \dfrac{\mathbf{F}}{m}$

$\Rightarrow \quad \mathbf{a} = \dfrac{(2t\hat{\mathbf{i}} + 3t^2\hat{\mathbf{j}})}{1} \quad (\because m = 1\text{ kg})$

$\Rightarrow \quad \mathbf{a} = (2t\hat{\mathbf{i}} + 3t^2\hat{\mathbf{j}})\text{ m/s}^2$

$\because$ acceleration, $a = \dfrac{dv}{dt}$

$\Rightarrow \quad dv = a\,dt$

Integrating both sides, we get

$$\int dv = \int a\,dt = \int (2t\hat{\mathbf{i}} + 3t^2\hat{\mathbf{j}})\,dt$$

$$\mathbf{v} = t^2\hat{\mathbf{i}} + t^3\hat{\mathbf{j}}$$

$\because$ Power developed by the force at the time t will be given as

$$P = \mathbf{F}.\mathbf{v} = (2t\hat{\mathbf{i}} + 3t^2\hat{\mathbf{j}}).(t^2\hat{\mathbf{i}} + t^3\hat{\mathbf{j}})$$

$$= (2t.t^2 + 3t^2.t^3)$$

$$P = (2t^3 + 3t^5)\text{ W}$$

06. *(a)* As the machine delivers a constant power. So, $F.v = \text{constant} = k$ (watts)

$\Rightarrow \quad m\dfrac{dv}{dt} \cdot v = k$

$\Rightarrow \quad \int v dv = \dfrac{k}{m}\int dt \Rightarrow \dfrac{v^2}{2} = \dfrac{k}{m}t$

$\Rightarrow \quad v = \sqrt{\dfrac{2k}{m}t}$

Now, force on the particle is given by

$$F = m\frac{dv}{dt} = m\frac{d}{dt}\left(\frac{2kt}{m}\right)^{\frac{1}{2}}$$

$$= \sqrt{2km}.\left(\frac{1}{2}.t^{-\frac{1}{2}}\right) = \sqrt{\frac{mk}{2}}.t^{-\frac{1}{2}}$$

07. *(a)* Given, pressure = 150 mm of Hg

Pumping rate of heart of a man

$$= \frac{dV}{dt} = \frac{5 \times 10^{-3}}{60}\text{ m}^3\text{/s}$$

Power of heart $= P \cdot \dfrac{dV}{dt} = \rho g h \cdot \dfrac{dV}{dt}$

$[p = \rho g h]$

$$= \frac{13.6 \times 10^3 \times 10 \times 0.15 \times 5 \times 10^{-3}}{60}$$

$= 1.70\text{ W}$

08. *(d)* Work done is the same in both cases.

Power is given by

$$P = \frac{\text{Work}(W)}{\text{Time}(t)}$$

Therefore, $\dfrac{P_1}{P_2} = \dfrac{t_2}{t_1} = \dfrac{30\text{ s}}{60\text{ s}}$

$\Rightarrow \quad \dfrac{P_1}{P_2} = \dfrac{1}{2} \Rightarrow 1:2$

09. *(b)* Given, instantaneous power,

$P_0 = F.v = mav$

$\Rightarrow \quad P_0 = mv\dfrac{dv}{dt} \Rightarrow P_0 dt = mvdv$

Integrating both sides

$\Rightarrow \quad \int mv\,dv = \int P_0 dt$

$\Rightarrow \quad \dfrac{mv^2}{2} = P_0 t \quad \Rightarrow v \propto \sqrt{t}$

10. *(b)* We know that, $P = F.v$

Since, the velocity is maximum when the body is about to touch the ground. So, power exerted by the instant just before the body hits the ground is greatest.

11. *(d)* Given, velocity of water $v = 2\text{ m/s}$

Mass per unit length of water in the pipe

$= 100\text{ kg/m}$

So, power = (mass per unit length of water in pipe) $\times v^3$

$$= \frac{m}{l} \times v^3 = 100 \times 2 \times 2 \times 2 = 800\text{ W}$$

12. *(d)* We know that power, $P = F \cdot v$

$= Ma.v$

or $\quad P = Mv\dfrac{dv}{dt}$

$\Rightarrow \quad P\,dt = Mv\,dv$

Integrating both sides, we get

$$Pt = \frac{1}{2}Mv^2 \Rightarrow P = \frac{1}{2}\frac{Mv^2}{t}$$

13. *(a)* As m is the mass per unit length, then rate of mass per second $= \dfrac{mx}{t} = mv$

$\therefore$ Rate of KE $= \dfrac{1}{2}(mv)v^2 = \dfrac{1}{2}mv^3$

14. *(a)* $P_{\text{generated}} = P_{\text{input}} \times \dfrac{90}{100}$

$= \dfrac{mgh}{t} \times \dfrac{90}{100} = \dfrac{15 \times 10 \times 60}{1} \times \dfrac{90}{100}$

$= 8.1 \text{ kW}$

15. *(b)* Given, force $\mathbf{F} = (60\hat{\mathbf{i}} + 15\hat{\mathbf{j}} - 3\hat{\mathbf{k}})$ N

Velocity, $\mathbf{v} = (2\hat{\mathbf{i}} - 4\hat{\mathbf{j}} + 5\hat{\mathbf{k}})$ m/s

Instantaneous power, $P = \mathbf{F} \cdot \mathbf{v}$

$= (60\hat{\mathbf{i}} + 15\hat{\mathbf{j}} - 3\hat{\mathbf{k}}) \cdot (2\hat{\mathbf{i}} - 4\hat{\mathbf{j}} + 5\hat{\mathbf{k}})$

$= 120 - 60 - 15 = 45 \text{ W}$

16. *(b)* Power of a body is defined as the rate at which the body can do the work, i.e.

$$\text{Power} = \frac{\text{Work}}{\text{Time}} = \frac{W}{t}$$

Given, power, $P = 2 \text{ kW} = 2000 \text{ W}$

$W = Mgh = M \times 10 \times 10$ $[\because g = 10 \text{ m/s}^2]$

$= 100\,M$

Time, $t = 60$ s

$\therefore \quad 2000 = \dfrac{100M}{60}$

$\therefore \quad M = 1200 \text{ kg}$ and $V = 1200$ L

Topic 5

01. *(c)* Velocity of point mass in vertical circle at lowest point, $v_l = \sqrt{7gr}$

$\therefore \quad v_l = \sqrt{7gr} > \sqrt{5gr}$

Hence, point mass will have completed the vertical circular path.

We know that,

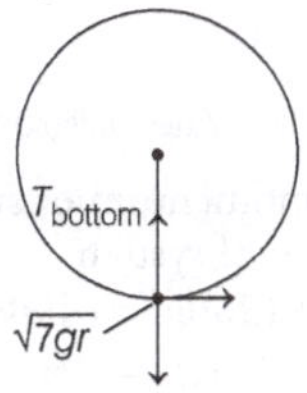

$$T_{\text{bottom}} - mg = \frac{mv^2}{r} = \frac{m}{r}(\sqrt{7gr})^2$$

$\Rightarrow \quad T_{\text{bottom}} - mg = 7mg$

$\Rightarrow \quad T_{\text{bottom}} = 8mg$

> **● Concept Enhancer**
>
> The tension in a string is defined as the force which holds something by the string against other forces.
>
> The force which makes any object to move in a circular motion with constant speed is known as centripetal force.
>
> The circular motion in the vertical plane, where we have the influence of gravity is known as vertical circular motion.

02. *(b)* Given, shown in the figure below.

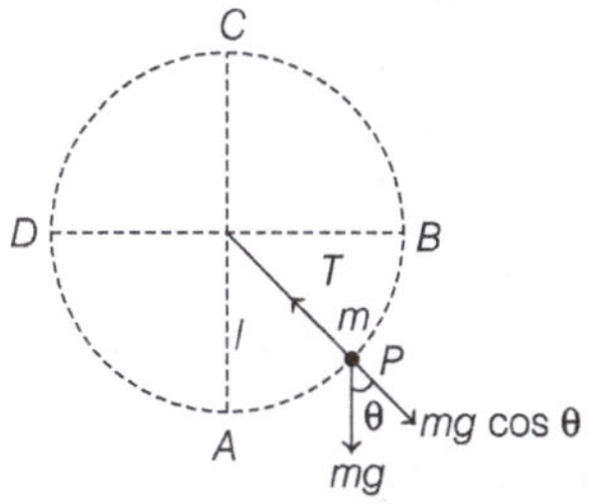

The tension in the string at any point P be T.

According to Newton's law of motion, In equilibrium, net force towards the centre = centripetal force

$\Rightarrow \quad T - mg\cos\theta = \dfrac{mv^2}{l}$

Here, l = length of wire and v = linear velocity of the particle whirling in a circle.

$\Rightarrow \quad T = mg\cos\theta + \dfrac{mv^2}{l}$

At $A, \theta = 0° \Rightarrow T_A = mg + \dfrac{mv^2}{l}$

At $B, \theta = 90° \Rightarrow T_B = \dfrac{mv^2}{l}$

At $C, \theta = 180° \Rightarrow T_C = -mg + \dfrac{mv^2}{l}$

At $D, \theta = 90° \Rightarrow T_D = T_B = \dfrac{mv^2}{l}$

So, from the above analysis, it can be concluded that the tension is maximum at A i.e. the lowest point of circle. So, chance of breaking is maximum.

03. *(d)* If a body is moving on a frictionless surface, then its total mechanical energy remains conserved.

According to the conservation of mechanical energy,

$$(\text{TE})_{\text{initial}} = (\text{TE})_{\text{final}}$$

$\Rightarrow (\text{KE})_i + (\text{PE})_i = (\text{KE})_f + (\text{PE})_f$

$0 + mgh = \dfrac{1}{2}mv_A^2 + 0$

$\Rightarrow \quad gh = \dfrac{v_A^2}{2}$

or $\quad h = \dfrac{v_A^2}{2g}$ $\quad$ ...(i)

In order to complete the vertical circle, the velocity of the body at point A should be

$$v_A = v_{\min} = \sqrt{5gR}$$

where, R is the radius of the body.

Here, $R = \dfrac{AB}{2} = \dfrac{D}{2}$

$\Rightarrow \quad v_{\min} = v_A = \sqrt{\dfrac{5}{2}gD}$

Substituting the value of v_A in Eq. (i), we get

$$h = \frac{\left(\sqrt{\left(\frac{5}{2}gD\right)}\right)^2}{2g} = \frac{5gD}{2 \times 2g} = \frac{5}{4}D$$

> **● Concept Enhancer**
>
> Mechanical energy is the sum total of kinetic energy and potential energy possessed by a body.
>
> Thus,
>
> $\text{ME} = \text{KE} + \text{PE} = \dfrac{mv^2}{2} + mgh$

04. *(a)* When stone is at its lowest position, it has only kinetic energy, given by

$$K = \frac{1}{2}mu^2$$

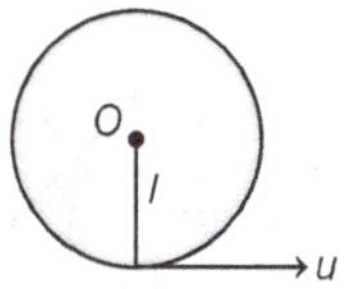

At the horizontal position, it has energy

$$E = U + K = \frac{1}{2}mu'^2 + mgl$$

According to conservation of mechanical energy, $K = E$

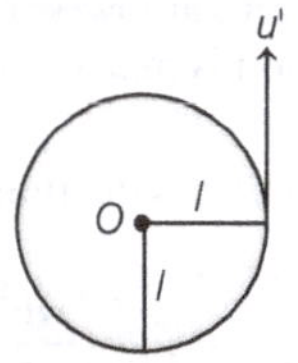

$\therefore \quad \dfrac{1}{2}mu^2 = \dfrac{1}{2}mu'^2 + mgl$

or $\quad \dfrac{1}{2}mu'^2 = \dfrac{1}{2}mu^2 - mgl$

or $\quad u'^2 = u^2 - 2gl$

or $\quad u' = \sqrt{u^2 - 2gl}$ $\quad$ ...(i)

So, the magnitude of change in velocity

$|\Delta\mathbf{u}| = |\mathbf{u}' - \mathbf{u}|$

$= \sqrt{u'^2 + u^2 + 2u'u\cos 90°}$

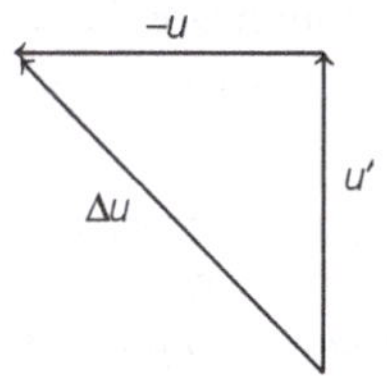

$$|\Delta \mathbf{u}| = \sqrt{u'^2 + u^2} = \sqrt{2(u^2 - gl)}$$
[from Eq. (i)]

Alternate Solution

From the conservation of energy, we get

$$\frac{1}{2}mu^2 - \frac{1}{2}mv^2 = mgl$$

$$\Rightarrow v = \sqrt{u^2 - 2gl}$$

Therefore, $|\mathbf{v} - \mathbf{u}| = \sqrt{u^2 + v^2}$

$$= \sqrt{u^2 + u^2 - 2gl} = \sqrt{2(u^2 - gl)}$$

05. *(b)* When string makes an angle θ with the vertical then

$$T - mg\cos\theta = \frac{mv^2}{l}$$

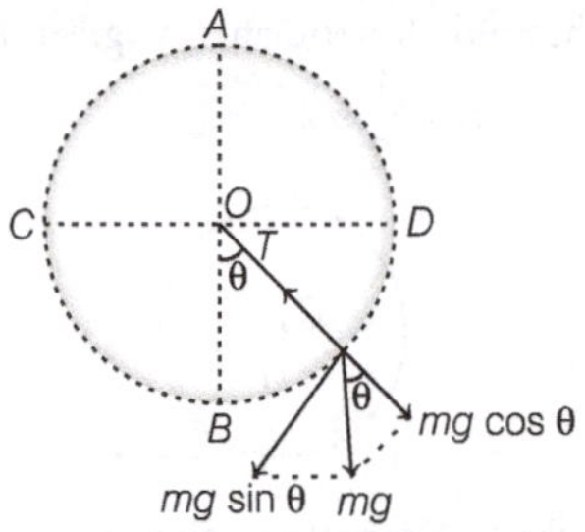

or $\quad T = mg\cos\theta + \dfrac{mv^2}{l}$

Tension is maximum when $\cos\theta = +1$

i.e. $\quad \theta = 0$

Thus, θ is zero at lowest point B. At this point tension is maximum. So, string will break at point B.

06. *(b)* At point B, equation of motion is given by

$$T_B = \frac{mv^2}{R} + mg$$

and at A and C, $T_C = T_A = \dfrac{mv^2}{R}$

At D, $T_D = \dfrac{mv^2}{R} - mg$

Thus, tension at point B is maximum and hence if average velocity is increased, the string will break at point B.

Topic 6

01. *(b)* Let both masses be m,

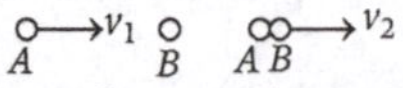

Thus, applying conservation of momentum, we get

$$m_1u_1 + m_2u_2 = m_1v_1 + m_2v_2$$

Both masses A and B stick together as a system.

So, $\quad mv_1 = 2mv_2 \qquad [\because u_2 = 0]$

$$v_1 = 2v_2$$

$$\Rightarrow \quad \frac{v_1}{v_2} = \frac{2}{1}$$

Hence, option (b) is correct.

02. *(a)*

key idea

As net external force applied on particles is zero, we can apply conservation of linear momentum equation, is

$$\Sigma m_i v_i = \Sigma m_f v_f$$

Let m be the mass of an object flying with velocity v in air. When it split into two pieces of masses in ratio 1 : 5, the mass of smaller piece is $m/6$ and of bigger piece is $\dfrac{5m}{6}$.

This situation can be interpreted diagrammatically as below

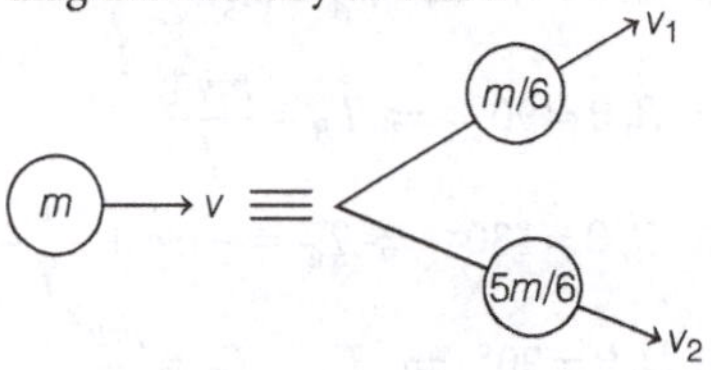

According to conservation of momentum,

The total momentum (before breaking) = total momentum (after breaking)

$$m\mathbf{v} = \frac{m}{6}\mathbf{v}_1 + \frac{5m}{6}\mathbf{v}_2$$

$$\Rightarrow \quad \mathbf{v} = \frac{\mathbf{v}_1}{6} + \frac{5\mathbf{v}_2}{6}$$

Here, $\quad \mathbf{v} = 20\hat{\mathbf{i}} + 25\hat{\mathbf{j}} - 12\hat{\mathbf{k}}$

$$\mathbf{v}_1 = 100\hat{\mathbf{i}} + 35\hat{\mathbf{j}} + 8\hat{\mathbf{k}}$$

$$\Rightarrow 20\hat{\mathbf{i}} + 25\hat{\mathbf{j}} - 12\hat{\mathbf{k}} = \frac{(100\hat{\mathbf{i}} + 35\hat{\mathbf{j}} + 8\hat{\mathbf{k}})}{6} + \frac{5\mathbf{v}_2}{6}$$

$$\Rightarrow (120\hat{\mathbf{i}} + 150\hat{\mathbf{j}} - 72\hat{\mathbf{k}}) = (100\hat{\mathbf{i}} + 35\hat{\mathbf{j}} + 8\hat{\mathbf{k}}) + 5\mathbf{v}_2$$

$$\Rightarrow \quad \mathbf{v}_2 = \frac{1}{5}(20\hat{\mathbf{i}} + 115\hat{\mathbf{j}} - 80\hat{\mathbf{k}})$$

$$= 4\hat{\mathbf{i}} + 23\hat{\mathbf{j}} - 16\hat{\mathbf{k}}$$

03. *(d)* The particle of mass 5m breaks in three fragments of mass m, m and 3m respectively. Two fragments of mass m each, move in perpendicular direction with velocity v and the left fragment will move in a direction with velocity $\mathbf{v}'$ such that the total momentum of the system must remain conserved.

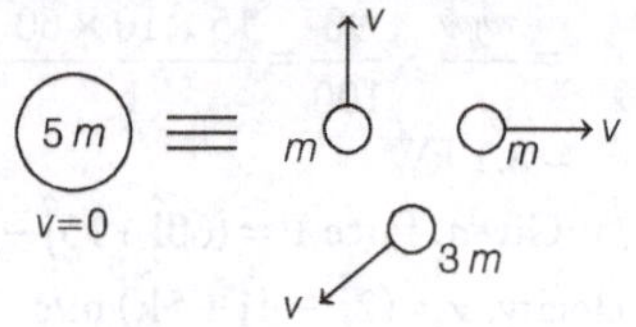

By law of conservation of momentum,

$$5m \times 0 = mv\hat{\mathbf{i}} + mv\hat{\mathbf{j}} + 3m\mathbf{v}'$$

$$\Rightarrow \quad \mathbf{v}' = -\frac{v}{3}\hat{\mathbf{i}} - \frac{v}{3}\hat{\mathbf{j}}$$

$$\therefore \quad |\mathbf{v}'| = \sqrt{\left(-\frac{v}{3}\right)^2 + \left(-\frac{v}{3}\right)^2} = \frac{v\sqrt{2}}{3}$$

$\therefore$ Energy released

$$E = \frac{1}{2}mv^2 + \frac{1}{2}mv^2 + \frac{1}{2} \times 3m\left(\frac{v\sqrt{2}}{3}\right)^2$$

$$= mv^2 + \frac{mv^2}{3} = \frac{4}{3}mv^2$$

04. *(a)* In head-on elastic collision, given situation of collision can be drawn as

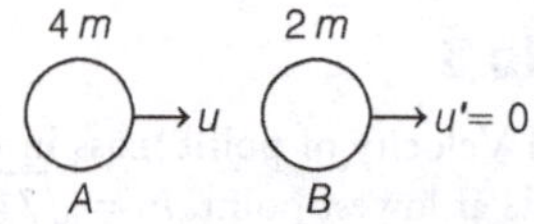

Before collision

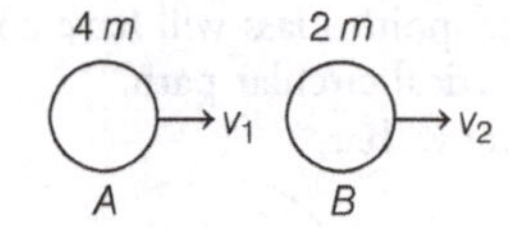

After collision

$\therefore$ Initial momentum of system = Final momentum of system

$$\Rightarrow (4m)u + (2m)u' = (4m)v_1 + (2m)v_2$$

$$4mu = 4mv_1 + 2mv_2$$

or $\qquad 2u = 2v_1 + v_2 \qquad \ldots$ (i)

The kinetic energy of A before collision is

$$\text{KE}_A = \frac{1}{2}(4m)u^2 = 2mu^2$$

Kinetic energy of B before collision,

$$\text{KE}_B = 0$$

The kinetic energy of A after collision is

$$\text{KE}'_A = \frac{1}{2}(4m)v_1^2 = 2mv_1^2$$

Kinetic energy of B after collision,

$$\text{KE}'_B = \frac{1}{2}(2m)v_2^2 = mv_2^2$$

As, Initial kinetic energy of the system = Final kinetic energy of the system

$\Rightarrow KE'_A + KE'_B = KE'_A + KE'_B$

$$2mu^2 + 0 = 2mv_1^2 + mv_2^2$$

$$2mu^2 = 2mv_1^2 + mv_2^2 \text{ or}$$

$$2u^2 = 2v_1^2 + v_2^2 \qquad \dots \text{(ii)}$$

Solving Eqs. (i) and (ii), we get

$$v_1 = \frac{1}{3}u \text{ and } v_2 = \frac{4}{3}u$$

or the final velocity of A can be directly calculated by using the formula.

The velocity after collision is given by

$$v_1 = \left(\frac{m_1 - m_2}{m_1 + m_2}\right)u_1 + \frac{2m_2u_2}{m_1 + m_2}$$

$$= \left(\frac{4m - 2m}{4m + 2m}\right)u + \frac{2(2m) \times 0}{(4m + 2m)}$$

$$[\because u_2 = u' = 0]$$

$$= \frac{2m}{6m}u = \frac{1}{3}u$$

∴ Net decreases in kinetic energy of A

$$\Delta KE = KE_A - KE'_A$$

$$= 2mu^2 - 2mv_1^2 = 2m(u^2 - v_1^2)$$

Substituting the value of v_1, we get

$$\Delta KE = 2m\left(u^2 - \frac{u^2}{9}\right) = \frac{16\,mu^2}{9}$$

∴ The fractional decreases in kinetic energy is

$$\frac{\Delta KE}{KE_A} = \frac{16mu^2}{9} \times \frac{1}{2mu^2} = \frac{8}{9}$$

Alternate Solution

Fractional loss of KE of colliding bodies for head on collision

$$\frac{\Delta K}{K} = \left[1 - \left(\frac{m_1 - m_2}{m_1 + m_2}\right)^2\right]$$

$$= \left[1 - \left(\frac{4m - 2m}{4m + 2m}\right)^2\right] = \left[1 - \left(\frac{1}{3}\right)^2\right] = \frac{8}{9}$$

05. *(b)* Since, the collision mentioned is an elastic head-on collision. Thus, according to the law of conservation of linear momentum, we get

$$m_1u_1 + m_2u_2 = m_1v_1 + m_2v_2$$

where, m_1 and m_2 are the masses of the two blocks, respectively and u_1 and u_2 are their initial velocities and v_1 and v_2 are their final velocities, respectively.

Here, $m_1 = m, m_2 = 4m$

$u_1 = v, u_2 = 0$ and $v_1 = 0$

$$mv + 4m \times 0 = 0 + 4mv_2$$

$$\Rightarrow \quad mv = 4mv_2$$

$$\text{or} \quad v_2 = \frac{v}{4} \qquad \dots \text{(i)}$$

As, the coefficient of restitution is given as,

$$e = \frac{\text{relative velocity of separation}}{\text{relative velocity of approach}}$$

$$= \frac{v_2 - v_1}{u_2 - u_1} = \frac{\frac{v}{u} - 0}{0 - v} \quad \text{[from Eq. (i)]}$$

$$= \frac{1}{4}$$

$$\therefore \quad e = 0.25$$

06. *(b)* It is given that mass of balls are same and collision is perfectly elastic ($e = 1$) so their velocities will be interchanged.

Thus, $v'_A = v_B = -0.3$ m/s,

$v'_B = v_A = 0.5$ m/s

07. *(c)* Given, mass of bullet,

$$m = 10\text{ g} = 10 \times 10^{-3}\text{ kg}$$

Velocity, $v = 400$ m/s

Mass of wooden block, $m = 2$ kg

Length of string, $l = 5$ m

Let the velocity of bullet and the block after collision be v_1 and v_2.

The block rises by = 10 cm = 0.1 m

PE at the maximum height = KE at bottom of the block

$$\Rightarrow \quad mgh = \frac{1}{2}mv_2^2$$

$$\Rightarrow \quad v_2 = \sqrt{2gh}$$

$$= \sqrt{2 \times 9.8 \times 0.1}$$

$$= 1.4 \text{ m/s}$$

Let u, be the initial velocity of the bullet, then according to the conservation of momentum

$$m_1u_1 = m_2v_2 + m_1v_1$$

$$\Rightarrow \quad v_1 = \frac{m_1u_1 - m_2v_2}{m_1}$$

$$= \frac{0.01 \times 400 - 2 \times 1.4}{0.01}$$

$$= 120 \text{ m/s}$$

08. *(c)* Total initial energy

$$= \frac{1}{2}m_1u_1^2 + \frac{1}{2}m_2u_2^2$$

Since, after collision one particle absorb energy ε.

∴ Total final energy

$$= \frac{1}{2}m_1v_1^2 + \frac{1}{2}m_2v_1^2 + \varepsilon$$

From conservation of energy,

$$\frac{1}{2}m_1u_1^2 + \frac{1}{2}m_2u_2^2$$

$$= \frac{1}{2}m_1v_1^2 + \frac{1}{2}m_2v_2^2 + \varepsilon$$

$$\Rightarrow \quad \frac{1}{2}m_1u_1^2 + \frac{1}{2}m_2u_2^2 - \varepsilon$$

$$= \frac{1}{2}m_1v_1^2 + \frac{1}{2}m_2v_2^2$$

09. *(c)* Let the particle A and B collide at time t. For their collision, the position vectors of both particles should be same at time t, is

$$\mathbf{r}_1 + \mathbf{v}_1t = \mathbf{r}_2 + \mathbf{v}_2t$$

$$\Rightarrow \quad \mathbf{r}_1 - \mathbf{r}_2 = \mathbf{v}_2t - \mathbf{v}_1t$$

$$= (\mathbf{v}_2 - \mathbf{v}_1)t \qquad \dots \text{(i)}$$

Also, $|\mathbf{r}_1 - \mathbf{r}_2| = |\mathbf{v}_2 - \mathbf{v}_1|t$

or $t = \left|\dfrac{\mathbf{r}_1 - \mathbf{r}_2}{\mathbf{v}_2 - \mathbf{v}_1}\right|$

Substituting the value of t in Eq. (i), we get

$$\mathbf{r}_1 - \mathbf{r}_2 = (\mathbf{v}_2 - \mathbf{v}_1)\left|\frac{\mathbf{r}_1 - \mathbf{r}_2}{\mathbf{v}_2 - \mathbf{v}_1}\right|$$

$$\text{or} \quad \frac{\mathbf{r}_1 - \mathbf{r}_2}{|\mathbf{r}_1 - r_2|} = \frac{(\mathbf{v}_2 - \mathbf{v}_1)}{|\mathbf{v}_2 - \mathbf{v}_1|}$$

10. *(a)*

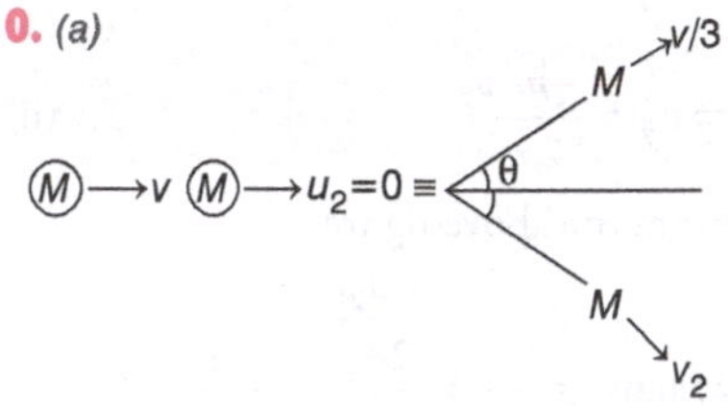

According to law of conservation of kinetic energy, we have

$$\frac{1}{2}Mv^2 + 0 = \frac{1}{2}M\left(\frac{v}{3}\right)^2 + \frac{1}{2}Mv_2^2$$

$$\Rightarrow v^2 = \frac{v^2}{9} + v_2^2 \quad \Rightarrow v^2 - \frac{v^2}{9} = v_2^2$$

$$\Rightarrow \quad v_2^2 = \frac{8v^2}{9}$$

Velocity of second block after collision

$$v_2 = \frac{2\sqrt{2}}{3}v$$

11. *(d)*

key idea

Use conservation of linear momentum in x and y direction and when use $\tan\theta = \dfrac{v_y}{v_x}$.

Given, the mass of sphere, $A = m_1$

the mass of sphere $B = m_2$

initial velocity of sphere, $A = u_A = 0$

initial velocity of sphere,

$B = u_B = v$ along the X-axis

final velocity of sphere B

$(v_B) = \frac{v}{2}$ along the Y-axis.

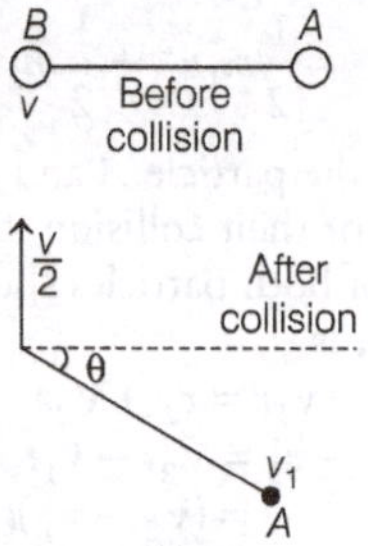

According to conservation of linear momentum in X-axis.

$\Rightarrow \quad m_A u_A + m_B u_B = m_A v_A + m_B v_B$

$\Rightarrow \quad m_1 \times 0 + m_2 v = m_1 v_x + m_2 \times 0$

$\Rightarrow \quad v_x = \frac{m_2 v}{m_1}$ ... (i)

Apply conservation of momentum in Y-axis

$m_A u_A + m_B u_B = m_A v_A + m_B v_B$

$\Rightarrow m_1 \times 0 + m_2 \times 0 = m_1 v_y + m_2 \left(\frac{v}{2}\right)$

$\Rightarrow v_y = \frac{-m_2 v}{2m_1}$ ... (ii)

From the above figure

$\Rightarrow \tan\theta = \frac{v_y}{v_x} = \frac{\frac{-m_2 v}{2m_1}}{\frac{m_2 v}{m_1}} = -\frac{1}{2}$

$\Rightarrow \theta = \tan^{-1}\left(-\frac{1}{2}\right)$ along X-axis.

12. *(b)* When mass m is moving with velocity v in x-direction.
It sticks to another particle of mass $3m$ moving in y-direction with velocity $2v$.
Apply conservation of linear momentum,

$mv\hat{i} + 3m(2v\hat{j}) = (m + 3m)\mathrm{v}$

$\Rightarrow mv\,\hat{i} + 6mv\,\hat{j} = 4m\,\mathrm{v}$

$\Rightarrow \quad \frac{v}{4}\hat{i} + \frac{3}{2}v\hat{j} = \mathrm{v}$

13. *(a)* If two bodies collide head on with coefficient of restitution

$e = \frac{v_2 - v_1}{u_1 - u_2}$ ...(i)

From, the law of conservation of linear momentum

$m_1 u_1 + m_2 u_2 = m_1 v_1 + m_2 v_2$

$\Rightarrow v_1 = \left[\frac{m_1 - em_2}{m_1 + m_2}\right] u_1 + \left[\frac{(1+e)\, m_2}{m_1 + m_2}\right] u_2$

Substituting

$u_1 = 2\ \mathrm{ms}^{-1}$, $u_2 = 0$, $m_1 = m$ and

$m_2 = 2m$, $e = 0.5$

we get, $\quad v_1 = \left[\frac{m - m}{m + 2m}\right] \times 2 \Rightarrow v_1 = 0$

Similarly,

$v_2 = \left[\frac{(1+e)\, m_1}{m_1 + m_2}\right] u_1 + \left[\frac{m_2 - em_1}{m_1 + m_2}\right] u_2$

$= \left[\frac{1.5 \times m}{3m}\right] \times 2 = 1\ \mathrm{ms}^{-1}$

14. *(b)* Applying conservation of linear momentum, we write,

$m_1 u_1 = m_2 u_2$

Here, $m_1 = 18$ kg

$m_2 = 12$ kg

$u_1 = 6\ \mathrm{ms}^{-1}$

$u_2 = ?$

$\therefore \quad 18 \times 6 = 12\, u_2$

$\Rightarrow \quad u_2 = \frac{18 \times 6}{12} = 9\ \mathrm{ms}^{-1}$

Thus, kinetic energy of 12 kg mass

$K_2 = \frac{1}{2} m_2 u_2^2$

$= \frac{1}{2} \times 12 \times (9)^2$

$= 6 \times 81 = 486$ J

15. *(d)* Given,

$u_1 = 3$ m/s

$u_2 = -5$ m/s

$m_1 = m_2 = m$

According to principle of conservation of linear momentum,

$m_1 u_1 + m_2 u_2 = m_1 v_1 + m_2 v_2$

$m \times 3 - m \times 5 = mv_1 + mv_2$

or $\quad v_1 + v_2 = -2$ ...(i)

In an elastic collision,

$e = \frac{v_2 - v_1}{u_1 - u_2}$

$\Rightarrow \quad v_2 - v_1 = e\,(u_1 - u_2)$

$\Rightarrow \quad v_2 - v_1 = (1)(3 + 5) \quad (\because e = 1)$

$\Rightarrow \quad v_1 - v_2 = -8$ ...(ii)

Adding Eqs. (i) and (ii), we obtain

$2v_1 = -10$

$\Rightarrow \quad v_1 = -5$ m/s

From Eq. (i),

$v_2 = -2 - v_1$

$= -2 + 5 = 3$ m/s

Thus, $\quad v_1 = -5$ m/s,

$v_2 = +3$ m/s

16. *(c)* Initial momentum = Final momentum

$\therefore \; m_1 v_1 + m_2 v_2 = (m_1 + m_2) v$

Given, $\quad v_1 = 36$ km/h

$= 36 \times \frac{5}{18} = 10$ m/s

$v_2 = 0$

$m_1 = 2$ kg

$m_2 = 3$ kg

$\therefore \quad v = \frac{m_1 v_1 + m_2 v_2}{m_1 + m_2} = \frac{2 \times 10 + 3 \times 0}{2 + 3}$

or $v = \frac{20}{5} = 4$ m/s

Loss in kinetic energy

$= \frac{1}{2} m_1 v_1^2 + \frac{1}{2} m_2 v_2^2 - \frac{1}{2}(m_1 + m_2) v^2$

$= \frac{1}{2} \times 2 \times (10)^2 + 0 - \frac{1}{2}(2 + 3) \times (4)^2$

$= 100 - 40 = 60$ J

17. *(a)*

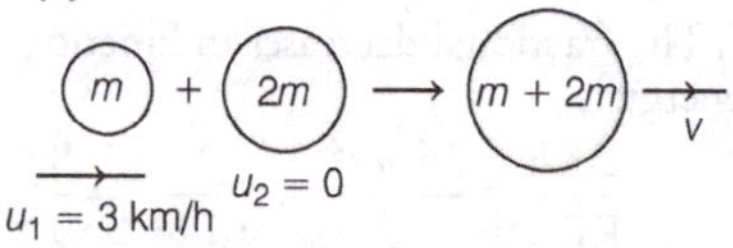

Let v be velocity of combined mass after collision.
Applying law of conservation of linear momentum
Initial momentum = Final momentum

$m \times 3 + 2m \times 0 = (m + 2m)\, v$

or $\quad 3m = 3mv$

or $\quad v = 1$ km /h

18. *(a)* It is defined as the ratio of relative velocity of separation after collision to the relative velocity of approach before collision. It is represented by e.

$e = \frac{\text{relative velocity of separation (after collision)}}{\text{relative velocity of approach (before collision)}}$

For a perfectly elastic collision, relative velocity of separation after collision is equal to relative velocity of approach before collision

$\therefore \quad e = 1$

C-06

NEET Chapterwise
Topicwise Physics

In NEET 2024, 2 questions were visible from this chapter. In past 5 years, 3 questions from topic-1, 2 questions from topic-2, 4 questions from topic-3, 2 questions from topic-4 and 1 question from topic-5 were asked.

SYSTEM OF PARTICLES AND ROTATIONAL MOTION

Topic 1 Rigid Body, Centre of Mass and its Motion

01 Two objects of mass 10 kg and 20 kg, respectively are connected to the two ends of a rigid rod of length 10 m with negligible mass. The distance of the center of mass of the system from the 10 kg mass is

[NCERT (New) Pg. 97, NEET 2022]

(a) $\frac{20}{3}$ m (b) 10 m (c) 5 m (d) $\frac{10}{3}$ m

02 Three identical spheres, each of mass M, are placed at the corners of a right angle triangle with the mutually perpendicular sides equal to 2 m (see figure). Taking the point of intersection of the two mutually perpendicular sides as the origin, find the position vector of centre of mass.

[NCERT (New) Pg. 97, NEET (Oct.) 2020]

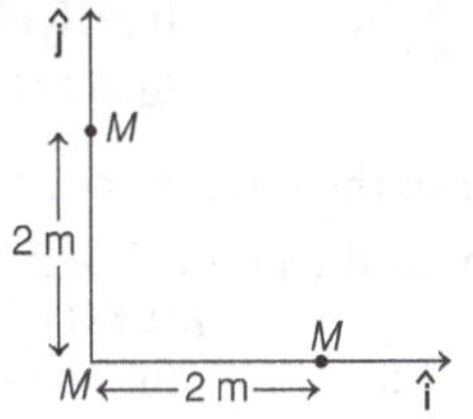

(a) $2(\hat{i}+\hat{j})$ (b) $(\hat{i}+\hat{j})$
(c) $\frac{2}{3}(\hat{i}+\hat{j})$ (d) $\frac{4}{3}(\hat{i}+\hat{j})$

03 Two particles of mass 5 kg and 10 kg, respectively are attached to the two ends of a rigid rod of length 1 m with negligible mass. The centre of mass of the system from the 5 kg particle is nearly at a distance of

[NCERT (New) Pg. 97, NEET (Sep.) 2020]

(a) 50 cm (b) 67 cm
(c) 80 cm (d) 33 cm

04 Which of the following statements are correct ?

(A) Centre of mass of a body always coincides with the centre of gravity of the body.
(B) Centre of mass of a body is the point at which the total gravitational torque on the body is zero.
(C) A couple on a body produce both translational and rotation motion in a body.
(D) Mechanical advantage greater than one means that small effort can be used to lift a large load.

[NCERT (New) Pg. 97, NEET 2017]

(a) (A) and (B) (b) (B) and (C)
(c) (C) and (D) (d) (B) and (D)

05 Two persons of masses 55 kg and 65 kg respectively, are at the opposite ends of a boat. The length of the boat is 3 m and weights 100 kg. The 55 kg man walks upto the 65 kg man and sits with him. If the boat is in still water the centre of mass of the system shifts by *[NCERT (New) Pg. 97, AIPMT 2012]*

(a) 3 m (b) 2.3 m
(c) zero (d) 0.75 m

06 Three masses are placed on the X-axis 300 g at origin, 500 g at $x = 40$ cm and 400 g at $x = 70$ cm. The distance of the centre of mass from the origin is

[NCERT (New) Pg. 97, AIPMT 2012]

(a) 40 cm (b) 45 cm
(c) 50 cm (d) 30 cm

07 A ball of mass M moving with a speed of 2 m/s hits another ball of mass 1 kg moving in the same direction with a speed of 1 m/s. If the kinetic energy of centre of mass is $\frac{4}{3}$ J, then magnitude of M is *[NCERT (New) Pg. 97, AIPMT 2010]*

(a) $\frac{1}{2}$ kg (b) 0.25 kg
(c) 0.050 kg (d) 2 kg

08 Two particles which are initially at rest, move towards each other under the action of their internal attraction. If their speeds are v and $2v$ at any instant, then the speed of centre of mass of the system will be *[NCERT (New) Pg. 97, AIPMT 2010]*

(a) $2v$ (b) 0 (c) $1.5v$ (d) v

09 Two bodies of mass 1 kg and 3 kg have position vectors $\hat{i}+2\hat{j}+\hat{k}$ and $-3\hat{i}-2\hat{j}+\hat{k}$, respectively. The centre of mass of this system has a position vector *[NCERT (New) Pg. 97, CBSE AIPMT 2009]*

(a) $-2\hat{i}+2\hat{k}$ (b) $-2\hat{i}-\hat{j}+\hat{k}$
(c) $2\hat{i}-\hat{j}-2\hat{k}$ (d) $-\hat{i}+\hat{j}+\hat{k}$

10 Consider a system of two particles having masses m_1 and m_2. If the particle of mass m_1 is pushed towards the centre of mass of particles through a distance d, by what distance would the particle of mass m_2 move so as to keep the centre of mass particles at the original position? *[NCERT (New) Pg. 97, AIPMT 2004]*

(a) $\frac{m_1}{m_1+m_2}d$ (b) $\frac{m_1}{m_2}d$ (c) d (d) $\frac{m_2}{m_1}d$

11 A rod is of length 3 m and its mass acting per unit length is directly proportional to distance x from its one end. The centre of gravity of the rod from that end will be at *[NCERT (New) Pg. 97, AIPMT 2002]*

(a) 1.5 m (b) 2 m
(c) 2.5 m (d) 3 m

12 A solid sphere of radius R is placed on a smooth horizontal surface. A horizontal force F is applied at height h from the lowest point. For the maximum acceleration of the centre of mass, *[NCERT (New) Pg. 97, AIPMT 2002]*

(a) $h=R$
(b) $h=2R$
(c) $h=0$
(d) the acceleration will be same whatever h may be

13 Three identical metal balls each of radius r are placed touching each other on a horizontal surface such that an equilateral triangle is formed with centres of three balls joined. The centre of mass of the system is located at *[NCERT (New) Pg. 97, AIPMT 1999]*

(a) horizontal surface
(b) centre of one of the balls
(c) line joining the centres of any two balls
(d) point of intersection of the medians

14 A cart of mass M is tied to one end of a massless rope of length 10 m. The other end of the rope is in the hands of a man of mass M. The entire system is on a smooth horizontal surface. The man is at $x=0$ and the cart at $x=10$ m. If the man pulls the cart by the rope, the man and the cart will meet at the point *[NCERT (New) Pg. 97, AIPMT 1997]*

(a) they will never meet (b) $x=10$ m
(c) $x=5$ m (d) $x=0$

15 In a carbon monoxide molecule, the carbon and the oxygen atoms are separated by a distance 1.12×10^{-10} m. The distance of the centre of mass from the carbon atom is *[NCERT (New) Pg. 97, AIPMT 1997]*

(a) 0.64×10^{-10} m (b) 0.56×10^{-10} m
(c) 0.51×10^{-10} m (d) 0.48×10^{-10} m

Topic 2 Torque and Equilibrium of Rigid Body

01 A uniform rod of length 200 cm and mass 500 g is balanced on a wedge placed at 40 cm mark. A mass of 2 kg is suspended from the rod at 20 cm and another unknown mass m is suspended from the rod at 160 cm mark as shown in the figure. Find the value of m such that the rod is in equilibrium. ($g=10$ m/s^2) *[NCERT (New) Pg. 109, NEET 2021]*

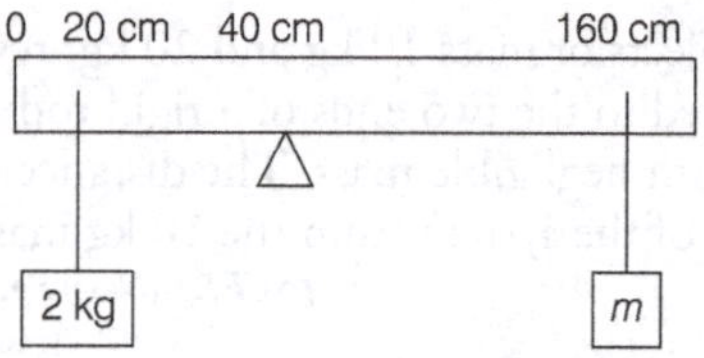

(a) $\frac{1}{2}$ kg (b) $\frac{1}{3}$ kg
(c) $\frac{1}{6}$ kg (d) $\frac{1}{12}$ kg

02 Find the torque about the origin when a force of $3\hat{j}$ N acts on the particle whose position vector is $2\hat{k}$ m. *[NCERT (New) Pg. 105, NEET (Sep.) 2020]*

(a) $6\hat{j}$ N-m (b) $-6\hat{i}$ N-m
(c) $6\hat{k}$ N-m (d) $6\hat{i}$ N-m

03 The moment of the force, $\mathbf{F}=4\hat{i}+5\hat{j}-6\hat{k}$ N at (2, 0, – 3), about the point (2, – 2, – 2), is given by *[NCERT (New) Pg. 105, NEET 2018]*

(a) $-7\hat{i}-8\hat{j}-4\hat{k}$ (b) $-4\hat{i}-\hat{j}-8\hat{k}$
(c) $-8\hat{i}-4\hat{j}-7\hat{k}$ (d) $-7\hat{i}-4\hat{j}-8\hat{k}$

04 A rod of weight w is supported by two parallel knife edges A and B and is in equilibrium in a horizontal position. The knives are at a distance d from each other. The centre of mass of the rod is at distance x from A. The normal reaction on A is *[AIPMT 2015]*

(a) $\frac{wx}{d}$ (b) $\frac{wd}{x}$
(c) $\frac{w(d-x)}{x}$ (d) $\frac{w(d-x)}{d}$

05 ABC is an equilateral triangle with O as its centre. $\mathbf{F_1}$, $\mathbf{F_2}$ and $\mathbf{F_3}$ represent three forces acting along the sides AB, BC and AC, respectively. If the total torque about O is zero, then the magnitude of $\mathbf{F_3}$ is *[NCERT (New) Pg. 105, AIPMT 2012]*

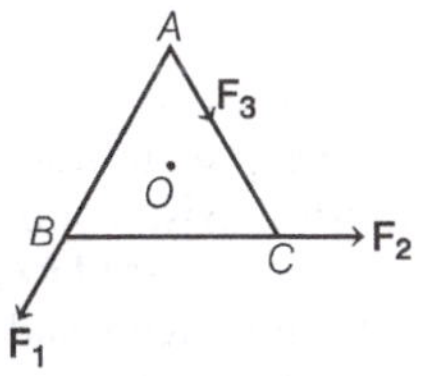

(a) $F_1 + F_2$ (b) $F_1 - F_2$ (c) $\frac{F_1 + F_2}{2}$ (d) $2(F_1 + F_2)$

06 If $\mathbf{F}$ is the force acting on a particle having position vector $\mathbf{r}$ and τ be the torque of this force about the origin, then *[NCERT (New) Pg. 105, AIPMT 2009]*

(a) $\mathbf{r}\cdot\tau \neq 0$ and $\mathbf{F}\cdot\tau = 0$ (b) $\mathbf{r}\cdot\tau > 0$ and $\mathbf{F}\cdot\tau < 0$
(c) $\mathbf{r}\cdot\tau = 0$ and $\mathbf{F}\cdot\tau = 0$ (d) $\mathbf{r}\cdot\tau = 0$ and $\mathbf{F}\cdot\tau \neq 0$

07 O is the centre of an equilateral ΔABC. F_1, F_2 and F_3 are three forces acting along the sides AB, BC and AC as shown in figure. What should be the magnitude of F_3, so that the total torque about O is zero? *[NCERT (New) Pg. 105, AIPMT 1998]*

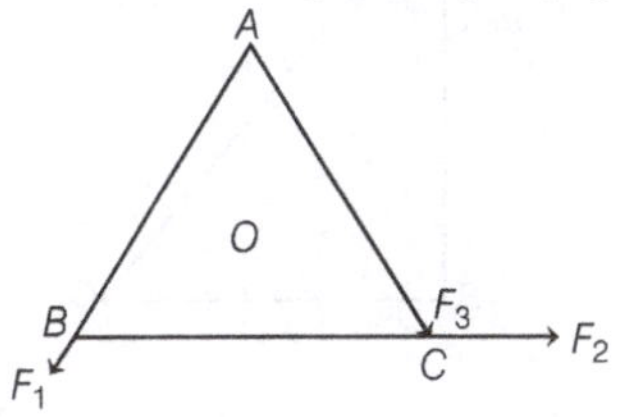

(a) $\frac{(F_1 + F_2)}{2}$ (b) $(F_1 - F_2)$
(c) $(F_1 + F_2)$ (d) $2(F_1 + F_2)$

08 A couple produces *[NCERT (New) Pg. 110, AIPMT 1997]*

(a) no motion
(b) linear and rotational motion
(c) purely rotational motion
(d) purely linear motion

09 Find the torque of a force $\mathbf{F} = -3\hat{i} + \hat{j} + 5\hat{k}$ acting at the point $\mathbf{r} = 7\hat{i} + 3\hat{j} + \hat{k}$. *[AIPMT 1997]*

(a) $-21\hat{i} + 3\hat{j} + 5\hat{k}$ (b) $-14\hat{i} + 3\hat{j} - 16\hat{k}$
(c) $4\hat{i} + 4\hat{j} + 6\hat{k}$ (d) $14\hat{i} - 38\hat{j} + 16\hat{k}$

Topic 3 Moment of Inertia

01 The moment of inertia of a thin rod about an axis passing through its mid-point and perpendicular to the rod is 2400 g cm^2. The length of the 400 g rod is nearly *[NCERT (New) Pg. 114, NEET 2024]*

(a) 8.5 cm (b) 17.5 cm
(c) 20.7 cm (d) 72.0 cm

02 The ratio of radius of gyration of a solid sphere of mass M and radius R about its own axis to the radius of gyration of the thin hollow sphere of same mass and radius about its axis is *[NCERT (New) Pg. 115, NEET 2023]*

(a) 5 : 3 (b) 2 : 5 (c) 5 : 2 (d) 3 : 5

03 The ratio of the radius of gyration of a thin uniform disc about an axis passing through its centre and normal to its plane to the radius of gyration of the disc about its diameter is *[NCERT (New) Pg. 115, NEET 2022]*

(a) $\sqrt{2} : 1$ (b) 4 : 1 (c) $1 : \sqrt{2}$ (d) 2 : 1

04 From a circular ring of mass M and radius R, an arc corresponding to a 90° sector is removed. The moment of inertia of the remaining part of the ring about an axis passing through the centre of the ring and perpendicular to the plane of the ring is K times MR^2. Then, the value of K is *[NEET 2021]*

(a) $\frac{3}{4}$ (b) $\frac{7}{8}$ (c) $\frac{1}{4}$ (d) $\frac{1}{8}$

05 From a disc of radius R and mass M, a circular hole of diameter R, whose rim passes through the centre is cut. What is the moment of inertia of the remaining part of the disc about a perpendicular axis, passing through the centre ? *[NCERT (New) Pg. 115, NEET 2016]*

(a) 13 $MR^2/32$ (b) 11 $MR^2/32$
(c) 9 $MR^2/32$ (d) 15 $MR^2/32$

06 A light rod of length l has two masses m_1 and m_2 attached to its two ends. The moment of inertia of the system about an axis perpendicular to the rod and passing through the centre of mass is *[NCERT (New) Pg. 115, NEET 2016]*

(a) $\frac{m_1 m_2}{m_1 + m_2} l^2$ (b) $\frac{m_1 + m_2}{m_1 m_2} l^2$
(c) $(m_1 + m_2) l^2$ (d) $\sqrt{m_1 m_2} l^2$

07 Three identical spherical shells, each of mass m and radius r are placed as shown in figure. Consider an axis XX', which is touching to two shells and passing through diameter of third shell.

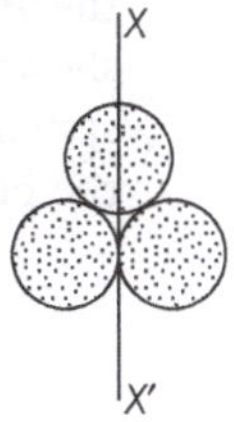

Moment of inertia of the system consisting of these three spherical shells about XX' axis is *[NCERT (New) Pg. 167, AIPMT 2015]*

(a) $\frac{11}{5} mr^2$ (b) $3\,mr^2$ (c) $\frac{16}{5} mr^2$ (d) $4\,mr^2$

08 The moment of inertia of a thin uniform rod of mass M and length L about an axis passing through its mid-point and perpendicular to its length is I_0. Its moment of inertia about an axis passing through one of its ends and perpendicular to its length is *[AIPMT 2011]*

(a) $I_0 + ML^2/4$ (b) $I_0 + 2ML^2$
(c) $I_0 + ML^2$ (d) $I_0 + ML^2/2$

09 Four identical thin rods each of mass M and length l, form a square frame. Moment of inertia of this frame about an axis through the centre of the square and perpendicular to its plane is *[NCERT (New) Pg. 115, AIPMT 2009]*

(a) $\frac{4}{3}Ml^2$ (b) $\frac{2}{3}Ml^2$
(c) $\frac{13}{3}Ml^2$ (d) $\frac{1}{3}Ml^2$

10 A thin rod of length L and mass M is bent at its mid-point into two halves so that the angle between them is 90°. The moment of inertia of the bent rod about an axis passing through the bending point and perpendicular to the plane defined by the two halves of the rod is *[NCERT (New) Pg. 115, AIPMT 2008]*

(a) $\frac{ML^2}{24}$ (b) $\frac{ML^2}{12}$
(c) $\frac{ML^2}{6}$ (d) $\frac{\sqrt{2}ML^2}{24}$

11 The ratio of the radii of gyration of a circular disc to that of a circular ring, each of same mass and radius, around their respective axes is *[AIPMT 2008]*

(a) $\sqrt{3}:\sqrt{2}$ (b) $1:\sqrt{2}$
(c) $\sqrt{2}:1$ (d) $\sqrt{2}:\sqrt{3}$

12 The moment of inertia of a uniform circular disc of radius R and mass M about an axis passing from the edge of the disc and normal to the disc is *[AIPMT 2006]*

(a) $\frac{1}{2}MR^2$ (b) MR^2
(c) $\frac{7}{2}MR^2$ (d) $\frac{3}{2}MR^2$

13 Three particles, each of mass m grams are situated at the vertices of an equilateral ΔABC of side l cm (as shown in the figure). The moment of inertia of the system about a line AX perpendicular to AB and in the plane of ABC in g-cm^2 units will be *[AIPMT 2004]*

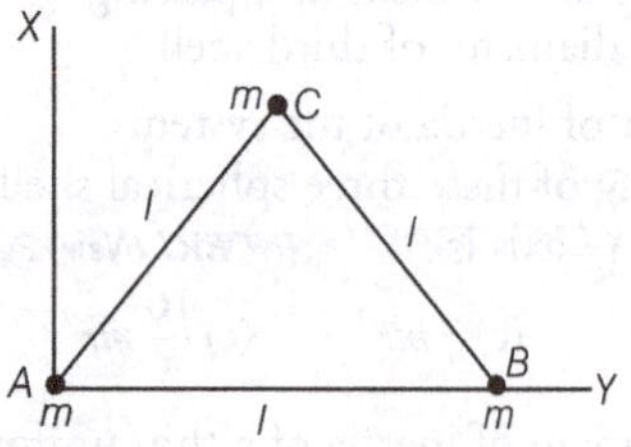

(a) $\left(\frac{3}{4}\right)ml^2$ (b) $2\,ml^2$
(c) $\left(\frac{5}{4}\right)ml^2$ (d) $\left(\frac{3}{2}\right)ml^2$

14 The ratio of the radii of gyration of a circular disc about a tangential axis in the plane of the disc and of a circular ring of the same radius about a tangential axis in the plane of the ring is *[AIPMT 2004]*

(a) 2 : 3 (b) 2 : 1
(c) $\sqrt{5}:\sqrt{6}$ (d) $1:\sqrt{2}$

15 A circular disc is to be made using iron and aluminium. To keep its moment of inertia maximum about a geometrical axis, it should be so prepared that *[NCERT (New) Pg. 114, AIPMT 2002]*

(a) aluminium is at the interior and iron surrounds it
(b) iron is at the interior and aluminium surrounds it
(c) aluminium and iron layers are in alternate order
(d) sheet of iron is used at both external surfaces and aluminium sheet as inner material

16 ABC is a right angled triangular plate of uniform thickness. The sides are such that $AB > BC$ as shown in figure. I_1, I_2, I_3 are moments of inertia about AB, BC and AC respectively. Then, which of the following relations is correct ? *[NCERT (New) Pg. 115, AIPMT 2000]*

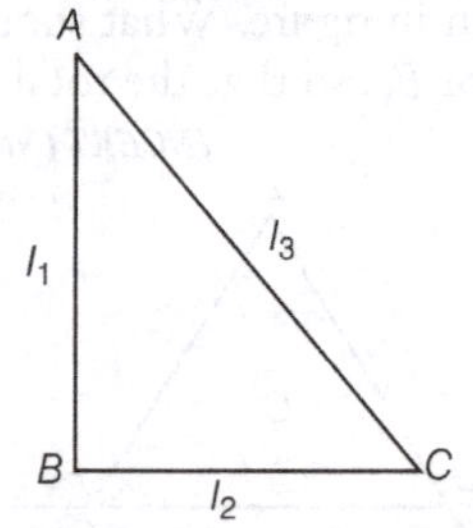

(a) $I_1 = I_2 = I_3$ (b) $I_2 > I_1 > I_3$
(c) $I_3 < I_2 < I_1$ (d) $I_3 > I_1 > I_2$

17 The moment of inertia of a disc of mass M and radius R about a tangent to its rim in its plane is *[AIPMT 1999]*

(a) $\frac{2}{3}MR^2$ (b) $\frac{3}{2}MR^2$ (c) $\frac{4}{5}MR^2$ (d) $\frac{5}{4}MR^2$

18 ABC is a triangular plate of uniform thickness. The sides are in the ratio shown in the figure. I_{AB}, I_{BC} and I_{CA} are the moments of inertia of the plate about AB, BC and CA as axes, respectively. Which one of the following relations is correct ? *[AIPMT 1995]*

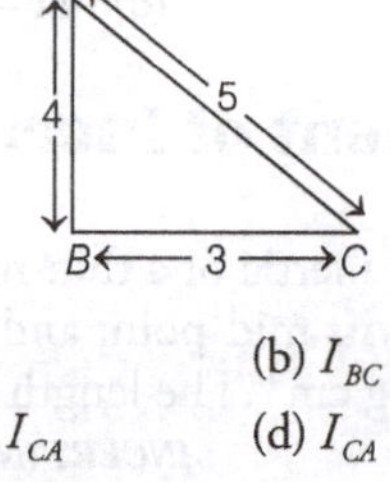

(a) $I_{AB} > I_{BC}$ (b) $I_{BC} > I_{AC}$
(c) $I_{AB} + I_{BC} = I_{CA}$ (d) I_{CA} is maximum

19 In a rectangle, $ABCD$ $(BC = 2AB)$. The moment of inertia is minimum along axis through *[AIPMT 1993]*

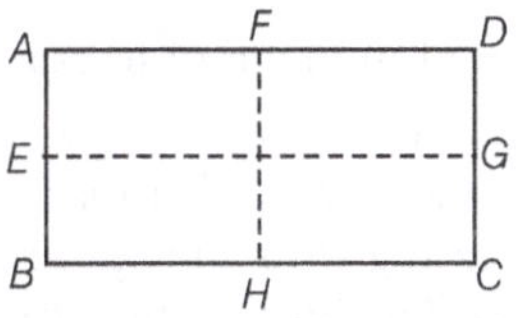

(a) BC (b) BD (c) HF (d) EG

Topic 4 Kinematics of Rotational Motion and Angular Velocity

01 The angular speed of a fly wheel moving with uniform angular acceleration changes from 1200 rpm to 3120 rpm in 16 s. The angular acceleration in rad/s^2 is *[NCERT (New) Pg. 117, NEET 2022]*
(a) 4π (b) 12π (c) 104π (d) 2π

02 The angular speed of the wheel of a vehicle is increased from 360 rpm to 1200 rpm in 14 s. Its angular acceleration is *[NCERT (New) Pg. 117, NEET (Oct.)2020]*
(a) 2π rad/s^2 (b) 28π rad/s^2
(c) 120π rad/s^2 (d) 1 rad/s^2

03 A particle starting from rest, moves in a circle of radius r. It attains a velocity of v_0 m/s in the nth round. Its angular acceleration will be *[NCERT (New) Pg. 117, NEET (Odisha) 2019]*
(a) $\frac{v_0}{n}$ rad/s^2 (b) $\frac{v_0^2}{2\pi nr^2}$ rad/s^2
(c) $\frac{v_0^2}{4\pi nr^2}$ rad/s^2 (d) $\frac{v_0^2}{4\pi nr}$ rad/s^2

04 A uniform circular disc of radius 50 cm at rest is free to turn about an axis which is perpendicular to its plane and passes through its centre. It is subjected to a torque which produces a constant angular acceleration of 2.0 rad s^{-2}. Its net acceleration in ms^{-2} at the end of 2.0 s is approximately. *[NEET 2016]*
(a) 8.0 (b) 7.0 (c) 6.0 (d) 3.0

05 An automobile moves on a road with a speed of 54 km h^{-1}. The radius of its wheels is 0.45 m and the moment of inertia of the wheel about its axis of rotation is 3 kg m^2. If the vehicle is brought to rest in 15 s, the magnitude of average torque transmitted by its brakes to the wheel is *[AIPMT 2015]*
(a) 6.66 kg m^2s^{-2} (b) 8.58 kg m^2s^{-2}
(c) 10.86 kg m^2s^{-2} (d) 2.86 kg m^2s^{-2}

06 The instantaneous angular position of a point on a rotating wheel is given by the equation $\theta(t) = 2t^3 - 6t^2$. The torque on the wheel becomes zero at *[NCERT (New) Pg. 117, AIPMT 2011]*
(a) $t = 0.5$ s (b) t=0.25 s
(c) $t = 2$ s (d) $t = 1$ s

07 A wheel has angular acceleration of 3 rad / s^2 and an initial angular speed of 2 rad/s. In a time of 2 s, it has rotated through an angle (in radian) of *[AIPMT 2007]*
(a) 6 (b) 10 (c) 12 (d) 4

08 A wheel having moment of inertia 2 kg m^2 about its vertical axis, rotates at the rate of 60 rpm about this axis. The torque which can stop the wheel's rotation in one minute would be *[NCERT (New) Pg. 117, AIPMT 2004]*
(a) $\frac{2\pi}{15}$ N m (b) $\frac{\pi}{12}$ N m (c) $\frac{\pi}{15}$ N m (d) $\frac{\pi}{18}$ N m

09 A wheel of radius 1 m rolls forward half a revolution on a horizontal ground. The magnitude of the displacement of the point of the wheel initially in contact with the ground is *[AIPMT 2002]*
(a) π (b) 2π
(c) $\sqrt{2}\pi$ (d) $\sqrt{\pi^2 + 4}$

10 A constant torque of 1000 N-m turns a wheel of moment of inertia 200 kg-m^2 about an axis through its centre. Its angular velocity after 3 s is *[AIPMT 2001]*
(a) 1 rad/s (b) 5 rad/s (c) 10 rad/s (d) 15 rad/s

11 What is the value of linear velocity, if $\mathbf{r} = 3\hat{i} - 4\hat{j} + \hat{k}$ and $\omega = 5\hat{i} - 6\hat{j} + 6\hat{k}$? *[NCERT (New) Pg. 104, AIPMT 1999]*
(a) $4\hat{i} - 13\hat{j} + 6\hat{k}$ (b) $18\hat{i} + 13\hat{j} - 2\hat{k}$
(c) $6\hat{i} + 2\hat{j} - 3\hat{k}$ (d) $6\hat{i} - 2\hat{j} + 8\hat{k}$

12 If a flywheel makes 120 rev/min, then its angular speed will be *[NCERT (New) Pg. 104, AIPMT 1996]*
(a) 8π rad / s (b) 6π rad / s
(c) 4π rad / s (d) 2π rad / s

13 The angular speed of an engine wheel making 90 rev/min is *[NCERT (New) Pg. 104, AIPMT 1995]*
(a) 1.5π rad / s (b) 3π rad / s
(c) 4.5π rad / s (d) 6π rad / s

Topic 5 Angular Momentum and Its Conservation

01 A bob is whirled in a horizontal plane by means of a string with an initial speed of ω rpm. The tension in the string is T. If speed becomes 2ω while keeping the same radius, the tension in the string becomes *[NCERT (New) Pg. 121, NEET 2024]*
(a) T (b) $4T$ (c) $T/4$ (d) $\sqrt{2}T$

02 A solid sphere is rotating freely about its symmetry axis in free space. The radius of the sphere is increased keeping its mass same. Which of the following physical quantities would remain constant for the sphere? *[NCERT (New) Pg. 121, NEET 2018]*
(a) Rotational kinetic energy
(b) Moment of inertia
(c) Angular velocity
(d) Angular momentum

03 A mass m moves in a circle on a smooth horizontal plane with velocity v_0 at a radius R_0. The mass is attached to a string which passes through a smooth hole in the plane as shown.

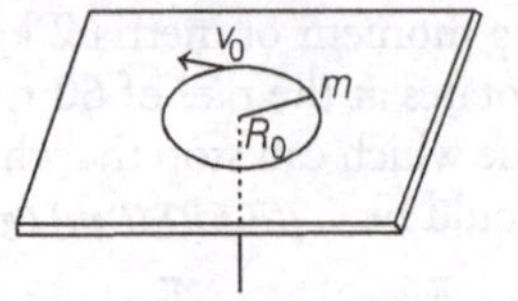

The tension in the string is increased gradually and finally m moves in a circle of radius $R_0/2$. The final value of the kinetic energy is *[AIPMT 2015]*

(a) mv_0^2 (b) $\frac{1}{4}mv_0^2$ (c) $2mv_0^2$ (d) $\frac{1}{2}mv_0^2$

04 A force $\mathbf{F}=\alpha\hat{i}+3\hat{j}+6\hat{k}$ is acting at a point $\mathbf{r}=2\hat{i}-6\hat{j}-12\hat{k}$. The value of α for which angular momentum about origin is conserved is *[AIPMT 2014]*

(a) -1 (b) 2 (c) zero (d) 1

05 Two discs are rotating about their axes, normal to the discs and passing through the centres of the discs. Disc D_1 has 2 kg mass and 0.2 m radius and initial angular velocity of 50 rad s^{-1}. Disc D_2 has 4 kg mass, 0.1 m radius and initial angular velocity of 200 rad s^{-1}. The two discs are brought in contact face to face, with their axes of rotation coincident. The final angular velocity (in rad s^{-1}) of the system is *[NCERT (New) Pg. 108, NEET 2013]*

(a) 40 (b) 60 (c) 100 (d) 120

06 A thin circular ring of mass M and radius r is rotating about its axis with constant angular velocity ω. Two objects each of mass m are attached gently to the opposite ends of a diameter of the ring. The ring now rotates with angular velocity given by *[NCERT (New) Pg. 108, AIPMT 2010, 2009, 1998]*

(a) $\frac{(M+2m)\omega}{2m}$ (b) $\frac{2M\omega}{M+2m}$

(c) $\frac{(M+2m)\omega}{M}$ (d) $\frac{M\omega}{M+2m}$

07 A particle of mass m in the XY-plane with a velocity v along the straight line AB. If the angular momentum of the particle with respect to origin O is L_A when it is at A and L_B when it is at B, then *[AIPMT 2007]*

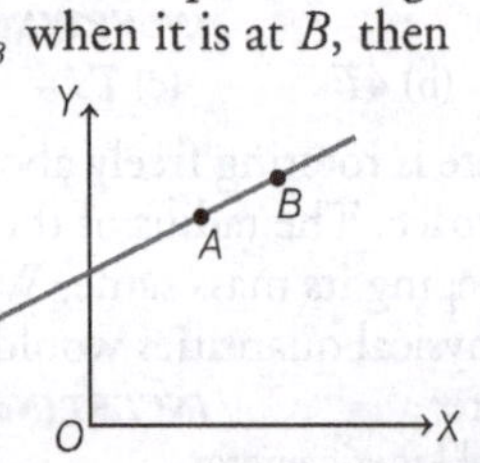

(a) $L_A > L_B$

(b) $L_A = L_B$

(c) the relationship between L_A and L_B depends upon the slope of the line AB

(d) $L_A < L_B$

08 A round disc of moment of inertia I_2 about its axis perpendicular to its plane and passing through its centre is placed over another disc of moment of inertia I_1 rotating with an angular velocity ω about the same axis. The final angular velocity of the combination of discs is *[NCERT (New) Pg. 107, AIPMT 2004]*

(a) $\frac{I_2\omega}{I_1+I_2}$ (b) ω

(c) $\frac{I_1\omega}{I_1+I_2}$ (d) $\frac{(I_1+I_2)\omega}{I_1}$

09 A thin circular ring of mass M and radius r is rotating about its axis with a constant angular velocity ω. Four objects each of mass m, are kept gently to the opposite ends of two perpendicular diameters of the ring. The angular velocity of the ring will be *[NCERT (New) Pg. 108, AIPMT 2003]*

(a) $\frac{(M+4m)\omega}{M}$ (b) $\frac{(M-4m)\omega}{M+4m}$

(c) $\frac{M\omega}{4m}$ (d) $\frac{M\omega}{M+4m}$

10 A disc is rotating with angular velocity ω. If a child sits on it, what is conserved ? *[AIPMT 2002]*

(a) Linear momentum

(b) Angular momentum

(c) Kinetic energy

(d) Moment of inertia

11 A boy suddenly comes and sits on a circular rotating table. What will remain conserved ? *[AIPMT 2002]*

(a) Angular velocity

(b) Angular momentum

(c) Linear momentum

(d) Kinetic energy

12 The angular momentum of a body with mass m moment of inertia I and angular velocity ω rad/s is equal to *[NCERT (New) Pg. 107, AIPMT 1996]*

(a) $I\omega$ (b) $I\omega^2$

(c) $\frac{I}{\omega}$ (d) $\frac{I}{\omega^2}$

13 Angular momentum is *[NCERT (New) Pg. 106, AIPMT 1994]*

(a) vector (axial) (b) vector (polar)

(c) scalar (d) None of these

14 A particle of mass $m = 5$ kg is moving with a uniform speed $v = 3\sqrt{2}$ in the XOY plane along the line $Y = X + 4$. The magnitude of the angular momentum of the particle about the origin is *[AIPMT 1991]*

(a) 60 unit (b) $40\sqrt{2}$ unit

(c) zero (d) 7.5 unit

15 A solid homogeneous sphere of mass M and radius R is moving on a rough horizontal surface, partly rolling and partly sliding. During this kind of motion of the sphere **[NCERT (New) Pg. 108, AIPMT 1988]**
(a) total kinetic energy is conserved
(b) the angular momentum of the sphere about the point of contact with the plane is conserved
(c) only the rotational kinetic energy about the centre of mass is conserved
(d) angular momentum about the centre of mass is conserved

Topic 6 Dynamics of Rotational Motion

01 A solid cylinder of mass 2 kg and radius 50 cm rolls up an inclined plane of angle inclination 30°. The centre of mass of cylinder has speed of 4 m/s. The distance travelled by the cylinder on the inclined surface will be (Take, $g = 10\ \text{m/s}^2$) **[NEET (Odisha) 2019]**
(a) 2.2 m (b) 1.6 m (c) 1.2 m (d) 2.4 m

02 A disc of radius 2 m and mass 100 kg rolls on a horizontal floor. Its centre of mass has speed of 20 cm/s. How much work is needed to stop it ? **[NCERT (Old) Pg. 174, NEET (National) 2019]**
(a) 30 kJ (b) 2 J (c) 1 J (d) 3 J

03 A solid cylinder of mass 2 kg and radius 4 cm is rotating about its axis at the rate of 3 rpm. The torque required to stop after 2π revolutions is **[NCERT (Old) Pg. 174, NEET (National) 2019]**
(a) 2×10^{-3} N-m (b) 12×10^{-4} N-m
(c) 2×10^{6} N-m (d) 2×10^{-6} N-m

04 Three objects, A (a solid sphere), B (a thin circular disk) and C (a circular ring), each have the same mass M and radius R. They all spin with the same angular speed ω about their own symmetry axes. The amounts of work W required to bring them to rest, would satisfy the relation **[NCERT (Old) Pg. 174, NEET 2018]**
(a) $W_B > W_A > W_C$ (b) $W_A > W_B > W_C$
(c) $W_C > W_B > W_A$ (d) $W_A > W_C > W_B$

05 A solid sphere is in rolling motion. In rolling motion, a body possesses translational kinetic energy K_t as well as rotational kinetic energy K_r simultaneously. The ratio $K_t : K_t + K_r$ for the sphere is **[NCERT (Old) Pg. 174, NEET 2018]**
(a) 10 : 7 (b) 5 : 7 (c) 7 : 10 (d) 2 : 5

06 Two discs of same moment of inertia rotating about their regular axis passing through centre and perpendicular to the plane of disc with angular velocities ω_1 and ω_2. They are brought into contact face to face coinciding the axis of rotation. The expression for loss of energy during this process is **[NCERT (Old) Pg. 174, NEET 2017]**
(a) $\frac{1}{2}I(\omega_1+\omega_2)^2$ (b) $\frac{1}{4}I(\omega_1-\omega_2)^2$
(c) $I(\omega_1-\omega_2)^2$ (d) $\frac{I}{8}(\omega_1-\omega_2)^2$

07 A rope is wound around a hollow cylinder of mass 3 kg and radius 40 cm. What is the angular acceleration of the cylinder, if the rope is pulled with a force of 30 N ? **[NCERT (New) Pg. 105, NEET 2017]**
(a) 25 m/s^2 (b) 0.25 rad/s^2
(c) 25 rad/s^2 (d) 5 m/s^2

08 Two rotating bodies A and B of masses m and $2m$ with moments of inertia I_A and $I_B (I_B > I_A)$ have equal kinetic energy of rotation. If L_A and L_B be their angular momenta respectively, then **[NEET 2016]**
(a) $L_A = \frac{L_B}{2}$ (b) $L_A = 2L_B$
(c) $L_B > L_A$ (d) $L_A > L_B$

09 A disc and a sphere of same radius but different masses roll off on two inclined planes of the same altitude and length. Which one of the two objects gets to the bottom of the plane first ? **[NEET 2016]**
(a) Sphere
(b) Both reach at the same time
(c) Depends on their masses
(d) Disc

10 A solid sphere of mass m and radius R is rotating about its diameter. A solid cylinder of the same mass and same radius is also rotating about its geometrical axis with an angular speed twice that of the sphere. The ratio of their kinetic energies of rotation $(E_{\text{Sphere}} / E_{\text{Cylinder}})$ will be **[NCERT (Old) Pg. 174, NEET 2016]**
(a) 2 : 3 (b) 1 : 5
(c) 1 : 4 (d) 3 : 1

11 Point masses m_1 and m_2 are placed at the opposite ends of a rigid rod of length L and negligible mass. The rod is to be set rotating about an axis perpendicular to it. The position of point P on this rod through which the axis should pass, so that the work required to set the rod rotating with angular velocity ω_0 is minimum, is given by **[AIPMT 2015]**

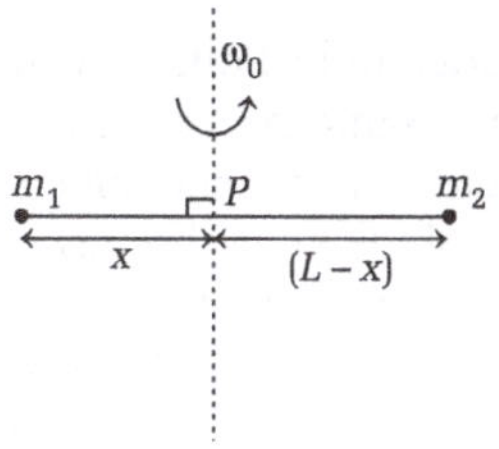

(a) $x = \frac{m_1 L}{m_1+m_2}$ (b) $x = \frac{m_1}{m_2}L$
(c) $x = \frac{m_2}{m_1}L$ (d) $x = \frac{m_2 L}{m_1+m_2}$

12 A solid cylinder of mass 50 kg and radius 0.5 m is free to rotate about the horizontal axis. A massless string is wound round the cylinder with one end attached to it and other hanging freely. Tension in the string required to produce an angular acceleration of 2 rev/s^2 is *[NCERT (New) Pg. 119, AIPMT 2014]*

(a) 25 N (b) 50 N
(c) 78.5 N (d) 157 N

13 The ratio of the accelerations for a solid sphere (mass m and radius R) rolling down an incline of angle θ without slipping and slipping down the incline without rolling is *[NCERT (Old) Pg. 174, AIPMT 2014]*

(a) 5 : 7 (b) 2 : 3
(c) 2 : 5 (d) 7 : 5

14 A small object of uniform density rolls up a curved surface with an initial velocity v. It reaches upto a maximum height of $\frac{3v^2}{4g}$ with respect to the initial position. The object is *[NEET 2013]*

(a) ring (b) solid sphere
(c) hollow sphere (d) disc

15 A rod PQ of mass M and length L is hinged at end P. The rod is kept horizontal by a massless string tied to a point Q as shown in figure. When string is cut, the initial angular acceleration of the rod is *[NEET 2013]*

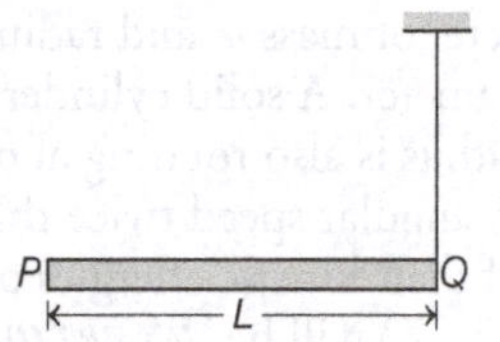

(a) $\frac{3g}{2L}$ (b) $\frac{g}{L}$ (c) $\frac{2g}{L}$ (d) $\frac{2g}{3L}$

16 A solid cylinder of mass 3 kg is rolling on a horizontal surface with velocity 4 ms^{-1}. If collides with a horizontal spring of force constant 200 N m^{-1}. The maximum compression produced in the spring will be *[NCERT (old) Pg. 174, AIPMT 2012]*

(a) 0.5 m (b) 0.6 m (c) 0.7 m (d) 0.2 m

17 A solid cylinder and a hollow cylinder both of the same mass and same external diameter are released from the same height at the same time on an inclined plane. Both roll down without slipping. Which one will reach the bottom first? *[AIPMT 2000, 2010]*

(a) Both together (b) Solid cylinder
(c) One with higher density (d) Hollow cylinder

18 A circular disc of moment of inertia I_t is rotating in a horizontal plane, about its symmetry axis, with a constant angular speed ω_i. Another disc of moment of inertia I_b is dropped coaxially onto the rotating disc. Initially the second disk has zero angular speed. Eventually both the discs rotate with a constant angular speed ω_f. The energy lost by initially rotating disc due to friction is *[NCERT (Old) Pg. 174, AIPMT 2010]*

(a) $\frac{1}{2}\frac{I_b^2}{(I_t+I_b)}\omega_i^2$ (b) $\frac{1}{2}\frac{I_t^2}{(I_t+I_b)}\omega_i^2$

(c) $\frac{1}{2}\frac{I_b-I_t}{(I_t+I_b)}\omega_i^2$ (d) $\frac{1}{2}\frac{I_bI_t}{(I_t+I_b)}\omega_i^2$

19 A uniform rod of length l and mass m is free to rotate in a vertical plane about A. The rod initially in horizontal position is released. The initial angular acceleration of the rod is (moment of inertia of rod about A is $\frac{ml^2}{3}$) *[NCERT (New) Pg. 115, AIPMT 2007]*

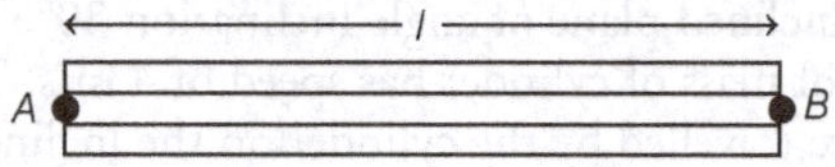

(a) $\frac{3g}{2l}$ (b) $\frac{2l}{3g}$ (c) $\frac{3g}{2l^2}$ (d) $mg\frac{l}{2}$

20 Two bodies have their moments of inertia I and $2I$ respectively about their axis of rotation. If their kinetic energies of rotation are equal, their angular momenta will be in the ratio *[AIPMT 2005]*

(a) 1 : 2 (b) $\sqrt{2}:1$ (c) 2 : 1 (d) $1:\sqrt{2}$

21 A ball rolls without slipping. The radius of gyration of the ball about an axis passing through its centre of mass is K. If radius of the ball be R, then the fraction of total energy associated with its rotational energy will be *[NCERT (Old) Pg. 174, AIPMT 2003]*

(a) $\frac{K^2}{K^2+R^2}$ (b) $\frac{R^2}{K^2+R^2}$

(c) $\frac{K^2+R^2}{R^2}$ (d) $\frac{K^2}{R^2}$

22 A wheel of bicycle is rolling without slipping on a level road. The velocity of the centre of mass is v_{CM}, then true statement is *[NCERT (Old) Pg. 174, AIPMT 2001]*

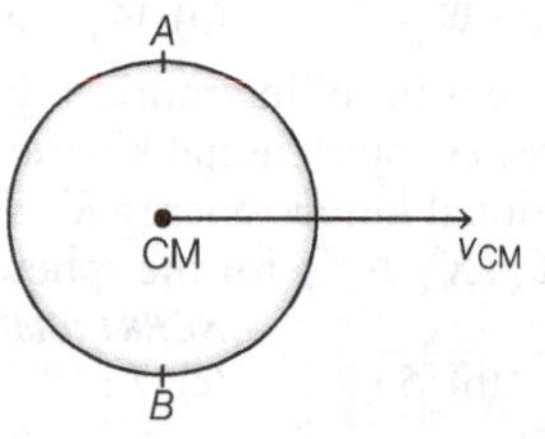

(a) The velocity of point A is $2v_{CM}$ and velocity of point B is zero.
(b) The velocity of point A is zero and velocity of point B is $2v_{CM}$.
(c) The velocity of point A is $2v_{CM}$ and velocity of point B is $-v_{CM}$.
(d) The velocities of both A and B are v_{CM}.

23 A disc is rolling, the velocity of its centre of mass is v_{cm}. Which one will be correct ?
[NCERT (Old) Pg. 174, AIPMT 2001]
(a) The velocity of highest point is $2v_{cm}$ and at point of contact is zero.
(b) The velocity of highest point is v_{cm} and at point of contact is v_{cm}.
(c) The velocity of highest point is $2v_{cm}$ and point of contact is v_{cm}.
(d) The velocity of highest point is $2v_{cm}$ and point of contact is $2v_{cm}$.

24 A spherical ball rolls on a table without slipping. Then, the fraction of its total energy associated with rotation is *[NCERT (Old) Pg. 174, AIPMT 1994]*
(a) 2/5 (b) 2/7 (c) 3/5 (d) 3/7

25 A thin uniform circular ring is rolling down an inclined plane of inclination 30° without slipping. Its linear acceleration along the inclined plane will be
[NCERT (Old) Pg. 174, AIPMT 1994]
(a) $\frac{g}{2}$ (b) $\frac{g}{3}$ (c) $\frac{g}{4}$ (d) $\frac{2g}{3}$

26 A solid sphere, disc and solid cylinder all of the same mass and made of the same material are allowed to roll down (from rest) on the inclined plane, then
[AIPMT 1993]
(a) solid sphere reaches the bottom first
(b) solid sphere reaches the bottom last
(c) disc will reach the bottom first
(d) all reach the bottom at the same time

27 The speed of a homogeneous solid sphere after rolling down an inclined plane of vertical height h from rest without sliding is *[NCERT (Old) Pg. 174, AIPMT 1992]*
(a) $\sqrt{\frac{10}{7}gh}$ (b) $\sqrt{gh}$
(c) $\sqrt{\frac{6}{5}gh}$ (d) $\sqrt{\frac{4}{3}gh}$

28 A flywheel rotating about a fixed axis has a kinetic energy of 360 J when its angular speed is 30 rad/s. The moment of inertia of the wheel about the axis of rotation is *[NCERT (Old) Pg. 174, AIPMT 1990]*
(a) $0.6\ kg\text{-}m^2$ (b) $0.15\ kg\text{-}m^2$
(c) $0.8\ kg\text{-}m^2$ (d) $0.75\ kg\text{-}m^2$

29 The moment of inertia of a body about a given axis is $1.2\ kg\text{-}m^2$. Initially, the body is at rest. In order to produce a rotational kinetic energy of 1500 J, an angular acceleration of $25\ rad/s^2$ must be applied about that axis for a duration of *[AIPMT 1990]*
(a) 4 s (b) 2 s
(c) 8 s (d) 10 s

30 At any instant, a rolling body may be considered to be in pure rotation about an axis through the point of contact. This axis is translating forward with speed
[NCERT (Old) Pg. 174, AIPMT 1989]
(a) equal to centre of mass
(b) zero
(c) twice of centre of mass
(d) None of the above

31 A solid cylinder of mass M and radius R rolls down an inclined plane of height h without slipping. The speed of its centre of mass when it reaches the bottom is *[NCERT (Old) Pg. 174, AIPMT 1989]*
(a) $\sqrt{2gh}$ (b) $\sqrt{\frac{4gh}{3}}$
(c) $\sqrt{\frac{3gh}{4}}$ (d) $\sqrt{\frac{4g}{h}}$

32 A ring of mass m and radius r rotates about an axis passing through its centre and perpendicular to its plane with angular velocity ω. Its kinetic energy is
[NCERT (Old) Pg. 174, AIPMT 1988]
(a) $\frac{1}{2}mr^2\omega^2$ (b) $mr\omega^2$
(c) $mr^2\omega^2$ (d) $\frac{1}{3}mr^2\omega^2$

Key Index

Topic 1

1 (a)	2 (c)	3 (b)	4 (d)	5 (c)	6 (a)	7 (a)	8 (b)	9 (b)	10 (b)
11 (b)	12 (d)	13 (d)	14 (c)	15 (a)					

Topic 2

1 (d)	2 (b)	3 (d)	4 (d)	5 (a)	6 (c)	7 (c)	8 (c)	9 (d)

Topic 3

1 (a)	2 (*)	3 (a)	4 (a)	5 (a)	6 (a)	7 (d)	8 (a)	9 (a)	10 (b)
11 (b)	12 (d)	13 (c)	14 (c)	15 (a)	16 (b)	17 (d)	18 (b)	19 (d)	

Topic 4

1 (a)	2 (a)	3 (c)	4 (a)	5 (a)	6 (d)	7 (b)	8 (c)	9 (d)	10 (d)
11 (b)	12 (c)	13 (b)							

Topic 5

1 (b)	2 (d)	3 (c)	4 (a)	5 (c)	6 (d)	7 (b)	8 (c)	9 (d)	10 (b)
11 (b)	12 (a)	13 (a)	14 (a)	15 (b)					

Topic 6

1 (d)	2 (d)	3 (d)	4 (c)	5 (b)	6 (b)	7 (c)	8 (c)	9 (a)	10 (b)
11 (d)	12 (d)	13 (a)	14 (d)	15 (a)	16 (b)	17 (b)	18 (d)	19 (a)	20 (d)
21 (a)	22 (a)	23 (a)	24 (b)	25 (c)	26 (a)	27 (a)	28 (c)	29 (b)	30 (a)
31 (b)	32 (a)								

Detailed Explanations

Topic 1

01. *(a)* The given situation is shown below.

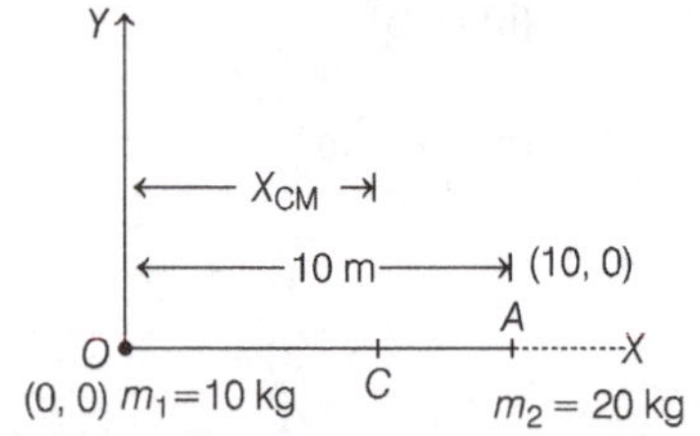

Let X_{CM} be the position of centre of mass from 10 kg mass.

$$\therefore X_{CM} = \frac{m_1x_1 + m_2x_2}{m_1 + m_2}$$

$$= \frac{10\times 0 + 20 \times 10}{10+20} = \frac{200}{30} = \frac{20}{3}\text{ m}$$

02. *(c)* The given situation is shown in the figure.

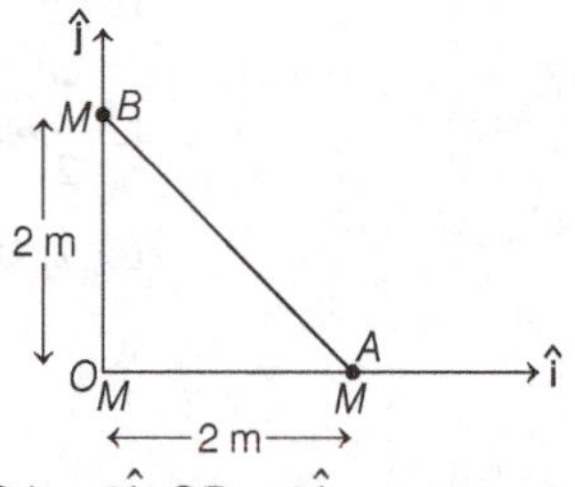

$OA = 2\hat{i}$, $OB = 2\hat{j}$

Position vector of centre of mass,

$$\mathbf{R}_{CM} = \frac{m_1\mathbf{r}_1 + m_2\mathbf{r}_2 + m_3\mathbf{r}_3}{m_1 + m_2 + m_3}$$

$$= \frac{M\,OA + M\,OB + M(0)}{M+M+M}$$

$$= \frac{M(2\hat{i}) + M(2\hat{j})}{3M}$$

$$= \frac{2M}{3M}(\hat{i}+\hat{j}) = \frac{2}{3}(\hat{i}+\hat{j})$$

03. *(b)* Given, $m_1 = 5$ kg, $m_2 = 10$ kg and $r = 1\text{ m} = 100$ cm

Let the centre of mass lies at origin O.

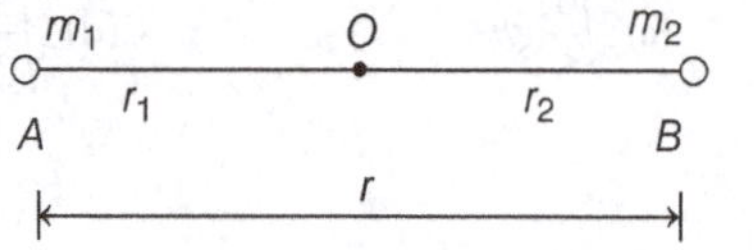

$$\therefore \frac{m_1r_1 + m_2r_2}{m_1+m_2} = 0$$

$$\Rightarrow -5r_1 + 10r_2 = 0$$

$$\Rightarrow r_2 = \frac{r_1}{2}$$

Also, $r_1 + r_2 = 100$

$$\Rightarrow r_1 + \frac{r_1}{2} = 100$$

$$\Rightarrow 3r_1 = 200$$

$$\Rightarrow r_1 = \frac{200}{3} \simeq 67\text{ cm}$$

04. *(d)* As we know that, mechanical advantage, $MA = \frac{\text{Load}}{\text{Effort}}$

If $MA > 1 \Rightarrow$ Load > Effort

Centre of mass may or may not coincide with centre of gravity.

Net torque of gravitational pull is zero about centre of mass.

$$\tau_g = \Sigma\tau_i = \Sigma r_i \times m_{ig} = 0$$

A couple produces rotational motion only. Hence, statements B and D are correct.

05. *(c)* Here on the entire system net external force on the system is zero hence centre of mass remains unchanged.

06. *(a)*

key idea

For rigid objects with uniform density, the centre of mass is located at the centroid.

$$CM_x = \frac{m_1x_1 + m_2x_2 + m_3x_3 \,.....}{m_1 + m_2 + m_3 \,.....}$$

$$CM_y = \frac{m_1y_1 + m_2y_2 + m_3y_3 \,....}{m_1 + m_2 + m_3 + ...}$$

Given, $m_1 = 300$ g, $m_2 = 500$ g

$m_3 = 400$ g, $x_2 = 40$ cm,

$x_3 = 70$ cm, $x_1 = 0$

The centre of mass will be given by

$$CM_x = \frac{m_1x_1 + m_2x_2 + m_3x_3}{m_1 + m_2 + m_3}$$

$$= \frac{300 \times 0 + 500 \times 40 + 400 \times 70}{300 + 500 + 400}$$

$$= \frac{48000}{1200} = 40 \text{ cm}$$

07. *(a)* Given, mass $m_1 = M$

Mass $m_2 = 1$ kg

As we know that,

$$v_{CM} = \frac{m_1v_1 + m_2v_2}{m_1 + m_2} = \frac{2M + 1}{M + 1}$$

Kinetic energy of centre of mass $= \frac{4}{3}$ J

i.e., $$\frac{4}{3} = \frac{1}{2}(M + 1)\left(\frac{2M + 1}{M + 1}\right)^2$$

$$\Rightarrow \quad M = 0.50 = \frac{1}{2} \text{ kg}$$

08. *(b)* As initially both the particles were at rest, therefore velocity of centre of mass was zero and there is no external force on the system so speed of centre of mass remains constant i.e., it should be equal to zero.

09. *(b)* The position vector of centre of mass

$$\mathbf{r} = \frac{m_1\mathbf{r}_1 + m_2\mathbf{r}_2}{m_1 + m_2}$$

$$= \frac{1(\hat{i} + 2\hat{j} + \hat{k}) + 3(-3\hat{i} - 2\hat{j} + \hat{k})}{1 + 3}$$

$$= \frac{1}{4}(-8\hat{i} - 4\hat{j} + 4\hat{k}) = -2\hat{i} - \hat{j} + \hat{k}$$

10. *(b)* The system of two given particles of masses m_1 and m_2 are shown in figure.

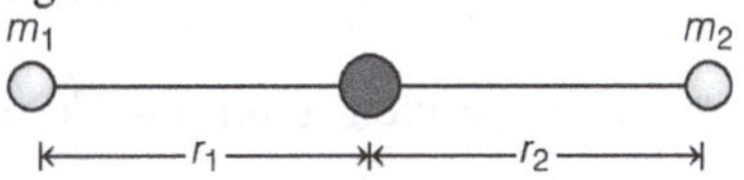

Initially, the centre of mass

$$r_{CM} = \frac{m_1r_1 + m_2r_2}{m_1 + m_2} \quad ...(i)$$

When mass m_1 moves towards centre of mass by a distance d, then let mass m_2 moves a distance d' away from CM to keep the CM in its initial position.

So, $$r_{CM} = \frac{m_1(r_1 - d) + m_2(r_2 + d')}{m_1 + m_2} \quad ...(ii)$$

Equating Eqs. (i) and (ii), we get

$$\frac{m_1r_1 + m_2r_2}{m_1 + m_2} = \frac{m_1(r_1 - d) + m_2(r_2 + d')}{m_1 + m_2}$$

$$\Rightarrow \quad -m_1d + m_2d' = 0$$

$$\Rightarrow \quad m_1d = m_2d'$$

$$d' = \frac{m_1}{m_2}d$$

Concept Enhancer

If both the masses are equal i.e., $m_1 = m_2$, then second mass will move a distance equal to the distance at which first mass is being displaced.

11. *(b)*

key idea

Assign a mass element dm and the

Use $x_{CG} = \frac{\int x\,dm}{\int dm}$

A rod lying along any of coordinate axes serves for us as continuous body. Suppose a rod of mass M and length L is lying along the X-axis with its one end at $x = 0$ and the other at $x = L$.

Mass per unit length of the rod $= \rho$

Therefore, $\rho \propto x$ or $\rho = kx$

where k is a constant.

Hence, the mass of the element PQ of length dx situated at x is $dm = kx\,dx$

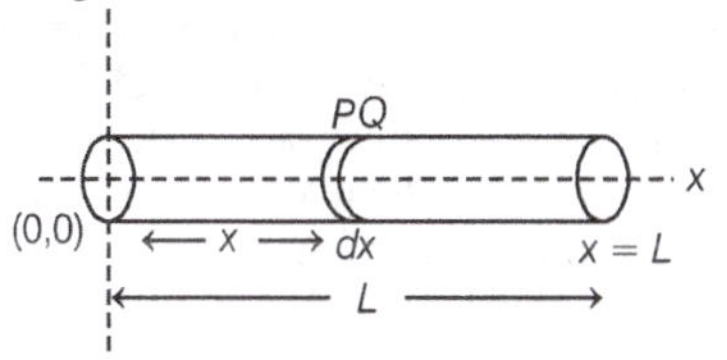

The coordinates of the element PQ are $(x, 0, 0)$. Therefore, x-coordinate of centre of gravity of the rod will be

$$x_{CG} = \frac{\int x\,dm}{\int dm} = \frac{\int_0^3 x(kx)\,dx}{\int_0^3 kx\,dx}$$

$$= \frac{\int_0^3 x^2\,dx}{\int_0^3 x\,dx} = \frac{\left[\frac{x^3}{3}\right]_0^3}{\left[\frac{x^2}{2}\right]_0^3}$$

$$= \frac{\frac{27}{3}}{\frac{9}{2}} = 2 \text{ m}$$

The y-coordinate of centre of gravity

$$y_{CG} = \frac{\int y\,dm}{\int dm} = 0 \, (\text{as } y = 0)$$

Similarly, $z_{CG} = 0$

i.e., the coordinates of centre of gravity of the rod are $(2, 0, 0)$ or it lies at the distance 2 m from one end.

12. *(d)* The linear acceleration of centre of mass will be $a = \frac{F}{m}$, wherever the force is applied. Hence, the acceleration will be same whatever the value of h may be.

13. *(d)* The whole mass of the ball will be concentrated at the centre of the ball. All the three balls are identical, i.e., the balls have same mass i.e., on each vertex of equilateral ΔPQR, same mass is kept.

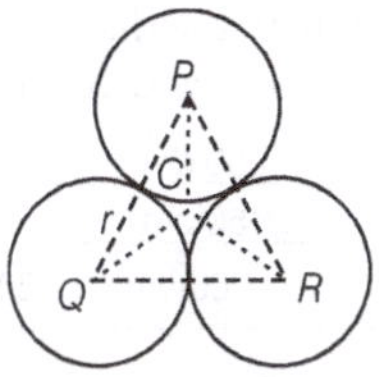

Therefore, centre of mass of the triangle is the centre of mass of the system which is point of intersection of the medians of the triangle.

14. *(c)* If the man pulls the cart by the rope, the force exerted on cart is in same direction and from Newton's third law, the opposite force will act on man due to cart. So, net external force will be zero, therefore net acceleration would be zero. The man and cart will meet at the centre of mass.

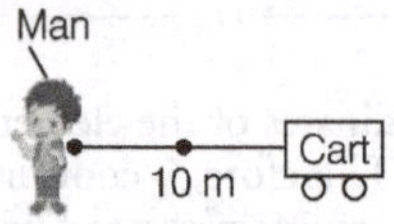

$$\therefore \quad x_{CM} = \frac{m_1x_1 + m_2x_2}{m_1 + m_2}$$

Taking axis at the point, where man is present

$$= \frac{M\times 0 + M\times 10}{M+M} \quad \begin{bmatrix} x_1 = 0, x_2 = 10 \\ m_1 = m_2 = M \end{bmatrix}$$

$$= \frac{10M}{2M} = 5\text{ m}$$

15. *(a)*

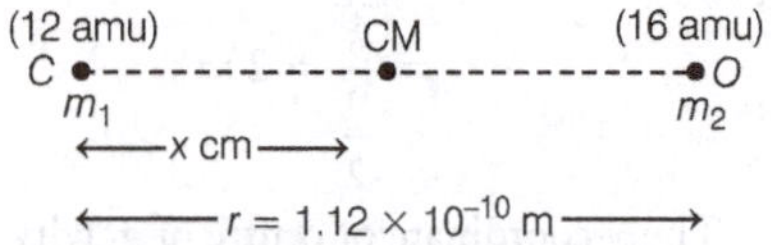

From definition of centre of mass

$$x_{CM} = \frac{m_1x_1 + m_2x_2}{m_1 + m_2}$$

$$= \frac{(12\text{ amu})\times 0 + (16\text{ amu})\times r}{12\text{ amu} + 16\text{ amu}}$$

$$= \frac{16}{28}r = \frac{16}{28}\times 1.12\times 10^{-10}\text{ m}$$

$$= 0.64\times 10^{-10}\text{ m}$$

Alternate Solution

Taking the position of C-atom to be origin.
Position of centre of mass

$$= \frac{12\times 16}{12+16} = \frac{12\times 16}{28} \simeq 0.64\text{ Å}$$

$$\simeq 0.64\times 10^{-10}\text{ m}$$

Topic 2

01. *(d)* Let's draw the diagram of the uniform rod suspended with mass.

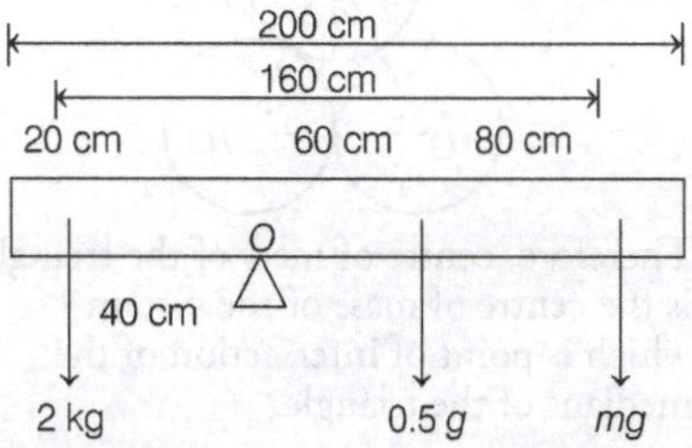

As we know in equilibrium net moment of force about the wedge is equals to zero.

$$\Rightarrow 0.5\,g\,(0.60) + mg\,(1.20) - 2g\,(0.20) = 0$$

$$\Rightarrow 0.3 + 1.20m - 0.4 = 0$$

$$\Rightarrow 1.20\text{ m} = 0.1 \Rightarrow m = \frac{1}{12}\text{ kg}$$

Alternate Solution

By balancing the torque

$$2g\times 20 = 0.5g\times 60 + mg\times 120$$

$$\Rightarrow \quad m = \frac{0.5}{6}\text{ kg} = \frac{1}{12}\text{ kg}$$

02. *(b)* Given, position vector, $\mathbf{r} = 2\hat{k}$ m

Force, $\mathbf{F} = 3\hat{j}$ N

As, torque, $\boldsymbol{\tau} = \mathbf{r}\times\mathbf{F} = 2\hat{k}\times 3\hat{j} = 6(-\hat{i})$

$$= -6\hat{i}\text{ N-m}$$

03. *(d)* Given, $\mathbf{F} = 4\hat{i} + 5\hat{j} - 6\hat{k}$ N

$$\mathbf{r}_1 = 2\hat{i} + 0\hat{j} - 3\hat{k}$$

$$\mathbf{r}_2 = 2\hat{i} - 2\hat{j} - 2\hat{k}$$

Moment of force, $\boldsymbol{\tau} = \mathbf{r}\times\mathbf{F}$

$$= (\mathbf{r}_1 - \mathbf{r}_2)\times\mathbf{F}$$

$$= [-(2\hat{i} - 2\hat{j} - 2\hat{k}) + (2\hat{i} + 0\hat{j} - 3\hat{k})] \times [4\hat{i} + 5\hat{j} - 6\hat{k}]$$

$$= [0\hat{i} + 2\hat{j} - 1\hat{k}]\times[4\hat{i} + 5\hat{j} - 6\hat{k}]$$

$$= \begin{vmatrix} \hat{i} & \hat{j} & \hat{k} \\ 0 & 2 & -1 \\ 4 & 5 & -6 \end{vmatrix} = \hat{i}[(-6\times 2) - (-1\times 5)] - \hat{j}[(-6\times 0) - (-1\times 4)] + \hat{k}[(0\times 5) - 2\times 4]$$

$$= -7\hat{i} - 4\hat{j} - 8\hat{k}$$

04. *(d)* As the weight w balances the normal reactions.

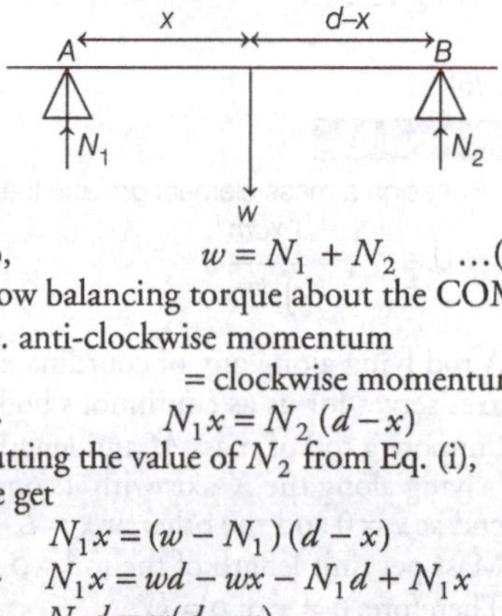

So, $\quad w = N_1 + N_2 \quad$ ...(i)

Now balancing torque about the COM, i.e. anti-clockwise momentum = clockwise momentum

$$\Rightarrow \quad N_1x = N_2(d - x)$$

Putting the value of N_2 from Eq. (i), we get

$$N_1x = (w - N_1)(d - x)$$

$$\Rightarrow N_1x = wd - wx - N_1d + N_1x$$

$$\Rightarrow N_1d = w(d - x)$$

$$\Rightarrow \quad N_1 = \frac{w(d-x)}{d}$$

05. *(a)* If we take clockwise torque

$$\tau_{net} = \tau_{F_1} + \tau_{F_2} + \tau_{F_3}$$

$$0 = F_1r + F_2r - F_3r$$

$$\Rightarrow \quad F_3 = F_1 + F_2$$

• Concept Enhancer

In the direction of clockwise, the torque is taken negative and anti-clockwise direction it taken as positive torque.

06. *(c)* $\boldsymbol{\tau} = \mathbf{r}\times\mathbf{F}$, where $\mathbf{r}$ = position vector

$\mathbf{F}$ = force

$\Rightarrow \boldsymbol{\tau} = |\mathbf{r}|\cdot|\mathbf{F}|\sin\theta$

Torque is perpendicular to both **r** and **F**. So, dot product of two vectors will be zero.

$$\boldsymbol{\tau}\cdot\mathbf{r} = 0 \Rightarrow \mathbf{F}\cdot\boldsymbol{\tau} = 0$$

07. *(c)*

key idea

For a body to be in equilibrium. Net torque about its centre of mass must be zero.

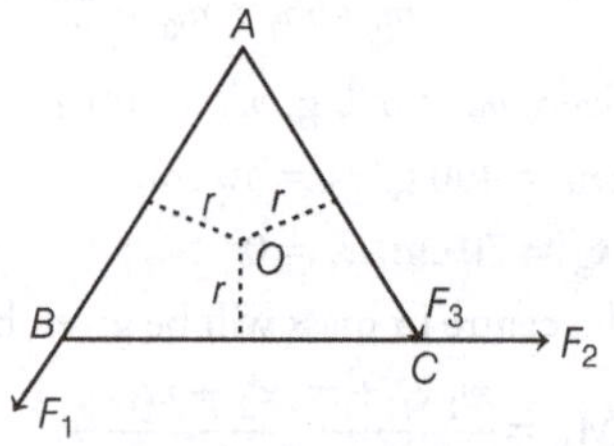

The torque of force F_3 about O is clockwise, while torque due to F_1 and F_2 are anticlockwise. For total torque to be zero about O, we must have

$$F_1r + F_2r - F_3r = 0$$

$$\Rightarrow \quad F_3 = F_1 + F_2$$

08. *(c)* A couple consists of two equal and opposite forces acting at a separation, so that net force becomes zero. When a couple acts on a body it rotates the body but does not produce any translatory motion. Hence, only rotational motion is produced.

• Concept Enhancer

Couple can only produce rotation. It cannot produce any translatory motion because forces are equal in magnitude and opposite in direction and hence, the net force acting on the object is zero. The net force is vector sum of all the forces acting on an object. Object will not experience any acceleration and will remain at rest or in uniform motion.

09. *(d)* Given,

$$\mathbf{r} = 7\hat{\mathbf{i}} + 3\hat{\mathbf{j}} + \hat{\mathbf{k}}$$

$$\mathbf{F} = -3\hat{\mathbf{i}} + \hat{\mathbf{j}} + 5\hat{\mathbf{k}}$$

$$\therefore \quad \tau = \mathbf{r} \times \mathbf{F}$$

$$= |\mathbf{r}||\mathbf{F}| \sin \theta$$

where, θ is the angle between $\mathbf{r}$ and $\mathbf{F}$

$$= (7\hat{\mathbf{i}} + 3\hat{\mathbf{j}} + \hat{\mathbf{k}}) \times (-3\hat{\mathbf{i}} + \hat{\mathbf{j}} + 5\hat{\mathbf{k}})$$

$$= \begin{vmatrix} \hat{\mathbf{i}} & \hat{\mathbf{j}} & \hat{\mathbf{k}} \\ 7 & 3 & 1 \\ -3 & 1 & 5 \end{vmatrix}$$

$$= \hat{\mathbf{i}}(15-1) - \hat{\mathbf{j}}(35+3) + \hat{\mathbf{k}}(7+9)$$

$$= 14\hat{\mathbf{i}} - 38\hat{\mathbf{j}} + 16\hat{\mathbf{k}}$$

Alternate Solution

$$\therefore \tau = \mathbf{r} \times \mathbf{F} = (7\hat{\mathbf{i}} + 3\hat{\mathbf{j}} + \hat{\mathbf{k}}) \times (-3\hat{\mathbf{i}} + \hat{\mathbf{j}} + 5\hat{\mathbf{k}})$$

$$= -21(\hat{\mathbf{i}} \times \hat{\mathbf{i}}) + 7(\hat{\mathbf{i}} \times \hat{\mathbf{j}}) + 35(\hat{\mathbf{i}} \times \hat{\mathbf{k}})$$

$$-9(\hat{\mathbf{j}} \times \hat{\mathbf{i}}) + 3(\hat{\mathbf{j}} \times \hat{\mathbf{j}}) + 15(\hat{\mathbf{j}} \times \hat{\mathbf{k}})$$

$$-3(\hat{\mathbf{k}} \times \hat{\mathbf{i}}) + (\hat{\mathbf{k}} \times \hat{\mathbf{j}}) + 5(\hat{\mathbf{k}} \times \hat{\mathbf{k}})$$

$$= 0 + 7\hat{\mathbf{k}} - 35\hat{\mathbf{j}} + 9\hat{\mathbf{k}} + 0 + 15\hat{\mathbf{i}} - 3\hat{\mathbf{j}} - \hat{\mathbf{i}} + 0$$

$$= 14\hat{\mathbf{i}} - 38\hat{\mathbf{j}} + 16\hat{\mathbf{k}}$$

Topic 3

01. *(a)* Given, moment of inertia

$$I = 2400 \text{ g cm}^2$$

mass of rod, $m = 400$ g

We know that moment of inertia of a thin rod,

$$I = \frac{ml^2}{12}$$

$$\Rightarrow \quad \frac{12 \times I}{m} = l^2 \Rightarrow l^2 = \frac{12 \times 2400}{400}$$

$$\Rightarrow \quad l^2 = 12 \times 6$$

$$\Rightarrow \quad l = \sqrt{72} = 8.48 \simeq 8.5 \text{ cm}$$

02. *(*)* Radius of gyration of solid sphere and hollow sphere are K_1 and K_2 respectively, then

$$MK_1^2 = \frac{2}{5} MR^2$$

$$\Rightarrow \quad K_1 = \sqrt{\frac{2}{5}} R$$

and $MK_2^2 = \frac{2}{3} MR^2 \Rightarrow K_2 = \sqrt{\frac{2}{3}} R$

$$\therefore \quad \frac{K_1}{K_2} = \frac{\sqrt{2/5}R}{\sqrt{2/3}R} = \sqrt{\frac{3}{5}}$$

No option is match.

03. *(a)* Radius of gyration of a body is given as

$$K = \sqrt{\frac{I}{m}}$$

where, I is moment of inertia and m is mass of body.

$$\therefore \quad \frac{K_1}{K_2} = \sqrt{\frac{I_1}{I_2}} \quad \ldots \text{(i)}$$

I_1 = Moment of inertia of thin uniform disc about an axis passing through its centre and normal to plane.

$$= \frac{MR^2}{2} \quad \left(\begin{array}{l}\text{where, } R = \text{radius of disc} \\ \text{and } M = \text{mass of disc}\end{array}\right)$$

I_2 = Moment of inertia of disc about its diameter.

$$= \frac{MR^2}{4}$$

$\therefore$ From Eq. (i),

$$\frac{K_1}{K_2} = \sqrt{\frac{MR^2/2}{MR^2/4}} = \sqrt{2}$$

$$\therefore \quad K_1 : K_2 = \sqrt{2} : 1$$

• Concept Enhancer

The radius of gyration is defined as the square root of the ratio of moment of inertia and mass and it is written as

$$K = \sqrt{\frac{I}{m}}$$

where I is moment of inertia and m is the mass of the body.

04. *(a)* An arc corresponding to a 90° sector in the circular ring is removed, means one-fourth part of circular ring is removed. Then, the mass of the removed circular ring,

$$M' = \frac{M}{4}$$

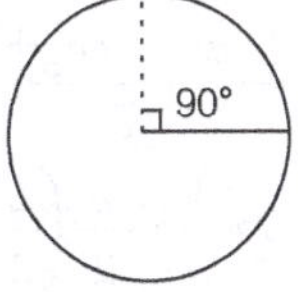

Now, the moment of inertia of the remaining part,

$$I'' = I - I' = MR^2 - \frac{MR^2}{4}$$

$$\Rightarrow \quad I'' = \frac{3MR^2}{4}$$

Comparing with $I'' = KMR^2$

The value of $K = 3/4$

05. *(a)* Considering the information given in the question, let us draw the figure

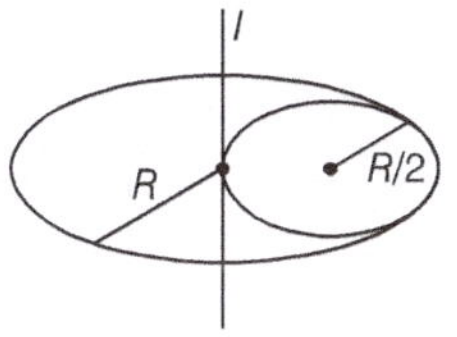

If the above figure is considered, then moment of inertia of disc will be given as

$$I = I_{\text{remain}} + I_{(R/2)}$$

$$\Rightarrow I_{\text{remain}} = I - I_{(R/2)}$$

Putting the values, we get

$$= \frac{MR^2}{2} - \left[\frac{\frac{M}{4}\left(\frac{R}{2}\right)^2}{2} + \frac{M}{4}\left(\frac{R}{2}\right)^2\right]$$

$$= \frac{MR^2}{2} - \left[\frac{MR^2}{32} + \frac{MR^2}{16}\right]$$

$$= \frac{MR^2}{2} - \left[\frac{MR^2 + 2MR^2}{32}\right]$$

$$= \frac{MR^2}{2} - \frac{3MR^2}{32}$$

$$= \frac{16MR^2 - 3MR^2}{32}$$

$$I_{\text{remain}} = \frac{13MR^2}{32}$$

06. *(a)* COM of m_1 and m_2 masses lies at

$$r = \frac{m_1 r_1 + m_2 r_2}{m_1 + m_2}$$

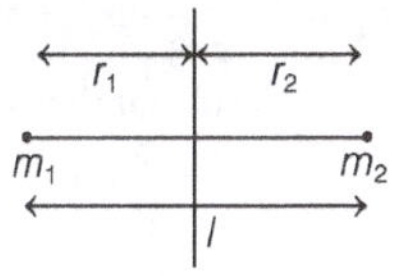

$\therefore$ Moment of inertia of the point masses about the given axis is

$$I = \Sigma m_i r_i^2$$

$$\Rightarrow I = m_1 r_1^2 + m_2 r_2^2$$

$$= m_1 \left(\frac{m_2 l}{m_1 + m_2}\right)^2 + m_2 \left(\frac{m_1 l}{m_1 + m_2}\right)^2$$

$$= \frac{m_1 m_2 l^2}{(m_1 + m_2)^2}(m_2 + m_1)$$

$$= \frac{m_1 m_2 l^2}{(m_1 + m_2)}$$

Alternate Solution

Here $l_1 + l_2 = l$

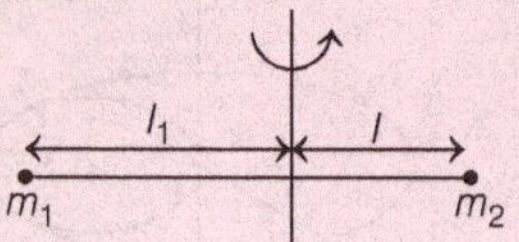

COM of the system,

$$l_1 = \frac{m_1 \times 0 + m_2 \times l}{m_1 + m_2} = \frac{m_2 l}{m_1 + m_2}$$

$$l_2 = l - l_1 = \frac{m_1 l}{m_1 + m_2}$$

Required moment of inertia of the system,

$$I = m_1 l_1^2 + m_2 l_2^2$$

$$= (m_1 m_2^2 + m_2 m_1^2)\frac{l^2}{(m_1 + m_2)^2}$$

$$= \frac{(m_1 m_2)(m_1 + m_2) l^2}{(m_1 + m_2)^2} = \frac{m_1 m_2}{m_1 + m_2} l^2$$

07. *(d)* The total moment of inertia of the system is

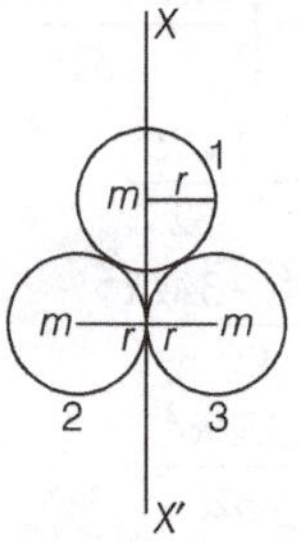

$$I = I_1 + I_2 + I_3 \quad \ldots \text{(i)}$$

Here, $I_1 = \frac{2}{3} mr^2$

$$I_2 = I_3 = \frac{2}{3} mr^2 + mr^2$$

[From parallel axis theorem]

$$= \frac{5}{3} mr^2$$

From Eq. (i), $I = \frac{2}{3} mr^2 + 2 \times \frac{5}{3} mr^2$

$$= mr^2 \left(\frac{2}{3} + \frac{10}{3}\right)$$

$$I = 4mr^2$$

08. *(a)*

key idea

Apply parallel axis theorem of moment of inertia.

i.e., Moment of inertia about an axis distance n from the COM is given by $I = I_{COM} + Mr^2$

According to parallel axes theorem of moment of inertia,

$$I = I_{CM} + MR^2$$

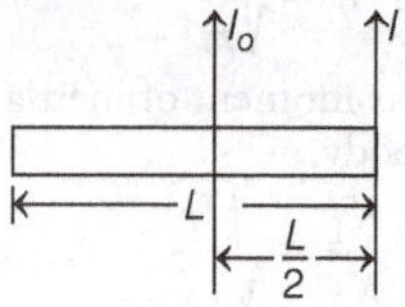

So, $I = I_0 + M\left(\frac{L}{2}\right)^2 \Rightarrow I = I_0 + \frac{ML^2}{4}$

09. *(a)* Moment of inertia of rod about an axis through its centre of mass and perpendicular to rod

$$= \frac{Ml^2}{12}$$

Using parallel axis theorem, moment of inertia of each rod about an axis through the centre of the square and perpendicular to its plane.

$$= \frac{Ml^2}{12} + M\left(\frac{l}{2}\right)^2 = \frac{Ml^2}{3}$$

Moment of inertia of the system

$$I = 4I' = \frac{Ml^2}{3} \times 4 = \frac{4}{3} Ml^2$$

10. *(b)* As the rod is bent into two equal halves, the mass and length of each half is $\frac{M}{2}$ and $\frac{L}{2}$, respectively.

The moment of inertia about an axis passing through its edge and perpendicular to the rod.

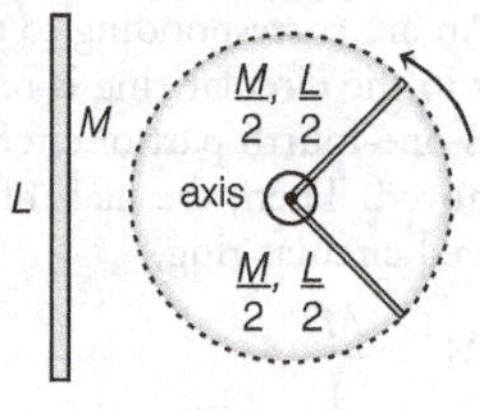

$$\text{Total MI} = \frac{\text{Mass} \times (\text{length})^2}{3}$$

$$\therefore \quad I = 2 \times \frac{1}{3} \times \frac{M}{2}\left(\frac{L}{2}\right)^2 = \frac{ML^2}{12}$$

11. *(b)* As we know that radius of gyration,

$$K = \sqrt{\frac{I}{m}}$$

So, for two different cases

$$\frac{K_{\text{ring}}}{K_{\text{disc}}} = \sqrt{\frac{I_{\text{ring}}}{I_{\text{disc}}}} = \sqrt{\frac{MR^2}{\frac{1}{2}MR^2}}$$

$$\therefore \quad \frac{K_{\text{ring}}}{K_{\text{disc}}} = \sqrt{2}$$

$$\Rightarrow \quad \frac{K_{\text{disc}}}{K_{\text{ring}}} = \frac{1}{\sqrt{2}}$$

• Concept Enhancer

The radius of gyration K of a body about an axis is the effective distance from the axis where the whole mass can be assumed to be concentrated keeping the moment of inertia same

$$I = MK^2$$

12. *(d)* $I_{AB} = \frac{1}{2} MR^2$

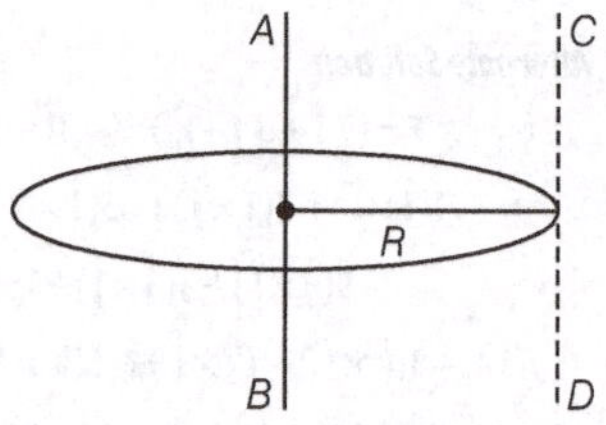

Using theorem of parallel axes, we have,

$$I_{CD} = I_{AB} + MR^2$$

$$= \frac{1}{2} MR^2 + MR^2$$

$$= \frac{3}{2} MR^2$$

13. *(c)* Moment of inertia of the system about AX is given by

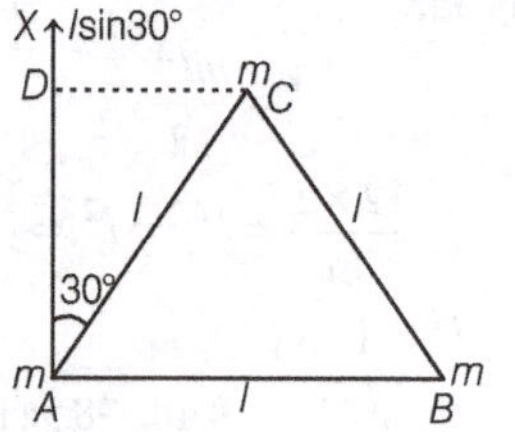

Moment of inertia

$$= m_A r_A^2 + m_B r_B^2 + m_C r_C^2$$

Perpendicular distance of mass $r_A = 0$ at A from axis AX perpendicular distance of mass $r_B = l$ at B from axis AX.

Perpendicular distance of mass at C from axis AX.

Moment of inertia

$$= m(0)^2 + m(l)^2 + m(l \sin 30°)^2$$

$$= ml^2 + \frac{ml^2}{4} = \frac{5}{4} ml^2$$

Alternate Solution

Moment of inertia of a system about a line OC perpendicular to AB in the plane of ABC is

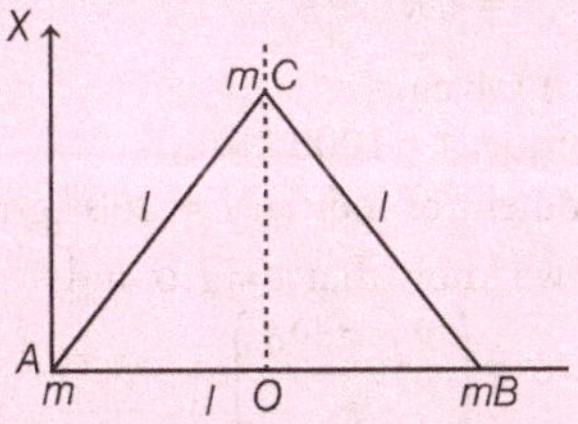

$$I_{CO} = m \times 0 + m \times \left(\frac{l}{2}\right)^2 + m \times \left(\frac{l}{2}\right)^2$$

$$\therefore \quad I_{CO} = \frac{ml^2}{4} + \frac{ml^2}{4} = \frac{ml^2}{2}$$

Now, by applying parallel axes theorem

$$I_{AX} = I_{CO} + Mx^2$$

where, x = distance of AX from CO

M = total mass of system

$$I_{AX} = \frac{ml^2}{2} + 3m \times \left(\frac{l}{2}\right)^2 = \frac{ml^2}{2} + \frac{3ml^2}{4} = \frac{5}{4}ml^2$$

14. *(c)* Moment of inertia of disc about tangential axis

$$I_d = \frac{5}{4} M_d R^2$$

Moment of inertia of ring about a tangential axis

$$I_r = \frac{3}{2} M_r R^2$$

but $\quad I = MK^2 \Rightarrow K = \sqrt{\frac{I}{M}}$

$$\therefore \quad \frac{K_d}{K_r} = \sqrt{\frac{I_d}{I_r} \times \frac{M_r}{M_d}}$$

or $\quad \frac{K_d}{K_r} = \sqrt{\frac{(5/4) M_d R^2}{(3/2) M_r R^2} \times \frac{M_r}{M_d}} = \sqrt{\frac{5}{6}}$

$$\therefore \quad K_d : K_r = \sqrt{5} : \sqrt{6}$$

15. *(a)* Moment of inertia depends on distribution of mass and about axis of rotation. Density of iron is more than that of aluminium, therefore for moment of inertia to be maximum, the iron should be far away from the axis. Thus, aluminium should be at interior and iron surrounds it.

16. *(b)* For a given body, mass is same, so it will depend only on the distribution of mass from the axis.

The mass is farthest from axis BC, so I_2 is maximum. Mass is nearest to axis AC, so I_3 is minimum.

Hence, the correct sequence will be

$$I_2 > I_1 > I_3$$

• Concept Enhancer

In a rotational motion, moment of inertia is also known as rotational inertia.

17. *(d)* Moment of inertia of a disc about its diameter is

$$I_d = \frac{1}{4} MR^2$$

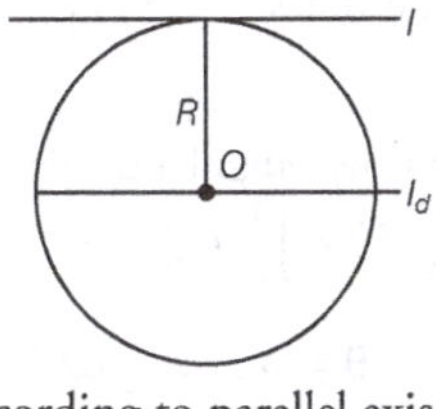

Now, according to parallel axis theorem, moment of inertia of disc about a tangent passing through rim and in the plane of disc is

$$I = I_d + MR^2$$

$$= \frac{1}{4} MR^2 + MR^2 = \frac{5}{4} MR^2$$

18. *(b)*

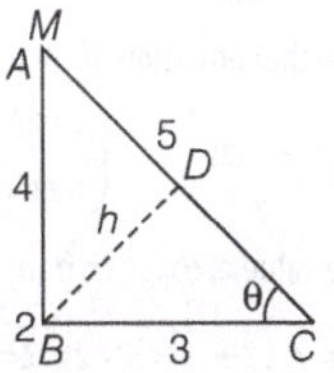

Moment of inertia of the triangular plate is maximum about the shortest side because effective distance of mass distribution about this side is maximum. Since, distances of centre of mass from the sides are related as

$$x_{BC} < x_{AB} < x_{AC}$$

Therefore, $I_{BC} > I_{AB} > I_{AC}$

or $\quad I_{BC} > I_{AC}$

19. *(d)*

key idea

The magnitude of moment of inertia depends on the distribution of mass taken from the axis.

From the axis EG, the distribution of masses is at minimum distance while from the axis BD the distribution of masses is at maximum distance. Hence, the moment of inertia is minimum along axis through EG.

Topic 4

01. *(a)* Given, initial angular velocity of fly wheel,

$$\omega_0 = 2\pi \text{ rad} \times 1200 \text{ rpm}$$

$$= 2\pi \text{ rad} \times \frac{1200}{60} \text{ rps} = 40\pi \text{ rad/s}$$

Similarly, final angular velocity of fly wheel,

$$\omega = 2\pi \text{ rad} \times 3120 \text{ rpm}$$

$$= 2\pi \text{ rad} \times \frac{3120}{60} \text{ rps} = 104\pi \text{ rad/s}$$

Time, $t = 16$ s

If α be the angular acceleration, then using the equation of rotational motion,

$$\omega = \omega_0 + \alpha t$$

$$\Rightarrow \quad 104\pi = 40\pi + \alpha \times 16$$

$$\Rightarrow \quad \alpha = \frac{104\pi - 40\pi}{16} = \frac{64\pi}{16}$$

$$= 4\pi \text{ rad/s}^2$$

02. *(a)* Initial angular speed of wheel,

$$\omega_0 = 2\pi f_0 = 2\pi \times \frac{360}{60} = 12\pi \text{ rad/s}$$

Final angular speed of wheel,

$$\omega = 2\pi f = 2\pi \times \frac{1200}{60} \text{ rad/s}$$

$$= 40\pi \text{ rad/s}$$

$$t = 14 \text{ s}$$

From the equation of rotational motion,

$$\omega = \omega_0 + \alpha t$$

$$\Rightarrow \alpha = \frac{\omega - \omega_0}{t} = \frac{40\pi - 12\pi}{14} = \frac{28\pi}{14}$$

$$= 2\pi \text{ rad/s}^2$$

03. *(c)* From third equation of motion for circular motion

$$\omega^2 - \omega_0^2 = 2\alpha\theta$$

$$\Rightarrow \quad \left(\frac{v_0}{r}\right)^2 - 0 = 2\alpha(2\pi n)$$

$$\Rightarrow \quad \alpha = \frac{v_0^2}{4\pi n r^2} \text{ rad/s}^2$$

04. *(a)*

key idea

The acceleration of particle moving in a circle has two components, tangential acceleration a_t which is along the tangent and radial acceleration (a_r) which is towards the centre of the circle. As the two components are mutually perpendicular therefore, net acceleration of the particle will be $a = \sqrt{a_t^2 + a_r^2}$.

Given, Radius of disc,
$R = 50 \text{ cm} = 0.5 \text{ m}$
Angular acceleration,
$\alpha = 2.0 \text{ rad s}^{-2}$, time $t = 2$ s
Let particle be at periphery and have both tangential and radial acceleration.
Angular speed, $\omega = \omega_0 + \alpha t$
$\omega = 0 + 2 \times 2 = 4$ rad/s
Centripetal accelration,
$a_c = \omega^2 R = (4)^2 \times 0.5$
$= 16 \times 0.5 = 8 \text{ m/s}^2$
Linear acceleration,
$a_t = \alpha . R = 0.5 \times 2 = 1 \text{ m/s}^2$
Net accelration,
$a_{\text{total}} = \sqrt{a_t^2 + a_c^2}$
$= \sqrt{1^2 + 8^2} \approx 8 \text{ m/s}^2$

05. *(a)* As velocity of an automobile vehicle,
$v = 54$ km/h
$= 54 \times \dfrac{5}{18} = 15$ m/s
Angular velocity of a vehicle,
$v = \omega_0 r$
$\Rightarrow \omega_0 = \dfrac{v}{R} = \dfrac{15}{0.45} = \dfrac{100}{3}$ rad/s
So, angular acceleration of an automobile,
$$\alpha = \frac{\Delta\omega}{t} = \frac{\omega_f - \omega_0}{t} = \frac{0 - \frac{100}{3}}{15}$$
$= \dfrac{-100}{45} \text{ rad/s}^2$
–ve sign represents retardation.
Thus, average torque transmitted by its brakes to wheel
$\tau = I\alpha$
$\Rightarrow \tau = 3 \times \dfrac{100}{45} = 6.66 \text{ kgm}^2\text{s}^{-2}$

06. *(d)* According to question, torque $\tau = 0$
It means that, $\alpha = 0$
$\alpha = \dfrac{d^2\theta}{dt^2}$
Given, $\theta(t) = 2t^3 - 6t^2$
So, $\dfrac{d\theta}{dt} = 6t^2 - 12t$
$\alpha = \dfrac{d^2\theta}{dt^2} = 12t - 12$
$12t - 12 = 0$
$\Rightarrow t = 1$ s

07. *(b)* By definition $\alpha = \dfrac{d\omega}{dt}$
i.e. $d\omega = \alpha \, dt$
So, if in time t the angular speed of a body changes from ω_0 to ω
$$\int_{\omega_0}^{\omega} d\omega = \int_0^t \alpha \, dt$$
If α is constant
$\omega - \omega_0 = \alpha t$
or $\omega = \omega_0 + \alpha t$ ...(i)
Now, as by definition $\omega = \dfrac{d\theta}{dt}$
Eq. (i) becomes $\dfrac{d\theta}{dt} = \omega_0 + \alpha t$
i.e. $d\theta = (\omega_0 + \alpha t)\, dt$
So, if in time t angular displacement is θ.
$$\int_0^{\theta} d\theta = \int_0^1 (\omega_0 + \alpha t)\, dt$$
or $\theta = \omega_0 t + \dfrac{1}{2}\alpha t^2$ ...(ii)
Given $\alpha = 3 \text{ rad/s}^2$
$\omega_0 = 2$ rad/s, $t = 2$ s
Here $\theta = 2 \times 2 + \dfrac{1}{2} \times 3 \times (2)^2$
or $\theta = 4 + 6 = 10$ rad

Alternate Solution
As we know that equation of circular motion
$\theta = \omega_0 t + \dfrac{1}{2}\alpha t^2$ (where symbols have their usual meaning)
Putting the value of ω_0, t, α from question.
So, $\theta = 2 \times 2 + \dfrac{1}{2} \times 3 \times 2 \times 2 = 10$ rad

08. *(c)* Given, moment of inertia,
$I = 2 \text{ kg-m}^2$
angular speed, $\omega = 60$ rpm
We know that,
$\omega_f = \omega_i - \alpha t \Rightarrow 0 = \omega_i - \alpha t$
$\therefore \alpha = \omega_i / t,$
where α is retardation.
The torque on the wheel is given by
$\tau = I\alpha = \dfrac{I\omega}{t} = \dfrac{I . 2\pi\upsilon}{t}$
$= \dfrac{2 \times 2 \times \pi \times 60}{60 \times 60} = \dfrac{\pi}{15}$ N-m

09. *(d)* Given, radius of wheel, $r = 1$ m
Linear distance covered by wheel in half revolution $= \pi r$.

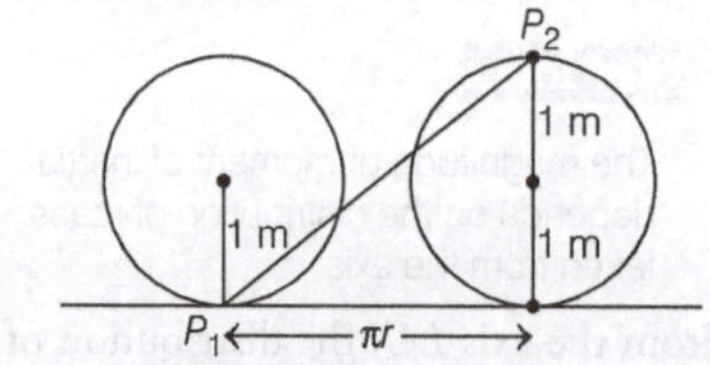

Point P_1 after half revolution reaches at P_2 vertically 2 m above the ground.
$\therefore$ Displacement P_1P_2
$= \sqrt{\pi^2 r^2 + 2^2}$
$= \sqrt{\pi^2 + 4}$ $[\because r = 1 \text{ m}]$

10. *(d)* Given,
Torque, $\tau = 1000$ N-m,
Moment of inertia, $I = 200 \text{ kg-m}^2$
As we know that $\tau = I . \alpha$ and
$\alpha = \left(\dfrac{\omega_f - \omega_0}{t}\right)$
$\Rightarrow \alpha = \dfrac{1000}{200} = 5 \text{ rad/s}^2$
$\omega_f = \omega_0 + \alpha t = 0 + 3 \times 5 = 15$ rad/s

11. *(b)* Given, $\mathbf{r} = 3\hat{i} - 4\hat{j} + \hat{k}$
$\omega = 5\hat{i} - 6\hat{j} + 6\hat{k}$
$$\mathbf{v} = \omega \times \mathbf{r} = \begin{vmatrix} \hat{i} & \hat{j} & \hat{k} \\ 5 & -6 & 6 \\ 3 & -4 & 1 \end{vmatrix}$$
$= 18\hat{i} + 13\hat{j} - 2\hat{k}$

12. *(c)* Angular velocity, $\omega = 2\pi\nu$
Here, $\nu = 120$ rev/min
$\therefore \omega = \dfrac{2\pi \times 120}{60}$
$= 4\pi$ rad/s

13. *(b)* Angular velocity,
$\therefore \omega = \dfrac{\theta}{t} = \dfrac{2\pi}{T} = 2\pi\nu$ $\left(\because T = \dfrac{1}{\nu}\right)$
Number of revolutions made by the engine wheel $(\nu) = 90$/min
$\therefore$ Angular velocity of the engine wheel,
$\omega = \dfrac{2\pi\nu}{60} = \dfrac{2\pi \times 90}{60}$
$= 3\pi$ rad/s

Topic 5

01. *(b)* The tension in the string will be equal to centripetal force is,
$F_c = \dfrac{mv^2}{r} = m\omega^2 r$
According to question, $T = m\omega^2 r$
and $T' = m(2\omega)^2 r$
$\dfrac{T'}{T} = \dfrac{m(4\omega^2)r}{m\omega^2 r}$
$\Rightarrow T' = 4T$

02. *(d)* Moment of inertia of a rotating solid sphere about its symmetrical (diametric) axis is given as, $I = \dfrac{2}{5}mR^2$

Rotational kinetic energy of solid sphere is

$$K_r = \frac{1}{2}I\omega^2 = \frac{1}{2}\times\frac{2}{5}mR^2\omega^2$$
$$= \frac{1}{5}mR^2\omega^2$$

Angular velocity, $\omega = v_{CM}R$

As, we know that external torque,

$$\tau_{ext} = \frac{dL}{dt}$$

where, L is the angular momentum.

Since, in the given condition, $\tau_{ext} = 0$

$$\Rightarrow \quad \frac{dL}{dt} = 0 \text{ or } L = \text{constant}$$

> • Concept **Enhancer**
> When the radius of the sphere is increased keeping its mass same, only the angular momentum remains constant. But other quantities like moment of inertia, rotational kinetic energy and angular velocity changes.

03. *(c)* According conservation of angular momentum

$$L_i = L_f$$
$$\Rightarrow mv_0R_0 = mv'\left(\frac{R_0}{2}\right)$$
$$\Rightarrow \quad v' = 2v_0$$

So, final kinetic energy of the particle is

$$K_f = \frac{1}{2}mv'^2 = \frac{1}{2}m(2v_0)^2$$
$$= 4\frac{1}{2}mv_0^2 = 2mv_0^2$$

04. *(a)* Given, force $\mathbf{F} = \alpha\hat{\mathbf{i}} + 3\hat{\mathbf{j}} + 6\hat{\mathbf{k}}$ is acting at a point

$$\mathbf{r} = 2\hat{\mathbf{i}} - 6\hat{\mathbf{j}} - 12\hat{\mathbf{k}}$$

As, angular momentum about origin is conserved.

i.e. $\quad \tau = \text{constant}$

$\Rightarrow$ Torque, $\tau = 0 \Rightarrow \mathbf{r}\times\mathbf{F} = 0$

$$\begin{vmatrix} \hat{\mathbf{i}} & \hat{\mathbf{j}} & \hat{\mathbf{k}} \\ 2 & -6 & -12 \\ \alpha & 3 & 6 \end{vmatrix} = 0$$

$$\Rightarrow (-36+36)\hat{\mathbf{i}} - (12+12\alpha)\hat{\mathbf{j}} + (6+6\alpha)\hat{\mathbf{k}} = 0$$
$$\Rightarrow \quad 0\hat{\mathbf{i}} - 12(1+\alpha)\hat{\mathbf{j}} + 6(1+\alpha)\hat{\mathbf{k}} = 0$$

On comparing

$$\Rightarrow \quad 6(1+\alpha) = 0$$
$$\Rightarrow \quad \alpha = -1$$

So, value of α for angular momentum about origin is conserved, $\alpha = -1$

> • Concept **Enhancer**
> When the resultant external torque acting on a system is zero, the total angular momentum of a system remains constant. This is the principle of the conservation of angular momentum.

05. *(c)* Given, mass $m_1 = 2$ kg

$$m_2 = 4 \text{ kg}$$

radius, $r_1 = 0.2$ m, $r_2 = 0.1$ m

$$\omega_1 = 50 \text{ rad s}^{-1}, \omega_2 = 200 \text{ rad s}^{-1}$$

As, angular momentum is given by

$$I_1\omega_1 + I_2\omega_2 = (I_1 + I_2)\omega_f$$
$$\therefore \omega_f = \frac{I_1\omega_1 + I_2\omega_2}{I_1 + I_2}$$
$$= \frac{\frac{1}{2}m_1r_1^2\omega_1 + \frac{1}{2}m_2r_2^2\omega_2}{\frac{1}{2}m_1r_1^2 + \frac{1}{2}m_2r_2^2}$$
$$= \frac{\frac{1}{2}\times 2\times(0.2)^2\times 50 + \frac{1}{2}\times 4\times(0.1)^2\times 200}{\frac{1}{2}\times 2\times(0.2)^2 + \frac{1}{2}\times 4\times(0.1)^2}$$
$$= 100 \text{ rad/s}$$

06. *(d)* As there is no external torque is acting about the axis, angular momentum of system remains conserved.

Therefore,

$$I_1\omega_1 = I_2\omega_2$$
$$\Rightarrow \quad \omega_2 = \frac{I_1\omega_1}{I_2} = \frac{Mr^2\omega}{(M+2m)r^2}$$
$$= \frac{M\omega}{(M+2m)}$$

07. *(b)* From the definition of angular momentum,

$$\mathbf{L} = \mathbf{r}\times\mathbf{p} = rmv \sin\phi\,(-\hat{\mathbf{k}})$$

$$\begin{bmatrix} \mathbf{r} = \text{position vector} \\ \mathbf{p} = \text{momentum} \end{bmatrix}$$

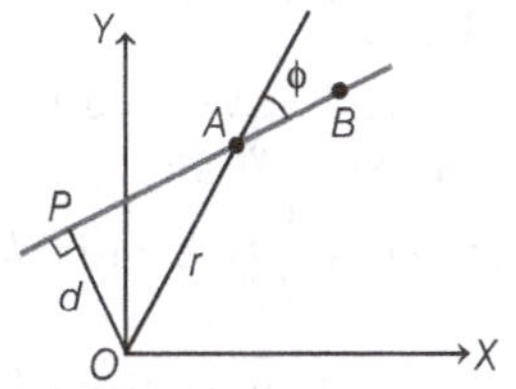

Therefore, the magnitude of L is

$$L = mvr\sin\phi = mvd$$

where, $d = r\sin\phi$ is the distance of closest approach of the particle to the origin.

As d is same for both the particles, hence $L_A = L_B$.

08. *(c)*

> **key idea**
> Apply conservation of angular momentum.

The angular momentum of a disc of moment of inertia I_1 and rotating about its axis with angular velocity ω is

$$L_1 = I_1\,\omega$$

When a round disc of moment of inertia I_2 is placed on first disc, then angular momentum of the combination is

$$L_2 = (I_1 + I_2)\,\omega'$$

In the absence of any external torque, angular momentum remains conserved

i.e., $\quad L_1 = L_2$

$$I_1\,\omega = (I_1 + I_2)\,\omega'$$
$$\Rightarrow \quad \omega' = \frac{I_1\,\omega}{I_1 + I_2}$$

09. *(d)* External torque $\tau_{ext} = 0$

So, $\quad \frac{dL}{dt} = 0$

Angular momentum,

$$L = \text{constant}$$

or $\quad I\omega = \text{constant}$

$$\therefore \quad I_1\,\omega_1 = I_2\,\omega_2 \quad \ldots\text{(i)}$$

So, for two different cases

Here, $I_1 = Mr^2$

$$\omega_1 = \omega$$
$$I_2 = Mr^2 + 4mr^2$$

Hence, Eq. (i) can be written as

$$Mr^2\omega = (Mr^2 + 4mr^2)\,\omega_2$$
$$\therefore \quad \omega_2 = \frac{M\omega}{M+4m}$$

10. *(b)* When a child sits on rotating disc, then no torque is applied (weight of child acts downward), so angular momentum will remain conserved.

11. *(b)* As net external torque is zero.

Therefore, $\tau = \frac{dL}{dt}$ i.e. $\tau_{ext} = 0$

Since, $\quad \frac{dL}{dt} = 0$

Therefore, L = constant.

i.e., L (angular momentum) remains conserved.

12. *(a)* Angular momentum,

$$L = I\omega$$

13. *(a)* The radial component of linear momentum does not contribute to angular momentum of the particle. It is only the transverse component of linear momentum (perpendicular to position vector **r**), which when multiplied by distance from the axis of rotation gives us angular momentum.

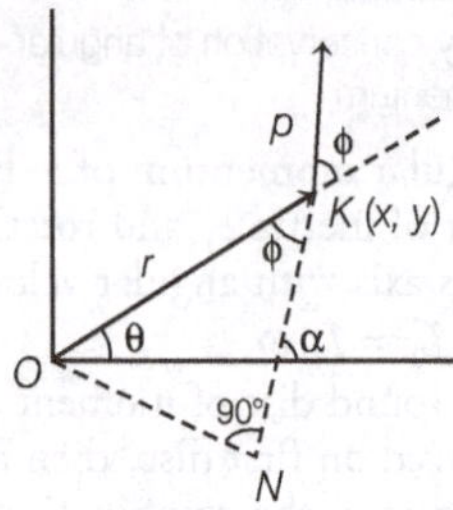

Hence, angular momentum is axial vector.

14. *(a)* The equation of the line is

$$Y = X + 4$$

or $X - Y + 4 = 0$

Length of perpendicular from origin on this line is

$$R = \frac{Ax_1 + Bx_2 + C}{\sqrt{A^2 + B^2}}$$

$$R = \frac{x - y + 4}{\sqrt{(1)^2 + (-1)^2}}$$

$$= \frac{0 - 0 + 4}{\sqrt{1^2 + 1^2}} = \frac{4}{\sqrt{2}}$$

$\therefore$ Angular momentum

$$L = mvR = 5 \times 3\sqrt{2} \times \frac{4}{\sqrt{2}}$$

$$= 60 \text{ unit}$$

Alternate Solution

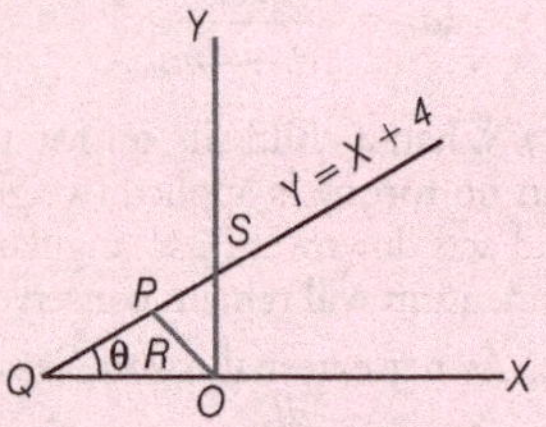

$Y = X + 4$ line is shown in the figure.

When $X = 0$, $Y = 4$, so $OS = 4$

To find slope of this line comparing this with equation of line

$$y = m'x + c$$

$\therefore$ Slope, $m' = \tan\theta = 1 \Rightarrow \theta = 45°$

Length of perpendicular $= OP$

In ΔPSO, $\frac{OP}{OS} = \sin 45°$

$\therefore$ $OP = OS \sin 45° = 4 \times \frac{1}{\sqrt{2}} = \frac{4}{\sqrt{2}}$

$\therefore$ Angular momentum of particle going along this line $= mvR = 5 \times 3\sqrt{2} \times \frac{4}{\sqrt{2}} = 60$ unit

15. *(b)* At the point of contact the frictional force acts tangentially and the weight of the sphere passes through it perpendicularly and there is no the sphere. So, as all forces pass through the point of contact, the moment of all forces acting on the body about the point of contact is zero. Hence, there is no torque about the point of contact which means angular momentum about the point of contact must be conserved.

Topic 6

01. *(d)*

key idea

Apply conservation of mechanical energy at initial and final point.

Therefore, kinetic energy at bottom + potential energy at bottom = kinetic energy at top + potential energy at top.

$$\Rightarrow \frac{1}{2}mv^2 + \frac{1}{2}I\omega^2 + 0 = 0 + mgh$$

When a body rolls i.e. have rotational motion, the total kinetic energy of the system will be

$$KE = \frac{1}{2}mv^2\left(1 + \frac{K^2}{R^2}\right)$$

where, m = mass of body,
v = velocity and
K = radius of gyration

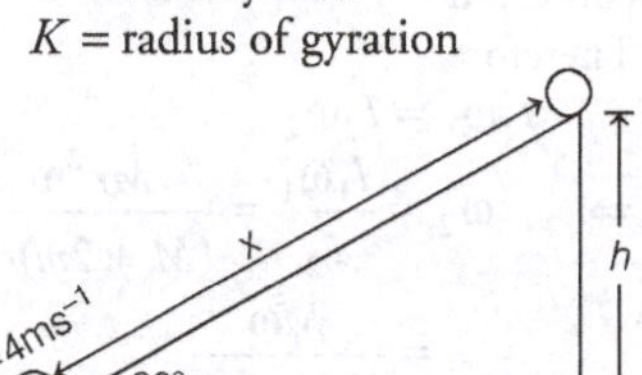

Given, $m = 2$ kg, $\theta = 30°$, $v = 4 \text{ ms}^{-1}$

Let h be the height of the inclined plane, then from law of conservation of energy,

$$KE = PE$$

$$\frac{1}{2}mv^2\left(1 + \frac{K^2}{R^2}\right) = mgh$$

Substituting the given values in the above equation, we get

$$\frac{1}{2} \times 2 \times 16\left(1 + \frac{1}{2}\right) = 2 \times 10 \times h$$

$$\left[\because \text{For cylinder } \frac{K^2}{R^2} = \frac{1}{2}\right]$$

$$\Rightarrow \quad 8 \times \frac{3}{2} = 10\,h$$

$$\Rightarrow \quad h = 1.2 \text{ m}$$

From the above diagram,

$$\sin\theta = \frac{h}{x}$$

$$\Rightarrow x = \frac{h}{\sin\theta} = \frac{1.2}{\sin 30°} = 1.2 \times 2 = 2.4 \text{ m}$$

$$\left[\because \sin 30° = \frac{1}{2}\right]$$

02. *(d)* Given, radius $R = 2$ m

mass, $m = 100$ kg and

v_{CM} (velocity centre of mass) $= v = 20$ cm/s $= 20 \times 10^{-2}$ m/s

Then, according to work energy theorem, the work done in stopping the disc is equal to the change in its kinetic energy, i.e.

$$W = KE_f - KE_i$$

As, the disc stops at the end, so final velocity is zero. Thus, $KE_f = 0$

Since, the disc is rolling so, its initial kinetic energy would have both rotational and translational kinetic energy component.

$$KE_i = KE_R + KE_T = \frac{1}{2}I\omega^2 + \frac{1}{2}mv^2$$

$$= \frac{1}{2}\left(\frac{1}{2}mR^2\right)\omega^2 + \frac{1}{2}mv^2$$

$$\left[\because \text{for disc, } I = \frac{1}{2}mR^2\right]$$

$$= \frac{1}{4}mR^2\omega^2 + \frac{1}{2}mv^2$$

$$= \frac{1}{4}mR^2\frac{v^2}{R^2} + \frac{1}{2}mv^2 \quad [\because v = r\omega]$$

$$= \frac{3}{4}mv^2$$

$$\therefore W = |KE_i| = \frac{3}{4}mv^2$$

Substituting the given values, we get

$$W = \frac{3}{4} \times 100 \times (20 \times 10^{-2})^2$$

$$= \frac{3}{4} \times 400 \times 100 \times 10^{-4} = 3 \text{ J}$$

Concept Enhancer

The work required to stop the rolling disc is equal to the final kinetic energy minus the initial kinetic energy or we can say that the work required to stop the rolling disc is equal to the total kinetic energy. It is written as $W = KE_f - KE_i$.

03. *(d)* Given, mass of cylinder, $m = 2$ kg

Radius of cylinder, $r = 4$ cm

$$= 4 \times 10^{-2} \text{ m}$$

Rotational velocity, $\omega = 3$ rpm

$$= 3 \times \frac{2\pi}{60} = \frac{\pi}{10} \text{ rad/s and } \theta = 2\pi$$

Revolution $= 2\pi \times 2\pi = 4\pi^2$ rad.

The work done $W = \tau\theta$

As the cylinder is brought to rest, so the work done will be negative.

According to work-energy theorem,

Work done = Change in rotational kinetic energy

$$-\tau\theta = \frac{1}{2}I\omega_f^2 - \frac{1}{2}I\omega_i^2$$

$$= \frac{1}{2}I(\omega_f^2 - \omega_i^2)$$

$$\Rightarrow -\tau = \frac{I(-\omega_i^2)}{2\theta} \quad [\because \omega_f = 0]$$

$$= \frac{1}{2}\left(\frac{1}{2}mr^2\right)\frac{\omega_i^2}{\theta}$$

$$\left[I = \frac{1}{2}MR^2 \text{ (for cylinder)}\right]$$

$$= \frac{1}{4}mr^2\frac{\omega^2}{\theta} \quad [\because \omega_i = \omega]$$

$$= \frac{1}{4}\times 2\times(4\times 10^{-2})^2\times\left(\frac{\pi}{10}\right)^2\times\frac{1}{4\pi^2}$$

$$= \frac{1}{4}\times 2\times 16\times 10^{-4}\times\frac{\pi^2}{100}\times\frac{1}{4\pi^2}$$

$$= \frac{2}{100}\times 10^{-4} = 2\times 10^{-6}\text{ N-m}$$

04. *(c)* Work done required to bring an object to rest is given as

$$W = \frac{1}{2}I\omega^2$$

where, I is the moment of inertia and ω is the angular velocity.

Since, here all the objects spin with the same ω, this means, $W \propto I$

As, I_A (for a solid sphere) $= \frac{2}{5}MR^2$

I_B (for a thin circular disk) $= \frac{1}{2}MR^2$

I_C (for a circular ring) $= MR^2$

$$\therefore W_A : W_B : W_C = I_A : I_B : I_C$$

$$= \frac{2}{5}MR^2 : \frac{1}{2}MR^2 : MR^2$$

$$= \frac{2}{5} : \frac{1}{2} : 1 = 4:5:10$$

$$\Rightarrow W_A < W_B < W_C$$

05. *(b)* Translational kinetic energy of a rolling body is

$$K_t = \frac{1}{2}mv_{CM}^2 \quad \ldots\text{(i)}$$

Total kinetic energy of a rolling body

$$= K_t + K_r$$

$$= \frac{1}{2}I\omega^2 + \frac{1}{2}mv_{CM}^2 \quad \ldots\text{(ii)}$$

For a solid sphere, $I = \frac{2}{5}MR^2$

Substituting the value of I in Eq. (ii), we get

$$K_t + K_r = \frac{1}{2}\left(\frac{2}{5}MR^2\right)\omega^2 + \frac{1}{2}mv_{CM}^2$$

$$= \frac{1}{2}\left(\frac{2}{5}MR^2\right)\left(\frac{v_{CM}}{R}\right)^2 + \frac{1}{2}mv_{CM}^2$$

$$[\because v_{CM} = R\omega]$$

$$= \frac{1}{5}mv_{CM}^2 + \frac{1}{2}mv_{CM}^2 = \left(\frac{1}{5}+\frac{1}{2}\right)mv_{CM}^2$$

$$= \frac{7}{10}mv_{CM}^2 \quad \ldots\text{(iii)}$$

$$\therefore \text{Ratio, } \frac{K_t}{K_t + K_r} = \frac{\frac{1}{2}mv_{CM}^2}{\frac{7}{10}mv_{CM}^2}$$

$$= \frac{1}{2}\times\frac{10}{7} = \frac{5}{7}$$

$$\therefore K_t : K_t + K_r = 5:7$$

Alternate Solution

Suppose, moment of inertia,

$$I = xMR^2 \quad \ldots\text{(i)}$$

For solid sphere, moment of inertia,

$$I = \frac{2}{5}MR^2 \quad \ldots\text{(ii)}$$

Thus, from Eqs. (i) and (ii), we get

$$x = \frac{2}{5}$$

Since, the ratio of translational energy to the total energy can be written as

$$\frac{K_t}{K_t + K_r} = \frac{\frac{1}{2}mv_{CM}^2}{\frac{1}{2}mv_{CM}^2\left(1+\frac{k^2}{R^2}\right)} \quad \ldots\text{(iii)}$$

where, k is called the radius of gyration.

As, $K = \sqrt{\frac{I}{m}}$ or $K^2 = \frac{I}{m}$

From Eq. (i), we get

$$K^2 = \frac{xmR^2}{m} = xR^2$$

Substituting the value of K^2 in Eq. (iii), we get

$$\frac{K_t}{K_t + K_r} = \frac{1}{\left(1+\frac{xR^2}{R^2}\right)} = \frac{1}{1+x}$$

Here, $x = \frac{2}{5}$

$$\Rightarrow \frac{K_t}{K_t + K_r} = \frac{1}{1+2/5} = \frac{5}{7}$$

06. *(b)*

key idea

When no external torque acts on system then, angular momentum of system remains constant.

Angular momentum before contact

$$= I_1\omega_1 + I_2\omega_2$$

Angular momentum after the discs brought into contact

$$= I_{net}\omega = (I_1 + I_2)\omega$$

So, final angular speed of system $= \omega$

$$= \frac{I_1\omega_1 + I_2\omega_2}{I_1 + I_2}$$

Now, to calculate loss of energy, we subtract initial and final energies of system.

$\Rightarrow$ Loss of energy

$$= \frac{1}{2}I\omega_1^2 + \frac{1}{2}I\omega_2^2 - \frac{1}{2}(2I)\omega^2$$

$$= \frac{1}{4}I(\omega_1 - \omega_2)^2$$

07. *(c)*

key idea

Torque τ acting on a body and angular acceleration α produced in it are related as

$$\tau = I\alpha$$

where, moment of inertia $I = mr^2$

Consider a hollow cylinder, around which a rope is wounded as shown in the figure.

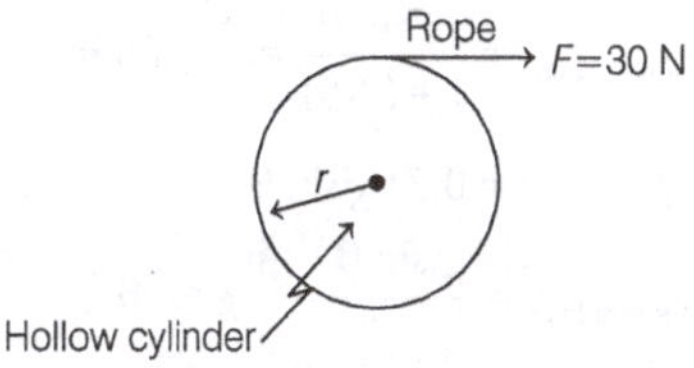

Torque acting on the cylinder due to the force F is

$$\tau = Fr$$

But, $\tau = I\alpha$

$$\Rightarrow \alpha = \frac{\tau}{I} = \frac{Fr}{mr^2} = \frac{F}{mr}$$

$$= \frac{30}{3\times 40\times 10^{-2}}$$

$$= \frac{100}{4} = 25\text{ rad/s}^2$$

08. *(c)* As we know that, the kinetic energy of a rotating body,

$$\text{KE} = \frac{1}{2}I\omega^2 = \frac{1}{2}\frac{I^2\omega^2}{I} = \frac{L^2}{2I}$$

Also, angular momentum, $L = I\omega$

Thus, $K_A = K_B$

$\Rightarrow \frac{1}{2}\frac{L_A^2}{I_A} = \frac{1}{2}\frac{L_B^2}{I_B}$

$\Rightarrow \left(\frac{L_A}{L_B}\right)^2 = \frac{I_A}{I_B} \Rightarrow \frac{L_A}{L_B} = \sqrt{\frac{I_A}{I_B}}$

$L \propto \sqrt{I}$

$\therefore \quad L_A < L_B \quad [\because I_B > I_A]$

09. *(a)* Acceleration of an object rolling down an inclined plane is given by

$$a = \frac{g \sin \theta}{1 + I/mr^2}$$

where, θ = angle of inclination of the inclined plane

m = mass of the object

I = moment of inertia about the axis through centre of mass

For disc, $\frac{I}{mr^2} = \frac{\left(\frac{1}{2}\right)mr^2}{mr^2} = \frac{1}{2}$

For solid sphere,

$$\frac{I}{mr^2} = \frac{(2/5)mr^2}{mr^2} = \frac{2}{5}$$

For hollow sphere,

$$\frac{I}{mr^2} = \frac{(2/3)mr^2}{mr^2} = \frac{2}{3}$$

$\therefore \quad a_{\text{disc}} = \frac{g \sin \theta}{1 + \frac{1}{2}} = \frac{2}{3} g \sin \theta$

$= 0.66\, g \sin \theta$

$a_{\text{solid sphere}} = \frac{g \sin \theta}{1 + (2/5)} = \frac{5}{7} g \sin \theta$

$= 0.71\, g \sin \theta$

$a_{\text{hollow sphere}} = \frac{g \sin \theta}{1 + \frac{2}{3}} = \frac{3}{5} g \sin \theta$

$= 0.6\, g \sin \theta$

Clearly, $a_{\text{solid sphere}} > a_{\text{disc}} > a_{\text{hollow sphere}}$

Type of sphere is not mentioned in the question. Therefore, we will assume the given sphere as solid sphere.

$\therefore a_{\text{solid sphere}} = a_{\text{hollow sphere}} > a_{\text{disc}}$

• Concept Enhancer

Whenever the block is rolling on a surface then there is no relative motion of the point of contact of the body w.r.t. surface. Then this type of motion is called pure rolling motion or rolling motion. Rolling is a type of motion that combines pure rotatory motion and translational motion of that object with respect to a surface..

10. *(b)* KE of a rotating rigid body,

$$\text{KE} = \frac{1}{2} I\omega^2$$

$\therefore$ KE of sphere,

$$E_{\text{Sphere}} = K_S = \frac{1}{2} I\omega_1^2 = \frac{1}{2}\left(\frac{2}{5}mR^2\right)\omega_1^2$$

$$= \frac{1}{5}mR^2\omega_1^2$$

KE of cylinder,

$$E_{\text{Cylinder}} = K_C = \frac{1}{2}\left(\frac{1}{2}mR^2\right)\omega_2^2$$

$$= \left(\frac{1}{4}mR^2\right)\omega_2^2$$

$$\frac{E_{\text{Sphere}}}{E_{\text{Cylinder}}} = \frac{K_S}{K_C} = \frac{\frac{mR^2\omega_1^2}{5}}{\frac{mR^2\omega_2^2}{4}}$$

$$= \frac{4}{5}\frac{\omega_1^2}{\omega_2^2} = \frac{4}{5}\frac{\omega_1^2}{(2\omega_1)^2}$$

$$= \frac{1}{5} \qquad (\text{given}, \omega_2 = 2\omega_1)$$

11. *(d)*

key idea

The position of point P on rod through which the axis should pass, so that the work required to set the rod rotating with minimum angular velocity ω_0 is their centre of mass, we have

$$m_1 x = m_2(L - x) \Rightarrow x = \frac{m_2 L}{m_1 + m_2}$$

As two point masses m_1 and m_2 are placed at opposite ends of a rigid rod of length L and negligible mass as shown in figure.

Total moment of inertia of the rod

$$I = m_1 x^2 + m_2 (L - x)^2$$

$$I = m_1 x^2 + m_2 L^2 + m_2 x^2 - 2m_2 Lx$$

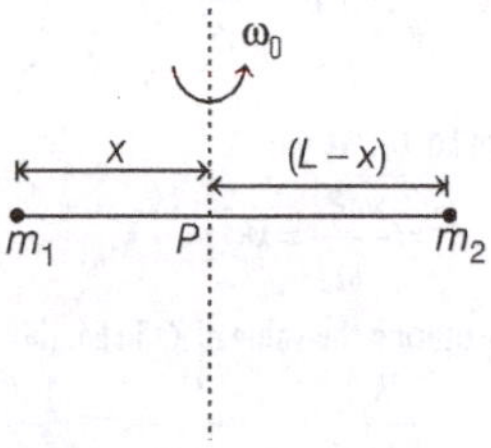

As, I is minimum i.e.

$$\frac{dI}{dx} = 2m_1 x + 0 + 2xm_2 - 2m_2 L = 0$$

$$\Rightarrow \quad x(2m_1 + 2m_2) = 2m_2 L$$

$$\Rightarrow \quad x = \frac{m_2 L}{m_1 + m_2}$$

12. *(d)*

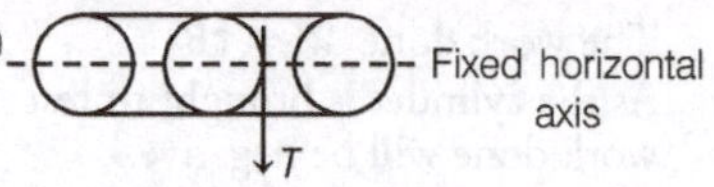

Given, $m = 50$ kg, $r = 0.5$ m,

$\alpha = 2$ rev/s^2 $= (2 \times 2\pi)$ rad/s^2

$\Rightarrow$ Torque produced by the tension in the string $\tau = Tr$

$$= T \times 0.5 = \frac{T}{2} \text{ N-m} \qquad \ldots(i)$$

We know $\tau = I\alpha \qquad \ldots(ii)$

From Eqs. (i) and (ii), $\frac{T}{2} = I\alpha$

$$= \left(\frac{MR^2}{2}\right) \times (2 \times 2\pi) \text{ rad/s}^2$$

$$\left[\text{because } I_{\text{Solid cylinder}} = \frac{MR^2}{2}\right]$$

$$\frac{T}{2} = \frac{50 \times (0.5)^2}{2} \times 4\pi$$

$$T = 50 \times \frac{1}{4} \times 4\pi = 50\,\pi = 157 \text{ N}$$

13. *(a)* A solid sphere rolling without slipping down an inclined plane

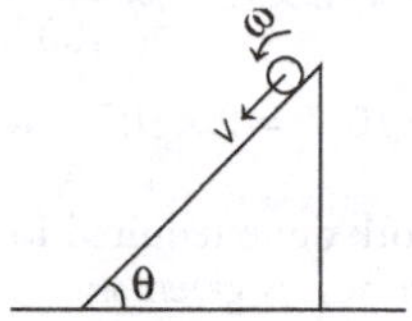

In this case,

$$a_1 = \frac{g \sin \theta}{1 + \frac{K^2}{R^2}} = \frac{g \sin \theta}{1 + \frac{(2/5)R^2}{R^2}}$$

$$\left[\therefore \text{ for solid sphere, } K^2 = \frac{2}{5}R^2\right]$$

$$= \frac{g \sin \theta}{7/5} \Rightarrow a_1 = \frac{5}{7} g \sin \theta$$

For a solid sphere slipping down without rolling an inclined plane

$\Rightarrow \quad a_{\text{slipping}} = g \sin \theta$

$\Rightarrow \quad \frac{a_1}{a_2} = \frac{5/7\, g \sin \theta}{g \sin \theta} \Rightarrow \frac{a_1}{a_2} = \frac{5}{7}$

14. *(d)* As, $v = \sqrt{\frac{2gh}{1 + (K^2/r^2)}}$

Given, $h = \frac{3v^2}{4g}$

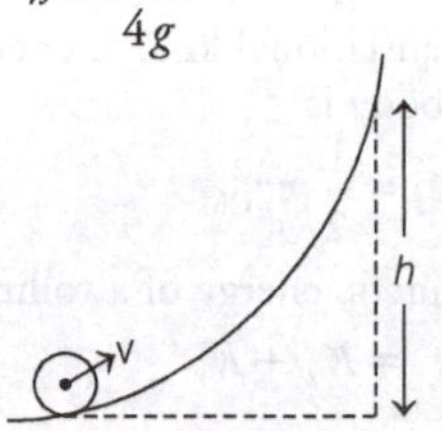

So, $v^2 = \dfrac{2gh}{1+\dfrac{K^2}{r^2}}$

$$= \frac{2g\,3v^2}{4g\left(1+\dfrac{K^2}{r^2}\right)} = \frac{6\,gv^2}{4\,g\left(1+\dfrac{K^2}{r^2}\right)}$$

$$1 = \frac{3}{2\left(1+\dfrac{K^2}{r^2}\right)}$$

or $1+\dfrac{K^2}{r^2} = \dfrac{3}{2}$ or $\dfrac{K^2}{r^2} = \dfrac{3}{2} - 1 = \dfrac{1}{2}$

$K^2 = \dfrac{1}{2}r^2$ (Equation of disc)

Hence, the object is disc.

15. *(a)*

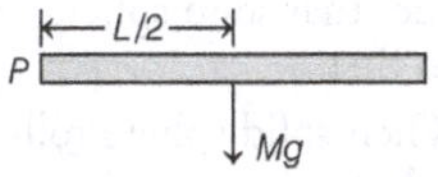

Torque on the rod = Moment of weight of the rod about P

$$\tau = Mg\frac{L}{2} \quad \ldots\text{(i)}$$

$\because$ Moment of inertia of rod about P

$$I = \frac{ML^2}{3} \quad \ldots\text{(ii)}$$

As $\tau = I\alpha$

From Eqs. (i) and (ii), we get

$$Mg\frac{L}{2} = \frac{ML^2}{3}\alpha$$

$$\Rightarrow \quad \alpha = \frac{3g}{2L}$$

16. *(b)* At maximum compression the solid cylinder will stop.

Therefore, loss in kinetic energy of cylinder = gain in potential of spring

$$\frac{1}{2}mv^2 + \frac{1}{2}I\omega^2 = \frac{1}{2}kx^2;$$

$$\frac{1}{2}mv^2 + \frac{1}{2}\left(\frac{mR^2}{2}\right)\left(\frac{v}{R}\right)^2 = \frac{1}{2}kx^2$$

($\because v = R\omega$ and for solid cylinder, $I = \frac{1}{2}mR^2$)

$$\frac{1}{2}mv^2 + \frac{1}{4}mv^2 = \frac{1}{2}kx^2$$

$$\frac{3}{4}mv^2 = \frac{1}{2}kx^2 \text{ or } x^2 = \frac{3}{2}\frac{mv^2}{k}$$

$$\Rightarrow x^2 = \frac{3\times3\times4\times4}{2\times200}$$

$$\Rightarrow x^2 = \frac{36}{100} \text{ or } x = 0.6 \text{ m}$$

17. *(b)*

key idea

Torque on the rod is equal to moment of inertia of rod about P.

The given situation is shown below,

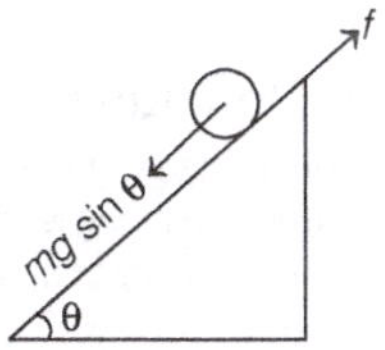

Torque, $I\alpha = f.R.$

Therefore, equation of motion is given by $mg\sin\theta - f = ma$

In case of pure rolling; $a = R\alpha$

Thus, $mg\sin\theta - \dfrac{I\alpha}{R} = ma$

$$\Rightarrow mg\sin\theta - \frac{Ia}{R^2} = ma\left(\because \alpha = \frac{a}{R}\right)$$

or, acceleration, $a = \dfrac{mg\sin\theta}{(I/R^2)+m}$

Using, 2nd equation of motion,

$$s = ut + \frac{1}{2}at^2$$

or, $s = \dfrac{1}{2}at^2 \Rightarrow t \propto \dfrac{1}{\sqrt{a}}$

$$I_{\text{solid}} < I_{\text{hollow}}$$

For minimum value of t, a should be more. This is possible when I is minimum which is the case for solid cylinder. Therefore, solid cylinder will reach the bottom first.

18. *(d)* As no external torque is applied to the system, the angular momentum of the system remains conserved.

$$L_i = L_f$$

According to given problem

$$I_t\omega_i = (I_t + I_b)\omega_f$$

Loss of energy is given by

$$\Delta E = \frac{1}{2}I_t\,\omega_i^2 - \frac{1}{2}\frac{I_t^2\,\omega_i^2}{(I_t+I_b)}$$

$$= \frac{1}{2}\frac{I_b\,I_t\,\omega_i^2}{(I_t+I_b)}$$

19. *(a)* The moment of inertia of the uniform rod about an axis through one end and perpendicular to length is

$$I = \frac{ml^2}{3}$$

where, m is mass of rod and l its length.

Torque ($\tau = I\alpha$) acting on centre of gravity of rod is given by

$$\tau = mg\frac{l}{2}$$

As we know that $\tau = I\alpha$

So $I\alpha = mg\dfrac{l}{2}$

or $\dfrac{ml^2}{3}\alpha = mg\dfrac{l}{2}$

$\therefore \quad \alpha = \dfrac{3g}{2l}$

20. *(d)* According to law of conservation of energy $K_A = K_B$

i.e. $\dfrac{1}{2}I_1\omega_1^2 = \dfrac{1}{2}I_2\,\omega_2^2$

$$\Rightarrow \quad \frac{1}{2I_1}(I_1\omega_1)^2 = \frac{1}{2I_2}(I_2\omega_2)^2$$

$$\Rightarrow \quad \frac{L_1^2}{I_1} = \frac{L_2^2}{I_2}$$

$$\Rightarrow \quad \frac{L_1}{L_2} = \sqrt{\frac{I_1}{I_2}}$$

but $\quad I_1 = I,\ I_2 = 2I$

$\therefore \quad \dfrac{L_1}{L_2} = \sqrt{\dfrac{I}{2I}} = \dfrac{1}{\sqrt{2}}$

or $\quad L_1 : L_2 = 1 : \sqrt{2}$

> • Concept **Enhancer**
>
> As for linear motion KE $= \dfrac{p^2}{2m}$
>
> Similarly, for rotational motion $KE_{rot} = \dfrac{L^2}{2I}$

21. *(a)* Kinetic energy of rotation is

$$K_{\text{rot}} = \frac{1}{2}I\omega^2 = \frac{1}{2}MK^2\frac{v^2}{R^2}$$

$$\left[K = \sqrt{\frac{I}{M}}\right]$$

where, K is radius of gyration.

Kinetic energy of translation is

$$K_{\text{trans}} = \frac{1}{2}Mv^2$$

Thus, total energy

$$E = K_{\text{rot}} + K_{\text{trans}}$$

$$= \frac{1}{2}MK^2\frac{v^2}{R^2} + \frac{1}{2}Mv^2$$

$$= \frac{1}{2}Mv^2\left(\frac{K^2}{R^2}+1\right)$$

$$= \frac{1}{2}\frac{Mv^2}{R^2}(K^2 + R^2)$$

Hence, $$\frac{K_{\text{rot.}}}{E} = \frac{\frac{1}{2}MK^2\frac{v^2}{R^2}}{\frac{1}{2}\frac{Mv^2}{R^2}(k^2+R^2)}$$

$$= \frac{K^2}{K^2+R^2}$$

22. *(a)*

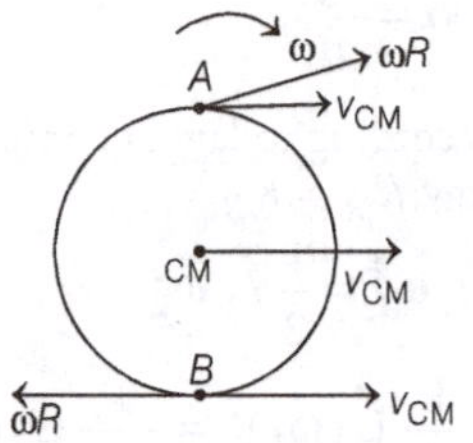

Velocity of point A is given by

v_A = velocity of centre of mass

v_{CM} + Linear velocity of point A $(R\omega)$

$$= v_{CM} + v_{CM} \quad (\because v_{CM} = R\omega)$$

$$= 2v_{CM}$$

Velocity of point B is,

$$v_B = v_{CM} - R\omega$$

$$= v_{CM} - v_{CM} = 0$$

Thus, the velocity of point A is $2v_{CM}$ and velocity of point B is zero.

23. *(a)* The given situation is shown below.

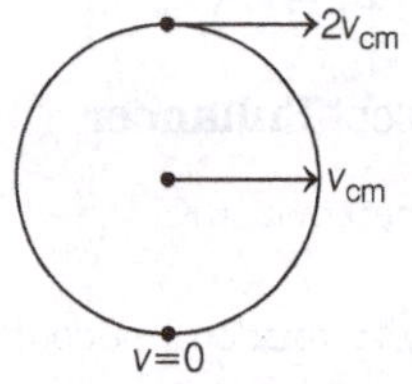

Therefore, the velocity of highest point is $2v_{cm}$ and at point of contact is zero.

24. *(b)* Total kinetic energy of spherical ball is given by

K = Kinetic energy rotational (K_{rot}) + Kinetic energy translational (K_{trans})

$$= \frac{1}{2}I\omega^2 + \frac{1}{2}mv^2$$

For sphere, moment of inertia about its diameter $I = \frac{2}{5}mr^2$

$$\therefore \quad K = \frac{1}{2}\left(\frac{2}{5}mr^2\right)\omega^2 + \frac{1}{2}mv^2$$

$$= \frac{1}{5}mr^2\omega^2 + \frac{1}{2}mv^2$$

$$= \frac{1}{5}mv^2 + \frac{1}{2}mv^2 \quad (\text{as } v = r\omega)$$

$$= \frac{7}{10}mv^2$$

$$\therefore \quad \frac{K_r}{K} = \frac{\frac{1}{5}mv^2}{\frac{7}{10}mv^2} = \frac{2}{7}$$

• Concept Enhancer

The total kinetic energy of the ball rolling on a table without slipping is equal to its rotational kinetic energy and translational kinetic energy

25. *(c)* Acceleration of the centre of mass of the rolling body is given by

$$a = \frac{g\sin\theta}{1 + \left(\frac{I}{MR^2}\right)}$$

Moment of inertia of the ring about an axis perpendicular to the plane of the ring and passing through its centre is given by

$$I = MR^2$$

$$\therefore \quad a = \frac{g\sin\theta}{1 + MR^2/MR^2}$$

$$= \frac{g\sin 30^\circ}{1+1} = \frac{g}{4}$$

26. *(a)* Let us consider that solid sphere, disc and solid cylinder are rolling on an inclined plane.

M, I and R be mass, moment of inertia and radius of the rolling section in each case.

(i) **Solid sphere** The moment of inertia of a solid sphere about its diameter is given by

$$I = \frac{2}{5}MR^2$$

or $$K = \frac{I}{MR^2} = \frac{2}{5}$$

As from the concept, acceleration

$$a = \frac{g\sin\theta}{1+K}$$

So, $$a = \frac{g\sin\theta}{1+\frac{2}{5}} = \frac{5}{7}g\sin\theta$$

(ii) **Disc** The moment of inertia of disc about an axis perpendicular to the plane of disc and passing through its centre is given by

$$I = \frac{1}{2}MR^2$$

or $$\frac{I}{MR^2} = \frac{1}{2}$$

$$\therefore \quad a = \frac{g\sin\theta}{1+\frac{1}{2}} = \frac{2}{3}g\sin\theta$$

(iii) **Solid cylinder** The moment of inertia of a cylinder about the axis passing through its centre and perpendicular to its plane is given by

$$I = \frac{1}{2}MR^2 \text{ or } \frac{I}{MR^2} = \frac{1}{2}$$

$$\therefore \quad a = \frac{g\sin\theta}{1+\frac{1}{2}} = \frac{2}{3}g\sin\theta$$

$$a_{\text{solid sphere}} > a_{\text{disc}} = a_{\text{solid cylinder}}$$

So, acceleration of solid sphere is more. It implies that solid sphere reaches the bottom first.

27. *(a)* When solid sphere rolls on inclined plane, then it has both rotational as well as translational kinetic energy

Total kinetic energy

$$K = K_{rot} + K_{trans}$$

$$= \frac{1}{2}I\omega^2 + \frac{1}{2}mv^2$$

For sphere, moment of inertia about its diameter

$$I = \frac{2}{5}mr^2$$

$$\therefore \quad K = \frac{1}{2}\left(\frac{2}{5}mr^2\right)\omega^2 + \frac{1}{2}mv^2$$

$$= \frac{1}{5}mr^2\omega^2 + \frac{1}{2}mv^2$$

$$= \frac{1}{5}mv^2 + \frac{1}{2}mv^2$$

(as $v = r\omega$)

$$= \frac{7}{10}mv^2$$

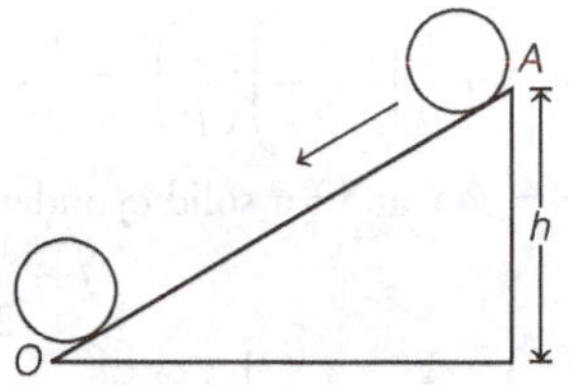

On reaching sphere at O, it has only kinetic energy

$\therefore$ PE = Total KE

$$mgh = \frac{7}{10}mv^2$$

$$\Rightarrow \quad v = \sqrt{\frac{10gh}{7}}$$

28. *(c)* A flywheel is a large heavy wheel with a long cylindrical axle supported on ball bearings. Its centre of mass lies on its axis of rotation, so that it remains at rest in any position. Rotational kinetic energy of flywheel is given by

$$K_{rot} = \frac{1}{2} I\omega^2$$

where, I = moment of inertia of the wheel about the axis of rotation

ω = angular velocity of flywheel

Given, Rotational kinetic energy

$K_r = 360$ J

Angular velocity

$\omega = 30$ rad/s

$$\therefore \quad I = \frac{2K_r}{\omega^2} = \frac{2 \times 360}{(30)^2}$$

$$= 0.8 \text{ kg-m}^2$$

29. *(b)* Given,

Moment of inertia,

$I = 1.2$ kg - m^2

Rotational kinetic energy,

$K_r = 1500$ J

Angular acceleration

$\alpha = 25$ rad / s^2, $\omega_0 = 0$,

Kinetic energy of rotation is given by

$$K_{rot} = \frac{1}{2} I\omega^2$$

$$\therefore \quad \omega = \sqrt{\frac{2K_r}{I}}$$

$$= \sqrt{\frac{2 \times 1500}{1.2}}$$

$$= 50 \text{ rad/s}$$

Now, from equation of rotational motion

$$\omega = \omega_0 + \alpha t$$

$$t = \frac{\omega - \omega_0}{\alpha}$$

$$= \frac{50 - 0}{25} = 2 \text{ s}$$

30. *(a)* Since, in this case, instantaneous axis of rotation is always below the centre of mass. This is possible only when point of contact moves with a velocity equal to centre of mass.

31. *(b)* When solid cylinder rolls down on an inclined plane, then it has both rotational and translational kinetic energy

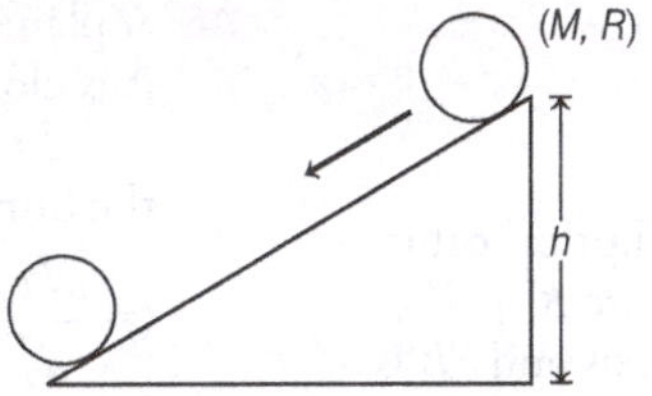

Total kinetic energy $K = K_{rot} + K_{trans}$

or $$K = \frac{1}{2} I\omega^2 + \frac{1}{2} mv^2$$

where, I = moment of inertia of solid cylinder about its axis

$$= \frac{1}{2} mr^2$$

$$\therefore \quad K = \frac{1}{2}\left(\frac{1}{2} mr^2\right)\omega^2 + \frac{1}{2} mv^2$$

$$= \frac{1}{4} mv^2 + \frac{1}{2} mv^2 \quad (\text{as } v = r\omega)$$

$$= \frac{3}{4} mv^2$$

Now, gain in KE = loss in PE

$$\therefore \quad \frac{3}{4} mv^2 = mgh$$

$$\Rightarrow \quad v = \sqrt{\left(\frac{4}{3} gh\right)}$$

32. *(a)* Kinetic energy of rotation

$$K_{rot} = \frac{1}{2} I\omega^2$$

Moment of inertia of the ring about an axis perpendicular to the plane of the ring and passing through its centre is

$$I = mr^2$$

So, $$K_{rot} = \frac{1}{2} mr^2\omega^2$$

C-07

NEET Chapterwise
Topicwise Physics

In NEET 2024, 2 questions were visible from this chapter. In past 5 years, 4 questions from topic-3, 2 questions from topic-4 and 3 questions from topic-5 were asked.

GRAVITATION

Topic 1 Kepler's Law

01 The time period of a geo-stationary satellite is 24 h, at a height $6R_E$ (R_E is the radius of Earth) from surface of Earth. The time period of another satellite whose height is 2.5 R_E from surface will be *[NCERT (New) Pg. 129, NEET (Odisha) 2019]*

(a) $6\sqrt{2}$ h (b) $12\sqrt{2}$ h
(c) $\frac{24}{2.5}$ h (d) $\frac{12}{2.5}$ h

02 The kinetic energies of a planet in an elliptical orbit about the Sun, at positions A, B and C are K_A, K_B and K_C, respectively. AC is the major axis and SB is perpendicular to AC at the position of the Sun S as shown in the figure. Then *[NEET 2018]*

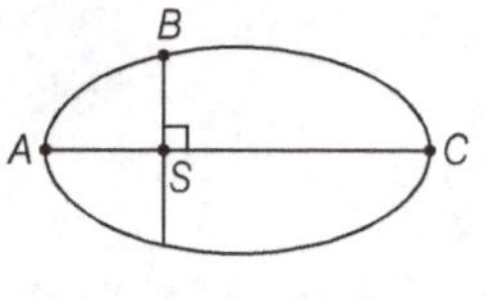

(a) $K_B < K_A < K_C$ (b) $K_A > K_B > K_C$
(c) $K_A < K_B < K_C$ (d) $K_B > K_A > K_C$

03 A geostationary satellite is orbiting the Earth at a height of 5 R above that surface of the Earth, R being the radius of the Earth. The time period of another satellite in hour at a height of 2 R from the surface of the Earth is *[NCERT (New) Pg. 129, AIPMT 2012]*

(a) 5 (b) 10 (c) $6\sqrt{2}$ (d) $6/\sqrt{2}$

04 A planet moving along an elliptical orbit is closest to the sun at a distance r_1 and farthest away at a distance of r_2. If v_1 and v_2 are the linear velocities at these points respectively, then the ratio v_1/v_2 is *[AIPMT 2011]*

(a) r_2/r_1 (b) $(r_2/r_1)^2$ (c) r_1/r_2 (d) $(r_1/r_2)^2$

05 The figure shows elliptical orbit of a planet m about the sun S. The shaded area SCD is twice the shaded area SAB. If t_1 is the time for the planet to move from C to D and t_2 is the time to move from A to B, then *[AIPMT 2009]*

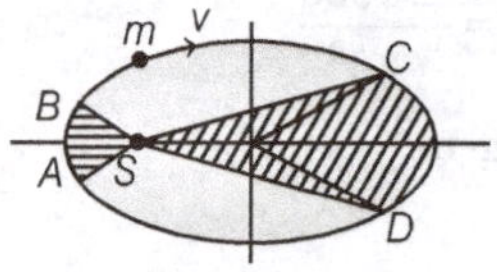

(a) $t_1 > t_2$ (b) $t_1 = 4t_2$ (c) $t_1 = 2t_2$ (d) $t_1 = t_2$

06 A planet moves around the Sun. At a given point P, it is closest from the Sun at a distance d_1 and has a speed v_1. At another point Q when it is farthest from the Sun at a distance d_2, its speed will be *[AIPMT 2002]*

(a) $\frac{d_1^2 v_1}{d_2^2}$ (b) $\frac{d_2 v_1}{d_1}$ (c) $\frac{d_1 v_1}{d_2}$ (d) $\frac{d_2^2 v_1}{d_1^2}$

07 The period of revolution of the planet A round the Sun is 8 times that of B. The distance of A from the Sun is how many times greater than that of B from the Sun ? *[NCERT (New) Pg. 129, AIPMT 1997]*

(a) 5 (b) 4 (c) 3 (d) 2

08 The orbital speed of Jupiter is *[AIPMT 1995]*

(a) greater than orbital speed of Earth
(b) less than the orbital speed of Earth
(c) equal to the orbital speed of Earth
(d) zero

09 The distance of Neptune and Saturn from the sun is nearly 10^{13} and 10^{12} m respectively. Assuming that they move in circular orbits, their periodic times will be in the ratio of *[AIPMT 1994]*

(a) 10 (b) 100
(c) $10\sqrt{10}$ (d) 1000

10 The largest and the shortest distance of the Earth from the Sun are r_1 and r_2. Its distance from the Sun when it is perpendicular to the major axis of the orbit drawn from the Sun *[AIPMT 1988]*

(a) $\frac{r_1 + r_2}{4}$ (b) $\frac{r_1 + r_2}{r_1 - r_2}$
(c) $\frac{2r_1 r_2}{r_1 + r_2}$ (d) $\frac{r_1 + r_2}{3}$

Topic 2 Universal Law of Gravitation

01 Two astronauts are floating in gravitational free space after having lost contact with their spaceship. The two will *[NCERT (New) Pg. 130, NEET 2017]*
(a) keep floating at the same distance between them
(b) move towards each other
(c) move away from each other
(d) will become stationary

02 Kepler's third law states that square of period of revolution T of a planet around the Sun, is proportional to third power of average distance r between the Sun and planet i.e. $T^2 = Kr^3$, here K is constant. If the masses of the Sun and planet are M and m respectively, then as per Newton's law of gravitation force of attraction between them is *[NCERT (New) Pg. 129, AIPMT 2015]*
$F = \frac{GMm}{r^2}$, here G is gravitational constant. The relation between G and K is described as
(a) $GK = 4\pi^2$
(b) $GMK = 4\pi^2$
(c) $K = G$
(d) $K = \frac{I}{G}$

03 Two spherical bodies of masses M and $5M$ and radii R and $2R$ are released in free space with initial separation between their centres equal to $12\,R$. If they attract each other due to gravitational force only, then the distance covered by the smaller body before collision is *[NCERT (New) Pg. 130, AIPMT 2015]*
(a) $2.5\,R$ (b) $4.5\,R$
(c) $7.5\,R$ (d) $1.5\,R$

04 A body projected vertically upward from the Earth reaches a height equal to Earth's radius before returning to the Earth. The power exerted by the gravitational force is greatest *[AIPMT 2011]*
(a) at the instant just before the body hits the Earth
(b) it remains constant all through
(c) at the instant just after the body is projected
(d) at the highest position of the body

05 The Earth (mass $= 6 \times 10^{24}$ kg) revolves around the Sun with an angular velocity of 2×10^{-7} rad/s in a circular orbit of radius 1.5×10^8 km. The force exerted by the Sun on the Earth, in Newton, is *[AIPMT 1995]*
(a) 36×10^{21} (b) 27×10^{39}
(c) zero (d) 10×10^{25}

Topic 3 Acceleration Due to Gravity and its Variations

01 The mass of a planet is $1/10$ th that of the Earth and its diameter is half that of the Earth. The acceleration due to gravity on that planet is *[NCERT (New) Pg. 132, NEET 2024]*
(a) $19.6\ ms^{-2}$ (b) $9.8\ ms^{-2}$
(c) $4.9\ ms^{-2}$ (d) $3.92\ ms^{-2}$

02 A body of mass 60 g experiences a gravitational force of 3.0 N, when placed at a particular point. The magnitude of the gravitational field intensity at that point is *[NCERT (New) Pg. 133, NEET 2022]*
(a) 50 N/kg (b) 20 N/kg
(c) 180 N/kg (d) 0.05 N/kg

03 What is the depth at which the value of acceleration due to gravity becomes $1/n$ times the value that the surface of Earth ? (Radius of earth $= R$) *[NEET (Oct.) 2020]*
(a) R/n^2 (b) $R(n-1)/n$
(c) $Rn/(n-1)$ (d) R/n

04 A body weighs 72 N on the surface of the Earth. What is the gravitational force on it, at a height equal to half of radius of the Earth ? *[NEET (Sep.) 2020]*
(a) 32 N (b) 30 N
(c) 24 N (d) 48 N

05 A body weighs 200 N on the surface of the Earth. How much will it weigh half way down to the centre of the Earth ? *[NCERT (New) Pg. 133, NEET (National) 2019]*
(a) 200 N (b) 250 N
(c) 100 N (d) 150 N

06 If the mass of the Sun were ten times smaller and the universal gravitational constant were ten times larger in magnitude, which of the following is not correct ? *[NEET 2018]*

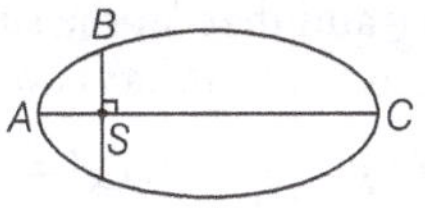

(a) Time period of a simple pendulum on the Earth would decrease
(b) Walking on the ground would become more difficult
(c) Raindrops will fall faster
(d) g on the Earth will not change

07 The acceleration due to gravity at a height 1 km above the Earth is the same as at a depth d below the surface of Earth. Then *[NEET 2017]*
(a) $d = \frac{1}{2}$ km (b) $d = 1$ km
(c) $d = \frac{3}{2}$ km (d) $d = 2$ km

08 Starting from the centre of the Earth having radius R, the variation of g (acceleration due to gravity) is shown by *[NCERT (New) Pg. 133, NEET 2016]*

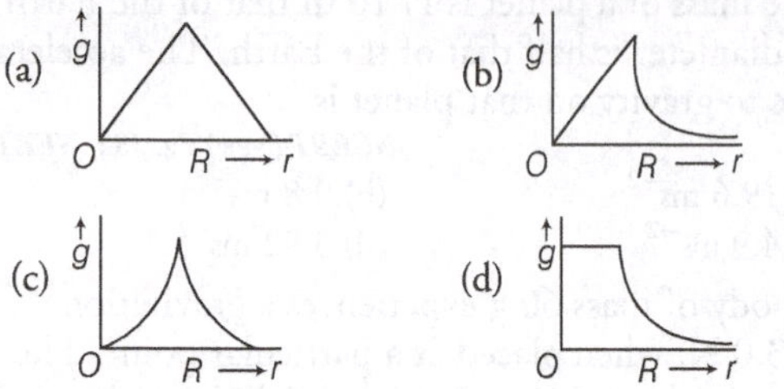

09 Dependence of intensity of gravitational field E of Earth with distance r from centre of Earth is correctly represented by *[NCERT (New) Pg. 133, AIPMT 2014]*

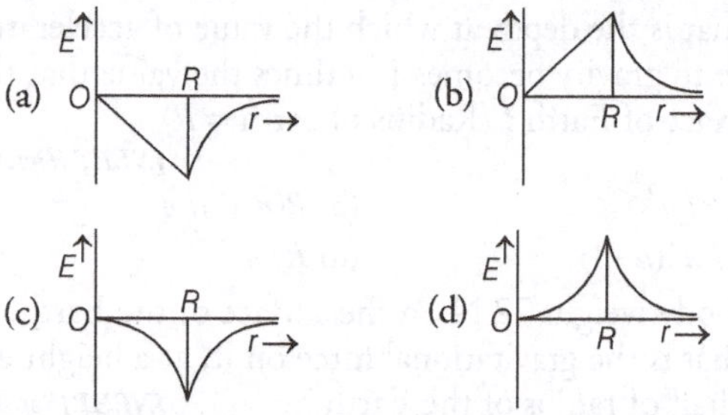

10 A spherical planet has a mass M_p and diameter D_p. A particle of mass m falling freely near the surface of this planet will experience an acceleration due to gravity, equal to *[AIPMT 2012]*

(a) $4GM_p/D_p^2$ (b) GM_pm/D_p^2
(c) GM_p/D_p^2 (d) $4GM_pm/D_p^2$

11 Imagine a new planet having the same density as that of the Earth but it is 3 times bigger than the Earth in size. If the acceleration due to gravity on the surface of the Earth is g and that on the surface of the new planet is g', then *[NCERT (New) Pg. 133, AIPMT 2005]*

(a) $g' = 3g$ (b) $g' = \frac{g}{9}$ (c) $g' = 9g$ (d) $g' = 27g$

12 The density of newly discovered planet is twice that of the Earth. The acceleration due to gravity at the surface of the planet is equal to that at the surface of the Earth. If the radius of the Earth is R, the radius of the planet would be *[AIPMT 2004]*

(a) $2R$ (b) $4R$ (c) $\frac{1}{4}R$ (d) $\frac{1}{2}R$

13 The acceleration due to gravity on the planet A is 9 times the acceleration due to gravity on the planet B. A man jumps to a height of 2 m on the surface of A. What is the height of jump by the same person on the planet B? *[NCERT (New) Pg. 133, AIPMT 2003]*

(a) 6 m (b) $\frac{2}{3}$ m (c) $\frac{2}{9}$ m (d) 18 m

14 Assuming Earth to be a sphere of uniform density, what is the value of g in a mine 100 km below the Earth's surface? (Given, $R = 6400$ km) *[AIPMT 2001]*

(a) $9.65\ m/s^2$ (b) $7.65\ m/s^2$
(c) $5.06\ m/s^2$ (d) $3.10\ m/s^2$

15 The acceleration due to gravity g and mean density of the Earth ρ are related by which of the following relations? (where G is the gravitational constant and R is the radius of the earth). *[AIPMT 1995]*

(a) $\rho = \frac{3g}{4\pi GR}$ (b) $\rho = \frac{3g}{4\pi GR^3}$
(c) $\rho = \frac{4\pi gR^2}{3G}$ (d) $\rho = \frac{4\pi gR^3}{3G}$

16 The radius of Earth is about 6400 km and that of Mars is 3200 km. The mass of the Earth is about 10 times mass of Mars. An object weighs 200 N on the surface of Earth. Its weight on the surface of Mars will be *[NCERT (New) Pg. 133, AIPMT 1994]*

(a) 20 N (b) 8 N
(c) 80 N (d) 40 N

Topic 4 Gravitational Potential and Gravitational Potential Energy

01 The minimum energy required to launch a satellite of mass m from the surface of Earth of mass M and radius R in a circular orbit at an altitude of $2R$ from the surface of the Earth is *[NCERT (New) Pg. 134, NEET 2024]*

(a) $\frac{5GmM}{6R}$ (b) $\frac{2GmM}{3R}$ (c) $\frac{GmM}{2R}$ (d) $\frac{GmM}{3R}$

02 Two bodies of mass m and $9m$ are placed at a distance R. The gravitational potential on the line joining the bodies where the gravitational field equals zero, will be (G = gravitational constant) *[NCERT (New) Pg. 135, NEET 2023]*

(a) $-\frac{12\,Gm}{R}$ (b) $-\frac{16\,Gm}{R}$ (c) $-\frac{20\,Gm}{R}$ (d) $-\frac{8\,Gm}{R}$

03 The work done to raise a mass m from the surface of the Earth to a height h, which is equal to the radius of the Earth, is *[NEET (National) 2019]*

(a) $2mgR$ (b) $\frac{1}{2}mgR$ (c) $\frac{3}{2}mgR$ (d) mgR

04 Assuming that the gravitational potential energy of an object at infinity is zero, the change in potential energy (final – initial) of an object of mass m, when taken to a height h from the surface of earth (of radius R) is given by, *[NCERT (New) Pg. 135, NEET (Odisha) 2019]*

(a) $-\frac{GMm}{R+h}$ (b) $\frac{GMmh}{R(R+h)}$ (c) mgh (d) $\frac{GMm}{R+h}$

05 At what height from the surface of Earth the gravitational potential and the value of g are -5.4×10^7 J kg^{-2} and 6.0 ms^{-2} respectively ? Take, the radius of Earth as 6400 km. *[NEET 2016]*
(a) 1600 km (b) 1400 km (c) 2000 km (d) 2600 km

06 Infinite number of bodies, each of mass 2 kg are situated on X-axis at distances 1m, 2 m, 4 m and 8 m, respectively from the origin. The resulting gravitational potential due to this system at the origin will be *[NCERT (New) Pg. 135, NEET 2013]*
(a) $-G$ (b) $-\frac{8}{3}G$ (c) $-\frac{4}{3}G$ (d) $-4G$

07 A body of mass m taken from the Earth's surface to the height equal to twice the radius R of the Earth. The change in potential energy of body will be *[NEET 2013]*
(a) $mg2R$ (b) $\frac{2}{3}mgR$ (c) $3mgR$ (d) $\frac{1}{3}mgR$

08 The height at which the weight of a body becomes 1/16th its weight on the surface of the Earth (radius R), is *[NCERT (New) Pg. 135, AIPMT 2012]*
(a) $5R$ (b) $15R$ (c) $3R$ (d) $4R$

09 A body of mass m is placed on the Earth's surface. It is then taken from the Earth's surface to a height $h = 3R$, then the change in gravitational potential energy is *[AIPMT 2002]*
(a) $\frac{mgh}{R}$ (b) $\frac{2}{3}mgR$
(c) $\frac{3}{4}mgR$ (d) $\frac{mgR}{2}$

10 With what velocity should a particle be projected so that its height becomes equal to radius of Earth ? *[NCERT (New) Pg. 135, AIPMT 2001]*
(a) $\left(\frac{GM}{R}\right)^{1/2}$ (b) $\left(\frac{8GM}{R}\right)^{1/2}$
(c) $\left(\frac{2GM}{R}\right)^{1/2}$ (d) $\left(\frac{4GM}{R}\right)^{1/2}$

11 A body attains a height equal to the radius of the Earth. The velocity of the body with which it was projected is *[AIPMT 2001]*
(a) $\sqrt{\frac{GM}{R}}$ (b) $\sqrt{\frac{2GM}{R}}$ (c) $\sqrt{\frac{5}{4}\frac{GM}{R}}$ (d) $\sqrt{\frac{3GM}{R}}$

12 A body of mass m rises to height $h = \frac{R}{5}$ from the Earth's surface, where R is Earth's radius. If g is acceleration due to gravity at Earth's surface, the increase in potential energy is *[AIPMT 1991]*
(a) $\frac{5}{6}mgh$ (b) $\frac{4}{5}mgh$ (c) mgh (d) $\frac{6}{7}mgh$

13 A planet is moving in an elliptical orbit around the Sun. If T, U, E and L stand for its kinetic energy, gravitational potential energy, total energy and magnitude of angular momentum about the centre of force, which of the following is correct ? *[AIPMT 1990]*
(a) T is conserved
(b) U is always positive
(c) E is always negative
(d) L is conserved but direction of vector L changes continuously

14 In a gravitational field, at a point where the gravitational potential is zero *[AIPMT 1990]*
(a) the gravitational field is necessarily zero.
(b) the gravitational field is not necessarily zero.
(c) nothing can be said definitely about gravitational field.
(d) None of the above

Topic 5 Escape Velocity and Motion of Satellite

01 A satellite is orbiting just above the surface of the Earth with period T. If d is the density of the Earth and G is the universal constant of gravitation, the quantity $\frac{3\pi}{Gd}$ represents *[NCERT (New) Pg. 136, NEET 2023]*
(a) T^2 (b) T^3 (c) $\sqrt{T}$ (d) T

02 The escape velocity from the Earth's surface is v. The escape velocity from the surface of another planet having a radius, four times that of Earth and same mass density is *[NCERT (New) Pg. 136, NEET 2021]*
(a) v (b) $2v$ (c) $3v$ (d) $4v$

03 A particle of mass m is projected with a velocity $v = kv_e$ $(k < 1)$ from the surface of the Earth.
(Here, v_e = escape velocity)
The maximum height above the surface reached by the particle is *[NCERT (New) Pg. 136, NEET 2021]*
(a) $R\left(\frac{k}{1-k}\right)^2$ (b) $R\left(\frac{k}{1+k}\right)^2$ (c) $\frac{R^2k}{1+k}$ (d) $\frac{Rk^2}{1-k^2}$

04 The ratio of escape velocity at Earth v_e to the escape velocity at a planet v_p whose radius and mean density are twice as that of Earth is *[NEET 2016]*
(a) $1:2\sqrt{2}$ (b) $1:4$ (c) $1:\sqrt{2}$ (d) $1:2$

05 A satellite of mass m is orbiting the Earth (of radius R) at a height h from its surface. The total energy of the satellite in terms of g_0, the value of acceleration due to gravity at the Earth's surface is *[NEET 2016]*
(a) $\frac{mg_0R^2}{2(R+h)}$ (b) $-\frac{mg_0R^2}{2(R+h)}$
(c) $\frac{2mg_0R^2}{R+h}$ (d) $-\frac{2mg_0R^2}{R+h}$

06 A remote sensing satellite of Earth revolves in a circular orbit at a height of 0.25×10^6 m above the surface of Earth. If Earth's radius is 6.38×10^6 m and $g = 9.8$ ms^{-2}, then the orbital speed of the satellite is *[NCERT (New) Pg. 137, AIPMT 2015]*

(a) 7.76 kms^{-1} (b) 8.56 kms^{-1}
(c) 9.13 kms^{-1} (d) 6.67 kms^{-1}

07 A satellite S is moving in an elliptical orbit around the Earth. The mass of the satellite is very small as compared to the mass of the Earth. Then, *[AIPMT 2015]*

(a) the angular momentum of S about the centre of the Earth changes in direction, but its magnitude remains constant
(b) the total mechanical energy of S varies periodically with time
(c) the linear momentum of S remains constant in magnitude
(d) the acceleration of S is always directed towards the centre of the Earth

08 A black hole is an object whose gravitational field is so strong that even light cannot escape from it. To what approximate radius would Earth (mass = 5.98×10^{24} kg) have to be compressed to be a black hole ? *[NCERT (New) Pg. 136, AIPMT 2014]*

(a) 10^{-9} m (b) 10^{-6} m
(c) 10^{-2} m (d) 10^{-7} m

09 A particle of mass m is kept at rest at a height $3R$ from the surface of Earth, where R is radius of Earth and M is mass of Earth. The minimum speed with which it should be projected, so that it does not return back, is (g is acceleration due to gravity on the surface of Earth) *[NCERT (New) Pg. 136, NEET 2013]*

(a) $\left(\frac{GM}{2R}\right)^{1/2}$ (b) $\left(\frac{gR}{4}\right)^{1/2}$
(c) $\left(\frac{2g}{R}\right)^{1/2}$ (d) $\left(\frac{GM}{R}\right)^{1/2}$

10 If v_e is escape velocity and v_0 is orbital velocity of a satellite for orbit close to the Earth's surface, then these are related by *[NCERT (New) Pg. 136, AIPMT 2012]*

(a) $v_0 = \sqrt{2}v_e$ (b) $v_0 = v_e$
(c) $v_e = \sqrt{2v_0}$ (d) $v_e = \sqrt{2}v_0$

11 A particle of mass m is thrown upwards from the surface of the Earth, with a velocity u. The mass and the radius of the Earth are respectively, M and R. G is gravitational constant and g is acceleration due to gravity on the surface of the Earth. The mininum value of u, so that the particle does not return back to Earth, is *[AIPMT 2011]*

(a) $\sqrt{\frac{2GM}{R^2}}$ (b) $\sqrt{\frac{2GM}{R}}$ (c) $\sqrt{\frac{2gM}{R^2}}$ (d) $\sqrt{2gR^2}$

12 The additional kinetic energy to be provided to a satellite of mass m revolving around a planet of mass M, to transfer it from a circular orbit of radius R_1 to another of radius $R_2 (R_2 > R_1)$ is *[AIPMT 2010]*

(a) $GmM\left(\frac{1}{R_1^2} - \frac{1}{R_2^2}\right)$ (b) $GmM\left(\frac{1}{R_1} - \frac{1}{R_2}\right)$
(c) $2GmM\left(\frac{1}{R_1} - \frac{1}{R_2}\right)$ (d) $\frac{1}{2}GmM\left(\frac{1}{R_1} - \frac{1}{R_2}\right)$

13 Two satellites of the Earth, S_1 and S_2 are moving in the same orbit. The mass of S_1 is four times the mass of S_2. Which one of the following statements is true ? *[NCERT (Old) Pg. 256, AIPMT 2007]*

(a) The time period of S_1 is four times that of S_2
(b) The potential energies of the earth and satellite in the two cases are equal
(c) S_1 and S_2 are moving with the same speed
(d) The kinetic energies of the two satellites are equal

14 The Earth is assumed to be a sphere of radius R. A platform is arranged at a height R from the surface of the Earth. The escape velocity of a body from this platform is $f v_e$, where v_e is its escape velocity from the surface of the Earth. The value of f is *[NCERT (New) Pg. 136, AIPMT 2006]*

(a) $\sqrt{2}$ (b) $1/\sqrt{2}$
(c) $1/3$ (d) $1/2$

15 For a satellite moving in an orbit around the earth, the ratio of kinetic energy to potential energy is *[AIPMT 2005]*

(a) 2 (b) 1/2
(c) $\frac{1}{\sqrt{2}}$ (d) $\sqrt{2}$

16 The potential energy of a satellite, having mass m and rotating at a height of 6.4×10^6 m from the Earth surface, is *[NCERT (New) Pg. 135, AIPMT 2002]*

(a) $-mgR_e$ (b) $-0.67mgR_e$
(c) $-0.5mgR_e$ (d) $-0.33mgR_e$

17 Escape velocity from the earth is 11.2 km/s. Another planet of same mass has radius 1/4 times that of the earth. What is the escape velocity from another planet ? *[NCERT (New) Pg. 136, AIPMT 2000]*

(a) 11.2 km/s (b) 44.8 km/s
(c) 22.4 km/s (d) 5.6 km/s

18 The escape velocity of a sphere of mass m is given by (G = universal gravitational constant, M_e = mass of the Earth and R_e = radius of the Earth) *[AIPMT 1999]*

(a) $\sqrt{\frac{GM_e}{R_e}}$ (b) $\sqrt{\frac{2\,GM_e}{R_e}}$
(c) $\sqrt{\frac{2\,Gm}{R_e}}$ (d) $\frac{GM_e}{R_e^2}$

19 A ball is dropped from a satellite revolving around the Earth at a height of 120 km. The ball will *[AIPMT 1996]*

(a) continue to move with same speed along a straight line tangentially to the satellite at that time

(b) continue to move with the same speed along the original orbit of satellite

(c) fall down to the earth gradually

(d) go far away in space

20 The escape velocity from the surface of the Earth is v_e. The escape velocity from the surface of a planet whose mass and radius are three times those of the earth, will be *[NCERT (New) Pg. 136, AIPMT 1995]*

(a) v_e (b) $3v_e$

(c) $9v_e$ (d) $\frac{1}{3v_e}$

21 A satellite in force free space sweeps stationary interplanetary dust at a rate $dM/dt = \alpha v$, where M is the mass and v is the velocity of the satellite and α is a constant. What is the deceleration of the satellite? *[AIPMT 1994]*

(a) $-\alpha v^2$ (b) $-\alpha v^2/2M$

(c) $-\alpha v^2/M$ (d) $-2\alpha v^2/M$

22 The mean radius of the earth is R, its angular speed on its own axis is ω and the acceleration due to gravity at the Earth's surface is g. What will be the radius of the orbit of a geostationary satellite ? *[NCERT (New) Pg. 137, AIPMT 1992]*

(a) $\left(\frac{R^2 g}{\omega^2}\right)^{1/3}$ (b) $\left(\frac{Rg}{\omega^2}\right)^{1/3}$

(c) $\left(\frac{R^2\omega^2}{g}\right)^{1/3}$ (d) $\left(\frac{R^2 g}{\omega}\right)^{1/3}$

23 The satellite of mass m is orbiting around the Earth in a circular orbit with a velocity v. What will be its total energy ? *[AIPMT 1991]*

(a) $\frac{3}{4}mv^2$ (b) $\frac{1}{2}mv^2$

(c) mv^2 (d) $-\left(\frac{1}{2}\right)mv^2$

Key Index

Topic 1

1 (a)	2 (b)	3 (c)	4 (a)	5 (c)	6 (c)	7 (b)	8 (b)	9 (c)	10 (c)

Topic 2

1 (b)	2 (b)	3 (c)	4 (a)	5 (a)

Topic 3

1 (d)	2 (a)	3 (b)	4 (a)	5 (c)	6 (d)	7 (d)	8 (b)	9 (a)	10 (a)
11 (a)	12 (d)	13 (d)	14 (a)	15 (a)	16 (c)				

Topic 4

1 (a)	2 (b)	3 (b)	4 (b)	5 (d)	6 (d)	7 (b)	8 (c)	9 (c)	10 (a)
11 (a)	12 (a)	13 (c)	14 (a)						

Topic 5

1 (a)	2 (d)	3 (d)	4 (a)	5 (b)	6 (a)	7 (d)	8 (c)	9 (a)	10 (d)
11 (b)	12 (d)	13 (c)	14 (b)	15 (b)	16 (c)	17 (c)	18 (b)	19 (b)	20 (a)
21 (c)	22 (a)	23 (d)							

Detailed **Explanations**

Topic 1

01. *(a)* From Kepler's third law, the time period of revolution of satellite around Earth is

$$T^2 \propto r^3 \quad \text{or} \quad T \propto r^{3/2} \qquad \ldots\text{(i)}$$

$$T \propto (R_E + h)^{3/2}$$

where, r is the radius of satellite's orbit.

Here, $r_1 = 6R_E + R_E, T_1 = 24$ h

$r_2 = 2.5R_E + R_E, T_2 = ?$

where R_E = radius of Earth

So, from Eq. (i), we get

$$\frac{T_1}{T_2} = \left(\frac{r_1}{r_2}\right)^{3/2}$$

$$\frac{24}{T_2} = \left(\frac{6R_E + R_E}{2.5R_E + R_E}\right)^{3/2} = \left(\frac{7}{3.5}\right)^{3/2}$$

$$\Rightarrow \quad T_2 = \frac{24}{(2)^{3/2}} = \frac{24}{2\sqrt{2}}$$

$$= \frac{12}{\sqrt{2}} = 6\sqrt{2} \text{ h}$$

02. *(b)* According to the question,

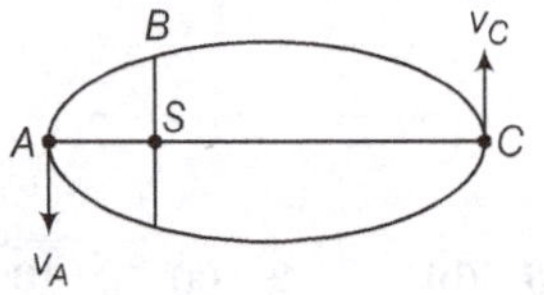

The above figure shows an ellipse traced by a planet around the Sun, S. The closed point A is known as perihelion (perigee) and the farthest point C is known as aphelion (apogee).

Since, as per the result of the Kepler's second law of area, the planet will move slowly (v_{min}) only when it is farthest from the Sun and more rapidly (v_{max}) when it is nearest to the Sun.

Thus, $\quad v_A = v_{max}, v_C = v_{min}$

Therefore, we can write

$$v_A > v_B > v_C \qquad \ldots\text{(i)}$$

Kinetic energy of the planet at any point is given as,

$$K = \frac{1}{2}mv^2$$

Thus, at point A, $K_A = \frac{1}{2}mv_A^2$

At point B, $\quad K_B = \frac{1}{2}mv_B^2$

At C, $\quad K_C = \frac{1}{2}mv_C^2$

From Eq. (i), we can write

$$K_A > K_B > K_C$$

• Concept Enhancer

The energy of a particle due to its motion is called kinetic energy of that particle.

kinetic energy, $KE = \frac{1}{2}mv^2$ and $v = \omega R$

$\Rightarrow \quad KE = \frac{1}{2}m\omega^2R^2$

03. *(c)* From Kepler's third law

$$T^2 \propto r^3$$

[where, T = time period of satellite
r = radius of elliptical orbit (semi major axis)]

Hence, $\quad T_1^2 \propto r_1^3$ and $T_2^2 \propto r_2^3$

So, $$\frac{T_2^2}{T_1^2} = \frac{r_2^3}{r_1^3} = \frac{(2R+R)^3}{(5R+R)^3} = \frac{(3R)^3}{(6R)^3}$$

or $$\frac{T_2^2}{T_1^2} = \frac{1}{8}$$

$$T_2^2 = \frac{1}{8}T_1^2 \Rightarrow T_2 = \frac{24}{2\sqrt{2}} = 6\sqrt{2} \text{ h}$$

04. *(a)*

key idea

Apply conservation of angular momentum.

From the law of conservation of angular momentum, $L_1 = L_2$

So, $\quad mr_1v_1 = mr_2v_2$

[where, m = mass the of planet
r = radius of orbit
v = velocity of the planet]

$$r_1v_1 = r_2v_2 \Rightarrow \frac{v_1}{v_2} = \frac{r_2}{r_1}$$

05. *(c)* $\frac{dA}{dt}$ = constant or $\frac{A_1}{t_1} = \frac{A_2}{t_2}$

where, A_1 = area under SCD

A_2 = area under ABS

$$\Rightarrow \quad t_1 = \frac{A_1}{A_2}t_2$$

Given, $A_1 = 2A_2$

$\therefore \quad t_1 = 2t_2$

• Concept Enhancer

The line joining the Sun to the planet sweeps out equal areas in equal time interval i.e. areal velocity remains constant.

06. *(c)* According to the Kepler's second law, angular momentum is conserved.

Therefore, $mv_1d_1 = mv_2d_2$

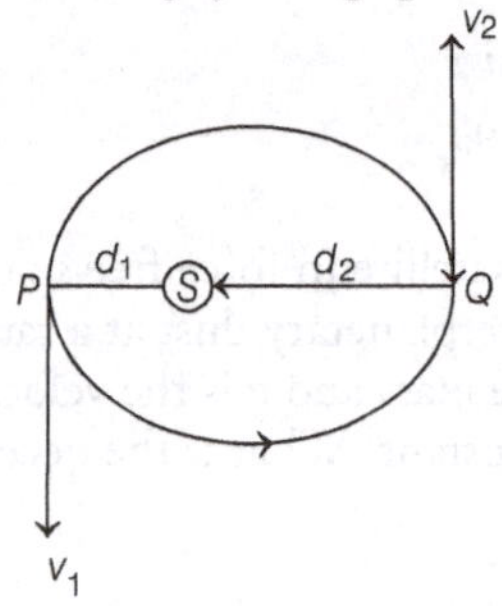

$$\Rightarrow \quad v_2 = \frac{v_1d_1}{d_2}$$

07. *(b)* According to Kepler's third law

$$T^2 \propto r^3$$

where, T = Time period of revolution

r = Semi major axis

$$\therefore \quad \frac{T_A^2}{T_B^2} = \frac{r_A^3}{r_B^3}$$

Given, period of revolution of planet A, $T_A = 8T_B$

$$\therefore \quad \frac{r_A}{r_B} = \left(\frac{T_A}{T_B}\right)^{2/3} = \left(\frac{8T_B}{T_B}\right)^{2/3}$$

$$= (8)^{2/3} = 2^{3 \times \frac{2}{3}} = 4$$

or $\quad r_A = 4r_B$

08. *(b)* As we know that orbital radius of Jupiter > orbital radius of Earth

$$\frac{v_J}{v_e} = \frac{r_e}{r_J}$$

As $\quad r_J > r_e \Rightarrow v_J < v_e$

09. *(c)*

key idea

Apply Kepler's third law and use

$$T^2 \propto R^3$$

From Kepler's third law,

$$T^2 \propto R^3$$

$$\Rightarrow \quad \left(\frac{T_N}{T_S}\right)^2 = \left(\frac{R_N}{R_S}\right)^3$$

$$\Rightarrow \quad \frac{T_N}{T_S} = \left(\frac{R_N}{R_S}\right)^{3/2}$$

$$= \left(\frac{10^{13}}{10^{12}}\right)^{3/2} = 10^{3/2} = 10\sqrt{10}$$

10. *(c)* From the property of ellipse,

$$\frac{2}{R} = \frac{1}{r_1} + \frac{1}{r_2}$$

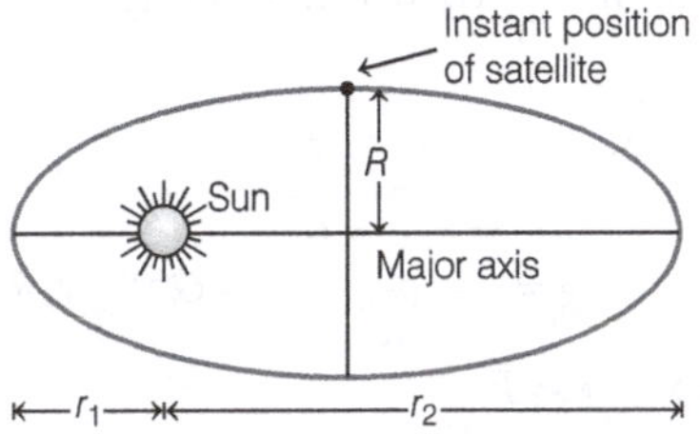

or $\quad \frac{2}{R} = \frac{r_1 + r_2}{r_1 r_2} \Rightarrow R = \frac{2 r_1 r_2}{r_1 + r_2}$

Topic 2

01. *(b)* In the space, there is no external gravity. Due to masses of the astronauts, there will be small gravitational attractive force between them. Thus, these astronauts will move towards each other.

02. *(b)* The gravitational force of attraction between the planet and Sun provide the centripetal force

i.e. $\quad \frac{GMm}{r^2} = \frac{mv^2}{r}$

$$\Rightarrow \quad v = \sqrt{\frac{GM}{r}}$$

The time period of planet will be

$$T = \frac{2\pi r}{v}$$

$$\Rightarrow \quad T^2 = \frac{4\pi^2 r^2}{\frac{GM}{r}} = \frac{4\pi^2 r^3}{GM} \quad \ldots \text{(i)}$$

Also from Kepler's third law

$$T^2 = Kr^3 \quad \ldots \text{(ii)}$$

From Eqs. (i) and (ii), we get

$$\frac{4\pi^2 r^3}{GM} = Kr^3 = GMK = 4\pi^2$$

03. *(c)* Suppose, the smaller body cover a distance x before collision, then

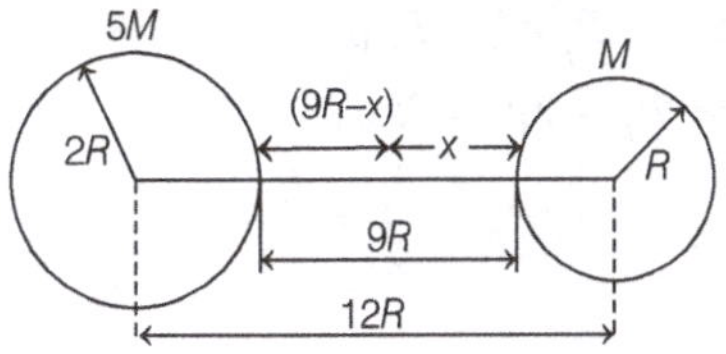

Using law of gravitation,

$$F = \frac{Gm_1 m_2}{r^2} \text{ and } F = ma$$

So, $a_{\text{small}} = \frac{F}{M} = \frac{G \times 5M}{(12R - x)^2}$

and $a_{\text{big}} = \frac{F}{5M} = \frac{G \times M}{(12R - x)^2}$

Using second equation of motion

$$x = \frac{1}{2}at^2 = \frac{a_{\text{small}}}{2}t^2 = \frac{5 \times GM \times t^2}{2(12R - x)^2} \quad \ldots \text{(i)}$$

$$9R - x = \frac{a_{\text{big}} t^2}{2} = \frac{GM \times t^2}{2(12R - x)^2} \quad \ldots \text{(ii)}$$

Dividing Eq. (i) by Eq. (ii)

$$x = 45R - 5x$$

$$\Rightarrow \quad 6x = 45R = x = 7.5\,R$$

04. *(a)* We know that, Power,

$$P = \mathbf{F} \cdot \mathbf{v} = Fv\cos\theta$$

where, F is gravitational force

So, just before hitting, θ is zero, power will be maximum.

05. *(a)* Given, mass, $m = 6 \times 10^{24}$ kg

angular velocity, $\omega = 2 \times 10^{-7}$ rad/s

Radius, $r = 1.5 \times 10^8$ km

Force exerted on Earth $= mR\omega^2$

$$= (6 \times 10^{24}) \times (1.5 \times 10^8 \times 10^3) \times (2 \times 10^{-7})^2$$

$$= 36 \times 10^{21} \text{ N}$$

Topic 3

01. *(d)* We know that

$$g = \frac{GM}{R^2}$$

According to question,

$$g = \frac{G\left(\frac{M}{10}\right)}{\left(\frac{R}{2}\right)^2} = \frac{GM \times 4}{R^2 \times 10} = \frac{GM}{R^2} \times \frac{2}{5}$$

Hence, $\frac{g'}{g} = \frac{\frac{GM}{R^2} \times \frac{2}{5}}{\frac{GM}{R^2}}$

$$\Rightarrow \quad g' = \frac{2}{5} \times g = \frac{2}{5} \times 9.8 = 3.92 \text{ ms}^{-2}$$

02. *(a)* Given, mass of body, $m = 60$ g

$$= 6 \times 10^{-2} \text{kg}$$

Gravitational force, $F = 3.0$ N

Magnitude of gravitational field intensity,

$$I = \frac{F}{m} = \frac{3}{6 \times 10^{-2}}$$

$$= 50 \text{ N/kg}$$

03. *(b)* Radius of Earth $= R$

Let at depth d, gravitational acceleration becomes $\frac{g}{n}$.

i.e., $\quad g_d = \frac{g}{n} \Rightarrow g\left(1 - \frac{d}{R}\right) = \frac{g}{n}$

$$\Rightarrow \quad 1 - \frac{d}{R} = \frac{1}{n} \Rightarrow 1 - \frac{1}{n} = \frac{d}{R}$$

$$\Rightarrow \quad \frac{n-1}{n} = \frac{d}{R} \Rightarrow d = \left(\frac{n-1}{n}\right)R$$

• Concept Enhancer

The force of attraction exerted by the Earth on a body is called gravitational pull or gravity.

We know that when a force acts on a body, it produces acceleration. Therefore, a body under effect of gravitational pull must accelerate.

Variation in g with depth is given by

$$g' = g\left[1 - \frac{d}{R}\right]$$

04. *(a)* Given, $w = mg = 72$ N (on the surface of Earth).

At height equal to half of radius of the Earth, $\left(\text{i.e. } h = \frac{R}{2}\right)$

Acceleration due to gravity,

$$g' = g\left(\frac{R}{R+h}\right)^2$$

$$= g\left(\frac{R}{R + R/2}\right)^2 = g\left(\frac{4R^2}{9R^2}\right)$$

$$\Rightarrow \quad g' = \frac{4}{9}g$$

$$\Rightarrow \quad mg' = \frac{4}{9}mg = \frac{4}{9} \times 72 = 32 \text{ N}$$

$$w' = 32 \text{ N}$$

05. *(c)* Given, weight of the body,

$$w = 200 \text{ N}$$

Gravitational acceleration at a depth d below the Earth's surface is given as

$$g' = g\left(1 - \frac{d}{R}\right) \quad \ldots \text{(i)}$$

Multiplying m on the both sides of Eq. (i), we get

$$mg' = mg\left(1 - \frac{d}{R}\right)$$

Thus, the weight of the body at half way down $\left(\text{i.e. } d = \frac{R}{2}\right)$ to the centre of the Earth is

$$mg' = 200 \times \left(1 - \frac{R/2}{R}\right)$$

$$= 200\left(1 - \frac{1}{2}\right) = 200 \times \frac{1}{2} = 100\text{N}$$

06. *(d)* Let the original mass of Sun was M_s and gravitational constant G'. According to the question,

New mass of Sun, $M_s' = \frac{M_s}{10}$

New gravitational constant, $G' = 10\,G$

As, the acceleration due to gravity is given as

$$g = \frac{GM_E}{R^2} \quad \ldots\text{(i)}$$

where, M_E is the mass of Earth and R is the radius of the Earth.

Now, new acceleration due to gravity,

$$g' = \frac{G'M_e}{R^2} = \frac{10\,M_e G}{R^2} \ldots\text{(ii)}$$

$\therefore \quad g' = 10\,g$ [from Eqs. (i) and (ii)]

This means that the acceleration due to gravity has been increased. Hence, force of gravity acting on a body placed on or surface of the Earth increases.

Due to this, rain drops will fall faster, walking on ground would become more difficult.

As, time period of the simple pendulum is

$$T = 2\pi\sqrt{\frac{l}{g}} \text{ or } T \propto \frac{1}{\sqrt{g}}$$

Thus, time period of the pendulum also decreases with the increase in g.

07. *(d)* g_h = Acceleration due to gravity at height h above earth's surface

$$= g\left(\frac{R}{R+h}\right)^2 = g\left(1 - \frac{2h}{R}\right)$$

g_d = Acceleration at depth d below earth's surface

$$= g\left(1 - \frac{d}{R}\right)$$

Given, when $h = 1$ km, $g_d = g_h$

or $\quad g\left(1 - \frac{d}{R}\right) = g\left(1 - \frac{2h}{R}\right)$

$\Rightarrow \quad d = 2h$ or $d = 2$ km

08. *(b)* Acceleration due to gravity at a depth d below the surface of the Earth is given by

$$g_{\text{depth}} = g_{\text{surface}}\left(1 - \frac{d}{R}\right)$$

Also, for a point at height h above surface,

$$g_{\text{height}} = g_{\text{surface}}\left[\frac{R^2}{(R+h)^2}\right]$$

Therefore, we can say that value of g increases from centre of maximum at the surface and then decreases as depicted in graph (b).

09. *(a)* For a point inside the Earth i.e. $r < R$, gravitational field intensity is given by $E = \frac{GM}{R^3} r$

where M and R be mass and radius of the Earth respectively.

At the centre, $r = 0$

$\therefore \quad E = 0$

For a point outside the Earth i.e. $r > R$, gravitational field intensity is given by

$$E = \frac{GM}{r^2}$$

On the surface of the Earth i.e. $r = R$,

$$E = -\frac{GM}{R^2}$$

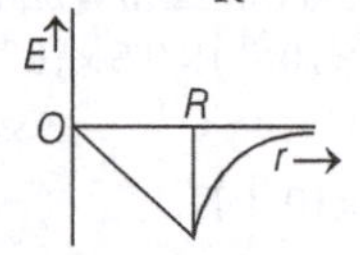

10. *(a)*

key idea

Apply Newton's law of gravitation

i.e. $\quad F = G\frac{Mm}{R^2}$

According to Newton's law of gravitational force,

$$F = \frac{GMm}{R^2}$$

Force on planet of mass M_p and body of mass m is given by

$$F = \frac{GM_p m}{(D_p/2)^2}$$

$\left[\begin{array}{l}\text{where, } D_p = \text{diameter of planet} \\ \text{and } R_p = \text{radius of planet} = \frac{D_p}{2}\end{array}\right]$

$$F = \frac{4GM_p m}{D_p^2}$$

As we know that, $F = ma$

So, acceleration due to gravity

$$a = \frac{F}{m} = \frac{4GM_p}{D_p^2}$$

11. *(a)* The acceleration due to gravity

$$g = \frac{GM}{R^2} \quad \ldots\text{(i)}$$

but $M = \frac{4}{3}\pi R^3 \rho$, where ρ being density.

Thus, Eq. (i) becomes

$$g = \frac{G \times \frac{4}{3}\pi R^3 \rho}{R^2} = G \times \frac{4}{3}\pi R \rho$$

$\Rightarrow \quad g \propto R$

$\therefore \quad \frac{g'}{g} = \frac{R'}{R}$

$\Rightarrow \quad \frac{g'}{g} = \frac{3R}{R} = 3$

$\Rightarrow \quad g' = 3g$

12. *(d)* The acceleration due to gravity on an object of mass m

$$g = \frac{F}{m}$$

but from Newton's law of gravitation

$$F = \frac{GMm}{R^2}$$

where, M is the mass of the earth and R is the radius of the Earth.

$$\therefore \quad g = \frac{GMm/R^2}{m} = \frac{GM}{R^2}$$

$\left[\because M_p = \frac{4}{3}\pi R_p^3 \rho_p \text{ and } M_e = \frac{4}{3}\pi R_e^3 \rho_e\right]$

Given, $\rho_{\text{planet}} = 2\,\rho_{\text{earth}}$

Also, $g_{\text{planet}} = g_{\text{earth}}$

$$\frac{GM_p}{R_p^2} = \frac{GM_e}{R_e^2}$$

As, Density $(\rho) = \frac{\text{Mass}\,(M)}{\text{Volume}\,(V)}$

So, $$\frac{G \times \frac{4}{3}\pi R_p^3 \rho_p}{R_p^2} = \frac{G \times \frac{4}{3}\pi R_e^3 \rho_e}{R_e^2}$$

or $\quad R_p \rho_p = R_e \rho_e$

or $\quad R_p \times 2\rho_e = R_e \rho_e$

or $\quad R_p = \frac{R_e}{2} = \frac{R}{2}$

13. *(d)* Here,

$$g_A = 9g_B \quad \text{...(i)}$$

From third equation of motion,

$$v^2 = 2gh$$

At planet A, $h_A = \dfrac{v^2}{2g_A}$ ...(ii)

At planet B, $h_B = \dfrac{v^2}{2g_B}$ ...(iii)

Dividing Eq. (ii) by Eq. (i), we have

$$\frac{h_A}{h_B} = \frac{g_B}{g_A}$$

From Eq. (i), $g_A = 9g_B$

$$\therefore \quad \frac{h_A}{h_B} = \frac{g_B}{9g_B} = \frac{1}{9}$$

or $\quad h_B = 9h_A = 9 \times 2 = 18 \text{ m}$

$(\because h_A = 2 \text{ m})$

14. *(a)* Given depth,

$$d = 100 \text{ km}$$

Radius of Earth,

$$R = 6400 \text{ km}$$

We know that effective gravity g' at depth below Earth surface is given by

$$g' = g\left(1 - \frac{d}{R}\right)$$

$$\therefore \quad g' = 9.8\left(1 - \frac{100}{6400}\right)$$

$$= 9.65 \text{ m/s}^2$$

15. *(a)* Acceleration due to gravity is given by

$$g = G \times \frac{M}{R^2} = G\frac{(4/3)\pi R^3 \times \rho}{R^2}$$

$$= G \times \frac{4}{3}\pi R \times \rho \quad (\because M = V \times \rho)$$

$$\Rightarrow \quad \rho = \frac{3g}{4\pi GR}$$

16. *(c)* Given radius of Earth,

$$R_e = 6400 \text{ km}$$

Radius of Mars, $R_m = 3200$ km,

Mass of Earth, $M_e = 10M_m$

and weight of the object on Earth,

$$w_e = 200 \text{ N}$$

$$\frac{w_m}{w_e} = \frac{mg_m}{mg_e} = \frac{M_m}{M_e} \times \left(\frac{R_e}{R_m}\right)^2$$

$$= \frac{1}{10} \times (2)^2 = \frac{2}{5}$$

$$\Rightarrow \quad w_m = w_e \times \frac{2}{5}$$

$$= 200 \times 0.4 = 80 \text{ N}$$

Topic 4

01. *(a)* Given, altitude, $h = 2R$

From surface, $r_1 = R$

and $\quad r_2 = 2R + R = 3R$

Then, energy required to launch a satellite from orbit r_1 to r_2 is sum of difference in energies in the orbit ΔE and energy on surface of Earth.

$$\Delta E = GMm\left(\frac{1}{r_1} - \frac{1}{r_2}\right) = GMm\left(\frac{1}{R} - \frac{1}{3R}\right)$$

$$= \frac{2}{3}\left(\frac{GMm}{R}\right)$$

Energy of surface $= \dfrac{1}{2}mv^2$

$$v^2 = \frac{GM}{r_{\text{orbit}}} = \frac{GM}{3R}$$

$$\therefore \text{ Minimum energy} = \Delta E + \frac{GMm}{6R}$$

$$= \frac{5}{6}GMm/R$$

02. *(b)* The given situation is shown below.

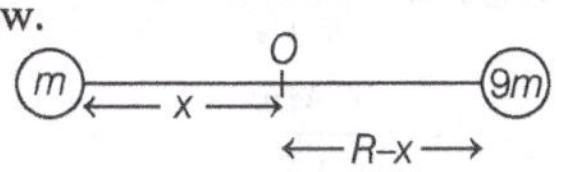

Since, gravitational field at point O is zero, hence

$$\frac{Gm}{x^2} = \frac{G(9m)}{(R-x)^2}$$

$$\Rightarrow \quad \left(\frac{1}{x}\right)^2 = \left(\frac{3}{R-x}\right)^2 \Rightarrow \frac{1}{x} = \frac{3}{R-x}$$

$$\Rightarrow \quad 3x = R - x \quad \Rightarrow x = \frac{R}{4}$$

$\therefore$ Gravitational potential at point O

$$V = \frac{-Gm}{x} + \left[\frac{-G(9m)}{R-x}\right]$$

$$= \frac{-Gm}{\frac{R}{4}} - \frac{9Gm}{R - \frac{R}{4}}$$

$$= -\frac{4Gm}{R} - \frac{12Gm}{R} = -\frac{16Gm}{R}$$

03. *(b)*

key idea

Amount of work done in moving a given body from one point to another against the gravitational force is equal to the change in potential energy of the body.

As we know, the potential energy of body of mass m of the surface of Earth is

$$U_1 = -\frac{GMm}{R} \quad \text{...(i)}$$

When the mass is raised to a height h from the surface of the Earth, then the potential energy of the body becomes

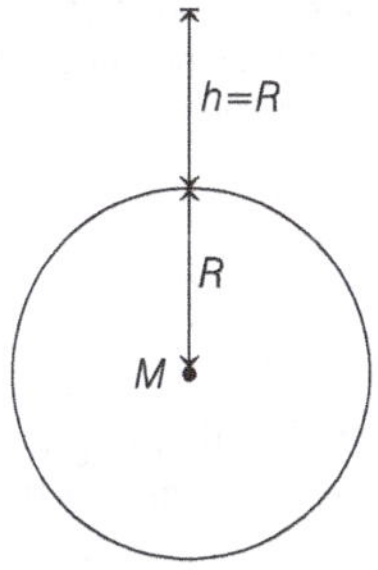

$$U_2 = -\frac{GMm}{(R+h)}$$

Here, $\quad h = R \quad$ (given)

$$\Rightarrow \quad U_2 = -\frac{GMm}{2R} \quad \text{... (ii)}$$

Thus, the change in potential energy,

$$\Delta U = U_2 - U_1$$

Substituting the values from Eqs. (i) and (ii), we get

$$\Delta U = -\frac{GMm}{2R} + \frac{GMm}{R}$$

$$= \frac{GMm}{2R} = \frac{gR^2m}{2R} \quad \left[\because g = \frac{GM}{R^2}\right]$$

$$= \frac{mgR}{2}$$

Thus, the work done in raising the mass to a height R is equals to $\dfrac{mgR}{2}$.

04. *(b)* The gravitational potential energy of an object placed at Earth's surface is

$$U_1 = -\frac{GMm}{R} \quad \text{...(i)}$$

The negative sign in the above relation indicates that it is the work done in bringing the object from infinity to a distance R.

The gravitational potential energy of object at a height h above the surface of earth is

$$U_2 = -\frac{GMm}{(R+h)} \quad \text{...(ii)}$$

So, the change in potential energy is

$$\Delta U = U_2 - U_1 = -\frac{GMm}{R+h} - \left(-\frac{GMm}{R}\right)$$

[From Eq. (i) and (ii)]

$$= -GMm\left[\frac{1}{(R+h)} - \frac{1}{R}\right]$$

$$= -GMm\left(-\frac{h}{R(R+h)}\right) = \frac{GMmh}{R(R+h)}$$

05. *(d)*

key idea

Equate the formula of gravitational potential energy and acceleration due to gravity and find the value of h.

Gravitational potential at some height h from the surface of the Earth is given by

$$V = -\frac{GM}{R+h} \quad \dots\text{(i)}$$

And acceleration due to gravity at some height h from the Earth surface can be given as

$$g' = \frac{GM}{(R+h)^2} \quad \dots\text{(ii)}$$

From Eqs. (i) and (ii), we get

$$\frac{|V|}{g'} = \frac{GM}{(R+h)} \times \frac{(R+h)^2}{GM}$$

$$\Rightarrow \frac{|V|}{g'} = R + h \quad \dots\text{(iii)}$$

$\because \quad V = -5.4 \times 10^7 \text{ J kg}^{-2}$

and $\quad g' = 6.0 \text{ ms}^{-2}$

Radius of Earth, $R = 6400$ km.

Substitute these values in Eq. (iii), we get

$$\frac{5.4 \times 10^7}{6.0} = R + h$$

$$\Rightarrow 9 \times 10^6 = R + h$$

$$\Rightarrow h = (9 - 6.4) \times 10^6 = 2.6 \times 10^6 \text{ m}$$

$$\Rightarrow h = 2600 \text{ km}$$

06. *(d)* The resulting gravitational potential,

$$V = -2G\left[\frac{1}{1} + \frac{1}{2} + \frac{1}{4} + \frac{1}{8} + \dots\right]$$

$$\Rightarrow V = -2G\left[1 + \frac{1}{2} + \frac{1}{2^2} + \frac{1}{2^3}\dots\right]$$

$$\Rightarrow V = -2G\left(1 + \frac{1}{2}\right)^{-1}$$

$$\Rightarrow V = -\frac{2G}{\left(1 - \frac{1}{2}\right)} = -\frac{2G}{\left(\frac{1}{2}\right)} = -4G$$

07. *(b)* Change in potential energy

So, $\Delta U = -\frac{GMm}{R + 2R} - \left(-\frac{GMm}{R}\right)$

Where, $U_{\text{Final}} = \frac{GMm}{R + 2R}$

$U_{\text{initial}} = \frac{-GMm}{R}$

$$\therefore \Delta U = -\frac{GMm}{3R} + \frac{GMm}{R}$$

$$= \frac{2\,GMm}{3R} = \frac{2}{3} mgR \left[\because g = \frac{GM}{R^2}\right]$$

08. *(c)* According to the question,

$$\frac{GMm}{(R+h)^2} = \frac{1}{16}\frac{GMm}{R^2}$$

where, $m =$ mass of the body

and $\frac{GM}{R^2} =$ gravitational acceleration

$$\frac{1}{(R+h)^2} = \frac{1}{16R^2} \text{ or } \frac{R}{R+h} = \frac{1}{4}$$

or $\frac{R+h}{R} = 4,\ h = 3R$

09. *(c)* Potential energy, $U = -\frac{GMm}{r}$

At the earth's surface, $r = R$

$$\therefore \quad U_e = -\frac{GMm}{R}$$

Now, if a body is taken to height $h = 3R$, then the potential energy is given by

$$U_h = -\frac{GMm}{R+h} \quad (\because r = h + R)$$

$$= -\frac{GMm}{4R}$$

Thus, change in gravitational potential energy,

$$\Delta U = U_h - U_e$$

$$= -\frac{GMm}{4R} - \left(-\frac{GMm}{R}\right)$$

$$= -\frac{GMm}{4R} + \frac{GMm}{R} = \frac{3}{4}\frac{GMm}{R}$$

$$\therefore \Delta U = \frac{3}{4}\frac{gR^2m}{R} \quad (\because GM = gR^2)$$

$$= \frac{3}{4} mgR$$

Alternate Solution

The gravitational potential energy at height h from the surface of earth is given by

$$\Delta U = \frac{mgh}{1 + \frac{h}{R}}$$

Here, $3R = h$

$$\Rightarrow \Delta U = \frac{mg(3R)}{1 + \frac{3R}{R}} = \frac{3}{4} mgR$$

10. *(a)* Let u be the initial velocity by which particle is projected and at maximum height, velocity becomes zero. So, from conservation of energy, we have

$$\frac{1}{2}mu^2 - \frac{GMm}{R} = \frac{1}{2}m \times (0)^2 - \frac{GMm}{(R+R)}$$

$$\Rightarrow \quad u^2 = \frac{2GM}{R} - \frac{2GM}{2R} = \frac{GM}{R}$$

$$\Rightarrow \quad u = \sqrt{\frac{GM}{R}}$$

11. *(a)* Energy at surface of the Earth = energy at maximum height

or $(K + U)$ at the Earth's surface $= (K + U)$ at maximum height

$$\therefore \frac{1}{2}mu^2 - \frac{GMm}{R} = \frac{1}{2}m \times (0)^2 - \frac{GMm}{R+h}$$

At maximum height, it has only potential energy,

or $\frac{1}{2}mu^2 = \frac{GMm}{R} - \frac{GMm}{R+R} \quad (\because h = R)$

or $u^2 = \frac{2GM}{R} - \frac{2GM}{2R}$ or $u^2 = \frac{GM}{R}$

$$\therefore \quad u = \sqrt{\frac{GM}{R}}$$

Alternate Solution

The expression for the speed with which a body should be projected so as to reach a height h is

$$u = \sqrt{\frac{2gh}{1 + (h/R)}} \quad \text{Here, } h = R \text{ (given)}$$

$$u = \sqrt{\frac{2gR}{1 + (R/R)}} = \sqrt{\frac{2 \times \frac{GM}{R^2} \times R}{2}} = \sqrt{\frac{GM}{R}}$$

12. *(a)* Gravitational potential energy at height h from the surface of Earth is given by

$$\Delta U = \frac{mgh}{1 + \frac{h}{R}}$$

Here, $\quad R = 5h$

$$\Rightarrow \quad \Delta U = \frac{mgh}{1 + \frac{1}{5}} = \frac{5}{6} mgh$$

13. *(c)*

key idea

Since net external torque is zero in closed orbits, therefore apply conservation of angular momentum.

When the planet moves in circular or elliptical orbit, then torque is always acting parallel to displacement or velocity. So, angular momentum is conserved. When the field is attractive, then potential energy is given by

$$U = -\frac{GMm}{R}$$

Negative sign shows that the potential energy is due to attractive gravitational force. Kinetic energy changes as velocity increases when distance is less. For planet to move in any orbit, its total energy must be bound. Thus, E must be negative always. Hence, option (c) is correct.

14. *(a)* Gravitational field intensity is given by $I = -\frac{dV}{dx}$

If $V = 0$, then gravitational field is necessarily zero.

Topic 5

01. *(a)* Time period of satellite,

$$T = \frac{2\pi r}{v_0} \Rightarrow T = \frac{2\pi(R_e + h)}{v_0} \quad \ldots\text{(i)}$$

Orbital velocity, $v_0 = \sqrt{\frac{GM_e}{r}}$

$$\Rightarrow \quad v_0 = \sqrt{\frac{GM_e}{(R_e + h)}} \quad \ldots\text{(ii)}$$

From Eq. (i) and Eq. (ii), we get

$$T = \frac{2\pi(R_e + h)}{\sqrt{\frac{GM_e}{R_e + h}}}$$

$$= 2\pi\sqrt{\frac{(R_e + h)^3}{GM_e}} \quad \ldots\text{(iii)}$$

Since, $M_e = \frac{4}{3}\pi R_e^3 d$

$\therefore$ Putting the value of M_e in Eq. (iii), we get

$$T = 2\pi\sqrt{\frac{(R_e + h)^3}{G\cdot\frac{4}{3}\pi R_e^3 d}} = \sqrt{\frac{3\pi(R_e + h)^3}{GdR_e^3}}$$

Since, satellite is orbiting just above the surface of the Earth, hence $h = 0$

$$\therefore \quad T = \sqrt{\frac{3\pi R_e^3}{GdR_e^3}} = \sqrt{\frac{3\pi}{Gd}}$$

02. *(d)* We know that, escape velocity from Earth's surface,

$$v_e = \sqrt{\frac{2GM_e}{R_e}}$$

Also, Density $= \frac{\text{Mass}}{\text{Volume}}$

$\Rightarrow$ Mass = Density × Volume

or $M_e = \rho \times V$

or $M_e = \rho \times \frac{4}{3}\pi R_e^3 \quad \left(\because V = \frac{4}{3}\pi R_e^3\right)$

Substituting the values in the escape velocity expression, we get

$$v_e = \sqrt{\frac{2G\rho \times \frac{4}{3}\pi R_e^3}{R_e}}$$

$$v_e = \sqrt{2G\rho \times \frac{4}{3}\pi R_e^2} \quad \ldots\text{(i)}$$

Given, radius of another planet is 4 times the radius of the Earth,

$$\Rightarrow v_p = \sqrt{2G\rho \times \frac{4}{3}\pi R_p^2}$$

$$v_p = \sqrt{2G\rho \times \frac{4}{3}\pi(4R_e)^2} \quad (\because R_p = 4R_e)$$

$$v_p = 4\sqrt{2G\rho \times \frac{4}{3}\pi(R_e)^2} \quad \ldots\text{(ii)}$$

On dividing Eq. (ii) by Eq. (i), we get

$$\frac{v_p}{v_e} = \frac{4\sqrt{2G\rho \times \frac{4}{3}\pi(R_e)^2}}{\sqrt{2G\rho \times \frac{4}{3}\pi R_e^2}}$$

$$\Rightarrow \quad v_p = 4v_e = 4v$$

• Concept Enhancer

Escape velocity is defined as the velocity at which an object travels to break free from the Earth's gravity or planet's gravity without any development of propulsion. It is written as

$$v_e = \sqrt{\frac{2GM}{R}}$$

03. *(d)* Given

Initial energy at the time of projection

$$= \frac{1}{2}mv^2 - \frac{GMm}{R}$$

Final energy at the maximum height h from surface of the Earth

$$= \frac{1}{2}mv^2 - \frac{GMm}{R+h} = \frac{1}{2}m(0)^2 - \frac{GMm}{R+h}$$

($\because$ final velocity is zero at height h from the surface of the Earth)

$$= -\frac{GMm}{R+h}$$

Using the law of conservation of energy, initial energy at the time of projection = final energy at the maximum height h from the surface of the Earth

$$\frac{1}{2}mv^2 - \frac{GMm}{R} = -\frac{GMm}{R+h}$$

Substituting the values in the above equation, we get

$$\frac{1}{2}m(kv_e)^2 - \frac{GMm}{R} = -\frac{GMm}{R+h}$$

$$\Rightarrow \frac{1}{2}mk^2\left(2\frac{GM}{R}\right) - \frac{GMm}{R} = -\frac{GMm}{R+h} \quad \left(\because v_e = \sqrt{\frac{2GM}{R}}\right)$$

$$\Rightarrow \quad \frac{k^2}{R} - \frac{1}{R} = -\frac{1}{R+h}$$

$$\Rightarrow \quad \frac{1}{R+h} = \frac{1}{R} - \frac{k^2}{R}$$

$$\Rightarrow \quad \frac{R}{1-k^2} = R + h$$

$$\Rightarrow \quad h = \frac{R}{1-k^2} - R$$

$$\Rightarrow \quad h = R\left(\frac{1}{1-k^2} - 1\right)$$

$$\Rightarrow \quad h = R\left(\frac{1-1+k^2}{1-k^2}\right)$$

$$\Rightarrow \quad h = R\left(\frac{k^2}{1-k^2}\right)$$

04. *(a)* Since, the escape velocity of Earth can be given as

$$v_e = \sqrt{2gR} = R\sqrt{\frac{8}{3}\pi G\rho}$$

[ρ = density of earth]

$$\Rightarrow \quad v_e = R\sqrt{\frac{8}{3}\pi G\rho} \quad \ldots\text{(i)}$$

As it is given that the radius and mean density of planet are twice as that of earth. So, escape velocity at planet will be

$$v_p = 2R\sqrt{\frac{8}{3}\pi G 2\rho} \quad \ldots\text{(ii)}$$

Divide, Eq. (i) by Eq. (ii), we get

$$\frac{v_e}{v_p} = \frac{R\sqrt{\frac{8}{3}\pi G\rho}}{2R\sqrt{\frac{8}{3}\pi G 2\rho}} = \frac{1}{2\sqrt{2}}$$

05. *(b)*

key idea

Use conservation of energy at initial time of projection and at maximum height.

i.e., $\frac{1}{2}mv^2 - \frac{GMm}{R} = -\frac{GMm}{R+h}$

∵ Total energy of a satellite at height h is

$$= \text{KE} + \text{PE} = \frac{GMm}{2(R+h)} - \frac{GMm}{(R+h)}$$

$$= \frac{-GMm}{2(R+h)} = \frac{-GMmR^2}{2R^2(R+h)} = \frac{-mg_0R^2}{2(R+h)}$$

$$\left(\because g_0 = \frac{GM}{R^2}\right)$$

06. *(a)* Given, height of a satellite

$h = 0.25 \times 10^6$ m

Earth's radius, $R_e = 6.38 \times 10^6$ m

For the satellite revolving around the earth, orbital velocity of the satellite

$$v_0 = \sqrt{\frac{GM_e}{R_e}} = \sqrt{\frac{GM_e}{R_e\left[1+\frac{h}{R_e}\right]}}$$

$$\Rightarrow v_0 = \sqrt{\frac{gR_e}{1+\frac{h}{R_e}}}$$

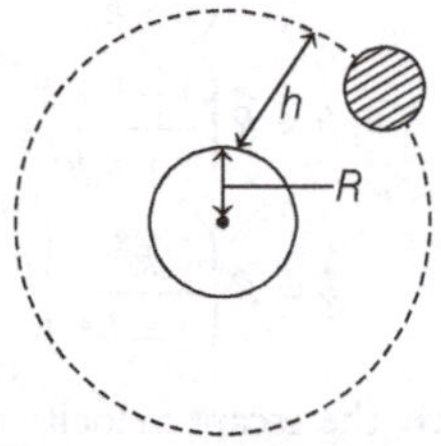

Substitutes the values of g, R_e and h, we get

$$v_0 = \sqrt{60 \times 10^6} \text{ m/s}$$

$$v_0 = 7.76 \times 10^3 = 7.76 \text{ km/s}$$

Alternate Solution

The orbital velocity of satellite is

$$v = \sqrt{\frac{GM}{R+h}}$$

$$= \sqrt{\frac{6.67 \times 10^{-11} \times 6 \times 10^{24}}{(6.4 \times 10^6) + (0.25 \times 10^6)}} = 7.76 \text{ km/s}$$

07. *(d)* As there is no external force, so according to conservating of energy, total mechanical energy of S is constant always. Also, as in the absence of external torque, angular momentum L is constant. Also, linear momentum is not constant. As we know that force on satellite is only gravitational force which will always be towards the centre of Earth. Thus, the acceleration of S is always directed towards the centre of the Earth.

08. *(c)*

key idea

For the black hole, the escape speed is more than c (speed of light). We should compare the escape speed with c (Note that the escape speed should be at least equal to c).

Escape velocity of an object mass M and radius R is given by

$$v_e = \sqrt{\frac{2GM}{R'}}$$

[R' = New radius of the earth]

$$c = \sqrt{\frac{2GM}{R'}} \qquad [v_e \approx c]$$

$$\Rightarrow c^2 = 2\frac{GM}{R'}$$

$$R' = \frac{2GM}{c^2}$$

$$= \frac{2 \times 6.67 \times 10^{-11} \times 5.98 \times 10^{24}}{9 \times 10^{16}}$$

$$= \frac{79.773}{9} \times 10^{-3}$$

$$= 8.863 \times 10^{-3} = 0.886 \times 10^{-2} = 10^{-2} \text{ m}$$

09. *(a)* Given, height $= 3R$

The minimum speed with which the particle should be projected from the surface of the earth so that it does not return back is known as escape speed and it is given by

$$v_e \sqrt{\frac{2GM}{(R+h)}}$$

$$\Rightarrow v_e = \sqrt{\frac{2GM}{(R+3R)}}$$

$$= \sqrt{\frac{2GM}{4R}} = \sqrt{\frac{GM}{2R}}$$

10. *(d)* Escape velocity is given by

$$v_e = \sqrt{\frac{2GM}{R}} \qquad \text{...(i)}$$

The orbital velocity of a satellite close to the Earth's surface is given by

$$v_0 = \sqrt{\frac{GM}{R}} \qquad \text{...(ii)}$$

From Eq. (i) and Eq. (ii), we get

$$v_e = \sqrt{2}v_0$$

11. *(b)* According to law of conservation of mechanical energy between the instants, the particle is at the surface of the Earth and at a very large distance is

$$u_i + k_i = u_f + k_f$$

$$\frac{1}{2}mu^2 - \frac{GMm}{R} = 0 \text{ or } u^2 = \frac{2GM}{R}$$

$$u = \sqrt{\frac{2GM}{R}} = \sqrt{2gR}$$

$$\left(\because g = \frac{GM}{R^2}\right)$$

12. *(d)* As we know that

$$\text{KE} = \left(\frac{-GMm}{2R_2}\right) - \left(\frac{GMm}{2R_1}\right)$$

$$= \frac{GMm}{2}\left(\frac{1}{R_1} - \frac{1}{R_2}\right)$$

13. *(c)* When two satellites of the Earth are moving in same orbit, then time period of both are equal.

From Kepler's third law, $T^2 \propto r^3$

Time period is independent of mass, hence their time periods will be equal. The potential energy and kinetic energy are mass dependent, hence the potential energy and kinetic energy of satellites are not equal.

But, if they are orbiting in a same orbit, then they have equal orbital speed.

14. *(b)* At a platform at a height h,

Escape energy = binding energy of sphere

$$\text{or} \quad \frac{1}{2}m(fv_e)^2 = \frac{GMm}{R+h}$$

$$\text{or} \quad fv_e = \sqrt{\frac{2GM}{R+h}} = \sqrt{\frac{2GM}{2R}} \qquad \text{...(i)}$$

$$(\because h = R)$$

But at surface of the Earth,

$$v_e = \sqrt{\frac{2GM}{R}} \qquad \text{...(ii)}$$

Dividing Eq. (ii) by Eq. (i).

$$\text{Hence,} \quad \frac{fv_e}{v_e} = \frac{\sqrt{\frac{GM}{R}}}{\sqrt{\frac{2GM}{R}}}$$

$$\Rightarrow \quad f = \frac{1}{\sqrt{2}}$$

15. *(b)* Potential energy, $U = -\dfrac{GM_em}{R_e}$

where, M_e = mass of the Earth

m = mass of satellite

R_e = radius of the Earth

G = gravitational constant

$$\text{or} \quad |U| = \frac{GM_em}{R_e}$$

$$\text{Kinetic energy, } K = \frac{1}{2}\frac{GM_em}{R_e}$$

$$\text{Thus, } \frac{K}{|U|} = \frac{1}{2}\frac{GM_em}{R_e} \times \frac{R_e}{GM_em} = \frac{1}{2}$$

16. *(c)* Given, Mass of the satellite = m
Height of satellite from Earth,
$h = 6.4 \times 10^6$ m
Gravitational potential energy of the satellite at height h is given by

$$U = -\frac{GM_e m}{R_e + h} = -\frac{gR_e^2 m}{2R_e}$$

$$= -\frac{gR_e m}{2} = -0.5mgR_e$$

17. *(c)*

key idea
Compare the equation of escape velocity of Earth and planet.

Escape velocity is given by,

$$v_{es} = \sqrt{\frac{2GM_e}{R_e}}$$

From a planet, $v'_{es} = \sqrt{\frac{2GM_p}{R_p}}$

Therefore, $\frac{v'_{es}}{v_{es}} = \sqrt{\frac{2GM_p}{R_p}} \times \sqrt{\frac{R_e}{2GM_e}}$

It is given that,
mass of the planet = mass of the Earth
i.e. $M_p = M_e$

So, $\frac{v'_{es}}{v_{es}} = \sqrt{\frac{R_e}{R_p}}$ ...(i)

Given, $R_p = \frac{R_e}{4} \Rightarrow \frac{R_p}{R_e} = \frac{1}{4}$

and $v_{es} = 11.2$ km/s
Substituting in Eq. (i), we have

$$\frac{v'_{es}}{11.2} = \sqrt{\frac{4}{1}} = 2,$$

$$v'_{es} = 11.2 \times 2 = 22.4 \text{ km/s}$$

18. *(b)* The binding energy of sphere of mass m (say) on the surface of the Earth kept at rest is $\frac{GM_e m}{R_e}$. To escape it from the Earth's surface, this much energy in the form of kinetic energy is supplied to it.

So, $\frac{1}{2}mv_e^2 = \frac{GM_e m}{R_e}$

or v_e = escape velocity = $\sqrt{\frac{2GM_e}{R_e}}$

where, R_e = radius of Earth,
M_e = mass of the Earth.

19. *(b)* The ball, when dropped from the orbiting satellite will not reach the surface of the Earth. When a ball is dropped from the satellite, the ball also starts moving with the same speed due to inertia. As the orbit of a satellite does not depend upon its mass, the ball continues to move along with the satellite in the same orbit.

20. *(a)* Escape velocity on surface of the Earth is given by

$$v_e = \sqrt{2gR_e} = \sqrt{\frac{2GM_e}{R_e}} \quad \left(\because g = \frac{GM_e}{R_e^2}\right)$$

where, M_e = mass of Earth
R_e = radius of the Earth
G = gravitational constant

$$\therefore \quad v_e \propto \sqrt{\frac{M_e}{R_e}}$$

If v_p is the escape velocity from the surface of the planet, then

$$\frac{v_e}{v_p} = \sqrt{\frac{M_e}{R_e}} \times \sqrt{\frac{R_p}{M_p}}$$

where, M_p is mass of the planet and R_p is radius of the planet.

but $R_p = 3R_e$ (given)
and $M_p = 3M_e$

$$\therefore \quad \frac{v_e}{v_p} = \sqrt{\frac{M_e}{R_e}} \times \sqrt{\frac{3R_e}{3M_e}} = \frac{1}{1} = 1$$

or $v_p = v_e$

21. *(c)* The force acting on the satellite is given by

$$F = \frac{d}{dt}(Mv) = \frac{dv}{dt}M + v\frac{dM}{dt}$$

$$= \frac{Mdv}{dt} + v(\alpha v)$$

We know that the net force is zero,
$F = 0$

$$M\frac{dv}{dt} = -v(\alpha v)$$

$$\frac{dv}{dt} = a = -\frac{\alpha v^2}{M}$$

22. *(a)* Let v_o be orbital speed and r be is the radius of orbit of a geostationary satellite. So, time period of satellite

$$T = \frac{2\pi r}{v_o}$$

As, $v_o = \sqrt{\frac{GM}{r}} = \sqrt{\frac{gR^2}{r}} \quad \left(\because g = \frac{GM}{R^2}\right)$

$$\therefore \quad T = \frac{2\pi r}{(gR^2/r)^{1/2}}$$

$$= \frac{2\pi r^{3/2}}{\sqrt{gR^2}}$$

but $T = \frac{2\pi}{\omega}$

$$\Rightarrow \quad T = \frac{2\pi r^{3/2}}{\sqrt{gR^2}} = \frac{2\pi}{\omega}$$

Hence, $r^{3/2} = \frac{\sqrt{gR^2}}{\omega}$

or $r^3 = \frac{gR^2}{\omega^2}$

or $r = \left(\frac{gR^2}{\omega^2}\right)^{1/3}$

23. *(d)* Let satellite of mass m be revolving closely around the earth of mass M and radius R.
Total energy of satellite

$$= \text{PE} + \text{KE}$$

$$= -\frac{GMm}{R} + \frac{1}{2}mv^2$$

$$= -\frac{GMm}{R} + \frac{m}{2}\frac{GM}{R} \quad \left[\text{as } v = \sqrt{\frac{GM}{R}}\right]$$

$$= -\frac{GMm}{2R}$$

$\therefore$ Total energy of satellite $= -\frac{1}{2}mv^2$

C-08

NEET Chapterwise Topicwise Physics

In NEET 2024, 1 question was visible from this chapter. In past 5 years, 4 questions from topic-1.
For detailed analysis scan QR code

MECHANICAL PROPERTIES OF SOLID

Topic 1 Elastic behaviour of Material, Hooke's Law and Elastic Moduli

01 The maximum elongation of a steel wire of 1 m length if the elastic limit of steel and its Young's modulus, respectively, are 8×10^8 Nm^{-2} and 2×10^{11} Nm^{-2}, is *[NCERT (New) Pg. 168, NEET 2024]*

(a) 4 mm (b) 0.4 mm
(c) 40 mm (d) 8 mm

02 Let a wire be suspended from the ceiling (rigid support) and stretched by a weight w attached at its free end. The longitudinal stress at any point of cross-sectional area A of the wire is *[NCERT (New) Pg. 168, NEET 2023]*

(a) w/A (b) $w/2A$
(c) zero (d) $2w/A$

03 Given below are two statements. One is labelled as Assertion (A) and the other is labelled as Reason (R)

Assertion (A) The stretching of a spring is determined by the shear modulus of the material of the spring.

Reason (R) A coil spring of copper has more tensile strength than a steel spring of same dimensions.

In the light of the above statements, choose the most appropriate answer from the options given below *[NCERT (New) Pg. 173, NEET 2022]*

(a) Both A and R are true but R is not the correct explanation of A.
(b) A is true but R is false.
(c) A is false but R is true.
(d) Both A and R are true and R is the correct explanation of A.

04 A wire of length L, area of cross-section A is hanging from a fixed support. The length of the wire changes to L_1 when mass M is suspended from its free end. The expression for Young's modulus is *[NCERT (New) Pg. 170, NEET (Sep.) 2020]*

(a) $\dfrac{Mg(L_1 - L)}{AL}$ (b) $\dfrac{MgL}{AL_1}$

(c) $\dfrac{Mg\,L}{A(L_1 - L)}$ (d) $\dfrac{MgL_1}{AL}$

05 Two wires are made of the same material and have the same volume. The first wire has cross-sectional area A and the second wire has cross-sectional area $3A$. If the length of the first wire is increased by Δl on applying a force F, how much force is needed to stretch the second wire by the same amount? *[NEET 2018]*

(a) $4F$ (b) $6F$ (c) $9F$ (d) F

06 The bulk modulus of a spherical object is B. If it is subjected to uniform pressure p, the fractional decrease in radius is *[NCERT (New) Pg. 173, NEET 2017]*

(a) $\dfrac{p}{B}$ (b) $\dfrac{B}{3p}$ (c) $\dfrac{3p}{B}$ (d) $\dfrac{p}{3B}$

07 The Young's modulus of steel is twice that of brass. Two wires of same length and of same area of cross-section, one of steel and another of brass are suspended from the same roof. If we want the lower ends of the wires to be at the same level, then the weights added to the steel and brass wires must be in the ratio of *[AIMPT 2015]*

(a) 4 : 1 (b) 1 : 1
(c) 1 : 2 (d) 2 : 1

08 The approximate depth of an ocean is 2700 m. The compressibility of water is 45.4×10^{-11} Pa^{-1} and density of water is 10^3 km/m^3. What fractional compression of water will be obtained at the bottom of the ocean ? *[NCERT (New) Pg. 173, AIMPT 2015 Cancelled]*

(a) 1.2×10^{-2} (b) 1.4×10^{-2} (c) 0.8×10^{-2} (d) 1.0×10^{-2}

09 The following four wires are made of same material. Which of these will have the largest extension when the same tension is applied? *[NEET 2013]*

(a) Length = 50 cm, diameter = 0.5 mm
(b) Length = 100 cm, diameter = 1 mm
(c) Length = 200 cm, diameter = 2 mm
(d) Length = 300 cm, diameter = 3 mm

10 If the ratio of diameters, lengths and Young's modulus of steel and copper wires shown in the figure are p, q and s respectively, then the corresponding ratio of increase in their lengths would be *[NCERT (New) Pg. 170, NEET 2013]*

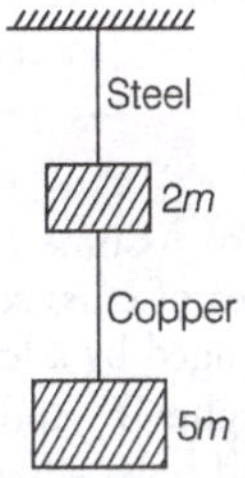

(a) $\frac{5q}{(7sp^2)}$ (b) $\frac{7q}{(5sp^2)}$ (c) $\frac{2q}{(5sp)}$ (d) $\frac{7q}{(5sp)}$

11 Two wires A and B are of the same material. Their lengths are in the ratio 1 : 2 and the diameter are in the ratio 2 : 1. If they are pulled by the same force, then increase in length will be in the ratio *[NCERT (New) Pg. 170, AIPMT 1988]*

(a) 2 : 1 (b) 1 : 4 (c) 1 : 8 (d) 8 : 1

Topic 2 Stress-Strain Curve's Elastic, Potential Energy and Thermal Stress

01 The stress-strain curves are drawn for two different materials X and Y. It is observed that the ultimate strength point and the fracture point are close to each other for material X but are far apart for material Y. We can say that materials X and Y are likely to be (respectively) *[NCERT (New) Pg. 169, NEET (Odisha) 2019]*

(a) ductile and brittle (b) brittle and ductile
(c) brittle and plastic (d) plastic and ductile

02 When a block of mass M is suspended by a long wire of length L, the length of the wire becomes $(L + l)$. The elastic potential energy stored in the extended wire is *[NEET (National) 2019]*

(a) MgL (b) $\frac{1}{2}Mgl$
(c) $\frac{1}{2}MgL$ (d) Mgl

03 Copper of fixed volume V is drawn into wire of length l. When this wire is subjected to a constant force F, the extension produced in the wire is Δl. Which of the following graph is a straight line ? *[NCERT (New) Pg. 169, AIPMT 2014]*

(a) Δl *versus* $\frac{1}{l}$
(b) Δl *versus* l^2
(c) Δl *versus* $\frac{1}{l^2}$
(d) Δl *versus* l

04 When an elastic materal with Young's modulus Y is subjected to stretching stress S, elastic energy stored per unit volume of the materials is *[AIPMT 1989]*

(a) $YS/2$ (b) $S^2Y/2$
(c) $S^2/2Y$ (d) $S/2Y$

• Key Index

Topic 1

1 (a)	2 (a)	3 (b)	4 (c)	5 (c)	6 (d)	7 (d)	8 (a)	9 (a)	10 (b)
11 (c)									

Topic 2

1 (b)	2 (b)	3 (b)	4 (c)

Detailed **Explanations**

Topic 1

01. *(a)* Length of wire = 1 m

Elastic limit, $E = 8\times10^{8}\ \text{Nm}^{-2}$

Young's modulus, $Y = 2\times10^{11}\ \text{Nm}^{-2}$

We know that, $Y = \frac{F}{A}\frac{l}{\Delta l}$

Here, $\frac{F}{A}$ = Elastic limit (E)

$$\Rightarrow \quad Y = E\frac{l}{\Delta l}$$

$$\Rightarrow \quad \Delta l = \frac{E}{Y}l$$

$$\Rightarrow \quad \Delta l = \frac{8\times10^{8}}{2\times10^{11}}\times1$$

$$= 4\times10^{-3}\ \text{m}$$

$$= 4\ \text{mm}$$

02. *(a)* Longitudinal stress $= \frac{\text{Weight}}{\text{Area}} = \frac{w}{A}$

03. *(b)* When a coil spring is stretched, neither its length nor its volume changes, but there is only the change in its shape. Therefore, stretching of a coil spring is determined by shear modulus.

Young's modulus of steel spring is more than Young's modulus of copper spring, due to which tensile strength of steel spring is more than tensile strength of copper spring.

Hence, Assertion is true but Reason is false.

04. *(c)* Here, change in length of wire,

$$\Delta L = (L_1 - L)$$

Area of cross-section = A

Force, $F = Mg$

Young's modulus,

$$Y = \frac{\text{Normal stress}}{\text{Longitudinal strain}}$$

$$\Rightarrow \quad Y = \frac{(F/A)}{\left(\frac{\Delta L}{L}\right)} = \frac{\left(\frac{Mg}{A}\right)}{\left(\frac{L_1 - L}{L}\right)}$$

$$= \frac{MgL}{A(L_1 - L)}$$

> **• Concept Enhancer**
>
> Young's modulus always inversely proportional to the longitudinal strain and directly proportional to the normal stress, measure the stifness of the material.

05. *(c)* According to the question,

For wire 1

$$\Rightarrow \quad Y_1 = \frac{F_1 l_1}{A_1\Delta l} \qquad \ldots\text{(i)}$$

For wire 2

Similarly, $$Y_2 = \frac{F_2 l_2}{A_2\Delta l} \qquad \ldots\text{(ii)}$$

$\because$ Volume, $V = Al$

or $$l = \frac{V}{A}$$

Substituting the value of l in Eqs. (i) and (ii), we get

$$Y_1 = \frac{F_1 V}{A_1^2\Delta l} \quad \text{and} \quad Y_2 = \frac{F_2 V}{A_2^2\Delta l}$$

As it is given that the wires are made up of same material, i.e. $Y_1 = Y_2$

$$\Rightarrow \quad \frac{F_1 V}{A_1^2\Delta l} = \frac{F_2 V}{A_2^2\Delta l}$$

$$\Rightarrow \quad \frac{F_1}{F_2} = \frac{A_1^2}{A_2^2} = \frac{A^2}{9A^2}$$

$$(\because A_1 = A \text{ and } A_2 = 3A)$$

$$= \frac{1}{9}$$

or $$F_2 = 9F_1 = 9F \quad (\text{given, } F_1 = F)$$

> ***Alternate Solution***
>
> Young's Modulus, $Y = \frac{Fl}{A\Delta l}$
>
> $$\Rightarrow \quad F = \frac{YA\Delta l}{l} = \frac{YA^2 Al}{V} \qquad (\because V = Al)$$
>
> $$\therefore \quad \frac{F_1}{F_2} = \left(\frac{A_1}{A_2}\right)^2 = \left(\frac{A}{3A}\right)^2 = \frac{1}{9}$$
>
> $$\Rightarrow \quad F_2 = 9F_1 = 9F$$

06. *(d)* Bulk modulus,

$$B = \frac{F/A}{\Delta V/V} = \frac{p}{\Delta V/V} \Rightarrow \frac{\Delta V}{V} = \frac{p}{B}$$

$$\Rightarrow \left|\frac{\Delta V}{V}\right| = \frac{p}{B}$$

Fractional decreases in volume

$$\Rightarrow \quad \frac{\Delta V}{V} = 3\frac{\Delta R}{R} \qquad \left[\because V = \frac{4}{3}\pi R^3\right]$$

Volume of the sphere decreases due to the decrease in its radius.

Hence, $$\frac{\Delta V}{V} = \frac{3\Delta R}{R} = \frac{p}{B} \Rightarrow \frac{\Delta R}{R} = \frac{p}{3B}$$

> **• Concept Enhancer**
>
> When pressure is applied on a body or an object, it is subjected to compression. The parameter related to compression is B. It shows the resistance offered by the object on being subjected to a pressure. Calculate the fractional decrease in radius using the given bulk modulus and applied pressure.
>
> $$B = -\frac{\Delta p}{\frac{\Delta V}{V}}$$

07. *(d)* Assume L and A are length and area of cross-section of each wire hanged by a leveled surface. Let wights W_s and W_b are added to steel and brass wires respectively.

Thus, the elongation produced in the steel wire is given by

$$\Delta L_s = \frac{W_s L}{Y_s A} \qquad \left(\text{as } Y = \frac{W/A}{\Delta L/L}\right)$$

Elongation produced in the brass wire is given by

$$\Delta L_b = \frac{W_b L}{Y_b A}$$

$\because \quad \Delta L_s = \Delta L_b$ [Given]

$$\therefore \quad \frac{W_s L}{Y_s A} = \frac{W_b L}{Y_b A} \text{ or } \frac{W_s}{W_b} = \frac{Y_s}{Y_b}$$

As given, $\frac{Y_s}{Y_b} = 2,$

$$\therefore \quad \frac{W_s}{W_b} = \frac{2}{1}$$

08. *(a)* Given,

Depth of an ocean, $d = 2700$ m

Density of water, $\rho = 10^3\ \text{kgm}^{-3}$

Compressibility of water,

$$K = 45.4\times10^{-11}\ \text{Pa}^{-1}$$

Excess pressure at the bottom, is given by

$$\Delta p = \rho g d = 10^3 \times 10 \times 2700$$

$$= 27\times10^6\ \text{Pa}$$

From bulk modulus of elasticity,

$$B = \frac{\Delta p}{(\Delta V / V)}$$

$$\Rightarrow \left(\frac{\Delta V}{V}\right) = \frac{\Delta p}{B} = K \cdot \Delta p \quad \left(\because K = \frac{1}{B}\right)$$

$$= 45.4 \times 10^{-11} \times 27 \times 10^{6}$$

$$= 1.2 \times 10^{-2}$$

09. *(a)* As $Y = \frac{F \times L}{\Delta L \times A} = \frac{mg \cdot L}{\Delta L \cdot A}$

or $\Delta L = \frac{mgL}{Y \cdot A}$

$$\Rightarrow \Delta L \propto \frac{L}{A^2} \propto \frac{L}{\pi\left(\frac{d^2}{4}\right)}$$

$$\Rightarrow \Delta L \propto \frac{1}{d^2}$$

For option (a)

$$\frac{L}{d^2} = \frac{50}{(0.05)^2} = 20000$$

For option (b)

$$\frac{L}{d^2} = \frac{100}{(0.1)^2} = 10000$$

For option (c)

$$\frac{L}{d^2} = \frac{200}{(0.2)^2} = 5000$$

For option (d)

$$\frac{L}{d^2} = \frac{300}{(0.3)^2} = 3333.33$$

Thus, $(a) > (b) > (c) > (d)$

SInce $\frac{L}{d^2}$ value is highest for the wire in option (a).

10. *(b)*

key idea

Apply Young's modulus of elasticity and divide the elongation produced in both wires.

Let length of a copper wire be L_C and length of steel wire be L_S, diameter of copper wire be D_C and diameter of steel wire be D_S.

Young's Modulus of elasticity is given by

$$Y = \frac{FL}{A\Delta L} = \frac{4FL}{\pi D^2 \Delta L}$$

$$\left(\because \text{Area of cross - section of wire } A = \pi\left(\frac{D}{2}\right)^2 = \frac{\pi D^2}{r}\right)$$

$$\Rightarrow \Delta L = \frac{4FL}{\pi D^2 Y}$$

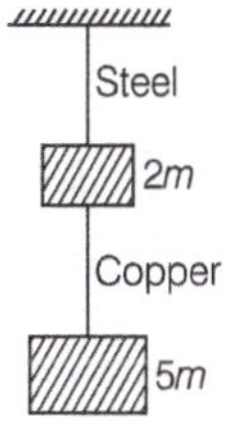

According to question

$$\frac{\Delta L_S}{\Delta L_C} = \frac{F_S}{F_C} \frac{L_S}{L_C} \frac{D_C^2}{D_S^2} \frac{Y_C}{Y_S}$$

Here,

$$F_S = (5m + 2m)g = 7mg$$

$$F_C = 5mg$$

$$\frac{L_S}{L_C} = q, \frac{D_S}{D_C} = p, \frac{Y_S}{Y_C} = s$$

$$\therefore \frac{\Delta L_S}{\Delta L_C} = \left(\frac{7mg}{5mg}\right)(q)\left(\frac{1}{p}\right)^2\left(\frac{1}{s}\right) = \frac{7q}{5p^2 s}$$

11. *(c)* We know that Young's modulus is given by

$$Y = \frac{F}{\pi r^2} \times \frac{L}{\Delta l}$$

Since, Y and F are same for both the wires

So, $l \propto \frac{L}{r^2}$

$$\Rightarrow \frac{\Delta l_1}{\Delta l_2} = \frac{r_2^2 \times L_1}{r_1^2 \times L_2} = \frac{(D_2/2)^2 \times L_1}{(D_1/2)^2 \times L_2}$$

$$\Rightarrow \frac{\Delta l_1}{\Delta l_2} = \frac{D_2^2 \times L_1}{D_1^2 \times L_2}$$

$$= \frac{D_2^2}{(2D_2)^2} \times \frac{L_2}{2L_2} = \frac{1}{8}$$

$$\Rightarrow \Delta l_1 : \Delta l_2 = 1 : 8$$

Topic 2

01. *(b)* The stress-strain curve for a material is shown

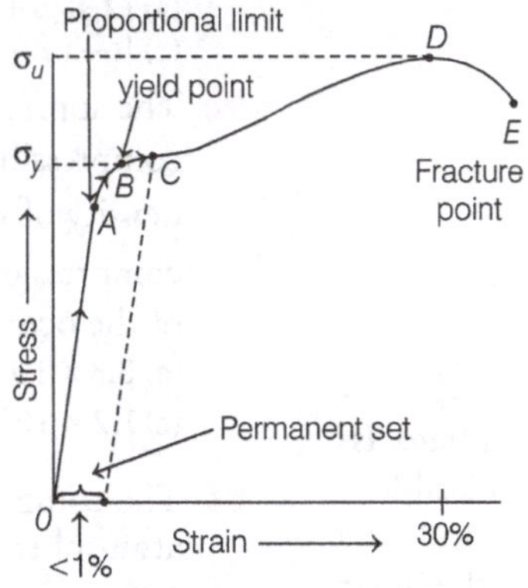

This curve specifies the behaviour of material.

For the material, if distance between strength point and fracture point is small, so it is brittle and will break easily on the application of some extra stress after point D.

For material Y, if the distance between strength point and fracture point is large, so it is a ductile material and can withstand for some extra stress beyond point D.

• Concept Enhancer

The permanent distortion which occurs when a material is subjected to compressive, bending and tensile stresses which exceed its strength and causes elongation, bending or twist.

Ductile is defined as property of the material drawn into a thin wire called ductility and it is the property of metal associated with the ability to be hammered thin or stretched into wire without breaking.

02. *(b)* In stretching a wire, the work done against internal restoring force is stored as elastic potential energy in wire and given by

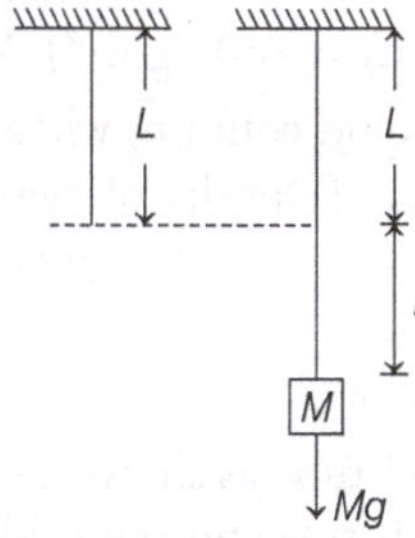

$$U = W = \frac{1}{2} \times \text{Force } (F) \times \text{Elongation } (l)$$

$$= \frac{1}{2} Fl = \frac{1}{2} \times Mg \times l = \frac{1}{2} Mgl$$

03. *(b)* Youngs' modulus is given by

$$Y = \frac{F \times l}{A \times \Delta l} \qquad \ldots(i)$$

As $V = A \times l =$ constant $\qquad \ldots(ii)$

From Eqs. (i) and (ii), we get

$$Y = \frac{F \times l^2}{V \times \Delta l} \Rightarrow \Delta l = \frac{F}{V \times Y} \times l^2$$

$$\Rightarrow \Delta l \propto l^2$$

04. *(c)* Given, Young's modulus $= Y$

Stretching stress $= S$

Energy stored per unit volume

$$= \frac{1}{2} \times \text{stress} \times \text{strain}$$

$$= \frac{1}{2} \times \text{stress} \times (\text{stress/Young's modulus})$$

$$= \frac{1}{2} \times (\text{stress})^2 / (\text{Young's modulus})$$

$$= \frac{S^2}{2Y}$$

C-09

NEET Chapterwise
Topicwise Physics

In NEET 2024, 1 question were visible from this chapter. In past 5 years, 1 question from topic-1, 3 questions from topic-2 and 5 questions from topic-3 were asked.
For detailed analysis scan QR code

MECHANICAL PROPERTIES OF FLUIDS

Topic 1 Pressure, Pascal's Law and Archimedes' Principle

01 A barometer is constructed using a liquid (density = 760 kg/m^3). What would be the height of the liquid column, when a mercury barometer reads 76 cm ? (Density of mercury = 13600 kg/m^3)

[NCERT (New) Pg. 184, NEET (Oct.) 2020]

(a) 1.36 m
(b) 13.6 m
(c) 136 m
(d) 0.76 m

02 In a U-tube as shown in a figure, water and oil are in the left side and right side of the tube, respectively. The heights from the bottom for water and oil columns are 15 cm and 20 cm, respectively. The density of the oil is [take $\rho_{water} = 1000$ kg/m^3]

[NEET (Odisha) 2019]

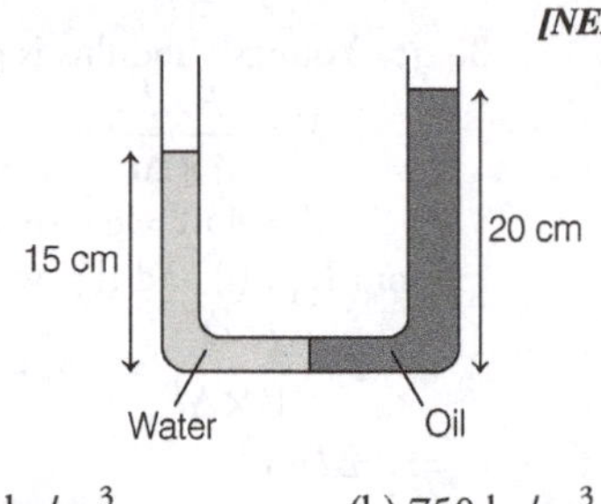

(a) 1200 kg/m^3
(b) 750 kg/m^3
(c) 1000 kg/m^3
(d) 1333 kg/m^3

03 A U-tube with both ends open to the atmosphere, is partially filled with water. Oil, which is immiscible with water, is poured into one side until it stands at a distance of 10 mm above the water level on the other side. Meanwhile the water rises by 65 mm from its original level (see diagram). The density of the oil is

[NCERT (New) Pg. 184, NEET 2017]

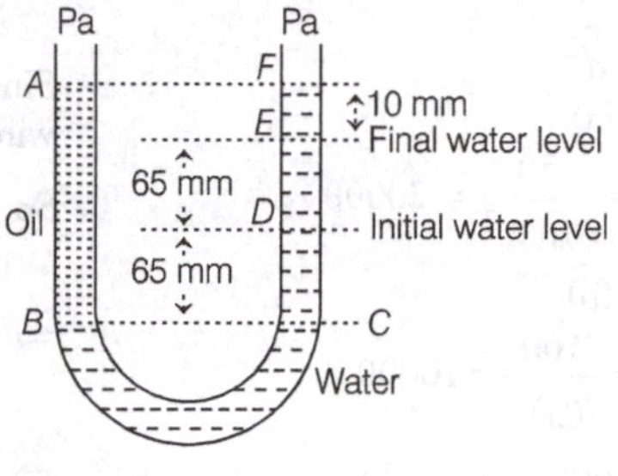

(a) 650 kg m^{-3}
(b) 425 kg m^{-3}
(c) 800 kg m^{-3}
(d) 928 kg m^{-3}

04 Two non-mixing liquids of densities ρ and $n\rho (n > 1)$ are put in a container. The height of each liquid is h. A solid cylinder of length L and density d is put in this container. The cylinder floats with its axis vertical and length pL ($p < 1$) in the denser liquid. The density d is equal to ***[NEET 2016]***

(a) $\{2+(n+1)p\}\rho$
(b) $\{2+(n-1)p\}\rho$
(c) $\{1+(n-1)p\}\rho$
(d) $\{1+(n+1)p\}\rho$

05 The approximate depth of an ocean is 2700 m. The compressibility of water is 45.4×10^{-11} Pa^{-1} and density of water is 10^3 kg / m^3. What fractional compression of water will be obtained at the bottom of the ocean ? ***[NCERT (New) Pg. 181, CBSE AIPMT 2015]***

(a) 0.8×10^{-2}
(b) 1.0×10^{-2}
(c) 1.2×10^{-2}
(d) 1.4×10^{-2}

06 The compressibility of water is 4×10^{-5} per unit atmospheric pressure. The decrease in volume of 100 cm^3 of water under a pressure of 100 atmosphere will be ***[NCERT (New) Pg. 181, AIPMT 1990]***

(a) 0.4 cm^3
(b) 4×10^{-5} cm^3
(c) 0.025 cm^3
(d) 0.004 cm^3

Topic 2 Fluid's Flow, Viscosity and Bernoulli's Principle

01 The venturimeter works on *[NEET 2023]*
(a) Bernoulli's principle
(b) the principle of parallel axes
(c) the principle of perpendicular axes
(d) Huygen's principle

02 A spherical ball is dropped in a long column of a highly viscous liquid. The curve in the graph shown, which represents the speed of the ball v as a function of time t is *[NCERT (New) Pg. 192, NEET 2022]*

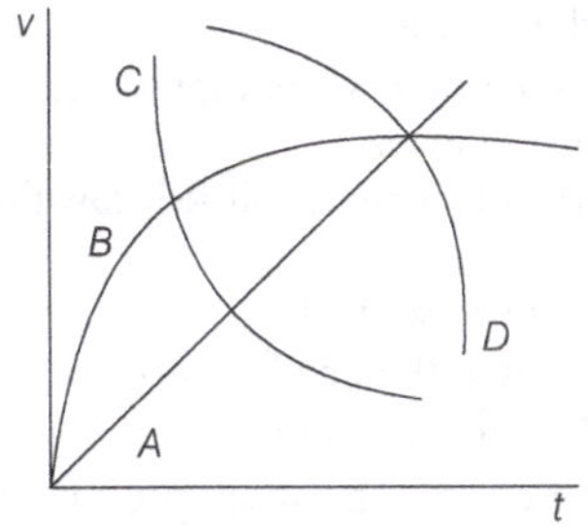

(a) B (b) C (c) D (d) A

03 The velocity of a small ball of mass M and density d when dropped in a container filled with glycerine becomes constant after some time. If the density of glycerine is $d/2$, then the viscous force acting on the ball will be *[NCERT (New) Pg. 191, NEET 2021]*
(a) $\frac{Mg}{2}$ (b) Mg (c) $\frac{3}{2}Mg$ (d) $2Mg$

04 Two small spherical metal balls, having equal masses, are made from materials of densities ρ_1 and ρ_2 $(\rho_1 = 8\rho_2)$ and have radii of 1 mm and 2 mm, respectively. They are made to fall vertically (from rest) in viscous medium whose coefficient of viscosity equals η and whose density is $0.1\,\rho_2$. The ratio of their terminal velocities would be *[NEET (Odisha) 2019]*
(a) $\frac{79}{72}$ (b) $\frac{19}{36}$ (c) $\frac{39}{72}$ (d) $\frac{79}{36}$

05 A small hole of area of cross-section 2 mm^2 is present near the bottom of a fully filled open tank of height 2 m. Taking $g = 10\text{ m/s}^2$, the rate of flow of water through the open hole would be nearly *[NCERT (New) Pg. 189, NEET (National) 2019]*
(a) $8.9\times10^{-6}\text{m}^3/\text{s}$ (b) $2.23\times10^{-6}\text{ m}^3/\text{s}$
(c) $6.4\times10^{-6}\text{ m}^3/\text{s}$ (d) $12.6\times10^{-6}\text{ m}^3/\text{s}$

06 A small sphere of radius r falls from rest in a viscous liquid. As a result, heat is produced due to viscous force. The rate of production of heat when the sphere attains its terminal velocity, is proportional to *[NEET 2018]*
(a) r^5 (b) r^2 (c) r^3 (d) r^4

07 A wind with speed 40 m/s blows parallel to the roof of a house. The area of the roof is 250 m^2. Assuming that the pressure inside the house is atmospheric pressure, the force exerted by the wind on the roof and the direction of the force will be $(\rho_{air} = 1.2\text{ kg/m}^3)$ *[NCERT (New) Pg. 188, AIPMT 2015]*
(a) 4.8×10^5 N, downwards (b) 4.8×10^5 N, upwards
(c) 2.4×10^5 N, upwards (d) 2.4×10^5 N, downwards

08 The cylindrical tube of a spray pump has radius R, one end of which has n fine holes, each of radius r. If the speed of the liquid in the tube is v, the speed of the ejection of the liquid through the holes is *[AIPMT 2015]*
(a) $\frac{vR^2}{n^2r^2}$ (b) $\frac{vR^2}{nr^2}$ (c) $\frac{vR^2}{n^3r^2}$ (d) $\frac{v^2R}{nr}$

09 A fluid in streamline flow across a horizontal pipe of variable area of cross-section. For this which of the following statements is correct ? *[NEET 2013]*
(a) The velocity is minimum at the narrowest part of the pipe and the pressure is minimum at the widest part of the pipe
(b) The velocity is maximum at the narrowest part of the pipe and pressure is maximum at the widest part of the pipe
(c) Velocity and pressure both are maximum at the narrowest part of the pipe
(d) Velocity and pressure both are maximum at the widest part of the pipe

10 The terminal velocity v_r of a small steel ball of radius r falling under gravity through a column of a viscous liquid of coefficient of viscosity η depends on mass of the ball m, acceleartion due to gravity g, coefficient of viscosity η and radius r.
Which of the following relations is dimensionally correct? *[AIPMT 1992]*
(a) $v_r \propto \frac{mgr}{\eta}$ (b) $v_r \propto mg\eta r$
(c) $v_r \propto \frac{mg}{r\eta}$ (d) $v_r \propto \frac{\eta mg}{r}$

Topic 3 Surface Tension and Capillarity

01 A thin flat circular disc of radius 4.5 cm is placed gently over the surface of water. If surface tension of water is 0.07 Nm^{-1}, then the excess force required to take it away from the surface is *[NCERT (New) Pg. 194, NEET 2024]*
(a) 19.8 mN (b) 198 N
(c) 1.98 mN (d) 99 N

02 The amount of energy required to form a soap bubble of radius 2 cm from a soap solution is nearly (surface tension of soap solution = 0.03 N m^{-1}) *[NEET 2023]*

(a) 5.06×10^{-4} J (b) 3.01×10^{-4} J
(c) 50.1×10^{-4} J (d) 30.16×10^{-4} J

03 If a soap bubble expands, the pressure inside the bubble *[NCERT (New) Pg. 194, NEET 2022]*

(a) increases
(b) remains the same
(c) is equal to the atmospheric pressure
(d) decreases.

04 A liquid does not wet the solid surface if angle of contact is *[NEET (Oct.) 2020]*

(a) equal to 45° (b) equal to 60°
(c) greater than 90° (d) zero

05 A capillary tube of radius r is immersed in water and water rises in it to a height h. The mass of the water in the capillary tube is 5 g. Another capillary tube of radius $2r$ is immersed in water. The mass of water that will rise in this tube is *[NEET (Sep.) 2020]*

(a) 5.0 g (b) 10.0 g (c) 20.0 g (d) 2.5 g

06 A soap bubble, having radius of 1 mm, is blown from a detergent solution having a surface tension of 2.5×10^{-2} N/m. The pressure inside the bubble equals at a point Z_0 below the free surface of water in a container. Taking $g = 10 \text{ m/s}^2$, density of water $= 10^3 \text{ kg/m}^3$, the value of Z_0 is *[NEET (National) 2019]*

(a) 10 cm (b) 1 cm (c) 0.5 cm (d) 100 cm

07 A rectangular film of liquid is extended from (4 cm × 2 cm) to (5 cm × 4 cm). If the work done is 3×10^{-4} J, the value of the surface tension of the liquid is *[NEET 2016]*

(a) 0.250 Nm^{-1} (b) 0.125 Nm^{-1}
(c) 0.2 Nm^{-1} (d) 8.0 Nm^{-1}

08 Three liquids of densities ρ_1, ρ_2 and ρ_3 (with $\rho_1 > \rho_2 > \rho_3$), having the same value of surface tension T, rise to the same height in three identical capillaries. The angles of contact θ_1, θ_2 and θ_3 obey *[NCERT (New) Pg. 197, NEET 2016]*

(a) $\frac{\pi}{2} > \theta_1 > \theta_2 > \theta_3 \geq 0$ (b) $0 \leq \theta_1 < \theta_2 < \theta_3 < \frac{\pi}{2}$

(c) $\frac{\pi}{2} < \theta_1 < \theta_2 < \theta_3 < \pi$ (d) $\pi > \theta_1 > \theta_2 > \theta_3 > \frac{\pi}{2}$

09 Water rises to height h in a capillary tube. If the length of capillary tube above the surface of water is made less than h then *[AIPMT 2015]*

(a) water rises upto the top of capillary tube and stays there without overflowing
(b) water rises upto a point a little below the top and stays there
(c) water does not rise at all.
(d) water rises upto the tip of capillary tube and then starts overflowing like fountain.

10 The angle of contact between pure water and pure glass, is *[AIPMT 2015]*

(a) 0° (b) 45°
(c) 90° (d) 135°

11 A certain number of spherical drops of a liquid of radius r coalesce to form a single drop of radius R and volume V. If T is the surface tension of the liquid, then *[NCERT (New) Pg. 195, AIPMT 2014]*

(a) energy $= 4VT\left(\frac{1}{r} - \frac{1}{R}\right)$ is released

(b) energy $= 3VT\left(\frac{1}{r} + \frac{1}{R}\right)$ is absorbed

(c) energy $= 3VT\left(\frac{1}{r} - \frac{1}{R}\right)$ is released

(d) energy is neither released nor absorbed

Key **Index**

Topic 1

1 (b)	2 (b)	3 (d)	4 (c)	5 (c)	6 (a)

Topic 2

1 (a)	2 (a)	3 (a)	4 (d)	5 (d)	6 (a)	7 (c)	8 (b)	9 (b)	10 (c)

Topic 3

1 (a)	2 (b)	3 (d)	4 (c)	5 (b)	6 (b)	7 (b)	8 (b)	9 (a)	10 (a)
11 (c)									

Detailed **Explanations**

Topic 1

01. *(b)* Density of a liquid,

$$\rho_l = 760 \text{ kg/m}^3$$

Density of mercury,

$$\rho_m = 13600 \text{ kg/m}^3$$

Height of liquid column in mercury barometer,

$$h_m = 76 \text{ cm} = 0.76 \text{ m}$$

Let height of liquid in liquid column be h_l, then

$$p_{\text{liquid}} = p_{\text{mercury}}$$

$$\Rightarrow \quad h_l \rho_l g = h_m \rho_m g$$

$$\Rightarrow \quad h_l = \frac{h_m \rho_m}{\rho_l} = \frac{0.76 \times 13600}{760}$$

$$= 13.6 \text{ m}$$

02. *(b)*

key idea

According to Pascal's law, pressure applied to an enclosed fluid is transmitted undiminished to every point of the fluid and the walls of the containing vessel.

According to the figure shown in the question, pressure due to water column of height 15 cm = Pressure due to oil column of height 20 cm

$$\Rightarrow \quad h_w \rho_w g = h_0 \rho_0 g$$

$$15 \rho_w = 20 \rho_0$$

$$\Rightarrow \quad \rho_0 = \frac{15}{20} \rho_\omega$$

$$\rho_0 = \frac{15}{20} \times 1000$$

$$(\because \text{given, } \rho_w = 1000 \text{ kg m}^{-3})$$

$$= 750 \text{ kgm}^{-3}$$

03. *(d)* Both ends of the U-tube are open, so the pressure on both the free surfaces must be equal.

i.e., $\quad p_1 = p_2$

$$h_{\text{oil}} \cdot \rho_{\text{oil}} \; g = h_{\text{water}} \cdot \rho_{\text{water}} \cdot g$$

ρ_{oil} = specific density of oil

$$\rho_{\text{oil}} = \frac{h_{\text{water}} \cdot \rho_{\text{water}} \cdot g}{h_{\text{oil}} \cdot g}$$

From figure, $\rho_{\text{oil}} = \dfrac{(65 + 65) \times 1000}{(65 + 65 + 10)}$

$$= 928 \text{ kgm}^{-3}$$

04. *(c)* According to question, the situation can be drawn as following.

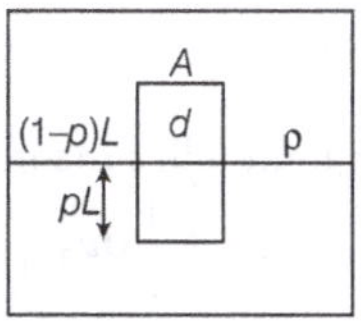

Applying Archimedes' principle
Weight of cylinder

$$= (\text{upthrust})_1 + (\text{upthrust})_2$$

i.e. $ALdg = (1 - p)\, LA\rho g + (pLA)\, n\rho g$

$$\Rightarrow \quad d = (1 - p)\,\rho + pn\rho$$

$$= \rho - p\rho + n\, p\rho$$

$$= \rho + (n - 1)\, p\rho$$

$$= \rho\,[1 + (n - 1)\, p]$$

05. *(c)* Given, $d = 2700$ m

$$\Rightarrow \quad \rho = 10^3 \text{ kg/m}^3$$

Compressibility of water,

$$= 45.4 \times 10^{-11} \text{ per Pascal}$$

The pressure at the bottom of ocean is given by

$$p = \rho g d$$

$$= 10^3 \times 10 \times 2700 = 27 \times 10^6 \text{ Pa}$$

So, fractional compression

$$= \text{compressibility} \times \text{pressure}$$

$$= 45.4 \times 10^{-11} \times 27 \times 10^6$$

$$= 1.2 \times 10^{-2}$$

06. *(a)* Given, $K = \dfrac{1}{B} = \dfrac{\Delta V / V}{p}$

Pressure, $p = 100$ atm,

$$K = 4 \times 10^{-5} \text{ atm}^{-1}$$

and $\quad V = 100 \text{ cm}^3$

$$\Rightarrow 4 \times 10^{-5} \times 100 = \frac{\Delta V}{100} \text{ cm}^3$$

$$\Rightarrow \quad \Delta V = 0.4 \text{ cm}^3$$

Topic 2

01. *(a)* Venturimeter is a device used to measure the flow speed of incompressible fluid. It works on the Bernoulli's principle.

02. *(a)* When a spherical ball is dropped in a long column of a highly viscous liquid, then its velocity first increases and after sometime, it moves with constant velocity, known as terminal velocity v. Hence, correct variation of speed of ball in liquid column with time is given as

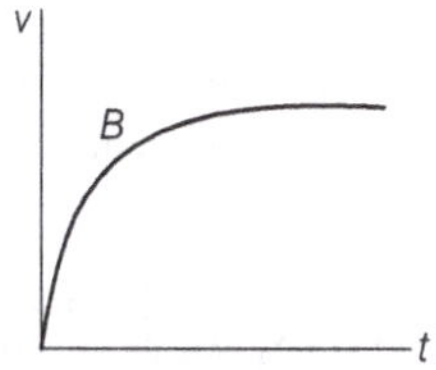

03. *(a)* As we know that,

Viscous force = weight – buoyant force

Viscous force $= Vd_1 g - Vd_2 g$

Here, V is the volume of submerged ball,

d_1 is the density of the small ball,

d_2 is the density of the glycerine,

$$d_1 = d$$

and $\quad d_2 = d / 2$

Substituting the given values in the viscous force expression, we get

$$\text{Viscous force} = Vdg - V\frac{d}{2}g$$

$$\text{Viscous force} = \frac{Vdg}{2} = \frac{Mg}{2}$$

$$(\because M = d \times V)$$

Concept Enhancer

When a body moves with constant velocity, then $Mg = F_B + F_V$ where F_B is buoyant force and F_V is viscous force.

04. *(d)* The terminal velocity achieved by ball in a viscous fluid is

$$v_t = \frac{2(\rho - \sigma) r^2 g}{9\eta}$$

where, ρ = density of metal of ball,

σ = density of viscous medium,

r = radius of ball and

η = coefficient of viscosity of medium

Terminal velocity of first ball,

$$v_{t_1} = \frac{2(\rho_1 - \sigma) r_1^2 g}{9\eta}$$

$$= \frac{2(8\rho_2 - \sigma) r_1^2 g}{9\eta} \quad \ldots \text{(i)}$$

$$[\because \rho_1 = 8\rho_2]$$

Similarly, for second ball

$$v_{t_2} = \frac{2(\rho_2 - \sigma) r_2^2 g}{9\eta} \quad \ldots \text{(ii)}$$

From Eq. (i) and (ii), we get

$$\frac{v_{t_1}}{v_{t_2}} = \frac{2(8\rho_2 - \sigma)r_1^2 g}{2(\rho_2 - \sigma)r_2^2 g} \times \frac{9\eta}{9\eta}$$

$$= \left(\frac{8\rho_2 - 0.1\rho_2}{\rho_2 - 0.1\rho_2}\right)\left(\frac{r_1}{r_2}\right)^2 \quad \ldots\text{(iii)}$$

$[\because \sigma = 0.1\rho_2]$

Here, $r_1 = 1$ mm and $r_2 = 2$ mm

Substituting these values in Eq. (iii), we get

$$\Rightarrow \frac{v_{t_1}}{v_{t_2}} = \left(\frac{7.9\rho_2}{0.9\rho_2}\right)\left(\frac{1}{2}\right)^2 = \frac{79}{36}$$

• Concept **Enhancer**

An object with a large surface area (like a parachute) will have a much lower terminal velocity than objects with a smaller surface area.

05. *(d)* The rate of water flow moving with velocity v through an area a is given by

Rate (R) = Area (a) × Velocity (v)

Given, area of cross-section of hole,

$$a = 2 \text{ mm}^2$$
$$= 2\times 10^{-6} \text{ m}^2$$

height of tank,

$$h = 2 \text{ m}$$

As the velocity of liquid flow is given as

$$v = \sqrt{2gh}$$

$$\therefore \quad R = av = a\sqrt{2gh}$$

Substituting the given values, we get,

$$R = 2\times10^{-6} \times \sqrt{2\times10\times2}$$
$$= 2\times10^{-6}\times 6.32$$
$$= 12.64\times10^{-6} \text{ m}^3/\text{s}$$
$$\simeq 12.6\times10^{-6} \text{ m}^3/\text{s}$$

06. *(a)* Rate of heat produced,

$$\frac{dQ}{dt} = F\times v_T$$

where, F is the viscous force and v_T is the terminal velocity.

As, $\quad F = 6\pi\eta r v_T$

$$\Rightarrow \frac{dQ}{dt} = 6\pi\eta r v_T \times v_T$$
$$= 6\pi\eta r v_T^2 \quad \ldots\text{(i)}$$

From the relation for terminal velocity,

$$v_T = \frac{2}{9}\frac{r^2(\rho-\sigma)}{\eta}g$$

we get

$$v_T \propto r^2 \quad \ldots\text{(ii)}$$

From Eq. (ii), we can rewrite Eq. (i) as

$$\frac{dQ}{dt} \propto r\cdot(r^2)^2$$

or $$\frac{dQ}{dt} \propto r^5$$

07. *(c)* From Bernoulli's theorem

$$p_1 + \frac{1}{2}\rho v_1^2 = p_2 + \frac{1}{2}\rho v_2^2$$

$$p_1 - p_2 = \frac{1}{2}\rho(v_2^2 - v_1^2)$$
$$= \frac{1}{2}\times 1.2\,(40^2 - 0)$$
$$= 960 \text{ N/m}^2$$

Force acting on the roof is given by

$$F = (p_1 - p_2)A$$
$$= 960\times 250$$
$$= 24\times10^4 \text{ N}$$
$$= 2.4\times10^5 \text{ N}$$

As the pressure inside the roof is more than outside to it. So the force will act in the upward direction,

i.e. $F = 2.4\times10^5$N- upwards.

08. *(b)*

key idea

During the streamline flow of viscous and incompressible fluid through a pipe of varying cross-section, the product of area of cross-section and normal fluid velocity (Av) remains constant throughout the flow.

According to equation of continuity,

$$Av = A'v'$$
$$\pi R^2 v = n\,\pi r^2 v'$$

$$\Rightarrow \quad v' = \frac{R^2 v}{nr^2}$$

09. *(b)* According to Bernoulli's theorem,

$$p + \frac{1}{2}\rho v^2 = \text{constant}$$

also Av = constant

If A is minimum, then v is maximum and p is minimum.

10. *(c)* According to stoke's law

$$F = 6\pi\eta r v_r$$

or $$mg = 6\pi\eta r v_r$$

$$\Rightarrow \quad v_r = \frac{mg}{6\pi\eta r}$$

$$\Rightarrow \quad v_r \propto \frac{mg}{\eta r}$$

Topic 3

01. *(a)* Radius of disc, $r = 4.5$ cm

$$= 4.5\times10^{-2} \text{ m}$$

Surface tension, $T = 0.07 \text{ Nm}^{-1}$

The force required to take away circular disc from the surface of water,

$$F = T\times 2\pi r$$
$$= 0.07\times2\times3.14\times4.5\times10^{-2}$$
$$= 1.9782\times10^{-2} \text{ N}$$
$$= 19.8 \text{ mN}$$

02. *(b)* Given, surface tension,

$$T = 0.03 \text{ Nm}^{-1}$$

Radius of soop bubble,

$$r = 2 \text{ cm} = 2\times10^{-2}\text{m}$$

∴ Amount of energy required,

$$E = 2TA$$
$$= 2\times0.03\times4\pi\,(2\times10^{-2})^2$$
$$= 3.01\times10^{-4} \text{ J}$$

03. *(d)* We know that pressure inside the soap bubble of radius r is given as,

$$p = \frac{4T}{r}$$

where, T is surface tension.

$$\Rightarrow \quad p \propto \frac{1}{r} \quad \ldots\text{(i)}$$

Therefore, when soap bubble expands, then its radius increases, hence from Eq. (i), pressure inside it will decrease.

• Concept **Enhancer**

In a liquid drop, we have only surface but in the air bubble we have two surfaces and a mathematical expression of the excess pressure inside an air bubble is calculated by

$$p_i - p_o = \frac{4T}{r}$$

04. *(c)* A liquid does not wet the solid surface, if the angle of contact is obtuse i.e., $\theta > 90°$.

05. *(b)*

key idea

The rise of a liquid in a capillary tube is given by

$$h = \frac{2T\cos\theta}{\rho g r}$$

and the mass of risen liquid is given by m = volume × density = $Ah\rho = \pi r^2 h\rho$

where r is the radius of the capillary.

Relation for height of water in capillary tube is

$$h = \frac{2T\cos\theta}{\rho g r} \Rightarrow h \propto \frac{1}{r}$$

$$\Rightarrow \quad \frac{h_1}{h_2} = \frac{r_2}{r_1} = \frac{2r}{r} = 2$$

As $\quad m = A \cdot h \cdot \rho$

$$\therefore \quad \frac{m_2}{m_1} = \frac{A_2 h_2 \rho}{A_1 h_1 \rho}$$

$$= \frac{\pi(r_2)^2}{\pi(r_1)^2} \frac{h_2}{h_1}$$

$$= \frac{4}{2} = 2$$

$$\Rightarrow \quad m_2 = 2 \times m_1 = 10 \text{ g}$$

06. *(b)* Given,

Surface tension

$T = 2.5 \times 10^{-2}$ N/m,

$\rho = 10^3$ kg/m^3,

$g = 10$ ms^{-2}

and $\quad r = 1$ mm $= 1 \times 10^{-3}$ m

Let p_0 be the outside pressure from the water, then total pressure inside the bubble becomes

$$p_1 = p_0 + \frac{4T}{r} \quad \ldots \text{(i)}$$

The pressure at the depth Z_0 below the water surface is

$$p_2 = p_0 + Z_0 \rho g \quad \ldots \text{(ii)}$$

As it is given that the pressure inside the bubble is same as the pressure at depth Z_0, then equating Eqs. (i) and (ii), we get

$$p_0 + \frac{4T}{r} = p_0 + Z_0 \rho g$$

$$\Rightarrow \quad Z_0 = \frac{4T}{r\rho g} \quad \ldots \text{(iii)}$$

Substituting these values in Eq. (iii), we get

$$\Rightarrow \quad Z_0 = \frac{4 \times 2.5 \times 10^{-2}}{1 \times 10^{-3} \times 10^3 \times 10}$$

$$= 10 \times 10^{-3} \text{ m} = 1 \text{ cm}$$

07. *(b)*

key idea

Increase in surface energy = change in surface area × surface tension

$$W = T \cdot \Delta A$$

Given, change in surface area,

$$\Delta A = (5 \times 4 - 4 \times 2) \times 2$$

($\because$ film has two surfaces)

$$= (20 - 8) \times 2 \text{ cm}^2$$

$$= 24 \text{ cm}^2$$

$$= 24 \times 10^{-4} \text{ m}^2$$

So, work done,

$$W = T \cdot \Delta A$$

$$3 \times 10^{-4} = T \times 24 \times 10^{-4}$$

$$\therefore \quad T = \frac{1}{8} = 0.125 \text{ N/m}$$

08. *(b)* According to ascent formula for capillary tube,

$$h = \frac{2T\cos\theta}{\rho g r}$$

$$\therefore \quad \frac{\cos\theta_1}{\rho_1} = \frac{\cos\theta_2}{\rho_2} = \frac{\cos\theta_3}{\rho_3}$$

Thus, $\cos\theta \propto \rho$

$$\therefore \quad \rho_1 > \rho_2 > \rho_3$$

$$\therefore \quad \cos\theta_1 > \cos\theta_2 > \cos\theta_3$$

$$0 \le \theta_1 < \theta_2 < \theta_3 < \frac{\pi}{2}$$

09. *(a)* Let R be the radius of the capillary tube or radius of meniscus, σ be the surface tension and ρ be the density of the liquid

Thus, $\quad h = \dfrac{2\sigma}{\rho g R}$

or $\quad R \propto \dfrac{1}{h}$

When height is reduced then the radius of meniscus increases.

Therefore water rises upto the top of capillary tube and stays there without overflowing.

Hence, option (a) is correct.

Concept Enhancer

In case of capillary of insufficient length i.e., $l < h$ the liquid will neither overflow from the upper end nor it will trickle along the vertical sides of the tube. The liquid after reaching the upper end will increase the radius of its menisucs without changing nature such that

$$hr = Lr'$$

$$\because \quad L < h \Rightarrow r' > r$$

10. *(a)* We know that the angle of contact is the angle between the tangent to liquid surface and the point of contact and solid surface inside the liquid. In case of pure water and pure glass, the angle of contact is zero.

11. *(c)* As energy released $= (A_f - A_i)T$

$$A_i = n \times 4\pi r^2 = \frac{R^3}{r^3} \times 4\pi r^2 = \frac{3V}{r}$$

$$A_f = 4\pi R^2 = \left(\frac{4}{3}\pi R^3\right)\frac{3}{R} = \frac{3V}{R}$$

decrease in surface area, $\Delta A = A_i - A_f$

$$= \frac{3V}{r} - \frac{3V}{R} = 3V\left(\frac{1}{r} - \frac{1}{R}\right)$$

Energy released = Surface tension × Decrease in surface area

$$= T \times \Delta A = 3VT\left(\frac{1}{r} - \frac{1}{R}\right)$$

C-10

NEET Chapterwise Topicwise Physics

In NEET 2024, 1 question were visible from this chapter. In past 5 years, 1 question from topic-1, 1 question from topic-2 and 1 question from topic-3.
For detailed analysis scan QR code

THERMAL PROPERTIES OF MATTER

Topic 1 Thermometry & Thermal Expansion

01 A metallic bar of Young's modulus, 0.5×10^{11} Nm^{-1} and coefficient of linear thermal expansion 10^{-5} $°C^{-1}$, length 1 m and area of cross-section 10^{-3} m^2 is heated from 0°C to 100°C without expansion or bending. The compressive force developed in it is *[NCERT (New) Pg. 205, NEET 2024]*
(a) 5×10^3 N (b) 50×10^3 N
(c) 100×10^3 N (d) 2×10^3 N

02 A copper rod of 88 cm and an aluminium rod of unknown length have their increase in length independent of increase in temperature. The length of aluminium rod is *[NCERT (New) Pg. 205, NEET (National) 2019]*
(a) 113.9 cm (b) 88 cm
(c) 68 cm (d) 6.8 cm

03 Coefficient of linear expansion of brass and steel rods are α_1 and α_2. Lengths of brass and steel rods are l_1 and l_2, respectively. If $(l_2 - l_1)$ is maintained same at all temperatures, which one of the following relations holds good ? *[NCERT (New) Pg. 205, NEET 2016, AIPMT 1999]*
(a) $\alpha_1 l_2^2 = \alpha_2 l_1^2$ (b) $\alpha_1^2 l_2 = \alpha_2^2 l_1$
(c) $\alpha_1 l_1 = \alpha_2 l_2$ (d) $\alpha_1 l_2 = \alpha_2 l_1$

04 The value of coefficient of volume expansion of glycerin is 5×10^{-4} K^{-1}. The fractional change in the density of glycerin for a rise of 40°C in its temperature is *[AIPMT 2015]*
(a) 0.015 (b) 0.020
(c) 0.025 (d) 0.010

05 If the cold junction of a thermo-couple is kept at 0°C and the hot juction is kept at T°C then the relation between neutral temperature T_n and temperature of inversion T_i is *[AIPMT 2015]*
(a) $T_n = 2T_i$ (b) $T_n = T_i - T$
(c) $T_n = T_i + T$ (d) $T_n = T_i / 2$

06 The density of water at 20 °C is 998 kg/m^3 and at 40 °C is 992 kg/m^3. The coefficient of volume expansion of water is *[NCERT (New) Pg. 205, NEET 2013]*
(a) 3×10^{-4} /°C (b) 2×10^{-4} /°C
(c) 6×10^{-4} /°C (d) 10^{-4} /°C

07 On a new scale of temperature (which is linear) and called the W scale, the freezing and boiling points of water are 39°W and 239°W, respectively. What will be the temperature on the new scale, corresponding to a temperature of 39°C on the celsius scale? *[AIPMT 2008]*
(a) 78°W (b) 117°W (c) 200°W (d) 139°W

08 The temperature of inversion of a thermocouple is 620°C and the neutral temperature is 300°C. what is the temperature of cold junction? *[AIPMT 2005]*
(a) 320°C (b) 20°C
(c) –20°C (d) 40°C

09 Mercury thermometer can be used to measure temperature upto *[AIPMT 1992]*
(a) 260°C (b) 100°C (c) 360°C (d) 500°C

10 A Centigrade and a Fahrenheit thermometer are dipped in boiling water. The water temperature is lowered until the Fahrenheit thermometer registers 140°. What is the fall in temperature as registered by the Centigrade thermometer ? *[AIPMT 1990]*
(a) 80° (b) 60° (c) 40° (d) 30°

Topic 2 Specific Heat Capacity, Change of State and Calorimetry

01 The quantities of heat required to raise the temperature of two solid copper spheres of radii r_1 and r_2 ($r_1 = 1.5\, r_2$) through 1 K are in the ratio *[NCERT (New) Pg. 208, NEET (Sep.) 2020]*

(a) $\frac{9}{4}$ (b) $\frac{3}{2}$ (c) $\frac{5}{3}$ (d) $\frac{27}{8}$

02 A piece of ice falls from a height h so that it melts completely. Only one-quarter of the heat produced is absorbed by the ice and all energy of ice gets converted into heat during its fall. The value of h is [Latent heat of ice is 3.4×10^5 J/kg and $g = 10$ N/kg] *[NCERT (New) Pg. 213, NEET 2016]*

(a) 544 km (b) 136 km (c) 68 km (d) 34 km

03 Two identical bodies are made of a material for which the heat capacity increases with temperature. One of these is at 100°C, while the other one is at 0°C. If the two bodies are brought into contact, then assuming no heat loss, the final common temperature is *[NEET 2016]*

(a) 50°C
(b) more than 50°C
(c) less than 50°C but greater than 0°C
(d) 0°C

04 Steam at 100°C is passed into 20 g of water at 10°C. When water acquires a temperature of 80°C, the mass of water present will be [Take specific heat of water $= 1 \text{ cal g}^{-1}\,{}^\circ\text{C}^{-1}$ and latent heat of steam $= 540 \text{ cal g}^{-1}$] *[NCERT (New) Pg. 210, AIPMT 2014]*

(a) 24 g (b) 31.5 g
(c) 42.5 g (d) 22.5 g

05 Liquid oxygen at 50 K is heated to 300 K at constant pressure of 1 atm. The rate of heating is constant. Which one of the following graphs represents the variation of temperature with time? *[AIPMT 2012]*

(a)
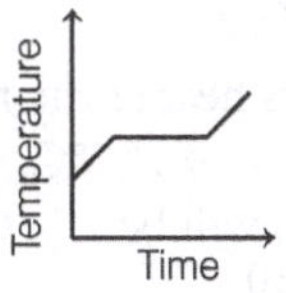

(c)
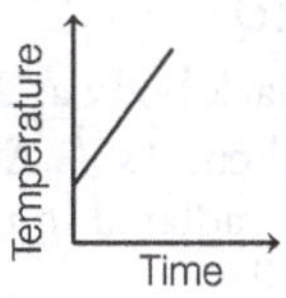

(b)
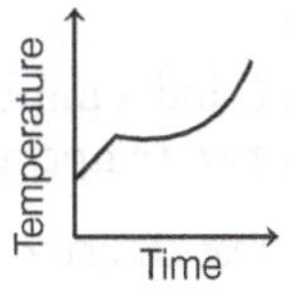

(d)
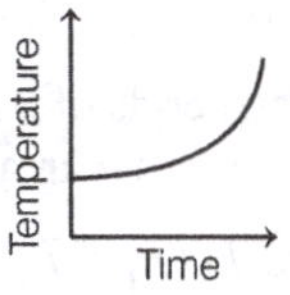

06 An electric kettle takes 4A current at 220 V. How much time will it take to boil 1 kg of water from temperature 20 °C? (The temperature of boiling water is 100°C) *[AIPMT 2008]*

(a) 6.3 min (b) 8.4 min
(c) 12.6 min (d) 4.2 min

07 If 1 g of steam is mixed with 1 g of ice, then the resultant temperature of the mixture is *[AIPMT 1999]*

(a) 270°C (b) 230°C
(c) 100°C (d) 50°C

08 Thermal capacity of 40 g of aluminium ($s = 0.2$ cal/g-K) is *[NCERT (New) Pg. 208, AIPMT 1990]*

(a) 168 J/°C (b) 672 J/°C
(c) 840 J/°C (d) 33.6 J/°C

09 Two containers A and B are partly filled with water and closed. The volume of A is twice that of B and it contains half the amount of water in B. If both are at the same temperature, the water vapour in the containers will have pressure in the ratio of *[AIPMT 1988]*

(a) 1 : 2 (b) 1 : 1 (c) 2 : 1 (d) 4 : 1

10 10 g of ice cubes at 0°C are released in a tumbler (water equivalent 55 g) at 40°C. Assuming that negligible heat is taken from the surroundings, the temperature of water in the tumbler becomes nearly ($L = 80$ cal/g) *[NCERT (New) Pg. 213, AIPMT 1988]*

(a) 31°C (b) 22°C
(c) 19°C (d) 15°C

Topic 3 Heat Transfer

01 Three stars A, B, C have surface temperatures T_A, T_B, T_C, respectively. Star A appears bluish, star B appears reddish and star C yellowish. Hence *[NCERT (New) Pg. 218, NEET (Oct.) 2020]*

(a) $T_A > T_B > T_C$ (b) $T_B > T_C > T_A$
(c) $T_C > T_B > T_A$ (d) $T_A > T_C > T_B$

02 A deep rectangular pond of surface area A, containing water (density = ρ, specific heat capacity = s), is located in a region where the outside air temperature is a steady value at the -26°C. The thickness of the frozen ice layer in this pond, at a certain instant is x. Taking the thermal conductivity of ice as K, and its specific latent heat of fusion as L, the rate of increase of the thickness of ice layer, at this instant would be given by *[NCERT (New) Pg. 215, NEET (Odisha) 2019]*

(a) $26K/\rho r(L-4s)$ (b) $26K/(\rho x^2 - L)$
(c) $26K/(\rho x L)$ (d) $26K/\rho r(L+4s)$

03 The power radiated by a black body is P and it radiates maximum energy at wavelength, λ_0. If the temperature of the black body is now changed, so that it radiates maximum energy at wavelength $3/4\ \lambda_0$, the power radiated by it becomes nP. The value of n is *[NCERT (New) Pg. 219, NEET 2018]*

(a) $\frac{256}{81}$ (b) $\frac{4}{3}$
(c) $\frac{3}{4}$ (d) $\frac{81}{256}$

04 Two rods A and B of different materials are welded together as shown in figure. Their thermal conductivities are K_1 and K_2. The thermal conductivity of the composite rod will be *[NEET 2017]*

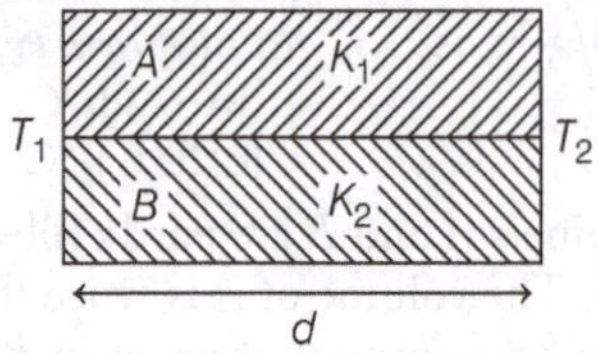

(a) $\frac{K_1 + K_2}{2}$ (b) $\frac{3(K_1 + K_2)}{2}$
(c) $K_1 + K_2$ (d) $2(K_1 + K_2)$

05 A spherical black body with a radius of 12 cm radiates 450 watt power at 500 K. If the radius were halved and the temperature doubled, the power radiated in watt would be *[NCERT (New) Pg. 219, NEET 2017]*
(a) 225 (b) 450 (c) 1000 (d) 1800

06 A metal rod at a temperature of 145°C radiates energy at a rate of 17W. If its temperature is increased to 273°C, then it will radiate at the rate of *[NEET 2017]*
(a) 17.5 W (b) 50.3 W (c) 49.6 W (d) 67.5 W

07 A black body is at a temperature of 5760 K. The energy of radiation emitted by the body at wavelength 250 nm is U_1, at wavelength 500 nm is U_2 and that at 1000 nm is U_3. Wien's constant, $b = 2.88 \times 10^6$ nm-K. Which of the following is correct ? *[NCERT (New) Pg. 218, NEET 2016]*
(a) $U_3 = 0$ (b) $U_1 > U_2$ (c) $U_2 > U_1$ (d) $U_1 = 0$

08 The two ends of a metal rod are maintained at temperatures 100°C and 110°C. The rate of heat flow in the rod is found to be 4.0 J/s. If the ends are maintained at temperatures 200°C and 210°C, the rate of heat flow will be *[CBSE AIPMT 2015]*
(a) 44.0 J/s (b) 16.8 J/s
(c) 8.0 J/s (d) 4.0 J/s

09 A piece of iron is heated in a flame. If first becomes dull red then becomes reddish yellow and finally turns to white hot. The correct explanation for the above observation is possible by using *[NEET 2013]*
(a) Stefan's law
(b) Wien's displacement law
(c) Kirchhoff's law
(d) Newton's law of cooling

10 Two metal rods 1 and 2 of same lengths have same temperature difference between their ends. Thier thermal conductivities are K_1 and K_2 and corss sectional areas A_1 and A_2, respectively. If the rate of heat conduction in 1 is four times that in 2, then *[NCERT (New) Pg. 215, NEET 2013]*
(a) $K_1A_1 = 4K_2A_2$ (b) $K_1A_1 = 2K_2A_2$
(c) $4K_1A_1 = K_2A_2$ (d) $K_1A_1 = K_2A_2$

11 If the radius of a star is R and it acts as a black body, what would be the temperature of the star, in which the rate of energy production is Q ? *[AIPMT 2012]*
(σ stands for Stefan's constant.)
(a) $Q/4\pi R^2\sigma$ (b) $(Q/4\pi R^2\sigma)^{-1/2}$
(c) $(4\pi R^2 Q/\sigma)^{1/4}$ (d) $(Q/4\pi R^2\sigma)^{1/4}$

12 A slab of stone of area 0.36m^2 and thickness 0.1 m is exposed on the lower surface to steam at 100°C. A block of ice at 0°C rests on the upper surface of the slab. In one hour 4.8 kg of ice is melted. The thermal conductivity of slab is *[NCERT (New) Pg. 215, AIPMT 2012]*
(Given, latent heat of fusion of ice $= 3.36 \times 10^5$ J kg^{-1})
(a) 1.24 J/m/s/°C (b) 1.29 J/m/s/°C
(c) 2.05 J/m/s/°C (d) 1.02 J/m/s/°C

13 The total radiant energy per unit area, normal to the direction of incidence, received at a distance R from the centre of a star of radius r, whose outer surface radiates as a black body at a temperature TK is given by *[NCERT (New) Pg. 219, AIPMT 2010]*
(a) $\frac{\sigma r^2 T^4}{R^2}$ (b) $\frac{\sigma r^2 T^4}{4\pi R^2}$
(c) $\frac{\sigma r^4 T^4}{R^4}$ (d) $\frac{4\pi\sigma r^2 T^4}{R^2}$
(where σ is Stefan's constant)

14 A cylindrical metallic rod in thermal contact with two reservoirs of heat at its two ends conducts an amount of heat Q in time t. The metallic rod is melted and the material is formed into a rod of half the radius of the original rod. What is the amount of heat conducted by the new rod when placed in thermal contact with the two reservoirs in time t ? *[NCERT (New) Pg. 215, AIPMT 2010]*
(a) $Q/4$ (b) $Q/16$
(c) $2Q$ (d) $Q/2$

15 A black body at 227°C radiates heat at the rate of 7 cal cm^{-2}s^{-1}. At a temperature of 727°C, the rate of heat radiated in the same units will be *[AIPMT 2009]*
(a) 60 (b) 50
(c) 112 (d) 80

16 The two ends of a rod of length L and a uniform cross-sectional area A are kept at two temperatures T_1 and $T_2 (T_1 > T_2)$. The rate of heat transfer, $\frac{dQ}{dt}$, through the rod in a steady state is given by *[NCERT (New) Pg. 215, AIPMT 2009]*
(a) $\frac{dQ}{dt} = \frac{KL(T_1 - T_2)}{A}$ (b) $\frac{dQ}{dt} = \frac{K(T_1 - T_2)}{LA}$
(c) $\frac{dQ}{dt} = KLA(T_1 - T_2)$ (d) $\frac{dQ}{dt} = \frac{KA(T_1 - T_2)}{L}$

17 Assuming the sun to have a spherical outer surface of radius r, radiating like a black body at temperature t° C, the power received by a unit surface, (normal to the incident rays) at a distance R from the centre of the sun is where, σ is the Stefan's constant. *[NCERT (New) Pg. 219, AIPMT 2007]*

(a) $\frac{4\pi r^2 t^4}{R^2}$ (b) $\frac{r^2\sigma(t+273)^4}{4\pi R^2}$
(c) $\frac{16\pi^2 r^2 \sigma t^4}{R^2}$ (d) $\frac{r^2\sigma(t+273)^4}{R^2}$

18 A black body is at 727°C. It emits energy at a rate which is proportional to *[AIPMT 2007]*
(a) $(727)^2$ (b) $(1000)^4$
(c) $(1000)^2$ (d) $(727)^4$

19 A black body at 1227°C emits radiations with maximum intensity at a wavelength of 5000 Å. If the temperature of the body is increased by 1000°C, the maximum intensity will be observed at *[AIPMT 2006]*
(a) 4000 Å (b) 5000 Å
(c) 6000 Å (d) 3000 Å

20 Which of the following circular rods, (given radius r and length l) each made of the same material and whose ends are maintained at the same temperature will conduct most heat ? *[NCERT (New) Pg. 215, AIPMT 2005]*
(a) $r = 2r_0, l = 2l_0$ (b) $r = 2r_0, l = l_0$
(c) $r = r_0, l = l_0$ (d) $r = r_0, l = 2l_0$

21 If λ_m denotes the wavelength at which the radiative emission from a black body at a temperature T K is maximum, then *[AIPMT 2004]*
(a) $\lambda_m \propto T^4$ (b) λ_m is independent of T
(c) $\lambda_m \propto T$ (d) $\lambda_m \propto T^{-1}$

22 We consider the radiation emitted by the human body. Which of the following statements is true ? *[NCERT (New) Pg. 215, AIPMT 2003]*
(a) The radiation is emitted during the summers and absorbed during the winters
(b) The radiation emitted lies in the ultraviolet region and hence is not visible
(c) The radiation emitted is in the infrared region
(d) The radiation is emitted only during the day

23 Consider a compound slab consisting of two different materials having equal thicknesses and thermal conductivities K and $2K$, respectively. The equivalent thermal conductivity of the slab is *[AIPMT 2003]*

(a) $3K$ (b) $\frac{4}{3}K$
(c) $\frac{2}{3}K$ (d) $\sqrt{2}K$

24 For a black body at temperature 727°C, its radiating power is 60 W and temperature of surrounding is 227°C. If the temperature of the black body is changed to 1227°C, then its radiating power will be *[NCERT (New) Pg. 219, AIPMT 2002]*
(a) 120 W (b) 240 W (c) 304 W (d) 320 W

25 Which of the following is close to an ideal black body ? *[AIPMT 2002]*
(a) Black lamp
(b) Cavity maintained at constant temperature
(c) Platinum black
(d) A lamp of charcoal heated to high temperature

26 Wien's displacement law expresses relation between *[NCERT (New) Pg. 218, AIPMT 2002]*
(a) wavelength corresponding to maximum energy and absolute temperature
(b) radiated energy and wavelength
(c) emissive power and temperature
(d) colour of light and temperature

27 Consider two rods of same length and different specific heats (s_1, s_2), thermal conductivities (K_1, K_2) and areas of cross-section (A_1, A_2) and both having temperatures (T_1, T_2) at their ends. If their rate of loss of heat due to conduction are equal, then *[NCERT (New) Pg. 220, AIPMT 2002]*

(a) $K_1A_1 = K_2A_2$ (b) $\frac{K_1A_1}{s_1} = \frac{K_2A_2}{s_2}$
(c) $K_2A_1 = K_1A_2$ (d) $\frac{K_2A_1}{s_2} = \frac{K_1A_2}{s_1}$

28 Rate of heat flow through a cylindrical rod is H_1. Temperatures of ends of rod are T_1 and T_2. If all the dimensions of rod become double and temperature difference remains same and rate of heat flow becomes H_2. Then, *[AIPMT 2001]*
(a) $H_2 = 2H_1$ (b) $H_2 = \frac{H_1}{2}$
(c) $H_2 = \frac{H_1}{4}$ (d) $H_2 = 4H_1$

29 The wavelength corresponding to maximum intensity of radiation emitted by a source at temperature 2000 K is λ, then what is the wavelength corresponding to maximum intensity of radiation at temperature 3000 K ? *[NCERT (New) Pg. 218, AIPMT 2001]*
(a) $\frac{2}{3}\lambda$ (b) $\frac{16}{81}\lambda$ (c) $\frac{81}{16}\lambda$ (d) $\frac{4}{3}\lambda$

30 A cylindrical rod having temperature T_1 and T_2 at its end. The rate of flow of heat is Q_1 cal/s. If all the linear dimensions are doubled keeping temperature constant, then the rate of flow of heat Q_2 will be *[AIPMT 2001]*

(a) $4Q_1$ (b) $2Q_1$
(c) $Q_1/4$ (d) $Q_1/2$

31 A black body has maximum wavelength λ_m at temperature 2000 K. Its corresponding wavelenght at temeperature 3000 K will be *[AIPMT 2001]*

(a) $\frac{3}{2}\lambda_m$ (b) $\frac{2}{3}\lambda_m$

(c) $\frac{4}{9}\lambda_m$ (d) $\frac{9}{4}\lambda_m$

32 The presence of gravitational field is required for the heat transfer by *[NCERT (New) Pg. 217, AIPMT 2000]*

(a) conduction
(b) stirring of liquids
(c) natural convection
(d) radiation

33 Which one of the following processes depends on gravity ? *[AIPMT 2000]*

(a) Conduction (b) Convection
(c) Radiation (d) None of these

34 The radiant energy from the sun, incident normally at the surface of earth is 20 kcal/m^2 min. What would have been the radiant energy, incident normally on the earth, if the sun had a temperature, twice of the present one ? *[AIPMT 1998]*

(a) 160 kcal/m^2 min (b) 40 kcal/m^2 min
(c) 320 kcal/m^2 min (d) 80 kcal/m^2 min

35 A black body is at temperature of 500 K. It emits energy at rate which is proportional to *[NCERT (New) Pg. 219, AIPMT 1997]*

(a) $(500)^4$ (b) $(500)^3$
(c) $(500)^2$ (d) 500

36 If the temperature of the Sun is doubled, the rate of energy received on earth will be increased by a factor of *[AIPMT 1993]*

(a) 2 (b) 4
(c) 8 (d) 16

Key Index

Topic 1

1 (b)	2 (c)	3 (c)	4 (b)	5 (d)	6 (a)	7 (b)	8 (c)	9 (c)	10 (c)

Topic 2

1 (d)	2 (b)	3 (b)	4 (d)	5 (a)	6 (a)	7 (c)	8 (d)	9 (b)	10 (b)

Topic 3

1 (d)	2 (c)	3 (a)	4 (a)	5 (d)	6 (c)	7 (c)	8 (d)	9 (b)	10 (a)
11 (d)	12 (a)	13 (a)	14 (b)	15 (c)	16 (d)	17 (d)	18 (b)	19 (d)	20 (b)
21 (d)	22 (c)	23 (b)	24 (d)	25 (b)	26 (a)	27 (a)	28 (a)	29 (a)	30 (b)
31 (b)	32 (c)	33 (b)	34 (c)	35 (a)	36 (d)				

Detailed **Explanations**

Topic 1

01. *(b)* Given,

Young's modulus, $Y = 0.5 \times 10^{11}\ \text{Nm}^{-2}$

Coefficient of linear thermal expansion,

$\alpha = 10^{-5}\ {}^\circ\text{C}^{-1}$

Length, $l = 1$ m

Area of cross-section, $A = 10^{-3}\ \text{m}^2$

$$\Delta T = 100^\circ\text{C}$$

We know that, stress $= Y \cdot \dfrac{\Delta l}{l}$

Here, $\Delta l = l \alpha \Delta T$

$$= 1 \times 10^{-5} \times 100 = 10^{-3}$$

$$\Rightarrow \quad \frac{F}{A} = Y \cdot \frac{10^{-3}}{1}$$

Compressive force,

$$F = 0.5 \times 10^{11} \times 10^{-3} \times 10^{-3}$$

$$= 0.5 \times 10^5 = 50 \times 10^3\ \text{N}$$

02. *(c)* Due to change in temperature, the thermal strain produced in a rod of length L is given by

$$\Delta L = L \alpha \Delta T$$

where L = original length of rod and α = coefficient of linear expansion of solid rod

ΔT is same for both copper and aluminium, Therefore,

$$L_{Cu} \alpha_{Cu} = L_{Al} \alpha_{Al} \quad \ldots \text{(i)}$$

Here, $\alpha_{Cu} = 1.7 \times 10^{-5}\ \text{K}^{-1}$

$\alpha_{Al} = 2.2 \times 10^{-5}\ \text{K}^{-1}$

and $L_{Cu} = 88$ cm

Substituting the given values in Eq. (i), we get

$$L_{Al} = \frac{L_{Cu} \alpha_{Cu}}{\alpha_{Al}}$$

$$= \frac{1.7 \times 10^{-5} \times 88}{2.2 \times 10^{-5}} \simeq 68\text{cm}$$

> **• Concept Enhancer**
>
> When a metal rod is heated such that its change in temperature is ΔT, then the metallic rod expands. This expansion is given by
>
> $$\frac{\Delta L}{L} = \alpha\ \Delta T$$
>
> where α is called coefficient of linear expansion. It depends on the nature of material and is different for each metal.

03. *(c)* According to question,

Coefficient of linear expansion of brass $= \alpha_1$

Coefficient of linear expansion of steel $= \alpha_2$

Length of brass and steel rods are l_1 and l_2, respectively.

As given difference increase in length $(l_2' - l_1')$ is same for all temperature.

So, $l_2' - l_1' = l_2 - l_1$

$\Rightarrow l_2 (1 + \alpha_2 \Delta T) - l_1 (1 + \alpha_1 \Delta T) = l_2 - l_1$

$\Rightarrow \quad l_2 \alpha_2 = l_1 \alpha_1$

04. *(b)* Given, $r = 5 \times 10^{-4}\ \text{K}^{-1}$

As, orginal density of glycerin,

$$\rho = \rho_0 (1 + \gamma \Delta T)$$

$\Rightarrow \rho - \rho_0 = \rho_0 \gamma \Delta T$

$\Delta T = 40^\circ\text{C}$

$$\frac{\rho - \rho_0}{\rho_0} = \gamma \Delta T = 5 \times 10^{-4} \times 40$$

$$= 200 \times 10^{-4} = 0.020$$

05. *(d)*

> **key idea**
>
> The neutral temperature of a thermocouple is given
>
> $$T_{\text{neutral}} = \frac{T_{\text{high}} + T_{\text{low}}}{2}$$

Neutral temperature,

$$T_n = \frac{T_i + T_c}{2}, \ T_n = \frac{T_i + 0}{2} = \frac{T_i}{2}$$

[$T_c = 0^\circ$C temperature of cold junctions]

06. *(a)* Given, $T_1 = 20^\circ\text{C}, T_2 = 40^\circ\text{C}$

$\rho_{T_1} = 998\ \text{kg/m}^3$

$\rho_{T_2} = 992\ \text{kg/m}^3$

As $\quad \rho_{T_2} = \dfrac{\rho_{T_1}}{(1 + \gamma \Delta T)} = \dfrac{\rho_{T_1}}{1 + \gamma (T_2 - T_1)}$

$\therefore \quad 992 = \dfrac{998}{1 + \gamma (40 - 20)}$

or, $\quad 992 = \dfrac{998}{1 + 20\gamma}$

$\Rightarrow \quad \gamma = \dfrac{6}{992} \times \dfrac{1}{20} = 3 \times 10^{-4} / {}^\circ\text{C}$

07. *(b)* The relation between true scale and new scale of temperature is given by

$$\left(\frac{t - \text{LFP}}{\text{UFP} - \text{LFP}}\right)_{\text{true}} = \left(\frac{t - \text{LFP}}{\text{UFP} - \text{LFP}}\right)_{\text{new}}$$

$$\frac{39^\circ \text{C} - 0^\circ \text{C}}{100^\circ \text{C} - 0^\circ \text{C}} = \frac{t - 39^\circ \text{W}}{239^\circ \text{W} - 39^\circ \text{W}}$$

$\Rightarrow \quad t = 117^\circ\text{W}$

08. *(c)* We know that nautral temperature

$$T_n = \frac{T_{\text{high}} + T_{\text{low}}}{2}$$

$$300^\circ\text{C} = \frac{620^\circ + T_{\text{low}}}{2}$$

$\Rightarrow 600^\circ\ \text{C} - 620^\circ\text{C} = T_{\text{low}}$

$\Rightarrow \quad T_{\text{low}} = -20^\circ\text{C}$

09. *(c)* Mercury thermometer is a liquid thermometer and it is based upon the uniform variation in volume of a liquid with temperature.

A mercury thermometer can be used to measure temperature upto 300°C or so, as before boiling at 367°C, the vaporisation of mercury will start.

10. *(c)* Relation between Celsius scale and Fahrenheit scale is

$$\frac{C}{100} = \frac{F - 32}{180}$$

Putting value of $F = 140^\circ$F

$\therefore \quad \dfrac{C}{100} = \dfrac{140 - 32}{180} = 0.6$

$\therefore \quad C = 60^\circ\text{C}$

Hence, fall in temperature

= Temperature of boiling water − final temperature

$100^\circ\ \text{C} - 60^\circ\ \text{C} = 40^\circ\ \text{C}$

> **• Concept Enhancer**
>
> Always remember this equation for quick interchange in temperature scale.
>
> $$\frac{C - 0}{100 - 0} = \frac{F - 32}{212 - 32} = \frac{K - 273.15}{373.15 - 273.15} = \frac{R - 491.67}{691.67 - 491.67}$$
>
> Here, C = Centigrade, F = Fahrenheit
> K = Kelvin, R = Reaumur

Topic 2

01. *(d)* Since, heat required,

$$Q = mc\Delta T = \left(\frac{4}{3}\pi r^3 \cdot \rho\right) c \Delta T$$

[$\because m = V_{\text{sphere}}\ \rho$]

Since, π, ρ, c and T are constants.

$\Rightarrow \quad Q \propto r^3$ or $\dfrac{Q_1}{Q_2} = \dfrac{r_1^3}{r_2^3}$

$$= \left(\frac{r_1}{r_2}\right)^3 = \left(\frac{1.5 r_2}{r_2}\right)^3 = \frac{27}{8}$$

02. (b)

key idea

Apply conservation of energy i.e., energy gained by the ice during its fall from height will be used to melt the ice.
So, $E = mgh = mL$

As given, only one quarter of its energy is absorbed by the ice.

So, $\dfrac{mgh}{4} = mL_f$

$$\Rightarrow \quad h = \frac{mL_f \times 4}{mg}$$

$$= \frac{L_f \times 4}{g} = \frac{3.4 \times 10^5 \times 4}{10 \times 1000} \text{ km}$$

$= 136$ km

03. (b) Heat lost by 1st body = heat gained by 2nd body. Body at 100°C temperature has greater heat capacity than body at 0°C. So, final temperature will be closer to 100°C.
i.e., $T_c > 50°$ C.

04. (d) Let m' be the amount of steam that converts into water.

$$m' \times L + m' s\,\Delta T = ms\,\Delta T$$

[s = Specific heat of water; L = Latent heat of water]

$$m' \times 540 + m' \times 1 \times (100 - 80) = 20 \times 1 \times (80 - 10)$$

$$m' = \frac{20 \times 70}{560} = 2.5\text{g}$$

Now, net mass of water
$= 20 + 2.5$
$= 22.5$ g

05. (a) Graph (a) shows the variation of temperature with time. At first temperature will increase then there will be state change from liquid to gas.

06. (a) Given,
Current, $I = 4$ A
Voltage, $V = 220$ V
Mass, $m = 1$ kg
Change in temperature
$\Delta T = 100° - 20°\text{C} = 80°\text{C}$
specific heat of water,
$s = 4200$ J/kg°C
Heat used to boil water

$$\Rightarrow V \times I \times t = ms\Delta T \Rightarrow t = \frac{ms\Delta T}{VI}$$

$$= \frac{1 \times 4200 \times 80}{220 \times 4} = 6.3 \text{ min}$$

07. (c) Heat required by 1g of ice at 0°C to melt into 1g of water at 0°C,

$Q_1 = mL$ (L = latent heat of fusion)
$= 1 \times 80 = 80$ cal (L = 80 cal/g)

Heat required by 1g of water at 0°C to boil at 100°C,

$Q_2 = mc\Delta\theta$
(c = specific heat of water)
$= 1 \times 1 (100 - 0)$ (c = 1 cal/g°C)
$= 100$ cal

Thus, total heat required by 1g of ice to reach a temperature of 100°C,

$Q = Q_1 + Q_2$
$= 80 + 100 = 180$ cal

Heat available with 1 g of steam to condense into 1g of water at 100°C,

$Q' = mL'$
(L' = latent heat of vaporisation)
$= 1 \times 536$ cal (L' = 536 cal/g)
$= 536$ cal

Obviously, the whole steam will not be condensed and ice will attain temperature of 100°C. Thus, the temperature of mixture is 100°C.

• Concept Enhancer

Principle of calorimetry states that heat lost by hot body is equal to heat gained by cold body.

08. (d) $\Delta Q = sm\,(\Delta T)$
where, s is specific heat of the body, when $\Delta T = 1\text{K}$, ΔQ = thermal capacity
∴ Thermal capacity
$= s \times m \times 1 = ms$
Here, $m = 40$ g,
$s = 0.2$ cal / g K
∴ Thermal capacity
$= 40 \times 0.2 = 8$ cal/°C
$= 4.2 \times 8$ J/°C $= 33.6$ J/°C

09. (b) Vapour pressure of a substance is independent of the amount of substance. It depends only on temperature. So, they have pressure in the ratio of 1 : 1.

10. (b) Let θ be the temperature when thermal equilibrium has reached. Using principle of calorimetry that heat gained = heat lost

$$mL + ms(\theta - 0) = 55(40 - \theta)$$

$$10 \times 80 + 10 \times 1 \times \theta = 55 \times (40 - \theta)$$

$$\theta = \frac{1400}{65} \approx 21.5°\text{C}$$

$\approx 22°$C

Topic 3

01. (d) According to Wein's displacement law,

$$\lambda = \frac{b}{T}$$

i.e., $\lambda \propto \dfrac{1}{T}$ ... (i)

We know that,

$$\lambda_{\text{bluish}} < \lambda_{\text{yellowish}} < \lambda_{\text{reddish}}$$

Hence, using Eq. (i), we have

$$T_A > T_C > T_B$$

02. (c)

key idea

If area of cross-section of a surface is not uniform or if the steady state condition is not reached, the heat flow equation can be applied to a thin layer of material perpendicular to direction of heat flow.

The rate of heat flow by conduction for growth of ice is given by,

$$\frac{dQ}{dt} = \frac{KA(\theta_0 - \theta_1)}{x}$$

where, $d\theta = \rho A dx L$, $\theta_0 = 0$ and $\theta_1 = -\theta$

Given, $\theta_0 = 0°$ C, $\theta_1 = -26°$ C

$$\frac{dQ}{dt} = \frac{KA(\theta_0 - \theta_1)}{x}$$

$$\Rightarrow \quad \frac{\rho A dx L}{dt} = \frac{KA(\theta_0 - \theta_1)}{x}$$

$$\Rightarrow \quad \frac{dx}{dt} = \frac{KA(\theta_0 - \theta_1)}{\rho A x L}$$

$$= \frac{K[0 - (-26)]}{\rho x L} = \frac{26K}{\rho x L}$$

03. (a) According to Wien's law,

$$\lambda_{\max} \propto \frac{1}{T}$$

i.e. $\lambda_{\max} T$ = constant

$$\therefore \quad \lambda_{\max_1} T_1 = \lambda_{\max_2} T_2$$

or $\dfrac{T_1}{T_2} = \dfrac{\lambda_{\max 2}}{\lambda_{\max 1}}$ ...(i)

Here, $\lambda_{\max_1} = \lambda_0$ and $\lambda_{\max_2} = \dfrac{3}{4}\lambda_0$

$$\therefore \quad \frac{T_1}{T_2} = \frac{\frac{3}{4}\lambda_0}{\lambda_0} = \frac{3}{4}$$

or $\frac{T_1}{T_2} = \frac{3}{4}$ ...(ii)

From Stefan's law,

$$P = \sigma A e T^4$$

i.e. $P \propto T^4$

$$\Rightarrow \frac{P_1}{P_2} = \frac{T_1^4}{T_2^4} = \left(\frac{T_1}{T_2}\right)^4$$

From Eq. (i), we get

$$\frac{P_1}{P_2} = \left(\frac{3}{4}\right)^4 = \frac{81}{256}$$

Given, $P_1 = P$ and $P_2 = nP$

$$\Rightarrow \frac{P_1}{P_2} = \frac{P}{nP} = \frac{81}{256}$$

or $n = \frac{256}{81}$

Alternate Solution

From Wien's displacement law,

$\lambda_{max} T = \text{constant}$

$$\Rightarrow \lambda_0 T = \frac{3\lambda_0}{4} T' \Rightarrow T' = \left(\frac{4}{3}\right) T$$

$$\Rightarrow \frac{P_2}{P_1} = \left(\frac{T'}{T}\right)^4 = \left(\frac{4}{3}\right)^4 = \frac{256}{81}$$

04. *(a)* In parallel arrangement of n rods, equivalent thermal conductivity is given by

$$K_{eq} = \frac{K_1 A_1 + K_2 A_2 + \ldots + K_n A_n}{A_1 + A_2 + \ldots + A_n}$$

If rods are of same area, then

$$K_{eq} = \frac{K_1 + K_2 + \ldots + K_n}{n}$$

∴ Equivalent thermal conductivity of the system of two rods

$$\Rightarrow K_{eq} = \frac{K_1 + K_2}{2}$$

05. *(d)* Radiated power of a black body,

$$P = \sigma A T^4$$

When radius of the sphere is halved, new area,

$$A' = \frac{A}{4}$$

∴ Power radiated,

$$P' = \sigma\left(\frac{A}{4}\right)(2T)^4 = \frac{16}{4} \cdot (\sigma A T^4)$$

$$= 4P = 4 \times 450 = 1800 \text{ W}$$

06. *(c)* Given inital temperatrue T

$= 145°\text{C} = 418 \text{ K}$

Power, $P_1 = 17$ W

Final temperature, $T_2 = 273°\text{C} = 546 \text{ K}$

From Stefan's Law,

$$E \propto T^4$$

$$\frac{E_1}{E_2} = \frac{P_1}{P_2} = \left(\frac{T_1}{T_2}\right)^4$$

$$\Rightarrow \frac{P_1}{P_2} = \left(\frac{418}{546}\right)^4 \Rightarrow P_2 = \frac{1}{0.343} \times 17$$

$$\Rightarrow P_2 = 49.6 \text{ W}$$

07. *(c)* Given, temperature, $T_1 = 5760$ K

According to Wien's law,

$$\lambda_m T = b$$

where, b = Wien's constant

$= 2.88 \times 10^6$ nm K

$$\Rightarrow \lambda_m = \frac{b}{T} = \frac{2.88 \times 10^6 \text{ nm K}}{5760 \text{ K}}$$

$$\Rightarrow \lambda_m = 500 \text{ nm}$$

∵ λ_m = wavelength corresponding to maximum energy, so, $U_2 > U_1$.

08. *(d)* Here, $\Delta T_1 = 110 - 100 = 10°$ C

$$\frac{dQ_1}{dt} = 4 \text{ J/s}$$

$$\Rightarrow \Delta T_2 = 210 - 200 = 10° \text{ C}$$

$$\frac{dQ_2}{dt} = ?$$

As, $\frac{dQ}{dt} \propto \Delta T$

Also, $\Delta T_1 = \Delta T_2$

Hence, $\frac{dQ_2}{dt} = 4$ J/s

09. *(b)* Equation of Wien's displacement law is given by $\lambda_m T$ = constant

i.e. $\lambda_m \propto \frac{1}{T}$, thus when temperature of iron rod is increased continuously, its wavelength keeps on decreasing continuously and this will cause visible change in colour in the piece of iron from dull red to reddish yellow to finally white hot.

10. *(a)*

key idea

Use the formula for heat transfer

i.e., $\frac{Q}{t} = \frac{KA\Delta T}{d}$

Let L be length of each rod.

For rod 1,

$$H_1 = \frac{K_1 A_1 \Delta T}{L}$$

For rod 2, $H_2 = \frac{K_2 A_2 \Delta T}{L}$

Therefore, $H_1 = 4H_2$

$$\Rightarrow \frac{K_1 A_1 \Delta T}{L} = 4 \frac{K_2 A_2 \Delta T}{L}$$

$$K_1 A_1 = 4 K_2 A_2$$

11. *(d)* From Stefan law,

$$E = \sigma T^4$$

So, the rate of energy production

$$Q = E \times A = \sigma T^4 \times 4\pi R^2$$

Temperature of star

$$T = \left(\frac{Q}{4\pi R^2 \sigma}\right)^{1/4}$$

12. *(a)*

key idea

The heat evolved is used to melt ice.

Thus, $Q = \frac{KA(\Delta T)t}{L} = m_{ice} L_f$

Given, area of stone slab, $A = 0.36$ m^2

Thickness, $L = 0.1$ m

Time, $t = 1$ hr $= 3600$ s

Mass of ice, $m = 4.8$ kg

$$Q = \frac{KA(T_1 - T_2)t}{L}$$

$$= \frac{K \times 0.36 \times (100 - 0) \times 3600}{0.1}$$

$$= \frac{K \times 0.36 \times 100 \times 3600}{0.1} \quad \ldots(i)$$

Heat required to melt ice is

$$Q = m_{ice} L_f = 4.8 \times 3.36 \times 10^5 \text{ J} \ldots(ii)$$

From (i) and (ii), we get

$$\frac{K \times 0.36 \times 100 \times 3600}{0.1} = 4.8 \times 3.36 \times 10^5$$

$$K = \frac{4.8 \times 3.36 \times 10^5 \times 0.1}{0.36 \times 100 \times 3600}$$

$$= 1.24 \text{ J/m/s/°C}$$

13. *(a)* According to the Stefan Boltzmann law, $P = \sigma 4\pi r^2 T^4$

where, r = radius of the star,

σ = Stefan's constant

The radiant power per unit area received at a distance R from the centre of a star is

$$S = \frac{P}{4\pi R^2} = \frac{\sigma 4\pi r^2 T^4}{4\pi R^2} = \frac{\sigma r^2 T^4}{R^2}$$

14. *(b)* We know that,

In steady state rate of heat transfer of material of rod will be

$$\Rightarrow \frac{Q}{t} \propto \frac{A}{l} \propto \frac{r^2}{l} \quad \ldots(i)$$

When the rod is melted

∴ Volume = constant, $V_1 = V_2$

$$\pi r_1^2 l_1 = \pi r_2^2 l_2 \qquad \left[\because r_2 = \frac{r_1}{2}\right]$$

$$\Rightarrow \quad l_1 = \frac{l_2}{4} \qquad \ldots\text{(ii)}$$

Now, from Eqs. (i) and (ii),

$$\frac{Q_1}{Q_2} = \frac{r_1^2}{l_1} \times \frac{l_2}{r_2^2} = \frac{r_1^2}{l_1} \times \frac{4l_1}{(r_1/2)^2}$$

$$\Rightarrow \quad Q_1 = 16\,Q_2$$

$$\Rightarrow \quad Q_2 = \frac{Q_1}{16}$$

15. *(c)* According to Stefan's law,
$E = \sigma T^4$

$$\frac{E_1}{E_2} = \left[\frac{T_1}{T_2}\right]^4$$

$$\Rightarrow E_2 = 7\left[\frac{273+727}{273+227}\right]^4 = \left[\frac{1000}{500}\right]^4 \times 7$$

$$= 112 \text{ cal-cm}^2\text{s}^{-1}$$

16. *(d)* The rate of heat flowing through the rod is

$$\frac{dQ}{dt} = \frac{KA(T_1 - T_2)}{L}$$

17. *(d)* From Stefan's law,

$$P = \sigma \times 4\pi r^2 T^4$$

[Sun is a perfectly black body as it emits radiations of all wavelengths and so for it $e = 1$]

The intensity of this power at the earth's surface (under the assumption $R >> r_0$) is

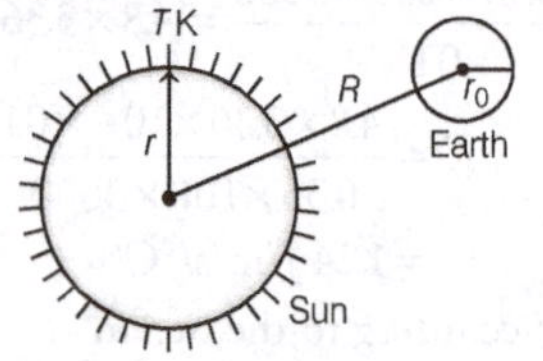

$$I = \frac{P}{4\pi R^2} = \frac{\sigma \times 4\pi r^2 T^4}{4\pi R^2}$$

$$= \frac{\sigma r^2 T^4}{R^2} = \frac{\sigma r^2 (t+273)^4}{R^2}$$

Alternate Solution

Total energy radiated by Stefan's law

$$E = \sigma 4\pi r^2 (t+273)^4$$

$$\text{Power} = \frac{E}{\text{Area}} = \frac{\sigma 4\pi r^2 (t+273)^4}{4\pi R^2}$$

$$= \frac{\sigma r^2 (t+273)^4}{R^2}$$

18. *(b)* According to Stefan's law,

$$E \propto T^4$$

Here, $E \propto (727 + 273)^4$

$\Rightarrow \quad E \propto (1000)^4$

19. *(d)*

key idea

Use Wien's displacement law, i.e. $\lambda_m T = \text{constant}$

According to Wien's law

$$\lambda_m T = \text{constant (say } b)$$

$$\therefore \quad \frac{\lambda'_m}{\lambda_m} = \frac{T}{T'}$$

Given, $T = 1227 + 273 = 1500$ K

$T' = 1227 + 1000 + 273 = 2500$ K

$\lambda_m = 5000$ Å

Hence, $\lambda'_m = \frac{1500}{2500} \times 5000 = 3000$ Å

20. *(b)* As from law of heat transfer through conduction

$$H = \frac{\Delta Q}{\Delta t} = KA\left(\frac{T_1 - T_2}{l}\right)$$

$$\Rightarrow \quad H \propto \frac{r^2}{l}$$

So, the rod with maximum radius r minimum length l will conduct most heat i.e. $r = 2r_0$, $l = l_0$

Alternate Solution

Heat is given by $H = KA\frac{\Delta T}{l} = K\pi r^2 \frac{\Delta T}{l}$

Thus for option (b) $\frac{\pi r^2}{l}$ will be greater than other options.

21. *(d)* According to Wien's displacement law,

i.e. $\quad \lambda_m T = \text{constant}$

or $\quad \lambda_m \propto T^{-1}$

22. *(c)* The heat radiation emitted by the human body is the infrared radiation. Their wavelength is of the order of 7.9×10^{-7} m to 10^{-3} m which is of course the range of infrared region.

23. *(b)* The quantity of heat flowing across a slab in time t,

$$Q = \frac{KA\Delta\theta}{l}$$

For same heat flow through each slab and (composite slab), we have

$$\frac{K_1 A(\Delta\theta_1)}{l} = \frac{K_2 A(\Delta\theta_2)}{l}$$

$$= \frac{K' A(\Delta\theta_1 + \Delta\theta_2)}{2l}$$

or $\quad K_1 \Delta\theta_1 = K_2 \Delta\theta_2$

$$= \frac{K'}{2}(\Delta\theta_1 + \Delta\theta_2) = C \text{ (say)}$$

So, $\quad \Delta\theta_1 = \frac{C}{K_1}, \; \Delta\theta_2 = \frac{C}{K_2}$

and $(\Delta\theta_1 + \Delta\theta_2) = \frac{2C}{K'}$

or $\quad \frac{C}{K_1} + \frac{C}{K_2} = \frac{2C}{K'}$

$\therefore \quad K' = \frac{2K_1 K_2}{K_1 + K_2}$

Given, $K_1 = K$, $K_2 = 2K$

So, $\quad K' = \frac{2K \times 2K}{K + 2K} = \frac{4}{3}K$

Alternate Solution

The thermal resistances can be added as they are in series. But, note that the width of the combined slab is twice the width of individual slab.

So, we have $\frac{2L}{K_{eq}A} = \frac{L}{KA} + \frac{L}{KA} \Rightarrow K_{eq} = \frac{4K}{3}$

24. *(d)* For two different cases ratio of radiation power is given by Stefan's law,

$$\text{i.e.,} \quad \frac{P_2}{P_1} = \left(\frac{T_2^4 - T_0^4}{T_1^4 - T_0^4}\right) \qquad \ldots\text{(i)}$$

Here, $P_1 = 60$ W,

$T_1 = 727°\text{C} = 1000$ K

$T_0 = 227°\text{C} = 500$ K,

$T_2 = 1227°\text{C} = 1500$ K

On substituting in Eq. (i), we get

$$P_2 = \frac{(1500)^4 - (500)^4}{(1000)^4 - (500)^4} \times 60$$

$$= 320 \text{ W}$$

• Concept Enhancer

Boltzmann corrected Stefan's law and stated that the amount of radiations emitted by the body, not only depends upon the temperature of the body, but also depends on the temperature of the surrounding. The radiated power by the body is given by

$$P = \sigma(T^4 - T_0^4)$$

where, T_0 is the absolute temperature of the surrounding and T is the temperature of body.

25. *(b)* Cavity approximating an ideal black body is shown in the figure. Radiation entering the cavity has little chance of leaving before it is completely absorbed.

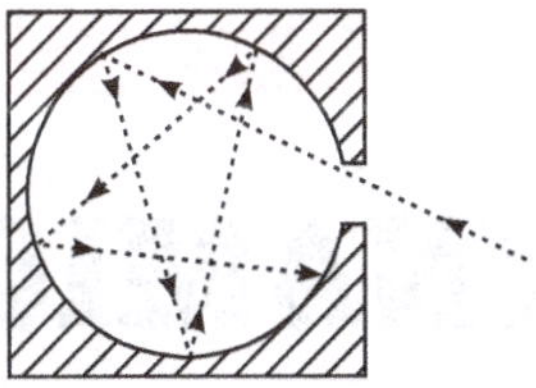

• **Concept Enhancer**
Materials like black velvet or lamp black come close to ideal black bodies, but the best practical realization of an ideal black body is a small hole leading into a cavity maintained at constant temperature as this absorbs 98% of the radiation incident on them.

26. *(a)* Wien's displacement law is

$$\lambda_m \cdot T = \text{constant}$$

• **Concept Enhancer**
According to Wien's displacement law, the quantity of energy radiated out by a body is not uniformly distributed over all the wavelengths emitted by it. It is maximum for a particular wavelength λ, which is different at different temperatures. As the temperature is increased, the value of the wavelength which carries maximum energy is decreased.

27. *(a)* Rate of loss of heat by conduction is,

$$H = \frac{\Delta Q}{\Delta t} = KA\left(\frac{T_1 - T_2}{l}\right)$$

For first rod,

$$H_1 = K_1 A_1 \left(\frac{T_1 - T_2}{l_1}\right)$$

For second rod,

$$H_2 = K_2 A_2 \left(\frac{T_1 - T_2}{l_2}\right)$$

but $l_1 = l_2$

i.e. of same length

and $H_1 = H_2$

or $K_1 A_1 (T_1 - T_2) = K_2 A_2 (T_1 - T_2)$

or $K_1 A_1 = K_2 A_2$

28. *(a)* Rate of heat flow w.r.t. time

or $H \propto \frac{A}{l}$

Since, dimensions of area, $A = [L^2]$

Dimensions of length, $l = [L]$

$\therefore \quad H \propto L$

or $\frac{H_2}{H_1} = \frac{L_2}{L_1} = \frac{2L_1}{L_1} \quad (\because L_2 = 2L_1)$

or $H_2 = 2H_1$

29. *(a)* Wien's displacement law is given by

$\lambda_m T = \text{constant}$

$\therefore \quad \lambda_1 T_1 = \lambda_2 T_2$

$$\lambda_2 = \lambda_1 \left(\frac{T_1}{T_2}\right)$$

Given, $T_1 = 2000$ K,

$T_2 = 3000$ K, $\lambda_1 = \lambda$

$$\therefore \quad \lambda_2 = \lambda \times \frac{2000}{3000} = \frac{2}{3}\lambda$$

30. *(b)* Rate of heat flow will be

$$Q = \frac{KA(T_1 - T_2)}{l}$$

i.e. $Q \propto \frac{A}{l}$

We know that dimensions of area

$A = [L^2]$

dimensions of distance $l = [L]$

$\therefore \quad Q \propto L$

$\Rightarrow \quad \frac{Q_2}{Q_1} = \frac{L_2}{L_1} = 2$

$\Rightarrow \quad Q_2 = 2Q_1$

31. *(b)* According to Wein's displacement law, we have

$$\lambda_m T = 2.88 \times 10^{-3}$$

When $T = 2000$ K,

$\lambda_m (2000) = 2.88 \times 10^{-3}$ ...(i)

when $T = 3000$ K,

$\lambda'_m (3000) = 2.88 \times 10^{-3}$ ...(ii)

Dividing (i) Eq. by Eq. (ii)

$$\frac{2}{3}\frac{\lambda_m}{\lambda'_m} = 1 \Rightarrow \frac{\lambda_m}{\lambda'_m} = \frac{3}{2}$$

$$\Rightarrow \quad \lambda'_m = \frac{2}{3}\lambda_m$$

32. *(c)* Natural convection occurs for transfer of heat in the presence of gravitational field.

33. *(b)* (a) Conduction is the process of transmission of heat in a body from the hotter part to the colder part without any bodily movement of constituent atoms or molecules of the body.

(b) In convection, the heated lighter particles move upward and colder heavier particles move downward to their place. This depends on weight and hence, on gravity.

(c) Radiation is the process of transmission of heat from one body to another body through electromagnetic waves even through vacuum, irrespective of their temperatures.

34. *(c)*

key idea
Use Stefan's law, $E = \sigma T^4$

According to Stefan's law,

$E = \sigma T^4$

or $E \propto T^4$

$$\therefore \quad \frac{E_1}{E_2} = \left(\frac{T_1}{T_2}\right)^4$$

Given, $T_1 = T, T_2 = 2T$,

$E_1 = 20$ kcal / m^{2}min

$$\therefore \quad \frac{20}{E_2} = \left(\frac{T}{2T}\right)^4$$

or $\frac{20}{E_2} = \frac{1}{16}$

$\therefore \quad E_2 = 20 \times 16$

$= 320$ kcal/m^{2}min

35. *(a)* According to Stefan's law,

$E \propto T^4$

$E = \sigma T^4$

$\therefore \quad E \propto (500)^4$

36. *(d)* According to Stefan-Boltzmann law,

$E \propto T^4$

If T is doubled, E becomes $(2)^4$ times (i.e. 16 times).

C-11

NEET Chapterwise
Topicwise Physics

In NEET 2024, 1 question was visible from this chapter. In past 5 years, 0 questions from topic-1, 3 questions from topic-2

For detailed analysis scan QR code

THERMODYNAMICS

Topic 1 Zeroth Law and First Law of Thermodynamics

01 1g of water of volume 1 cm^3 at 100°C is converted into steam at same temperature under normal atmospheric pressure ($\simeq 1 \times 10^5$ Pa). The volume of steam formed equals 1671 cm^3. If the specific latent heat of vaporisation of water is 2256 J/g, the change in internal energy is *[NCERT (New) Pg. 231, NEET (Odisha) 2019]*

(a) 2423 J (b) 2089 J (c) 167 J (d) 2256 J

02 A sample of 0.1 g of water at 100°C and normal pressure (1.013×10^5 Nm^{-2}) requires 54 cal of heat energy to convert to steam at 100°C. If the volume of the steam produced is 167.1 cc, the change in internal energy of the sample is *[NEET 2018]*

(a) 42.2 J (b) 208.7 J (c) 104.3 J (d) 84.5 J

03 The internal energy change in a system that has absorbed 2 kcal of heat and done 500 J of work is *[AIPMT 2009]*

(a) 8900 J (b) 6400 J (c) 5400 J (d) 7900 J

04 First law of thermodynamics is a consequence of conservation of *[NCERT (New) Pg. 230, AIPMT 1988]*

(a) work (b) energy (c) heat (d) All of these

Topic 2 Thermodynamic State Variable & Thermodynamic Processes

01 A thermodynamic system is taken through the cycle *abcda*. The work done by the gas along the path *bc* is *[NCERT (New) Pg. 235, NEET 2024]*

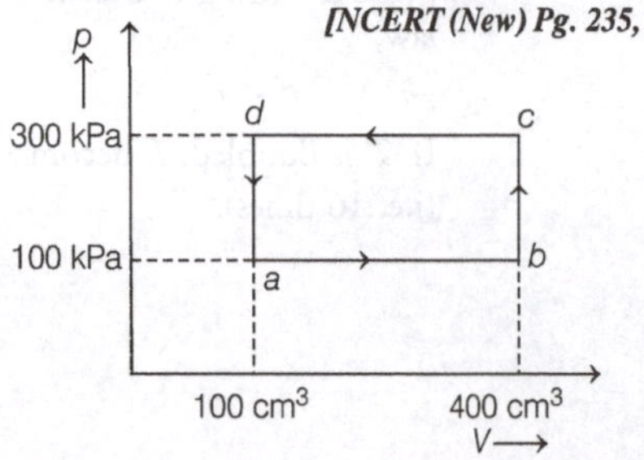

(a) Zero (b) 30 J
(c) −90 J (d) −60 J

02 An ideal gas undergoes four different processes from the same initial state as shown in the figure below. Those processes are adiabatic, isothermal, isobaric and isochoric. The curve which represents the adiabatic process among 1, 2, 3 and 4 is *[NCERT (New) Pg. 234, NEET 2022]*

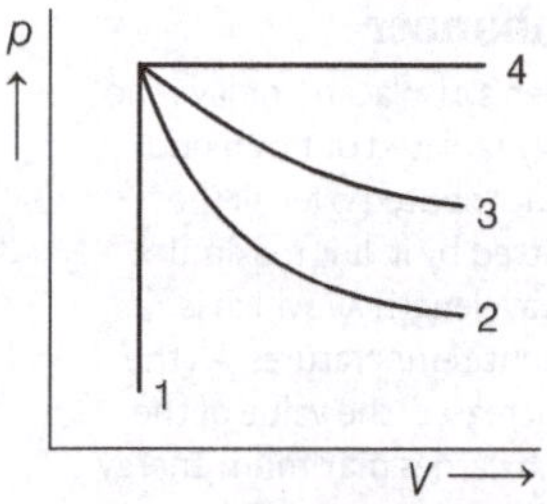

(a) 2 (b) 3
(c) 4 (d) 1

03 The *p-V* diagram for an ideal gas in a piston cylinder assembly undergoing a thermodynamic process is shown in the figure. The process is *[NCERT (New) Pg. 235, NEET (Oct.) 2020]*

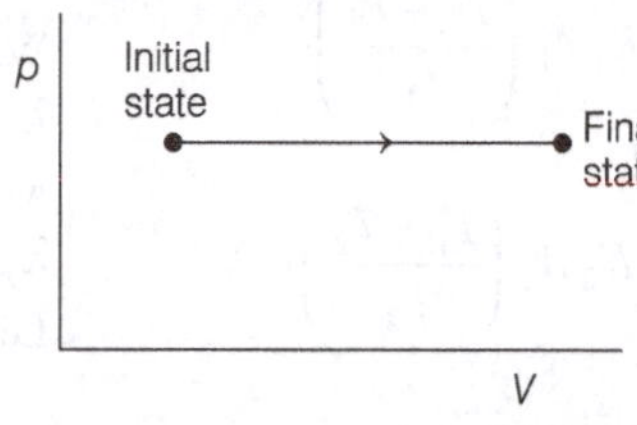

(a) adiabatic (b) isochoric
(c) isobaric (d) isothermal

04 In which of the following processes, heat is neither absorbed nor released by a system ? *[NEET (National) 2019]*

(a) Adiabatic
(b) Isobaric
(c) Isochoric
(d) Isothermal

05 The volume V of a monoatomic gas varies with its temperature T, as shown in the graph. The ratio of work done by the gas, to the heat absorbed by it, when it undergoes a change from state A to state B, is *[NCERT (New) Pg. 231, NEET 2018]*

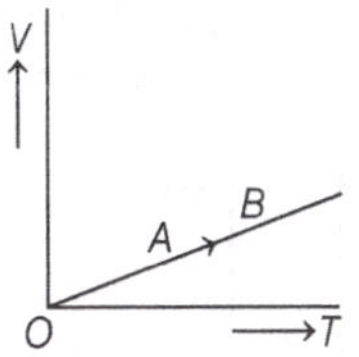

(a) 1/3 (b) 2/3 (c) 2/5 (d) 2/7

06 Thermodynamic processes are indicated in the following diagram *[NCERT (New) Pg. 234, NEET 2017]*

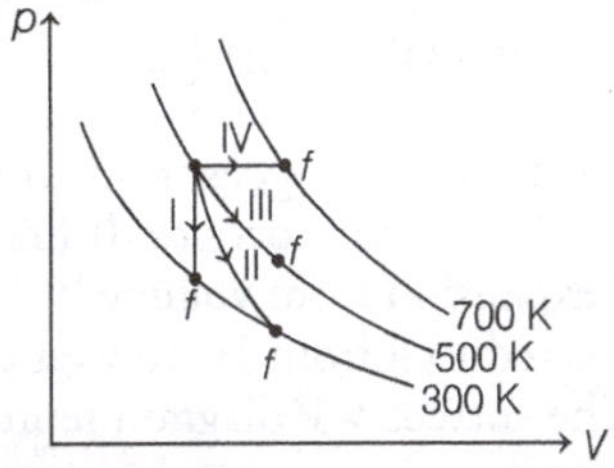

Match the following.

Column I		Column II
P. Process I	a.	Adiabatic
Q. Process II	b.	Isobaric
R. Process III	c.	Isochoric
S. Process IV	d.	Isothermal

(a) P→ a, Q→ c, R→ d, S→ b
(b) P→ c, Q→ a, R→ d, S→ b
(c) P→ c, Q→ d, R→ b, S→ a
(d) P→ d, Q→ b, R→ a, S→ c

07 A gas is compressed isothermally to half of its initial volume. The same gas is compressed separately through an adiabatic process until its volume is again reduced to half. Then, *[NEET 2016]*

(a) compressing the gas through adiabatic process will require more work to be done.
(b) compressing the gas isothermally or adiabatically will require the same amount of work.
(c) which of the case (whether compression through isothermal or through adiabatic process) requires more work will depend upon the atomicity of the gas.
(d) compressing the gas isothermally will require more work to be done.

08 One mole of an ideal monoatomic gas undergoes a process described by the equation pV^3 = constant. The heat capacity of the gas during this process is *[NCERT (New) Pg. 235, NEET 2016]*

(a) $\frac{3}{2}R$ (b) $\frac{5}{2}R$ (c) $2R$ (d) R

09 Figure below shows two paths that may be taken by a gas to go from a state A to a state C.

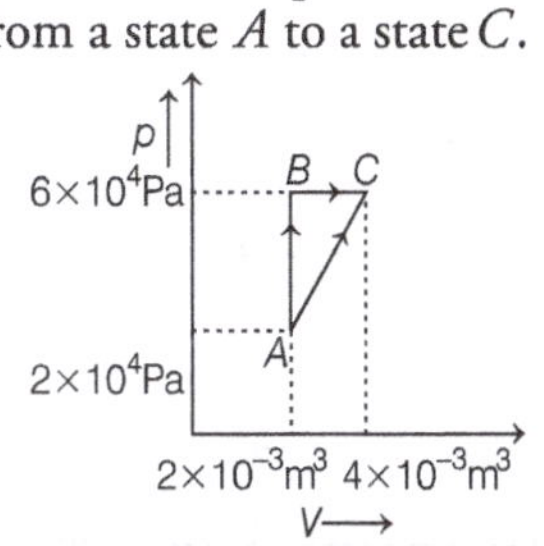

In process AB, 400 J of heat is added to the system and in process BC, 100 J of heat is added to the system. The heat absorbed by the system in the process AC will be *[NCERT (New) Pg. 235, AIPMT 2015]*

(a) 380 J (b) 500 J (c) 460 J (d) 300 J

10 One mole of an ideal diatomic gas undergoes a transition from A to B along a path AB as shown in the figure. *[NCERT (New) Pg. 231, AIPMT 2015]*

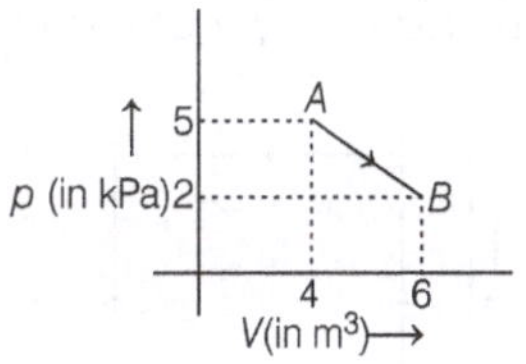

The change in internal energy of the gas during the transition is

(a) 20 kJ (b) – 20 kJ (c) 20 J (d) – 12 kJ

11 An ideal gas is compressed to half of its initial volume by means of several process. Which of the process results in the maximum work done on the gas ? *[AIPMT 2015]*

(a) Adiabatic (b) Isobaric
(c) Isochoric (d) Isothermal

12 A thermodynamic system undergoes cyclic process $ABCDA$ as shown in figure. The work done by the system in the cycle is *[AIPMT 2014]*

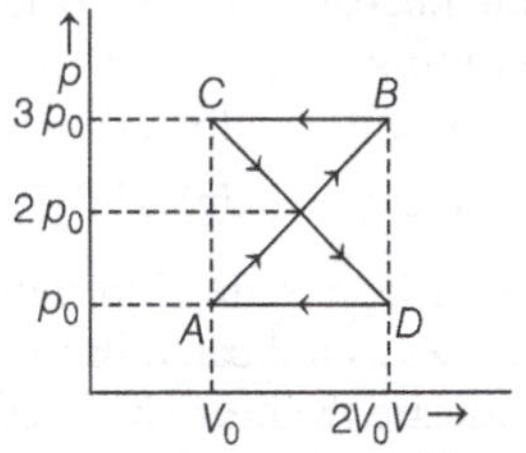

(a) p_0V_0 (b) $2p_0V_0$ (c) $\frac{p_0V_0}{2}$ (d) zero

13 A monoatomic gas at a pressure p, having a volume V expands isothermally to a volume $2V$ and then adiabatically to a volume $16V$. The final pressure of the gas is $\left(\text{take } \gamma = \frac{5}{3}\right)$ *[NCERT (New) Pg. 234, AIPMT 2014]*

(a) $64p$ (b) $32p$ (c) $\frac{p}{64}$ (d) $16p$

14 A gas is taken through the cycle $A \rightarrow B \rightarrow C \rightarrow A$, as shown. What is the net work done by the gas? **[NEET 2013]**

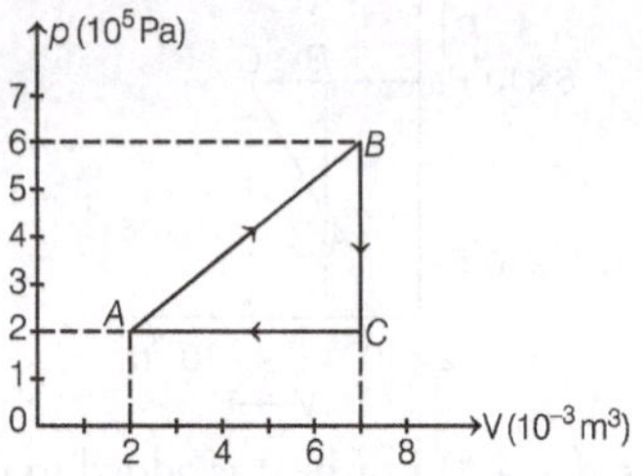

(a) 2000 J (b) 1000 J (c) Zero (d) −2000 J

15 A system is taken from state *a* to state *c* by two paths *adc* and *abc* as shown in the figure. The internal energy at *a* is $U_a = 10$ J. Along the path *adc* the amount of heat absorbed $\delta Q_1 = 50$ J and the work done $\delta W_1 = 20$ J whereas along the path *abc* the heat absorbed $\delta Q_2 = 36$ J. The amount of work done along the path *abc* is **[NCERT (New) Pg. 235, NEET 2013]**

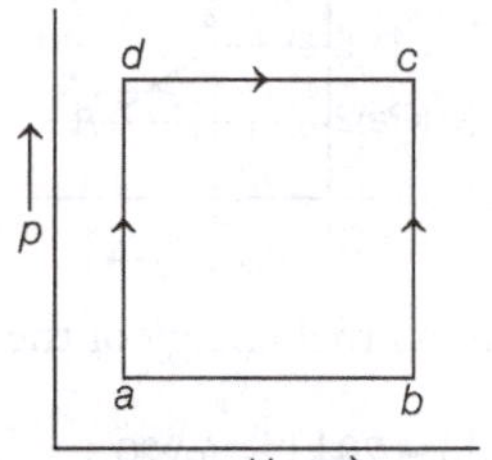

(a) 6 J (b) 10 J (c) 12 J (d) 36 J

16 During an adiabatic process, the pressure of a gas is found to be proportional to the cube of its temperature. The ratio of C_p/C_V for the gas is **[NEET 2013]**

(a) 5/3 (b) 3/2
(c) 4/3 (d) 2

17 Which of the following relations does not give the equation of an adiabatic process, where terms have their usual meaning? **[NEET 2013]**

(a) $p^{1-\gamma}T^{\gamma}$ = constant (b) pV^{γ} = constant
(c) $TV^{\gamma-1}$ = constant (d) $p^{\gamma}T^{1-\gamma}$ = constant

18 An ideal gas goes from state *A* to state *B* via three different processes as indicated in the *p-V* diagram. If Q_1, Q_2, Q_3 indicate the heat absorbed by the gas along the three processes and $\Delta U_1, \Delta U_2, \Delta U_3$ indicate the change in internal energy along the three processes respectively, then **[AIPMT 2012]**

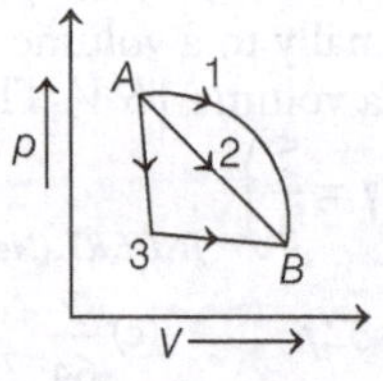

(a) $Q_1 > Q_2 > Q_3$ and $\Delta U_1 = \Delta U_2 = \Delta U_3$
(b) $Q_3 > Q_2 > Q_1$ and $\Delta U_1 = \Delta U_2 = \Delta U_3$
(c) $Q_1 = Q_2 = Q_3$ and $\Delta U_1 > \Delta U_2 > \Delta U_3$
(d) $Q_3 > Q_2 > Q_1$ and $\Delta U_1 > \Delta U_2 > \Delta U_3$

19 A thermodynamic system is taken through the cycle *ABCD* as shown in figure. Heat rejected by the gas during the cycle is **[NCERT (New) Pg. 235, AIPMT 2012]**

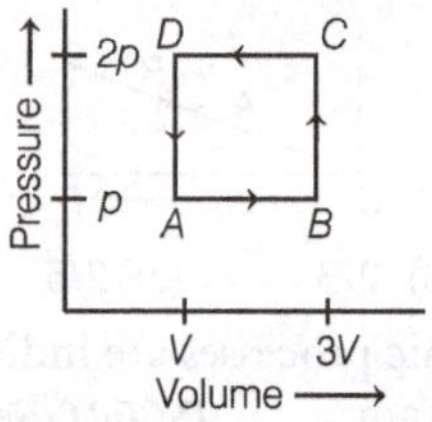

(a) $2\,pV$ (b) $4\,pV$ (c) $\frac{1}{2}pV$ (d) pV

20 One mole of an ideal gas goes from an initial state *A* to final state *B* *via* two processes. It first undergoes isothermal expansion from volume *V* to 3*V* and then its volume is reduced from 3*V* to *V* at constant pressure. The correct *p-V* diagram representing the two processes is **[AIPMT 2012]**

(a)
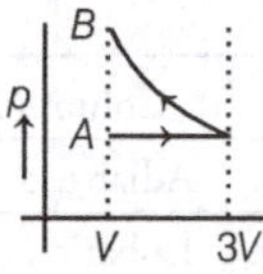

(b)
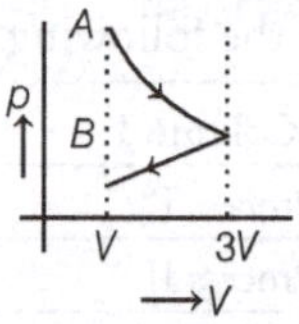

(c)
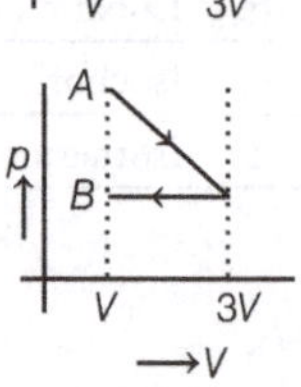

(d)
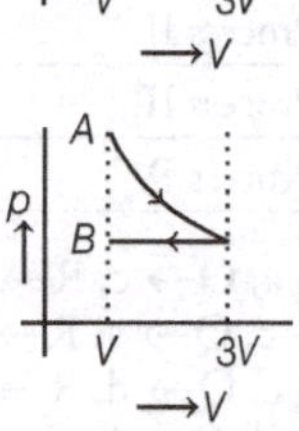

21 A mass of diatomic gas ($\gamma = 1.4$) at a pressure of 2 atmospheres is compressed adiabatically so that its temperature rises from 27°C to 927°C. The pressure of the gas in the final state is **[AIPMT 2011]**

(a) 8 atm (b) 28 atm
(c) 68.7 atm (d) 256 atm

22 During an isothermal expansion, a confined ideal gas does 150 J of work against its surroundings. This implies that **[NCERT (New) Pg. 234, AIPMT 2011]**

(a) 300 J of heat has been added to the gas
(b) no heat is transferred because the process is isothermal
(c) 150 J of heat has been added to the gas
(d) 150 J of heat has been removed from the gas

23 When 1 kg of ice at 0°C melts to water at 0°C, the resulting change in its entropy, taking latent heat of ice to be 80 cal/°C, is **[AIPMT 2011]**

(a) 273 cal/K (b) 8×104 cal/K
(c) 80 cal/K (d) 293 cal/K

24 If ΔU and ΔW represent the increase in internal energy and work done by the system, respectively in a thermodynamical process, which of the following is true ? *[NCERT (New) Pg. 230, AIPMT 2010, 1998]*
(a) $\Delta U = -\Delta W$, in an adiabatic process
(b) $\Delta U = \Delta W$, in an isothermal process
(c) $\Delta U = \Delta W$, in an adiabatic process
(d) $\Delta U = -\Delta W$, in an isothermal process

25 In thermodynamic processes which of the following statements is not true ? *[AIPMT 2009]*
(a) In an adiabatic process the system is insulated from the surroundings.
(b) In an isochoric process pressure remains constant.
(c) In an isothermal process the temperature remains constant.
(d) In an adiabatic process pV^{γ} = constant.

26 If Q, E and W denote respectively the heat added, change in internal energy and the work done in a closed cycle process, then *[AIPMT 2008]*
(a) $W = 0$ (b) $Q = W = 0$
(c) $E = 0$ (d) $Q = 0$

27 Which of the following processes is reversible ? *[NCERT (New) Pg. 234, AIPMT 2005]*
(a) Transfer of heat by radiation
(b) Electrical heating of a nichrome wire
(c) Transfer of heat by conduction
(d) Isothermal compression

28 One mole of an ideal gas at an initial temperature of T K does $6R$ J of work adiabatically. If the ratio of specific heats of this gas at constant pressure and at constant volume is 5/3, the final temperature of gas will be *[AIPMT 2004]*
(a) $(T + 2.4)$ K (b) $(T - 2.4)$ K
(c) $(T + 4)$ K (d) $(T - 4)$ K

29 An ideal gas at 27°C is compressed adiabatically to $8/27$ of its original volume. The rise in temperature is $\left(\gamma = \frac{5}{3}\right)$ *[NCERT (New) Pg. 235, AIPMT 1999]*
(a) 475°C (b) 402°C (c) 275°C (d) 175°C

30 One mole of an ideal gas at 300 K is expanded isothermally from an initial volume 1 L to 10 L. The ΔE for this process is *[AIPMT 1998]*
(a) 163.7 cal (b) zero
(c) 1381.1 cal (d) 9 L atm

31 If the ratio of specific heat of a gas at constant pressure to that at constant volume is γ, the change in internal energy of a mass of gas when the volume changes from V to $2V$ at constant pressure p is *[AIPMT 1998]*
(a) $\frac{R}{(\gamma - 1)}$ (b) pV
(c) $\frac{pV}{(\gamma - 1)}$ (d) $\frac{\gamma pV}{(\gamma - 1)}$

32 A sample of gas expands from volume V_1 to V_2. The amount of work done by the gas is greatest when the expansion is *[NCERT (New) Pg. 234, AIPMT 1997]*
(a) adiabatic (b) isobaric
(c) isothermal (d) Equal in all above cases

33 An ideal gas undergoing adiabatic change has the following pressure-temperature relationship *[AIPMT 1996]*
(a) $p^{\gamma - 1}T^{\gamma}$ = constant (b) $p^{\gamma}T^{\gamma - 1}$ = constant
(c) $p^{\gamma}T^{1-\gamma}$ = constant (d) $p^{1-\gamma}T^{\gamma}$ = constant

34 A diatomic gas initially at 18°C is compressed adiabatically to one of eighth of its original volume. The temperature after compression will be *[NCERT (New) Pg. 235, AIPMT 1996]*
(a) 18°C (b) 668.4°K
(c) 395.4°C (d) 144°C

35 An ideal gas A and a real gas B have their volumes increased from V to $2V$ under isothermal conditions. The increase in internal energy *[AIPMT 1993]*
(a) will be same in both A and B
(b) will be zero in both the gases
(c) of B will be more than that of A
(d) of A will be more than that of B

36 Which of the following is not thermodynamical function ? *[NCERT (New) Pg. 234, AIPMT 1993]*
(a) Enthalpy (b) Work done
(c) Gibb's energy (d) Internal energy

37 A thermodynamic system is taken from state A to B along ACB and is brought back to A along BDA as shown in the p-V diagram. The net work done during the complete cycle is given by the area *[AIPMT 1992]*

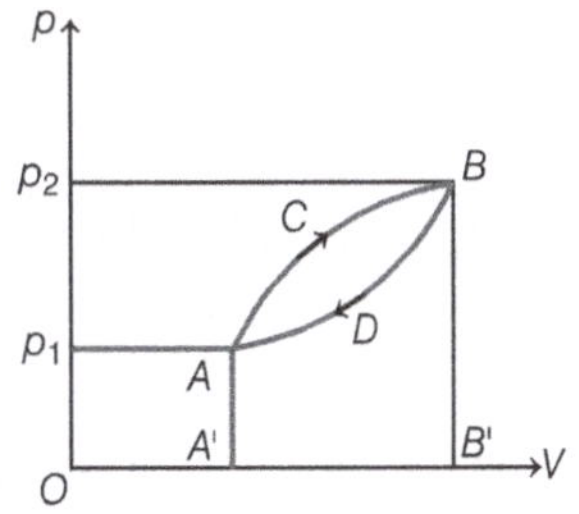

(a) $p_1ACBp_2p_1$ (b) $ACBB'A'A$
(c) $ACBDA$ (d) $ADBB'A'A$

38 A thermodynamic process is shown in the figure. The pressure and volumes corresponding to some points in the figure are

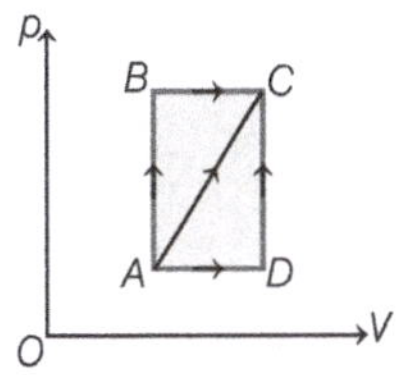

$p_A = 3 \times 10^4$ pa, $V_A = 2 \times 10^{-3}$ m^3

$p_B = 8 \times 10^4$ pa, $V_B = 5 \times 10^{-3}$ m^3

In process AB, 600 J of heat is added to the system and in process BC, 200 J of heat is added to the system. The change in internal energy of the system in process AC would be *[AIPMT 1991]*
(a) 560 J (b) 800 J (c) 600 J (d) 640 J

39 One mole of an ideal gas require 207 J heat to rise the temperature by 10 K when heated at constant pressure. If the same gas is heated at constants volume to raise the temperature by the same 10 K, the heat required is *[AIPMT 1990]*
(Given the gas constant $R = 8.3$ J/mole K)
(a) 198.7 J (b) 29 J
(c) 215.3 J (d) 124 J

40 At 27° C a gas is compressed suddenly such that its pressure becomes (1/8) of original pressure. Final temperature will be ($\gamma = 5/3$) *[AIPMT 1989]*
(a) 420 K (b) 300 K
(c) −142°C (d) 327°C

• Key Index

Topic 1

1 (b)	2 (b)	3 (d)	4 (b)

Topic 2

1 (a)	2 (a)	3 (c)	4 (a)	5 (c)	6 (b)	7 (a)	8 (d)	9 (c)	10 (b)
11 (a)	12 (d)	13 (c)	14 (b)	15 (a)	16 (b)	17 (d)	18 (a)	19 (a)	20 (d)
21 (d)	22 (c)	23 (d)	24 (a)	25 (b)	26 (c)	27 (d)	28 (d)	29 (b)	30 (b)
31 (c)	32 (b)	33 (d)	34 (b)	35 (b)	36 (b)	37 (c)	38 (a)	39 (d)	40 (c)

Detailed **Explanations**

Topic 1

01. *(b)*

key idea

Find heat supplied $\Delta Q = mL$ and work done, $\Delta W = p\Delta V$. Then, apply first law of thermodynamics, $\Delta Q = \Delta U + \Delta W$

Given, mass of water,

$$m = 1\,g$$

Volume of 1 g of water

$$V_1 = 1\,cm^3 = 10^{-6}\ m^3$$

Volume of 1 g of steam

$$= 1671\,cm^3$$

$$V_2 = 1671 \times 10^{-6}\ m^3$$

Pressure, $p = 1 \times 10^5$ Pa

Latent heat of vaporization of water,

$$L = 2256\ J/g$$

Change in volume, $\Delta L = (V_2 - V_1)$

$$\Delta V = (1671 - 1) \times 10^{-6}\ m^3$$

$$= 1670 \times 10^{-6} m^3 \quad ...(i)$$

Heat supplied,

$$\Delta Q = mL = 1 \times 2256 = 2256\ J \ ...(ii)$$

As the steam expands, the work done in expansion is

$$\Delta W = p\Delta V$$

$$= 1 \times 10^5 \times 1670 \times 10^{-6} \quad \text{[From Eq. (i)]}$$

$$= 167\ J \quad ...(iii)$$

According to first law of thermodynamics,

$$\Delta Q = \Delta U + \Delta W$$

$$\Rightarrow \Delta U = \Delta Q - \Delta W = 2256 - 167$$

[From Eq. (ii) and (iii)]

$$= 2089\ J$$

02. *(b)* According to the question,

Heat spent during the conversion of sample of water at $100°C$ to steam is,

$$\Delta Q = 54\ cal = 54 \times 4.18\ J$$

$$= 225.72\ J$$

Normal pressure,

$$p = 1.013 \times 10^5 Nm^{-2}$$

Net work done during the conversion would be given as

$$\Delta W = p\Delta V$$

$$= p[V_{steam} - V_{water}]$$

Here, $V_{steam} = 167.1$ cc

$$= 167.1 \times 10^{-6}\ m^3$$

$$V_{steam} = 0.1\ g$$

$$= 0.1 cc = 0.1 \times 10^{-6}\ m^3$$

$$\therefore\ \Delta W = 1.013 \times 10^5\ [(167.1 - 0.1) \times 10^{-6}]$$

$$= 1.013 \times 167 \times 10^{-1} = 16.917\ J$$

Now, by the first law of thermodynamics,

$$\Delta Q = \Delta U + \Delta W$$

where, ΔU is the change in internal energy of the sample.

$$\Rightarrow \Delta U = \Delta Q - \Delta W$$

Substituting the values in the above equation, we get

$$\Delta U = 225.72 - 16.917 = 208.7\ J$$

03. *(d)* According to first law of thermodynamics

$$\Delta Q = U + W$$

or $\quad \Delta U = Q - W$

$$\therefore\ \Delta U = 2 \times 4.2 \times 1000 - 500$$

$$= 8400 - 500 = 7900\ J$$

• Concept Enhancer

Internal energy is defined as the energy associated with the random disordered motion of molecules. It is a state function that defines the energy of substance in the absence of effect due to external energy.

04. *(b)* According to the first law of thermodynamics,

$$dQ = dU + dW$$

This law, which is basically the law of conservation of energy applies to every process in nature.

Topic 2

01. *(a)* Work done in an isochoric process is always zero.

02. *(a)* Curve 1 is isochoric process because volume is constant.

In curve 2 and 3, curve 3 has smaller slope than curve 2.

Hence, curve 3 represents isothermal process and curve 2 represents adiabatic process.

• Concept Enhancer

For isobaric process ⟶ Pressure is constant

For isochoric process ⟶ Volume is constant.

For isothermal process ⟶ Temperature is constant.

For adiabatic process ⟶ Heat is not exchanged.

03. *(c)* From the pV diagram, it is clear that pressure of ideal gas in the piston cylinder is constant during thermodynamic process. Hence, this process is isobaric.

04. *(a)* In an adiabatic process, the system is completely insulated from the surroundings. Thus, heat is neither absorbed nor released by the system to the surroundings. So, $\Delta Q = 0$.

05. *(c)* According to the given graph,

Volume $(V) \propto$ Temperature (T)

or $\quad \dfrac{V}{T} = \text{constant}$

Thus, the process is isobaric.

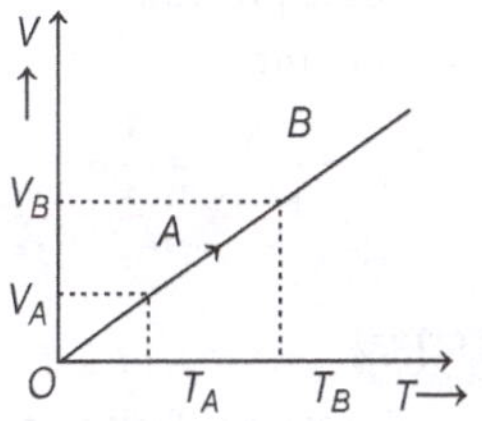

$\therefore$ Work done,

$$\Delta W = p\Delta V$$

$$= nR\Delta T = nR(T_B - T_A) \ ...(i)$$

Heat absorbed,

$$\Delta Q = nC_p\Delta T$$

$$= nC_p(T_B - T_A) \quad ...(ii)$$

For a monoatomic gas,

$$\Rightarrow \quad C_p = \left(R + \frac{3}{2}R\right) = \frac{5}{2}R$$

Substituting the value of C_p in Eq. (ii), we get

$$\Delta Q = n\left(\frac{5}{2}R\right)(T_B - T_A)$$

Hence, $\dfrac{\Delta W}{\Delta Q} = \dfrac{nR(T_B - T_A)}{n\left(\dfrac{5}{2}R\right)(T_B - T_A)} = \dfrac{2}{5}$

Alternate Solution

$$\frac{\text{Work done}}{\text{Heat absorbed}} = \frac{nC_p\Delta T - nC_v dT}{nC_p\Delta T} = 1 - \frac{1}{r} = \frac{2}{5}$$

06. *(b)* In isochoric process, the curve is parallel to Y-axis because volume is constant. Isobaric is parallel to X-axis because pressure is constant. Along the curve, it will be isothermal because temperature is constant.

Slope of an adiabatic process is more than isothermal process.

So,
P → c, Q → a, R → d, S → b

07. *(a)*

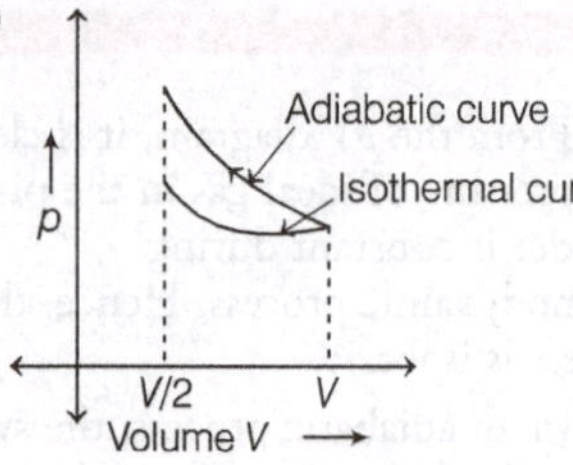

Since, the isothermal curve is less steeper than the adiabatic curve. So, area under the p-V curve for adiabatic process has more magnitude than isothermal curve.
Hence, work done in adiabatic process will be more than in isothermal process.

08. *(d)* Given, $pV^3 = \text{constant}$
For a polytropic process,

$$pV^{\alpha} = \text{constant}$$

$$\Rightarrow \quad C = C_V + \frac{R}{1-\alpha} = \frac{3}{2}R + \frac{R}{1-3} = R$$

09. *(c)*

key idea
Find work done for all processes and then find heat supplied for $A \to C$.
$A \to B$ is isochoric, $B \to C$ is isobaric.

Since, initial and final points are same
So, $\Delta U_{A \to B \to C} = \Delta U_{A \to C}$ ...(i)
Also $A \to B$ is isochoric process
So $dW_{A \to B} = 0$
and $dQ = dU + dW$
So, $dQ_{A \to B} = dU_{A \to B} = 400 \text{ J}$
Next $B \to C$ is isobaric process
So, $dQ_{B \to C} = dU_{B \to C} + dW_{B \to C}$

$$= dU_{B \to C} + p\Delta V_{B \to C}$$

$$\Rightarrow 100 = dU_{B \to C} + 6 \times 10^4 (2 \times 10^{-3})$$

$$\Rightarrow dU_{B \to C} = 100 - 120 = -20 \text{ J}$$

From Eq. (i),

$$\because \Delta U_{A \to B \to C} = \Delta U_{A \to C}$$

$$\Rightarrow \Delta U_{A \to B} + \Delta U_{B \to C} = dQ_{A \to C} - dW_{A \to C}$$

$$\Rightarrow 400 + (-20) = dQ_{A \to C} - (p\Delta V_A + \text{Area of } \Delta ABC)$$

$$dQ_{A \to C} = 380 + \begin{pmatrix} 2 \times 10^4 \times 2 \times 10^{-3} + \frac{1}{2} \\ \times 2 \times 10^{-3} \times 4 \times 10^4 \end{pmatrix}$$

$$= 380 + (40 + 40)$$

$$dQ_{A \to C} = 460 \text{ J}$$

10. *(b)* The change in internal energy of gas in the transition from A to B is

$$\Delta U = nC_V dT = n\left(\frac{5R}{2}\right)(T_B - T_A)$$

$$= nR\frac{5}{2}\left(\frac{p_B V_B}{nR} - \frac{p_A V_A}{nR}\right)$$

$$= \frac{5}{2}(2 \times 10^3 \times 6 - 5 \times 10^3 \times 4)$$

$$= \frac{5}{2} \times (-8 \times 10^3)$$

$$= 5 \times (-4 \times 10^3) = -20 \text{ kJ}$$

11. *(a)* Given, ideal gas is compressed to half its initial volume i.e.

$$V_0 = \frac{V}{2}$$

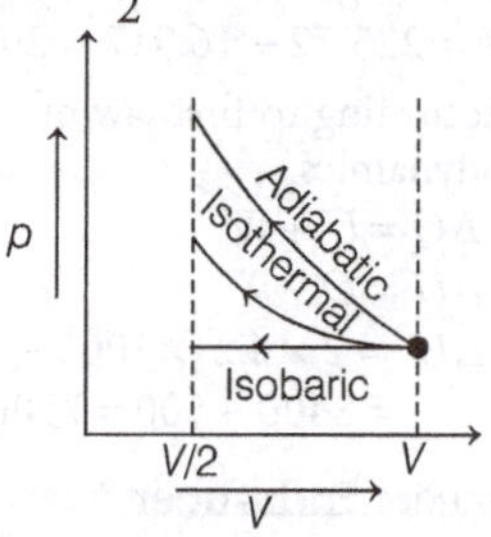

The isochoric process is one in which volume is kept constant, meaning that work done by the system will be zero.
i.e. $W_{\text{isochoric}} = 0$
As we know, work done on the gas = Area under curve, i.e.

$$W_{\text{adiabatic}} > W_{\text{isothermal}} > W_{\text{isobaric}}$$

12. *(d)* Work done in the cyclic process
= Area bounded by the closed configuration
= Area of closed configuration

$$= \frac{1}{2} \times V_0 \times p_0 - \frac{1}{2} \times V_0 \times p_0$$

= 0 (zero).

13. *(c)* For isothermal expansion process

$$pV = p' \times 2V \qquad [\because V' = 2V]$$

$$p' = \frac{p}{2}$$

For adiabatic expansion,

$$pV^{\gamma} = \text{constant}$$

$$\Rightarrow \quad p'V^{\gamma} = p''V''^{\gamma}$$

$$\Rightarrow \frac{p}{2}(2V)^{5/3} = p''(16V)^{5/3}$$

$$\Rightarrow \quad p'' = \frac{p}{2}\left[\frac{2V}{16V}\right]^{5/3} = \frac{p}{2}\left(\frac{1}{8}\right)^{5/3}$$

$$= \frac{p}{2}\left(\frac{1}{32}\right) = p/64$$

14. *(b)* Net work done = Area enclosed in pV curve i.e. ΔABC
Area of ΔABC

$$= \frac{1}{2} \times 5 \times 10^{-3} \times 4 \times 10^5 \text{ J}$$

$$= 10^3 \text{ J} = 1000 \text{ J}$$

15. *(a)* For process adc,

$$\Delta Q_{adc} = \Delta U_{adc} + W_{adc}$$

$$\Rightarrow \quad 50 \text{ J} = \Delta U_{adc} + 20 \text{ J}$$

$$\Delta U_{adc} = 30 \text{ J}$$

For process abc,

$$\Delta Q_{abc} = \Delta U_{abc} + W_{abc}$$

$$W_{abc} = Q_{abc} - \Delta U_{abc}$$

$$= 36 \text{ J} - 30 \text{ J} = 6 \text{ J}$$

16. *(b)* We know that, $p \propto T^3$

$$\therefore \quad pT^{-3} = \text{constant} \quad \text{...(i)}$$

For an adiabatic process;

$$pT^{\gamma/1-\gamma} = \text{constant} \quad \text{...(ii)}$$

On comparing Eqs. (i) and (ii), we get

$$\frac{\gamma}{1-\gamma} = -3$$

$$\gamma = -3 + 3\gamma \text{ or } \gamma = \frac{3}{2}$$

$$\gamma = \frac{C_p}{C_V} = \frac{3}{2}$$

17. *(d)* For an adiabatic process,

$$pV^{\gamma} = \text{constant} \quad \text{...(i)}$$

Ideal gas equation is given as

$$pV = nRT$$

$$\Rightarrow \quad p = \frac{nRT}{V}$$

On putting value of p in (i), we get

$$\frac{nRT}{V}V^{\gamma} = \text{constant}$$

$$\therefore TV^{\gamma-1} = \text{constant}$$

Again from the ideal gas equation,
we have $V = \dfrac{nRT}{p}$
On putting value of V in (i), we get

$$p\left(\frac{nRT}{p}\right)^{\gamma} = \text{constant}$$

$$p^{1-\gamma}T^{\gamma} = \text{constant}$$

18. *(a)* Since, the initial and final states are the same throughout the process.
Therefore, $\Delta U_1 = \Delta U_2 = \Delta U_3$
Workdone, W = Area under p-V graph
As area under curve 1 > area under curve 2 > area under curve 3

$$\therefore \quad W_1 > W_2 > W_3$$

According to first law of thermodynamics,

$$Q = W + \Delta U$$

As $W_1 > W_2 > W_3$

and $\Delta U_1 = \Delta U_2 = \Delta U_3$

$\Rightarrow \quad Q_1 > Q_2 > Q_3$

19. (a) For given cyclic process,

$$\Delta U = 0$$

$\Rightarrow \quad Q = W$

Also, $W = -$ area enclosed by the curve

$$= -AB \times AD$$
$$= -(2p - p)(3V - V)$$
$$= -p \times 2V$$

$\therefore$ Heat rejected $= 2pV$

20. (d) According to question, firstly gas expands from volume V to $3V$ and after this volume is reduced from $3V$ to V at constant pressure.

In isothermal expansion, p-V curve is rectangular hyperbola.

> **• Concept Enhancer**
> For isothermal expansion, T = constant
> $\Rightarrow pV = nRT$ = constant
> $\Rightarrow pV$ = constant
> Hence, it is a hyperbola.
> For isobaric compression, p = constant
> $pV = nRT \Rightarrow \frac{V}{T}$ = constant

21. (d) For an adiabatic process, gas equation is given as $\frac{T^\gamma}{p^{\gamma-1}}$ = constant

$$\therefore \left(\frac{T_i}{T_f}\right)^\gamma = \left(\frac{p_i}{p_f}\right)^{\gamma-1},$$

$$p_f = p_i \left(\frac{T_f}{T_i}\right)^{\frac{\gamma}{\gamma-1}} \quad \ldots(i)$$

$$\Rightarrow p_f = (2)\left(\frac{1200}{300}\right)^{\frac{1.4}{1.4-1}}$$

$$= (2)(4)^{1.4/0.4} = 2(2^2)^{7/2} = (2)(2)^7$$
$$= 2^8 = 256 \text{ atm}$$

22. (c) According to first law of thermodynamics,

$$\Delta U = \Delta Q - \Delta W$$

For isothermal process,

$$\Delta U = 0$$

So, $\Delta Q = \Delta W$

Given, $\Delta W = 150$ J

So, $\Delta Q = +150$ J

When Q is positive, the heat is added to the gas.

> **• Concept Enhancer**
> When ΔQ is positive, the heat is added to the system and when ΔQ is negative, the heat is extracted from the system.

23. (d) Given, Mass of ice, $M_{\text{ice}} = 1$ kg

temperature, $T = 0°\text{C} = 273$ K

Latent heat of ice,

$$L = 80 \text{ cal/°C}$$

Change in entropy is given by

$$\Delta S = \frac{dQ}{T}$$

or $\quad \Delta S = \frac{\Delta Q}{T} = \frac{mL_f}{273}$

$$\Rightarrow \quad \Delta S = \frac{1000 \times 80}{273} = 293 \text{ cal/K}$$

24. (a) From first law of thermodynamics

$$\Delta Q = \Delta U + \Delta W$$

For adiabatic process,

$$\Delta Q = 0$$

So, $\Delta U = -\Delta W$

25. (b) For an isochoric process, volume remain constant. So, option (b) is not correct statement.

26. (c) For a cyclic process, as initial and final states are same, so change in internal energy is zero. i.e.

$$\Delta U = 0 \text{ or } E = 0$$

27. (d) Isothermal compression is reversible, for example-Carnot cycle, Heat engine.

> **• Concept Enhancer**
> Not all isothermal process are reversible but an isothermal expansion is reversible in which there is an infinitesimal slow increase in the volume of the substance at constant temperature.

28. (d) In an adiabatic process,

$$Q = 0$$

So, from Ist law of thermodynamics,

$$\Delta Q = \Delta U + \Delta W$$

As $\quad \Delta Q = 0$

so, $\quad W = -\Delta U = -nC_V \Delta T$

$$= -n\left(\frac{R}{\gamma-1}\right)(T_f - T_i)$$

$$= \frac{nR}{\gamma-1}(T_i - T_f) \quad \ldots(i)$$

Given, work done,

$$W = 6R \text{ J}, n = 1 \text{ mol},$$
$$R = 8.31 \text{ J/mol-K},$$
$$\gamma = \frac{5}{3}, T_i = T \text{ K}$$

On substituting given values in Eq. (i), we get

$$\therefore \quad 6R = \frac{R}{(5/3 - 1)}(T - T_f)$$

$$\Rightarrow \quad 6R = \frac{3R}{2}(T - T_f)$$

$\Rightarrow T - T_f = 4$

$\therefore \quad T_f = (T - 4)$K

29. (b) For adiabatic process,

$$T_1 V_1^{\gamma-1} = T_2 V_2^{\gamma-1}$$

$$\frac{T_2}{T_1} = \left(\frac{V_1}{V_2}\right)^{\gamma-1}$$

$$= \left(\frac{27}{8}\right)^{\frac{5}{3}-1}$$

$$\frac{T_2}{T_1} = \frac{9}{4}$$

$$\Rightarrow \quad T_2 = \frac{9}{4} \times T_1$$

$$= \frac{9}{4} \times 300 = 675 \text{ K}$$

$$T_2 = 675 - 273°\text{C}$$
$$= 402°\text{C}$$

30. (b) Isothermal process means temperature is constant. At constant temperature, change in internal energy ΔE remains constant.

So $\quad \Delta E = 0$

31. (c) Change in internal energy of a gas having atomicity γ is given by

$$\Delta U = \frac{1}{(\gamma-1)}(p_2V_2 - p_1V_1)$$

Given, $\quad V_1 = V, V_2 = 2V$

So, $\quad \Delta U = \frac{1}{\gamma-1}[p \times 2V - p \times V]$

$$= \frac{1}{\gamma-1} \times pV = \frac{pV}{\gamma-1}$$

> ***Alternate Solution***
> At constant pressure, change in internal energy,
> $\Delta U = nC_v dT$
> Now, $\frac{C_p}{C_V} = \gamma \Rightarrow 1 + \frac{R}{C_V} = \gamma \Rightarrow C_V = \frac{R}{\gamma-1}$
> Using, Charle's law, final temperature
> $= 2 \times$ initial temperature $= 2 \times T$
> Thus, $\Delta U = nC_v(2T - T) = nC_V T = \frac{nRT}{\gamma-1} = \frac{pV}{\gamma-1}$

32. *(b)* The *p-V* diagram for isobaric, isothermal and adiabatic processes of an ideal gas is shown in graph below

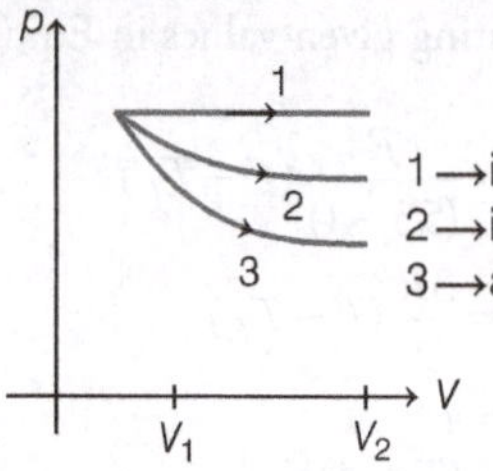

In thermodynamics, for some change in volume, the work done is maximum for the curve having maximum area enclosed with the volume axis.

33. *(d)* The adiabatic relation between p and V for a perfect gas is

$$pV^{\gamma} = k \qquad \ldots(i)$$

From standard gas equation

$$pV = RT$$

or $$V = \frac{RT}{p}$$

On putting the value of V in Eq. (i), we get

$$p\left(\frac{RT}{p}\right)^{\gamma} = k$$

i.e., $p^{1-\gamma}T^{\gamma}$ = constant

34. *(b)* Given initial temperature,

$$T_1 = 18°\text{ C} = 291\text{ K}$$

Let initial volume be $V_1 = V$

and final volume be $V_2 = \frac{V}{8}$

For an adiabatic process,

$$TV^{\gamma-1} = \text{constant}$$

Therefore,

$$T_1V_1^{\gamma-1} = T_2V_2^{\gamma-1}$$

$$\Rightarrow \quad T_2 = 291\left(\frac{V_1}{V_2}\right)^{\gamma-1}$$

$$\Rightarrow \quad T_2 = 291(8)^{\frac{7}{5}-1}$$

$$= 291 \times 2.297 = 668.4\text{ K}$$

$$\left[\text{For diatomic gas } \gamma = \frac{C_p}{C_V} = \frac{7}{5}\right]$$

35. *(b)* In isothermal process, there is a free exchange of heat between the gas and its surroundings.

$\therefore \quad T$ = constant

$$\Delta T = 0$$

So, internal energy remains constant.

36. *(b)* There are four principal thermodynamic functions

(i) Internal energy (U)
(ii) Helmholtz function (F)
(iii) Enthalpy (H)
(iv) Gibb's energy (G)

Hence, work done is not thermodynamic function.

37. *(c)* Work done during path ACB

= area $ACBB'\,A'\,A$

Work done during path BDA

= area $BDAA'\,B'\,B$

$\therefore$ Work done during going from ACB and then to BDA path is

= area $ACB\,B'\,A'\,A$ − area $BDAA'\,B'\,B$

= area $ACBDA$

Note Net work done in cyclic process is given by area under the cycle.

38. *(a)* For path AB, applying first law of thermodynamics

$$dQ = dU + dW$$

or $$dQ = U_B - U_A + dW$$

or $$600 = U_B - U_A + 0$$

(for isochoric process $dV = 0$ so, $dW = 0$)

$$U_B - U_A = 600 \qquad \ldots(i)$$

For path BC,

$$dQ = dU + dW$$

$$\therefore \quad 200 = U_C - U_B + p_B\,(V_C - V_B)$$

(as BC is isobaric process)

$$\therefore \quad 200 = U_C - U_B + 8 \times 10^4\,(5 \times 10^{-3} - 2 \times 10^{-3})$$

or $$200 = U_C - U_B + 240$$

$$\therefore \quad U_C - U_B = -40\text{ J} \qquad \ldots(ii)$$

For AC, change in internal energy can be calculated by adding Eqs. (i) and (ii),

$$= U_C - U_A$$
$$= U_C - U_B + U_B - U_A$$
$$= -40 + 600 = 560\text{ J}$$

Alternate Solution

No work is done during isochoric process $A \rightarrow B$.

Work done during isochoric process $B \rightarrow C$

i.e. given by, $W = p_B(V_C - V_B)$

$$= p_B(V_D - V_A) = 240\text{ J}$$

From Conservation of energy,

$$\Delta Q = \Delta U + \Delta W$$

$$\Rightarrow \quad \Delta U = \Delta Q - \Delta W$$

$$= (600 + 200) - 240 = 560\text{ J}$$

39. *(d)* Using Mayer's formula

$$C_p - C_V = R,$$

C_p is heat needed for raising by 10 K.

$$Q = nC_p\Delta T$$

$$207 = C_p \times 10$$

$$\therefore \quad C_p = 20.7\text{ J/mol K}$$

Given $R = 8.3$ J/mole K

$$\therefore \quad C_V = 20.7 - 8.3$$

$$= 12.4\text{ J/mol K}$$

$\therefore$ For raising temperature by 10 K heat required will be, $Q = 124$ J.

40. *(c)* Given,

$$T_1 = 27°\text{C} = 300°\text{ K}$$

$$p_1 = p$$

$$p_2 = \frac{p}{8}$$

For an adiabatic process,

$$T_1^{\gamma}p_1^{1-\gamma} = T_2^{\gamma}p_2^{1-\gamma}$$

$$\Rightarrow \quad \left(\frac{T_2}{T_1}\right)^{\gamma} = \left(\frac{p_1}{p_2}\right)^{1-\gamma}$$

$$\Rightarrow \quad T_2 = T_1 \cdot \left(\frac{p_1}{p_2}\right)^{\frac{1-\gamma}{\gamma}}$$

$$= 300 \times (8)^{-2/5}$$

$$= 131\text{ K}$$

$$T_2 = 131 - 273 = -142°\text{C}$$

In NEET 2024, 1 question was visible from this chapter. In past 5 years, 5 questions from topic-1, 2 questions from topic-2 and 2 questions from topic-3 were asked.
For detailed analysis scan QR code

KINETIC THEORY OF GASES

Topic 1 Kinetic Theory of Gases and Gas Laws

01 The following graph represents the *T*-*V* curves of an ideal gas (where *T* is the temperature and *V* the volume) at three pressures p_1, p_2 and p_3 compared with those of Charles's law represented as dotted lines. ***[NCERT (New) Pg. 247, NEET 2024]***

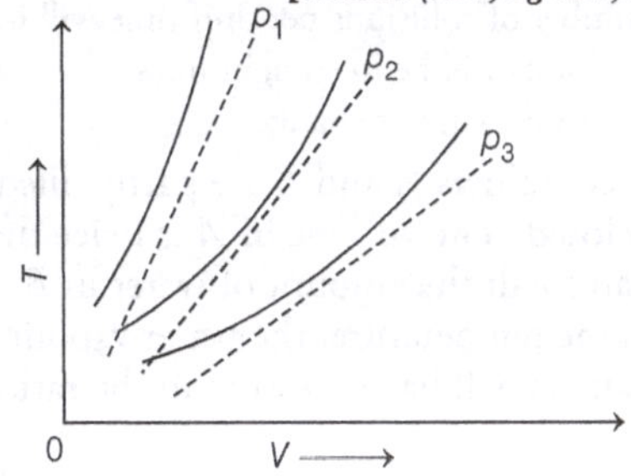

Then the correct relation is
(a) $p_3 > p_2 > p_1$
(b) $p_1 > p_3 > p_2$
(c) $p_2 > p_1 > p_3$
(d) $p_1 > p_2 > p_3$

02 The temperature of a gas is –50°C. To what temperature the gas should be heated, so that the rms speed is increased by 3 times ? ***[NEET 2022]***
(a) 3295°C (b) 3097 K
(c) 223 K (d) 669°C

03 The volume occupied by the molecules contained in 4.5 kg water at STP, if the intermolecular forces vanish away is ***[NCERT (New) Pg. 246, NEET 2022]***
(a) $5.6 \times 10^3\ m^3$ (b) $5.6 \times 10^{-3}\ m^3$
(c) $5.6\ m^3$ (d) $5.6 \times 10^6\ m^3$

04 A cylinder contains hydrogen gas at pressure of 249 kPa and temperature 27°C.
Its density is ($R = 8.3\ J\ mol^{-1}\ K^{-1}$) ***[NEET (Sep.) 2020]***
(a) 0.2 kg/m^3 (b) 0.1 kg/m^3
(c) 0.02 kg/m^3 (d) 0.5 kg/m^3

05 An ideal gas equation can be written as $p = \frac{\rho RT}{M_0}$ where, ρ and M_0 are respectively, ***[NCERT (New) Pg. 246, NEET (Oct.) 2020]***
(a) mass density, mass of the gas
(b) number density, molar mass
(c) mass density, molar mass
(d) number density, mass of the gas

06 At what temperature will the rms speed of oxygen molecules become just sufficient for escaping from the Earth's atmosphere ?
(Given, mass of oxygen molecule,
$m = 2.76 \times 10^{-26}$ kg, Boltzmann's constant
$k_B = 1.38 \times 10^{-23}\ J\ K^{-1}$) ***[NCERT (New) Pg. 250, NEET 2018]***
(a) 5.016×10^4 K (b) 8.326×10^4 K
(c) 2.508×10^4 K (d) 1.254×10^4 K

07 A given sample of an ideal gas occupies a volume *V* at a pressure *p* and absolute temperature *T*. The mass of each molecule of the gas is *m*. Which of the following gives the density of the gas ? ***[NCERT (New) Pg. 246, NEET 2016]***
(a) $p/(k_BT)$ (b) $pm/(k_BT)$
(c) $p/(k_BTV)$ (d) mk_BT

08 The molecules of a given mass of a gas have rms velocity of 200 ms^{-1} at 27°C and $1.0 \times 10^5\ Nm^{-2}$ pressure. When the temperature and pressure of the gas are respectively, 127°C and $0.05 \times 10^5\ Nm^{-2}$, the rms velocity of its molecules in ms^{-1} is ***[NEET 2016]***
(a) $\frac{400}{\sqrt{3}}$ (b) $\frac{100\sqrt{2}}{3}$ (c) $\frac{100}{3}$ (d) $100\sqrt{2}$

09 Two vessels separately contain two ideal gases *A* and *B* at the same temperature, the pressure of *A* being twice that of *B*. Under such conditions, the density of *A* is found to be 1.5 times the density of *B*. The ratio of molecular weight of *A* and *B* is ***[NCERT (New) Pg. 246, AIPMT 2015]***
(a) 1/3 (b) 3/4 (c) 2 (d) 1/2

10 In the given (*V-T*) diagram, what is the relation between pressures p_1 and p_2? ***[NEET 2013]***

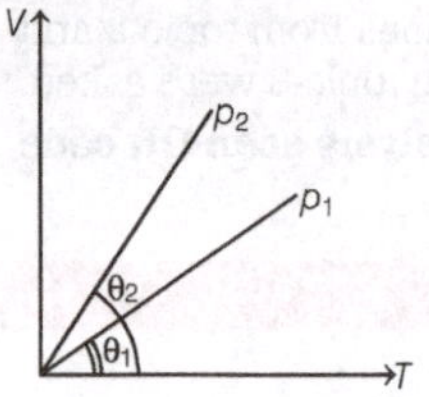

(a) $p_2 = p_1$ (b) $p_2 > p_1$
(c) $p_2 < p_1$ (d) Cannot be predicted

11 In a vessel, the gas is at a pressure p. If the mass of all the molecules is halved and their speed is doubled. then the resultant pressure will be ***[NEET 2013]***
(a) $4p$ (b) $2p$ (c) p (d) $p/2$

12 At 10°C the value of the density of a fixed mass of an ideal gas divided by its pressure is x. At 110°C this ratio is ***[NCERT (New) Pg. 246, AIPMT 2008]***
(a) x (b) $\frac{383}{283}x$ (c) $\frac{10}{110}x$ (d) $\frac{283}{383}x$

13 When volume of system is increased to twice and temperature is decreased to half of its initial temperature, then pressure becomes ***[NCERT (New) Pg. 246, AIPMT 2006]***
(a) 2 times (b) 4 times (c) 1/2 times (d) 1/4 times

14 The equation of state for 5 g of oxygen at a pressure p and temperature T, when occupying a volume V, will be ***[NCERT (New) Pg. 246, AIPMT 2004]***
(a) $pV = \left(\frac{5}{32}\right)RT$ (b) $pV = 5RT$
(c) $pV = \left(\frac{5}{2}\right)RT$ (d) $pV = \left(\frac{5}{16}\right)RT$

15 A gas at 27°C temperature and 30 atmospheric pressure is allowed to expand to atmospheric pressure. If the volume becomes 10 times its initial volume, then the final temperature becomes ***[AIPMT 2001]***
(a) 100°C (b) 173°C (c) 273°C (d) −173°C

16 At 0 K which of the, following properties of a gas will be zero ? ***[AIPMT 1996]***
(a) Kinetic energy (b) Potential energy
(c) Density (d) Mass

17 The equation of state, corresponding to 8g of O_2 is ***[NCERT (New) Pg. 246, AIPMT 1994]***
(a) $pV = 8RT$ (b) $pV = RT/4$
(c) $pV = RT$ (d) $pV = RT/2$

18 The temperature of a gas is raised from 27°C to 927°C. The root mean square speed ***[AIPMT 1994]***
(a) is $\sqrt{\left(\frac{927}{27}\right)}$ times the earlier value
(b) remains the same
(c) gets halved
(d) gets doubled

19 N molecules each of mass m of a gas A and $2N$ molecules each of mass $2m$ of gas B are contained in the same vessel which is maintained at temperature T. The mean square velocity of molecules of B type is v^2 and the mean square rectangular component of the velocity of A type is denoted by ω^2. Then ω^2/v^2 ***[AIPMT 1991]***
(a) 2 (b) 1 (c) 1/3 (d) 2/3

20 Three containers of the same volume contain three different gases. The masses of the molecules are m_1, m_2 and m_3 and the number of molecules in their respective containers are N_1, N_2 and N_3. The gas pressure in the containers are p_1, p_2 and p_3 respectively. All the gases are now mixed and put in one of these containers. The pressure p of the mixture will be ***[AIPMT 1991]***
(a) $p < (p_1 + p_2 + p_3)$ (b) $p = \frac{p_1 + p_2 + p_3}{3}$
(c) $p = p_1 + p_2 + p_3$ (d) $p > (p_1 + p_2 + p_3)$

21 At constant volume temperature is increased, then ***[AIPMT 1989]***
(a) collision on walls will be less
(b) number of collisions per unit time will increase
(c) collisions will be in straight lines
(d) collisions will not change

22 Two containers A and B are partly filled with water and closed. The volume of A is twice that of B and it contains half the amount of water in B. If both are at the same temperature, the water vapour in the containers will have pressure in the ratio of ***[AIPMT 1988]***
(a) 1 : 2 (b) 1 : 1 (c) 2 : 1 (d) 4 : 1

Topic 2 Degree of Freedom and Law of Equipartition of Energy

01 Match Column I with Column II and choose the correct match from the given choices. ***[NCERT (New) Pg. 250, NEET 2021]***

	Column I		Column II
A.	Root mean square of gas molecules	1.	$\frac{1}{3}nm\bar{v}^2$
B.	Pressure exerted by ideal gas	2.	$\sqrt{\frac{3RT}{M}}$
C.	Average kinetic energy of a molecule	3.	$\frac{5}{2}RT$
D.	Total internal energy of 1 mole of a diatomic gas	4.	$\frac{3}{2}k_BT$

Codes

	A	B	C	D		A	B	C	D
(a)	3	1	4	2	(b)	2	3	4	1
(c)	2	1	4	3	(d)	3	2	1	4

02 The average thermal energy for a monoatomic gas is (where, k_B is Boltzmann constant and T is absolute temperature.) *[NEET (Sep.) 2020]*

(a) $\frac{3}{2}k_BT$ (b) $\frac{5}{2}k_BT$
(c) $\frac{7}{2}k_BT$ (d) $\frac{1}{2}k_BT$

03 Increase in temperature of a gas filled in a container would lead to *[NEET (National) 2019]*

(a) increase in its kinetic energy
(b) decrease in its pressure
(c) decrease in intermolecular distance
(d) increase in its mass

04 A gas mixture consists of 2 moles of O_2 and 4 moles of Ar at temperature T. Neglecting all vibrational modes, the total internal energy of the system is *[NEET 2017]*

(a) $4RT$ (b) $15RT$
(c) $9RT$ (d) $11RT$

05 The amount of heat energy required to raise the temperature of 1 g of helium at NTP, from T_1K to T_2K is *[NEET 2013]*

(a) $\frac{3}{8}N_ak_B(T_2-T_1)$ (b) $\frac{3}{2}N_ak_B(T_2-T_1)$
(c) $\frac{3}{4}N_ak_B(T_2-T_1)$ (d) $\frac{3}{4}N_ak_B\left(\frac{T_2}{T_1}\right)$

06 The gases carbon-monoxide (CO) and nitrogen at the same temperature have kinetic energies E_1 and E_2 respectively. Then *[NCERT (New) Pg. 253, AIPMT 2000]*

(a) $E_1 = E_2$
(b) $E_1 > E_2$
(c) $E_1 < E_2$
(d) E_1 and E_2 cannot be compared

07 To find out degree of freedom, the expression is *[AIPMT 2000]*

(a) $f=\frac{2}{\gamma-1}$ (b) $f=\frac{\gamma+1}{2}$
(c) $f=\frac{2}{\gamma+1}$ (d) $f=\frac{1}{\gamma+1}$

08 The degrees of freedom of a molecule of a triatomic gas are *[NCERT (New) Pg. 253, AIPMT 1999]*

(a) 2 (b) 4
(c) 6 (d) 8

09 The number of translational degree of freedom for a diatomic gas is *[AIPMT 1993]*

(a) 2 (b) 3 (c) 5 (d) 6

10 A polyatomic gas with n degrees of freedom has a mean energy per molecule given by *[AIPMT 1989]*

(a) $\frac{nk_BT}{N}$ (b) $\frac{nk_BT}{2N}$
(c) $\frac{nk_BT}{2}$ (d) $\frac{3k_BT}{2}$

Topic 3 Specific Heat Capacity and Mean Free Path

01 The mean free path λ for a gas, with molecular diameter d and number density n can be expressed as *[NCERT (New) Pg. 255, NEET (Sep.) 2020]*

(a) $\frac{1}{\sqrt{2}\,n\pi d^2}$ (b) $\frac{1}{\sqrt{2}\,n^2\pi d^2}$
(c) $\frac{1}{\sqrt{2}\,n^2\pi^2 d^2}$ (d) $\frac{1}{\sqrt{2}\,n\pi d}$

02 The mean free path l for a gas molecule depends upon diameter, d of the molecule as *[NCERT (New) Pg. 255, NEET (Oct.) 2020]*

(a) $l\propto\frac{1}{d^2}$ (b) $l\propto d$ (c) $l\propto d^2$ (d) $l\propto\frac{1}{d}$

03 One mole of an ideal monoatomic gas undergoes a process described by the equation $pV^3=$ constant. The heat capacity of the gas during this process is *[NCERT (New) Pg. 253, NEET 2016]*

(a) $\frac{3}{2}R$ (b) $\frac{5}{2}R$ (c) $2R$ (d) R

04 4.0 g of a gas occupies 22.4 L at NTP. The specific heat capacity of the gas at constant volume is 5.0 JK^{-1} mol^{-1}. If the speed of sound in this gas at NTP is 952 ms^{-1}, then the heat capacity at constant pressure is (Take gas constant $R=8.3$ JK^{-1} mol^{-1}) *[AIPMT 2015]*

(a) 8.0 JK^{-1} mol^{-1} (b) 7.5 JK^{-1} mol^{-1}
(c) 7.0 JK^{-1} mol^{-1} (d) 8.5 JK^{-1} mol^{-1}

05 The ratio of the specific heats $\frac{C_p}{C_V}=\gamma$ in terms of degrees of freedom n is given by *[AIPMT 2015]*

(a) $\left(1+\frac{1}{n}\right)$ (b) $\left(1+\frac{n}{3}\right)$
(c) $\left(1+\frac{2}{n}\right)$ (d) $\left(1+\frac{n}{2}\right)$

06 The mean free path of molecules of a gas, (radius r) is inversely proportional to *[NCERT (New) Pg. 255, AIPMT 2014]*

(a) r^3 (b) r^2 (c) r (d) $\sqrt{r}$

07 The molar specific heats of an ideal gas at constant pressure and volume are denoted by C_p and C_V respectively. If $\gamma=\frac{C_p}{C_V}$ and R is the universal gas constant, then C_V is equal to *[NCERT (New) Pg. 253, NEET 2013]*

(a) $\frac{1+\gamma}{1-\gamma}$ (b) $\frac{R}{(\gamma-1)}$ (c) $\frac{(\gamma-1)}{R}$ (d) γR

08 During an adiabatic process, the pressure of a gas is found to be proportional to the cube of its temperature. The ratio of $\frac{C_p}{C_V}$ for the gas is **[NEET 2013]**

(a) $\frac{4}{3}$ (b) 2 (c) $\frac{5}{3}$ (d) $\frac{3}{2}$

09 If c_p and c_V denote the specific heats (per unit mass) of an ideal gas of molecular weight M **[AIPMT 2010]**

(a) $c_p - c_V = R/M^2$ (b) $c_p - c_V = R$

(c) $c_p - c_V = R/M$ (d) $c_p - c_V = MR$

Where R is the molar gas constant

10 The molar specific heat at constant pressure of an ideal gas is $(7/2)R$. The ratio of specific heat at constant pressure to that at constant volume is **[NCERT (New) Pg. 253, AIPMT 2006]**

(a) 7/5 (b) 8/7 (c) 5/7 (d) 9/7

11 If γ be the ratio of specific heats of a perfect gas, the number of degrees of freedom of a molecule of the gas is **[AIPMT 2000]**

(a) $\frac{25}{2}(\gamma-1)$ (b) $\frac{3\gamma-1}{2\gamma-1}$

(c) $\frac{2}{\gamma-1}$ (d) $\frac{9}{2}(\gamma-1)$

12 If for a gas, $\frac{R}{C_V} = 0.67$, this gas is made up of molecules which are **[AIPMT 1992]**

(a) diatomic
(b) mixture of diatomic and polyatomic molecules
(c) monoatomic
(d) polyatomic

13 For hydrogen gas $C_p - C_V = a$ and for oxygen gas $C_p - C_V = b$, so the relation between a and b is given by **[NCERT (New) Pg. 253, AIPMT 1991]**

(a) $a = 16b$ (b) $16b = a$

(c) $a = 4b$ (d) $a = b$

14 One mole of an ideal gas requires 207 J heat to raise the temperature by 10 K when heated at constant pressure. If the same gas is heated at constant volume to raise the temperature by the same 10 K, the heat required is (Given the gas constant $R = 8.3$ J/mol-K) **[AIPMT 1990]**

(a) 198.7 J (b) 29 J (c) 215.3 J (d) 124 J

15 For a certain gas the ratio of specific heats is given to be $\gamma = 1.5$, for this gas **[CBSE AIPMT 1990]**

(a) $C_V = \frac{3R}{J}$ (b) $C_p = \frac{3R}{J}$

(c) $C_p = \frac{5R}{J}$ (d) $C_p = \frac{5R}{J}$

• Key **Index**

Topic 1

1 (d)	2 (a)	3 (c)	4 (a)	5 (c)	6 (b)	7 (b)	8 (a)	9 (b)	10 (c)
11 (b)	12 (d)	13 (d)	14 (a)	15 (d)	16 (a)	17 (b)	18 (d)	19 (d)	20 (c)
21 (b)	22 (b)								

Topic 2

1 (c)	2 (a)	3 (a)	4 (d)	5 (a)	6 (a)	7 (a)	8 (c)	9 (b)	10 (c)

Topic 3

1 (a)	2 (a)	3 (d)	4 (a)	5 (c)	6 (b)	7 (b)	8 (d)	9 (c)	10 (a)
11 (c)	12 (c)	13 (a)	14 (d)	15 (b)					

Detailed Explanations

Topic 1

01. *(d)* Charle's law states that volume of a gas is proportional to its temperature on kelvin scale at constant pressure.

It is clear for p_1, T is higher.

Thus, $p_1 > p_2 > p_3$

Alternate Solution

We know that $pV = nRT$

$\frac{T}{V} = \frac{p}{nR}$

Slope $= \frac{p}{nR}$

i.e., slope $\propto p$

Hence, $p_1 > p_2 > p_3$

02. *(a)* Initial temperature of the gas,

$T_1 = -50°C = (-50 + 273)K = 223K$

Final temperature of the gas,

$T_2 = ?$

$(v_{rms})_1 = v,$

$(v_{rms})_2 = (v_{rms})_1 + 3(v_{rms})_1$

$= v + 3v = 4v$

We know that, $v_{rms} = \sqrt{\frac{3RT}{m}}$

$\Rightarrow \quad v_{rms} \propto \sqrt{T} \Rightarrow \frac{(v_{rms})_2}{(v_{rms})_1} = \sqrt{\frac{T_2}{T_1}}$

$\Rightarrow \quad \frac{4v}{v} = \sqrt{\frac{T_2}{223}} \Rightarrow 16 = \frac{T_2}{223}$

$\Rightarrow \quad T_2 = 3568\text{ K}$

$\Rightarrow \quad T_2 = (3568 - 273)°C = 3295°C$

03. *(c)*

key idea

First find the number of moles for water and then apply ideal gas equation.

$pV = nRT$

Molecular weight of water

$= 18\text{ g} = 1.8 \times 10^{-2}\text{ kg}$

$\therefore$ Mass of water, $M = 4.5$ kg

$\therefore$ Number of moles of water,

$$n = \frac{\text{Mass of water}}{\text{Molecular weight of water}}$$

$$= \frac{4.5}{1.8 \times 10^{-2}} = 250$$

At STP, $T = 273$ K,

$p = 10^5\text{ N/m}^2$

Using equation,

$pV = nRT$

$\Rightarrow \quad V = \frac{nRT}{p} = \frac{250 \times 8.3 \times 273}{10^5}$

$= 5.6\text{ m}^3$

04. *(a)* Given,

pressure, $p = 249\text{ kPa} = 249 \times 10^3\text{ Pa}$

Temperature, $T = 27°C$

$= 273 + 27K = 300K$

As, from ideal gas equation,

$pV = nRT$

$\Rightarrow \quad pV = \frac{m}{M}RT \qquad \left[\text{as } n = \frac{m}{M}\right]$

$\Rightarrow \quad pVM = mRT$

$\Rightarrow \quad pM = \frac{m}{V}RT = \rho RT \qquad \left[\text{as } \frac{m}{V} = \rho\right]$

$\Rightarrow \quad \rho = \frac{pM}{RT} = \frac{249 \times 10^3 \times 2 \times 10^{-3}}{8.3 \times 300}$

[$\because$ for hydrogen gas, $M = 2$ g $= 2 \times 10^{-3}$ kg]

$\Rightarrow \quad \rho = 0.2\text{ kg/m}^3$

05. *(c)* Ideal gas equation is given as

$p = \frac{\rho RT}{M_0} \Rightarrow p \cdot \frac{M_0}{\rho} = RT$

$\Rightarrow \quad pV = RT$

where, $\quad V = \frac{M_0}{\rho}$

Ideal gas equation is

$pV = nRT$

$\Rightarrow \quad pV = \frac{m}{M_0}RT \qquad \left[\because n = \frac{m}{M_0}\right]$

$p = \frac{m}{V}\frac{RT}{M_0} = \frac{\rho RT}{M_0} \qquad \left[\because \rho = \frac{M}{V}\right]$

Hence, ρ and M_0 are mass density and molar mass, respectively.

06. *(b)* Escape velocity on surface of earth is given by

$v_e = \sqrt{2gR}$

$v_e = \sqrt{2 \times 9.8 \times 6.4 \times 10^6}$

$\cong 11.2\text{ km s}^{-1} = 11200\text{ ms}^{-1}$

According to the question, $v_{rms} = v_e$

where, v_{rms} is the rms speed of the oxygen molecule.

$\Rightarrow \quad \sqrt{\frac{3k_BT}{m_{O_2}}} = 11.2 \times 10^3$

or $\quad T = \frac{(11.2 \times 10^3)^2 (m_{O_2})}{(3k_B)}$

Substituting the given values, i.e.,

$k_B = 1.38 \times 10^{-23}\text{ JK}^{-1}$

and $m_{O_2} = m = 2.76 \times 10^{-26}$ kg

we get,

$T = \frac{(11.2 \times 10^3)^2 (2.76 \times 10^{-26})}{(3 \times 1.38 \times 10^{-23})}$

$= 8.326 \times 10^4$ K

• Concept Enhancer

The minimum velocity with which the body must be projected vertically upwards, so that it could escape from the Earth's atmosphere, is its escape velocity (v_e).

07. *(b)* As we know that

Pressure, $p = \frac{1}{3} \cdot \frac{nm}{V} v_{rms}^2$

$\because$ nm = mass of the gas,

V = volume of the gas

$\therefore \quad \frac{mn}{V}$ = density of the gas.

Thus, $p = \frac{1}{3}\rho v_{rms}^2 = \frac{1}{3}\rho\frac{3RT}{M_0} = \frac{\rho RT}{M_0}$

$\left(\because v_{rms} = \sqrt{\frac{3RT}{M_0}}\right)$

$\rho = \frac{pM_0}{RT} = \frac{pmN_A}{k_B N_A T}$

[$\because$ $R = N_A k_B$ and $M_0 = mN_A$]

$\rho = \frac{pm}{k_BT}$

Alternate Solution

Pressure $= \frac{F}{A} = \frac{[MLT^{-2}]}{[L^2]} = [ML^{-1}T^{-2}]$

Volume $= [L^3]$

Mass $= [M]$

K_BT = Energy $= [ML^2T^{-2}]$

Therefore, $\frac{pm}{K_BT} = \frac{[ML^{-1}T^{-2}][M]}{[ML^2T^{-2}]} = [ML^{-3}]$

Which is the dimensional formula of density.

Only option (b) gives the dimensional formula of density hence option (b) is correct.

08. *(a)* It is given that

$$v_{rms} = 200\ ms^{-1}, T_1 = 300\ K,$$
$$p_1 = 10^5\ N/m^2$$
$$T_2 = 400\ K,$$
$$p_2 = 0.05 \times 10^5\ N/m^2$$

As, rms velocity of gas molecules,

$$\because\ v_{rms} \propto \sqrt{T} \quad \left(\because v_{rms} = \sqrt{\frac{3RT}{m}}\right)$$

For two different cases

$$\Rightarrow \frac{(v_{rms})_1}{(v_{rms})_2} = \sqrt{\frac{T_1}{T_2}}$$

$$\Rightarrow \frac{200}{(v_{rms})_2} = \sqrt{\frac{300}{400}} = \sqrt{\frac{3}{4}}$$

$$\Rightarrow (v_{rms})_2 = \frac{2}{\sqrt{3}} \times 200 = \frac{400}{\sqrt{3}}\ ms^{-1}$$

09. *(b)*

Vessel-I	Vessel-II
Ideal Gas A	Ideal Gas B
T	T

$$\rho_A = 1.5\,\rho_B$$
$$p_A = 2p_B$$

$$\because \text{ Pressure, } p = \frac{\rho RT}{M},$$

$$\text{Such that, } \frac{p}{\rho} = \frac{RT}{M} \Rightarrow M = \frac{\rho RT}{p}$$

$$\text{So, } \quad M \propto \frac{\rho}{p} \Rightarrow \frac{M_A}{M_B} = \frac{\rho_A}{\rho_B} \times \frac{p_B}{p_A}$$

$$= 1.5 \times \frac{1}{2} = 0.75 = \frac{3}{4}$$

10. *(c)* According to question,

$$\text{Slope of the graph} \propto \frac{1}{\text{Pressure } p}$$

$$\text{So,} \quad p_2 < p_1$$

11. *(b)* Pressure due to N molecules of mass m and volume V, gas is given by

$$p = \frac{1}{3}\frac{mN}{V} v_{rms}^2$$

When mass is halved and speed is doubled then,

Resultant pressure,

$$p' = \frac{1}{3} \times \left(\frac{m}{2}\right) \times \frac{N}{V}(2v_{rms})^2 = 2p$$

12. *(d)*

key idea

Use ideal gas equation to find the ratio between density of a fixed mass of an ideal gas and its pressure.

Ideal gas equation is given by

$$pV = nRT$$

$$\frac{pV}{m} = \frac{1}{M} RT \quad \left(\because n = \frac{m}{M}\right)$$

$$\frac{p}{\rho} = \frac{RT}{M} \quad \left(\because \frac{V}{m} = \frac{1}{\rho}\right)$$

$$\therefore \quad \frac{\rho}{p} \propto \frac{1}{T}$$

For two different situations i.e. at two different temperatures and densities

$$\therefore \quad \frac{\rho_1/p_1}{\rho_2/p_2} = \frac{T_2}{T_1}$$

$$\Rightarrow \quad \frac{x}{(\rho_2/p_2)} = \frac{383\ K}{283\ K} \Rightarrow \frac{\rho_2}{p_2} = \frac{283}{383}x$$

13. *(d)* Since, $\frac{pV}{T}$ = constant

$$\text{Therefore } \frac{p_1V_1}{T_1} = \frac{p_2V_2}{T_2}$$

$$\Rightarrow \quad \frac{p_1}{p_2} = \left(\frac{T_1}{T_2}\right)\left(\frac{V_2}{V_1}\right)$$

$$\Rightarrow \quad \frac{p_1}{p_2} = 4 \quad \left[\because V_2 = 2V_1,\ T_2 = T_1/2\right]$$

$$\Rightarrow \quad p_2 = \frac{1}{4}p_1$$

Hence, the pressure will become 1/4 times.

14. *(a)* Number of moles,

$$n = \frac{m}{\text{molecular weight}} = \frac{5}{32}$$

As, from ideal gas equation

$$pV = nRT \Rightarrow pV = \frac{5}{32}RT$$

15. *(d)* Equation of gas is given by

$$\frac{p_1V_1}{T_1} = \frac{p_2V_2}{T_2}$$

$$\text{or,} \quad \frac{30 \times V}{300} = \frac{1 \times 10 \times V}{T_2}$$

$$\Rightarrow \quad T_2 = 100\ K$$

$$\Rightarrow \quad T_2 = -173°C$$

16. *(a)* At 0 K, all molecular motion seizes. Hence, kinetic energy of molecules becomes zero.

17. *(b)* 8 g of oxygen is equivalent to (1/4) mole.

($\because O_2$ is a diatomic molecule)

From ideal gas equation $pV = nRT$

$$pV = \frac{1}{4}RT \quad \left(\because n = \frac{1}{4} \text{ moles}\right)$$

18. *(d)*

key idea

RMS speed is defined as the square root of the mean of the squares of the random velocities of the individual molecules of a gas. From Maxwell distribution law, rms speed is given by

$$v_{rms} = \sqrt{\left(\frac{3kT}{m}\right)}$$

$$\because \quad \frac{(v_{rms})_1}{(v_{rms})_2} = \sqrt{\frac{T_1}{T_2}}$$

Here, $T_1 = 27°C = 300\ K$

$T_2 = 927°C = 1200\ K$

$$\therefore \quad \frac{(v_{rms})_1}{(v_{rms})_2} = \sqrt{\frac{300}{1200}} = \frac{1}{2}$$

$$\Rightarrow (v_{rms})_2 = 2\,(v_{rms})_1$$

Hence, root mean square speed will be doubled.

19. *(d)* The mean square speed of type a molecule will be

$$\omega_x^2 + \omega_y^2 + \omega_z^2 = 3\omega^2$$

$$\text{Therefore, } \frac{1}{2}m(3\omega^2) = \frac{1}{2}(2m)v^2$$

$$\Rightarrow \quad \frac{\omega^2}{v^2} = \frac{2}{3}$$

20. *(c)* According to Dalton's law of partial pressure, the total pressure exerted by a mixture of gases, which do not interact with each other, is equal to sum of the partial pressures which each would exert, if alone occupied the same volume at the given temperature. When gases are put in one container, then pressure p of the mixture will be

$$p = p_1 + p_2 + p_3$$

21. *(b)* On raising the temperature, the average velocity of the gas molecules increases. As a result of which more molecules collide with the walls or number of collisions per unit time will increase.

22. *(b)* Vapour pressure does not depend on the amount of substance. It depends only on the temperature.

Hence, the pressure in the containers will be the same.

Topic 2

01. *(c)* We know that,

$$v_{rms} = \sqrt{3RT/M}$$

Pressure exerted by an ideal gas,

$$p = \frac{1}{3}nm\bar{v}^2$$

$\bar{v}$ is the average speed of the gas molecules. The average kinetic energy of a molecule,

$$KE_{avg} = \frac{3}{2} k_B T$$

For diatomic gas, degree of freedom, $f = 5$

As, total internal energy of 1 mole of diatomic gas,

$$\Delta U = \frac{nfRT}{2}$$

$$\Rightarrow \quad \Delta U = \frac{1(5)RT}{2} = \frac{5RT}{2}$$

The correct match is A → 2, B → 1, C → 4 and D → 3.

02. *(a)* The average thermal energy of a system with degree of freedom f is equals to its average energy, which is given as $= \frac{f}{2} k_B \cdot T$

For monoatomic gas, $f = 3$

∴ Average thermal energy $= \frac{3}{2} k_B \cdot T$

> • Concept **Enhancer**
> (i) Degree of freedom of a monoatomic gas (He, Ne, Ar) = 3
> (ii) Degree of freedom of a diatomic gas $(O_2, N_2, CO, Cl_2) = 5$
> (iii) Degree of freedom of a triatomic gas $(H_2O, SO_2) = 6$

03. *(a)* As the temperature of gas in the container is increased, the kinetic energy also increases. This is because the average kinetic energy of a gas is given by

$$KE = \frac{f}{2} nRT \quad \text{... (i)}$$

From Eq. (i), KE $\propto T$

04. *(d)* Total internal energy of system = Internal energy of oxygen molecules + Internal energy of argon molecules

$$= \frac{f_1}{2} n_1 RT + \frac{f_2}{2} n_2 RT$$

$$= \frac{5}{2} \times 2RT + \frac{3}{2} \times 4RT = 11RT$$

05. *(a)* We know that,

$$Q = \frac{f}{2} nR\Delta T$$

∴ Amount of heat required,

$$Q = \frac{3}{2} \times \frac{1}{4} \times k_B N_a \Delta T$$

$$= \frac{3}{8} N_a k_B (T_2 - T_1)$$

06. *(a)* The gases carbon-monoxide (CO) and nitrogen (N_2) are diatomic, so both have equal kinetic energy $\frac{5}{2} k_B T$,

i.e. $E_1 = E_2$

07. *(a)* We know that, $\gamma = 1 + \frac{2}{f}$ where f is the degree of freedom

$$\Rightarrow \frac{2}{f} = \gamma - 1 \text{ or } f = \frac{2}{\gamma - 1}$$

08. *(c)* For a triatomic molecule the motion is given below.

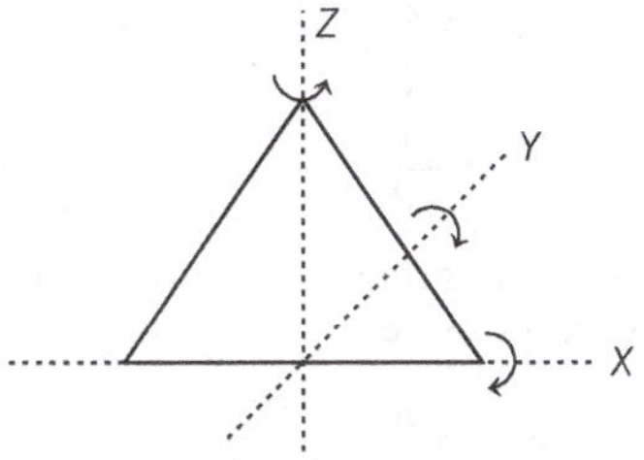

(3 translational + 3 rotational) at room temperature.

Thus, $f = 6$

> • Concept **Enhancer**
> The molecule of a triatomic gas has a tendency of rotating about any of three coordinate axes. So, it has 6 degrees of freedom, 3 translational and 3 rotational. At high enough temperature, a triatomic molecule has 2 vibrational degree of freedom. But as temperature requirement is not given, so we answer simply by assuming triatomic gas molecule at room temperature.

09. *(b)* Let A = number of particles in the system,

R = number of independent relations among the particles,

N = number of degree of freedom of the system, then

Then $\quad N = 3A - R$

Each monoatomic, diatomic and triatomic gas has three translatory degree of freedom.

∴ $\quad N = 3(3) - 6 = 3$

> • Concept **Enhancer**
> Number of degree of freedom of a dynamical system is obtained by subtracting the number of independent relations from the total number of coordinates required to specify the positions of constituent particles of the system.

10. *(c)* For a polyatomic gas with n degrees of freedom the mean energy per molecule $= \frac{1}{2} nk_B T$.

k_B = Boltzmann constant

n = degree of freedom

T = Temperature

> • Concept **Enhancer**
> If there is sudden compression without exchange of heat the process will be adiabatic.

Topic 3

01. *(a)* The mean free path λ for a gas, with molecular diameter d and number density n is given by the relation

$$\lambda = \frac{1}{\sqrt{2}\, n\pi d^2}$$

02. *(a)* The mean free path l for a gas molecule is given as

$$l = \frac{1}{\sqrt{2}\pi n d^2}$$

$$\Rightarrow \quad l \propto \frac{1}{d^2}$$

where, d = diameter of molecule of gas.

03. *(d)* As we know that for polytropic process of index α specific heat capacity

$$= C_V + \frac{R}{1-\alpha}$$

∵ Process, pV^3 = constant $\Rightarrow \alpha = 3$

$$\therefore \quad C = C_V + \frac{R}{1-\alpha}$$

$$= \frac{fR}{2} + \frac{R}{1-3}$$

where, $C_V = \frac{fR}{2} = \frac{3R}{2}$

For monatomic gas, $f = 3$

$$\Rightarrow \quad C = \frac{3R}{2} - \frac{R}{2} = R$$

04. *(a)* Given, $M = 4$ g, $V = 22.4$ L

$$C_V = 5 \text{ JK}^{-1}\text{mol}^{-1}$$

$$v_{sound} = 952 \text{ m/s},$$

As, velocity of sound,

$$v_{sound} = \sqrt{\frac{\gamma pV}{M}}$$

$$\Rightarrow \quad \gamma = \frac{M}{pV} v_{sound}^2 = \frac{C_p}{C_V}$$

So, heat capacity at constant pressure,

$$C_p = C_V \left[\frac{M}{pV}\right] v_{sound}^2$$

$$= 5\left[\frac{4\times10^{-3}}{10^5\times22.4\times10^{-3}}\right](952)^2$$

$$= \frac{20}{22.4}\times(952)^2\times10^{-5}$$

$$= 809200\times10^{-5} = 8.09 \text{ J/mol K}$$

05. *(c)* The specific heat of gas at constant volume in terms of degree of freedom n is

$$C_V = \frac{n}{2}R$$

Also $C_p - C_V = R$

So $\quad C_p = \frac{n}{2}R + R = R\left(1+\frac{n}{2}\right)$

Now $\quad \gamma = \frac{C_p}{C_V} = \frac{R\left(1+\frac{n}{2}\right)}{\frac{n}{2}R} = \frac{2}{n}+1$

06. *(b)* Mean free path (l) is given by

$$l = \frac{1}{\sqrt{2}n\pi d^2} \Rightarrow l \propto \frac{1}{d^2}$$

So, $\quad l \propto \frac{1}{r^2}$

07. *(b)* As we know that, $C_p - C_V = R$

$$C_p = R + C_V$$

and $\quad \frac{C_p}{C_V} = \gamma \quad$ (given)

So, $\quad \frac{R + C_V}{C_V} = \gamma \Rightarrow \gamma C_V = R + C_V$

$$\Rightarrow \gamma C_V - C_V = R$$

$$\Rightarrow \quad C_V = \frac{R}{\gamma - 1}$$

08. *(d)* According to question,

$$p \propto T^3 \quad \ldots(i)$$

and we know that

$$pV = nRT$$

and $\quad pV \propto T \quad \ldots(ii)$

So, putting Eq. (ii) in (i),

$$p \propto (pV)^3$$

$$\Rightarrow \quad p^2V^3 = \text{constant}$$

$$\Rightarrow \quad pV^{3/2} = \text{constant} \quad \ldots(iii)$$

$\Rightarrow$ Comparing Eq. (iii) with

$$pV^\gamma = \text{constant}$$

$$\gamma = 3/2$$

and $\quad \frac{C_p}{C_V} = \gamma = \frac{3}{2}$

09. *(c)* From Mayer's formula, we have

$$C_p - C_V = R$$

$$Mc_p - Mc_V = R$$

$$\Rightarrow c_p - c_V = \frac{R}{M}$$

10. *(a)* We have given molar specific heat at instant pressure

$$C_p = \frac{7}{2}R$$

Mayer's relation can be written as

i.e. $C_p - C_V = R \Rightarrow C_V = C_p - R$

$$= \frac{7}{2}R - R = \frac{5}{2}R\left[\because C_p = \frac{7}{2}R\right]$$

Hence, required ratio is

$$\gamma = \frac{C_p}{C_V} = \frac{\left(\frac{7}{2}\right)R}{\left(\frac{5}{2}\right)R} = \frac{7}{5}$$

11. *(c)* We know that ratio of specific heats, is given by

$$\gamma = 1 + \frac{2}{f} \quad \text{or} \quad f = \frac{2}{\gamma - 1}$$

12. *(c)* $C_V = \frac{R}{0.67} \approx 1.5\,R = \frac{3}{2}R$

This is the case of monoatomic gases.

when $C_V = \frac{3}{2}R$

13. *(a)* If it was the case of specific heat of 1g $C_p - C_V = r = \frac{R}{m}$

$\therefore \quad C_p - C_V = \frac{R}{2} \quad$ (for H, $\frac{R}{2} = a$)

$$C_p - C_V = \frac{R}{32} \quad (\text{for } O_2, \frac{R}{32} = b)$$

$$R = 2a = 32b$$

$$a = 16b$$

14. *(d)* As $(dQ)_p = \mu C_p dT \quad \ldots(i)$

(At constant pressure)

and $\quad (dQ)_V = \mu C_V dT \quad \ldots(ii)$

(At constant volume)

Given, $(dQ)_p = 207$ J

$$R = 8.3 \text{ J/mol-K}$$

$$dT = 10 \text{ K}$$

Putting value in Eq. (i),

$$207 = 1 \times C_p \times 10$$

$\therefore \quad C_p = 20.7$ J/kg

As $\quad C_p - C_V = R = 8.3$

$$C_V = 20.7 - 8.3 = 12.4 \text{ J}$$

$\therefore \quad (dQ)_V = 1 \times 12.4 \times 10$

$$= 124 \text{ J}$$

15. *(b)* Given, $\quad \gamma = \frac{C_p}{C_V} = 1.5 = \frac{3}{2}$

$\therefore \quad C_V = \frac{2}{3}C_p$

Again from Mayer's formula

$$C_p - C_V = \frac{R}{J}$$

$\therefore \quad C_p - \frac{2}{3}C_p = \frac{R}{J}$

$$\Rightarrow \quad \frac{C_p}{3} = \frac{R}{J}$$

$$\Rightarrow \quad C_p = \frac{3R}{J}$$

In NEET 2024, 2 question was visible from this chapter. In past 5 years, 4 questions from topic-1, 1 question from topic 2 and 3 questions from topic-3 were asked.
For detailed analysis scan QR code

OSCILLATIONS

Topic 1 Simple Harmonic Motion

01 If $x = 5\sin\left(\pi t + \frac{\pi}{3}\right)$ m represents the motion of a particle executing simple harmonic motion, the amplitude and time period of motion, respectively, are *[NCERT (New) Pg. 262, NEET 2024]*

(a) 5 cm, 2 s (b) 5 m, 2 s (c) 5 cm, 1 s (d) 5 m, 1 s

02 The *x-t* graph of a particle performing simple harmonic motion is shown in the figure. The acceleration of the particle at $t = 2$ s is *[NEET 2023]*

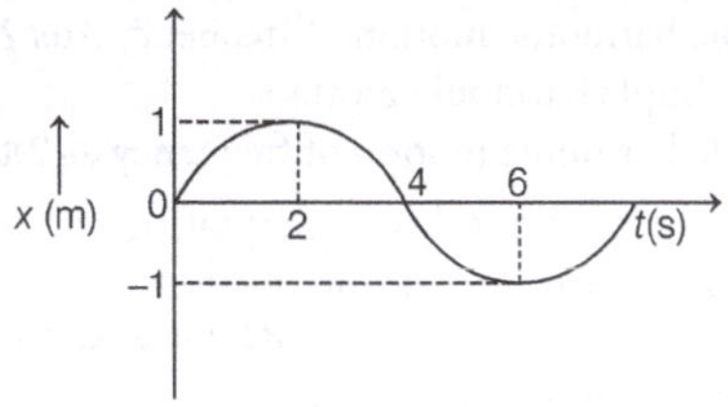

(a) $-\frac{\pi^2}{8}$ ms^{-2} (b) $\frac{\pi^2}{16}$ ms^{-2} (c) $-\frac{\pi^2}{16}$ ms^{-2} (d) $\frac{\pi^2}{8}$ ms^{-2}

03 Identify the function which represents a periodic motion. *[NCERT (New) Pg. 260, NEET (Oct.) 2020]*

(a) $e^{\omega t}$ (b) $\log_e(\omega t)$
(c) $\sin\omega t + \cos\omega t$ (d) $e^{-\omega t}$

04 The phase difference between displacement and acceleration of a particle in a simple harmonic motion is *[NCERT (New) Pg. 266, NEET (Sep.) 2020]*

(a) $\frac{3\pi}{2}$ rad (b) $\frac{\pi}{2}$ rad
(c) zero (d) π rad

05 The distance covered by a particle undergoing SHM in one time period is (amplitude = A) *[NEET (Odisha) 2019]*

(a) zero (b) A
(c) $2A$ (d) $4A$

06 Average velocity of a particle executing SHM in one complete vibration is *[NEET (National) 2019]*

(a) $A\omega$ (b) $\frac{A\omega^2}{2}$
(c) zero (d) $\frac{A\omega}{2}$

07 The displacement of a particle executing simple harmonic motion is given by

$$y = A_0 + A\sin\omega t + B\cos\omega t$$

Then, the amplitude of its oscillation is given by *[NEET (National) 2019]*

(a) $\sqrt{A^2 + B^2}$
(b) $\sqrt{A_0^2 + (A+B)^2}$
(c) $A + B$
(d) $A_0 + \sqrt{A^2 + B^2}$

08 The radius of circle, the period of revolution, initial position and sense of revolution are indicated in the below figure. *[NCERT (New) Pg. 265, NEET (National) 2019]*

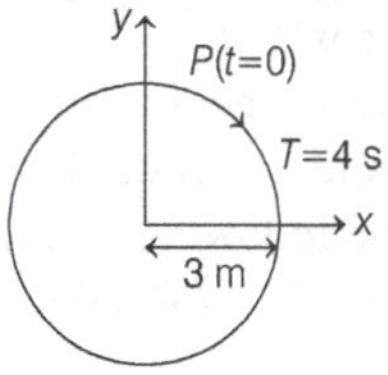

y-projection of the radius vector of rotating particle P is

(a) $y(t) = 4\sin\left(\frac{\pi t}{2}\right)$, where y in metre
(b) $y(t) = 3\cos\left(\frac{3\pi t}{2}\right)$, where y in metre
(c) $y(t) = 3\cos\left(\frac{\pi t}{2}\right)$, where y in metre
(d) $y(t) = -3\cos 2\pi t$, where y in metre

09 A particle executes linear simple harmonic motion with an amplitude of 3 cm. When the particle is at 2 cm from the mean position, the magnitude of its velocity is equal to that of its acceleration. Then, its time period in seconds is *[NEET 2017]*

(a) $\frac{\sqrt{5}}{\pi}$ (b) $\frac{\sqrt{5}}{2\pi}$ (c) $\frac{4\pi}{\sqrt{5}}$ (d) $\frac{2\pi}{\sqrt{3}}$

10 When two displacements represented by $y_1 = a \sin(\omega t)$ and $y_2 = b \cos(\omega t)$ are superimposed, the motion is *[AIPMT 2015]*

(a) not a simple harmonic

(b) simple harmonic with amplitude $\frac{a}{b}$

(c) simple harmonic with amplitude $\sqrt{a^2 + b^2}$

(d) simple harmonic with amplitude $\frac{(a+b)}{2}$

11 A particle is executing SHM along a straight line. Its velocities at distances x_1 and x_2 from the mean position are v_1 and v_2 respectively. Its time period is *[NCERT (New) Pg. 267, AIPMT 2015]*

(a) $2\pi\sqrt{\frac{x_1^2 + x_2^2}{v_1^2 + v_2^2}}$ (b) $2\pi\sqrt{\frac{x_2^2 - x_1^2}{v_1^2 - v_2^2}}$

(c) $2\pi\sqrt{\frac{v_1^2 + v_2^2}{x_1^2 + x_2^2}}$ (d) $2\pi\sqrt{\frac{v_1^2 - v_2^2}{x_1^2 - x_2^2}}$

12 A particle is executing a simple harmonic motion. Its maximum acceleration is α and maximum velocity is β. Then, its time period of vibration will be *[NCERT (New) Pg. 267, AIPMT 2015]*

(a) $\frac{\beta^2}{\alpha^2}$ (b) $\frac{\alpha}{\beta}$ (c) $\frac{\beta^2}{\alpha}$ (d) $\frac{2\pi\beta}{\alpha}$

13 The oscillation of a body on a smooth horizontal surface is represented by the equation,

$x = A \cos(\omega t)$

where, x = displacement at time t

ω = frequency of oscillation

Which one of the following graphs shows correctly the variation of a with t? *[NCERT (New) Pg. 264, AIPMT 2014]*

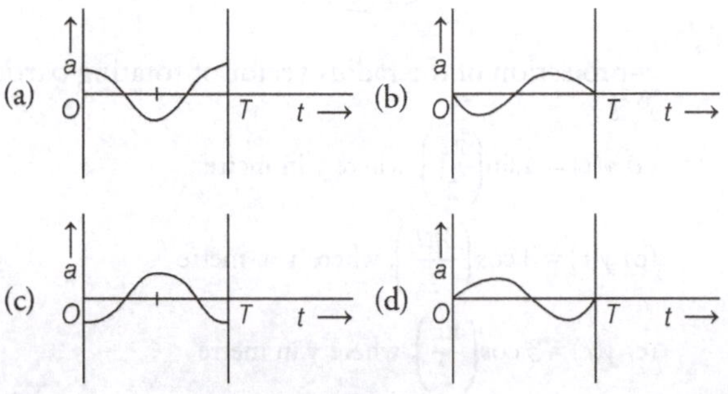

Here, a = acceleration at time t

T = time period

14 Out of the following functions representing motion of a particle which represents SHM? *[AIPMT 2011]*

I. $y = \sin \omega t - \cos \omega t$

II. $y = \sin^3 \omega t$

III. $y = 5\cos\left(\frac{3\pi}{4} - 3\omega t\right)$

IV. $y = 1 + \omega t + \omega^2 t^2$

(a) Only (IV) does not represent SHM

(b) (I) and (III)

(c) (I) and (II)

(d) Only (I)

15 Two particles are oscillating along two close parallel straight lines side by side, with the same frequency and amplitudes. They pass each other, moving in opposite directions, when their displacement is half of the amplitude. The mean positions of the two particles lie on a straight line perpendicular to the paths of the two particles. The phase difference is *[NCERT (New) Pg. 263, AIPMT 2011]*

(a) $\frac{\pi}{6}$ (b) 0 (c) $\frac{2\pi}{3}$ (d) π

16 The displacement of a particle along the X-axis is given by $x = a \sin^2 \omega t$. The motion of the particle corresponds to *[AIPMT 2010]*

(a) simple harmonic motion of frequency ω/π

(b) simple harmonic motion of frequency $3\omega/2\pi$

(c) non-simple harmonic motion

(d) simple harmonic motion of frequency $\omega/2\pi$

17 Which one of the following equations of motion represents simple harmonic motion? *[NCERT (New) Pg. 267, AIPMT 2009]*

(a) Acceleration $= -k_0 x + k_1 x^2$

(b) Acceleration $= -k(x + a)$

(c) Acceleration $= k(x + a)$

(d) Acceleration $= kx$

(where, k, k_0, k_1 and a are all positive.)

18 Two simple harmonic motions of angular frequency 100 rad s^{-1} and 1000 rad s^{-1} have the same displacement amplitude. The ratio of their maximum accelerations is *[NCERT (New) Pg. 267, AIPMT 2008]*

(a) 1 : 10 (b) $1 : 10^2$

(c) $1 : 10^3$ (d) $1 : 10^4$

19 A point performs simple harmonic oscillation of period T and the equation of motion is given by $x = a \sin\left(\omega t + \frac{\pi}{6}\right)$. After the elapse of what fraction of the time period, the velocity of the point will be equal to half of its maximum velocity? *[AIPMT 2008]*

(a) $\frac{T}{8}$ (b) $\frac{T}{6}$ (c) $\frac{T}{3}$ (d) $\frac{T}{12}$

20 A particle executes simple harmonic oscillation with an amplitude a. The period of oscillation is T. The minimum time taken by the particle to travel half of the amplitude from the equilibrium position is *[NCERT (New) Pg. 266, CBSE AIPMT 2007]*

(a) $\frac{T}{4}$ (b) $\frac{T}{8}$
(c) $\frac{T}{12}$ (d) $\frac{T}{2}$

21 A particle executing simple harmonic motion of amplitude 5 cm has maximum speed of 31.4 cm/s. The frequency of its oscillation is *[AIPMT 2005]*

(a) 3 Hz (b) 2 Hz
(c) 4 Hz (d) 1 Hz

22 Which one of the following statements is true for the speed v and the acceleration α of a particle executing simple harmonic motion? *[AIPMT 2004]*

(a) When v is maximum, α is maximum
(b) Value of α is zero, whatever may be the value of v
(c) When v is zero, α is zero
(d) When v is maximum, α is zero

23 Two strings A and B have lengths l_A and l_B and carry masses M_A and M_B at their lower ends, the upper ends being supported by rigid supports. If n_A and n_B are the frequencies of their vibrations and $n_A = 2n_B$, then *[NCERT (New) Pg. 283, AIPMT 2000]*

(a) $l_A = 4l_B$, regardless of masses
(b) $l_B = 4l_A$, regardless of masses
(c) $M_A = 2M_B, l_A = 2l_B$
(d) $M_B = 2M_A, l_B = 2l_A$

24 Two simple harmonic motions given by,

$x = a\sin(\omega t + \delta)$ and $y = a\sin\left(\omega t + \delta + \frac{\pi}{2}\right)$ act on a particle simultaneously, then the motion of particle will be *[AIPMT 2000]*

(a) circular anti-clockwise (b) circular clockwise
(c) elliptical anti-clockwise (d) elliptical clockwise

25 A particle executing SHM has amplitude 0.01 m and frequency 60 Hz. The maximum acceleration of the particle is *[NCERT (New) Pg. 267, AIPMT 1999]*

(a) $144\pi^2$ m/s^2 (b) $120\pi^2$ m/s^2
(c) $80\pi^2$ m/s^2 (d) $60\pi^2$ m/s^2

26 Two simple harmonic motions with the same frequency act on a particle at right angles i.e. along X-axis and Y-axis. If the two amplitudes are equal and the phase difference is $\pi/2$, the resultant motion will be *[NCERT (New) Pg. 267, AIPMT 1997]*

(a) a circle
(b) an ellipse with the major axis along Y-axis
(c) an ellipse with the major axis along X-axis
(d) a straight line inclined at 45° to the X-axis

27 A particle starts simple harmonic motion from the mean position. Its amplitude is a and time period is T. What is its displacement when its speed is half of its maximum speed? *[NCERT (New) Pg. 264, AIPMT 1996]*

(a) $\frac{\sqrt{2}}{3}a$ (b) $\frac{\sqrt{3}}{2}a$ (c) $\frac{2}{\sqrt{3}}a$ (d) $\frac{a}{\sqrt{2}}$

28 A particle starts with SHM from the mean position as shown in the figure. Its amplitude is A and its time period is T. At one time, its speed is half that of the maximum speed. What is the displacement of the particle at that time? *[AIPMT 1996]*

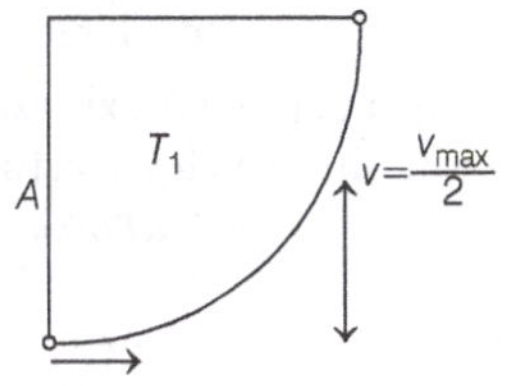

(a) $\frac{2A}{\sqrt{3}}$ (b) $\frac{3A}{\sqrt{2}}$ (c) $\frac{\sqrt{2}A}{3}$ (d) $\frac{\sqrt{3}A}{2}$

29 A particle is subjected to two mutually perpendicular simple harmonic motions such that its x and y coordinates are given by

$x = 2\sin\omega t,\ y = 2\sin\left(\omega t + \frac{\pi}{4}\right)$

The path of the particle will be *[AIPMT 1994]*

(a) a straight line (b) a circle
(c) an ellipse (d) a parabola

30 Which one of the following is a simple harmonic motion? *[NCERT (New) Pg. 262, AIPMT 1994]*

(a) Ball bouncing between two rigid vertical walls
(b) Particle moving in a circle with uniform speed
(c) Wave moving through a string fixed at both ends
(d) Earth spinning about its own axis

31 A simple harmonic oscillator has an amplitude a and time period T. The time required by it to travel from $x = a$ to $x = \frac{a}{2}$ is *[NCERT (New) Pg. 264, AIPMT 1992]*

(a) $\frac{T}{6}$ (b) $\frac{T}{4}$
(c) $\frac{T}{3}$ (d) $\frac{T}{2}$a

32 If a simple harmonic oscillator has got a displacement of 0.02 m and acceleration equal to 2.0 m/s^2 at any time, the angular frequency of the oscillator is equal to *[NCERT (New) Pg. 262, AIPMT 1992]*

(a) 10 rad/s (b) 0.1 rad/s
(c) 100 rad/s (d) 1 rad/s

33 A body is executing SHM. When the displacements from the mean position is 4 cm and 5 cm, the corresponding velocities of the body is 10 cm/s and 8 cm/s. Then, the time period of the body is *[AIPMT 1991]*

(a) 2π s (b) $\frac{\pi}{2}$ s (c) π s (d) $\frac{3\pi}{2}$ s

34 The composition of two simple harmonic motions of equal periods at right angle to each other and with a phase difference of π results in the displacement of the particle along *[AIPMT 1990]*

(a) circle (b) figure of eight
(c) straight line (d) ellipse

35 A particle moving along the *X*-axis executes simple harmonic motion, then the force acting on it is given by *[NCERT (New) Pg. 268, AIPMT 1988]*

(a) $-AKx$ (b) $A\cos Kx$
(c) $A\exp(-Kx)$ (d) AKx

where, A and K are positive constants.

Topic 2 Energy in SHM

01 A body is executing simple harmonic motion with frequency *n*, the frequency of its potential energy is *[NEET 2021]*

(a) n (b) $2n$ (c) $3n$ (d) $4n$

02 The particle executing simple harmonic motion has a kinetic energy $K_0\cos^2\omega t$. The maximum values of the potential energy and the total energy are respectively *[NCERT (New) Pg. 268, AIPMT 2007]*

(a) 0 and $2K_0$ (b) $\frac{K_0}{2}$ and K_0
(c) K_0 and $2K_0$ (d) K_0 and K_0

03 A particle of mass *m* oscillates with simple harmonic motion between points x_1 and x_2, the equilibrium position being *O*. Its potential energy is plotted. It will be as given below in the graph *[AIPMT 2003]*

(a)

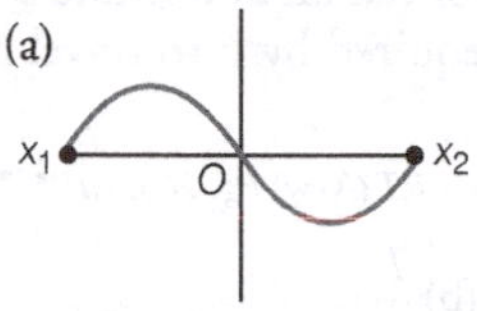

(b)

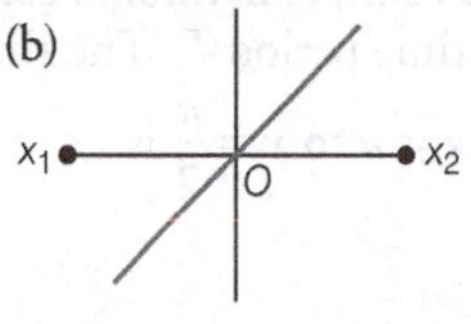

(c)

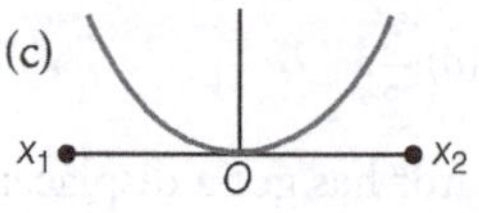

(d)

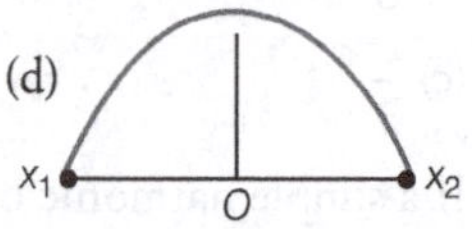

04 The potential energy of a simple harmonic oscillator when the particle is half way to its end point is *[NCERT (New) Pg. 268, AIPMT 2003]*

(a) $\frac{1}{4}E$ (b) $\frac{1}{2}E$ (c) $\frac{2}{3}E$ (d) $\frac{1}{8}E$

05 The displacement of particle between maximum potential energy position and maximum kinetic energy position in simple harmonic motion is *[AIPMT 2002]*

(a) $\pm\frac{a}{2}$ (b) $\pm a$ (c) $\pm 2a$ (d) ± 1

06 In SHM restoring force is $F = -kx$, where k is force constant, x is displacement and a is amplitude of motion, then total energy depends upon *[AIPMT 2001]*

(a) k, a and m (b) k, x, m (c) k, a (d) k, x

07 In a simple harmonic motion, when the displacement is one-half the amplitude, what fraction of the total energy is kinetic ? *[AIPMT 1996]*

(a) Zero (b) $\frac{1}{4}$ (c) $\frac{1}{2}$ (d) $\frac{3}{4}$

08 A linear harmonic oscillator of force constant 2×10^6 N/m and amplitude 0.01 m has a total mechanical energy of 160 J. Its *[AIPMT 1996]*

(a) maximum potential energy is 160 J
(b) maximum potential energy is 100 J
(c) maximum potential energy is zero
(d) minimum potential energy is 100 J

09 A body executes SHM with an amplitude *a*. At what displacement from the mean position, the potential energy of the body is one-fourth of its total energy ? *[AIPMT 1995]*

(a) $\frac{a}{4}$ (b) $\frac{a}{2}$
(c) $\frac{3a}{4}$ (d) Some other fraction of *a*

10 The angular velocity and the amplitude of a simple pendulum is ω and a respectively. At a displacement x from the mean position, if its kinetic energy is T and potential energy is U, then the ratio of T to U is *[NCERT (New) Pg. 268, AIPMT 1991]*

(a) $\left(\frac{a^2 - x^2\omega^2}{x^2\omega^2}\right)$ (b) $\frac{x^2\omega^2}{(a^2 - x^2\omega^2)}$
(c) $\frac{(a^2 - x^2)}{x^2}$ (d) $\frac{x^2}{(a^2 - x^2)}$

Topic 3 Some Systems Executing SHM

01 If the mass of the bob in a simple pendulum is increased to thrice its original mass and its length is made half its original length, then the new time period of oscillation is $x/2$ times its original time period. Then, the value of x is *[NCERT (New) Pg. 270, NEET 2024]*

(a) $\sqrt{3}$ (b) $\sqrt{2}$
(c) $2\sqrt{3}$ (d) 4

02 Two pendulums of length 121 cm and 100 cm start vibrating in phase. At some instant, the two are at their mean position in the same phase. The minimum number of vibrations of the shorter pendulum after which the two are again in phase at the mean position is *[NCERT (New) Pg. 271, NEET 2022]*
(a) 9 (b) 10 (c) 8 (d) 11

03 A spring is stretched by 5 cm by a force 10 N. The time period of the oscillations when a mass of 2 kg is suspended by it is *[NCERT (New) Pg. 268, NEET 2021]*
(a) 0.0628 s (b) 6.28 s
(c) 3.14 s (d) 0.628 s

04 A mass falls from a height h and its time of fall t is recorded in terms of time period T of a simple pendulum. On the surface of earth it is found that $t = 2T$. The entire set up is taken on the surface of another planet whose mass is half of earth and radius the same. Same experiment is repeated and corresponding times noted as t' and T'. *[NEET (Odisha) 2019]*
(a) $t' = \sqrt{2}T'$ (b) $t' > 2T'$
(c) $t' < 2T'$ (d) $t' = 2T'$

05 A pendulum is hung from the roof of a sufficiently high building and is moving freely to and fro like a simple harmonic oscillator. The acceleration of the bob of the pendulum is 20 m/s^2 at a distance of 5 m from the mean position. The time period of oscillation is *[NEET 2018]*
(a) 2 s (b) π s (c) 2π s (d) 1 s

06 A spring of force constant k is cut into lengths of ratio 1 : 2 : 3. They are connected in series and the new force constant is k'. If they are connected in parallel and force constant is k'', then $k' : k''$ is *[NEET 2017]*
(a) 1 : 6 (b) 1 : 9
(c) 1 : 11 (d) 1 : 14

07 A body of mass m is attached to the lower end of a spring whose upper end is fixed. The spring has negligible mass. When the mass m is slightly pulled down and released, it oscillates with a time period of 3 s. When the mass m is increased by 1 kg, the time period of oscillations becomes 5 s. The value of m in kg is *[NCERT (New) Pg. 268, NEET 2016]*
(a) $\frac{3}{4}$ (b) $\frac{4}{3}$ (c) $\frac{16}{9}$ (d) $\frac{9}{16}$

08 The period of oscillation of a mass M suspended from a spring of negligible mass is T. If along with it another mass M is also suspended, the period of oscillation will now be *[NCERT (New) Pg. 268, AIPMT 2010]*
(a) T (b) $T/\sqrt{2}$
(c) $2T$ (d) $\sqrt{2}T$

09 A simple pendulum performs simple harmonic motion about $x = 0$ with an amplitude a and time period T. The speed of the pendulum at $x = \frac{a}{2}$ will be *[NCERT (New) Pg. 266, AIPMT 2009]*
(a) $\frac{\pi a\sqrt{3}}{2T}$ (b) $\frac{\pi a}{T}$ (c) $\frac{3\pi^2 a}{T}$ (d) $\frac{\pi a\sqrt{3}}{T}$

10 A mass of 2.0 kg is put on a flat pan attached to a vertical spring fixed on the ground as shown in the figure. The mass of the spring and the pan is negligible. When pressed slightly and released the mass executes a simple harmonic motion. The spring constant is 200 N / m. What should be the minimum amplitude of the motion, so that the mass gets detached from the pan? (Take, $g = 10\ m/s^2$) *[NCERT (New) Pg. 268, AIPMT 2007]*

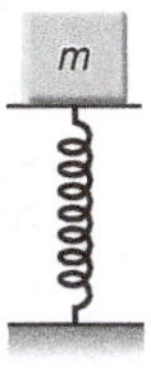

(a) 8.0 cm
(b) 10.0 cm
(c) Any value less than 12.0 cm
(d) 4.0 cm

11 A rectangular block of mass m and area of cross-section A floats in a liquid of density ρ. If it is given a small vertical displacement from equilibrium, it undergoes oscillation with a time period T. Then, *[AIPMT 2006]*
(a) $T \propto \sqrt{\rho}$ (b) $T \propto \frac{1}{\sqrt{A}}$ (c) $T \propto \frac{1}{\rho}$ (d) $T \propto \frac{1}{\sqrt{m}}$

12 Two springs of spring constants k_1 and k_2 are joined in series. The effective spring constant of the combination is given by *[AIPMT 2004]*
(a) $\sqrt{k_1 k_2}$ (b) $\frac{(k_1 + k_2)}{2}$
(c) $k_1 + k_2$ (d) $\frac{k_1 k_2}{(k_1 + k_2)}$

13 A mass is suspended separately by two springs of spring constants k_1 and k_2 in successive order. The time periods of oscillations in the two cases are T_1 and T_2, respectively. If the same mass be suspended by connecting the two springs in parallel, (as shown in figure) then the time period of oscillations is T. The correct relation is *[CBSE AIPMT 2002]*

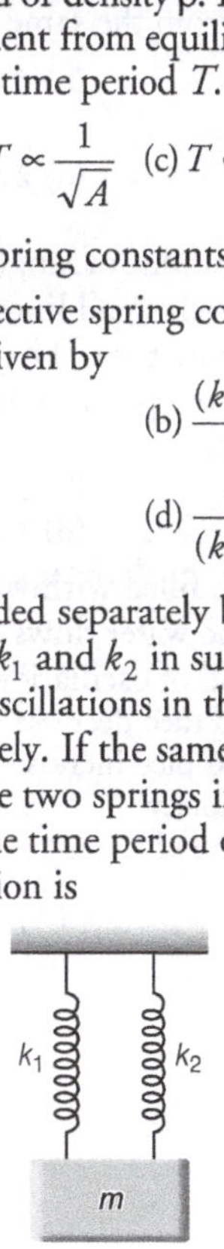

(a) $T^2 = T_1^2 + T_2^2$ (b) $T^{-2} = T_1^{-2} + T_2^{-2}$
(c) $T^{-1} = T_1^{-1} + T_2^{-1}$ (d) $T = T_1 + T_2$

14 Masses M_A and M_B hanging from the ends of strings of lenghts L_A and L_B are executing simple harmonic motions. If thier frequencies are $f_A = 2f_B$, then *[NCERT (New) Pg. 271, AIPMT 2000]*
(a) $L_A = 2L_B$ and $M_A = M_B/2$
(b) $L_A = 4L_B$ regardless of masses
(c) $L_B = 4L_A$ regardless of mass
(d) $L_A = L_B$ and $M_A = M_B$

15 A pendulum is displaced to an angle θ from its equilibrium position, then it will pass through its mean position with a velocity v equal to *[AIPMT 2000]*
(a) $\sqrt{2gl}$ (b) $\sqrt{2gl \sin\theta}$
(c) $\sqrt{2gl \cos\theta}$ (d) $\sqrt{2gl(1-\cos\theta)}$

16 The time period of a simple pendulum is 2 s. If its length is increased by 4 times, then its period becomes *[NCERT (New) Pg. 271, AIPMT 1999]*
(a) 16 s (b) 12 s
(c) 8 s (d) 4 s

17 A mass m is vertically suspended from a spring of negligible mass, the system oscillates with a frequency n. What will be the frequency of the system, if a mass $4m$ is suspended from the same spring ? *[AIPMT 1998]*
(a) $\frac{n}{4}$ (b) $4n$
(c) $\frac{n}{2}$ (d) $2n$

18 Two simple pendulums of length 0.5 m and 2.0 m respectively are given small linear displacement in one direction at the same time. They will again be in the same phase when the pendulum of shorter length has completed oscillations *[AIPMT 1998]*
(a) 5 (b) 1
(c) 2 (d) 3

19 A hollow sphere is filled with water. It is hung by a long thread. As the water flows out of a hole at the bottom, the period of oscillation will *[AIPMT 1997]*
(a) first increase and then decrease
(b) first decrease and then increase
(c) increase continuously
(d) decrease continuously

20 A simple pendulum is suspended from the roof of a trolley which moves in a horizontal direction with an acceleration α, then the time period is given by $T = 2\pi\sqrt{\left(\frac{l}{g}\right)}$, where g is equal to *[AIPMT 1991]*
(a) g (b) $g - \alpha$
(c) $g + \alpha$ (d) $\sqrt{(g^2 + \alpha^2)}$

21 A mass m is suspended from the two coupled springs connected in series. The force constant for springs are k_1 and k_2. The time period of the suspended mass will be *[AIPMT 1990]*
(a) $T = 2\pi\sqrt{\frac{m}{k_1 - k_2}}$ (b) $T = 2\pi\sqrt{\frac{mk_1k_2}{k_1 + k_2}}$
(c) $T = 2\pi\sqrt{\frac{m}{k_1 + k_2}}$ (d) $T = 2\pi\sqrt{\frac{m(k_1 + k_2)}{k_1k_2}}$

Topic 4 Free, Forced and Damped Oscillations

01 In case of a forced vibration, the resonance peak becomes very sharp when the *[AIPMT 2003]*
(a) damping force is small
(b) restoring force is small
(c) applied periodic force is small
(d) quality factor is small

02 When a damped harmonic oscillator completes 100 oscillations, its amplitude is reduced to 1/3 of its initial value. What will be its amplitude when it completes 200 oscillations ? *[NCERT (New) Pg. 256, AIPMT 2002]*
(a) $\frac{1}{5}$ (b) $\frac{2}{3}$
(c) $\frac{1}{6}$ (d) $\frac{1}{9}$

03 Resonance is an example of *[AIPMT 1999]*
(a) tuning fork (b) forced vibration
(c) free vibration (d) damped vibration

• Key Index

Topic 1

1	(b)	2	(c)	3	(c)	4	(d)	5	(d)	6	(c)	7	(a)	8	(c)	9	(c)	10	(c)
11	(b)	12	(d)	13	(c)	14	(b)	15	(c)	16	(c)	17	(b)	18	(b)	19	(d)	20	(c)
21	(d)	22	(d)	23	(b)	24	(b)	25	(a)	26	(a)	27	(b)	28	(d)	29	(c)	30	(c)
31	(a)	32	(a)	33	(c)	34	(c)	35	(a)										

Topic 2

1	(b)	2	(d)	3	(c)	4	(a)	5	(b)	6	(c)	7	(d)	8	(a)	9	(b)	10	(c)

Topic 3

1	(b)	2	(d)	3	(d)	4	(d)	5	(b)	6	(c)	7	(d)	8	(d)	9	(d)	10	(b)
11	(b)	12	(d)	13	(b)	14	(c)	15	(d)	16	(d)	17	(c)	18	(c)	19	(a)	20	(d)
21	(d)																		

Topic 4

1	(a)	2	(d)	3	(b)

Detailed Explanations

Topic 1

01. *(b)* Given, $x = 5\sin\left(\pi t + \frac{\pi}{3}\right)$ m ...(i)

The standard equation for SHM is

$$x = A\sin(\omega t + \phi) \quad \text{...(ii)}$$

Thus, comparing Eqs. (i) and (ii), we get

$$A = 5 \text{ m and } \omega = \pi$$

$$\Rightarrow \quad \frac{2\pi}{T} = \pi \Rightarrow T = 2\text{ s}$$

Hence, option (b) is correct.

02. *(c)* The motion of the particle performing SHM is represented by

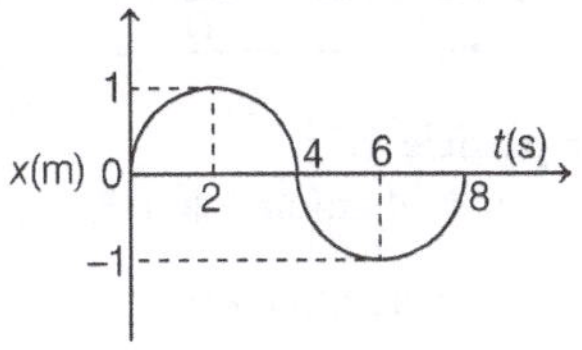

$$x = A\sin\omega t = 1\sin\frac{2\pi}{T}t = 1\sin\frac{2\pi}{8}t$$

$$\Rightarrow x = \sin\left(\frac{\pi}{4}t\right)$$

$$\therefore \text{ velocity, } v = \frac{dx}{dt} = \frac{d}{dt}\sin\left(\frac{\pi}{4}\right)t$$

$$= \frac{\pi}{4}\cos\left(\frac{\pi}{4}\right)t$$

$\therefore$ Acceleration of the particle,

$$a = \frac{dv}{dt} = \frac{d}{dt}\left[\frac{\pi}{4}\cos\left(\frac{\pi}{4}\right)t\right]$$

$$= -\frac{\pi}{4}\cdot\frac{\pi}{4}\cdot\sin\left(\frac{\pi}{4}t\right)$$

$$\Rightarrow \quad a = -\frac{\pi^2}{16}\sin\left(\frac{\pi}{4}\cdot t\right)$$

At $\quad t = 2$ s

$$a = -\frac{\pi^2}{16}\cdot\sin\left(\frac{\pi}{4}\cdot 2\right)$$

$$= -\frac{\pi^2}{16}\text{ ms}^{-2}$$

03. *(c)* $\sin\omega t$ and $\cos\omega t$, both are periodic function of period $\frac{2\pi}{\omega}$.

We know that sum of two periodic functions is also a periodic function, hence, $\sin\omega t + \cos\omega t$ represents periodic motion.

04. *(d)* In SHM, equation of displacement of a particle is $y = a\sin\omega t$ and equation of acceleration of a particle is

$$A = a\omega^2\sin\omega t$$

$$= a\omega^2\sin(\omega t + \pi)$$

$\therefore$ Phase difference between displacement and acceleration of a particle is

$$= (\omega t + \pi) - \omega t$$

$$= \pi \text{ rad}$$

05. *(d)* Distance covered in one time period

$$x = OP + PO + OQ + QO$$

$$= A + A + A + A$$

$$= 4A$$

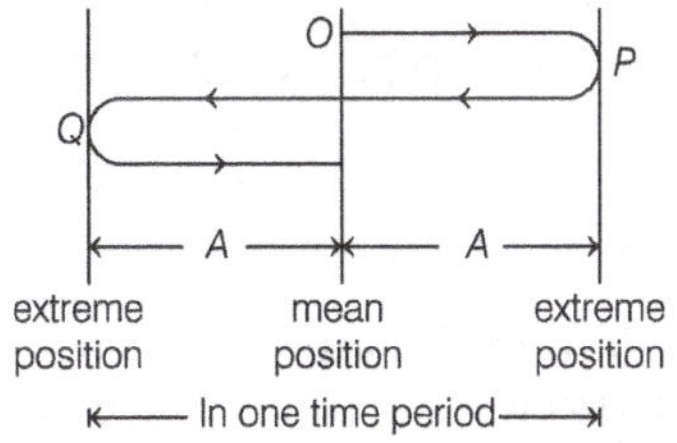

06. *(c)* The average velocity of a particle executing simple harmonic motion (SHM) is

$$v_{avg} = \frac{\text{Total displacement}}{\text{Time interval}}$$

$$= \frac{x_f - x_i}{T}$$

where, x_f and x_i are the initial and final position of the particle executing SHM.

$\because$ Displacement,

$$x_f - x_i = 0$$

$$\therefore \quad v_{av} = \frac{0}{T} = 0$$

Hence, the average velocity is zero.

07. *(a)*

key idea

If two waves executing simple harmonic motion, travelling in same direction with amplitudes A_1 and A_2, then you can find resultant amplitude with the help of following formula.

$$A = \sqrt{A_1^2 + A_2^2 + 2A_1A_2\cos\phi}$$

where ϕ is phase difference.

The displacement of given particle is

$$y = A_0 + A\sin\omega t + B\cos\omega t \quad \text{...(i)}$$

The general equation of SHM can be given as

$$x = a\sin\omega t + b\cos\omega t \quad \text{...(ii)}$$

So, from Eqs. (i) and (ii), we can say that A_0 is the value of mean position, at which $y = 0$.

$\therefore$ Amplitude,

$$R = \sqrt{A^2 + B^2 + 2AB\cos\theta}$$

As two function sine and cosine have phase shift to 90°.

$$\therefore \quad R = \sqrt{A^2 + B^2} \quad [\because \cos 90° = 0]$$

08. *(c)*

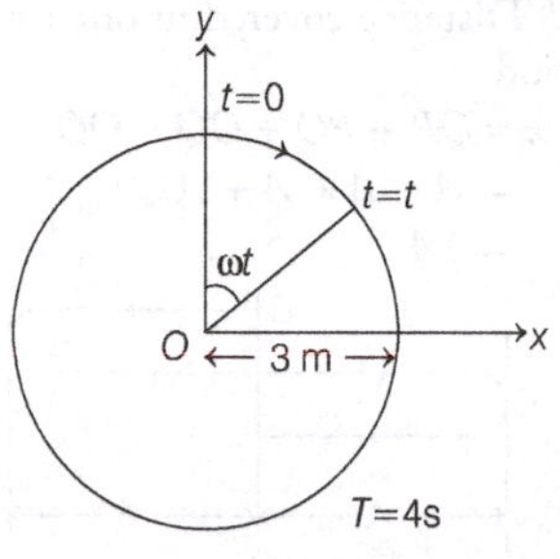

As the general equation of displacement of a particle will be in the form

$$y = A\cos\omega t$$

Here,

$$A = 3\text{ m}$$

Then, $\omega = \frac{2\pi}{T} = \frac{2\pi}{4}$ [Given, $T = 4$ s]

$$= \frac{\pi}{2}$$

$$\therefore \quad y = 3\cos\left(\frac{\pi}{2}t\right) \text{ (in metre)}$$

09. *(c)* Given, when $x = 2$ cm

$$|\mathbf{v}| = |\mathbf{a}|$$

$$\Rightarrow \omega\sqrt{A^2 - x^2} = \omega^2 x$$

$$\Rightarrow \quad \omega = \frac{\sqrt{A^2 - x^2}}{x} = \frac{\sqrt{9-4}}{2}$$

$$\Rightarrow \text{Angular velocity } \omega = \frac{\sqrt{5}}{2}$$

$\therefore$ Time period of motion

$$T = \frac{2\pi}{\omega} = \frac{4\pi}{\sqrt{5}}\text{ s}$$

• Concept Enhancer

Magnitude of velocity of particle when it is at displacement x from mean position $= \omega\sqrt{A^2 - x^2}$

Also, magnitude of acceleration of particle in SHM $= \omega^2 x$

10. *(c)* The resultant displacement is given by

$$y = y_1 + y_2$$

$$= \sqrt{a^2 + b^2}\sin(\omega t + \phi)$$

Hence, the motion of superimposed wave is simple harmonic with amplitude $\sqrt{a^2 + b^2}$.

11. *(b)* Let A be the amplitude of oscillation, then

$$v_1^2 = \omega^2(A^2 - x_1^2) \quad \text{...(i)}$$

$$v_2^2 = \omega^2(A^2 - x_2^2) \quad \text{...(ii)}$$

On subtracting Eq. (ii) from Eq. (i), we get

$$v_1^2 - v_2^2 = \omega^2(x_2^2 - x_1^2)$$

$$\Rightarrow \quad \omega = \sqrt{\frac{v_1^2 - v_2^2}{x_2^2 - x_1^2}}$$

$$\Rightarrow \quad \frac{2\pi}{T} = \sqrt{\frac{v_1^2 - v_2^2}{x_2^2 - x_1^2}}$$

$$\Rightarrow \quad T = 2\pi\sqrt{\frac{x_2^2 - x_1^2}{v_1^2 - v_2^2}}$$

12. *(d)* For a particle executing SHM, we have maximum acceleration,

$$\alpha = A\omega^2 \quad \text{...(i)}$$

Maximum velocity,

$$\beta = A\omega \quad \text{...(ii)}$$

On dividing Eq. (i) by Eq. (ii), we get

$$\frac{\alpha}{\beta} = \frac{A\omega^2}{A\omega} \Rightarrow \frac{\alpha}{\beta} = \omega = \frac{2\pi}{T}$$

i.e. $$T = \frac{2\pi\beta}{\alpha}$$

13. *(c)* As, $x = A\cos\omega t$

$$\therefore \quad v = \frac{dx}{dt} = -A\omega\sin\omega t \quad \text{...(i)}$$

and

$$a = \frac{d^2x}{dt^2} = -A\omega^2\cos\omega t \quad \text{...(ii)}$$

We can find the correct graph by putting different values of t in Eq. (ii).

At $t = 0$, $a = -A\omega^2$

At $t = \frac{T}{4}$, $a = -A\omega^2\cos\left(\frac{2\pi}{T} \times \frac{T}{4}\right) = 0$

At $t = \frac{T}{2}$, $a = -A\omega^2\cos\left(\frac{2\pi}{T} \times \frac{T}{2}\right)$

$$= A\omega^2$$

At $t = \frac{3T}{4}$,

$$a = -A\omega^2\cos\left(\frac{2\pi}{T} \times \frac{3T}{4}\right) = 0$$

At $t = T$, $a = -A\omega^2\cos\left(\frac{2\pi}{T} \times T\right)$

$$= -A\omega^2$$

This condition is represented by graph in option (c).

14. *(b)* For a simple harmonic motion,

$$a \propto \frac{d^2y}{dt^2} \propto -y$$

Hence, equations $y = \sin\omega t - \cos\omega t$ and $y = 5\cos\left(\frac{3\pi}{4} - 3\omega t\right)$ are satisfying this condition of SHM.

15. *(c)*

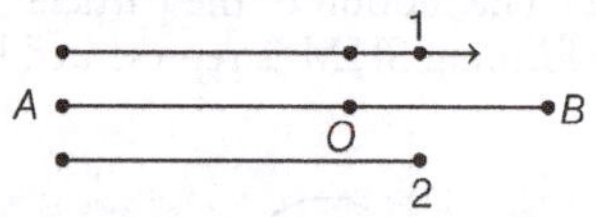

For particle 1,

$$x_1 = A\sin(\omega t + \phi_1)$$

$$\frac{A}{2} = A\sin(\omega t + \phi_1)$$

$$\omega t + \phi_1 = \frac{\pi}{6} \quad \text{...(i)}$$

For particle 2,

$$x_2 = A\sin(\omega t + \phi_2)$$

$$\frac{A}{2} = A\sin(\omega t + \phi_2)$$

$$(\omega t + \phi_2) = \left(\pi - \frac{\pi}{6}\right) \quad \text{...(ii)}$$

[∵ partilce 2 moving towards mean position]

Phase difference,

$$\Delta\phi = \phi_2 - \phi_1 = (\omega t + \phi_2) - (\omega t + \phi_1)$$

Using Eqs (i) and (ii), we get

$$\Delta\phi = \pi - \frac{\pi}{6} - \frac{\pi}{6} = \frac{2\pi}{3}$$

16. *(c)* For a particle executing SHM

Acceleration $(a) \propto -$ displacement ...(i)

Given $x = a\sin^2 \omega t$ ...(ii)

On differentiating the above equation w.r.t. t, we get

$$\frac{dx}{dt} = 2a\omega(\sin \omega t)(\cos\omega t)$$

Again differentiating, we get

$$\frac{d^2x}{dt^2} = a = 2a\omega^2 [\cos^2 \omega t - \sin^2 \omega t]$$

$$= 2a\omega^2 \cos 2\omega t$$

The given equation does not satisfy the condition for SHM [Eq. (i)]. Therefore, motion is not simple harmonic.

17. *(b)* As we know that the condition for a body executing SHM is $F = -kx$

So, $a = \frac{F}{m} = -\frac{k}{m}x$

or $a = -\omega^2 x$

Acceleration $\propto -$ (displacement)

$$A \propto -y$$

$$A = -\omega^2 y$$

$$A = -\frac{k}{m}y$$

$$A = -ky$$

Here, $y = x + a$

∴ Acceleration $= -k(x + a)$

18. *(b)* Maximum acceleration of body executing SHM is given by

$$\alpha_{max} = \omega^2 a$$

So, for two different cases,

$$\frac{\alpha_{max_1}}{\alpha_{max_2}} = \frac{\omega_1^2}{\omega_2^2} \quad (\because a \text{ is same})$$

$$= \frac{(100)^2}{(1000)^2} = \frac{1}{10^2}$$

19. *(d)* According to the question, equation of motion of SHM is

$$x = a\sin\left(\omega t + \frac{\pi}{6}\right)$$

velocity of body is given by

$$v = \frac{dx}{dt} = a\omega\cos\left(\omega t + \frac{\pi}{6}\right)$$

$$\frac{a\omega}{2} = a\omega\cos\left(\omega t + \frac{\pi}{6}\right)$$

$$\frac{1}{2} = \cos\left(\omega t + \frac{\pi}{6}\right)$$

$$\omega t + \frac{\pi}{6} = \frac{\pi}{3} \quad \left[\because \cos\frac{\pi}{3} = \frac{1}{2}\right]$$

$$\Rightarrow \omega t = \frac{\pi}{6}$$

$$\frac{2\pi}{T}t = \frac{\pi}{6}$$

$$\Rightarrow t = \frac{T}{12}$$

20. *(c)* Let displacement equation of particle executing SHM is

$$x = a\sin \omega t$$

As particle travels half of the amplitude from the equilibrium position, so

$$x = \frac{a}{2}$$

Therefore, $\frac{a}{2} = a\sin \omega t$

or $\sin \omega t = \frac{1}{2} = \sin\frac{\pi}{6}$

or $\omega t = \frac{\pi}{6}$ or $t = \frac{\pi}{6\omega}$

or $t = \frac{\pi}{6\left(\frac{2\pi}{T}\right)} \quad \left(\text{as, } \omega = \frac{2\pi}{T}\right)$

or $t = \frac{T}{12}$

21. *(d)* Maximum speed of a particle executing SHM is given by,

$$v_{max} = a\omega = a(2\pi n)$$

$$\Rightarrow n = \frac{v_{max}}{2\pi a}$$

Here, $v_{max} = 31.4$ cm/s, $a = 5$ cm

On substituting, the given values, we get

$$n = \frac{31.4}{2 \times 3.14 \times 5} = 1 \text{ Hz}$$

22. *(d)* In simple harmonic motion, the displacement equation is, $x = a\sin \omega t$.

Velocity, $v = \frac{dx}{dt} = a\omega\cos\omega t$

$$v = a\omega\sqrt{1 - \sin^2 \omega t}$$

$$v = \omega\sqrt{a^2 - x^2} \quad \text{...(i)}$$

Acceleration, $\alpha = \frac{dv}{dt} = \frac{d}{dt}(a\omega\cos\omega t)$

$$\alpha = -\omega^2 x \quad \text{...(ii)}$$

Hence, it is clear that when v is maximum, then α is minimum (i.e. zero) or *vice-versa.*

23. *(b)* The frequency of vibrations of string is

$$n = \frac{1}{2}\sqrt{\frac{g}{l}} \quad \text{...(i)}$$

Given, $n_A = 2n_B$

$$\therefore \frac{1}{2}\sqrt{\frac{g}{l_A}} = 2\cdot\frac{1}{2}\sqrt{\frac{g}{l_B}}$$

or $\frac{1}{l_A} = \frac{4}{l_B}$

or $l_B = 4l_A$

24. *(b)* Two simple harmonic motions can be written as

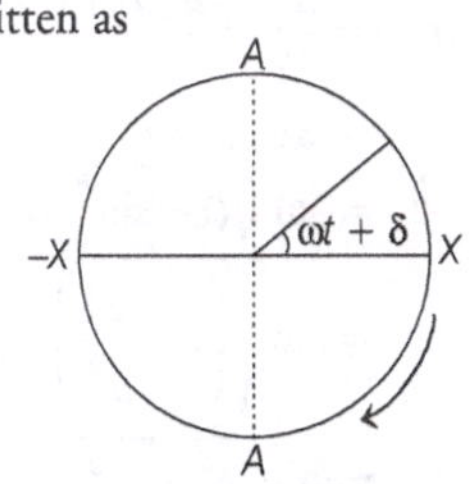

$$x = a\sin(\omega t + \delta) \quad \text{...(i)}$$

and $y = a\sin\left(\omega t + \delta + \frac{\pi}{2}\right)$

or $y = a\cos(\omega t + \delta)$ ...(ii)

On squaring and adding Eqs. (i) and (ii), we get

$$x^2 + y^2 = a^2 [\sin^2(\omega t + \delta) + \cos^2(\omega t + \delta)]$$

or $x^2 + y^2 = a^2$

$$(\because \sin^2\theta + \cos^2\theta = 1)$$

This is the equation of a circle.

At $(\omega t + \delta) = 0$; $x = 0$, $y = a$

At $(\omega t + \delta) = \frac{\pi}{2}$; $x = a$, $y = 0$

At $(\omega t + \delta) = \pi$; $x = 0$, $y = -a$

At $(\omega t + \delta) = \frac{3\pi}{2}$; $x = -a$, $y = 0$

At $(\omega t + \delta) = 2\pi$; $x = 0$, $y = a$

Thus, it is obvious that motion of particle is traversed in clockwise direction.

25. *(a)* Maximum acceleration

$$= A\omega^2 = 0.01 \times (2\pi\nu)^2$$

$$= 0.01 \times 4\pi^2 \times 60 \times 60$$

$$= 144\pi^2 \text{ m/s}^2$$

26. *(a)* The two simple harmonic motions can be written as

$$x = a\sin\omega t \quad \text{...(i)}$$

and $$y = a\sin\left(\omega t + \frac{\pi}{2}\right)$$

$$y = a\cos\omega t \quad \text{...(ii)}$$

On squaring and adding Eqs. (i) and (ii), we get

$$x^2 + y^2 = a^2(\sin^2\omega t + \cos^2\omega t)$$

or $x^2 + y^2 = a^2$

This is the equation of a circular motion with radius a.

27. *(b)* Velocity of the particle executing SHM at any instant is defined as the time rate of change of its displacement at that instant. Let the displacement of the particle at an instant t is given by

$$x = a\sin\omega t$$

$\therefore$ Velocity $v = \frac{dx}{dt} = \frac{d(a\sin\omega t)}{dt}$

$$= a\omega\cos\omega t$$

$$= a\omega\sqrt{(1-\sin^2\omega t)}$$

$$= a\omega\sqrt{\left(1-\frac{x^2}{a^2}\right)}$$

$$= \omega\sqrt{(a^2 - x^2)}$$

At mean position, $x = 0$

$\therefore$ $v_{max} = \omega a$

According to problem,

$$v = \frac{v_{max}}{2} = \frac{a\omega}{2}$$

But, $v = \omega\sqrt{a^2 - x^2}$

$\therefore$ $\frac{a\omega}{2} = \omega\sqrt{a^2 - x^2}$ or $x = \frac{\sqrt{3}}{2}a$

28. *(d)* We know that maximum velocity is given by

$$v_{max} = A\omega$$

According to the question,

$$\frac{v_{max}}{2} = \frac{A\omega}{2} = \omega\sqrt{A^2 - y^2}$$

$$\frac{A^2}{4} = A^2 - y^2$$

$$\Rightarrow \quad y^2 = A^2 - \frac{A^2}{4} \Rightarrow y = \frac{\sqrt{3}A}{2}$$

29. *(c)* In transverse wave motion individual particles of the medium execute simple harmonic motion about their mean position in a direction perpendicular to the direction of propagation of wave motion. Wave moving through a string fixed at both ends executes SHM.

30. *(c)* Here, the phase difference between waves is $\frac{\pi}{4}$. So, the resultant path of particle will be ellipse.

Alternate Solution

$$x = 2\sin\omega t$$

$$y = 2\sin\left(\omega t + \frac{\pi}{4}\right)$$

$$\sin\omega t = \frac{x}{2} \quad \text{...(i)}$$

$$\cos\omega t = \sqrt{1-\sin^2\omega t}$$

$$\cos\omega t = \sqrt{1-\left(\frac{x}{2}\right)^2} = \sqrt{1-\frac{x^2}{2}} \quad \text{...(ii)}$$

$$y = 2\sin\left(\omega t + \frac{\pi}{4}\right) = \frac{2(\sin\omega t + \cos\omega t)}{\sqrt{2}}$$

Using the values from Eqs. (i) and (ii), we get

$$y = \sqrt{2}\left(\frac{x}{2} + \sqrt{\frac{1-x^2}{4}}\right)$$

$$\Rightarrow \frac{y}{\sqrt{2}} - \frac{x}{2} = \sqrt{1-\frac{x^2}{4}}$$

$$\Rightarrow \frac{y^2}{2} + \frac{x^2}{4} - \frac{x^4}{\sqrt{2}} = 1 - \frac{x^2}{4}$$

$$\Rightarrow \frac{x^2}{2} + \frac{y^2}{2} - \frac{xy}{\sqrt{2}} - 1 = 0$$

$$\Rightarrow x^2 + y^2 - \sqrt{2}xy - 2 = 0$$

$$\Rightarrow x^2 + y^2 - \sqrt{2}xy = 2 \Rightarrow x^2 + y^2 - \sqrt{2}xy = 2$$

Which is an equation of ellipse.

31. *(a)* Equation of SHM is

$$x = a\sin\omega t \text{ or } x = a\sin\left(\frac{2\pi}{T}\right)t,$$

when $x = a$, then $a = a\sin\left(\frac{2\pi}{T}\right)t$

$$\Rightarrow \quad t = \frac{T}{4}$$

when $x = \frac{a}{2}$, then $\frac{a}{2} = a\sin\left(\frac{2\pi}{T}\cdot t\right)$

$$t = \frac{T}{12}$$

Hence, time taken to travel from

$$x = a \text{ to } x = \frac{a}{2} = \frac{T}{4} - \frac{T}{12} = \frac{T}{6}$$

32. *(a)* Time period of body executing SHM is given by

$$T = \frac{2\pi}{\omega} = 2\pi\sqrt{\frac{x}{a}} \quad \text{...(i)}$$

From Eq. (i) $\omega = \sqrt{\frac{a}{x}}$ or $\omega^2 = \frac{a}{x}$

Here, $a = 2.0\text{ m/s}^2$, $x = 0.02$ m

$\therefore$ $\omega^2 = \frac{2.0}{0.02}$ or $\omega^2 = 100$

or $\omega = 10$ rad/s

33. *(c)* Velocity of the particle executing SHM at any instant is

$$v = \omega\sqrt{(a^2 - x^2)}$$

Case I $\quad 10 = \omega\sqrt{a^2 - 16} \quad$ ...(i)

Case II $\quad 8 = \omega\sqrt{a^2 - 25} \quad$ ...(ii)

On dividing Eq. (ii) by Eq. (i), we get

$$\frac{5}{4} = \frac{\sqrt{a^2-16}}{\sqrt{a^2-25}} \text{ or } \frac{25}{16} = \frac{a^2-16}{a^2-25}$$

or $16a^2 - 256 = 25a^2 - 625$

or $a^2 = \frac{369}{9}$

On putting value of a^2 in Eq. (i), we get

$$10 = \omega\sqrt{\left(\frac{369}{9} - 16\right)}$$

or $\omega = \frac{10 \times 3}{15} = 2$ rad/s

$\therefore$ Time period, $T = \frac{2\pi}{\omega} = \frac{2\pi}{2} = \pi$ s

34. *(c)* $x = A_1\sin\omega t$

$$y = A_2\sin(\omega t + \pi)$$

$$y = -A_2\sin(\omega t)$$

$\therefore$ $\frac{y}{x} = \frac{-A_2}{A_1}$, $y = -\frac{A_2 x}{A_1}$

This is represent a straight line.

35. *(a)* The restoring force F acting on the particle at that instant is given by

$$F = -kx$$

where, k is known as force constant. Hence, in given options, option (a) is correct.

$$F = -AKx$$

Here, $k = AK$

Topic 2

01. *(b)* In simple harmonic motion, both kinetic energy and potential energy attain their maximum value two times in one complete oscillation.

Hence, frequency of kinetic energy and potential energy is 2 for one complete oscillation.

So, the frequency of the potential energy of a body executing SHM with frequency n is $2n$.

02. *(d)*

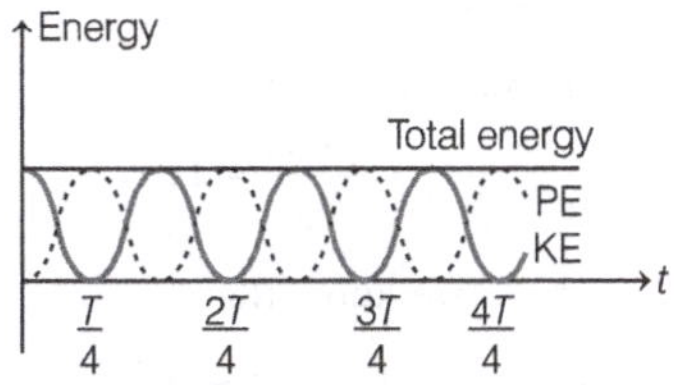

The variation of PE and KE with time is shown in figure by dotted parabolic curve and solid parabolic curve respectively.

Figure indicates that maximum values of total energy, KE and PE of SHM are equal.

Now, $\text{KE} = K_0 \cos^2 \omega t$

$\therefore \quad \text{KE}_{max} = K_0$

So, $\text{PE}_{max} = K_0$

and $(E)_{\text{Total}} = K_0$

• Concept Enhancer

In simple harmonic motion, kinetic energy and potential energy are periodic function of time and the time period of each being half the time period of oscillation.

03. *(c)* Potential energy is given by

$$U = \frac{1}{2} kx^2$$

The corresponding graph is shown in figure.

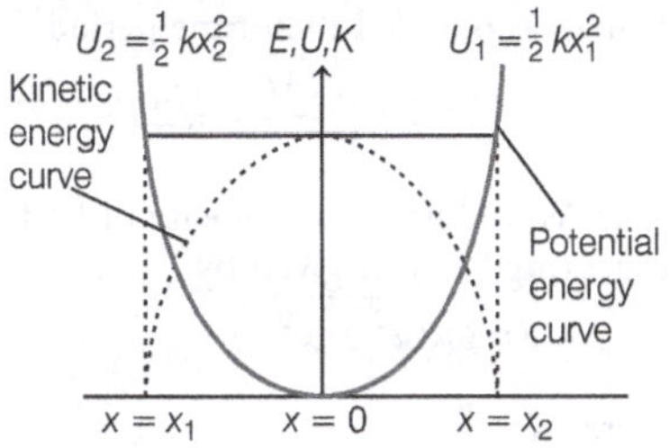

04. *(a)* Total energy is

$$E = \frac{1}{2} m\omega^2 a^2$$

When the particle is half way to its end point i.e. at half of its amplitude, then

$$x = \frac{a}{2}$$

Hence, potential energy

$$U = \frac{1}{2} m\omega^2 \left(\frac{a}{2}\right)^2$$

$$= \frac{1}{4}\left(\frac{1}{2} m\omega^2 a^2\right)$$

$$\Rightarrow \quad U = \frac{E}{4}$$

(where, E is the total energy)

• Concept Enhancer

In simple harmonic motion, magnitude of velocity is maximum, where magnitude of acceleration is minimum and *vice versa*.

05. *(b)* Expression of kinetic energy is

$$K = \frac{1}{2} k(a^2 - x^2) \quad \text{...(i)}$$

Expression of potential energy is

$$U = \frac{1}{2} kx^2 \quad \text{...(ii)}$$

where, $k = m\omega^2$

We observe that at mean position ($x = 0$), kinetic energy is maximum $\left(\frac{1}{2} ka^2\right)$ and potential energy is minimum (zero). Also at extreme positions ($x = \pm a$), kinetic energy is zero and potential energy is maximum $\left(\frac{1}{2} ka^2\right)$. Thus, displacement between positions of maximum potential energy and maximum kinetic energy is $\pm a$.

• Concept Enhancer

Kinetic energy is zero at extreme positions but potential energy at mean position need not be zero. It is minimum at mean position.

06. *(c)*

key idea

In simple harmonic motion, kinetic energy is maximum at mean position (due to its maximum velocity) and is minimum at extreme postion (due to its zero velocity)

In SHM, the total energy

$$E = U + K$$

$$= \frac{1}{2} m\omega^2 x^2 + \frac{1}{2} m\omega^2 (a^2 - x^2)$$

$$= \frac{1}{2} m\omega^2 a^2 = \frac{1}{2} ka^2,$$

where $k =$ force constant $= m\omega^2$

Thus, total energy depends on k *and* a.

07. *(d)* Total energy of the particle executing SHM at instant t is given by

$$E = \frac{1}{2} m\omega^2 a^2 \quad \text{...(i)}$$

And kinetic energy of the particle at instant t is given by

$$E_K = \frac{1}{2} m\omega^2 (a^2 - x^2) \quad \text{...(ii)}$$

When, $x = \frac{a}{2}$, $E_K = \frac{1}{2} m\omega^2 \left(a^2 - \frac{a^2}{4}\right)$

$$= \frac{1}{2} m\omega^2 \times \frac{3}{4} a^2$$

or $\quad E_K = \frac{1}{2} \times \frac{3}{4} m\omega^2 a^2 \quad \text{...(iii)}$

From Eqs. (i) and (iii), we get

$$\frac{E_K}{E} = \frac{3}{4}$$

$$\Rightarrow \quad E_K = \frac{3}{4} E$$

08. *(a)* The maximum potential energy of a particle executing SHM is given by,

$$U_{\text{max}} = \frac{1}{2} m\omega^2 a^2 \quad \text{...(i)}$$

Also, total energy of the particle at instant t is given by

$$E = \frac{1}{2} m\omega^2 a^2 \quad \text{...(ii)}$$

So, when $E = 160$ J, then maximum potential energy of particle will also be 160 J.

Alternate Solution

$(\text{KE})_{\text{max}} = (\text{PE})_{\text{max}}$

$= \text{Total mechanical energy}$

So, Total mechanical energy = 160 J

09. *(b)* Potential energy of the body executing SHM is given by

$$U = \frac{1}{2} m\omega^2 x^2$$

Total energy of the body executing SHM is

$$E = \frac{1}{2} m\omega^2 a^2$$

According to problem,

$$U = \frac{1}{4} E$$

$$\therefore \quad \frac{1}{2} m\omega^2 x^2 = \frac{1}{4} \times \frac{1}{2} m\omega^2 a^2$$

or $\quad x^2 = \frac{a^2}{4} \quad$ or $\quad x = \frac{a}{2}$

10. *(c)* Potential energy of particle is

$$U = \frac{1}{2} m\omega^2 x^2 \quad \text{...(i)}$$

and kinetic energy of particle is

$$T = \frac{1}{2} m\omega^2 (a^2 - x^2) \quad \text{...(ii)}$$

From Eqs. (i) and (ii), we get

$$\frac{T}{U} = \frac{a^2 - x^2}{x^2}$$

Topic 3

01. *(b)* Time period of a bob is given by,

$$T = 2\pi\sqrt{\frac{l}{g}}$$

According to question, $T' = 2\pi\sqrt{\frac{l}{2g}}$

$$= \frac{2\pi\sqrt{l}}{\sqrt{2g}}$$

Thus, $T' = \frac{T}{\sqrt{2}}$

$$T' = \frac{T}{\sqrt{2}} = \frac{x}{2}T$$

Hence, $x = \sqrt{2}$

02. *(d)* Given, $l_1 = 121$ cm $= 1.21$ m

$l_2 = 100$ cm $= 1$ m

Let T_1 and T_2 be the time periods of longer and shorter pendulum, respectively.

Since, $T = 2\pi\sqrt{l/g}$

$$\Rightarrow \frac{T_1}{T_2} = \sqrt{\frac{l_1}{l_2}} = \sqrt{\frac{1\cdot 21}{1}} = 1\cdot 1 = \frac{11}{10}$$

$\Rightarrow \quad 10\,T_1 = 11\,T_2$

$\therefore$ 10 vibrations of longer pendulum $= 11$ vibrations of shorter pendulum

$\therefore$ Minimum number of vibrations of shorter pendulum $= 11$

03. *(d)* Given,

$m = 2$ kg

$x = 5$ cm $= 0.05$ m

$F = 10$ N

As we know that magnitude of spring force,

$F = kx$

$\Rightarrow \quad 10\text{ N} = k\,(0.05\text{ m})$

$\Rightarrow \quad k = 200$ N/m

Now, time period of the oscillation,

$$T = 2\pi\sqrt{\frac{m}{k}} \Rightarrow T = 2\pi\sqrt{\frac{2}{200}}$$

Time period, $T = 0.628$ s

04. *(d)* Time of fall t is given by

$$t = \sqrt{\frac{2h}{g}} \quad \ldots\text{(i)}$$

The time period of simple pendulum is

$$T = 2\pi\sqrt{\frac{l}{g}} \quad \ldots\text{(ii)}$$

where, l is the length of the pendulum. From Eq. (i) and (ii), since h and l are constant, so we can conclude that

$$t \propto \frac{1}{\sqrt{g}} \text{ and } T \propto \frac{1}{\sqrt{g}}$$

$$\therefore \quad \frac{t}{T} = 1$$

Thus, the ratio of time of fall and time period of pendulum is independent of value of gravity (g) or any other parameter like mass and radius of the planet. Thus, the relation between t' and T' on another planet irrespective of its mass or radius will remains same as it was on earth i.e.

$$t' = 2T'$$

05. *(b)* The acceleration of particle executing SHM at any instant (at position x) is given as

$$a = -\omega^2 x$$

$$\Rightarrow \quad |a| = \omega^2 x \quad \ldots\text{(i)}$$

Here, $x = 5$ m, $|a| = 20$ ms^{-2}

On substituting the given values in Eq. (i), we get

$$20 = \omega^2 \times 5$$

$$\Rightarrow \quad \omega^2 = \frac{20}{5} = 4$$

or $\quad \omega = 2$ rad s^{-1}

As, we know that

$$\text{Time period, } T = \frac{2\pi}{\omega} \quad \ldots\text{(ii)}$$

On substituting the value of ω in Eq. (ii), we get

$$T = \frac{2\pi}{2} = \pi \text{ s}$$

06. *(c)*

key idea

When two springs of spring constant k_1 and k_2 are connected in (i) series and (ii) parallel, then their effective time constant is calculated by following formulae.

In series, $\frac{1}{k_s} = \frac{1}{k_1} + \frac{1}{k_2}$. In parallel, $k_p = k_1 + k_2$

When the spring is cut into pieces, they will have the new force constant. The spring is divided into 1 : 2 : 3 ratio. When the pieces are connected in series, the resultant force constant

$$\frac{1}{k'} = \frac{1}{k_1} + \frac{1}{k_2} + \frac{1}{k_3} = \frac{1}{x} + \frac{1}{2x} + \frac{1}{3x}$$

$$k' = \frac{6x}{11}$$

In parallel, the net force constant

$$K'' = x + 2x + 3x = 6x$$

The required ratio

$$\frac{K'}{K''} = \frac{6x/11}{6x} = 1:11$$

07. *(d)* As we know that

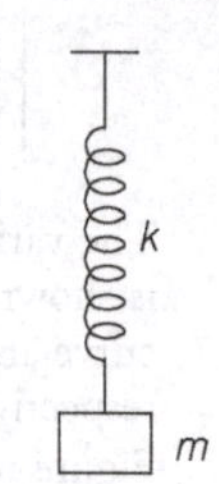

Time period, $T = 2\pi\sqrt{\frac{m}{k}}$

Case I $\quad T_1 = 2\pi\sqrt{\frac{m}{k}}$ ...(i)

Case II When the mass m is increased by 1 kg, then $T_2 = 2\pi\sqrt{\frac{m+1}{k}}$ ...(ii)

From Eqs. (ii) and (i), we get

$$\frac{T_2}{T_1} = \sqrt{\frac{m+1}{m}}$$

$$\Rightarrow \quad \frac{5}{3} = \sqrt{\frac{m+1}{m}} \Rightarrow \frac{25}{9} = \frac{m+1}{m}$$

$$\Rightarrow \quad \frac{25}{9} = 1 + \frac{1}{m} \Rightarrow \frac{1}{m} = \frac{16}{9}$$

$$\therefore \quad m = \frac{9}{16} \text{ kg}$$

08. *(d)* Time period of spring pendulum,

$$T = 2\pi\sqrt{\frac{M}{k}}.$$

If mass is doubled then time period

$$T' = 2\pi\sqrt{\frac{2M}{k}} = \sqrt{2}T$$

09. *(d)* As we know, the velocity of body executing SHM is given by

$$v = \omega\sqrt{a^2 - x^2}$$

Here, $x = \frac{a}{2}$

$$\therefore \quad v = \omega\sqrt{a^2 - \frac{a^2}{4}} = \omega\sqrt{\frac{3a^2}{4}}$$

$$= \frac{2\pi}{T}\frac{a\sqrt{3}}{2} = \frac{\pi a\sqrt{3}}{T}$$

• Concept Enhancer

Use the equation of motion of a body executing SHM.

i.e. $\quad x = a\sin\omega t$

10. *(b)* Let the minimum amplitude of SHM be a. Restoring force on spring

$$F = ka$$

Restoring force is balanced by weight mg of block. For mass to execute simple harmonic motion of amplitude a.

$\therefore \quad ka = mg \quad \text{or} \quad a = \dfrac{mg}{k}$

Here, $m = 2\text{ kg}, k = 200\text{ N/m}$

$g = 10\text{ m/s}^2$

$$\therefore \quad a = \frac{2 \times 10}{200} = \frac{10}{100}\text{ m}$$

$$= \frac{10}{100} \times 100 = 10\text{ cm}$$

Hence, minimum amplitude of the motion should be 10 cm so that the mass gets detached from the pan.

11. *(b)* Applied force = Upthrust

$\therefore \quad ma = -Ax\rho g$

or $\quad a = -\dfrac{A\rho g}{m}x = -\omega^2 x$

This is the equation of simple harmonic motion. Time period of oscillation,

$$T = \frac{2\pi}{\omega} = 2\pi\sqrt{\frac{m}{A\rho g}} \Rightarrow T \propto \frac{1}{\sqrt{A}}$$

12. *(d)*

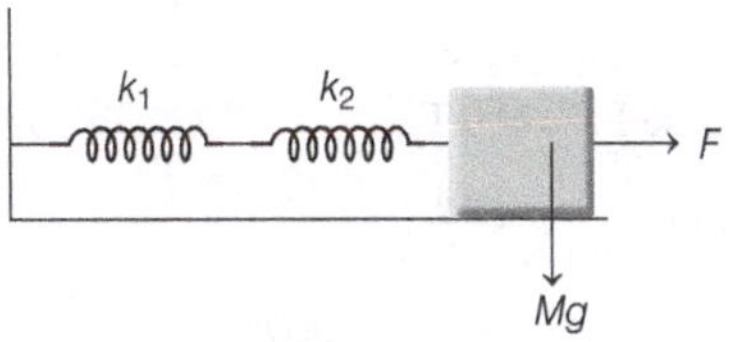

Here, $y = y_1 + y_2$ or $\dfrac{F}{k} = \dfrac{F_1}{k_1} + \dfrac{F_2}{k_2}$

But, as springs are massless, so force on them must be same

i.e. $\quad F_1 = F_2 = F$

So, $\quad \dfrac{1}{k} = \dfrac{1}{k_1} + \dfrac{1}{k_2}$ or $k = \dfrac{k_1 k_2}{k_1 + k_2}$

13. *(b)* In equilibrium position,

$$kl = mg$$

$$\Rightarrow \quad \frac{m}{k} = \frac{l}{g}$$

$$\because \quad T = 2\pi\sqrt{\frac{m}{k}}$$

$$\therefore \quad T_1 = 2\pi\sqrt{\frac{m}{k_1}}$$

$$\Rightarrow \quad k_1 = 4\pi^2 \frac{m}{T_1^2} \qquad \text{...(i)}$$

Similarly $T_2 = 2\pi\sqrt{\dfrac{m}{k_2}}$

$$\Rightarrow \quad k_2 = 4\pi^2 \frac{m}{T_2^2} \qquad \text{...(ii)}$$

Since, springs are in parallel, effective force constant

$$k = k_1 + k_2$$

$$\therefore \quad T = 2\pi\sqrt{\frac{m}{k_1 + k_2}}$$

$$\Rightarrow \quad k_1 + k_2 = 4\pi^2 \frac{m}{T^2} \qquad \text{...(iii)}$$

On substituting values of k_1 and k_2 from Eqs. (i) and (ii) in Eq. (iii), we get

$$4\pi^2 \frac{m}{T_1^2} + 4\pi^2 \frac{m}{T_2^2} = 4\pi^2 \frac{m}{T^2}$$

$$\Rightarrow \quad \frac{1}{T^2} = \frac{1}{T_1^2} + \frac{1}{T_2^2}$$

or $\quad T^{-2} = T_1^{-2} + T_2^{-2}$

14. *(c)* For each case,

$$f_A = \frac{1}{2\pi}\sqrt{\frac{g}{L_A}}$$

and $f_B = \dfrac{f_A}{2} = \dfrac{1}{2\pi}\sqrt{\dfrac{g}{L_B}}$

$$\Rightarrow \quad 2 = \sqrt{\frac{L_B}{L_A}}$$

$$\Rightarrow \quad 4 = \frac{L_B}{L_A} \Rightarrow L_B = 4L_A$$

In above relation, the mass is irrelevant. Hence, mass of a simple pendulum does not play any role.

15. *(d)*

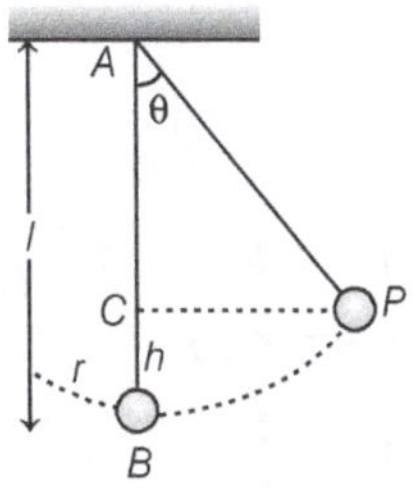

$$h = AB - AC = l - l\cos\theta$$
$$= l(1 - \cos\theta) \qquad \text{...(i)}$$

At point P (maximum displacement position i.e. extreme position), potential energy is maximum and kinetic energy is zero. At point B (mean or equilibrium position) potential energy is minimum and kinetic energy is maximum, so from principle of conservation of energy.

$$(\text{PE} + \text{KE})\text{ at } P = (\text{KE} + \text{PE})\text{ at } B$$

or $\quad mgh + 0 = \dfrac{1}{2}mv^2 + 0$

or $\quad v = \sqrt{2gh} \qquad \text{...(ii)}$

On substituting the value of h from Eq. (i) into Eq. (ii), we get

$$v = \sqrt{2gl(1 - \cos\theta)}$$

16. *(d)* Time period of simple pendulum

$$T = 2\pi\sqrt{\frac{l}{g}}$$

i.e. $\quad T \propto \sqrt{l}$

Hence, $\quad \dfrac{T_2}{T_1} = \sqrt{\dfrac{l_2}{l_1}} \qquad \text{...(i)}$

Given, $\quad l_2 = 4l_1, T_1 = 2\text{ s}$

On substituting the values in Eq. (i), we get

$$T_2 = \sqrt{\frac{4l_1}{l_1}} \times 2 = 2 \times 2 = 4\text{ s}$$

17. *(c)* Time period of spring-mass system, is given by

$$T = 2\pi\sqrt{\left(\frac{\text{displacement}}{\text{acceleration}}\right)}$$

$\therefore$ Frequency,

$$n = \frac{1}{T} = \frac{1}{2\pi}\sqrt{\frac{\text{acceleration}}{\text{displacement}}}$$

$$n = \frac{1}{2\pi}\sqrt{\frac{g}{l}} \qquad \text{...(i)}$$

In case of vertical spring-mass system, in equilibrium position

$$kl = mg \quad \Rightarrow \quad \frac{g}{l} = \frac{k}{m}$$

$\therefore$ From Eq. (i), we get

$$n = \frac{1}{2\pi}\sqrt{\frac{k}{m}}$$

or $\quad n \propto \dfrac{1}{\sqrt{m}}$ or $\dfrac{n_1}{n_2} = \sqrt{\dfrac{m_2}{m_1}}$

But, $m_1 = m, \; m_2 = 4m, \; n_1 = n$ [Given]

$$\therefore \quad \frac{n}{n_2} = \sqrt{\frac{4m}{m}} = 2$$

or $\quad n_2 = \dfrac{n}{2}$

Alternate Solution

As we know that

$$T = 2\pi\sqrt{\frac{m}{k}} \quad \text{(for spring mass system)}$$

$$n = \frac{1}{2\pi}\sqrt{\frac{k}{m}}$$

So, for two different masses suspended with same spring.

$$n_1 = \frac{1}{2\pi}\sqrt{\frac{k}{m_1}} \quad \left[\begin{array}{l} k \text{ is same for both the} \\ \text{cases as spring is same} \end{array}\right]$$

$$n_2 = \frac{1}{2\pi}\sqrt{\frac{k}{m_2}}$$

so, $\dfrac{n_1}{n_2} = \sqrt{\dfrac{m_2}{m_1}}$

Here, $m_2 = 4m_1$

so, $\dfrac{n_1}{n_2} = \sqrt{\dfrac{4m_1}{m_1}} = \dfrac{2}{1} \Rightarrow n_1 = 2n_2$

$$\Rightarrow n_2 = \frac{n_1}{2} = \frac{n}{2} \qquad [n_1 = n]$$

18. *(c)* For the pendulum to be again in the same phase, there should be difference of one complete oscillation. If smaller pendulum completes n oscillations the larger pendulum will complete $(n-1)$ oscillations.
Time period of n oscillations of first = Time period of $(n-1)$ oscillations of second

i.e. $nT_1 = (n-1)T_2$

or $n\,2\pi\sqrt{\dfrac{l_1}{g}} = (n-1)\,2\pi\sqrt{\dfrac{l_2}{g}}$

or $n\sqrt{l_1} = (n-1)\sqrt{l_2}$

or $\dfrac{n}{n-1} = \sqrt{\dfrac{l_2}{l_1}} = \sqrt{\dfrac{2.0}{0.5}}$

or $\dfrac{n}{n-1} = 2$ or $n = 2n - 2$

$\therefore$ $n = 2$

19. *(a)* Given,

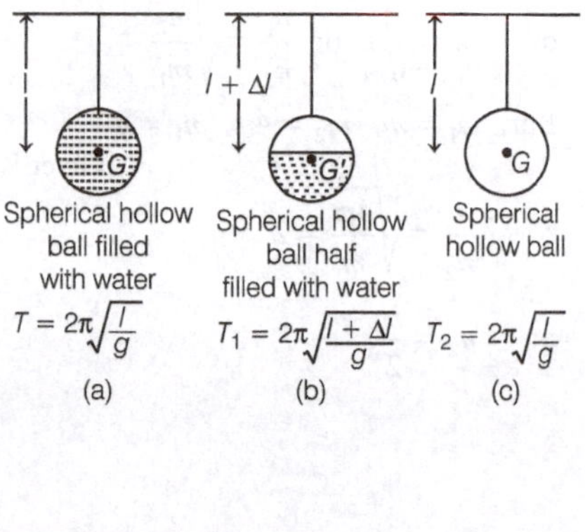

Initially, centre of gravity is at the centre of sphere [Fig. (a)]. When water leaks the centre of gravity goes down until it is half-filled [Fig. (b)], then it begins to go up and finally it again goes at the centre [Fig. (c)]. That is, effective length first increases and then decreases. As $T \propto \sqrt{l}$, so time period first increases and then decreases.

20. *(d)* Apply vector formula to determine resultant acceleration of the both.

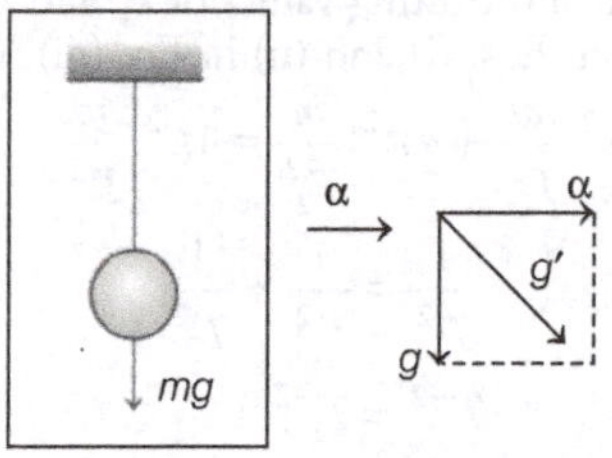

The bob is now under the combined action of two accelerations, g vertically downwards and α along the horizontal.

$\therefore$ Resultant acceleration

$$g' = \sqrt{g^2 + \alpha^2}$$

21. *(d)* The restoring force is same in each spring.

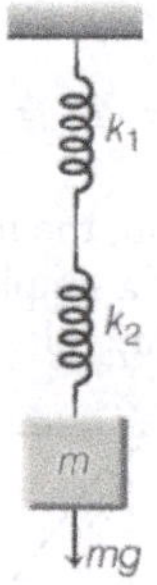

$\therefore$ $F = -k_1 y_1$

and $F = -k_2 y_2$

or $y_1 = -\dfrac{F}{k_1}$

and $y_2 = -\dfrac{F}{k_2}$

$\therefore$ Total extension,

$$y = y_1 + y_2$$
$$= -\frac{F}{k_1} - \frac{F}{k_2}$$
$$= -F\left(\frac{k_1 + k_2}{k_1 k_2}\right)$$

or $F = -\left(\dfrac{k_1 k_2}{k_1 + k_2}\right) y$

If k is the spring constant of series combination of springs then

$$F = -ky$$

$\therefore$ $k = \dfrac{k_1 k_2}{k_1 + k_2}$

If the body is left free after pulling down, it will execute SHM of period

$$T = 2\pi\sqrt{\frac{m}{k}}$$
$$= 2\pi\sqrt{\frac{m(k_1 + k_2)}{k_1 k_2}}$$

Topic 4

01. *(a)* Smaller damping gives a taller and narrower resonance peak.

02. *(d)* In case of damped vibration, amplitude at any instant t is given by

$$a = a_0 e^{-bt}$$

Case I $t = 100\,T$

and $a = \dfrac{a_0}{3}$

$\therefore$ $\dfrac{a_0}{3} = a_0 e^{-b(100\,T)}$

$\Rightarrow e^{-100\,bT} = \dfrac{1}{3}$

Case II $t = 200\,T$

$$a = a_0 e^{-bt}$$
$$= a_0 e^{-b(200\,T)}$$
$$= a_0 (e^{-100\,bT})^2$$
$$= a_0 \times \left(\frac{1}{3}\right)^2 = \frac{a_0}{9}$$

Thus, after 200 oscillations, amplitude will become $\dfrac{1}{9}$ times.

03. *(b)* We know that the frequency of an external forced oscillation is equal to the natrual frequency of the oscillator, then the amplitude of the force oscillation.
So, the body become very large. this phenomenon is called resonance.
Thus, resonance is an example of forced vibration.

In NEET 2024, no question was visible from this chapter. In past 5 years, 1 question from topic-1, 2 questions from topic-3 and 1 question from topic-4 were asked.
For detailed analysis scan QR code

WAVES

Topic 1 Types of Wave & its Motion

01 If the initial tension on a stretched string is doubled, then the ratio of the initial and final speeds of a transverse wave along the string is *[NCERT (New) Pg. 284, NEET 2022]*

(a) $\sqrt{2}:1$ (b) $1:\sqrt{2}$ (c) $1:2$ (d) $1:1$

02 A uniform rope of length L and mass m_1 hangs vertically from a rigid support. A block of mass m_2 is attached to the free end of the rope. A transverse pulse of wavelength λ_1 is produced at the lower end of the rope. The wavelength of the pulse when it reaches the top of the rope is λ_2. The ratio λ_2/λ_1 is *[NEET 2016]*

(a) $\sqrt{\dfrac{m_1+m_2}{m_2}}$ (b) $\sqrt{\dfrac{m_2}{m_1}}$

(c) $\sqrt{\dfrac{m_1+m_2}{m_1}}$ (d) $\sqrt{\dfrac{m_1}{m_2}}$

03 Sound waves travel at 350 m/s through a warm air and at 3500 m/s through brass. The wavelength of a 700 Hz acoustic wave as it enters brass from warm air *[AIPMT 2011]*

(a) increases by a factor 20 (b) increases by a factor 10
(c) decreases by a factor 20 (d) decreases by a factor 10

04 Which one of the following statements is true ? *[AIPMT 2006]*

(a) Both light and sound waves in air are transverse
(b) The sound waves in air are longitudinal while the light waves are transverse
(c) Both light and sound waves in air are longitudinal
(d) Both light and sound waves can travel in vacuum

05 The time of reverberation of a room A is 1s. What will be the time (in seconds) of reverberation of a room, having all the dimensions double of those of room A ? *[AIPMT 2006]*

(a) 2 (b) 4
(c) 1/2 (d) 1

06 A point source emits sound equally in all directions in a non-absorbing medium. Two points P and Q are at distance of 2m and 3m, respectively from the source. The ratio of the intensities of the waves at P and Q is *[AIPMT 2005]*

(a) 9 : 4 (b) 2 : 3 (c) 3 : 2 (d) 4 : 9

07 A wave enters water from air. In air frequency, wavelength, intensity and velocity are n_1, λ_1, I_1 and v_1, respectively. In water the corresponding quantities are n_2, λ_2, I_2 and v_2, respectively, then *[AIPMT 2001]*

(a) $I_1 = I_2$ (b) $n_1 = n_2$
(c) $v_1 = v_2$ (d) $\lambda_1 = \lambda_2$

08 What is the effect of humidity on sound waves when humidity increases ? *[NCERT (New) Pg. 287, AIPMT 1996]*

(a) Speed of sound waves increases
(b) Speed of sound waves decreases
(c) Speed of sound waves remains same
(d) Speed of sound waves becomes zero

09 The speed of a wave in a medium is 760 m/s. If 3600 waves are passing through a point in the medium in 2 min, then their wavelength is *[AIPMT 1995]*

(a) 13.8 m (b) 25.3 m
(c) 41.5 m (d) 57.2 m

10 A hospital uses an ultrasonic scanner to locate tumours in a tissue. The operating frequency of the scanner is 4.2 MHz. The speed of sound in a tissue is 1.7 km/s. The wavelength of sound in tissue is close to *[NCERT (New) Pg. 284, AIPMT 1995]*

(a) 4×10^{-4} m
(b) 8×10^{-4} m
(c) 4×10^{-3} m
(d) 8×10^{-3} m

11 If c_s be the velocity of sound in air and c be the rms velocity, then *[NCERT (New) Pg. 287, AIPMT 1994]*

(a) $c_s < c$ (b) $c_s = c$

(c) $c_s = c\left(\dfrac{\gamma}{3}\right)^{1/2}$ (d) None of these

12 With the propagation of a longitudinal wave through a material medium, the quantities transmitted in the propagation direction are *[AIPMT 1992]*
(a) energy, momentum and mass
(b) energy
(c) energy and mass
(d) energy and linear momentum

13 A 5.5 m length of string has a mass of 0.035 kg. If the tension in the string is 77 N, the speed of a wave on the string is *[AIPMT 1989]*
(a) 110 ms^{-1} (b) 165 ms^{-1}
(c) 77 ms^{-1} (d) 102 ms^{-1}

14 If the amplitude of sound is doubled and the frequency reduced to one-fourth, the intensity of sound at the same point will *[AIPMT 1989]*
(a) increase by a factor of 2 (b) decrease by a factor of 2
(c) decrease by a factor of 4 (d) remains unchanged

15 The velocity of sound in any gas depends upon *[NCERT (New) Pg. 287, AIPMT 1988]*
(a) wavelength of sound
(b) density and elasticity of gas
(c) intensity of sound waves
(d) amplitude and frequency of sound

Topic 2 Displacement Relation in Progressive Wave

01 A wave travelling in the positive x-direction having displacement along y-direction as 1 m, wavelength 2π m and frequency of $1/\pi$ Hz is represented by *[NCERT (New) Pg. 283, NEET 2013]*
(a) $y = \sin(x - 2t)$ (b) $y = \sin(2\pi x - 2\pi t)$
(c) $y = \sin(10\pi x - 20\pi t)$ (d) $y = \sin(2\pi x + 2\pi t)$

02 Two waves are represented by the equations $y_1 = a\sin(\omega t + kx + 0.57)$ m and $y_2 = a\cos(\omega t + kx)$ m, where x is in metre and t in second. The phase difference between them is *[NCERT (New) Pg. 282, AIPMT 2011]*
(a) 1.25 rad (b) 1.57 rad (c) 0.57 rad (d) 1 rad

03 A transverse wave is represented by $y = A\sin(\omega t - kx)$. For what value of the wavelength is the wave velocity equal to the maximum particle velocity? *[AIPMT 2010]*
(a) $\pi A/2$ (b) πA
(c) $2\pi A$ (d) A

04 A wave in a string has an amplitude of 2 cm. The wave travels in the positive direction of X-axis with a speed of 128 ms^{-1} and it is noted that 5 complete waves fit in 4 m length of the string. The equation describing the wave is *[AIPMT 2009]*
(a) $y = (0.02)$ m $\sin(7.85x + 1005t)$
(b) $y = (0.02)$ m $\sin(15.7x - 2010t)$
(c) $y = (0.02)$ m $\sin(15.7x + 2010t)$
(d) $y = (0.02)$ m $\sin(7.85x - 1005t)$

05 The wave described by $y = 0.25\sin(10\pi x - 2\pi t)$, where x and y are in metre and t in second, is a wave travelling along the *[NCERT (New) Pg. 283, AIPMT 2008]*
(a) negative x-direction with frequency 1 Hz
(b) positive x-direction with frequency π Hz and wavelength $\lambda = 0.2$ m
(c) positive x-direction with frequency 1 Hz and wavelength $\lambda = 0.2$ m
(d) negative x-direction with amplitude 0.25 m and wavelength $\lambda = 0.2$ m

06 A transverse wave propagating along X-axis is represented by

$$y(x, t) = 8\sin\left(0.5\pi x - 4\pi t - \frac{\pi}{4}\right),$$

where x is in metre and t is in second. The speed of the wave is *[NCERT (New) Pg. 284, AIPMT 2006]*
(a) 4π m/s (b) 0.5π m/s
(c) $\frac{\pi}{4}$ m/s (d) 8 m/s

07 The phase difference between two waves, represented by

$$y_1 = 10^{-6}\sin\left\{100t + \left(\frac{x}{50}\right) + 0.5\right\} \text{ m}$$

$$y_2 = 10^{-6}\cos\left\{100t + \left(\frac{x}{50}\right)\right\} \text{ m},$$

where x is expressed in metre and t is expressed in second, is approximately *[NCERT (New) Pg. 282, AIPMT 2004]*
(a) 1.07 rad (b) 2.07 rad
(c) 0.5 rad (d) 1.5 rad

08 A wave of amplitude $a = 0.2$ m, velocity $v = 360$ m/s and wavelength 60 m is travelling along positive X-axis, then the correct expression for the wave is *[NCERT (New) Pg. 281, AIPMT 2002]*
(a) $y = 0.2\sin 2\pi\left(6t + \frac{x}{60}\right)$ (b) $y = 0.2\sin\pi\left(6t + \frac{x}{60}\right)$
(c) $y = 0.2\sin 2\pi\left(6t - \frac{x}{60}\right)$ (d) $y = 0.2\sin\pi\left(6t - \frac{x}{60}\right)$

09 The equation of a wave is given by $y = a\sin\left(100t - \frac{x}{10}\right)$, where x and y are in metre and t in second, then velocity of wave is *[AIPMT 2001]*
(a) 0.1 m/s (b) 10 m/s
(c) 100 m/s (d) 1000 m/s

10 In a sinusoidal wave, the time required for a particular point, to move from maximum displacement to zero displacement is 0.170 s. The frequency of the wave is *[NCERT (New) Pg. 283, AIPMT 1998]*
(a) 1.47 Hz (b) 0.36 Hz
(c) 0.73 Hz (d) 2.94 Hz

11 A transverse wave is represented by the equation

$$y = y_0 \sin \frac{2\pi}{\lambda}(vt - x)$$

For what value of λ is the maximum particle velocity equal to two times the wave velocity? *[AIPMT 1998]*

(a) $\lambda = 2\pi y_0$ (b) $\lambda = \frac{\pi y_0}{3}$
(c) $\lambda = \frac{\pi y_0}{2}$ (d) $\lambda = \pi y_0$

12 The equation of a sound wave is given as $y = 0.005 \sin(62.4x + 316t)$. The wavelength of this wave is *[NCERT (New) Pg. 283, AIPMT 1996]*

(a) 0.4 unit (b) 0.3 unit
(c) 0.2 unit (d) 0.1 unit

13 From a wave equation $y = 0.5 \sin \frac{2\pi}{3.2}(64t - x)$, the frequency of the wave is *[AIPMT 1995]*

(a) 5 Hz (b) 15 Hz (c) 20 Hz (d) 25 Hz

14 Which of the following equation represents a wave ? *[AIPMT 1994]*

(a) $y = a \sin \omega t$ (b) $y = a \cos kx$
(c) $y = a \sin(\omega t - bx + c)$ (d) $y = a \sin(\omega t - kx)$

15 The frequency of sinusoidal wave, $0.40 \cos(2000t + 0.80)$ would be *[AIPMT 1992]*

(a) 1000π Hz (b) 2000 Hz
(c) 20 Hz (d) $\frac{1000}{\pi}$ Hz

16 The transverse wave represented by the equation

$$y = 4 \sin \frac{\pi}{6} \sin (15t - 3x)$$

[AIPMT 1990]

(a) amplitude $= 4\pi$ (b) wavelength $= \frac{4\pi}{3}$
(c) speed of propagation $= 5$ (d) period $= \frac{\pi}{15}$

17 Velocity of sound waves in air is 330 m/s. For a particular sound wave in air, path difference of 40 cm is equivalent to phase difference of 1.6π. The frequency of this wave is *[NCERT (New) Pg. 284, AIPMT 1990]*

(a) 165 Hz (b) 150 Hz
(c) 660 Hz (d) 330 Hz

18 Equation of progressive wave is given by

$$y = 4 \sin\left[\pi\left(\frac{t}{5} - \frac{x}{9}\right) + \frac{\pi}{6}\right]$$

Then, which of the following is correct ? *[NCERT (New) Pg. 284, AIPMT 1988]*

(a) $v = 5$ cm (b) $\lambda = 18$ cm
(c) $a = 0.04$ cm (d) $f = 50$ Hz

Topic 3 Principle of Superposition of Waves and Organ Pipe

01 The ratio of frequencies of fundamental harmonic produced by an open pipe to that of closed pipe having the same length is *[NEET 2023]*

(a) 2 : 1 (b) 1 : 3
(c) 3 : 1 (d) 1 : 2

02 The length of the string of a musical instrument is 90 cm and has a fundamental frequency of 120 Hz. Where should it be pressed to produce fundamental frequency of 180 Hz ? *[NCERT (New) Pg. 290, NEET (Oct.) 2020]*

(a) 75 cm (b) 60 cm
(c) 45 cm (d) 80 cm

03 A tuning fork with frequency 800 Hz produces resonance in a resonance column tube with upper end open and lower end closed by water surface. Successive resonance are observed at length 9.75 cm, 31.25 cm and 52.75 cm. The speed of sound in air is *[NEET (Odisha) 2019]*

(a) 500 m/s (b) 156 m/s
(c) 344 m/s (d) 172 m/s

04 The fundamental frequency in an open organ pipe is equal to the third harmonic of a closed organ pipe. If the length of the closed organ pipe is 20 cm, the length of the open organ pipe is *[NEET 2018]*

(a) 12.5 cm (b) 8 cm
(c) 13.3 cm (d) 16 cm

05 A tuning fork is used to produce resonance in a glass tube. The length of the air column in this tube can be adjusted by a variable piston. At room temperature of 27°C, two successive resonances are produced at 20 cm and 73 cm of column length. If the frequency of the tuning fork is 320 Hz, the velocity of sound in air at 27°C is *[NCERT (New) Pg. 292, NEET 2018]*

(a) 350 m/s (b) 339 m/s
(c) 330 m/s (d) 300 m/s

06 The two nearest harmonics of a tube closed at one end and open at other end are 220 Hz and 260 Hz. What is the fundamental frequency of the system? *[NCERT (New) Pg. 292, NEET 2017]*

(a) 10 Hz (b) 20 Hz
(c) 30 Hz (d) 40 Hz]

07 The second overtone of an open organ pipe has the same frequency as the first overtone of a closed pipe L metre long. The length of the open pipe will be *[NCERT (New) Pg. 291, NEET 2016]*

(a) L (b) $2L$
(c) $L/2$ (d) $4L$

08 The fundamental frequency of a closed organ pipe of length 20 cm is equal to the second overtone of an organ pipe open at both the ends. The length of organ pipe open at both the ends is *[AIPMT 2015]*
(a) 80 cm (b) 100 cm
(c) 120 cm (d) 140 cm

09 An air column, closed at one end and open at the other, resonates with a tunning fork when the smallest length of the column is 50 cm. The next larger length of the column resonating with the same tunning fork is *[NCERT (New) Pg. 292, AIPMT 2015]*
(a) 100 cm (b) 150 cm
(c) 200 cm (d) 66.7 cm

10 A string is stretched between fixed points separated by 75.0 cm. It is observed to have resonant frequencies of 420 Hz and 315 Hz. There are no other resonant frequencies between these two. The lowest resonant frequency for this strings is *[AIPMT 2015]*
(a) 155 Hz (b) 205 Hz
(c) 10.5 Hz (d) 105 Hz

11 If n_1, n_2 and n_3 are the fundamental frequencies of three segments into which a string is divided, then the original fundamental frequency n of the string is given by *[AIPMT 2014]*
(a) $\frac{1}{n} = \frac{1}{n_1} + \frac{1}{n_2} + \frac{1}{n_3}$
(b) $\frac{1}{\sqrt{n}} = \frac{1}{\sqrt{n_1}} + \frac{1}{\sqrt{n_2}} + \frac{1}{\sqrt{n_3}}$
(c) $\sqrt{n} = \sqrt{n_1} + \sqrt{n_2} + \sqrt{n_3}$
(d) $n = n_1 + n_2 + n_3$

12 The number of possible natural oscillations of air column in a pipe closed at one end of length 85 cm whose frequencies lie below 1250 Hz are (velocity of sound = 340 ms^{-1}) *[NCERT (New) Pg. 292, AIPMT 2014]*
(a) 4 (b) 5
(c) 7 (d) 6

13 If we study the vibration of a pipe open at both ends, which of the following statements is not true? *[NEET 2013]*
(a) Open end will be antinode
(b) Odd harmonics of the fundamental frequency will be generated
(c) All harmonics of the fundamental frequency will be generated
(d) Pressure change will be maximum at both ends

14 When a string is divided into three segments of lengths l_1, l_2 and l_3, the fundamental frequencies of these three segments are ν_1, ν_2 and ν_3, respectively. The original fundamental frequency (ν) of the string is *[NCERT (New) Pg. 291, AIPMT 2012]*
(a) $\sqrt{\nu} = \sqrt{\nu_1} + \sqrt{\nu_2} + \sqrt{\nu_3}$
(b) $\nu = \nu_1 + \nu_2 + \nu_3$
(c) $\frac{1}{\nu} = \frac{1}{\nu_1} + \frac{1}{\nu_2} + \frac{1}{\nu_3}$
(d) $\frac{1}{\sqrt{\nu}} = \frac{1}{\sqrt{\nu_1}} + \frac{1}{\sqrt{\nu_2}} + \frac{1}{\sqrt{\nu_3}}$

15 Two periodic waves of intensities I_1 and I_2 pass through a region at the same time in the same direction. The sum of the maximum and minimum intensities is *[AIPMT 2008]*
(a) $I_1 + I_2$ (b) $(\sqrt{I_1} + \sqrt{I_2})^2$
(c) $(\sqrt{I_1} - \sqrt{I_2})^2$ (d) $2(I_1 + I_2)$

16 Equations of two progressive waves are given by $y_1 = a \sin(\omega t + \phi_1)$ and $y_2 = a \sin(\omega t + \phi_2)$. If amplitude and time period of resultant wave are same as that of both the waves, then $(\phi_1 - \phi_2)$ is *[AIPMT 2001]*
(a) $\frac{\pi}{3}$ (b) $\frac{2\pi}{3}$
(c) $\frac{\pi}{6}$ (d) $\frac{\pi}{4}$

17 A sonometer wire when vibrated in full length has frequency n. Now, it is divided by the help of bridges into a number of segments of lengths $l_1, l_2, l_3, \ldots$ When vibrated these segments have frequencies $n_1, n_2, n_3, \ldots$ then the correct relation is *[AIPMT 2000]*
(a) $n = n_1 + n_2 + n_3 + \ldots$ (b) $n^2 = n_1^2 + n_2^2 + n_3^2 + \ldots$
(c) $\frac{1}{n} = \frac{1}{n_1} + \frac{1}{n_2} + \frac{1}{n_3} + \ldots$ (d) $\frac{1}{\sqrt{n}} = \frac{1}{\sqrt{n_1}} + \frac{1}{\sqrt{n_2}} + \frac{1}{\sqrt{n_3}} + \ldots$

18 A standing wave having 3 node and 2 antinode is formed between two atoms having a distance 1.21 Å between them. The wavelength of the standing wave is *[NCERT (New) Pg. 290, AIPMT 1998]*
(a) 1.21 Å (b) 1.42 Å
(c) 6.05 Å (d) 3.63 Å

19 A cylindrical resonance tube open at both ends has a fundamental frequency f, in air. If half of the length is dipped vertically in water, the fundamental frequency of the air column will be *[AIPMT 1997]*
(a) $2f$ (b) $\frac{3f}{2}$ (c) f (d) $\frac{f}{2}$

20 A pulse of a wave train travels along a stretched string and reaches the fixed end of the string. It will be reflected back with *[NCERT (New) Pg. 290, AIPMT 1997]*
(a) a phase change of 180° with velocity reversed
(b) the same phase as the incident pulse with no reversal of velocity
(c) a phase change of 180° with no reversal of velocity
(d) the same phase as the incident pulse but with velocity reversed

21 Standing waves are produced in a 10 m long stretched string. If the string vibrates in 5 segments and the wave velocity is 20 m/s, the frequency is *[AIPMT 1997]*

(a) 10 Hz (b) 5 Hz (c) 4 Hz (d) 2 Hz

22 Two waves of same frequency and intensity superimpose on each other in opposite phases. After the super- position, the intensity and frequency of waves will *[AIPMT 1996]*

(a) increase (b) decrease
(c) remain constant (d) become zero

23 Two waves are said to be coherent, if they have *[AIPMT 1995]*

(a) same phase but different amplitude
(b) same frequency but different amplitude
(c) same frequency, phase and amplitude
(d) different frequency, phase and amplitude

24 Two waves are approaching each other with a velocity of 20 m/s and frequency n. The distance between two successive nodes is *[AIPMT 1995]*

(a) $\frac{20}{n}$ (b) $\frac{10}{n}$ (c) $\frac{5}{n}$ (d) $\frac{n}{10}$

25 A wave of frequency 100 Hz is sent along a string towards a fixed end. When this wave travels back after reflection, a node is formed at a distance of 10 cm from the fixed end of the string. The speed of incident (and reflected) wave are *[AIPMT 1994]*

(a) 5 m/s (b) 10 m/s (c) 20 m/s (d) 40 m/s

26 A standing wave is represented by $y = a\sin(100t)\cos(0.01)x$, where y and a are in millimetre, t in second and x is in metre. Velocity of wave is *[NCERT (New) Pg. 284, AIPMT 1994]*

(a) 10^4 m/s (b) 1 m/s
(c) 10^{-4} m/s (d) None of these

27 A wave has SHM (simple harmonic motion) whose period is 4s while another wave which also possesses SHM has its period 3 s. If both are combined, then the resultant wave will have the period equal to *[AIPMT 1993]*

(a) 4 s (b) 5 s (c) 12 s (d) 3 s

28 A stretched string resonates with tuning fork of frequency 512 Hz when length of the string is 0.5 m. The length of the string required to vibrate resonantly with a tuning fork of frequency 256 Hz would be *[AIPMT 1993]*

(a) 0.25 m (b) 0.5 m (c) 1 m (d) 2 m

29 A closed organ pipe (closed at one end) is excited to support the third overtone. It is found that air in the pipe has *[NCERT (New) Pg. 292, AIPMT 1991]*

(a) three nodes and three antinodes
(b) three nodes and four antinodes
(c) four nodes and three antinodes
(d) four nodes and four antinodes

Topic 4 Beats & Doppler Effect

01 In a guitar, two strings A and B made of same material are slightly out of tune and produce beats of frequency 6 Hz. When tension in B is slightly decreased, the beat frequency increases to 7 Hz. If the frequency of A is 530 Hz, the original frequency of B will be *[NCERT (New) Pg. 293, NEET (Sep.) 2020]*

(a) 524 Hz (b) 536 Hz (c) 537 Hz (d) 523 Hz

02 Two cars moving in opposite directions approach each other with speed of 22 m/s and 16.5 m/s, respectively. The driver of the first car blows a horn having a frequency 400 Hz. The frequency heard by the driver of the second car is [velocity of sound 340 m/s] *[NEET 2017]*

(a) 350 Hz (b) 361 Hz (c) 411 Hz (d) 448 Hz

03 A siren emitting a sound of frequency 800 Hz moves away from an observer towards a cliff at a speed of 15 ms^{-1}. Then, the frequency of sound that the observer hears in the echo reflected from the cliff is (Take, velocity of sound in air = 330 ms^{-1}) *[NEET 2016]*

(a) 800 Hz (b) 838 Hz
(c) 885 Hz (d) 765 Hz

04 Three sound waves of equal amplitudes have frequencies $(n-1)$, n, $(n+1)$. They superimpose to give beats. The number of beats produced per second will be *[NCERT (New) Pg. 293, NEET 2016]*

(a) 1 (b) 4
(c) 3 (d) 2

05 A source of sound S emitting waves of frequency 100 Hz and an observer O are located at some distance from each other. The source is moving with a speed of 19.4 ms^{-1} at an angle of 60° with the source observer line as shown in the figure. The observer is at rest. The apparent frequency observed by the observer (velocity of sound in air is 330 ms^{-1}), is *[NCERT (New) Pg. 385, AIPMT 2015]*

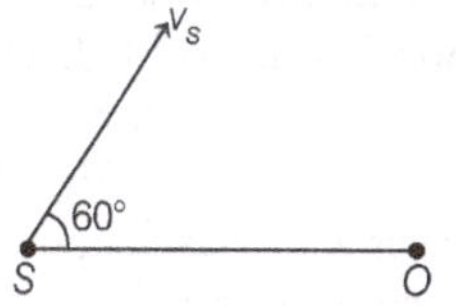

(a) 100 Hz (b) 103 Hz
(c) 106 Hz (d) 97 Hz

06 A speeding motorcyclist sees a traffic jam ahead of him. He slows down to 36 km/h. He finds that traffic has eased and a car moving ahead of him at 18 km/h is honking at a frequency of 1392 Hz. If the speed of sound is 343 m/s, the frequency of the honk as heard by him will be *[AIPMT 2014]*

(a) 1332 Hz (b) 1372 Hz
(c) 1412 Hz (d) 1454 Hz

07 A source of unknown frequency gives 4 beat/s when sounded with a source of known frequency 250 Hz. The second harmonic of the source of unknown frequency gives 5 beat/s when sounded with a source of frequency 513 Hz. The unknown frequency is ***[NCERT (New) Pg. 293, NEET 2013]***

(a) 254 Hz (b) 246 Hz
(c) 240 Hz (d) 260 Hz

08 Two sources P and Q produce notes of frequency 660 Hz each. A listener moves from P to Q with a speed of 1 ms^{-1}. If the speed of sound is 330 m/s, then the number of beats heard by the listener per second will be ***[NCERT (New) Pg. 293, NEET 2013]***

(a) 4 (b) 8
(c) 2 (d) zero

09 Two sources of sound placed closed to each other are emitting progressive waves given by $y_1 = 4\sin 600\pi t$ and $y_2 = 5\sin 608\pi t$.
An observer located near these two sources of sound will hear ***[AIPMT 2012]***

(a) 4 beat/s with intensity ratio 25 : 16 between waxing and waning
(b) 8 beat/s with intensity ratio 25 : 16 between waxing and waning
(c) 8 beat/s with intensity ratio 81 : 1 between waxing and waning
(d) 4 beat/s with intensity ratio 81 : 1 between waxing and waning

10 A tuning fork of frequency 512 Hz makes 4 beat/s with the vibrating string of a piano. The beat frequency decreases to 2 beat/s when the tension in the piano string is slightly increased. The frequency of the piano string before increasing the tension was ***[NCERT (New) Pg. 293, AIPMT 2010]***

(a) 510 Hz (b) 514 Hz
(c) 516 Hz (d) 508 Hz

11 The driver of a car travelling with speed 30 ms^{-1} towards a hill sounds a horn of frequency 600 Hz. If the velocity of sound in air is 330 ms^{-1}, the frequency of reflected sound as heard by driver is ***[AIPMT 2009]***

(a) 550 Hz (b) 555.5 Hz
(c) 720 Hz (d) 500 Hz

12 Two sound waves with wavelengths 5 m and 5.5 m respectively, each propagate in a gas with velocity 330 m/s. We expect the following number of beat per second ***[NCERT (New) Pg. 293, AIPMT 2006]***

(a) 12 (b) zero
(c) 1 (d) 6

13 Two vibrating tuning forks produce progressive waves given by $y_1 = 4\sin 500\,\pi t$ and $y_2 = 2\sin 506\,\pi t$. Number of beat produced per minute is ***[AIPMT 2005]***

(a) 360 (b) 180
(c) 3 (d) 60

14 A car is moving towards a high cliff. The car driver sounds a horn of frequency f. The reflected sound heard by the driver has a frequency $2f$. If v be the velocity of sound, then the velocity of the car, in the same velocity units, will be ***[AIPMT 2004]***

(a) $\frac{v}{\sqrt{2}}$ (b) $\frac{v}{3}$
(c) $\frac{v}{4}$ (d) $\frac{v}{2}$

15 An observer moves towards a stationary source of sound with a speed 1 / 5th of the speed of sound. The wavelength and frequency of the source emitted are λ and f, respectively. The apparent frequency and wavelength recorded by the observer are respectively ***[NCERT (New) Pg. 385, AIPMT 2003]***

(a) $f, 1.2\lambda$ (b) $0.8f, 0.8\lambda$
(c) $1.2f, 1.2\lambda$ (d) $1.2f, \lambda$

16 A whistle revolves in a circle with angular velocity $\omega = 20$ rad/s using a string of length 50 cm. If the actual frequency of sound from the whistle is 385 Hz, then the minimum frequency heard by the observer far away from the centre is (velocity of sound $v = 340$ m/s) ***[AIPMT 2002]***

(a) 385 Hz (b) 374 Hz
(c) 394 Hz (d) 333 Hz

17 Two sources are at a finite distance apart. They emit sounds of wavelength λ. An observer situated between them in line joining approaches one source with speed u. Then, the number of beat heard/second by observer will be ***[NCERT (New) Pg. 293, AIPMT 2000]***

(a) $\frac{2u}{\lambda}$ (b) $\frac{u}{\lambda}$
(c) $\frac{u}{2\lambda}$ (d) $\frac{\lambda}{u}$

18 Two waves of wavelength 50 cm and 51 cm produce 12 beat/s. The speed of sound is ***[AIPMT 1999]***

(a) 306 m/s (b) 331 m/s
(c) 340 m/s (d) 360 m/s

19 A vehicle, with a horn of frequency n, is moving with a velocity of 30 m/s in a direction perpendicular to the straight line joining the observer and the vehicle. The observer perceives the sound to have a frequency $n + n_1$. Then (If the sound velocity in air is 300 m/s) ***[NCERT (New) Pg. 385, AIPMT 1998]***

(a) $n_1 = 10n$ (b) $n_1 = 0$
(c) $n_1 = 0.1\,n$ (d) $n_1 = -0.1\,n$

20 A source of sound gives 5 beats per seond, when sounded with another source of frequency 100/s. The second harmonic of the source, together with a source of frequency 205/sec gives 5 beats per second. What is the frequency of the soruce? ***[NCERT (New) Pg. 293, AIPMT 1995]***

(a) 95 s^{-1} (b) 100 s^{-1}
(c) 105 s^{-1} (d) 205 s^{-1}

21 For production of beats the two sources must have *[AIPMT 1992]*

(a) different frequencies and same amplitude
(b) different frequencies
(c) different frequencies, same amplitude and same phase
(d) different frequencies and same phase

22 Two trains move towards each other with the same speed. The speed of sound is 340 m/s. If the height of the tone of the whistle of one of them heard on the other changes 9/8 times, then the speed of each train should be *[NCERT (Old) Pg. 386, AIPMT 1991]*

(a) 20 m/s (b) 2 m/s (c) 200 m/s (d)2000 m/s

• Key Index

Topic 1

1 (b)	**2** (a)	**3** (b)	**4** (b)	**5** (a)	**6** (a)	**7** (b)	**8** (a)	**9** (b)	**10** (a)
11 (c)	**12** (b)	**13** (a)	**14** (c)	**15** (b)					

Topic 2

1 (a)	**2** (d)	**3** (c)	**4** (d)	**5** (c)	**6** (d)	**7** (a)	**8** (c)	**9** (d)	**10** (a)
11 (d)	**12** (d)	**13** (c)	**14** (d)	**15** (d)	**16** (c)	**17** (c)	**18** (b)		

Topic 3

1 (a)	**2** (b)	**3** (c)	**4** (c)	**5** (b)	**6** (b)	**7** (b)	**8** (c)	**9** (b)	**10** (d)
11 (a)	**12** (d)	**13** (d)	**14** (c)	**15** (d)	**16** (b)	**17** (c)	**18** (a)	**19** (c)	**20** (a)
21 (b)	**22** (d)	**23** (c)	**24** (b)	**25** (c)	**26** (a)	**27** (c)	**28** (c)	**29** (d)	

Topic 4

1 (a)	**2** (d)	**3** (b)	**4** (d)	**5** (b)	**6** (c)	**7** (a)	**8** (a)	**9** (d)	**10** (d)
11 (c)	**12** (d)	**13** (b)	**14** (b)	**15** (d)	**16** (b)	**17** (a)	**18** (a)	**19** (b)	**20** (c)
21 (b)	**22** (a)								

Detailed **Explanations**

Topic 1

01. *(b)* Velocity of transverse wave in the string, $v \propto \sqrt{T}$

$$\therefore \quad \frac{v_1}{v_2} = \sqrt{\frac{T_1}{T_2}} = \sqrt{\frac{T_1}{2T_1}} \quad [\because T_2 = 2T_1]$$

$$= \frac{1}{\sqrt{2}}$$

$$v_1 : v_2 = 1 : \sqrt{2}$$

02. *(a)* Wavelength of transverse pulse

$$\lambda = \frac{v}{f} \quad \ldots \text{(i)}$$

As we know, $v = \sqrt{\frac{T}{\mu}}$ ...(ii)

From Eqs. (i) and (ii), we get

$$\lambda = \frac{1}{f}\sqrt{\frac{T}{\mu}} \Rightarrow \lambda \propto \sqrt{T}$$

So, for two different case, we get

$$\frac{\lambda_2}{\lambda_1} = \sqrt{\frac{T_2}{T_1}} = \sqrt{\frac{m_1 + m_2}{m_2}}$$

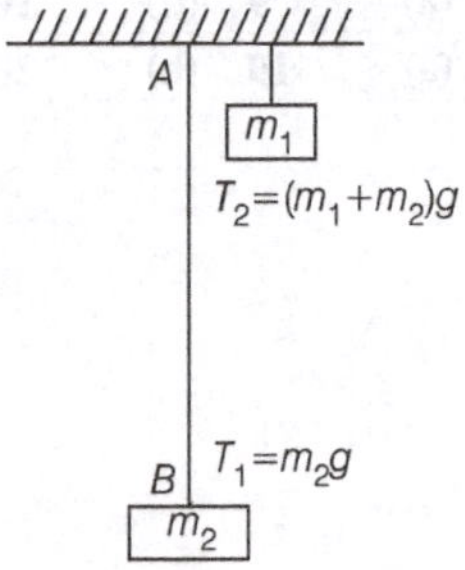

03. *(b)* Velocity of a wave is given by

$$v = n\lambda$$

So, for two different cases,

$$v_1 = n_1\lambda_1$$
$$v_2 = n_2\lambda_2$$
$$\lambda_2 = \lambda_1 \frac{v_2}{v_1} = \lambda_1 \times \frac{3500}{350}$$
$$= \lambda_1 \times 10 \quad [\because n_1 = n_2]$$
$$\lambda_2 = 10\,\lambda_1$$

The wavelength of a 700 Hz acoustic wave as it enters brass from warm air, increased by a factor 10.

04. *(b)* Sound waves are longitudinal in nature.

Light waves being electromagnetic are transverse waves.

Hence, option (b) is correct.

05. *(a)* Sabine's formula for reverberation time is

$$T = \frac{0.16\,V}{\Sigma as} \quad \text{or} \quad T \propto \frac{V}{s},$$

where V is volume of hall in m^3.

$$\Sigma as = a_1 s_1 + a_2 s_2 + \ldots$$
= Total absorption of the hall (room)

Here, s_1, s_2, s_3 ... are surface areas of the absorbers and a_1, a_2, a_3 ... are their respective absorption coefficients.

So, for two different cases of reverberation.

$$\therefore \quad \frac{T'}{T} = \frac{V'}{s'} \times \frac{s}{V} = \frac{(2)^3}{(2)^2} = \frac{8}{4} = 2$$

Hence, $T' = 2T = 2 \times 1 = 2$ s

06. *(a)*

key idea

You can find the intensity of sound wave using

$$I = \frac{P}{4\pi r^2}$$

where, P = power

r = distance between source and the point

Intensity of sound,

$$I = \frac{P}{4\pi r^2}$$

or $\quad I \propto \frac{1}{r^2} \quad$ or $\quad \frac{I_1}{I_2} = \left(\frac{r_2}{r_1}\right)^2$

Here, $\quad r_1 = 2$ m, $r_2 = 3$ m

On substituting the values, we get

$$\frac{I_1}{I_2} = \left(\frac{3}{2}\right)^2 = \frac{9}{4}$$

07. *(b)* When a wave enters from one medium to another, its frequency remains unchanged, i.e. $n_1 = n_2$ but wavelength, intensity and velocity get changed.

08. *(a)* As velocity of wave in moist air is given by

$$\therefore \quad v_m = \sqrt{\frac{\gamma p}{\rho_m}} \text{ and } v_d = \sqrt{\frac{\gamma p}{\rho_d}}$$

On dividing, we get $\frac{v_m}{v_d} = \sqrt{\frac{\rho_d}{\rho_m}}$

The presence of water vapours reduces the density of air.

i.e., $\quad \rho_m < \rho_d$

Hence, velocity of sound in moist air is greater, then the velocity of sound in dry air.

> • Concept **Enhancer**
>
> The presence of water vapour in air changes its density. That is why, the velocity of sound changes with humidity of air.

09. *(b)* Given speed of wave, $v = 760$ m/s

Number of waves = 3600

Time, $\quad t = 2$ min
$= 2 \times 60 = 120$ s

$\therefore$ Frequency of waves,

$$\nu = \frac{\text{Total number of waves}}{\text{Time taken}}$$
$$= \frac{3600}{120} = 30 \text{ Hz}$$

$\therefore$ Wavelength of waves,

$$\lambda = \frac{v}{\nu} = \frac{760}{30} = 25.3 \text{ m}$$

10. *(a)* Wavelength of a wave is

$$\lambda = \frac{v}{\nu}$$

Given, $v = 1.7 \times 10^3$ m/s

$\nu = 4.2 \times 10^6$ Hz

$$\therefore \quad \lambda = \frac{1.7 \times 10^3}{4.2 \times 10^6} = 4 \times 10^{-4} \text{ m}$$

11. *(c)* Velocity of sound c_s is given by

$$c_s = \sqrt{\frac{\gamma p}{\rho}} \quad \ldots \text{(i)}$$

rms velocity of gas molecules is given by

$$c = \sqrt{\left(\frac{3p}{\rho}\right)} \quad \ldots \text{(ii)}$$

From Eqs. (i) and (ii), we get

$$\frac{c_s}{c} = \sqrt{\frac{\gamma p}{\rho} \times \frac{\rho}{3p}} = \sqrt{\frac{\gamma}{3}}$$

$$\Rightarrow \quad c_s = c \times \sqrt{\left(\frac{\gamma}{3}\right)}$$

12. *(b)* In longitudinal waves, energy is propagated along with the wave motion without any net transport of the mass of the medium.

13. *(a)* The velocity of propagation of a transverse wave on a stretched string is given by

$$v = \sqrt{\left(\frac{T}{\mu}\right)}$$

Here, $\mu = \frac{0.035}{5.5}$ kg/m

$T = 77$ N

$\therefore \quad v = \sqrt{\frac{77 \times 5.5}{0.035}} = 110$ m/s

14. *(c)* As intensity $I \propto a^2$ and $I \propto \nu^2$

Therefore, intensity becomes $\frac{2^2}{4^2} = \frac{1}{4}$th.

15. *(b)* From purely theoretical considerations, Newton came to the conclusion that velocity of longitudinal waves through any medium, solid, liquid or gas depends upon the elasticity and density of the medium.

Topic 2

01. *(a)* As $y = a \sin(kx - \omega t)$

Given, $a = 1$m, $\lambda = 2\pi$m, $f = \frac{1}{\pi}$Hz

and we know that, $k = \frac{2\pi}{\lambda}$ and $\omega = 2\pi f$

So, $y = \sin\left(\frac{2\pi}{2\pi} - 2\pi \times \frac{1}{\pi} t\right)$

$= \sin(x - 2t)$

02. *(d)* According to question,

$y_1 = a \sin(\omega t + kx + 0.57)$

and $y_2 = a \cos(\omega t + kx)$

or $y_2 = a \sin\left(\frac{\pi}{2} + \omega t + kx\right)$

As phase difference,

$\Delta\phi = \phi_2 - \phi_1 = \frac{\pi}{2} - 0.57$

$= 1.57 - 0.57 = 1$ rad

03. *(c)* As we know that wave velocity is given by

$v_w = \frac{\lambda}{T} = \frac{\omega\lambda}{2\pi}$ ...(i) $\left[T = \frac{2\pi}{\omega}\right]$

And maximum particle velocity is given by

$v_p = A\omega$ ...(ii)

So, as Eq. (i) is equal to Eq. (ii),

$A\omega = \frac{\omega\lambda}{2\pi}, \ \lambda = 2\pi A$

04. *(d)* Given, amplitude of wave,

$A = 2$ cm

direction = +ve x -direction

Velocity of wave

$v = 128 \text{ ms}^{-1}$

and length of string,

$5\lambda = 4$

We know that

$k = \frac{2\pi}{\lambda} = \frac{2\pi \times 5}{4} = 7.85$

and $v = \frac{\omega}{k} = 128 \text{ ms}^{-1}$

[ω = Angular frequency]

$\Rightarrow \quad \omega = v \times k$

$= 128 \times 7.85 = 1005$

As, the wave travelling towards + x-axis is given by

$y = A \sin(kx - \omega t)$

So, $y = 2 \sin(7.85x - 1005t)$

$y = (0.02) \text{ m} \sin(7.85x - 1005t)$

05. *(c)* $y = 0.25 \sin(10\pi x - 2\pi t)$

Compare the above equation with

$y = A \sin(kx - \omega t)$

As, $2\pi t = \omega t$

$\Rightarrow \quad \omega = 2\pi = 2\pi\nu$

$\Rightarrow \quad \nu = 1$ Hz

Also, $kx = 10\pi x$

$k = 10\pi = \frac{2\pi}{\lambda}$

$\lambda = \frac{2\pi}{10\pi} = 0.2$

06. *(d)* The given equation is

$y(x,t) = 8.0 \sin\left(0.5\pi x - 4\pi t - \frac{\pi}{4}\right)$ ...(i)

Compare it with the standard wave equation

$y = a \sin(kx - \omega t + \phi)$ ...(ii)

On comparing the Eqs. (i) and (ii), we have

$k = 0.5\pi, \ \omega = 4\pi$

$\therefore$ Speed of transverse wave,

$v = \frac{\omega}{k} = \frac{4\pi}{0.5\pi} = 8$ m/s

07. *(a)* The given waves are

$y_1 = 10^{-6} \sin\left[100t + \left(\frac{x}{50}\right) + 0.5\right]$ m ...(i)

and $y_2 = 10^{-6} \cos\left[100t + \left(\frac{x}{50}\right)\right]$ m ...(ii)

Eq. (ii) can be written as

$\Rightarrow y_2 = 10^{-6} \sin\left[100t + \left(\frac{x}{50}\right) + \frac{\pi}{2}\right]$ m

$\left[\because \sin\left(\frac{\pi}{2} + \theta\right) = \cos\theta\right]$

Hence, the phase difference between the waves is

$\Delta\phi = \left(\frac{\pi}{2} - 0.5\right) \text{rad} = \left(\frac{3.14}{2} - 0.5\right) \text{rad}$

$= (1.57 - 0.5)$ rad

$= 1.07$ rad

> **Concept Enhancer**
>
> The given waves are sine and cosine functions, so they are plane progressive harmonic waves.

08. *(c)* The general expression of travelling wave can be written as

$y = a \sin(\omega t \pm kx)$ ...(i)

For travelling wave along positive X-axis we should use minus (–) sign only.

$\therefore \quad y = a \sin(\omega t - kx)$

But, $\omega = \frac{2\pi v}{\lambda}$ and $k = \frac{2\pi}{\lambda}$

So, $y = a \sin \frac{2\pi}{\lambda}(vt - x)$ ...(ii)

Given, $a = 0.2$ m,

$v = 360$ m/s

$\lambda = 60$ m

On substituting in Eq. (ii), we get

$y = 0.2 \sin \frac{2\pi}{60}(360t - x)$

or $y = 0.2 \sin 2\pi\left(6t - \frac{x}{60}\right)$

09. *(d)* The given wave equation is

$y = a \sin\left(100t - \frac{x}{10}\right)$

Compare it with the standard wave equation, we get

$\omega = 100, \ k = \frac{1}{10}$

Velocity of the wave,

$v = \frac{\omega}{k} = \frac{100}{1/10}$

$= 100 \times 10 = 1000$ m/s

10. *(a)* If T is the time period, then time required for a point to move from maximum displacement to zero displacement is $\frac{T}{4}$.

So, $\frac{T}{4} = 0.170$

or $T = 0.170 \times 4 = 0.680$ s

Therefore, the frequency of wave is

$n = \frac{1}{T} = \frac{1}{0.680} = 1.47$ Hz

11. *(d)* The given wave equation is

$$y = y_0 \sin \frac{2\pi}{\lambda}(vt - x) \quad \ldots\text{(i)}$$

Differentiating Eq. (i) w.r.t. t, we get

$$u = \frac{dy}{dt} = y_0 \frac{2\pi v}{\lambda} \cos \frac{2\pi(vt-x)}{\lambda}$$

maximum particle velocity,

$$u_{\max} = y_0 \frac{2\pi v}{\lambda}$$

Now, it is given that maximum particle velocity

$$= 2 \times \text{wave velocity}$$

or $\quad y_0 \dfrac{2\pi v}{\lambda} = 2v$ or $\lambda = \pi y_0$

12. *(d)* Equation of plane progressive harmonic wave is

$$y = a \sin(\omega t + kx) \quad \ldots\text{(i)}$$

Given equation is

$$y = 0.005 \sin(62.4x + 316t) \ldots\text{(ii)}$$

On comparing Eq. (ii) with Eq. (i), we get

$$\omega = 316, k = 62.4$$

$$\Rightarrow \quad k = \frac{2\pi}{\lambda} = 62.4$$

$$\therefore \quad \lambda = \frac{2\pi}{62.4} = \frac{2 \times 3.14}{62.4}$$

$$= 0.1 \text{ unit}$$

13. *(c)* Standard equation of plane progressive harmonic wave is

$$y = a \sin \frac{2\pi}{\lambda}(vt - x) \quad \ldots\text{(i)}$$

Given equation is

$$y = 0.5 \sin \frac{2\pi}{3.2}(64t - x) \quad \ldots\text{(ii)}$$

On comparing Eq. (ii) with Eq. (i), we get

$$v = 64 \quad \text{and} \quad \lambda = 3.2$$

$$\therefore \text{ Frequency } \nu = \frac{v}{\lambda} = \frac{64}{3.2} = 20 \text{ Hz}$$

14. *(d)* A wave equation travelling in +ve x-direction is represented as

$$y = a \sin \omega \left(t - \frac{x}{v}\right)$$

Other forms of wave equations are

$$y = a \sin(\omega t - kx)$$

15. *(d)* Equation of harmonic wave in cosine function is

$$y = a \cos(2\pi \nu t + \phi) \quad \ldots\text{(i)}$$

Given equation is

$$= 0.40 \cos(2000t + 0.80) \ldots\text{(ii)}$$

On comparing Eq. (i) with Eq. (ii), we get

$$2\pi\nu = 2000$$

$$\therefore \quad \nu = \frac{2000}{2\pi} = \frac{1000}{\pi} \text{ Hz}$$

16. *(c)* The standard equation of transverse wave is

$$y = a \sin\left[\frac{2\pi t}{T} - \frac{2\pi x}{\lambda}\right] \quad \ldots\text{(i)}$$

Given equation is

$$y = 4 \sin \frac{\pi}{6} \sin(15t - 3x) \ldots\text{(ii)}$$

On comparing Eq. (ii) with Eq. (i), we get

$$\frac{2\pi}{\lambda} = 3$$

$$\therefore \quad \lambda = \frac{2\pi}{3}$$

and $\quad \dfrac{2\pi}{T} = 15$

$$\therefore \quad T = \frac{2\pi}{15}$$

∴ Speed of propagation wave,

$$v = \frac{\lambda}{T} = \frac{2\pi/3}{2\pi/15} = 5$$

17. *(c)* At a given time (t = constant), the phase changes with position x. The phase change $\Delta\phi$ at a given time for a wavelength λ for a distance Δx is given by

$$\Delta\phi = \frac{2\pi}{\lambda} \Delta x \quad \ldots\text{(i)}$$

From Eq. (i),

$$\Delta x = \frac{\lambda}{2\pi} \cdot \Delta\phi$$

or $\quad \lambda = 2\pi \cdot \dfrac{\Delta x}{\Delta\phi}$

Here, $\Delta x = 0.4$ m, $\Delta\phi = 1.6\,\pi$

$$\therefore \quad \lambda = 2\pi \cdot \frac{0.4}{1.6\pi} = 0.5$$

∴ Frequency of wave is

$$\nu = \frac{v}{\lambda} = \frac{330}{0.5} = 660 \text{ Hz}$$

18. *(b)* Equation of plane progressive simple harmonic wave is

$$y = a \sin\left[2\pi\left(\frac{t}{T} - \frac{x}{\lambda}\right) + \phi\right] \quad \ldots\text{(i)}$$

The given equation is

$$y = 4 \sin\left[\pi\left(\frac{t}{5} - \frac{x}{9}\right) + \frac{\pi}{6}\right] \ldots\text{(ii)}$$

Comparing Eqs. (i) and (ii), we get

$$a = 4 \text{ cm}, T = 10 \text{ s}, \lambda = 18 \text{ cm}$$

and $\quad \phi = \dfrac{\pi}{6}$

Topic 3

01. *(a)* Fundamental frequency of an open pipe,

$$f_0 = \frac{v}{2l}$$

and fundamental frequency of an closed pipe,

$$f_c = \frac{v}{4l}$$

$$\therefore \quad \frac{f_0}{f_c} = \frac{v/2l}{v/4l} = \frac{2}{1}$$

$$\therefore \quad f_0 : f_c = 2:1$$

02. *(b)* Length of string of musical instrument, $l = 90$ cm $= 0.9$ m

Fundamental frequency, $f_1 = 120$ Hz

$$f_2 = 180 \text{ Hz}$$

∴ We know that $f \propto \dfrac{1}{l}$

$$\Rightarrow \quad \frac{f_1}{f_2} = \frac{l_2}{l_1} \Rightarrow l_2 = \frac{f_1 l_1}{f_2} = \frac{120 \times 0.9}{180}$$

$$= \frac{2}{3} \times 0.9 = 0.6 \text{ m} = 60 \text{ cm}$$

03. *(c)* For vibrating tunning fork over a resonance tube, the first resonance is obtained at the length

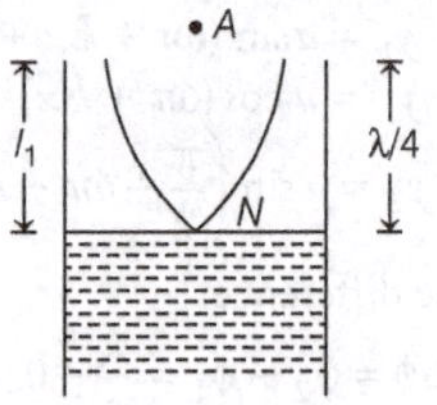

and for second resonance,

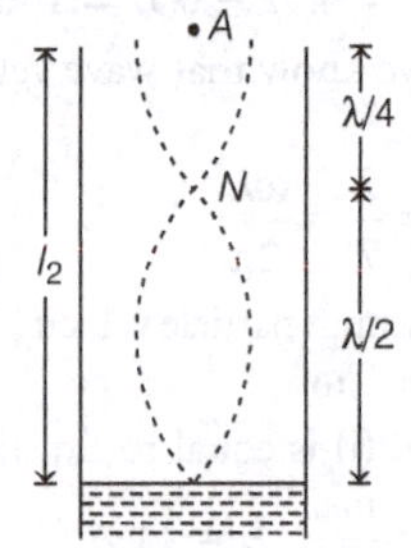

$$l_1 = \frac{\lambda}{4} \quad \ldots\text{(i)}$$

$$l_2 = \frac{\lambda}{4} + \frac{\lambda}{2} = \frac{3\lambda}{4} \quad \ldots\text{(ii)}$$

From Eq. (i) and (ii), we get

$$l_2 - l_1 = \frac{3\lambda}{4} - \frac{\lambda}{4} = \frac{\lambda}{2}$$

$$\Rightarrow \quad \lambda = 2(l_2 - l_1)$$

$$\Rightarrow \quad v = 2f(l_2 - l_1) \quad \ldots\text{(iii)}$$

$$\left(\because \lambda = \frac{v}{f}\right)$$

Here, $f = 800$ Hz, $l_1 = 9.75$ cm, $l_2 = 31.25$ cm

On substituting the given values in Eq. (iii), we get

$$\Rightarrow \quad v = 2 \times 800(31.25 - 9.75)$$
$$= 34400 \text{ cm/s} = 344 \text{ m/s}$$

04. *(c)* Fundamental frequency for an open organ pipe is given as

$$f_1 = \frac{v}{2L}$$

Third harmonic for a closed organ pipe is given as $f' = \dfrac{3v}{4L'}$

According to the question,

$$f = f' \Rightarrow \frac{v}{2L} = \frac{3v}{4L'}$$

$$L = \frac{2}{3}L'$$

Given, $L' = 20$ cm

$$\Rightarrow L = \frac{2}{3} \times 20 \text{ cm} = \frac{40}{3} \text{ cm} = 13.3 \text{ cm}$$

05. *(b)* For first resonance, $l_1 = \dfrac{\lambda}{4}$

For second resonance, $l_2 = \dfrac{3\lambda}{4}$

$$\therefore \quad (l_2 - l_1) = \frac{3\lambda}{4} - \frac{\lambda}{4}$$

$$\text{or} \quad \lambda = 2(l_2 - l_1) \quad \ldots\text{(i)}$$

As, velocity of sound wave is given as,

$$v = \nu\lambda$$

where, ν is the frequency.

$$\Rightarrow \quad v = \nu[2(l_2 - l_1)]$$

[From Eq. (i)]

Here, $\nu = 320$ Hz, $l_2 = 0.73$ m, $l_1 = 0.20$ m

$$\Rightarrow \quad v = 2\,[320(0.73 - 0.20)]$$
$$= 2 \times 320 \times 0.53$$
$$= 339.2 \text{ ms}^{-1} \simeq 339 \text{ ms}^{-1}$$

06. *(b)*

key idea

Frequency of nth harmonic in a closed end tube

$$\Rightarrow \quad f = \frac{(2n-1)v}{4l}, \; n = 1, 2, 3, \ldots$$

Only odd harmonics exists in a closed end tube. Now, given two nearest harmonics are of frequency 220 Hz and 260 Hz.

Frequency of nth harmonic occurs.

$$\therefore \quad \frac{(2n-1)v}{4l} = 220 \text{ Hz} \quad \ldots\text{(i)}$$

Next frequency of $(n+1)$th harmonic occurs at

$$\frac{(2n+1)v}{4l} = 260 \text{ Hz} \quad \ldots\text{(ii)}$$

On subtracting Eq. (i) from Eq. (ii), we get

$$\frac{\{(2n+1)-(2n-1)\}v}{4l} = 260 - 220$$

$$2\left(\frac{v}{4l}\right) = 40$$

$$\Rightarrow \quad \frac{v}{4l} = 20 \text{ Hz}$$

$\therefore$ Fundamental frequency of the system $= \dfrac{v}{4l} = 20$ Hz

07. *(b)* For an open organ pipe,

$$\nu_n = \frac{n}{2L}v, \text{ where } n = 1, 2, 3, \ldots$$

For second overtons $n = 3$,

$$v_{2O} = \frac{3}{2L_1}v \quad \ldots\text{(i)}$$

For closed organ pipe

$$\nu_n = \left(\frac{2n+1}{4L}\right)v,$$

where, $n = 0, 1, 2, 3, \ldots$

Ist overtone for closed organ pipe, $n = 1$

$$\nu_{1C} = \frac{3}{4L}v \quad \ldots\text{(ii)}$$

$$\because \quad \nu_{2O} = \nu_{1C}$$

$$\Rightarrow \quad \frac{3v}{2L_1} = \frac{3}{4L}v$$

$$\Rightarrow \quad L_1 = 2L$$

08. *(c)* The fundamental frequencies of closed and open organ pipe are givan as

$$\nu_c = \frac{v}{4l}$$

$$\Rightarrow \quad \nu_o = \frac{v}{2l'}$$

Given the second overtone (i.e. third harmonic) of open pipe is equal to the fundamental frequency of closed pipe

$$\text{i.e.} \quad 3\nu_o = \nu_c$$

$$\Rightarrow \quad 3\frac{v}{2l'} = \frac{v}{4l}$$

$$\Rightarrow \quad l' = 6l$$
$$= 6 \times 20 = 120 \text{ cm}$$

09. *(b)* The smallest length of the air column is associated with fundamental mode of vibration of the air column as shown in the diagram.

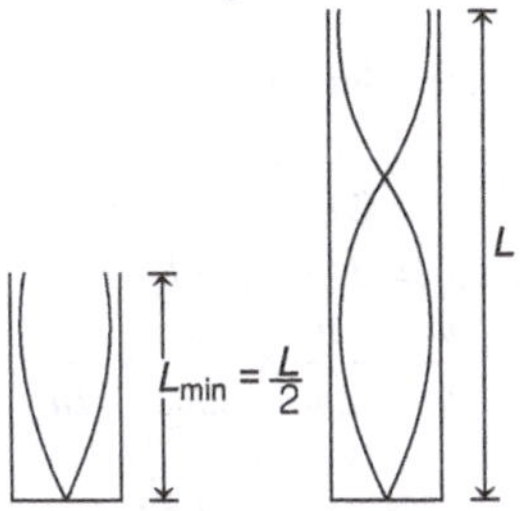

$$\because \quad L_{min} = \frac{\lambda}{4} \Rightarrow 50 \text{ cm} = \frac{\lambda}{4}$$

$$\Rightarrow \quad \lambda = 200 \text{ cm}$$

The next higher length of the air column is

$$L = \frac{\lambda}{4} + \frac{\lambda}{2} = \frac{\lambda + 2\lambda}{4} = \frac{3\lambda}{4}$$
$$= \frac{3}{4} \times 200 = 150 \text{ cm}$$

10. *(d)* Given $l = 75$ cm,

$f_1 = 420$ Hz

and $f_2 = 315$ Hz.

As, two consecutive resonant frequencies for a string fixed at both ends will be

$$f_1 = \frac{nv}{2l} \text{ and } f_2 = \frac{(n+1)v}{2l}$$

$$\Rightarrow \quad f_2 - f_1 = 420 - 315$$

$$\Rightarrow \frac{(n+1)v}{2l} - \frac{nv}{2l} = 105 \text{ Hz}$$

$$\Rightarrow \quad \frac{v}{2l} = 105 \text{ Hz}$$

11. *(a)*

key idea

In this problem, the fundamental frequencies of each part could be found. The fundamental frequency of the complete wire could be found. One should check each option for the given values.

Given,

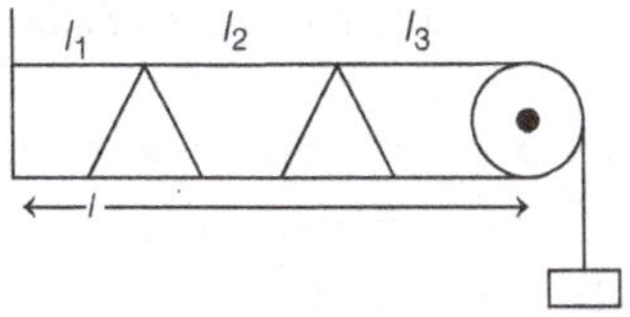

For Ist part, $n_1 = \dfrac{v}{2l_1}$

$$\Rightarrow \quad l_1 = \frac{v}{2n_1}$$

For IInd part, $n_2 = \frac{v}{2l_2} \Rightarrow l_2 = \frac{v}{2n_2}$

For IIIrd part, $n_3 = \frac{v}{2l_3} \Rightarrow l_3 = \frac{v}{2n_3}$

For the complete wire,

$$n = \frac{v}{2l} \Rightarrow l = \frac{v}{2n}$$

We have, $l = l_1 + l_2 + l_3$

$$\frac{v}{2n} = \frac{v}{2n_1} + \frac{v}{2n_2} + \frac{v}{2n_3}$$

$$\frac{1}{n} = \frac{1}{n_1} + \frac{1}{n_2} + \frac{1}{n_3}$$

12. *(d)* For pipe closed at one end,

$f_n = n\left(\frac{v}{4l}\right)$, where n is an odd number.

$$= n\left[\frac{340}{4 \times 85 \times 10^{-2}}\right] = n[100]$$

Here, n is an odd number, so for the given condition, n can go upto $n = 11$

i.e. $n = 1, 3, 5, 7, 9, 11$

So, number of possible natural oscillations could be 6, which are below 1250 Hz.

13. *(d)* Statement (d) is not true because at the open end pressure change will be zero.

14. *(c)* The fundamental frequency of string

$$\nu = \frac{1}{2l}\sqrt{\frac{T}{m}}$$

$\therefore \quad \nu_1 l_1 = \nu_2 l_2 = \nu_3 l_3 = k \quad$ ...(i)

From Eq. (i),

$$l_1 = \frac{k}{\nu_1}, l_2 = \frac{k}{\nu_2}, l_3 = \frac{k}{\nu_3}$$

Original length,

Here, $\quad l = l_1 + l_2 + l_3$

$$\frac{k}{\nu} = \frac{k}{\nu_1} + \frac{k}{\nu_2} + \frac{k}{\nu_3}$$

$$\frac{1}{\nu} = \frac{1}{\nu_1} + \frac{1}{\nu_2} + \frac{1}{\nu_3}$$

15. *(d)* As intensity is directly proportional to the square of amplitude

i.e. $\quad I \propto a^2$

So, maximum intensity is given by

$$I_{max} = (\sqrt{I_1} + \sqrt{I_2})^2$$

and $\quad I_{min} = (\sqrt{I_1} - \sqrt{I_2})^2$

$$\therefore I_{max} + I_{min} = (\sqrt{I_1} + \sqrt{I_2})^2 + (\sqrt{I_1} - \sqrt{I_2})^2$$

$$= 2(I_1 + I_2)$$

16. *(b)* The given progressive waves are

$y_1 = a \sin(\omega t + \phi_1)$

$y_2 = a \sin(\omega t + \phi_2)$

According to principle of super position, the resultant of two waves is

$$y = y_1 + y_2$$
$$= a[\sin(\omega t + \phi_1) + \sin(\omega t + \phi_2)]$$

If A is the amplitude of resultant wave, then

$$A = a \qquad \text{[Given]}$$

$\therefore \quad A^2 = a^2 + a^2 + 2a^2 \cos\phi$

or $\quad a^2 = a^2 + a^2 + 2a^2 \cos\phi$

or $\quad \cos\phi = -\frac{1}{2} = \cos 120°$

$\therefore \quad \phi = 120° = \frac{2\pi}{3}$

Thus, $\phi_1 - \phi_2 = \frac{2\pi}{3}$

17. *(c)* From law of length, the frequency of vibrating sonometer wire is inversely proportional to its length,

i.e. $\quad n \propto \frac{1}{l}$ or nl = constant (say k)

or $\quad l = \frac{k}{n}$

Total length of sonometer wire is l.

So, $\quad l = l_1 + l_2 + l_3 + \ldots$

$\therefore \quad \frac{k}{n} = \frac{k}{n_1} + \frac{k}{n_2} + \frac{k}{n_3} + \ldots$

or $\quad \frac{1}{n} = \frac{1}{n_1} + \frac{1}{n_2} + \frac{1}{n_3} + \ldots$

18. *(a)* The given standing wave is shown in the figure.

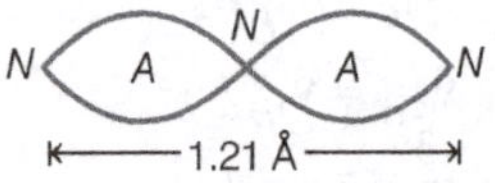

As length of one loop or segment is $\frac{\lambda}{2}$,

so length of 2 segments is $2\left(\frac{\lambda}{2}\right)$.

So, according to question

$\therefore \quad 2\frac{\lambda}{2} = 1.21 \text{ Å} \Rightarrow \lambda = 1.21 \text{ Å}$

19. *(c)* Fundamental frequency of open pipe,

$$f = \frac{v}{2l} \qquad \text{...(i)}$$

When half length of tube is dipped vertically in water then length of the air column becomes half $\left(l' = \frac{l}{2}\right)$ and the pipe becomes closed.

So, new fundamental frequency of closed pipe

$$f' = \frac{v}{4l'} = \frac{v}{4\left(\frac{l}{2}\right)} = \frac{v}{2l} \qquad \text{...(ii)}$$

From Eqs. (i) and (ii), we get

$$f' = f$$

20. *(a)* A pulse of a wave train travels along a stretched string and reaches the fixed end of the string is then reflected back to the same medium and the reflected ray suffers a phase change of π with the incident wave and wave velocity after reflection will reverse.

21. *(b)* In the case of standing wave, the length of one segment is $\frac{\lambda}{2}$.

There are 5 segments and total length of string is 10 m.

$\therefore \quad 5\frac{\lambda}{2} = 10 \Rightarrow \lambda = 4$ m

Frequency, $\quad n = \frac{v}{\lambda} = \frac{20}{4} = 5$ Hz

$(\because v = 20$ m/s$)$

22. *(d)* Interference phenomenon is common to sound and light. In sound, the interference is said to be constructive at points where resultant intensity is maximum (are in phase) and destructive at points where resultant intensity is minimum or zero (are in opposite phase).

• Concept Enhancer

Destructive interference means node and constructive interference means antinode.

23. *(c)* Two wave are said to be coherent, when they have same frequency, amplitude and constant phase difference.

24. *(b)* Distance between two successive nodes $= \frac{\lambda}{2}$

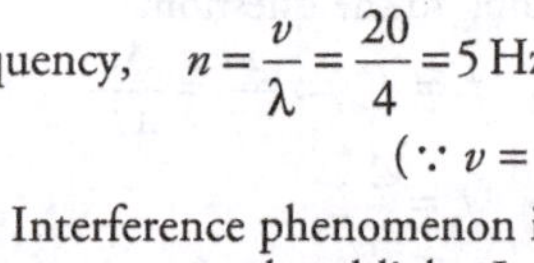

but we know that, $v = \nu\lambda$

$$\therefore \quad \frac{\lambda}{2} = \frac{v}{2\nu}$$

Given, $\quad v = 20$ m/s

frequency, $\quad \nu = n$

So, $\quad \frac{\lambda}{2} = \frac{20}{2n} = \frac{10}{n}$

25. *(c)* As fixed end is a node, therefore distance between two consecutive nodes,

$$\frac{\lambda}{2} = 10 \text{ cm}$$

[λ = wavelength of wave sent]

$$\Rightarrow \quad \lambda = 20 \text{ cm} = 0.2 \text{ m}$$

As we know, $v = \nu\lambda$

$$\therefore \; v = 100 \times 0.2 = 20 \text{ m/s}$$

26. *(a)* The standard equation of standing wave is

$$y = a \sin(\omega t)\cos(kx) \qquad \ldots\text{(i)}$$

Given equation is

$$y = a \sin(100t)\cos(0.01x) \qquad \ldots\text{(ii)}$$

Comparing Eqs. (i) and (ii)

$$\omega = 100 \quad \text{and} \quad k = 0.01$$

$\therefore$ Velocity of wave is

$$v = \frac{\lambda}{T} = \frac{\omega}{k} = \frac{100}{0.01} = 10^4 \text{ m/s}$$

27. *(c)* When both waves are combined, then beats are produced. Frequency of beats will be $= \nu_1 - \nu_2$

$$= \frac{1}{T_1} - \frac{1}{T_2}$$

$$= \frac{1}{3} - \frac{1}{4} = \frac{1}{12}$$

Hence, time period = 12 s

28. *(c)* The frequency of fundamental note of the stretched string is given by

$$\nu = \frac{1}{2L}\sqrt{\left(\frac{T}{\mu}\right)} \qquad \ldots\text{(i)}$$

From Eq. (i) $\nu \propto \frac{1}{L}$

For two different case

$$\therefore \quad \frac{\nu_1}{\nu_2} = \frac{L_2}{L_1}$$

Here, $\nu_1 = 512$ Hz, $L_1 = 0.5$ m

$\nu_2 = 256$ Hz, $L_2 = ?$

$$\therefore \quad \frac{512}{256} = \frac{L_2}{0.5}$$

$$\Rightarrow \quad L_2 = 0.5 \times 2 = 1 \text{ m}$$

29. *(d)* In a closed organ pipe, only alternate harmonics of frequencies $\nu_1, 3\nu_1, 5\nu_1, \ldots$ etc are present. The harmonics of frequencies $2\nu_1, 4\nu_1, 6\nu_1, \ldots$ are missing. In general, the frequency of node produced in *n*th normal mode of vibration of closed organ pipe would be

$$\nu_n = \frac{(2n-1)v}{4L} = (2n-1)\nu_1$$

This is $(2n-1)$ th harmonic or $(n-1)$ th overtone.

Third overtone has a frequency $7\nu_1$, which means

$$L = \frac{7\lambda}{4} = \frac{\lambda}{2} + \frac{\lambda}{2} + \frac{\lambda}{2} + \frac{\lambda}{4}$$

which is three full loops and a half loop, which is equal to four nodes and four antinodes.

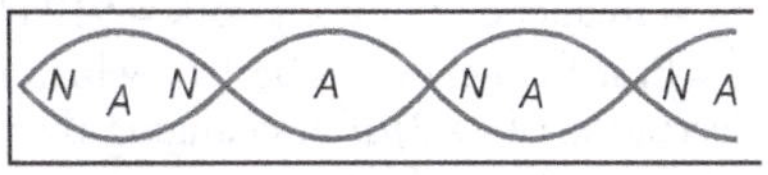

Topic 4

01. *(a)* In case of beats formation unknown frequency $(\nu_B) = \nu_A \pm$ beats

where, $\nu_A = 530$ Hz and beats = 6 Hz.

$$\Rightarrow \quad \nu_B = 530 \pm 6 = 536$$

or 524 Hz

When tension in *B* is slightly decreased, then beats frequency increases to 7 Hz. This is possible if we take original frequency of *B* as 524 Hz.

02. *(d)*

key idea

When both source and observer are moving towards each other, apparent frequency is given by

$$f_a = f_0\left(\frac{v + v_0}{v - v_s}\right)$$

Frequency of the horn,

$$f_0 = 400 \text{ Hz}$$

Speed of observer in the second car,

$$v_0 = 16.5 \text{ m/s}$$

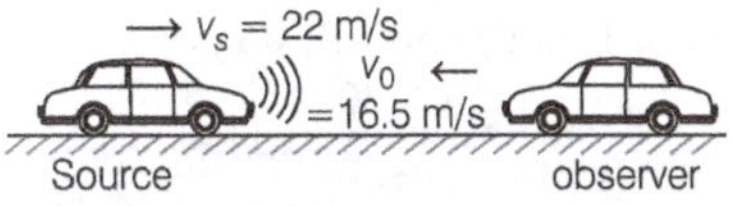

Speed of source,

v_s = speed of first car = 22 m/s

Frequency heard by the driver in the second car

$$f_a = f_0\left(\frac{v + v_0}{v - v_s}\right)$$

$$= 400\left(\frac{340 + 16.5}{340 - 22}\right) = 448 \text{ Hz}$$

03. *(b)* According to question, situation can be drawn as follows

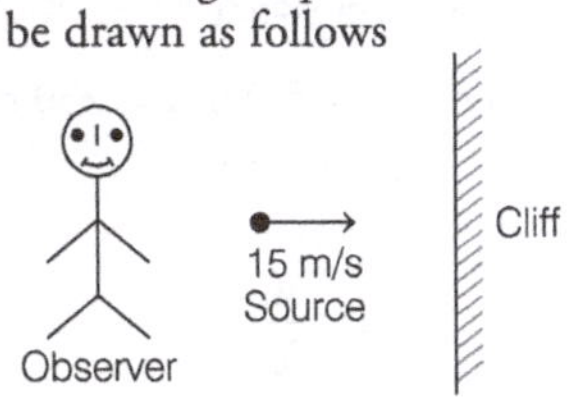

Frequency of sound that the observer hears in the echo reflected from the cliff is given by

$$f' = \left(\frac{v}{v - v_s}\right) f$$

where f = original frequency of source;

v = velocity of sound

v_s = velocity of source

So,

$$f' = \left(\frac{330}{330 - 15}\right) 800$$

$$= 838 \text{ Hz}$$

04. *(d)* As we know that

Beat frequency $= f_2 - f_1$

$$= n - (n-1) = 1$$

and similarly for n and $n+1$

Beat frequency $= n + 1 - n = 1$

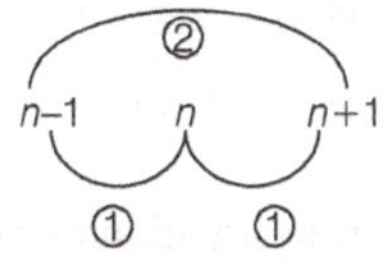

Given,

$f_1 = n - 1$

$f_2 = n$

$f_3 = n + 1$

The number of beats produced per/s

$$= f_3 - f_1$$

$$= (n+1) - (n-1)$$

$$= 2 \text{ beats/s}$$

05. *(b)* Given,

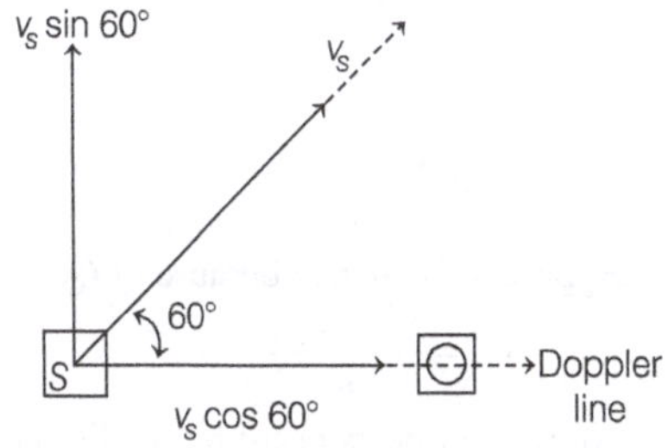

The apparent frequency heard by observer

$$f_0 = f_s\left[\frac{v}{v - v_s \cos 60°}\right]$$

$$= 100\left[\frac{330}{330 - 19.4 \times \frac{1}{2}}\right]$$

$$= 100\left[\frac{330}{300 - 9.7}\right] = 100\left[\frac{330}{320.3}\right]$$

$$= 103.02 \text{ Hz}$$

$$\simeq 103 \text{ Hz}$$

06. *(c)*

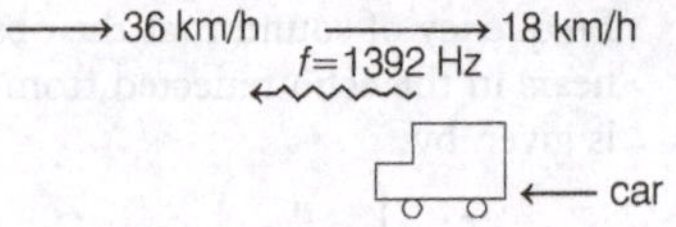

⇒ As both observer and source are moving, we can use the formula of apparent frequency as

$$f = f_0\left(\frac{v+v_0}{v+v_s}\right) = 1392\left[\frac{343+10}{343+5}\right]$$

$[\because v_0 = 36 \text{ km/h} = 10 \text{ m/s and } v_s = 18 \text{ km/h} = 5 \text{ m/s}]$

$$= 1392\left[\frac{353}{348}\right] = 1412 \text{ Hz}$$

07. *(a)* Given,

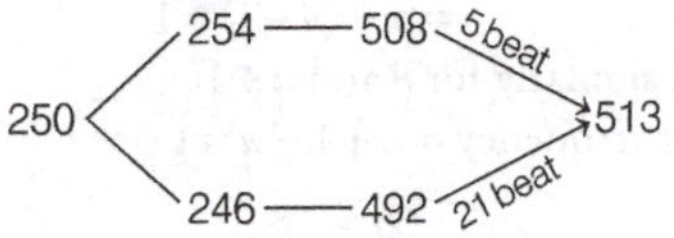

Hence, unknown frequency is 254 Hz.

08. *(a)* The given situation as shown below, speed of listener,

$$v_L = 1 \text{ ms}^{-1}$$

Speed of sound,

$$v = 330 \text{ ms}^{-1}$$

Frequency of source,

$$\nu = 660 \text{ Hz}$$

Apparent frequency because of p

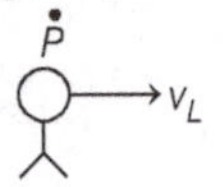

$$\nu' = \frac{\nu(v - v_L)}{v}$$

Apparent frequency because of Q,

$$\nu'' = \frac{\nu(v + v_L)}{v}$$

Number of beats heard by the listener per second is given by

$$\nu'' - \nu' = \frac{\nu(v+v_L)}{v} - \nu\frac{(v-v_L)}{v}$$

$$= \frac{2\nu v_L}{v} = \frac{2\times 660\times 1}{330} = 4$$

09. *(d)* Given, $y_1 = 4\sin 600\pi t$

and $y_2 = 5\sin 608\pi t$

On comparing with general equation

$$y = a\sin 2\pi f t$$

We get, $f_1 = 300$ Hz

and $f_2 = 304$ Hz

So, number of beats $= f_2 - f_1$

$= 4$ beats/s

We know that,

$$\frac{I_{max}}{I_{min}} = \left(\frac{a_1 + a_2}{a_1 - a_2}\right)^2 = \left(\frac{4+5}{4-5}\right)^2 = 81$$

10. *(d)* Let n_p be the frequency of piano.

As $(n_p \propto \sqrt{T})$,

n_f = frequency of tuning fork = 512 Hz

x = Beat frequency = 4 beats/s, which is decreasing $(4 \to 2)$ after changing the tension of piano wire.

Also, tension of piano wire is increasing so $n_p \uparrow$

Hence, $n_p \uparrow - n_f = x\downarrow \longrightarrow$ wrong

$n_f - n_p \uparrow = x\downarrow \longrightarrow$ correct

$$n_p = n_f - x$$

$$= 512 - 4 = 508 \text{ Hz}$$

11. *(c)*

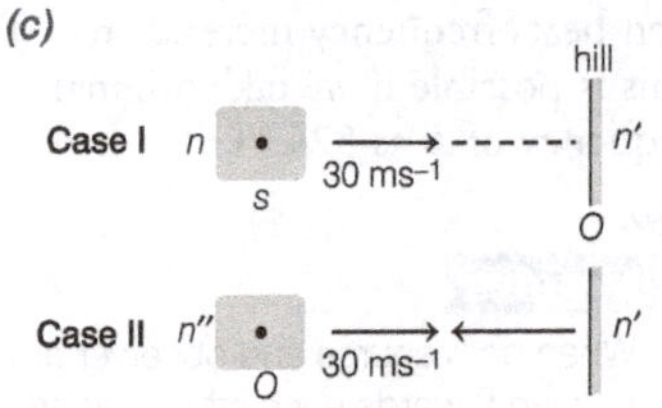

For case I, $n' = \dfrac{v}{v-30} n$ ...(i)

[n = frequency emitted by car
v = velocity of sound]

For case II, $n'' = \dfrac{v+30}{v} n'$ ...(ii)

[n'' = frequency heard by the driver after reflection]

From Eqs. (i) and (ii), we get

$$n'' = \frac{v+30}{v-30}$$

$$n = \frac{360}{300} \times 600$$

$$= 720 \text{ Hz}$$

• Concept Enhancer

According to Doppler's effect, whenever there is a relative motion between a source of sound and the observer (listener), the frequency of sound heard by the observer is different from the actual frequency of sound emitted by source.

12. *(d)* Given, $\lambda_1 = 5.0$ m, $v = 330$ m/s

and $\lambda_2 = 5.5$ m

$\therefore \quad v = n\lambda$

$\Rightarrow \quad n = \dfrac{v}{\lambda}$ ....(i)

The frequency corresponding to wavelength λ_1,

$$n_1 = \frac{v}{\lambda_1} = \frac{330}{5.0} = 66 \text{ Hz}$$

The frequency corresponding to wavelength λ_2,

$$n_2 = \frac{v}{\lambda_2} = \frac{330}{5.5} = 60 \text{ Hz}$$

Hence, number of beats per second

$= n_1 - n_2$

$= 66 - 60 = 6$

13. *(b)*

key idea

You can find beat frequency by using following formula, $f_b = f_2 - f_1$.

where, f_1 and f_2 are frequencies of two waves.

We have,

$$\omega_1 = 500\pi$$

$\Rightarrow \quad n_1 = \dfrac{500\pi}{2\pi} = 250$ beats/s

and $\omega_2 = 506\pi$

$\Rightarrow \quad n_2 = \dfrac{506\pi}{2\pi}$

$= 253$ beats/s

Thus, number of beats produced

$= n_2 - n_1$

$= 253 - 250$

$= 3$ beats/s

$= 3 \times 60$ beats/min

$= 180$ beats/min

14. *(b)* Using doppler effect,

$$f' = f\left(\frac{v+v_o}{v-v_s}\right) \quad ...(i)$$

where, v = velocity of sound,

v_o = velocity of car $= v_s$

Thus, Eq. (i) becomes

$$\therefore \quad 2f = f\left(\frac{v+v_o}{v-v_o}\right)$$

or $2v - 2v_o = v + v_o$

or $3v_o = v$

or $v_o = \dfrac{v}{3}$

15. *(d)* When an observer moves towards a stationary source of sound, then apparent frequency,

$$f' = \left(\frac{v+v_o}{v-v_s}\right) f$$

As source is stationary hence,

$$v_s = 0$$

$\therefore \quad f' = \left(\frac{v + v_o}{v}\right) f$

Given, $\quad v_o = \frac{v}{5}$

On substituting in the relation for f', we get

$$f' = \left(\frac{v + v/5}{v}\right) f$$

$$= \frac{6}{5} f = 1.2 f$$

Wavelength remains same i.e. λ.

• Concept Enhancer

Motion of observer does not affect the wavelength reaching the observer, hence, wavelength remains λ.

16. *(b)* Velocity of source (whistle) is given by

$$v_s = r\omega = (0.5 \text{ m})(20 \text{ rad/s})$$
$$= 10 \text{ m/s}$$

The frequency of sound observed by the observer will be minimum when the whistle is at point A. Thus, at this point minimum frequency of source as observed by observer is

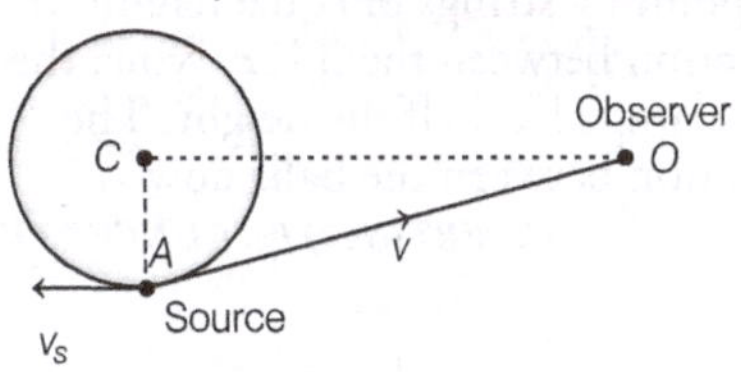

$$f_{\min} = \left(\frac{v}{v + v_s}\right) n$$

$$f_{\min} = \frac{340}{340 + 10} \times 385$$

$$= \frac{34}{35} \times 385$$

$$= 34 \times 11 = 374 \text{ Hz}$$

17. *(a)* Let v be the speed of sound and n the original frequency of each source. They emit sounds of wavelength λ.

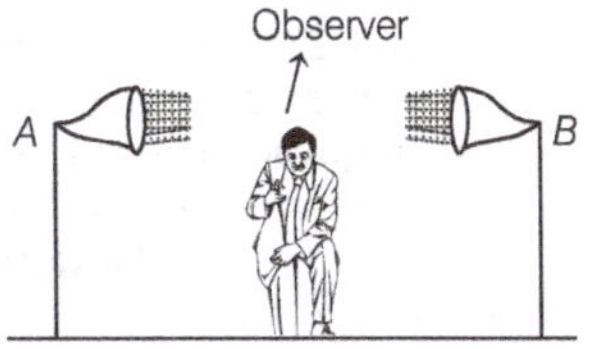

When observer moves towards one source (say A), the apparent frequency of A as observed by the observer will be

$$n' = n\left(\frac{v + u}{v}\right)$$

[u = speed of observer towards A]

The observer is now receding source B, so the apparent frequency of B observed will be

$$n'' = n\left(\frac{v - u}{v}\right)$$

[u = speed of observer going away from B]

Thus, number of beats,

$$x = n' - n'' = n\left[\frac{v + u}{v} - \frac{v - u}{v}\right]$$

$$= \frac{n}{v}[v + u - v + u] = \frac{2nu}{v}$$

but $\quad v = n\lambda$

Thus, $\quad x = \frac{2nu}{n\lambda} = \frac{2u}{\lambda}$

18. *(a)* Beats produced due to the two frequencies is given by

$$n_1 - n_2$$

Here, number of beats = 12/s

$$\lambda_1 = 50 \text{ cm} = 0.50 \text{ m}$$
$$\lambda_2 = 51 \text{ cm} = 0.51 \text{ m}$$

$$n_1 - n_2 = 12$$

or $\quad \frac{v}{\lambda_1} - \frac{v}{\lambda_2} = 12 \quad \left[n = \frac{v}{\lambda}\right]$

or $\quad v\left(\frac{\lambda_2 - \lambda_1}{\lambda_1 \lambda_2}\right) = 12$

or $\quad v = \frac{12\lambda_1\lambda_2}{\lambda_2 - \lambda_1} = \frac{12 \times 0.50 \times 0.51}{(0.51 - 0.50)}$

$$= \frac{12 \times 0.50 \times 0.51}{0.01}$$

$$= 306 \text{ m/s}$$

Thus, speed of sound is 306 m/s.

19. *(b)* When velocity of source (vehicle) is perpendicular to the line joining the observer and source, then there is no Doppler's effect of sound as the component of velocity either towards or away from the observer. So, there is no change in apparent frequency.

Therefore, $n_1 = 0$.

20. *(c)* Frequency of source one with 5 beats/s = 100 Hz

Frequency of source two with 5 beats/s = 205 Hz

Therefore, frequency of first source

$$f_1 = 100 \pm 5 \text{ Hz}$$
$$= 105 \text{ or } 95 \text{ Hz}$$

Similarly for f_2,

$$f_2 = 205 \pm 5 \text{ Hz}$$
$$= 200 \text{ or } 210 \text{ Hz}$$

As the second harmonics gives 5 beats/s with the sound of frequency 205 Hz, therefore frequency of second harmonic should be 210 Hz. So, frequency of source should be 105 Hz.

21. *(b)* When two sound waves of nearly equal frequencies (but not equal) superimpose on each other they produce beats.

22. *(a)* Apparent frequency of sound wave heard by the listener is

$$\nu' = \frac{v - v_l}{v - v_s} \times \nu$$

According to problem, $\nu' = (9/8)\,\nu$ and source and observer are moving in opposite directions with same speed (say v), then apparent frequency

$$\nu' = \nu \times \left(\frac{v + v_l}{v - v_s}\right)$$

$\therefore \quad \frac{9}{8}\nu = \nu \times \frac{340 + v}{340 - v}$

$\therefore \quad 17v = 340$

or $\quad v = \frac{340}{17} = 20 \text{ m/s}$

C-15

NEET Chapterwise Topicwise Physics

In NEET 2024, no questions were visible from this chapter. In past 5 years, 1 question from topic-1, 0 questions from topic-2, 4 questions from topic-3 and 2 questions from topic-4 were asked.

For detailed analysis scan QR code

ELECTRIC CHARGES AND FIELDS

Topic 1 Electric Charges and Coulomb's Law

01 The acceleration of an electron due to the mutual attraction between the electron and a proton when they are 1.6 Å apart is, ($m_e \simeq 9 \times 10^{-31}$ kg, $e = 1.6 \times 10^{-19}$ C) $\left(\text{Take, } \frac{1}{4\pi\varepsilon_0} = 9 \times 10^9 \text{ Nm}^2\text{C}^{-2}\right)$

[NCERT (New) Pg. 08, NEET (Oct.) 2020]

(a) 10^{24} m/s^2 (b) 10^{23} m/s^2

(c) 10^{22} m/s^2 (d) 10^{25} m/s^2

02 Two point charges A and B, having charges $+Q$ and $-Q$ respectively, are placed at certain distance apart and force acting between them is F. If 25% charge of A is transferred to B, then force between the charges becomes ***[NCERT (New) Pg. 08, NEET (National) 2019]***

(a) $\frac{9F}{16}$ (b) $\frac{16F}{9}$

(c) $\frac{4F}{3}$ (d) F

03 Suppose the charge of a proton and an electron differ slightly. One of them is $-e$ and the other is $(e + \Delta e)$. If the net of electrostatic force and gravitational force between two hydrogen atoms placed at a distance d (much greater than atomic size) apart is zero, then Δe is of the order [Given mass of hydrogen, $m_h = 1.67 \times 10^{-27}$ kg] ***[NCERT (New) Pg. 08, NEET 2017]***

(a) 10^{-20} C (b) 10^{-23} C

(c) 10^{-37} C (d) 10^{-47} C

04 Two identical charged spheres suspended from a common point by two massless strings of lengths l, are initially at a distance d $(d << l)$ apart because of their mutual repulsion. The charges begin to leak from both the spheres at a constant rate. As a result, the spheres approach each other with a velocity v. Then, v varies as a function of the distance x between the sphere, as ***[NCERT (New) Pg. 08, NEET 2016]***

(a) $v \propto x$ (b) $v \propto x^{-1/2}$

(c) $v \propto x^{-1}$ (d) $v \propto x^{1/2}$

05 Two pith balls carrying equal charges are suspended from a common point by strings of equal length, the equilibrium separation between them is r. Now, the strings are rigidly clamped at half the height. The equilibrium separation between the balls now becomes ***[NCERT (New) Pg. 08, NEET 2013]***

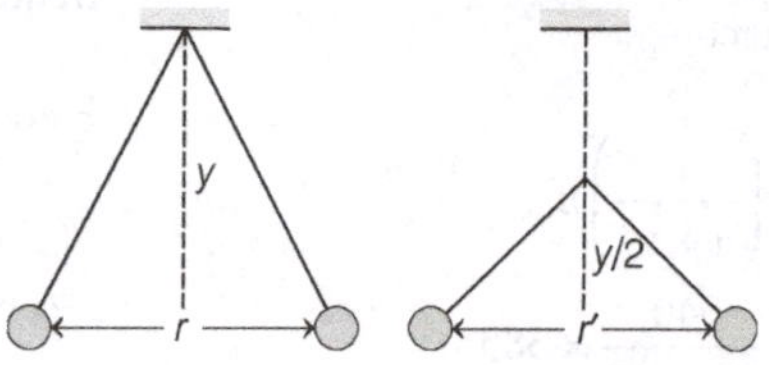

(a) $\left(\frac{1}{\sqrt{2}}\right)^2$ (b) $\left(\frac{r}{\sqrt[3]{2}}\right)$

(c) $\left(\frac{2r}{\sqrt{3}}\right)$ (d) $\left(\frac{2r}{3}\right)$

06 Two positive ions, each carrying a charge q, are separated by a distance d. If F is the force of repulsion between the ions, the number of electrons missing from each ion will be (e being the charge on an electron) ***[NCERT (New) Pg. 08, AIPMT 2010]***

(a) $\frac{4\pi\varepsilon_0 Fd^2}{e^2}$ (b) $\sqrt{\frac{4\pi\varepsilon_0 Fe^2}{d^2}}$

(c) $\sqrt{\frac{4\pi\varepsilon_0 Fd^2}{e^2}}$ (d) $\frac{4\pi\varepsilon_0 Fd^2}{q^2}$

07 An electron is moving round the nucleus of a hydrogen atom in a circular orbit of radius r. The coulomb force F between the two is *[AIPMT 2003]*

(a) $K\frac{e^2}{r^3}\mathbf{r}$ (b) $-K\frac{e^2}{r^3}\mathbf{r}$

(c) $K\frac{e^2}{r^2}\hat{\mathbf{r}}$ (d) $-K\frac{e^2}{r^3}\hat{\mathbf{r}}$ (where, $K=\frac{1}{4\pi\varepsilon_0}$)

08 A simple pendulum has a metal bob, which is negatively charges. If it is allowed to oscillate above a positively charged metallic plate, then its time period will *[NCERT (New) Pg. 271, AIPMT 2001]*

(a) increase (b) decrease
(c) become zero (d) remian the same

09 When air is replaced by a dielectric medium of constant K, the maximum force of attraction between two charges, separated by a distance *[AIPMT 1999]*

(a) decreases K times (b) increases K times
(c) remains unchanged (d) becomes $\frac{1}{K^2}$ times

10 A charge q is placed at the centre of the line joining two exactly equal positive charges Q. The system of three charges will be in equilibrium, if q is equal to *[NCERT (New) Pg. 08, AIPMT 1995]*

(a) $-\frac{Q}{4}$ (b) $+Q$ (c) $-Q$ (d) $\frac{Q}{2}$

11 Point charges $+4q, -q$ and $+4q$ are kept on the X-axis at points $x=0, x=a$ and $x=2a$, respectively. Then, *[NCERT (New) Pg. 12, AIPMT 1988]*

(a) only $-q$ is in stable equilibrium
(b) None of the charges is in equilibrium
(c) all the charges are in unstable equilibrium
(d) all the charges are in stable equilibrium

Topic 2 Electric Field

01 An electron falls from rest through a vertical distance h in a uniform and vertically upward directed electric field E. The direction of electric field is now reversed, keeping its magnitude the same. A proton is allowed to fall from rest in it through the same vertical distance h. The time of fall of the electron, in comparison to the time of fall of the proton is *[NCERT (New) Pg. 14, NEET 2018]*

(a) 10 times greater (b) 5 times greater
(c) smaller (d) equal

02 A particle of mass m and charge q is placed at rest in a uniform electric field E and then released. The kinetic energy attained by the particle after moving a distance y is *[AIPMT 1998]*

(a) qEy^2 (b) qE^2y (c) qEy (d) q^2Ey

03 A pendulum bob of mass 30.7×10^{-6} kg and carrying a charge 2×10^{-8} C is at rest in a horizontal uniform electric field of 20000 V/m. The tension in the thread of the pendulum is ($g=9.8$ m/s^2) *[NCERT (New) Pg. 14, AIPMT 1990]*

(a) 3×10^4 N (b) 4×10^{-4} N
(c) 5×10^{-4} N (d) 6×10^{-4} N

Topic 3 Electric Dipole

01 An electric dipole is placed at an angle of 30° with an electric field of intensity 2×10^5 NC^{-1}. It experiences a torque equal to 4 N m. Calculate the magnitude of charge on the dipole, if the dipole length is 2 cm. *[NCERT (New) Pg. 27, NEET 2023, 2016]*

(a) 6 mC (b) 4 mC (c) 2 mC (d) 8 mC

02 Two point charges $-q$ and $+q$ are placed at a distance of L, as shown in the figure.

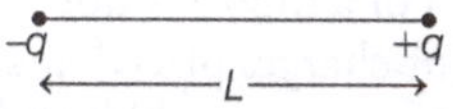

The magnitude of electric field intensity at a distance $R(R>>L)$ varies as *[NCERT (New) Pg. 24, NEET 2022]*

(a) $\frac{1}{R^3}$ (b) $\frac{1}{R^4}$
(c) $\frac{1}{R^6}$ (d) $\frac{1}{R^2}$

03 A dipole is placed in an electric field as shown. In which direction will it move ? *[NCERT (New) Pg. 23, NEET 2021]*

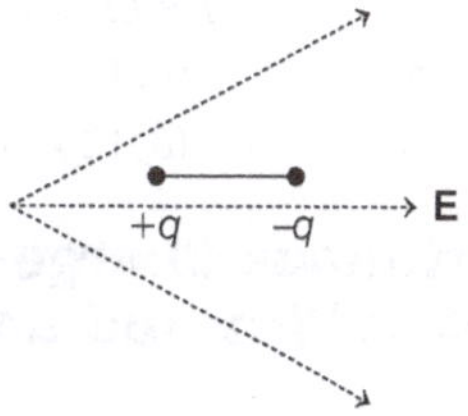

(a) Towards the left as its potential energy will increase.
(b) Towards the right as its potential energy will decrease.
(c) Towards the left as its potential energy will decrease.
(d) Towards the right as its potential energy will increase.

04 The electric field at a point on the equatorial plane at a distance r from the centre of a dipole having dipole moment $\mathbf{p}$ is given by
($r>>$ separation of two charges forming the dipole, ε_0 = permittivity of free space) *[NEET (Oct.) 2020]*

(a) $\mathbf{E}=\frac{\mathbf{p}}{4\pi\varepsilon_0 r^3}$ (b) $\mathbf{E}=\frac{2\mathbf{p}}{4\pi\varepsilon_0 r^3}$

(c) $\mathbf{E}=-\frac{\mathbf{p}}{4\pi\varepsilon_0 r^2}$ (d) $\mathbf{E}=-\frac{\mathbf{p}}{4\pi\varepsilon_0 r^3}$

05 Three point charges $+q$, $-2q$ and $+q$ are placed at points $(x=0, y=a, z=0)$, $(x=0, y=0, z=0)$ and $(x=a, y=0, z=0)$, respectively. The magnitude and direction of the electric dipole moment vector of this charge assembly are *[AIPMT 2007]*

(a) $\sqrt{2}\, qa$ along $+y$-direction

(b) $\sqrt{2}\, aq$ along the line joining points $(x=0, y=0, z=0)$ and $(x=a, y=a, z=0)$

(c) qa along the line joining points $(x=0, y=0, z=0)$ and $(x=a, y=a, z=0)$

(d) $\sqrt{2}\, aq$ along $+x$-direction

06 A point Q lies on the perpendicular bisector of an electric dipole of dipole moment p. If the distance of Q from the dipole is r, (much larger than the size of the dipole) then electric field at Q is proportional to *[NCERT (New) Pg. 24, AIPMT 1998]*

(a) p^{-1} and r^{2} (b) p and r^{-2}

(c) p^{2} and r^{-3} (d) p and r^{-3}

07 The formation of a dipole is due to two equal and dissimilar point charges placed at a *[AIPMT 1996]*

(a) short distance (b) long distance

(c) above each other (d) None of these

08 Intensity of an electric field E depends on distance r due to a dipole, is related as *[AIPMT 1996]*

(a) $E \propto \frac{1}{r}$ (b) $E \propto \frac{1}{r^2}$ (c) $E \propto \frac{1}{r^3}$ (d) $E \propto \frac{1}{r^4}$

09 An electric dipole, consisting of two opposite charges of 2×10^{-6}C each separated by a distance 3 cm is placed in an electric field of 2×10^{5} N/C. Torque on the dipole is *[NCERT (New) Pg. 27, AIPMT 1995]*

(a) 12×10^{-1} N-m (b) 12×10^{-2} N-m

(c) 12×10^{-3} N-m (d) 12×10^{-4} N-m

Topic 4 Continuous Charge Distribution, Electric Flux and Gauss's Laws

01 If $\oint \mathbf{E}\cdot d\mathbf{S} = 0$ over a surface, then *[NCERT (New) Pg. 28, NEET 2023]*

(a) the magnitude of electric field on the surface is constant.

(b) all the charges must necessarily be inside the surface.

(c) the electric field inside the surface is necessarily uniform.

(d) the number of flux lines entering the surface must be equal to the number of flux lines leaving it.

02 A spherical conductor of radius 10 cm has a charge of 3.2×10^{-7} C distributed uniformly. What is the magnitude of electric field at a point 15 cm from the centre of the sphere ? *[NCERT (New) Pg. 14, NEET (Sep.) 2020]*

$\left(\frac{1}{4\pi\varepsilon_0} = 9\times10^{9}\ \text{Nm}^2/\text{C}^2\right)$

(a) 1.28×10^{5} N/C (b) 1.28×10^{6} N/C

(c) 1.28×10^{7} N/C (d) 1.28×10^{4} N/C

03 A sphere encloses an electric dipole with charge $\pm3\times10^{-6}$ C. What is the total electric flux across the sphere ? *[NCERT (New) Pg. 28, NEET (Odisha) 2019]*

(a) -3×10^{-6} N-m^2/C

(b) Zero

(c) 3×10^{6} N-m^2/C

(d) 6×10^{-6} N-m^2/C

04 Two parallel infinite line charges with linear charge densities $+\lambda$ C/m and $-\lambda$ C/m are placed at a distance of $2R$ in free space. What is the electric field mid-way between the two line charges ? *[NCERT (New) Pg. 28, NEET (National) 2019]*

(a) $\frac{2\lambda}{\pi\varepsilon_0 R}$ N/C (b) $\frac{\lambda}{\pi\varepsilon_0 R}$ N/C

(c) $\frac{\lambda}{2\pi\varepsilon_0 R}$ N/C (d) Zero

05 A hollow metal sphere of radius R is uniformly charged. The electric field due to the sphere at a distance r from the centre *[NCERT (New) Pg. 28, NEET (National) 2019]*

(a) zero as r increases for $r < R$, decreases as r increases for $r > R$

(b) zero as r increases for $r < R$, increases as r increases for $r > R$

(c) decreases as r increases for $r < R$ and for $r > R$

(d) increases as r increases for $r < R$ and for $r > R$

06 The electric field in a certain region is acting radially outward and is given by $E = Ar$. A charge contained in a sphere of radius a centred at the origin of the field' will be given by *[NCERT (New) Pg. 28, AIPMT 2015]*

(a) $4\pi\varepsilon_0 Aa^2$ (b) $A\varepsilon_0 a^2$

(c) $4\pi\varepsilon_0 Aa^3$ (d) $\varepsilon_0 Aa^3$

07 What is the flux through a cube of side a if a point charge of q is at one of its corner ? *[NCERT (New) Pg. 22, AIPMT 2012]*

(a) $\frac{2q}{\varepsilon_0}$ (b) $\frac{q}{8\varepsilon_0}$

(c) $\frac{q}{\varepsilon_0}$ (d) $\frac{q}{2\varepsilon_0}6a^2$

08 A charge Q is enclosed by a Gaussian spherical surface of radius R. If the radius is doubled, then the outward electric flux will *[AIPMT 2011]*

(a) be reduced to half (b) remain the same

(c) be doubled (d) increase four times

09 A square surface of side L metre in the plane of the paper is placed in a uniform electric field E (V/m) acting along the same place at an angle θ with the horizontal side of the square as shown in figure.

The electric flux linked to the surface in unit of V-m, is **[AIPMT 2010]**

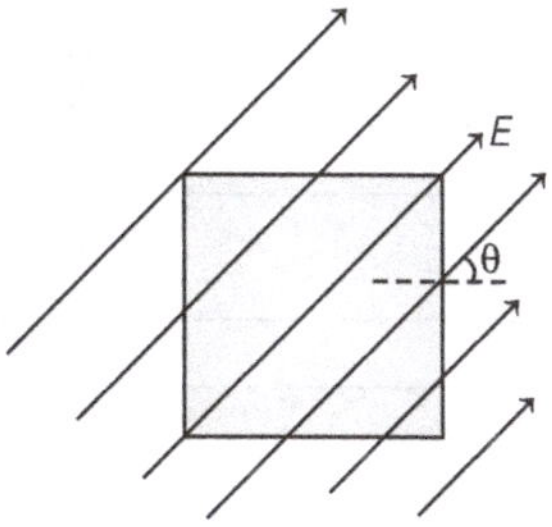

(a) EL^2 (b) $EL^2 \cos\theta$
(c) $EL^2 \sin\theta$ (d) 0

10

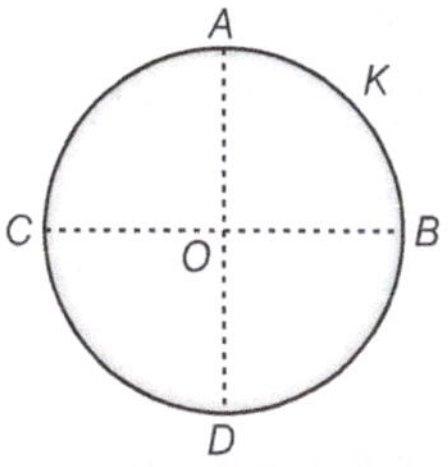

A thin conducting ring of radius R is given a charge $+Q$. The electric field at the centre O of the ring due to the charge on the part AKB of the ring is E. The electric field at the centre due to the charge on the part $ACDB$ of the ring is **[NCERT (New) Pg. 29, AIPMT 2008]**

(a) 3 E along KO
(b) E along OK
(c) E along KO
(d) 3 E along OK

11 A hollow cylinder has a charge q coulomb within it. If ϕ is the electric flux in unit of voltmeter associated with the curved surface B, the flux linked with the plane surface A in unit of voltmeter will be **[AIPMT 2007]**

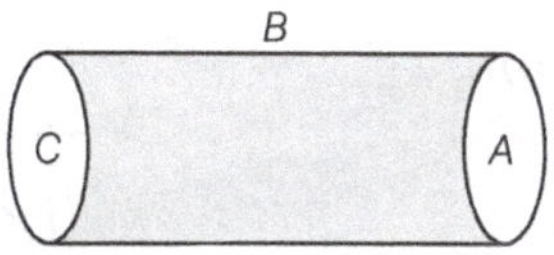

(a) $\frac{1}{2}\left(\frac{q}{\varepsilon_0}-\phi\right)$ (b) $\frac{q}{2\varepsilon_0}$
(c) $\frac{\phi}{3}$ (d) $\frac{q}{\varepsilon_0}-\phi$

12 A square surface of side L metre is in the plane of the paper. A uniform electric field **E** (V/m), also in the plane of the paper, is limited only to the lower half of the square surface, (see figure). The electric flux in SI units associated with the surface is **[NCERT (New) Pg. 29, AIPMT 2006]**

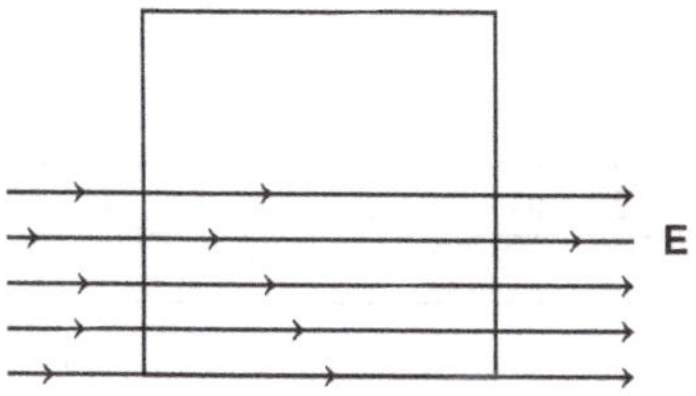

(a) $\frac{EL^2}{(2\varepsilon_0)}$ (b) $\frac{EL^2}{2}$ (c) zero (d) EL^2

13 A charge q is located at the centre of a cube. The electric flux through any face is **[NCERT (New) Pg. 22, AIPMT 2003]**

(a) $\frac{\pi q}{6(4\pi\varepsilon_0)}$ (b) $\frac{q}{6(4\pi\varepsilon_0)}$ (c) $\frac{2\pi q}{6(4\pi\varepsilon_0)}$ (d) $\frac{4\pi q}{6(4\pi\varepsilon_0)}$

14 A charge q μC is placed at the centre of a cube of a side 0.1 m, then the electric flux diverging from each face of the cube is **[NCERT (New) Pg. 22, AIPMT 2001]**

(a) $\frac{q\times10^{-6}}{24\varepsilon_0}$ (b) $\frac{q\times10^{-4}}{\varepsilon_0}$ (c) $\frac{q\times10^{-6}}{6\varepsilon_0}$ (d) $\frac{q\times10^{-4}}{12\varepsilon_0}$

15 A charge q is placed at the corner of a cube of side a. The electric flux through the cube is **[AIPMT 2000]**

(a) $\frac{q}{\varepsilon_0}$ (b) $\frac{q}{3\varepsilon_0}$ (c) $\frac{q}{6\varepsilon_0}$ (d) $\frac{q}{8\varepsilon_0}$

16 A charged wire is bent in the form of a semicircular arc of radius a. If charge per unit length is λ coulomb/metre, the electric field at the centre O is **[NCERT (New) Pg. 28, AIPMT 2000]**

(a) $\frac{\lambda}{2\pi a^2\varepsilon_0}$ (b) $\frac{\lambda}{4\pi^2\varepsilon_0 a}$ (c) $\frac{\lambda}{2\pi\varepsilon_0 a}$ (d) zero

17 A hollow insulated conducting sphere is given a positive charge of 10 μC. What will be the electric field at the centre of the sphere if its radius is 2 m? **[AIPMT 1998]**

(a) Zero (b) $5\,\mu Cm^{-2}$
(c) $20\,\mu Cm^{-2}$ (d) $8\,\mu Cm^{-2}$

18 A point charge $+q$ is placed at mid-point of a cube of side L. The electric flux emerging from the cube is **[AIPMT 1996]**

(a) $\frac{q}{\varepsilon_0}$ (b) $\frac{6\,qL^2}{\varepsilon_0}$ (c) $\frac{q}{6L^2\,\varepsilon_0}$ (d) zero

19 The electric field strength in air at NTP is 3×10^6 V / m. The maximum charge that can be given to a spherical conductor of radius 3 m is **[NCERT (New) Pg. 29, AIPMT 1993]**

(a) 3×10^4 C (b) 3×10^{-3} C
(c) 3×10^{-2} C (d) 3×10^{-1} C

• Key Index

Topic 1

1 (c)	2 (a)	3 (c)	4 (b)	5 (b)	6 (c)	7 (b)	8 (b)	9 (a)	10 (a)
11 (c)									

Topic 2

1 (c)	2 (c)	3 (c)

Topic 3

1 (c)	2 (a)	3 (b)	4 (d)	5 (b)	6 (d)	7 (a)	8 (c)	9 (c)

Topic 4

1 (d)	2 (a)	3 (b)	4 (b)	5 (a)	6 (c)	7 (b)	8 (b)	9 (d)	10 (b)
11 (a)	12 (c)	13 (d)	14 (c)	15 (d)	16 (c)	17 (a)	18 (a)	19 (b)	

Detailed **Explanations**

Topic 1

01. *(c)* Force of mutual attraction between the electron and proton.
(when, $r = 1.6\ \text{Å} = 1.6 \times 10^{-10}$ m) is given as

$$F = 9 \times 10^9 \times \frac{e^2}{r^2}$$
$$= 9 \times 10^9 \times \frac{(1.6 \times 10^{-19})^2}{(1.6 \times 10^{-10})^2}$$
$$= 9 \times 10^{-9}\ \text{N}$$

∴ Acceleration of electron

$$= \frac{F}{m_e} = \frac{9 \times 10^{-9}}{9 \times 10^{-31}} = 10^{22}\ \text{m/s}^2$$

02. *(a)* The force between two point charges A and B having charge $+Q$ and $-Q$ respectively is given by

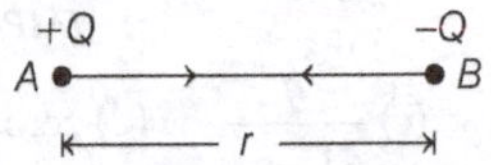

$$F = \frac{KQ_AQ_B}{r^2}$$
$$= \frac{KQ(Q)}{r^2} = \frac{KQ^2}{r^2} \quad \ldots\text{(i)}$$

When 25% charge of A is transferred to B, then new amount of charge on A and B respectively become

$$Q'_A = \frac{3}{4}Q$$
$$Q'_B = \left(\frac{25}{100}Q_A + Q_B\right)$$
$$= \left(\frac{1}{4}Q - Q\right) = \frac{-3}{4}Q$$
$$|Q'_B| = \frac{3Q}{4}$$

So, the force between the two charges now becomes

$$F' = \frac{KQ'_A|Q'_B|}{r^2} = \frac{K\left(\frac{3Q}{4}\right)\left(\frac{3}{4}Q\right)}{r^2}$$
$$= \frac{9KQ^2}{16r^2} = \frac{9}{16}F \quad \text{[From Eq. (i)]}$$

Thus, the new force between the charges is 9/16 times the initial force between the charges.

03. *(c)* Net charge on one H-atom $q = -e + e + \Delta e = \Delta e$
Net electrostatic repulsive force between two H-atoms

$$F_r = \frac{Kq^2}{d^2} = \frac{K(\Delta e)^2}{d^2}$$

Similarly, net gravitational attractive force between two H-atoms

$$F_G = \frac{Gm_r^2}{d^2}$$

It is given that,

$$F_r - F_G = 0$$
$$\Rightarrow \frac{K(\Delta e)^2}{d^2} - \frac{Gm_r^2}{d^2} = 0$$
$$\Rightarrow (\Delta e)^2 = \frac{Gm_r^2}{K}$$
$$(\Delta e)^2 = \frac{(6.67 \times 10^{-11})(1.67 \times 10^{-27})^2}{9 \times 10^9}$$
$$\Rightarrow \Delta e = 1.437 \times 10^{-37}\ \text{C}$$

04. *(b)* According to question, two identical charged spheres suspended from a common point by two massless strings of length l.

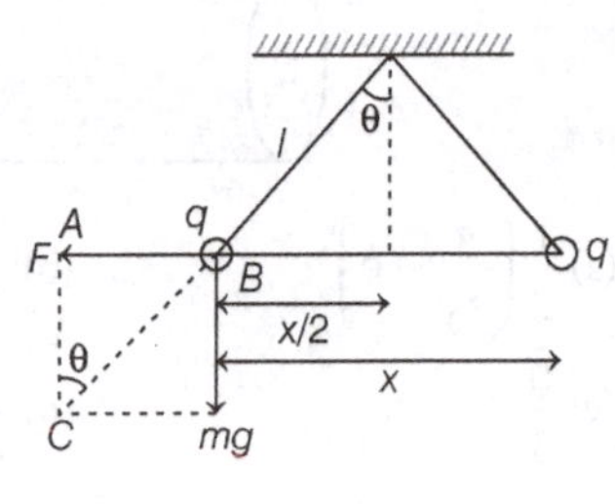

∵ In ΔABC,

$$\frac{F}{mg} = \tan\theta \quad \ldots\text{(i)}$$

Since, the charges begins to leak from both the spheres at a constant rate. As a result, the spheres approach each other with velocity v.

Therefore, Eq. (i) can be rewritten as

$$\frac{kq^2}{x^2 mg} = \frac{x/2}{\sqrt{l^2 - \frac{x^2}{4}}} \quad [\because l >>> x]$$

$$\Rightarrow \quad \frac{kq^2}{x^2 mg} = \frac{x}{2l} \quad \text{or} \quad q^2 \propto x^3$$

$$\Rightarrow \quad q \propto x^{3/2}$$

$$\Rightarrow \quad \frac{dq}{dt} \propto \frac{d(x^{3/2})}{dx} \cdot \frac{dx}{dt}$$

$$\Rightarrow \quad \frac{dq}{dt} \propto x^{1/2} . v$$

$$\Rightarrow \quad v \propto \frac{1}{x^{1/2}} \quad \text{or} \quad v \propto x^{-1/2}$$

05. *(b)* **Case I** $F_e \cos\theta = mg \sin\theta$

$$\Rightarrow \quad \frac{F_e}{mg} = \tan\theta$$

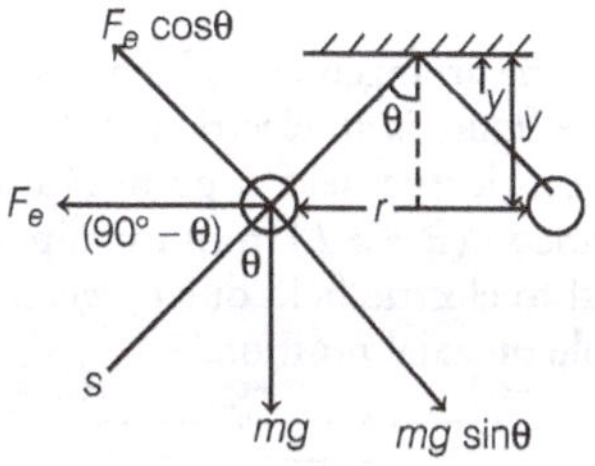

$$\Rightarrow \quad mg = \frac{F_e}{\tan\theta} \quad \ldots\text{(i)}$$

Case II $F_e' \cos\theta_1 = mg \sin\theta_1$

$$\Rightarrow \quad \frac{F_e'}{mg} = \tan\theta_1$$

$$\Rightarrow \quad mg = \frac{F_e'}{\tan\theta_1} \quad \ldots\text{(ii)}$$

From Eqs. (i) and (ii), we get

$$\frac{F_e}{\tan\theta} = \frac{F_e'}{\tan\theta_1} \Rightarrow \frac{F_e}{F_e'} = \frac{\tan\theta}{\tan\theta_1}$$

As, $\tan\theta = \dfrac{P\,(\text{perpendicular})}{b\,(\text{base})} = \dfrac{r}{2y}$

$$\tan\theta_1 = P/b = \frac{r'}{2 \times y} \times 2 = \frac{r'}{y}$$

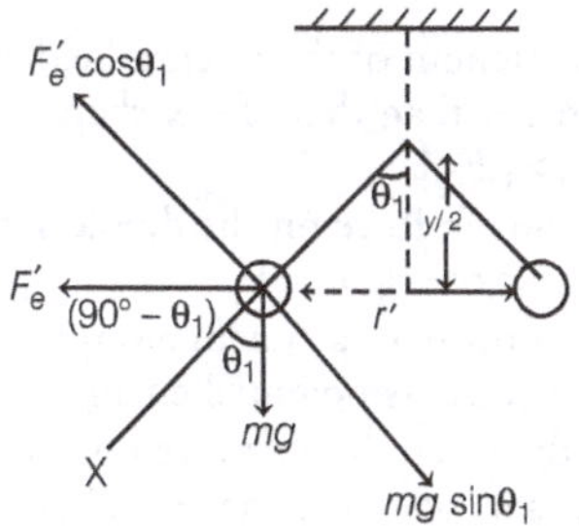

$$\frac{F_e}{F_e'} = \frac{r}{2y \times r'} \times y \Rightarrow \frac{F_e'}{r'} = \frac{2F_e}{r}$$

$$\text{So,} \quad \frac{kq^2}{r'^3} = \frac{2kq^2}{r^3}$$

$$\therefore \quad r' = \frac{r}{\sqrt[3]{2}}$$

Alternate Solution

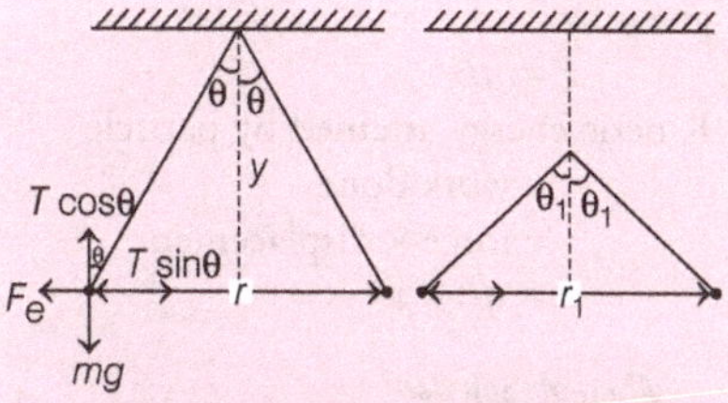

At equilibrium, $T\cos\theta = mg$, $T\sin\theta = F_e$

$$\therefore \tan\theta = \frac{F}{mg} \Rightarrow \frac{r/2}{y} = \frac{\frac{kq^2}{r^2}}{mg}$$

$$\Rightarrow \quad r^3 \propto y \quad \ldots\text{(i)}$$

When string is clamped at half the height

$$r'^3 \propto \frac{y}{2} \quad \ldots\text{(ii)}$$

On dividing Eq. (ii) from Eq. (i), we get

$$\frac{r'}{r} = \frac{1}{2^{1/3}} \Rightarrow r' = \frac{r}{\sqrt[3]{2}}$$

06. *(c)* Two positive ions each carrying a charge q are kept at a distance d, then it is found that force of repulsion between them is

$$F = \frac{kqq}{d^2} = \frac{1}{4\pi\varepsilon_0} \frac{qq}{d^2}$$

where, $q = ne$

$$\therefore \ F = \frac{1}{4\pi\varepsilon_0} \frac{n^2 e^2}{d^2} \quad \Rightarrow n = \sqrt{\frac{4\pi\varepsilon_0 Fd^2}{e^2}}$$

07. *(b)* Let charges on an electron and hydrogen nucleus be q_1 and q_2. Then, Coulomb's force between them at a distance r is,

$$\mathbf{F} = -\frac{1}{4\pi\varepsilon_0} \frac{q_1 q_2}{r^2} \hat{\mathbf{r}}$$

Putting, $\dfrac{1}{4\pi\varepsilon_0} = K$ [Given]

$$\mathbf{F} = -K \frac{q_1 q_2}{r^2} \hat{\mathbf{r}}$$

Since, the nucleus of hydrogen atom has one proton, so charge on nucleus is e i.e. $q_2 = +e$

also $q_1 = e$ for electron

$$\text{So,} \quad \mathbf{F} = -K \frac{e.e}{r^2} \hat{\mathbf{r}} = -K \frac{e^2}{r^2} \hat{\mathbf{r}}$$

but $\quad \hat{\mathbf{r}} = \dfrac{\mathbf{r}}{|\mathbf{r}|} = \dfrac{\mathbf{r}}{r}.$

Hence, $\quad \mathbf{F} = -K \dfrac{e^2}{r^2} . \dfrac{\mathbf{r}}{r} = -K \dfrac{e^2}{r^3} . \mathbf{r}$

08. *(b)*

key idea

You can use following formula to calculate time period of simple pendulum.

$T = 2\pi\sqrt{l/g}$

We know that the time period T of a simple pendulum is given by

$$= 2\pi\sqrt{\frac{l}{g'}} \propto \frac{1}{\sqrt{g'}}$$

$$g' = g_{\text{effective}}$$

Since, the negative charged bob is attracted by the positively charged plate, therefore acceleration due to gravity will increase and time period will decrease.

09. *(a)* According to Coulomb's law, force between two charges is

$$F = \frac{1}{4\pi\varepsilon_0 K} \frac{q_1 q_2}{r^2} \quad \ldots\text{(i)}$$

If a dielectric medium of constant K is placed between them, then new force between them,

$$F_1 = \frac{1}{4\pi\varepsilon_0 K} \cdot \frac{q_1 q_2}{r^2} \quad \ldots\text{(ii)}$$

Dividing Eq. (ii) by Eq. (i), we have

$$\frac{F_1}{F} = \frac{1}{K} \text{ or } F' = \frac{F}{K}$$

Thus, new force decreases K times.

10. *(a)* Let two equal charges Q each be held at A and B, where $AB = 2x$. C is the centre of AB, where charge q is held. Net force on q is zero. So, q is already in equilibrium.

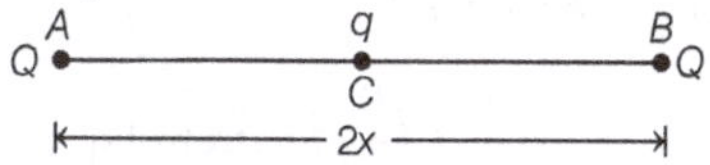

For the three charges to be in equilibrium, net force on each charge must be zero.

Now, total force on Q at B is

$$\frac{1}{4\pi\varepsilon_0} \cdot \frac{Qq}{x^2} + \frac{1}{4\pi\varepsilon_0} \cdot \frac{QQ}{(2x)^2} = 0$$

$$\text{or} \quad \frac{1}{4\pi\varepsilon_0} \cdot \frac{Qq}{x^2} = -\frac{1}{4\pi\varepsilon_0} \cdot \frac{Q^2}{4x^2}$$

$$\text{or} \quad q = -\frac{Q}{4}$$

11. *(c)* Net force on charge placed at A due to charges placed at C and B

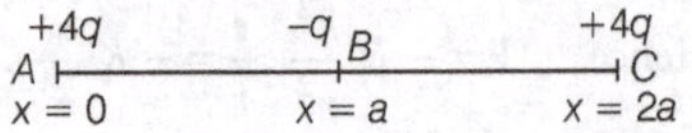

$$F_A = \frac{1}{4\pi\varepsilon_0}\frac{(+4q)(q)}{a^2} - \frac{1}{4\pi\varepsilon_0}\frac{(+4q)(+4q)}{(2a)^2}$$

$$= \frac{1}{4\pi\varepsilon_0}\frac{4q^2}{a^2} - \frac{1}{4\pi\varepsilon_0}\frac{4q^2}{a^2} = 0$$

Similarly, F_B and F_C will be zero. As net force on each charge is zero, therefore all the charges are in equilibrium. If we were to displace $-q$ to the right, (in figure), net force of attraction will be to the right which will displace it further. Therefore, equilibrium is unstable.

Topic 2

01. *(c)* Force on a charged particle in the presence of an electric field is given as

$$F = qE \quad \text{...(i)}$$

From Newton's second law of motion, force on a particle with mass m is given as

$$F = ma \quad \text{...(ii)}$$

where, a is the acceleration.

From Eqs. (i) and (ii), we get

$$F = ma = qE$$

$$\Rightarrow \quad a = \frac{qE}{m} \quad \text{...(iii)}$$

Now, consider that a particle falls from rest through a vertical distance h. Therefore, $u = 0$ and the second equation of motion becomes

$$s = ut + \frac{1}{2}at^2$$

or $$h = 0 \times t + \frac{1}{2}at^2$$

$$= \frac{1}{2} \times \frac{qE}{m}t^2 \quad \text{[from Eq. (iii)]}$$

$$\Rightarrow \quad t^2 = \frac{2hm}{qE} \text{ or } t = \sqrt{\frac{2hm}{qE}}$$

Since, the particles given in the question is electron and proton; and the quantity $\sqrt{\frac{2h}{qE}}$ (here, $q_p = q_e = e$) for both of them is constant. Thus, we can write, $t = k\sqrt{m}$

where, $k = \sqrt{\frac{2h}{qE}}$ or $t \propto \sqrt{m}$

As, mass of proton $(m_p) >>$ mass of electron (m_e).

Thus, the time of fall of an electron would be smaller than the time of fall of a proton.

02. *(c)* Electric force on charged particle is given by

$$F = qE$$

Kinetic energy attained by particle

= work done

= force × displacement

$= qE \times y$

Alternate Solution

Force on charged particle in a uniform electric field is

$$F = ma = Eq \text{ or } a = \frac{Eq}{m} \quad \text{...(i)}$$

From the equation of motion, we have

$$v^2 = u^2 + 2ay = 0 + 2 \times \frac{Eq}{m} \times y \quad [u = 0]$$

$$= \frac{2Eqy}{m}$$

Now, kinetic energy of the particle

$$K = \frac{1}{2}mv^2 = \frac{m}{2} \times \frac{2Eqy}{m} = qEy$$

03. *(c)* There are 2 forces acting on pendulum (i) its weight (ii) electric force

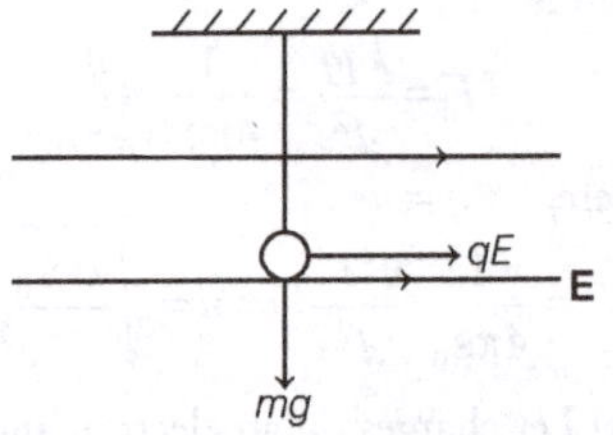

(i) Weight, $mg = 30.7 \times 10^{-6} \times 9.8$

$= 3 \times 10^{-4}$ N

vertically downward, and

(ii) Force, $F = qE$

$= 2 \times 10^{-8} \times 20000$

$= 4 \times 10^{-4}$ N

In the horizontal direction.

So, net tension,

$$T = \sqrt{(mg)^2 + F^2}$$

$$= \sqrt{(3 \times 10^{-4})^2 + (4 \times 10^{-4})^2}$$

$$= 5 \times 10^{-4} \text{ N}$$

Topic 3

01. *(c)* Given, $\theta = 30°$

$$E = 2 \times 10^5 \text{ NC}^{-1}$$

Dipole length, $2l = 2$ cm $= 2 \times 10^{-2}$ m

Torque, $\tau = 4$ N-m

We know that, $\tau = pE \sin\theta$

$$\Rightarrow \quad p = \frac{\tau}{E\sin\theta} = \frac{4}{2 \times 10^5 \times \sin 30°}$$

$$\Rightarrow \quad p = 4 \times 10^{-5} \text{ C-m}$$

$$\Rightarrow \quad 2l \cdot q = 4 \times 10^{-5}$$

$$\Rightarrow \quad q = \frac{4 \times 10^{-5}}{2l} = \frac{4 \times 10^{-5}}{2 \times 10^{-2}}$$

$$= 2 \times 10^{-3} \text{ C} = 2 \text{ mC}$$

02. *(a)* The arrangement of charges shown in the figure is an electric dipole. Hence, electric field at point P at a distance $R(R >> L)$ from the dipole is equal to electric field due to electric dipole on axial position.

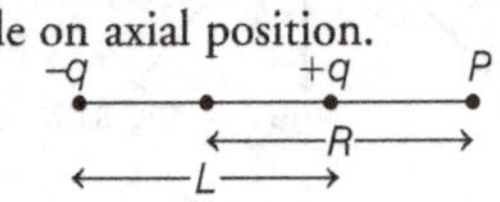

i.e., $$E = \frac{1}{4\pi\varepsilon_0} \cdot \frac{2p}{R^3}$$

where, $p = qL$ (Electric dipole moment)

$$\therefore \quad E \propto \frac{1}{R^3}$$

03. *(b)* We know that, the direction of electric dipole moment is from negative charge to positive charge.

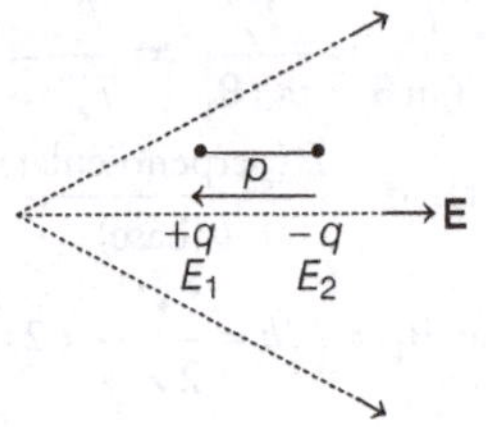

The strength of the electric field at $+q$ is greater than that of $-q$ charge, i.e. $|E_1| > |E_2|$.

So, the net force on the dipole act towards the right side.

We know that, a system always moves to decrease its potential energy.

So, the given dipole move towards right side as its potential energy will decrease.

04. *(d)* Electric field due to electric dipole on equatorial plane at a distance r from the centre of dipole is given as

$$\mathbf{E} = -\frac{1}{4\pi\varepsilon_0} \cdot \frac{\mathbf{p}}{r^3}$$

05. *(b)* Choose the three coordinate axes as X, Y and Z and plot the charges with the given coordinates as shown. O is the origin at which $-2q$ charge is placed.

The system is equivalent to two dipoles along x-and y-directions respectively. The dipole moments of two dipoles are shown in figure.

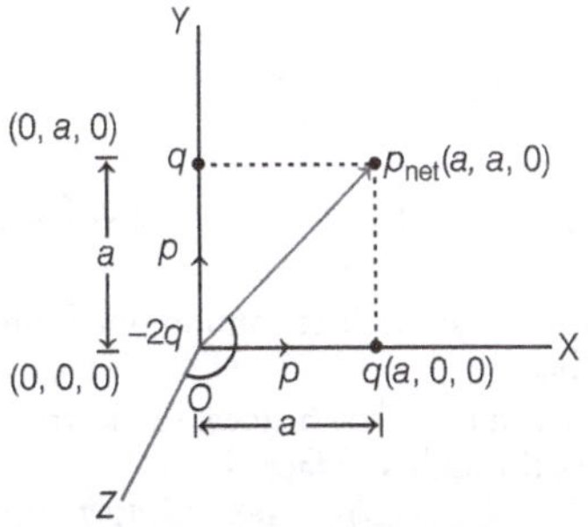

The resultant dipole moment will be directed along OP where coordinate of $\mathbf{p}_{net}$ is given by $(a, a, 0)$. The magnitude of resultant dipole moment is

$$\mathbf{p}_{net} = \sqrt{p^2 + p^2}$$
$$= \sqrt{(qa)^2 + (qa)^2} = \sqrt{2}\, qa$$

06. *(d)* Electric field due to a dipole at bisector or at a point on its broad side on position or equatorial position is given by

$$E = \frac{1}{4\pi\varepsilon_0} \cdot \frac{p}{r^3} \text{ or } E \propto \frac{p}{r^3} \quad \text{...(i)}$$

where, r is the distance of that point from centre of dipole and p is dipole moment.

So, from Eq. (i)

$$E \propto p \text{ and } E \propto r^{-3}$$

> **• Concept Enhancer**
> An electric dipole is an arrangement of two equal and opposite charges placed at distance $2l$.

07. *(a)* An electric dipole consists of a pair of equal and opposite point charges separated by a very small distance. .

08. *(c)* Field intensity on axial line of electric dipole is given by

$$E = \frac{1}{4\pi\varepsilon_0} \cdot \frac{2p}{r^3} \quad \text{...(i)}$$

and electric field at equatorial position is given by

$$E = \frac{1}{4\pi\varepsilon_0} \times \frac{p}{r^3} \quad \text{...(ii)}$$

where, p is electric dipole moment.

From Eqs. (i) and (ii), we get

$$E \propto \frac{1}{r^3}$$

> **• Concept Enhancer**
> Atoms or molecules of ammonia, water, alcohol, carbon dioxide, HCl etc are some of the examples of electric dipoles, because in these cases, the centres of positive and negative charge distributions are separated by some small distance.

09. *(c)* When a dipole of dipole moment $\mathbf{p}$ is placed in a uniform external electric field $\mathbf{E}$, then torque acting on dipole is

$$\tau = \mathbf{p} \times \mathbf{E} = |p| \times |E| \sin\theta$$

where, $\mathbf{p} = q \times 2l$

($2l$ is length of dipole)

Given, $q = 2 \times 10^{-6}$ C

$$2l = 3 \text{ cm} = 3 \times 10^{-2} \text{ m}$$
$$E = 2 \times 10^5 \text{ N/C}$$

As, $\tau = pE \sin\theta \quad (\theta = 90° \; p \perp \mathbf{E})$

So, $\tau = pE$

$\therefore$

$$\tau = (2 \times 10^{-6}) \times (3 \times 10^{-2}) \times (2 \times 10^5)$$
$$= 12 \times 10^{-3} \text{ N-m}$$

Topic 4

01. *(d)* According to Gauss's law, $\oint \mathbf{E} \cdot d\mathbf{S}$ represents total electric flux passing through a closed surface.

If $\oint \mathbf{E} \cdot d\mathbf{S} = 0$, then it signifies that the number of electric flux lines entering the surface must be equal to the number of flux lines leaving the surface.

02. *(a)* Given, radius, $r = 10$ cm

$$= 10 \times 10^{-2} \text{ m}$$

Charge, $q = 3.2 \times 10^{-7}$ C

Electric field at a point ($x = 15$ cm) from the centre of the sphere is

$$E = \frac{1}{4\pi\varepsilon_0} \cdot \frac{q}{x^2}$$
$$= 9 \times 10^9 \times \frac{3.2 \times 10^{-7}}{(15 \times 10^{-2})^2}$$
$$= 1.28 \times 10^5 \text{ N/C}$$

Hence, correct option is (a).

03. *(b)* When a sphere encloses a charged dipole,

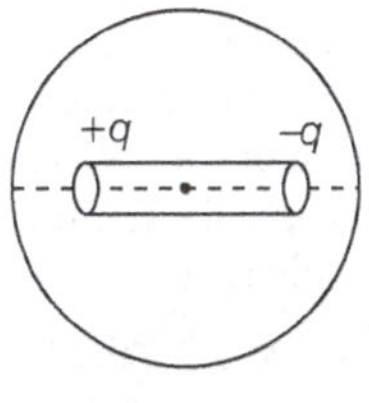

Here, $q = \pm 3 \times 10^{-6}$ C

Thus, according to Gauss's law, the net electric flux across the closed surface is equal to the net charge enclosed by it divided by ε_0, i.e.

$$\phi_E = \frac{q_{in}}{\varepsilon_0} = \frac{+3 \times 10^{-6} - 3 \times 10^{-6}}{\varepsilon_0} = 0$$

Hence, electric flux across the sphere is zero.

Note For a dipole or quadrupole, net electric flux will always be zero.

04. *(b)* Consider two infinite line charges with linear charge densities $+\lambda$ C/m and $-\lambda$ C/m respectively, which are lying in y-direction as shown in the figure below.

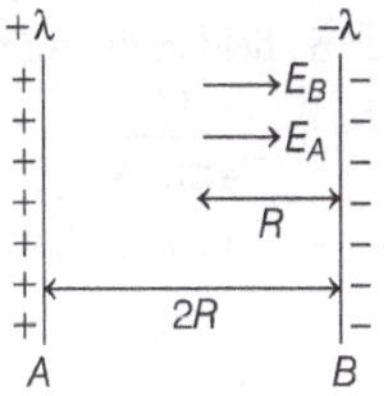

Then, the electric field due to line A at the mid way between the two line charges, i.e. at R is

$$|\mathbf{E}_A| = \frac{\lambda}{2\pi\varepsilon_0 R} \text{ N/C} \quad \text{... (i)}$$

which lies along +ve X-axis (outward), i.e. from A to B. Similarly, the electric field due to line B at the mid-way between the two line charges, i.e. at R is

$$|\mathbf{E}_B| = \frac{\lambda}{2\pi\varepsilon_0 R} \text{N/C} \quad \text{... (ii)}$$

Due to negative charge on B, $\mathbf{E}_B$ also lies along +ve X-axis (inward), i.e. from A to B.

So, the resultant electric field at R is given as

$$|\mathbf{E}_R| = |\mathbf{E}_A| + |\mathbf{E}_B|$$

Substituting the values from Eqs. (i) and (ii), we get

$$|\mathbf{E}_R| = \frac{\lambda}{2\pi\varepsilon_0 R} + \frac{\lambda}{2\pi\varepsilon_0 R}$$

$$= \frac{\lambda}{\pi\varepsilon_0 R} \text{ N/C}$$

which also lies along the + ve X-axis, i.e. from A to B.

05. *(a)* As the hollow sphere is uniformly charged, so the net charge will appear on the surface of the sphere.

(i) The electric field at a point outside the hollow sphere is

$$\phi = \oint_S \mathbf{E} \cdot d\mathbf{S} = \frac{Q_{\text{enclosed}}}{\varepsilon_0}$$

[from Gauss' law]

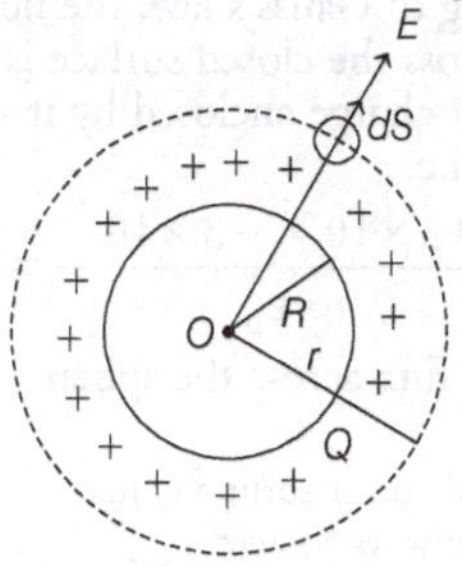

$$\Rightarrow \quad E(4\pi r^2) = \frac{Q}{\varepsilon_0}$$

$$\Rightarrow \quad E = \frac{Q}{4\pi\varepsilon_0 r^2} \Rightarrow E \propto \frac{1}{r^2}$$

(ii) The electric field at the surface ($r = R$),

$$E = \frac{Q}{4\pi\varepsilon_0 R}$$

(iii) The electric field inside hollow sphere is

$$E = \frac{Q}{4\pi\varepsilon_0 r} = 0 \quad [\because Q_{\text{inside}} = 0]$$

Thus, the electric field is zero inside the hollow sphere maximum at the surface and decreases as r increases for $r > R$. This can be shown graphically as

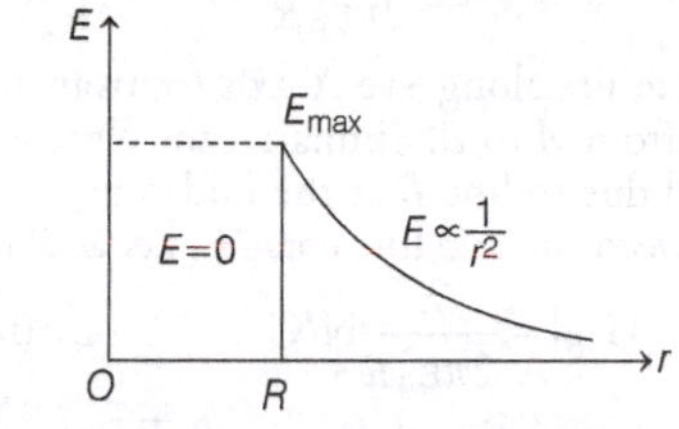

06. *(c)* Given, $\quad E = Ar \quad$ ...(i)

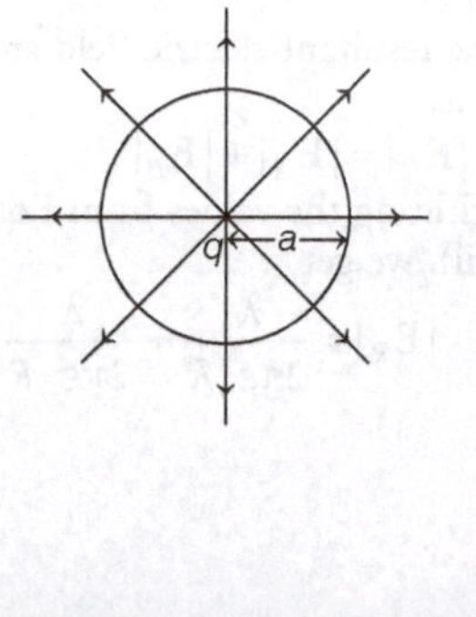

Here, $\quad r = a$

$$\Rightarrow \quad E = \frac{1}{4\pi\varepsilon_0} \cdot \frac{q}{a^2}$$

From Eq. (i), we get

$$\frac{1}{4\pi\varepsilon_0} \cdot \frac{q}{a^2} = Aa$$

$$\Rightarrow \quad q = 4\pi\varepsilon_0 A a^3$$

07. *(b)* According to Gauss's law, the electric flux through a closed surface is equal to $\frac{1}{\varepsilon_0}$ times the net charge enclosed by the surface.

As the charge enclosed $= q/8$

So, electric flux $= \frac{q_{\text{enclosed}}}{\varepsilon_0} \Rightarrow \phi = \frac{q}{8\varepsilon_0}$

08. *(b)* Total flux through any enclosed surface is given by,

$$\phi_{\text{net}} = \frac{\text{net charge enclosed}}{\varepsilon_0}$$

Hence, we can say that the electric flux depends only on net enclosed charge by surface.

09. *(d)* Flux of electric field $\mathbf{E}$ through any area A is defined as $\phi = E \cdot A \cos\theta$ or $\phi = \mathbf{E} \cdot \mathbf{A} = 0$, the lines are parallel to the surface.

10. *(b)* $\because \quad \mathbf{E}_{\text{total}} = 0$

$$\mathbf{E}_{AKB} + \mathbf{E}_{ACDB} = 0$$

$$\mathbf{E}_{ACDB} = -\mathbf{E}_{AKB}$$

$$\mathbf{E}_{ACDB} = \mathbf{E} \text{ along } OK$$

> • **Concept Enhancer**
>
> Net electric field at the centre of thin conducting ring is zero.

11. *(a)* Gauss's law states that the net electric flux through any closed surface is equal to the net charge inside the surface divided by ε_0.

i.e. $\quad \phi_{\text{total}} = \frac{q_{\text{inside}}}{\varepsilon_0}$

Let electric flux linked with surfaces A, B and C are ϕ_A, ϕ_B and ϕ_C respectively, i.e.

$$\phi_{\text{total}} = \phi_A + \phi_B + \phi_C$$

Since, $\quad \phi_C = \phi_A$

$$\therefore \; 2\phi_A + \phi_B = \phi_{\text{total}} = \frac{q}{\varepsilon_0}$$

or $\quad \phi_A = \frac{1}{2}\left(\frac{q}{\varepsilon_0} - \phi_B\right)$

But $\quad \phi_B = \phi \quad$ (given)

Hence, $\quad \phi_A = \frac{1}{2}\left(\frac{q}{\varepsilon_0} - \phi\right)$

12. *(c)* As we know, the electric flux (ϕ) through any surface area is given by,

$$\phi = \mathbf{E} \cdot d\mathbf{S} = |E|\,|dS|\cos\theta$$

As according to question, surface area is in plane of paper and $\mathbf{E}$ is also in plane of paper. So, angle between area vector and $\mathbf{E}$ is 90°

So, $\quad \phi = |E|\,|dS|\cos 90° = 0°$

13. *(d)* As we know expression of Gauss's law is

$$\oint \mathbf{E} \cdot d\mathbf{S} = \frac{q_{\text{inside}}}{\varepsilon_0}$$

So, $\quad \phi = \frac{q}{\varepsilon_0} \quad [\phi = \oint \mathbf{E} \cdot d\mathbf{S}]$

This is the net flux coming out from cube.

Since, a cube has 6 sides, so electric flux through any face is

$$\phi' = \frac{\phi}{6} = \frac{q}{6\varepsilon_0} = \frac{4\pi q}{6(4\pi\varepsilon_0)}$$

14. *(c)* The electric flux emerging from the cube is

$$\phi = \frac{1}{\varepsilon_0} \times \text{charge enclosed } (q_{\text{inside}})$$

$$\phi = \frac{1}{\varepsilon_0} \times q \times 10^{-6}$$

$$[q_{\text{inside}} = q \times 10^{-6}]$$

Since, a cube has six faces, so electric flux through each face is,

$$\phi' = \frac{\phi}{6} = \frac{1}{6\varepsilon_0} \times q \times 10^{-6} = \frac{q \times 10^{-6}}{6\varepsilon_0}$$

15. *(d)* Since, q is the charge enclosed by the surface, then electric flux, $\phi = \frac{q}{\varepsilon_0}$

If charge q is placed at a corner of cube, it will be divided into 8 such cubes. Therefore, electric flux through the cube is

$$\phi' = \frac{1}{8}\left(\frac{q}{\varepsilon_0}\right)$$

> • **Concept Enhancer**
>
> According to Gauss's law, the electric flux through a closed surface is equal to $\frac{1}{\varepsilon_0}$ times the net charge enclosed by the surface.

16. *(c)* Considering symmetric elements each of length dl at A and B, we know that electric fields perpendicular to PO are cancelled and those along PO are added. The electric field due to an element of length $dl\,(= a d\theta)$ along PO.

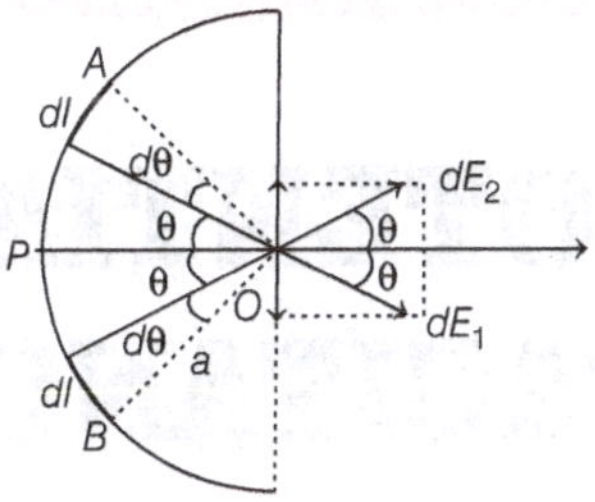

$$dE = \frac{1}{4\pi\varepsilon_0}\frac{dq}{a^2}\cos\theta$$

$$= \frac{1}{4\pi\varepsilon_0}\frac{\lambda dl}{a^2}\cos\theta$$

$$= \frac{1}{4\pi\varepsilon_0}\frac{\lambda(a\,d\theta)}{a^2}\cos\theta \qquad (\because dl = a d\theta)$$

Net electric field at O

$$E = \int_{-\pi/2}^{\pi/2} dE$$

$$= 2\int_0^{\pi/2}\frac{1}{4\pi\varepsilon_0}\frac{\lambda\, a\cos\theta\, d\theta}{a^2}$$

$$= 2.\frac{1}{4\pi\varepsilon_0}\frac{\lambda}{a}[\sin\theta]_0^{\pi/2}$$

$$= 2\cdot\frac{1}{4\pi\varepsilon_0}\cdot\frac{\lambda}{a}\cdot 1 = \frac{\lambda}{2\pi\varepsilon_0 a}$$

17. *(a)* Charge resides on the outer surface of a conducting hollow or solid sphere of radius R (say). We consider a spherical surface of radius $r < R$.

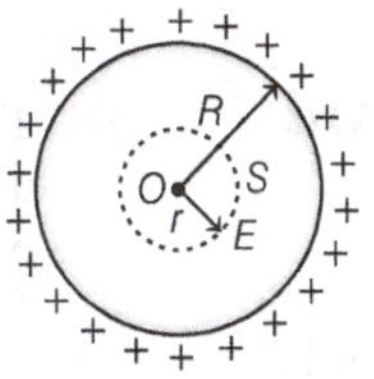

By Gauss' theorem,

$$\sum \mathbf{E}\cdot d\mathbf{S} = \frac{q_{\text{inside}}}{\varepsilon_0}$$

$$\text{or } E\times 4\pi r^2 = \frac{1}{\varepsilon_0}\times q_{\text{inside}}$$

and we know that $q_{\text{inside}} = 0$

So, $E = 0$

i.e. electric field inside a hollow sphere is zero.

18. *(a)* By Gauss's theorem, total electric flux over the closed surface is $1/\varepsilon_0$ times the total charges contained inside surface.

$\therefore$ Total electric flux

$$= \frac{\text{total charge inside cube}}{\varepsilon_0}$$

$$\text{or} \quad \phi = \frac{q}{\varepsilon_0}$$

19. *(b)* Given, $E_{max} = 3\times 10^6$ V/m

and $R = 3$ m

We know that,

$$E = \frac{1}{4\pi\varepsilon_0}\times\frac{Q}{R^2}$$

$$\Rightarrow Q_{max} = 4\pi\varepsilon_0 R^2 E_{max}$$

$$= \frac{3\times 3\times 3\times 10^6}{9\times 10^9} = 3\times 10^{-3}\,\text{C}$$

C-16

NEET Chapterwise
Topicwise Physics

In NEET 2024, 3 questions were visible from this chapter. In past 5 years, 7 questions from topic-1, 4 questions from topic-2, 2 questions from topic-3 and 5 questions from topic-4 were asked.
For detailed analysis scan QR code

ELECTROSTATICS POTENTIAL AND CAPACITANCE

Topic 1 Electrostatic Potential and Equipotential Surface

01 A thin spherical shell is charged by some source. The potential difference between the two points C and P (in V) shown in the figure is

(Take, $\frac{1}{4\pi\varepsilon_0} = 9\times10^9$ SI units)
[NCERT (New) Pg. 48, NEET 2024]

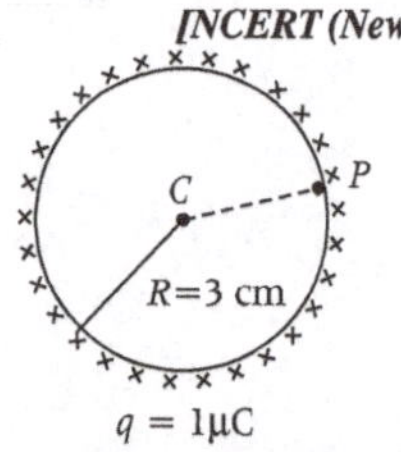

$q = 1\mu C$

(a) 3×10^5 (b) 1×10^5 (c) 0.5×10^5 (d) Zero

02 The angle between the electric lines of force and the equipotential surface is *[NCERT (New) Pg. 54, NEET 2022]*
(a) 45° (b) 90° (c) 180° (d) 0°

03 Two hollow conducting spheres of radii R_1 and $R_2 (R_1 > R_2)$ have equal charges. The potential would be *[NCERT (New) Pg. 52, NEET 2022]*
(a) more on smaller sphere
(b) equal on both the spheres
(c) dependent on the material property of the sphere
(d) more on bigger sphere

04 Twenty seven drops of same size are charged at 220 V each. They combine to form a bigger drop. Calculate the potential of the bigger drop. *[NEET 2021]*
(a) 660 V (b) 1320 V (c) 1520 V (d) 1980 V

05 Two charged spherical conductors of radii R_1 and R_2 are connected by a wire. Then, the ratio of surface charge densities of the spheres (σ_1/σ_2) is *[NEET 2021]*

(a) $\frac{R_1}{R_2}$ (b) $\frac{R_2}{R_1}$ (c) $\sqrt{\left(\frac{R_1}{R_2}\right)}$ (d) $\frac{R_1^2}{R_2^2}$

06 The variation of electrostatic potential with radial distance r from the centre of a positively charged metallic thin shell of radius R is given by the graph
[NCERT (New) Pg. 52, NEET (Oct.) 2020]

(a)
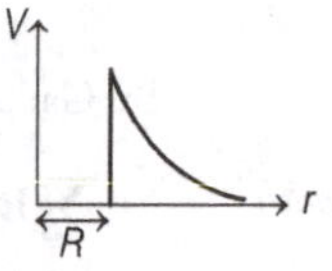

(b)
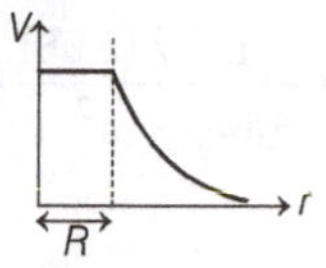

(c)
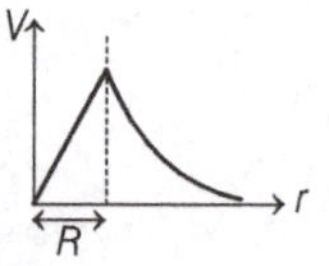

(d)
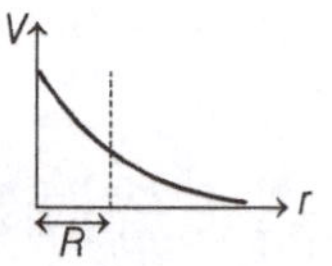

07 In a certain region of space with volume $0.2\ m^3$, the electric potential is found to be 5 V throughout. The magnitude of electric field in this region is
[NCERT (New) Pg. 55, NEET (Sep.) 2020]
(a) 0.5 N/C (b) 1 N/C
(c) 5 N/C (d) zero

08 Two metal spheres, one of radius R and the other of radius $2R$, respectively have the same surface charge density σ. They are brought in contact and separated. What will be the new surface charge densities on them ? *[NCERT (New) Pg. 52, NEET (Odisha) 2019]*

(a) $\sigma_1 = \frac{5}{6}\sigma,\ \sigma_2 = \frac{5}{2}\sigma$ (b) $\sigma_1 = \frac{5}{2}\sigma,\ \sigma_2 = \frac{5}{6}\sigma$

(c) $\sigma_1 = \frac{5}{2}\sigma,\ \sigma_2 = \frac{5}{3}\sigma$ (d) $\sigma_1 = \frac{5}{3}\sigma,\ \sigma_2 = \frac{5}{6}\sigma$

09 The diagrams below show regions of equipotentials.

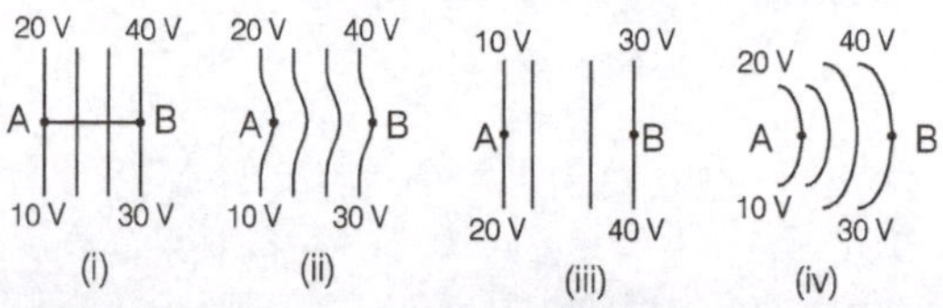

A positive charge is moved from A to B in each diagram. *[NCERT (New) Pg. 54, NEET 2017]*

(a) Maximum work is required to move q in figure (iii)
(b) In all the four cases, the work done is the same
(c) Minimum work is required to move q in figure (i)
(d) Maximum work is required to move q in figure (ii)

10 If potential (in volts) in a region is expressed as $V(x, y, z) = 6xy - y + 2yz$, the electric field (in N/C) at point (1, 1, 0) is *[NCERT (New) Pg. 55, AIPMT 2015]*

(a) $-(3\hat{i}+5\hat{j}+3\hat{k})$ (b) $-(6\hat{i}+5\hat{j}+2\hat{k})$
(c) $-(2\hat{i}+3\hat{j}+\hat{k})$ (d) $-(6\hat{i}+9\hat{j}+\hat{k})$

11 A conducting sphere of radius R is given a charge Q. The electric potential and the electric field at the centre of the sphere, respectively are *[AIPMT 2014]*

(a) zero and $\frac{Q}{4\pi\varepsilon_0 R^2}$ (b) $\frac{Q}{4\pi\varepsilon_0 R}$ and zero
(c) $\frac{Q}{4\pi\varepsilon_0 R}$ and $\frac{Q}{4\pi\varepsilon_0 R^2}$ (d) Both are zero

12 In a region, the potential is represented by $V(x, y, z) = 6x - 8xy - 8y + 6yz$, where V is in volt and x, y, z are in metres. The electric force experienced by a charge of 2 C situated at point (1, 1, 1) is *[NCERT (New) Pg. 55, AIPMT 2014]*

(a) $6\sqrt{5}$ N (b) 30 N
(c) 24 N (d) $4\sqrt{35}$ N

13 A, B and C are three points in a uniform electric field. The electric potential is *[NCERT (New) Pg. 55, NEET 2013]*

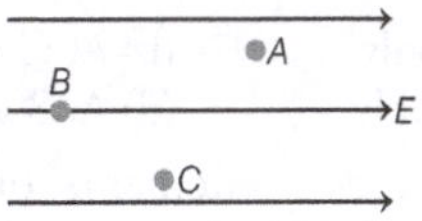

(a) maximum at A (b) maximum at B
(c) maximum at C
(d) same at all the three points A, B and C

14 Four point charges $-Q, -q, 2q$ and $2Q$ are placed, one at each corner of the square. The relation between Q and q for which the potential at the centre of the square is zero, is *[NCERT (New) Pg. 51, AIPMT 2012]*

(a) $Q = -q$ (b) $Q = -\frac{1}{q}$ (c) $Q = q$ (d) $Q = \frac{1}{q}$

15 Four electric charges $+q, +q, -q$ and $-q$ are placed at the corners of a square of side $2L$ (see figure). The electric potential at point A, mid-way between the two charges $+q$ and $+q$ is *[AIPMT 2011]*

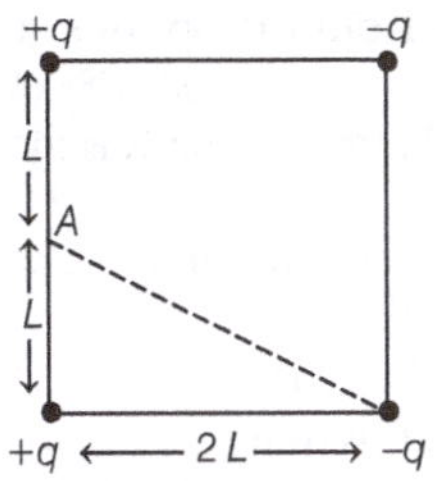

(a) $\frac{1}{4\pi\varepsilon_0}\frac{2q}{L}\left(1+\frac{1}{\sqrt{5}}\right)$ (b) $\frac{1}{4\pi\varepsilon_0}\frac{2q}{L}\left(1-\frac{1}{\sqrt{5}}\right)$
(c) zero (d) $\frac{1}{4\pi\varepsilon_0}\frac{2q}{L}(1+\sqrt{5})$

16 The electric potential V at any point (x, y, z), all in metres in space is given by $V = 4x^2$ V. The electric field at the point (1, 0, 2) in volt/meter, is *[NCERT (New) Pg. 55, AIPMT 2011]*

(a) 8 along negative X-axis (b) 8 along positive X-axis
(c) 16 along negative X-axis (d) 16 along positive X-axis

17 Three charges, each $+q$, are placed at the corners of an isosceles triangle ABC of sides BC and AC, $2a$. D and E are the mid points of BC and CA. The work done in taking a charge Q from D to E is *[AIPMT 2011]*

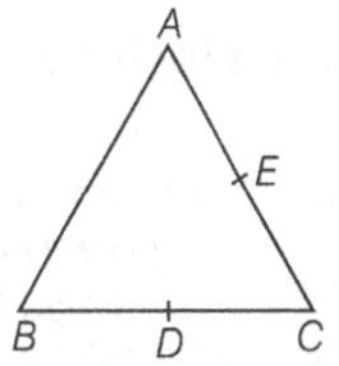

(a) $\frac{3qQ}{4\pi\varepsilon_0 a}$ (b) $\frac{3qQ}{8\pi\varepsilon_0 a}$
(c) $\frac{qQ}{4\pi\varepsilon_0 a}$ (d) zero

18 The electric potential at a point (x, y, z) is given by
$V = -x^2y - xz^3 + 4$
The electric field E at that point is *[NCERT (New) Pg. 55, AIPMT 2009]*

(a) $\mathbf{E} = (2xy + z^3)\hat{i} + x^2\hat{j} + 3xz^2\hat{k}$
(b) $\mathbf{E} = 2xy\hat{i} + (x^2 + y^2)\hat{j} + (3xz - y^2)\hat{k}$
(c) $\mathbf{E} = z^3\hat{i} + xyz\hat{j} + z^2\hat{k}$
(d) $\mathbf{E} = (2xy - z^3)\hat{i} + xy^2\hat{j} + 3z^2x\hat{k}$

19 Three concentric spherical shells have radii a, b and c $(a < b < c)$ and have surface charge densities $\sigma, -\sigma$ and σ, respectively. If V_A, V_B and V_C denote the potentials of the three shells, then for $c = a + b$, we have *[AIPMT 2009]*

(a) $V_C = V_A \neq V_B$ (b) $V_C = V_B \neq V_A$
(c) $V_C \neq V_B \neq V_A$ (d) $V_C = V_B = V_A$

20 The electric potential at a point in free space due to a charge Q coulomb is $Q \times 10^{11}$ V. The electric field at that point is *[AIPMT 2008]*

(a) $4\pi\varepsilon_0 Q \times 10^{22}$ V/m
(b) $12\pi\varepsilon_0 Q \times 10^{20}$ V/m
(c) $4\pi\varepsilon_0 Q \times 10^{20}$ V/m
(d) $12\pi\varepsilon_0 Q \times 10^{22}$ V/m

21 As per this diagram a point charge $+q$ is placed at the origin O. Work done in taking another point charge $-Q$ from the point A [coordinates $(0, a)$] to another point B [coordinates $(a, 0)$] along the straight path AB is *[AIPMT 2005]*

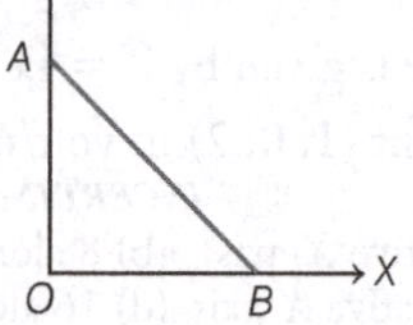

(a) zero (b) $\left(\frac{-qQ}{4\pi\varepsilon_0}\frac{1}{a^2}\right)\sqrt{2}a$

(c) $\left(\frac{qQ}{4\pi\varepsilon_0}\frac{1}{a^2}\right)\cdot\frac{a}{\sqrt{2}}$ (d) $\left(\frac{qQ}{4\pi\varepsilon_0}\frac{1}{a^2}\right)\sqrt{2}a$

22 A bullet of mass 2 g is having a charge of 2 μC. Through what potential difference must it be accelerated, starting from rest, to acquire a speed of 10 m/s ? *[NCERT (New) Pg. 49, AIPMT 2004]*

(a) 5 kV (b) 50 kV
(c) 5 V (d) 50 V

23 Some charge is being given to a conductor, then its potential is *[AIPMT 2002]*

(a) maximum at surface
(b) maximum at centre
(c) same throughout the conductor
(d) maximum somewhere between surface and centre

24 An electron of mass m and charge e is accelerated from rest through a potential difference of V volt in vacuum. Its final speed will be *[NCERT (New) Pg. 49, AIPMT 1996]*

(a) $\frac{eV}{2m}$ (b) $\frac{eV}{m}$ (c) $\sqrt{\frac{2eV}{m}}$ (d) $\sqrt{\frac{eV}{2m}}$

25 There is an electric field E in x-direction. If the work done on moving a charge of 0.2 C through a distance of 2 m along a line making an angle 60° with X-axis is 4 J, then what is the value of E ? *[NCERT (New) Pg. 55, AIPMT 1995]*

(a) 3 N/C (b) 4 N/C
(c) 5 N/C (d) 20 N/C

26 A hollow metal sphere of radius 10 cm is charged such that the potential on its surface is 80 V. The potential at the centre of the sphere is *[AIPMT 1994]*

(a) zero (b) 80 V
(c) 800 V (d) 8 V

27 Charge q_2 is at the centre of a circular path with radius r. Work done in carrying charge q_1, once around this equipotential path, would be *[AIPMT 1994]*

(a) $\frac{1}{4\pi\varepsilon_0}\times\frac{q_1q_2}{r^2}$ (b) $\frac{1}{4\pi\varepsilon_0}\times\frac{q_1q_2}{r}$

(c) zero (d) infinite

28 Two spherical conductors A and B of radii 1 mm and 2 mm are separated by a distance of 5 cm and are uniformly charged. If the spheres are connected by a conducting wire, then in equilibrium condition, the ratio of the magnitude of the electric fields at the surfaces of spheres A and B is *[AIPMT 1992]*

(a) 4 : 1 (b) 1 : 2 (c) 2 : 1 (d) 1 : 4

29 Two concentric spheres of radii R and r have similar charges with equal surface charge densities σ. What is the electric potential at their common centre ? *[NCERT (New) Pg. 52, AIPMT 1991]*

(a) $\frac{\sigma}{\varepsilon_0}$ (b) $\frac{\sigma}{\varepsilon_0}(R-r)$

(c) $\frac{\sigma}{\varepsilon_0}(R+r)$ (d) None of these

Topic 2 Electric Dipole and Potential Energy

01 If the plates of a parallel plate capacitor connected to a battery are moved close to each other, then *[NCERT (New) Pg. 49, NEET 2024]*

A. the charge stored in it, increases.
B. the energy stored in it, decreases.
C. its capacitance increases.
D. the ratio of charge to its potential remains the same.
E. the product of charge and voltage increases.

Choose the most appropriate answer from the options given below.

(a) A, B and E only (b) A, C and E only
(c) B, D and E only (d) A, B and C only

02 Given below are two statements. one is labelled as Assertion (A) and the other is labelled as Reason (R).

Assertion (A) The potential V at any axial point, at 2 m distance r from the centre of the dipole of dipole moment vector **p** of magnitude, 4×10^{-6} Cm, is $\pm 9\times10^3 V$.

(Take, $\frac{1}{4\pi\varepsilon_0} = 9\times10^9$ SI units)

Reason (R) $V = \pm\frac{2p}{4\pi\varepsilon_0 r^2}$, where r is the distance of any axial point, situated at 2 m from the centre of the dipole.

In the light of the above statements, choose the correct answer from the options given below. *[NCERT (New) Pg. 49, NEET 2024]*

(a) Both A and R are true and R is the correct explanation of A.
(b) Both A and R are true but R is not the correct explanation of A.
(c) A is true but R is false.
(d) A is false but R is true.

03 An electric dipole is placed as shown in the figure.

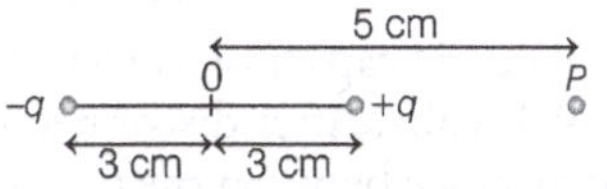

The electric potential (in 10^2 V) at point P due to the dipole is (ε_0 = permittivity of free space and $\frac{1}{4\pi\varepsilon_0} = K$) *[NEET 2023]*

(a) $\left(\frac{5}{8}\right)qK$ (b) $\left(\frac{8}{5}\right)qK$ (c) $\left(\frac{8}{3}\right)qK$ (d) $\left(\frac{3}{8}\right)qK$

04 Polar molecules are the molecules *[NCERT (New) Pg. 23, NEET 2021]*

(a) having zero dipole moment
(b) acquire a dipole moment only in the presence of electric field due to displacement of charges
(c) acquire a dipole moment only when magnetic field is absent
(d) having a permanent electric dipole moment

05 A short electric dipole has a dipole moment of 16×10^{-9} C-m. The electric potential due to the dipole at a point at a distance of 0.6 m from the centre of the dipole, situated on a line making an angle of 60° with the dipole axis is

$$\left(\frac{1}{4\pi\varepsilon_0} = 9 \times 10^9 \text{ Nm}^2/\text{C}^2\right)$$

[NCERT (New) Pg. 51, NEET (Sep.) 2020]

(a) 200 V (b) 400 V
(c) zero (d) 50 V

06 An electric dipole of moment p is placed in an electric field of intensity E. The dipole acquires a position such that the axis of the dipole makes an angle θ with the direction of the field. Assuming that the potential energy of the dipole to be zero when $\theta = 90°$, the torque and the potential energy of the dipole will respectively be *[AIPMT 2012]*

(a) $pE\sin\theta, -pE\cos\theta$ (b) $pE\sin\theta, -2pE\cos\theta$
(c) $pE\sin\theta, 2pE\cos\theta$ (d) $pE\cos\theta, -pE\sin\theta$

07 Charges $+q$ and $-q$ are placed at points A and B, respectively which are at a distance $2L$ apart, C is the midpoint between A and B. The work done in moving a charge $+Q$ along the semicircle CRD is *[NCERT (New) Pg. 56, AIPMT 2007]*

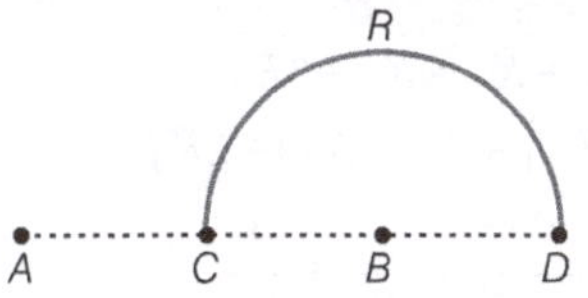

(a) $\frac{qQ}{4\pi\varepsilon_0 L}$ (b) $\frac{qQ}{2\pi\varepsilon_0 L}$ (c) $\frac{qQ}{6\pi\varepsilon_0 L}$ (d) $-\frac{qQ}{6\pi\varepsilon_0 L}$

08 An electric dipole of moment **p** is lying along a uniform electric field **E**. The work done in rotating the dipole by 90° is *[AIPMT 2006]*

(a) $\sqrt{2}\,pE$ (b) $pE/2$ (c) $2pE$ (d) pE

09 Two charges q_1 and q_2 are placed 30 cm apart, as shown in the figure. A third charge q_3 is moved along the arc of a circle of radius 40 cm from C to D. The change in the potential energy of the system is $\frac{q_3}{4\pi\varepsilon_0}k$, where k is *[NCERT (New) Pg. 56, AIPMT 2005]*

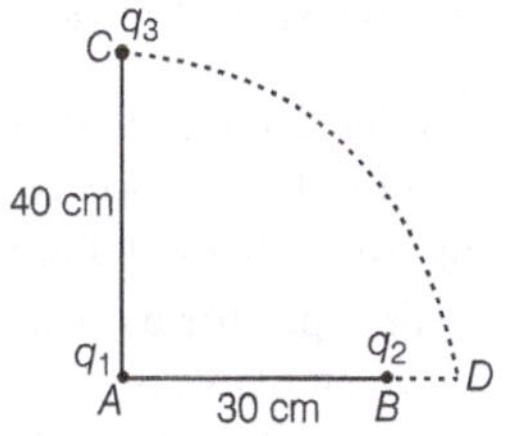

(a) $8q_2$ (b) $8q_1$ (c) $6q_2$ (d) $6q_1$

10 An electric dipole has the magnitude of its charge as q and its dipole moment is p. It is placed in a uniform electric field E. If its dipole moment is along the direction of the field, the force on it and its potential energy are respectively *[AIPMT 2004]*

(a) $2qE$ and minimum (b) qE and pE
(c) zero and minimum (d) qE and maximum

11 Identical charges $(-q)$ are placed at each corners of a cube of side b, then the electrostatic potential energy of charge $(+q)$ placed at the centre of the cube will be *[NCERT (New) Pg. 57, AIPMT 2002]*

(a) $-\frac{4\sqrt{2}q^2}{\pi\varepsilon_0}$ (b) $\frac{8\sqrt{2}q^2}{\pi\varepsilon_0 b}$
(c) $-\frac{4q^2}{\sqrt{3}\pi\varepsilon_0 b}$ (d) $\frac{8\sqrt{2}q^2}{4\pi\varepsilon_0 b}$

12 In bringing an electron towards another electron, the electrostatic potential energy of the system *[NCERT (New) Pg. 56, AIPMT 1999]*

(a) decreases (b) increases
(c) remains same (d) becomes zero

Topic 3 Capacitors and its Capacitance

01 A parallel plate capacitor having cross-sectional area A and separation d has air in between the plates. Now, an insulating slab of same area but thickness $d/2$ is inserted between the plates as shown in figure having dielectric constant $K(=4)$. The ratio of new capacitance to its original capacitance will be *[NEET (Oct.) 2020]*

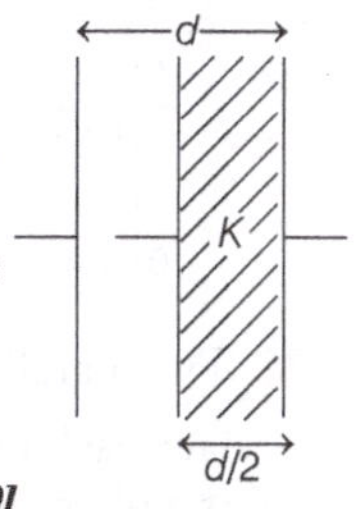

(a) 2 : 1 (b) 8 : 5 (c) 6 : 5 (d) 4 : 1

02 The capacitance of a parallel plate capacitor with air as medium is $6\,\mu F$. With the introduction of a dielectric medium, the capacitance becomes $30\,\mu F$. The permittivity of the medium is ($\varepsilon_0 = 8.85 \times 10^{-12}\, C^2N^{-1}m^{-2}$) *[NEET (Sep.) 2020]*

(a) $1.77 \times 10^{-12}\, C^2N^{-1}m^{-2}$ (b) $0.44 \times 10^{-10}\, C^2N^{-1}m^{-2}$
(c) $5.00\, C^2N^{-1}m^{-2}$ (d) $0.44 \times 10^{-13}\, C^2N^{-1}m^{-2}$

03 The electrostatic force between the metal plates of an isolated parallel plate capacitor C having a charge Q and area A, is *[NEET 2018]*

(a) proportional to the square root of the distance between the plates
(b) linearly proportional to the distance between the plates
(c) independent of the distance between the plates
(d) inversely proportional to the distance between the plates

04 A parallel plate air capacitor has capacity C, distance of separation between plates is d and potential difference V is applied between the plates. Force of attraction between the plates of the parallel plate air capacitor is *[AIPMT 2015]*

(a) $\frac{C^2V^2}{2d}$ (b) $\frac{CV^2}{2d}$
(c) $\frac{CV^2}{d}$ (d) $\frac{C^2V^2}{2d^2}$

05 Two thin dielectric slabs of dielectric constants K_1 and K_2 ($K_1 < K_2$) are inserted between plates of a parallel plate capacitor, as shown in the figure.

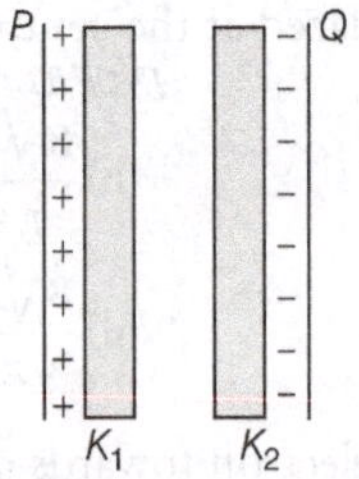

The variation of electric field E between the plates with distance d as measured from plate P is correctly shown by *[AIPMT 2014]*

(a)
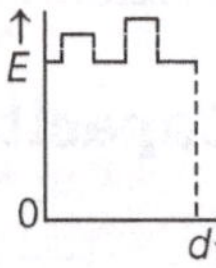

(b)
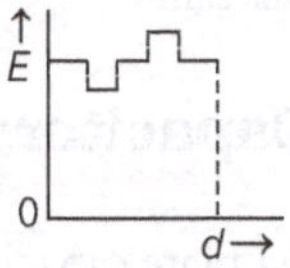

(c)
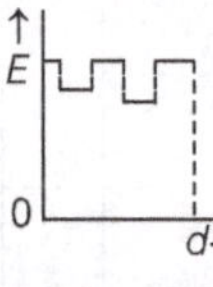

(d)
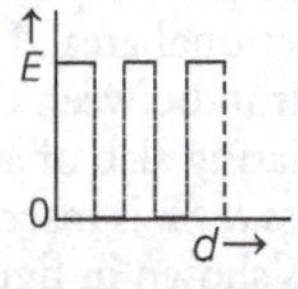

06 Two parallel metal plates having charges $+Q$ and $-Q$ face each other at a certain distance between them. If the plates are now dipped in kerosene oil tank, the electric field between the plates will *[AIPMT 2010]*

(a) become zero (b) increase
(c) decrease (d) remain same

07 A parallel plate air capacitor is charged to a potential difference of V volts. After disconnecting the charging battery the distance between the plates of the capacitor is increased using an insulating handle. As a result the potential difference between the plates *[AIPMT 2006]*

(a) decreases
(b) does not change
(c) becomes zero
(d) increases

08 A parallel plate condenser with oil (dielectric constant 2) between the plates has capacitance C. If oil is removed, the capacitance of capacitor becomes *[AIPMT 1999]*

(a) $\sqrt{2}\,C$ (b) $2\,C$
(c) $C/\sqrt{2}$ (d) $C/2$

Topic 4 Combination of Capacitors and Energy Stored in Capacitor

01 The equivalent capacitance of the system shown in the following circuit is *[NEET 2023]*

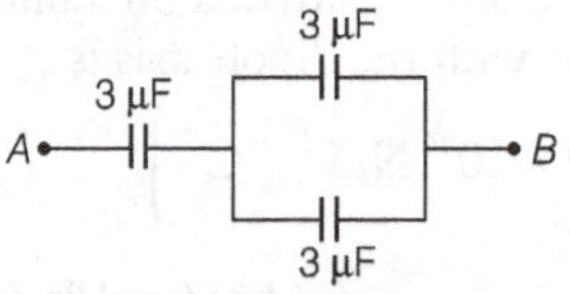

(a) $3\,\mu F$ (b) $6\,\mu F$
(c) $9\,\mu F$ (d) $2\,\mu F$

02 A parallel-plate capacitor of area A, plate separation d and capacitance C is filled with four dielectric materials having dielectric constants K_1, K_2, K_3 and K_4 as shown in the figure below. If a single dielectric material is to be used to have the same capacitance C in this capacitor, then its dielectric constant K is given by *[NCERT (New) Pg. 70, NEET 2021]*

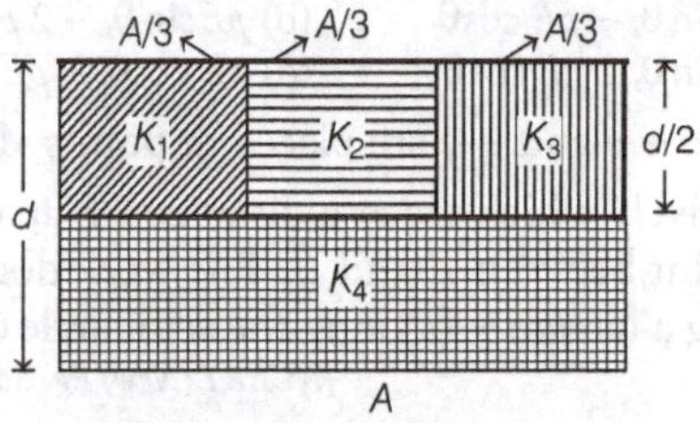

(a) $K = K_1 + K_2 + K_3 + 3K_4$
(b) $K = \frac{2}{3}(K_1 + K_2 + K_3) + 2K_4$
(c) $\frac{2}{K} = \frac{3}{K_1 + K_2 + K_3} + \frac{1}{K_4}$
(d) $\frac{1}{K} = \frac{1}{K_1} + \frac{1}{K_2} + \frac{1}{K_3} + \frac{3}{2K_4}$

03. A capacitor of capacitance $C = 900\text{pF}$ is charged fully by 100 V battery B as shown in figure (a). Then, it is disconnected from the battery and connected to another uncharged capacitor of capacitance $C = 900\ \text{pF}$ as shown in figure (b). The electrostatic energy stored by the system (b) is *[NCERT (New) Pg. 74, NEET 2021]*

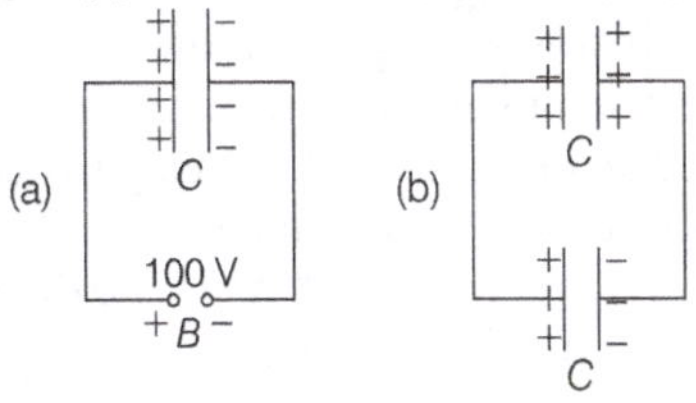

(a) 3.25×10^{-6} J (b) 2.25×10^{-6} J
(c) 1.5×10^{-6} J (d) 4.5×10^{-6} J

04 The equivalent capacitance of the combination shown in the figure is *[NCERT (New) Pg. 72, NEET 2021]*

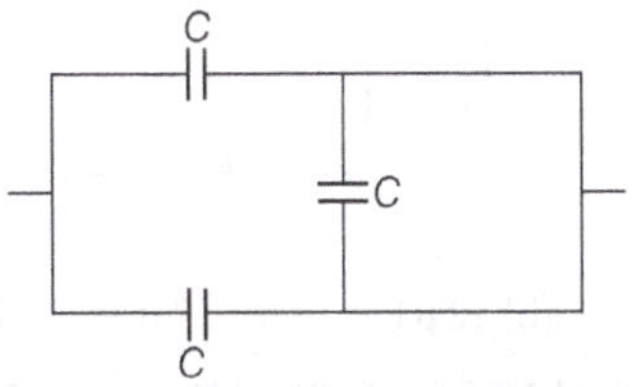

(a) $3C$ (b) $2C$
(c) $C/2$ (d) $3C/2$

05 A parallel plate capacitor has a uniform electric field **E** in the space between the plates. If the distance between the plates is d and the area of each plate is A, the energy stored in the capacitor is (ε_0 = permittivity of free space). *[NCERT (New) Pg. 74-75, NEET 2021, AIPMT 2011]*

(a) $\frac{1}{2}\varepsilon_0 E^2$ (b) $\varepsilon_0 EAd$
(c) $\frac{1}{2}\varepsilon_0 E^2 Ad$ (d) $\frac{E^2 Ad}{\varepsilon_0}$

06 Two identical capacitors C_1 and C_2 of equal capacitance are connected as shown in the circuit. Terminals a and b of the key k are connected to charge capacitor C_1 using battery of emf V volt. Now, disconnecting a and b the terminals b and c are connected. Due to this, what will be the percentage loss of energy? *[NCERT (New) Pg. 74, NEET (Odisha) 2019]*

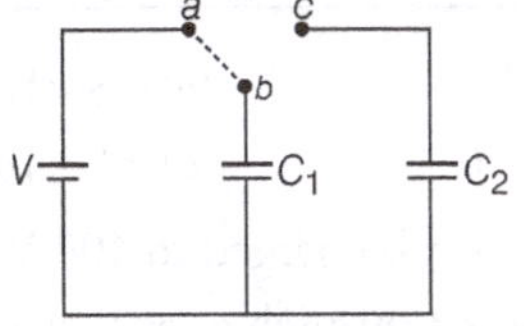

(a) 75% (b) 0%
(c) 50% (d) 25%

07 A capacitor is charged by a battery. The battery is removed and another identical uncharged capacitor is connected in parallel. The total electrostatic energy of resulting system *[NCERT (New) Pg. 74, NEET 2017]*
(a) increases by a factor of 4 (b) decreases by a factor of 2
(c) remains the same (d) increases by a factor of 2

08 A capacitor of $2\,\mu\text{F}$ is charged as shown in the figure. When the switch S is turned to position 2, the percentage of its stored energy dissipated is *[NCERT (New) Pg. 74, NEET 2016]*

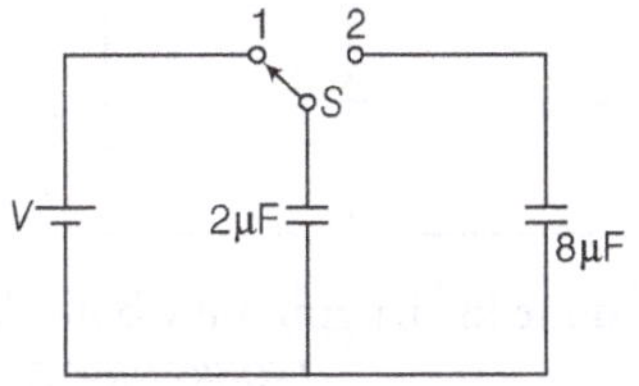

(a) 20% (b) 75%
(c) 80% (d) 0%

09 A parallel plate air capacitor of capacitance C is connected to a cell of emf V and then disconnected from it. A dielectric slab of dielectric constant K, which can just fill the air gap of the capacitor, is now inserted in it. Which of the following is incorrect ? *[NCERT (New) Pg. 74, AIPMT 2015]*
(a) The potential difference between the plates decreases K times
(b) The energy stored in the capacitor decreases K times
(c) The change in energy stored is $\frac{1}{2}CV^2\left(\frac{1}{K}-1\right)$
(d) The charge on the capacitor is not conserved

10 A series combination of n_1 capacitors, each of value C_1, is charged by a source of potential difference $4V$. When another parallel combination of n_2 capacitors, each of value C_2, is charged by a source of potential difference V, it has the same (total) energy stored in it, as the first combination has. The value of C_2, in terms of C_1, is then *[NCERT (New) Pg. 72, AIPMT 2010]*
(a) $\frac{2C_1}{n_1 n_2}$ (b) $16\frac{n_2}{n_1}C_1$
(c) $2\frac{n_2}{n_1}C_1$ (d) $\frac{16C_1}{n_1 n_2}$

11 Three capacitors each of capacitance C and of breakdown voltage V are joined in series. The capacitance and breakdown voltage of the combination will be *[NCERT (New) Pg. 72, AIPMT 2009]*
(a) $\frac{C}{3}, \frac{V}{3}$ (b) $3C, \frac{V}{3}$
(c) $\frac{C}{3}, 3V$ (d) $3C, 3V$

12 The energy required to charge a parallel plate condenser of plate separation d and plate area of cross-section A such that the uniform electric field between the plates E, is **[AIPMT 2008]**

(a) $\frac{1}{2}\frac{\varepsilon_0 E^2}{Ad}$ (b) $\frac{\varepsilon_0 E^2}{Ad}$ (c) $\varepsilon_0 E^2 Ad$ (d) $\frac{1}{2}\frac{\varepsilon_0 E^2}{Ad}$

13 Two condensers, one of capacity C and the other of capacity $C/2$, are connected to a V volt battery, as shown.

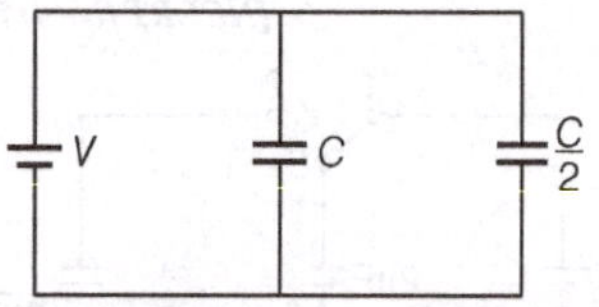

The work done in charging fully both the condensers is **[NCERT (New) Pg. 74, AIPMT 2007]**

(a) $2CV^2$ (b) $\frac{1}{4}CV^2$ (c) $\frac{3}{4}CV^2$ (d) $\frac{1}{2}CV^2$

14 A network of four capacitors of capacity equal to $C_1 = C, C_2 = 2C, C_3 = 3C$ and $C_4 = 4C$ are connected to a battery as shown in the figure. The ratio of the charges on C_2 and C_4 is **[AIPMT 2005]**

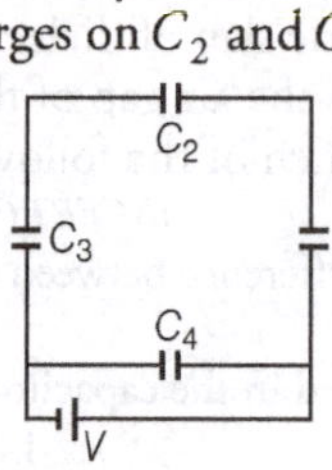

(a) 22/3 (b) 3/22 (c) 7/4 (d) 4/7

15 Three capacitors each of capacity 4 μF are to be connected in such a way that the effective capacitance is 6 μF. This can be done by **[NCERT (New) Pg. 72, AIPMT 2003]**

(a) connecting two in series and one in parallel
(b) connecting two in parallel and one in series
(c) connecting all of them in series
(d) connecting all of them in parallel

16 A capacitor of capacity C_1 is charged upto potential V volt and then connected in parallel to an uncharged capacitor of capacity C_2. The final potential difference across each capacitor will be **[NCERT (New) Pg. 72, AIPMT 2002]**

(a) $\frac{C_2 V}{C_1 + C_2}$ (b) $\frac{C_1 V}{C_1 + C_2}$

(c) $\left(1 + \frac{C_2}{C_1}\right)V$ (d) $\left(1 - \frac{C_2}{C_1}\right)V$

17 In a parallel plate capacitor, the distance between the plates is d and potential difference across plates is V. Energy stored per unit volume between the plates of capacitor is **[AIPMT 2001]**

(a) $\frac{Q^2}{2V^2}$ (b) $\frac{1}{2}\frac{\varepsilon_0 V^2}{d^2}$

(c) $\frac{1}{2}\frac{V^2}{\varepsilon_0 d^2}$ (d) $\frac{1}{2}\varepsilon_0 \frac{V^2}{d}$

18 A capacitor is charged by connecting a battery across its plates. It stores energy U. Now the battery is disconnected and another identical capacitor is connected across it, then the energy stored by both capacitors of the system will be **[NCERT (New) Pg. 74, AIPMT 2000]**

(a) U (b) $\frac{U}{2}$ (c) $2U$ (d) $\frac{3}{2}U$

19 The effective capacitance between points X and Y of figure shown is **[NCERT (New) Pg. 72, AIPMT 1999]**

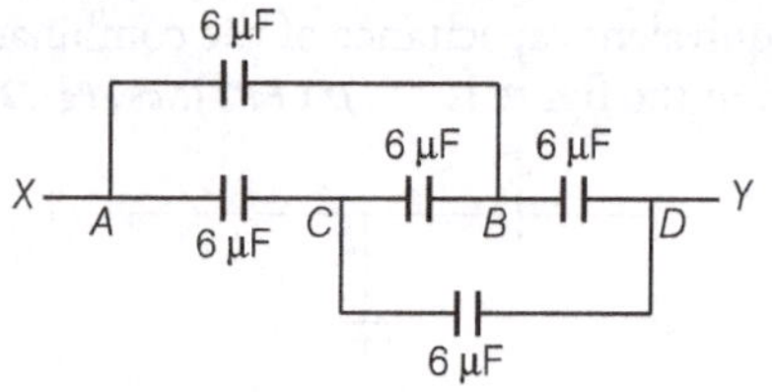

(a) 6 μF (b) 12 μF (c) 18 μF (d) 24 μF

20 The energy stored in a capacitor of capacity C and potential V is given by **[NCERT (New) Pg. 74, AIPMT 1996]**

(a) $\frac{CV}{2}$ (b) $\frac{C^2V^2}{2}$ (c) $\frac{C^2V}{2}$ (d) $\frac{CV^2}{2}$

21 If the potential of a capacitor having capacity 6 μF is increased from 10 V to 20 V, then increase in its energy will be **[NCERT (New) Pg. 74, AIPMT 1995]**

(a) 4×10^{-4} J (b) 4×10^{-14} J
(c) 9×10^{-4} J (d) 12×10^{-6} J

22 The four capacitors, each of 25 μF are connected as shown in figure. The DC voltmeter reads 200 V. The charge on each plate of capacitor is **[NCERT (New) Pg. 72, AIPMT 1994]**

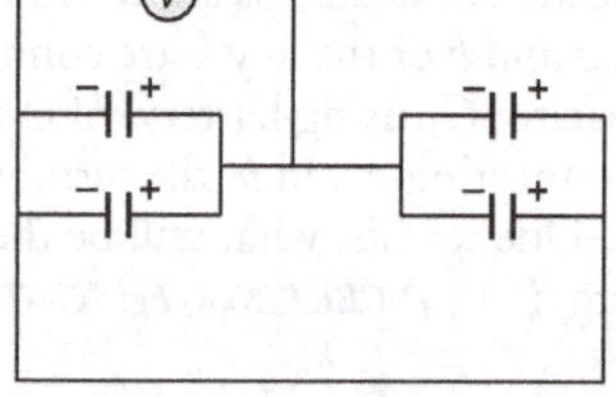

(a) $\pm 2 \times 10^{-3}$ C (b) $\pm 5 \times 10^{-3}$ C
(c) $\pm 2 \times 10^{-2}$ C (d) $\pm 5 \times 10^{-2}$ C

23 A 4 μF capacitor is charged to 400 V and then its plates are joined through a resistance of 1 kΩ. The heat produced in the resistance is **[AIPMT 1989]**

(a) 0.16 J (b) 1.28 J
(c) 0.64 J (d) 0.32 J

Key Index

Topic 1

1 (d)	2 (b)	3 (a)	4 (d)	5 (b)	6 (b)	7 (d)	8 (d)	9 (b)	10 (b)
11 (b)	12 (d)	13 (b)	14 (a)	15 (b)	16 (a)	17 (d)	18 (a)	19 (a)	20 (a)
21 (a)	22 (b)	23 (c)	24 (c)	25 (d)	26 (b)	27 (c)	28 (c)	29 (c)	

Topic 2

1 (b)	2 (c)	3 (d)	4 (d)	5 (a)	6 (a)	7 (d)	8 (d)	9 (a)	10 (c)
11 (c)	12 (b)								

Topic 3

1 (b)	2 (b)	3 (c)	4 (b)	5 (c)	6 (c)	7 (d)	8 (d)

Topic 4

1 (d)	2 (c)	3 (b)	4 (b)	5 (c)	6 (c)	7 (b)	8 (c)	9 (c)	10 (d)
11 (c)	12 (c)	13 (c)	14 (b)	15 (a)	16 (b)	17 (b)	18 (b)	19 (a)	20 (d)
21 (c)	22 (b)	23 (d)							

Detailed **Explanations**

Topic 1

01. *(d)* Since, there is no electric field inside the shell the potential at any point inside the shell is equal to the potential on the surface of the shell is

$$V = \frac{1}{4\pi\varepsilon_0}\frac{q}{r}$$

$$V_C - V_P = 0$$

02. *(b)* Work done to move a charge q particle between any two points on equipotential surface is zero.

i.e. $W = q(V_2 - V_1)$

$\Rightarrow \quad \mathbf{F}\cdot ds = q(V - V) \quad [\because V_1 = V_2 = V]$

$\Rightarrow q(\mathbf{E}\cdot ds) = 0 \quad [\because \mathbf{F} = \mathbf{E}\cdot ds]$

$\Rightarrow \quad \mathbf{E}\cdot ds = 0$

Therefore, $\mathbf{E} \perp ds$

Since, ds lies in the plane of equipotential surface.

Thus, angle between the electric lines of force and the equipotential surface is 90°.

> **Concept Enhancer**
>
> Electric field lines are perpendicular to equipotential surface. Work done to move a charge particle on equipotential surface is always zero.

03. *(a)* Potential on the hollow conducting sphere of radius R due to charge Q is

$$V = \frac{1}{4\pi\varepsilon_0}\cdot\frac{Q}{R}$$

$\Rightarrow \quad V \propto \frac{1}{R}$ [For same charge Q]

$\Rightarrow \quad \frac{V_1}{V_2} = \frac{R_2}{R_1}$

Since, $R_1 > R_2$

$\therefore \quad \frac{R_2}{R_1} < 1 \Rightarrow \frac{V_1}{V_2} < 1$

$\therefore \quad V_1 < V_2$

Hence, potential will more on smaller sphere.

04. *(d)* According to the question,

$$V_{bigger} = 27 \times V_{small}$$

$\Rightarrow \quad \frac{4}{3}\pi R^3 = 27 \times \frac{4}{3}\pi r^3$

$\Rightarrow \quad R^3 = 27 \times r^3$

$\Rightarrow \quad R = 3r$

Now, the potential of the small drop,

$$V = \frac{Kq}{r} \quad \ldots\text{(i)}$$

The potential of the bigger drop,

$$V' = \frac{KQ}{R}$$

$$Q = 27q$$

So, the potential of the bigger drop,

$$V' = \frac{K \times 27q}{3r} = 9\frac{Kq}{r}$$

$V' = 9V$ [From Eq. (i)]

$= 9 \times 220 = 1980$ V

05. *(b)* When two charged spherical conductors are connected by a conducting wire, then the potential becomes same in both the spherical conductor, i.e.

$$V_1 = V_2$$

$\Rightarrow \quad \frac{Kq_1}{R_1} = \frac{Kq_2}{R_2} \Rightarrow \frac{q_1}{q_2} = \frac{R_1}{R_2} \quad \ldots\text{(i)}$

$$\sigma = \frac{q}{4\pi R^2}$$

$\therefore \quad \frac{\sigma_1}{\sigma_2} = \frac{\frac{q_1}{4\pi R_1^2}}{\frac{q_2}{4\pi R_2^2}} \Rightarrow \frac{\sigma_1}{\sigma_2} = \frac{q_1}{q_2}\frac{R_2^2}{R_1^2}$

$$\Rightarrow \quad \frac{\sigma_1}{\sigma_2} = \frac{R_1}{R_2} \frac{R_2^2}{R_1^2} \quad \text{[From Eq. (i)]}$$

$$\Rightarrow \quad \frac{\sigma_1}{\sigma_2} = \frac{R_2}{R_1}$$

06. *(b)* For metallic spherical shell,

$$V_{\text{inside}} = V_{\text{surface}} = \frac{1}{4\pi\varepsilon_0} \cdot \frac{q}{R} = \text{constant}$$

Outside the spherical shell, $V \propto \frac{1}{r}$

Hence, variation of potential V with distance r is given as

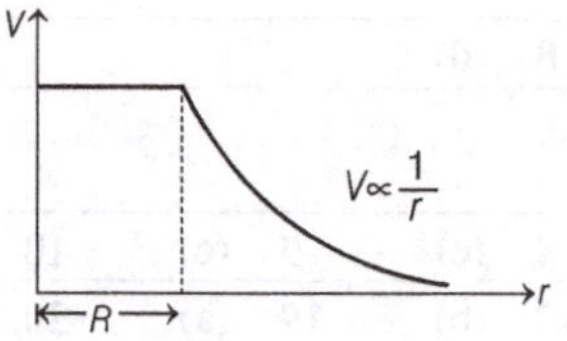

07. *(d)* Given, volume, $V = 0.2 \text{ m}^3$

Electric potential = 5 V = constant

$\because$ Electric field $E = \frac{-dV}{dr} = \frac{-d(5)}{dr} = 0$

08. *(d)* Surface charge density,

$$\sigma = \frac{\text{Charge}}{\text{Area}} = \frac{Q}{A} \quad \text{or} \quad Q = \sigma A$$

$$Q_P = \sigma \times 4\pi R^2 = 4\pi\sigma R^2 \quad \ldots\text{(i)}$$

and $Q_Q = \sigma \times 4\pi(2R)^2$

$$= 16\pi\sigma R^2 \quad \ldots\text{(ii)}$$

When they are brought in contact with each other, the total charge will be

$$Q_t = Q_P + Q_Q$$

$$= 4\pi\sigma R^2 + 16\pi\sigma R^2$$

[From Eq. (i) and (ii)]

$$= 20\pi\sigma R^2 \quad \ldots\text{(iii)}$$

When two charged bodies are connected

$$\therefore \quad V_1 = V_2$$

$$\frac{Q_P}{4\pi\varepsilon_0 R} = \frac{Q_Q}{4\pi\varepsilon_0 2R}$$

$$\Rightarrow \quad \frac{Q_P}{R} = \frac{Q_Q}{2R} \Rightarrow \frac{Q_P}{Q_Q} = \frac{1}{2}$$

$$\therefore \quad Q_P' = \frac{1}{3} Q_t \text{ and } Q_Q' = \frac{2}{3} Q_t$$

After separation, the new surface charge densities on P and Q will be

$$\sigma_P = \frac{Q_P'}{\text{Area}} = \frac{1}{3} \frac{Q_t}{\text{Area}}$$

$$\Rightarrow \quad \sigma_1 = \frac{1}{3} \frac{20\pi\sigma R^2}{4\pi R^2} = \frac{5}{3}\sigma \; [\because \sigma_P = \sigma_1]$$

and $\sigma_Q = \frac{Q_Q'}{\text{Area}} = \frac{2}{3} \frac{Q_t}{\text{Area}}$

$$\Rightarrow \quad \sigma_2 = \frac{2}{3} \times \frac{20\pi\sigma R^2}{4\pi(2R)^2} \quad [\because \sigma_Q = \sigma_2]$$

$$= \frac{2}{3} \times \frac{5}{4}\sigma = \frac{5}{6}\sigma$$

09. *(b)* We know that,

Work done $(W) = q\,\Delta V$

ΔV is same in all the cases. So, work done will be same in the all cases.

10. *(b)* Given, potential in a region,

$$V = 6xy - y + 2yz.$$

Electric field in a region,

$$\mathbf{E} = -\frac{\partial V}{\partial x}\hat{\mathbf{i}} - \frac{\partial V}{\partial y}\hat{\mathbf{j}} - \frac{\partial V}{\partial z}\hat{\mathbf{k}}$$

$$\Rightarrow \mathbf{E} = -6y\hat{\mathbf{i}} - (6x - 1 + 2z)\hat{\mathbf{j}} - 2y\hat{\mathbf{k}}$$

At, (1, 1, 0), electric field can be expressed,

$$E = -(6 \times 1\hat{\mathbf{i}}) - (6 \times 1 - 1 + 2 \times 0)\hat{\mathbf{j}} - (2 \times 1)\hat{\mathbf{k}}$$

$$= -(6\hat{\mathbf{i}} + 5\hat{\mathbf{j}} + 2\hat{\mathbf{k}}) \text{ N/C}$$

11. *(b)* A conducting solid sphere is equivalent to spherical shell.

$$V_{\text{inside}} = V_{\text{surface}}$$

$$= \frac{1}{4\pi\varepsilon_0} \frac{Q}{R}$$

Electric field inside a conducting shell is zero i.e. [E = 0]

12. *(d)* As we know, $\mathbf{E} = -\frac{dV}{dr}$

As $\quad V = 6x - 8xy - 8y + 6yz$

So, $\quad \mathbf{E} = -\frac{dV}{dx}\hat{\mathbf{i}} - \frac{\partial V}{\partial y}\hat{\mathbf{j}} - \frac{dV}{\partial z}\hat{\mathbf{k}}$

$$= -[(6 - 8y)\hat{\mathbf{i}} + (-8x - 8 + 6z)\hat{\mathbf{j}} + 6y\hat{\mathbf{k}}]$$

The value of **E** at coordinate (1, 1, 1)

$$\mathbf{E} = -[-2\hat{\mathbf{i}} - 10\hat{\mathbf{j}} + 6\hat{\mathbf{k}}]$$

So, $\mathbf{E}_{\text{net}} = \sqrt{(-2)^2 + (-10)^2 + 6^2}$

$$= 2\sqrt{35} \text{ N/C}$$

and force on charge q due to $\mathbf{E}_{\text{net}}$ is given by

$$F = q\,\mathbf{E}_{\text{net}} = 2 \times 2\sqrt{35}$$

$$= 4\sqrt{35} \text{ N}$$

13. *(b)* The electric field is maximum at B, because electric field is directed along decreasing potential $V_B > V_C > V_A$.

14. *(a)* As, shown in figure

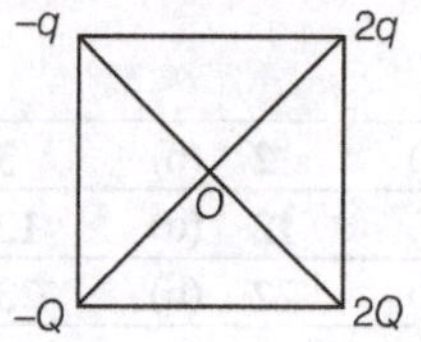

If potential at centre is zero, then

$$V_1 + V_2 + V_3 + V_4 = 0$$

$$\Rightarrow -\frac{KQ}{r} - \frac{Kq}{r} + \frac{K2Q}{r} + \frac{K2q}{r} = 0$$

$$\Rightarrow \quad -Q - q + 2q + 2Q = 0$$

$$\therefore \quad Q = -q$$

15. *(b)* Potential at any distance r due to a point charge is given by,

$$V = \frac{Kq}{r} \quad \left[K = \frac{1}{4\pi\varepsilon_0}\right]$$

Given, $V = 2V_{\text{positive}} + 2V_{\text{negative}}$

$$= \frac{1}{4\pi\varepsilon_0}\left[\frac{2q}{L} - \frac{2q}{L\sqrt{5}}\right]$$

$$V = \frac{2q}{4\pi\varepsilon_0 L}\left(1 - \frac{1}{\sqrt{5}}\right)$$

16. *(a)* We know that,

$$\mathbf{E} = -\left[\hat{\mathbf{i}}\frac{\partial V}{\partial x} + \hat{\mathbf{j}}\frac{\partial V}{\partial y} + \hat{\mathbf{k}}\frac{\partial V}{\partial z}\right]$$

Here, $V = 4x^2$

$$\therefore \quad E = -8x\hat{\mathbf{i}}$$

$$\mathbf{E}_{(1,\,0,\,2)} = -8\hat{\mathbf{i}} \text{ Vm}^{-1} \{\text{at point } [1, 0, 2]\}$$

So electric field is along the negative X-axis.

17. *(d)* Given, $AC = BC = 2a$

$$AE = EC = a \text{ and } BD = DC = a$$

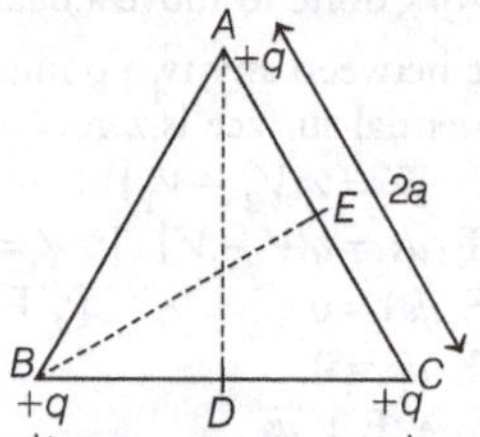

In ΔADC,

$$(AD)^2 = (AC)^2 - (DC)^2$$

$$= (2a)^2 - (a)^2 = 4a^2 - a^3 = 3a^2$$

$$\Rightarrow AD = a\sqrt{3}$$

Potential at point D due to the given charge configuration is given as

$$V_D = \frac{1}{4\pi\varepsilon_0}\left[\frac{q}{BD} + \frac{q}{DC} + \frac{q}{AD}\right]$$

$$= \frac{q}{4\pi\varepsilon_0}\left[\frac{1}{a}+\frac{1}{a}+\frac{1}{\sqrt{3}a}\right]$$

$$= \frac{q}{4\pi\varepsilon_0 a}\left[2+\frac{1}{\sqrt{3}}\right] \quad \ldots\text{(i)}$$

Similarly,

$$V_E = \frac{1}{4\pi\varepsilon_0}\left[\frac{q}{AE}+\frac{q}{EC}+\frac{q}{BE}\right]$$

$$= \frac{q}{4\pi\varepsilon_0}\left[\frac{1}{a}+\frac{1}{a}+\frac{1}{a\sqrt{3}}\right]$$

$$\frac{q}{4\pi\varepsilon_0 a}\left[2+\frac{1}{\sqrt{3}}\right] \ldots\text{(ii)}$$

From (i) and (ii), it is clear that

$V_D = V_E$

The work done in taking a charge Q from D to E is

$$W = Q(V_E - V_D) = 0 \quad (\because V_D = V_E)$$

18. *(a)* Potential gradient relates with electric field according to the following relation,

$$E = \frac{-dV}{dr}, \quad \mathbf{E} = -\frac{dV}{dr}$$

As $V = -x^2y - xz^3 + 4$

So, $\mathbf{E} = -\frac{dV}{dx}\hat{\mathbf{i}} - \frac{dV}{dy}\hat{\mathbf{j}} - \frac{dV}{dz}\hat{\mathbf{k}}$

$$\mathbf{E} = (2xy + z^3)\hat{\mathbf{i}} + x^2\hat{\mathbf{j}} + 3xz^2\hat{\mathbf{k}}$$

19. *(a)* $V_A = \frac{1}{4\pi\varepsilon_0}\cdot\frac{\sigma 4\pi a^2}{a} - \frac{1}{4\pi\varepsilon_0}\cdot\frac{\sigma 4\pi b^2}{b} + \frac{1}{4\pi\varepsilon_0}\cdot\frac{\sigma 4\pi c^2}{c}$

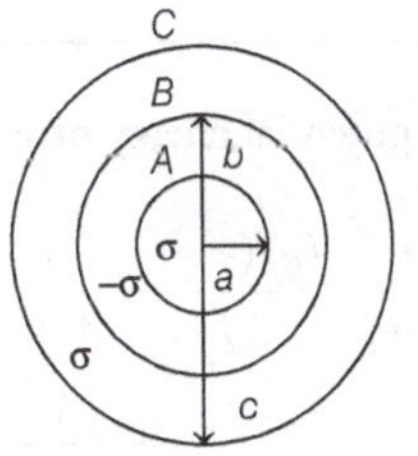

$$= \frac{\sigma}{\varepsilon_0}(a - b + c) = \frac{\sigma}{\varepsilon_0}(2a)$$

$$(\because c = a + b)$$

$$V_B = \frac{1}{4\pi\varepsilon_0}\cdot\frac{\sigma 4\pi a^2}{b} - \frac{1}{4\pi\varepsilon_0}\cdot\frac{\sigma 4\pi b^2}{b} + \frac{1}{4\pi\varepsilon_0}\cdot\frac{\sigma 4\pi c^2}{c}$$

$$= \frac{\sigma}{\varepsilon_0}\left(\frac{a^2}{b} - b + c\right)$$

and

$$V_C = \frac{1}{4\pi\varepsilon_0}\cdot\frac{\sigma 4\pi a^2}{c} - \frac{1}{4\pi\varepsilon_0}\cdot\frac{\sigma 4\pi b^2}{c} + \frac{1}{4\pi\varepsilon_0}\cdot\frac{\sigma 4\pi c^2}{c}$$

$$V_C = \frac{\sigma}{\varepsilon_0}\left(\frac{a^2}{c} - \frac{b^2}{c} + c\right)$$

$$V_C = \frac{\sigma}{\varepsilon_0}\left[\frac{(a+b)(a-b)}{c} + c\right]$$

$$V_c = \frac{\sigma}{\varepsilon_0}[a - b + c]$$

$$= \frac{\sigma}{\varepsilon_0}(2a) \quad (\because c = a + b)$$

Hence, $V_C = V_A \neq V_B$

20. *(a)* As potential at any point due to a point charge is given by,

$$V = \frac{KQ}{r} \quad \left[K = \frac{1}{4\pi\varepsilon_0}\right]$$

$$V = \frac{1}{4\pi\varepsilon_0}\times\frac{Q}{r}$$

$$E = \frac{1}{4\pi\varepsilon_0}\times\frac{Q}{r^2}$$

$$E = \frac{4\pi\varepsilon_0 V^2}{Q} = 4\pi\varepsilon_0 \times \frac{Q^2\times 10^{22}}{Q}$$

$$E = 4\pi\varepsilon_0 Q \times 10^{22} \text{ V/m}$$

21. *(a)* Potential at A,

$$V_A = \frac{1}{4\pi\varepsilon_0}\frac{q}{a}$$

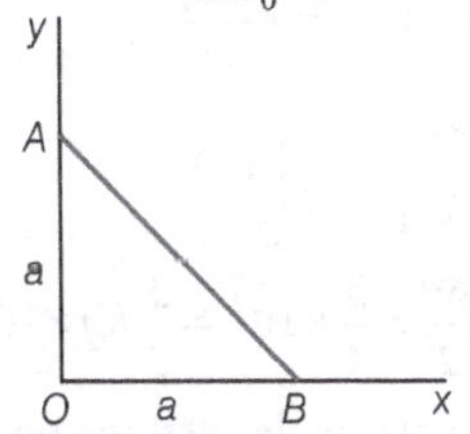

Potential at B,

$$V_B = \frac{1}{4\pi\varepsilon_0}\frac{q}{a}$$

Thus, work done in carrying a test charge $-Q$ from A to B

$$W = (V_A - V_B)(-Q) = 0$$

22. *(b)* Kinetic energy of bullet $= qV$

From energy conservation,

$$\frac{1}{2}mv^2 = qV \quad \Rightarrow V = \frac{mv^2}{2q}$$

$$\Rightarrow \quad V = \frac{2\times 10^{-3}\times(10)^2}{2\times 2\times 10^{-6}}$$

$$= 50\times 10^3 \text{ V} = 50 \text{ kV}$$

23. *(c)* An equipotential surface has a constant value of potential at all points on its surface. The surface and interior of a charged conductor is equipotential. Therefore, the potential is same throughout the charged conductor.

24. *(c)* According to conservation of energy, we have

$$eV = \frac{1}{2}mv^2$$

$$\therefore \quad v = \sqrt{\left(\frac{2eV}{m}\right)}$$

25. *(d)* Work done in moving the charge,

$$W = Fd\cos\theta$$

As $\quad F = qE$

$$\therefore \quad W = qEd\cos\theta \text{ or } E = \frac{W}{q\,d\cos\theta}$$

Here, $\quad q = 0.2$ C, $d = 2$ m

$\theta = 60°$, $W = 4$ J

$$\therefore \quad E = \frac{4}{0.2\times 2\times\cos 60°}$$

$$= 20 \text{ N/C}$$

Alternate Solution

As we know that potential at any point in the direction of θ and electric field $\mathbf{E}$ is given by

$dV = -\mathbf{E}\cdot dr$

(negative sign indicates decreasing potential in direction of electric field)

So, for the given situation

$dr = d\cos\theta$

So, $\quad dV = Ed\cos\theta$

Now, work done for a charge moving in potential difference dV is given by

$W = q\,dV \Rightarrow W = qEd\cos\theta$

Given, $\quad q = 0.2$ C, $d = 2$ m, $\theta = 60°$, $W = 4$ J

So, $\quad 4 \text{ J} = 0.2\times E\times 2\times\cos 60°$

$\Rightarrow \quad E = \frac{4}{0.2\times 2}\times 2 = 20$ N/C

26. *(b)* In case of spherical metal conductor hollow or solid for an internal point (i.e. $r < R$) potential everywhere inside is same.

It is maximum at the surface of sphere and further going out of sphere its value decreases.

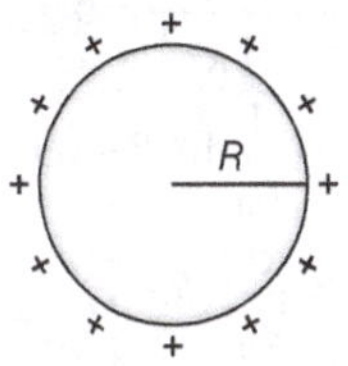

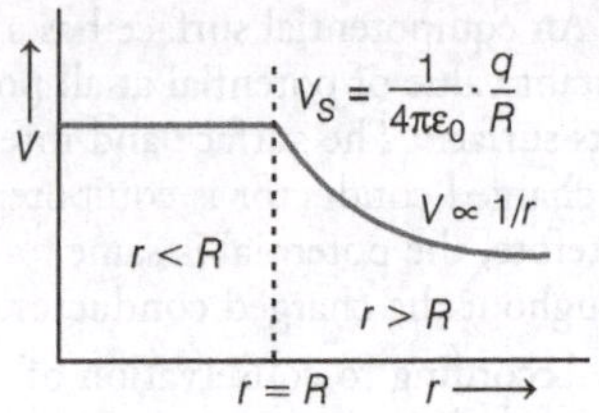

So, according to above graph

$V_{in} = V_{centre} = V_{surface}$

$= \frac{1}{4\pi\varepsilon_0} \times \frac{q}{R} = 80 \text{ V} \quad [\because V_{surface} = 80 \text{ V}]$

27. *(c)* Work done on carrying a charge from one place to another on an equipotential surface is zero

$\therefore \quad W = q(V_1 - V_2)$

$= q \times 0 \quad [\because V_1 = V_2]$

$= 0$

28. *(c)* When the two conducting spheres are connected by a conducting wire, charge will flow from one sphere (having higher potential) to other (having lower potential) till both acquire the same potential.

After connection, $V_1 = V_2$

$\Rightarrow K\frac{Q_1}{r_1} = K\frac{Q_2}{r_2}$

$\Rightarrow \frac{Q_1}{r_1} = \frac{Q_2}{r_2} \Rightarrow \frac{Q_1}{Q_2} = \frac{r_1}{r_2}$

$\therefore \frac{E_1}{E_2} = \frac{KQ_1/r_1^2}{KQ_2/r_2^2} = \frac{Q_1}{Q_2}\frac{r_2^2}{r_1^2}$

$= \frac{r_1}{r_2} \times \frac{r_2^2}{r_1^2} = \frac{r_2}{r_1} = \frac{2}{1}$

> **• Concept Enhancer**
>
> The electric field at any point, outside or inside, the conducting sphere can depend only on *r* (the radial distance from the centre of the sphere to the point).

29. *(c)* Let Q and q be the charges on the spheres. The potential at the common centre will be

$$V = \frac{1}{4\pi\varepsilon_0}\left(\frac{Q}{R}\right) + \frac{1}{4\pi\varepsilon_0}\left(\frac{q}{r}\right)$$

$$= \frac{1}{\varepsilon_0}\left[\frac{Q}{4\pi R^2} \times R + \frac{q}{4\pi r^2} \times r\right]$$

But, $\frac{Q}{4\pi R^2} = \frac{q}{4\pi r^2} = \sigma$

$\therefore \quad V = \frac{1}{\varepsilon_0}[\sigma R + \sigma r]$

$= \frac{\sigma}{\varepsilon_0}(R + r)$

Topic 2

01. *(b)* We know that,

$$C = \frac{\varepsilon_0 A}{d}$$

$$E = \frac{1}{2}CV^2 \text{ and } Q = C \cdot V$$

As the distance between the plates decreases capacitance increases, therefore energy increases and also charge stored is increased.

Hence, A, C, and E are correct.

02. *(c)* We know that, potential at point due to an ideal point at any point on axial line is given

$$V = \pm \frac{1}{4\pi\varepsilon_0}\frac{p}{r^2}$$

Putting the values of p and r, we get

$$V = \pm 9 \times 10^9 \times \frac{4 \times 10^{-6}}{(2)^2}$$

$$= \pm 9 \times 10^3 \text{ V}$$

Hence, A is true but R is false.

03. *(d)*

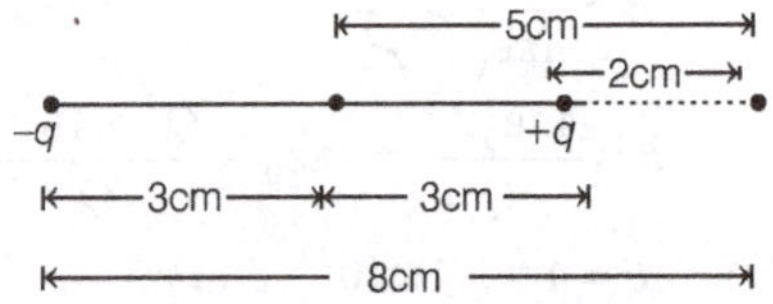

$$V_1 = \frac{Kq}{2 \times 10^{-2}}, V_2 = -\frac{Kq}{8 \times 10^{-2}}$$

$$V_{net} = V_1 + V_2 = \frac{Kq}{2 \times 10^{-2}} - \frac{Kq}{8 \times 10^{-2}}$$

$$= \frac{Kq}{2}\left[1 - \frac{1}{4}\right] \times 10^2$$

$$V_{net} = \frac{Kq}{2} \times \frac{3}{4} \times 10^2 = \frac{3}{8}Kq \times 10^2$$

04. *(d)* In polar molecules, the positive charge and negative charge do not overlap each other. So, the total charge on the polar molecule is zero. Thus, these types of molecules have permanent electric dipole moment. e.g. Water is polar molecule.

05. *(a)* Given, electric dipole moment,

$$p = 16 \times 10^{-9} \text{ C-m}$$

Distance, $r = 0.6$ m

Angle, $\theta = 60° \Rightarrow \cos 60° = \frac{1}{2}$

Electric potential at a point which is at a distance r at some angle θ from electric dipole is

$$V = \frac{p\cos\theta}{4\pi\varepsilon_0 r^2} = \frac{9 \times 10^9 \times 16 \times 10^{-9} \times \frac{1}{2}}{(0.6)^2}$$

$$= 2 \times 10^2 = 200 \text{ V}$$

06. *(a)* Here, torque, $\tau = pE\sin\theta$

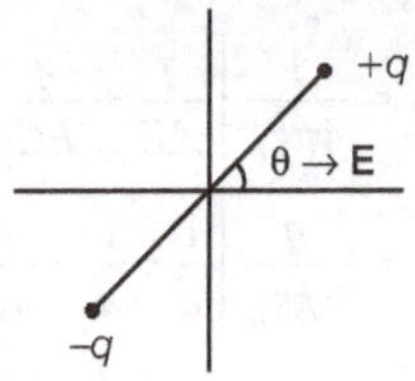

Potential energy of the dipole,

$U = \int \tau\, d\theta$

$= \int_{\pi/2}^{0} pE\sin\theta\, d\theta = -pE[\cos\theta]_{\pi/2}^{\theta}$

$= -pE\cos\theta$

07. *(d)* In case I, when charge $+Q$ is situated at C.

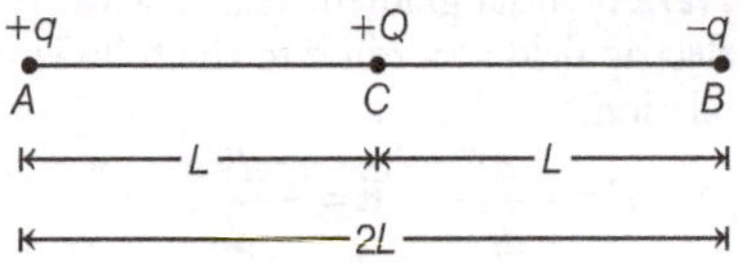

Electric potential energy of system,

$$U_1 = \frac{1}{4\pi\varepsilon_0}\frac{(q)(-q)}{2L} + \frac{1}{4\pi\varepsilon_0}\frac{(-q)Q}{L} + \frac{1}{4\pi\varepsilon_0}\frac{qQ}{L}$$

In case II, when charge $+Q$ is moved from C to D.

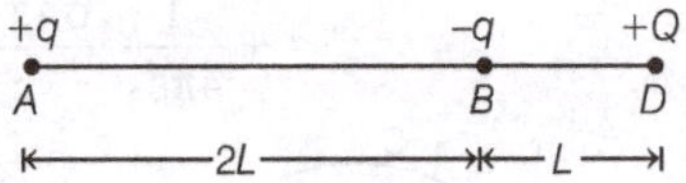

Electric potential energy of system in that case,

$$U_2 = \frac{1}{4\pi\varepsilon_0} \cdot \frac{(q)(-q)}{2L} + \frac{1}{4\pi\varepsilon_0} \cdot \frac{qQ}{3L} + \frac{1}{4\pi\varepsilon_0}\frac{(-q)(Q)}{L}$$

Work done,

$\Delta U = U_2 - U_1$

$$= \left(-\frac{1}{4\pi\varepsilon_0}\frac{q^2}{2L} + \frac{1}{4\pi\varepsilon_0} \cdot \frac{qQ}{3L} - \frac{1}{4\pi\varepsilon_0}\frac{qQ}{L}\right) - \left(-\frac{1}{4\pi\varepsilon_0}\frac{q^2}{2L} - \frac{1}{4\pi\varepsilon_0} \cdot \frac{qQ}{L} + \frac{1}{4\pi\varepsilon_0}\frac{qQ}{L}\right)$$

$$= -\frac{qQ}{6\pi\varepsilon_0 L}$$

08. *(d)* When an electric dipole is placed in an electric field $\mathbf{E}$, a torque $\tau = \mathbf{p} \times \mathbf{E}$ acts on it. This torque tries to rotate the dipole. If the dipole is rotated from an angle θ_1 to θ_2, then work done by external force is given by

$$W = pE(\cos\theta_1 - \cos\theta_2) \quad \text{...(i)}$$

Putting $\theta_1 = 0°, \theta_2 = 90°$ in the Eq. (i), we get

$$W = pE(\cos 0° - \cos 90°)$$
$$= pE(1 - 0) = pE$$

09. *(a)* When charge q_3 is at C, then its potential energy is

$$U_C = \frac{1}{4\pi\varepsilon_0}\left(\frac{q_1 q_3}{0.4} + \frac{q_2 q_3}{0.5}\right)$$

When charge q_3 is at D, then potential energy is

$$U_D = \frac{1}{4\pi\varepsilon_0}\left(\frac{q_1 q_3}{0.4} + \frac{q_2 q_3}{0.1}\right)$$

Hence, change in potential energy

$$\Delta U = U_D - U_C$$
$$= \frac{1}{4\pi\varepsilon_0}\left(\frac{q_2 q_3}{0.1} - \frac{q_2 q_3}{0.5}\right)$$

but $\Delta U = \dfrac{q_3}{4\pi\varepsilon_0} k$

$$\frac{q_3}{4\pi\varepsilon_0} k = \frac{1}{4\pi\varepsilon_0}\left(\frac{q_2 q_3}{0.1} - \frac{q_2 q_3}{0.5}\right)$$
$$k = q_2(10 - 2) = 8q_2$$

10. *(c)* The dipole is placed in electric field as such its dipole moment is in direction of electric field as shown in figure. Direction of dipole moment is from negative to positive charge.

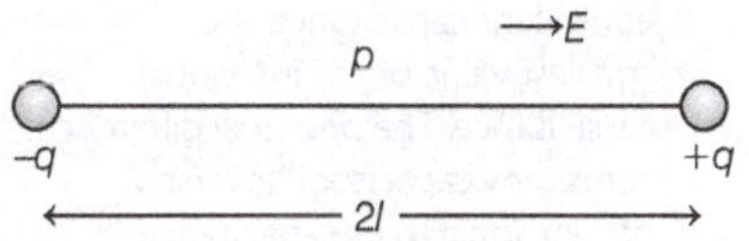

Now, force on the charge q is $F_2 = qE$ along the direction of E and force on charge $-q$ is $F_1 = -qE$ in the direction opposite to E.

Since, forces on the dipole are equal and opposite, so net force on the electric dipole is zero.

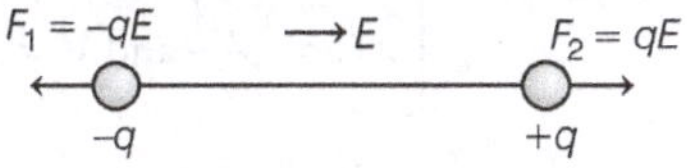

Now, potential energy of the dipole,

$$U = -pE\cos\theta$$

where, θ is the angle between direction of electric field and direction of dipole moment.

$\therefore \quad \theta = 0°$

Hence, $U = -pE\cos 0° = -pE$ (minimum)

11. *(c)* Electrostatic potential energy of charge $(+q)$ placed at the centre of cube is

$$U = 8 \times \frac{1}{4\pi\varepsilon_0} \times \frac{q(-q)}{\text{half - diagonal distance}}$$
$$= 8 \times \frac{1}{4\pi\varepsilon_0} \frac{-q^2}{b\frac{\sqrt{3}}{2}}$$

$$\begin{bmatrix}\text{diagonal of cube} = \sqrt{3}b \\ \text{where, } b = \text{side of cube}\end{bmatrix}$$

$$= \frac{-4q^2}{\sqrt{3}\pi\varepsilon_0 b}$$

• Concept Enhancer

The potential energy of two unlike charges is negative. Negative potential energy indicates that an external agency will have to do work to seperate the charges infinite distance apart while positive potential energy implies that work can be obtained by releasing the charges.

12. *(b)* The electron has negative charge. When an electron is brought towards another electron, then due to same negative charges repulsive force is produced between them. So, to bring them closer a work is done against this repulsive force. This work is stored in the form of electrostatic potential energy. Thus, electrostatic potential energy of system increases.

Alternate Solution

Electrostatic potential energy of system of two electrons

$$U = \frac{1}{4\pi\varepsilon_0}\frac{(-e)(-e)}{r} = \frac{1}{4\pi\varepsilon_0}\frac{e^2}{r}$$

Thus, as r decreases, potential energy increases.

Topic 3

01. *(b)*

key idea

You can use following formula to calculate the value of capacitance, when dielectric material is partially filled.

$$C = \frac{\varepsilon_0 A}{(d - t) + \frac{t}{K}}$$

where, t is thickness of dielectric material.

Capacitance of parallel plate capacitor when medium is air

$$C_0 = \frac{\varepsilon_0 A}{d} \quad \text{... (i)}$$

According to second condition,

$$A' = A, t = d/2, K = 4$$

$\therefore$ Capacitance, $C = \dfrac{\varepsilon_0 A}{(d - t) + \frac{t}{K}}$

$$= \frac{\varepsilon_0 A}{\left(d - \frac{d}{2}\right) + \frac{d/2}{4}} = \frac{8}{5} \cdot \frac{\varepsilon_0 A}{d}$$

$$\therefore \frac{C}{C_0} = \frac{\frac{8}{5} \cdot \frac{\varepsilon_0 A}{d}}{\frac{\varepsilon_0 A}{d}} \Rightarrow C : C_0 = 8 : 5$$

02. *(b)* Given, $C_0 = 6\,\mu\text{F}, C_m = 30\,\mu\text{F}$

$\therefore$ As, dielectric constant

$$K = \varepsilon_r = \frac{C_m}{C_0} = \frac{30}{6} = 5$$

Permittivity of the medium,

$$\varepsilon_m = K \times \varepsilon_0 = 5 \times \varepsilon_0$$
$$= 5 \times 8.85 \times 10^{-12}$$
$$= 0.44 \times 10^{-10}\,\text{C}^2\text{N}^{-1}\text{m}^{-2}$$

03. *(c)* As we know that, the total work done in transferring a charge to a parallel plate capacitor is given as

$$W = \frac{Q^2}{2C} \quad \text{...(i)}$$

Since, $\quad W = F \cdot d \quad$ ...(ii)

where, F is the electrostatic force between the plates of capacitor and d is the distance between the plates.

From Eqs. (i) and (ii), we get

$$W = \frac{Q^2}{2C} = Fd \Rightarrow F = \frac{Q^2}{2Cd} \quad \text{...(iii)}$$

As, the capacitance of a parallel plate is given as, $\quad C = \dfrac{\varepsilon_0 A}{d}$

Substituting the value of C in Eq. (iii), we get,

$$F = \frac{Q^2 d}{2\varepsilon_0 A d} = \frac{Q^2}{2\varepsilon_0 A}$$

This means, electrostatic force is independent of the distance between the plates.

04. *(b)* Force between plates of parallel capacitor,

$$F = qE = q\left[\frac{\sigma}{2\varepsilon_0}\right]$$

$\because$ Surface charge density

$$\sigma = q/A$$

$\therefore \quad F = q\left[\frac{q}{2A\varepsilon_0}\right] \Rightarrow F = \frac{q^2}{2A\varepsilon_0}$

So, net charge across a capacitor,

$$q = CV$$

$$F = \frac{C^2V^2}{2A\varepsilon_0} \qquad \left[C = \frac{A\varepsilon_0}{d}\right]$$

$$\Rightarrow \quad F = \frac{\left(\frac{A\varepsilon_0}{d}\right)\times CV^2}{2A\varepsilon_0} = \frac{CV^2}{2d}$$

05. *(c)* Graph (c) will be the right graph, the electric field inside the dielectrics will be less than the electric field outside the dielectrics. The electric field inside the dielectrics could not be zero.

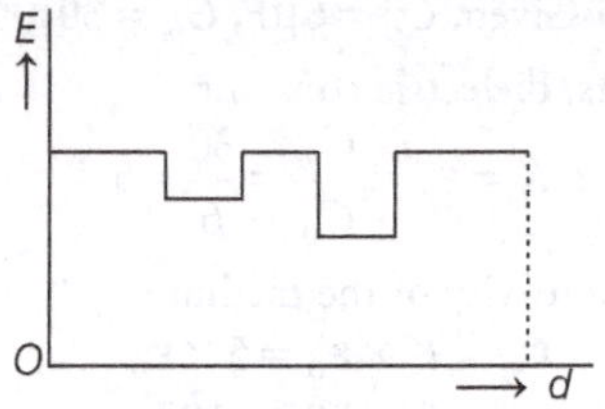

As $K_2 > K_1$, the drop in electric field for K_2 dielectric must be more than K_1.

06. *(c)* Electric field between two plates of parallel plate capacitor in vacuum is given by $E = \frac{\sigma}{\varepsilon_0}$.

In a medium of dielectric constant

$$K, E' = \frac{\sigma}{\varepsilon_0 K}$$

For kerosene oil $K > 1$

$$\Rightarrow \quad E' < E$$

07. *(d)* If the battery is removed after charging, then the charge stored in the capacitor remains constant.

$$q = \text{constant}$$

Change in capacitance,

$$C' = \frac{\varepsilon_0 A}{d'}$$

As $\quad d' > d$

Hence, $C' < C$

As, potential difference between the plates of capacitor is given by

$$V = q / C$$

So, for the new capacitor formed

$$V' \propto \frac{1}{C'} \qquad [q = \text{constant}]$$

As capacitance decreases, so potential difference increases.

08. *(d)* The capacitance of a parallel plate capacitor with dielectric (oil) between its plates is

$$C = K\varepsilon_0 A / d \qquad \text{...(i)}$$

When dielectric (oil) is removed, so capacitance of capacitor becomes,

$$C_0 = \varepsilon_0 A / d \qquad \text{...(ii)}$$

Comparing Eqs. (i) and (ii), we get

$$C = KC_0$$

$$\Rightarrow \quad C_0 = \frac{C}{K} = \frac{C}{2} \Rightarrow (K = 2)$$

Topic 4

01. *(d)* Equivalent capacitance of the system,

$$C_{AB} = \frac{3\times(3+3)}{3+(3+3)} = \frac{18}{9} = 2\,\mu\text{F}$$

02. *(c)* $C_1 = \dfrac{\left(\frac{A}{3}\right)K_1\varepsilon_0}{d/2} = \dfrac{2K_1}{3K}C \qquad \left[\because C = \dfrac{A\varepsilon_0 K}{d},\ \dfrac{C}{K} = \dfrac{A\varepsilon_0}{d}\right]$

$$C_2 = \frac{\left(\frac{A}{3}\right)K_2\varepsilon_0}{d/2} = \frac{2K_2}{3K}C,$$

$$C_3 = \frac{\left(\frac{A}{3}\right)K_3\varepsilon_0}{d/2} = \frac{2K_3}{3K}C,$$

$$C_4 = \frac{(A)K_4\varepsilon_0}{d/2} = \frac{2K_4}{K}C \qquad \left[\because C = C_{eq},\ \frac{1}{C} = \frac{1}{C_{eq}}\right]$$

Equivalent capacitance

$$\frac{1}{C_{eq}} = \frac{1}{(C_1 + C_2 + C_3)} + \frac{1}{C_4}$$

$$\text{or} \quad \frac{1}{C_{eq}} = \frac{3K}{2C}\left[\frac{1}{K_1 + K_2 + K_3}\right] + \frac{K}{2K_4 C}$$

$$\frac{2}{K} = \frac{3}{K_1 + K_2 + K_3} + \frac{1}{K_4}$$

03. *(b)* The given situation is shown below.

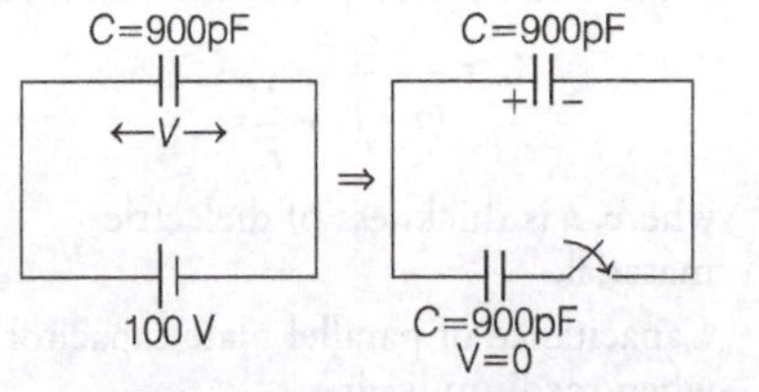

After combination,
Common potential,

$$V = \frac{C_1V_1 + C_2V_2}{C_1 + C_2} = \frac{C\times 100 + C\times 0}{C + C} = 50\text{ V}$$

$\therefore$ Electrostatic stored potential energy,

$$U = 2\times\frac{1}{2}CV^2 = CV^2$$

$$= 9\times 10^{-10}\times 50^2 = 2.25\times 10^{-6}\text{ J}$$

04. *(b)* Consider the nodes be A, B, E and F as shown in the figure

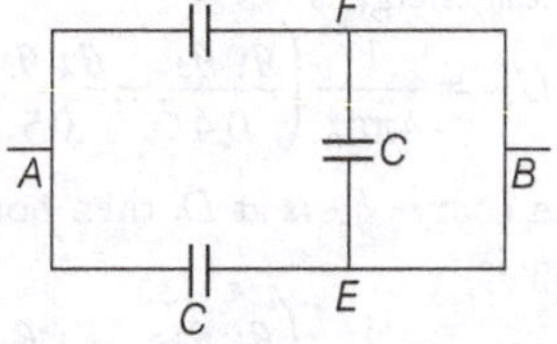

The potential at F is equal to the potential at node E.
So, EF behave as open circuit.

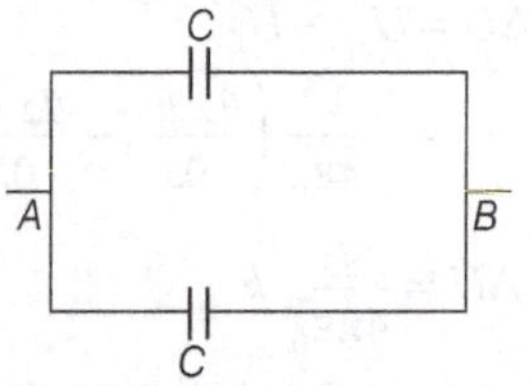

Now, the two capacitors are arranged in parallel. The net equivalent capacitors,

$$C_{eq} = C_1 + C_2$$

$$\Rightarrow \quad C_{eq} = C + C$$

$$\Rightarrow \quad C_{eq} = 2C$$

> **Concept Enhancer**
> In series combination of capacitors, the equivalent capacitance is smaller than the smallest value of any individual capacitance. The potential difference across any capacitor is inversely proportional to its capacitance.

05. *(c)* The energy stored in the capacitor,

$$U = \frac{1}{2}CV^2$$

$$U = \frac{1}{2}\left(\frac{\varepsilon_0 A}{d}\right)(Ed)^2 \qquad \left[\because C = \frac{\varepsilon_0 A}{d} \text{ and } V = Ed\right]$$

$$U = \frac{1}{2}(\varepsilon_0 A)(E)^2 d$$

$$= \frac{1}{2}\varepsilon_0 E^2 Ad$$

06. *(c)* When C_1 is connected to voltage source, it is charged to a potential V and this will be stored as a potential energy in the capacitor given by

$$U = \frac{1}{2}CV^2$$

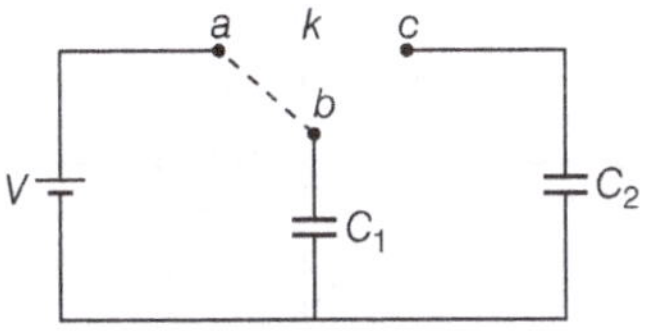

When key is disconnected from battery and b and c are connected, the charge will be transformed from the capacitor C_1 to capacitor C_2, then

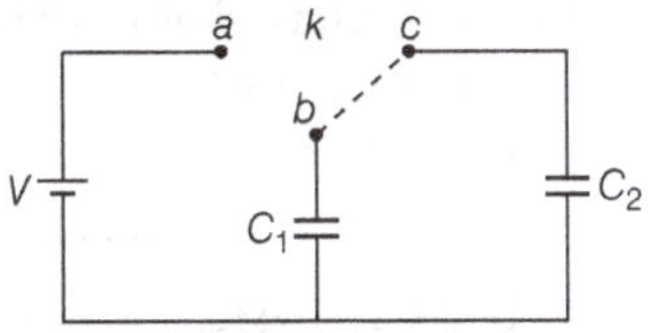

The loss of energy due to redistribution of charge is given by

$$\Delta U = \frac{C_1C_2}{2(C_1 + C_2)}(V_1 - V_2)^2$$

$$= \frac{C \times C}{2(C + C)}(V - 0)^2 = \frac{1}{4}CV^2$$

$[\because C_1 = C_2]$

$\therefore$ Percentage loss $= \dfrac{\Delta U}{U} \times 100$

$$= \frac{\frac{1}{4}CV^2}{\frac{1}{2}CV^2} \times 100 = 50\%$$

07. *(b)* **Thinking Process**

Energy stored in a system of capacitors

$$= \Sigma \frac{1}{2}CV^2$$

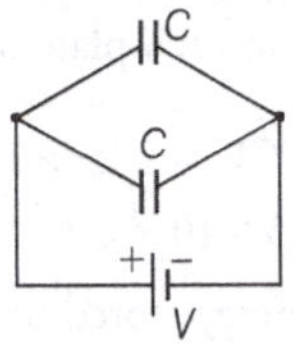

Also, potential drop remains same in parallel across both capacitors.

Initially stored energy,

$$U_1 = \frac{1}{2}CV^2$$

Charge on capacitor $q = CV$

When it is connected with another uncharged capacitor,

$$V_c = \frac{q_1 + q_2}{C_1 + C_2} = \frac{q + 0}{C + C} = \frac{V}{2}$$

Final energy

$$U_2 = \frac{1}{2}C\left(\frac{V}{2}\right)^2 + \frac{1}{2}C\left(\frac{V}{2}\right)^2$$

$$U_2 = \left(\frac{CV^2}{4}\right) \Rightarrow V_2 = \frac{1}{2} \times \frac{1}{2}CV^2$$

$$U_2 = \frac{U_1}{2}$$

08. *(c)* Consider the given figure,

When the switch S is connected to point 1, then initial energy stored in the capacitor can be given as

$$U = \frac{1}{2}(2\mu\text{F}) \times V^2$$

When the switch S is connected to point 2, energy dissipated on connection across 8 μF will be

$$\Delta U = \frac{1}{2}\left(\frac{C_1C_2}{C_1 + C_2}\right).V^2$$

$$= \frac{1}{2} \times \frac{2\mu\text{F} \times 8\mu\text{F}}{10\mu\text{F}} \times V^2$$

$$= \frac{1}{2} \times (1.6\,\mu\text{F}) \times V^2$$

Therefore, % loss of energy

$$\frac{\Delta U}{U} \times 100 = \frac{1.6}{2} \times 100 = 80\%.$$

09. *(c)* When a parallel plate air capacitor connected to a cell of emf V, then charge stored will be

$$q = CV \quad \Rightarrow V = q/C$$

Also energy stored is

$$U = \frac{1}{2}CV^2 = \frac{q^2}{2C}$$

As the battery is disconnected from the capacitor the charge will not be destroyed, i.e. $q' = q$ with the introduction of dielectric in the gap of capacitor the new capacitance will be

$$C' = CK \Rightarrow V' = q/C' = q/CK$$

The new energy stored will be

$$U' = \frac{q^2}{2CK} \Rightarrow \Delta U = U' - U$$

$$= \frac{q^2}{2C}\left(\frac{1}{K} - 1\right) = \frac{1}{2}CV^2\left(\frac{1}{K} - 1\right)$$

10. *(d)* **Case I** When the capacitors are joined in series,

$$U_{\text{series}} = \frac{1}{2}\frac{C_1}{n_1}(4V)^2$$

Case II When the capacitors are joined in parallel,

$$U_{\text{parallel}} = \frac{1}{2}(n_2\,C_2)V^2$$

Given, $U_{\text{series}} = U_{\text{parallel}}$

So, $\dfrac{1}{2}\dfrac{C_1}{n_1}(4V)^2 = \dfrac{1}{2}(n_2\,C_2)V^2$

$\Rightarrow \qquad C_2 = 16C_1/n_2\,n_1$

11. *(c)*

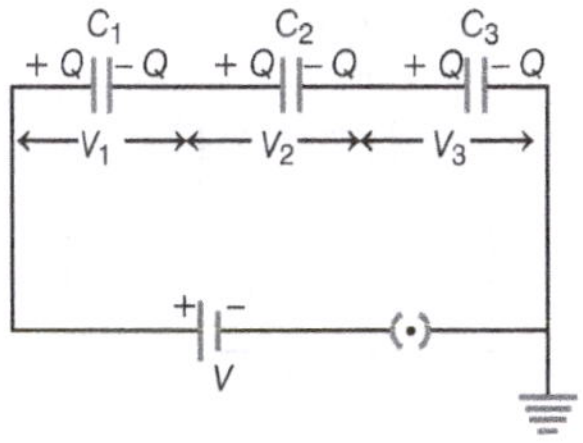

$$V = V_1 + V_2 + V_3$$

$[\because V_1 = V_2 = V_3 = V]$

Here, $V = 3V$

The equivalent capacitance C_s is given by

$$\frac{1}{C_s} = \frac{1}{C_1} + \frac{1}{C_2} + \frac{1}{C_3}$$

$[\because C_1 = C_2 = C_3 = C]$

$$C_s = \frac{C}{3}$$

12. *(c)* Energy of charged capacitor

$$= \frac{1}{2}CV^2$$

Energy given by cell

$$= CV^2 = \frac{A\varepsilon_0}{d} \times (Ed)^2 \quad [\text{As, } V = Ed]$$

$$= A\varepsilon_0E^2d$$

13. *(c)* The two condensers in the circuit are in parallel order, hence

$$C' = C + \frac{C}{2} = \frac{3C}{2}$$

The work done in charging the equivalent capacitor is stored in the form of potential energy.

Hence, $W = U = \dfrac{1}{2}C'V^2$

$$= \frac{1}{2}\left(\frac{3C}{2}\right)V^2 = \frac{3}{4}CV^2$$

14. *(b)* The charge flowing through C_4 is

$$q_4 = C_4 \times V = 4CV$$

The series combination of C_1, C_2 and C_3 gives

$$\frac{1}{C_{\text{eq}}} = \frac{1}{C} + \frac{1}{2C} + \frac{1}{3C}$$

$$= \frac{6 + 3 + 2}{6C} = \frac{11}{6C} \Rightarrow C_{\text{eq}} = \frac{6C}{11}$$

$$q_2 = C_{\text{eq}}V = \frac{6C}{11} \times V$$

Now, ratio of charge on C_4 and C_2 is given by,

$$\frac{q_4}{q_2} = \frac{4CV \times 11}{6CV} = \frac{22}{3} \Rightarrow \frac{q_2}{q_4} = \frac{3}{22}$$

15. *(a)* Given, $C_1 = C_2 = C_3 = 4\ \mu F$

(a) The network of three capacitors can be shown as

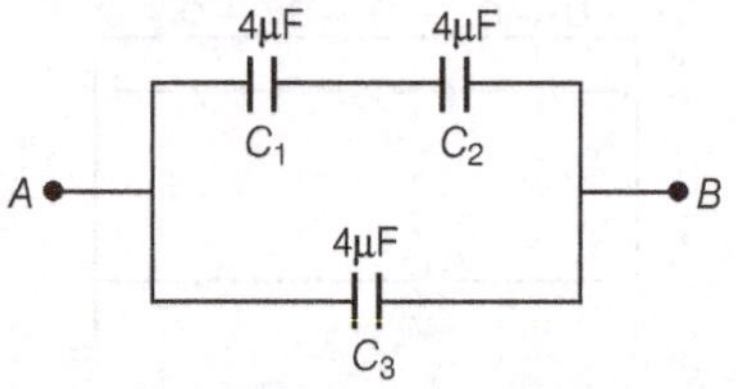

$$C_{\text{net}} = \frac{C_1 C_2}{C_1 + C_2} + C_3 = \left(\frac{4 \times 4}{4+4}\right) + 4$$

$$= 2 + 4 = 6\mu F$$

(b) The corresponding network is shown in figure below

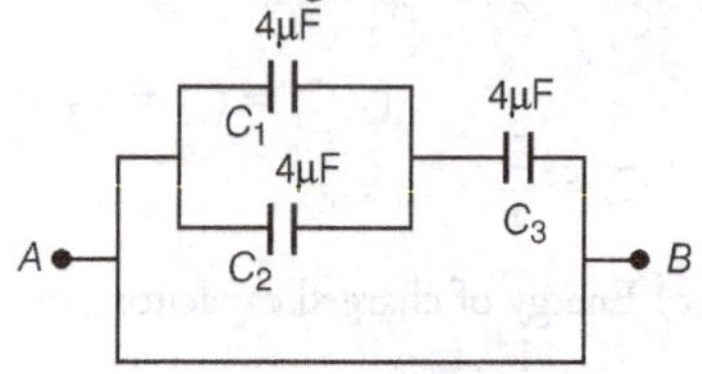

So, $C_{\text{net}} = \dfrac{(C_1 + C_2) \times C_3}{(C_1 + C_2) + C_3}$

$$= \frac{(4+4) \times 4}{(4+4) + 4} = \frac{32}{12} = \frac{8}{3}\mu F$$

(c) The corresponding network is shown below.

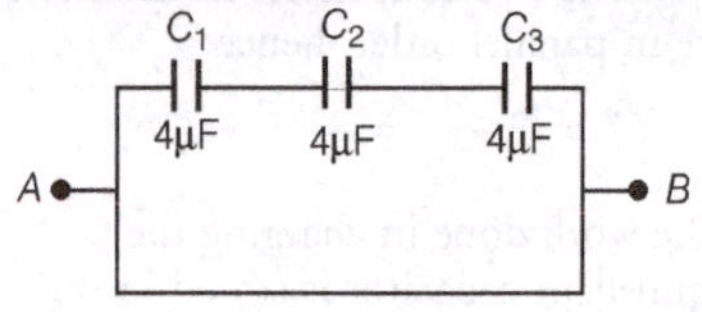

So, $\dfrac{1}{C_{net}} = \dfrac{1}{C_1} + \dfrac{1}{C_2} + \dfrac{1}{C_3}$

$$= \frac{1}{4} + \frac{1}{4} + \frac{1}{4} = \frac{3}{4}$$

$\therefore \quad C = \dfrac{4}{3}\mu F$

(d) The corresponding network is shown below.

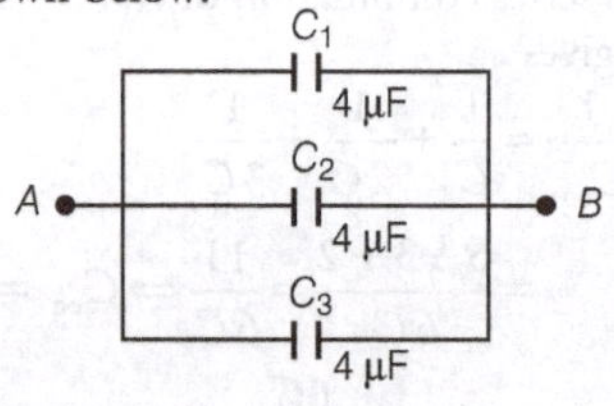

So, $C_{\text{net}} = C_1 + C_2 + C_3$

$$= 4 + 4 + 4 = 12\,\mu F$$

Thus, options (a) is correct.

16. *(b)* The common potential difference across two capacitors connected in parallel.

$$V_C = \frac{C_1 V_1 + C_2 V_2}{C_1 + C_2}$$

Here, potential of charged capacitor

$V_1 = V,$

potential of uncharged capacitor

$V_2 = 0$

$\therefore \quad V_C = \dfrac{C_1 V}{C_1 + C_2}$

17. *(b)* Energy stored, in parallel plate capacitor is given by

$$U = \frac{1}{2}\frac{q^2}{C}$$

but $\sigma = \dfrac{q}{A}$ and $C = \dfrac{\varepsilon_0 A}{d}$

$\therefore \quad U = \dfrac{1}{2}\dfrac{(\sigma A)^2}{\left(\dfrac{\varepsilon_0 A}{d}\right)} = \dfrac{A\sigma^2 d}{2\varepsilon_0}$

or $\quad = \dfrac{1}{2}\left(\dfrac{\sigma}{\varepsilon_0}\right)^2 \times \varepsilon_0 A d$

or $\quad U = \dfrac{1}{2}E^2 \varepsilon_0 A d$

Energy stored per unit volume i.e. energy density is thus given by

$$u = \frac{U}{V} = \frac{U}{Ad} = \frac{1}{2}\varepsilon_0 E^2$$

$$\Rightarrow \quad = \frac{1}{2}\varepsilon_0 \left(\frac{V}{d}\right)^2 = \frac{1}{2}\varepsilon_0 \frac{V^2}{d^2}$$

18. *(b)*

key idea

You can find the energy stored in the capacitor using following formula.

$$U = \frac{1}{2}CV^2 = \frac{1}{2}\frac{q^2}{C}$$

When a capacitor is charged by connecting a battery across its plates, the initial energy stored,

$$U = \frac{q^2}{2C}$$

When the battery is disconnected, then the charge remains constant i.e. q = constant. Now, another identical capacitor is connected across it i.e. the capacitors are connected in parallel, so the equivalent capacitance

$$C_{\text{eq}} = C_1 + C_2 = C + C = 2C$$

Thus, final energy stored by the system of capacitors,

$$U' = \frac{q^2}{2C_{\text{eq}}} \Rightarrow U' = \frac{q^2}{2(2C)}$$

$$U' = \frac{1}{2}U = \frac{U}{2}$$

19. *(a)* The given circuit can be redrawn as,

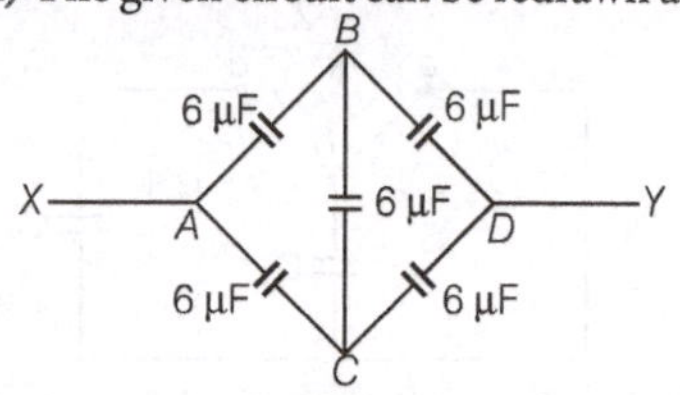

It is a balanced Wheatstone's bridge $\left(\text{as } \dfrac{C_{AB}}{C_{BD}} = \dfrac{C_{AC}}{C_{CD}} = \dfrac{6}{6}\right)$.

The simplified circuit is shown as below.

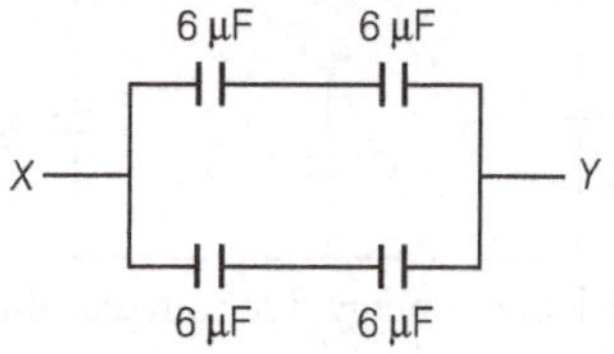

$$C_{\text{net}} = \frac{6 \times 6}{6+6} = \frac{6 \times 6}{6+6} = 3 + 3 = 6\,\mu F$$

20. *(d)* Energy stored in a capacitor,

$$U = \frac{1}{2}CV^2.$$

21. *(c)* This energy stored in the capacitor is given by

$$U = \frac{1}{2}CV^2$$

If initial potential is V_1 and final potential is V_2, then increase in energy ΔU

$$\Delta U = \frac{1}{2}C(V_2^2 - V_1^2)$$

$$= \frac{1}{2} \times (6 \times 10^{-6}) \times [(20)^2 - (10)^2]$$

$$= (3 \times 10^{-6}) \times 300 = 9 \times 10^{-4}\ \text{J}$$

22. *(b)* $V = 200$ V

So, charge on each plate of capacitor is given by

$$Q = \pm CV = \pm 25 \times 10^{-6} \times 200$$

$$= \pm 5 \times 10^{-3}\,\text{C}$$

23. *(d)* The energy stored in the capacitor

$$= \frac{1}{2}CV^2$$

This energy will be converted into heat in the resistor.

$\therefore$ Heat produced = energy stored

$$= \frac{1}{2}CV^2$$

$$= \frac{1}{2} \times 4 \times 10^{-6} \times (400)^2 = 0.32\ \text{J}$$

C-17

NEET Chapterwise Topicwise Physics

In NEET 2024, 4 questions were visible from this chapter. In past 5 years, 2 questions from topic-1, 5 questions from topic-2, 5 questions from topic-3, 5 questions from topic-4, 2 questions from topic-5 and 4 questions from topic-6 were asked.

For detailed analysis scan QR code

CURRENT ELECTRICITY

Topic 1 Electric Current, Drift Velocity and Mobility

01 **Column I** Gives certain physical terms associated with flow of current through a metallic conductor. **Column II** Gives some mathematical relations involving electrical quantities. Match Column I and Column II with appropriate relations.

[NCERT (New) Pg. 86, NEET 2021]

Column I		Column II	
A.	Drift velocity	1.	$\frac{m}{ne^2\rho}$
B.	Electrical resistivity	2.	nev_d
C.	Relaxation period	3.	$\frac{eE}{m}\tau$
D.	Current density	4.	E/J

Codes

	A	B	C	D		A	B	C	D
(a)	3	4	1	2	(b)	3	4	2	1
(c)	3	1	4	2	(d)	3	2	4	1

02 A charged particle having drift velocity of 7.5×10^{-4} ms^{-1} in an electric field of 3×10^{-10} Vm^{-1}, has a mobility (in m^{2}V^{-1}s^{-1}) of

[NCERT (New) Pg. 86, NEET (Sep.) 2020]

(a) 2.5×10^{6} (b) 2.5×10^{-6}
(c) 2.25×10^{-15} (d) 2.25×10^{15}

03 Across a metallic conductor of non-uniform cross-section, a constant potential difference is applied. The quantity which remain constant along the conductor is *[NCERT (New) Pg. 82, AIPMT 2015]*

(a) current density
(b) current
(c) drift velocity
(d) electric field

04 The velocity of charge carriers of current (about 1 A) in a metal under normal conditions is of the order of

[AIPMT 1991]

(a) a fraction of mm/s
(b) velocity of light
(c) several thousand m/s
(d) a few hundred m/s

Topic 2 Ohm's Law, Resistance and Resistivity

01 The resistance of platinum wire at 0°C is 2 Ω and 6.8 Ω at 80°C. The temperature coefficient of resistance of the wire is *[NEET 2023]*

(a) 3×10^{-3} °C^{-1} (b) 3×10^{-2} °C^{-1}
(c) 3×10^{-1} °C^{-1} (d) 3×10^{-4} °C^{-1}

02 A copper wire of length 10m and radius $(10^{-2}/\sqrt{\pi})$ m has electrical resistance of 10 Ω. The current density in the wire for an electric field strength of 10(V/m) is

[NCERT (New) Pg. 86, NEET 2022]

(a) 10^4 A/m^2 (b) 10^6 A/m^2
(c) 10^{-5} A/m^2 (d) 10^5 A/m^2

03 As the temperature increases, the electrical resistance

[NCERT (New) Pg. 91, NEET 2022]

(a) decreases for both conductors and semiconductors.
(b) increases for conductors but decreases for semiconductors.
(c) decreases for conductors but increases for semiconductors.
(d) increases for both conductors and semiconductors.

04 Two solid conductors are made up of same material, have same length and same resistance. One of them has a circular cross-section of area A_1 and the other one has a square cross-section of area A_2. The ratio A_1/A_2 is *[NCERT (New) Pg. 84, NEET (Oct.) 2020]*

(a) 1.5 (b) 1
(c) 0.8 (d) 2

05 Which of the following graph represents the variation of resistivity ρ with temperature T for copper ? *[NEET (Sep.) 2020]*

(a)
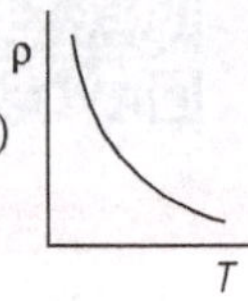

(b)
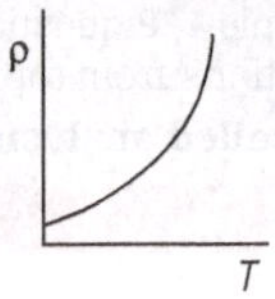

(c)
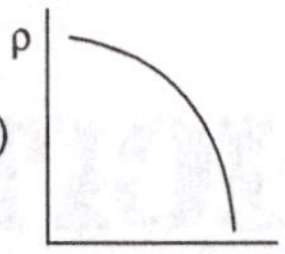

(d)
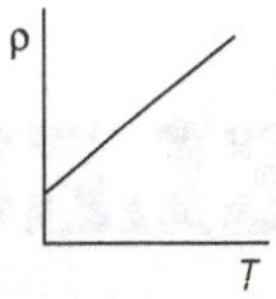

06 In the circuits shown below, the readings of voltmeters and the ammeters will be *[NCERT (New) Pg. 84, NEET (National) 2019]*

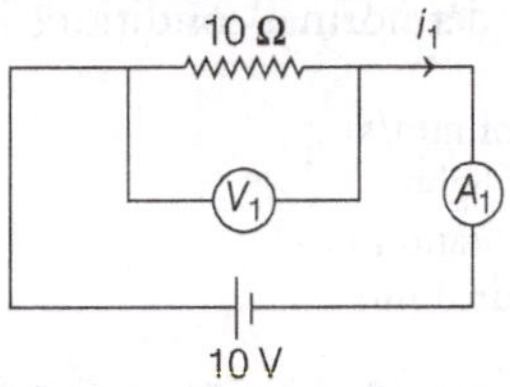

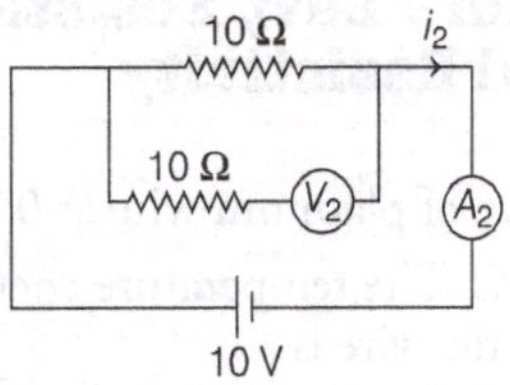

(a) $V_1 = V_2$ and $i_1 > i_2$
(b) $V_1 = V_2$ and $i_i = i_2$
(c) $V_2 > V_1$ and $i_1 > i_2$
(d) $V_2 > V_1$ and $i_1 = i_2$

07 Which of the following acts as a circuit protection device ? *[NEET (National) 2019]*
(a) Inductor (b) Switch
(c) Fuse (d) Conductor

08 The resistance of a wire is $R\,\Omega$. If it is melted and stretched to n times its original length, its new resistance will be *[NCERT (New) Pg. 84, NEET 2017]*
(a) nR (b) $\frac{R}{n}$
(c) n^2R (d) $\frac{R}{n^2}$

09 A wire of resistance 4Ω is stretched to twice its original length. The resistance of stretched wire would be *[NCERT (New) Pg. 84, NEET 2013]*
(a) 2 Ω (b) 4 Ω
(c) 8 Ω (d) 16 Ω

10 The mean free path of electrons in a metal is 4×10^{-8} m. The electric field which can give on an average 2 eV energy to an electron in the metal will be in unit of Vm^{-1} *[AIPMT 2009]*
(a) 8×10^7 (b) 5×10^{-11}
(c) 8×10^{-11} (d) 5×10^7

11 A wire of a certain material is stretched slowly by 10 percent. Its new resistance and specific resistance become, respectively *[NCERT (New) Pg. 84, AIPMT 2008]*
(a) 1.2 times, 1.1 times
(b) 1.21 times, same
(c) Both remain the same
(d) 1.1 times, 1.1 times

12 The electric resistance of a certain wire of iron *is R*. If its length and radius are both doubled, then *[AIPMT 2004]*
(a) the resistance will be doubled and the specific resistance will be halved
(b) the resistance will be halved and the specific resistance will remain unchanged
(c) the resistance will be halved and the specific resistance will be doubled
(d) the resistance and the specific resistance will both remain unchanged

13 A 6 V battery is connected to the terminals of a three metre long wire of uniform thickness and resistance of 100 Ω. The difference of potential between two points on the wire separated by a distance of 50 cm will be *[NCERT (New) Pg. 84, AIPMT 2004]*
(a) 2 V (b) 3 V
(c) 1 V (d) 1.5 V

14 Fuse wire is a wire of *[AIPMT 2003]*
(a) low resistance and low melting point
(b) low resistance and high melting point
(c) high resistance and high melting point
(d) high resistance and low melting point

15 The specific resistance of a conductor increases with *[AIPMT 2002]*
(a) increase in temperature
(b) increase in cross-sectional area
(c) decrease in length
(d) decrease in cross-sectional area

16 Copper and silicon is cooled from 300 K to 60 K, the specific resistance *[NCERT (New) Pg. 90, AIPMT 2001]*
(a) decreases in copper but increases in silicon
(b) increases in copper but decreases in silicon
(c) increases in both
(d) decreases in both

17 The resistance of a discharge tube is *[AIPMT 1999]*
(a) zero (b) ohmic
(c) non-ohmic (d) infinity

18 From the graph between current I and voltage V shown in figure, identify the portion corresponding to negative resistance. *[NCERT (New) Pg. 84, AIPMT 1997]*

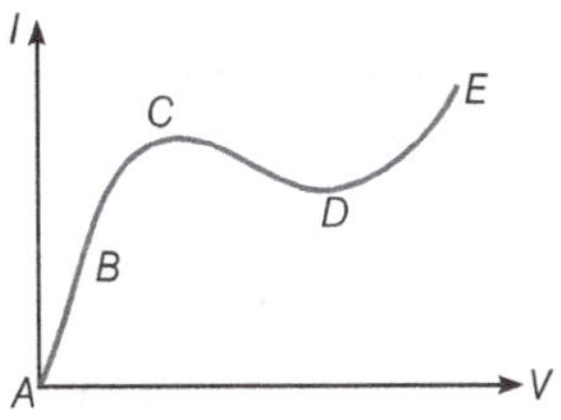

(a) DE (b) CD
(c) BC (d) AB

19 There are three copper wires of length and cross-sectional area (L, A), $(2L, A/2)$ $(L/2, 2A)$. In which case is the resistance minimum? *[AIPMT 1997]*
(a) It is the same in all three cases
(b) Wire of cross-sectional area $2A$
(c) Wire of cross-sectional area A
(d) Wire of cross-sectional area $\frac{1}{2}A$

20 If a neglegibly small current is passed through a wire of length 15 m and of resistance 5 Ω having uniform cross-section of 6×10^{-7} m^2, then coefficient of resistivity of material is *[NCERT (New) Pg. 84, AIPMT 1996]*
(a) 1×10^{-7} Ω-m (b) 2×10^{-7} Ω-m
(c) 3×10^{-7} Ω-m (d) 4×10^{-7} Ω-m

21 If the resistance of a conductor is 5 Ω at 50°C and 7 Ω at 100°C, then the mean temperature coefficient of resistance (of the material) is *[AIPMT 1996]*
(a) 0.01/°C (b) 0.04/°C
(c) 0.06/°C (d) 0.08/°C.

22 If a wire of resistance R is melted and recasted to half of its length, then the new resistance of the wire will be *[NCERT (New) Pg. 84, AIPMT 1995]*
(a) $\frac{R}{4}$ (b) $\frac{R}{2}$
(c) R (d) $2R$

23 A wire 50 cm long and 1 mm^2 in cross-section carries a current of 4 A when connected to a 2 V battery. The resistivity of the wire is *[AIPMT 1994]*
(a) 4×10^{-6} Ω-m (b) 1×10^{-6} Ω-m
(c) 2×10^{-7} Ω-m (d) 5×10^{-7} Ω-m

24 The masses of the three wires of copper are in the ratio of 1 : 3 : 5 and their lengths are in the ratio of 5 : 3 : 1. The ratio of their electrical resistance is *[AIPMT 1988]*
(a) 1 : 3 : 5 (b) 5 : 3 : 1
(c) 1 : 25 : 125 (d) 125 : 15 : 1

Topic 3 Combination of Resistors

01 A wire of length l and resistance 100 Ω is divided into 10 equal parts. The first 5 parts are connected in series while the next 5 parts are connected in parallel. The two combinations are again connected in series. The resistance of this final combination is *[NEET 2024]*
(a) 26 Ω (b) 52 Ω
(c) 55 Ω (d) 60 Ω

02 10 resistors, each of resistance R are connected in series to a battery of emf E and negligible internal resistance. Then those are connected in parallel to the same battery, the current is increased n times. The value of n is *[NEET 2023]*
(a) 100 (b) 1
(c) 1000 (d) 10

03 The effective resistance of a parallel connection that consists of four wires of equal length, equal area of cross-section and same material is 0.25 Ω. What will be the effective resistance if they are connected in series? *[NCERT (New) Pg. 109, NEET 2021]*
(a) 0.25 Ω (b) 0.5 Ω
(c) 1 Ω (d) 4 Ω

04 Three resistors having resistances r_1, r_2 and r_3 are connected as shown in the given circuit. The ratio i_3 / i_1 of currents in terms of resistances used in the circuit is *[NCERT (New) Pg. 109, NEET 2021]*

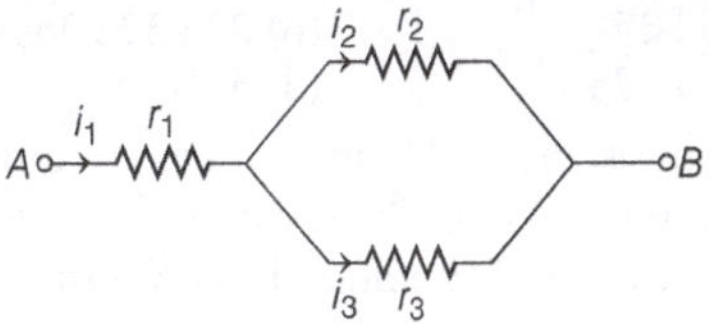

(a) $\frac{r_1}{r_2 + r_3}$ (b) $\frac{r_2}{r_2 + r_3}$
(c) $\frac{r_1}{r_1 + r_2}$ (d) $\frac{r_2}{r_1 + r_3}$

05 The equivalent resistance between A and B for the mesh shown in the figure is *[NCERT (New) Pg. 109, NEET (Oct.) 2020]*

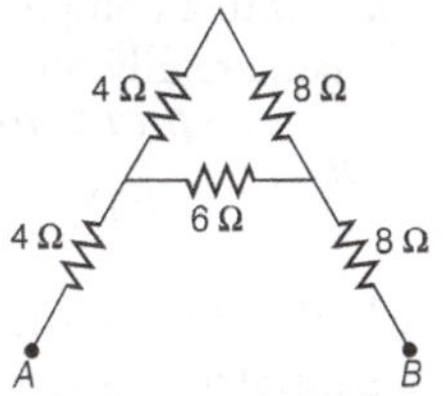

(a) 7.2 Ω (b) 16 Ω
(c) 30 Ω (d) 4.8 Ω

06 Two metal wires of identical dimensions are connected in series. If σ_1 and σ_2 are the conductivities of the metal wires respectively, the effective conductivity of the combination is *[AIPMT 2015]*

(a) $\frac{2\sigma_1\sigma_2}{\sigma_1+\sigma_2}$ (b) $\frac{\sigma_1+\sigma_2}{2\sigma_1\sigma_2}$ (c) $\frac{\sigma_1+\sigma_2}{\sigma_1\sigma_2}$ (d) $\frac{\sigma_1\sigma_2}{\sigma_1+\sigma_2}$

07 A, B and C are voltmeters of resistance R, $1.5R$ and $3R$ respectively as shown in the figure. When some potential difference is applied between X and Y, the voltmeter readings are V_A, V_B and V_C respectively. Then, *[AIPMT 2015]*

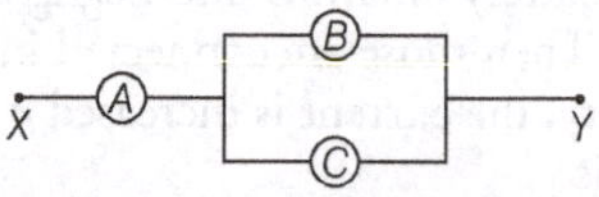

(a) $V_A = V_B = V_C$ (b) $V_A \neq V_B = V_C$
(c) $V_A = V_B \neq V_C$ (d) $V_A \neq V_B \neq V_C$

08 A 12 cm wire is given a shape of a right angled triangle ABC having sides 3 cm, 4 cm and 5 cm as shown in the figure. The resistance between two ends (AB, BC, CA) of the respective sides are measured one by one by a multimeter. The resistances will be in the ratio *[NCERT (Old) Pg. 108, NEET 2013]*

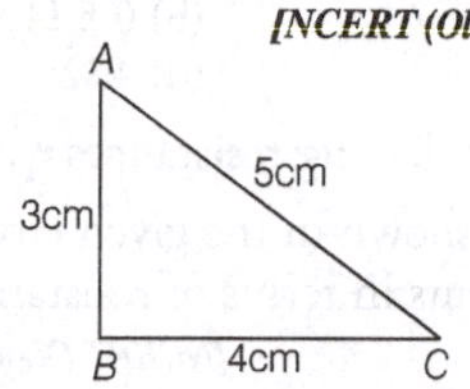

(a) 9 : 16 : 25 (b) 27 : 32 : 35
(c) 21 : 24 : 25 (d) 3 : 4 : 5

09 A wire of resistance $12\,\Omega\,\text{m}^{-1}$ is bent to form a complete circle of radius 10 cm. The resistance between its two diametrically opposite points A and B as shown in the figure is *[AIPMT 2009]*

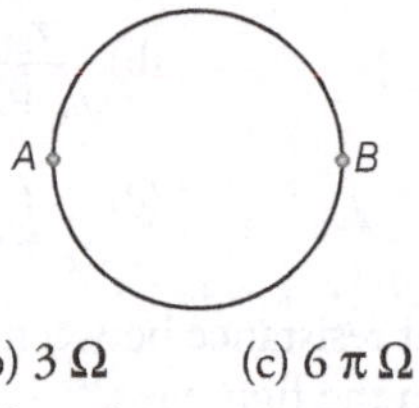

(a) $0.6\pi\,\Omega$ (b) $3\,\Omega$ (c) $6\pi\,\Omega$ (d) $6\,\Omega$

10 When a wire of uniform cross-section a, length l and resistance R is bent into a complete circle, resistance between two of diametrically opposite points will be *[NCERT (Old) Pg. 109, AIPMT 2005]*

(a) $\frac{R}{4}$ (b) $\frac{R}{8}$ (c) $4R$ (d) $\frac{R}{2}$

11 n resistances each of r ohm, when connected in parallel give an equivalent resistance of $R\,\Omega$. If these resistances were connected in series, the combination would have a resistance in ohms, equal to *[NCERT (Old) Pg. 109, AIPMT 2004]*

(a) n^2R (b) $\frac{R}{n^2}$ (c) $\frac{R}{n}$ (d) nR

12 What will be the equivalent resistance of circuit shown in figure between two points A and D? *[AIPMT 1996]*

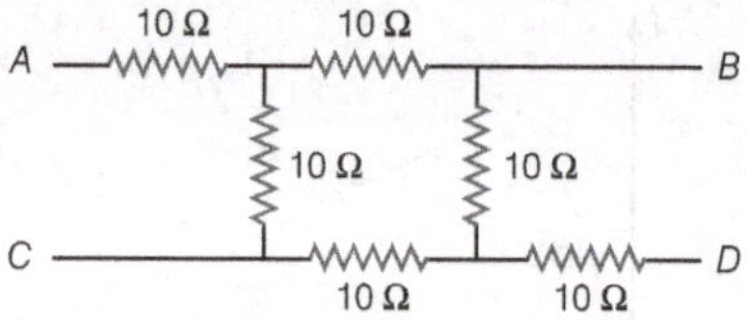

(a) $10\,\Omega$ (b) $20\,\Omega$
(c) $30\,\Omega$ (d) $40\,\Omega$

13 Two wires of the same metal have same length, but their cross-sections are in the ratio 3 : 1. They are joined in series. The resistance of thicker wire is $10\,\Omega$. The total resistance of the combination will be *[NCERT (Old) Pg. 108, AIPMT 1995]*

(a) $10\,\Omega$ (b) $20\,\Omega$
(c) $40\,\Omega$ (d) $100\,\Omega$

14 Three resistances each of $4\,\Omega$ are connected to form a triangle. The resistance between any two terminals is *[AIPMT 1993]*

(a) $12\,\Omega$ (b) $2\,\Omega$
(c) $6\,\Omega$ (d) $\frac{8}{3}\,\Omega$

15 You are given several identical resistances each of value $R = 10\,\Omega$ and each capable of carrying a maximum current of 1A. It is required to make a suitable combination of these resistances of $5\,\Omega$ which can carry a current of 4 A. The minimum number of resistances of the type R that will be required for this job is *[NCERT (Old) Pg. 109, AIPMT 1990]*

(a) 4 (b) 10
(c) 8 (d) 20

16 In the network shown in figure each resistance is $1\,\Omega$. The effective resistance between A and B is *[AIPMT 1990]*

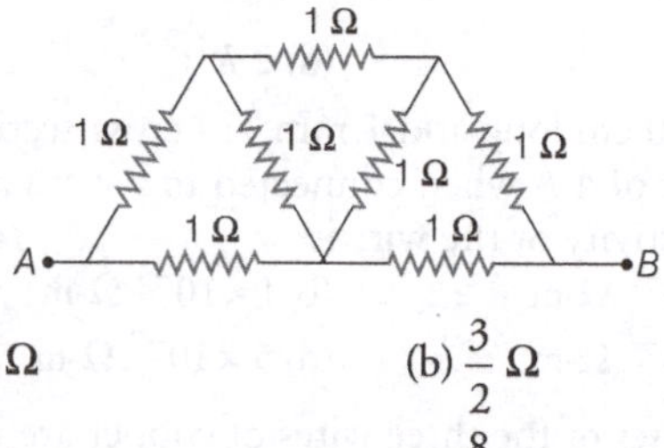

(a) $\frac{4}{3}\,\Omega$ (b) $\frac{3}{2}\,\Omega$
(c) $7\,\Omega$ (d) $\frac{8}{7}\,\Omega$

17 n equal resistors are first connected in series and then connected in parallel. What is the ratio of the maximum to the minimum resistance? *[AIPMT 1989]*

(a) n (b) $1/n^2$
(c) n^2 (d) $1/n$

Topic 4 Cells, its Combination and Kirchhoff's Law

01 The terminal voltage of the battery, whose emf is 10 V and internal resistance 1 Ω when connected through an external resistance of 4 Ω as shown in the figure is *[NCERT (New) Pg. 94, NEET 2024]*

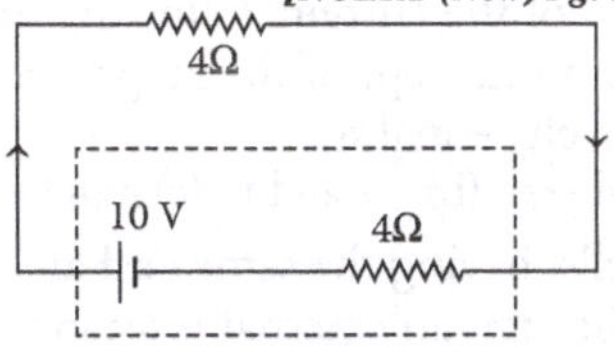

(a) 4 V (b) 6 V (c) 8 V (d) 10 V

02 If the galvanometer G does not show any deflection in the circuit shown, the value of R is given by *[NEET 2023]*

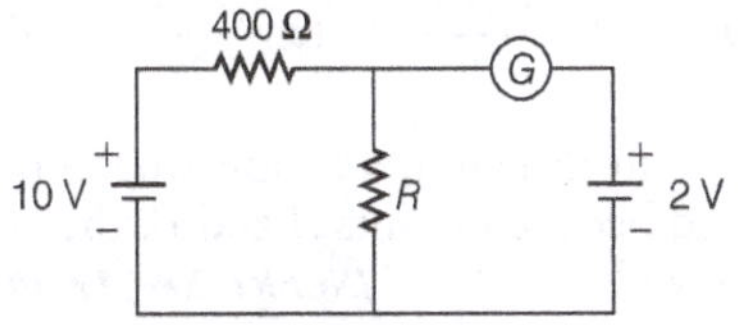

(a) 50 Ω (b) 100 Ω (c) 400 Ω (d) 200 Ω

03 The magnitude and direction of the current in the following circuit is *[NEET 2023]*

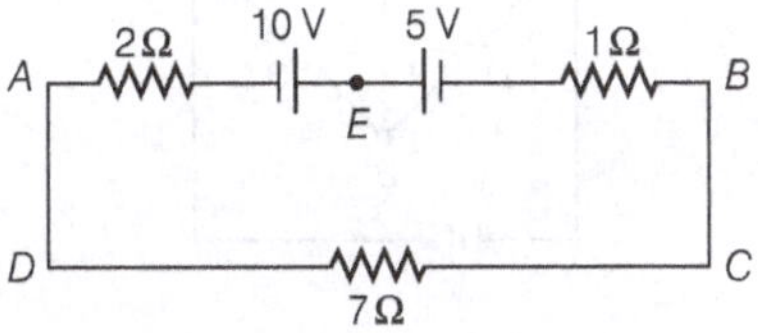

(a) 0.5 A from A to B through E
(b) 5/9 A from A to B through E
(c) 1.5 A from B to A through E
(d) 0.2 A from B to A through E

04 For the circuit shown in the figure, the current I will be *[NCERT (New) Pg. 98, NEET (Oct.) 2020]*

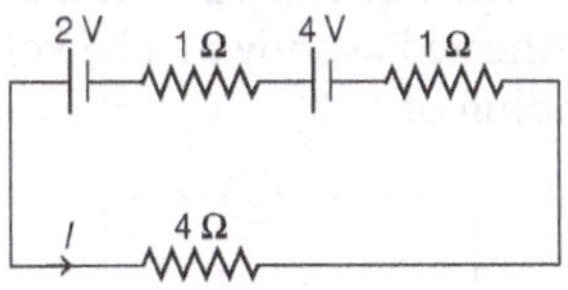

(a) 0.75 A (b) 1 A (c) 1.5 A (d) 0.5 A

05 For the circuit given below, the Kirchhoff's loop rule for the loop $BCDEB$ is given by the equation *[NEET (Oct.) 2020]*

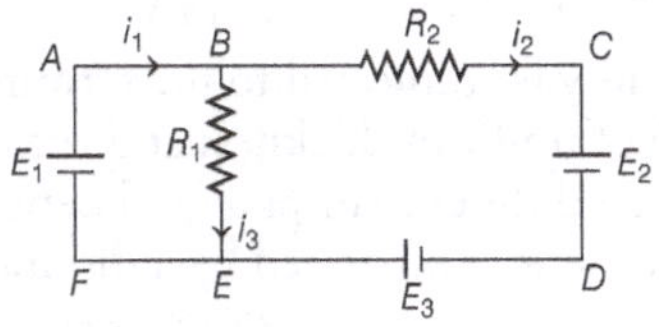

(a) $-i_2R_2 + E_2 - E_3 + i_3R_1 = 0$
(b) $i_2R_2 + E_2 - E_3 - i_3R_1 = 0$
(c) $i_2R_2 + E_2 + E_3 + i_3R_1 = 0$
(d) $-i_2R_2 + E_2 + E_3 + i_3R_1 = 0$

06 The reading of an ideal voltmeter in the circuit shown is *[NCERT (New) Pg. 109, NEET (Odisha) 2019]*

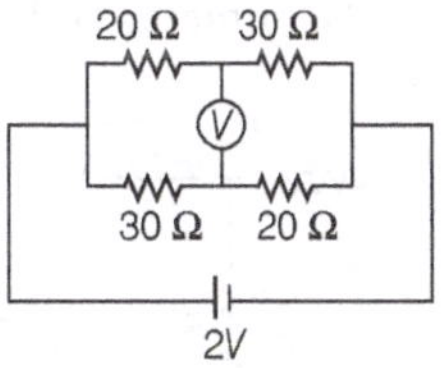

(a) 0.6 V (b) 0 V (c) 0.5 V (d) 0.4 V

07 A set of n equal resistors, of value R each are connected in series to a battery of emf E and internal resistance R. The current drawn is I. Now, the n resistors are connected in parallel to the same battery. Then, the current drawn from battery becomes $10I$. The value of n is *[NCERT (New) Pg. 96, NEET 2018]*
(a) 20 (b) 11 (c) 10 (d) 9

08 A battery consists of a variable number n of identical cells (having internal resistance r each) which are connected in series. The terminals of the battery are short-circuited and the current I is measured. Which of the graphs shows the correct relationship between I and n? *[NCERT (New) Pg. 96, NEET 2018]*

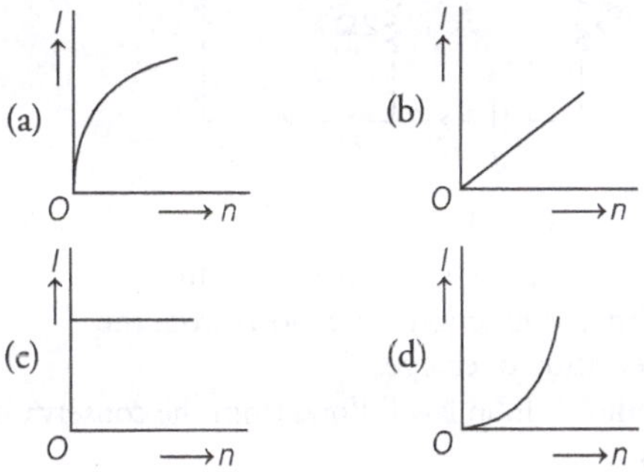

09 The potential difference $(V_A - V_B)$ between the points A and B in the given figure is *[NEET 2016]*

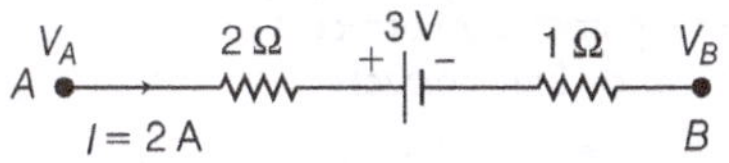

(a) −3 V (b) +3 V
(c) +6 V (d) +9 V

10 A circuit contains an ammeter, a battery of 30 V and a resistance 40.8 Ω all connected in series. If the ammeter has a coil of resistance 480 Ω and a shunt of 20 Ω, then reading in the ammeter will be *[AIPMT 2015]*
(a) 0.5 A (b) 0.25 A
(c) 2 A (d) 1 A

11 The internal resistance of a 2.1 V cell which gives a current of 0.2 A through a resistance of 10 Ω is *[NCERT (New) Pg. 96, NEET 2013]*

(a) 0.2 Ω (b) 0.5 Ω (c) 0.8 Ω (d) 1.0 Ω

12 In the circuit shown, the cells *A* and *B* have negligible resistances. For $V_A = 12$ V, $R_1 = 500\ \Omega$ and $R = 100\ \Omega$, the galvanometer *G* shows no deflection. The value of V_B is *[AIPMT 2012]*

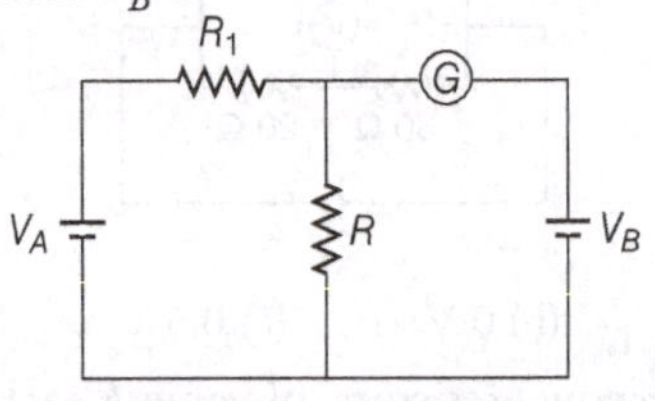

(a) 4 V (b) 2 V (c) 12 V (d) 6 V

13 A current of 2 A flows through a 2 Ω resistor when connected across a battery. The same battery supplies a current of 0.5 A when connected across a 9 Ω resistor. The internal resistance of the battery is *[NCERT (New) Pg. 96, AIPMT 2011]*

(a) 1/3 Ω (b) 1/4 Ω (c) 1 Ω (d) 0.5 Ω

14 In the circuit shown in the figure, if the potential at point *A* is taken to be zero, the potential at point *B* is *[NCERT (New) Pg. 98, AIPMT 2011]*

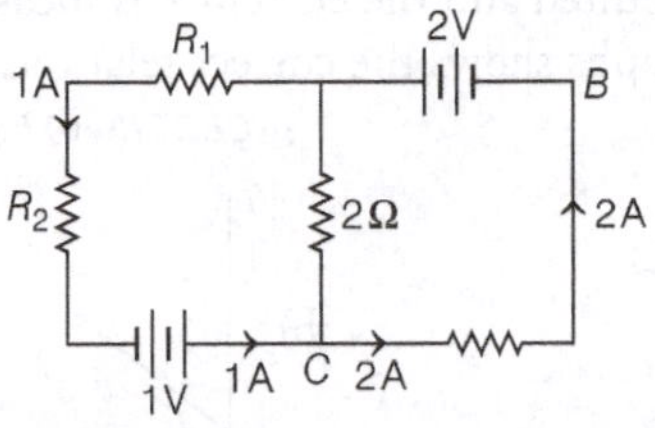

(a) +1 V (b) −1 V (c) + 2 V (d) − 2 V

15 Consider the following two statements.

I. Kirchhoff's junction law follows from the conservation of charge.

II. Kirchhoff's loop law follows from the conservation of energy.

Which of the following is correct ? *[AIPMT 2010]*

(a) Both I and II are wrong
(b) I is correct and II is wrong
(c) I is wrong and II is correct
(d) Both I and II are correct

16 See the electrical circuit shown in this figure. Which of the following equations is a correct equation for it ? *[NCERT (New) Pg. 98, AIPMT 2009]*

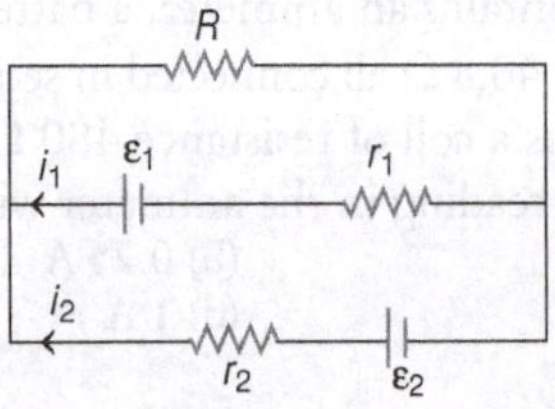

(a) $\varepsilon_1 - (i_1 + i_2)R - i_1 r_1 = 0$
(b) $\varepsilon_2 - i_2 r_2 - \varepsilon_1 - i_1 r_1 = 0$
(c) $-\varepsilon_2 - (i_1 + i_2)R + i_2 r_2 = 0$
(d) $\varepsilon_1 - (i_1 + i_2)R + i_1 r_1 = 0$

17 A student measures the terminal potential difference *V* of a cell (of emf ε and internal resistance *r*) as a function of the current *I* flowing through it. The slope and intercept of the graph between *V* and *I*, respectively, equal to *[AIPMT 2009]*

(a) ε and − *r* (b) − *r* and ε (c) *r* and − ε (d) −ε and *r*

18 Two cells, having the same emf are connected in series through an external resistance *R*. Cells have internal resistances r_1 and r_2 ($r_1 > r_2$) respectively. When the circuit is closed, the potential difference across the first cell is zero. The value of *R* is *[NCERT (New) Pg. 96, AIPMT 2006]*

(a) $r_1 - r_2$ (b) $\frac{r_1 + r_2}{2}$ (c) $\frac{r_1 - r_2}{2}$ (d) $r_1 + r_2$

19 In the circuit shown, if a conducting wire is connected between points *A* and *B*, the current in this wire will *[NCERT (New) Pg. 109, AIPMT 2006]*

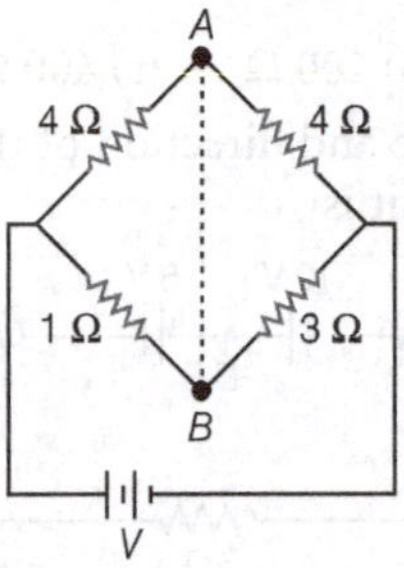

(a) flow from *A* to *B*
(b) flow in the direction which will be decided by the value of *V*
(c) be zero
(d) flow from *B* to *A*

20 Two batteries, one of emf 18 V and internal resistance 2 Ω and the other of emf 12 V and internal resistance 1 Ω, are connected as shown. The voltmeter *V* will record a reading of *[AIPMT 2005]*

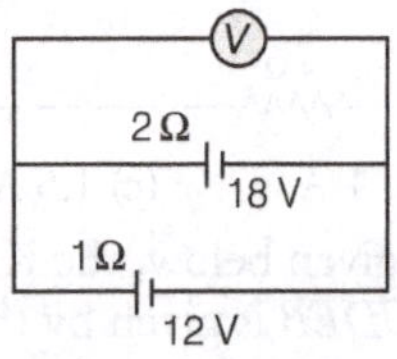

(a) 15 V (b) 30 V (c) 14 V (d) 18 V

21 A 6 V battery is connected to the terminals of a 3 m long wire of uniform thickness and resistance of 100 Ω. The difference of potential between two points on the wire separated by a distance of 50 cm will be *[NCERT (New) Pg. 96, AIPMT 2004]*

(a) 2 V (b) 3 V (c) 1 V (d) 1.5 V

22 For a cell, the terminal potential difference is 2.2 V when circuit is open and reduces to 1.8 V when cell is connected to a resistance $R = 5\ \Omega$, the internal resistance r of cell is **[AIPMT 2002]**

(a) $\frac{10}{9}\ \Omega$ (b) $\frac{9}{10}\ \Omega$
(c) $\frac{11}{9}\ \Omega$ (d) $\frac{5}{9}\ \Omega$

23 A cell has an emf 1.5 V. When connected across an external resistance of 2 Ω, the terminal potential difference falls to 1.0 V. The internal resistance of the cell is **[NCERT (New) Pg. 96, AIPMT 2000]**

(a) 2 Ω (b) 1.5 Ω
(c) 1.0 Ω (d) 0.5 Ω

24 The current i in the given circuit is **[AIPMT 1999]**

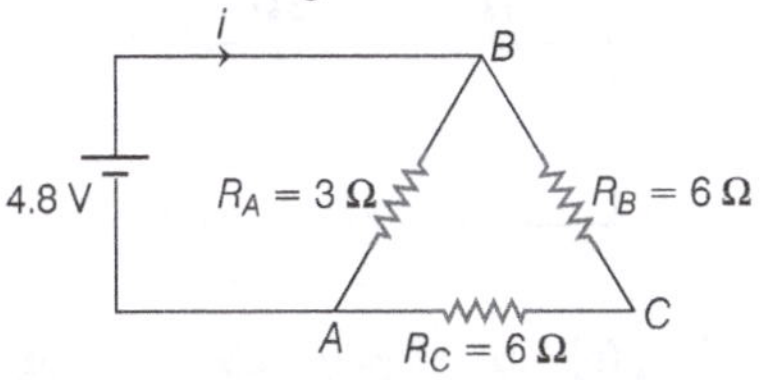

(a) 1.6 A (b) 2 A
(c) 0.32 A (d) 3.2 A

25 The current in the following circuit is **[NCERT (Old) Pg. 109, AIPMT 1997]**

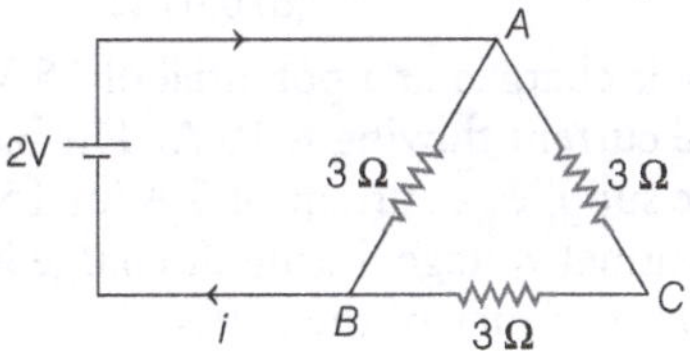

(a) 1 A (b) $\frac{2}{3}$ A
(c) $\frac{2}{9}$ A (d) $\frac{1}{8}$ A

26 Kirchhoff's first law, i.e. $\Sigma i = 0$ at a junction, deals with the conservation of **[AIPMT 1997]**

(a) angular momentum (b) linear momentum
(c) energy (d) charge

27 In the circuit of figure, the current in 4 Ω resistance is 1.2 A, what is the potential difference between B and C ? **[NCERT (Old) Pg. 109, AIPMT 1994]**

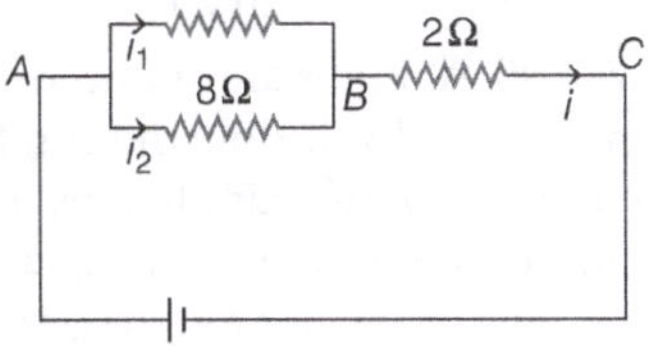

(a) 3.6 V (b) 6.3 V
(c) 1.8 V (d) 2.4 V

28 Current through 3 Ω resistor is 0.8 A, then potential drop through 4 Ω resistor is **[AIPMT 1993]**

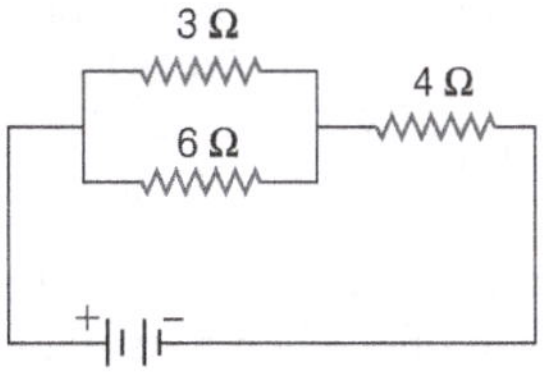

(a) 9.6 V (b) 2.6 V (c) 4.8 V (d) 1.2 V

29 Kirchhoff's first law of electricity follows **[AIPMT 1992]**

(a) only law of conservation of energy
(b) only law of conservation of charge
(c) law of conservation of both energy and charge
(d) sometimes law of conservation of energy and some other times law of conservation of charge

30 Two batteries of emf 4 V and 8 V with internal resistance 1 Ω and 2 Ω are connected in a circuit with a resistance of 9 Ω as shown in figure. The current and potential difference between the points P and Q are **[NCERT (New) Pg. 98, AIPMT 1988]**

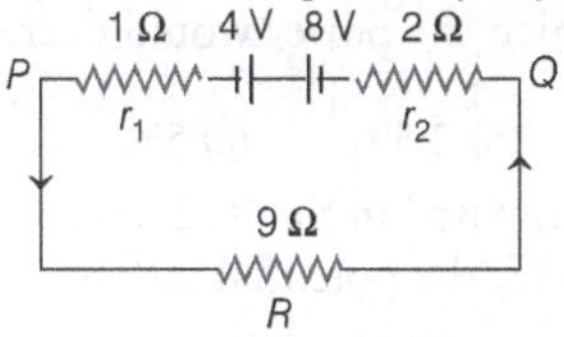

(a) $\frac{1}{3}$ A and 3 V (b) $\frac{1}{6}$ A and 4 V
(c) $\frac{1}{9}$ A and 9 V (d) $\frac{1}{12}$ A and 12 V

Topic 5 Electrical Energy, Heating Effect of Current and Electrical Power

01 Two resistors of resistance, 100 Ω and 200 Ω are connected in parallel in an electrical circuit, The ratio of the thermal energy developed in 100 Ω to that in 200 Ω in a given time is **[NCERT (New) Pg. 93, NEET 2022]**

(a) 2 : 1 (b) 1 : 4 (c) 4 : 1 (d) 1 : 2

02 The energy that will be ideally radiated by a 100 kW transmitter in 1 h is **[NEET 2022]**

(a) 36×10^4 J (b) 36×10^5 J
(c) 1×10^5 J (d) 36×10^7 J

03 Six similar bulbs are connected as shown in the figure with a DC source of emf E and zero internal resistance. The ratio of power consumption by the bulbs when (i) all are glowing and (ii) in the situation when two from section A and one from section B are glowing, will be **[NEET (National) 2019]**

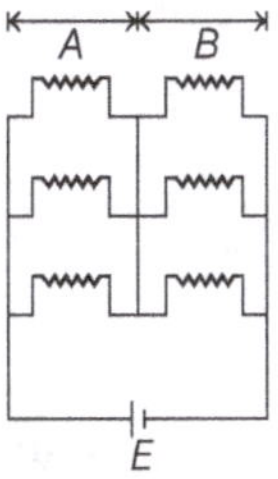

(a) 9 : 4 (b) 1 : 2 (c) 2 : 1 (d) 4 : 9

04 The charge following through a resistance R varies with time t as $Q = at - bt^2$, where a and b are positive constants. The total heat produced in R is *[NCERT (New) Pg. 93, NEET 2016]*

(a) $\frac{a^3 R}{3b}$ (b) $\frac{a^3 R}{2b}$ (c) $\frac{a^3 R}{b}$ (d) $\frac{a^3 R}{6b}$

05 A filament bulb (500 W, 100 V) is to be used in a 230 V main supply. When a resistance R is connected in series, it works perfectly and the bulb consumes 500 W. The value of R is *[NEET 2016]*

(a) 230 Ω (b) 46 Ω
(c) 26 Ω (d) 13 Ω

06 Two cities are 150 km apart. Electric power is sent from one city to another city through copper wires. The fall of potential per km is 8 V and the average resistance per km is 0.5 Ω. The power loss in the wire is *[NCERT (New) Pg. 93, AIPMT 2014]*

(a) 19.2 W (b) 19.2 kW
(c) 19.2 J (d) 12.2 kW

07 If voltage across a bulb rated 220 V-100 W drops by 2.5% of its rated value, the percentage of the rated value by which the power would decrease is *[CBSE AIPMT 2012]*

(a) 20% (b) 2.5% (c) 5% (d) 10%

08 If power dissipated in the 9 Ω resistor in the circuit shown is 36W, the potential difference across the 2 Ω resistor is *[AIPMT 2011]*

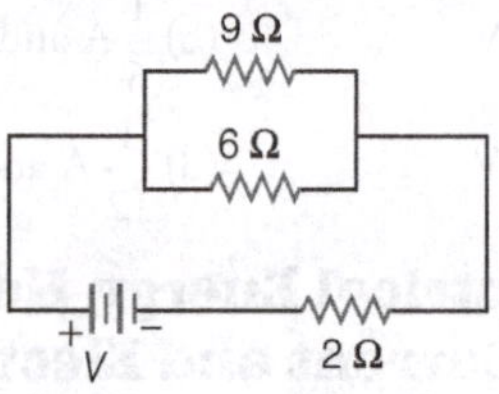

(a) 8 V (b) 10 V (c) 2 V (d) 4 V

09 An electric kettle takes 4 A current at 220 V. How much time will it take to boil 1 kg of water from temperature 20°C ? *[AIPMT 2008]*

(a) 6.3 min (b) 8.4 min
(c) 12.6 min (d) 4.2 min

10 A current of 3 A flows through the 2 Ω resistor shown in the circuit. The power dissipated in the 5 Ω resistor is *[NCERT (New) Pg. 93, AIPMT 2008]*

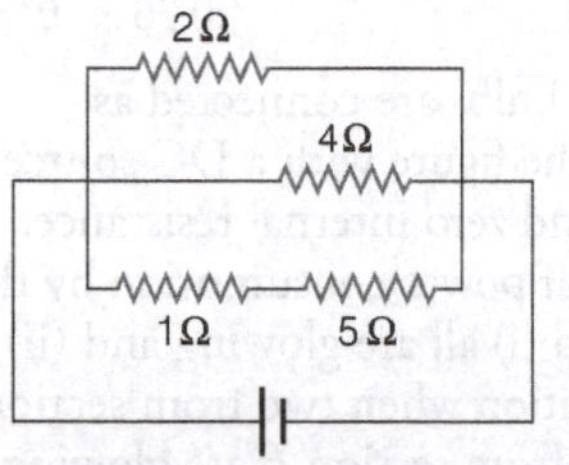

(a) 4 W (b) 2 W
(c) 1 W (d) 5 W

11 The total power dissipated in watts in the circuit shown here is *[NCERT (New) Pg. 93, AIPMT 2007]*

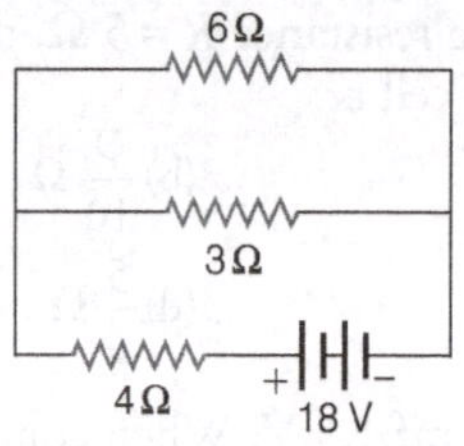

(a) 16 (b) 40
(c) 54 (d) 4

12 Power dissipated across the 8 Ω resistor in the circuit shown here is 2 W. The power dissipated in watt units across the 3 Ω resistor is *[AIPMT 2006]*

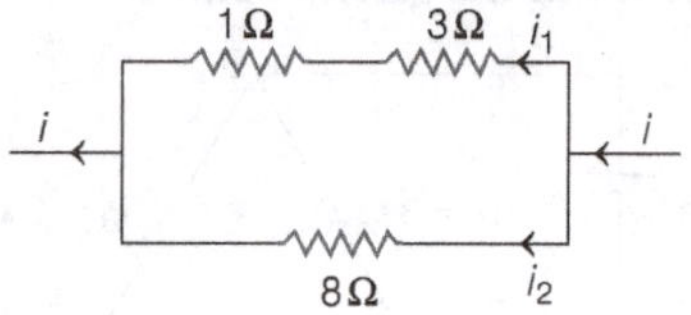

(a) 2.0 (b) 1.0 (c) 0.5 (d) 3.0

13 A 5 A fuse wire can withstand a maximum power of 1 W in circuit. The resistance of the fuse wire is *[NCERT (New) Pg. 93, AIPMT 2005]*

(a) 0.2 Ω (b) 5 Ω
(c) 0.4 Ω (d) 0.04 Ω

14 A battery is charged at a potential of 15 V for 8 h when the current flowing is 10 A. The battery on discharge supplies a current of 5 A for 15 h. The mean terminal voltage during discharge is 14 V. The watt-hour efficiency of the battery is *[AIPMT 2004]*

(a) 82.5% (b) 80%
(c) 90% (d) 87.5%

15 In India, electricity is supplied for domestic use at 220 V. It is supplied at 110 V in USA. If the resistance of a 60 W bulb for use in India is R, the resistance of a 60 W bulb for use in USA will be *[AIPMT 2004]*

(a) R (b) $2R$ (c) $\frac{R}{4}$ (d) $\frac{R}{2}$

16 When three identical bulbs of 60 W, 200 V rating are connected in series to a 200 V supply, the power drawn by them will be *[AIPMT 2004]*

(a) 60 W (b) 180 W
(c) 10 W (d) 20 W

17 Two 220 V, 100 W bulbs are connected first in series and then in parallel. Each time the combination is connected to a 220 V AC supply line. The power drawn by the combination in each case respectively will be *[NCERT (New) Pg. 93, AIPMT 2003]*

(a) 200 W, 150 W (b) 50 W, 200 W
(c) 50 W, 100 W (d) 100 W, 50 W

18 An electric kettle has two heating coils. When one of the coils is connected to an AC source, the water in the kettle boils in 10 min. When the other coil is used the water boils in 40 min. If both the coils are connected in parallel, the time taken by the same quantity of water to boil will be *[AIPMT 2003]*
(a) 25 min (b) 15 min
(c) 8 min (d) 4 min

19 Two bulbs 25 W, 220 V and 100 W, 220 V are given. Which has higher resistance ? *[AIPMT 2000]*
(a) 25 W bulb
(b) 100 W bulb
(c) Both bulbs will have equal resistance
(d) Resistance of bulbs cannot be compared

20 A 5°C rise in temperature is observed in a conductor by passing a current. When the current is doubled, the rise in temperature will be approximately *[AIPMT 1998]*
(a) 16°C (b) 10°C (c) 20°C (d) 12°C

21 Three equal resistors connected in series across a source of emf together dissipate 10 W of power. What will be the power dissipated in watt if the same resistors are connected in parallel across the same source of emf ? *[AIPMT 1998]*
(a) 10/3 (b) 10 (c) 30 (d) 90

22 A 100 W 200 V bulb is connected to a 160 V power supply. The power consumption would be *[NCERT (New) Pg. 93, AIPMT 1997]*
(a) 125 W (b) 100 W
(c) 80 W (d) 64 W

23 A heating coil is labelled 100 W, 220 V. The coil is cut in two equal halves and the two pieces are joined in parallel to the same source. The energy now liberated per second is *[AIPMT 1995]*
(a) 25 J (b) 50 J
(c) 200 J (d) 400 J

24 A 4 μF conductor is charged to 400 V and then its plates are joined through a resistance of 1 kΩ. The heat produced in the resistance is *[AIPMT 1994]*
(a) 0.16 J (b) 1.28 J
(c) 0.64 J (d) 0.32 J

25 40 electric bulbs are connected in series across a 220 V supply. After one bulb is fused, the remaining 39 are connected again in series across the same supply. The illumination will be *[AIPMT 1989]*
(a) more with 40 bulbs than with 39
(b) more with 39 bulbs than with 40
(c) equal in both the cases
(d) in the ratio $40^2 : 39^2$

26 A current of 2 A, passing through a conductor produces 80 J of heat in 10 s. The resistance of the conductor (in ohm) is *[AIPMT 1989]*
(a) 0.5 (b) 2 (c) 4 (d) 20

Topic 6 Measuring Instruments

01 In the following circuit, the equivalent capacitance between terminal A and terminal B is
[NCERT (New) Pg. 101, NEET 2024]

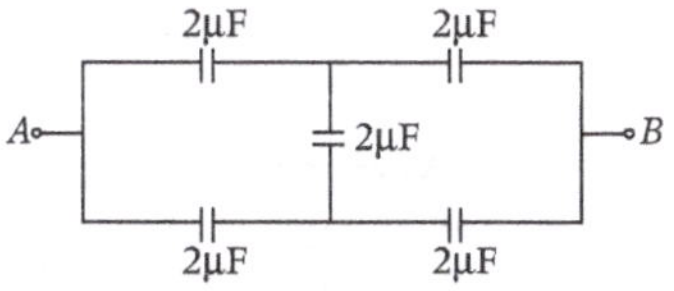

(a) 2 μF (b) 1 μF
(c) 0.5 μF (d) 4 μF

02 Choose the correct circuit which can achieve the bridge balance. *[NCERT (New) Pg. 101, NEET 2024]*

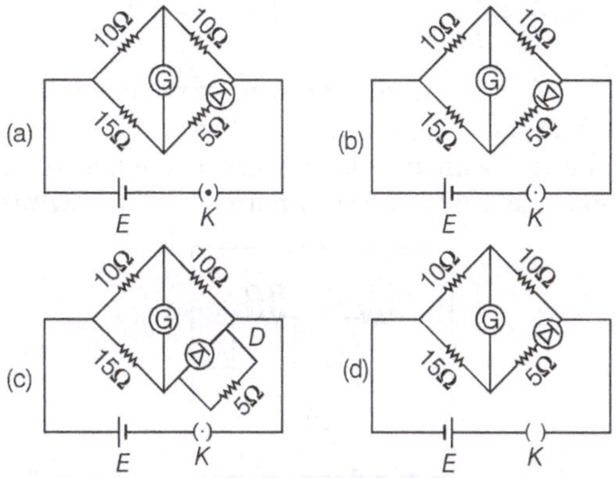

03 A wheatstone bridge is used to determine the value of unknown resistance X by adjusting the variable resistance Y as shown in the figure. For the most precise measurement of X, the resistances P and Q
[NCERT (New) Pg. 101, NEET 2022]

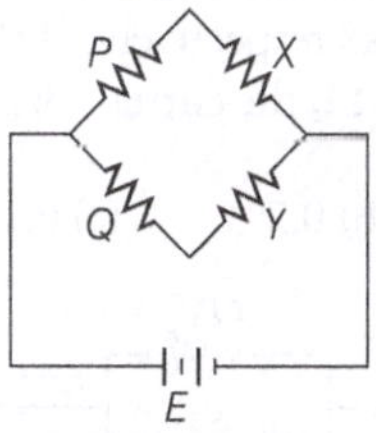

(a) should be approximately equal and are small
(b) should be very large and unequal
(c) do not play any significant role
(d) should be approximately equal to $2X$

04 A resistance wire connected in the left gap of a metre bridge balances a 10 Ω resistance in the right gap at a point which divides the bridge wire in the ratio 3 : 2. If the length of the resistance wire is 1.5 m, then the length of 1 Ω of the resistance wire is
[NEET (Sep.) 2020]
(a) 1.0×10^{-1} m (b) 1.5×10^{-1} m
(c) 1.5×10^{-2} m (d) 1.0×10^{-2} m

05 The meter bridge shown in the balance position with $\frac{P}{Q} = \frac{l_1}{l_2}$. If we now interchange the positions of galvanometer and cell, will the bridge work ? If yes, that will be balanced condition? *[NEET (Odisha) 2019]*

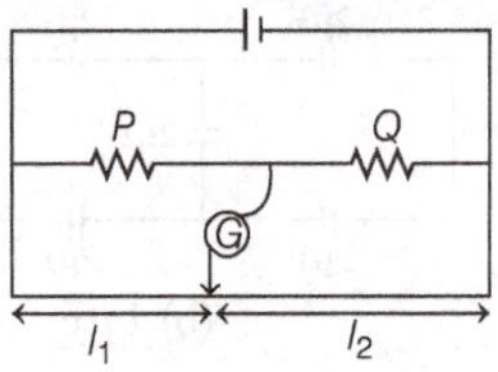

(a) yes, $\frac{P}{Q} = \frac{l_2 - l_1}{l_2 + l_1}$ (b) no, no null point
(c) yes, $\frac{P}{Q} = \frac{l_2}{l_1}$ (d) yes, $\frac{P}{Q} = \frac{l_1}{l_2}$

06 The resistances in the two arms of the meter bridge are 5 Ω and R Ω, respectively. When the resistance R is shunted with an equal resistance, the new balance point is at $1.6\, l_1$. The resistance R, is *[AIPMT 2014]*

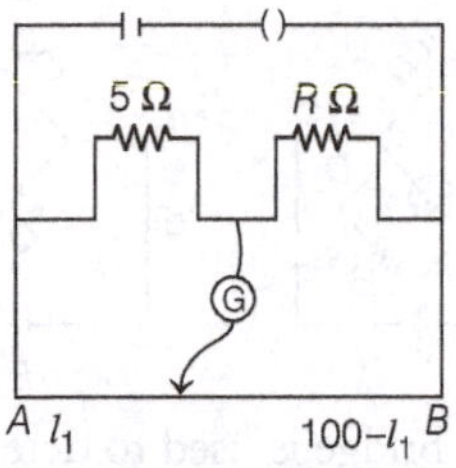

(a) 10 Ω (b) 15 Ω (c) 20 Ω (d) 25 Ω

07 The resistances of the four arms P, Q, R and S in a Wheatstone bridge are 10 Ω, 30 Ω, 30 Ω and 90 Ω, respectively. The emf and internal resistance of the cell are 7 V and 5 Ω respectively. If the galvanometer resistance is 50 Ω, the current drawn from the cell will be *[NEET 2013]*
(a) 1.0 A (b) 0.2 A (c) 0.1 A (d) 2.0 A

08

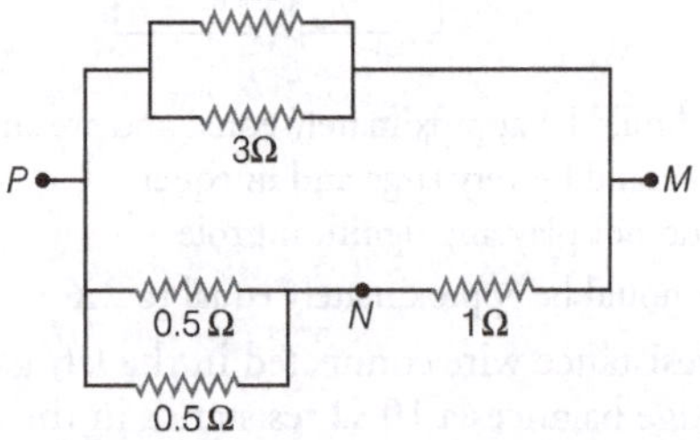

In the circuit shown, the current through the 4 Ω resistor is 1 A when the points P and M are connected to a DC voltage source. The potential difference between the points M and N is *[AIPMT 2008]*
(a) 1.5 V (b) 1.0 V
(c) 0.5 V (d) 3.2 V

09 Three resistance P, Q, R each of 2 Ω and an unknown resistance S form the four arms of a Wheatstone bridge circuit. When a resistance of 6 Ω is connected in parallel to S, the bridge gets balanced. What is the value of S ? *[NCERT (New) Pg. 101, AIPMT 2007]*
(a) 2 Ω (b) 3 Ω
(c) 6 Ω (d) 1 Ω

10 For the network shown in the figure the value of the current i is *[NCERT (New) Pg. 101, AIPMT 2005]*

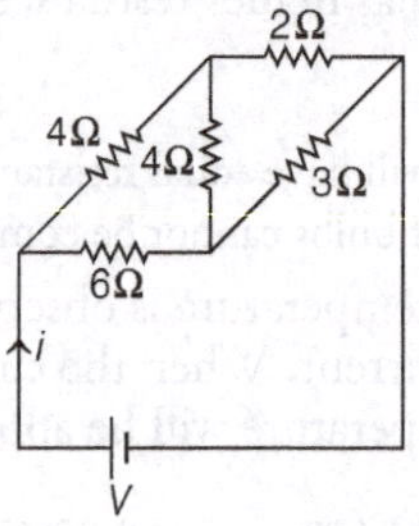

(a) $\frac{9V}{35}$ (b) $\frac{18V}{5}$
(c) $\frac{5V}{9}$ (d) $\frac{5V}{18}$

11 Five equal resistances each of resistance R are connected as shown in the figure. A battery of $4V$ volts is connected between A and B. The current flowing in $AFCEB$ will be *[AIPMT 2004]*

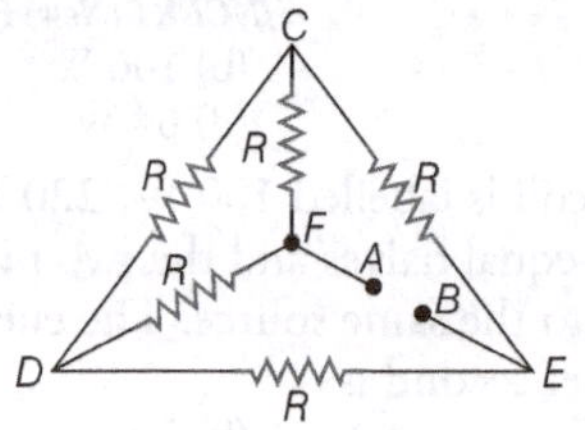

(a) $\frac{3V}{R}$ (b) $\frac{V}{R}$
(c) $\frac{V}{2R}$ (d) $\frac{2V}{R}$

12 In a Wheatstone bridge, all the four arms have equal resistance R. If the resistance of the galvanometer arm is also R, the equivalent resistance of the combination as seen by the battery is *[AIPMT 2003]*
(a) R (b) $2R$
(c) $\frac{R}{4}$ (d) $\frac{R}{2}$

13 In a Wheatstone bridge, resistance of each of the four sides is 10 Ω. If the resistance of the galvanometer is also 10 Ω, then effective resistance of the bridge will be *[AIPMT 2001]*
(a) 10 Ω (b) 5 Ω
(c) 20 Ω (d) 40 Ω

14 A bridge circuit is shown in figure. The equivalent resistance between A and B will be *[AIPMT 2000]*

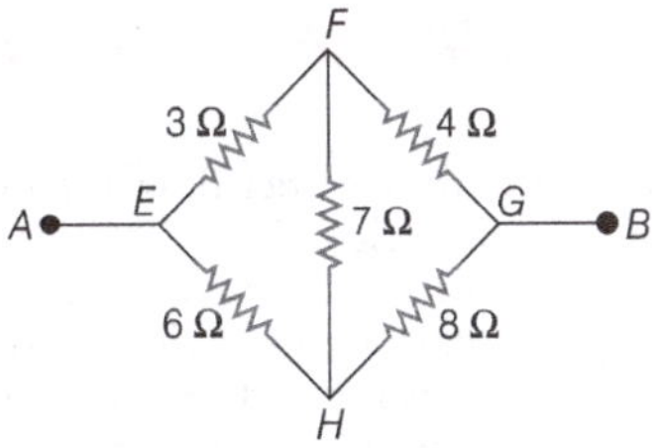

(a) 21 Ω (b) 7 Ω (c) $\frac{252}{85}$ Ω (d) $\frac{14}{3}$ Ω

15 In meter bridge, the balancing length from left is found to be 20 cm when standard resistance of 1 Ω is in right gap. The value of unknown resistance is *[NCERT (Old) Pg. 121, AIPMT 1999]*

(a) 0.25 Ω (b) 0.4 Ω
(c) 0.5 Ω (d) 4 Ω

16 A battery of emf 10 V and internal resistance 0.5 Ω is connected across a variable resistance R. The value of R for which the power delivered in it is maximum, is given by *[NCERT (New) Pg. 98, AIPMT 1992]*

(a) 0.5 Ω (b) 1.0 Ω
(c) 2.0 Ω (d) 0.25 Ω

17 Two identical batteries each of emf 2 V and internal resistance 1 Ω are available to produce heat in an external resistance by passing a current through it. The maximum power that can be developed across R using these batteries is *[AIPMT 1990]*

(a) 3.2 W (b) 2 W
(c) 1.28 W (d) 8/9 W

Key Index

Topic 1

1	(a)	2	(a)	3	(b)	4	(a)

Topic 2

1	(b)	2	(d)	3	(b)	4	(b)	5	(b)	6	(b)	7	(c)	8	(c)	9	(d)	10	(d)
11	(b)	12	(b)	13	(c)	14	(d)	15	(a)	16	(a)	17	(c)	18	(b)	19	(b)	20	(b)
21	(a)	22	(a)	23	(b)	24	(d)												

Topic 3

1	(b)	2	(a)	3	(d)	4	(b)	5	(b)	6	(a)	7	(a)	8	(b)	9	(a)	10	(a)
11	(a)	12	(c)	13	(c)	14	(d)	15	(c)	16	(d)	17	(c)						

Topic 4

1	(c)	2	(b)	3	(a)	4	(b)	5	(b)	6	(d)	7	(c)	8	(c)	9	(d)	10	(a)
11	(b)	12	(b)	13	(a)	14	(a)	15	(d)	16	(a)	17	(b)	18	(a)	19	(d)	20	(c)
21	(c)	22	(a)	23	(c)	24	(b)	25	(a)	26	(d)	27	(a)	28	(c)	29	(b)	30	(a)

Topic 5

1	(a)	2	(d)	3	(a)	4	(d)	5	(c)	6	(b)	7	(c)	8	(b)	9	(a)	10	(d)
11	(c)	12	(d)	13	(d)	14	(d)	15	(c)	16	(d)	17	(b)	18	(c)	19	(a)	20	(c)
21	(d)	22	(d)	23	(d)	24	(d)	25	(b)	26	(b)								

Topic 6

1	(a)	2	(a)	3	(a)	4	(a)	5	(d)	6	(b)	7	(b)	8	(d)	9	(b)	10	(d)
11	(c)	12	(a)	13	(a)	14	(d)	15	(a)	16	(a)	17	(b)						

Detailed **Explanations**

Topic 1

01. *(a)*

key idea

Try to remind the concepts of drift velocity, electrical resistivity, relaxation period and current density.

As we know that, the expression of the drift velocity,

$$v_d = \frac{eE}{m}\tau$$

Here, e is the electric charge,
E is the electric field,
m is the mass of an electron,
τ is the relaxation time.
Consider the conductor having length l, area of the cross-section A and the charge density n.
Electrical resistivity,

$$\rho = \frac{m}{ne^2\tau}$$

Relaxation period,

$$\tau = \frac{m}{ne^2\rho}$$

Current density,

$$J = \frac{I}{A} = \frac{neAv_d}{A} = nev_d$$

Again, $\frac{E}{J} = \frac{E}{\sigma E} = \frac{1}{\sigma} = \rho$

∴ Electrical resistivity,

$$\rho = \frac{E}{J}$$

The correct match is
$A \to 3, B \to 4, C \to 1, D \to 2$.

02. *(a)* Given, drift velocity,

$$v_d = 7.5 \times 10^{-4} \text{ m/s}$$

Electric field, $E = 3 \times 10^{-10}$ V-m

As, Mobility,

$$\mu = \frac{v_d}{E} = \frac{7.5 \times 10^{-4}}{3 \times 10^{-10}} = 2.5 \times 10^6 \text{ m}^2\text{V}^{-1}\text{s}^{-1}$$

Hence, correct option is (a).

03. *(b)* As the cross-sectional area of the conductor is non-uniform, so current density will be different.

As $\quad I = JA \quad$ ...(i)

It is clear from Eq. (i), when area increases, the current density decreases so the number of flow of electrons will be same and thus, the current will be constant.

04. *(a)* In metals the valence electrons of the atoms do not remain attached to individual atoms but are free to move throughout the volume of the conductor. Their velocity under normal conditions is of the order of a fraction of mm/s.

Topic 2

01. *(b)* Given, $R_0 = 2\ \Omega$

At $t = 80°$C, $R_t = 6.8\ \Omega$

We know that,

$$R_t = R_0(1 + \alpha t)$$

$$\Rightarrow \quad R_t = R_0 + R_0\alpha t$$

$$\therefore \quad \alpha = \frac{R_t - R_0}{R_0 t} = \frac{6.8 - 2}{2 \times 80} = \frac{4.8}{2 \times 80} = 0.03 = 3 \times 10^{-2}\ °\text{C}^{-1}$$

02. *(d)* Given, length, $l = 10$ m

radius, $r = \frac{10^{-2}}{\sqrt{\pi}}$ m

The current density,

$$j = \sigma E = \frac{E}{\rho} \quad \text{...(i)}$$

So, $$\rho = \frac{RA}{l} = \frac{10 \times \pi \times \frac{10^{-4}}{\pi}}{10} = 10^{-4}\ \Omega\text{ m}$$

From equation (i), we get

$$j = \frac{10}{10^{-4}} = 10^5 \text{ A/m}^2$$

03. *(b)* Coefficient of thermal resistance α is positive for conductor and negative for semiconductor. Thus, on increasing temperature, resistance of conductor increases and resistance of semiconductor decreases.

04. *(b)* Given, $R_1 = R_2, l_1 = l_2$

Since, resistance, $R = \rho \cdot \frac{l}{A}$

$$\Rightarrow \quad \frac{R_1}{R_2} = \frac{l_1}{l_2} \cdot \frac{A_2}{A_1}$$

$$\Rightarrow \quad \frac{R_1}{R_1} = \frac{l_1}{l_1} \cdot \frac{A_2}{A_1}$$

$$\Rightarrow \quad 1 = \frac{A_2}{A_1} \quad \left[\because R_1 = R_2 \text{ and } l_1 = l_2\right]$$

$$\Rightarrow \quad \frac{A_1}{A_2} = 1$$

05. *(b)* Resistivity of copper (a metal) as a function of temperature increases with the increase in temperature as shown below.

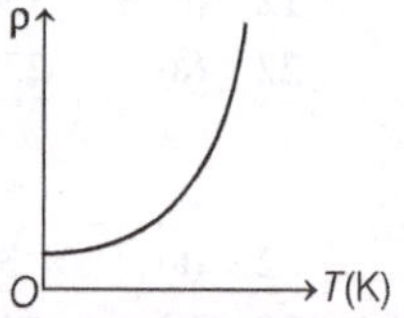

Concept Enhancer

Resistivity is the resistance that is offered by a material and resistance is the nature of material for opposing the flow of electric current.

06. *(b)* For an ideal voltmeter, the resistance is infinite and for an ideal ammeter, the resistance is zero.

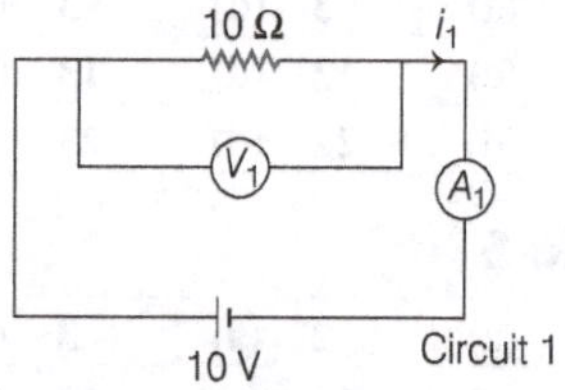

So, the current in circuit 1 is

$$R \times i = V$$

or $$10\,i_1 = 10$$

$$\Rightarrow \quad i_1 = \frac{10}{10} = 1 \text{ A}$$

$\therefore \quad V_1 = i_1 \times R$
$= 1 \times 10 = 10$ V

Similarly, for circuit 2, the addition of $10\,\Omega$ to voltmeter does not affect the current and hence,

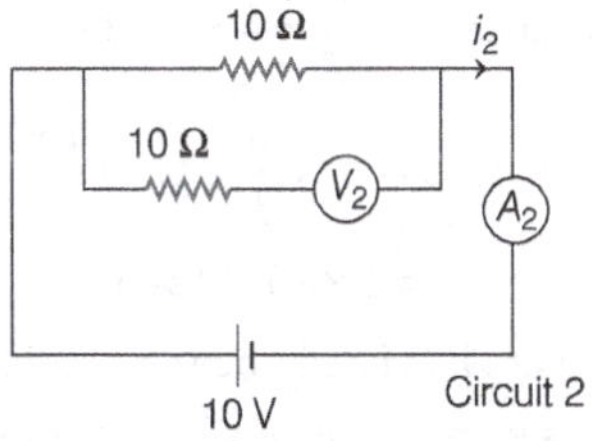

$10 i_2 = 10$

$\Rightarrow \quad i_2 = \frac{10}{10} = 1$ A

$V_2 = i_2 R = 1 \times 10 = 10$ V

$\therefore \quad V_1 = V_2$

and $\quad i_1 = i_2$

07. *(c)* Among given devices, fuse is used in electric circuit as a protective device. It helps in preventing excessive amount of current to flow in the circuit or from short circuiting.
It has low melting point and low resistivity, so when excess amount of current flows in the circuit, it melts and breaks the circuit.

• Concept **Enhancer**

Protection is required to prevent damage of electric components and if a circuit is overload due to excessive current flow, you can use fuses, circuit breakers and thermal limiters as a circuit protection device.

08. *(c)* As volume remains same,

$A_1 l_1 = A_2 l_2$

Now, given $l_2 = n l_1$

$\therefore$ New area, $A_2 = \frac{A_1 l_1}{l_2} = \frac{A_1}{n}$ ...(i)

Resistance of wire after stretching

$R_2 = \rho \frac{l_2}{A_2} = \rho \cdot \frac{n l_1}{A_1 / n}$ [Using Eq. (i)]

$= \left(\rho \frac{l_1}{A_1}\right) \cdot n^2 = n^2 \cdot R$

$\left[\because R = \left(\rho \frac{l_1}{A_1}\right)\right]$

09. *(d)* As the resistance of stretched wire to length n times of its original length is

$R' = n^2 R = 2^2 \times 4$

$= 4 \times 4 = 16\,\Omega$

where, R = original resistance
R' = final resistance

10. *(d)* Energy = 2 eV

$eV_0 = 2$ eV $\Rightarrow V_0 = 2$ V

So, electric field,

$$E = \frac{2}{4 \times 10^{-8}} = 0.5 \times 10^8$$

$$= 5 \times 10^7 \text{ V/m}$$

11. *(b)* After stretching, specific resistance (ρ) will remain same.

Original resistance of wire, $R = \frac{\rho l}{A}$

As volume remain same,

$V_1 = V_2$

$A_1 l_1 = A_2 l_2$

$\frac{A_1}{A_2} = \frac{l_2}{l_1}$ ...(i)

Ratio of resistance before and after streching,

$\frac{R_2}{R_1} = \frac{l_2}{l_1} \times \frac{A_1}{A_2} = \left[\frac{l_2}{l_1}\right]^2$ [using Eq. (i)]

$\frac{R_2}{R_1} = \frac{(l + 10\% l)^2}{l^2} = \frac{\left(\frac{11}{10} l\right)^2}{l^2}$

$R_2 = 1.21 R_1$

12. *(b)*

key idea

To solve this question, you can use following formula

$$\frac{R_1}{R_2} = \frac{l_1}{l_2} \times \frac{r_2^2}{r_1^2}$$

The formula for resistance of wire is

$$R = \frac{\rho l}{A}$$

where, ρ = specific resistance of the wire

$\Rightarrow \quad R \propto \frac{l}{A}$

$\Rightarrow \quad R \propto \frac{l}{r^2} \quad (\because A = \pi r^2)$

$\therefore \quad \frac{R_1}{R_2} = \frac{l_1}{l_2} \times \frac{r_2^2}{r_1^2}$ ...(i)

Given, $l_1 = l, l_2 = 2l,$
$r_1 = r, r_2 = 2r, R_1 = R.$

Substituting these values in Eq. (i), we have

$$\frac{R_1}{R_2} = \frac{l}{2l} \times \frac{(2r)^2}{r^2}$$

$$\frac{R_1}{R_2} = \frac{l}{2l} \times \frac{(2r)^2}{r^2}$$

$$\frac{R_1}{R_2} = 2 \Rightarrow R_2 = \frac{R}{2}$$

Therefore, resistance will be halved.
Now, the specific resistance of the wire does not depend on the geometry of the wire. Hence, it remains unchanged.

13. *(c)* We know that,

$R = \rho \frac{l}{A} \Rightarrow 100\,\Omega = \rho \frac{3}{A}$

$\Rightarrow \quad \frac{\rho}{A} = \frac{100}{3}$

Thus, resistance of 50 cm wire is

$R_1 = \frac{\rho}{A} l = \frac{100}{3} \times 0.5 = \frac{50}{3}\,\Omega$

The current in the wire, $I = \frac{6}{100}$ A.

$\therefore \quad V = IR_1 = \frac{50}{3} \times \frac{6}{100} = 1$ V

14. *(d)* The electric fuse is a device which is used to limit the current in an electric circuit. Thus, the use of fuse safeguards the circuit and the appliances connected in the circuit from being damaged. It is always connected with the live (or phase) wire. The fuse wire is a short piece of wire made of a material of high resistance and low melting point so that it may easily melt due to overheating when excessive current passes through it.

15. *(a)* The specific resistance (resistivity) of a metallic conductor nearly increases with increasing temperature as shown in figure. This is because, with the increase in temperature, the ions of the conductors vibrate with greater amplitude and the collisions between electrons and ions become more frequent, over a small temperature range (upto 100°C). The resistivity of a metal can be represented approximately by the equation,

$$\rho_t = \rho_0 (1 + \alpha t)$$

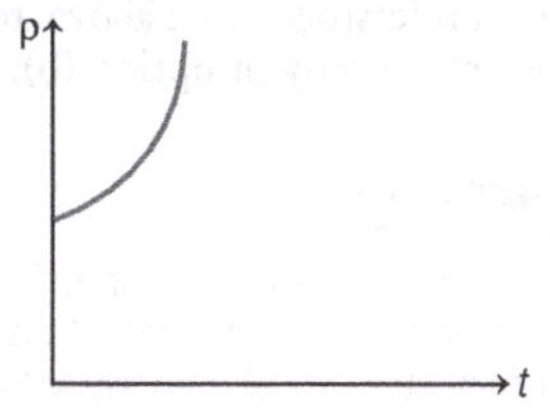

The factor α is called the temperature coefficient of resistivity.

16. *(a)* For metal or conductor specific resistance decreases with decrease in temperature whereas for semiconductor material, specific resistance increases with decrease in temperature.

17. *(c)* In discharge tube, the current is due to flow of positive ions and electrons. Moreover, secondary emission of electrons is also possible. So, *V-I* curve is non-linear, hence its resistance is non-ohmic.

18. *(b)* From Ohm's law, resistance

$$R = \frac{\Delta V}{\Delta I}$$

Resistance is said to be negative, if on increasing voltage or temperature, current decreases.

In *V-I* graph, for portion *CD* of graph, the current decreases with increasing voltage. Thus, portion *CD* corresponds to negative resistance.

Alternate Solution

We know that the slope of graph *V-I* will give the resistance, since slope of *CD* curve is negative. So it has negative resistance.

19. *(b)* The relation between length and area is

$$R = \frac{\rho l}{A} \quad \ldots(i)$$

where, ρ being specific resistance is the proportionality constant and depends on nature of material.

(i) Length = L, area = A

Putting in Eq. (i), we have

$$R = \frac{\rho L}{A}$$

(ii) Length = $2L$, area = $\frac{A}{2}$

Putting in Eq. (i), we have

$$R = \rho \frac{2L}{A/2} = \frac{4\rho L}{A}$$

(iii) Length = $\frac{L}{2}$, area = $2A$

Putting in Eq. (i), we have

$$R = \frac{\rho(L/2)}{2A} = \frac{\rho L}{4A}$$

As it is understood from above, resistance is minimum only in option (b).

20. *(b)*

key idea

To find out the value of specific resistance of the material of the conductor, you should use following formula :

$$\rho = \frac{RA}{l}$$

Resistance of a given conducting wire is given by

$$R = \rho \cdot \frac{l}{A}$$

where, ρ is the specific resistance of the material of the conductor.

Here, $l = 15$ m

$$A = 6 \times 10^{-7} \text{ m}^2$$

$$R = 5\,\Omega$$

$$\therefore \quad \rho = \frac{RA}{l} = \frac{5 \times 6 \times 10^{-7}}{15}$$

$$= 2 \times 10^{-7}\ \Omega\text{-m}$$

21. *(a)* Temperature coefficient of resistance is defined as the increase in resistance per unit original resistance per degree rise of temperature and is given by

$$\alpha = \frac{R_t - R_o}{R_o \times t}$$

or $R_t = R_o(1 + \alpha t)$

R_t = Resistance at final temperature

R_o = Resistance at initial temperature

t = Change in temperature

Case I $5 = R_o[1 + \alpha(50)]$ ...(i)

Case II $7 = R_o[1 + \alpha(100)]$ ...(ii)

Dividing Eq. (i) by Eq. (ii)

$$\frac{5}{7} = \frac{1 + 50\alpha}{1 + 100\alpha}$$

$$\therefore \quad 5 + 500\alpha = 7 + 350\alpha$$

$$\therefore \quad \alpha = \frac{2}{150} = 0.01/°\text{C}$$

22. *(a)* Let initial resistance of wire be R, its initial length be l_1 and final length be l_2. According to problem, $l_2 = 0.5\,l_1$.

Thus, volume of the wire = lA.

Since, the volume of wire remains the same after recasting, therefore

$$l_1 A_1 = l_2 A_2$$

$$\therefore \quad \frac{l_1}{l_2} = \frac{A_2}{A_1} \text{ or } \frac{l_1}{0.5\,l_1} = \frac{A_2}{A_1}$$

$$\therefore \quad \frac{A_2}{A_1} = 2$$

As resistance of wire, $R \propto \frac{l}{A}$

$$\therefore \quad \frac{R_1}{R_2} = \frac{l_1}{l_2} \times \frac{A_2}{A_1} = \frac{l_1}{0.5\,l_1} \times 2 = 4$$

or $$R_2 = \frac{R_1}{4} = \frac{R}{4}$$

• Concept Enhancer

As we know that the resistance R of wire of length l and area of cross-section, A is given by $R = \rho l / A$

23. *(b)* Area, $A = 1\text{ mm}^2 = 1 \times 10^{-6}\text{ m}^2$,

Current, $I = 4$ A and

Voltage, $V = 2$ V

According to Ohm's law,

$$\text{Resistance, } R = \frac{V}{I} = \frac{2}{4} = 0.5\,\Omega$$

$$\text{Resistivity, } \rho = R \times \frac{A}{l} = 0.5 \times \frac{1 \times 10^{-6}}{0.5}$$

$$= 1 \times 10^{-6}\ \Omega\text{-m}$$

24. *(d)* Let A_1, A_2, A_3 be the area of cross-section of three wires of copper of masses m_1, m_2, m_3 and length l_1, l_2, l_3 respectively.

Given $m_1 = m, m_2 = 3m,$

$m_3 = 5m, l_1 = 5l, l_2 = 3l, l_3 = l$

Mass = volume × density,

So, $m = A_1 \times 5l \times \rho$ ...(i)

$3m = A_2 \times 3l \times \rho$ ...(ii)

$5m = A_3 \times l \times \rho$ ...(iii)

From Eqs. (i) and (ii), we get

$$A_2 = 5A_1$$

From Eqs. (i) and (iii),

$$A_3 = 25A_1$$

$$\therefore \quad R_1 = \rho\frac{l_1}{A_1} = \rho\frac{5l}{A_1}$$

$$R_2 = \rho\frac{l_2}{A_2} = \rho \times \frac{3l}{5A_1}$$

$$= \frac{3}{25}R_1$$

$$R_3 = \rho\frac{l_3}{A_3} = \frac{\rho \times l}{25A_1} = \frac{R_1}{125}$$

$$\therefore \quad R_1 : R_2 : R_3 = R_1 : \frac{3}{25}R_1 : \frac{R_1}{125}$$

$$= 125 : 15 : 1$$

Topic 3

01. *(b)* Given,

wire of length l is divided into 10 parts each having $\frac{100}{10}\,\Omega = 10\,\Omega$ resistance.

According to question, 5 parts are connected in series

i.e., $R_1 = 5 \times 10 = 50\,\Omega$

5 parts are connected in parallel

i.e., $R_2 = \frac{R}{5} = \frac{10}{5} = 2\,\Omega$

Then, both R_1 and R_2 are connected in series

Thus, $R_{net} = R_1 + R_2$

$= 50 + 2 = 52\,\Omega$

02. (a) When 10 resistors, each of resistance R is connected in series, then equivalent resistance,

$$R_s = R + R + R + \ldots 10 \text{ times}$$

$$\Rightarrow \quad R_s = 10R$$

$\therefore$ Current drawn from the battery,

$$I_s = \frac{E}{R_S} = \frac{E}{10R}$$

$$\Rightarrow \quad I_s = \frac{E}{10R} \qquad \ldots(i)$$

In second case, when resistors are connected in parallel, then equivalent resistance,

$$\frac{1}{R_p} = \frac{1}{R} + \frac{1}{R} + \frac{1}{R} + \ldots 10 \text{ times}$$

$$= \frac{10}{R} \Rightarrow R_p = \frac{R}{10}$$

$\therefore$ Current drawn from the battery,

$$I_p = \frac{E}{R_p} = \frac{E}{R/10} = 10 \times \frac{E}{R} = 100 \times \frac{E}{10R}$$

$$\Rightarrow \quad I_p = 100 I_s$$

$$\therefore \quad n = 100$$

03. (d) The four resistances have equal length, equal cross-sectional area and same material.

So, $R_1 = R_2 = R_3 = R_4 = R$ (say)

Given, the effective resistance,

$$R_{eq} = 0.25\,\Omega$$

For parallel arrangement,

$$\frac{1}{R_{eq}} = \frac{1}{R_1} + \frac{1}{R_2} + \frac{1}{R_3} + \frac{1}{R_4}$$

$$\Rightarrow \quad \frac{1}{R_{eq}} = \frac{1}{R} + \frac{1}{R} + \frac{1}{R} + \frac{1}{R}$$

$$\Rightarrow \quad \frac{1}{0.25\,\Omega} = \frac{4}{R} \Rightarrow R = 1\,\Omega$$

For series combination,

$$R_{eq} = R_1 + R_2 + R_3 + R_4$$

$$\Rightarrow \quad R_{eq} = R + R + R + R$$

$$\Rightarrow \quad R_{eq} = 4R = 4(1) = 4\,\Omega$$

04. (b) According to the given circuit diagram in question,

$$i_1 = i_2 + i_3 \qquad \ldots(i)$$

In parallel arrangement of the electrical circuit, the voltage remains same.

$\therefore \quad V = ir$ (using Ohm's law)

$$\Rightarrow \quad i_2 r_2 = i_3 r_3 \Rightarrow i_2 = \frac{i_3 r_3}{r_2}$$

Substituting the values in the Eq. (i), we get

$$i_1 = \frac{i_3 r_3}{r_2} + i_3$$

$$\Rightarrow \quad \frac{i_1}{i_3} = \frac{r_3}{r_2} + 1$$

$$\Rightarrow \quad \frac{i_3}{i_1} = \frac{r_2}{r_3 + r_2}$$

05. (b) Equivalent resistance between points A and B is given as

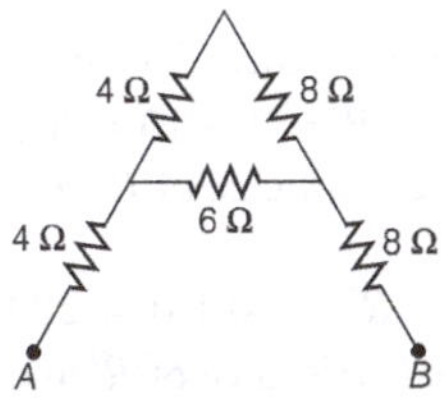

$$R_{AB} = [(4+8)\,||\,6] + 4 + 8$$

$$= [12\,||\,6] + 12 = \left[\frac{12 \times 6}{12 + 6}\right] + 12$$

$$= [4] + 12 = 16\,\Omega$$

06. (a) Net resistance of a metal wire having resistivity ρ, we have

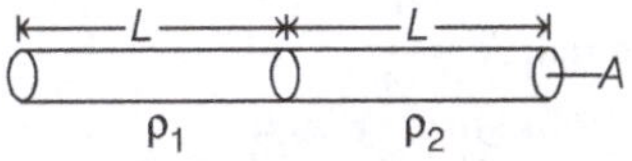

$$R_1 = \rho_1 \frac{L}{A}$$

Similarly, $R_2 = \rho_2 \dfrac{L}{A}$

Then, net effective resistance of two metal wires,

$$R_{eq} = R_1 + R_2$$

$$\Rightarrow \quad \rho \frac{2L}{A} = \rho_1 \frac{L}{A} + \rho_2 \frac{L}{A}$$

$$\Rightarrow \quad 2\rho = \rho_1 + \rho_2$$

As, conductivity, $\sigma = \dfrac{1}{\rho}$, we have

$$\frac{2}{\sigma} = \frac{1}{\sigma_1} + \frac{1}{\sigma_2} \Rightarrow \frac{2}{\sigma} = \frac{\sigma_1 + \sigma_2}{\sigma_1 \sigma_2}$$

$\Rightarrow$ Net effective conductivity of combined wires,

$$\sigma = \frac{2\sigma_1 \sigma_2}{\sigma_1 + \sigma_2}$$

07. (a) The equivalent resistance between Q and S is given by

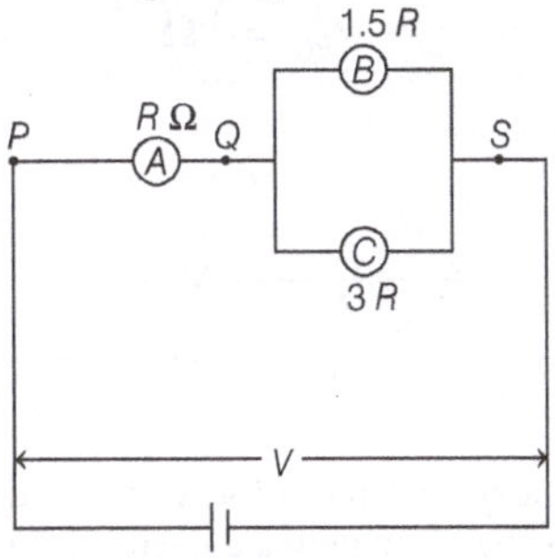

$$\frac{1}{R'} = \frac{1}{1.5R} + \frac{1}{3R} = \frac{2+1}{3R}$$

$$\Rightarrow \quad R' = R$$

Now, $V_{PQ} = V_A = IR$

Also $V_{QS} = V_B = V_C = IR$

Hence, $V_A = V_B = V_C$

08. (b) Resistance of side AB is $R_1 = \dfrac{3\rho}{A}$

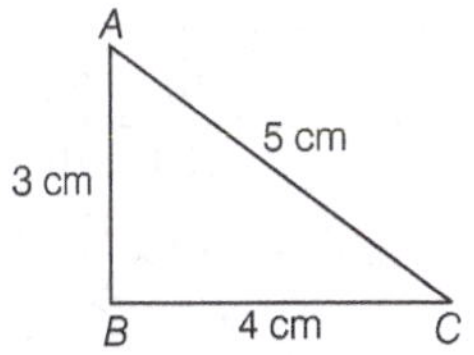

Resistance of side BC, $R_2 = \dfrac{4\rho}{A}$

Resistance of side AC, $R_3 = \dfrac{5\rho}{A}$

$\therefore$ The resistance between the ends A and B is given as

$$R_{AB} = \frac{R_1(R_2 + R_3)}{R_1 + R_2 + R_3}$$

$$= \frac{\frac{3\rho}{A}\left(\frac{4\rho}{A} + \frac{5\rho}{A}\right)}{\frac{3\rho}{A} + \left(\frac{4\rho}{A} + \frac{5\rho}{A}\right)}$$

$$= \frac{27}{12}\frac{\rho}{A}$$

The resistance between the ends B and C is given as

$$R_{BC} = \frac{R_2(R_1 + R_3)}{R_2 + R_1 + R_3}$$

$$= \frac{\frac{4\rho}{A}\left(\frac{3\rho}{A} + \frac{5\rho}{A}\right)}{\frac{4\rho}{A} + \frac{3\rho}{A} + \frac{5\rho}{A}} = \frac{32}{12}\frac{\rho}{A}$$

The resistance between the ends A and C is given as,

$$R_{AC} = \frac{R_3(R_1 + R_2)}{R_3 + R_1 + R_2} = \frac{\frac{5\rho}{A}\left(\frac{3\rho}{A} + \frac{4\rho}{A}\right)}{\frac{5\rho}{A} + \frac{3\rho}{A} + \frac{4\rho}{A}}$$

$$= \frac{35}{12}\frac{\rho}{A}$$

$$\therefore \quad R_{AB} : R_{BC} : R_{AC} = \frac{27}{12} : \frac{32}{12} : \frac{35}{12}$$

$$= 27 : 32 : 35$$

09. *(a)*

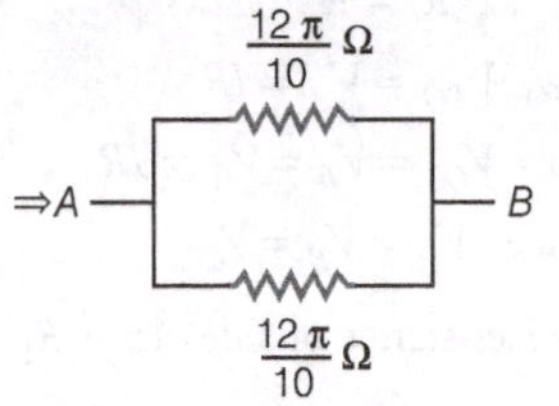

Circumference of circle

$$= 2\pi r = 2\times\pi\frac{10}{100} = \frac{2\pi}{10} = \frac{\pi}{5}$$

Resistance of wire $= 12\times\frac{\pi}{5} = \frac{12\pi}{5}$

Resistance of each section $= \frac{12\pi}{10}\,\Omega$

$$\therefore \text{ Equivalent resistance} = \frac{\frac{12\pi}{10}\times\frac{12\pi}{10}}{\frac{12\pi}{10}+\frac{12\pi}{10}}$$

$$\Rightarrow \qquad = \frac{6\pi}{10} = 0.6\,\pi\,\Omega$$

10. *(a)* When wire is bent to form a complete circle, then

Total circumference,

$$2\pi r = \text{Total length, } R$$

$$\Rightarrow \qquad r = \frac{R}{2\pi}$$

Resistance of each semicircle $= \pi r$

$$= \frac{\pi R}{2\pi} = \frac{R}{2} \quad \text{[from Eq. (i)]}$$

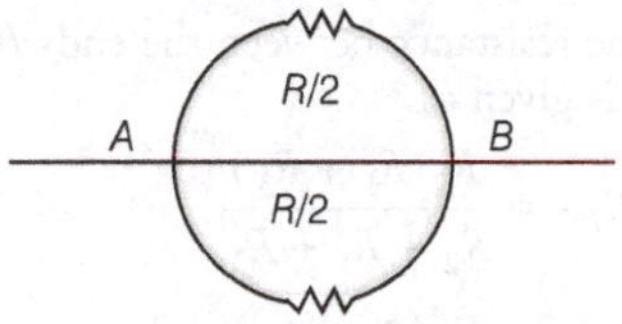

Thus, net resistance in parallel combination of two semicircular resistances

$$R' = \frac{\frac{R}{2}\times\frac{R}{2}}{\frac{R}{2}+\frac{R}{2}} = \frac{\frac{R^2}{4}}{R} = \frac{R}{4}$$

11. *(a)* Equivalent resistance of n resistances each of $r\Omega$ in parallel is given by

$$\frac{1}{R} = \frac{1}{r}+\frac{1}{r}+\ldots+n\text{ times} = \frac{n}{r}$$

So, $\quad r = nR$

When these resistances are connected in series, effective resistance is

$$R' = r + r + \ldots + n\text{ times} = nr$$

$$\therefore \qquad R' = n\,(nR) = n^2 R.$$

12. *(c)*

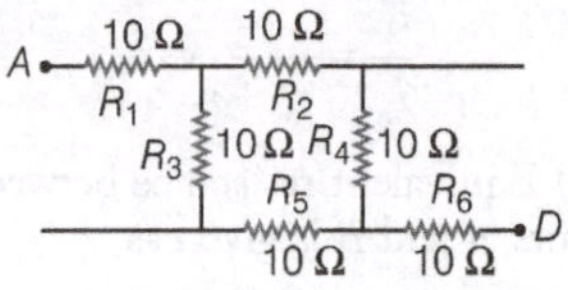

Effective resistance of R_2 and R_4 in series,

$$R' = 10 + 10 = 20\,\Omega$$

Effective resistance of R_3 and R_5 in series,

$$R'' = 10 + 10 = 20\,\Omega$$

Net total resistance of R' and R'' in parallel is

$$R_p = \frac{20\times 20}{20+20} = 10\,\Omega$$

$\therefore$ Total resistance between A and D

$$= 10 + 10 + 10 = 30\,\Omega$$

13. *(c)* For the same length and same material, $R \propto \frac{1}{A}$

$$\frac{R_2}{R_1} = \frac{A_1}{A_2} = \frac{3}{1} \text{ or } R_2 = 3R_1$$

The resistance of thick wire,

$$R_1 = 10\,\Omega$$

The resistance of thin wire

$$= 3\,R_1 = 3\times 10 = 30\,\Omega$$

Total resistance $= 10 + 30 = 40\,\Omega$

14. *(d)*

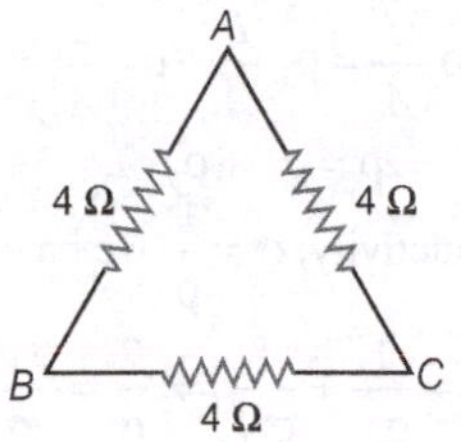

Between any two terminals, two resistors of two arms are in series i.e. between B and C, equivalent resistance is

$$\frac{1}{R_{BC}} = \frac{1}{4}+\frac{1}{8} = \frac{2+1}{8}$$

$$\therefore \qquad R_{BC} = \frac{8}{3}\,\Omega$$

15. *(c)*

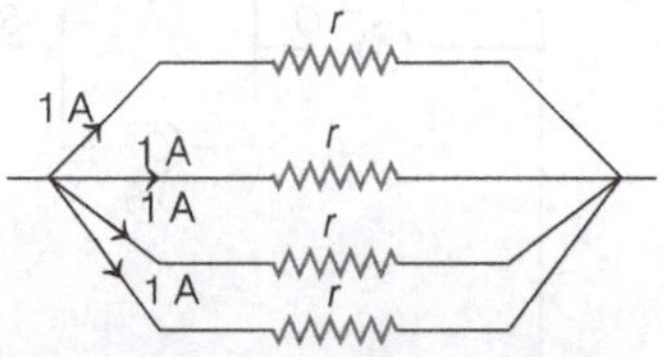

To carry a current of 4 A, we need four path, each carrying a current of 1A.

Let r be the resistance of each path. These resistances are connected in parallel. So, their equivalent resistance.

$$\frac{1}{r_p} = \frac{1}{r}+\frac{1}{r}+\frac{1}{r}+\frac{1}{r} \text{ or } r_p = \frac{r}{4}$$

But, $\quad r_p = \frac{r}{4} = 5 \qquad$ (given)

$$\therefore \qquad r = 20\,\Omega$$

For this purpose, two resistances should be connected is series. There are four such combinations in parallel.

Hence, the total number of resistances

$$= 4\times 2 = 8.$$

16. *(d)* The distribution of currents in the circuit is shown in the Fig. (a). Due to symmetry, current in arm AE is equal to current in the arm EB.

Since, current in the arm CE is equal to the current in the arm ED, therefore the resistance of network will not change, if the wires CED and AEB are disconnected at E, as shown in Fig. (b).

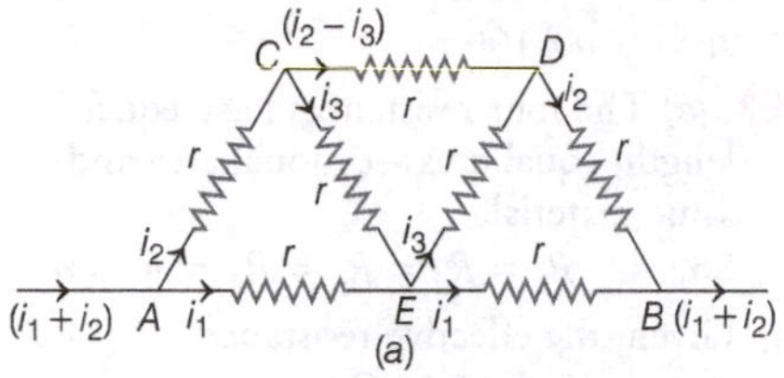

(a)

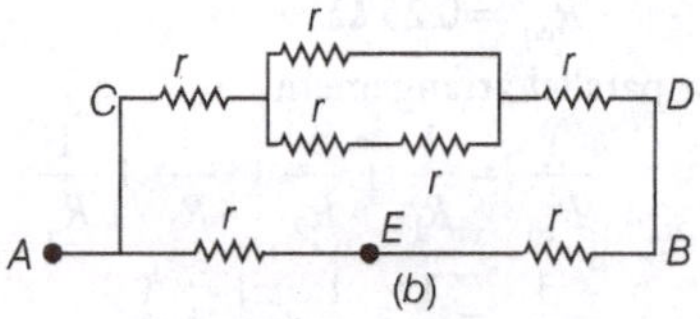

(b)

Now, resistance of path

$$AEB = r + r = 2r \qquad [\because r = 1\Omega]$$

Resistance of path

$$ACDB = r + \frac{(2r)\times r}{(2r)+r} + r = \frac{8r}{3}$$

The paths AEB and $ACDB$ are in parallel, therefore the effective resistance between A and B will be

$$\frac{1}{R} = \frac{1}{2r}+\frac{3}{8r}$$

$$= \frac{4+3}{8r} = \frac{7}{8r} \text{ or } R = \frac{8r}{7}$$

Therefore, $\quad R = \frac{8\times 1}{7} = \frac{8}{7}\,\Omega$

17. *(c)* When resistors are connected in series, then effective resistance of series combination

$$R_S = R + R + \ldots + n\text{ terms}$$

$$= nR \qquad \ldots\text{(i)}$$

When resistors are connected in parallel, then effective resistance

$$\frac{1}{R_P} = \frac{1}{R} + \frac{1}{R} + \ldots + n \text{ terms}$$

or $$\frac{1}{R_P} = \frac{n}{R} \quad \ldots\text{(ii)}$$

$$R_p = \frac{R}{n}$$

From Eqs. (i) and (ii), we get

$$\frac{R_S}{R_P} = \frac{n^2}{1}$$

Topic 4

01. (c) Given,

EMF, $\varepsilon = 10$ V

Internal resistance, $r = 1\,\Omega$

External resistance, $R = 4\,\Omega$

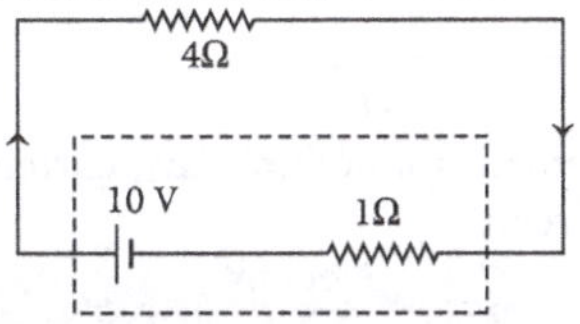

Terminal voltage, $V = \varepsilon - Ir$

and $I = \dfrac{\varepsilon}{R+r} = \dfrac{10}{4+1} = 2$ A

Thus, $V = 10 - 2 \times 1 = 8$ V

02. *(b)* The given situation is shown below.

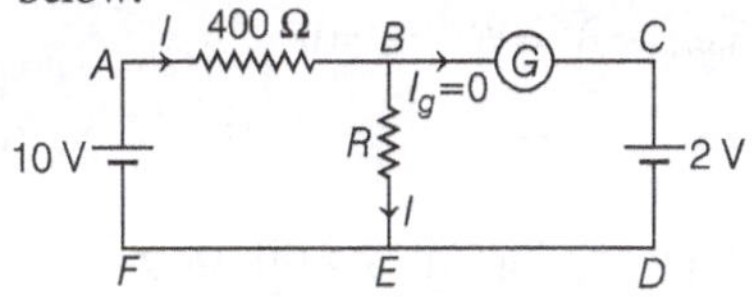

Applying Kirchhoff's voltage law in the loop *ABCDEFA*, we get

$$400I + 2 - 10 = 0$$

$$\Rightarrow \quad I = \frac{8}{400} = \frac{1}{50} \text{ A}$$

Applying Kirchhoff's voltage law in loop *ABEFA*, we get

$$400I + RI - 10 = 0$$

$$\Rightarrow \quad (400 + R)I = 10$$

$$\Rightarrow \quad (400 + R) \times \frac{1}{50} = 10$$

$$\Rightarrow \quad 400 + R = 500$$

$$\Rightarrow \quad R = 100\,\Omega$$

03. *(a)* The circuit diagram is shown as

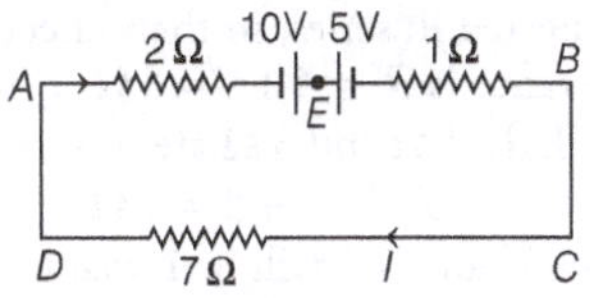

Applying KVL in the closed loop *AEBCDA*,

$$2I - 10 + 5 + I \cdot 1 + 7I = 0$$

$$\Rightarrow \quad 10I = 5$$

$$\Rightarrow \quad I = 0.5 \text{ A}$$

Since, current is positive, hence, direction of current is from *A* to *B* through *E*.

04. *(b)* The circuit diagram is shown below.

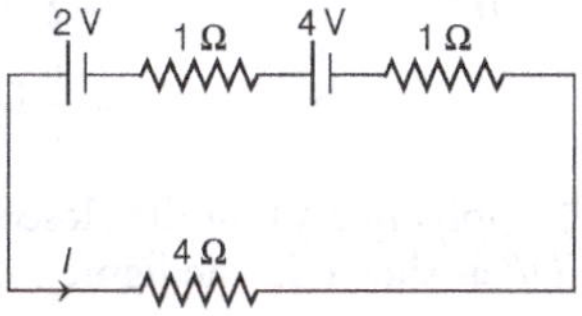

Applying KVL in the loop, we get

$$4I + I \cdot 1 - 4 + I \cdot 1 - 2 = 0$$

$$\Rightarrow \quad 6I = 6 \Rightarrow I = 1 \text{ A}$$

05. *(b)* The circuit diagram is given below.

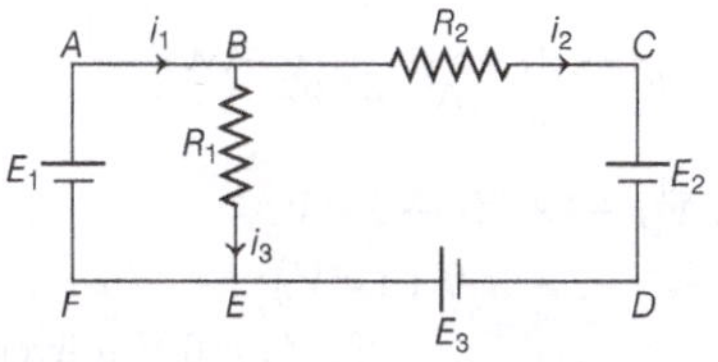

Applying KVL rule in loop *BCDEB*,

$$R_2 i_2 + E_2 - E_3 - i_3 R_1 = 0$$

06. *(d)* The given circuit diagram can be drawn as shown below

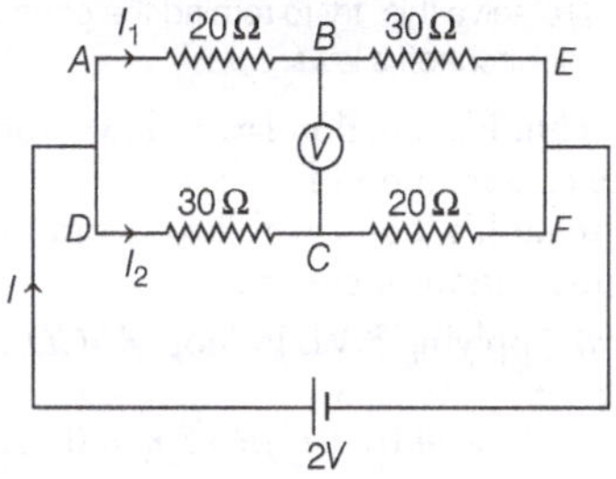

The equivalent resistance of circuit is given by

$$\frac{1}{R_{eq}} = \frac{1}{R_{AE}} + \frac{1}{R_{DF}}$$

$$= \frac{1}{(20+30)} + \frac{1}{(30+20)}$$

$$= \frac{1}{50} + \frac{1}{50} = \frac{2}{50}$$

$$\Rightarrow \quad R_{eq} = 25\,\Omega$$

The current in circuit,

$$I = \frac{V}{R} = \frac{2}{25} \text{ A}$$

As the resistance of two branches is same i.e. 50 Ω. So, the current,

$$I_1 = I_2$$

$$\Rightarrow \quad I = I_1 + I_2$$

$$\frac{2}{25} = 2I_1$$

$$\Rightarrow \quad I_2 = I_1 = \frac{1}{25} \text{ A}$$

∴ The voltage across *AB*

$$V_1 = I_1 R_1 = \frac{1}{25} \times 20$$

and voltage across *CD*,

$$V_2 = I_2 R_2 = \frac{1}{25} \times 30$$

∴ Voltmeter reading $= V_2 - V_1$

$$= \frac{30}{25} - \frac{20}{25} = \frac{10}{25} = 0.4 \text{ V}$$

07. *(c)* When n equal resistors of resistance R are connected in series, then the current drawn is given as

$$I = \frac{E}{nR + r}$$

where, nR = equivalent resistance of n resistors in series and r = internal resistance of battery.

Given, $r = R$

$$\Rightarrow \quad I = \frac{E}{nR + R} = \frac{E}{R(n+1)} \quad \ldots\text{(i)}$$

Similarly, when n equal resistors are connected in parallel, then the current drawn is given as

$$I' = \frac{E}{\frac{R}{n} + R}$$

where, $\dfrac{R}{n}$ = equivalent resistance of n resistors in parallel.

Given, $I' = 10I$

$$\Rightarrow \quad 10I = \frac{E}{\frac{R}{n} + R} = \frac{nE}{(n+1)R} \quad \ldots\text{(ii)}$$

Substituting the value of I from Eq. (i) in Eq. (ii), we get

$$10\left(\frac{E}{R(n+1)}\right) = \frac{nE}{R(n+1)}$$

$$\Rightarrow \quad n = 10$$

08. *(c)* If n identical cells are connected in series, then

Equivalent emf of the combination,

$$E_{eq} = nE$$

Equivalent internal resistance,

$$r_{eq} = nr$$

$$\therefore \text{ Current, } I = \frac{E_{eq}}{r_{eq}} = \frac{nE}{nr}$$

or $\quad I = \dfrac{E}{r} = \text{constant}$

Thus, current I is independent of the number of cells n present in the circuit. Therefore, option (c) is correct.

09. *(d)*

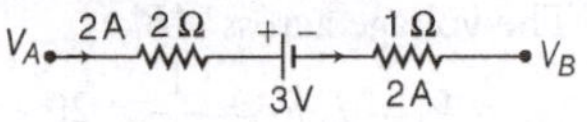

Applying KVL,

$$V_A + \Sigma V = V_B + 2\times 2 + 2\times 1$$
$$V_A - V_B - 3 = 4 + 2;$$
$$V_A - V_B = 9\ \text{V}$$

10. *(a)* Effective resistance of a circuit,

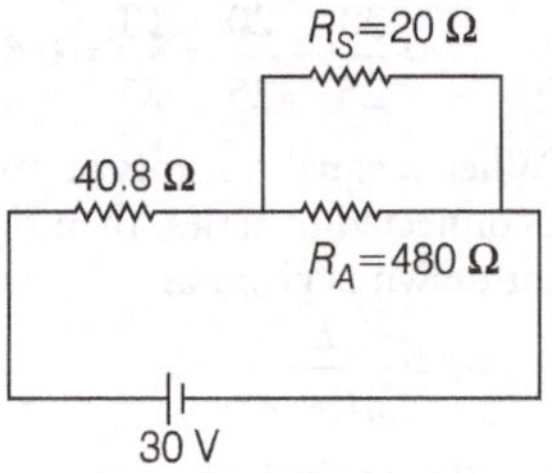

$$R_{\text{eff}} = 40.8 + \frac{480\times 20}{480+20}$$
$$= 40.8 + 19.2 = 60\ \Omega$$

So, current flowing across ammeter,

$$I = \frac{V}{R} = \frac{30}{60} = \frac{1}{2} = 0.5\ \text{A}$$

Hence, reading of ammeter = 0.5 A

11. *(b)* As, $I = \dfrac{E}{R+r}$

E = emf of cell
R = external resistance
r = internal resistance
I = current in circuit

or $\quad E = I\,(R+r)$,

$$2.1 = 0.2\,(10+r)$$
$$10 + r = \frac{2.1}{2}\times 10$$
$$\therefore \quad r = 10.5 - 10 = 0.5\ \Omega$$

12. *(b)* Applying Kirchhoff's law,

$$500I + 100I = 12$$

So, $\quad I = \dfrac{12\times 10^{-2}}{6} = 2\times 10^{-2}$ A

Hence, $V_B = 100\,(2\times 10^{-2}) = 2$ V

> **• Concept Enhancer**
> If potential difference across R Ω resistor is equal to potential difference of cell B, galvanometer shows no deflection.

13. *(a)* Current in circuit connected with battery of emf E with internal resistance r is given by

Current, $\quad i = \dfrac{E}{R+r}$

Case I $\quad 2 = \dfrac{E}{2+r}$ ...(i)

Case II $\quad 0.5 = \dfrac{E}{9+r}$ ...(ii)

From Eqs. (i) and (ii), we have,

$$\frac{2}{0.5} = \frac{9+r}{2+r} \Rightarrow 4 = \frac{9+r}{2+r}$$
$$\Rightarrow \quad 3r = 1 \Rightarrow r = \frac{1}{3}\ \Omega$$

14. *(a)* Applying KVL in the closed path $ACDB$ as shown in the figure.

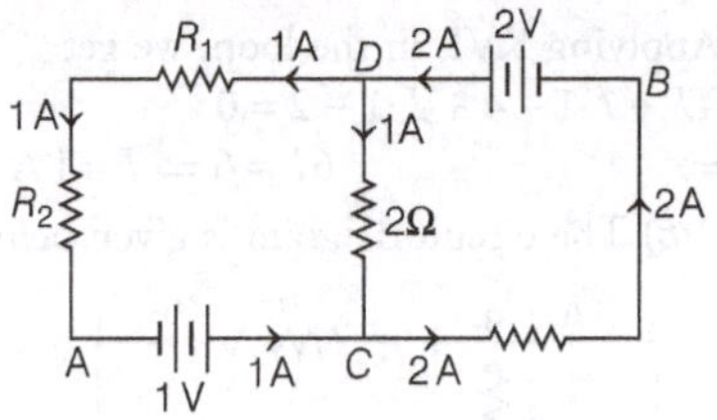

$$\therefore\ V_A + 1 + 2(1) - 2 = V_B$$
$$0 + 1 = V_B$$
$$[\because V_A = 0\ \text{V (Given)}]$$
$$V_B = +1\ \text{V}$$

15. *(d)*

key idea
To solve this, try to remind the concept of Kirchhoff's laws.

Kirchhoff's junction law follows from the conservation of charge.
Kirchhoff's loop law follows from the conservation of energy.

16. *(a)* Applying KVL in loop $ABCDA$, we get

$$-\varepsilon_1 + (i_1 + i_2)R + i_1 r_1 = 0 \quad \text{...(i)}$$

Applying KVL in loop $ADEFA$,

$$-\varepsilon_2 + i_2 r_2 + \varepsilon_1 - i_1 r_1 = 0$$
$$-\varepsilon_2 = -i_2 r_2 - \varepsilon_1 + i_1 r_1 \quad \text{...(ii)}$$

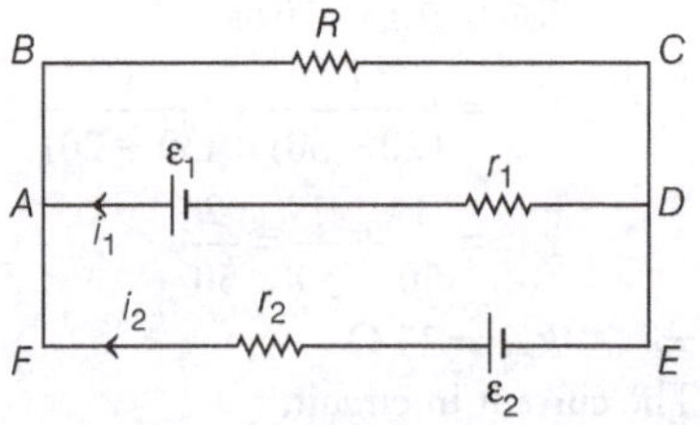

Again applying KVL in loop $BCDEFAB$

$$(i_1 + i_2)R - \varepsilon_2 + i_2 r_2 = 0$$
$$\Rightarrow (i_1 + i_2)R - i_2 r_2 - \varepsilon_1 + i_1 r_1 + i_2 r_2 = 0$$
[From Eq. (ii)]
$$\Rightarrow \varepsilon_1 - (i_1 + i_2)R - i_1 r_1 = 0$$

17. *(b)* According to Ohm's law

$$\frac{dV}{dI} = -r$$

and $\quad V = \varepsilon$ if $I = 0 \quad$ [As $V + Ir = \varepsilon$]

Compare it with

$$y = mx + c$$

So, slope of the graph $= -r$
and intercept $= \varepsilon$

18. *(a)* Net resistance of the circuit

$$= r_1 + r_2 + R$$

Net emf in series $= E + E = 2E$

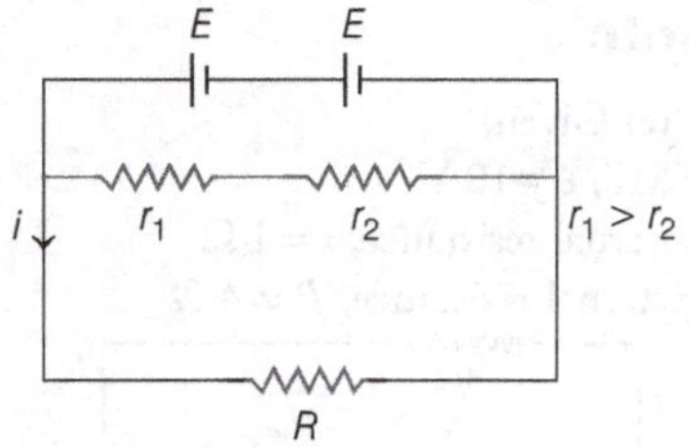

Therefore, from Ohm's law, current in the circuit

$$i = \frac{\text{Net emf}}{\text{Net resistance}}$$
$$\Rightarrow \quad i = \frac{2E}{r_1 + r_2 + R} \quad \text{...(i)}$$

It is given that, as circuit is closed, potential difference across the first cell is zero.

i.e., $\quad V = E - ir_1 = 0$

$$\Rightarrow \quad i = \frac{E}{r_1} \quad \text{...(ii)}$$

Equating Eqs. (i) and (ii), we get

$$\frac{E}{r_1} = \frac{2E}{r_1 + r_2 + R}$$
$$\Rightarrow \quad 2r_1 = r_1 + r_2 + R$$
$$\therefore \quad R = \text{external resistance}$$
$$\Rightarrow \quad R = r_1 - r_2$$

Note The question is wrong as the statement is when the circuit is closed, the potential difference across the first cell is zero which implies that in a series circuit, one part cannot conduct current which is wrong, Kirchhoff's law is violated. The question must have been modified.

19. *(d)* Resistances 4 Ω and 4 Ω are connected in series, so their effective resistance is $R' = 4 + 4 = 8\ \Omega$

Similarly, 1 Ω and 3 Ω are in series

So, $\quad R'' = 1 + 3 = 4\ \Omega$

Now R' and R'' will be in parallel, hence effective resistance

$$R = \frac{R' \times R''}{R' + R''} = \frac{8 \times 4}{8 + 4} = \frac{32}{12} = \frac{8}{3}\,\Omega$$

Current through the circuit, from Ohm's law, $i = \frac{V}{R} = \frac{3V}{8}$ A

Let currents i_1 and i_2 flow in the branches as shown below. As voltage remains same in parallel combination,

i.e. $V_1 = V_2$

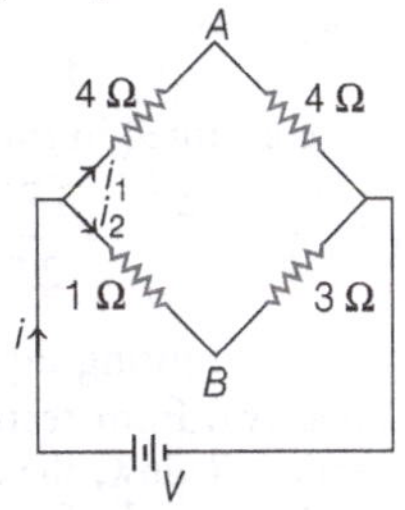

$\therefore \quad 8i_1 = 4i_2$

$\Rightarrow \quad i_2 = 2i_1 \quad$ ...(i)

Also, $\quad i = i_1 + i_2 \Rightarrow \frac{3V}{8} = i_1 + 2i_1$

$\Rightarrow \quad i_1 = \frac{V}{8}$ A and $i_2 = \frac{V}{4}$ A

Potential drop at A,

$$V_A = 4 \times i_1 = \frac{4V}{8} = \frac{V}{2}$$

Potential drop at B,

$$V_B = 1 \times i_2 = 1 \times \frac{V}{4} = \frac{V}{4}$$

Since, drop of potential is greater in 4 Ω resistance so, it will be at lower potential than B. Hence, on connecting wire between points A and B, the current will flow from B to A.

20. *(c)* It is clear that the two cells oppose each other hence, the effective emf in closed circuit is $18 - 12 = 6$ V and net resistance is $1 + 2 = 3\,\Omega$ (because in the closed circuit, the internal resistances of two cells are in series).

The current in circuit will be in direction of arrow shown in figure.

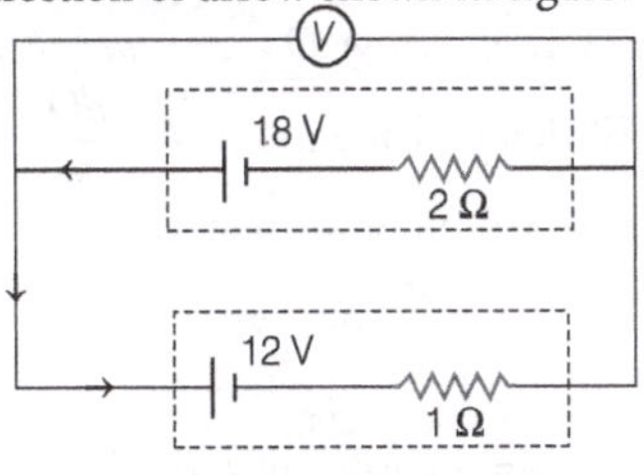

$$I = \frac{\text{Effective emf}}{\text{Total resistance}} = \frac{6}{3} = 2\text{ A}$$

The potential difference across V will be same as the terminal voltage of either cell. Since, current is drawn from the cell of 18 V, hence,

$$V_1 = E_1 - ir_1$$
$$= 18 - (2 \times 2) = 18 - 4 = 14\text{ V}$$

Similarly, current enters in the cell of 12 V, hence,

$$V_2 = E_2 + ir_2 = 12 + 2 \times 1$$
$$= 12 + 2 = 14\text{ V}$$

Hence, $V = 14$ V

21. *(c)* Total current drawn from the battery,

$$i = \frac{E}{R + r} = \frac{6}{100 + 0} = 0.06\text{ A}$$

Resistance of 50 cm wire is

$$R' = \frac{\rho l'}{A} = \left(\frac{\rho}{A}\right) l' = \left(\frac{R}{l}\right) l' \qquad \left(\because R = \frac{\rho l}{A}\right)$$

$$= \frac{100}{300} \times 50$$

So, $\quad R' = \frac{50}{3}\,\Omega$

Hence, the potential difference between two points on the wire separated by a distance l' is given by Ohm's law

i.e. $\quad V = iR' = 0.06 \times \frac{50}{3} = 1$ V

22. *(a)* In an open circuit, emf of cell,

$$E = 2.2\text{ V}$$

In a closed circuit, terminal potential difference

$$V = 1.8\text{ V}$$

External resistance, $R = 5\,\Omega$

Thus, internal resistance of cell is

$$r = \left(\frac{E}{V} - 1\right) R = \left(\frac{2.2}{1.8} - 1\right) 5$$
$$= \left(\frac{11}{9} - 1\right) 5 = \frac{2}{9} \times 5 = \frac{10}{9}\,\Omega$$

23. *(c)* Internal resistance of the cell is given by

$$r = \left(\frac{E - V}{V}\right) R$$

Given, $E = 1.5$ V, $\quad V = 1.0$ V,

$R = 2\,\Omega$

$$\therefore \quad r = \left(\frac{1.5 - 1.0}{1.0}\right) \times 2 = \frac{0.5}{1.0} \times 2 = 1\,\Omega$$

24. *(b)* In the given circuit, resistances R_B and R_C are in series order, so their effective resistance,

$$R' = R_B + R_C = 6 + 6 = 12\,\Omega$$

Now, R_A and R' are in parallel order, hence net resistance of the circuit

$$R = \frac{R' \times R_A}{R' + R_A} = \frac{12 \times 3}{12 + 3} = \frac{36}{15}\,\Omega$$

The current flowing in the circuit,

$$i = \frac{V}{R} = 4.8 \times \frac{15}{36} = 2\text{ A}$$

25. *(a)* From the given figure, the resistances in the arms AC and BC are in series.

$\therefore \quad R' = R_{AC} + R_{BC}$
$= 3\,\Omega + 3\,\Omega = 6\,\Omega$

Now, R' is in parallel with the resistance in arm AB,

So, $R = \frac{R' \times R_{AB}}{R' + R_{AB}} = \frac{6\,\Omega \times 3\,\Omega}{6\,\Omega + 3\,\Omega} = 2\,\Omega$

Current, $i = \frac{V}{R}$

Substituting the values, we get

$$i = \frac{2}{2} = 1\text{ A} \qquad (\because V = 2\text{ V})$$

26. *(d)* Kirchhoff's law states that the algebraic sum of currents meeting at a point (say at a junction) is equals to zero i.e.,

$$\Sigma i = 0$$

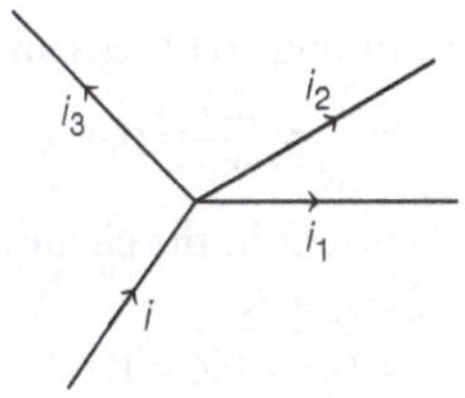

or $\quad i = i_1 + i_2 + i_3$

$$\frac{dQ}{dt} = \frac{dQ_1}{dt} + \frac{dQ_2}{dt} + \frac{dQ_3}{dt}$$

or, $\quad dQ = dQ_1 + dQ_2 + dQ_3$

So, we can say that when a steady current flows through circuit, then neither accumulation of charges takes place at the junction in the circuit nor any charge is removed from there. That's why Kirchhoff's first law deals with the conservation of charge.

27. *(a)*

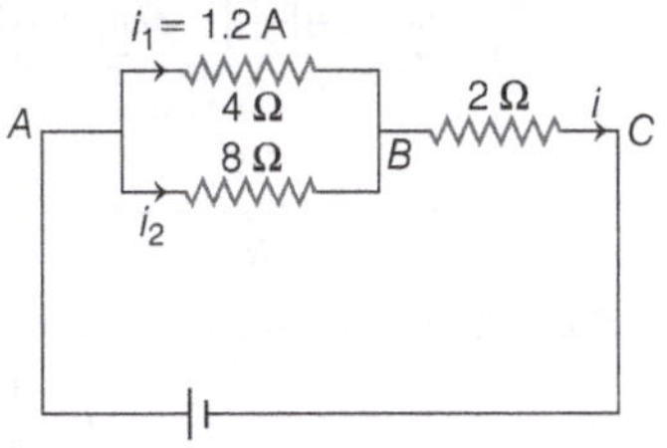

The potential difference across 4 Ω resistance is given by Ohm's law

$$= 4 \times i_1 = 4 \times 1.2 = 4.8\text{ V}$$
$$(\text{as } i_1 = 1.2\text{ A})$$

As resistances 4 Ω and 8 Ω are in parallel, so potential difference across 8 Ω resistance will also be 4.8 V.

∴ Current through 8 Ω resistance

$$i_2 = \frac{V}{R} = \frac{4.8}{8} = 0.6 \text{ A}$$

$$\therefore \quad i = i_1 + i_2 = 1.2 + 0.6 = 1.8 \text{ A}$$

∴ Potential difference across 2 Ω resistance $V_{BC} = i \times 2$

$$= 1.8 \times 2 = 3.6 \text{ V}$$

28. *(c)*

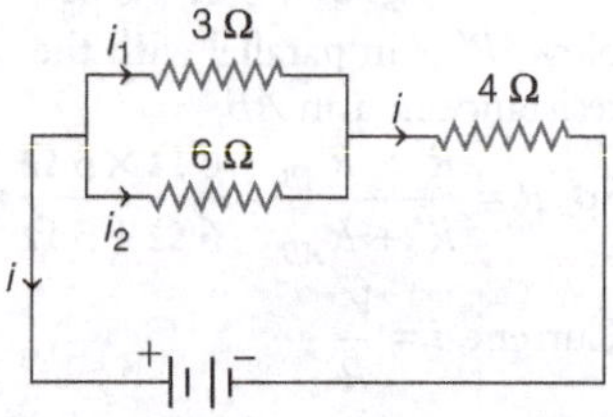

Voltage across 3 Ω resistance is given by Ohm's law

i.e. $V = IR = 3 \times i_1$

$$= 3 \times 0.8 = 2.4 \text{ V}$$

$$(\text{as } i_1 = 0.8 \text{ A})$$

As 3 Ω and 6 Ω are in parallel, hence voltage across 6 Ω resistance will also be 2.4 V.

∴ Current through 6 Ω resistance

$$i_2 = \frac{V}{R} = \frac{2.4}{6} = 0.4 \text{ A}$$

∴ Total current in the circuit,

$$i = i_1 + i_2$$
$$= 0.8 + 0.4 = 1.2 \text{ A}$$

∴ Potential drop across 4 Ω resistance,

$$= i \times 4 = 1.2 \times 4$$
$$= 4.8 \text{ V}$$

29. *(b)* Kirchhoff's first law supports law of conservation of charge. This is because a point in a circuit cannot act as a source or sink of charge.

30. *(a)* Applying Kirchhoff's voltage law in the given loop and going in direction of current *PSTQ* total voltage is equal to zero

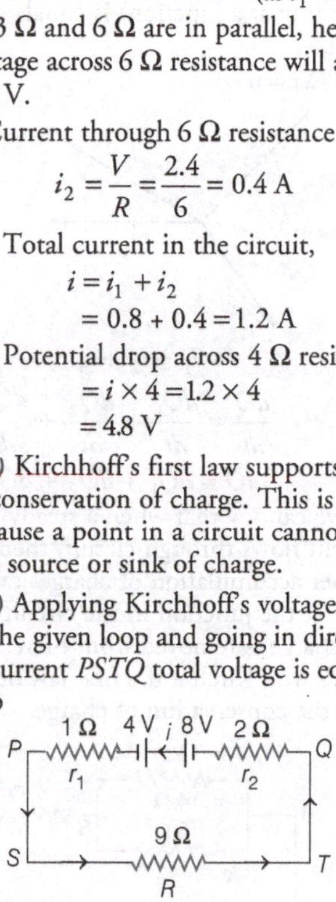

So, $-2i + 8 - 4 - 1 \times i - 9i = 0$

$$\therefore \quad i = \frac{1}{3} \text{ A}$$

Potential difference across $PQ = \frac{1}{3} \times 9$

$$= 3 \text{ V}$$

Topic 5

01. *(a)*

key idea

To find the ratio of thermal energy, you can use following formula

$$\frac{H_1}{H_2} = \frac{R_2}{R_1}$$

The given situation is shown in the following circuit diagram.

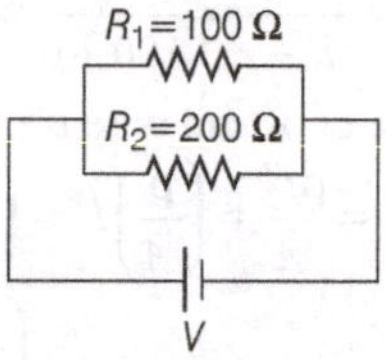

Let, these two resistors are connected with a battery of voltage *V* volts. Hence, potential difference across R_1, and R_2 are given as,

$$V_1 = V_2 = V \text{ V}$$

If H_1 and H_2 are thermal energy produced through resistances R_1 and R_2 in time *t*, then

$$H_1 = \frac{V_1^2}{R_1} t = \frac{V^2 t}{100}$$

and $$H_2 = \frac{V_2^2 t}{R_2} = \frac{V^2 t}{200}$$

Hence, $$\frac{H_1}{H_2} = \frac{V^2 t/100}{V^2 t/200} = \frac{200}{100} = \frac{2}{1}$$

$$\Rightarrow H_1 : H_2 = 2 : 1$$

02. *(d)* Given, power radiated by transmitter, $P = 100 \text{ kW} = 10^5 \text{ W}$

∴ Time, $t = 1 \text{ h} = 60 \times 60 \text{ s} = 3 \cdot 6 \times 10^3 \text{ s}$

∴ Energy radiated by the transmitter,

$$E = P \times t$$
$$= 10^5 \times 3 \cdot 6 \times 10^3$$
$$= 3 \cdot 6 \times 10^8 \text{ J} = 36 \times 10^7 \text{ J}$$

03. *(a)* Case I When all bulbs are glowing, then the circuit can be realised as shown in the figure.

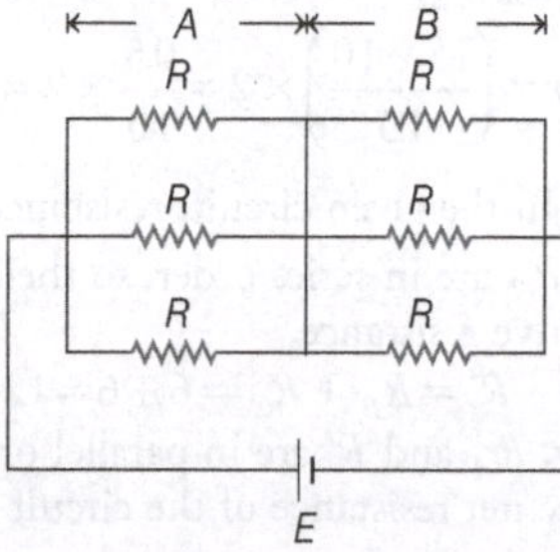

∴ The equivalent resistance of this circuit is

$$R_{eq} = R_A + R_B$$

As, section *A* has three parallel resistance, so equivalent resistance,

$$R_A = \frac{R}{3}$$

Similarly, for section *B*, equivalent resistance,

$$R_B = \frac{R}{3} \Rightarrow R_{eq} = \frac{R}{3} + \frac{R}{3} = \frac{2R}{3} \quad \text{... (i)}$$

Thus, power consumed in this circuit,

$$P_1 = \frac{V^2}{R} = \frac{E^2}{R_{eq}} = \frac{3E^2}{2R}$$

[using Eq. (i)] ...(ii)

Case II When two from section *A* and one from section *B* glow, the circuit can be realised as shown in the figure below.

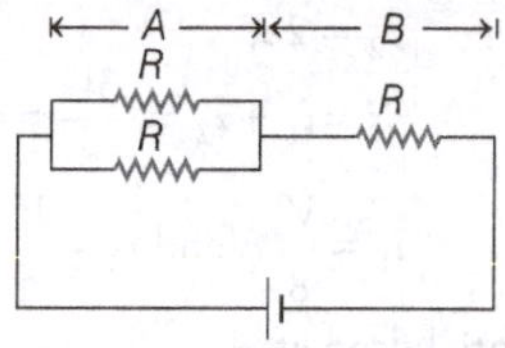

∴ Equivalent resistance of section *A*,

$$R_A = \frac{R}{2}$$

and of section *B*, $R_B = R$

Thus, equivalent resistance of the entire circuit becomes

$$R_{eq} = R_A + R_B = \frac{R}{2} + R = \frac{3R}{2} \quad \text{...(iii)}$$

∴ Power consumed by this circuit,

$$P_2 = \frac{V^2}{R} = \frac{E^2}{R_{eq}} = \frac{2E^2}{3R}$$

[using Eq. (iii)] ...(iv)

So, ratio of power of two cases is obtained from Eqs. (ii) and (iv), we get

$$\frac{P_1}{P_2} = \frac{3E^2}{2R} \times \frac{3R}{2E^2} = \frac{9}{4} \text{ or } 9:4$$

04. *(d)* Given, charge $Q = at - bt^2$ ...(i)

∵ We know that current, $I = \frac{dQ}{dt}$

So, Eq. (i) can be written as

$$I = \frac{d}{dt}(at - bt^2)$$

$$\Rightarrow \quad I = a - 2bt \quad \text{...(ii)}$$

For maximum value of *t*, till the current exist is given by

$$\Rightarrow a - 2bt = 0$$

$$\therefore \quad t = \frac{a}{2b} \quad \text{...(iii)}$$

∵ The total heat produced H can be given as

$$H = \int_0^t I^2 R\, dt$$

$$= \int_0^{a/2b} (a - 2bt)^2 R . dt \qquad \left\{\because t = \frac{a}{2b}\right\}$$

$$= \int_0^{a/2b} (a^2 + 4b^2t^2 - 4abt)\, Rdt$$

$$H = \left[a^2 t + 4b^2 \frac{t^3}{3} - \frac{4abt^2}{2}\right]_0^{a/2b} R$$

Solving above equation, we get

$$\Rightarrow \quad H = \frac{a^3 R}{6b}$$

05. *(c)* $P_{rated} = \dfrac{V_{rated}^2}{R}$

∴ Current in the bulb, $i = \dfrac{P}{V}$ ($\because P = Vi$)

$$i = \frac{500}{100} = 5 \text{ A}$$

∴ Resistance of bulb, $R_b = \dfrac{V^2}{P}$

$$R_b = \frac{100 \times 100}{500} = 20\ \Omega$$

∵ Resistance R is connected in series.

∴ Current, $i = \dfrac{E}{R_{net}} = \dfrac{230}{R + R_b}$

$$\Rightarrow R + 20 = \frac{230}{5} = 46$$

$$\therefore \quad R = 26\ \Omega$$

06. *(b)* Potential drop between two cities is

$$= 150 \times 8 = 1200 \text{ V}$$

Average resistance of total wire

$$= 0.5 \times 150 = 75\ \Omega$$

So, power loss, $P = \dfrac{V^2}{R}$

$$= \frac{1200 \times 1200}{75}$$

$$= 19200 \text{ W} = 19.2 \text{ kW}$$

07. *(c)* Power, $P = \dfrac{V^2}{R}$

For small variation,

$$\frac{\Delta P}{P} \times 100 = 2 \times \frac{\Delta V}{V} \times 100$$

$$= 2 \times 2.5 = 5\%$$

Therefore, power would decrease by 5%.

08. *(b)* Electric power,

$$P = i^2 R$$

∴ Current, $i = \sqrt{\dfrac{P}{R}}$

For resistance of 9 Ω,

$$i_1 = \sqrt{\frac{36}{9}} = \sqrt{4} = 2 \text{ A}$$

$$i_2 = \frac{i_1 \times R}{6} = \frac{2 \times 9}{6} = 3 \text{ A}$$

$$I = i_1 + i_2 = 2 + 3 = 5 \text{ A}$$

So, $\quad V_2 = IR_2 = 5 \times 2 = 10$ V

09. *(a)* From conservation of heat energy,

$$Vit = ms\,\Delta t$$

$$\Rightarrow \quad t = \frac{ms\,\Delta t}{Vi}$$

$$= \frac{1 \times 4200 \times 80}{220 \times 4}$$

$$= 381.82 \text{ s} = 6.3 \text{ min}$$

10. *(d)* Voltage across 2 Ω,

$$= 3 \times 2 = 6 \text{ V}$$

Voltage across 4 Ω and (5 Ω + 1 Ω) resistor is same.

So, current across 5 Ω $= \dfrac{6}{1+5} = 1$ A $\quad \left[i = \dfrac{V}{R}\right]$

Power across 5 Ω $= P = i^2 R$

$$= (1)^2 \times 5 = 5 \text{ W}$$

11. *(c)* The resistance of 6 Ω and 3 Ω are in parallel in the given circuit, their equivalent resistance is

$$\frac{1}{R_1} = \frac{1}{6} + \frac{1}{3} = \frac{1+2}{6} = \frac{1}{2}$$

or $\quad R_1 = 2\ \Omega$

Again, R_1 is in series with 4 Ω resistance, hence

$$R = R_1 + 4$$

$$= 2 + 4 = 6\ \Omega$$

Thus, the total power dissipated in the circuit

$$P = \frac{V^2}{R}$$

$$= \frac{(18)^2}{6} = 54 \text{ W}$$

12. *(d)* **Problem Solving Strategy** Find the equivalent resistance of the circuit and then calculate the power dissipated by the circuit.

Resistances 1 Ω and 3 Ω are connected in series, so, effective resistance

$$R' = 1 + 3 = 4\ \Omega$$

Now, R' and 8 Ω are in parallel. We know that potential difference across resistances in parallel is same.

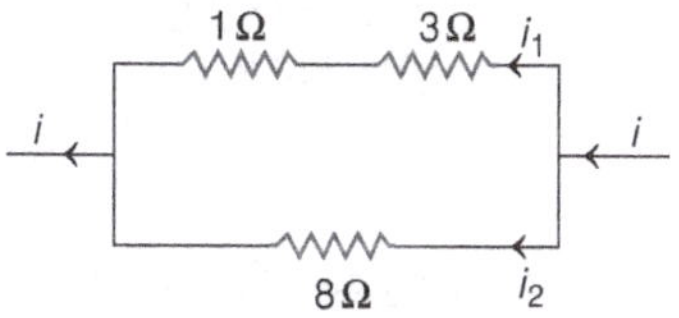

So, from Kirchhoff's law, $V_1 = V_2$

$$R' \times i_1 = 8 i_2$$

or $\quad 4 \times i_1 = 8 i_2$

or $\quad i_1 = \dfrac{8}{4} i_2 = 2 i_2$

or $\quad i_1 = 2 i_2 \quad$ ...(i)

Power dissipated across 8 Ω resistance is

$$i_2^2 (8) t = 2 \text{ W} \qquad [\because H = i^2 Rt]$$

or $\quad i_2^2 t = \dfrac{2}{8} = 0.25$ W $\quad$ ...(ii)

Power dissipated across 3 Ω resistance is

$$H = i_1^2 (3) t$$

$$= (2i_2)^2 (3) t = 12\, i_2^2\, t$$

but $\quad i_2^2\, t = 0.25$ W

$$H = 12 \times 0.25 = 3 \text{ W}$$

13. *(d)* As we know that,

Power, $\quad P = i^2 R$

$$R = \frac{P}{i^2}$$

Given, $\quad P = 1$ W

$$i = 5 \text{ A}$$

$$R = \frac{1}{(5)^2} = 0.04\ \Omega$$

14. *(d)* Input energy when the battery is charged,

$$E_{in} = Vit = 15 \times 10 \times 8$$

$$= 1200 \text{ Wh}$$

Energy released when the battery is discharged

$$E_{out} = 14 \times 5 \times 15 = 1050 \text{ Wh}$$

Hence, watt hour efficiency of battery is given by

$$= \frac{\text{Energy output}}{\text{Energy input}} = \frac{1050}{1200}$$

$$= 0.875 = 87.5\%$$

15. *(c)* Since, power rating of bulb in both the countries India and USA is same, so

$$\frac{V_1^2}{R_1} = \frac{V_2^2}{R_2} \qquad \left[P = \frac{V^2}{R}\right]$$

$$\Rightarrow \quad \frac{220 \times 220}{R_1} = \frac{110 \times 110}{R_2}$$

$$\Rightarrow \quad \frac{R_2}{R_1} = \frac{110 \times 110}{220 \times 220}$$

$$\Rightarrow \quad R_2 = \frac{R}{4} \qquad (\because R_1 = R)$$

16. *(d)* Let R_1, R_2 and R_3 are the resistances of three bulbs respectively.

In series order, $R = R_1 + R_2 + R_3$

but, $R = \frac{V^2}{P}$ and supply voltage in series order is the same as the rated voltage.

$$\therefore \quad \frac{V^2}{P} = \frac{V^2}{P_1} + \frac{V^2}{P_2} + \frac{V^2}{P_3}$$

$$\text{or} \quad \frac{1}{P} = \frac{1}{60} + \frac{1}{60} + \frac{1}{60}$$

$$\text{or} \quad P = \frac{60}{3} = 20 \text{ W}$$

Alternate Solution

As three bulbs have same power and voltage so, they have equal resistance. So, power equivalent when connected in series is given by,

$$\frac{1}{P_{EQ}} = \frac{1}{P_1} + \frac{1}{P_2} + \frac{1}{P_3}$$

$$\frac{1}{P_{EQ}} = \frac{1}{P} + \frac{1}{P} + \frac{1}{P} \quad (\text{as } P_1 = P_2 = P_3 = P)$$

So, $P_{EQ} = \frac{P}{3} \Rightarrow \frac{60}{3} = 20 \text{ W}$

17. *(b)* Power, $P = 100$ W,

Voltage, $V = 220$ V

$$P = \frac{V^2}{R}$$

$$\therefore \quad R = \frac{V^2}{P} = \frac{(220)^2}{100}$$

$$= \frac{220 \times 220}{100} \, \Omega$$

As both the bulb have same voltage and power so, resistance of bulbs will also be same.

Case I When two bulbs are connected in series.

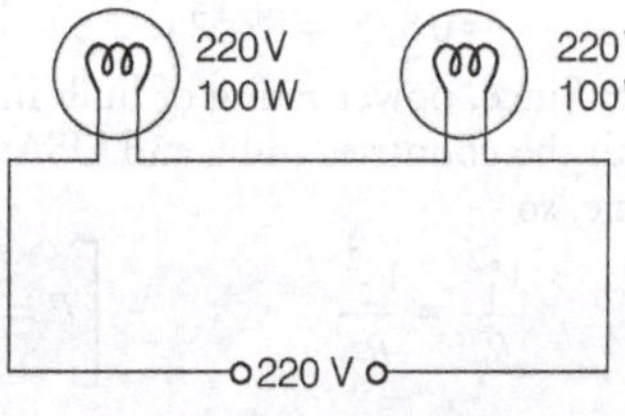

In series, $R_{eq} = R_1 + R_2$

$$= \left(\frac{220 \times 220}{100}\right) \times 2$$

Hence, $P_{eq} = \frac{V^2}{R_{eq}}$

$$= \frac{220 \times 220}{\left(\frac{220 \times 220}{100} \times 2\right)} = \frac{100}{2} = 50 \text{ W}$$

Case II When two bulbs are connected in parallel.

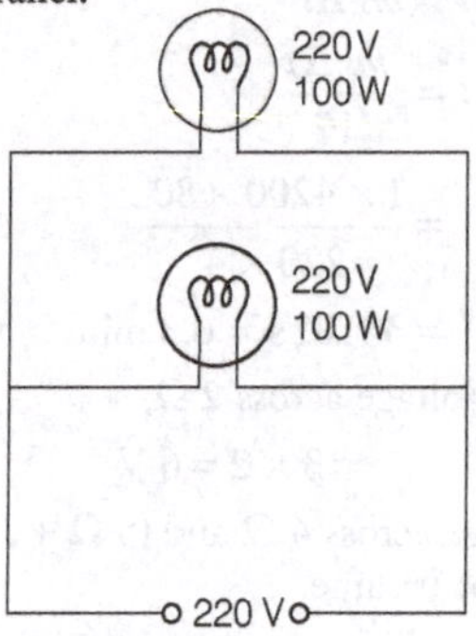

In parallel,

$$R_{eq} = \frac{R_1 R_2}{R_1 + R_2} = \frac{\left(\frac{220 \times 220}{100}\right)^2}{\frac{220 \times 220}{100} \times 2}$$

$$R_{eq} = \frac{220 \times 220}{100} \times \frac{1}{2}$$

Hence, $P_{eq} = \frac{V^2}{R_{eq}} = \frac{220 \times 220}{\frac{220 \times 220}{100} \times \frac{1}{2}}$

$$= 200 \text{ W}$$

Alternate Solution

For series, $P_{eq} = \frac{P_1 P_2}{P_1 + P_2} = \frac{100 \times 100}{200} = 50 \text{ W}$

For parallel, $P_{eq} = P_1 + P_2 = 100 + 100 = 200 \text{ W}$

Note Power equivalent of two or more resistance in series is given by

$\frac{1}{P_{eq}} = \frac{1}{P_1} + \frac{1}{P_2}$ and for parallel combination, $P_{eq} = P_1 + P_2$.

18. *(c)* Let R_1 and R_2 be the resistances of the coils, V be the supply voltage, H be the heat required to boil the water.

For first coil, $H = \frac{V^2 t_1}{R_1}$ ...(i)

For second coil, $H = \frac{V^2 t_2}{R_2}$ ...(ii)

Equating Eqs. (i) and (ii), we get

$$\frac{t_1}{R_1} = \frac{t_2}{R_2}$$

i.e. $\frac{R_2}{R_1} = \frac{t_2}{t_1} = \frac{40}{10} = 4 \quad \left[\begin{array}{l} t_1 = 10 \text{ min} \\ t_2 = 40 \text{ min} \end{array}\right]$

$\Rightarrow \quad R_2 = 4R_1$ ...(iii)

When the two heating coils are in parallel, equivalent resistance is given by

$$R = \frac{R_1 R_2}{R_1 + R_2} = \frac{R_1 \times 4R_1}{R_1 + 4R_1} = \frac{4R_1}{5}$$

and $H = \frac{V^2 t}{R}$ ...(iv)

Comparing Eqs. (i) and (iv), we get

$$\frac{V^2 t_1}{R_1} = \frac{V^2 t}{R}$$

$\Rightarrow \quad t = \frac{R}{R_1} \times t_1 \qquad [t_1 = 10 \text{ min}]$

$$\therefore \quad t = \frac{4}{5} \times 10 = 8 \text{ min}$$

19. *(a)* Power of electric bulb, $P = \frac{V^2}{R}$

So, resistance of electric bulb, $R = \frac{V^2}{P}$

Given, $P_1 = 25$ W, $P_2 = 100$ W

$V_1 = V_2 = 220$ V

Therefore, for same potential difference V,

$$R \propto \frac{1}{P}$$

Thus, we observe that for minimum power, resistance will be maximum and *vice-versa*. Hence, resistance of 25 W bulb is maximum and 100 W bulb is minimum.

20. *(c)* Energy loss in conductor, $Q = i^2 Rt$

where, i = current flowing through it

R = resistance of conductor

t = time for which current is passed

Heat developed = $ms\,\Delta\theta$

$$\therefore \quad ms\,\Delta\theta = i^2 Rt$$

Since m, s, R, t remains constant.

So, $\Delta\theta \propto i^2$

So, for two different cases

$$\frac{\Delta\theta_2}{\Delta\theta_1} = \frac{i_2^2}{i_1^2}$$

$$\text{or} \quad \Delta\theta_2 = \left(\frac{i_2}{i_1}\right)^2 \Delta\theta_1 \quad \text{... (i)}$$

Given, $i_2 = 2i_1$, $\Delta\theta_1 = 5°C$

So, from Eq. (i),

$$\therefore \quad \Delta\theta_2 = \left(\frac{2i_1}{i_1}\right)^2 \times 5$$

$$= 4 \times 5 = 20°\ C$$

21. *(d)* Power, $= Vi$

or $$P = Vi = \frac{V^2}{R} \qquad (\because V = iR)$$

When resistors are in series, then

$$R_1 = R + R + R = 3R$$

$\therefore$ Power dissipated,

$$P_1 = \frac{V^2}{R_1} = \frac{V^2}{3R} \qquad \ldots(i)$$

When resistors are in parallel, then

$$\frac{1}{R_2} = \frac{1}{R} + \frac{1}{R} + \frac{1}{R} = \frac{3}{R}$$

$$\Rightarrow \quad R_2 = \frac{R}{3}$$

$$\therefore \quad P_2 = \frac{V^2}{R_2} = \frac{V^2}{R/3} = \frac{3V^2}{R} \qquad \ldots(ii)$$

By taking ratio of Eqs. (i) and (ii)

$$\frac{P_2}{P_1} = \frac{3V^2}{R} \times \frac{3R}{V^2} = 9$$

$$P_2 = 9P_1$$

$$= 9 \times 10 = 90\ W$$

22. *(d)* Power consumed, $P = \frac{V^2}{R}$

and $$P' = \frac{V'^2}{R}$$

(As resistance is same for both the cases)

Given, $V = 200$ V

$V' = 160$ V, $P = 100$ W

Comparing two different cases of voltage supplied.

So, $$\frac{P'}{P} = \left(\frac{V'}{V}\right)^2 = \left(\frac{160}{200}\right)^2 = (0.8)^2$$

or $$P' = (0.8)^2\ P$$

$$= 0.64 \times 100 = 64\ W$$

23. *(d)* When heating coil is cut into two equal parts and these parts are joined in parallel, then the resistance of the coil is reduced to $\frac{1}{4}$ of the previous value. As $\left(H \propto \frac{1}{R}\right)$, for constant voltage so, energy liberated per second becomes 4 times, i.e.

$$4 \times 100 = 400\ J.$$

24. *(d)* The energy stored in the capacitor $= \frac{1}{2}CV^2$.

This energy will be converted into heat in the resistor.

$$\therefore \quad H = \frac{1}{2}CV^2$$

where, C = capacitance of capcitor

V = voltage across the plate of capacitor

$$\Rightarrow \quad H = \frac{1}{2} \times 4 \times 10^{-6} \times (400)^2$$

$$= 0.32\ J$$

25. *(b)* As the voltage is same for both 40 and 39 bulbs combination, therefore, heat produced is given by $H = \frac{V^2 t}{R}$ and $H \propto \frac{1}{R}$. As equivalent resistance decreases, the combination of 39 bulbs will glow more.

26. *(b)*

key idea

To find out resistance of the conductor, you should use following formula :

$$R = \frac{H}{i^2 t}$$

Amount of heat produced in a conductor is equal to work done in carrying a charge q from one end of conductor to other end of conductor having potential difference V.

$$\therefore \quad H = W = Vq = Vit = i^2 Rt$$

[as $V = IR$]

$$\therefore \quad H = i^2 Rt\ J \Rightarrow R = \frac{H}{(i^2 t)}$$

Given, $H = 80$ J, $i = 2$ A, $t = 10$ s,

So, $$R = \frac{80}{(2)^2 \times 10} = 2\ \Omega$$

Topic 6

01. *(a)* Given combination of capacitors represent Wheatstone bridge, thus central capacitor can be removed.

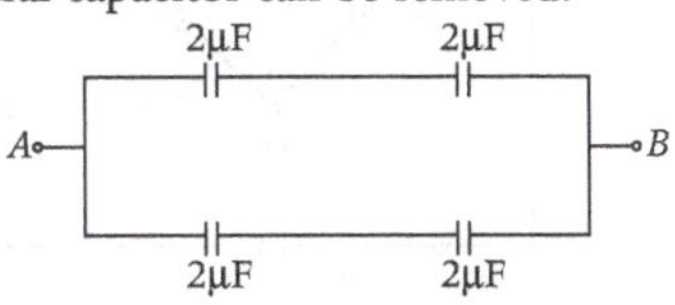

Capacitance of each branch,

$$C = \frac{2}{2} = 1\mu F$$

Capacitance between A and B,

$$C_{net} = 1 + 1 = 2\mu F$$

02. *(a)* For a diode to be active, it must be connected in forward biased. In option (b) and (d) the diode is reverse biased. Hence, option (b) and (d) can not achieve bridge balance condition.

For option (a), a balance bridge condition is,

$$\frac{10}{15} = \frac{10}{5 + r}$$

Here, r is the resistance of diode.

In this case if $r = 10\Omega$, then bridge can be balanced.

For option (c), $\frac{10}{15} = \frac{10}{5 || r}$

In this case the resistane of 5Ω branch can only decrease. This circuit will not be able to achieve balance bridge condition.

03. *(a)* For the most precise measurement of unknown resistance X, the resistances P and Q should be approximately equal and should be small so that it could decrease error in experiment.

04. *(a)* According to the question, the metre bridge is shown below,

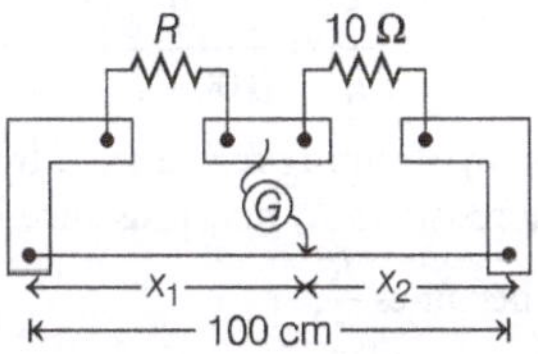

Given, $\frac{x_1}{x_2} = \frac{3}{2}$

At balance condition in metre bridge,

$$\frac{R}{10} = \frac{x_1}{x_2}$$

$$\Rightarrow \quad R = \frac{x_1}{x_2} \times 10 = \frac{3}{2} \times 10 = 15\ \Omega$$

Now, length of given wire whose resistance $15\ \Omega$ is 1.5 m.

Therefore, length of $1\ \Omega$ resistance wire is

$$= \frac{1.5}{15} = \frac{1}{10}$$

$$= 0.1 = 1 \times 10^{-1}\ m$$

Hence, correct option is (a).

05. *(d)* For balanced position in a meter bridge,

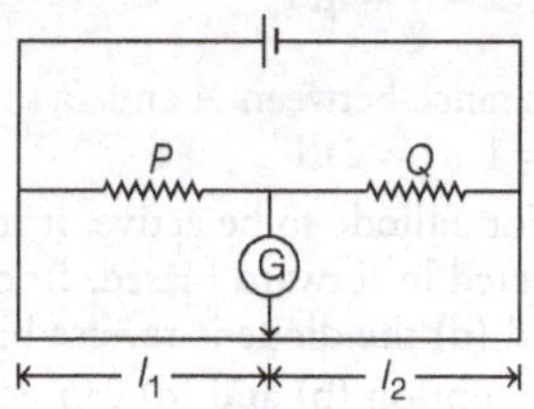

$$\frac{P}{Q}=\frac{l_1}{l_2}$$

Now, if position of G and cell is interchanged,

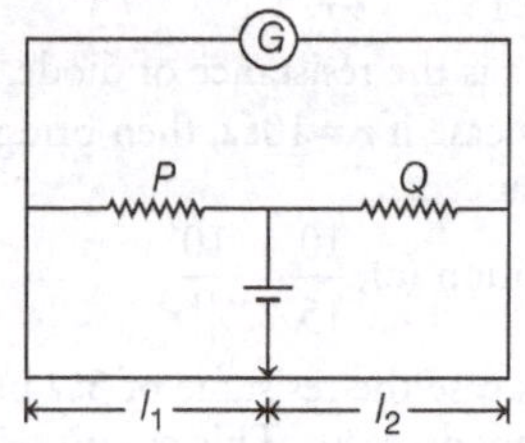

The balance condition still remains the same, if the jockey points at the same point as given in the initial condition, for which there is no deflection in the galvanometer or no current will be drawn from the cell. Thus, the bridge will work as usual and balance condition is same, $P/Q=l_1/l_2$

06. *(b)* For first case, balanced condition of meter bridge will be

$$\frac{5}{l_1}=\frac{R}{(100-l_1)} \quad \text{...(i)}$$

Now, by shunting resistance R by an equal resistance$R$, new resistance in that arm becomes $\frac{R}{2}$.

So, new balanced condition will be

$$\frac{5}{1.6\,l_1}=\frac{R/2}{(100-1.6\,l_1)} \quad \text{...(ii)}$$

From Eqs. (i) and (ii),

$$\frac{1.6}{1}=\frac{(100-1.6\,l_1)}{100-l_1}\times 2$$

$$\Rightarrow \quad 160-1.6l_1=200-3.2\,l_1$$

$$1.6\,l_1=40$$

$$l_1=\frac{40}{1.6}=25\text{ m}$$

$$\Rightarrow \text{From Eq. (i), } \frac{5}{25}=\frac{R}{75}$$

$$\Rightarrow \quad R=15\ \Omega$$

07. *(b)* Effective resistance,

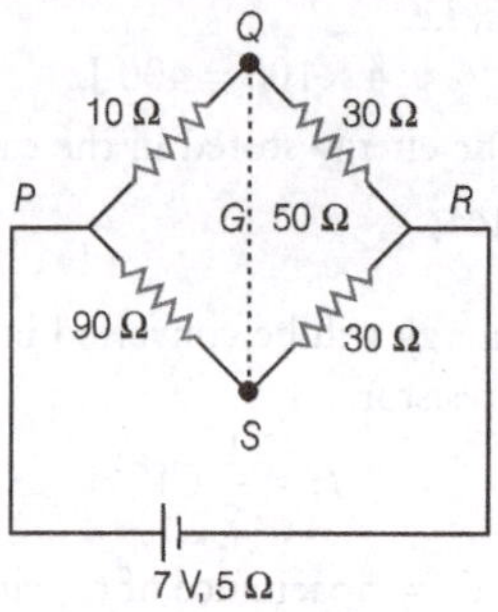

$$\frac{1}{R_{\text{eff}}}=\frac{1}{R_1}+\frac{1}{R_2} \quad \text{...(i)}$$

then, $R_1=10+30=40\ \Omega$

Now, $R_2=90+30=120\ \Omega$

By Eq. (i),

$$\frac{1}{R_{\text{eff}}}=\frac{1}{40}+\frac{1}{120}$$

$$R_{\text{eff}}=\frac{40\times 120}{120+40}=\frac{4800}{160}=30\ \Omega$$

In the balancing condition,

$$\therefore \text{ Current, } I=\frac{7}{(30+5)}=\frac{7}{35}=0.2\text{ A}$$

$$\left[\because I=\frac{E}{R+r}\right]$$

08. *(d)* Potential across PM,

$$V_{PM}=4\times 1=4\text{ V}$$

Now, equivalent resistance across PN

$$\frac{1}{R_{\text{eq}}}=\frac{1}{0.5}+\frac{1}{0.5}=\frac{0.5}{2}=0.25\ \Omega$$

Effective resistance between P and M

$$R_{PM}=0.25+1=1.25\ \Omega$$

For balancing condition,

$$\frac{V_{MN}}{V_{PM}}=\frac{R_{MN}}{R_{PM}}$$

$$V_{MN}=\frac{V_{PM}\times R_{MN}}{R_{PM}}=\frac{1}{1.25}\times 4$$

$$=3.2\text{ V}$$

09. *(b)*

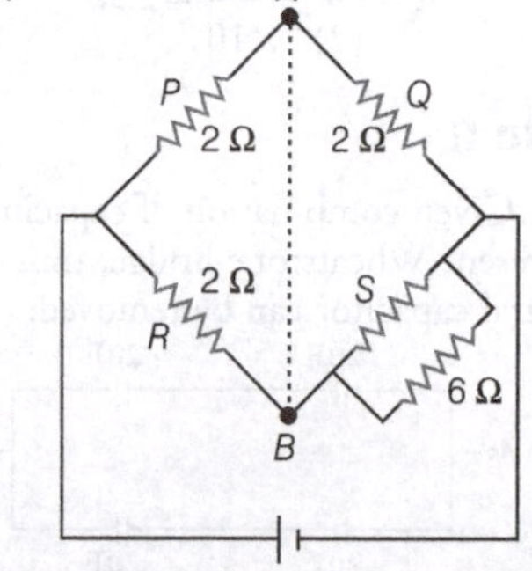

As resistances S and $6\ \Omega$ are in parallel, their effective resistance is

$$\frac{6S}{6+S}\ \Omega$$

For balancing condition,

$$\frac{P}{Q}=\frac{R}{\left(\frac{6S}{6+S}\right)} \text{ or } \frac{2}{2}=\frac{2(6+S)}{6S}$$

or $\quad 3S=6+S$ or $S=3\ \Omega$

10. *(d)* Since given circuit is in the form of Wheatstone bridge, therefore,

$$\frac{1}{R_{\text{eq}}}=\frac{1}{(4+2)}+\frac{1}{(6+3)}$$

$$R_{\text{eq}}=18/5\ \Omega,\ V=iR_{\text{eq}}$$

$$\Rightarrow \quad i=\frac{V}{R_{\text{eq}}}=\frac{5V}{18}$$

11. *(c)* The given circuit can be redrawn as shown.

From circuit, $\frac{FC}{CE}=\frac{FD}{DE}=1$

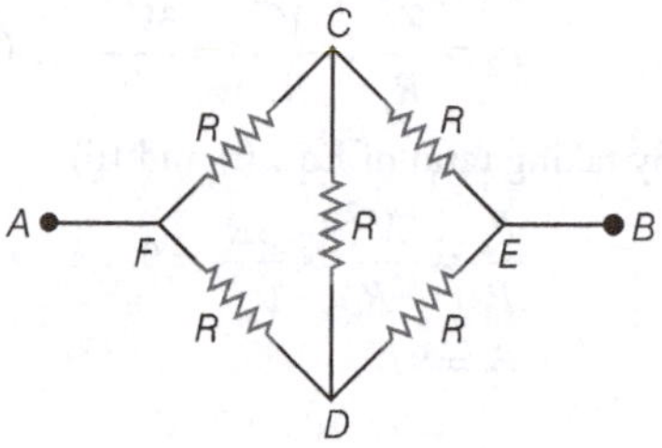

Thus, it is a balanced Wheatstone bridge, so, resistance in arm CD is ineffective and so no current flows in this arm.

Net resistance of the circuit is

$$\frac{1}{R'}=\frac{1}{(R+R)}+\frac{1}{(R+R)}$$

$$=\frac{1}{2R}+\frac{1}{2R}$$

$$=\frac{2}{2R}=\frac{1}{R}$$

$$\therefore \quad R'=R$$

So, net current drawn from the battery is $i'=\frac{V}{R'}=\frac{V}{R}$

As from symmetry, upper circuit $AFCEB$ is half of the whole circuit and is equal to $AFDEB$.

So, in both the halves half of the total current will flow. Hence, in $AFCEB$, the current flowing is

$$i=\frac{i'}{2}=\frac{V}{2R}$$

12. (a) $\dfrac{R_{AB}}{R_{BC}} = \dfrac{R_{AD}}{R_{DC}}$

As bridge is in balanced condition, no current will flow through BD.

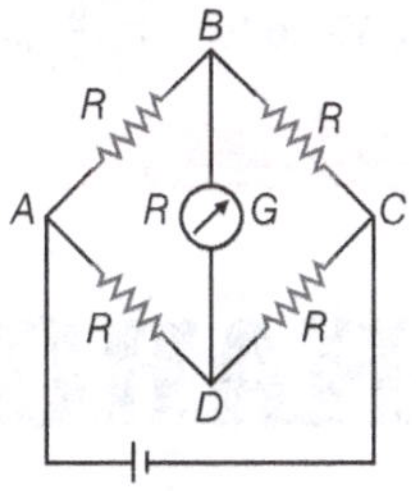

$$R_1 = R_{AB} + R_{BC} = R + R = 2R$$
$$R_2 = R_{AD} + R_{CD} = R + R = 2R$$

R_1 and R_2 are in parallel combination. Hence, equivalent resistance between A and C will be

$$\therefore\ R_{eq} = \frac{R_1 R_2}{R_1 + R_2} = \frac{4R^2}{4R} = R$$

13. (a) The given circuit can be shown as,

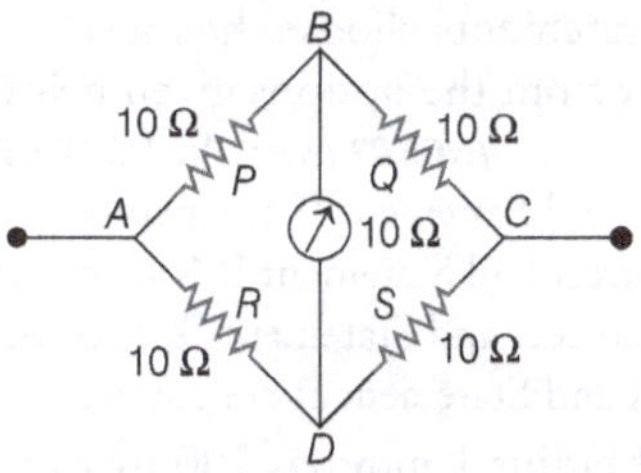

From figure, $\dfrac{P}{Q} = \dfrac{10}{10} = 1$

$\Rightarrow \qquad \dfrac{R}{S} = \dfrac{10}{10} = 1$

$\therefore \qquad \dfrac{P}{Q} = \dfrac{R}{S}$

Hence, Wheatstone bridge is balanced. Therefore, the galvanometer will be ineffective.

The above Wheatstone bridge can be redrawn as

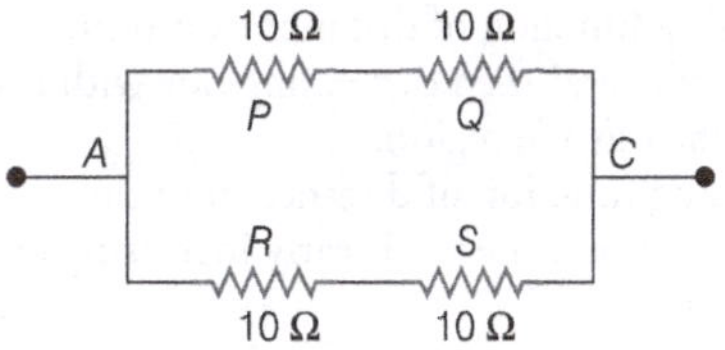

Resistances P and Q are in series, so
$$R' = 10 + 10 = 20\ \Omega$$
Resistances R and S are in series, so
$$R'' = 10 + 10 = 20\ \Omega$$
Now, R' and R'' are in parallel hence, net resistance of the circuit
$$= \frac{R' \times R''}{R' + R''}$$
$$= \frac{20 \times 20}{20 + 20} = 10\ \Omega$$

14. (d) The bridge circuit can be shown as

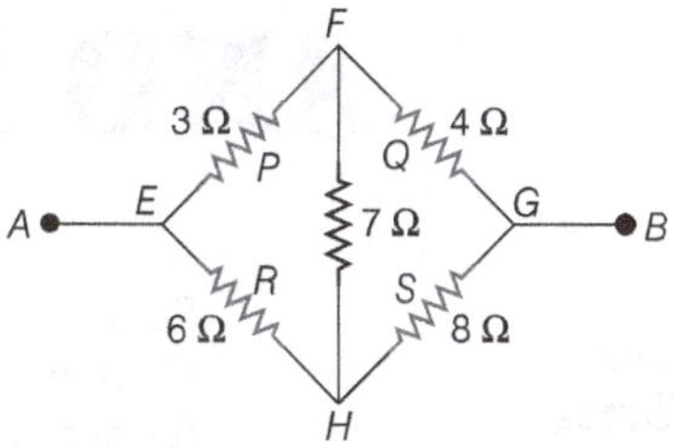

The balanced condition of bridge circuit is given by

$$\frac{P}{Q} = \frac{3}{4},\ \frac{R}{S} = \frac{6}{8} = \frac{3}{4}$$
$$\Rightarrow \qquad \frac{P}{Q} = \frac{R}{S}$$

Thus, it is balanced Wheatstone bridge, so potential at F is equal to potential at H. Therefore, no current will flow through 7 Ω resistance. So, circuit can be redrawn as

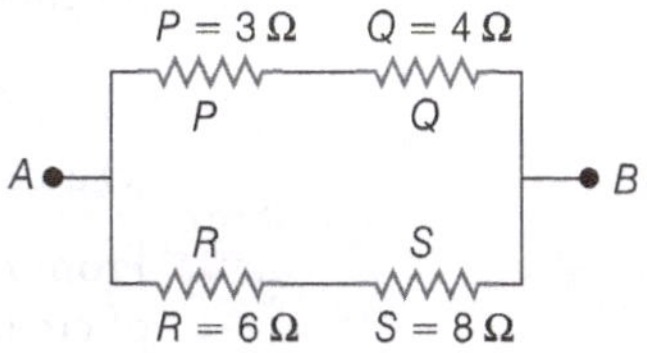

P and Q are in series, so their equivalent resistance = 3 + 4 = 7 Ω

R and S are also in series, so their equivalent resistance = 6 + 8 = 14 Ω

Now, 7 Ω and 14 Ω resistances are in parallel, so

$$R_{AB} = \frac{7 \times 14}{7 + 14}$$
$$= \frac{7 \times 14}{21} = \frac{14}{3}\ \Omega$$

- **Concept Enhancer**

Normally, in Wheatstone bridge, in middle arm galvanometer must be connected. In Wheatstone bridge, cell and galvanometer arms are interchangeable.

In both the cases, condition of balanced bridge is $\dfrac{P}{Q} = \dfrac{R}{S}$

15. (a) Let unknown resistance be X.

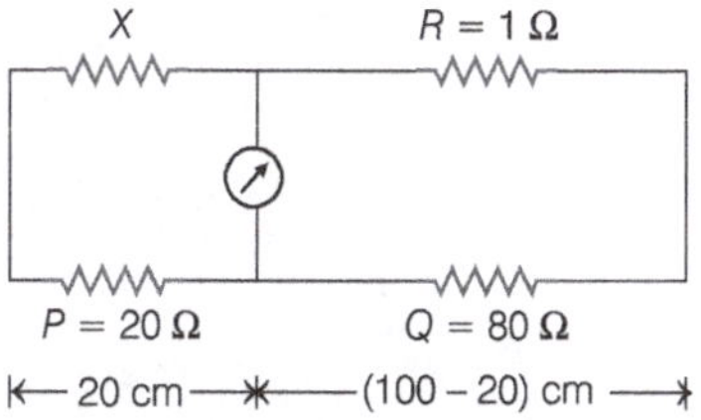

Then condition of balanced Wheatstone bridge gives, $\dfrac{X}{R} = \dfrac{20}{80}$

where, X = unknown resistance

R = known resistance

Hence, unknown resistance is

$$X = \frac{20}{80} \times R = \frac{1}{4} \times 1 \quad (\because R = 1\ \Omega)$$
$$= 0.25\ \Omega$$

16. (a) According to maximum power transfer theorem, the power output across load due to a cell or battery is maximum, if the load resistance is equal to the internal resistance of cell or battery. Hence, value of R will be 0.5 Ω.

17. (b) To receive maximum current, the two batteries should be connected in series.

Given, $R = 1\ \Omega + 1\ \Omega = 2\ \Omega$.

Hence, power developed across the resistance R with the batteries in series is

$$P = i^2 R = \left(\frac{2E}{R + 2r}\right)^2 R \qquad \left[I = \frac{E}{R_{eq}}\right]$$
$$= \left(\frac{2 \times 2}{2 + 2}\right) \times 2 = 2\ \text{W} \qquad [\because r = 1\ \Omega]$$

Note In case of batteries connected in series, equivalent emf is given by

$$E_{eq} = E_1 + E_2$$

In NEET 2024, 2 questions were visible from this chapter. In past 5 years, 7 questions from topic-1, 3 questions from topic-2 and 1 question from topic-3 were asked.
For detailed analysis scan QR code

MOVING CHARGES AND MAGNETISM

Topic 1 Biot Savart's Law and Ampere's Circuital Law

01 A tightly wound 100 turns coil of radius 10 cm carries a current of 7 A. The magnitude of the magnetic field at the centre of the coil is (Take, permeability of free space as $4\pi \times 10^{-7}$ SI units) ***[NCERT (New) Pg. 116, NEET 2024]***

(a) 44 mT (b) 4.4 T (c) 4.4 mT (d) 44 T

02 A very long conducting wire is bent in a semi-circular shape from A to B as shown in figure. The magnetic field at point P for steady current configuration is given by ***[NEET 2023]***

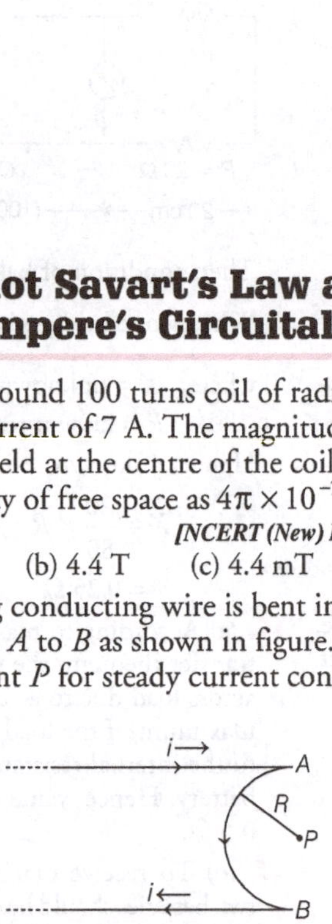

(a) $\frac{\mu_0 i}{4R}$ pointed away from the page

(b) $\frac{\mu_0 i}{4R}\left[1-\frac{2}{\pi}\right]$ pointed away from page

(c) $\frac{\mu_0 i}{4R}\left[1-\frac{2}{\pi}\right]$ pointed into the page

(d) $\frac{\mu_0 i}{4R}$ pointed into the page

03 Given below are two statements.

Statement I Biot-Savart's law gives us the expression for the magnetic field strength of an infinitesimal current element Idl of a current carrying conductor only.

Statement II Biot-Savart's law is analogous to Coulomb's inverse square law of charge q, with the former being related to the field produced by a scalar source, Idl while the latter being produced by a vector source, q.

In light of above statements choose the most appropriate answer from the options given below ***[NCERT (New) Pg. 113, NEET 2022]***

(a) Both Statement I and Statement II are incorrect.
(b) Statement I is correct and Statement II is incorrect.
(c) Statement I is incorrect and Statement II is correct.
(d) Both Statement I and Statement II are correct.

04 A long solenoid of radius 1 mm has 100 turns per mm. If 1A current flows in the solenoid, the magnetic field strength at the centre of the solenoid is ***[NCERT (New) Pg. 122, NEET 2022]***

(a) 12.56×10^{-2} T (b) 12.56×10^{-4} T
(c) 6.28×10^{-4} T (d) 6.28×10^{-2} T

05 From Ampere's circuital law for a long straight wire of circular cross-section carrying a steady current, the variation of magnetic field in the inside and outside region of the wire is ***[NCERT (New) Pg. 118, NEET 2022]***

(a) a linearly increasing function of distance upto the boundary of the wire and then linearly decreasing for the outside region.
(b) a linearly increasing function of distance r upto the boundary of the wire and then decreasing one with $1/r$ dependence for the outside region.
(c) a linearly decreasing function of distance upto the boundary of the wire and then a linearly increasing one for the outside region.
(d) uniform and remains constant for both the regions.

06 A thick current carrying cable of radius R carries current I uniformly distributed across its cross-section. The variation of magnetic field B due to the cable with the distance r from the axis of the cable is represented by *[NCERT (New) Pg. 116, NEET 2021]*

(a) 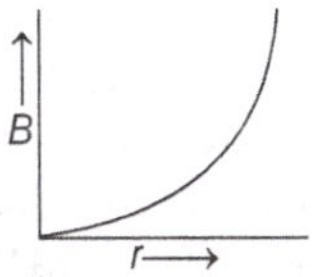

(b) 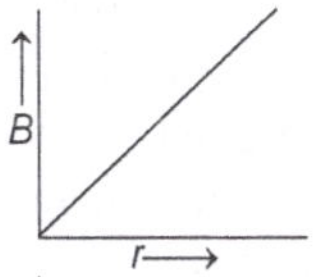

(c) 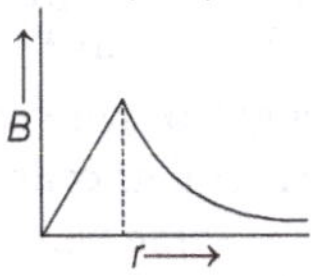

(d) 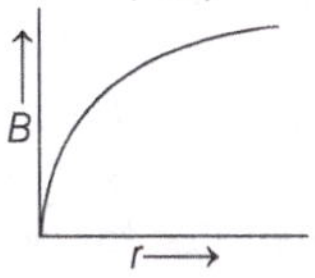

07 A long solenoid of 50 cm length having 100 turns carries a current of 2.5 A. The magnetic field at the centre of solenoid is
(Take, $\mu_0 = 4\pi \times 10^{-7}$ T m A^{-1}) *[NEET (Sep.) 2020]*

(a) 3.14×10^{-4} T
(b) 6.28×10^{-5} T
(c) 3.14×10^{-5} T
(d) 6.28×10^{-4} T

08 Two toroids 1 and 2 have total number of turns 200 and 100, respectively with average radii 40 cm and 20 cm, respectively. If they carry same current I, the ratio of the magnetic fields along the two loops is *[NCERT (New) Pg. 152, NEET (Odisha) 2019]*

(a) 1 : 1
(b) 4 : 1
(c) 2 : 1
(d) 1 : 2

09 A straight conductor carrying current i splits into two parts as shown in the figure. The radius of the circular loop is R. The total magnetic field at the centre P of the loop is *[NEET (Odisha) 2019]*

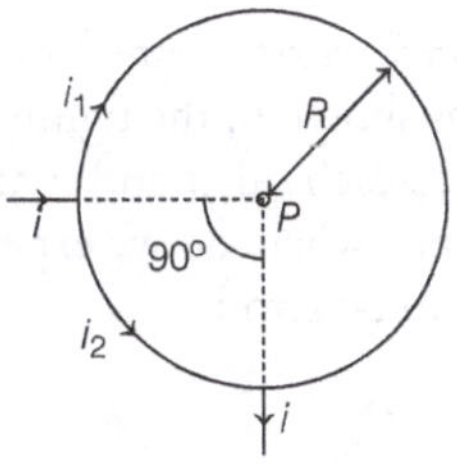

(a) zero
(b) $3\mu_0 i/32R$, outward
(c) $3\mu_0 i/32R$, inward
(d) $\frac{\mu_0 i}{2R}$, inward

10 A cylindrical conductor of radius R is carrying a constant current. The plot of the magnitude of the magnetic field B with the distance d from the centre of the conductor, is correctly represented by the figure *[NCERT (New) Pg. 116, NEET NEET (National) 2019]*

(a) 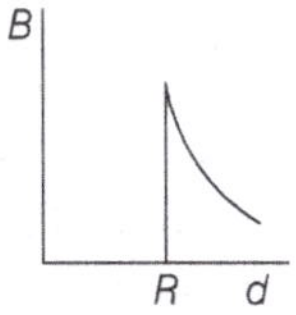

(b) 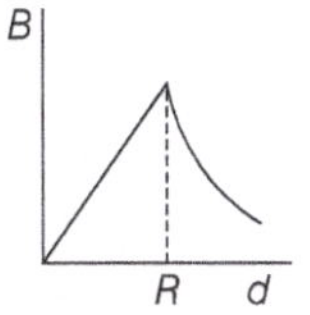

(c) 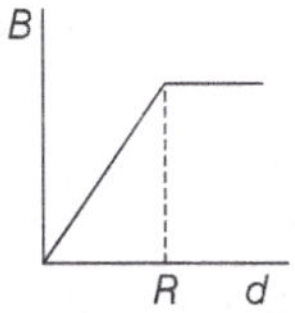

(d) 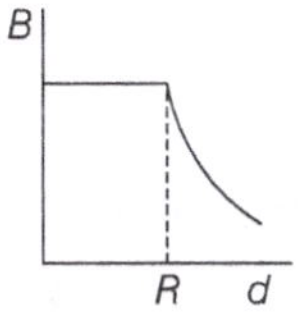

11 A long straight wire of radius a carries a steady current I. The current is uniformly distributed over its cross-section. The ratio of the magnetic fields B and B' at radial distances $a/2$ and $2a$ respectively, from the axis of the wire is *[NEET 2016]*

(a) $\frac{1}{2}$
(b) 1
(c) 4
(d) $\frac{1}{4}$

12 A long wire carrying a steady current is bent into a circular loop of one turn. The magnetic field at the centre of the loop is B. It is then bent into a circular coil of n turns. The magnetic field at the centre of this coil of n turns will be *[NEET 2016]*

(a) nB
(b) $n^2 B$
(c) $2nB$
(d) $2n^2 B$

13 A wire carrying current I has the shape as shown in adjoining figure. Linear parts of the wire are very long and parallel to X-axis while semicircular portion of radius R is lying in YZ-plane. Magnetic field at point O is *[NCERT (New) Pg. 116, AIPMT 2015]*

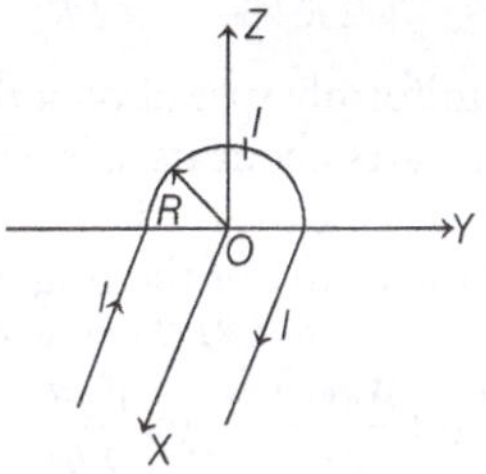

(a) $\mathbf{B} = \frac{\mu_0}{4\pi}\frac{I}{R}(\pi\hat{i} + 2\hat{k})$
(b) $\mathbf{B} = -\frac{\mu_0}{4\pi}\frac{I}{R}(\pi\hat{i} - 2\hat{k})$
(c) $\mathbf{B} = -\frac{\mu_0}{4\pi}\frac{I}{R}(\pi\hat{i} + 2\hat{k})$
(d) $\mathbf{B} = \frac{\mu_0}{4\pi}\frac{I}{R}(\pi\hat{i} - 2\hat{k})$

14 An electron moving in a circular orbit of radius r makes n rotations per second. The magnetic field produced at the centre has magnitude *[AIPMT 2015]*

(a) $\frac{\mu_0 ne}{2\pi r}$
(b) zero
(c) $\frac{\mu_0 n^2 e}{r}$
(d) $\frac{\mu_0 ne}{2r}$

15 Two identical long conducting wires AOB and COD are placed at right angle to each other, such that one is above the other and O is their common point. The wires carry I_1 and I_2 currents, respectively. Point P is lying at distance d from O along a direction perpendicular to the plane containing the wires. The magnetic field at the point P will be **[AIPMT 2014]**

(a) $\frac{\mu_0}{2\pi d}\left(\frac{I_1}{I_2}\right)$ (b) $\frac{\mu_0}{2\pi d}(I_1 + I_2)$

(c) $\frac{\mu_0}{2\pi d}(I_1^2 - I_2^2)$ (d) $\frac{\mu_0}{2\pi d}(I_1^2 + I_2^2)^{1/2}$

16 When a proton is released from rest in a room, it starts with an initial acceleration a_0 towards West. When it is projected towards North with a speed v_0 it moves with an initial acceleration $3a_0$ towards West. The electric and magnetic fields in the room are **[NCERT (Old) Pg. 162, NEET 2013]**

(a) $\frac{ma_0}{e}$ West, $\frac{2ma_0}{ev_0}$ up (b) $\frac{ma_0}{e}$ West, $\frac{2ma_0}{ev_0}$ down

(c) $\frac{ma_0}{e}$ East, $\frac{3ma_0}{ev_0}$ up (d) $\frac{ma_0}{e}$ East, $\frac{3ma_0}{ev_0}$ down

17 Two similar coils of radius R are lying concentrically with their planes at right angles to each other. The currents flowing in them are I and $2I$, respectively. The resultant magnetic field induction at the centre will be **[AIPMT 2012]**

(a) $\frac{\sqrt{5}\mu_0 I}{2R}$ (b) $\frac{3\mu_0 I}{2R}$ (c) $\frac{\mu_0 I}{2R}$ (d) $\frac{\mu_0 I}{R}$

18 Charge q is uniformly spread on a thin ring of radius R. The ring rotates about its axis with a uniform frequency f Hz. The magnitude of magnetic induction at the center of the ring is **[NCERT (New) Pg. 114, AIPMT 2011, 2010]**

(a) $\frac{\mu_0 qf}{2\pi R}$ (b) $\frac{\mu_0 qf}{2R}$ (c) $\frac{\mu_0 q}{2fR}$ (d) $\frac{\mu_0 q}{2\pi fR}$

19 A current loop consists of two identical semicircular parts each of radius R, one lying in the XY-plane and the other in XZ-plane. If the current in the loop is i. The resultant magnetic field due to the two semicircular parts at their common centre is **[AIPMT 2010]**

(a) $\frac{\mu_0 i}{2\sqrt{2}R}$ (b) $\frac{\mu_0 i}{2R}$ (c) $\frac{\mu_0 i}{4R}$ (d) $\frac{\mu_0 i}{\sqrt{2}R}$

20 Two wires are held perpendicular to the plane of paper and are 5 m apart. They carry currents of 2.5 A and 5 A in same direction. Then, the magnetic field strength B at a point mid-way between the wires will be **[AIPMT 2008]**

(a) $\frac{\mu_0}{4\pi}$ T (b) $\frac{\mu_0}{2\pi}$ T (c) $\frac{3\mu_0}{2\pi}$ T (d) $\frac{3\mu_0}{4\pi}$ T

21 Two circular coils 1 and 2 are made from the same wire but the radius of the 1st coil is twice that of the 2nd coil. What is the ratio of potential difference applied across them so that the magnetic field at their centres is the same ? **[AIPMT 2006]**

(a) 3 (b) 4 (c) 6 (d) 2

22 A long solenoid carrying a current produces a magnetic field B along its axis. If the current is doubled and the number of turns per cm is halved, the new value of the magnetic field is **[AIPMT 2003]**

(a) $2B$ (b) $4B$ (c) $B/2$ (d) B

23 The magnetic field of a given length of wire carrying a current for a single turn circular coil at centre is B, then its value for two turns for the same wire when same current passing through it is **[AIPMT 2002]**

(a) $B/4$ (b) $B/2$ (c) $2B$ (d) $4B$

24 Magnetic field due to 0.1A current flowing through a circular coil of radius 0.1m and 1000 turns at the centre of the coil is **[AIPMT 1999]**

(a) 0.2 T (b) 2×10^{-4} T

(c) 6.28×10^{-4} T (d) 9.8×10^{-4} T

25 If a long hollow copper pipe carries a current, then magnetic field is produced **[AIPMT 1999]**

(a) inside the pipe only
(b) outside the pipe only
(c) both inside and outside the pipe
(d) no where

26 A coil of one turn is made of a wire of certain length and then from the same length a coil of two turns is made. If the same current is passed in both the cases, then the ratio of the magnetic induction at their centres will be **[AIPMT 1998]**

(a) 2 : 1 (b) 1 : 4 (c) 4 : 1 (d) 1 : 2

27 Two equal electric currents are flowing perpendicular to each other as shown in the figure. AB and CD are perpendicular to each other and symmetrically placed w.r.t the currents, where do we expect the resultant magnetic field to be zero ? **[AIPMT 1996]**

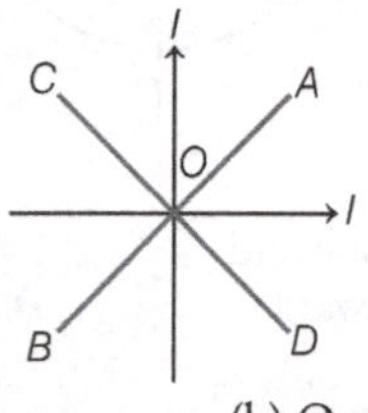

(a) On AB (b) On CD
(c) On both AB and CD (d) On both OD and BO

28 The magnetic field $d\mathbf{B}$ due to a small element at a distance r and carrying current i is **[AIPMT 1996]**

(a) $d\mathbf{B} = \frac{\mu_0}{4\pi} i\left(\frac{d\mathbf{l} \times \mathbf{r}}{r}\right)$ (b) $d\mathbf{B} = \frac{\mu_0}{4\pi} i^2\left(\frac{d\mathbf{l} \times \mathbf{r}}{r^2}\right)$

(c) $d\mathbf{B} = \frac{\mu_0}{4\pi} i^2\left(\frac{d\mathbf{l} \times \mathbf{r}}{r}\right)$ (d) $d\mathbf{B} = \frac{\mu_0}{4\pi} i\left(\frac{d\mathbf{l} \times \mathbf{r}}{r^3}\right)$

29 At what distance from a long straight wire carrying a current of 12 A will the magnetic field be equal to 3×10^{-5} Wb / m^2 ? *[NCERT (New) Pg. 114, AIPMT 1995]*
(a) 8×10^{-2} m (b) 12×10^{-2} m
(c) 18×10^{-2} m (d) 24×10^{-2} m

30 A straight wire of diameter 0.5 mm carrying a current of 1 A is replaced by another wire of 1mm diameter carrying same current. The strength of magnetic field far away is *[NCERT (New) Pg. 114, AIPMT 1995]*
(a) twice the earlier value
(b) same as the earlier value
(c) one-half of the earlier value
(d) one-quarter of the earlier value

31 The magnetic field at a distance r from a long wire carrying current i is 0.4 T. The magnetic field at a distance $2r$ is *[AIPMT 1992]*
(a) 0.2 T (b) 0.8 T
(c) 0.1 T (d) 1.6 T

32 The magnetic induction at a point P which is at the distance of 4 cm from a long current carrying wire is 10^{-3} T. The field of induction at a distance 12 cm from the current will be *[AIPMT 1990]*
(a) 3.33×10^{-4} T (b) 1.11×10^{-4} T
(c) 3×10^{-3} T (d) 9×10^{-3} T

33 Tesla is the unit of *[AIPMT 1988]*
(a) magnetic flux (b) magnetic field
(c) magnetic induction (d) magnetic moment

Topic 2 Magnetic Force on Charged Particle in Magnetic Field and Motion in Magnetic Field

01 A sheet is placed on a horizontal surface in front of a strong magnetic pole. A force is needed to *[NCERT (New) Pg. 122, NEET 2024]*
A. hold the sheet there if it is magnetic.
B. hold the sheet there if it is non-magnetic.
C. move the sheet away from the pole with uniform velocity if it is conducting.
D. move the sheet away from the pole with uniform velocity if it is both, non-conducting and non-polar.
Choose the correct statement(s) from the options given below
(a) B and D only (b) A and C only
(c) A, C and D only (d) C only

02 In the product $\mathbf{F} = q(\mathbf{v}\times\mathbf{B}) = q\mathbf{v}\times(B\hat{i} + B\hat{j} + B_0\hat{k})$
For $q = 1$ C and $\mathbf{v} = 2\hat{i}+4\hat{j}+6\hat{k}$
and $\mathbf{F} = 4\hat{i}-20\hat{j}+12\hat{k}$
What will be the complete expression for **B** ? *[NCERT (New) Pg. 109, NEET 2021]*
(a) $-8\hat{i}-8\hat{j}-6\hat{k}$ (b) $-6\hat{i}-6\hat{j}-8\hat{k}$
(c) $8\hat{i}+8\hat{j}-6\hat{k}$ (d) $6\hat{i}+6\hat{j}-8\hat{k}$

03 An infinitely long straight conductor carries a current of 5 A as shown. An electron is moving with a speed of 10^5 m/s parallel to the conductor. The perpendicular distance between the electron and the conductor is 20 cm at an instant. Calculate the magnitude of the force experienced by the electron at that instant *[NCERT (New) Pg. 114, NEET 2021]*

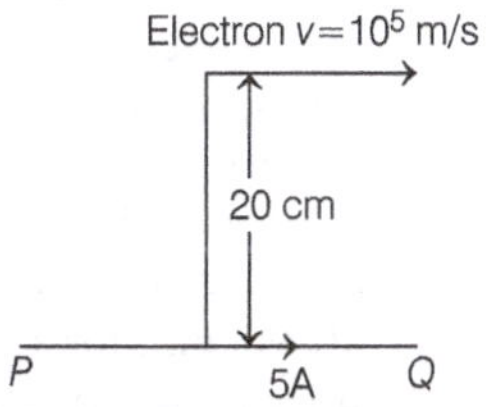

(a) 8×10^{-20} N (b) 4×10^{-20} N
(c) $8\pi\times10^{-20}$ N (d) $4\pi\times10^{-20}$ N

04 Ionised hydrogen atoms and α -particles with same momenta enters perpendicular to a constant magnetic field, B. The ratio of their radii of their paths $r_H : r_\alpha$ will be *[NEET (National) 2019]*
(a) 1 : 2 (b) 4 : 1
(c) 1 : 4 (d) 2 : 1

05 An electron is moving in a circular path under the influence of a transverse magnetic field of 3.57×10^{-2} T. If the value of e/m is 1.76×10^{11} C/kg, the frequency of revolution of the electron is *[NEET 2016]*
(a) 1 GHz (b) 100 MHz
(c) 62.8 MHz (d) 6.28 MHz

06 A proton and an alpha particle both enter a region of uniform magnetic field B, moving at right angles to field B. If the radius of circular orbits for both the particles is equal and the kinetic energy acquired by proton is 1 MeV the energy acquired by the alpha particle will be *[AIPMT 2015]*
(a) 0.5 MeV (b) 1.5 MeV
(c) 1 MeV (d) 4 MeVs

07 A long straight wire carries a certain current and produces a magnetic field of 2×10^{-4} Wb/m^2 at a perpendicular distance of 5 cm from the wire. An electron situated at 5 cm from the wire moves with a velocity 10^7 m/s towards the wire along perpendicular to it. The force experienced by the electron will be *[NCERT (New) Pg. 109, NEET 2013]*
(charge on electron = 1.6×10^{-19} C)
(a) zero (b) 3.2 N
(c) 3.2×10^{-16} N (d) 1.6×10^{-16} N

08 A proton carrying 1 MeV kinetic energy is moving in a circular path of radius R in uniform magnetic field. What should be the energy of an α-particle to describe a circle of same radius in the same field ? *[AIPMT 2012]*
(a) 2 MeV (b) 1 MeV
(c) 0.5 MeV (d) 4 MeV

09 A uniform electric field and a uniform magnetic field are acting along the same direction in a certain region. If an electron is projected in the region such that its velocity is pointed along the direction of fields, then the electron *[NCERT (Old) Pg. 140, AIPMT 2011]*
(a) speed will decrease
(b) speed will increase
(c) will turn towards left of direction of motion
(d) will turn towards right of direction of motion

10 A beam of cathode rays is subjected to crossed electric E and magnetic fields B. The fields are adjusted such that the beam is not deflected. The specific charge of the cathode rays is given by *[AIPMT 2010]*
(a) $\frac{B^2}{2VE^2}$ (b) $\frac{2VB^2}{E^2}$ (c) $\frac{2VE^2}{B^2}$ (d) $\frac{E^2}{2VB^2}$

11 A particle having a mass of 10^{-2} kg carries a charge of 5×10^{-8} C. The particle is given an initial horizontal velocity of 10^5 m s^{-1} in the presence of electric field **E** and magnetic field **B**. To keep the particle moving in a horizontal direction, it is necessary that
(1) **B** should be perpendicular to the direction of velocity and **E** should be along the direction of velocity
(2) Both **B** and **E** should be along the direction of velocity
(3) Both **B** and **E** are mutually perpendicular and perpendicular to the direction of velocity.
(4) **B** should be along the direction of velocity and **E** should be perpendicular to the direction of velocity *[NCERT (Old) Pg. 140, AIPMT 2010]*

Which one of the following pairs of statements is possible ?
(a) (1) and (3) (b) (3) and (4)
(c) (2) and (3) (d) (2) and (4)

12 The magnetic force acting on a charged particle of charge $-2\,\mu$C in a magnetic field of 2T acting in y-direction, when the particle velocity is $(2\hat{i}+3\hat{j})\times10^6$ m/s is *[NCERT (New) Pg. 109, AIPMT 2009]*
(a) 4 N in z-direction (b) 8 N in y-direction
(c) 8 N in z-direction (d) 8 N in $-z$-direction

13 A particle of mass m charge q and kinetic energy T enters a transverse uniform magnetic field of induction **B**. After 3 s, the kinetic energy of the particle will be *[AIPMT 2008]*
(a) $3T$ (b) $2T$
(c) T (d) $4T$

14 A beam of electrons passes undeflected through mutually perpendicular electric and magnetic fields. If the electric field is switched OFF and the same magnetic field is maintained, the electrons move *[AIPMT 2007]*
(a) in an elliptical orbit (b) in a circular orbit
(c) along a parabolic path (d) along a straight line

15 Under the influence of a uniform magnetic field a charged particle is moving in a circle of radius R with constant speed v. The time period of the motion *[AIPMT 2007]*
(a) depends on v and not on R
(b) depends on both R and v
(c) is independent of both R and v
(d) depends on R and not on v

16 In a mass spectrometer used for measuring the masses of ions, the ions are initially accelerated by an electric potential V and then made to describe semicircular path of radius R using a magnetic field B. If V and B are kept constant, the ratio $\left(\frac{\text{charge on the ion}}{\text{mass of the ion}}\right)$ will be proportional to *[AIPMT 2007]*
(a) $1/R^2$ (b) R^2 (c) R (d) $1/R$

17 When a charged particle moving with velocity **v** is subjected to a magnetic field of induction **B**, the force on it is non-zero. This implies that *[AIPMT 2006]*
(a) angle between **v** and **B** is necessarily 90°
(b) angle between **v** and **B** can have any value other than 90°
(c) angle between **v** and **B** can have any value other than zero and 180°
(d) angle between **v** and **B** is either zero or 180°

18 An electron moves in a circular orbit with a uniform speed v. It produces a magnetic field B at the centre of the circle. The radius of the circle is proportional to *[NCERT (Old) Pg. 162, AIPMT 2005]*
(a) $\frac{B}{v}$ (b) $\frac{v}{B}$ (c) $\sqrt{\frac{v}{B}}$ (d) $\sqrt{\frac{B}{v}}$

19 A charged particle moves through a magnetic field in a direction perpendicular to it. Then, the *[AIPMT 2003]*
(a) acceleration remains unchanged
(b) velocity remains unchanged
(c) speed of the particle remains unchanged
(d) direction of the particle remains unchanged

20 A charge q moves in a region where electric field **E** and magnetic field **B** both exist, then the force on it is *[AIPMT 2002]*
(a) $q(\mathbf{v}\times\mathbf{B})$ (b) $q\,\mathbf{E}+q(\mathbf{v}\times\mathbf{B})$
(c) $q\,\mathbf{B}+q(\mathbf{B}\times\mathbf{v})$ (d) $q\,\mathbf{B}+q(\mathbf{E}\times\mathbf{v})$

21 A charged particle of charge q and mass m enters perpendicularly in a magnetic field B. Kinetic energy of the particle is E, then frequency of rotation is *[AIPMT 2001]*
(a) $\frac{qB}{m\pi}$ (b) $\frac{qB}{2\pi m}$
(c) $\frac{qBE}{2\pi m}$ (d) $\frac{qB}{2\pi E}$

22 In a certain region of space electric field **E** and magnetic field **B** are perpendicular to each other and an electron enters in region perpendicular to the direction of **B** and **E** both and moves undeflected, then velocity of electron is *[NCERT (Old) Pg. 140, AIPMT 2001]*

(a) $\frac{|\mathbf{E}|}{|\mathbf{B}|}$ (b) $\mathbf{E} \times \mathbf{B}$
(c) $\frac{|\mathbf{B}|}{|\mathbf{E}|}$ (d) $\mathbf{E} \cdot \mathbf{B}$

23 A proton moving with a velocity 3×10^5 m/s enters a magnetic field of 0.3 T at an angle of 30° with the field. The radius of curvature of its path will be (e/m for proton $= 10^8$ C/kg) *[AIPMT 2000]*

(a) 2 cm (b) 0.5 cm
(c) 0.02 cm (d) 1.25 cm

24 A positively charged particle moving due east enters a region of uniform magnetic field directed vertically upwards. The particle will *[NCERT (New) Pg. 112, AIPMT 1997]*

(a) continue to move due East
(b) move in a circular orbit with its speed unchanged
(c) move in a circular orbit with its speed increased
(d) gets deflected vertically upwards

25 A beam of electrons is moving with constant velocity in a region having simultaneous perpendicular electric and magnetic fields of strength 20 Vm^{-1} and 0.5 T, respectively at right angles to the direction of motion of the electrons. Then, the velocity of electrons must be *[AIPMT 1996]*

(a) 8 m/s (b) 20 m/s
(c) 40 m/s (d) $\frac{1}{40}$ m/s

26 A 10 eV electron is circulating in a plane at right angle to a uniform field of magnetic induction 10^{-4} Wb/m^2 (= 1.0 G). The orbital radius of the electron is *[NCERT (New) Pg. 112, AIPMT 1996]*

(a) 12 cm (b) 16 cm
(c) 11 cm (d) 18 cm

27 An electron enters a region where magnetic field B and electric field E are mutually perpendicular, then *[AIPMT 1994]*

(a) it will always move in the direction of B
(b) it will always move in the direction of E
(c) it always possess circular motion
(d) it can go undeflected also

28 A charge moving with velocity v in x-direction is subjected to a field of magnetic induction in negative x-direction. As a result, the charge will *[AIPMT 1993]*

(a) remain unaffected
(b) start moving in a circular YZ-plane
(c) retard along X-axis
(d) move along a helical path around X-axis

29 A uniform magnetic field acts right angles to the direction of motion of electrons. As a result, the electron moves in a circular path of radius 2 cm. If the speed of electrons is doubled, then the radius of the circular path will be *[NCERT (New) Pg. 109, AIPMT 1991]*

(a) 2.0 cm (b) 0.5 cm (c) 4.0 cm (d) 1.0 cm

30 A deutron of kinetic energy 50 keV is describing a circular orbit of radius 0.5 m in a plane perpendicular to magnetic field B. The kinetic energy of the proton that describes a circular orbit of radius 0.5 m in the same plane with the same magnetic field B is *[AIPMT 1991]*

(a) 25 keV (b) 50 keV (c) 200 keV (d) 100 keV

Topic 3 Force and Torque on Current Carrying Conductor

01 A wire carrying a current I along the positive X-axis has length L. It is kept in a magnetic field $\mathbf{B} = (2\hat{\mathbf{i}} + 3\hat{\mathbf{j}} - 4\hat{\mathbf{k}})$ T. The magnitude of the magnetic force acting on the wire is. *[NCERT (New) Pg. 128, NEET 2023]*

(a) $\sqrt{5}\, IL$ (b) $5\, IL$ (c) $\sqrt{3}\, IL$ (d) $3\, IL$

02 A metallic rod of mass per unit length 0.5 kg m^{-1} is lying horizontally on a smooth inclined plane which makes an angle of 30° with the horizontal. The rod is not allowed to slide down by flowing a current through it when a magnetic field of induction 0.25 T is acting on it in the vertical direction. The current flowing in the rod to keep it stationary is *[NCERT (New) Pg. 126, NEET 2018]*

(a) 14.76 A (b) 5.98 A (c) 7.14 A (d) 11.32 A

03 An arrangement of three parallel straight wires placed perpendicular to plane of paper carrying same current I along the same direction is shown in figure. Magnitude of force per unit length on the middle wire B is given by *[NEET 2017]*

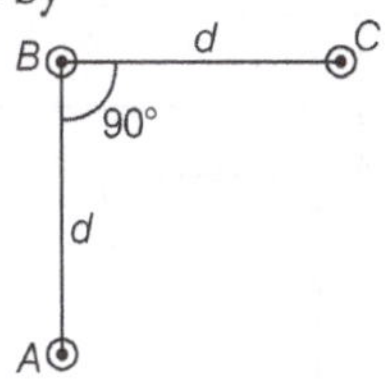

(a) $\frac{\mu_0 i^2}{2\pi d}$ (b) $\frac{2\mu_0 i^2}{\pi d}$
(c) $\frac{\sqrt{2}\mu_0 i^2}{\pi d}$ (d) $\frac{\mu_0 i^2}{\sqrt{2}\, \pi d}$

04 A square loop $ABCD$ carrying a current i, is placed near and coplanar with a long straight conductor XY carrying a current I, the net force on the loop will be *[NCERT (New) Pg. 128, NEET 2016]*

(a) $\frac{\mu_0 Ii}{2\pi}$ (b) $\frac{2\mu_0 IiL}{3\pi}$ (c) $\frac{\mu_0 IiL}{2\pi}$ (d) $\frac{2\mu_0 Ii}{3\pi}$

05 A rectangular coil of length 0.12 m and width 0.1 m having 50 turns of wire is suspended vertically in a uniform magnetic field of strength 0.2 Wb/m^2. The coil carries a current of 2 A. If the plane of the coil is inclined at an angle of 30° with the direction of the field, the torque required to keep the coil in stable equilibrium will be ***[AIPMT 2015]***

(a) 0.15 Nm (b) 0.20 Nm
(c) 0.24 Nm (d) 0.12 Nm

06 A current loop in a magnetic field ***[NCERT (New) Pg. 128, NEET 2013]***

(a) experiences a torque whether the field is uniform or non-uniform in all orientations
(b) can be in equilibrium in one orientation
(c) can be in equilibrium in two orientations, both the equilibrium states are unstable
(d) can be in equilibrium in two orientations, one stable while other is unstable

07 A current carrying closed loop in the form of a right angled isosceles $\Delta\, ABC$ is placed in a uniform magnetic field acting along AB. If the magnetic force on the arm BC is F, the force on the arm AC is ***[NCERT (New) Pg. 128, AIPMT 2011]***

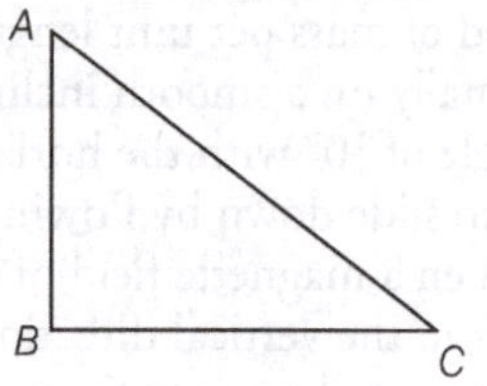

(a) −F (b) F
(c) $\sqrt{2}$ F (d) $-\sqrt{2}$ F

08 A square loop, carrying a steady current I, is placed in a horizontal plane near a long straight conductor carrying a steady current I_1 at a distance d from the conductor as shown in figure. The loop will experience ***[AIPMT 2011]***

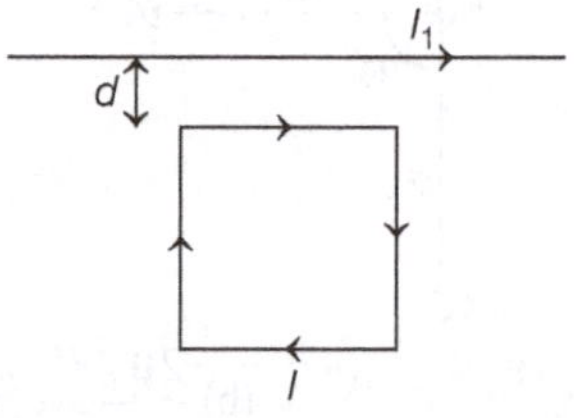

(a) a net repulsive force away from the conductor
(b) a net torque acting upward perpendicular to the horizontal plane
(c) a net torque acting downward normal to the horizontal plane
(d) a net attractive force towards the conductor

09 A closely wound solenoid of 2000 turns and area of cross-section $1.5\times10^{-4}\ m^2$ carries a current of 2.0 A. It is suspended through its centre and perpendicular to its length, allowing it to turn in a horizontal plane in a uniform magnetic field 5×10^{-2} tesla making an angle of 30° with the axis of the solenoid. The torque on the solenoid will be ***[NCERT (New) Pg. 126, AIPMT 2010]***

(a) 3×10^{-3} Nm (b) 1.5×10^{-3} Nm
(c) 1.5×10^{-2} Nm (d) 3×10^{-2} Nm

10 A square current carrying loop is suspended in a uniform magnetic field acting in the plane of the loop. If the force on one arm of the loop is F, the net force on the remaining three arms of the loop is ***[AIPMT 2010]***

(a) 3 F (b) −F (c) −3 F (d) F

11 A circular coil $ABCD$ carrying a current i is placed in a uniform magnetic field. If the magnetic force on the segment AB is F, the force on the remaining segment $BCDA$ is ***[AIPMT 2010]***

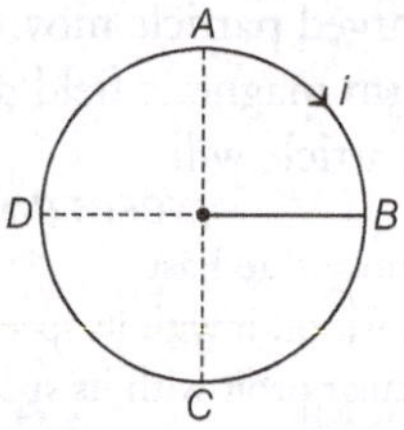

(a) F (b) − F (c) 3F (d) − 3F

12 A closed loop $PQRS$ carrying a current is placed in a uniform magnetic field. If the magnetic forces on segments PS, SR and RQ are F_1, F_2 and F_3 respectively and are in the plane of the paper and along the directions shown in figure, the force on the segment QP is ***[NCERT (New) Pg. 128, AIPMT 2008]***

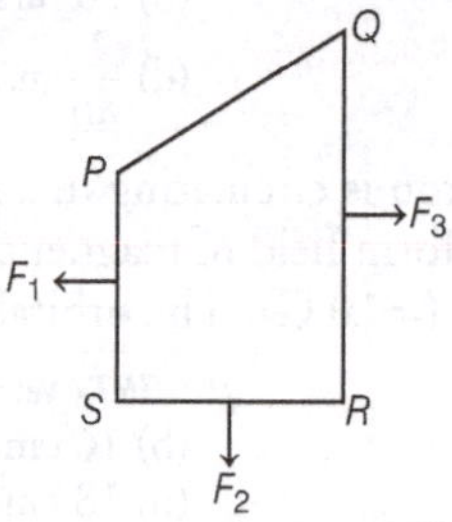

(a) $F_3 - F_1 - F_2$ (b) $\sqrt{(F_3 - F_1)^2 + F_2^2}$
(c) $\sqrt{(F_3 - F_1)^2 - F_2^2}$ (d) $F_3 - F_1 + F_2$

13 A coil in the shape of an equilateral triangle of side l is suspended between the pole pieces of a permanent magnet such that **B** is in plane of the coil. If due to a current i in the triangle a torque τ acts on it, the side l of the triangle is ***[AIPMT 2005]***

(a) $\frac{2}{\sqrt{3}}\left(\frac{\tau}{Bi}\right)^{1/2}$ (b) $\frac{2}{\sqrt{3}}\left(\frac{\tau}{Bi}\right)$

(c) $2\left(\frac{\tau}{\sqrt{3}\,Bi}\right)^{1/2}$ (d) $\frac{1}{\sqrt{3}}\frac{\tau}{Bi}$

14 Current is flowing in a coil of area A and number of turns N, then magnetic moment of the coil, M is equal to *[AIPMT 2001]*

(a) NiA (b) $\frac{Ni}{A}$

(c) $\frac{Ni}{\sqrt{A}}$ (d) $N^2 Ai$

15 Two long parallel wires are at a distance of 1 m. Both of them carry 1A of current. The force of attraction per unit length between the two wires is *[AIPMT 1998]*

(a) 2×10^{-7} N/m (b) 2×10^{-8} N/m

(c) 5×10^{-8} N/m (d) 10^{-7} N/m

16 A straight wire of length 0.5 m and carrying a current of 1.2 A is placed in uniform magnetic field of induction 2 T. The magnetic field is perpendicular to the length of the wire. The force on the wire is *[NCERT (New) Pg. 110, AIPMT 1992]*

(a) 2.4 N (b) 1.2 N

(c) 3.0 N (d) 2.0 N

17 A current carrying coil is subjected to a uniform magnetic field. The coil will orient so that its plane becomes *[AIPMT 1988]*

(a) inclined at 45° to the magnetic field

(b) inclined at any arbitrary angle to the magnetic field

(c) parallel to the magnetic field

(d) perpendicular to magnetic field

Topic 4 Moving Coil Galvanometer

01 Current sensitivity of a moving coil galvanometer is 5 div/mA and its voltage sensitivity (angular deflection per unit voltage applied) is 20 div/V. The resistance of the galvanometer is *[NCERT (New) Pg. 130, NEET 2018]*

(a) 250 Ω (b) 25 Ω (c) 40 Ω (d) 500 Ω

02 In an ammeter 0.2% of main current passes through the galvanometer. If resistance of galvanometer is G, the resistance of ammeter will be *[AIPMT 2014]*

(a) $\frac{1}{499}G$ (b) $\frac{499}{500}G$ (c) $\frac{1}{500}G$ (d) $\frac{500}{499}G$

03 A millivoltmeter of 25 mV range is to be converted into an ammeter of 25 A range. The value (in ohm) of necessary shunt will be *[AIPMT 2012]*

(a) 0.001 (b) 0.01 (c) 1 (d) 0.05

04 A galvanometer of resistance, G is shunted by a resistance $S\Omega$. To keep the main current in the circuit unchanged, the resistance to be put in series with the galvanometer is *[NCERT (New) Pg. 130, AIPMT 2011]*

(a) $\frac{S^2}{(S+G)}$ (b) $\frac{SG}{(S+G)}$

(c) $\frac{G^2}{(S+G)}$ (d) $\frac{G}{(S+G)}$

05 A galvanometer has a coil of resistance 100 ohm and gives a full-scale deflection for 30 mA current. It is to work as a voltmeter of 30 V range, the resistance required to be added will be *[AIPMT 2010]*

(a) 900 Ω (b) 1800 Ω

(c) 500 Ω (d) 1000 Ω

06 A galvanometer having a coil resistance of 60 Ω shows full scale deflection when a current of 1.0 A passes through it. It can be converted into an ammeter to read currents upto 5.0 A by *[AIPMT 2009]*

(a) putting in series a resistance of 15 Ω

(b) putting in series a resistance of 240 Ω

(c) putting in parallel a resistance of 15 Ω

(d) putting in parallel a resistance of 240 Ω

07 A galvanometer of resistance 50 Ω is connected to battery of 3V along with a resistance of 2950 Ω in series. A full scale deflection of 30 divisions is obtained in the galvanometer. In order to reduce this deflection to 20 divisions, the resistance in series should be *[NCERT (New) Pg. 130, AIPMT 2008]*

(a) 5050 Ω (b) 5550 Ω

(c) 6050 Ω (d) 4450 Ω

08 The resistance of an ammeter is 13 Ω and its scale is graduated for a current upto 100 A. After an additional shunt has been connected to this ammeter it becomes possible to measure currents upto 750 A by this meter. The value of shunt resistance is *[AIPMT 2007]*

(a) 20 Ω (b) 2 Ω (c) 0.2 Ω (d) 2 kΩ

09 A galvanometer of 50Ω resistance has 25 divisions. A current of 4×10^{-4} A gives a deflection of one per division. To convert this galvanometer into a voltmeter having a range of 25 V, it should be connected with a resistance of *[AIPMT 2004, 2002]*

(a) 2450 Ω in series (b) 2500 Ω in series

(c) 245 Ω in series (d) 2550 Ω in series

10 A galvanometer acting as a voltmeter will have *[AIPMT 2004, 2002]*

(a) a low resistance in series with its coil

(b) a high resistance in parallel with its coil

(c) a high resistance in series with its coil

(d) a low resistance in parallel with its coil

11 A galvanometer having a resistance of 8 Ω is shunted by a wire of resistance 2 Ω. If the total current is 1 A, the part of it passing through the shunt will be *[AIPMT 1998]*

(a) 0.25 A (b) 0.8 A

(c) 0.2 A (d) 0.5 A

• Key **Index**

Topic 1

1 (c)	**2** (b)	**3** (b)	**4** (a)	**5** (b)	**6** (c)	**7** (d)	**8** (a)	**9** (a)	**10** (b)
11 (b)	**12** (b)	**13** (c)	**14** (d)	**15** (d)	**16** (b)	**17** (a)	**18** (b)	**19** (a)	**20** (b)
21 (b)	**22** (d)	**23** (d)	**24** (c)	**25** (b)	**26** (b)	**27** (a)	**28** (d)	**29** (a)	**30** (b)
31 (a)	**32** (a)	**33** (c)							

Topic 2

1 (b)	**2** (b)	**3** (a)	**4** (d)	**5** (a)	**6** (c)	**7** (c)	**8** (b)	**9** (a)	**10** (d)
11 (c)	**12** (d)	**13** (c)	**14** (b)	**15** (c)	**16** (a)	**17** (c)	**18** (c)	**19** (c)	**20** (b)
21 (b)	**22** (a)	**23** (b)	**24** (b)	**25** (c)	**26** (c)	**27** (d)	**28** (a)	**29** (c)	**30** (d)

Topic 3

1 (b)	**2** (d)	**3** (d)	**4** (d)	**5** (b)	**6** (d)	**7** (a)	**8** (d)	**9** (c)	**10** (b)
11 (b)	**12** (b)	**13** (c)	**14** (a)	**15** (a)	**16** (b)	**17** (d)			

Topic 4

1 (a)	**2** (c)	**3** (a)	**4** (c)	**5** (a)	**6** (c)	**7** (d)	**8** (b)	**9** (a)	**10** (c)
11 (b)									

Detailed **Explanations**

Topic 1

01. *(c)* Given, number of turns $N = 100$

radius, $r = 10 \text{ cm} = 10 \times 10^{-2}$ m

current, $I = 7\text{A}$

Magnetic field at the centre of a solenoid,

$$B = \frac{\mu_0 NI}{2r}$$

$$= \frac{4\pi \times 10^{-7} \times 100 \times 7}{2 \times 10 \times 10^{-2}}$$

$$= 44 \times 10^{-4}$$

$$= 4.4 \times 10^{-3} \text{ T}$$

$$= 4.4 \text{ mT}$$

02. *(b)*

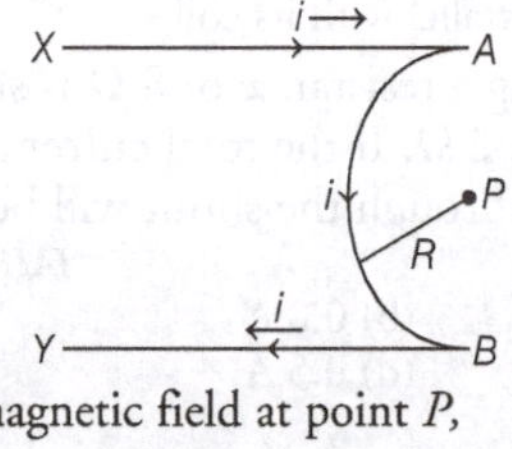

Net magnetic field at point P,

$$B = B_{\text{semicircle}} - B_{XA} - B_{YB}$$

$$= \frac{\mu_0 i}{4R} - \frac{\mu_0 i}{4\pi R} - \frac{\mu_0 i}{4\pi R}$$

$$= \frac{\mu_0 i}{4R}\left[1 - \frac{2}{\pi}\right]$$

pointed away from the page.

03. *(b)* According to Biot-Savart's law, magnetic field due to small current element Idl, at a distance r from it is given as

$$dB = \frac{\mu_0 (Idl \times r)}{4\pi r^3}$$

Thus, current element Idl is a vector quantity. Hence, Statement I is correct and Statement II is incorrect.

04. *(a)*

key idea

To find out the magnetic field at the center of the solenoid, you can use following formula.

$B = \mu_0 nI$, where, n = Number of turns per metre.

Given, radius of solenoid,

$$r = 1 \text{ mm}$$

$$\text{Number of turns per mm} = \frac{100}{1 \text{ mm}}$$

$\therefore$ Number of turns per metre

$$= \frac{100}{1 \times 10^{-3} \text{ m}}$$

i.e., $n = 10^5$ turns/m

Current flowing through the solenoid,

$$I = 1 \text{ A}$$

$\therefore$ Magnetic field strength at the centre of the solenoid $B = \mu_0 nI$

$$= 4\pi \times 10^{-7} \times 10^5 \times 1$$

$$= 4\pi \times 10^{-2} \text{ T} = 12.56 \times 10^{-2} \text{ T}$$

05. *(b)* According to Ampere's circuital law, magnetic field inside the current carrying long straight wire of circular cross-section is a linearly increasing function of distance $r\,(r < R)$ upto the boundary of the wire and magnetic field outside the wire at distance

$r(r > R)$ from its axis is decreasing one with $\frac{1}{r}$ dependence as shown in figure.

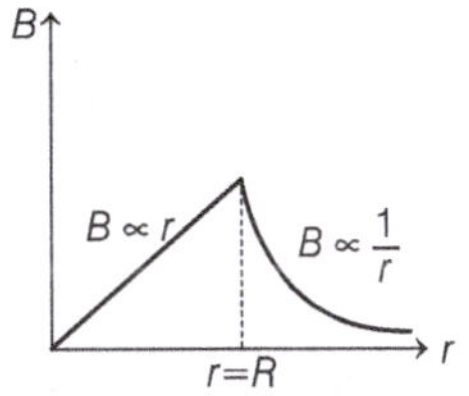

where, R is radius of circular cross-section of wire.

06. *(c)* Magnetic field inside the conducting cylindrical cable,

$$B = \frac{\mu_0 I}{2\pi R^2} r$$

Here, R is the radius of the cylindrical cable, r is the distance from the axis of the cylinder, I is the current carrying in the cylindrical cable.

$$\Rightarrow \quad B \propto r$$

$\therefore$ The graph of magnetic field B with r is a straight line passing through origin.

For a point outside the cylinder,

$$B = \frac{\mu_0 I}{2\pi r} \Rightarrow B \propto \frac{1}{r}$$

The graph of magnetic field (B) with r is a rectangular hyperbola passing through the outer surface of the cylinder.

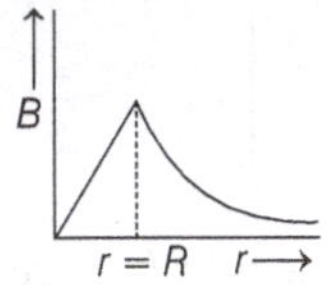

$\therefore$ The variation of the magnetic field B due to the cable with the distance r from the axis of the cylindrical cable is as shown in the figure.

07. *(d)*

key idea

To find the magnetic field at the center of the solenoid, you can use following formula.

$$B = \mu_0 \left(\frac{N}{l}\right) I$$

where, N = Number of turns in solenoid.
l = Length of solenoid.

Given, $l = 50$ cm $= 0.5$ m,
$N = 100$ turns and $I = 2.5$ A

$\therefore$ Magnetic field at the centre of solenoid is

$$= \mu_0 nI = \mu_0 \left(\frac{N}{l}\right) \cdot I$$

$$= 4\pi \times 10^{-7} \times \frac{100}{0.5} \times 2.5$$

$$= 6.28 \times 10^{-4} \text{ T}$$

Hence, correct option is (d).

08. *(a)* The magnetic field within the turns of toroid is

$$B = \frac{\mu_0 NI}{2\pi r}$$

where, N = number of turns,
I = current in loops and
r = radius of each turn

Here, $N_1 = 200$, $N_2 = 100$, $r_1 = 40$ cm, $r_2 = 20$ cm

and current I is same, then

$$\frac{B_1}{B_2} = \frac{\mu_0 N_1 I}{2\pi r_1} \times \frac{2\pi r_2}{\mu_0 N_2 I}$$

Substituting the given values in the above relation, we get

$$\frac{B_1}{B_2} = \left(\frac{N_1}{N_2}\right)\left(\frac{r_2}{r_1}\right)$$

$$= \left(\frac{200}{100}\right)\left(\frac{20}{40}\right) = 2 \times \frac{1}{2} = 1$$

$$\therefore \quad B_1 : B_2 = 1 : 1$$

09. *(a)*

key idea

To find solution of this question, you can use following steps :

(i) First of all, find out the magnetic field due to larger arc and smaller arc using formula,

$$B = \frac{\mu_0 I}{2R} \times \frac{\theta}{2\pi}$$

(ii) Now, the resultant magnetic field is $B_R = B_1 + B_2$

(iii) Since, wire is uniform, so $\frac{R_1}{R_2} = \frac{R \times 270}{R \times 90}$, and $\frac{I_1}{I_2} = \frac{R_2}{R_1} \Rightarrow \frac{I_1}{I_2} = \frac{1}{3}$

where, R_1 and R_2 are resistance of segments.

(iv) Now, the value of current I_1 and I_2 put in equation of resultant magnetic field and solve.

The magnetic field at the centre of an arc subtended at an angle θ is given by

$$B = \frac{\mu_0 i}{2R} \times \frac{\theta}{2\pi}$$

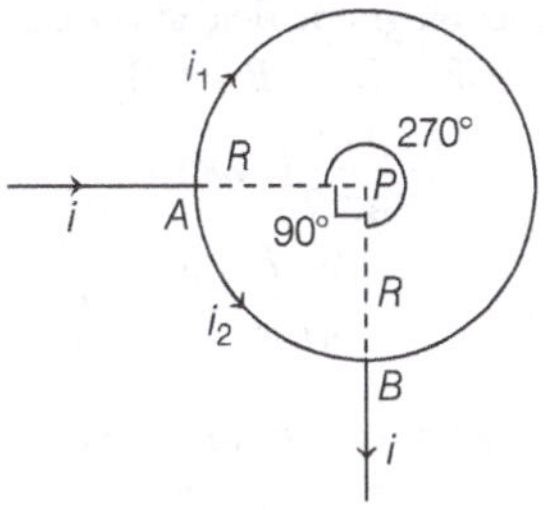

Then, the magnetic field due to larger arc AB is

$$B_1 = \frac{\mu_0 i_1}{2R} \times \frac{270}{2\pi} \quad \ldots\text{(i)}$$

which acts in inward direction according to right hand thumb rule.

Magnetic field due to smaller arc AB is

$$B_2 = \frac{\mu_0 i_2}{2R} \times \frac{90}{2\pi} \quad \ldots\text{(ii)}$$

which acts in outward direction.

The resultant magnetic field

$$B_R = B_1 + B_2$$

$$= -\frac{\mu_0 i_1 \times 270}{4\pi R} + \frac{\mu_0 i_2 \times 90}{4\pi R}$$

[From Eq. (i) and (ii)] ...(iii)

which acts in inward direction as $B_1 > B_2$.

Two arcs can also be seen as the two resistances in parallel combination.

So, the potential across them will be same i.e.,

$$V_1 = V_2$$

$$i_1 R_1 = i_2 R_2 \quad \ldots\text{(iv)}$$

where, R_1 and R_2 = Resistance of respective segments

The wire is uniform so

$$\frac{R_1}{R_2} = \frac{L_1}{L_2} = \frac{R \times 270}{R \times 90}$$

[$\because$ length of arc = radius $\times$ angle]

From Eq. (iv), we get

$$\Rightarrow \quad \frac{i_1}{i_2} = \frac{R_2}{R_1} = \frac{90}{270} = \frac{1}{3}$$

or $\quad 3i_1 = i_2 \quad \ldots\text{(v)}$

From Eq. (iii) and (v), we get

$$B_R = \frac{\mu_0}{4\pi R}(-270 i_1 + 90 i_2)$$

$$= \frac{\mu_0}{4\pi R}[-270 i_1 + 90(3 i_1)]$$

$$= \frac{\mu_0}{4\pi R}(-270 i_1 + 270 i_1) = 0$$

10. *(b)* The cylinder can be considered to be made from concentric circles of radius R.

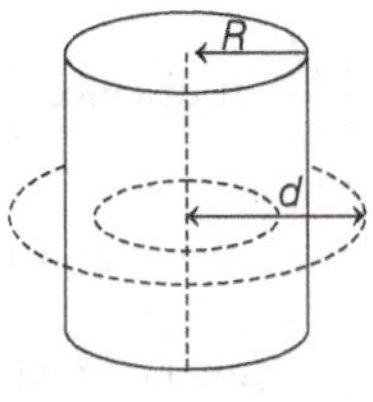

(i) The magnetic field at point outside cylinder, i.e.

$$d > R$$

$$\Rightarrow \quad B = \frac{\mu_0 I}{2\pi d}$$

where, μ_0 = permeability of free space.

(ii) The magnitude field at surface, i.e. $d = R$

$$B = \frac{\mu_0 I}{2\pi R}$$

(iii) The magnetic field at inside point. Current at inside point

$$= \frac{I}{\pi R^2}\pi d^2 = \frac{Id^2}{R^2}$$

$$\therefore \; B = \frac{\mu_0 I}{2\pi R^2} d$$

So, the variation of magnetic field can be plotted as

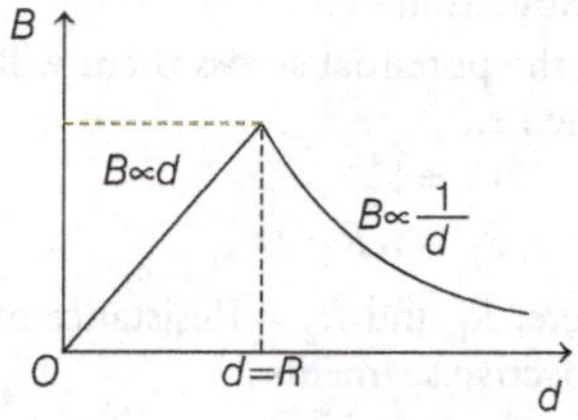

11. *(b)* Consider two amperian loops of radius $\frac{a}{2}$ and $2a$ as shown in the diagram.
Applying Ampere's circuital law for these loops we get,

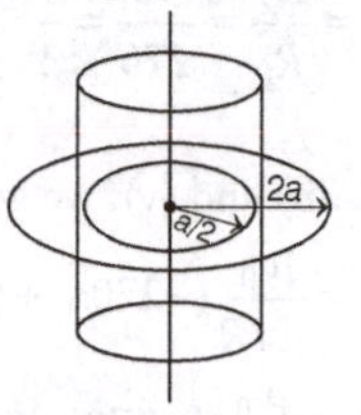

$$\oint \mathbf{B} \, . \, dL = \mu_0 I_{\text{enclosed}}$$

For the smaller loop

$$\Rightarrow B \times 2\pi\frac{a}{2} = \mu_0 \times \frac{I}{\pi a^2} \times \pi\left(\frac{a}{2}\right)^2$$

$$= \mu_0 I \times \frac{1}{4} = \frac{\mu_0 I}{4}$$

$\Rightarrow \; B = \frac{\mu_0 I}{4\pi a}$, at distance $\frac{a}{2}$ from the axis of the wire.

Similarly, for bigger amperian loop.

$$B' \times 2\pi\,(2a) = \mu_0 I$$

[total current enclosed by Amperian loop is 2]

$\Rightarrow \quad B' = \frac{\mu_0 I}{4\pi a}$,

at distance $2a$ from the axis of the wire.

So, ratio of $\frac{B}{B'} = \frac{\mu_0 I}{4\pi a} \times \frac{4\pi a}{\mu_0 I} = 1$

12. *(b)* $B_{\text{centre}} = \frac{n \cdot \mu_0 i}{2R}$ (for a circular coil)

where, n = Number of turns in circular coil

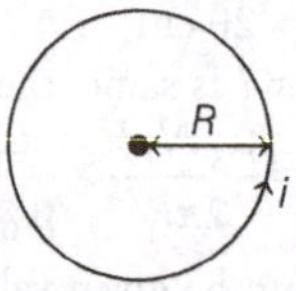

For one turn,

$$B = \frac{\mu_0 i}{2R} = \frac{\mu_0 i(2\pi)}{2(l)} = \frac{\mu_0 \pi i}{l}$$

$[\because l = 2\pi R]$

For n truns

$$B' = \frac{\mu_0 ni}{2R'}$$

$$2\pi R = n \times 2\pi R'$$

$$\therefore \quad R' = \frac{R}{n}$$

$$B' = \frac{\mu_0 in \times n}{2R} = n^2 B$$

13. *(c)* The magnetic field in the different regions is given by

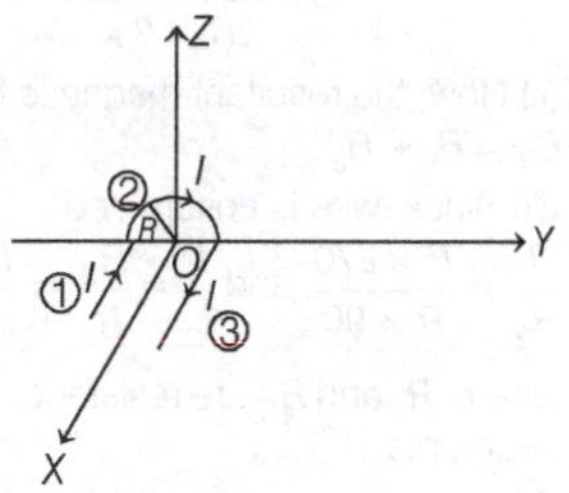

$$\mathbf{B}_1 = \frac{\mu_0}{4\pi} \times \frac{I}{R}(-\hat{\mathbf{k}})$$

$$\mathbf{B}_3 = \frac{\mu_0 I}{4\pi R}(-\hat{\mathbf{k}})$$

$$\mathbf{B}_2 = \frac{\mu_0 I}{4R}(-\hat{\mathbf{i}})$$

The net magnetic field at the centre O is

$$\mathbf{B} = \mathbf{B}_1 + \mathbf{B}_2 + \mathbf{B}_3$$

$$= \frac{\mu_0 I}{4\pi R}(-2\hat{\mathbf{k}}) + \frac{\mu_0 I}{4R}(-\hat{\mathbf{i}})$$

$$= -\frac{\mu_0 I}{4\pi R}(2\hat{\mathbf{k}} + \pi\hat{\mathbf{i}})$$

14. *(d)* As $I = \frac{q}{t}$. So, for an electron revolving in a circular orbit of radius r

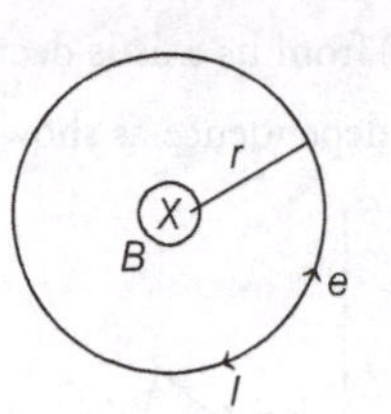

$$q = e \text{ and } t = T$$

$$\Rightarrow \quad I = \frac{e}{T} = \frac{e}{2\pi/\omega} = \frac{\omega e}{2\pi} = \frac{2\pi ne}{2\pi} = ne$$

The magnetic field produced at the centre is

$$B = \frac{\mu_0 I}{2R} = \frac{\mu_0 ne}{2r}$$

15. *(d)* As from question

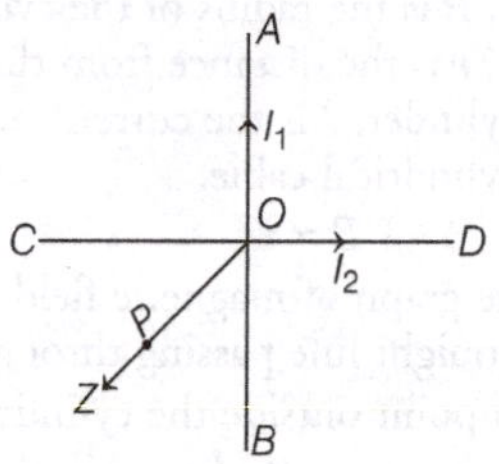

The point P is lying at a distance d along the Z-axis.

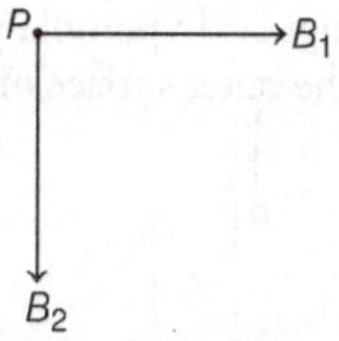

As magnetic field B_1 is given by

$$= \frac{\mu_0}{2\pi}\frac{I_1}{d}$$

and magnetic field B_2 is given by

$$= \frac{\mu_0}{2\pi}\frac{I_2}{d}$$

B_1 and B_2 are $\perp$ to each other

So, B_{net} is given by

$$B_{\text{net}} = \sqrt{B_1^2 + B_2^2} = \frac{\mu_0}{2\pi}\frac{1}{d}(I_1^2 + I_2^2)^{1/2}$$

16. *(b)* Case I Initial acceleration is given by

$$a_0 = \frac{eE}{m} \qquad (F = eE)$$

$$\Rightarrow \quad E = \frac{a_0 m}{e} \qquad \ldots\text{(i)}$$

along west

Case II

$$\therefore \quad \frac{ev_0 B + eE}{m} = 3a_0$$

or $ev_0B + eE = 3a_0m$

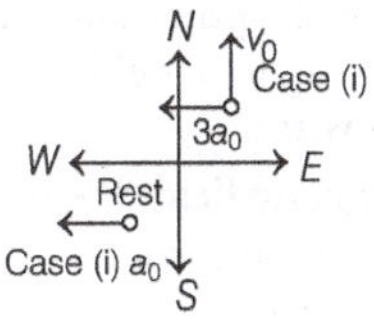

$\therefore ev_0B = 3ma_0 - eE$

$\Rightarrow \quad = 3ma_0 - ma_0$ [from Eq. (i)]

$\therefore \quad B = \dfrac{2ma_0}{ev_0}$,

in vertically downward direction .

17. (a) The magnetic field (B) at the centre of circular current carrying coil of radius R and current I is $B = \dfrac{\mu_0 I}{2R}$

Similarly, if current is $2I$, then

Magnetic field $= \dfrac{\mu_0 2I}{2R} = 2B$

So, resultant magnetic field

$$= \sqrt{B^2 + (2B)^2} = \sqrt{5B^2}$$

$$= \sqrt{5}B = \frac{\mu_0 I\sqrt{5}}{2R}$$

18. (b) The current flowing in the ring is given as

$$I = \frac{q}{T} = qf \quad \text{...(i)}$$

The magnetic induction at the centre of the ring is

$$B = \frac{\mu_0 I}{2R} = \frac{\mu_0 qf}{2R} \quad \text{(Using (i))}$$

19. (a) Magnetic field at the centre due to semicircular loop lying in XY-plane,

$B_{XY} = \dfrac{1}{2}\left(\dfrac{\mu_0 i}{2R}\right)$ negative z-direction.

Similarly, field due to loop in XZ-plane, $B_{XZ} = \dfrac{1}{2}\left(\dfrac{\mu_0 i}{2R}\right)$ in negative y-direction.

Since, $B_{XY} \perp B_{XZ}$

$\therefore$ Magnetic of resultant magnetic field.

$$B = \sqrt{B_{XY}^2 + B_{XY}^2}$$

$$= \sqrt{\left(\frac{\mu_0 i}{4R}\right)^2 + \left(\frac{\mu_0 i}{4R}\right)^2}$$

$$= \frac{\mu_0 i}{4R}\sqrt{2} = \frac{\mu_0 i}{2\sqrt{2}R}$$

20. (b) According to Maxwell's right handed screw rule, the magnetic field at right hand of wire 1 is perpendicular to the current carrying wire in plane of paper going inwards shown by ⊗. Similarly, the magnetic field at left hand of wire 2 is perpendicular to current carrying wire in plane of paper opposite to first wire shown by ⊙. Thus, the two fields are opposite to each other.

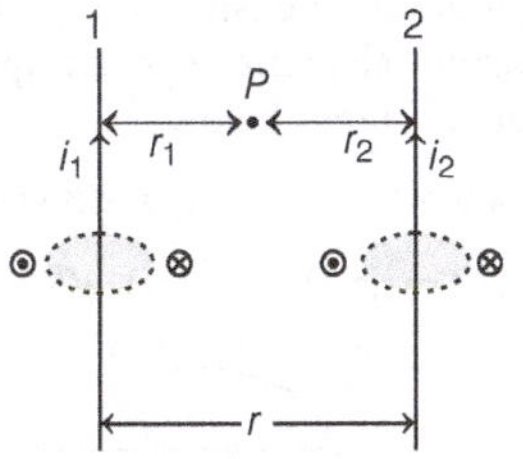

Therefore, net magnetic field at point P

$$B = B_1 - B_2 = \frac{\mu_0 i_1}{2\pi r_1} - \frac{\mu_0 i_2}{2\pi r_2}$$

At mid-point, $r_1 = r_2 = \dfrac{r}{2} = \dfrac{5}{2} = 2.5$ cm

Hence, $B = \dfrac{\mu_0}{2\pi}\left(\dfrac{i_1}{r/2} - \dfrac{i_2}{r/2}\right)$

$$= \frac{\mu_0}{2\pi}\left(\frac{5}{2.5} - \frac{2.5}{2.5}\right) = \frac{\mu_0}{2\pi}(2-1) = \frac{\mu_0}{2\pi}\text{ T}$$

21. (b) Magnetic field at the centre of a circular coil is

$$B = \frac{\mu_0}{2\pi} \times \frac{i}{r}$$

where, i is current flowing in the coil and r is radius of coil.

At the centre of coil-1,

$$B_1 = \frac{\mu_0}{2\pi} \times \frac{i_1}{r_1} \quad \text{...(i)}$$

At the centre of coil-2

$$B_2 = \frac{\mu_0}{2\pi} \times \frac{i_2}{r_2} \quad \text{...(ii)}$$

But $\quad B_1 = B_2$

$\therefore \quad \dfrac{\mu_0}{2\pi}\dfrac{i_1}{r_1} = \dfrac{\mu_0}{2\pi}\dfrac{i_2}{r_2}$ or $\dfrac{i_1}{r_1} = \dfrac{i_2}{r_2}$

As given $r_1 = 2r_2$

$\therefore \quad \dfrac{i_1}{2r_2} = \dfrac{i_2}{r_2}$

or $\quad i_1 = 2i_2 \quad$ ...(iii)

Now, ratio of potential differences

$$\frac{V_2}{V_1} = \frac{i_2 \times R_2}{i_1 \times R_1}$$

$$= \frac{i_2 \times R_2}{2i_2 \times 2R_2} = \frac{1}{4}$$

$[R \propto r]$

Here, R_1 and R_2 are resistance of coil 1 and coil 2, respectively.

$\therefore \quad \dfrac{V_1}{V_2} = \dfrac{4}{1}$

• Concept Enhancer

If wire of circular coil are made of same material, then resistance of coil is proportional to the radius of coil i.e. $R \propto r$ so, $R \propto 2\pi r$.

22. (d)

key idea

To find the new value of magnetic field, when current is changed. You can use following relation

$$\frac{B_1}{B_2} = \frac{n_1 i_1}{n_2 i_2}$$

For a solenoid magnetic field is given by $B = \mu_0 ni$

where, n = number of turns per unit length and i = current through the coil or so for two different cases $B \propto ni$

$$\therefore \quad \frac{B_1}{B_2} = \frac{n_1\, i_1}{n_2\, i_2}$$

Here, $\quad n_1 = n, \quad n_2 = \dfrac{n}{2}$,

$i_1 = i, \quad i_2 = 2i, \quad B_1 = B$

Hence, $\quad \dfrac{B}{B_2} = \dfrac{n}{n/2} \times \dfrac{i}{2i} = 1$ or $B_2 = B$

23. (d) Magnetic field at the centre of circular coil carrying current i with N number of turns is given by

$$B = \frac{\mu_0 Ni}{2r}$$

Case I $\; N = 1, L = 2\pi r \quad \Rightarrow \quad r = \dfrac{L}{2\pi}$

$$\therefore \quad B = \frac{\mu_0 \times 1 \times i}{2r} = \frac{\mu_0 i}{2r}$$

Case II $\; N = 2, L = 2 \times 2\pi r'$

$$\Rightarrow \quad r' = \frac{L}{4\pi} = \frac{r}{2}$$

$$\therefore \quad B' = \frac{\mu_0 \times 2 \times i}{2r'}$$

Putting the value of r'

$$B' = \frac{\mu_0 \times 2i}{2 \times (r/2)} = \frac{4\mu_0 i}{2r} = 4B$$

Note Magnetic field at the centre of circular coil is maximum and decreases as we move away from the centre (on the axis of coil).

24. (c) At the centre of current carrying, circular coil, the magnetic field is,

$$B = \frac{\mu_0 Ni}{2r}$$

Given, $N = 1000$, $i = 0.1$ A, $r = 0.1$ m
Substituting the values, we have

$$B = \frac{4\pi \times 10^{-7} \times 1000 \times 0.1}{2 \times 0.1}$$
$$= 2\pi \times 10^{-4} = 6.28 \times 10^{-4} \text{ T}$$

25. *(b)* According to Ampere's circuital law,

$$\int B \cdot dl = \mu_0 \, i_{\text{enclosed}}$$

So, $B(2\pi r) = \mu_0 \times 0$ $\quad [i_{\text{enclosed}} = 0]$

$\therefore \quad B = 0$

So, inside a hollow metallic (copper) pipe there is no current inside the Ampere's surface so, the magnetic field is zero.
But for external points, the whole current behaves as if it were concentrated at the axis only, so outside

$$B_0 = \frac{\mu_0 i}{2\pi r}$$

Thus, the magnetic field is produced outside the pipe only.

26. *(b)* Magnetic induction at the centre of current carrying coil of N turns carrying current is given by

$$B = \frac{\mu_0 N i}{2r} \quad \text{...(i)}$$

Suppose the length of the wire be L.
Case I For coil of one turn, let radius be r_1.

$\therefore \quad L = 2\pi r_1 \times N$

or $\quad r_1 = \frac{L}{2\pi \times N} = \frac{L}{2\pi} \quad (\because N = 1)$

Case II For coil of two turns, let radius be r_2.

$\therefore \quad L = 2\pi r_2 \times N$

or $\quad r_2 = \frac{L}{2\pi \times N} = \frac{L}{2\pi \times 2} \quad (\because N = 2)$

or $\quad r_2 = \frac{r_1}{2}$

By comparing two different cases from Eq. (i),

$$\frac{B_1}{B_2} = \frac{N_1}{r_1} \times \frac{r_2}{N_2} \text{ or } \frac{B_1}{B_2} = \frac{1 \times \frac{r_1}{2}}{r_1 \times 2}$$

$$\therefore \quad \frac{B_1}{B_2} = \frac{1}{4}$$

27. *(a)* Applying right hand grip rule and considering AB, the direction of magnetic field due to one current is upwards and that due to other is downwards.
Both the magnetic fields cancel out each other and the resultant magnetic field is zero.
Considering CD and applying right hand grip rule for the two currents, the direction of magnetic field is in the same direction in both the cases giving non-zero resultant.

28. *(d)* According to Biot-Savart law, the magnetic field induction $d\mathbf{B}$ (also called magnetic flux density) at a point P due to current element depends upon the factors as stated below.

(i) $dB \propto i$ $\qquad$ (ii) $dB \propto dl$

(iii) $dB \propto \sin\theta$ $\qquad$ (iv) $dB \propto \frac{1}{r^2}$

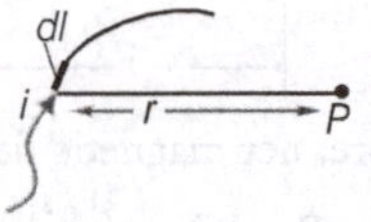

Combining these factors, we get magnitude of $d\mathbf{B}$

i.e., $\quad d\mathbf{B} = \frac{\mu_0}{4\pi} \cdot \frac{i \, dl \sin\theta}{r^2}$

In vector form,

$$d\mathbf{B} = \frac{\mu_0}{4\pi} i \frac{(d\mathbf{l} \times \mathbf{r})}{r^3}$$

$$\left[\frac{\mu_0}{4\pi} = 10^{-7} \text{ T - m / A}\right]$$

29. *(a)* Total magnetic field due to current carrying straight wire at any point P is given by

$$B = \frac{\mu_0 i}{4\pi r}(\sin\phi_1 + \sin\phi_2)$$

When the conductor is of infinite length and point P lies near the centre of conductor, then $\phi_1 = \phi_2 = 90°$

$$\therefore \quad B = \frac{\mu_0 i}{4\pi r}(\sin 90° + \sin 90°)$$

$$= \frac{\mu_0}{4\pi} \cdot \frac{2i}{r} \Rightarrow r = \frac{\mu_0 i}{2\pi B}$$

Here, current $i = 12$ A,
magnetic field, $B = 3 \times 10^{-5}$ Wb / m^2
$\therefore$ Perpendicular distance from wire to

the point, $r = \frac{4\pi \times 10^{-7} \times 12}{2 \times \pi \times (3 \times 10^{-5})}$

$$= 8 \times 10^{-2} \text{ m}$$

30. *(b)* Magnetic field due to straight wire is given by

$$B = \frac{\mu_0}{4\pi} \frac{2i}{r}$$

From above expression magnetic field due to current carrying conductor doesn't depends on the diameter of wire, it only depends on distance of wire from the point and current in the wire so, magnetic field reamaining same for both wires.

31. *(a)* Magnetic field due to a long current carrying wire at distance r at point P is given by

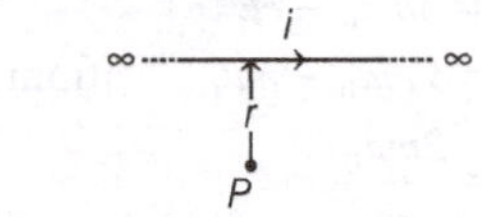

$$B = \frac{\mu_0}{4\pi} \cdot \frac{2i}{r}$$

So, $\quad B \propto \frac{1}{r}$

when r is doubled, the magnetic field becomes halved.

i.e., $\quad B' = \frac{B}{2} \Rightarrow B' = \frac{0.4}{2} = 0.2$ T

32. *(a)* Magnetic field due to a long straight conductor carrying current i at a distance r is given by

$$B = \frac{\mu_0}{4\pi} \frac{2i}{r}$$

Given, $\quad r_1 = 4$ cm, $r_2 = 12$ cm

As $\quad B \propto \frac{1}{r}$

and distance becomes 3 times, field is reduced to its one-third value.

Hence, $\quad B' = \frac{B}{3} = \frac{10^{-3}}{3}$

$$= 3.33 \times 10^{-4} \text{ T}$$

33. *(c)* SI unit of magnetic induction is Tesla (T).
Magnetic field induction at a point is said to be one tesla if a charge of one coulomb while moving at right angle to a magnetic field, with a velocity of 1 ms^{-1} experiences a force of 1 N, at that point.

$\therefore \quad 1\text{T} = 1\text{NA}^{-1} \text{ m}^{-1}$

Topic 2

01. *(b)* If the sheet is magnetic in nature. then the flux will be linked through the sheet and a small amount of force will be needed to held the sheet. The pole will apply a force on the sheet.

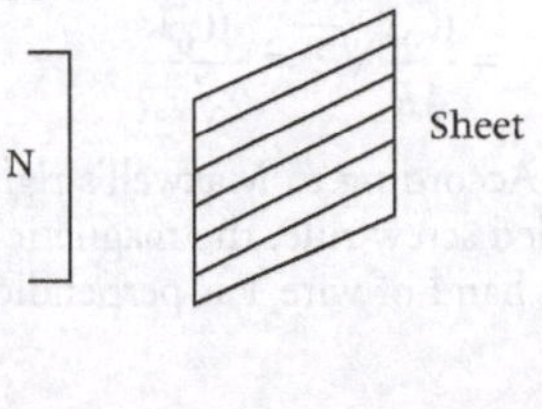

Also, to move the sheet towards or away from the magnetic pole, a force will be required.
If sheet is non-magnetic then no force will be required either to hold it or move it when the sheet is non-conducting.

02. *(b)* Given, velocity,

$$\mathbf{v} = 2\hat{\mathbf{i}} + 4\hat{\mathbf{j}} + 6\hat{\mathbf{k}}$$

Force, $\mathbf{F} = 4\hat{\mathbf{i}} - 20\hat{\mathbf{j}} + 12\hat{\mathbf{k}}$

As we know, $\mathbf{F} = q(\mathbf{v} \times \mathbf{B})$

Here, $q = 1\,\text{C}$ (given)

Substituting the values in the above equation, we get

$$4\hat{\mathbf{i}} - 20\hat{\mathbf{j}} + 12\hat{\mathbf{k}} = (1)[(2\hat{\mathbf{i}} + 4\hat{\mathbf{j}} + 6\hat{\mathbf{k}}) \times (B\hat{\mathbf{i}} + B\hat{\mathbf{j}} + B_0\hat{\mathbf{k}})]$$

$$4\hat{\mathbf{i}} - 20\hat{\mathbf{j}} + 12\hat{\mathbf{k}} = \begin{vmatrix} \hat{\mathbf{i}} & \hat{\mathbf{j}} & \hat{\mathbf{k}} \\ 2 & 4 & 6 \\ B & B & B_0 \end{vmatrix}$$

$$\Rightarrow 4\hat{\mathbf{i}} - 20\hat{\mathbf{j}} + 12\hat{\mathbf{k}} = \hat{\mathbf{i}}(4B_0 - 6B) - \hat{\mathbf{j}}(2B_0 - 6B) + \hat{\mathbf{k}}(2B - 4B)$$

Comparing the LHS and RHS of the above equation, we get

$\hat{\mathbf{i}}$ terms:

$$4B_0 - 6B = 4 \quad \ldots(\text{i})$$

$\hat{\mathbf{j}}$ terms: $2B_0 - 6B = 20 \quad \ldots(\text{ii})$

$\hat{\mathbf{k}}$ terms: $2B - 4B = 12$

$$\Rightarrow B = -6$$

Substituting the value of B in the Eq. (ii), we get

$$2B_0 - 6(-6) = 20$$

$$\Rightarrow B_0 = -8$$

Thus, the magnetic field vector,

$$B = -6\hat{\mathbf{i}} - 6\hat{\mathbf{j}} - 8\hat{\mathbf{k}}$$

03. *(a)* Magnetic field due to a current carrying wire at a distance r from the wire.

$$\text{or, } B = \frac{\mu_0 2i}{4\pi r} = \frac{10^{-7} \times 2 \times 5}{20 \times 10^{-2}}$$

$$= \frac{1}{2} \times 10^{-5}\,\text{T}$$

upward to the plane of paper

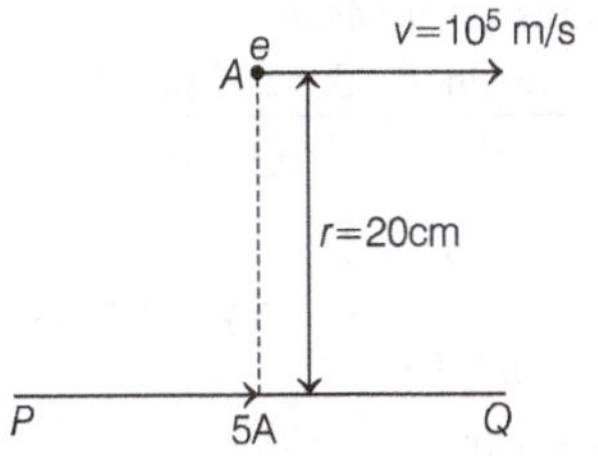

Therefore, force acting on electron

$$\mathbf{F} = q(\mathbf{v} \times \mathbf{B})$$

$$|\mathbf{F}| = 1.6 \times 10^{-19} \times 10^5 \times \frac{1}{2} \times 10^{-5}$$

$$= 8 \times 10^{-20}\,\text{N}$$

04. *(d)*

key idea

If momenta of hydrogen atom and α-particle are same then the ratio of their radii of their paths are given as

$$\frac{r_H}{r_\alpha} = \frac{q_\alpha}{q_H}$$

The centripetal force required for circular motion is provided by magnetic force

$$\Rightarrow \frac{mv_p^2}{r} = Bqv_p$$

$$\Rightarrow r = \frac{mv_p}{qB} \quad \ldots(\text{i})$$

where, v_p = perpendicular velocity of particle and
q = charge on particle.

As, momentum, $p = mv_p$

$$\therefore r = \frac{p}{qB} \quad [\text{from Eq. (i)}]$$

According to the question, moment of both particle is same.

$$\Rightarrow r \propto \frac{1}{q}$$

For ionised hydrogen atom, $q_H = e$ and for α-particle, $q_\alpha = 2e$

$$\Rightarrow \frac{r_H}{r_\alpha} = \frac{q_\alpha}{q_H} = \frac{2e}{e} = \frac{2}{1} \text{ or } 2:1$$

05. *(a)* As we know that, radius of a charged particle in a magnetic field B is given by

$$r = \frac{mv}{qB} \quad \ldots(\text{i})$$

$\therefore$ The time taken to complete the circle,

$$T = \frac{2\pi r}{v} \Rightarrow \frac{T}{2\pi} = \frac{m}{qB}$$

[from Eq. (i)]

$$\therefore \omega = \frac{2\pi}{T} = \frac{qB}{m}$$

$$\because q = e \text{ and } \frac{e}{m} = 1.76 \times 10^{11}\,\text{C/kg}$$

$$B = 3.57 \times 10^{-2}\,\text{T}$$

$$\Rightarrow \frac{2\pi}{T} = \frac{eB}{m}$$

$$\Rightarrow f = \frac{1}{2\pi}\frac{e}{m}B \quad \left(\because \frac{1}{T} = f\right)$$

$$= \frac{1}{2\pi} \times 1.76 \times 10^{11} \times 3.57 \times 10^{-2}$$

$$= 1.0 \times 10^9\,\text{Hz} = 1\,\text{GHz}$$

06. *(c)* $F = qvB = \dfrac{mv^2}{r}$

$$\therefore r = \frac{mv}{qB} = \frac{\sqrt{2m(\text{KE})}}{qB}$$

Since r is same so, $\text{KE} \propto \dfrac{q^2}{m}$

Therefore

$$\frac{\text{KE}_\alpha}{\text{KE}_p} = \frac{q_\alpha^2}{m_\alpha} \times \frac{m_p}{q_p^2}$$

$$= \frac{(2e)^2}{4m_p} \times \frac{m_p}{e^2} = 1$$

$$\text{KE}_\alpha = \text{KE}_p = 1\,\text{MeV}$$

07. *(c)* Given,

Magnetic field,

$$B = 2 \times 10^{-4}\,\text{Wb/m}^2$$

Velocity of electron,

$$v = 10^7\,\text{m/s}$$

Lorentz force, $F = qvB\sin\theta$

$$= 1.6 \times 10^{-19} \times 10^7 \times 2 \times 10^{-4} \quad (\because \theta = 90^\circ)$$

$$= 3.2 \times 10^{-16}\,\text{N}$$

08. *(b)* According to given situation,

$$F_c = F_m \Rightarrow \frac{mv^2}{r} = qVB$$

$$\Rightarrow r = \frac{mv}{qB} = \frac{p}{qB} = \frac{\sqrt{2m.K}}{qB}$$

$$r_\alpha = \frac{\sqrt{2(4m)K'}}{2qB} \Rightarrow \frac{r}{r_\alpha} = \sqrt{\frac{K}{K'}}$$

but $r = r_\alpha$ (given)

Thus $K = K' = 1\,\text{MeV}$

09. *(a)* Magnetic field B will not apply any force. Only electric field E will apply a force opposite to velocity of the electron hence, speed decreases.

10. *(d)* As the electron beam is not deflected,

then $F_m = F_e$ or $Bev = Ee$

$$\text{or } v = \frac{E}{B} \quad \ldots(\text{i})$$

According to law of conservation of energy,

$$\frac{1}{2}mv^2 = eV \text{ or } v = \sqrt{\frac{2eV}{m}} \quad \ldots(\text{ii})$$

From Eqs. (i) and (ii), we have

$$\sqrt{\frac{2eV}{m}} = \frac{E}{B}$$

or $$\frac{e}{m} = \frac{E^2}{2VB^2}$$

11. *(c)* To keep the particle moving in horizontal direction, it is necessary that both **B** and **E** should be along the direction of velocity and also perpendicular to the direction of velocity.

12. *(d)* The magnetic force,

$$\mathbf{F} = q(\mathbf{v} \times \mathbf{B})$$
$$= (-2\times10^{-6})[\{(2\hat{i}+3\hat{j})\times10^{6}\}\times(2\hat{j})]$$
$$= -4(2\hat{k}) = -8\text{N}\hat{k}$$

13. *(c)* Magnetic field can never increase the energy of a charged particle so, its kinetic energy will remain same.

14. *(b)* If both electric and magnetic fields are present and are perpendicular to each other and the particle is moving perpendicular to both of them with $F_e = F_m$.

In this situation $\mathbf{E} \neq 0$ and $\mathbf{B} \neq 0$ and $F_e + F_m = 0$.

But if electric field becomes zero, then only force due to magnetic field exists. And **E** is perpendicular to the **B** so the charge moves along a circle.

15. *(c)*

key idea

To find the period of the motion, you can use following formula .

$$T = \frac{2\pi m}{Bq}$$

When magnetic field is perpendicular to motion of charged particle, then particle performs circular motion.

So, centripetal force = magnetic force

i.e. $$\frac{mv^2}{R} = Bqv \text{ or } R = \frac{mv}{Bq}$$

Further, time period of the motion

$$T = \frac{2\pi R}{v} = \frac{2\pi\left(\frac{mv}{Bq}\right)}{v} = \frac{2\pi m}{Bq}$$

16. *(a)* In mass spectrometer, when ions are accelerated through potential V, then

$$\frac{1}{2}mv^2 = qV \quad \text{...(i)}$$

As the magnetic field curves the path of the ions in a semicircle orbit, hence

$$Bqv = \frac{mv^2}{R}$$

$$\Rightarrow \quad v = \frac{BqR}{m} \quad \text{...(ii)}$$

Substituting (ii) in (i)

$$\frac{1}{2}m\left[\frac{BqR}{m}\right]^2 = qV \text{ or } \frac{q}{m} = \frac{2V}{B^2R^2}$$

$$\Rightarrow \quad \frac{q}{m} \propto \frac{1}{R^2}$$

17. *(c)* When a charged particle q is moving in a uniform magnetic field **B** with velocity **v** such that angle between **v** and **B** is θ, then the charge q experiences a force which is given by

$$F = q(\mathbf{v}\times\mathbf{B}) = qvB\sin\theta$$

If $\theta = 0°$ or $180°$, then $\sin\theta = 0$

$\therefore \quad F = qvB\sin\theta = 0$

Since, force on charged particle is non-zero, so angle between **v** and **B** can have any value other than 0° and 180°.

Note Force experienced by the charged particle is the Lorentz force.

18. *(c)* The time period of electron moving in a circular orbit,

$$T = \frac{\text{Circumference of circular path}}{\text{Speed}} = \frac{2\pi r}{v}$$

Now, equivalent current due to flow of electron is given by

$$i = \frac{q}{T} = \frac{e}{(2\pi r/v)} = \frac{ev}{2\pi r} \quad [q = e]$$

Magnetic field at centre of circle

$$B = \frac{\mu_0 i}{2r} = \frac{\mu_0 ev}{4\pi r^2} \quad \left(i = \frac{ev}{2\pi r}\right)$$

$$\Rightarrow \quad r \propto \sqrt{\frac{v}{B}}$$

19. *(c)* When a charged particle moves through a perpendicular magnetic field, then a magnetic force acts on it which changes the direction of particle but does not alter the magnitude of its velocity (i.e., speed).

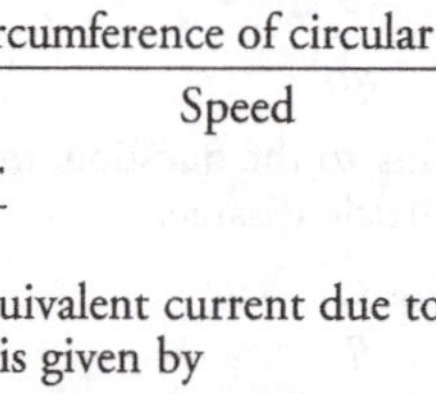

So, speed of charged particle remains unchanged i.e., of velocity magnitude remains constant.

Note If a charged particle moves at 45° to magnetic field, then path of the particle will be a helix whose circular part has radius according to relation,

$$r = \frac{mv\sin\theta}{qB}.$$

20. *(b)* If **E** is the electric field strength and **B** is the magnetic field strength and q is the charge on a particle, then electric force on the charge

$$\mathbf{F}_e = q\mathbf{E}$$

and magnetic force on the charge

$$\mathbf{F}_m = q(\mathbf{v}\times\mathbf{B})$$

The net force on the charge

$$\mathbf{F} = \mathbf{F}_e + \mathbf{F}_m = q\mathbf{E} + q(\mathbf{v}\times\mathbf{B})$$

Alternate Solution

According to Lorentz force if a charged particle is in both electric field **E** and magnetic field **B**, force is given by

$$\mathbf{F} = q[\mathbf{E} + (\mathbf{v}\times\mathbf{B})]$$

21. *(b)* Magnetic force = centripetal force

i.e. $$qvB = \frac{mv^2}{r} \text{ or } qvB = mr\omega^2$$

$(v = r\omega)$

or $$\omega^2 = \frac{qvB}{mr} = \frac{q(r\omega)B}{mr}$$

Angular frequency, $$\omega = \frac{qB}{m}$$

If ν is the frequency of rotation, then

$$\omega = 2\pi\nu \Rightarrow \nu = \frac{\omega}{2\pi}$$

$$\therefore \quad \nu = \frac{qB}{2\pi m}$$

Note In the resultant expression q/m is known as specific charge. It is sometimes denoted by α. So, in terms of α, the above formula can be written as

$$\omega = B\alpha \text{ and } \nu = \frac{B\alpha}{2\pi}$$

22. *(a)* Electron moves undeflected if force exerted due to electric field is equal to force exerted due to magnetic field.

i.e., $$q|\mathbf{v}||\mathbf{B}| = q|\mathbf{E}| \Rightarrow |\mathbf{v}| = \frac{|\mathbf{E}|}{|\mathbf{B}|}$$

23. *(b)* Radius of curvature,

$$r = \frac{mv\sin\theta}{Be} = \frac{3\times10^5\sin30°}{0.3\times10^8}$$

$$= \frac{3\times10^5\times\frac{1}{2}}{3\times10^7} = 0.5\times10^{-2}\text{ m}$$

$$= 0.5\text{ cm}$$

24. *(b)*

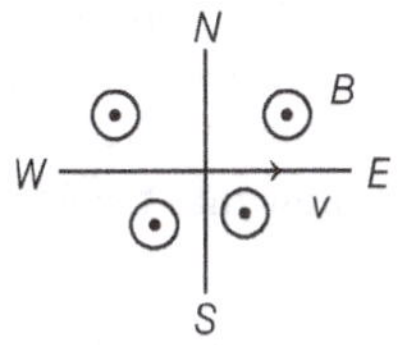

According to Fleming's left hand rule, the force acts perpendicular to the velocity of the particle. This force in magnitude remains same but the direction of charged particle goes on changing and always perpendicular to the velocity of the particle, so the particle will move in a circular orbit. The magnetic force does not make any change in its kinetic energy which implies that speed is constant or unchanged.

25. *(c)* According to Lorentz force,

$$F_{net} = q[\mathbf{E} + (\mathbf{v} \times \mathbf{B})]$$

When **v**, **E** and **B** are mutually perpendicular to each other, in this situation if **E** and **B** are such that $\mathbf{F} = \mathbf{F}_e + \mathbf{F}_m = 0$, then acceleration in the particle, $\mathbf{a} = \frac{\mathbf{F}}{m} = 0$. It means particle will pass undeflected.

Here, $F_e = F_m$

So, $qE = qvB, \begin{bmatrix} F_e = qE \\ F_M = qvB \end{bmatrix}$ or $v = \frac{E}{B}$

Given, $E = 20 \text{ Vm}^{-1}, B = 0.5\text{T}$

$\therefore \quad v = \frac{20}{0.5} = 40 \text{ m/s}$

26. *(c)* If charged particle is moving perpendicular to the direction of **B**, it experiences a maximum force which acts perpendicular to the direction of **B** as well as v. Hence, this force will provide the required centripetal force and the charged particle will describe a circular path in the magnetic field of radius r and is given by

$$\frac{mv^2}{r} = qvB$$

Now, KE of electron = 10 eV

$\Rightarrow \quad \frac{1}{2}mv^2 = 10 \text{ eV}$

$\therefore \frac{1}{2} \times (9.1 \times 10^{-31}) v^2 = 10 \times 1.6 \times 10^{-19}$

$\Rightarrow \quad v^2 = \frac{2 \times 10 \times 1.6 \times 10^{-19}}{9.1 \times 10^{-31}}$

$\Rightarrow \quad v^2 = 3.52 \times 10^{12}$

or $\quad v = 1.88 \times 10^6$ m

Now, radius of circular path,

$$r = \frac{mv}{qB} = \frac{9.1 \times 10^{-31} \times 1.88 \times 10^6}{1.6 \times 10^{-19} \times 10^{-4}}$$

$= 11\text{cm}$

27. *(d)* The force experienced by a charged particle moving in space where both electric and magnetic fields exist is called Lorentz force.

Due to both electric and magnetic fields, the total force experienced by the charged particle will be given by,

$$\mathbf{F} = \mathbf{F}_e + \mathbf{F}_m = q\mathbf{E} + q(\mathbf{v} \times \mathbf{B})$$
$$= q(\mathbf{E} + \mathbf{v} \times \mathbf{B})$$

When **v**, **E** and **B** are mutually perpendicular to each other. In this situation, if **E** and **B** are such that $\mathbf{F} = \mathbf{F}_e + \mathbf{F}_m = 0$, then acceleration in the particle, $\mathbf{a} = \frac{\mathbf{F}}{m} = 0$.

It means particle will go undeflected.

28. *(a)* Force on a charged particle in the magnetic field is

$$|\mathbf{F}| = q|\mathbf{v} \times \mathbf{B}| \text{ or } F = qvB \sin\theta$$

when angle between velocity v and magnetic induction B is 180° or 0°, then

$$F = qvB \sin 180° = 0$$

[as sin 180° or sin 0° = 0]

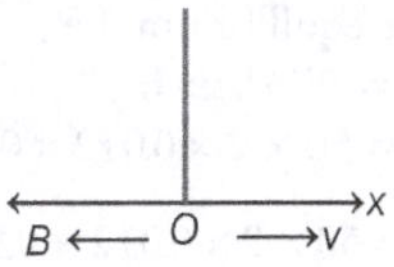

So, the charged particle remains unaffected.

29. *(c)* The force F on the charged particle due to external magnetic field provides the required centripetal force $(= mv^2/r)$ necessary for motion along the circular path of radius r.

So, $\quad qvB = \frac{mv^2}{r} \quad$ or $\quad r = \frac{mv}{qB}$

$\therefore \quad r \propto v \quad \left[\frac{m}{qB} = \text{constant}\right]$

As v is doubled, the radius also becomes double. Hence, radius = 2 × 2 = 4 cm.

30. *(d)* When charged particle moves on circular path, the kinetic energy will be

$$E_K = \frac{B^2q^2r^2}{2m}$$

where, m = mass of particle
v = velocity of particle
q = charge on particle
B = external magnetic field
r = radius of circular path

For deutron, $E_1 = \frac{B^2q^2r^2}{2 \times (2m)}$ (mass = 2m)

For proton, $E_2 = \frac{B^2q^2r^2}{2m}$ (mass = m)

$\therefore \quad \frac{E_1}{E_2} = \frac{1}{2} \Rightarrow \frac{50 \text{ keV}}{E_2} = \frac{1}{2}$

or $\quad E_2 = 100$ keV

Topic 3

01. *(b)* Given, $\mathbf{L} = L\hat{\mathbf{i}}$

$\mathbf{B} = 2\hat{\mathbf{i}} + 3\hat{\mathbf{j}} - 4\hat{\mathbf{k}}$

$\therefore \mathbf{F} = I(\mathbf{L} \times \mathbf{B})$

$= I[L\hat{\mathbf{i}} \times (2\hat{\mathbf{i}} + 3\hat{\mathbf{j}} - 4\hat{\mathbf{k}})]$

$= I[2L(\hat{\mathbf{i}} \times \hat{\mathbf{i}}) + 3L(\hat{\mathbf{i}} \times \hat{\mathbf{j}}) - 4L(\hat{\mathbf{i}} \times \hat{\mathbf{k}})]$

$= I[0 + 3L\hat{\mathbf{k}} + 4L\hat{\mathbf{j}}]$

$= I[4L\hat{\mathbf{j}} + 3L\hat{\mathbf{k}}]$

$\therefore F = |\mathbf{F}| = \sqrt{(4LI)^2 + (3LI)^2} = 5LI$

02. *(d)* As, the system is in equilibrium,

$$\Sigma F_x = 0$$

or $\quad mg \sin\theta = F \cos\theta \quad \ldots(i)$

where, F is the magnitude of force experienced by the rod when placed in a magnetic field and current I is flowing through it.

But the force experienced by the given rod in a uniform magnetic field is

$$F = ILB$$

$\therefore$ Eq. (i) becomes,

$mg \sin\theta = ILB \cos\theta$

$\Rightarrow \quad I = \frac{mg \sin\theta}{LB \cos\theta} = \frac{mg}{LB} \tan\theta$

$I = \left(\frac{m}{L}\right)\frac{g \tan\theta}{B} \quad \ldots(ii)$

According to the question,

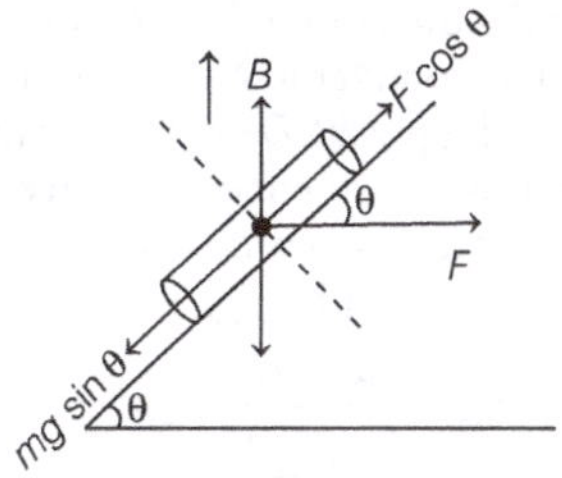

Here, $\frac{m}{L} = 0.5 \text{ kg m}^{-1}, g = 9.8 \text{ ms}^{-2}$,

$\theta = 30°, \; B = 0.25\text{T}$

Substituting the given values in Eq. (ii), we get

$$I = \frac{0.5 \times 9.8}{0.25} \tan 30^\circ$$

$$= \frac{0.5 \times 9.8}{0.25} \times \frac{1}{\sqrt{3}}$$

$$= 11.32 \text{ A}$$

• Concept **Enhancer**

Firstly, make a free body diagram of the system and indicate the magnitude and direction of all the forces acting on the body. Then, choose any two mutually perpendicular axes say X and Y in the plane of forces in case of coplanar forces.

03. *(d)* As force on wire B due to A and C are attractive, so we have following condition

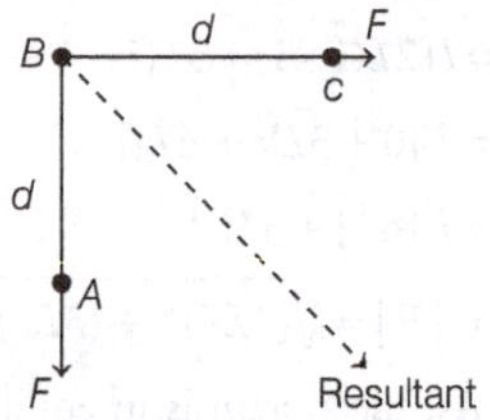

$$F = \frac{\mu_0 I^2}{2\pi d}$$

Resultant force on B

$$= \sqrt{F_1^2 + F_2^2} = \sqrt{2}\, F$$

$$= \sqrt{2} \times \frac{\mu_0 I^2}{2\pi d} = \frac{\mu_0 I^2}{\sqrt{2}\pi d}$$

04. *(d)* Consider the given figure,

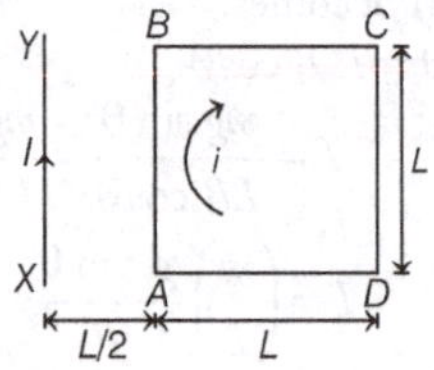

From the above figure, it can be seen that the direction of currents in a long straight conductor XY and arm AB of a square loop $ABCD$ are in the same direction. So, there exist a force of attraction between the two, which will be experienced by F_{BA} as

$$F_{BA} = \frac{\mu_0 IiL}{2\pi\left(\frac{L}{2}\right)}$$

In the case of XY and arm CD, the direction of currents are in the opposite direction. So, there exist a force of repulsion which will be experienced by CD as $F_{CD} = \frac{\mu_0 IiL}{2\pi\left(\frac{3L}{2}\right)}$

Therefore, net force on the loop $ABCD$ will be

$$F_{loop} = F_{BA} - F_{CD}$$

$$= \frac{\mu_0 IiL}{2\pi}\left[\frac{1}{(L/2)} - \frac{1}{(3L/2)}\right]$$

$$F_{loop} = \frac{2\mu_0 iI}{3\pi}$$

05. *(b)* Given, $N = 50$

$B = 0.2 \text{ Wb/m}^2$, $I = 2\text{A}$

$\theta = 60^\circ$, $A = 0.12 \times 0.1 = 0.012 \text{ m}^2$

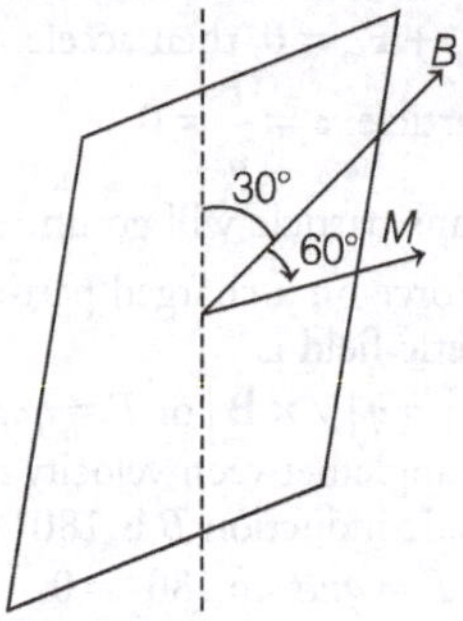

Thus, torque required to keep the coil in stable equilibrium, i.e.,

$$\tau = NIAB \sin\theta$$

$$= 50 \times 2 \times 0.012 \times 0.2 \times \sin 60^\circ$$

$$= 50 \times 2 \times 0.012 \times 0.2 \times \frac{\sqrt{3}}{2}$$

$$= 0.20 \text{ Nm}$$

06. *(d)* For parallel, M is stable and for antiparallel, it is unstable.

07. *(a)* Force on AB is given by,

$$F_{AB} = 0$$

According to the question,

$$\mathbf{F}_{AB} = 0$$

$$\Rightarrow \mathbf{F}_{AB} + \mathbf{F}_{BC} + \mathbf{F}_{CA} = 0$$

$$\mathbf{F}_{BC} + \mathbf{F}_{CA} = 0$$

$$\mathbf{F}_{CA} = -\mathbf{F}_{BC} = -\mathbf{F}$$

08. *(d)* Given situation is shown below,

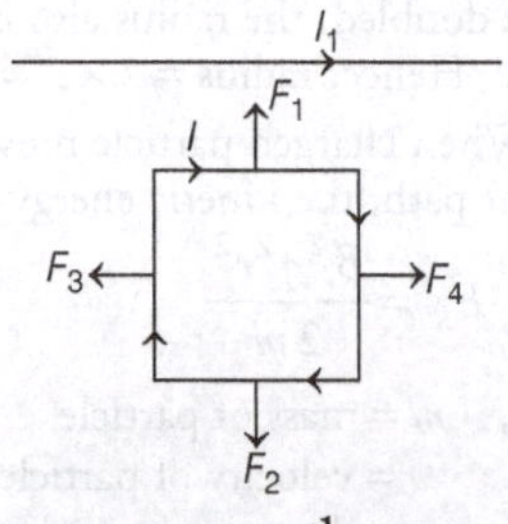

$F_1 > F_2$ as $F \propto \frac{1}{d}$

and F_3 and F_4 are equal and opposite. Therefore, the net attraction force will be towards the conductor.

09. *(c)* We know that $\tau = MB\sin\theta$

$= NIAB\sin\theta$ $[\because M = NIA]$

$= 2000 \times 2 \times 1.5 \times 10^{-4} \times 5 \times 10^{-2} \times \frac{1}{2}$ $\left[\because \sin 30^\circ = \frac{1}{2}\right]$

$= 0.6 \times 5 \times 10^{-2} \times \frac{1}{2}$

$= 1.5 \times 10^{-2}$ Nm

10. *(b)* When a current carrying loop is placed in a magnetic field, the coil experiences a torque given by

$$\tau = NBi\,A\sin\theta$$

Torque is maximum when $\theta = 90^\circ$, i.e., the plane of the coil is parallel to the field.

$$\tau_{max} = NBiA$$

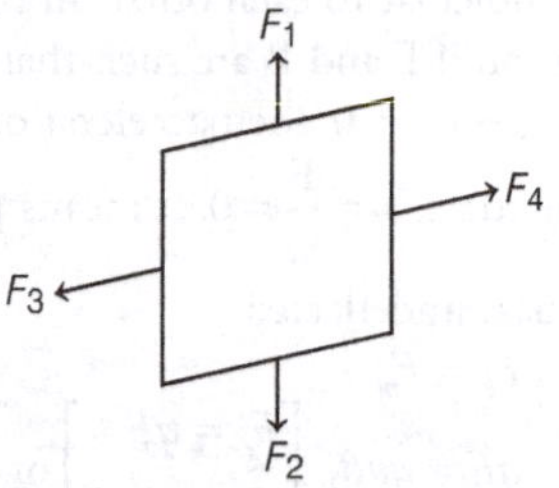

Forces $\mathbf{F}_1$ and $\mathbf{F}_2$ acting on the coil are equal in magnitude and opposite in direction. As the forces $\mathbf{F}_1$ and $\mathbf{F}_2$ have the same line of action, their resultant effect on the coil is zero.

The two forces $\mathbf{F}_3$ and $\mathbf{F}_4$ are equal in magnitude and opposite in direction. As the two forces have different lines of action, they constitute a torque.

Thus, if the force on one arc of the loop is F, the net force on the remaining three arms of the loop is –F.

11. *(b)* According to given situation,

$\mathbf{F}_{AB} + \mathbf{F}_{BCDA} = 0$

$\Rightarrow \mathbf{F}_{BCDA} = -\mathbf{F}_{AB} = -\mathbf{F}$ $(\because F_{AB} = \mathbf{F})$

12. *(b)* As the net force on closed loop is equal to zero.

So, force on QP will be equal and opposite to sum of forces on other 3 sides.

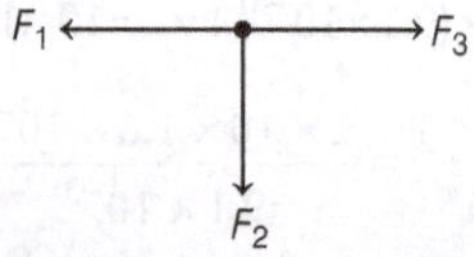

So, from vector laws,

$$F_{QP} = \sqrt{(F_3 - F_1)^2 + F_2^2}$$

13. *(c)* Torque acting on equilateral triangle in a magnetic field **B** is

$$\tau = \mathbf{M} \times \mathbf{B}$$

$$\tau = iAB \sin\theta \qquad [\mathrm{M} = iA]$$

Area of $\Delta\, LMN$

$$A = \frac{\sqrt{3}}{4} l^2$$

and $\theta = 90°$ [l = sides of triangle]

Substituting the given values in the expression for torque, we have

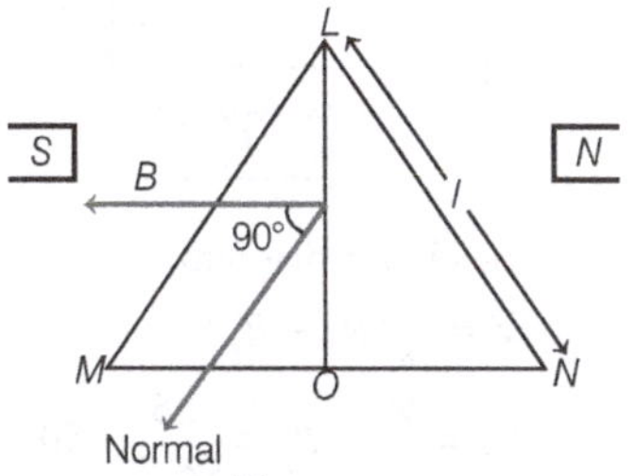

$$\tau = i \times \frac{\sqrt{3}}{4} l^2\, B \sin 90°$$

$$= \frac{\sqrt{3}}{4} il^2 B \qquad (\because \sin 90° = 1)$$

Hence, $l = 2\left(\dfrac{\tau}{\sqrt{3}\, Bi}\right)^{1/2}$

14. *(a)* If there are N turns in a coil, i is the current flowing and A is the area of the coil, then magnetic dipole moment or simply magnetic moment of the coil is $M = NiA$

As we know when velocity of charged particle entering to magnetic field region is perpendicular to **B**, then it follows circular path.

15. *(a)* Magnetic force between parallel wires per unit length is given by

$$\frac{F}{l} = \frac{\mu_0}{2\pi} \times \frac{i_1 i_2}{r}$$

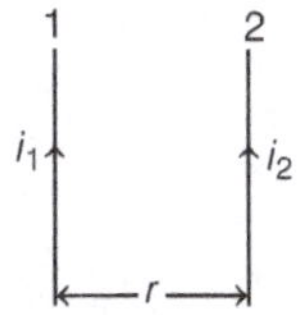

where, i_1 and i_2 are the currents in wires 1 and 2 respectively and r is the distance between them. Since, it is given that between two wires there is a force of attraction, so, the direction of currents in both will be the same.

Given,

$$i_1 = i_2 = 1\text{A}, \quad r = 1\text{ m}$$

$$\mu_0 = 4\pi \times 10^{-7}\text{ T-m/A}$$

$$\therefore \quad \frac{F}{l} = \frac{4\pi \times 10^{-7}}{2\pi} \times \frac{1 \times 1}{1}$$

$$= 2 \times 10^{-7}\text{ N/m}$$

• Concept Enhancer

When current is in same direction in both the wires there will be attraction and if current in opposite direction there is repulsion.

16. *(b)* Force on a current carrying conductor placed in a magnetic field is given by

$$F = i(l \times B) = il\, B \sin\theta$$

where, θ = angle between current elements and magnetic field.

If linear conductor carrying current is placed perpendicular to the direction of magnetic field, ($\theta = 90°$) it will experience maximum force.

i.e., $F_{\text{max}} = ilB$

Given, $i = 1.2$ A,

$l = 0.5$ m and $B = 2$ T

$$\therefore \quad F = 2 \times 1.2 \times 0.5 = 1.2\text{ N}$$

17. *(d)* The coil must orient so that its magnetic moment becomes parallel to the field. So that the magnetic force on the coil is zero.

Topic 4

01. *(a)* Current sensitivity of a moving coil galvanometer is the deflection θ per unit current I flowing through it, i.e.

$$I_S = \frac{\theta}{I} = \frac{NAB}{k} \qquad \ldots\text{(i)}$$

where, N = number of turns in the coil,

A = Area of each turn of coil,

B = magnetic field

k = restoring torque per unit twist of the fibre strip.

Similarly, voltage sensitivity is the deflection per unit voltage, i.e.

$$V_S = \frac{\theta}{V} = \left(\frac{NAB}{k}\right)\frac{I}{V} = \frac{NAB}{kR_G} \qquad \ldots\text{(ii)}$$

where, R_G is the resistance of the galvanometer.

From Eqs. (i) and (ii), we get

$$R_G = \frac{I_S}{V_S} \qquad \ldots\text{(iii)}$$

Here, $I_S = 5$ div/mA

$= 5 \times 10^{+3}$ div/A

and $V_S = 20$ div/V

Substituting the given values in Eq. (iii), we get

$$R_G = \frac{5 \times 10^3}{20} = 250$$

$\therefore$ The resistance of the galvanometer is 250 Ω.

02. *(c)* For ammeter,

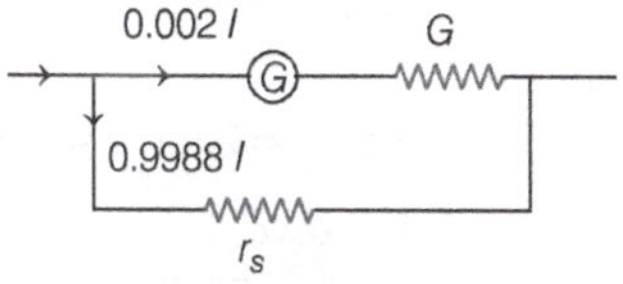

$$0.002\, I \times G = 0.998\, I \times r_s$$

$$r_s = \frac{0.002}{0.998} G$$

$$\Rightarrow \quad r_s = \frac{1}{499} \times G$$

Equivalent resistance of ammeter,

$$\frac{1}{R} = \frac{1}{G} + \frac{1}{r_s}$$

$$\therefore \quad \frac{1}{R} = \frac{1}{G} + \frac{1}{G/499}$$

$$\Rightarrow \quad R = \frac{G}{500}$$

03. *(a)* The full scale deflection current

$$i_g = \frac{25\text{mV}}{G}\text{ A}$$

where, G is the resistance of the meter. The value of shunt required for converting it into ammeter of range 25 A is $S = \dfrac{i_g G}{i - i_g}$

$$\Rightarrow \quad S = i_g \frac{G}{i} \qquad (\text{as } i >> i_g)$$

So that,

$$S \approx \frac{25\text{ mV}}{G} \cdot \frac{G}{i}$$

$$= \frac{25\text{ mV}}{25} = 0.001\,\Omega$$

04. *(c)* For the proper operation of galvanometer, the resistance of the galvanometer should be equal to the net the resistance.

$$\therefore \quad G = \left(\frac{GS}{G+S}\right) + S'$$

$$\Rightarrow G - \frac{GS}{G+S} = S'$$

$$\therefore \quad S' = \frac{G^2}{G+S}$$

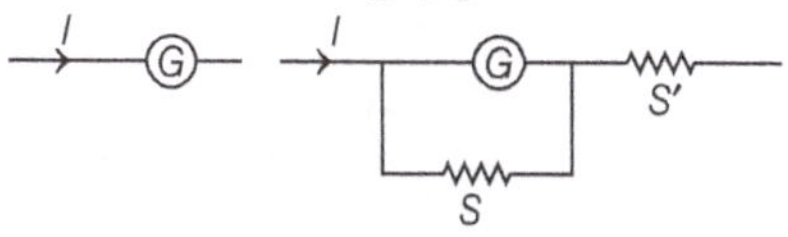

05. *(a)* If R be the required added resistance, then

$30 = I_g(r + R)$

$\therefore \; R = \frac{30}{I_g} - r = \frac{30}{30 \times 10^{-3}} - 100$

$= 1000 - 100 = 900\ \Omega$

06. *(c)* Given,

$G = 60\ \Omega, I_g = 1.0\ \text{A}, I = 5\ \text{A}$

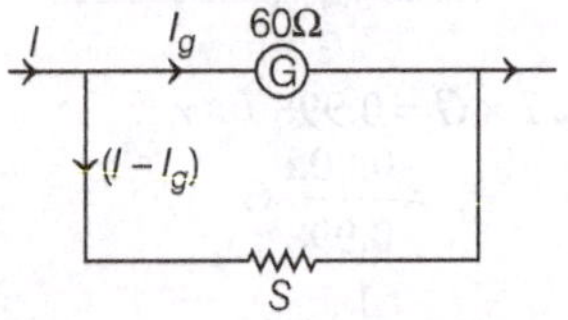

Let S be the shunt resistance, then

$I_g G = (I - I_g) S,$

$\Rightarrow \; S = \frac{I_g G}{I - I_g}$

$= \frac{1}{5 - 1} \times 60 = 15\ \Omega$

07. *(d)* According to given situation, total internal resistance

$= (50 + 2950)\ \Omega = 3000\ \Omega, \varepsilon = 3\ \text{V}$

$I = \frac{\varepsilon}{R} = \frac{3}{3000} = 1 \times 10^{-3}\ \text{A} = 1.0\ \text{mA}$

$\therefore$ Current for full scale deflection of 30 divisions is 1.0 mA

$\therefore$ Current for a deflection of 20 divisions.

$I = \left(\frac{20}{30} \times 1\right) \text{mA or } I = \frac{2}{3}\ \text{mA}$

Let the resistance be $p\ \Omega$. Then

$p = \frac{\varepsilon}{I} = \frac{3V}{\left(\frac{2}{3} \times 10^{-3}\ \text{A}\right)}$

$= \frac{3 \times 3 \times 10^3}{2}\ \Omega = 4500\ \Omega$

But the resistance of the galvanometer is 50 Ω.

$\therefore$ Resistance to be added

$= (4500 - 50)\ \Omega$

$= 4450\ \Omega$

08. *(b)* Let i_a be the current flowing through ammeter and i be the total current. So, a current $i - i_a$ will flow through shunt resistance.

Potential difference across ammeter and shunt resistance is same.

i.e. $\quad i_a \times R = (i - i_a) \times S$

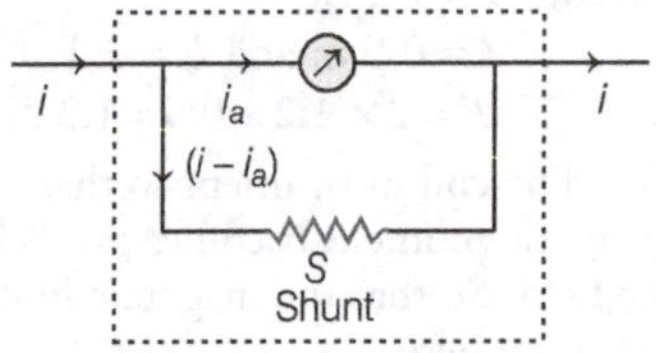

High reading ammeter

or $\quad S = \frac{i_a R}{i - i_a} \quad \ldots\text{(i)}$

Given,

$i_a = 100\ \text{A}, i = 750\ \text{A},$

$R = 13\ \Omega$

Hence, $S = \frac{100 \times 13}{750 - 100} = 2\ \Omega$

09. *(a)* Given, $R_g = 50\ \Omega,$

$I_g = 25 \times 4 \times 10^{-4}\ \text{A} = 10^{-2}\ \text{A}$

Range of $V = 25\ \text{V}$

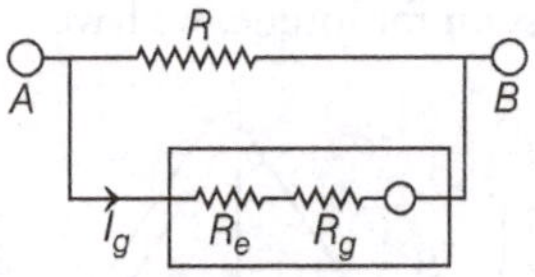

From the circuit diagram,

$V = I_g(R_e + R_g)$

$\therefore \quad R_e = \frac{V}{I_g} - R_g = \frac{25}{10^{-2}} - 50$

$= 2450\ \Omega$

10. *(c)* A galvanometer can be converted into a voltmeter by connecting the high resistance in series with it so that only a small amount of current passes through it for its proper operation.

11. *(b)* For the galvanometer,

$I_s = I \times \frac{G}{S + G}$

$= 1 \times \frac{8}{2 + 8} = \frac{8}{10} = 0.8\ \text{A}$

C-19

NEET Chapterwise
Topicwise Physics

In NEET 2024,3 questions was visible from this chapter. In past 5 years, 3 questions from topic-1, 2 questions from topic-3 and 2 questions from topic-4 were asked.
For detailed analysis scan QR code

MAGNETISM AND MATTER

Topic 1 Bar Magnet and Magnetic Dipole Moment

01 An iron bar of length L has magnetic moment M. It is bent at the middle of its length such that the two arms make an angle 60° with each other. The magnetic moment of this new magnet is *[NCERT (New) Pg. 139, NEET 2024]*

(a) M (b) $M/2$ (c) $2M$ (d) $M/\sqrt{3}$

02 A uniform conducting wire of length $12a$ and resistance R is wound up as a current I carrying coil in the shape of

1. an equilateral triangle of side a.
2. a square of side a.

The magnetic dipole moments of the coil in each case respectively are *[NCERT (New) Pg. 141, NEET 2021]*

(a) $\sqrt{3}\ Ia^2$ and $3\ Ia^2$ (b) $3\ Ia^2$ and Ia^2
(c) $3\ Ia^2$ and $4\ Ia^2$ (d) $4\ Ia^2$ and $3\ Ia^2$

03 A wire of length L metre carrying a current of I ampere is bent in the form of a circle. Its magnetic moment is *[NEET (Oct.) 2020]*

(a) $(I\,L^2/4)\,\text{Am}^2$ (b) $(I\,\pi L^2/4)\,\text{Am}^2$
(c) $(2I\,L^2/\pi)\,\text{Am}^2$ (d) $(I\,L^2/4\pi)\,\text{Am}^2$

04 Following figures show the arrangement of bar magnets in different configurations. Each magnet has magnetic dipole moment M. Which configuration has highest net magnetic dipole moment ? *[NCERT (New) Pg. 137, AIPMT 2014]*

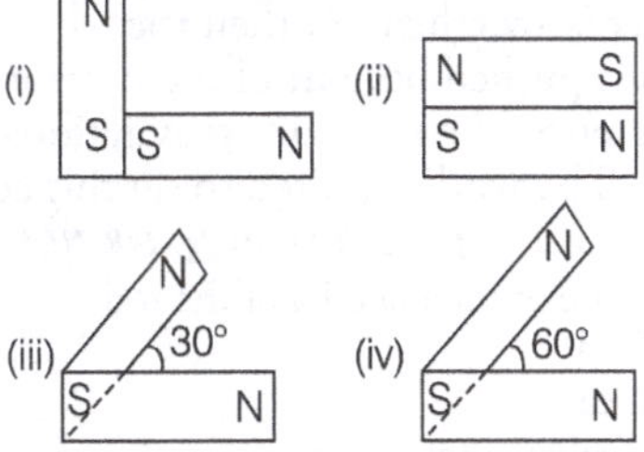

(a) (i) (b) (ii) (c) (iii) (d) (iv)

05 A bar magnet of length l and magnetic dipole moment M is bent in the form of an arc as shown in figure. The new magnetic dipole moment will be *[NEET 2013]*

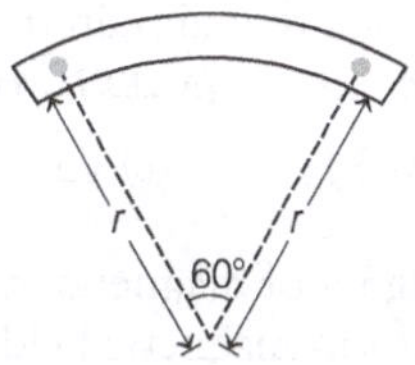

(a) M (b) $\frac{3}{\pi}M$ (c) $\frac{2}{\pi}M$ (d) $\frac{M}{2}$

06 A compass needle which is allowed to move in a horizontal plane is taken to a geomagnetic pole. It *[NCERT (New) Pg. 138, AIPMT 2012]*

(a) will become rigid showing no movement
(b) will stay in any position
(c) will stay in North-South direction only
(d) will stay in East-West direction only

07 Two identical bar magnets are fixed with their centres at a distance d apart. A stationary charge Q is placed at P in between the gap of the two magnets at a distance D from the centre O as shown in the figure *[NCERT (New) Pg. 137, AIPMT 2010]*

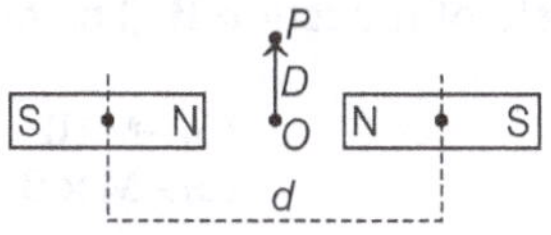

The force,on the charge Q is

(a) zero (b) directed along OP
(c) directed along PO
(d) directed perpendicular to the plane of paper

08 A charged particle (charge q) is moving in a circle of radius R with uniform speed v. The associated magnetic moment μ is given by *[AIPMT 2007]*

(a) $\frac{qvR}{2}$ (b) qvR^2 (c) $\frac{qvR^2}{2}$ (d) qvR

Topic 2 Magnetic Dipole in Uniform Magnetic Field

01 A 250 turn rectangular coil of length 2.1 cm and width 1.25 cm carries a current of 85 μA and subjected to a magnetic field of strength 0.85 T. Work done for rotating the coil by 180° against the torque is *[NCERT (New) Pg. 139, NEET 2017]*

(a) 9.1 μJ (b) 4.55 μJ (c) 2.3 μJ (d) 1.5 μJ

02 A bar magnet is hung by a thin cotton thread in a uniform horizontal magnetic field and is in equilibrium state. The energy required to rotate it by 60° is W. Now the torque required to keep the magnet in this new position is *[NEET 2016]*

(a) $\frac{W}{\sqrt{3}}$ (b) $\sqrt{3}W$ (c) $\frac{\sqrt{3}W}{2}$ (d) $\frac{2W}{\sqrt{3}}$

03 A magnetic needle suspended parallel to a magnetic field requires $\sqrt{3}$ J of work to turn it through 60°. The torque needed to maintain the needle in this position will be *[NCERT (New) Pg. 139, AIPMT 2012]*

(a) $2\sqrt{3}$ J (b) 3 J (c) $\sqrt{3}$ J (d) $\frac{3}{2}$ J

04 A short bar magnet of magnetic moment 0.4 J T^{-1} is placed in a uniform magnetic field of 0.16 T. The magnet is in stable equilibrium when the potential energy is *[AIPMT 2011]*

(a) 0.064 J (b) −0.064 J
(c) zero (d) −0.082 J

05 A bar magnet having a magnetic moment of 2×10^4 J T^{-1} is free to rotate in a horizontal plane. A horizontal magnetic field $B = 6\times 10^{-4}$ T exists in the space. The work done in taking the magnet slowly from a direction parallel to the field to a direction 60° from the field is *[NCERT (New) Pg. 139, AIPMT 2009]*

(a) 0.6 J (b) 12 J
(c) 6 J (d) 2 J

06 A bar magnet of magnetic moment **M** is placed in a magnetic field of induction **B**. The torque exerted on it is *[AIPMT 1999]*

(a) $\mathbf{M}\cdot\mathbf{B}$ (b) $-\mathbf{M}\cdot\mathbf{B}$
(c) $\mathbf{M}\times\mathbf{B}$ (d) $-\mathbf{M}\times\mathbf{B}$

Topic 3 Gauss's Law in Magnetism

01 In a uniform magnetic field of 0.049 T, a magnetic needle performs 20 complete oscillations in 5 s as shown. The moment of inertia of the needle is 9.8×10^{-6} kg m^2. If the magnitude of magnetic moment of the needle is $x\times 10^{-5}$ Am^2, then the value of x is *[NCERT (New) Pg. 139, NEET 2024]*

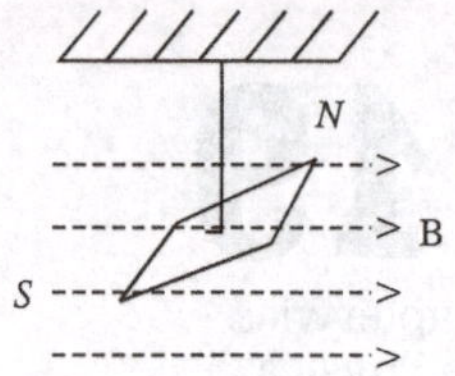

(a) $5\pi^2$ (b) $128\pi^2$ (c) $50\pi^2$ (d) $1280\pi^2$

02 The net magnetic flux through any closed surface is *[NCERT (New) Pg. 142, NEET 2023]*

(a) positive (b) infinity
(c) negative (d) zero

03 Two bar magnets having same geometry with magnetic moments M and $2M$, are firstly placed in such a way that their similar poles are on the same side, then its period of oscillation is T_1. Now, the polarity of one of the magnets is reversed the time period of oscillations becomes T_2. Then, *[AIPMT 2002]*

(a) $T_1 < T_2$ (b) $T_1 > T_2$ (c) $T_1 = T_2$ (d) $T_2 = \infty$

Topic 4 Magnetic Materials and Its Properties

01 Match List I with List II. *[NCERT (New) Pg. 147, NEET 2024]*

	List I (Material)		List II (Susceptibility (χ))
A	Diamagnetic	I.	$\chi = 0$
B	Ferromagnetic	II.	$0 > \chi \geq -1$
C	Paramagnetic	III.	$\chi >> 1$
D	Non-magnetic	IV.	$0 < \chi < \varepsilon$ (a small positive number)

Choose the correct answer from the options given below.

(a) A-II, B-III, C-IV, D-I (b) A-II, B-I, C-III, D-IV
(c) A-III, B-II, C-I, D-IV (d) A-IV, B-III, C-II, D-I

02 An iron rod of susceptibility 599 is subjected to a magnetising field of 1200 A m^{-1}. The permeability of the material of the rod is
(Take, $\mu_0 = 4\pi\times 10^{-7}$ T m A^{-1}) *[NEET (Sep.) 2020]*

(a) 8.0×10^{-5} T m A^{-1} (b) $2.4\pi\times 10^{-5}$ T m A^{-1}
(c) $2.4\pi\times 10^{-7}$ T m A^{-1} (d) $2.4\pi\times 10^{-4}$ T m A^{-1}

03 A thin diamagnetic rod is placed vertically between the poles of an electromagnet. When the current in the electromagnet is switched on, then the diamagnetic rod is pushed up, out of the horizontal magnetic field. Hence, the rod gains gravitational potential energy. The work required to do this comes from *[NCERT (New) Pg. 148, NEET 2018]*

(a) the lattice structure of the material of the rod
(b) the magnetic field
(c) the current source
(d) the induced electric field due to the changing magnetic field

04 The magnetic susceptibility is negative for *[NCERT (New) Pg. 148, NEET 2016]*
(a) paramagnetic material only
(b) ferromagnetic material only
(c) paramagnetic and ferromagnetic materials
(d) diamagnetic material only

05 There are four light weight rod samples *A, B, C* and *D* separately suspended by thread. A bar magnet is slowly brought near each sample and the following observations are noted
(i) *A* is feebly repelled (ii) *B* is feebly attracted
(iii) *C* is strongly attracted (iv) *D* remains unaffected
Which one of the following is true ? *[AIPMT 2011]*
(a) *C* is of a diamagnetic material
(b) *D* is of a ferromagnetic material
(c) *A* is of a non-magnetic material
(d) *B* is of a paramagnetic material

06 If a diamagnetic substance is brought near the North or the South pole of a bar magnet, it is *[AIPMT 2009]*
(a) repelled by both the poles
(b) repelled by the North pole and attracted by the South pole
(c) attracted by the North pole and repelled by the South pole
(d) attracted by both the poles

07 Nickel shows ferromagnetic property at room temperature. If the temperature is increased beyond Curie temperature, then it will show *[AIPMT 2007]*
(a) paramagnetism (b) anti-ferromagnetism
(c) no magnetic property (d) diamagnetism

08 Above Curie temperature *[AIPMT 2006]*
(a) a ferromagnetic substance becomes paramagnetic
(b) a paramagnetic substance becomes diamagnetic
(c) a diamagnetic substance becomes paramagnetic
(d) a paramagnetic substance becomes ferromagnetic

09 If the magnetic dipole moment of an atom of diamagnetic material, paramagnetic material and ferromagnetic material are denoted by μ_d, μ_p and μ_f respectively, then *[NCERT (New) Pg. 148, AIPMT 2005]*
(a) $\mu_d \neq 0$ and $\mu_f \neq 0$ (b) $\mu_p = 0$ and $\mu_f \neq 0$
(c) $\mu_d = 0$ and $\mu_p \neq 0$ (d) $\mu_d \neq 0$ and $\mu_p = 0$

10 According to Curie's law, the magnetic susceptibility of a paramagnetic substance at an absolute temperature T is proportional to *[AIPMT 2003]*
(a) $\frac{1}{T^2}$ (b) T^2 (c) $\frac{1}{T}$ (d) T

11 A diamagnetic material in a magnetic field moves *[AIPMT 2003]*
(a) perpendicular to the field
(b) from weaker to the stronger parts of the field
(c) from stronger to the weaker parts of the field
(d) None of the above

12 In which type of material the magnetic susceptibility does not depend on temperature ? *[AIPMT 2001]*
(a) Diamagnetic (b) Paramagnetic
(c) Ferromagnetic (d) Ferrite

13 A diamagnetic substance is brought near a strong magnet, then it is *[AIPMT 1999]*
(a) attracted by a magnet
(b) repelled by a magnet
(c) repelled by North pole and attracted by South pole
(d) attracted by North pole and repelled by South pole

14 For protecting a sensitive equipment from the external magnetic field, it should be *[AIPMT 1998]*
(a) placed inside an aluminium can
(b) placed inside an iron can
(c) wrapped with insulation around it when passing current through it
(d) surrounded with fine copper sheet

Key Index

Topic 1

1 (b)	2 (a)	3 (d)	4 (c)	5 (b)	6 (b)	7 (a)	8 (a)

Topic 2

1 (a)	2 (b)	3 (b)	4 (b)	5 (c)	6 (c)

Topic 3

1 (d)	2 (d)	3 (a)

Topic 4

1 (a)	2 (d)	3 (c)	4 (d)	5 (d)	6 (a)	7 (a)	8 (a)	9 (c)	10 (c)
11 (c)	12 (a)	13 (b)	14 (b)						

Detailed **Explanations**

Topic 1

01. *(b)*

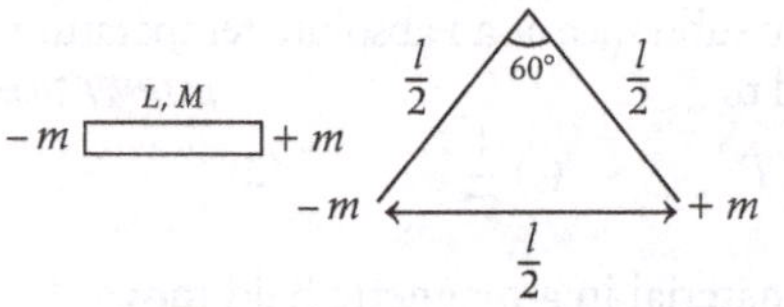

The magnetic moment is given by

$M = m \cdot L$

New magnetic moment, $M' = m \cdot L'$

$$= m \cdot \frac{l}{2} = \frac{ml}{2}$$

Thus, $M' = \frac{M}{2}$

02. *(a)* We know that, magnetic dipole moment,

$$M = nIA$$

For case (1)

An equilateral triangle of side a.

Total wire length

$= n \times$ Perimeter of the triangle

$$12a = n \times 3a$$

$$\Rightarrow \quad n = 4$$

Area of an equilateral triangle,

$$A = \frac{\sqrt{3}}{4} a^2$$

Magnetic dipole moment,

$$M = nIA$$

$$\Rightarrow \quad M = 4I \times \frac{\sqrt{3}}{4} a^2$$

$$\Rightarrow \quad M = \sqrt{3} I a^2$$

For case (2) A square of side a.

Total wire length $= n \times$ Perimeter of the square

$$12a = n \times 4a$$

$$\Rightarrow \quad n = 3$$

Area of the square loop,

$$A = a^2$$

Magnetic dipole moment,

$$M = nIA$$

$$\Rightarrow \quad M = 3Ia^2$$

03. *(d)* When wire of length L is bent in the form of a circle of radius R, then

$$L = 2\pi R$$

$$\Rightarrow \quad R = \frac{L}{2\pi} \quad \text{...(i)}$$

$\therefore$ Magnetic moment,

$$M = IA = I(\pi R^2)$$

$$= I \cdot \pi \left(\frac{L}{2\pi}\right)^2 \quad \text{[From Eq. (i)]}$$

$$= \frac{I\pi L^2}{4\pi^2} = \frac{IL^2}{4\pi} \text{ A-m}^2$$

04. *(c)* Magnetic moment is from S to N

So, $M_{net} = \sqrt{M^2 + M^2 + 2M^2 \cos\theta}$

M_{net} will be maximum if $\cos\theta$ is maximum. $\cos\theta$ will be maximum when θ will be minimum.

So, at $\theta = 30°$, M_{net} will be maximum.

05. *(b)* The magnetic moment,

$$M = ml$$

According to question,

$$l = \frac{\pi}{3} \times r$$

$$\text{So,} \quad r = \frac{3l}{\pi}$$

New magnetic moment,

$$M' = m \times r$$

$$= m \times \frac{3l}{\pi} = \frac{3}{\pi} \cdot ml = \frac{3M}{\pi}$$

06. *(b)* A compass needle which is allowed to move in a horizontal plane is taken to geometric pole. It will stay in any position as the horizontal component of earth's magnetic field becomes zero at the geometic pole.

07. *(a)* Magnetic field due to bar magnets exerts force on moving charges only. Since, charge is stationary, hence no force acts on it.

08. *(a)* As revolving charge is equivalent to a current, so

$$= qf = q \times \frac{\omega}{2\pi}$$

$$\text{But,} \quad \omega = \frac{v}{R}$$

$$\text{Therefore, } i = \frac{qv}{2\pi R}$$

Now, magnetic moment

$$M = iA = i \times \pi R^2$$

$$\text{or} \quad M = \frac{qv}{2\pi R} \times \pi R^2$$

$$= \frac{1}{2} qvR$$

Alternate Solution

Current produced due to circular motion of charge q is given by

$$i = \frac{q}{T} \quad [T = \text{Time period of revolution}]$$

$$\text{Now} \quad T = \frac{2\pi R}{v}$$

$$\text{So,} \quad i = \frac{q}{2\pi R} \times v$$

Now, magnetic moment (μ) is given by

$$M = iA$$

$$\text{So,} \quad M = \frac{qv}{2\pi R} \times \pi R^2 \Rightarrow M = \frac{qvR}{2}$$

Topic 2

01. *(a)* Work done for rotating the coil

$$W = MB(\cos\theta_1 - \cos\theta_2)$$

where, M = magnetic moment

B = magnetic field

Given, $\theta_1 = 0°, \theta_2 = 180°$

$$\Rightarrow \quad W = MB(\cos 0° - \cos 180°)$$

$$= 2MB = 2 \times NIA \times B$$

$$= 2 \times 250 \times 85 \times 10^{-6} \times (2.1 \times 1.25 \times 10^{-4}) \times 0.85$$

$$= 9.48 \times 10^{-6} \text{ J}$$

$$\approx 9.5 \times 10^{-6} \text{ J} = 9.5 \ \mu\text{J}$$

The closest option is (a).

02. *(b)* $\because$ Work done in rotating the magnet,

$$W = MB(\cos\theta_0 - \cos\theta)$$

where, M = magnetic moment of the magnet

B = magnetic field

$$W = MB(\cos 0° - \cos 60°)$$

$$= MB\left(1 - \frac{1}{2}\right) = \frac{MB}{2}$$

$$\therefore \quad MB = 2W \quad \text{...(i)}$$

Torque on a magnet in this position is given by,

$$\tau = M \times B$$

$$= MB \cdot \sin\theta = 2W \cdot \sin 60° \quad \text{[from Eq. (i)]}$$

$$= 2W \frac{\sqrt{3}}{2} = W\sqrt{3}$$

03. *(b)* Work done,

$$W = MB(\cos\theta_1 - \cos\theta_2)$$

Here, $\theta_1 = 0°, \theta_2 = 60°$

$$= MB(\cos 0° - \cos 60°)$$

$$= MB\left(1 - \frac{1}{2}\right) = \frac{MB}{2} \quad \ldots(i)$$

The torque on the needle, $\tau = \mathbf{M} \times \mathbf{B}$

In magnitude,

$$\tau = MB\sin\theta = MB\sin 60° = \frac{\sqrt{3}}{2}MB \quad \ldots(ii)$$

Dividing Eq. (ii) by (i), we get

$$\frac{\tau}{W} = \sqrt{3}$$

or $\tau = \sqrt{3}W = \sqrt{3} \times \sqrt{3}\text{ J} = 3\text{ J}$

04. *(b)* Given, $M = 0.4\text{ J T}^{-1}$

$$B = 0.16\text{ T}$$

Potential energy of bar magnet,

$$U = \mathbf{M} \cdot \mathbf{B} = -MB\cos\theta$$

For stable equilibrium,

$$\theta = 0°$$

$\therefore$ $U = -MB = -(0.4) \times 0.16$

$$= -0.064\text{ J}$$

05. *(c)* When magnetic dipole is rotated from initial position θ_1 to final position θ_2, then, work done

$$= MB(\cos\theta_1 - \cos\theta_2)$$

Given, $\theta_1 = 0°, \theta_2 = 60°$

Magnetic moment,

$$M = 2 \times 10^4\text{ J/T}$$

Magnetic field, $B = 6 \times 10^{-4}$ T

So, $W = MB\left(1 - \frac{1}{2}\right)$

$$\left[\because \cos 0° = 1 \text{ and } \cos 60° = 1/2\right]$$

$$= \frac{2 \times 10^4 \times 6 \times 10^{-4}}{2}$$

$$= 6\text{ J}$$

06. *(c)* When a bar magnet is placed in an external magnetic field **B**, a magnetic torque τ acts on it, which is given by $\tau = \mathbf{M} \times \mathbf{B} = |\mathbf{M}| \times |\mathbf{B}| \sin\theta$

(θ = angle between **M** and **B**)

Topic 3

01. *(d)* Given, magnetic field

$$B = 0.049\text{ T}$$

Time period, $T = \frac{5}{20} = \frac{1}{4}$ s

Moment of inertia,

$$I = 9.8 \times 10^{-6}\text{ kg m}^2$$

The time period of oscillation of a magnetic needle in a magnetic field is given by $T = 2\pi\sqrt{\frac{I}{MB}}$

where, M is the magnetic moment of the needle.

Thus, $T = 2\pi\sqrt{\frac{9.8 \times 10^{-6}}{M \times 0.049}}$

$$\Rightarrow \left(\frac{1}{4}\right)^2 = (2\pi)^2\left(\frac{9.8 \times 10^{-6}}{M \times 4.9 \times 10^{-2}}\right)$$

$$\Rightarrow \frac{1}{16} = \frac{4\pi^2 \times 2 \times 10^{-4}}{M}$$

$$\Rightarrow M = 16 \times 8 \times \pi^2 \times 10^{-4}$$

$$= 128\pi^2 \times 10^{-4}\text{ Am}^2$$

$$= 1280\pi^2 \times 10^{-5}\text{ Am}^2$$

02. *(d)* Net magnetic flux through a closed surface is zero because the number of field lines leaving the surface are equal to the number of field lines entering the surface.

03. *(a)*

key idea

You can find the time period of oscillation of a freely suspended bar magnet in magnetic field B using following formula,

$$T = 2\pi\sqrt{\frac{I}{MB}}$$

where, $I \rightarrow$ Moment of inertia, $M \rightarrow$ Magnetic dipole moment

The time period of bar magnet is

$$T = 2\pi\sqrt{\frac{I}{MH}}$$

where, M = magnetic moment of magnet

I = moment of inertia

and H = horizontal component of magnetic field

When same poles of magnets are placed on same side, then net magnetic moment

$$M_1 = M + 2M = 3M$$

$$\therefore \quad T_1 = 2\pi\sqrt{\frac{I}{M_1 H}}$$

$$= 2\pi\sqrt{\frac{I}{3MH}} \quad \ldots(i)$$

When opposite poles of magnets are placed on same side, then net magnetic moment

$$M_2 = 2M - M = M$$

$$\therefore \quad T_2 = 2\pi\sqrt{\frac{I}{M_2 H}}$$

$$= 2\pi\sqrt{\frac{I}{MH}} \quad \ldots(ii)$$

From Eqs. (i) and (ii), we observe that

$$T_1 < T_2$$

Topic 4

01. *(a)* For a diamagnetic material magnetic susceptibility χ is small and negative, is, $0 > \chi \geq -1$

For a ferromagnetic material, $\chi >> 1$.

For a paramagnetic material, $0 < \chi < \varepsilon$ and for non-magnetic material, $\chi = 0$

Hence, correct option is (a).

02. *(d)* Given, susceptibility, $\chi = 599$

Magnetic field, $B = 1200\text{ Am}^{-1}$

Permeability of the material of the rod = ?

As, $\mu_m = \mu_0(1 + \chi)$

$$= 4\pi \times 10^{-7}(1 + 599)$$

$$= 2.4\pi \times 10^{-4}\text{ TmA}^{-1}$$

03. *(c)* As the source of current is switched on, a magnetic field sets up in between the poles of the electromagnet. As we know that a diamagnetic substance when placed in a magnetic field acquires a feeble magnetism opposite to the direction of magnetic field.

Also, in the presence of the field (non-uniform), these substances are attracted towards the weaker field, i.e. they move from stronger to weaker magnetic field.

Due to these reasons, the rod is repelled by the field produced to the current source. Hence, it is pushed up, out of horizontal field and gains gravitational potential energy.

04. *(d)* As we know the relation between the magnetic permeability and susceptibility of material, i.e.

$$\mu_r = 1 + \chi_m \quad \ldots(i)$$

$\because$ For diamagnetic substances, $\mu_r < 1$

So, according to equation (i), the magnetic susceptibility (χ_m) of diamagnetic substance will be negative.

While in the case of para and ferromagnetic substances, diamagnetic susceptibility is positive.

05. *(d)* Paramagnetic material will be feebly attracted, diamagnetic material will be feebly repelled and ferromagnetic material will be strongly attracted.

06. *(a)* Diamagnetic substances are weakly magnetised in a direction opposite to that of applied magnetic field.

These are repelled in an external magnetic field i.e. have a tendency to move from high to low field region, i.e. it is repelled by both North and South poles of a bar magnet.

07. *(a)* Ferromagnetic substances (nickle, cobalt etc.) behave like paramagnetic substances when these are heated above curie temperature.

08. *(a)* Above the Curie temperature, a ferromagnetic substance becomes paramagnetic. This is because the thermal energy at the temperature above Curie point is sufficient to disrupt the alignment of the magnetic dipoles within the material , causing if to lose its strong magnetic properties and behave like a paramagnetic substance.

09. *(c)* In diamagnetic substances, in each pair of electrons, the spin of both the electrons are in opposite directions. Hence, the electrons of each pair completely cancel the magnetic moment of each other.

Thus, the net magnetic moment of each atom of such substances is zero, i.e. $\mu_d = 0$.

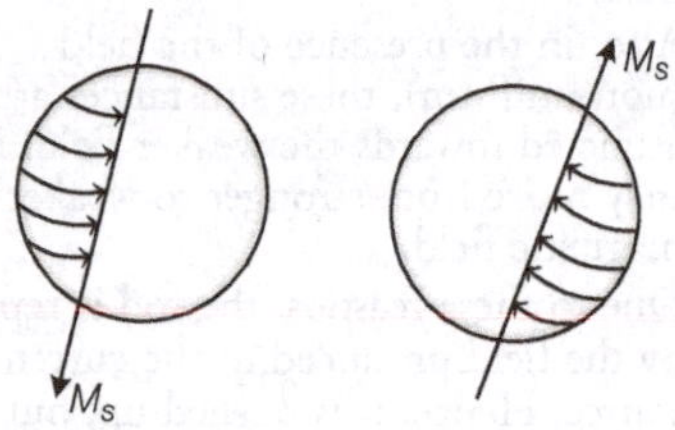

The property of paramagnetism is bound in those substances whose atoms or molecules have an excess of electrons spinning in same direction. Hence, atoms of paramagnetic substances have permanent magnetic moment i.e. $\mu_p \neq 0$.

The property of ferromagnetism is found in substances which acquire very strong magnetism when placed in an external magnetic field. Like the paramagnetic substances, each atom of ferromagnetic substances also has a permanent magnetic moment i.e. $\mu_f \neq 0$.

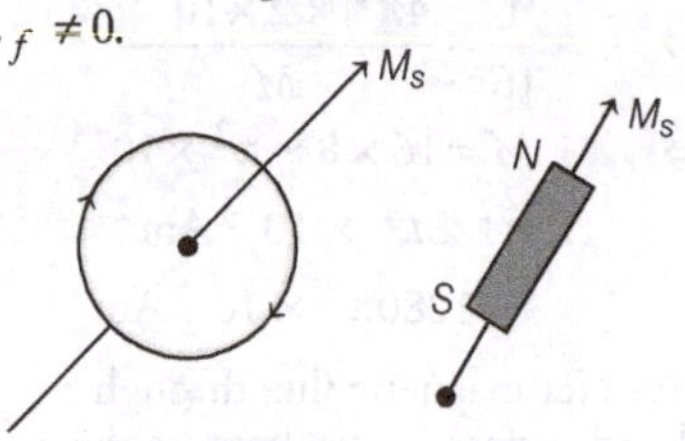

10. *(c)* According to Curie's law, magnetic susceptibility χ_m of a paramagnetic substance is inversely proportional to absolute temperature T i.e.

$$\chi_m \propto \frac{1}{T}$$

11. *(c)* When a diamagnetic material is placed in an external magnetic field, the spin motion of electrons is so modified that the electrons which produce the magnetic moments in the direction of external field slow down, while the electrons which produce magnetic moments in opposite direction get accelerated.

Thus, a net magnetic moment is induced in the opposite direction of applied magnetic field.

Hence, the substance is magnetised opposite to the external field. Thus, it moves from stronger to weaker parts of the magnetic field.

Diamagnetism is present in all the substances.

However, its effect is so weak in most cases that it gets shifted by other effects like paramagnetism, ferromagmetism, etc.

12. *(a)* The magnetic susceptibility of a material is a measure of the ease with which a specimen of that material can be magnetised in a magnetising field. For a diamagnetic substance, magnetic susceptibility (χ_m) is independent of temperature.

> • Concept **Enhancer**
>
> Among the three types of magnetic materials (Diamagnetic, paramagnetic and ferromagnetic), only diamagnetic substance has negative value of susceptibility.

13. *(b)* When diamagnetic substances are placed in magnetic field of a strong magnet, then it is feebly magnetised in the opposite to the direction of field or it is repelled by strong magnet.

14. *(b)* Iron is a ferromagnetic substance. There are no magnetic lines of force inside a ferromagnetic substance.

So, equipment may be protected by placing it inside the can made of a ferromagnetic substance.

Hence, it is placed inside an iron can.

C-20

NEET Chapterwise Topicwise Physics

In NEET 2024, 1 question was visible from this chapter. In past 5 years, 4 questions from topic-1, 1 question from topic-2, 1 question from topic-3 and 1 question from topic-4 were asked.

For detailed analysis scan QR code

ELECTROMAGNETIC INDUCTION

Topic 1 Magnetic Flux, Faraday's Law and Lenz's Law

01

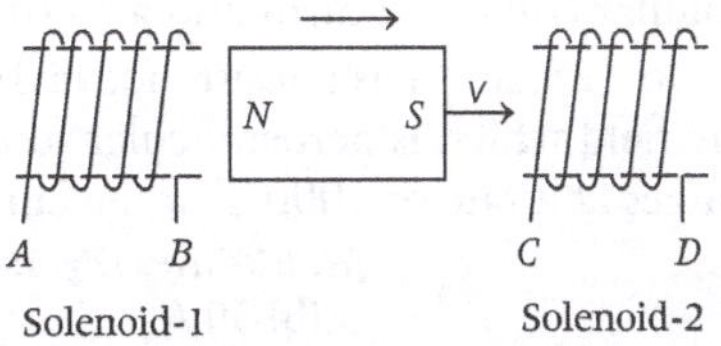

In the above diagram, a strong bar magnet is moving towards solenoid-2 from solenoid-1. The direction of induced current in solenoid-1 and that in solenoid-2, respectively, are through the directions. *[NCERT (New) Pg. 160, NEET 2024]*

(a) *AB* and *DC* (b) *BA* and *CD*
(c) *AB* and *CD* (d) *BA* and *DC*

02 A square loop of side 1 m and resistance 1 Ω placed in a magnetic field of 0.5 T. If the plane of loop is perpendicular to the direction of magnetic field, the magnetic flux through the loop is *[NCERT (New) Pg. 157, NEET 2022]*

(a) 0.5 Wb (b) 1 Wb
(c) zero Wb (d) 2 Wb

03 A big circular coil of 1000 turns and average radius 10 m is rotating about its horizontal diameter at 2 rad s^{-1}. If the vertical component of earth's magnetic field at that place is 2×10^{-5} T and electrical resistance of the coil is 12.56 Ω, then the maximum induced current in the coil will be *[NCERT (New) Pg. 158, NEET 2022]*

(a) 0.25 A (b) 1.5 A
(c) 1 A (d) 2 A

04 The magnetic flux linked with a coil (in Wb) is given by the equation $\phi = 5t^2 + 3t + 16$

The magnitude of induced emf in the coil at the fourth second will be *[NEET (Oct.) 2020]*

(a) 33 V (b) 43 V
(c) 108 V (d) 10 V

05 A coil of 800 turns effective area 0.05 m^2 is kept perpendicular to a magnetic field 5×10^{-5} T. When the plane of the coil is rotated by 90° around any of its co-planar axis in 0.1 s, the emf induced in the coil will be *[NCERT (New) Pg. 158, NEET (National) 2019]*

(a) 0.2 V (b) 2×10^{-3} V
(c) 0.02 V (d) 2 V

06 A uniform magnetic field is restricted within a region of radius *r*. The magnetic field changes with time at a rate $\frac{d\mathbf{B}}{dt}$. Loop 1 of radius $R > r$ encloses the region *r* and loop 2 of radius *R* is outside the region of magnetic field as shown in the figure. Then, the emf generated is *[NCERT (New) Pg. 158, NEET 2016]*

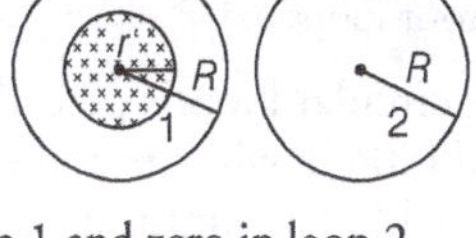

(a) zero in loop 1 and zero in loop 2
(b) $-\frac{d\mathbf{B}}{dt}\pi r^2$ in loop 1 and $-\frac{d\mathbf{B}}{dt}\pi r^2$ in loop 2
(c) $-\frac{d\mathbf{B}}{dt}\pi R^2$ in loop 1 and zero in loop 2
(d) $-\frac{d\mathbf{B}}{dt}\pi r^2$ in loop 1 and zero in loop 2

07 An electron moves on a straight line path *XY* as shown. The *abcd* is a coil adjacent in the path of electron. What will be the direction of current, if any induced in the coil ? *[NCERT (New) Pg. 160, AIPMT 2015]*

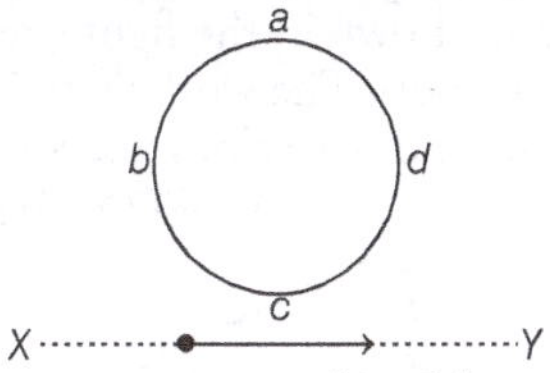

(a) *abcd* (b) *adcb*
(c) The current will reverse its direction as the electron goes past the coil
(d) No current induced

08 A wire loop is rotated in a magnetic field. The frequency of change of direction of the induced emf is *[NEET 2013]*
(a) once per revolution (b) twice per revolution
(c) four times per revolution (d) six times per revolution

09 A coil of resistance 400 Ω is placed in a magnetic field. If the magnetic flux ϕ (Wb) linked with the coil varies with time t (second) as $\phi = 50t^2 + 4$. The current in the coil at $t = 2$ s is *[NCERT (New) Pg. 158, AIPMT 2012]*
(a) 0.5 A (b) 0.1 A (c) 2 A (d) 1 A

10 A conducting circular loop is placed in a uniform magnetic field, $B = 0.025$ T with its plane perpendicular to the loop. The radius of the loop is made to shrink at a constant rate of 1 mm s^{-1}. The induced emf when the radius is 2 cm, is *[AIPMT 2010]*
(a) $2\pi\,\mu V$ (b) $\pi\,\mu V$ (c) $\frac{\pi}{2}\,\mu V$ (d) $2\,\mu V$

11 A rectangular, a square, a circular and an elliptical loop, all in the XY-plane, are moving out of a uniform magnetic field with a constant velocity, $\mathbf{v} = v\hat{\mathbf{i}}$. The magnetic field is directed along the negative Z-axis direction. The induced emf, during the passage of these loops, out of the field region, will not remain constant for *[NCERT (New) Pg. 158, AIPMT 2009]*
(a) the rectangular, circular and elliptical loops
(b) the circular and the elliptical loops
(c) only the elliptical loop
(d) any of the four loops

12 A conducting circular loop is placed in a uniform magnetic field 0.04 T with its plane perpendicular to the magnetic field. The radius of the loop starts shrinking at 2 mm s^{-1}. The induced emf in the loop when the radius is 2 cm is *[AIPMT 2009]*
(a) $3.2\,\pi\,\mu V$ (b) $4.8\,\pi\,\mu V$ (c) $0.8\,\pi\,\mu V$ (d) $1.6\,\pi\,\mu V$

13 A circular disc of radius 0.2 m is placed in a uniform magnetic field of induction $\frac{1}{\pi}$ (Wb/m^2) in such a way that its axis makes an angle of 60° with **B** The magnetic flux linked with the disc is *[AIPMT 2008]*
(a) 0.02 Wb (b) 0.06 Wb (c) 0.08 Wb (d) 0.01 Wb

14 As a result of change in the magnetic flux linked to the closed loop shown in the figure, an emf V volt is induced in the loop. The work done (joule) in taking a charge q coulomb once along the loop is *[NCERT (New) Pg. 163, AIPMT 2005]*

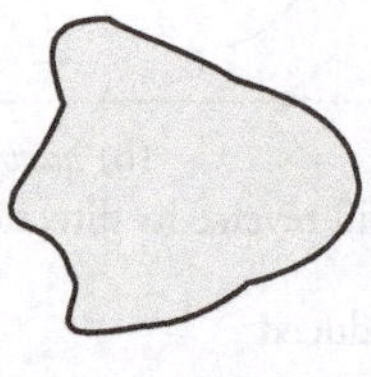

(a) qV (b) zero
(c) $2\,qV$ (d) $qV/2$

15 The magnetic flux through a circuit of resistance R changes by an amount $\Delta\phi$ in a time Δt. Then the total quantity of electric charge q that passes any point in the circuit during the time Δt is represented by *[NCERT (New) Pg. 158, AIPMT 2004]*
(a) $q = \frac{1}{R}\cdot\frac{\Delta\phi}{\Delta t}$ (b) $q = \frac{\Delta\phi}{R}$
(c) $q = \frac{\Delta\phi}{\Delta t}$ (d) $q = R\cdot\frac{\Delta\phi}{\Delta t}$

16 The total charge induced in a conducting loop when it is moved in magnetic field depends on *[AIPMT 1992]*
(a) the rate of change of magnetic flux
(b) initial magnetic flux
(c) the total change in magnetic flux
(d) final magnetic flux

17 A rectangular coil of 20 turns and area of cross-section 25 cm^2 has a resistance of 100 Ω. If a magnetic field which is perpendicular to the plane of coil changes at a rate of 1000 T/s, the current in the coil is *[NCERT (New) Pg. 158, AIPMT 1992]*
(a) 1 A (b) 50 A
(c) 0.5 A (d) 5 A

18 A magnetic field of 2×10^{-2} T acts at right angles to a coil of area 100 cm^2, with 50 turns. The average emf induced in the coil is 0.1 V, when it is removed from the field in t second. The value of t is *[NCERT (New) Pg. 158, AIPMT 1991]*
(a) 10 s (b) 0.1 s (c) 0.01 s (d) 1 s

Topic 2 Motional EMF and Eddy Current

01 A wheel with 20 metallic spokes each 1 m long is rotated with a speed of 120 rpm in a plane perpendicular to a magnetic field of 0.4 G. The induced emf between the axle and rim of the wheel will be (1 G = 10^{-4} T) *[NCERT (New) Pg. 162, NEET (Oct.) 2020]*
(a) 2.51×10^{-4} V (b) 2.51×10^{-5} V
(c) 4.0×10^{-5} V (d) 2.51 V

02 A cycle wheel of radius 0.5 m is rotated with constant angular velocity of 10 rad/s in a region of magnetic field of 0.1 T which is perpendicular to the plane of the wheel. The emf generated between its centre and the rim is *[NCERT (New) Pg. 162, NEET (Odisha) 2019]*
(a) 0.25 V (b) 0.125 V
(c) 0.5 V (d) zero

03 In which of the following devices, the eddy current effect is not used ? *[NEET (National) 2019]*
(a) Magnetic braking in train (b) Electromagnet
(c) Electric heater (d) Induction furnace

04 A thin semicircular conducting ring PQR of radius r is falling with its plane vertical in a horizontal magnetic field B, as shown in figure. The potential difference developed across the ring when its speed is v, is

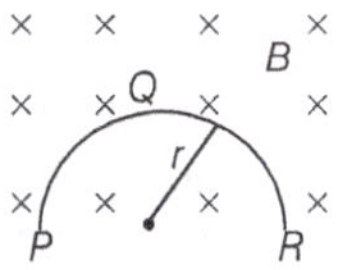

[NCERT (New) Pg. 163, AIPMT 2014]

(a) zero
(b) $Bv\pi r^2/2$ and P is at higher potential
(c) πrBv and R is at higher potential
(d) $2rBv$ and R is at higher potential

05 A conductor of length 0.4 m is moving with a speed of 7 m/s perpendicular to a magnetic field of intensity 0.9 Wb/m^2. The induced emf across the conductor is *[NCERT (New) Pg. 163, AIPMT 1995]*
(a) 1.26 V (b) 2.52 V (c) 5.04 V (d) 25.2 V

06 Eddy currents are produced when *[AIPMT 1988]*
(a) a metal is kept in varying magnetic field
(b) a metal is kept in steady magnetic field
(c) a circular coil is placed in a magnetic field
(d) current is passed through a circular coil

Topic 3 Mutual-Inductance

01 Two conducting circular loops of radii R_1 and R_2 are placed in the same plane with their centres coinciding. If $R_1 >> R_2$, the mutual inductance M between them will be directly proportional to *[NCERT (New) Pg. 167, NEET 2021]*
(a) $\frac{R_1}{R_2}$ (b) $\frac{R_2}{R_1}$ (c) $\frac{R_1^2}{R_2}$ (d) $\frac{R_2^2}{R_1}$

02 A long solenoid of diameter 0.1 m has 2×10^4 turns per metre. At the centre of the solenoid, a coil of 100 turns and radius 0.01 m is placed with its axis coinciding with the solenoid axis. The current in the solenoid reduces at a constant rate to 0 A from 4 A in 0.05 s. If the resistance of the coil is $10\pi^2\ \Omega$, the total charge flowing through the coil during this time is *[NCERT (New) Pg. 168, NEET 2017]*
(a) $32\pi\ \mu C$ (b) $16\ \mu C$ (c) $32\ \mu C$ (d) $16\pi\ \mu C$

03 Two coils of self-inductances 2 mH and 8 mH are placed so close together that the effective flux in one coil is completely linked with the other. The mutual inductance between these coils is *[AIPMT 2006]*
(a) 10 mH (b) 6 mH (c) 4 mH (d) 16 mH

04 Two coils have a mutual inductance of 0.005 H. The current changes in the first coil according to equation $i = i_0 \sin \omega t$, $i_0 = 10\ A$ and $\omega = 100\ \pi$ rad/s. The maximum value of emf in the second coil is *[NCERT (New) Pg. 167, AIPMT 1998]*
(a) 2π (b) 5π (c) π (d) 4π

Topic 4 Self-Inductance

01 The magnetic energy stored in an inductor of inductance 4 μH carrying a current of 2 A is *[NCERT (New) Pg. 169, NEET 2023]*
(a) 4 mJ (b) 8 mJ
(c) 8 μJ (d) 4 μJ

02 A light bulb and an inductor coil are connected to AC source through a key as shown in the figure below. The key is closed and after sometime an iron rod is inserted into the interior of the inductor. The glow of the light bulb *[NEET (Oct.) 2020]*

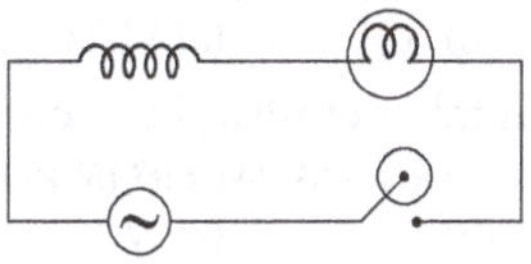

(a) decreases (b) remains unchanged
(c) will fluctuate (d) increases

03 The magnetic potential energy stored in a certain inductor is 25 mJ, when the current in the inductor is 60 mA. This inductor is of inductance *[NCERT (New) Pg. 169, NEET 2018]*
(a) 1.389 H (b) 138.88 H
(c) 0.138 H (d) 13.89 H

04 A long solenoid has 1000 turns. When a current of 4A flows through it, the magnetic flux linked with each turn of the solenoid is 4×10^{-3} Wb. The self-inductance of the solenoid is *[NEET 2016]*
(a) 3 H (b) 2 H
(c) 1 H (d) 4 H

05 The current I in the inductance is varying with time according to the plot shown in figure. *[NCERT (New) Pg. 168, AIPMT 2012]*

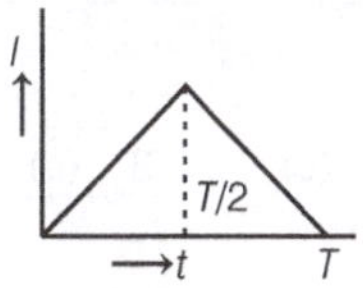

Which one of the following is the correct variation of voltage with time in the coil ?

(a)
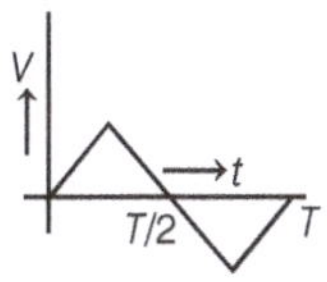

(b)
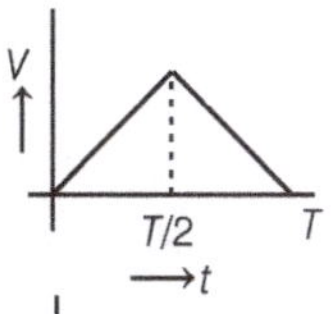

(c)
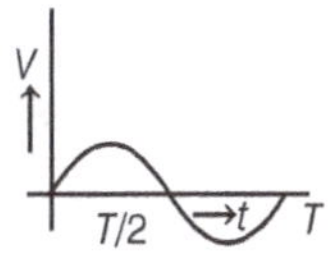

(d)
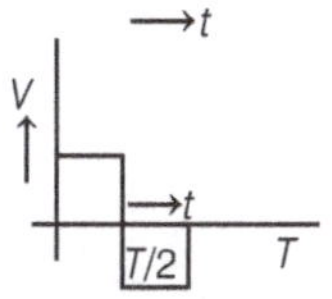

06 A long solenoid has 500 turns. When a current of 2 A is passed through it, the resulting magnetic flux linked with each turn of the solenoid is 4×10^{-3} Wb. The self-inductance of the solenoid is *[AIPMT 2008]*
(a) 2.5 H (b) 2 H (c) 1 H (d) 4 H

07 In an inductor of self-inductance $L = 2$ mH, current changes with time according to relation $i = t^2 e^{-t}$. At what time emf is zero ? *[NCERT (New) Pg. 168, AIPMT 2001]*
(a) 4 s (b) 3 s (c) 2 s (d) 1 s

08 A varying current in a coil changes from 10 A to zero in 0.5 s. If the average emf induced in the coil is 220 V, the self-inductance of the coil is *[AIPMT 1995]*
(a) 5 H (b) 6 H (c) 11 H (d) 12 H

09 If N is the number of turns in a coil, the value of self-inductance varies as *[NCERT (New) Pg. 168, AIPMT 1993]*
(a) N^0 (b) N (c) N^2 (d) N^{-2}

10 What is the self-inductance of a coil which produces 5 V when the current changes from 3 A to 2 A in one millisecond ? *[AIPMT 1993]*
(a) 5000 H (b) 5 mH (c) 50 H (d) 5 H

11 A 100 mH coil carries a current of 1 A. Energy stored in its magnetic field is *[AIPMT 1991]*
(a) 0.5 J (b) 1 A
(c) 0.05 J (d) 0.1 J

12 If the number of turns per unit length of a coil of solenoid is doubled, the self-inductance of the solenoid will *[NCERT (New) Pg. 168, AIPMT 1991]*
(a) remain unchanged (b) be halved
(c) be doubled (d) become four times

13 An inductor may store energy in *[AIPMT 1990]*
(a) its electric field
(b) its coils
(c) its magnetic field
(d) Both in electric and magnetic fields

14 In the circuit of figure, the bulb will become suddenly bright, if *[NCERT (New) Pg. 168, AIPMT 1989]*

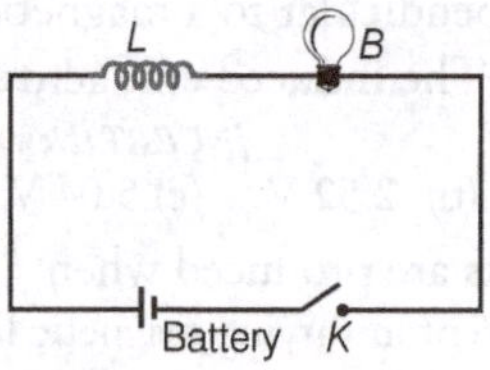

(a) contact is made or broken (b) contact is made
(c) contact is broken (d) None of these

15 Energy in a current carrying coil is stored in the form of *[AIPMT 1988]*
(a) electric field (b) magnetic field
(c) dielectric strength (d) heat

• Key Index

Topic 1

1 (a)	2 (a)	3 (c)	4 (d)	5 (c)	6 (d)	7 (c)	8 (b)	9 (a)	10 (b)
11 (b)	12 (a)	13 (a)	14 (a)	15 (b)	16 (c)	17 (c)	18 (b)		

Topic 2

1 (a)	2 (b)	3 (c)	4 (d)	5 (b)	6 (a)

Topic 3

1 (d)	2 (c)	3 (c)	4 (b)

Topic 4

1 (c)	2 (a)	3 (d)	4 (c)	5 (d)	6 (c)	7 (c)	8 (c)	9 (c)	10 (b)
11 (c)	12 (d)	13 (c)	14 (c)	15 (b)					

Detailed **Explanations**

Topic 1

01. *(a)* The direction of induced current is always such that it opposes the cause (which created it). For solenoid-1, the magnet is moving away from the solenoid-1 thus near the *B*-point. *S*-pole will be generated.

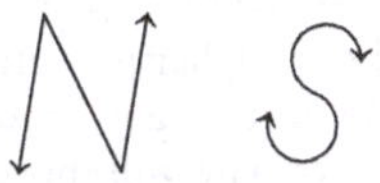

Thus, the current in solenoid-1 will be from *A* to *B*.

Similarly, the current in the solenoid-2 will be from *D* to *C*.

02. *(a)* Side of square loop, $a = 1$ m

$\therefore$ Area of square loop, $A = 1\ \text{m}^2$

Resistance of square loop, $R = 1\ \Omega$

Magnetic field, $B = 0.5$ T

$\therefore$ Magnetic flux passing through the loop,

$\phi = BA\cos\theta = 0.5 \times 1 \times \cos 0° = 0.5$ Wb

03. *(c)* Given, $N = 1000$, $r = 10$ m

$$\omega = 2\ \text{rad s}^{-1}$$

$$B = 2 \times 10^{-5}\ \text{T}$$

$$R = 12.56\ \Omega$$

Maximum induced emf $= N\omega AB$

Here area of the circular coil

$$A = \pi r^2$$

$$\varepsilon = N\omega\pi r^2 B$$

$$= 1000 \times 2 \times 3.14 \times (10)^2 \times 2 \times 10^{-5}$$

$$\varepsilon = 12.56\ \text{V}$$

The maximum induced current,

$$i_{\max} = \frac{\varepsilon}{R} \Rightarrow i_{\max} = \frac{12.56}{12.56} = 1\ \text{A}$$

04. *(d)*

key idea

If magnetic flux linked with a coil is given as a function of time *t*, then you can find induced emf by differentiating it with respect to time *t*.

i.e. $|e| = \dfrac{d\phi}{dt}$

Magnetic flux linked with coil,

$$\phi = (5t^2 + 3t + 16)\ \text{Wb}$$

Magnitude of induced emf,

$$e = \left|-\frac{d\phi}{dt}\right| = \frac{d}{dt}(5t^2 + 3t + 16)$$

$$= 10t + 3$$

For $t = 3$ s,

$$e_3 = 10 \times 3 + 3 = 33\ \text{V}$$

For $t = 4$ s

$$e_4 = 10 \times 4 + 3 = 43\ \text{V}$$

$\therefore$ Induced emf in coil at the fourth second is given as

$$e = e_4 - e_3$$

$$= 43 - 33 = 10\ \text{V}$$

05. *(c)* Given, area of coil, $A = 0.05\ \text{m}^2$

Magnetic field, $B = 5 \times 10^{-5}$ T

and number of turns, $N = 800$.

The magnetic flux linked with the coil is

$$\phi = N(\mathbf{B} \cdot \mathbf{A}) = NBA\cos\theta \quad \ldots\text{(i)}$$

where, θ is the angle between **B** and **A**.

The emf induced when coil is rotated from $\theta_1 = 0°$ to $\theta_2 = 90°$ is

$$e = -\frac{\Delta\phi}{\Delta t} = -\frac{\Delta}{\Delta t}(NBA\cos\theta)$$

[using Eq. (i)]

$$= -\frac{NBA}{\Delta t}(\cos\theta_2 - \cos\theta_1) \ldots\text{(ii)}$$

Here, $\Delta t = 0.1$ s

Thus, substituting the given values in Eq. (ii), we get

$$e = -\frac{800 \times 5 \times 10^{-5} \times 0.05 \times [\cos 90° - \cos 0°]}{0.1}$$

$$= 2000 \times 10^{-5} = 0.02\ \text{V}$$

06. *(d)* Induced emf in the region is given by

$$|e| = \frac{d\phi}{dt}$$

where, $\phi = \mathbf{B}A = \pi r^2 \mathbf{B}$

$$\Rightarrow \quad \frac{d\phi}{dt} = -\pi r^2 \frac{d\mathbf{B}}{dt}$$

Rate of change of magnetic flux associated with loop 1

$$e_1 = -\frac{d\phi_1}{dt} = -\pi r^2 \frac{d\mathbf{B}}{dt}$$

Similarly e_2 = emf associated with loop 2

$$= -\frac{d\phi_2}{dt} = 0 \qquad (\because \phi_2 = 0)$$

07. *(c)* First current develops in direction of *abcd* but when electron moves away then magnetic field inside loop decreases and current changes its direction.

08. *(b)* If a wire loop is rotated in a magnetic field, the frequency of change in the direction of the induced emf is twice per revolution.

09. *(a)* Induced emf in a coil is given by

$$E = \left|-\frac{d\phi}{dt}\right|$$

Given, $\phi = 50t^2 + 4$

and resistance, $R = 400\ \Omega$

So, $E = \left|-\dfrac{d\phi}{dt}\right|_{t=2} = |100t|_{t=2} = 200$ V

So, current in the coil will be

$$I = \frac{E}{R} = \frac{200}{400} = \frac{1}{2} = 0.5\ \text{A}$$

10. *(b)* Magnetic flux ϕ linked with magnetic field **B** and area **A** is given by

$$\phi = \mathbf{B} \cdot \mathbf{A} = |\mathbf{B}||\mathbf{A}|\cos\theta$$

Here, $\theta = 0°$

So, $\phi = BA = B\pi r^2$

Now, Induced emf,

$$|e| = \left|\frac{-d\phi}{dt}\right| = B\pi(2r)\frac{dr}{dt}$$

$$= 0.025 \times \pi \times 2 \times 2 \times 10^{-2} \times 1 \times 10^{-3}$$

$$= \pi\,\mu\text{V}$$

11. *(b)* Area coming out per second from the magnetic field is not constant for elliptical and circular loops, so induced emf, during the passage out of these loops, from the field region will not remain constant.

12. *(a)* Magnetic field, $B = 0.04$ T

and rate of change of radius of coil due to shrinkage,

$$\frac{-dr}{dt} = 2\ \text{mm s}^{-1}$$

Induced emf,

$$e = \frac{-d\phi}{dt} = -B\frac{dA}{dt} = -B\frac{d(\pi r^2)}{dt}$$

$$= -B\pi 2r\frac{dr}{dt}$$

Now, if $r = 2$ cm

$$e = -0.04 \times \pi \times 2 \times 2 \times 10^{-2} \times 2 \times 10^{-3}$$

$$= 3.2\,\pi\,\mu\text{V}$$

13. *(a)* Magnetic flux $\phi = \mathbf{B} \cdot \mathbf{A}$

$$\phi = BA\cos\theta = \frac{1}{\pi} \times \pi(0.2)^2 \cos 60^\circ$$

$$= 0.02 \text{ Wb}$$

14. *(a)* Work done in moving a charge through potential difference V is given by $W = qV$

15. *(b)* From Faraday's second law, emf induced in the circuit

$$e = \frac{\Delta\phi}{\Delta t}$$

If R is the resistance of the circuit, then

$$i = \frac{e}{R} = \frac{\Delta\phi}{R\Delta t}$$

Thus, charge passing through the circuit,

$$q = i \times \Delta t$$

$$\Rightarrow \quad q = \frac{\Delta\phi}{R\Delta t} \cdot \Delta t \Rightarrow q = \frac{\Delta\phi}{R}$$

16. *(c)* Total charge induced in a conducting loop is

$$q = \int i \, dt$$

As, $i = \dfrac{e}{R}$

$$\therefore \quad q = \int \frac{e}{R} dt = \frac{1}{R}\int e \, dt$$

Induced emf e is given by

$$e = -\frac{d\phi}{dt}$$

$$\therefore \quad q = \frac{1}{R}\int\left(-\frac{d\phi}{dt}\right)dt = \frac{1}{R}\int d\phi$$

Hence, total charge induced in the conducting loop depends upon resistance of loop and change in magnetic flux.

17. *(c)* Total number of turns, $N = 20$

Area of coil, $A = 25 \text{ cm}^2$

$$= 25 \times 10^{-4} \text{ m}^2$$

Change in magnetic field w.r.t. t

$$\frac{dB}{dt} = 1000 \text{ T/s}$$

Resistance of coil $R = 100\ \Omega$

$\therefore$ Induced current,

$$i = \frac{e}{R} = \frac{NA\dfrac{dB}{dt}}{R} \quad \left(\because e = NA\frac{dB}{dt}\right)$$

$$= \frac{20 \times 25 \times 10^{-4} \times 1000}{100}$$

$$= 0.5 \text{ A}$$

18. *(b)* Emf induced in the coil due to change in magnetic flux

$$e = -\frac{d\phi}{dt} = -\frac{(\phi_2 - \phi_1)}{dt}$$

When magnetic field is perpendicular to coil

$$\phi_1 = NBA$$

When coil is removed, $\phi_2 = 0$

So, $\quad e = -\dfrac{(0 - NBA)}{dt}$ or $dt = \dfrac{NBA}{e}$

Here, $N = 50$, $B = 2 \times 10^{-2}$ T,

$A = 100 \text{ cm}^2$

$= 10^{-2} \text{ m}^2$ and $e = 0.1$ V

$$\therefore \quad dt = \frac{50 \times 2 \times 10^{-2} \times 10^{-2}}{0.1} = 0.1 \text{s}$$

Topic 2

01. *(a)*

key idea

You can find induced emf between the axle and rim of the wheel with the help of following formula

i.e. $\quad e = \dfrac{1}{2}B\omega l^2$

where, symbols are there usual meanings.

Given, magnetic field,

$$B = 0.4 \text{ G} = 0.4 \times 10^{-4} \text{ T}$$

$$l = 1 \text{ m}$$

Frequency, $f = 12 \text{ rpm} = \dfrac{120}{60}$ rps

$$= 2 \text{ Hz}$$

Induced emf between the axle and rim of the wheel is given as

$$e = \frac{1}{2}B\omega l^2 = \frac{1}{2}B(2\pi f)l^2 = \pi B f l^2$$

$$= 3.14 \times 0.4 \times 10^{-4} \times 2 \times 1^2$$

$$= 2.51 \times 10^{-4} \text{ V}$$

02. *(b)*

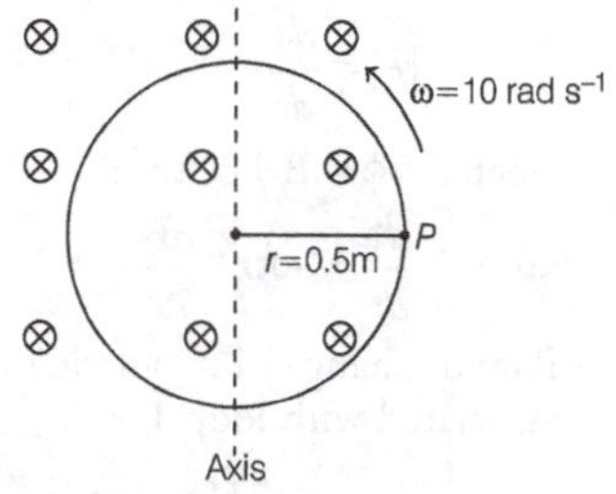

Induced emf is given by,

$$e = \frac{1}{2}B\omega r^2 \quad \ldots(\text{i})$$

Here, $B = 0.1$ T, $\omega = 10$ rad/s,

$r = 0.5$ m

Substituting these values in Eq. (i), we get

$$\therefore e = \frac{1}{2} \times 0.1 \times 10 \times (0.5)^2 = \frac{1}{8}$$

$$= 0.125 \text{ V}$$

03. *(c)* Electric heaters are not based on the eddy current effect. Rather their working is based on Joule's heating effect of current.

04. *(d)* For induced emf,

$$e = Bv(L_{\text{eff}}) = Bv \times (2r)$$

$$= 2Bvr \ (\because L_{\text{eff}} = \text{diameter} = 2r)$$

R will be at higher potential, we can find it by using right hand rule. The electrons of wire will move towards end P due to electric force and at end R the excess positive charge will be left.

Concept Enhancer

An induced emf (BLv) called motional emf is produced by moving a conductor instead of varying the magnetic field.

05. *(b)*

key idea

Motional emf is determined by using following formula.

$e = Bvl\sin\theta$

where, symbols are there usual meanings.

Given, length of conductor, l

$$= 0.4 \text{ m}$$

speed, $v = 7$ m/s

Magnetic field, $B = 0.9 \text{ Wb/m}^2$

Induced emf,

$$e = Blv \sin\theta$$

$[\theta = 90^\circ$ as $\mathbf{B}$ is $\perp$ v$]$

$$= 0.9 \times 0.4 \times 7 \times \sin 90^\circ$$

$$= 2.52 \text{ V}$$

06. *(a)* Eddy currents are the currents induced in the body of a conductor when the amount of magnetic flux linked with the conductor changes.

Topic 3

01. *(d)* Since, both conducting circular loops are in same plane and their centres are coinciding.

Hence, magnetic flux, $\phi = Mi \quad \ldots(\text{i})$

Here, M is the mutual inductance.

Also, the magnetic flux, $\phi = BA$

Here, B is the magnetic field and $A\ (= \pi R_2^2)$ is the area of the inner circular loop. If the current passing through the outer loop is i, then the magnetic field,

$$B = \frac{\mu_0 i}{2R_1}$$

Magnetic flux, $\phi = BA$

$$\Rightarrow \quad \phi = \frac{\mu_0 i}{2R_1} \pi R_2^2 \quad \ldots\text{(ii)}$$

Comparing Eqs. (i) and (ii), we get

$$M = \frac{\mu_0}{2R_1} \pi R_2^2$$

Thus, the mutual inductance is directly proportional to the $\frac{R_2^2}{R_1}$.

02. *(c)* Current induced in the coil is given by

$$i = \frac{1}{R}\left(\frac{d\phi}{dt}\right) \Rightarrow \frac{\Delta q}{\Delta t} = \frac{1}{R}\left(\frac{\Delta\phi}{\Delta t}\right)$$

Given, resistance of the solenoid,

$$R = 10\pi^2\ \Omega$$

Radius of second and coil $r = 10^{-2}$

$$\Delta t = 0.05\text{ s}$$

$$\Delta i = 4 - 0 = 4\text{ A}$$

Charge flowing through the coil is given by

$$\Delta q = \left(\frac{\Delta\phi}{\Delta t}\right)\frac{1}{R}(\Delta t)$$

$$= \mu_0 N_1 N_2 \pi r^2 \left(\frac{\Delta i}{\Delta t}\right)\frac{1}{R}\Delta t$$

$$= 4\pi \times 10^{-7} \times 2 \times 10^4 \times 100 \times \pi$$

$$\times (10^{-2})^2 \times \left(\frac{4}{0.05}\right) \times \frac{1}{10\pi^2} \times 0.05$$

$$= 32 \times 10^{-6}\text{ C} = 32\ \mu\text{C}$$

03. *(c)* When the total flux associated with one coil links with the other i.e. a case of maximum flux linkage, then mutual induction in coil 1 due coil 2 is

$$M_{12} = \frac{N_2 \phi_{B_2}}{i_1}$$

and mutual induction in coil 2 due to coil 1 is

$$M_{21} = \frac{N_1 \phi_{B_1}}{i_2}$$

Similarly, self-inductance in coil 1 is

$$L_1 = \frac{N_1 \phi_{B_1}}{i_1}$$

and self-inductance in coil 2 is

$$L_2 = \frac{N_2 \phi_{B_2}}{i_2}$$

If all the flux of coil 2 links coil 1 and *vice-versa,* then

$$\phi_{B_2} = \phi_{B_1}$$

Since, $M_{12} = M_{21} = M$, hence we have

$$M_{12} M_{21} = M^2$$

$$= \frac{N_1 N_2 \phi_{B_1} \phi_{B_2}}{i_1 i_2} = L_1 L_2$$

$$\therefore \quad M_{max} = \sqrt{L_1 L_2}$$

Given, $L_1 = 2$ mH, $L_2 = 8$ mH

$$\therefore \quad M_{max} = \sqrt{2 \times 8} = \sqrt{16} = 4\text{ mH}$$

04. *(b)*

key idea

Differentiate the given equation of current changing in first coil and find out the maximum change in di/dt.

The given equation of current changing in the first coil is

$$i = i_0 \sin \omega t \quad \ldots\text{(i)}$$

Differentiating Eq. (i) w.r.t. t, we have

$$\frac{di}{dt} = \frac{d}{dt}(i_0 \sin \omega t)$$

or $$\frac{di}{dt} = i_0\, \omega \cos \omega t$$

For maximum $\frac{di}{dt}$, the value of $\cos \omega t$ should be equal to 1.

So, $$\left(\frac{di}{dt}\right)_{max} = i_0\, \omega$$

The maximum value of emf is given by

$$\therefore \quad e_{max} = M\left(\frac{di}{dt}\right)_{max} = M i_0 \omega$$

As, $M = 0.005$ H, $i_0 = 10$ A,

$$\omega = 100\pi\text{ rad/s}$$

$$\therefore \quad e_{max} = 0.005 \times 10 \times 100\pi = 5\pi$$

Topic 4

01. *(c)* Stored magnetic energy,

$$U = \frac{1}{2} LI^2$$

Here, $L = 4\mu\text{H} = 4 \times 10^{-6}$ H

$$I = 2\text{ A}$$

$$\therefore \quad U = \frac{1}{2} \times 4 \times 10^{-6} \times 2^2$$

$$= 8 \times 10^{-6}\text{ J} = 8\ \mu\text{J}$$

02. *(a)* When an iron rod is inserted into the interior of the inductor, then inductance L of the coil increases.

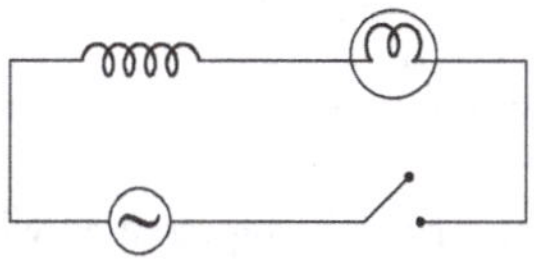

Hence, inductive reactance ($X_L = \omega L$) also increases.

$\therefore$ Current in the circuit is given as

$$I = \frac{e}{X_L}$$

Hence, when X_L increases, then current I decreases. Therefore, glow of the light bulb will decrease.

03. *(d)* Given, magnetic potential energy stored in an inductor,

$$U = 25\text{ mJ} = 25 \times 10^{-3}\text{ J}$$

Current in an inductor,

$$I_0 = 60\text{ mA}$$

$$= 60 \times 10^{-3}\text{ A}$$

As, the expression for energy stored in an inductor is given as

$$U = \frac{1}{2} LI_0^2$$

where, L is the inductance of the inductor.

Substituting the given values in above equation., we get

$$(25 \times 10^{-3}) = \frac{1}{2} \times L \times (60 \times 10^{-3})^2$$

$$\Rightarrow \quad L = \frac{2 \times 25 \times 10^{-3}}{3600 \times 10^{-6}} = \frac{500}{36}$$

or $$L = 13.89\text{ H}$$

04. *(c)* Given, Number of turns of solenoid, $N = 1000$

Current, $I = 4$A

Magnetic flux,

$$\phi_B = 4 \times 10^{-3}\text{ Wb}$$

$\because$ Self-inductance of solenoid is given by

$$L = \frac{\phi_B . N}{I} \quad \ldots\text{(i)}$$

Substitute the given values in Eq. (i), we get

$$L = \frac{4 \times 10^{-3} \times 1000}{4} = 1\text{ H}$$

05. *(d)* For inductor, as we know induced voltage for $t = 0$ to $t = T/2$,

$$V = L\frac{dI}{dt} = L\frac{d}{dt}\left(\frac{2I_0 t}{T}\right) = \text{constant}$$

For $t = T/2$ to $t = T$,

$$V = L\frac{dI}{dt} = \left(\frac{-2I_0 t}{T}\right) = -\text{ constant}$$

So, answer can be represented with graph (d).

06. *(c)* Net flux through solenoid is,

$$\phi_{net} = N\phi$$

$$\therefore \quad \phi_{net} = 500 \times 4 \times 10^{-3} = 2 \text{ Wb}$$

where, ϕ = flux through each turn, and N = total number of turns

Also, $\phi_{net} = Li = 2$ Wb

Now, $L \times 2 = 2$

$\Rightarrow$ Self-inductance, $L = 1$ H

07. *(c)* It is given that emf is zero i.e.,

$$e = -L\frac{di}{dt} = 0 \text{ or } L\frac{di}{dt} = 0$$

$$\text{or } \frac{d}{dt}(t^2e^{-t}) = 0 \qquad (\text{As, } i = t^2e^{-t})$$

$$\text{or } 2t \times e^{-t} + t^2 \times (-1)e^{-t} = 0$$

$$\text{or } te^{-t}(2-t) = 0 \text{ or } t = 2 \text{ s } (\because te^{-t} \neq 0)$$

08. *(c)* Emf induced in the coil of self-inductance L is given by

$$e = -\frac{d\phi}{dt} = -\frac{d}{dt}(Li) \text{ or } e = -L\frac{di}{dt}$$

$$\left(\frac{di}{dt} = \text{rate of flow of current in coil}\right)$$

As, $di = i_2 - i_1 = 0 - 10 = -10$ A

$dt = 0.5$ s

$e = 220$ V

$$\therefore \quad 220 = -L\frac{(-10)}{0.5} \text{ or } L = \frac{220}{20} = 11 \text{ H}$$

09. *(c)* Magnetic flux, $\phi = BA$

and magnetic field due to circular coil is

$$B = \frac{\mu_0 Ni}{2R}$$

As self-inductance,

$$L = \frac{N\phi}{i}$$

$$\therefore \quad L = \frac{N}{i}(BA) = \frac{N}{i}\left(\frac{\mu_0 Ni}{2R}\right)A$$

$$= \frac{\mu_0 N^2 A}{2R}$$

$$\therefore \quad L \propto N^2$$

10. *(b)* Emf induced in the coil is given by

$$e = -\frac{d\phi}{dt}$$

If coil has self-inductance L and current i, then induced emf is given by

$$e = -\frac{d}{dt}(Li) \text{ or } e = -L\frac{di}{dt}$$

$$\therefore \quad L = \frac{|e|}{\frac{di}{dt}}$$

Given, $|e| = 5$ V, $di = 3 - 2 = 1$ A

$dt = 1 \text{ ms} = 1 \times 10^{-3}$ s

$$\therefore \quad L = \frac{5 \times 10^{-3}}{1} = 5 \text{mH}$$

11. *(c)* Energy stored in coil is $E = \frac{1}{2}Li^2$

where, L is self-inductance of coil and i is current induced.

Here, $L = 100$ mH

$= 100 \times 10^{-3}$ H and $i = 1$ A

$$\therefore \quad E = \frac{1}{2} \times (100 \times 10^{-3}) \times (1)^2$$

$$= 0.05 \text{ J}$$

> **• Concept Enhancer**
>
> Energy stored in the coil is given as,
>
> $$E = \frac{1}{2}LI^2$$
>
> where, $I \rightarrow$ current, $L \rightarrow$ self-inductance.

12. *(d)* Self-inductance of solenoid is given by

$$L = \frac{\mu_0 N^2 A}{l}$$

$$\Rightarrow \quad L = \mu_0 n^2 Al$$

(n = number of turns per unt length)

So, $\quad L \propto n^2$

When n^2 is doubled, L becomes 4 times.

13. *(c)* When the magnetic flux linked with a coil changes, an induced emf acts in the coil which is given by

$$e = -\frac{d\phi}{dt}$$

The magnetic flux linked with a coil carrying a current i, is proportional to i.

or $\quad \phi \propto i$ or $\phi = Li$

$$\therefore \quad e = -\frac{d\phi}{dt} = -L\frac{di}{dt}$$

The work done in maintaining the current for time dt

$$= -e\,i\,dt = L\frac{di}{dt}i\,dt$$

and the total work done while the current i_0 is being established

$$W = \int_0^t L\frac{di}{dt}i\,dt$$

$$= \int_0^{i_0} Li\,di$$

$$= \frac{1}{2}Li_0^2$$

Thus, an inductor may store energy in its magnetic field.

14. *(c)* When the contact is suddenly broken, self induced current flow in the direction of main current. Therefore, the bulb B will become suddenly bright.

15. *(b)* Energy stored in a current carrying coil is in the form of magnetic field.

C-21

NEET Chapterwise Topicwise Physics

In NEET 2024, 2 questions were visible from this chapter. In past 5 years, 1 question from topic-1, 5 questions from topic-2, 3 questions from topic-3 and 3 questions from topic-4 were asked.

For detailed analysis scan QR code

ALTERNATING CURRENT (AC)

Topic 1 Introduction to Alternating Current and Voltage

01 The peak voltage of the AC source is equal to *[NCERT (New) Pg. 180, NEET 2022]*

(a) the rms value of the AC source.
(b) $\sqrt{2}$ times the rms value of the AC source.
(c) $1/\sqrt{2}$ times the rms value of the AC source.
(d) the value of voltage supplied to the circuit.

02 The variation of EMF with time for four types of generators are shown in the figures. Which amongst them can be called AC ? *[NEET (Odisha) 2019]*

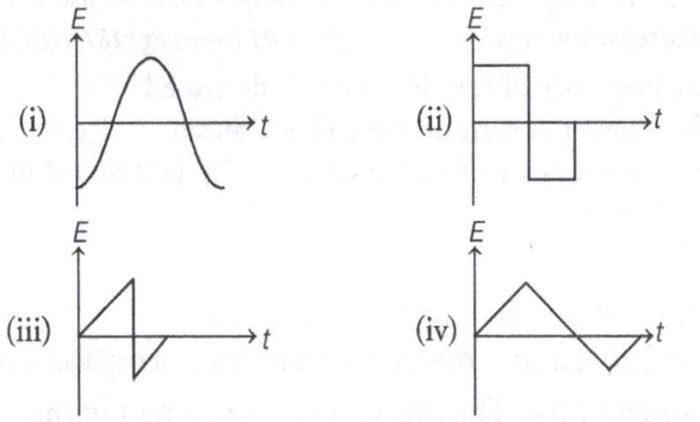

(a) (i) and (ii) (b) (i), (ii), (iii) and (iv)
(c) (i) and (iv) (d) Only (i)

03 The rms value of potential difference V shown in the figure is *[NCERT (New) Pg. 180, AIPMT 2011]*

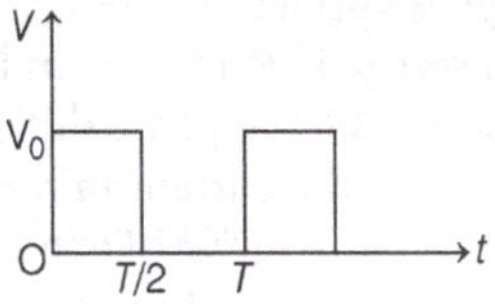

(a) $\frac{V_0}{\sqrt{3}}$ (b) V_0 (c) $\frac{V_0}{\sqrt{2}}$ (d) $\frac{V_0}{2}$

04 Two cables of copper are of equal lengths. One of them has a single wire of area of cross-section A, while other has 10 wires of cross-sectional area $A/10$ each. Give their suitability for transporting AC and DC. *[AIPMT 1994]*

(a) Only multiple strands for AC, either for DC.
(b) Only multiple strands for AC, only single strand for DC.
(c) Only single strand for DC, either for AC.
(d) Only single strand for AC, either for DC.

05 In an AC circuit, the rms value of current, i_{rms} is related to the peak current, i_0 by the relation *[NCERT (New) Pg. 180, AIPMT 1994]*

(a) $i_{rms} = \sqrt{2}\, i_0$ (b) $i_{rms} = \pi i_0$
(c) $i_{rms} = \frac{i_0}{\pi}$ (d) $i_{rms} = \frac{1}{\sqrt{2}} i_0$

Topic 2 AC Circuit and Power in AC Circuit

01 A 10 μF capacitor is connected to a 210 V, 50 Hz source as shown in figure. The peak current in the circuit is nearly ($\pi = 3.14$) *[NCERT (New) Pg. 184, NEET 2024]*

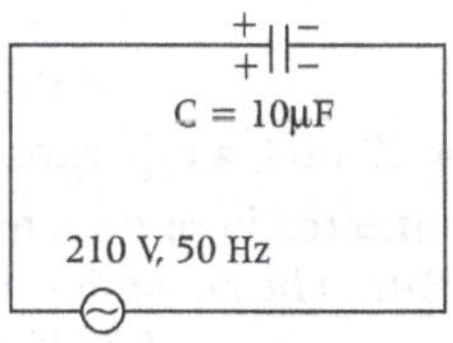

(a) 0.58 A (b) 0.93 A
(c) 1.20 A (d) 0.35 A

02 The net impedance of circuit (as shown in figure) will be *[NCERT (New) Pg. 189, NEET 2023]*

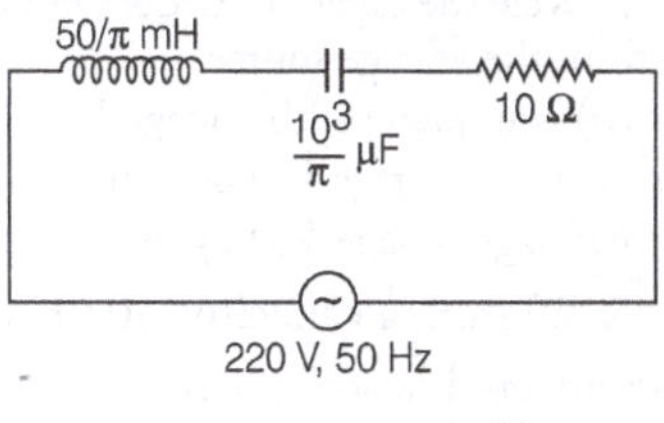

(a) 15 Ω (b) $5\sqrt{5}$ Ω
(c) 25 Ω (d) $10\sqrt{2}$ Ω

03 An inductor of inductance L, a capacitor of capacitance C and a resistor of resistance R are connected in series to an AC source of potential difference V volts as shown in figure.

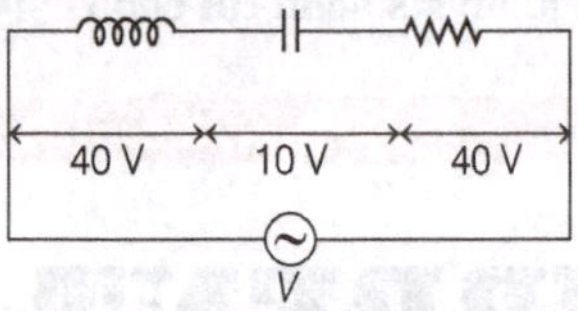

Potential difference across L, C and R is 40 V, 10 V and 40 V, respectively. The amplitude of current flowing through L-C-R series circuit is $10\sqrt{2}$ A. The impedance of the circuit is *[NCERT (New) Pg. 178, NEET 2021]*

(a) $4\sqrt{2}\ \Omega$ (b) $5\sqrt{2}\ \Omega$ (c) $4\ \Omega$ (d) $5\ \Omega$

04 A series L-C-R circuit is connected to an AC voltage source. When L is removed from the circuit, the phase difference between current and voltage is $\pi/3$. If instead C is removed from the circuit, the phase difference is again $\pi/3$ between current and voltage. The power factor of the circuit is *[NCERT (New) Pg. 191, NEET (Sep.) 2020, AIPMT 2012]*

(a) 0.5 (b) 1.0
(c) −1.0 (d) zero

05 A 40 μF capacitor is connected to a 200 V, 50 Hz AC supply. The rms value of the current in the circuit is, nearly *[NEET (Sep.) 2020]*

(a) 2.05 A (b) 2.5 A (c) 25.1 A (d) 1.7 A

06 A circuit when connected to an AC source of 12 V gives a current of 0.2 A. The same circuit when connected to a DC source of 12 V, gives a current of 0.4 A. The circuit is *[NEET (Odisha) 2019]*

(a) series L-R (b) series R-C
(c) series L-C (d) series L-C-R

07 An inductor 20 mH, a capacitor 100 μF and a resistor 50 Ω are connected in series across a source of emf, $V = 10\sin 314t$. The power loss in the circuit is *[NCERT (New) Pg. 191, NEET 2018]*

(a) 0.79 W (b) 0.43 W
(c) 2.74 W (d) 1.13 W

08 A small signal voltage $V(t) = V_0 \sin \omega t$ is applied across an ideal capacitor C *[NEET 2016]*

(a) over a full cycle the capacitor C does not consume any energy from the voltage source
(b) current $I(t)$ is in phase with voltage $V(t)$
(c) current $I(t)$ leads voltage $V(t)$ by 180°
(d) current $I(t)$, lags voltage $V(t)$ by 90°

09 An inductor 20 mH, a capacitor 50 μF and a resistor 40 Ω are connected in series across a source of emf $V = 10\sin 340\,t$. The power loss in AC circuit is *[NEET 2016]*

(a) 0.67 W (b) 0.76 W
(c) 0.89 W (d) 0.51 W

10 The potential differences across the resistance, capacitance and inductance are 80 V, 40 V and 100 V, respectively in an L-C-R circuit. The power factor of this circuit is *[NCERT (New) Pg. 191, NEET 2016]*

(a) 0.4 (b) 0.5
(c) 0.8 (d) 1.0

11 A resistance R draws power P when connected to an AC source. If an inductance is now placed in series with the resistance, such that the impedance of the circuit becomes Z the power drawn will be *[AIPMT 2015]*

(a) $P\left(\frac{R}{Z}\right)^2$ (b) $P\sqrt{\frac{R}{Z}}$
(c) $P\left(\frac{R}{Z}\right)$ (d) P

12 A series R-C circuit is connected to an alternating voltage source. Consider two situations. *[AIPMT 2015]*
1. When capacitor is air filled.
2. When capacitor is mica filled.

Current through resistor is i and voltage across capacitor is V then

(a) $V_a < V_b$ (b) $V_a > V_b$
(c) $i_a > i_b$ (d) $V_a = V_b$

13 A coil of self-inductance L is connected in series with a bulb B and an AC source. Brightness of the bulb decreases when *[NCERT (New) Pg. 187, NEET 2013]*

(a) frequency of the AC source is decreased
(b) number of turns in the coil is reduced
(c) a capacitance of reactance $X_C = X_L$ is included in the same circuit
(d) an iron rod is inserted in the coil

14 In an AC circuit an alternating voltage $e = 200\sqrt{2}\sin 100\,t$ V is connected to a capacitor of capacity 1 μF. The rms value of the current in the circuit is *[AIPMT 2011]*

(a) 100 mA (b) 200 mA
(c) 20 mA (d) 10 mA

15 An AC voltage is applied to a resistance R and an inductor L in series. If R and the inductive reactance are both equal to 3 Ω, the phase difference between the applied voltage and the current in the circuit is *[NCERT (New) Pg. 188, AIPMT 2011]*

(a) $\pi/4$ (b) $\pi/2$
(c) zero (d) $\pi/6$

16 A coil has resistance 30 Ω and inductive reactance 20 Ω at 50 Hz frequency. If an AC source, of 200 V, 100 Hz, is connected across the coil, the current in the coil will be *[AIPMT 2011]*

(a) 2.0 A (b) 4.0 A
(c) 8.0 A (d) $20/\sqrt{13}$ A

17 Power dissipated in an L-C-R series circuit connected to an AC source of emf ε is *[NCERT (New) Pg. 191, AIPMT 2009]*

(a) $\dfrac{\varepsilon^2 R}{\left[R^2 + \left(L\omega - \dfrac{1}{C\omega}\right)^2\right]}$ (b) $\dfrac{\varepsilon^2 \sqrt{R^2 + \left(L\omega - \dfrac{1}{C\omega}\right)^2}}{R}$

(c) $\dfrac{\varepsilon^2 \left[R^2 + \left(L\omega - \dfrac{1}{C\omega}\right)^2\right]}{R}$ (d) $\dfrac{\varepsilon^2 R}{\sqrt{R^2 + \left(L\omega - \dfrac{1}{C\omega}\right)^2}}$

18 In an AC circuit the emf V and the current i at any instant are given respectively by

$$V = V_0 \sin \omega t, \; i = i_0 \sin(\omega t - \phi)$$

The average power in the circuit over one cycle of AC is *[AIPMT 2008]*

(a) $\dfrac{V_0 i_0}{2}$ (b) $\dfrac{V_0 i_0}{2} \sin \phi$

(c) $\dfrac{V_0 i_0}{2} \cos \phi$ (d) $V_0 i_0$

19 A coil of inductive reactance 31 Ω has a resistance of 8 Ω. It is placed in series with a condenser of capacitative reactance 25 Ω. The combination is connected to an AC source of 110 V. The power factor of the circuit is *[AIPMT 2006]*

(a) 0.56 (b) 0.64 (c) 0.80 (d) 0.33

20 In a circuit, L, C and R are connected in series with an alternating voltage source of frequency f. The current leads the voltage by 45°. The value of C is *[NCERT (New) Pg. 191, AIPMT 2005]*

(a) $\dfrac{1}{2\pi f(2\pi fL + R)}$ (b) $\dfrac{1}{\pi f(2\pi fL + R)}$

(c) $\dfrac{1}{2\pi f(2\pi fL - R)}$ (d) $\dfrac{1}{\pi f(2\pi fL - R)}$

21 A coil of 40 H inductance is connected in series with a resistance of 8Ω and the combination is joined to the terminals of a 2 V battery. The time constant of the circuit is *[AIPMT 2004]*

(a) 5 s (b) 1/5 s (c) 40 s (d) 20 s

22 The reactance of a capacitor of capacitance C is X. If both the frequency and capacitance be doubled, then new reactance will be *[AIPMT 2001]*

(a) X (b) $2X$ (c) $4X$ (d) $X/4$

23 In a circuit inductance L and capacitance C are connected as shown in figure. A_1 and A_2 are ammeters. When key K is pressed to complete the circuit, then just after closing key K, the reading of current will be *[AIPMT 1999]*

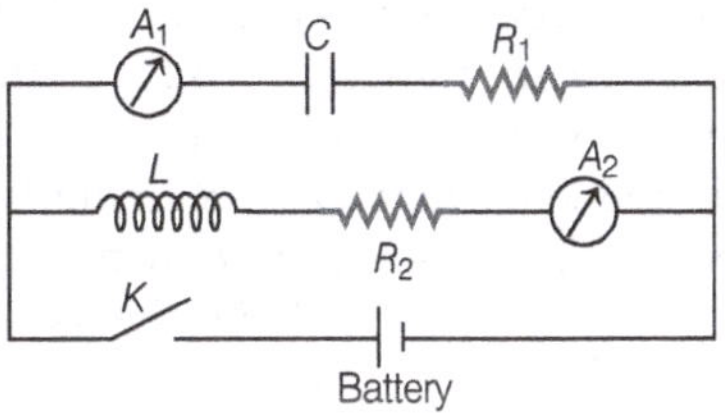

(a) zero in both A_1 and A_2
(b) maximum in both A_1 and A_2
(c) zero in A_1 and maximum in A_2
(d) maximum in A_1 and zero in A_2

24 In an AC circuit with voltage V and current i the power dissipated is *[NCERT (New) Pg. 191, AIPMT 1997]*

(a) depends on the phase between V and i

(b) $\dfrac{1}{\sqrt{2}} Vi$

(c) $\dfrac{1}{2} Vi$

(d) Vi

25 The current I in an AC circuit with inductance coil varies with time according to the graph given below. *[NCERT (New) Pg: 181, AIPMT 1994]*

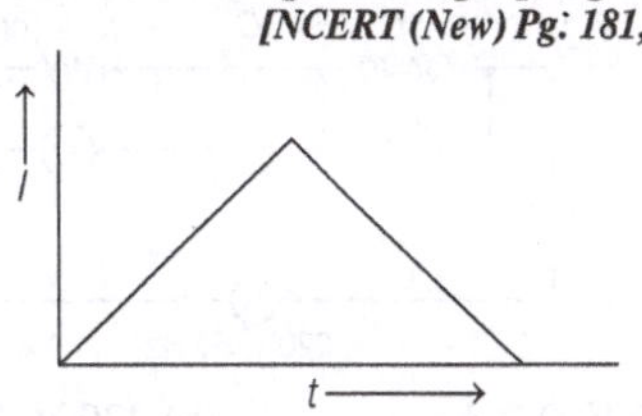

Which one of the following graphs gives the variation of voltage with time ?

(a)
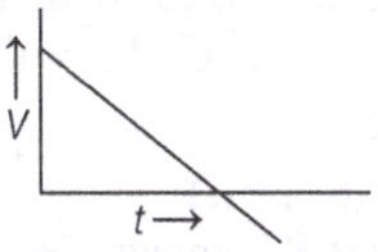

(b)
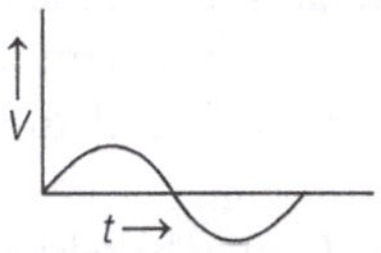

(c)
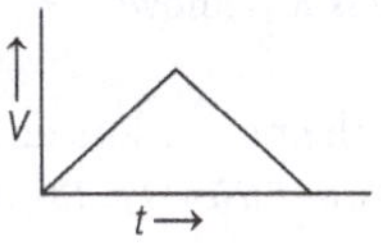

(d)
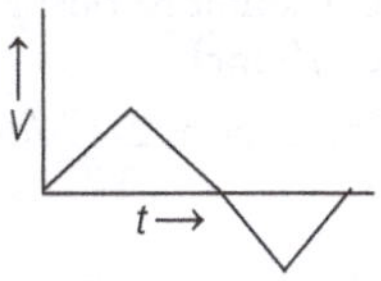

26 The time constant of C-R circuit is *[AIPMT 1992]*

(a) $\dfrac{1}{CR}$ (b) $\dfrac{C}{R}$

(c) CR (d) $\dfrac{R}{C}$

Topic 3 Resonance

01 In a series L-C-R circuit, the inductance L is 10 mH, capacitance C is 1 μF and resistance R is 100 Ω. The frequency at which resonance occurs is *[NEET 2023]*

(a) 15.9 kHz (b) 1.59 rad/s

(c) 1.59 kHz (d) 15.9 rad/s

02 A series *L-C-R* circuit with inductance 10 H, capacitance 10 μF, resistance 50 Ω is connected to an AC source of voltage, $V = 200 \sin(100\,t)$ V. If the resonant frequency of the *L-C-R* circuit is ν_0 and the frequency of the AC source is ν, then *[NCERT (New) Pg. 189, NEET 2022]*

(a) $\nu_0 = \nu = \frac{50}{\pi}$ Hz (b) $\nu_0 = \frac{50}{\pi}$ Hz, $\nu = 50$ Hz
(c) $\nu = 100$ Hz, $\nu_0 = \frac{100}{\pi}$ Hz (d) $\nu_0 = \nu = 50$ Hz

03 A series *L-C-R* circuit containing 5.0 H inductor, 80 μF capacitor and 40 Ω resistor is connected to 230 V variable frequency AC source. The angular frequencies of the source at which power transferred to the circuit is half the power at the resonant angular frequency are likely to be *[NEET 2021]*

(a) 25 rad/s and 75 rad/s (b) 50 rad/s and 25 rad/s
(c) 46 rad/s and 54 rad/s (d) 42 rad/s and 58 rad/s

04 In the given circuit, the reading of voltmeter V_1 and V_2 are 200 V each. The reading to the voltmeter V_3 and ammeter *A* are respectively *[AIPMT 2010]*

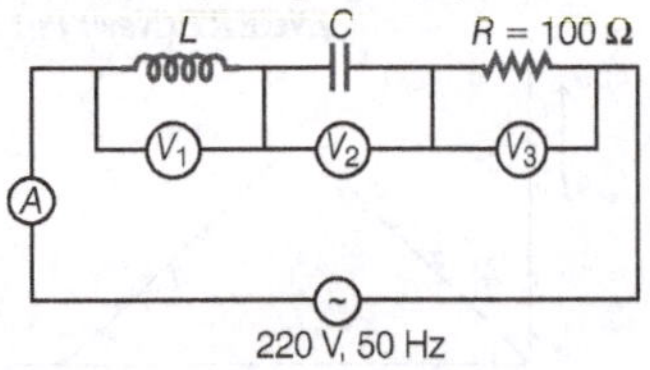

(a) 150 V, 2.2 A (b) 220 V, 2.2 A
(c) 220 V, 2.0 A (d) 100 V, 2.0 A

05 What is the value of inductance *L* for which the current is maximum in a series *L-C-R* circuit with $C = 10\,\mu$F and $\omega = 1000\,s^{-1}$? *[AIPMT 2007]*

(a) 100 mH (b) 1 mH
(c) Cannot be calculated unless *R* is known
(d) 10 mH

06 For a series *L-C-R* circuit, the power loss at resonance is *[NCERT (New) Pg. 189, AIPMT 2002]*

(a) $\frac{V^2}{\omega L - \frac{1}{\omega C}}$ (b) $i^2 C\omega$ (c) $i^2 R$ (d) $\frac{V^2}{\omega C}$

07 In an experiment, 200 V AC is applied at the ends of an *L-C-R* circuit. The circuit consists of an inductive reactance $X_L = 50\ \Omega$, capacitive reactance $X_C = 50\ \Omega$ and ohmic resistance $R = 10\ \Omega$. The impedance of the circuit is *[NCERT (New) Pg. 189, AIPMT 1996]*

(a) 10 Ω (b) 20 Ω (c) 30 Ω (d) 40 Ω

08 An *L-C-R* series circuit is connected to a source of alternating current. At resonance, the applied voltage and the current flowing through the circuit will have a phase difference of *[AIPMT 1994]*

(a) π (b) π/2 (c) π/4 (d) zero

Topic 4 Transformer and AC Generator

01 In an ideal transformer, the turns ratio is $\frac{N_p}{N_s} = \frac{1}{2}$.
The ratio $V_s : V_p$ is equal to (the symbols carry their usual meaning) : *[NCERT (New) Pg. 195, NEET 2024]*

(a) 1 : 2 (b) 2 : 1
(c) 1 : 1 (d) 1 : 4

02 A 12 V, 60 W lamp is connected to the secondary of a step down transformer, whose primary is connected to AC mains of 220 V. Assuming the transformer to be ideal, what is the current in the primary winding? *[NCERT (New) Pg. 195, NEET 2023]*

(a) 2.7 A (b) 3.7 A
(c) 0.37 A (d) 0.27 A

03 A step down transformer connected to an AC mains supply of 220 V is made to operate at 11 V, 44 W lamp. Ignoring power losses in the transformer, what is the current in the primary circuit? *[NCERT (New) Pg. 195, NEET 2021]*

(a) 0.2 A (b) 0.4 A
(c) 2 A (d) 4 A

04 A transformer having efficiency of 90% is working on 200 V and 3 kW power supply. If the current in the secondary coil is 6 A, the voltage across the secondary coil and the current in the primary coil respectively are *[AIPMT 2014]*

(a) 300 V, 15 A (b) 450 V, 15 A
(c) 450 V, 13.5 A (d) 600 V, 15 A

05 The primary of a transformer when connected to a DC battery of 10 V draws a current of 1 mA. The number of turns of the primary and secondary windings are 50 and 100, respectively. The voltage in the secondary and the current drawn by the circuit in the secondary are respectively *[NEET 2013]*

(a) 20 V and 2.0 mA
(b) 10 V and 0.5 mA
(c) zero volt and therefore no current
(d) 20 V and 0.5 mA

06 A 220 V input is supplied to a transformer. The output circuit draws a current of 2.0 A at 440 V. If the efficiency of the transformer is 80%, the current drawn by the primary windings of the transformer is *[NCERT (New) Pg. 195, AIPMT 2010]*

(a) 3.6 A (b) 2.8 A
(c) 2.5 A (d) 5.0 A

07 A transformer is used to light a 100 W and 110 V lamp from a 220 V mains. If the main current is 0.5 A, the efficiency of the transformer is approximately *[AIPMT 2007]*

(a) 30% (b) 50%
(c) 90% (d) 10%

08 The primary and secondary coils of a transformer have 50 and 1500 turns, respectively. If the magnetic flux ϕ linked with the primary coil is given by $\phi = \phi_0 + 4t$, where ϕ is in weber, t is in second and ϕ_0 is a constant, the output voltage across the secondary coil is *[NCERT (New) Pg. 195, AIPMT 2007]*
(a) 90 V (b) 120 V (c) 220 V (d) 30 V

09 The core of a transformer is laminated because *[AIPMT 2006]*
(a) energy losses due to eddy currents may be minimised
(b) the weight of the transformer may be reduced
(c) rusting of the core may be prevented
(d) ratio of voltage in primary and secondary may be increased

10 A step-up transformer operates on a 230 V line and supplies current of 2 A to a load. The ratio of the primary and secondary windings is 1 : 25. The current in the primary coil is *[AIPMT 1998]*
(a) 15 A (b) 50 A
(c) 25 A (d) 12.5 A

11 The primary winding of transformer has 500 turns whereas its secondary has 5000 turns. The primary is connected to an AC supply of 20 V-50 Hz. The secondary will have an output of *[NCERT (New) Pg. 195, AIPMT 1997]*
(a) 2 V, 5 Hz (b) 200 V, 500 Hz
(c) 2 V, 50 Hz (d) 200 V, 50 Hz

Key Index

Topic 1

1 (b)	2 (b)	3 (c)	4 (a)	5 (d)

Topic 2

1 (b)	2 (b)	3 (d)	4 (b)	5 (b)	6 (a)	7 (a)	8 (a)	9 (d)	10 (c)
11 (a)	12 (b)	13 (d)	14 (c)	15 (a)	16 (b)	17 (a)	18 (c)	19 (c)	20 (a)
21 (a)	22 (d)	23 (d)	24 (a)	25 (a)	26 (c)				

Topic 3

1 (c)	2 (a)	3 (c)	4 (b)	5 (a)	6 (c)	7 (a)	8 (d)

Topic 4

1 (b)	2 (d)	3 (a)	4 (b)	5 (c)	6 (d)	7 (c)	8 (b)	9 (a)	10 (b)
11 (d)									

Detailed **Explanations**

Topic 1

01. *(b)*

key idea

You can use the following relation to solve this question.

$$V_0 = \sqrt{2}\, V_{rms}$$

We know that, peak voltage V_0 and rms voltage V_{rms} are related as,

$$\therefore \quad V_0 = \sqrt{2}\, V_{rms}$$

02. *(b)* The emf generated due to a rotating conductor in a generator is given by $E = -\dfrac{d\phi_B}{dt}$

where, ϕ_B = magnetic flux linked with conductor.

From the above equation we can conclude that the emf generated is a varying function of time with opposite polarity.

So, all the graph are correct for the given variations.

03. *(c)* According to figure, we observe that,

$$V = V_0 \text{ for } 0 \le t \le \frac{T}{2}$$

$$\Rightarrow V = 0 \text{ for } \frac{T}{2} \le t \le T$$

$$V_{rms} = \left[\frac{\int_0^T V^2 dt}{\int_0^T dt}\right]^{1/2} = \left[\frac{\int_0^{T/2} V_0^2 dt + \int_{T/2}^T (0) dt}{\int_0^T dt}\right]^{1/2}$$

$$= \left[\frac{V_0^2}{T}[t]_0^{T/2}\right]^{\frac{1}{2}} = \left[\frac{V_0^2}{T}\left(\frac{T}{2}\right)\right]^{\frac{1}{2}}$$

$$\therefore \quad V_{rms} = \frac{V_0}{\sqrt{2}}$$

04. *(a)* The major portion of the AC flows on the surface of the conducting wire. So where a thick wire is required, a number of thin wires are joined together to give an equivalent effect of a thick wire.

Therefore, multiple strands are suitable for transporting wire AC. Similarly multiple strands can also be used for DC.

05. *(d)* $\overline{i^2} = \dfrac{\int_0^{2\pi/\omega} i^2\, dt}{\dfrac{2\pi}{\omega}}$

$= \dfrac{\int_0^{2\pi/\omega} i_0^2 \sin^2 \omega t\, dt}{\dfrac{2\pi}{\omega}}$

$= \dfrac{i_0^2\omega}{2\pi}\int_0^{2\pi/\omega} \dfrac{1}{2}(1 - \cos 2\omega t)\, dt$

$= \dfrac{i_0^2\omega}{4\pi}\left[t - \dfrac{\sin 2\omega t}{2\omega}\right]_0^{2\pi/\omega}$

$= \dfrac{i_0^2\omega}{4\pi}\left(\dfrac{2\pi}{\omega}\right) = \dfrac{i_0^2}{2}$

$\therefore \quad i_{rms} = \sqrt{\overline{i^2}} = \dfrac{i_0}{\sqrt{2}}$

Topic 2

01. *(b)* Given,

$C = 10\mu F = 10 \times 10^{-6} F$

Potential, $V = 210$ V

Frequency, $f = 50$ Hz

Reactance of circuit, $X_C = \dfrac{1}{\omega C}$

$= \dfrac{1}{2\pi f C}$

$= \dfrac{1}{2 \times 3.14 \times 50 \times 10 \times 10^{-6}}$

$= \dfrac{10^3}{3.14}$

Peak current, $I_m = \dfrac{V\sqrt{2}}{X_C} = \dfrac{210 \times \sqrt{2}}{\dfrac{10^3}{3.14}}$

$= \dfrac{3.14 \times 210 \times \sqrt{2}}{1000} \simeq 0.93$ A

02. *(b)* Given, $L = \dfrac{50}{\pi}$ mH $= \dfrac{5}{\pi} \times 10^{-2}$ H

$C = \dfrac{10^3}{\pi}\mu F = \dfrac{1}{\pi} \times 10^{-3}$ F

$R = 10\,\Omega,\ f = 50$ Hz, $V = 220$ V

$\therefore \quad X_L = 2\pi f L$

$= 2\pi \times 50 \times \dfrac{5}{\pi} \times 10^{-2} = 5\,\Omega$

$X_C = \dfrac{1}{\omega C} = \dfrac{1}{2\pi f C}$

$= \dfrac{1}{2\pi \times 50 \times \dfrac{1}{\pi} \times 10^{-3}} = \dfrac{1}{10^{-1}}$

$= 10\,\Omega$

$\therefore$ Net impedance the circuit,

$Z = \sqrt{R^2 + (X_C - X_L)^2}$

$= \sqrt{10^2 + (10-5)^2}$

$= \sqrt{125} = 5\sqrt{5}\,\Omega$

03. *(d)* The given circuit diagram as shown below.

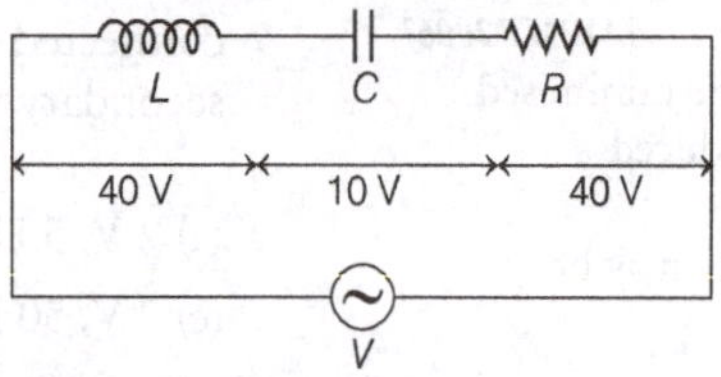

Given, $V_L = 40$ V, $V_C = 10$ V

and $\quad V_R = 40$ V

$I_0 = 10\sqrt{2}$ A $\quad$ ...(i)

$\therefore \quad I_{rms} = \dfrac{I_0}{\sqrt{2}}$

$\Rightarrow \quad I_{rms} = \dfrac{10\sqrt{2}}{\sqrt{2}}$ $\quad$ [From Eq. (i)]

$\Rightarrow \quad I_{rms} = 10$ A

$\therefore \quad V_{rms} = \sqrt{V_R^2 + (V_L - V_C)^2}$

$\Rightarrow \quad V_{rms} = \sqrt{(40)^2 + (40-10)^2}$

$\Rightarrow \quad V_{rms} = 50$ V

The impedance of the *L-C-R* series circuit,

$Z = \dfrac{V_{rms}}{I_{rms}} = \dfrac{50\text{ V}}{10\text{ A}} = 5\,\Omega$

04. *(b)* For *L-C-R* circuit, phase difference,

$\phi = \tan^{-1}\left(\dfrac{X_L - X_C}{R}\right)$

When L is removed, then $X_L = 0$

$\therefore \quad \phi = \tan^{-1}\left(\dfrac{-X_C}{R}\right)$

$\Rightarrow \quad \tan\phi = \left|\dfrac{X_C}{R}\right|$

$\tan\dfrac{\pi}{3} = \dfrac{X_C}{R}$

$\sqrt{3} = \dfrac{X_C}{R} \Rightarrow X_C = R\sqrt{3}$ $\quad$ ...(i)

When C is removed, then $X_C = 0$

$\therefore \quad \phi = \tan^{-1}\left(\dfrac{X_L}{R}\right)$

$\Rightarrow \quad \tan\phi = \dfrac{X_L}{R}$

$\tan\dfrac{\pi}{3} = \sqrt{3} = \dfrac{X_L}{R}$

$X_L = R\sqrt{3}$ $\quad$ ...(ii)

From Eqs. (i) and (ii), we get

$X_L = X_C$

$\therefore$ Impedance,

$Z = \sqrt{R^2 + (X_L - X_C)^2} = R$

Power factor, $\cos\phi = \dfrac{R}{Z} = \dfrac{R}{R} = 1$

• **Concept Enhancer**

Power factor of *L-C-R* series circuit is easily determined by impedance triangle.

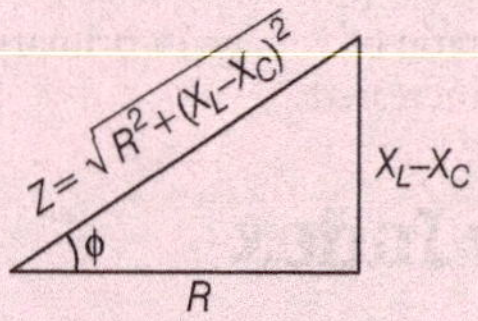

Impedance triangle

Here, $\cos\phi = \dfrac{R}{Z} = \dfrac{R}{\sqrt{R^2 + (X_L - X_C)^2}}$

05. *(b)* Given, $C = 40\,\mu F = 40 \times 10^{-6}$ F

$V_{rms} = 200$ V, $\nu = 50$ Hz

As, $X_C = \dfrac{1}{2\pi\nu C}$

$= \dfrac{1}{2\pi \times 50 \times 40 \times 10^{-6}} = \dfrac{250}{\pi}\,\Omega$

$\therefore \quad I_{rms} = \dfrac{V_{rms}}{X_C} = \dfrac{200}{\left(\dfrac{250}{\pi}\right)} = 2.5$ A

06. *(a)* When the circuit is connected to AC source,

Voltage, $V = 12$ V

Current, $I = 0.2$ A

$\Rightarrow$ Impedance $Z = \dfrac{V}{I} = \dfrac{12}{0.2} = 60\,\Omega$

When it is connected to DC source,

Voltage, $V = 12$ V, Current, $I = 0.4$ A

$\Rightarrow$ Resistance, $R = \dfrac{V}{I} = \dfrac{12}{0.4} = 30\,\Omega$

As in case of DC supply, the capacitor act as an open circuit and no current flows through the circuit.

So the given circuit will not have capacitor in series combination.

Therefore the circuit should be a series *L-R* circuit.

07. *(a)* Impedance Z is an ac circuit is

$Z = \sqrt{R^2 + (X_C - X_L)^2}$;

where X_C = capacitive reactance and X_L = inductive reactance.

Also $X_C = \dfrac{1}{\omega C}$ and $X_L = \omega L$

$\therefore$

$$Z = \sqrt{(50)^2 + \left(\frac{1}{314 \times 100 \times 10^{-6}} - 314 \times 20 \times 10^{-3}\right)^2}$$

or $Z = 56\ \Omega$

The power loss in the circuit is

$$P_{av} = \left(\frac{V_{rms}}{Z}\right)^2 R$$

$$\therefore\ P_{av} = \left(\frac{10}{(\sqrt{2})56}\right)^2 \times 50 = 0.79\ \text{W}$$

08. *(a)* For purely capacitance circuit,

$$\phi = \frac{\pi}{2}\ \text{rad}$$

In this case current is ahead of voltage by $\frac{\pi}{2}$. Hence, power in this case is given by $P = VI \cos\phi = VI \cos 90° = 0$

Therefore, no power consumption in one complete cycle across a capacitor i.e. does not consume any energy.

09. *(d)* Given,

Inductance $L = 20$ mH

Capacitance, $C = 50\ \mu$F

Resistance, $R = 40\ \Omega$

emf, $V = 10 \sin 340\, t$

$\because$ Power loss in AC circuit will be given as

$$P_{av} = I_V^2 R = \left[\frac{E_V}{Z}\right]^2 .R$$

$$P_{av} = \left(\frac{E_V}{\sqrt{R^2 + (X_C - X_L)^2}}\right)^2 .R$$

$$P_{av} = \left(\frac{10}{\sqrt{2}}\right)^2 .40$$

$$\frac{1}{\sqrt{40^2 + \left(\frac{1}{340 \times 50 \times 10^{-6}} - (340 \times 20 \times 10^{-3})\right)^2}}$$

$\approx 0.46\text{W} \approx 0.51$ W

10. *(c)* Power factor of the L-C-R circuit

$$= \cos\phi = \frac{R}{Z}$$

$$= \frac{IR}{IZ} = \frac{80}{I\sqrt{(X_L - X_C)^2 + R^2}}$$

$$= \frac{80}{\sqrt{(IX_L - IX_C)^2 + (IR)^2}}$$

$$= \frac{80}{\sqrt{(100 - 40)^2 + (80)^2}} = 0.8$$

11. *(a)*

key idea

You can use the following formula to calculate average power in AC circuit.

$$P_{av} = V_{rms} \times I_{rms} \times \cos\phi$$

When a resistor is connected to an AC source. The power drawn will be

$$P = V_{rms} \cdot I_{rms} = V_{rms} \cdot \frac{V_{rms}}{R}$$

$$\Rightarrow\ V_{rms}^2 = PR$$

When an inductor is connected in series with the resistor, then the power drawn will be

$$P' = V_{rms} \cdot I_{rms} \cos\phi$$

where, ϕ = phase difference

$$\therefore\ P' = \frac{V_{rms}^2}{R} \cdot \frac{R^2}{Z^2} = P \cdot R \cdot \frac{R}{Z^2}$$

$$\Rightarrow\ P' = \frac{P \cdot R^2}{Z^2} = P\left(\frac{R}{Z}\right)^2$$

12. *(b)* Net reactive capacitance,

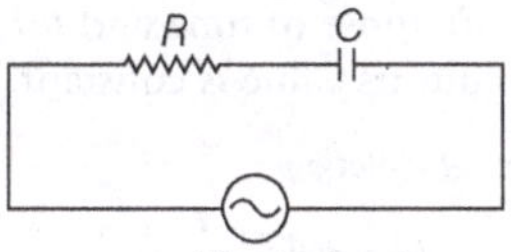

$V = V_0 \sin \omega t$

$$X_C = \frac{1}{2\pi fC}$$

So, current in circuit, $I = \frac{V}{Z}$

$$= \frac{V}{\sqrt{R^2 + \left(\frac{1}{2\pi fC}\right)^2}}$$

$$\Rightarrow\ I = \frac{2\pi fC}{\sqrt{4\pi^2 f^2 C^2 R^2 + 1}} \times V$$

Voltage drop across capacitor,

$$V_C = I \times X_C$$

$$= \frac{2\pi fC}{\sqrt{4\pi^2 f^2 C^2 R^2 + 1}} \times \frac{1}{2\pi fC} \times V$$

$$\text{i.e. } V_C = \frac{V}{\sqrt{4\pi^2 f^2 C^2 R^2 + 1}}$$

When mica is introduced, capacitance will increase hence, voltage across capacitor get decrease.

13. *(d)* When a bulb of resistance R is connected in series with a coil of self-inductance L, then current in the circuit is given by

$$I = \frac{E}{\sqrt{\omega^2 L^2 + R^2}}$$

where E is the voltage of an AC source

$$\text{As}\quad L = \frac{\mu_0 \mu_r N^2 A}{l} \Rightarrow L \propto \mu_r$$

When iron rod is inserted, L increases, therefore current I decreases.

14. *(c)* Compare the given equation with the equation of alternating voltage i.e.

$$e = e_m \sin \omega t \text{ where, } e_m = e_{rms}\sqrt{2}$$

Given, emf, $e = 200\sqrt{2} \sin 100\, t$ V

and $C = 1\ \mu\text{F} = 1 \times 10^{-6}$F

As $e_{rms} = 200\text{V}$ and $\omega = 100$

$$\therefore\ X_C = \frac{1}{\omega C} = \frac{1}{1 \times 10^{-6} \times 100} = 10^4\ \Omega$$

$$i_{rms} = \frac{e_{rms}}{X_C} = \frac{200}{10^4}$$

$$= 2 \times 10^{-2}\ \text{A} = 20\ \text{mA}$$

15. *(a)* As we know that

$$\tan\phi = \frac{X_L}{R} = \frac{\omega L}{R} \Rightarrow \tan\phi = \frac{3}{3}$$

$$\therefore\quad \tan\phi = 1 \Rightarrow \phi = 45°$$

So, phase difference $= \frac{\pi}{4}$ rad

16. *(b)* Here, resistance, $R = 30\ \Omega$

Inductive reactance, $X_L = 20\ \Omega$ at 50 Hz

$$X_L = 2\pi\nu L$$

$$X_L' = \frac{\nu'}{\nu} \times X_L = \left(\frac{100}{50}\right) \times 20\ \Omega$$

$$= 40\ \Omega$$

Impedance, $Z = \sqrt{R^2 + (X_L')^2}$

$$= \sqrt{(30)^2 + (40)^2} = 50\ \Omega$$

Current in the coil, $I = \frac{V}{Z} = \frac{200\text{V}}{50\ \Omega}$

$$= 4\ \text{A}$$

17. *(a)* Power dissipated in series L-C-R.

$$P = I_{rms}^2 R = \frac{\varepsilon_{rms}^2 R}{|Z|^2}$$

$$= \frac{\varepsilon^2 R}{\left[R^2 + \left(\omega L - \frac{1}{\omega C}\right)^2\right]}$$

As $I_{rms} = \frac{V_{rms}}{Z}$

18. *(c)* $P_{av} = V_{rms} \cdot i_{rms} \cos\phi = \frac{1}{2} V_0\, i_0 \cos\phi$

$$\left[\because\ V_{rms} = \frac{V_0}{\sqrt{2}},\ i_{rms} = \frac{i_0}{\sqrt{2}}\right]$$

where, $\cos\phi$ = power factor

19. (c) Power factor of AC circuit is given by

$$\cos\phi = \frac{R}{Z} \quad ...(i)$$

where, R is resistance and Z is the impedance of the circuit and is given by

$$Z = \sqrt{R^2 + (X_L - X_C)^2} \quad ...(ii)$$

Eqs. (i) and (ii) meet to give,

$$\cos\phi = \frac{R}{\sqrt{R^2 + (X_L - X_C)^2}} \quad ...(iii)$$

Given, $R = 8\,\Omega$, $X_L = 31\,\Omega$

$X_C = 25\,\Omega$

$$\cos\phi = \frac{8}{\sqrt{(8)^2 + (31-25)^2}}$$

Hence, $\cos\phi = 0.80$

20. (a) Phase difference between current and voltage in L-C-R series circuit is given by

$$\tan\phi = \frac{\frac{1}{\omega C} - \omega L}{R}$$

ϕ being the angle by which the current leads the voltage.

Given, $\phi = 45°$

$$\tan 45° = \frac{\frac{1}{\omega C} - \omega L}{R}$$

$$\Rightarrow \quad R = \frac{1}{\omega C} - \omega L \Rightarrow \omega C = \frac{1}{R + \omega L}$$

$$\Rightarrow \quad C = \frac{1}{2\pi f(R + 2\pi f)}$$

21. (a) Time constant of L-R circuit is

$$\tau = L/R$$

$$\therefore \quad \tau = \frac{40}{8} = 5\text{ s}$$

22. (d) If a capacitor of capacitance C is connected with an AC signal, then reactance of that circuit is purely capacitive. The capacitive reactance is

$$X = \frac{1}{\omega C} = \frac{1}{2\pi f C} \quad (\omega = 2\pi f)$$

or $\quad X \propto \dfrac{1}{fC}$

Considering two different situations of frequency and capacitance, we have

$$\frac{X'}{X} = \frac{fC}{f'C'} = \frac{f \times C}{2f \times 2C}$$

$$[\because f' = 2f \text{ and } C' = 2C]$$

or $\quad \dfrac{X'}{X} = \dfrac{1}{4}$ or $X' = \dfrac{X}{4}$

23. (d) There is no DC current in inductive circuit because it does not allow DC current to flow and maximum DC current in capacitive circuit. Hence, the current is zero in A_2 and maximum in A_1.

24. (a) In an AC circuit with voltage V and current i, the power dissipated is given by $P = Vi\cos\phi$

where, ϕ is the phase and $\cos\phi$ is the power factor. Thus, the power dissipated, depends upon the phase between voltage V and current i.

25. (a) In an AC circuit with inductance coil, the voltage V leads the current I by a phase difference of 90° or the current I lags behind the voltage V by a phase difference of 90°. Thus, the voltage goes on decreasing with the increase in time as shown in the graph (a).

26. (c) The quantity $\tau = CR$ is called time constant or capacitive time constant of CR circuit. This is because dimensions of RC are those of time and for a given CR circuit, its value is constant.

Alternate Solution

As $\quad R = \dfrac{V}{i}$ and $C = \dfrac{q}{V}$

$$\therefore \quad RC = \frac{V}{i}\frac{q}{V} = \frac{q}{i} = \frac{i \times t}{i} = t$$

$$\therefore \quad [RC] = [t] = [T]$$

Topic 3

01. (c) In series L-C-R circuit,

$$L = 10\text{ mH} = 10^{-2}\text{ H}$$

$$C = 1\text{ F} = 10^{-6}\text{ F}, R = 100\,\Omega$$

$\therefore$ Resonance frequency,

$$f = \frac{1}{2\pi\sqrt{LC}} = \frac{1}{2\pi\sqrt{10^{-2} \times 10^{-6}}}$$

$$= \frac{1}{2\pi \times 10^{-4}} = \frac{10^4}{2\pi}$$

$$= 1.59 \times 10^3\text{ Hz} = 1.59\text{ kHz}$$

02. (a) Given, in series L-C-R circuit,

$$L = 10\text{ H}, C = 10\,\mu\text{F} = 10^{-5}\text{F}$$

$$R = 50\,\Omega$$

Source voltage, $V = 200\sin(100\,t)$ V

$$\omega = 100\text{ rad/s}$$

$$\therefore \quad 2\pi\nu = 100 \Rightarrow \nu = \frac{100}{2\pi} = \frac{50}{\pi}\text{ Hz}$$

Resonance frequency,

$$\nu_0 = \frac{1}{2\pi\sqrt{LC}} = \frac{1}{2\pi\sqrt{10 \times 10^{-5}}}$$

$$= \frac{1}{2\pi \times 10^{-2}} = \frac{50}{\pi}\text{ Hz}$$

Hence, $\nu = \nu_0 = \dfrac{50}{\pi}$ Hz

03. (c) Given, in the L-C-R series circuit,

$$L = 5\text{ H},$$

$$C = 80\,\mu\text{F}, R = 40\,\Omega$$

Supply voltage, $V = 230$ V

We know that, resonance frequency,

$$\omega_r = \frac{1}{\sqrt{LC}}$$

Substituting the values in the above equation, we get

$$\omega_r = \frac{1}{\sqrt{5 \times 80 \times 10^{-6}}} = 50\text{ rad/s}$$

Therefore, the angular frequencies of the source at which power transferred to the circuit is half the power at the resonant angular frequency are

$$\omega = \omega_r \pm \Delta\omega \quad ...(i)$$

We know that,

$$\Delta\omega = \frac{R}{2L} \Rightarrow \Delta\omega = \frac{40}{2(5)}$$

$$\Rightarrow \quad \Delta\omega = 4$$

Using the Eq. (i), we get $\omega = \omega_r \pm \Delta\omega$

$$\omega = (50 \pm 4)\text{ rad/s}$$

So, the angular frequency is likely to be 46 rad/s and 54 rad/s.

04. (b) For series L-C-R circuit

Voltage, $\quad V = \sqrt{V_R^2 + (V_L - V_C)^2}$

Since, $\quad V_L = V_C$

Hence $\quad V = V_R = 220$ V

Also, current $i = \dfrac{V}{R} = \dfrac{220}{100} = 2.2$A

05. (a) Current in L-C-R series circuit,

$$i = \frac{V}{\sqrt{R^2 + (X_L - X_C)^2}}$$

For current to be maximum, at resonance

$$X_L = X_C \quad \text{i.e.} \quad \omega L = \frac{1}{\omega C}$$

or $\quad L = \dfrac{1}{\omega^2 C} \quad ...(i)$

Given, $\omega = 1000\text{ s}^{-1}$, $C = 10\,\mu$F

$$= 10 \times 10^{-6}\text{ F}$$

Hence, $L = \dfrac{1}{(1000)^2 \times 10 \times 10^{-6}}$

$$= 0.1\text{ H} = 100\text{ mH}$$

06. (c) In series L-C-R circuit at resonance, capacitive reactance (X_C) = inductive reactance (X_L)

i.e. $\frac{1}{\omega C} = \omega L$

Total impedance of the circuit

$$Z = \sqrt{R^2 + (X_L - X_C)^2}$$

$$= \sqrt{R^2 + \left(\omega L - \frac{1}{\omega C}\right)^2}$$

i.e. $Z = R$

So, power factor, $\cos\phi = \frac{R}{Z} = \frac{R}{R} = 1$

Thus, power loss at resonance is given by

$$P = V_{rms}\, i_{rms} \cos\phi \qquad [\cos\phi = 1]$$

$$= V_{rms}\, i_{rms} \times 1 = (i_{rms} R)\, i_{rms}$$

$$= (i_{rms})^2 R = i^2 R$$

07. *(a)*

key idea

A series *L-C-R* circuit is said to be in resonance condition if $X_L = X_C$

Since, $X_L = X_C = 50\,\Omega$

$\therefore$ It is a series *L-C-R* resonance circuit.

$\therefore$ Impedance,

$$Z = R = 10\,\Omega$$

08. *(d)* The impedance Z of an *L-C-R* circuit is given by

$$Z = \sqrt{R^2 + \left(\omega L - \frac{1}{\omega C}\right)^2}$$

At resonance $X_L = X_C$

i.e. $\omega L = \frac{1}{\omega C}$, $Z = R$

So, circuit behaves as if it contains R only. So, phase difference = 0.

Frequency of resonating *L-C-R* circuit is given by

$$\omega^2 = \frac{1}{LC}$$

$$\Rightarrow \quad f = \frac{1}{2\pi\sqrt{LC}}$$

Topic 4

01. *(b)* We know that, transformation ratio,

$$r = \frac{N_s}{N_p} = \frac{V_s}{V_p}$$

$$\because \quad \frac{N_p}{N_s} = \frac{1}{2} = \frac{V_p}{V_s} \Rightarrow V_s : V_p = 2:1$$

02. *(d)* According to given situation,

$$V_s = 12\text{ V},$$

$$\therefore \quad I_s = \frac{P}{V_s} = \frac{60}{12} = 5\text{ A}$$

$\therefore$ Given, $V_p = 220$ V

For ideal transformer.

$$I_p V_p = I_s V_s$$

$$\Rightarrow \quad I_p = \frac{I_s V_s}{V_p} = \frac{5 \times 12}{220} = 0.27\text{ A}$$

03. *(a)* Given, the main supply line voltage in transformer,

$$V = 220\text{ V}$$

The rating of the lamp = 11 V, 44 W

We know that, $P = VI_P$ ...(i)

Here, P is the power that operates the lamp,

V is the supply line voltage,

I_P is the primary current in the transformer.

From Eq. (i), we get

$$\Rightarrow \quad 44 = I_P \times 220 \Rightarrow I_P = 0.2\text{ A}$$

04. *(b)* Initial power = 3000 W

As efficiency is 90%, then final power

$$= 3000 \times \frac{90}{100} = 2700\text{ W}$$

$$\Rightarrow \quad \left.\begin{array}{l} V_1 I_1 = 3000\text{W} \\ V_2 I_2 = 2700\text{ W} \end{array}\right] \quad \text{...(i)}$$

$$V_2 = \frac{2700}{6} = \frac{900}{2} \qquad [\because I_2 = 6\text{ A}]$$

$$\Rightarrow \quad V_2 = 450\text{ V}$$

$$\text{and} \quad I_1 = \frac{3000}{200} \qquad [\because V_1 = 200\text{ V}]$$

$$\Rightarrow \quad I_1 = 15\text{ A}$$

05. *(c)* Transformer cannot work on DC.

$$\therefore \quad V_s = 0$$

$$\text{and} \quad I_s = 0$$

06. *(d)* Efficiency is defined as the ratio of output power and input power

$$\text{i.e} \quad \eta\% = \frac{P_{out}}{P_{input}} \times 100 = \frac{V_s\, i_s}{V_p\, i_p} \times 100$$

$$80 = \frac{2 \times 440}{220 \times i_p} \times 100$$

$$\Rightarrow \quad i_p = 5\text{ A}$$

07. *(c)* $\eta = \frac{\text{Output power}}{\text{Input power}}$ or $\eta = \frac{V_s I_s}{V_p I_p}$

[as power = VI]

Given, $V_s I_s = 100$ W, $V_p = 220$ V

$$I_p = 0.5\text{ A}$$

$$\text{Hence,} \quad \eta = \frac{100}{220 \times 0.5} = 0.90 = 90\%$$

08. *(b)* The magnetic flux linked with the primary coil is given by $\phi = \phi_0 + 4t$

So, voltage across primary

$$V_p = \frac{d\phi}{dt} = \frac{d}{dt}(\phi_0 + 4t)$$

$$= 4\text{ V} \quad (\text{as } \phi_0 = \text{constant})$$

Also, we have

$$N_p = 50 \text{ and } N_s = 1500$$

$$\frac{V_s}{V_p} = \frac{N_s}{N_p} \text{ or } V_s = V_p \frac{N_s}{N_p}$$

$$= 4\left(\frac{1500}{50}\right) = 120\text{ V}$$

09. *(a)* The core of a transformer is laminated in order to minimise energy lost in the form of heat due to eddy currents.

10. *(b)* As, $\phi \propto N$

$$\text{So,} \quad \frac{\phi_p}{N_p} = \frac{\phi_s}{N_s}$$

$$\text{or} \quad \frac{1}{N_p} \cdot \frac{d\phi_p}{dt} = \frac{1}{N_s} \frac{d\phi_s}{dt}$$

$$\therefore \quad \frac{V_s}{V_p} = \frac{N_s}{N_p} \qquad \left(\text{as } V \propto \frac{d\phi}{dt}\right)$$

For no loss of power, Vi = constant

$$\therefore \quad i = \frac{1}{V} \times \text{constant}$$

$$\text{or} \quad \frac{i_p}{i_s} = \frac{V_s}{V_p} \text{ or } \frac{i_p}{i_s} = \frac{N_s}{N_p}$$

i_p and i_s are currents in primary and secondary coils

$$\text{Here,} \quad \frac{N_p}{N_s} = \frac{1}{25}$$

$$i_s = 2\text{ A}$$

$$\therefore \quad \frac{i_p}{2} = \frac{25}{1}$$

$$\text{or} \quad i_p = 25 \times 2 = 50\text{ A}$$

Concept Enhancer

For a transformer, $\frac{N_s}{N_p} = \frac{e_s}{e_p} = \frac{I_s}{I_p}$

For step-up transformer,

$N_s > N_p, e_s > e_p, I_s < I_p$

For step-down transformer,

$N_s < N_p, e_s < e_p, I_s > I_p$.

11. *(d)* For a transformer,

$$\frac{V_s}{V_p} = \frac{N_s}{N_p}$$

$$V_s = \frac{N_s}{N_p} V_p = \frac{5000}{500} \times 20$$

$$= 200\text{ V}$$

and frequency remains same

Thus, output has voltage 200 V and frequency 50 Hz.

C-22

NEET Chapterwise
Topicwise Physics

In NEET 2024, 2 questions were visible from this chapter. In past 5 years, 9 questions from topic-1,and 2 questions from topic-2 were asked.

For detailed analysis scan QR code

ELECTROMAGNETIC WAVES

Topic 1 Displacement Current, Electromagnetic Wave & its Characteristic

01 A parallel plate capacitor is charged by connecting it to a battery through a resistor. If I is the current in the circuit, then in the gap between the plates.

[NCERT (New) Pg. 203, NEET 2024]

(a) There is no current.
(b) Displacement current of magnitude equal to I flows in the same direction as I.
(c) Displacement current of magnitude equal to I flows in a direction opposite to that of I.
(d) Displacement current of magnitude greater than I flows but can be in any direction.

02 The property which is not of an electromagnetic wave travelling in free space is that.

[NCERT (New) Pg. 206, NEET 2024]

(a) They are transverse in nature.
(b) The energy density in electric field is equal to energy density in magnetic field.
(c) They travel with a speed equal to $\frac{1}{\sqrt{\mu_0 \varepsilon_0}}$.
(d) They originate from charges moving with uniform speed.

03 In a plane electromagnetic wave travelling in free space, the electric field component oscillates sinusoidally at a frequency of 2.0×10^{10} Hz and amplitude 48 V m^{-1}. Then the amplitude of oscillating magnetic field is (Speed of light in free space $= 3 \times 10^8\ \text{m s}^{-1}$)

[NEET 2023]

(a) 1.6×10^{-8} T (b) 1.6×10^{-7} T
(c) 1.6×10^{-6} T (d) 1.6×10^{-9} T

04 When light propagates through a material medium of relative permittivity ε_r and relative permeability μ_r, the velocity of light, v is given by (c velocity of light in vacuum)

[NCERT (New) Pg. 207, NEET 2022]

(a) $v = \sqrt{\frac{\mu_r}{\varepsilon_r}}$ (b) $v = \sqrt{\frac{\varepsilon_r}{\mu_r}}$ (c) $v = \frac{c}{\sqrt{\varepsilon_r \mu_r}}$ (d) $v = c$

05 A capacitor of capacitance C, is connected across an AC source of voltage V, given by $V = V_0 \sin \omega t$
The displacement current between the plates of the capacitor, would then be given by

[NEET 2021]

(a) $I_d = V_0\, \omega C \cos \omega t$
(b) $I_d = \frac{V_0}{\omega C} \cos \omega t$
(c) $I_d = \frac{V_0}{\omega C} \sin \omega t$
(d) $I_d = V_0 \omega C \sin \omega t$

06 For a plane electromagnetic wave propagating in x-direction, which one of the following combination gives the correct possible directions for electric field E and magnetic field B respectively ?

[NCERT (New) Pg. 206, NEET 2021]

(a) $\hat{j}+\hat{k}, \hat{j}+\hat{k}$ (b) $-\hat{j}+\hat{k}, -\hat{j}-\hat{k}$
(c) $\hat{j}+\hat{k}, -\hat{j}+\hat{k}$ (d) $-\hat{j}+\hat{k}, -\hat{j}+\hat{k}$

07 The magnetic field in a plane electromagnetic wave is given by $B_y = 2 \times 10^{-7} \sin(\pi \times 10^3 x + 3\pi \times 10^{11} t)$T
Calculate the wavelength.

[NEET (Oct.) 2020]

(a) $\pi \times 10^3$ m (b) 2×10^{-3} m
(c) 2×10^3 m (d) $\pi \times 10^{-3}$ m

08 The ratio of contributions made by the electric field and magnetic field components, to the intensity of an electromagnetic wave is (where, c = speed of electromagnetic waves)

[NEET (Sep.) 2020]

(a) $1:1$ (b) $1:c$
(c) $1:c^2$ (d) $c:1$

09 Light with an average flux of 20 W/cm^2 falls on a non-reflecting surface at normal incidence having surface area 20 cm^2. The energy received by the surface during time span of 1 min is

[NCERT (New) Pg. 203, NEET (Sep.) 2020]

(a) 12×10^3 J (b) 24×10^3 J
(c) 48×10^3 J (d) 10×10^3 J

10 A parallel plate capacitor of capacitance 20μF is being charged by a voltage source whose potential is changing at the rate of 3 V/s. The conduction current through the connecting wires and the displacement current through the plates of the capacitor, would be, respectively. *[NEET (National) 2019]*
(a) 60 μA, 60 μA (b) 60 μA, zero
(c) zero, zero (d) zero, 60 μA

11 For a transparent medium relative permeability and permittivity, μ_r and ε_r, are 1.0 and 1.44 respectively. The velocity of light in this medium would be *[NCERT (New) Pg. 207, NEET 2019]*
(a) 2.5×10^8 m/s (b) 3×10^8 m/s
(c) 2.08×10^8 m/s (d) 4.32×10^8 m/s

12 An EM wave is propagating in a medium with a velocity $\mathbf{v} = v\hat{\mathbf{i}}$. The instantaneous oscillating electric field of this EM wave is along $+Y$-axis. Then, the direction of oscillating magnetic field of EM wave will be along *[NEET 2018]*
(a) $-y$-direction (b) $+z$-direction
(c) $-z$-direction (d) $-x$-direction

13 In an electromagnetic wave in free space the root mean square value of the electric field is $E_{rms} = 6\ \text{V m}^{-1}$. The peak value of the magnetic field is *[NCERT (New) Pg. 207, NEET 2017]*
(a) 2.83×10^{-8} T (b) 0.70×10^{-8} T
(c) 4.23×10^{-8} T (d) 1.41×10^{-8} T

14 A 100 Ω resistance and a capacitor of 100 Ω reactance are connected in series across a 220 V source. When the capacitor is 50% charged, the peak value of the displacement current is *[NEET 2016]*
(a) 2.2 A (b) 11 A
(c) 4.4 A (d) $11\sqrt{2}$ A

15 Out of the following options which one can be used to produce a propagating electromagnetic wave?
(a) A stationary charge *[NCERT (New) Pg. 205, NEET 2016]*
(b) A chargeless particle
(c) An accelerating charge
(d) A charge moving at constant velocity

16 A radiation of energy E falls normally on a perfectly reflecting surface. The momentum transferred to the surface is (c = velocity of light) *[AIPMT 2015]*
(a) $\frac{E}{c}$ (b) $\frac{2E}{c}$ (c) $\frac{2E}{c^2}$ (d) $\frac{E}{c^2}$

17 Light with an energy flux of $25 \times 10^4\ \text{Wm}^{-2}$ falls on a perfectly reflecting surface at normal incidence. If the surface area is $15\ \text{cm}^2$, the average force exerted on the surface is *[NCERT (Old) Pg. 277, AIPMT 2014]*
(a) 1.25×10^{-6} N (b) 2.50×10^{-6} N
(c) 1.20×10^{-6} N (d) 3.0×10^{-6} N

18 An electromagnetic wave of frequency $\nu = 3.0$ MHz passes from vacuum into a dielectric medium with relative permittivity $\varepsilon = 4.0$. Then, *[NEET 2013]*
(a) wavelength is doubled and frequency becomes half
(b) wavelength is halved and frequency remains unchanged.
(c) wavelength and frequency both remains unchanged
(d) wavelength is doubled and frequency unchanged

19 The electric field associated with an electro magnetic wave in vacuum is given by $\mathbf{E} = \hat{\mathbf{i}}\,40 \cos(kz - 6 \times 10^8 t)$, where E, z and t are in V/m, metre and second respectively. The value of wave vector k is *[NCERT (New) Pg. 278, AIPMT 2012]*
(a) $2\ \text{m}^{-1}$ (b) $0.5\ \text{m}^{-1}$
(c) $6\ \text{m}^{-1}$ (d) $3\ \text{m}^{-1}$

20 The electric and the magnetic field, associated with an electromagnetic wave, propagating along the $+Z$-axis, can be represented by *[AIPMT 2011]*
(a) $\mathbf{E} = E_0\hat{\mathbf{k}},\ \mathbf{B} = B_0\hat{\mathbf{i}}$
(b) $\mathbf{E} = E_0\hat{\mathbf{j}},\ \mathbf{E} = B_0\hat{\mathbf{j}}$
(c) $\mathbf{E} = E_0\hat{\mathbf{j}},\ \mathbf{B} = B_0\hat{\mathbf{k}}$
(d) $\mathbf{E} = E_0\hat{\mathbf{i}},\ \mathbf{B} = B_0\hat{\mathbf{j}}$

21 Which of the following statement is false for the properties of electromagnetic waves? *[AIPMT 2010]*
(a) Both electric and magnetic field vectors attain the maxima and minima at the same place and same time
(b) The energy in electromagnetic wave is divided equally between electric and magnetic vectors
(c) Both electric and magnetic field vectors are parallel to each other and perpendicular to the direction of propagation of wave
(d) These waves do not require any material medium for propagation

22 The electric field part of an electromagnetic wave in a medium is represented by $E_x = 0$,
$$E_y = 2.5\frac{\text{N}}{\text{C}}\cos\left[\left(2\pi \times 10^6 \frac{\text{rad}}{\text{m}}\right)t - \left(\pi \times 10^{-2}\frac{\text{rad}}{\text{s}}\right)x\right],\ E_z = 0.$$
The wave is *[AIPMT 2009]*
(a) moving along y-direction with frequency $2\pi \times 10^6$ Hz and wavelength 200 m
(b) moving along x-direction with frequency 10^6 Hz and wavelength 100 m
(c) moving along x-direction with frequency 10^6 Hz and wavelength 200 m
(d) moving along $-x$-direction with frequency 10^6 Hz and wavelength 200 m

23 The velocity of electromagnetic radiation in a medium of permittivity ε_0 and permeability μ_0 is given by *[NCERT (New) Pg. 207, AIPMT 2008]*

(a) $\sqrt{\dfrac{\varepsilon_0}{\mu_0}}$ (b) $\sqrt{\mu_0\varepsilon_0}$ (c) $\dfrac{1}{\sqrt{\mu_0\varepsilon_0}}$ (d) $\sqrt{\dfrac{\mu_0}{\varepsilon_0}}$

24 The velocity of electromagnetic wave is along the direction of *[NCERT (New) Pg. 206, AIPMT 2002]*

(a) $\mathbf{B}\times\mathbf{E}$ (b) $\mathbf{E}\times\mathbf{B}$ (c) $\mathbf{E}$ (d) $\mathbf{B}$

25 In a certain region of space electric field **E** and magnetic field **B** are perpendicular to each other and an electron enters in region perpendicular to the direction of **E** and **B** both and moves undeflected, then velocity of electron is *[AIPMT 2001]*

(a) $\dfrac{|\mathbf{E}|}{|\mathbf{B}|}$ (b) $\mathbf{E}\times\mathbf{B}$ (c) $\dfrac{|\mathbf{B}|}{|\mathbf{E}|}$ (d) $\mathbf{E}\cdot\mathbf{B}$

26 The electromagnetic radiations are caused by *[AIPMT 1999]*

(a) a stationary charge (b) uniformly moving charges
(c) accelerated charges (d) All of the above

27 The wavelength of light of frequency 100 Hz is *[NCERT (New) Pg. 207, AIPMT 1999]*

(a) 2×10^6 m (b) 3×10^6 m
(c) 4×10^6 m (d) 5×10^6 m

28 If ε_0 and μ_0 are respectively the electric permittivity and magnetic permeability of free space, ε and μ are the corresponding quantities in a medium, the index of refraction of the medium is *[AIPMT 1997]*

(a) $\sqrt{\dfrac{\varepsilon_0\mu_0}{\varepsilon\mu}}$ (b) $\sqrt{\dfrac{\varepsilon\mu}{\varepsilon_0\mu_0}}$
(c) $\sqrt{\dfrac{\varepsilon_0\mu}{\varepsilon\mu_0}}$ (d) $\sqrt{\dfrac{\varepsilon}{\varepsilon_0}}$

29 The oscillating electric and magnetic field vectors of electromagnetic wave are oriented along *[AIPMT 1995]*

(a) the same direction and in phase
(b) the same direction but have a phase difference of 90°
(c) mutually perpendicular directions and are in phase
(d) mutually perpendicular directions but has a phase difference of 90°

Topic 2 Electromagnetic Spectrum

01 Match List I with List II.

List I (Electromagnetic waves)	List II (Wavelength)
(A) AM radio waves	(i) 10^{-10} m
(B) Microwaves	(ii) 10^{2} m
(C) Infrared radiations	(iii) 10^{-2} m
(D) X-rays	(iii) 10^{-4} m

Choose the correct answer from the options given below *[NCERT (New) Pg. 208, NEET 2022]*

(a) (A)-(iv), (B)-(iii), (C)-(ii), (D)-(i)
(b) (A)-(iii), (B)-(ii), (C)-(i), (D)-(iv)
(c) (A)-(iii), (B)-(iv), (C)-(ii), (D)-(i)
(d) (A)-(ii), (B)-(iii), (C)-(iv), (D)-(i)

02 The electromagnetic wave with shortest wavelength among the following is *[NEET (Oct.) 2020]*

(a) UV-rays (b) X-rays
(c) γ-rays (d) microwaves

03 The energy of the EM waves is of the order of 15 keV. To which part of the spectrum does it belong ? *[NCERT (New) Pg. 211, AIPMT 2015]*

(a) X-rays (b) Infrared rays
(c) Ultravioiet rays (d) γ-rays

04 The condition under which a microwave oven heats up a food item containing water molecules most efficiently is *[NEET 2013]*

(a) the frequency of the microwave must match the resonant frequency of the water molecules
(b) the frequency of the microwave has no relation with natural frequency of water molecules
(c) microwave are heat waves, so always produce heating
(d) infra-red waves produce heating in a microwave oven

05 The decreasing order of wavelength of infrared, microwave, ultraviolet and gamma rays is *[AIPMT 2011]*

(a) gamma rays, ultraviolet, infrared, microwaves
(b) microwaves, gamma rays, infrared, ultraviolet
(c) infrared, microwave, ultraviolet, gamma rays
(d) microwave, infrared, ultraviolet, gamma rays

06 If λ_v, λ_x and λ_m represent the wavelengths of visible light, X-rays and microwaves respectively, then *[NCERT (New) Pg. 208, AIPMT 2005]*

(a) $\lambda_m>\lambda_x>\lambda_v$
(b) $\lambda_v>\lambda_m>\lambda_x$
(c) $\lambda_m>\lambda_v>\lambda_x$
(d) $\lambda_v>\lambda_x>\lambda_m$

07 Which of the following rays are not electromagnetic waves ? *[AIPMT 2003]*

(a) β-rays (b) Heat rays (c) X-rays (d) γ-rays

08 Which of the following has minimum wavelength ? *[AIPMT 2002]*

(a) X-rays (b) Ultraviolet rays
(c) γ-rays (d) Cosmic rays

09 What is the cause of "Green house effect"? *NCERT (New) Pg. 210, [AIPMT 2002]*

(a) Infrared rays (b) Ultraviolet rays
(c) X-rays (d) Radio-waves

10 The frequency of γ-rays, X-rays and ultraviolet rays are a, b and c respectively. Then, *[AIPMT 2000]*

(a) $a>b>c$ (b) $a<b<c$
(c) $a=b=c$ (d) $a>c>b$

11 Ozone layer blocks the radiations of wavelength *[AIPMT 1999]*

(a) less than 3×10^{-7} m (b) equal to 3×10^{-7} m

(c) more than 3×10^{-7} m (d) All of the above

12 The structure of solids is investigated by using *[NCERT (New) Pg. 211, AIPMT 1992]*

(a) cosmic rays (b) X-rays

(c) γ-rays (d) infrared radiations

13 The frequency of electromagnetic wave, which is best suited to observe a particle of radius 3×10^{-4} cm, is of the order of *[NCERT (New) Pg. 211, AIPMT 1991]*

(a) 10^{15} (b) 10^{14}

(c) 10^{13} (d) 10^{12}

14 Pick out the longest wavelength from the following types of radiations *[AIPMT 1990]*

(a) blue light (b) gamma rays

(c) X-rays (d) red light

15 Which of the following is the longest wave ? *[NCERT (New) Pg. 208, AIPMT 1989]*

(a) X-rays

(b) γ-rays

(c) Microwaves

(d) Radiowaves

• Key **Index**

Topic 1

1 (b)	2 (d)	3 (b)	4 (c)	5 (a)	6 (b)	7 (b)	8 (a)	9 (b)	10 (a)
11 (a)	12 (b)	13 (a)	14 (a)	15 (c)	16 (b)	17 (b)	18 (b)	19 (a)	20 (d)
21 (c)	22 (c)	23 (c)	24 (b)	25 (a)	26 (c)	27 (b)	28 (b)	29 (c)	

Topic 2

1 (d)	2 (c)	3 (a)	4 (a)	5 (d)	6 (c)	7 (a)	8 (d)	9 (a)	10 (a)
11 (a)	12 (b)	13 (b)	14 (d)	15 (d)					

Detailed **Explanations**

Topic 1

01. *(b)*

key idea

Capacitor blocks DC

When a capacitor is charged through a battery, its opposite plates are charged to a maximum value. There is displacement current as the capacitor is being charged,

$$I_d = \varepsilon \cdot \frac{d\phi_E}{dt}$$

Due to charging, ϕ_E changes and hence displacement current equal to conduction current arises while charging. When capacitor gets fully charged, the displacement current became zero.

02. *(d)* Electromagnetic waves are generated by accelerated charged particles.

Hence, option (d) is incorrect.

03. *(b)* Given, amplitude of electric field,

$$E_0 = 48 \text{ Vm}^{-1}$$

As we know, $\dfrac{|E|}{|B|} = c = \dfrac{E_0}{B_0}$

where, E_0 = Amplitude of electric field.

B_0 = Amplitude of magnetic field.

$$\therefore \quad B_0 = \frac{E_0}{c} = \frac{48 \text{ Vm}^{-1}}{3 \times 10^8 \text{ ms}^{-1}}$$

$$= 1.6 \times 10^{-7} \text{ T}$$

04. *(c)* When light (EM wave) propagates through a material medium of relative permittivity ε_r and relative permeability μ_r, then velocity of light (EM wave) is given by

$$v = \frac{c}{\sqrt{\mu_r \varepsilon_r}}$$

where, c is speed of light in vacuum.

05. *(a)* Given, AC source voltage,

$$V = V_0 \sin \omega t \quad \ldots\text{(i)}$$

We know that,

$$Q = CV \quad \ldots\text{(ii)}$$

On differentiate Eq. (ii) w.r.t. time, we get

$$\frac{dQ}{dt} = \frac{d(CV)}{dt} \Rightarrow \frac{dQ}{dt} = \frac{Cd(V_0 \sin \omega t)}{dt}$$

[From Eq. (i)]

$$\Rightarrow \frac{dQ}{dt} = C\omega V_0 \cos \omega t$$

As we know, the displacement current,

$$I_d = \frac{dQ}{dt} = V_0 \, \omega \, C \cos \omega t$$

06. *(b)* We know that, in electromagnetic wave, the electric field E and magnetic field B are perpendicular to each other, $\mathbf{E} \cdot \mathbf{B} = 0$

Consider the option (a),

$(\hat{j} + \hat{k}) \cdot (\hat{j} + \hat{k}) = 1 + 1 = 2 \neq 0$

So, it is incorrect option.

Consider the option (b);

$$(-\hat{j} + \hat{k}) \cdot (-\hat{j} - \hat{k}) = 1 - 1 = 0$$

Hence, it satisfies the condition $\mathbf{E} \cdot \mathbf{B} = 0$

Similarly, options (c) and (d) are incorrect.

07. *(b)* Magnetic field in plane electromagnetic wave is given as

$$B_y = 2\times10^{-7}\sin(\pi\times10^3 x + 3\pi\times10^{11} t)\text{T}$$

Comparing with,

$B_y = B_0 \sin(kx - \omega t)$, we get

$$k = \pi\times10^3$$

$$\Rightarrow \frac{2\pi}{\lambda} = \pi\times10^3 \Rightarrow \lambda = \frac{2}{10^3}$$

$$= 2\times10^{-3}\text{ m}$$

08. *(a)* The intensity of electric field is

$$U_{av} = \frac{1}{2}\varepsilon_0 E_0^2 \quad \ldots\text{(i)}$$

and magnetic field

$$U'_{av} = \frac{1}{2}\frac{B_0^2}{\mu_0} \quad \ldots\text{(ii)}$$

Also, $E_0 = cB_0$

On putting this value in Eq. (i), we get

$$U_{av} = \frac{1}{2}\varepsilon_0 c^2 B_0^2 \quad \ldots\text{(iii)}$$

where, $c = \frac{1}{\sqrt{\mu_0\varepsilon_0}}$

$$U_{av} = \frac{1}{2}\varepsilon_0 B_0^2 \times \frac{1}{\mu_0\varepsilon_0}$$

$$= \frac{1}{2}\frac{B_0^2}{\mu_0} \quad \ldots\text{(iv)}$$

On dividing Eqs. (ii) and (iv), we get

$$\frac{U_{av}}{U'_{av}} = \frac{1}{1} \text{ or } 1:1$$

09. *(b)* Given,

average flux = 20 W/cm^2

Surface area = 20 cm^2

Time = 1 min = 60 s

For non-reflecting surface,

energy received = average flux × surface area × time

$$= 20\times20\times60 = 24\times10^3\text{ J}$$

10. *(a)*

key idea

You can calculate the value of displacement current with the help of the following formula.

$$I_d = C\frac{dV}{dt}$$

where, the symbols have there usual meaning.

Given, $C = 20\mu\text{F} = 20\times10^{-6}\text{ F}$

and $\frac{dV}{dt} = 3\text{ V/s}$

$$\therefore \quad I_d = C\frac{dV}{dt}$$

Substituting the given values, we get

$$I_d = 20\times10^{-6}\times3$$

$$= 60\times10^{-6}\text{ A} = 60\,\mu\text{A}$$

As displacement current is in between the plates of capacitor and conduction current is in the connecting wires which are equal to each other. So,

$$I_c = I_d = 60\,\mu\text{A}$$

11. *(a)* Given, $\varepsilon_r = 1.44, \mu_r = 1$

We know that, $\varepsilon_r = \frac{\varepsilon}{\varepsilon_0}$

$$\Rightarrow \quad \varepsilon = \varepsilon_r\varepsilon_0 \text{ and } \mu_r = \frac{\mu}{\mu_0}$$

$$\Rightarrow \quad \mu = \mu_r\mu_0$$

∴ Velocity of light in the medium will be

$$v = \frac{1}{\sqrt{\mu\varepsilon}} = \frac{1}{\sqrt{\mu_r\mu_0\varepsilon_r\varepsilon_0}}$$

$$= \frac{c}{\sqrt{\mu_r\varepsilon_r}} = \frac{3\times10^8}{\sqrt{1\times1.44}}$$

$$= 2.5\times10^8\text{ m/s}$$

• Concept Enhancer

When an EM wave travels, then its electric field component and magnetic field component vibrate perpendicular to each other and also perpendicular to direction of propagation of EM wave.

12. *(b)* Here, velocity of EM wave,

$$\mathbf{v} = v\hat{\mathbf{i}}$$

Instantaneous oscillating electric field,

$$\mathbf{E} = E\hat{\mathbf{j}}$$

i.e. $\quad \mathbf{E}\times\mathbf{B} = v$

$$\Rightarrow \quad (E\hat{\mathbf{j}})\times\mathbf{B} = v\hat{\mathbf{i}} \quad \ldots\text{(i)}$$

As we know that from vector algebra,

$$\hat{\mathbf{j}}\times\hat{\mathbf{k}} = \hat{\mathbf{i}} \quad \ldots\text{(ii)}$$

Comparing Eqs. (i) and (ii), we get

$$\mathbf{B} = B\hat{\mathbf{k}},$$

where B (say) be the magnitude of magnetic field.

Thus, we can say that the direction of oscillating magnetic field of the em wave will be along $+z$-direction.

13. *(a)* We know that,

$$\frac{E_{rms}}{B_{rms}} = c \text{ or } B_{rms} = \frac{E_{rms}}{c}$$

$$\Rightarrow \quad B_{rms} = \frac{6}{3\times10^8} = 2\times10^{-8}\text{ T}$$

Since, $B_{rms} = \frac{B_0}{\sqrt{2}}$

$$\therefore \quad B_0 = B_{rms}\sqrt{2} = 2\times10^{-8}\times\sqrt{2}\text{ T}$$

$$B_0 \approx 2.83\times10^{-8}\text{ T}$$

14. *(a)* We know that,

$$Z = \sqrt{R^2 + X_C^2} = 100\sqrt{2}\,\Omega$$

Peak value of displacement current = Maximum conduction current in the circuit

$$= \frac{\varepsilon_0}{Z} = \frac{220\sqrt{2}}{100\sqrt{2}} = 2.2\text{ A}$$

15. *(c)* It known that an electric charge at rest has electric field in the region around it, but no magnetic field. A moving charge produces both the electric and magnetic fields.

If a charge is moving with a constant velocity, the electric and magnetic fields will not change with time, hence no EM wave will be produced.

But if the charge is moving with a non-zero acceleration, both the electric and magnetic field will change with space and time, it then produces EM wave. This shows that an accelerated charge emits electromagnetic waves.

16. *(b)* The radiation energy is given by

$$E = \frac{hc}{\lambda}$$

Initial momentum of the radiation is

$$\mathbf{p}_i = \frac{h}{\lambda} = \frac{E}{c}$$

The reflected momentum is

$$\mathbf{p}_r = -\frac{h}{\lambda} = -\frac{E}{c}$$

So, the change in momentum of light is

$$\Delta\mathbf{p}_{light} = \mathbf{p}_r - \mathbf{p}_i = -\frac{2E}{c}$$

Thus, the momentum transferred to the surface is $\Delta\mathbf{p}_{light} = \frac{2E}{c}$

17. *(b)* As $F_{average} = \frac{2IA}{c}$

where, $\quad I$ = energy flux of light $= 25\times10^4\text{ Wm}^{-2}$

A = Surface area of reflecting surface

and $\quad c$ = speed of light $= 3\times10^8$ m/s

$$\therefore \quad F_{av} = \frac{2\times25\times10^4\times15\times10^{-4}}{3\times10^8}$$

$$= 2.50\times10^{-6}\text{ N}$$

18. *(b)* Frequency of electromagnetic wave remains unchanged in medium but wavelength and velocity of wave changes with change in medium.

We know that

$$c = \frac{1}{\sqrt{\mu_0 \varepsilon_0}} = \nu\lambda_{\text{vacuum}} \quad \ldots(i)$$

Velocity of electromagnetic wave in the medium

$$v_{\text{medium}} = \frac{1}{\sqrt{\mu_0 \mu_r \varepsilon_0 \varepsilon_r}} = \frac{c}{\sqrt{\mu_r \varepsilon_r}}$$

For dielectric medium, $\mu_r = 1$

$$\therefore \quad v_{\text{medium}} = \frac{c}{\sqrt{\varepsilon_r}}$$

Here, $\varepsilon_r = 4.0 \quad \ldots(ii)$

wavelength of the wave in medium

$$\lambda_{\text{medium}} = \frac{v_{\text{medium}}}{v} = \frac{c}{2v} = \frac{\lambda_{\text{vacuum}}}{2}$$

[Using (i) and (ii)]

19. *(a)* Electromagnetic wave equation is given by

$$E = E_0 \cos(kz - \omega t) \quad \ldots(i)$$

Speed of electromagnetic wave, $v = \frac{\omega}{k}$

Given, equation is

$$\mathbf{E} = \hat{\mathbf{i}}\, 40 \cos(kz - 6 \times 10^8 t) \ldots(ii)$$

Comparing Eqs. (i) and (ii), we get

$$\omega = 6 \times 10^8 \text{ and } E_0 = 40\hat{\mathbf{i}}$$

Here, wave factor,

$$k = \frac{\omega}{v} = \frac{6 \times 10^8}{3 \times 10^8} = 2 \text{ m}^{-1}$$

20. *(d)* As we know that

$$\mu = \mathbf{E} \times \mathbf{B} = E_0 \hat{\mathbf{i}} + B_0 \hat{\mathbf{j}}$$

$\mathbf{E} \times \mathbf{B}$ points in the direction of wave propagation.

21. *(c)* The time varying electric and magnetic fields are mutually perpendicular to each other and also perpendicular to the direction of propagation.

22. *(c)* Comparing the given equation

$$E_y = 2.5 \frac{\text{N}}{\text{C}} \cos\left[\left(2\pi \times 10^6 \frac{\text{rad}}{\text{m}}\right)t - \left(\pi \times 10^{-2} \frac{\text{rad}}{\text{s}}\right)x\right]$$

With the standard equation

$$E_y = E_0 \cos(\omega t - kx)$$

we get $\omega = 2\pi f = 2\pi \times 10^6$

$$\therefore \quad f = 10^6 \text{ Hz}$$

Moreover, we know that

$$\frac{2\pi}{\lambda} = k = \pi \times 10^{-2} \text{ m}^{-1} \Rightarrow \lambda = 200 \text{ m}$$

As only the direction of the electric field (Y-axis) is given, the wave could be travelling in either X or Z-axis.

23. *(c)*

key idea

Using dimensions of μ_0 and ε_0, you can find the relation between μ_0, ε_0 and c.

The velocity of electromagnetic waves in free space is given by

$$c = \frac{1}{\sqrt{\mu_0 \varepsilon_0}}$$

24. *(b)* An electromagnetic wave is the wave composed of the oscillations of electric and magnetic fields in mutually perpendicular planes and these oscillations are perpendicular to the direction of propagation of wave.

The direction of propagation of electromagnetic wave is given by poynting vector

$$\mathbf{S} = \mathbf{E} \times \mathbf{H} = \frac{\mathbf{E} \times \mathbf{B}}{\mu_0}$$

This is parallel to $\mathbf{E} \times \mathbf{B}$.

25. *(a)* For electron to pass undeflected, electric force on electron

= magnetic force on electron

i.e. $eE = evB$ or $v = \frac{E}{B}$ or $v = \frac{|\mathbf{E}|}{|\mathbf{B}|}$

26. *(c)* A stationary charge produces electric field only; a uniformly moving charge produces localised electromagnetic field. An accelerated charge produces electro- magnetic radiations. The reason is that due to accelerated charges, magnetic field is produced around accelerating charges. As the velocity of charge changes, the magnetic field produced due to it also changes with time. This varying magnetic field produces the electric field.

The electric field, so produced also changes with time. These two varying fields are mutually perpendicular and also perpendicular to the direction of propagation of wave and both the fields are in same phase and of same frequency. The frequency of these fields is same as the frequency of oscillations of the charged particle. The wave associated with these oscillations is called the electromagnetic wave.

27. *(b)* The relation between velocity of light c, frequency ν and wavelength λ is $c = \nu\lambda$

Thus, wavelength $\lambda = \frac{c}{\nu}$

Given, $c = 3 \times 10^8$ m/s, $\nu = 100$ Hz

$$\therefore \quad \lambda = \frac{3 \times 10^8}{100} = 3 \times 10^6 \text{ m}$$

28. *(b)* Refractive index of medium is given by $n = \sqrt{\mu_r \varepsilon_r}$.

Here, $\mu = \mu_0 \mu_r \Rightarrow \mu_r = \frac{\mu}{\mu_0}$

and $\varepsilon = \varepsilon_0 \varepsilon_r \Rightarrow \varepsilon_r = \frac{\varepsilon}{\varepsilon_0}$

$$\therefore \quad n = \sqrt{\frac{\mu}{\mu_0} \cdot \frac{\varepsilon}{\varepsilon_0}} = \sqrt{\frac{\varepsilon\mu}{\varepsilon_0 \mu_0}}$$

29. *(c)* According to Maxwell, the electromagnetic waves are those waves in which there are sinusoidal variations of electric and magnetic field vectors at right angles to each other as well as right angles to the direction of wave propagation. Both these fields vary with time and space and have the same frequency. In figure, the electric field vector **E** and magnetic field vector **B** are vibrating along y and z-directions and propagation of electromagnetic wave is shown in x-direction.

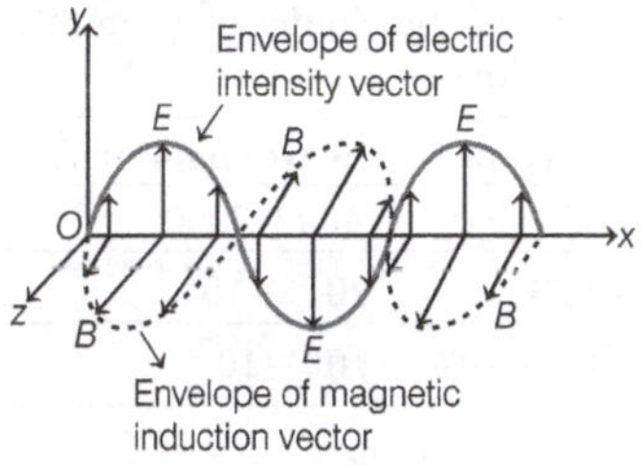

From figure it is clear that electric and magnetic fields oscillate in same phase.

Topic 2

01. *(d)* The wavelength of AM radio waves is 10^2 m. The wavelength of microwaves ranges between 10^{-3} m to 10^{-1} m.

Infrared radiations wavelength lines between 4×10^{-7} m to 7×10^{-3} m.

X-rays wavelength ranges from 10^{-8} m to 10^{-12} m.

02. *(c)* γ-rays has the shortest wavelength because it has higher frequency than UV-rays, microwaves and X-rays.

03. *(a)* Given, energy of EM waves is of the order of 15 keV

i.e. $E = h\nu = h \times \frac{c}{\lambda}$

$$\Rightarrow \lambda = \frac{h \times c}{E}$$

$$= \frac{6.624 \times 10^{-34} \times 3 \times 10^{8}}{15 \times 10^{3} \times 1.6 \times 10^{-19}}$$

$$= \frac{1.3248 \times 10^{-29}}{1.6 \times 10^{-19}}$$

$$= 0.828 \times 10^{-10} \text{ m}$$

$$= 0.828 \text{ Å} \quad [\because 1 \text{Å} = 10^{-10} \text{ m}]$$

$$\lambda = 0.828 \text{ Å}$$

Thus, this spectrum is a part of X-rays.

04. *(a)* It is an electromagnetic wave. The frequency of the microwave oven must match the resonant frequency of the water molecules.

• Concept Enhancer

In the presence of microwaves, water molecules oscillates with frequency of microwaves and large amount of heat is developed.

05. *(d)* Decreasing order of wavelength of various rays is

Microwave > Infrared > Ultraviolet > Gamma rays

06. *(c)* Wavelength order of given rays are listed below

Waves	Wavelength (in Å)
Visible light	4000–7000
X-rays	$10^{-3} - 10^{2}$
Microwaves	$10^{7} - 10^{9}$

So, $\lambda_x < \lambda_v < \lambda_m$

07. *(a)* (a) β-rays are fast moving electrons. So, they are not electromagnetic waves.

(b) Heat rays can travel through vaccum *via* radiation process. They are electromagnetic waves.

(c) X-rays are electromagnetic waves having wavelengths from about 10^{-8} m to 10^{-12} m.

(d) γ-rays are electromagnetic waves having wavelengths ranging from about 10^{-16} m to 10^{-14} m.

Hence, choice (a) is correct.

08. *(d)* The wavelength order of waves are given below

Waves	Wavelength (in Å)
(a) X-rays	0.001 Å to 100 Å
(b) Ultraviolet rays	10 Å to 4000 Å
(c) γ-rays	0.0001 Å to 1 Å
(d) Cosmic rays	upto 4×10^{-3} Å

Thus, cosmic rays have the minimum wavelength.

09. *(a)* The green house is a room made of glass which is constructed to grow plants in open space. The glass transmits the infrared radiations of short wavelength and the visible light, but it absorbs the infrared radiations of long wavelength. During day time, the light and the infrared radiations of short wavelength enter inside the green house through the roof and the walls and they are absorbed by the plants. At night, plants emit infrared radiations through the glass walls and roof. As a result a green house remains warm. This is called green house effect.

10. *(a)* Frequency of radiations given are listed below.

Waves	Frequency (in Hz)
1. γ-rays	(a) 3×10^{21} to 3×10^{18}
2. X-rays	(b) 3×10^{18} to 3×10^{16}
3. Ultraviolet radiation	(c) 3×10^{16} to 7.5×10^{14}

Thus, correct order is $a > b > c$.

11. *(a)* Ozone layer extends from 30 km to nearly 50 km above the earth's surface in ozone sphere.

This layer absorbs the major part of ultraviolet radiations coming from the sun and does not allow them to reach the earth's surface.

The range of ultraviolet radiations is 100 Å to 4000 Å. Thus, it blocks the radiations of wavelength less than 3×10^{-7} m (or 3000 Å).

• Concept Enhancer

γ-rays are used in radio theory for the treatment of malignant tumours and ultraviolet rays can help in the study of invisible writings.

12. *(b)* Due to high penetrating power of X-rays, X-rays are used for investigation of structure of solids.

Lane spot method and rotating cylinder method are used for this purpose.

X-rays fall on solid under investigation and their structure is received on photographic plate.

13. *(b)* Size of particle of any wave is given in terms of wavelength

$$\lambda = \frac{c}{\nu}$$

Here, $\lambda = 3 \times 10^{-4}$ cm,

Velocity of light in vacuum,

$$c = 3 \times 10^{10} \text{ cm/s}$$

$$\therefore 3 \times 10^{-4} = \frac{3 \times 10^{10}}{\nu}$$

∴ Frequency of electromagnetic wave

$$\nu = 10^{14} \text{ Hz}$$

14. *(d)* γ-rays have wavelength range 6×10^{-14} m to 1×10^{-10} m, X-rays have wavelength range 1×10^{-13} m to 3×10^{-8} m. Blue light and red light lies in visible range of spectrum which extends from 4000Å to 7800 Å. Hence, wavelength of red light is longest.

15. *(d)* Wavelength range of various waves are as follows

Name	Wavelength range (m)
Gamma rays	6×10^{-14} to 1×10^{-10}
X-rays	1×10^{-13} to 3×10^{-8}
Radio waves	greater than 0.1
Microwaves	10^{-3} to 0.3

So, radiowaves are the longest waves.

C-23

NEET Chapterwise Topicwise Physics

In NEET 2024, 2 questions were visible from this chapter. In past 5 years, 1 question from topic-1, 6 questions from topic-2, 6 questions from topic-3 and 2 question from topic-4 were asked.

For detailed analysis scan QR code

RAY OPTICS AND OPTICAL INSTRUMENTS

Topic 1 Reflection of Light

01 An object is placed on the principal axis of a concave mirror at a distance of $1.5\ f$ (f is the focal length). The image will be at *[NCERT (New) Pg. 225, NEET (Oct.) 2020]*

(a) $-3f$ (b) $1.5f$ (c) $-1.5f$ (d) $3f$

02 An object is placed at a distance of 40 cm from a concave mirror of focal length 15 cm. If the object is displaced through a distance of 20 cm towards the mirror, the displacement of the image will be *[NEET 2018]*

(a) 30 cm towards the mirror
(b) 36 cm away from the mirror
(c) 30 cm away from the mirror
(d) 36 cm towards the mirror

03 A beam of light from a source L is incident normally on a plane mirror fixed at a certain distance x from the source. The beam is reflected back as a spot on a scale placed just above the source L. When the mirror is rotated through a small angle θ, the spot of the light is found to move through a distance y on the scale. The angle θ is given by *[NEET 2017]*

(a) $\frac{y}{2x}$ (b) $\frac{y}{x}$ (c) $\frac{x}{2y}$ (d) $\frac{x}{y}$

04 Match the corresponding entries of Column I with Column II. [Where m is the magnification produced by the mirror] *[NCERT (New) Pg. 225, NEET 2016]*

	Column I		Column II
A.	$m = -2$	a.	Convex mirror
B.	$m = -\frac{1}{2}$	b.	Concave mirror
C.	$m = +2$	c.	Real image
D.	$m = +\frac{1}{2}$	d.	Virtual image

(a) A→ a and c, B→ a and d, C→ a and b, D→ c and d
(b) A→ a and d, B→ b and c, C→ b and d, D→ b and c
(c) A→ c and d, B→ b and d, C→ b and c, D→ a and d
(d) A→ b and c, B→ b and c, C→ b and d, D→ a and d

05 A concave mirror of focal length f_1 is placed at a distance of d from a convex lens of focal length f_2. A beam of light coming from infinity and falling on this convex lens- concave mirror combination returns to infinity. The distance d must be equal *[AIPMT 2012]*

(a) $f_1 + f_2$
(b) $-f_1 + f_2$
(c) $2f_1 + f_2$
(d) $-2f_1 + f_2$

06 A man is 6 ft tall. In order to see his entire image, he requires a plane mirror of minimum length equal to *[AIPMT 2000]*

(a) 6 ft (b) 12 ft
(c) 2 ft (d) 3 ft

07 If two mirrors are kept inclined at 60° to each other and a body is placed at the middle, then total number of images formed, is *[AIPMT 1995]*

(a) six
(b) five
(c) four
(d) three

08 Ray optics is valid, when characteristic dimensions are *[AIPMT 1989]*

(a) of the same order as the wavelength of light
(b) much smaller than the wavelength of light
(c) of the order of one millimetre
(d) much larger than the wavelength of light

Topic 2 Refraction, TIR and Prism

01 A light ray enters through a right angled prism at point P with the angle of incidence $30°$ as shown in figure. It travels through the prism parallel to its base BC and emerges along the face AC. The refractive index of the prism is *[NCERT (New) Pg. 240, NEET 2024]*

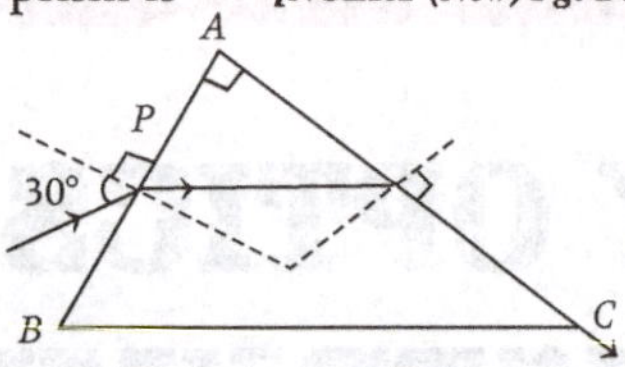

(a) $\frac{\sqrt{5}}{4}$ (b) $\frac{\sqrt{5}}{2}$ (c) $\frac{\sqrt{3}}{4}$ (d) $\frac{\sqrt{3}}{2}$

02 Light travels a distance x in time t_1 in air and $10x$ in time t_2 in another denser medium. What is the critical angle for this medium ? *[NEET 2023]*

(a) $\sin^{-1}\left(\frac{10t_2}{t_1}\right)$ (b) $\sin^{-1}\left(\frac{t_1}{10t_2}\right)$

(c) $\sin^{-1}\left(\frac{10t_1}{t_2}\right)$ (d) $\sin^{-1}\left(\frac{t_2}{t_1}\right)$

03 Two transparent media A and B are separated by a plane boundary. The speed of light in those media are 1.5×10^8 m/s and 2.0×10^8 m / s, respectively. The critical angle for a ray of light for these two media is *[NCERT (New) Pg. 230, NEET 2022]*

(a) $\sin^{-1}(0.750)$ (b) $\tan^{-1}(0.500)$

(c) $\tan^{-1}(0.750)$ (d) $\sin^{-1}(0.500)$

04 Find the value of the angle of emergence from the prism. Refractive index of the glass is $\sqrt{3}$. *[NCERT (New) Pg. 230, NEET 2021]*

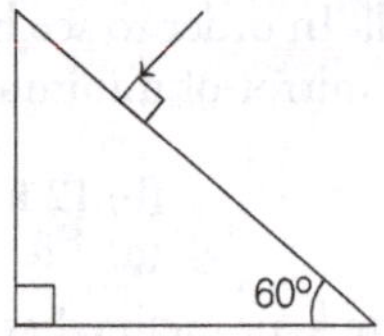

(a) 60° (b) 30° (c) 45° (d) 90°

05 If the critical angle for total internal reflection from a medium to vacuum is 45°, then velocity of light in the medium is *[NCERT (New) Pg. 230, NEET (Oct.) 2020]*

(a) 1.5×10^8 m/s (b) $\frac{3}{\sqrt{2}} \times 10^8$ m/s

(c) $\sqrt{2} \times 10^8$ m/s (d) 3×10^8 m/s

06 A ray is incident at an angle of incidence i on one surface of a small angle prism (with angle of prism A) and emerges normally from the opposite surface. If the refractive index of the material of the prism is μ, then the angle of incidence is nearly equal to *[NCERT (New) Pg. 240, NEET (Sep.) 2020]*

(a) $\frac{2A}{\mu}$ (b) μA (c) $\frac{\mu A}{2}$ (d) $\frac{A}{2\mu}$

07 Pick the wrong answer in the context with rainbow. *[NEET (National) 2019]*

(a) The order of colours is reversed in the secondary rainbow
(b) An observer can see a rainbow when his front is towards the sun
(c) Rainbow is a combined effect of dispersion refraction and reflection of sunlight
(d) When the light rays undergo two internal reflections in a water drop, a secondary rainbow is formed

08 Which colour of the light has the longest wavelength ? *[NEET (National) 2019]*

(a) Blue (b) Green (c) Violet (d) Red

09 In total internal reflection when the angle of incidence is equal to the critical angle for the pair of media in contact, what will be angle of refraction ? *[NCERT (New) Pg. 230, NEET (National) 2019]*

(a) 0°
(b) Equal to angle of incidence
(c) 90°
(d) 180°

10 The refractive index of the material of a prism is $\sqrt{2}$ and the angle of the prism is 30°. One of the two refracting surfaces of the prism is made a mirror inwards, by silver coating. A beam of monochromatic light entering the prism from the other face will retrace its path (after reflection from the silvered surface) if its angle of incidence on the prism is *[NCERT (New) Pg. 240, NEET 2018]*

(a) 30° (b) 45° (c) 60° (d) zero

11 A thin prism having refracting angle 10° is made of glass of refractive index 1.42. This prism is combined with another thin prism of glass of refractive index 1.7. This combination produces dispersion without deviation. The refracting angle of second prism should be *[NCERT (New) Pg. 240, NEET 2017]*

(a) 4° (b) 6° (c) 8° (d) 10°

12 The angle of incidence for a ray of light at a refracting surface of a prism is 45°. The angle of prism is 60°. If the ray suffers minimum deviation through the prism, the angle of minimum deviation and refractive index of the material of the prism respectively, are *[NCERT (New) Pg. 240, NEET 2016]*

(a) 30°, $\sqrt{2}$ (b) 45°, $\sqrt{2}$ (c) 30°, $\frac{1}{\sqrt{2}}$ (d) 45°, $\frac{1}{\sqrt{2}}$

13 An air bubble in a glass slab with refractive index 1.5 (near normal incidence) is 5 cm deep when viewed from one surface and 3 cm deep when viewed from the opposite face. The thickness (in cm) of the slab is *[NCERT (New) Pg. 233, NEET 2016]*

(a) 8 (b) 10
(c) 12 (d) 16

14 The refracting angle of a prism is A, and refractive index of the material of the prism is cot $(A/2)$. The angle of minimum deviation is *[AIPMT 2015]*

(a) $180° - 3A$ (b) $180° - 2A$
(c) $90° - A$ (d) $180° + 2A$

15 A beam of light consisting of red, green and blue colours is incident on a right angled prism. The refractive index of the material of the prism for the above red, green and blue wavelengths are 1.39, 1.44 and 1.47, respectively. *[NCERT (New) Pg. 240, AIPMT 2015]*

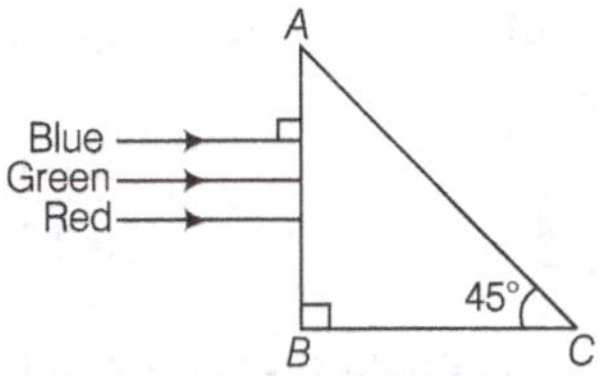

The prism will

(a) separate the blue colour part from the red and green colours
(b) separate all the three colours from one another
(c) not separate the three colours at all
(d) separate the red colour part from the green and blue colours

16 The angle of a prism is A. One of its refracting surfaces is silvered. Light rays falling at an angle of incidence $2A$ on the first surface returns back through the same path after suffering reflection at the silvered surface. The refractive index μ, of the prism is *[NCERT (New) Pg. 240, AIPMT 2014]*

(a) $2 \sin A$ (b) $2 \cos A$ (c) $\frac{1}{2} \cos A$ (d) $\tan A$

17 A ray of light is incident at an angle of incidence, i, on one face of a prism of angle A (assumed to be small) and emerges normally from the opposite face. If the refractive index of the prism is μ, the angle of incidence i, is nearly equal to *[AIPMT 1989, 2012]*

(a) μA (b) $\frac{\mu A}{2}$
(c) A/μ (d) $A/2\mu$

18 Which of the following is not due to total internal reflection? *[NCERT (New) Pg. 230, AIPMT 2011]*

(a) Difference between apparent and real depth of a pond
(b) Mirage on hot summer days
(c) Brilliance of diamond
(d) Working of optical fibre

19 A ray of light travelling in a transparent medium of refractive index μ, falls on a surface separating the medium from air at an angle of incidence of 45°. For which of the following value of μ the ray can undergo total internal reflection? *[NCERT (New) Pg. 230, AIPMT 2010]*

(a) $\mu = 1.33$ (b) $\mu = 1.40$
(c) $\mu = 1.50$ (d) $\mu = 1.25$

20 The frequency of a light wave in a material is 2×10^{14} Hz and wavelength is 5000 Å. The refractive index of material will be *[NCERT (New) Pg. 228, AIPMT 2007]*

(a) 1.40 (b) 1.50 (c) 3.00 (d) 1.33

21 A small coin is resting on the bottom of a beaker filled with a liquid. A ray of light from the coin travels upto the surface of the liquid and moves along its surface (see figure).

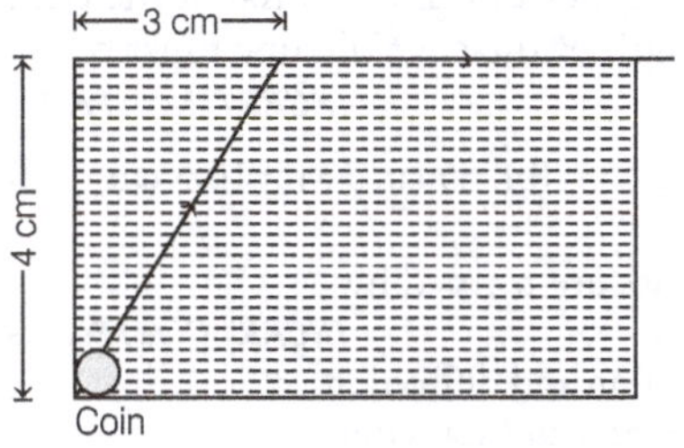

How fast is the light travelling in the liquid? *[NCERT (New) Pg. 230, AIPMT 2007]*

(a) 1.8×10^8 m/s (b) 2.4×10^8 m/s
(c) 3.0×10^8 m/s (d) 1.2×10^4 m/s

22 The refractive index of the material of a prism is $\sqrt{2}$ and its refracting angle is 30°. One of the refracting surfaces of the prism is made a mirror inwards. A beam of monochromatic light entering the prism from the other face will retrace its path after reflection from the mirrored surface, if its angle of incidence on the prism is *[NCERT (New) Pg. 240, AIPMT 2004]*

(a) 45° (b) 60° (c) 0° (d) 30°

23 A beam of light composed of red and green rays is incident obliquely at a point on the face of a rectangular glass slab. When coming out on the opposite parallel face, the red and green rays emerge from *[NCERT (New) Pg. 230, AIPMT 2004]*

(a) two points propagating in two different non-parallel directions
(b) two points propagating in two different parallel directions
(c) one point propagating in two different directions
(d) one point propagating in the same direction

24 For the given incident ray as shown in figure, the condition of total internal reflection of the ray will be satisfied if the refractive index of block will be *[NCERT (New) Pg. 230, AIPMT 2002]*

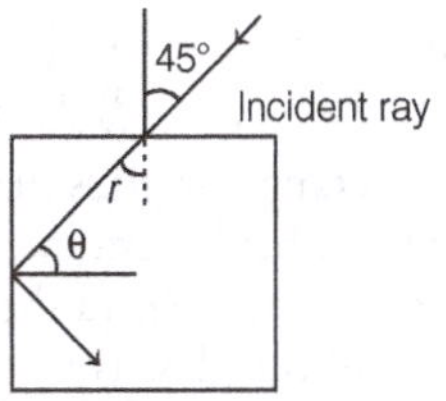

(a) $\frac{\sqrt{3}+1}{2}$ (b) $\frac{\sqrt{2}+1}{2}$ (c) $\sqrt{\frac{3}{2}}$ (d) $\sqrt{\frac{7}{6}}$

25 Transmission of light in optical fibre is due to *[NCERT (New) Pg. 232, AIPMT 2001]*
(a) scattering
(b) diffraction
(c) polarisation
(d) multiple total internal reflections

26 A transparent cube contains a small air bubble. Its apparent distance is 2 cm when seen through one face and 5 cm when seen through other face. If the refractive index of the material of the cube is 1.5, the real length of the edge of cube must be *[NCERT (New) Pg. 229, AIPMT 2000]*
(a) 7 cm (b) 7.5 cm (c) 10.5 cm (d) $\frac{14}{3}$ cm

27 Rainbows are formed by *[NCERT (New) Pg. 229, AIPMT 2000]*
(a) reflection and diffraction
(b) refraction and scattering
(c) dispersion and total internal reflection
(d) interference only

28 The refractive index of the material of the equilateral prism is $\sqrt{3}$, then the angle of minimum deviation of the prism is *[NCERT (New) Pg. 240, AIPMT 1999]*
(a) 30° (b) 45° (c) 60° (d) 75°

29 Light enters at an angle of incidence in a transparent rod of refractive index μ. For what value of the refractive index of the material of the rod the light once entered into it will not leave it through its lateral face whatsoever be the value of angle of incidence? *[NCERT (New) Pg. 230, AIPMT 1998]*
(a) $\mu > \sqrt{2}$ (b) $\mu = 1$
(c) $\mu = 1.1$ (d) $\mu = 1.3$

30 Electromagnetic radiation of frequency ν, velocity v and wavelength λ, in air, enters a glass slab of refractive index μ. The frequency, wavelength and velocity of light in the glass slab will be, respectively *[NCERT (New) Pg. 228, AIPMT 1997]*
(a) $\frac{\nu}{\mu}, \frac{\lambda}{\mu}, v$ (b) $\nu, \lambda, \frac{v}{\mu}$ (c) $\nu, \frac{\lambda}{\mu}, \frac{v}{\mu}$ (d) $\frac{\nu}{\mu}, \frac{\lambda}{\mu}, \frac{v}{\mu}$

31 If f_V and f_R are the focal lengths of a convex lens for violet and red light respectively and F_V and F_R are the focal lengths of concave lens for violet and red light respectively, then we have *[NCERT (New) Pg. 234, AIPMT 1996]*
(a) $f_V < f_R$ and $F_V > F_R$ (b) $f_V < f_R$ and $F_V < F_R$
(c) $f_V > f_R$ and $F_V > F_R$ (d) $f_V > f_R$ and $F_V < F_R$

32 One face of a rectangular glass plate 6 cm thick is silvered. An object held 8 cm in front of the first face, forms an image 12 cm behind the silvered face. The refractive index of the glass is *[NCERT (New) Pg. 230, AIPMT 1996]*
(a) 0.4 (b) 0.8
(c) 1.2 (d) 1.6

33 Light travels through a glass plate of thickness t and refractive index μ. If c is the speed of light in vacuum, the time taken by light to travel this thickness of glass is *[NCERT (New) Pg. 230, AIPMT 1996]*
(a) μtc (b) $\frac{tc}{\mu}$ (c) $\frac{1}{\mu t}$ (d) $\frac{\mu t}{c}$

34 Angle of deviation δ by a prism (refractive index $= \mu$, and supposing the angle of prism A to be small) can be given by *[NCERT (New) Pg. 240, AIPMT 1994]*
(a) $\delta = (\mu - 1) A$ (b) $\delta = (\mu + 1) A$
(c) $\delta = \frac{\sin \frac{A+\delta}{2}}{\sin \frac{A}{2}}$ (d) $\delta = \frac{\mu - 1}{\mu + 1} A$

35 A point source of light is placed 4 m below the surface of water of refractive index $\frac{5}{3}$. The minimum diameter of a disc, which should be placed over the source, on the surface of water to cut off all light coming out of water is *[NCERT (New) Pg. 230, AIPMT 1994]*
(a) infinite (b) 6 m (c) 4 m (d) 3 m

36 Time taken by sunlight to pass through a window of thickness 4 mm whose refractive index is 3/2, is *[NCERT (New) Pg. 230, AIPMT 1993]*
(a) 2×10^{-4} s (b) 2×10^{8} s
(c) 2×10^{-11} s (d) 2×10^{11} s

37 There is a prism with refractive index equal to $\sqrt{2}$ and the refracting angle equal to 30°. One of the refracting surface of the prism is polished. A beam of monochromatic light will retrace its path if its angle of incidence over the refracting surface of the prism is *[NCERT (New) Pg. 240, AIPMT 1992]*
(a) 0° (b) 30°
(c) 45° (d) 60°

38 A beam of monochromatic light is refracted from vacuum into a medium of refractive index 1.5. The wavelength of refracted light will be *[AIPMT 1991, 1992]*
(a) dependent on intensity of refracted light
(b) same
(c) smaller
(d) larger

Topic 3 Lenses

01 Two thin lenses are of same focal lengths f, but one is convex and the other one is concave. When they are placed in contact with each other, the equivalent focal length of the combination will be *[NEET 2023]*
(a) $f/4$ (b) $f/2$
(c) infinite (d) zero

02 In the figure shown here, what is the equivalent focal length of the combination of lenses (Assume that all layers are thin) ? *[NEET 2023]*

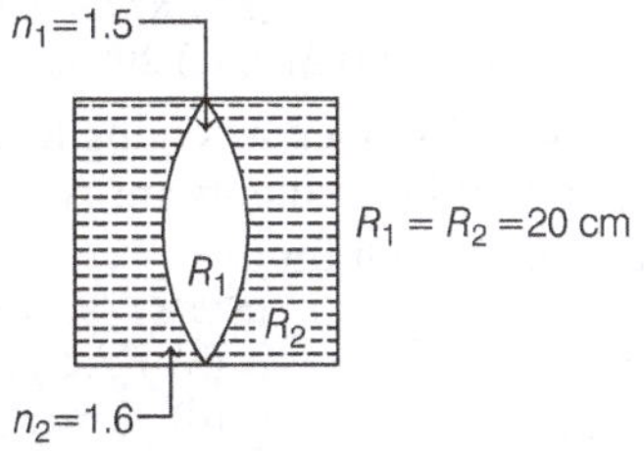

(a) – 40 cm (b) – 100 cm (c) – 50 cm (d) 40 cm

03 A biconvex lens has radii of curvature, 20cm each. If the refractive index of the material of the lens is 1.5, the power of the lens is *[NCERT (New) Pg. 236, NEET 2022]*

(a) + 20 D (b) + 5 D
(c) infinity (d) + 2 D

04 A convex lens *A* of focal length 20 cm and a concave lens *B* of focal length 5 cm are kept along the same axis with a distance *d* between them. If a parallel beam of light falling on *A* leaves *B* as a parallel beam, then the distance *d* (in cm) will be *[NEET 2021]*

(a) 25 (b) 15 (c) 50 (d) 30

05 A plano-convex lens of unknown material and unknown focal length is given. With the help of a spherometer we can measure the *[NEET (Oct.) 2020]*

(a) focal length of the lens
(b) radius of curvature of the curved surface
(c) aperture of the lens
(d) refractive index of the material

06 The power of a biconvex lens is 10 D and the radius of curvature of each surface is 10 cm. Then, the refractive index of the material of the lens is *[NEET (Oct.) 2020]*

(a) $\frac{4}{3}$ (b) $\frac{9}{8}$ (c) $\frac{5}{3}$ (d) $\frac{3}{2}$

07 An equi-convex lens has power *P* it is cut into two symmetrical halves by a plane containing the principal axis. The power of one part will be *[NCERT (New) Pg. 238, NEET (Odisha) 2019]*

(a) 0 (b) $\frac{P}{2}$ (c) $\frac{P}{4}$ (d) P

08 A double convex lens has focal length 25 cm. The radius of curvature of one of the surfaces is doubled of the other. Find the radii, if the refractive index of the material of the lens is 1.5. *[NEET (Odisha) 2019]*

(a) 100 cm, 50 cm (b) 25 cm, 50 cm
(c) 18.75 cm, 37.5 cm (d) 50 cm, 100 cm

09 Two similar thin equi-convex lenses, of focal length f each, are kept coaxially in contact with each other such that the focal length of the combination is F_1. When the space between the two lenses is filled with glycerine (which has the same refractive index ($\mu = 1.5$) as that of glass) then the equivalent focal length is F_2. The ratio $F_1 : F_2$ will be *[NCERT (New) Pg. 238, NEET (National) 2019]*

(a) 1 : 2 (b) 2 : 3 (c) 3 : 4 (d) 2 : 1

10 Two identical glass ($\mu_g = 3/2$) equi-convex lenses of focal length f each are kept in contact. The space between the two lenses is filled with water ($\mu_w = 4/3$). The focal length of the combination is *[NEET 2016]*

(a) $f/3$ (b) f (c) $\frac{4f}{3}$ (d) $\frac{3f}{4}$

11 Two identical thin plano-convex glass lenses (refractive index 1.5) each having radius of curvature of 20 cm are placed with their convex surfaces in contact at the centre. The intervening space is filled with oil of refractive index 1.7. The focal length of the combination is *[NCERT (New) Pg. 235, AIPMT 2015]*

(a) – 20 cm (b) – 25 cm
(c) – 50 cm (d) 50 cm

12 A plano-convex lens fits exactly into a plano-concave lens. Their plane surfaces are parallel to each other. If lenses are made of different materials of refractive indices μ_1 and μ_2 and R is the radius of curvature of the curved surface of the lenses, then the focal length of the combination is *[NCERT (New) Pg. 238, NEET 2013]*

(a) $\frac{R}{2(\mu_1 + \mu_2)}$ (b) $\frac{R}{2(\mu_1 - \mu_2)}$

(c) $\frac{R}{(\mu_1 - \mu_2)}$ (d) $\frac{2R}{(\mu_2 - \mu_1)}$

13 When a biconvex lens of glass having refractive index 1.47 is dipped in a liquid, it acts as a plane sheet of glass. This implies that the liquid must have refractive index *[NCERT (New) Pg. 235, AIPMT 2012]*

(a) equal to that of glass (b) less than one
(c) greater than that of glass (d) less than that of glass

14 A biconvex lens has a radius of curvature of magnitude 20 cm. Which one of the following options describe best the image formed of an object of height 2 cm placed 30 cm from the lens? *[NCERT (New) Pg. 235, AIPMT 2011]*

(a) Virtual, upright, height = 0.5 cm
(b) Real, inverted, height = 4 cm
(c) Real, inverted, height = 1 cm
(d) Virtual, upright, height = 1 cm

15 A lens having focal length f and aperture of diameter d forms an image of intensity I. Aperture of diameter $d/2$ in central region of lens is covered by a black paper. Focal length of lens and intensity of image now will be respectively *[AIPMT 2010]*

(a) f and $\frac{I}{4}$ (b) $\frac{3f}{4}$ and $\frac{I}{2}$

(c) f and $\frac{3I}{4}$ (d) $\frac{f}{2}$ and $\frac{I}{2}$

16 A boy is trying to start a fire by focusing sunlight on a piece of paper using an equiconvex lens of focal length 10 cm. The diameter of the sun is 1.39×10^9 m and its mean distance from the earth is 1.5×10^{11} m. What is the diameter of the sun's image on the paper ? *[NCERT (New) Pg. 236, AIPMT 2008]*

(a) 9.2×10^{-4} m (b) 6.5×10^{-4} m
(c) 6.5×10^{-5} m (d) 12.4×10^{-4} m

17 Two thin lenses of focal lengths f_1 and f_2 are in contact and coaxial. The power of the combination is *[NCERT (New) Pg. 238, AIPMT 2008]*

(a) $\sqrt{\frac{f_1}{f_2}}$ (b) $\sqrt{\frac{f_2}{f_1}}$ (c) $\frac{f_1+f_2}{2}$ (d) $\frac{f_1+f_2}{f_1 f_2}$

18 A convex lens and a concave lens, each having same focal length of 25 cm, are put in contact to form a combination of lenses. The power in diopters of the combination is *[NCERT (New) Pg. 235, AIPMT 2006]*

(a) 25 (b) 50 (c) infinite (d) zero

19 A convex lens is dipped in a liquid whose refractive index is equal to the refractive index of the lens. Then its focal length will *[NCERT (New) Pg. 235, AIPMT 2003]*

(a) become small, but non-zero
(b) remain unchanged
(c) become zero
(d) become infinite

20 An equiconvex lens is cut into two halves along (i) XOX' and (ii) YOY' as shown in the figure. Let f, f', f'' be the focal lengths of the complete lens, of each half in case (i), and of each half in case (ii), respectively.

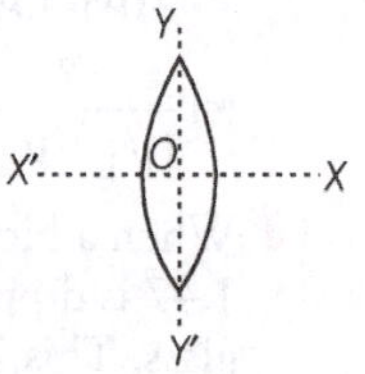

Choose the correct statement from the following *[NCERT (New) Pg. 238, AIPMT 2003]*

(a) $f' = f, f'' = f$ (b) $f' = 2f, f'' = 2f$
(c) $f' = f, f'' = 2f$ (d) $f' = 2f, f'' = f$

21 A body is located on a wall. Its image of equal size is to be obtained on a parallel wall with the help of a convex lens. The lens is placed at a distance d ahead of second wall, then the required focal length will be *[NCERT (New) Pg. 235, AIPMT 2002]*

(a) only $d/2$
(b) only $d/2$
(c) more than $d/4$ but less than $d/2$
(d) less than $d/4$

22 A planoconvex lens is made of a material of refractive index $\mu = 1.5$. The radius of curvature of curved surface of the lens is 20 cm. If its plane surface is silvered, the focal length of the silvered lens will be *[NCERT (New) Pg. 237, AIPMT 2000]*

(a) 10 cm (b) 20 cm (c) 40 cm (d) 80 cm

23 A planoconvex lens is made of material of refractive index 1.6. The radius of curvature of the curved surface is 60 cm. The focal length of the lens is *[NCERT (New) Pg. 237, AIPMT 1999]*

(a) 50 cm (b) 100 cm (c) 200 cm (d) 400 cm

24 The focal lengths of a converging lens measured for violet, green and red colours are f_V, f_G, f_R respectively. We will find *[NCERT (New) Pg. 232, AIPMT 1997]*

(a) $f_G > f_R$ (b) $f_V < f_R$
(c) $f_V > f_R$ (d) $f_V = f_R$

25 A convex lens of focal length 80 cm and a concave lens of focal length 50 cm are combined together. What will be their resulting power ? *[AIPMT 1996]*

(a) + 6.5 D (b) – 6.5 D (c) + 7.5 D (d) – 0.75 D

26 A lens is placed between a source of light and a wall. It forms images of area A_1 and A_2 on the wall, for its two different positions, the area of the source of light is *[AIPMT 1995]*

(a) $\sqrt{A_1 A_2}$ (b) $\frac{A_1 + A_2}{2}$ (c) $\frac{A_1 - A_2}{2}$ (d) $\frac{1}{A_1} + \frac{1}{A_2}$

27 An achromatic combination of lenses is formed by joining *[AIPMT 1995]*

(a) 2 convex lenses (b) 2 concave lenses
(c) 1 convex, 1 concave lens (d) 1 convex and 1 plane mirror

28 Focal length of a convex lens will be maximum for *[NCERT (New) Pg. 232, AIPMT 1994]*

(a) blue light (b) yellow light
(c) green light (d) red light

29 Focal length of a convex lens of refractive index 1.5 is 2 cm. Focal length of lens when immersed in a liquid of refractive index 1.25 will be *[AIPMT 1988]*

(a) 10 cm (b) 2.5 cm
(c) 5 cm (d) 7.5 cm

Topic 4 Optical Instruments

01 A small telescope has an objective of focal length 140 cm and an eye piece of focal length 5.0 cm. The magnifying power of telescope for viewing a distant object is *[NCERT (New) Pg. 244, NEET 2024]*

(a) 34 (b) 28
(c) 17 (d) 32

02 A lens of large focal length and large aperture is best suited as an objective of an astronomical telescope, since *[NCERT (New) Pg. 242, NEET 2021]*

(a) a large aperture contributes to the quality and visibility of the images
(b) a large area of the objective ensures better light gathering power
(c) a large aperture provides a better resolution
(d) All of the above

03 An astronomical telescope has objective and eyepiece of focal lengths 40 cm and 4 cm, respectively. To view an object 200 cm away from the objective, the lenses must be separated by a distance *[NEET 2016]*
(a) 46.0 cm (b) 50.0 cm
(c) 54.0 cm (d) 37.3 cm

04 A person can see clearly objects only when they lie between 50 cm and 400 cm from his eyes. In order to increase the maximum distance of distinct vision to infinity, the type and power of the correcting lens, the person has to use, will be *[NEET 2016]*
(a) convex, + 2.25 D (b) concave, – 0.25 D
(c) concave – 0.2 D (d) convex, + 0.15 D

05 In an astronomical telescope in normal adjustment a straight black line of length L is drawn on inside part of objective lens. The eye-piece forms a real image of this line. The length of this image is I. The magnification of the telescope is *[NCERT (New) Pg. 242, AIPMT 2015]*
(a) $\frac{L}{I}+1$ (b) $\frac{L}{I}-1$ (c) $\frac{L+1}{L-1}$ (d) $\frac{L}{I}$

06 If the focal length of objective lens is increased, then magnifying power of *[NCERT (New) Pg. 242, AIPMT 2014]*
(a) microscope will increase but that of telescope decrease
(b) microscope and telescope both will increase
(c) microscope and telescope both will decrease
(d) microscope will decrease but that of telescope will increase

07 For a normal eye, the cornea of eye provides a converging power of 40 D and the least converging power of the eye lens behind the cornea is 20 D. Using this information, the distance between the retina and the cornea, eye lens can be estimated to be *[NEET 2013]*
(a) 5 cm (b) 2.5 cm
(c) 1.67 cm (d) 1.5 cm

08 The magnifying power of a telescope is 9. When it is adjusted for parallel rays the distance between the objective and eyepiece is 20 cm. The focal length of lenses are *[NCERT (New) Pg. 242, AIPMT 2012]*
(a) 10 cm, 10 cm (b) 15 cm, 5 cm
(c) 18 cm, 2 cm (d) 11 cm, 9 cm

09 A microscope is focussed on a mark on a piece of paper and then a slab of glass of thickness 3 cm and refractive index 1.5 is placed over the mark. How should the microscope be moved to get the mark in focus again ? *[NCERT (New) Pg. 242, AIPMT 2006]*
(a) 1 cm upward
(b) 4.5 cm downward
(c) 1 cm downward
(d) 2 cm upward

10 An astronomical telescope of ten-fold angular magnification has a length of 44 cm. The focal length of the objective is *[NCERT (New) Pg. 242, AIPMT 1997]*
(a) 440 cm (b) 44 cm
(c) 40 cm (d) 4 cm

• Key Index

Topic 1

1 (a)	2 (b)	3 (a)	4 (d)	5 (c)	6 (d)	7 (b)	8 (d)

Topic 2

1 (b)	2 (c)	3 (a)	4 (a)	5 (b)	6 (b)	7 (b)	8 (d)	9 (c)	10 (b)
11 (b)	12 (a)	13 (c)	14 (b)	15 (d)	16 (b)	17 (a)	18 (a)	19 (c)	20 (c)
21 (a)	22 (a)	23 (b)	24 (c)	25 (d)	26 (c)	27 (c)	28 (c)	29 (a)	30 (c)
31 (a)	32 (c)	33 (d)	34 (a)	35 (b)	36 (c)	37 (c)	38 (c)		

Topic 3

1 (c)	2 (b)	3 (b)	4 (b)	5 (b)	6 (d)	7 (d)	8 (c)	9 (a)	10 (d)
11 (c)	12 (c)	13 (a)	14 (b)	15 (c)	16 (a)	17 (d)	18 (d)	19 (d)	20 (c)
21 (b)	22 (b)	23 (b)	24 (b)	25 (d)	26 (a)	27 (c)	28 (d)	29 (c)	
31 (c)									

Topic 4

1 (b)	2 (d)	3 (c)	4 (b)	5 (d)	6 (d)	7 (c)	8 (c)	9 (a)	10 (c)

Detailed **Explanations**

Topic 1

01. *(a)* Object distance, $u = -1.5f$

By mirror formula, $\frac{1}{v} + \frac{1}{u} = \frac{1}{f}$

$$\Rightarrow \frac{1}{v} + \frac{1}{-1.5f} = \frac{1}{-f}$$

$$\Rightarrow \frac{1}{v} = -\frac{1}{f} + \frac{1}{1.5f} = \frac{1}{f}\left[-1 + \frac{1}{1.5}\right]$$

$$= \frac{1}{f}\left[-1 + \frac{2}{3}\right]$$

$$\Rightarrow \frac{1}{v} = \frac{1}{f}\left(-\frac{1}{3}\right) \Rightarrow v = -3f$$

02. *(b)* Case I When the object distance,

$u_1 = -40$ cm

Focal length of mirror, $f = -15$ cm

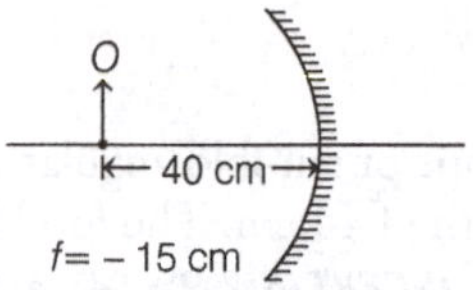

Using the mirror formula, we get

$$\frac{1}{f} = \frac{1}{v_1} + \frac{1}{u_1}$$

Substituting the given values, we get

$$-\frac{1}{15} = \frac{1}{v_1} + \left(\frac{-1}{40}\right)$$

$$\Rightarrow \frac{1}{v_1} = \frac{1}{40} - \frac{1}{15} = \frac{3-8}{120} = \frac{-5}{120}$$

$$\Rightarrow v_1 = \frac{-120}{5} = -24 \text{ cm}$$

Case II When the object distance,

$u_2 = -20$ cm

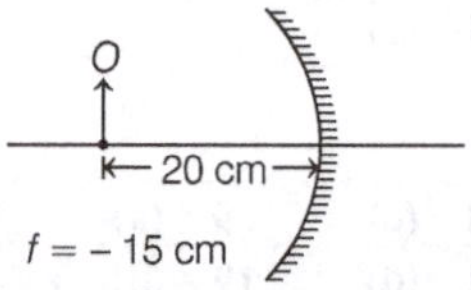

Using the mirror formula, we get

$$\frac{1}{f} = \frac{1}{v_2} + \frac{1}{u_2}$$

Substituting the given values, we get

$$-\frac{1}{15} = \frac{1}{v_2} + \left(-\frac{1}{20}\right)$$

$$\Rightarrow \frac{1}{v_2} = \frac{1}{20} - \frac{1}{15} = \frac{3-4}{60} = \frac{-1}{60}$$

$$\Rightarrow v_2 = -60 \text{ cm}$$

$\therefore$ The displacement of the image is

$$= v_2 - v_1 = -60 - (-24)$$
$$= -60 + 24 = -36 \text{ cm}$$

i.e. 36 cm away from the mirror.

03. *(a)* According to the question

L = Light source

When the light beam is incident normally on the plane mirror, it is reflected back to the point from which it was coming. When the plane mirror is rotated by an angle θ, the reflected ray or beam of light must rotate by angle 2θ, from refraction at plane surface theory.

Angle of refraction is 2θ

$$\tan 2\theta = \frac{y}{x}$$

$$2\theta = \frac{y}{x}$$

$$\theta = \frac{y}{2x}$$

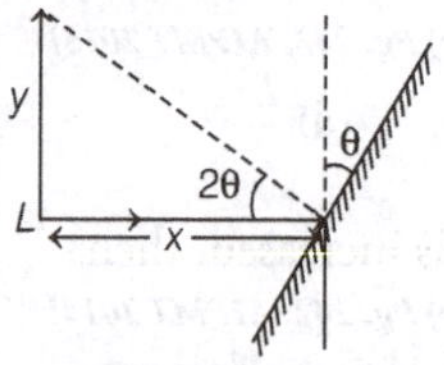

04. *(d)* A concave mirror forms real and virtual images, whose magnification can be negative or positive depending upon the position of the object.

If object is placed between focus and pole the image obtained will be virtual and its magnification will be positive.

In all other cases concave mirror forms real images whose magnification will be negative. A convex mirror always forms a virtual image whose magnification will always be positive.

05. *(c)* According to question, the ray diagram will be

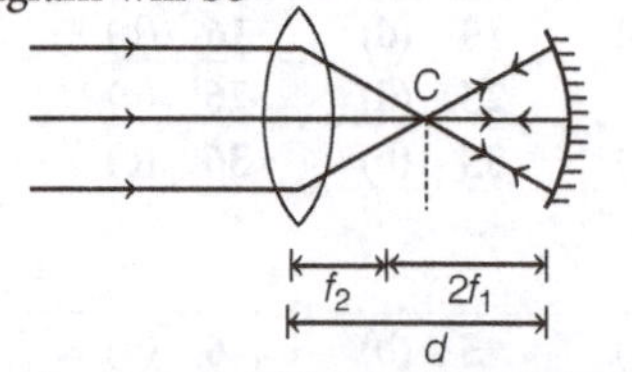

So, distance d between convex lens and concave mirror is given by

$$d = 2f_1 + f_2$$

06. *(d)* The minimum size of plane mirror required to see full length of a man

$$= \frac{\text{height of man}}{2}$$

Given, height of man = 6 ft

Thus, minimum size of plane mirror

$$= \frac{6}{2} = 3 \text{ ft}$$

07. *(b)*

key idea

If an object is kept between the two plane mirrors oriented at an angle θ, then number of images $= \frac{360°}{\theta} - 1$, if $\frac{360°}{\theta}$ is even and number of images $= \frac{360°}{\theta}$, if $\frac{360°}{\theta}$ is odd.

When an object is held in between two plane mirrors M_1 and M_2 inclined at $\angle\theta$, more than one image is formed on account of multiple reflections of light from the mirrors.

In general, total number of images (n) formed is given by

$$n = \frac{360°}{\theta} - 1$$

Here, $\theta = 60°$

$$\therefore \quad n = \frac{360°}{60°} - 1 = 6 - 1 = 5$$

08. *(d)* Ray optics uses the geometry of straight lines to account for the macroscopic phenomena like rectilinear propagation, reflection, refraction etc. Ray optics can be taken as a limiting case of wave optics. This is primarily because wavelength of light is small.

Topic 2

01. *(b)* Given, the rays in the prism is parallel to base.

$$A = r_1 + r_2$$

i.e., $r_2 = 90 - r_1$ ...(i)

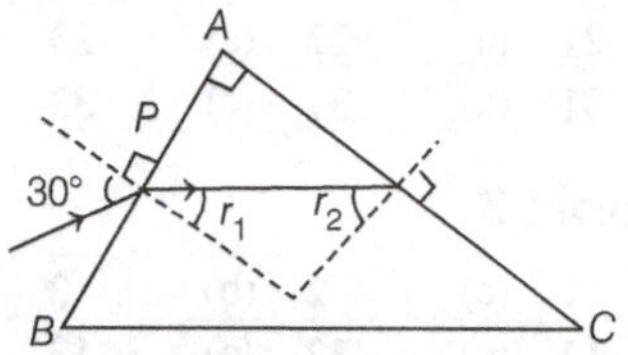

For AB interface, $\sin 30° = \mu \sin r_1$

$$\Rightarrow \quad \sin r_1 = \frac{1}{2\mu} \quad \text{...(ii)}$$

For AC interface;

$$\mu \sin r_2 = 1 \sin 90°$$

$$\Rightarrow \quad \sin r_2 = \frac{1}{\mu} \Rightarrow \sin(90 - r_1) = \frac{1}{\mu}$$

$$\cos r_1 = \frac{1}{\mu} \quad \text{...(iii)}$$

We know that, $\sin^2\theta + \cos^2\theta = 1$

From Eqs. (ii) and (iii), we get

$\sin^2 r_1 + \cos^2 r_1 = 1$

$$\Rightarrow \left(\frac{1}{2\mu}\right)^2 + \left(\frac{1}{\mu}\right)^2 = 1$$

$$\Rightarrow \frac{1}{4\mu^2} + \frac{1}{\mu^2} = 1 \Rightarrow \frac{1}{\mu^2}\left(\frac{1}{4} + \frac{1}{1}\right) = 1$$

$$\Rightarrow \mu^2 = \frac{5}{4} \Rightarrow \mu = \frac{\sqrt{5}}{2}$$

02. *(c)* According to given situation,

$$c = \frac{x}{t_1} \text{ and } v = \frac{10x}{t_2}$$

$$\text{Since, } \sin i_c = \frac{1}{\mu} = \frac{1}{(c/v)} = \frac{v}{c} = \frac{\frac{10x}{t_2}}{\frac{x}{t_1}}$$

$$= \frac{10t_1}{t_2} \Rightarrow i_c = \sin^{-1}\left(\frac{10t_1}{t_2}\right)$$

03. *(a)*

key idea

If speed of light in rarer medium and denser medium are known as v_A and v_B respectively, then refractive index of denser medium

$$\mu = \frac{1}{\sin i_C} = \frac{v_B}{v_A}$$

Given, $v_A = 1.5 \times 10^8$ m/s

$v_B = 2 \times 10^8$ m/s

Refractive index μ and critical angle i_c are related as

$$\mu = \frac{1}{\sin i_c}$$

$$\Rightarrow \sin i_c = \frac{1}{\mu} = \frac{1}{(v_B/v_A)} \quad \left[\because \mu = \frac{v_B}{v_A}\right]$$

$$= \frac{v_A}{v_B} = \frac{1.5 \times 10^8}{2 \times 10^8} = 0.750$$

$$\Rightarrow i_c = \sin^{-1}(0\cdot750)$$

04. *(a)* Given, the refractive index of the glass,

$n_2 = \sqrt{3}$

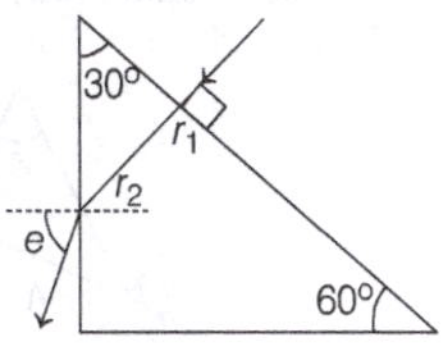

The refractive index of the air,

$n_1 = 1$

The path of ray incident on the prism is as shown below.

From the given figure, $r_1 = 0°$

As, $A = r_1 + r_2$

where, A is the angle of prism .

$$30° = 0° + r_2 \Rightarrow r_2 = 30°$$

Using the Snell's law, in glass and air interference,

$$n_2 \sin\theta_2 = n_1 \sin\theta_1$$

$$\Rightarrow n_2 \sin r_2 = n_1 \sin e$$

$$\Rightarrow \sqrt{3}\sin 30° = 1 \times \sin e \Rightarrow \sin e = \frac{\sqrt{3}}{2}$$

$$\Rightarrow \sin e = \sin 60° \Rightarrow e = 60°$$

05. *(b)* Critical angle,

$i_C = 45°$

We know that,

$$\mu = \frac{1}{\sin i_c} = \frac{1}{\sin 45°} = \frac{1}{1/\sqrt{2}} = \sqrt{2}$$

$$\Rightarrow \mu = \sqrt{2}$$

$$\Rightarrow \frac{\text{Velocity of light in air}}{\text{Velocity of light in medium}} = \sqrt{2}$$

$$\Rightarrow \frac{3 \times 10^8}{v_m} = \sqrt{2} \Rightarrow v_m = \frac{3}{\sqrt{2}} \times 10^8 \text{ m/s}$$

06. *(b)* According to the question, the ray diagram can be shown as

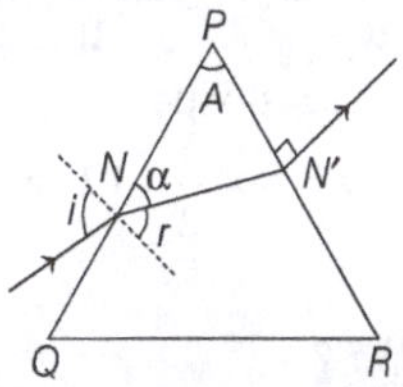

From figure in $\Delta PNN'$,

$$A + \alpha + 90° = 180°$$

$$\Rightarrow \alpha = 90° - A \quad \ldots\text{(i)}$$

Also, $r + \alpha = 90°$

$$\Rightarrow r = 90° - \alpha$$

$$= 90° - (90° - A) = A$$

[$\because$ from Eq. (i)]

$$\Rightarrow r = A$$

From Snell's law,

$$\mu_1 \sin i = \mu_2 \sin r$$

$$\Rightarrow \sin i = \mu \sin A$$

(here, $\mu_1 = 1$ and $\mu_2 = \mu$)

For small angle, $\sin\theta \simeq \theta$

$$\Rightarrow i = \mu A$$

07. *(b)* The necessary conditions for the rainbow to take place is

(i) Sun should be shining in part of the sky while it is raining in opposite part of the sky.

(ii) The observer must stand with his back towards the sun.

$\therefore$ Statement in option (b) is wrong.

However, rest statements regarding the rainbow are correct.

08. *(d)* Different colours of white light have different wavelengths. The descending order of the wavelength of the component of white light is

$$\lambda_{Red} > \lambda_{Green} > \lambda_{Blue} > \lambda_{Violet}$$

> • Concept **Enhancer**
>
> Speed of red colour of light is maximum among all other colours of light, hence it deviates least.

09. *(c)* The total internal reflection is the phenomenon of reflection back of light in the denser medium when it travel from denser to rarer medium, when the angle of incidence is greater than the critical angle. While the critical angle for a pair of given media in contact is the angle of incidence in denser medium for which the angle of refraction in rarer medium is 90°.

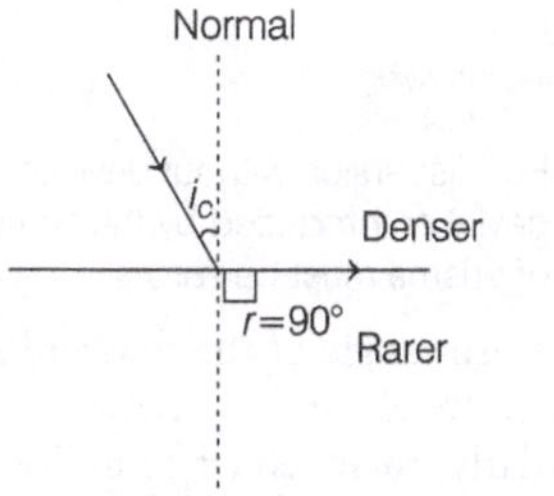

10. *(b)* According to the question, the figure of mentioned prism is given as

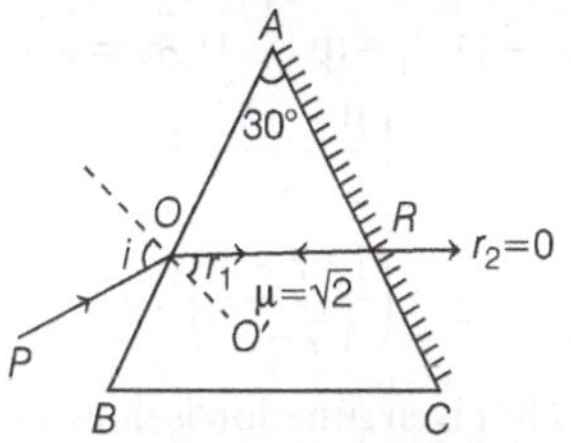

(since, there is no refraction at the face AC)

Given,

Refractive index of the material of prism, $\mu = \sqrt{2}$

Angle of prism, $A = 30°$

If the ray OR has to retrace its path after reflection (as per the given condition), then the ray has to fall normally on the surface AC.

This means

$$\angle ARO = \angle ORC = 90°$$

In ΔAOR,

$$\angle AOR + \angle ARO + \angle OAR = 180°$$

$$\Rightarrow \angle AOR + 90° + 30° = 180°$$

$$\Rightarrow \angle AOR = 180° - 120° = 60° \quad \ldots\text{(i)}$$

As we know,

$$\angle AOR + \angle r_1 = 90°$$

$\Rightarrow \quad \angle r_1 = 90° - 60° = 30°$ [From Eq. (i)]

Applying Snell's law at the face AB, we get

$$\mu = \frac{\sin i}{\sin r_1}$$

Substituting the given values, we get

$$\sqrt{2} = \frac{\sin i}{\sin 30°}$$

$$\Rightarrow \quad \sin i = \sin 30° \times \sqrt{2} = \frac{1}{2} \times \sqrt{2} \quad \left(\because \sin 30° = \frac{1}{2}\right)$$

$$= \frac{1}{\sqrt{2}} \text{ or } i = \sin^{-1}\left(\frac{1}{\sqrt{2}}\right)$$

$$= 45° \quad \left(\because \sin 45° = \frac{1}{\sqrt{2}}\right)$$

11. *(b)*

key idea

For dispersion without deviation, net deviation produced by the combination of prisms must be zero.

Let prism angle of the first and second prisms are A_1 and A_2 respectively. Similarly, their refractive indices are μ_1 and μ_2. Condition for dispersion without deviation is

$$\delta_1 - \delta_2 = 0$$

$$\Rightarrow (\mu_1 - 1) A_1 - (\mu_2 - 1) A_2 = 0$$

$$\Rightarrow \quad A_2 = \left(\frac{\mu_1 - 1}{\mu_2 - 1}\right) A_1$$

$$A_2 = \left(\frac{1.42 - 1}{1.7 - 1}\right)(10°) = 6°$$

12. *(a)* The given situation is shown below.

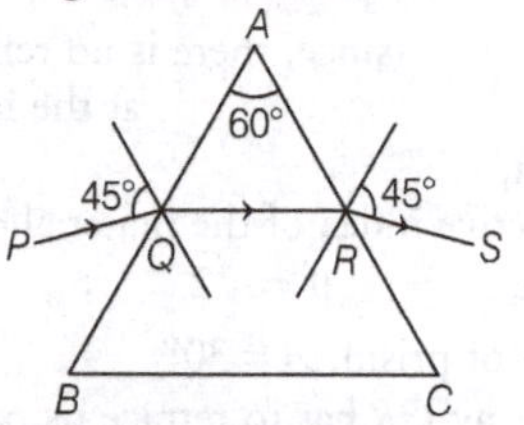

angle of prism $= 60°$

For minimum deviation $i = e$

angle of emergence, $e = 45°$

Therefore, minimum deviation suffered by the ray is

$$\delta_{min} = i + e - A = 90° - 60° = 30°$$

Also we know that

$$\mu = \frac{\sin\left(\frac{A + \delta_m}{2}\right)}{\sin \frac{A}{2}}$$

where, μ = refractive index of the material of the prism.

A = angle of prism $= 60°$

$$\therefore \quad \mu = \frac{\sin\left(\frac{60° + 30°}{2}\right)}{\sin \frac{60°}{2}} = \frac{\sin 45°}{\sin 30°}$$

$$= \frac{1/\sqrt{2}}{1/2} = \frac{2}{\sqrt{2}} = \sqrt{2}$$

13. *(c)* Let thickness of the given slab is t. According to the question, when viewed from both the surfaces

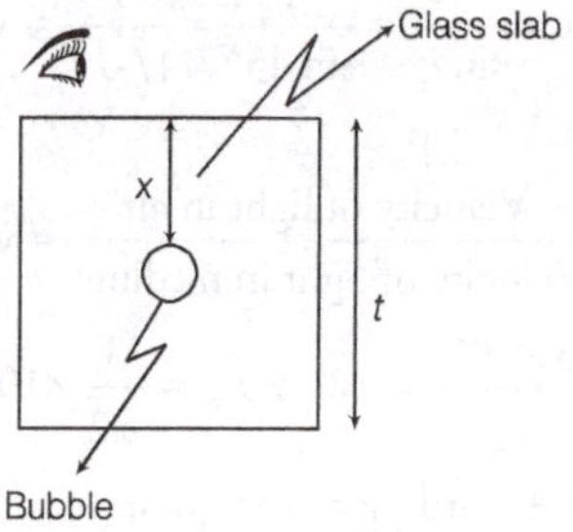

$$\frac{x}{\mu} + \frac{t - x}{\mu} = 3 + 5 \Rightarrow \frac{t}{\mu} = 8 \text{ cm}$$

$$\Rightarrow \quad t = 8 \times \mu$$

$$\Rightarrow \quad t = 8 \times \frac{3}{2} = 12 \text{ cm}$$

14. *(b)*

key idea

Use the following formula

$$\mu = \frac{\sin \frac{A + D_m}{2}}{\sin \frac{A}{2}}$$

As, we know that

$$\mu = \frac{\sin\left(\frac{A + D_m}{2}\right)}{\sin \frac{A}{2}}$$

$$\Rightarrow \quad \cot \frac{A}{2} = \frac{\sin\left(\frac{A + D_m}{2}\right)}{\sin \frac{A}{2}}$$

$$\Rightarrow \quad \frac{\cos \frac{A}{2}}{\sin \frac{A}{2}} = \frac{\sin\left(\frac{A + D_m}{2}\right)}{\sin \frac{A}{2}}$$

$$\sin\left(\frac{\pi}{2} - \frac{A}{2}\right) = \sin\left(\frac{A + D_m}{2}\right)$$

$$\Rightarrow \quad \frac{\pi}{2} - \frac{A}{2} = \frac{A}{2} + \frac{D_m}{2}$$

$$\Rightarrow \quad D_m = \pi - 2A$$

$$D_m = 180° - 2A$$

15. *(d)* For refractive index of a material,

$$\mu = \frac{1}{\sin i_c} = \frac{1}{\sin 45°} = \sqrt{2}$$

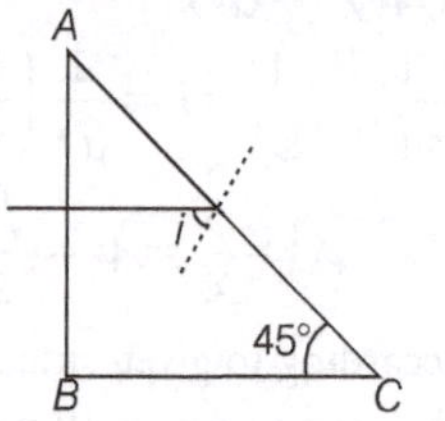

As, $\mu_{red} = 1.39, \mu_{green} = 1.44$

and $\mu_{blue} = 1.47$

$\therefore (\mu_{red} = 1.39) < \mu, \mu_{green} > \mu, \mu_{blue} > \mu$

Thus, only red colour do not suffer total internal reflection.

16. *(b)* According to question, diagram is shown below.

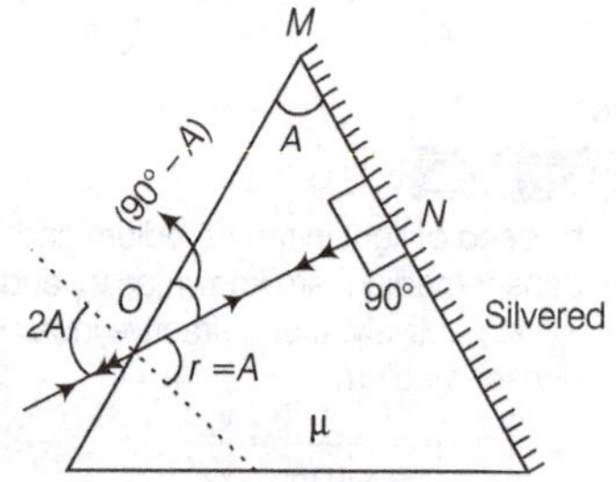

So, $\angle MON = 90° - A$

and $\angle r = 90° - (90° - A)$

$\Rightarrow \quad \angle r = A$

By Snell's law, $\frac{\sin i}{\sin r} = \mu$

$$\frac{\sin(2A)}{\sin(A)} = \mu$$

$$\frac{2 \sin A \cos A}{\sin A} = \mu \Rightarrow \mu = 2 \cos A$$

17. *(a)* Refractive index

$$\mu = \frac{\sin i}{\sin r}, \quad \mu = \frac{\sin i}{\sin A}$$

In case of small angle, $\sin i \approx i$ and $\sin A \approx A$

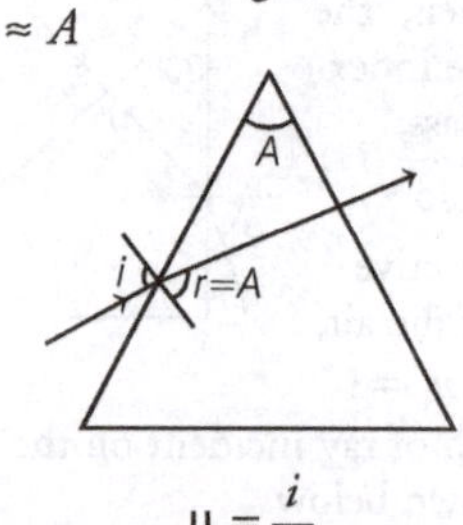

$$\mu = \frac{i}{A}$$

$$\Rightarrow \quad i = \mu A$$

18. *(a)* Real and apparent depth are explained on the basis of refraction only. The concept of TIR is not involved here.

19. *(c)* For total internal reflection,

$i > c$ (initial angle)

So, $\sin i > \sin c$

$\Rightarrow \quad \sin 45° > \dfrac{1}{\mu}$

$\Rightarrow \quad \mu > \sqrt{2} \Rightarrow \mu > 1.4$

20. *(c)* Velocity of light waves in material is

$v = \nu\lambda$ ...(i)

Refractive index of material is

$\mu = \dfrac{c}{v}$ ...(ii)

where, c is speed of light in vacuum or air.

or $\mu = \dfrac{c}{\nu\lambda}$ ...(iii)

Given, $\nu = 2 \times 10^{14}$ Hz

$\lambda = 5000$ Å

$= 5000 \times 10^{-10}$ m,

and $c = 3 \times 10^8$ m/s

Hence, from Eq. (iii), we get

$$\mu = \frac{3 \times 10^8}{2 \times 10^{14} \times 5000 \times 10^{-10}} = 3.00$$

21. *(a)* As shown in figure, a light ray from the coin will not emerge out of liquid, if $i > C$.

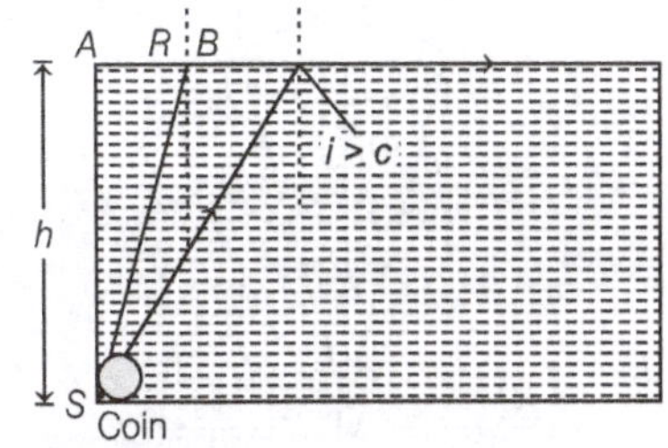

Therefore, minimum radius R corresponds to $i = c$.

In ΔSAB, $\dfrac{R}{h} = \tan c$

or $R = h \tan c$

or $R = \dfrac{h}{\sqrt{\mu^2 - 1}}$

Given, $R = 3$ cm

$h = 4$ cm

Hence, $\dfrac{3}{4} = \dfrac{1}{\sqrt{\mu^2 - 1}}$

or $\mu^2 = \dfrac{25}{9}$ or $\mu = \dfrac{5}{3}$

But $\mu = \dfrac{c}{v}$ or $v = \dfrac{c}{\mu} = \dfrac{3 \times 10^8}{5/3}$

$= 1.8 \times 10^8$ m/s

22. *(a)* According to the given condition, the beam of light will retrace its path after reflection from BC.

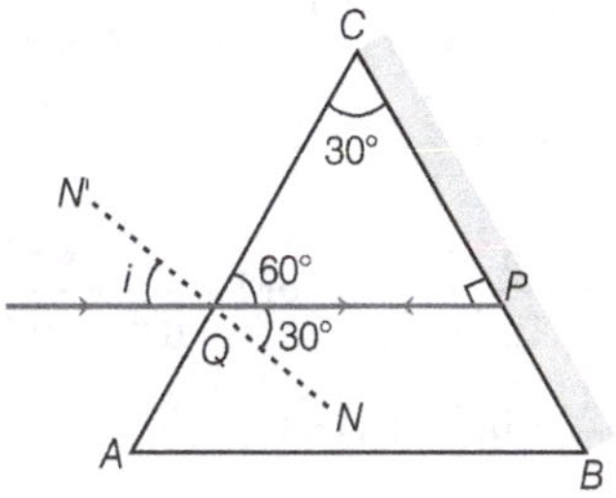

So, $\angle CPQ = 90°$

Thus, angle of refraction at surface AC

$\angle PQN = \angle r$

$= 90° - 60° = 30°$

By Snell's law

$\mu = \dfrac{\sin i}{\sin r}$

$\Rightarrow \sqrt{2} = \dfrac{\sin i}{\sin 30°}$

$\therefore \sqrt{2} \times \sin 30° = \sin i$

$\Rightarrow \quad \sqrt{2} \times \dfrac{1}{2} = \sin i$

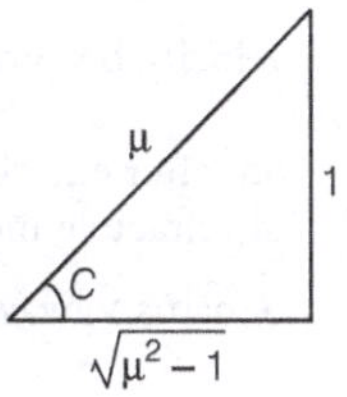

$\Rightarrow$

$\sin i = \dfrac{1}{\sqrt{2}} = \sin 45°$

$\therefore \quad i = 45°$

23. *(b)* In any medium other than air or vacuum, the velocities of different colours are different. Therefore, both red and green colours are refracted at different angles of refraction.
Hence, after emerging from the glass slab through the opposite parallel face, they appear at two different points and move in two different parallel directions.

24. *(c)* For total internal reflection to take place, angle of incidence > critical angle i.e. $\theta > c$ or $\sin\theta > \sin c$
But for the case of total internal reflection,

$$\sin c = \frac{1}{\mu}$$

and according to question

$\theta = 90° - r$

So, $\sin(90° - r) > \dfrac{1}{\mu}$

i.e. $\mu > \dfrac{1}{\cos r}$

[$\because \sin(90 - r) = \cos r$] ...(i)

From Snell's law,

$\dfrac{\sin 45°}{\sin r} = \mu \Rightarrow \sin r = \dfrac{1}{\sqrt{2}\mu}$

$\therefore \quad \cos r = \sqrt{1 - \sin^2 r} = \sqrt{1 - \dfrac{1}{2\mu^2}}$

Thus, Eq. (i) becomes

$$\mu > \frac{1}{\sqrt{1 - \frac{1}{2\mu^2}}}$$

$\therefore \quad \mu^2 = \dfrac{1}{1 - \dfrac{1}{2\mu^2}}$

or $\mu^2 - \dfrac{1}{2} = 1$ or $\mu = \sqrt{\dfrac{3}{2}}$

25. *(d)*

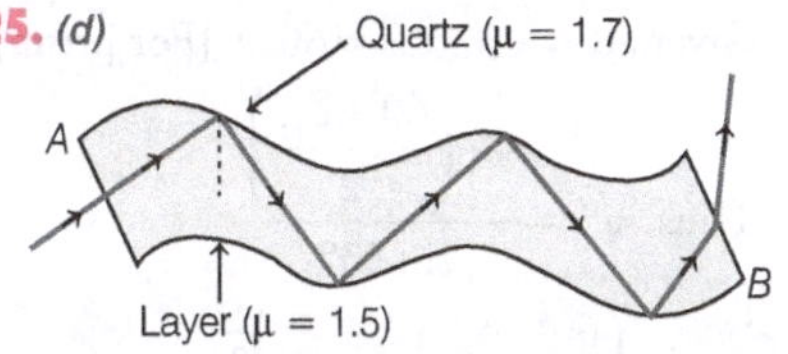

When a light ray is incident at one end A of fibre making a small angle of incidence. It suffers multiple total internal reflections and finally it reaches the point B.

> **• Concept Enhancer**
> In optical fiber, refractive index of material of core is greater than refractive index of material of cladding.

26. *(c)* As light travels from denser to rarer medium, so

refractive index $(\mu) = \dfrac{\text{real depth}}{\text{apparent depth}}$

Refractive index $(\mu) = 1.5$

Net apparent depth $= 2 + 5 = 7$ cm

And real depth = apparent depth $\times \mu$

$\therefore \quad$ Real depth $= 1.5 \times 7 = 10.5$ cm

27. *(c)* When white light from sun falls on raindrops, sometimes a band of different colours in form of a circular arc is seen in the sky. This is called the rainbow.
The reason of origin of rainbow is that the small drops of water behave like a prism for the white sunlight due to which refraction, dispersion and total

internal reflection of white light occurs from the water drops.

The rainbow is not seen after every rain, but is seen only when the light rays of particular colour suffer minimum deviation after one or two total internal reflections inside the small water drops.

28. *(c)* The refractive index of material of prism (from Snell's law) is

$$\mu = \frac{\sin i}{\sin r}$$

Here, $i = \frac{A+\delta_m}{2}$ and $r = \frac{A}{2}$

where, A is the angle of prism and δ_m the angle of minimum deviation.

In case of minimum deviation, refractive index of prism is given by

$$\mu = \frac{\sin\left(\frac{A+\delta_m}{2}\right)}{\sin\frac{A}{2}}$$

Given, $\mu = \sqrt{3}$, $A = 60°$ [For prism]

Thus, $\sqrt{3} = \frac{\sin\left(\frac{60+\delta_m}{2}\right)}{\sin 30°}$

or $\sin\left(\frac{60+\delta_m}{2}\right) = \frac{1}{2}\times\sqrt{3}$

or $\sin\left(\frac{60+\delta_m}{2}\right) = \sin 60°$

or $\frac{60+\delta_m}{2} = 60$

or $\delta_m = 2\times 60 - 60 = 60°$

29. *(a)* Suppose a light ray enters at A and refracted beam is AB. At the lateral face, the angle of incidence is θ. For no refraction at this face, $\theta > c$

$$\sin\theta > \sin c$$

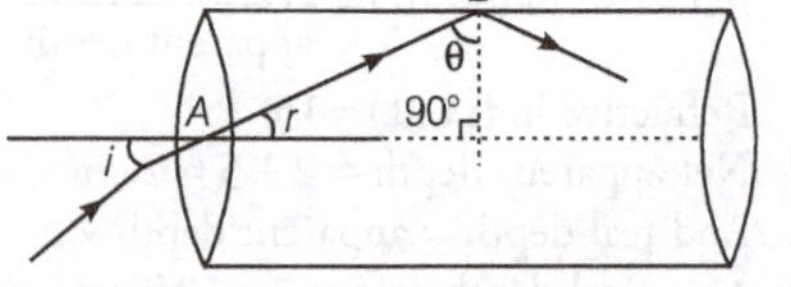

but $\theta + r = 90°$

(According to geometry of figure)

$\Rightarrow \quad \theta = (90° - r)$

$\therefore \quad \sin(90° - r) > \sin c$

or $\quad \cos r > \sin c \quad$ ...(i)

Now from Snell's law,

$$\mu = \frac{\sin i}{\sin r} \Rightarrow \sin r = \frac{\sin i}{\mu}$$

As from trigonometry,

$$\cos r = \sqrt{1 - \sin^2 r}$$

$\therefore \quad \cos r = \sqrt{\left(1 - \frac{\sin^2 i}{\mu^2}\right)}$

$\therefore$ Eq. (i) gives, $\sqrt{1 - \frac{\sin^2 i}{\mu^2}} > \sin c$

$\Rightarrow \quad 1 - \frac{\sin^2 i}{\mu^2} > \sin^2 c$

Also $\sin c = \frac{1}{\mu}$

$\therefore \; 1 - \frac{\sin^2 i}{\mu^2} > \frac{1}{\mu^2}$ or $1 > \frac{1}{\mu^2} + \frac{\sin^2 i}{\mu^2}$

or $\frac{1}{\mu^2}(\sin^2 i + 1) < 1$

or $\quad \mu^2 > \sin^2 i + 1$

The maximum value of $\sin i$ is 1. So,

$\therefore \quad \mu^2 > 2$ or $\mu > \sqrt{2}$

30. *(c)* When electromagnetic wave enters in other medium, frequency remains unchanged while wavelength and velocity become $\frac{1}{\mu}$ times.

So, after entering from air to glass slab of refractive index (μ), frequency remains ν, wavelength $\lambda' = \frac{\lambda}{\mu}$ and velocity of light $v' = \frac{v}{\mu}$.

31. *(a)* According to Cauchy relation,

$$\mu = A + \frac{B}{\lambda^2} + \frac{C}{\lambda^4} + \ldots \Rightarrow \mu \propto \frac{1}{\lambda}$$

Hence, focal length $f \propto \lambda$

For a convex lens,

$$f_R > f_V \text{ or } f_V < f_R.$$

For a concave lens, focal length is negative.

So, focal length of concave lens for violet light

$F_V >$ Focal length of concave lens for red light F_R.

32. *(c)* Given,

Thickness of rectangular glass plate,

$$t = 6 \text{ cm}$$

Distance of the object, $u = 8$ cm

Distance of the image, $v = 12$ cm

Let y = apparent position of the silvered surface.

From property of mirror,

Image distance of object from the mirror = distance of image from the mirror

i.e. $\quad y + 8 = 12 + 6 - y$

$\therefore \quad y = 5$ cm

$\therefore \quad \mu = \frac{\text{real depth}}{\text{apparent depth}} = \frac{6}{5} = 1.2$

33. *(d)* Here, total thickness $= t$

Refractive index $= \mu$

Speed of light in glass plate $= \frac{c}{\mu}$

$\left[\because v = \frac{\text{speed of light in vacuum}}{\text{refractive index of medium}}\right]$

$\therefore$ Time taken by light to travel this thickness of glass $= \frac{t}{\left(\frac{c}{\mu}\right)} = \frac{\mu t}{c}$

34. *(a)* When refracting angle of a prism is small ($\angle 10°$), the deviation δ is calculated from the relation

$\delta = (\mu - 1) A$.

For prisms with bigger refracting angles, we use the relation

$$\delta = (i_1 + i_2) - A$$

35. *(b)* In figure, O is the point source of light, K is centre of disc of radius r, $OK = h$.

The source will not be seen at all when the height is such that $\angle KOL = c$. (i.e. critical angle between water and air.)

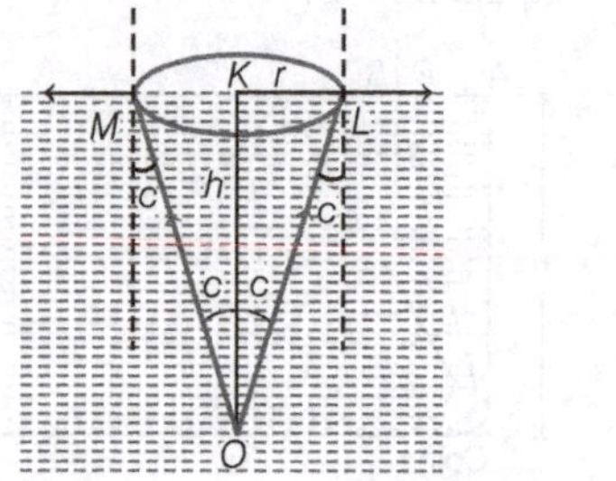

From figure,

$$\sin c = \frac{KL}{OL} = \frac{r}{\sqrt{r^2 + h^2}}$$

For total internal reflection of light,

$$\sin c = \frac{1}{\mu} = \frac{r}{\sqrt{r^2 + h^2}}$$

$\therefore \quad r^2 + h^2 = \mu^2 r^2$

or $\quad h^2 = r^2(\mu^2 - 1)$

Given, $\quad h = 4$ m, $\mu = \frac{5}{3}$

or $r^2 = \frac{h^2}{\mu^2 - 1} = \frac{(4)^2}{\left(\frac{5}{3}\right)^2 - 1}$

So, $r^2 = 9$

$\therefore$ $r = 3$ m

$\therefore$ Diameter of disc $= 2r = 6$ m

36. *(c)* Let x be thickness of window, v be velocity of light entering in window, so time taken by sunlight to pass through the window.

$$t = \frac{x}{v} = \frac{x}{\frac{c}{\mu}} = \frac{\mu x}{c} \qquad \left[v = \frac{c}{\mu}\right]$$

$$\therefore \quad t = \frac{1.5 \times 4 \times 10^{-3}}{3 \times 10^8} = 2 \times 10^{-11} \text{ s}$$

37. *(c)* The ray QR will retrace its path, when

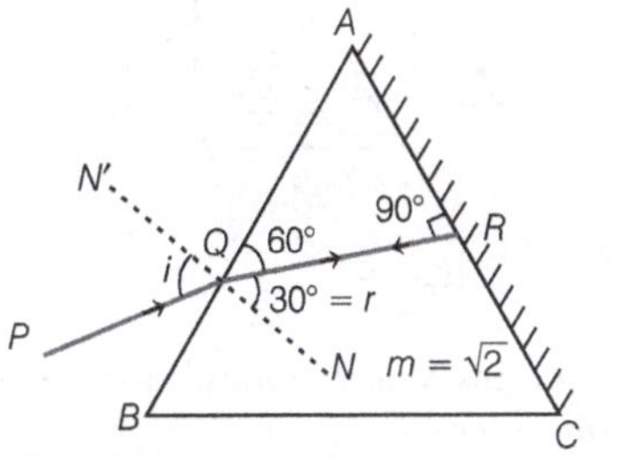

$\angle ARQ = 90°, \quad \angle r = 30°$

$\therefore \quad \angle AQR = 90° - 30° = 60°$

As from Snell's law,

$$\sin i \times 1 = \sin r \times \mu$$

$$\sin i = \mu \sin r = \sqrt{2} \sin 30°$$

[Refractive index of air = 1]

$$= \sqrt{2} \times \frac{1}{2} = \frac{1}{\sqrt{2}}$$

$\therefore \quad \angle i = 45°$

38. *(c)* Refractive index, $\mu = \frac{c}{v} = \frac{\nu\lambda_v}{\nu\lambda_m}$

As, c = velocity of light in vacuum

v = velocity of light in medium

$v = \nu\lambda$ and ν remains constant during refraction

$\therefore \lambda_m = \frac{\lambda_v}{\mu}$

$\Rightarrow \lambda_m < \lambda_v$ $\quad$ ($\because \mu = 1$, given)

Hence, the wavelength decreases in second medium.

Topic 3

01. *(c)* Focal length of convex lens,

$$f_1 = +f$$

Focal length of concave lens,

$$f_2 = -f$$

When both lenses are kept in contact, then equivalent focal length (F) is given by

$$\frac{1}{F} = \frac{1}{f_1} + \frac{1}{f_2} = \frac{1}{f} + \frac{1}{-f} = 0$$

$\Rightarrow \quad F = \infty$

02. *(b)* The given situation is shown below.

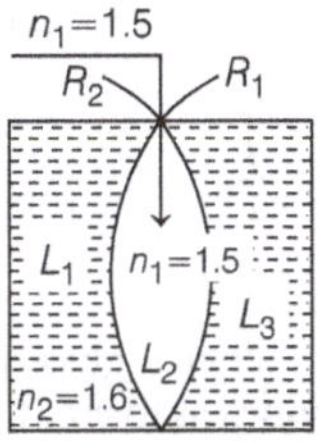

$\therefore \quad R_1 = 20$ cm, $R_2 = -20$ cm

Lens L_1 and L_3 are plano concave lens.

Focal length of lens L_1 is given as

$$\frac{1}{f_1} = (n_2 - 1)\left(\frac{1}{\infty} - \frac{1}{R_1}\right)$$

$$= (1.6 - 1)\left(-\frac{1}{20}\right)$$

$$= -\frac{3}{100}$$

$$\Rightarrow \quad \frac{1}{f_1} = \frac{-3}{100} \text{ cm}$$

Similarly, focal length of lens L_3,

$$\frac{1}{f_3} = \frac{-3}{100} \text{ cm}$$

Now, focal length of convex lens L_2 is given as

$$\frac{1}{f_2} = (n_1 - 1)\left(\frac{1}{R_1} - \frac{1}{R_2}\right)$$

$$= (1.5 - 1)\left(\frac{1}{20} - \frac{1}{-20}\right) = \frac{1}{20}$$

$$\Rightarrow \quad \frac{1}{f_2} = \frac{1}{20} \text{ cm}$$

If F be the focal length of combination, then

$$\frac{1}{F} = \frac{1}{f_1} + \frac{1}{f_2} + \frac{1}{f_3}$$

$$= \frac{-3}{100} + \frac{1}{20} - \frac{3}{100}$$

$$= \frac{-3 + 5 - 3}{100} = \frac{-1}{100}$$

$\therefore \quad F = -100$ cm

03. *(b)* For a biconvex lens,

$R_1 = +20$ cm

$R_2 = -20$cm and $\mu = 1.5$

By using lens maker's formula, we have,

$$\frac{1}{f} = (\mu - 1)\left(\frac{1}{R_1} - \frac{1}{R_2}\right)$$

$$= (1.5 - 1)\left(\frac{1}{20} - \frac{1}{-20}\right)$$

$$= 0.5\left(\frac{2}{20}\right)$$

$$\Rightarrow \quad \frac{1}{f} = 0.5 \times \frac{1}{10} \Rightarrow f = \frac{10}{0.5}$$

$\Rightarrow \quad f = 20$ cm $= 0.2$ m

$\therefore$ Power of the lens, $P = \frac{1}{f}$ (in metre)

$$= \frac{1}{0.2} = +5 \text{ D}$$

04. *(b)* Given, the focal length of convex lens A,

$f_1 = +20$ cm

The focal length of concave lens B,

$f_2 = -5$ cm

The convex lens is the converging lens and the concave lens is the diverging lens.

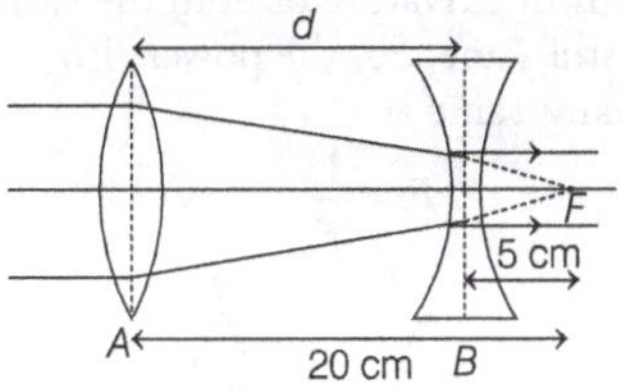

When the parallel beam of light passes through the convex lens, it converges at the focal point F and the distance between lens A and F point is 20 cm. Now, after emerging from the lens B, the beam is still parallel in nature. So, the net focal length of the lens A and B will be infinite.

As we know,

$$\frac{1}{f} = \frac{1}{f_1} + \frac{1}{f} - \frac{d}{f_1 f_2}$$

$$\Rightarrow \quad \frac{1}{\infty} = \frac{1}{20} - \frac{1}{5} + \frac{d}{20 \times 5}$$

$$\Rightarrow \quad \frac{3}{20} = \frac{d}{20 \times 5}$$

or $\quad d = 3 \times 5 = 15$ cm

05. *(b)* Spherometer is used to measure the radius of curvature of an item such as a lens and curved mirrors that are spherical in shape.

06. *(d)*

key idea
Use the following formula to solve this problem.

$$P=\frac{1}{f}=(\mu-1)\left(\frac{1}{R_1}-\frac{1}{R_2}\right)$$

Power of biconvex lens,

$$P=10\text{D}$$

$$\therefore \quad f=\frac{1}{P}=\frac{1}{10}=0.1 \text{ m}=10 \text{ cm}$$

$$R_1=R_2=10 \text{ cm}$$

By lens Maker's formula,

$$\frac{1}{f}=(\mu-1)\left(\frac{1}{R_1}-\frac{1}{R_2}\right)$$

$$\Rightarrow \quad \frac{1}{10}=(\mu-1)\left(\frac{1}{10}-\frac{1}{-10}\right)$$

$$\Rightarrow \quad \frac{1}{10}=(\mu-1)\left(\frac{2}{10}\right)$$

$$\Rightarrow \quad 1=(\mu-1)\times 2$$

$$\Rightarrow \quad \mu-1=\frac{1}{2} \Rightarrow \mu=1+\frac{1}{2}=\frac{3}{2}$$

07. *(d)* When the lens is cut along its principal axis, the focal length of the two halves will remain same because the radius of curvature of both the surfaces are still same. So, the power also remains same as

$$P=\frac{1}{f}$$

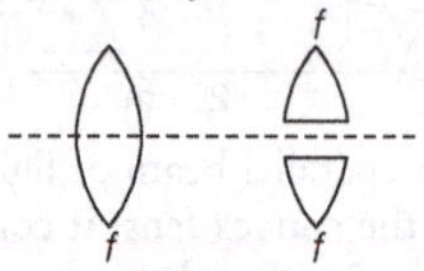

08. *(c)* Using the lens Maker's formula

$$\frac{1}{f}=\left(\frac{\mu_2-\mu_1}{\mu_1}\right)\left(\frac{1}{R_1}-\frac{1}{R_2}\right)$$

Here, $f=25$ cm, $\mu_2=1.5$, $\mu_1=1$ (for air)

let $\quad R_1=R$ and $R_2=-2R$

$$\Rightarrow \quad \frac{1}{25}=\left(\frac{1.5-1}{1}\right)\left[\frac{1}{R}-\left(-\frac{1}{2R}\right)\right]$$

$$\frac{1}{25\times 0.5}=\frac{1}{R}+\frac{1}{2R}$$

$$\Rightarrow \quad R=\frac{3}{2}\times 25\times 0.5=18.75 \text{ cm}$$

$$\therefore \quad R_1=18.75 \text{ cm}$$

$$R_2=2\times 18.75=37.5 \text{ cm}$$

09. *(a)* **Case I** When two equi-convex lens of focal length f_1 and f_2 respectively, are kept co-axially in contact, then the equivalent focal length of combination is

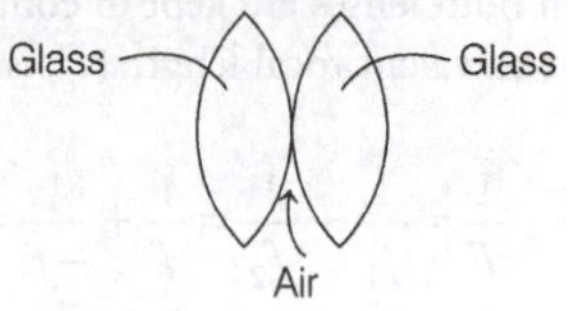

$$\frac{1}{F_1}=\frac{1}{f_1}+\frac{1}{f_2}=\frac{1}{f}+\frac{1}{f} \quad [\because \text{Here, } f_1=f_2]$$

$$=\frac{2}{f}$$

$$\Rightarrow \quad F_1=\frac{f}{2} \quad \dots \text{(i)}$$

Case II When glycerine of same refractive index as that of the glass is filled in the space between two lens, then the combination will now comprises of three lenses; first bi-convex, second bi-concave and third is bi-convex.

So, the focal length of the combination now is given as

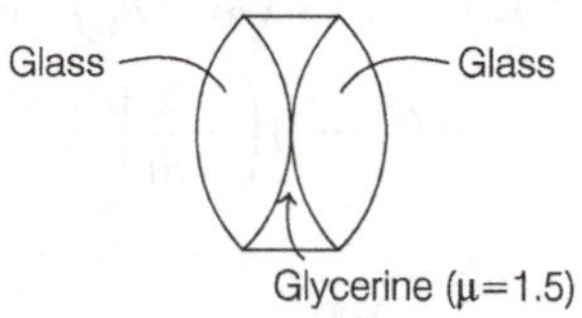

$$\frac{1}{F_2}=\frac{1}{f}+\frac{1}{(-f)}+\frac{1}{f}=\frac{1}{f}$$

$$\Rightarrow \quad F_2=f \quad \dots \text{(ii)}$$

From Eqs. (i) and (ii), we get

$$F_1 : F_2=1:2$$

10. *(d)* Consider the situation shown is figure. Let radius of curvature of lens surfaces is R. The combination is equivalent to three lenses in contact.

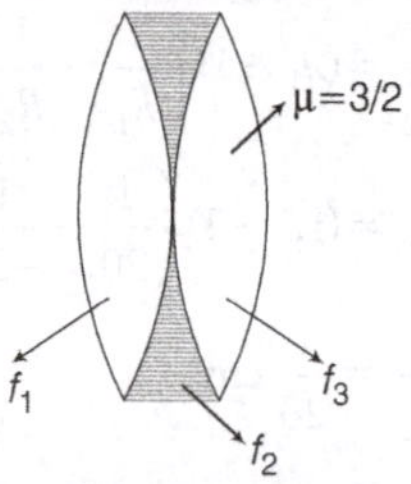

$$\therefore \quad \frac{1}{f_{eq}}=\frac{1}{f_1}+\frac{1}{f_2}+\frac{1}{f_3}$$

$$=\frac{2}{f_1}+\frac{1}{f_2} \quad (\because f_1=f_3)$$

$$\text{Now } \frac{1}{f_1}=\frac{1}{f_3}=(\mu-1)\left(\frac{2}{R}\right)=\frac{1}{f}$$

$$\frac{1}{f_2}=(\mu_w-1)\left(-\frac{2}{R}\right)$$

$$=\left(\frac{4}{3}-1\right)\left(\frac{-2}{R}\right)$$

$$=\left(\frac{1}{3}\right)\left(-\frac{2}{R}\right)=\left(\frac{-2}{3}\right)\left(\frac{1}{2(\mu-1)f}\right)$$

$$\Rightarrow \frac{1}{f_2}=\left(-\frac{1}{3}\right)\left(\frac{1}{\frac{3}{2}-1}\right)\left(\frac{1}{f}\right)=-\frac{2}{3}\times\frac{1}{f}$$

$$\therefore \frac{1}{f_{eq}}=\frac{2}{f}-\frac{2}{3}\times\frac{1}{f}=\frac{6-2}{3f}=\frac{4}{3f}$$

$$\Rightarrow f_{eq}=\frac{3f}{4}$$

11. *(c)* Given $\mu_g=1.5$

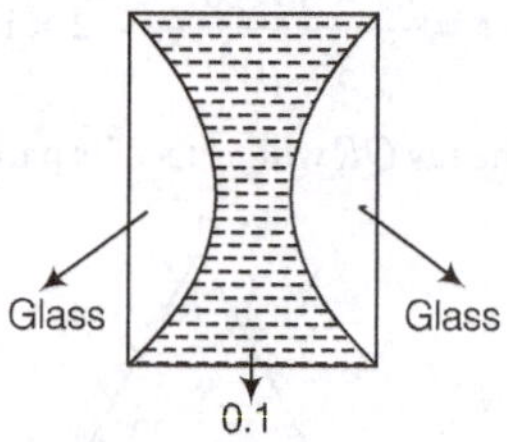

$$\mu_{oil}=1.7$$

$$\Rightarrow \quad R=20 \text{ cm}$$

From lens Maker's formula for the plano convex lens

$$\frac{1}{f}=(\mu-1)\left[\frac{1}{R_1}-\frac{1}{R_2}\right]$$

Here, $\quad R_1=R$

and for plane surface $R_2=\infty$

$$\therefore \quad \frac{1}{f_{lens}}=(1.5-1)\left(\frac{1}{R}-0\right)$$

$$\Rightarrow \quad \frac{1}{f_{lens}}=\frac{0.5}{R}$$

When the intervening medium is filled with oil, then focal length of the concave lens formed by the oil

$$\frac{1}{f_{concave}}=(1.7-1)\left(-\frac{1}{R}-\frac{1}{R}\right)$$

$$=-0.7\times\frac{2}{R}=\frac{-1.4}{R}$$

Here, we have two concave surfaces

$$\text{So, } \frac{1}{f_{eq}}=2\times\frac{1}{f_{planoconvex}}+\frac{1}{f_{concave}}$$

$$=2\times\frac{0.5}{R}+\left(\frac{-1.4}{R}\right)$$

$$=\frac{1}{R}-\frac{1.4}{R}=-\frac{0.4}{R}$$

$$\therefore \quad f_{eq}=-\frac{R}{0.4}=-\frac{20}{0.4}=-50 \text{ cm}$$

12. *(c)* Focal length of the combination

$$\frac{1}{f}=\frac{1}{f_1}+\frac{1}{f_2} \quad \text{...(i)}$$

We have

$$\frac{1}{f_1}=(\mu_1-1)\left(\frac{1}{\infty}-\frac{1}{-R}\right)=\frac{\mu_1-1}{R}$$

and

$$\frac{1}{f_2}=(\mu_2-1)\left(\frac{1}{-R}-\frac{1}{\infty}\right)$$

$$=-\frac{(\mu_2-1)}{R}$$

Putting these values of $\frac{1}{f_1}$ and $\frac{1}{f_2}$ in Eq. (i)

$$\frac{1}{f}=\frac{(\mu_1-1)}{R}-\frac{(\mu_2-1)}{R}$$

$$=\frac{[\mu_1-1-\mu_2+1]}{R}$$

$$=\frac{\mu_1-\mu_2}{R}$$

$$f=\frac{R}{\mu_1-\mu_2}$$

13. *(a)* If biconvex lens behaves like a plane sheet of glass, a ray will pass undeviated through it only when the medium has same refractive index as that of the biconvex lens.

- **Concept Enhancer**

When a convex lens of refractive index (μ_g) is dipped in a liquid of refractive index μ_l, then if,

(i) $\mu_l>\mu_g$, convex lens will behave as a concave lens is liquid.

(ii) $\mu_l<\mu_g$, then convex lens will behave as convex lens.

(iii) $\mu_l=\mu_g$, then convex lens will behave like a plane glass in liquid.

14. *(b)* Given, $R=20$ cm

$$h_0=2\text{ cm and } u=-30\text{ cm}$$

In general we have assumed $\mu=1.5$

As $\frac{1}{f}=(1.5-1)\times\frac{2}{20}=\frac{1}{20}$

So, $f=20$ cm

Now, as $\frac{1}{f}=\frac{1}{v}-\frac{1}{u}$

$$\frac{1}{20}=\frac{1}{v}-\frac{1}{-30}$$

$$\frac{1}{v}=\frac{1}{20}-\frac{1}{30}=\frac{10}{600}$$

$\therefore$ $v=60$ cm

As $m=\frac{v}{u}=\frac{60}{-30}=-2$

$\Rightarrow$ $m=\frac{h_i}{h_o}=-2$

$\therefore$ $h_i=-2\times2=-4$ cm

Here, image is real, inverted, magnified and height of image is 4 cm.

15. *(c)* As we know that

Intensity, $I\propto A$ (Area exposed)

$$\Rightarrow \frac{I_2}{I_1}=\left[\frac{A_2}{A_1}\right]=\frac{\frac{\pi d^2}{4}-\frac{\pi d^2/4}{4}}{\frac{\pi d^2}{4}}=\frac{3}{4}$$

$$\Rightarrow I_2=\frac{3}{4}I_1$$

and focal length remains unchanged.

16. *(a)* The diameter of the sun, $O=1.39\times10^9$ m and its image is I. As the distance of sun from lens $u=1.5\times10^{11}$ m and from paper is $v=0.1$ m

Then by using relation $\frac{I}{O}=\frac{v}{u}$

$$\Rightarrow \frac{I}{1.39\times10^9}=\frac{0.1}{1.5\times10^{11}}$$

we get, $I=9.2\times10^{-4}$ m

17. *(d)* As and we know that

$$P_{eq}=P_1+P_2$$

$$\frac{1}{F_{eq}}=\frac{1}{f_1}+\frac{1}{f_2}$$

$$\therefore \quad F_{eq}=\frac{f_1f_2}{f_1+f_2}$$

As $P=\frac{1}{F}$

$$\therefore \quad P_{eq}=\frac{f_1+f_2}{f_1f_2}$$

18. *(d)* Focal length of combination of lenses placed in contact is

$$\frac{1}{F}=\frac{1}{f_1}+\frac{1}{f_2}$$

For convex lens $f_1=25$ cm

For concave lens, $f_2=-25$ cm

Hence, $\frac{1}{F}=\frac{1}{25}+\frac{1}{-25}=\frac{1}{25}-\frac{1}{25}=0$

$\therefore$ $F=\frac{1}{0}=\infty$

Hence, power of combination,

$$P=\frac{1}{F}=0\text{D}$$

Alternate Solution

Given, $f_1=25$ cm, $f_2=-25$ cm

$\therefore$ $P_1=\frac{100}{f_1}\text{D}=\frac{100}{25}=+4\text{D}$

$P_2=\frac{100}{f_2}\text{D}=\frac{100}{-25}\text{D}=-4\text{D}$

$\therefore$ **Combined power**

$P=P_1+P_2=4-4=0\text{D}$

19. *(d)* From lens maker's formula

$$\frac{1}{f}=(\mu_g-1)\left(\frac{1}{R_1}-\frac{1}{R_2}\right) \quad \text{...(i)}$$

When convex lens is dipped in a liquid of refractive index (μ_l), then its focal length becomes

$$\frac{1}{f_l}=\left(\frac{\mu_g}{\mu_l}-1\right)\left(\frac{1}{R_1}-\frac{1}{R_2}\right)$$

or $$\frac{1}{f_l}=\frac{(\mu_g-\mu_l)}{\mu_l}\left(\frac{1}{R_1}-\frac{1}{R_2}\right) \quad \text{...(ii)}$$

Dividing Eq. (i) by Eq. (ii), we get

$$\frac{f_l}{f}=\frac{(\mu_g-1)\mu_l}{(\mu_g-\mu_l)} \quad \text{...(iii)}$$

But it is given that refractive index of lens is equal to refractive index of liquid i.e. $\mu_g=\mu_l$.

Hence, Eq. (iii) gives,

$$\frac{f_l}{f}=\frac{(\mu_g-1)\mu_l}{0}=\infty \quad \text{(infinity)}$$

20. *(c)* Initially, the focal length of equiconvex lens is

$$\frac{1}{f}=(\mu-1)\left(\frac{1}{R_1}-\frac{1}{R_2}\right) \quad \text{...(i)}$$

$$\frac{1}{f}=(\mu-1)\left(\frac{1}{R}-\frac{1}{-R}\right)=\frac{2(\mu-1)}{R}$$

Case I When lens is cut along XOX', then each half is again equiconvex with $R_1=R$, $R_2=-R$

Thus, $\frac{1}{f}=(\mu-1)\left[\frac{1}{R}-\frac{1}{(-R)}\right]$

$$=(\mu-1)\left[\frac{1}{R}+\frac{1}{R}\right]=(\mu-1)\frac{2}{R}=\frac{1}{f'}$$

$\Rightarrow$ $f'=f$

Case II When lens is cut along YOY', then each half becomes planoconvex with $R_1=R$, $R_2=\infty$

Thus, $\frac{1}{f''}=(\mu-1)\left(\frac{1}{R_1}-\frac{1}{R_2}\right)$

$$=(\mu-1)\left(\frac{1}{R}-\frac{1}{\infty}\right)$$

$$= \frac{(\mu - 1)}{R} = \frac{1}{2f}$$

Hence, $f' = f, \quad f'' = 2f$

• Concept Enhancer

When we cut a convex lens along principal axis both the lenses formed are convex lens of same focal length as that of original. When we cut a convex lens vertical to principal axis, each lens has focal length twice of original.

21. *(b)* **Concept** For equal size of image and object, object must be placed of centre of curvature of lens i.e. $u = v$.
The lens formula can be written as

$$\frac{1}{f} = \frac{1}{v} - \frac{1}{u} \quad \text{...(i)}$$

Given, $v = d$
For equal sized image,

$$|v| = |u| = d$$

By sign convention,

$$u = -d$$

$$\therefore \quad \frac{1}{f} = \frac{1}{d} + \frac{1}{d} \quad \text{or} \quad f = \frac{d}{2}$$

22. *(b)* When a ray falls on convex surface of a planoconvex lens, then it is first refracted and reflected from plane surface and then finally refracted from convex surface. Thus, two refractions and one reflection take place.
Since, refraction takes place two times and reflection takes place one time, focal length of planoconvex lens is

$$\frac{1}{F} = \frac{2}{f_l} + \frac{1}{f_m} \quad \text{...(i)}$$

If plane surface is silvered, so

$$f_m = \frac{R_2}{2} = \frac{\infty}{2} = \infty$$

And from lens maker formula

$$\frac{1}{f_l} = (\mu - 1)\left(\frac{1}{R_1} - \frac{1}{R_2}\right)$$

$$= (\mu - 1)\left(\frac{1}{R} - \frac{1}{\infty}\right) = \frac{(\mu - 1)}{R}$$

$$\therefore \quad \frac{1}{F} = \frac{2(\mu - 1)}{R} + \frac{1}{\infty} = \frac{2(\mu - 1)}{R}$$

$$\text{or} \quad F = \frac{R}{2(\mu - 1)} \quad \text{...(ii)}$$

Given, $R = 20$ cm

$\mu = 1.5$

$$\text{Hence, } F = \frac{20}{2(1.5 - 1)} = \frac{20}{2 \times 0.5} = 20 \text{ cm}$$

23. *(b)* According to Lens maker's formula, focal length of lens is given by

$$\frac{1}{f} = (\mu - 1)\left(\frac{1}{R_1} - \frac{1}{R_2}\right) \quad \text{...(i)}$$

We know that for planoconvex lens, the radius of curvature of plane surface is infinite,
i.e. $R_2 = \infty$.
Given,

$$R_1 = 60 \text{ cm}, \mu = 1.6$$

Substituting the given values in Eq. (i), we get

$$\frac{1}{f} = (1.6 - 1)\left(\frac{1}{60} - \frac{1}{\infty}\right) = 0.6 \times \frac{1}{60}$$

$\therefore$ Focal length of plane convex lens

$$f = \frac{60}{0.6} = 100 \text{ cm}$$

24. *(b)* Lens maker's formula is

$$\frac{1}{f} = (\mu - 1)\left(\frac{1}{R_1} - \frac{1}{R_2}\right)$$

$$\text{or} \quad \frac{1}{f} \propto \mu \quad \text{or } f \propto \frac{1}{\mu} \quad \text{...(i)}$$

According to Cauchy's formula,

$$\mu \propto \frac{1}{\lambda} \quad \text{...(ii)}$$

From Eqs. (i) and (ii), we get

$$f \propto \lambda$$

Hence, focal length of a converging lens is maximum for red colour (highest wavelength) and minimum for violet colour (lowest wavelength)
i.e. $f_V < f_R$

25. *(d)* Power of a lens is the ability of the lens to converge a beam of light falling on the lens. It is measured as the reciprocal of focal length of the lens.

$$\text{i.e.} \quad P = \frac{1}{f_{(\text{in m})}}$$

$$\text{When } f \text{ is in cm, } P = \frac{100}{f} \text{ D}$$

Here, $f_1 = 80$ cm

$f_2 = -50$ cm

Combined power of two lenses in contact is given by

$$P_{eq} = P_1 + P_2$$

$$\Rightarrow \quad P_{eq} = \frac{1}{f_1(\text{m})} + \frac{1}{f_2(\text{m})}$$

[f_1 and f_2 are with sign]

$$\therefore \quad P = \frac{100}{80} - \frac{100}{50}$$

$$= -0.75 \text{ D}$$

26. *(a)* In displacement method, total magnification $m = \sqrt{m_1 m_2}$.
Therefore, area of source is given by $A = \sqrt{A_1 A_2}$.

27. *(c)* When two or more lenses are combined together in such a way that the combination is free from chromatic aberration, then such a combination is called achromatic combination of lenses.
For this purpose, one lens should be convex and other a concave lens.

28. *(d)* As wavelength of violet light $\lambda_{\text{violet}} <$ Wavelength of red light λ_{red}, therefore, refractive index of violet light $\mu_{\text{violet}} >$ Refractive index of red light μ_{red}.
Hence, $\quad f_{\text{red}} > f_{\text{violet}}$
So, focal length of lens for red light is maximum than other visible spectrum of light.

29. *(c)* Focal length of convex lens in air is given by

$$\frac{1}{f_a} = ({}_a\mu_g - 1)\left(\frac{1}{R_1} - \frac{1}{R_2}\right) \quad \text{...(i)}$$

Focal length of convex lens when immersed in liquid of refractive index μ_l is given by

$$\frac{1}{f_l} = ({}_l\mu_g - 1)\left(\frac{1}{R_1} - \frac{1}{R_2}\right)$$

${}_l\mu_g$ = refractive index of glass w.r.t. liquid
R_1, R_2 = radius of curvature of lens spherical surface

$$\text{or} \quad \frac{1}{f_l} = \left(\frac{\mu_g}{\mu_l} - 1\right)\left(\frac{1}{R_1} - \frac{1}{R_2}\right) \quad \text{...(ii)}$$

From Eqs. (i) and (ii),

$$\frac{\frac{1}{f_a}}{\frac{1}{f_l}} = \frac{(\mu_g - 1)}{\left(\frac{\mu_g}{\mu_l} - 1\right)}$$

$$\text{or} \quad \frac{f_l}{f_a} = \frac{(\mu_g - 1)}{\left(\frac{\mu_g}{\mu_l} - 1\right)}$$

$$\text{or} \quad \frac{f_l}{f_a} = \frac{(1.5 - 1)}{\left(\frac{1.5}{1.25} - 1\right)} = \frac{1/2}{1/5} = \frac{5}{2}$$

$$\therefore \quad f_l = \frac{5}{2} f_a = \frac{5}{2} \times 2 = 5 \text{ cm}$$

Topic 4

01. *(b)* Given,

Focal length of objective, $f_0 = 140$ cm

Focal length of eyepiece, $f_e = 5$ cm

Magnifying power, $M = \left[\frac{f_0}{f_e}\right]$

$= \left[\frac{140}{5}\right] = 28$

02. *(d)* The objective of an astronomical telescope has large focal length and large aperture. Because the lens used is a convex lens, the magnification of an astronomical telescope is directly proportional to the focal length of the objective lens.

This large aperture also contributes to the better quality and visibility of the images. Thus, it provides better resolution.

Due to large focal length of the objective, it covers large area which ensures better light gathering power.

Thus, all options (a), (b) and (c) are correct.

03. *(c)* According to question,

Focal length of objective lens,

$F_0 = +40$ cm

Focal length of eyepiece lens F_e

$= 4$ cm

Object distance for objective lens ,

$u_0 = -200$ cm

Applying lens formula for objective lens

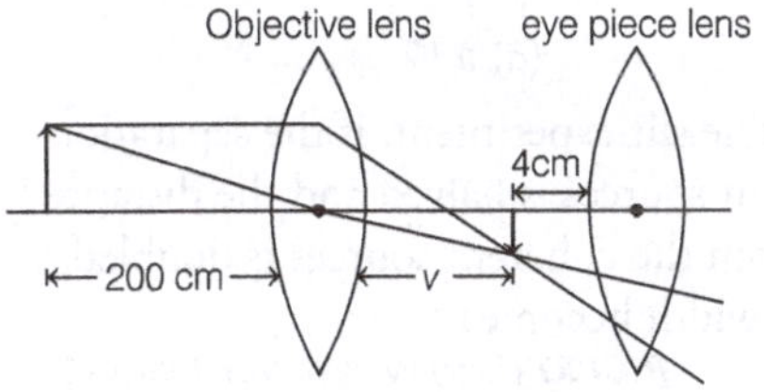

$$\frac{1}{v} - \frac{1}{u} = \frac{1}{f}$$

$$\Rightarrow \frac{1}{v} - \frac{1}{-200} = \frac{1}{40}$$

$$\Rightarrow \frac{1}{v} = \frac{1}{40} - \frac{1}{200} = \frac{5-1}{200} = \frac{4}{200}$$

$$\Rightarrow v = 50 \text{ cm}$$

Image will be form at first focus of eyepiece lens.

So, for normal adjustment distance between objectives and eye piece lense (length of tube) will be

$$v + F_e \Rightarrow 50 + 4 \Rightarrow 54 \text{ cm}$$

04. *(b)*

key idea

Image of object at ∞ must lie within distance upto which person can view clearly.

Image distance,

$$v = -400 \text{ cm} = -4 \text{ m}$$

$$\Rightarrow u = \infty$$

Using lens equation,

$$\frac{1}{v} - \frac{1}{u} = \frac{1}{f}$$

$$\Rightarrow \frac{1}{-4} - \frac{1}{\infty} = \frac{1}{f} \Rightarrow f = -4 \text{ m}$$

Now power of the required lens is,

$$P = \frac{1}{f} = \frac{1}{-4} = -0.25 \text{ D}$$

Thus, the person require a concave lens of power -0.25 D.

05. *(d)*

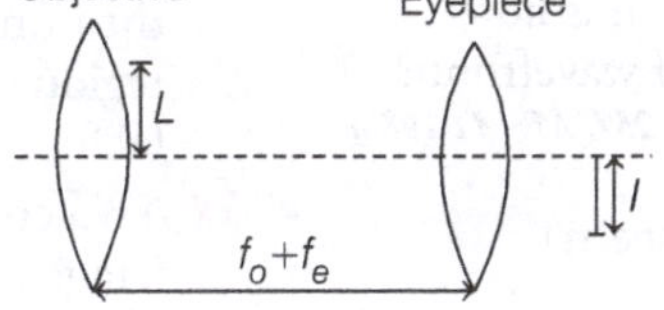

We know, magnification of telescope, we have

$$M = \frac{f_o}{f_e},$$

Here $\frac{f_e}{f_e + u} = \frac{-I}{L}$

$$\Rightarrow \frac{f_e}{f_e - (f_o + f_e)} = \frac{-I}{L} \Rightarrow \frac{f_e}{f_o} = \frac{I}{L}$$

i.e. $M = \frac{L}{I}$

06. *(d)* For microscope,

$$m = \frac{L}{f_o}\frac{D}{f_e} \Rightarrow m \propto \frac{1}{f_o}$$

For telescope, $m = \frac{f_o}{f_e}$

$$m \propto f_o$$

The magnifying power of microscope will decrease but the magnifying power of telescope will increase.

07. *(c)* Given, power $P_1 = 40$ D and Power, $P_2 = 20$ D

We have $P_{eq} = P_1 + P_2$

$= 40 + 20 = 60$ D

So, $\frac{1}{f_{eq}} = \frac{1}{f_1} + \frac{1}{f_2}$

$\Rightarrow f_{eq} = \frac{100}{P_{eq}} = \frac{100}{60} = 1.67$ cm

08. *(c)* Given, magnification $= \frac{f_o}{f_e} = 9$

and $f_o + f_e = 20$

$f_o = 9f_e$

So, $9f_e + f_e = 20$

$f_e = 2$ cm

$\therefore$ $f_o = 9 \times 2$

$f_o = 18$ cm

09. *(a)* Apparent depth of mark as seen through a glass slab of thickness x and refractive index μ is

Apparent depth $= \frac{\text{real depth}}{\text{refractive index}}$

or $x' = \frac{x}{\mu} = \frac{3}{1.5} = 2$ cm

As image appears to be raised by 1 cm, therefore, microscope must be moved upward by 1 cm.

10. *(c)* For an astronomical telescope,

where magnification, $m = \frac{f_o}{f_e}$

f_0 = focal length of objective lens

f_e = focal length of eye piece lens

Length of telescope tube

$$L = f_o + f_e$$

Given, $m = 10$, $L = 44$ cm

$\therefore$ $\frac{f_o}{f_e} = 10$ and $f_o + f_e = 44$

$\Rightarrow$ $f_e = \frac{f_o}{10}$

So, $f_o + \frac{f_o}{10} = 44$ or $\frac{11 f_o}{10} = 44$

or $f_o = 40$ cm

C-24

NEET Chapterwise Topicwise Physics

In NEET 2024, 2 questions was visible from this chapter. In past 5 years, 6 questions from topic-2, 1 question from topic-3 and 3 questions from topic-4 were asked.

For detailed analysis scan QR code

WAVE OPTICS

Topic 1 Huygen's Principle and Doppler's Effect of Light

01 A star, which is emitting radiation at a wavelength of 5000 Å, is approaching the earth with a velocity of 1.5×10^4 m/s. The change in wavelength of the radiation as received on the earth is *[NCERT (New) Pg. 259, AIPMT 1995]*

(a) 25 Å (b) 100 Å (c) zero (d) 2.5 Å

02 Which one of the following phenomenon is not explained by Huygen's consctruction of wavefront ? *[NCERT (New) Pg. 257, AIPMT 1988]*

(a) Refraction (b) Reflection
(c) Diffraction (d) Origin of spectra

Topic 2 Interference and Young's Double Slit Experiment

01 An unpolarised light beam strikes a glass surface at Brewster's angle. Then *[NCERT (New) Pg. 264, NEET 2024]*

(a) the reflected light will be partially polarised.
(b) the refracted light will be completely polarised.
(c) both the reflected and refracted light will be completely polarised.
(d) the reflected light will be completely polarised but the refracted light will be partially polarised.

02 For Young's double slit experiment, two statements are given below. *[NCERT (New) Pg. 266, NEET 2023]*

Statement I If screen is moved away from the plane of slits, angular separation of the fringes remains constant.

Statement II If the monochromatic source is replaced by another monochromatic source of larger wavelength, the angular separation of fringes decreases.

In the light of the above statements, choose the correct answer from the options given below.

(a) Both Statement I and Statement II are false.
(b) Statement I is true but Statement II is false.
(c) Statement I is false but Statement II is true.
(d) Both Statement I and Statement II are true.

03 In a Young's double slit experiment, a student observes 8 fringes in a certain segment of screen when a monochromatic light of 600 nm wavelength is used. If the wavelength of light is changed to 400 nm, then the number of fringes he would observe in the same region of the screen is *[NEET 2022]*

(a) 8 (b) 9 (c) 12 (d) 6

04 Two coherent sources of light interfere and produce fringe pattern on a screen. For central maximum, the phase difference between the two waves will be *[NCERT (New) Pg. 264, NEET (Oct.) 2020]*

(a) zero (b) π
(c) $3\pi/2$ (d) $\pi/2$

05 In Young's double slit experiment, if the separation between coherent sources is halved and the distance of the screen from the coherent sources is doubled, then the fringe width becomes *[NCERT (New) Pg. 266, NEET (Sep.) 2020]*

(a) half (b) four times
(c) one-fourth (d) double

06 In a Young's double slit experiment, if there is no initial phase-difference between the light from the two slits, a point on the screen corresponding to the fifth minimum has path difference. *[NCERT (New) Pg. 266, NEET (Odisha) 2020]*

(a) $5\frac{\lambda}{2}$ (b) $10\frac{\lambda}{2}$
(c) $9\frac{\lambda}{2}$ (d) $11\frac{\lambda}{2}$

07 In a double slit experiment, when light of wavelength 400 nm was used, the angular width of the first minima formed on a screen placed 1 m away, was found to be 0.2°. What will be the angular width of the first minima, if the entire experimental apparatus is immersed in water ? ($\mu_{water} = 4/3$)
[NCERT (New) Pg. 266, NEET (National) 2019]
(a) 0.15° (b) 0.051° (c) 0.1° (d) 0.266°

08 In Young's double slit experiment the separation d between the slits is 2 mm, the wavelength λ of the light used is 5896 Å and distance D between the screen and slits is 100 cm. It is found that the angular width of the fringes is 0.20°. To increase the fringe angular width to 0.21° (with same λ and D) the separation between the slits needs to be changed to
[NCERT (New) Pg. 266, NEET 2018]
(a) 1.8 mm (b) 1.9 mm (c) 2.1 mm (d) 1.7 mm

09 Young's double slit experiment is first performed in air and then in a medium other than air. It is found that 8th bright fringe in the medium lies where 5th dark fringe lies in air. The refractive index of the medium is nearly *[NCERT (New) Pg. 266, NEET 2017]*
(a) 1.25 (b) 1.59 (c) 1.69 (d) 1.78

10 The intensity at the maximum in a Young's double slit experiment is I_0. Distance between two slits is $d = 5\lambda$, where λ is the wavelength of light used in the experiment. What will be the intensity infront of one of the slits on the screen placed at a distance D = 10 d? *[NCERT (New) Pg. 266, NEET 2016]*
(a) $\frac{I_0}{4}$ (b) $\frac{3}{4}I_0$ (c) $\frac{I_0}{2}$ (d) I_0

11 The interference pattern is obtained with two coherent light sources of intensity ratio n. In the interference pattern, the ratio $\frac{I_{max} - I_{min}}{I_{max} + I_{min}}$ will be
[NEET 2016]
(a) $\frac{\sqrt{n}}{n+1}$ (b) $\frac{2\sqrt{n}}{n+1}$ (c) $\frac{\sqrt{n}}{(n+1)^2}$ (d) $\frac{2\sqrt{n}}{(n+1)^2}$

12 In a double slit experiment, the two slits are 1 mm apart and the screen is placed 1 m away. A monochromatic light of wavelength 500 nm is used. What will be the width of each slit for obtaining ten maxima of double slit within the central maxima of single slit pattern? *[NCERT (New) Pg. 266, AIPMT 2015]*
(a) 0.2 mm (b) 0.1 mm (c) 0.5 mm (d) 0.02 mm

13 Two slits in Youngs experiment have widths in the ratio 1 : 25. The ratio of intensity at the maxima and minima in the interference pattern $\frac{I_{max}}{I_{min}}$ is
[NCERT (New) Pg. 266, AIPMT 2015]
(a) $\frac{9}{4}$ (b) $\frac{121}{49}$ (c) $\frac{49}{121}$ (d) $\frac{4}{9}$

14 In the Young's double-slit experiment, the intensity of light at a point on the screen (where the path difference is λ) is K, (λ being the wavelength of light used). The intensity at a point where the path difference is $\lambda/4$, will be *[NCERT (New) Pg. 266, AIPMT 2014]*
(a) K (b) $K/4$ (c) $K/2$ (d) zero

15 In Young's double slit experiment, the slits are 2 mm apart and are illuminated by photons of two wavelengths $\lambda_1 = 12000$ Å and $\lambda_2 = 10000$ Å. At what minimum distance from the common central bright fringe on the screen 2 m from the slit will a bright fringe from one interference pattern coincide with a bright fringe from the other ?
[NCERT (New) Pg. 266, NEET 2013]
(a) 8 mm (b) 6 mm (c) 4 mm (d) 3 mm

16 In Young's double slit experiment the distance between the slits and the screen is doubled. The separation between the slits is reduced to half. As a result the fringe width *[NEET 2013]*
(a) is halved (b) becomes four times
(c) remains unchanged (d) is doubled

17 Colours of thin soap bubbles are due to *[AIPMT 1999]*
(a) refraction (b) dispersion
(c) interference (d) diffraction

18 Interference was observed in interference chamber where air was present, now the chamber is evacuated, and if the same light is used, a careful observer will see *[AIPMT 1993]*
(a) no interference
(b) interference with brighter bands
(c) interference with dark bands
(d) interference with larger bands

19 In Young's double slit experiment carried out with light of wavelength (λ) = 5000 Å, the distance between the slits is 0.2 mm and the screen is at 200 cm from the slits. The central maximum is at $x = 0$. The third maximum (taking the central maximum as zeroth maximum) will be at x equal to
[AIPMT 1992]
(a) 1.67 cm (b) 1.5 cm (c) 0.5 cm (d) 5.0 cm

20 If yellow light emitted by sodium lamp in Young's double slit experiment is replaced by monochromatic blue light of the same intensity *[AIPMT 1992]*
(a) fringe width will decrease
(b) fringe width will increase
(c) fringe width will remain unchanged
(d) fringes will becomes less intense

21 In Young's experiment, two coherent sources are placed 0.90 mm apart and fringes are observed one metre away. If it produces second dark fringe at a distance of 1 mm from central fringe, the wavelength of monochromatic light is used would be *[AIPMT 1991]*
(a) 60×10^{-4} cm (b) 10×10^{-4} cm
(c) 10×10^{-5} cm (d) 6×10^{-5} cm

22 Ratio of intensitities of two waves are given by 4 : 1. Then ratio of the amplitudes of the two waves is *[NCERT (New) Pg. 264, AIPMT 1991]*
(a) 2:1 (b) 1 : 2 (c) 4 :1 (d) 1 : 4

23 In Young's double slit experiment is performed with blue and with green light of wavelengths 4360 Å and 5460 Å respectively. If x is the distance of 4th maxima from the central one, then *[AIPMT 1990]*
(a) x (blue) = x (green) (b) x (blue) > x (green)
(c) x (blue) < x (green) (d) $\frac{x\text{ (blue)}}{x\text{ (green)}}=\frac{5460}{4360}$

24 In Young's double slit experiment, the fringes width is found to be 0.4 mm. If the whole apparatus is immersed in water of refractive index 4/3, without distrubing the geometrical arrangement, the new fringe width will be *[AIPMT 1990]*
(a) 0.30 mm (b) 0.40 mm
(c) 0.53 mm (d) 450 micron

25 Interference is possible in *[AIPMT 1989]*
(a) light waves only
(b) sound waves only
(c) both light and sound waves
(d) neight light nor sound waves

Topic 3 Diffraction

01 Assume that, light of wavelength 600 nm is coming from a star. The limit of resolution of telescope whose objective has a diameter of 2 m is *[NCERT (Old) Pg. 373, NEET (Sep.) 2020]*
(a) 1.83×10^{-7} rad (b) 7.32×10^{-7} rad
(c) 6.00×10^{-7} rad (d) 3.66×10^{-7} rad

02 Angular width of the central maxima in the Fraunhoffer diffraction for $\lambda = 6000$ Å is θ_0. When the same slit is illuminated by another monochromatic light, the angular width decreases by 30%. The wavelength of this light is *[NCERT (Old) Pg. 369, NEET (Odisha) 2019]*
(a) 1800 Å (b) 4200 Å
(c) 6000 Å (d) 420 Å

03 An astronomical refracting telescope will have large angular magnification and high angular resolution, when it has an objective lens of *[NEET 2018]*
(a) large focal length and large diameter
(b) large focal length and small diameter
(c) small focal length and large diameter
(d) small focal length and small diameter

04 The ratio of resolving powers of an optical microscope for two wavelengths $\lambda_1 = 4000$ Å and $\lambda_2 = 6000$ Å is *[NCERT (Old) Pg. 373, NEET 2017]*
(a) 8 : 27 (b) 9 : 4
(c) 3 : 2 (d) 16 : 81

05 In a diffraction pattern due to a single slit of width a, the first minimum is observed at an angle 30° when light of wavelength 5000 Å is incident on the slit. The first secondary maximum is observed at an angle of *[NCERT (Old) Pg. 369, NEET 2016]*
(a) $\sin^{-1}\left(\frac{2}{3}\right)$ (b) $\sin^{-1}\left(\frac{1}{2}\right)$
(c) $\sin^{-1}\left(\frac{3}{4}\right)$ (d) $\sin^{-1}\left(\frac{1}{4}\right)$

06 A linear aperture whose width is 0.02 cm is placed immediately in front of a lens of focal length 60 cm. The aperture is illuminated normally by a parallel beam of wavelength 5×10^{-5} cm. The distance of the first dark band of the diffraction pattern from the centre of the screen is *[NCERT (Old) Pg. 369, NEET 2016]*
(a) 0.10 cm (b) 0.25 cm
(c) 0.20 cm (d) 0.15 cm

07 For a parallel beam of monochromatic light of wavelength λ diffraction is produced by a single slit whose width a is of the order of the wavelength of the light. If D is the distance of the screen from the slit, the width of the central maxima will be *[NCERT (Old) Pg. 369, AIPMT 2015]*
(a) $\frac{2D\lambda}{a}$ (b) $\frac{D\lambda}{a}$ (c) $\frac{Da}{\lambda}$ (d) $\frac{2Da}{\lambda}$

08 At the first minimum adjacent to the central maximum of a single slit diffraction pattern, the phase difference between the Huygen's wavelet from the edge of the slit and the wavelet from the midpoint of the slit is *[NCERT (Old) Pg. 369, AIPMT 2015]*
(a) $\frac{\pi}{4}$ rad (b) $\frac{\pi}{2}$ rad
(c) π rad (d) $\frac{\pi}{8}$ rad

09 A beam of light of $\lambda = 600$ nm from a distant source falls on a single slit 1 mm wide and the resulting diffraction pattern is observed on a screen 2 m away. The distance between first dark fringes on either side of the central bright fringe is *[NCERT (Old) Pg. 369, AIPMT 2014]*
(a) 1.2 cm (b) 1.2 mm (c) 2.4 cm (d) 2.4 mm

10 The angular resolution of a 10 cm diameter telescope at a wavelength of 5000 Å is of the order of *[AIPMT 2005]*
(a) 10^6 rad (b) 10^{-2} rad (c) 10^{-4} rad (d) 10^{-6} rad

11 A telescope has an objective lens of 10 cm diameter and is situated at a distance of one kilometre from two objects. The minimum distance between these two objects, which can be resolved by the telescope, when the mean wavelength of light is 5000 Å, is of the order of *[AIPMT 2004]*
(a) 0.5 m (b) 5 m
(c) 5 mm (d) 5 cm

12 Diameter of human eye lens is 2 mm. What will be the minimum distance between two points to resolve them, which are situated at a distance of 50 m from eye ? (The wavelength of light is 5000 Å.) *[NCERT (Old) Pg. 381, AIPMT 2002]*

(a) 2.32 m (b) 4.28 mm
(c) 1.25 cm (d) 12.48 cm

Topic 4 Polarisation

01 If the monochromatic source in Young's double slit experiment is replaced by white light, then *[NCERT (New) Pg. 266, NEET 2024]*

(a) interference pattern will disappear
(b) there will be a central dark fringe surrounded by a few coloured fringes
(c) there will be a central bright white fringe surrounded by a few coloured fringes
(d) all bright fringes will be of equal width

02 A light ray falls on a glass surface of refractive index $\sqrt{3}$ at an angle 60°. The angle between the refracted and reflected rays would be *[NCERT, NEET 2022]*

(a) 60° (b) 90° (c) 120° (d) 30°

03 The Brewster's angle i_b for an interface should be *[NCERT (Old) Pg. 381, NEET (Sep.) 2020]*

(a) $30° < i_b < 45°$ (b) $45° < i_b < 90°$
(c) $i_b = 90°$ (d) $0° < i_b < 30°$

04 Unpolarised light is incident from air on a plane surface of a material of refractive index μ. At a particular angle of incidence i, it is found that the reflected and refracted rays are perpendicular to each other. Which of the following options is correct for this situation ? *[NCERT (Old) Pg. 380, NEET 2018]*

(a) $i = \sin^{-1}\left(\frac{1}{\mu}\right)$
(b) Reflected light is polarised with its electric vector perpendicular to the plane of incidence
(c) Reflected light is polarised with its electric vector parallel to the plane of incidence
(d) $i = \tan^{-1}\left(\frac{1}{\mu}\right)$

05 Two polaroids P_1 and P_2 are placed with their axis perpendicular to each other. Unpolarised light I_0 is incident on P_1. A third polaroid P_3 is kept in between P_1 and P_2 such that its axis makes an angle 45° with that of P_1. The intensity of transmitted light through P_2 is *[NCERT (Old) Pg. 271, NEET 2017]*

(a) $\frac{I_0}{2}$ (b) $\frac{I_0}{4}$ (c) $\frac{I_0}{8}$ (d) $\frac{I_0}{16}$

06 Which of the phenomenon is not common to sound and light waves ? *[NCERT (Old) Pg. 269, AIPMT 1988]*

(a) Interference (b) Diffraction
(c) Coherence (d) Polarisation

Key Index

Topic 1

1 (a)	2 (d)								

Topic 2

1 (d)	2 (b)	3 (c)	4 (a)	5 (b)	6 (c)	7 (a)	8 (b)	9 (d)	10 (c)
11 (b)	12 (a)	13 (a)	14 (c)	15 (b)	16 (b)	17 (c)	18 (d)	19 (b)	20 (a)
21 (d)	22 (a)	23 (c)	24 (a)	25 (c)					

Topic 3

1 (d)	2 (b)	3 (a)	4 (c)	5 (c)	6 (d)	7 (a)	8 (c)	9 (d)	10 (d)
11 (c)	12 (c)								

Topic 4

1 (c)	2 (b)	3 (b)	4 (b)	5 (c)	6 (d)				

Detailed **Explanations**

Topic 1

01. *(a)*

key idea

To determine the change in wavelength of radiation, you can use following formula

$$\Delta\lambda = \frac{\lambda v}{c}$$

Here, wavelength, $\lambda = 5000$ Å and velocity, $v = 1.5 \times 10^4$ m/s

Wavelength of the approaching star,

$$\lambda' = \lambda \frac{c - v}{c}$$

or $$\frac{\lambda'}{\lambda} = 1 - \frac{v}{c}$$

or, $$\frac{v}{c} = 1 - \frac{\lambda'}{\lambda} = \frac{\lambda - \lambda'}{\lambda} = \frac{\Delta\lambda}{\lambda}$$

Therefore

$$\Delta\lambda = \lambda \times \frac{v}{c}$$

$$= 5000\ \text{Å} \times \frac{1.5 \times 10^6}{3 \times 10^8}$$

$$= 25\ \text{Å}$$

02. *(d)* Origin of spectra is not explained by Huygen's construction of wavefront. It is explained by quantum theory.

Topic 2

01. *(d)* At Brewster's angle, the angle between refracted and reflected rays is 90°. The reflected ray is completely linearly polarised and the refracted rays is partially polarised.

02. *(b)* Angular separation of fringes,

$$\theta = \frac{\lambda}{d}$$

i.e., Angular separation does not depend on the distance between screen and plane of slits. Thus, statement I is correct.

Since,

$$\theta \propto \lambda$$

Thus, if the monochromatic source is replaced by another monochromatic source of larger wavelength, then angular separation of fringes increases. Hence, Statement II is incorrect.

03. *(c)* In Young's double slit experiment, wavelength of light used is inversely proportional to the number of fringes observed.

i.e. $\lambda_1 n_1 = \lambda_2 n_2$

$$n_2 = \frac{n_1 \lambda_1}{\lambda_2}$$

Here, $\lambda_1 = 600\ \text{nm} = 6 \times 10^{-7}$ m

$\lambda_2 = 400\ \text{nm} = 4 \times 10^{-7}$ m

$n_1 = 8$

$$\therefore \quad n_2 = \frac{8 \times 6 \times 10^{-7}}{4 \times 10^{-7}} = 12$$

04. *(a)* For central maximum, path difference is zero for both coherent sources in interference.

Hence, phase difference

$$= \frac{2\pi}{\lambda} \times \text{path difference}$$

$$= \frac{2\pi}{\lambda} \times 0 = 0$$

05. *(b)* Fringe width,

$$\beta = \frac{\lambda D}{d}$$

$$\therefore \quad \frac{\beta_2}{\beta_1} = \frac{\dfrac{\lambda_2 D_2}{d_2}}{\dfrac{\lambda_1 D_1}{d_1}}$$

[As $\lambda_1 = \lambda_2$, $D_2 = 2D_1$ and $d_2 = \frac{d_1}{2}$]

$$\therefore \quad \frac{\beta_2}{\beta_1} = \frac{2D_1}{\left(\dfrac{d_1}{2}\right)} \times \frac{d_1}{D_1} = 4$$

$\Rightarrow \quad \beta_2 = 4\beta_1$

i.e., fringe width becomes four times.

06. *(c)* In a YDSE, the path difference for nth minima is given by

$$\Delta y = (2n - 1)\frac{\lambda}{2}$$

For 5th minima, $n = 5$

$$\therefore \quad \Delta y = [2(5) - 1]\frac{\lambda}{2} = \frac{9\lambda}{2}$$

07. *(a)* The angular width in YDSE is given by

$$\theta = \frac{\beta}{D}$$

If YDSE apparatus is immersed in a liquid of refractive index μ, then the wavelength of light and hence the angular width decreases by μ times.

i.e. and $\theta' = \frac{\beta}{\mu D} = \frac{\theta}{\mu}$

Here, μ (for water) $= 4/3$ and $\theta = 0.2°$

$$\Rightarrow \quad \theta' = \frac{0.2}{4/3} = 0.15°$$

08. *(b)*

key idea

Here, you can use following relation to solve this question

$$\frac{\theta_1}{\theta_2} = \frac{d_2}{d_1}$$

Here, $\theta_1 = 0.20°, \theta_2 = 0.21°$

$d_1 = 2$ mm

We know that,

Angular width, $\theta = \frac{\lambda}{d}$

$$\Rightarrow \quad \theta \propto \frac{1}{d}$$

[$\because$ λ same for both]

$$\therefore \quad \frac{\theta_1}{\theta_2} = \frac{d_2}{d_1}$$

$$d_2 = \frac{\theta_1}{\theta_2} \times d_1 = \frac{0.20}{0.21} \times 2$$

$= 1.9$ mm

Alternate Solution

Angular width $= \frac{\lambda}{d}$

$0.20° = \frac{\lambda}{2\ \text{mm}}$ and $0.21° = \frac{\lambda}{d}$

On dividing we get, $\frac{0.20}{0.21} = \frac{d}{2\ \text{mm}}$

$\therefore \quad d = 1.9$ mm

09. *(d)* According to question,

5th dark fringe in air = 8 bright fringe in the medium

$$(2 \times 5 - 1)\frac{\lambda D}{2d} = 8\frac{\lambda D}{\mu d}$$

$$\Rightarrow \quad 9\frac{\lambda D}{2d} = 8\frac{\lambda D}{\mu d}$$

$$\Rightarrow \quad \frac{9}{2} = \frac{8}{\mu} \Rightarrow \mu = \frac{8 \times 2}{9}$$

$$\mu = \frac{16}{9} = 1.7777 \approx 1.78$$

10. *(c)*

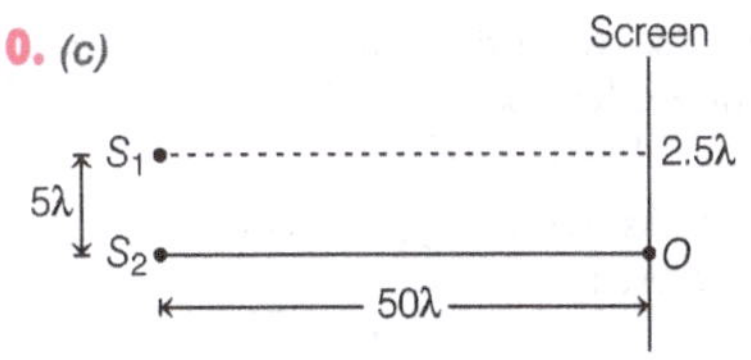

In the above figure, S_1 and S_2 are the two different slits.

Given, distance between slits S_1 and S_2, $d = 5\lambda$

distance between screen and slits,

$$D = 10d = 50\lambda$$

Here, λ is the wavelength of light used in the experiment.

According to question, the intensity at maximum in this Young's double slit experiment is I_0.

$\Rightarrow I_{max} = I_0$

$\because$ Path difference

$$= \frac{dY_n}{D} = \frac{d \times \frac{d}{2}}{10d} = \frac{d}{20} = \frac{\lambda}{4}$$

$$\{\because d = 5\lambda\}$$

A path difference of λ corresponds to phase difference 2π. So, for path difference $\lambda/4$, phase difference

$$\phi = \frac{2\pi}{\lambda} \times \frac{\lambda}{4}$$

$$= \pi/2 = 90°$$

As we know,

$$I = I_0 \cos^2 \frac{\phi}{2}$$

$$\Rightarrow \quad I = I_0 \cos^2 \frac{90°}{2}$$

$$\Rightarrow \quad I = I_0 \times \left(\frac{1}{\sqrt{2}}\right)^2 \Rightarrow I = \frac{I_0}{2}$$

11. *(b)* It is given that,

$$\frac{I_2}{I_1} = n$$

$\Rightarrow \quad I_2 = nI_1$

$\therefore$ Ratio of intensities is given by

$$\frac{I_{max} - I_{min}}{I_{max} + I_{min}}$$

$$= \frac{(\sqrt{I_2} + \sqrt{I_1})^2 - (\sqrt{I_2} - \sqrt{I_1})^2}{(\sqrt{I_1} + \sqrt{I_2})^2 + (\sqrt{I_2} - \sqrt{I_1})^2)}$$

$$= \frac{\left(\sqrt{\frac{I_2}{I_1}} + 1\right)^2 - \left(\sqrt{\frac{I_2}{I_1}} - 1\right)^2}{\left(\sqrt{\frac{I_2}{I_1}} + 1\right)^2 + \left(\sqrt{\frac{I_2}{I_1}} - 1\right)^2}$$

$$= \frac{(\sqrt{n} + 1)^2 - (\sqrt{n} - 1)^2}{(\sqrt{n} + 1)^2 + (\sqrt{n} - 1)^2}$$

$$= \frac{2\sqrt{n}}{n + 1}$$

12. *(a)* Given, $d = 1\text{ mm} = 1 \times 10^{-3}$ m

$$D = 1\text{ m}, \lambda = 500\text{ nm}$$

$$= 5 \times 10^{-7}\text{ m}$$

As width of central maxima = width of 10 maxima

$$\therefore \quad \frac{2D\lambda}{a} = 10\left(\frac{\lambda D}{d}\right)$$

$$\Rightarrow \quad a = \frac{d}{5} = \frac{10^{-3}}{5}$$

$$= 0.2 \times 10^{-3}\text{ m}$$

$$= 0.2\text{ mm}$$

13. *(a)* Given, YDSE experiment, having two slits of width are in the ratio of 1 : 25.

So, ratio of intensity,

$$\frac{I_1}{I_2} = \frac{W_1}{W_2} = \frac{1}{25}$$

$$\Rightarrow \quad \frac{I_2}{I_1} = \frac{25}{1}$$

$$\therefore \quad \frac{I_{max}}{I_{min}} = \frac{(\sqrt{I_2} + \sqrt{I_1})^2}{(\sqrt{I_2} - \sqrt{I_1})^2}$$

$$= \left[\frac{\sqrt{\frac{I_2}{I_1}} + 1}{\sqrt{\frac{I_2}{I_1}} - 1}\right]^2$$

$$\Rightarrow \quad \left[\frac{5+1}{5-1}\right]^2 = \left(\frac{6}{4}\right)^2 = \frac{36}{16} = \frac{9}{4}$$

Thus, $\frac{I_{max}}{I_{min}} = \frac{9}{4}$

14. *(c)* For net intensity,

$$I' = 4I_0 \cos^2 \frac{\phi}{2}$$

For the first case,

$$K = 4I_0 \cos^2[\pi]$$

$$\because \quad \left(\phi = \frac{2\pi}{\lambda} \times \lambda\right)$$

$$K = 4I_0 \quad \text{...(i)}$$

For the second case,

$$K' = 4I_0 \cos^2\left(\frac{\pi/2}{2}\right)$$

$$\because \quad \left(\phi = \frac{2\pi}{\lambda} \times \frac{\lambda}{4}\right)$$

$$K' = 2I_0 \quad \text{...(ii)}$$

Comparing Eqs. (i) and (ii), we get

$$K' = \frac{K}{2}$$

15. *(b)* Given, $\lambda_1 = 12000$ Å

and $\lambda_2 = 10000$ Å, $D = 2$ m

and $d = 2\text{ mm} = 2 \times 10^{-3}$ m.

Fringe-width of first wavelength,

$$\beta_1 = \frac{\lambda_1 D}{d}$$

$$= \frac{12000 \times 10^{-10} \times 2}{2 \times 10^{-3}}$$

$$= 1.2\text{ mm}$$

Fringe-width of second wavelength,

$$\beta = \frac{\lambda_2 D}{d} = \frac{10000 \times 10^{-10} \times 2}{2 \times 10^{-3}}$$

$$= 1\text{ mm}$$

At 6 mm distance from central bright fringe, 5th fringe of first wavelength coincide with 6th fringe of second wavelength.

16. *(b)* We know that,

Fringe width,

$$\beta = \frac{\lambda D}{d}$$

When D is doubled and d is reduced to half, then fringe width becomes

$$\beta' = \frac{\lambda\,(2D)}{(d/2)} = \frac{4\lambda D}{d} = 4\beta$$

17. *(c)* When white light is incident on a soap bubble it is partly reflected from upper surface and partly reflected from lower surface. These two reflected beams superpose to cause interference. The colours which satisfy the condition of maxima are visible in reflected light. So, colours of soap bubbles are caused due to interference.

18. *(d)* As we know that, $\beta \propto \lambda$

$\because$ In vacuum, λ increases very slightly compared to that in air. Therefore, width of interference fringe increase slightly.

19. *(b)*

key idea

To solve this question, you can use following formula

$$x = \frac{n\lambda D}{d}$$

Here, $\lambda = 5000$ Å

$$d = 0.2\text{ mm} = 0.2 \times 10^{-3}\text{ m}$$

$$D = 200\text{ cm} = 2\text{ m}$$

$n = 3$

We know that,

$$x = (n)\lambda \frac{D}{d}$$

$$= 3 \times 5000 \times 10^{-10} \times \frac{2}{0.2 \times 10^{-3}}$$

$$= 1.5 \times 10^{-2} \text{ m} = 1.5 \text{ cm}$$

20. *(a)* As we know that,

$$\beta \propto \lambda$$

and wavelength of blue light is less than wavelength of yellow light.

Therefore, fringe width β will decrease.

21. *(d)*

key idea

To find out the wavelength of monochromatic light, you can use following formula

$$\lambda = \frac{2xd}{(2n-1)D}$$

Here, $d = 0.90$ mm

$$= 0.9 \times 10^{-3} \text{ m}$$

$$x = 1\text{mm} = 10^{-3} \text{ m}$$

$$D = 1 \text{ m}$$

$$n = 2$$

For dark fringe,

$$x = (2n-1)\frac{\lambda D}{2d}$$

$$\lambda = \frac{2xd}{(2n-1)D}$$

$$= \frac{2 \times 10^{-3} \times 0.9 \times 10^{-3}}{(2 \times 2 - 1) \times 1}$$

$$\lambda = 0.6 \times 10^{-6} \text{ m}$$

$$= 6 \times 10^{-5} \text{ cm}$$

22. *(a)* Here, $\frac{I_1}{I_2} = \frac{4}{1}$

We know, $\frac{I_1}{I_2} = \frac{a^2}{b^2} = \frac{4}{1}$

$$\therefore \quad \frac{a}{b} = \frac{2}{1}$$

23. *(c)* As we know that, distance of *n*th maxima, $x = n\lambda \frac{D}{d} \propto \lambda$

$\because \quad \lambda_{blue} < \lambda_{green}$

$\therefore x$ (blue) $< x$ (green)

24. *(a)* Here, $\beta = 0.4$ mm, $\mu = \frac{4}{3}$

We know that

$$\beta' = \frac{\beta}{\mu} = \frac{0.4}{4/3} = 0.3 \text{ mm}$$

25. *(c)* Interference is possible in both light and sound waves.

Topic 3

01. *(d)* Given, light of wavelength,

$$\lambda = 600 \text{ nm}$$

$$= 600 \times 10^{-9} \text{ m}$$

Diameter, $d = 2$ m

As, limit of resolution of telescope,

$$d\theta = \frac{1.22\lambda}{d}$$

$$= \frac{1.22 \times 600 \times 10^{-9}}{2}$$

$$= 3.66 \times 10^{-7} \text{ rad}$$

Hence, correct option is (d).

02. *(b)* The angular width of central maxima is given by

$$2\theta = \frac{2\lambda}{a} \quad \ldots(i)$$

where, λ = wavelength of light used

a = width of the slit

For $\lambda_1 = 6000$ Å, $2\theta = \theta_0$ (given)

For another light of wavelength λ_2 (says), the angular width decreases by 30% so,

$$2\theta = \left(\frac{100-30}{100}\right)\theta_0 = \frac{70}{100}\theta_0 = 0.7\theta_0$$

As slit width is constant, so using Eq. (i) for these values, we get

$$\frac{\theta_0}{0.7\theta_0} = \frac{\lambda_1}{\lambda_2}$$

$$\Rightarrow \quad \lambda_2 = \lambda_1 \times 0.7$$

$$= 6000 \times 0.7$$

$$= 4200 \text{ Å}$$

03. *(a)* Angular magnification of an astronomical refracting telescope is given as

$$M = \frac{f_0}{f_e}$$

where, f_0 and f_e are the focal length of objective and eye-piece, respectively.

From the given relation, it is clear that for large magnification either f_0 has to be large or f_e has to be small.

Angular resolution of an astronomical refracting telescope is given as

$$R = \frac{a}{1.22\lambda}$$

where, a is the diameter of the objective. Thus, to have large resolution, the diameter of the objective should be large.

Hence, from the above objective lens should have large focal length (f_0) and large diameter (a).

04. *(c)* As, resolving power of a microscope,

$$(\text{RP}) \propto \frac{1}{\lambda_{(\text{wavelength})}}$$

$$\therefore \quad \frac{\text{RP}_1}{\text{RP}_2} = \frac{\lambda_2}{\lambda_1}$$

$$= \frac{6000}{4000} = \frac{3}{2}$$

05. *(c)* As the first minimum is observed at an angle of 30° in a diffraction pattern due to a single slit of width *a*.

i.e. $n = 1$, $\theta = 30°$

Condition for *n*th minima in single slit diffraction pattern is,

$$a \sin\theta = n\lambda$$

$$\Rightarrow a \sin 30° = (1)\lambda \quad (n = 1)$$

$$\Rightarrow \quad a = 2\lambda \quad \ldots(i)$$

$$\left\{\because \sin 30° = \frac{1}{2}\right\}$$

For Ist secondary maxima

$$\Rightarrow a \sin\theta_1 = \frac{3\lambda}{2}$$

$$\Rightarrow \sin\theta_1 = \frac{3\lambda}{2a} \quad \ldots(ii)$$

Substitute value of *a* from Eq. (i) to Eq. (ii), we get

$$\sin\theta_1 = \frac{3\lambda}{4\lambda}$$

$$\Rightarrow \quad \sin\theta_1 = \frac{3}{4}$$

$$\Rightarrow \quad \theta_1 = \sin^{-1}\left(\frac{3}{4}\right)$$

06. *(d)* For the distance of the first dark band of the diffraction pattern from the centre of the screen is given by positon of Ist minima.

i.e. $Y = \frac{\lambda D}{a}$

where, λ = wavelength of parallel beams

D = focal length

a = width of linear aperture.

$$\Rightarrow \quad Y = \frac{(5 \times 10^{-5})(0.6)}{0.02 \times 10^{-2}} \quad \text{(given)}$$

$$\Rightarrow \quad Y = 0.15 \text{ cm}$$

07. (a) For the condition of maxima

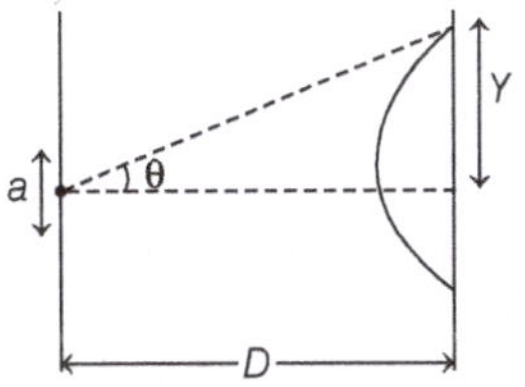

$$\sin\theta = \frac{\lambda}{a}$$

From the geometry,

$$\tan\theta \simeq \sin\theta = \theta = \frac{Y}{D} \text{ (for small angle)}$$

So, $\frac{Y}{D} = \frac{\lambda}{a}$

$\Rightarrow$ $Y = \frac{\lambda D}{a}$

Hence, width of central maxima

$$= 2Y = \frac{2\lambda D}{a}$$

08. (c) For first minima at P,

$a\sin\theta = n\lambda$

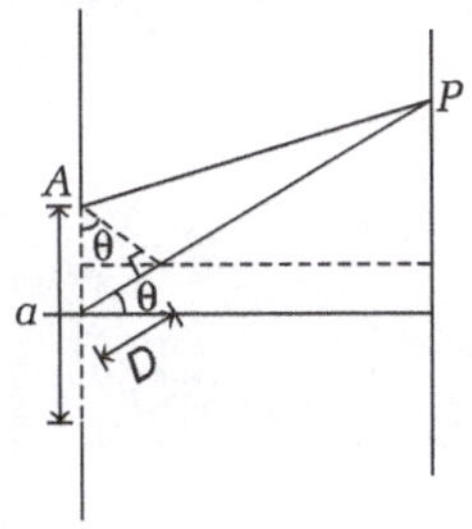

where, $n = 1 \Rightarrow a\sin\theta = \lambda$

So, phase difference,

$$\Delta\phi_1 = \frac{\Delta x_1}{\lambda} \times 2\pi = \frac{(a/2)\sin\theta}{\lambda} \times 2\pi$$

$$= \frac{\lambda}{2\lambda} \times 2\pi = \pi \text{ rad}$$

09. (d) According to question diagram is shown as

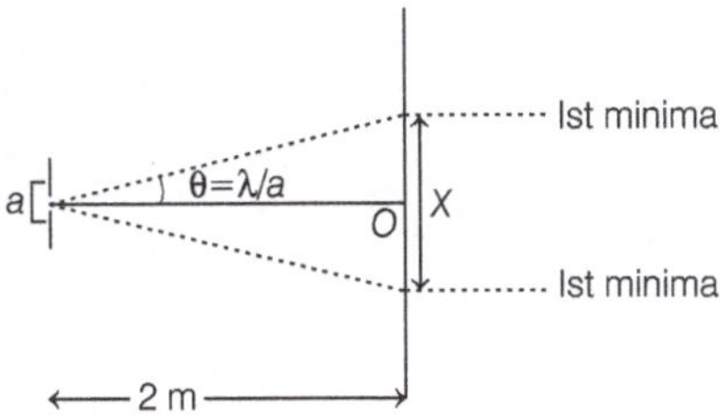

$$\tan\theta = \frac{x/2}{2}$$

For small θ and when θ is counted in rad, $\tan\theta \approx \theta$

So, $\theta = \frac{x/2}{2}$

$\Rightarrow$ $\frac{\lambda}{a} = \frac{x}{4}$

$\Rightarrow$ $x = \frac{4\lambda}{a} = \frac{4 \times 600 \times 10^{-9}}{10^{-3}}$

$= 24 \times 10^{-4}$ m

$= 2.4 \times 10^{-3}$ m

$= 2.4$ mm

10. (d) Here, $\lambda = 5000$ Å

$= 5000 \times 10^{-10}$ m

$D = 10 \text{ cm} = 10 \times 10^{-2}$ m

The angular resolution,

$$\Delta\theta = \frac{1.22\lambda}{D}$$

$$= \frac{1.22 \times 5000 \times 10^{-10}}{0.1}$$

$$= 6.1 \times 10^{-6} \simeq 10^{-6} \text{ rad}$$

11. (c) Angular resolution of telescope

$$d\theta = 1.22\frac{\lambda}{D}$$

$$= 1.22 \times \frac{5000 \times 10^{-8}}{10}$$

$$x = d\theta \times d$$

$$= \frac{1.22 \times 5000 \times 10^{-8} \times 10^5}{10}$$

$$= 6.1 \times 10^{-1} \text{ cm} \simeq 5 \text{ mm}$$

12. (c) Here, $d = 2 \text{ mm} = 2 \times 10^{-1}$ cm

$\lambda = 5000 \text{ Å} = 5000 \times 10^{-8}$ cm

Resolving power of eye lens

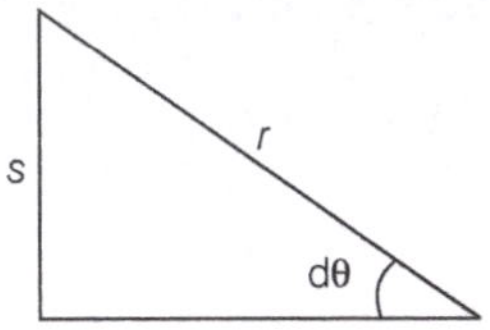

$$= \frac{d}{\lambda} = \frac{2 \times 10^{-1}}{5000 \times 10^{-8}} = \frac{1}{d\theta}$$

Let s be the minimum distance between two points, so that it may be resolved.

$\therefore$ $s = r\,d\theta$.

Here $r = 50 \text{ m} = 5000$ cm

$$\therefore \quad s = 5000 \times \frac{5000 \times 10^{-8}}{2 \times 10^{-1}}$$

$= 1.25$ cm

Topic 4

01. (c) When YDSE is performed in white light instead of monochromatic light, all wavelengths shows their maxima and minima in order of their wavelength. Thus a central bright is observed along with few fringes that will be different colours.

02. (b) Given, refractive index of glass surface

$$\mu = \sqrt{3}$$

Angle of incidence, $i = 60°$

Since, above situation follows Brewster's law because,

$$\mu = \tan i = \tan 60° = \sqrt{3}$$

Hence, angle i is equal to polarising angle i_p.

i.e., $i_p = i = 60°$

By snell's law $\mu = \frac{\sin i_p}{\sin r}$

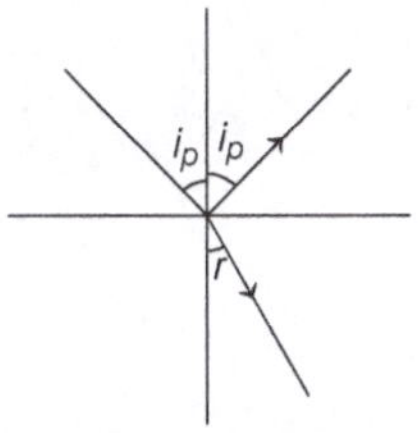

$\Rightarrow$ $\tan i_p = \frac{\sin i_p}{\sin r}$

[Since, $\mu = \tan i_p$]

$\Rightarrow$ $\frac{\sin i_p}{\cos i_p} = \frac{\sin i_p}{\sin r}$

$\Rightarrow$ $\cos i_p = \sin r$

$\Rightarrow$ $\cos i_p = \cos(90° - r)$

$\Rightarrow$ $i_p = 90° - r \Rightarrow r + i_p = 90°$

Hence, angle between the refracted and reflected rays

$= 180° - (r + i_p)$

$= 180° - (90°) = 90°$

It is also called Brewster's law.

03. (b) The Brewster's angle i_b for an interface should lies between 45° to 90°, i.e. $45° < i_b < 90°$.

Hence, correct option is (b).

04. (b) The figure shown below represents the course of path an unpolarised light follows when it is incident from air on plane surface of material of refractive index μ.

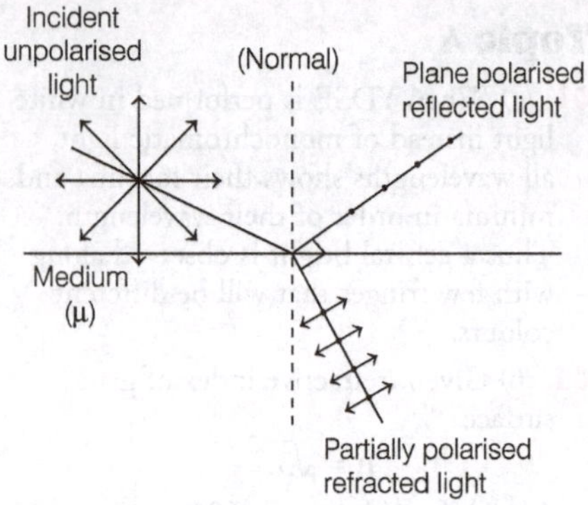

When the beam of unpolarised light is reflected from a medium (refractive index = μ) and if reflected and refracted light are perpendicular to each other. Then, the reflected light is completely plane polarised at a certain angle of incidence.

This means, the reflected light has electric vector perpendicular to incidence plane.

05. *(c)* According to the question,

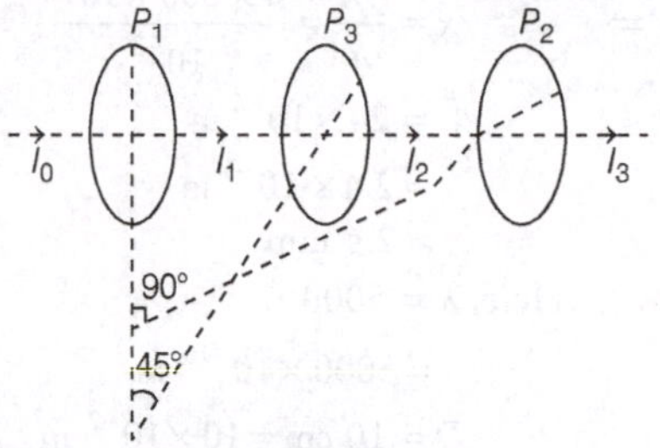

From the above diagram, intensity transmitted through P_3

$$I_2 = \frac{I_0}{2}\cos^2 45°$$

$$\Rightarrow \quad I_2 = \frac{I_0}{2} \times \left(\frac{1}{\sqrt{2}}\right)^2$$

$$\Rightarrow \quad I_2 = \frac{I_0}{4}$$

Similarly, intensity transmitted through P_2,

$$I_3 = \frac{I_0}{4}\cos^2 45°$$

$$\Rightarrow \quad I_3 = \frac{I_0}{4} \times \left(\frac{1}{\sqrt{2}}\right)^2$$

$$\Rightarrow \quad I_3 = \frac{I_0}{4} \times \frac{1}{2}$$

$$\Rightarrow \quad I_3 = \frac{I_0}{8}$$

06. *(d)* Sound waves can not be polarised as they are longitudinal. Light waves can be polarised as they are transverse.

C-25

NEET Chapterwise Topicwise Physics

In NEET 2024, 2 question was visible from this chapter. In past 5 years, 3 questions from topic-1, 2 question from topic-2 and 6 questions from topic-3 were asked.
For detailed analysis scan QR code

DUAL NATURE OF RADIATION AND MATTER

Topic 1 Photoelectric Effect & Einstein's Photoelectric Equation

01 The work functions of Caesium (Cs), Potassium (K) and Sodium (Na) are 2.14 eV, 2.30 eV and 2.75 eV respectively. If incident electromagnetic radiation has an incident energy of 2.20 eV. Which of these photosensitive surfaces may emit photoelectrons? ***[NEET 2023]***

(a) Both Na and K (b) K only
(c) Na only (d) Cs only

02 When two monochromatic lights of frequency, ν and $\nu/2$ are incident on a photoelectric metal, their stopping potential becomes $V_s/2$ and V_s, respectively. The threshold frequency for this metal is : ***[NCERT (New) Pg. 281, NEET 2022]***

(a) 3ν (b) $\frac{2}{3}\nu$ (c) $\frac{3}{2}\nu$ (d) 2ν

03 Light of frequency 1.5 times the threshold frequency is incident on a photosensitive material. What will be the photoelectric current if the frequency is halved and intensity is doubled? ***[NEET (Sep.) 2020]***

(a) Four times (b) One-fourth
(c) Zero (d) Doubled

04 The work function of a photosensitive material is 4.0 eV. This longest wavelength of light that can cause photon emission from the substance is (approximately) ***[NCERT (New) Pg. 281, NEET (Odisha) 2019]***

(a) 3100 nm (b) 966 nm (c) 31 nm (d) 310 nm

05 When the light of frequency $2\nu_0$ (where, ν_0 is threshold frequency), is incident on a metal plate, the maximum velocity of electrons emitted is v_1. When the frequency of the incident radiation is increased to $5\nu_0$, the maximum velocity of electrons emitted from the same plate is v_2. The ratio of v_1 to v_2 is ***[NCERT (New) Pg. 281, NEET 2018]***

(a) 4 : 1 (b) 1 : 4
(c) 1 : 2 (d) 2 : 1

06 The photoelectric threshold wavelength of silver is 3250×10^{-10} m. The velocity of the electron ejected from a silver surface by ultraviolet light of wavelength 2536×10^{-10} m is (Given, $h = 4.14 \times 10^{-15}$ eVs and $c = 3 \times 10^8$ ms^{-1}) ***[NEET 2017]***

(a) $\approx 6 \times 10^5$ ms^{-1} (b) $\approx 0.6 \times 10^6$ ms^{-1}
(c) $\approx 61 \times 10^3$ ms^{-1} (d) $\approx 0.3 \times 10^6$ ms^{-1}

07 When a metallic surface is illuminated with radiation of wavelength λ, the stopping potential is V. If the same surface is illuminated with radiation of wavelength 2λ, the stopping potential is $V/4$. The threshold wavelength for the metallic surface is ***[NCERT (New) Pg. 281, NEET 2016]***

(a) 5λ (b) $\frac{5}{2}\lambda$
(c) 3λ (d) 4λ

08 Photons with energy 5 eV are incident on a cathode C in a photoelectric cell. The maximum energy of emitted photoelectrons is 2 eV. When photons of energy 6 eV are incident on C, no photoelectrons will reach the anode A, if the stopping potential of A relative to C is ***[NCERT (New) Pg. 281, NEET 2016]***

(a) + 3 V (b) + 4 V
(c) − 1 V (d) − 3 V

09 A certain metallic surface is illuminated with monochromatic light of wavelength λ. The stopping potential for photoelectric current for this light is $3V_0$. If the same surface is illuminated with light of wavelength 2λ, the stopping potential is V_0. The threshold wavelength for this surface for photoelectric effect is ***[AIPMT 2015]***

(a) 6λ (b) 4λ (c) $\lambda/4$ (d) $\lambda/6$

10 A photoelectric surface is illuminated successively by monochromatic light of wavelength λ and $\lambda/2$. If the maximum kinetic energy of the emitted photoelectrons in the second case is 3 times that in the first case, the work function of the surface of the material is *[NCERT (New) Pg. 281, AIPMT 2015]*
(h = Planck's constant, c = speed of light)
(a) $\frac{hc}{2\lambda}$ (b) $\frac{hc}{\lambda}$ (c) $\frac{2hc}{\lambda}$ (d) $\frac{hc}{3\lambda}$

11 When the energy of the incident radiation is increased by 20%, the kinetic energy of the photoelectrons emitted from a metal surface increased from 0.5 eV to 0.8 eV. The work function of the metal is *[AIPMT 2014]*
(a) 0.65 eV (b) 1.0 eV (c) 1.3 eV (d) 1.5 eV

12 For photoelectric emission from certain metal, the cut-off frequency is ν. If radiation of frequency 2ν impinges on the metal plate, the maximum possible velocity of the emitted electron will be (m is the electron mass) *[NCERT (New) Pg. 281, NEET 2013]*
(a) $\sqrt{\frac{h\nu}{(2m)}}$ (b) $\sqrt{\frac{h\nu}{m}}$ (c) $\sqrt{\frac{2h\nu}{m}}$ (d) $2\sqrt{\frac{h\nu}{m}}$

13 A source of light is placed at a distance of 50 cm from a photo cell and the stopping potential is found to be V_0. If the distance between the light source and photo cell is made 25 cm, the new stopping potential will be *[NEET 2013]*
(a) $V_0/2$ (b) V_0 (c) $4V_0$ (d) $2V_0$

14 The threshold frequency for a photosensitive metal is 3.3×10^{14} Hz. If light of frequency 8.2×10^{14} Hz is incident on this metal, the cut-off voltage for the photoelectron emission is nearly *[AIPMT 2011]*
(a) 1 V (b) 2 V
(c) 3 V (d) 4 V

15 Light of two different frequencies whose photons have energies 1 eV and 2.5 eV respectively illuminate a metallic surface whose work function is 0.5 eV successively. Ratio of maximum speeds of emitted electrons will be *[NCERT (New) Pg. 281, AIPMT 2011]*
(a) 1 : 2 (b) 1 : 1
(c) 1 : 5 (d) 1 : 4

16 Photoelectric emission occurs only when the incident light has more than a certain minimum *[AIPMT 2011]*
(a) wavelength (b) intensity
(c) frequency (d) power

17 In photoelectric emission process from a metal of work function 1.8 eV the kinetic energy of most energetic electrons is 0.5 eV. The corresponding stopping potential is *[NCERT (New) Pg. 279, AIPMT 2011]*
(a) 1.3 V (b) 0.5 V
(c) 2.3 V (d) 1.8 V

18 When monochromatic radiation of intensity I falls on a metal surface, the number of photoelectrons and their maximum kinetic energy are N and T respectively. If the intensity of radiation is $2I$, the number of emitted electrons and their maximum kinetic energy are respectively *[AIPMT 2010]*
(a) N and $2T$ (b) $2N$ and T
(c) $2N$ and $2T$ (d) N and T

19 The potential difference that must be applied to stop the fastest photoelectrons emitted by a nickel surface, having work function 5.01 eV, when ultraviolet light of 200 nm falls on it, must be *[AIPMT 2010]*
(a) 2.4 V (b) –1.2 V
(c) –2.4 V (d) 1.2 V

20 The number of photoelectrons emitted for light of a frequency ν (higher than the threshold frequency ν_0) is proportional to *[NCERT (New) Pg. 278, AIPMT 2009]*
(a) $\nu - \nu_0$ (b) threshold frequency (ν_0)
(c) intensity of light (d) frequency of light (ν)

21 The figure shows a plot of photocurrent *versus* anode potential for a photo sensitive surface for three different radiations. Which one of the following is a correct statement ? *[AIPMT 2009]*

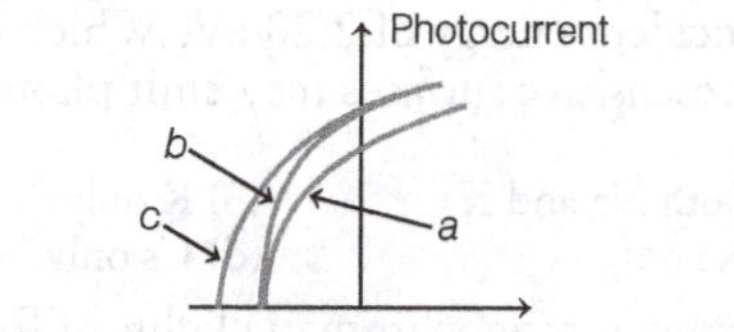

(a) Curves a and b represent incident radiations of different frequencies and different intensities
(b) Curves a and b represent incident radiations of same frequency but of different intensities
(c) Curves b and c represent incident radiations of different frequencies and different intensities
(d) Curves b and c represent incident radiations of same frequency having same intensity

22 In the phenomenon of electric discharge through gases at low pressure, the coloured glow in the tube appears as a result of *[AIPMT 2008]*
(a) excitation of electrons in the atoms
(b) collision between the atoms of the gas
(c) collisions between the charged particles emitted from the cathode and the atoms of the gas
(d) collision between different electrons of the atoms of the gas

23 The work function of a surface of a photosensitive material is 6.2 eV. The wavelength of the incident radiation for which the stopping potential is 5 V lies in the *[NCERT (New) Pg. 281, AIPMT 2008]*
(a) ultraviolet region (b) visible region
(c) infrared region (d) X-ray region

24 A 5 W source emits monochromatic light of wavelength 5000 Å. When placed 0.5 m away, it liberates photoelectrons from a photosensitive metallic surface. When the source is moved to a distance of 1.0 m, the number of photoelectrons liberated will be reduced by a factor of *[AIPMT 2007]*
(a) 4 (b) 8 (c) 16 (d) 2

25 A photocell employs photoelectric effect to convert *[NCERT (New) Pg. 278, AIPMT 2006]*
(a) change in the frequency of light into a change in electric voltage
(b) change in the intensity of illumination into a change in photoelectric current
(c) change in the intensity of illumination into a change in the work function of the photocathode
(d) change in the frequency of light into a change in the electric current

26 A photosensitive metallic surface has work function, $h\nu_0$. If photons of energy $2h\nu_0$ fall on this surface, the electrons come out with a maximum velocity of 4×10^6 m/s. When the photon energy is increased to $5h\nu_0$, then maximum velocity of photoelectrons will be *[AIPMT 2005]*
(a) 2×10^6 m/s (b) 2×10^7 m/s
(c) 8×10^5 m/s (d) 8×10^6 m/s

27 The work functions for metals *A*, *B* and *C* are respectively 1.92 eV, 2.0 eV and 5 eV. According to Einstein's equation, the metals which will emit photoelectrons for a radiation of wavelength 4100 Å is/are *[NCERT (New) Pg. 275, AIPMT 2005]*
(a) None of these (b) *A* only
(c) *A* and *B* only (d) All the three metals

28 According to Einstein's photoelectric equation, the graph between the kinetic energy of photoelectrons ejected and the frequency of incident radiation is *[NCERT (New) Pg. 281, AIPMT 2004]*

(a) 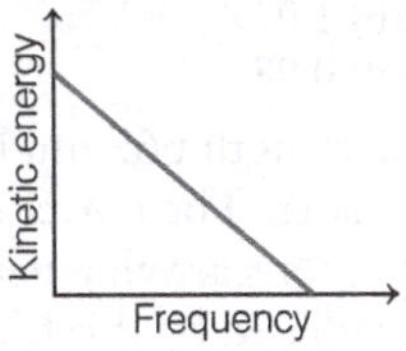

(b) 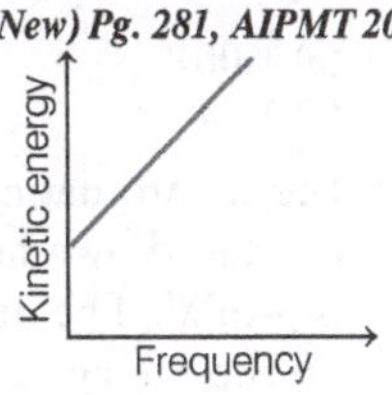

(c) 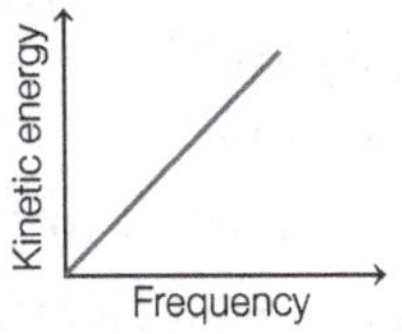

(d) 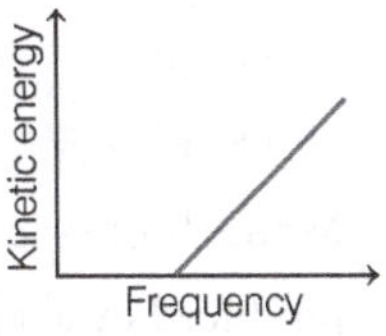

29 A photoelectric cell is illuminated by a point source of light 1 m away. When the source is shifted to 2 m, then *[NCERT (New) Pg. 278, AIPMT 2003]*
(a) each emitted electron carries half the initial energy
(b) number of electrons emitted is a quarter of the initial number
(c) each emitted electron carries one quarter of the initial energy
(d) number of electrons emitted is half the initial number

30 The value of Planck's constant is *[AIPMT 2002]*
(a) 6.63×10^{-34} J/s (b) 6.63×10^{-34} kg m^2/s
(c) 6.63×10^{-34} kg m^2 (d) 6.63×10^{-34} J s

31 When ultraviolet rays are incident on metal plate, the photoelectric effect does not occur. It occurs by incidence of *[AIPMT 2002]*
(a) infrared rays (b) X-rays
(c) radiowaves (d) light waves

32 Which of the following is not the property of cathode rays? *[AIPMT 2002]*
(a) It produces heating effect
(b) It does not deflect in electric field
(c) Its casts shadow
(d) It produces fluorescence

33 A light source is at a distance *d* from a photoelectric cell, then the number of photoelectrons emitted from the cell is *n*. If the distance of light source and cell is reduced to half, then the number of photoelectrons emitted will become *[AIPMT 2001]*
(a) $\frac{n}{2}$ (b) $2n$ (c) $4n$ (d) n

34 Einstein's work on photoelectric effect gives support to *[NCERT (New) Pg. 281, AIPMT 2000]*
(a) $E = mc^2$ (b) $E = h\nu$
(c) $h\nu = \frac{1}{2}mv^2$ (d) $E = \frac{h}{\lambda}$

35 When intensity of incident light increases *[AIPMT 1999]*
(a) photocurrent increases
(b) photocurrent decreases
(c) kinetic energy of emitted photoelectrons increases
(d) kinetic energy of emitted photoelectrons decreases

36 The photoelectric work function for a metal surface is 4.125 eV. The cut-off wavelength for this surface is *[NCERT (New) Pg. 281, AIPMT 1999]*
(a) 4125 Å (b) 3000 Å (c) 6000 Å (d) 2062.5 Å

37 In a photoemissive cell, with exciting wavelength λ, the fastest electron has speed v. If the exciting wavelength is changed to $3\lambda/4$, the speed of the fastest emitted electron will be *[AIPMT 1998]*
(a) $v\left(\frac{3}{4}\right)^{1/2}$ (b) $v\left(\frac{4}{3}\right)^{1/2}$
(c) less than $v\left(\frac{4}{3}\right)^{1/2}$ (d) greater than $v\left(\frac{4}{3}\right)^{1/2}$

38 Light of wavelength 5000 Å falls on a sensitive plate with photoelectric work function of 1.9 eV. The kinetic energy of the photoelectron emitted will be *[NCERT (New) Pg. 400, AIPMT 1998]*
(a) 0.58 eV (b) 2.48 eV (c) 1.24 eV (d) 1.16 eV

39 Which of the following is true? *[AIPMT 1997]*
(a) The stopping potential increases with increasing intensity of incident light
(b) The photocurrent increases with increasing intensity of light
(c) The current in photocell increases with increasing frequency of light
(d) The photocurrent is proportional to applied voltage

40 If the threshold wavelength for a certain metal is 2000 Å, then the work function of the metal is *[AIPMT 1995]*
(a) 6.2 J (b) 6.2 eV (c) 6.2 MeV (d) 6.2 keV

41 In photoelectric effect, the work function of a metal is 3.5 eV. The emitted electrons can be stopped by applying a potential of – 1.2 V. Then, *[AIPMT 1994]*
(a) the energy of the incident photons is 4.7 eV
(b) the energy of the incident photons is 2.3 eV
(c) if higher frequency photons be used, the photoelectric current will rise
(d) when the energy of photons is 3.5 eV, the photoelectric current will be maximum

42 Number of ejected photoelectron increases with increase *[NCERT (New) Pg. 278, AIPMT 1993]*
(a) in intensity of light
(b) in wavelength of light
(c) in frequency of light
(d) Never

43 The cathode of a photoelectric cell is changed such that the work function changes from W_1 to W_2 ($W_2 > W_1$). If the current before and after changes are I_1 and I_2, all other conditions remaining unchanged, then (assuming $h\nu > W_2$) *[AIPMT 1992]*
(a) $I_1 = I_2$ (b) $I_1 < I_2$
(c) $I_1 > I_2$ (d) $I_1 < I_2 < 2I_1$

44 Photoelectric work function of a metal is 1 eV, light of wavelength $\lambda = 3000$ Å falls on it. The photoelectrons come out with velocity *[AIPMT 1991]*
(a) 10 m/s (b) 10^2 m/s
(c) 10^4 m/s (d) 10^6 m/s

45 Ultraviolet radiation of 6.2 eV falls on an aluminium surface. KE of fastest electron emitted is (work function = 4.2 eV) *[NCERT (New) Pg. 281, AIPMT 1989]*
(a) 3.2×10^{-21} J (b) 3.2×10^{-19} J
(c) 7×10^{-25} J (d) 9×10^{-32} J

46 The threshold frequency for photoelectric effect on sodium corresponds to a wavelength of 5000 Å. Its work function is *[NCERT (New) Pg. 279, AIPMT 1988]*
(a) 4×10^{-19} J (b) 1 J
(c) 2×10^{-19} J (d) 3×10^{-19} J

47 Which of the following are thermions? *[AIPMT 1988]*
(a) Protons (b) Electrons
(c) Photons (d) Positrons

Topic 2 Particle Nature of Light-The Photon

01 If c is the velocity of light in free space, the correct statements about photon among the following are: *[NCERT (New) Pg. 283, NEET 2024]*
A. The energy of a photon is $E = h\nu$.
B. The velocity of a photon is c.
C. The momentum of a photon, $p = \frac{h\nu}{c}$
D. In a photon-electron collision, both total energy and total momentum are conserved.
E. Photon possesses positive charge.
Choose the correct answer from the options given below:
(a) A and B only (b) A, B, C and D only
(c) A, C and D only (d) A, B, D and E only

02 The number of photons per second on average emitted by the source of monochromatic light of wavelength 600 nm, when it delivers the power of 3.3×10^{-3} W will be ($h = 6.6 \times 10^{-34}$ J-s) *[NCERT (New) Pg. 283, NEET 2021]*
(a) 10^{18} (b) 10^{17}
(c) 10^{16} (d) 10^{15}

03 A 200 W sodium street lamp emits yellow light of wavelength 0.6 µm. Assuming it to be 25% efficient in converting electrical energy to light, the number of photons of yellow light it emits per second is *[AIPMT 2012]*
(a) 1.5×10^{20} (b) 6×10^{18}
(c) 62×10^{20} (d) 3×10^{19}

04 A source S_1 is producing, 10^{15} photons/s of wavelength 5000 Å. Another source S_2 is producing 1.02×10^{15} photons per second of wavelength 5100 Å. Then, (power of S_2)/ (power of S_1) is equal to *[NCERT (New) Pg. 283, AIPMT 2010]*
(a) 1.00 (b) 1.02
(c) 1.04 (d) 0.98

05 Monochromatic light of wavelength 667 nm is produced by a helium neon laser. The power emitted is 9 mW. The number of photons arriving per second on the average at a target irradiated by this beam is *[AIPMT 2009]*
(a) 9×10^{17} (b) 3×10^{16}
(c) 9×10^{15} (d) 3×10^{19}

06 Monochromatic light of frequency 6.0×10^{14} Hz is produced by a laser. The power emitted is 2×10^{-3} W. The number of photons emitted, on the average, by the source per second is *[AIPMT 2007]*
(a) 5×10^{15} (b) 5×10^{16}
(c) 5×10^{17} (d) 5×10^{14}

07 The momentum of a photon of energy 1 MeV in kg m/s, will be *[NCERT (New) Pg. 285, AIPMT 2006]*
(a) 0.33×10^{6} (b) 7×10^{-24}
(c) 10^{-22} (d) 5×10^{-22}

08 Which one among the following shows particle nature of light? *[NCERT (New) Pg. 281, AIPMT 2001]*
(a) Photoelectric effect (b) Interference
(c) Refraction (d) Polarization

09 The 21 cm radiowave emitted by hydrogen in interstelar space is due to the interaction called the hyperfine interaction in atomic hydrogen. The energy of the emitted wave is nearly *[AIPMT 1998]*
(a) 10^{-17} J (b) 1 J
(c) 7×10^{-6} J (d) 10^{-24} J

10 The velocity of photons is proportional to (where ν = frequency) *[AIPMT 1996]*
(a) $1/\sqrt{\nu}$ (b) ν^2
(c) ν (d) $\sqrt{\nu}$

11 The nature of ions knocked out from hot surfaces is *[AIPMT 1995]*
(a) protons (b) electrons
(c) neutrons (d) nuclei

12 Momentum of a photon of wavelength λ is *[NCERT (New) Pg. 285, AIPMT 1993]*
(a) $\frac{h}{\lambda}$ (b) zero
(c) $\frac{h\lambda}{c^2}$ (d) $\frac{h\lambda}{c}$

13 The wavelength of a 1 keV photon is 1.24×10^{-9} m. What is the frequency of 1 MeV photon? *[AIPMT 1991]*
(a) 1.24×10^{15} Hz (b) 2.4×10^{20} Hz
(c) 1.24×10^{18} Hz (d) 2.4×10^{23} Hz

14 The momentum of a photon of an electro- magnetic radiation is 3.3×10^{-29} kg-ms^{-1}. What is the frequency of the associated waves? *[AIPMT 1990]*
($h = 6.6\times10^{-34}$ J-s, $c = 3\times10^{8}$ ms^{-1})
(a) 1.5×10^{13} Hz (b) 7.5×10^{12} Hz
(c) 6.0×10^{13} Hz (d) 3.0×10^{3} Hz

15 A radio transmitter operates at a frequency 880 kHz and a power of 10 kW. The number of photons emitted per second is *[NCERT (New) Pg. 283, AIPMT 1990]*
(a) 1.72×10^{31} (b) 1.327×10^{25}
(c) 1.327×10^{37} (d) 1.327×10^{45}

16 The energy of a photon of wavelength λ is *[NCERT (New) Pg. 285, AIPMT 1988]*
(a) $hc\lambda$ (b) $\frac{hc}{\lambda}$
(c) $\frac{\lambda}{hc}$ (d) $\frac{\lambda h}{c}$

Topic 3 Matter Wave and Davisson-Germer Experiment

01 The graph which shows the variation of $\frac{1}{\lambda^2}$ and its kinetic energy, E is (where, λ is de-Broglie wavelength of a free particle): *[NCERT (New) Pg. 285, NEET 2024]*

(a) 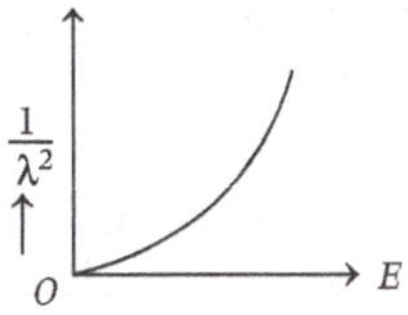

(b) 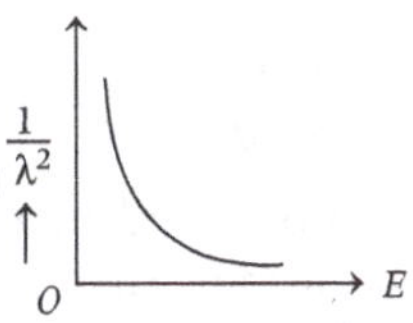

(c) 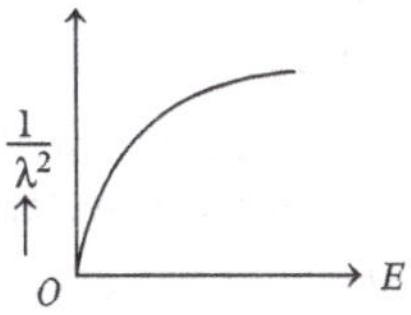

(d) 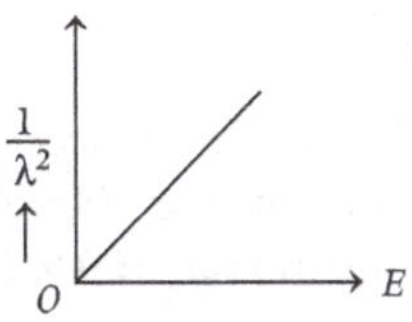

02 The graph which shows the variation of the de-Broglie wavelength λ of a particle and its associated momentum p is *[NEET 2022]*

(a) 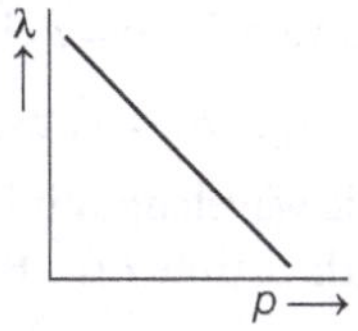

(b) 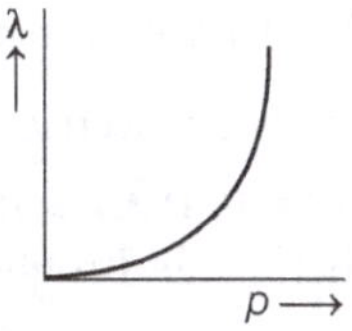

(c) 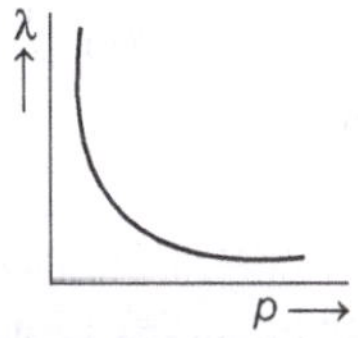

(d) 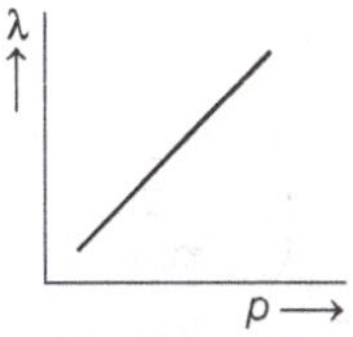

03 An electromagnetic wave of wavelength λ is incident on a photosensitive surface of negligible work function. If m mass is of photoelectron emitted from the surface has de-Broglie wavelength λ_d, then *[NCERT (New) Pg. 285, NEET 2021]*
(a) $\lambda = \left(\frac{2h}{mc}\right)\lambda_d^2$ (b) $\lambda = \left(\frac{2m}{hc}\right)\lambda_d^2$
(c) $\lambda = \left(\frac{2mc}{h}\right)\lambda^2$ (d) $\lambda = \left(\frac{2mc}{h}\right)\lambda_d^2$

04 The de-Broglie wavelength of an electron moving with kinetic energy of 144 eV is nearly *[NEET (Oct.) 2020]*
(a) 102×10^{-3} nm
(b) 102×10^{-4} nm
(c) 102×10^{-5} nm
(d) 102×10^{-2} nm

05 The wave nature of electrons was experimentally verified by *[NEET (Oct.) 2020]*
(a) de-Broglie (b) Hertz
(c) Einstein (d) Davisson and Germer

06 An electron is accelerated from rest through a potential difference of V volt. If the de-Broglie wavelength of the electron is 1.227×10^{-2} nm, the potential difference is *[NCERT (New) Pg. 400, NEET (Sep.) 2020]*
(a) 10^2 V (b) 10^3 V
(c) 10^4 V (d) 10 V

07 A proton and an α-particle are accelerated from rest to the same energy. The de-Broglie wavelengths λ_p and λ_α are in the ratio *[NEET (Odisha) 2019]*
(a) 2:1 (b) 1:1
(c) $\sqrt{2}:1$ (d) 4:1

08 An electron is accelerated through a potential difference of 10000 V. Its de-Broglie wavelength is (nearly) $(m_e = 9 \times 10^{-31}$ kg) *[NCERT (Old) Pg. 400, NEET (National) 2019]*
(a) 12.2×10^{-12} m (b) 12.2×10^{-14} m
(c) 12.2 nm (d) 12.2×10^{-13} m

09 An electron of mass m with a velocity $\mathbf{v} = v_0\hat{\mathbf{i}}\ (v_0 > 0)$ enters an electric field $\mathbf{E} = -E_0\hat{\mathbf{i}}\ (E_0 = \text{constant} > 0)$ at $t = 0$. If λ_0 is its de-Broglie wavelength initially, then its de-Broglie wavelength at time t is *[NEET 2018]*
(a) $\lambda_0 t$ (b) $\lambda_0\left(1 + \frac{eE_0}{mv_0}t\right)$
(c) $\frac{\lambda_0}{\left(1 + \frac{eE_0}{mv_0}t\right)}$ (d) λ_0

10 The de-Broglie wavelength of a neutron in thermal equilibrium with heavy water at a temperature T (Kelvin) and mass m, is *[NEET 2017]*
(a) $\frac{h}{\sqrt{mkT}}$ (b) $\frac{h}{\sqrt{3mkT}}$
(c) $\frac{2h}{\sqrt{3mkT}}$ (d) $\frac{2h}{\sqrt{mkT}}$

11 An electron of mass m and a photon have same energy E. The ratio of de-Broglie wavelengths associated with them is *[NCERT (Old) Pg. 400, NEET 2016]*
(a) $\left(\frac{E}{2m}\right)^{\frac{1}{2}}$ (b) $c(2mE)^{\frac{1}{2}}$
(c) $\frac{1}{c}\left(\frac{2m}{E}\right)^{\frac{1}{2}}$ (d) $\frac{1}{c}\left(\frac{E}{2m}\right)^{\frac{1}{2}}$
(c being velocity of light)

12 Electrons of mass m with de-Broglie wavelength λ fall on the target in an X-ray tube. The cut-off wavelength λ_0 of the emitted X-ray is *[NEET 2016]*
(a) $\lambda_0 = \frac{2mc\lambda^2}{h}$ (b) $\lambda_0 = \frac{2h}{mc}$
(c) $\lambda_0 = \frac{2m^2c^2\lambda^3}{h^2}$ (d) $\lambda_0 = \lambda$

13 Which of the following figures represent the variation of particle momentum and the associated de-Broglie wavelength? *[NCERT (New) Pg. 285, AIPMT 2015]*
(a) 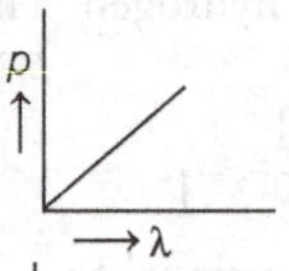

(b) 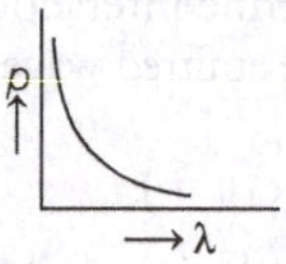

(c) 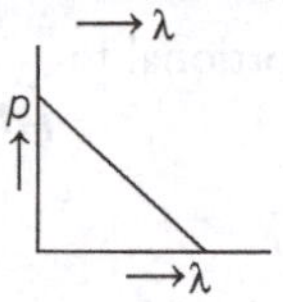

(d) 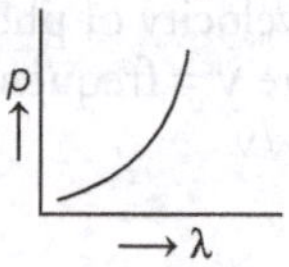

14 Light of wavelength 500 nm is incident on a metal with work function 2.28 eV. The de-Broglie wavelength of the emitted electron is *[AIPMT 2015]*
(a) $\geq 2.8 \times 10^{-9}$ m (b) $\leq 2.8 \times 10^{-12}$ m
(c) $< 2.8 \times 10^{-10}$ m (d) $< 2.8 \times 10^{-9}$ m

15 If the kinetic energy of the particle is increased to 16 times its previous value, the percentage change in the de-Broglie wavelength of the particle is *[AIPMT 2014]*
(a) 25 (b) 75 (c) 60 (d) 50

16 The wavelength λ_e of an electron and λ_p of a photon of same energy E are related by *[NEET 2013]*
(a) $\lambda_p \propto \lambda_e^2$ (b) $\lambda_p \propto \lambda_e$
(c) $\lambda_p \propto \sqrt{\lambda_e}$ (d) $\lambda_p \propto \frac{1}{\sqrt{\lambda_e}}$

17 An α-particle moves in a circular path of radius 0.83 cm in the presence of a magnetic field of 0.25 Wb/m^2. The de-Broglie wavelength associated with the particle will be *[AIPMT 2012]*
(a) 1 Å (b) 0.1 Å (c) 10 Å (d) 0.01 Å

18 If the momentum of an electron is changed by p, then the de-Broglie wavelength associated with it changes by 0.5%. The initial momentum of electron will be *[NCERT (New) Pg. 285, AIPMT 2012]*
(a) 200 P (b) 400 P
(c) P/200 (d) 100 P

19 Electrons used in an electron microscope are accelerated by a voltage of 25 kV. If the voltage is increased to 100 kV then the de-Broglie wavelength associated with the electrons would *[AIPMT 2011]*
(a) increase by 2 times (b) decrease by 2 times
(c) decrease by 4 times (d) increase by 4 times

20 A particle of mass 1 mg has the same wavelength as an electron moving with a velocity of 3×10^{6} ms^{-1}. The velocity of the particle is (mass of electron = 9.1×10^{-31} kg) *[AIPMT 2008]*
(a) 2.7×10^{-18} ms^{-1} (b) 9×10^{-2} ms^{-1}
(c) 3×10^{-31} ms^{-1} (d) 2.7×10^{-21} ms^{-1}

21 The following particles are moving with the same velocity, then maximum de-Broglie wavelength will be for *[NCERT (New) Pg. 282, AIPMT 2002]*
(a) proton (b) α-particle
(c) neutron (d) β-particle

22 The energy of a photon of light is 3 eV. Then the wavelength of photon must be *[AIPMT 2000]*
(a) 4125 nm (b) 412.5 nm
(c) 41250 nm (d) 4 nm

23 The wavelength associated with an electron, accelerated through a potential difference of 100 V, is of the order of *[NCERT (Old) Pg. 400, AIPMT 1996]*
(a) 1000 Å (b) 100 Å (c) 10.5 Å (d) 1.2 Å

24 An electron beam has a kinetic energy equal to 100 eV. Find its wavelength associated with a beam, if mass of electron $= 9.1\times 10^{-31}$ kg and 1 eV $= 1.6\times 10^{-19}$ J. (Planck's constant $= 6.6\times 10^{-34}$ Js) *[AIPMT 1996]*
(a) 24.6 Å (b) 0.12 Å (c) 1.2 Å (d) 6.3 Å

25 The de-Broglie wave corresponding to a particle of mass m and velocity v has a wavelength associated with it *[NCERT (New) Pg. 285, AIPMT 1989]*
(a) $\frac{h}{mv}$ (b) hmv
(c) $\frac{mh}{v}$ (d) $\frac{m}{hv}$

Key Index

Topic 1

1 (d)	2 (c)	3 (c)	4 (d)	5 (c)	6 (a, b)	7 (c)	8 (d)	9 (b)	10 (a)
11 (b)	12 (c)	13 (b)	14 (b)	15 (a)	16 (c)	17 (b)	18 (b)	19 (b)	20 (c)
21 (b)	22 (c)	23 (a)	24 (a)	25 (b)	26 (d)	27 (c)	28 (d)	29 (b)	30 (d)
31 (b)	32 (b)	33 (c)	34 (b)	35 (a)	36 (b)	37 (d)	38 (a)	39 (b)	40 (b)
41 (a)	42 (a)	43 (a)	44 (d)	45 (b)	46 (a)	47 (b)			

Topic 2

1 (b)	2 (c)	3 (a)	4 (a)	5 (b)	6 (a)	7 (d)	8 (a)	9 (d)	10 (c)
11 (b)	12 (a)	13 (b)	14 (a)	15 (a)	16 (b)				

Topic 3

1 (d)	2 (c)	3 (d)	4 (d)	5 (a)	6 (c)	7 (a)	8 (a)	9 (c)	10 (b)
11 (d)	12 (a)	13 (b)	14 (a)	15 (b)	16 (a)	17 (d)	18 (a)	19 (b)	20 (a)
21 (d)	22 (b)	23 (d)	24 (c)	25 (a)					

Detailed **Explanations**

Topic 1

01. *(d)* For photoelectric emission, energy of incident electromagnetic radiation must be greater than or equal to work function of photosensitive surface. Thus, only Cs can emit photoelectron.

02. *(c)* Using Einstein's photoelectric equation,

$$eV' = h\nu' - h\nu_0$$

when $\nu' = \nu$

and $V' = V_{s/2}$, then

$$\therefore \quad \frac{eV_s}{2} = h\nu - h\nu_0 \quad \ldots\text{(i)}$$

Again when $\nu' = \dfrac{\nu}{2}$ and $V' = V_s$ then

$$\therefore \quad eV_s = \frac{h\nu}{2} - h\nu_0 \quad \ldots\text{(ii)}$$

Dividing Eq. (i) by Eq. (ii), we get

$$\frac{eV_s/2}{eV_s} = \frac{h\nu - h\nu_0}{\dfrac{h\nu}{2} - h\nu_0}$$

$$\frac{1}{2} = \frac{(\nu - \nu_0)}{\dfrac{\nu}{2} - \nu_0}$$

$$\frac{\nu}{2} - \nu_0 = 2\nu - 2\nu_0$$

$$\Rightarrow \quad \nu_0 = \frac{3}{2}\nu$$

Hence, correct option is (c).

03. *(c)* Initially, frequency of light,

$$\nu = 1.5\nu_0$$

But when the frequency of incident light is halved, then

$\nu' = \dfrac{\nu}{2} = 0.75\nu_0$. Thus, it becomes less than the threshold frequency. In that case, no photoelectric effect takes place.

Hence, photoelectric current becomes zero.

Hence, correct option is (c).

04. *(d)* The work function of material is given by

$$\phi = h\nu$$

$$\phi = \frac{hc}{\lambda} \quad \ldots\text{(i)} \quad \left[\because \nu = \frac{c}{\lambda}\right]$$

where, h = Planck's constant $= 6.63 \times 10^{-34}$ J-s

c = speed of light $= 3 \times 10^{8}\ \text{ms}^{-1}$

and λ = wavelength of light

Here, $\phi = 4\ \text{eV} = 4 \times 1.6 \times 10^{-19}$ J

Substituting the given values in Eq. (i), we get

$$\Rightarrow \quad 4 \times 1.6 \times 10^{-19} = \frac{6.63 \times 10^{-34} \times 3 \times 10^{8}}{\lambda}$$

$$\text{or} \quad \lambda = \frac{6.63 \times 10^{-34} \times 3 \times 10^{8}}{4 \times 1.6 \times 10^{-19}}$$

$$= 3.108 \times 10^{-7}\ \text{m} \simeq 310\ \text{nm}$$

05. *(c)*

key idea

For the calculation of maximum kinetic energy of emitted photoelectron, you can use Einstein's photoelectric equation given as,

$$K_{max} = h\nu - \phi_0 = \frac{hc}{\lambda} - \phi_0$$

where, symbols are their usual meaning.

According to the Einstein's photoelectric equation,

$$K_{max} = \frac{1}{2}mv_{max}^2 = hv - \phi_0$$

$$= hv - hv_0 \quad \ldots\text{(i)}$$

When incident frequency of light,

$$v = 2v_0$$

Substituting the value of ν in Eq. (i), we get

$$\frac{1}{2}mv_1^2 = h(2v_0) - hv_0$$

$$= 2hv_0 - hv_0 = hv_0 \quad \ldots\text{(ii)}$$

If incident frequency of radiation,

$$\nu = 5\nu_0$$

Substituting the value of ν in Eq. (i), we get

$$\frac{1}{2}mv_2^2 = h(5v_0) - hv_0$$

$$= 5hv_0 - hv_0 = 4hv_0 \quad \ldots\text{(iii)}$$

On dividing Eq. (ii) by Eq (iii), we get

$$\frac{\frac{1}{2}mv_1^2}{\frac{1}{2}mv_2^2} = \frac{hv_0}{4hv_0}$$

$$\Rightarrow \quad \frac{v_1^2}{v_2^2} = \frac{1}{4} \quad \text{or} \quad \frac{v_1}{v_2} = \frac{1}{2}$$

$$\therefore \quad v_1 : v_2 = 1:2$$

06. *(a, b)*

key idea

Applying Einstein's photoelectric equation, kinetic energy of emitted electron can be given by

$$\frac{1}{2}mv^2 = h\nu - h\nu_0$$

$$K = \frac{1}{2}mv^2 = h\nu - h\nu_0 = \frac{hc}{\lambda} - \frac{hc}{\lambda_0}$$

Given,

$$\lambda_0 = 3250 \times 10^{-10}\ \text{m}$$

$$\lambda = 2536 \times 10^{-10}\ \text{m}$$

Let, velocity of ejected electron be v. Now, applying Einstein's photoelectric equation, we have

$$E = K + \phi_0$$

$$\Rightarrow \quad K = E - \phi$$

$$\Rightarrow \quad \frac{1}{2}m_e v^2 = h\nu - h\nu_0$$

$$= hc\left(\frac{1}{\lambda} - \frac{1}{\lambda_0}\right)$$

$\Rightarrow$ Velocity of electron

$$v = \sqrt{\frac{2hc}{m_e}\left(\frac{1}{\lambda} - \frac{1}{\lambda_0}\right)}$$

$$= \sqrt{\frac{2 \times 4.14 \times 10^{-15} \times 1.6 \times 10^{-19} \times 3 \times 10^{8}}{9.1 \times 10^{-31}}\left(\frac{3250 - 2536}{3250 \times 2536}\right)}$$

$$\approx 0.6 \times 10^{6}\ \text{ms}^{-1} \approx 6 \times 10^{5}\ \text{ms}^{-1}$$

07. *(c)* In Ist case, when a metallic surface is illuminated with radiation of wavelength λ, the stopping potential is V.

So, photoelectric equation can be written as

$$eV = \frac{hc}{\lambda} - \frac{hc}{\lambda_0} \quad \ldots\text{(i)}$$

In IInd case, when the same surface is illuminated with radiation of wavelength 2λ, the stopping potential is $\frac{V}{4}$. So, photoelectric equation can be written as

$$\frac{eV}{4} = \frac{hc}{2\lambda} - \frac{hc}{\lambda_0}$$

$$\Rightarrow \quad eV = \frac{4hc}{2\lambda} - \frac{4hc}{\lambda_0} \quad \text{...(ii)}$$

From Eqs. (i) and (ii), we get

$$\Rightarrow \frac{hc}{\lambda} - \frac{hc}{\lambda_0} = \frac{4hc}{2\lambda} - \frac{4hc}{\lambda_0}$$

$$\Rightarrow \frac{1}{\lambda} - \frac{1}{\lambda_0} = \frac{2}{\lambda} - \frac{4}{\lambda_0}$$

$$\Rightarrow \quad \lambda_0 = 3\lambda$$

• Concept Enhancer

The stopping potential varies linearly with the frequency of incident radiation for a given photosensitive material.

08. *(d)*

key idea

Use equation of photoelectric effect, $E = (KE)_{max} + \phi$

We know that,

$$E = (KE)_{max} + \text{Work function } (\phi)$$

where, $\phi = h\nu_0$, $E = h\nu$

$$(KE)_{max} = \frac{1}{2} m v_0^2$$

$$\Rightarrow \quad (KE)_{max} = h\nu - \phi$$

$$\Rightarrow \quad 2\text{eV} = 5\text{ eV} - \phi \quad \text{(given)}$$

$$\Rightarrow \quad \phi = 3\text{ eV}$$

Thus, $V_{cathode} - V_{anode} = 3\text{ V}$

$$\Rightarrow \quad V_{anode} - V_{cathode} = -3\text{ V}$$

09. *(b)* From photoelectric equation

$$h\nu = W + eV_0$$

(where, W = work function)

So $\quad \frac{hc}{\lambda} = W + 3eV_0 \quad \text{...(i)}$

Also, $\quad \frac{hc}{2\lambda} = W + eV_0$

$$\Rightarrow \quad \frac{hc}{\lambda} = 2W + 2eV_0 \quad \text{...(ii)}$$

Subtracting Eq. (i) from Eq. (ii), we get

$$0 = W - eV_0$$

$$\Rightarrow \quad W = eV_0$$

From Eq. (i),

$$\frac{hc}{\lambda} = eV_0 + 3eV_0 = 4eV_0$$

The threshold wavelength is given by

$$\lambda_{th} = \frac{hc}{W} = \frac{4eV_0\lambda}{eV_0} = 4\lambda$$

10. *(a)* According to Einstein's photoelectric equation,

$$E = K_{max} + W$$

$$K_{max} = E - W = h\nu - W$$

$$K_{max} = \frac{hc}{\lambda} - W \quad \text{...(i)}$$

Similarly, in second case, maximum kinetic energy of emitted electron is 3 times that in first case, we get

$$3K_{max} = \frac{hc}{\frac{\lambda}{2}} - W \quad \text{...(ii)}$$

Solving Eqs. (i) and (ii), we get work function of an emitted electron from a metal surface.

$$W = \frac{hc}{2\lambda}$$

11. *(b)* For photoelectric equation, Einstein's equation can be written as

$$(KE)_{max} = h\nu - \phi_0$$

For the first condition,

$$0.5 = E - \phi_0 \quad \text{...(i)}$$

For the second condition,

$$0.8 = 1.2E - \phi_0 \quad \text{...(ii)}$$

From Eqs. (i) and (ii), we get

$$-0.3 = -0.2E$$

$$E = \frac{0.3}{0.2} = 1.5\text{ eV}$$

From Eq. (i), we get

$$0.5 = 1.5 - \phi_0$$

$$\phi_0 = 1.5 - 0.5 = 1\text{ eV}$$

12. *(c)* As we know that,

$$\frac{1}{2} m (v_{max})^2 = 2h\nu - h\nu$$

So, $\quad v_{max} = \sqrt{\frac{2h\nu}{m}}$

13. *(b)* When position of source of light from photo cell is changed then intensity of light falling on photo cell is changed.

As stopping potential is independent of the intensity of the incident light, hence stopping potential remains same i.e., V_0.

14. *(b)* We know that,

$$eV_0 = h\nu - h\nu_0$$

or $\quad V_0 = \frac{h}{e}(\nu - \nu_0)$

Substituting the given values, we get

$$V_0 = \frac{6.63 \times 10^{-34} (8.2 \times 10^{14} - 3.3 \times 10^{14})}{1.6 \times 10^{-19}}$$

$$\approx 2\text{V}$$

15. *(a)* Kinetic energy in photoelectric effect can also be written as

$$KE = \phi - \phi_0 \quad \left[\begin{array}{l}\phi = \text{incident energy} \\ \phi_0 = \text{work function}\end{array}\right]$$

Given, $KE_1 = 1 - 0.5 = 0.5$ eV

$$KE_2 = 2.5 - 0.5 = 2\text{ eV}$$

So, $\quad \frac{KE_1}{KE_2} = \frac{0.5}{2} = \frac{1}{4}$

or $\quad \frac{v_1^2}{v_2^2} = \frac{1}{4} \quad \left[\because KE = \frac{1}{2}mv^2\right]$

or $\quad \frac{v_1}{v_2} = \sqrt{\frac{1}{4}} = \frac{1}{2}$

16. *(c)* According to the concept of thresholds recency minimum frequency needed for photoelectric emission i.e.

$$KE = h\nu - \phi_0$$

or $\quad \frac{1}{2}mv^2 = h\nu - h\nu_0$

So, $\quad \nu \geq \nu_0$

17. *(b)* As we know that stopping potential gives the maximum KE of ejected electrons, so

$$KE_{max} = eV_0$$

So, $1.6 \times 10^{-19} \times V_0 = 0.5 \times 1.6 \times 10^{-19}$

$$\Rightarrow \quad V_0 = 0.5\text{ V}$$

18. *(b)* The number of photoelectrons ejected by metal surface is directly proportional to the intensity of incident light. Maximum kinetic energy is independent of intensity of incident light but depends upon the frequency of light.

19. *(b)* Given, $\lambda = 200$ nm

$$\phi_0 = 5.01\text{ eV}$$

According to Einstein's photoelectric equation

$$eV_s = h\nu - \phi_0$$

or $\quad eV_s = \frac{hc}{\lambda} - \phi_0$

$$eV_s = \frac{(1240\text{ eV nm})}{(200\text{ nm})} - 5.01\text{ eV}$$

$$= 6.2\text{ eV} - 5.01\text{ eV} = 1.2\text{ eV}$$

or $\quad V_s = 1.2$ eV

The potential difference that must be applied to stop photoelectrons

$$= -V_s = -1.2\text{ V}$$

20. *(c)* Independent of frequency (ν) of light, it only depends on the intensity of incident light. If intensity increases, number of photo electrons increases.

21. (b)

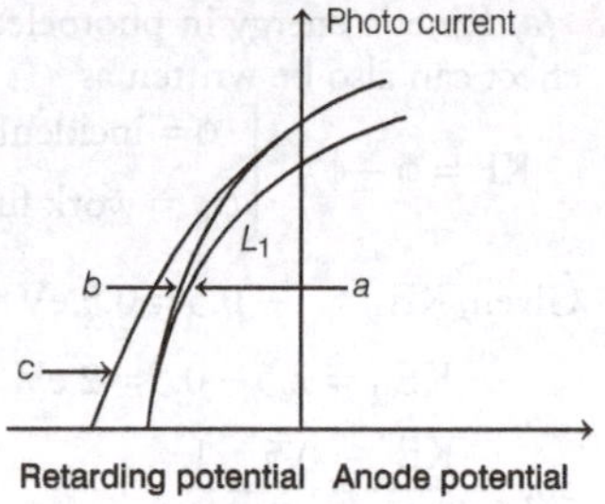

Since in the graph of retarding potential is same in graph (a) and (b) and photo current is different so, for curves they have same frequency but different intensity of light.

> • Concept **Enhancer**
>
> The value of saturation current depends on the intensity of incident radiation but is independent of the frequency of the incident radiation.
> The photoelectric emission starts instantaneously without any apparent time lag ($\sim 10^{-8}$ s), even when the incident radiation has low intensity.

22. (c) In the phenomenon of electric discharge through gases at low pressure, as the charged particles emitted from the cathode collides with the atoms of the gas, coloured glow appears in the tube.

23. (a) According to Einstein's photoelectric equation, kinetic energy of photoelectron

$$KE = h\nu - W_0$$

or $\quad h\nu = KE + W_0$

As maximum KE of ejected electrons is given by

$$KE = eV_0$$

where, V_0 is stopping potential.

$$h\nu = 5\text{ eV} + 6.2\text{ eV} \quad [\because eV_0 = 5\text{ eV}]$$
$$= 11.2\text{ eV}$$

$$\frac{hc}{\lambda} = 11.2\text{ eV} \qquad \left[\because \nu = \frac{c}{\lambda}\right]$$

$$\therefore \lambda = \frac{hc}{11.2 \times 1.6 \times 10^{-19}}$$

$$= \frac{6.62 \times 10^{-34} \times 3 \times 10^8}{11.2 \times 1.6 \times 10^{-19}} = 110\text{ nm}$$

Wavelength of visible region ranges from 380 nm-700nm.
Wavelength in infrared region ranges from 700nm-1000nm.
Wavelength of in X-ray region ranges from 0.01nm-10nm and UV region covers 100-400nm.
[Which is lies in UV region]

24 (a) Intensity of light is inversely proportional to square of distance of source

i.e. $\quad I \propto \dfrac{1}{d^2}$

For two different situations,

$$\frac{I_2}{I_1} = \frac{(d_1)^2}{(d_2)^2}$$

Given, $\quad d_1 = 0.5$ m, $d_2 = 1.0$ m

Therefore, $\dfrac{I_2}{I_1} = \dfrac{(0.5)^2}{(1)^2} = \dfrac{1}{4}$

Since number of photoelectrons emitted per second is directly proportional to intensity, so number of electrons emitted would decrease by factor of 4.

25. (b) In a photoelectric effect, it is found that the photoelectric current increases linearly with the intensity of incident light as shown in figure.

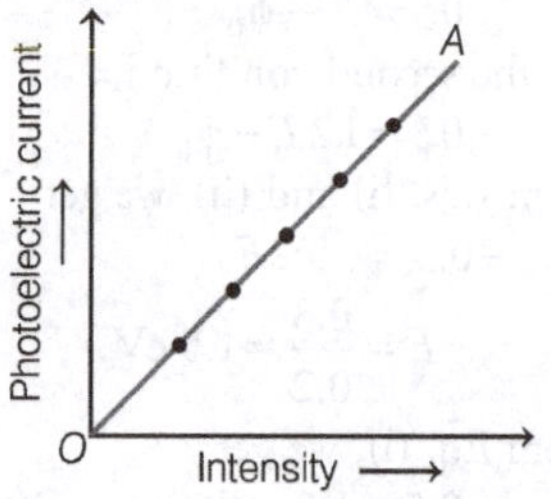

Hence, a photocell employs photoelectric effect to convert change in the intensity of illumination into a change in photoelectric current.

> • Concept **Enhancer**
>
> If we change intensity of incident radiation, then neither slope of the graph nor the y-intercept cut by graph will change.

26. (d) Einstein's photoelectric equation can be written as

$$KE = \frac{1}{2}mv^2 = h\nu - W_0$$

where, [W_0 = work function]

When photon of energy $2h\nu_0$ falls then

$$\Rightarrow \frac{1}{2}m \times (4 \times 10^6)^2 = 2h\nu_0 - h\nu_0 \quad \text{...(i)}$$

When photon of energy $5h\nu_0$ falls then

$$\frac{1}{2}m \times v^2 = 5h\nu_0 - h\nu_0 \quad \text{...(ii)}$$

Dividing Eq. (ii) by (i), we get

$$\frac{v^2}{(4 \times 10^6)^2} = \frac{4h\nu_0}{h\nu_0}$$

or $\quad v^2 = 4 \times 16 \times 10^{12}$

or $\quad v^2 = 64 \times 10^{12}$

$\therefore \quad v = 8 \times 10^6$ m/s

27. (c) Work function for wavelength of 4100 Å is given by

$$W_0 = \frac{hc}{\lambda}$$

$$= \frac{6.62 \times 10^{-34} \times 3 \times 10^8}{4100 \times 10^{-10}}$$

$$= 4.8 \times 10^{-19}\text{ J}$$

Energy in eV is given by

$$= \frac{4.8 \times 10^{-19}}{1.6 \times 10^{-19}}\text{ eV} = 3\text{ eV}$$

Now, we have

$$W_A = 1.92\text{ eV}$$
$$W_B = 2.0\text{ eV}$$
$$W_C = 5\text{ eV}$$

Since, $W_A < W$ and $W_B < W$, hence, A and B will emit photoelectrons.

28. (d) Einstein's photoelectric equation is

$$KE = h\nu - W_0 \quad \text{...(i)}$$

where,
W_0 = work function of metal, (= $h\nu_0$)
Comparing above Eq. (i) with equation of a straight line

$$y = mx + c$$

we get, $\quad m = h, c = -W_0$

Therefore, graph (d) is correct.

29. (b) Intensity of light source is inversely proportional to square of the distance (d)

i.e. $\quad I \propto \dfrac{1}{d^2}$

When distance is doubled, intensity becomes one-fourth. As number of photoelectrons ∝ intensity, so number of photoelectrons is quarter of the initial number.

30. (d) The value of Planck's constant,

$$h = 6.63 \times 10^{-34}\text{ J-s}$$

31. (b) Out of the given radiations, X-rays have wavelength less than that of ultraviolet rays. Thus, X-rays can cause photoelectric emission.

32. (b) Cathode rays are negatively charged particles called electrons. Outside the discharge tube, if an electric field is applied, the cathode rays bend towards the positive plate. Thus, (b) is right option.

33. *(c)* Intensity of light source is given by

$$I \propto \frac{1}{d^2}$$

where, d is the distance of light source from the cell.

So, for two different situations for intensities,

or $$\frac{I_1}{I_2} = \left(\frac{d_2}{d_1}\right)^2 = \left(\frac{1}{2}\right)^2 = \frac{1}{4}$$

or $$I_2 = 4I_1$$

As number of photoelectrons emitted is directly proportional to intensity, so number of photoelectrons emitted will become 4 times, i.e. 4 n.

34. *(b)* Einstein's work on photoelectric effect gives support to $E = h\nu$.

35. *(a)* According to Einstein's theory of photoelectric effect, a single incident photon ejects a single electron.

Therefore, when intensity increases, the number of incident photons increases, so number of ejected electrons increases, hence, photocurrent increases.

36. *(b)* As we know that,

$$\text{cut-off wavelength} = \frac{hc}{\text{work function}}$$

$$\therefore \quad \lambda_0 = \frac{hc}{W_0} \quad \text{...(i)}$$

Given, $h = 6.6 \times 10^{-34}$ J-s

$c = 3 \times 10^8$ m/s

$W_0 = 4.125$ eV

$= 4.125 \times 1.6 \times 10^{-19}$ J

Substituting the given values in Eq. (i), we get

$$\lambda_0 = \frac{6.6 \times 10^{-34} \times 3 \times 10^8}{4.125 \times 1.6 \times 10^{-19}} \text{ Å}$$

$$= 3 \times 10^{-7} \text{ m} = 3000 \text{ Å}$$

37. *(d)* Einstein's photoelectric equation is given by

$$\text{KE} = E - W_0$$

As we know that

$$\text{KE} = \frac{1}{2}mv^2 \text{ and } E = \frac{hc}{\lambda}$$

$$\therefore \quad \frac{1}{2}mv^2 = \frac{hc}{\lambda} - W_0 \quad \text{...(i)}$$

Suppose v' be the new speed, when λ is changed to $\frac{3\lambda}{4}$.

The new equation can be written as

$$\frac{1}{2}mv'^2 = \frac{hc}{(3\lambda/4)} - W_0$$

or $$\frac{1}{2}mv'^2 = \frac{4}{3}\frac{hc}{\lambda} - W_0 \quad \text{...(ii)}$$

Dividing Eq. (ii) by Eq. (i), we get

$$\frac{v'^2}{v^2} = \frac{\frac{4}{3}\frac{hc}{\lambda} - W_0}{\frac{hc}{\lambda} - W_0}$$

$$= \frac{\left(\frac{4}{3}\frac{hc}{\lambda} - \frac{4}{3}W_0\right) + \frac{1}{3}W_0}{\frac{hc}{\lambda} - W_0}$$

$$= \frac{4}{3} + \frac{W_0}{3\left(\frac{hc}{\lambda} - W_0\right)} > \frac{4}{3}$$

$$\therefore \quad \frac{v'}{v} > \sqrt{\frac{4}{3}} \text{ or } v' > \sqrt{\frac{4}{3}}\,v$$

38. *(a)* Energy of photon is given by

$$E = \frac{hc}{\lambda} = \frac{12375}{\lambda(\text{Å})} \text{ eV}$$

$$\therefore \quad E = \frac{12375}{5000} = 2.48 \text{ eV}$$

According to Einstein's photoelectric equation

$$\text{KE} = E - W_0$$

$$= 2.48 \text{ eV} - 1.9 \text{ eV}$$

$$= 0.58 \text{ eV}$$

39. *(b)* If intensity of incident light is increased, we can say that the number of photons incident per unit area per unit time will be increased.

Therefore, more electrons will be emitted per second.

Hence, photo-current increases. Thus, choice (b) is correct.

40. *(b)* Work function is given by

$$W_0 = h\nu_0 = \frac{hc}{\lambda_0}$$

Given wavelength,

$$\lambda_0 = 2000 \text{ Å}$$

$$= 2000 \times 10^{-10} \text{ m}$$

$$\therefore \quad W_0 = \frac{6.6 \times 10^{-34} \times 3 \times 10^8}{2000 \times 10^{-10}}$$

$$= 9.9 \times 10^{-19} \text{ J} = \frac{9.9 \times 10^{-19}}{1.6 \times 10^{-19}}$$

$$[1 \text{ eV} = 1.6 \times 10^{-19} \text{ J}]$$

$$= 6.2 \text{ eV}$$

> **Concept Enhancer**
> Maximum wavelength of incident radiation above which no emission of photoelectrons take place called threshold wavelength.

41. *(a)* When a photon of light of frequency ν is incident on a photosensitive metal surface. Then, according to Einstein's photoelectric equation

$$h\nu = W_0 + \frac{1}{2}mv^2$$

where, W_0 is work function of the metal and $\frac{1}{2}mv^2$ is KE of the photoelectron.

Given, $W_0 = 3.5$ eV, KE = 1.2 eV

$$\therefore \quad h\nu = 3.5 + 1.2 = 4.7 \text{ eV}$$

> **Concept Enhancer**
> Stopping potential always gives maximum kinetic energy of ejected electrons.

42. *(a)* It is found that the photoelectric current increases linearly with the intensity of incident light.

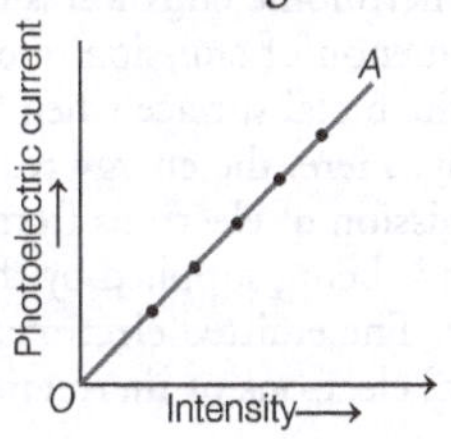

It means number of photoelectrons emitted per second from photosensitive plate is directly proportional to the intensity of the incident radiation.

> **Concept Enhancer**
> One photon can emit only one electron from a photosensitive material, no matter how much its energy is.

43. *(a)* The work function has no effect on photoelectric current as long as $h\nu > W_0$.

The photoelectric current is proportional to the intensity of incident light.

Since, there is no change in the intensity of light, hence $I_1 = I_2$

44. *(d)* According to Einstein's photoelectric equation, KE of the photoelectron

$$\frac{1}{2}mv^2 = \frac{hc}{\lambda} - W_0$$

Given, $\lambda = 3000 \text{ Å} = 3000 \times 10^{-10}$ m

$W_0 = 1 \text{ eV} = 1.6 \times 10^{-19}$ J

$m = 9.1 \times 10^{-31}$ kg

$\therefore \frac{1}{2} \times 9.1 \times 10^{-31} \times v^2$

$= \frac{6.6 \times 10^{-34} \times 3 \times 10^8}{3000 \times 10^{-10}} - 1.6 \times 10^{-19}$

$\Rightarrow v = 10^6$ m/s

45. (b) According to Einstein photoelectric equation

$$KE = E - W_0$$

Here, $E = 6.2$ eV, $W_0 = 4.2$ eV

$\therefore \quad KE = 6.2 - 4.2 = 2.0$ eV

$= 2 \times 1.6 \times 10^{-19}$

$= 3.2 \times 10^{-19}$ J

46. (a) We know, $W_0 = h\nu_0$

(where, ν_0 is threshold frequency)

or $\quad W_0 = \frac{hc}{\lambda_0}$

Here, $\lambda_0 = 5000$ Å $= 5000 \times 10^{-10}$ m

$\therefore \quad W_0 = \frac{6.63 \times 10^{-34} \times 3 \times 10^8}{5000 \times 10^{-10}}$

$= 4 \times 10^{-19}$ J

47. (b) Thermionic emission is the phenomenon of emission of electrons from the metal surface when heated suitably. Here, the energy required for the emission of electrons from metal surface is being supplied by thermal energy. The emitted electrons are called thermal electrons or thermions.

Topic 2

01. (b) Photon is quanta of energy. It is a massless and chargeless particle. The rest mass of photon is zero. In free space, it moves with velocity 'c' and energy of photon is equal to $h\nu$. The momentum of the photon is given by

$p = \frac{E}{c} = \frac{h\nu}{c}$.

02. (c) Given, the monochromatic light of the wavelength,

$\lambda = 600$ nm

The power of the source,

$P = 3.3 \times 10^{-3}$ W

We know that, $P = \frac{nhc}{\lambda}$

Substituting the values in the above equation, we get

$3.3 \times 10^{-3} = \frac{n \times 6.6 \times 10^{-34} \times 3 \times 10^8}{600 \times 10^{-9}}$

$\Rightarrow \quad n = 10^{16}$

03. (a) Efficient power (P) is given by

$$P = \frac{N}{t} \times \frac{hc}{\lambda}$$

(N = total number of photons)

$\frac{N}{t} = \frac{P \times \lambda}{hc}$

$= \frac{50 \times 0.6 \times 10^{-6}}{6.6 \times 10^{-34} \times 3 \times 10^8}$

[$\because$ 25% of 200W = 50W]

$= 1.5 \times 10^{20}$

04. (a) Power is givne by $P = \frac{nhc}{\lambda}$

So, for two different situations,

$\Rightarrow \quad \frac{P_2}{P_1} = \frac{n_2 \lambda_1}{n_1 \lambda_2}$

$= \frac{1.02 \times 10^{15} \times 5000}{10^{15} \times 5100} = 1$

05. (b) Here, $\lambda = 667 \times 10^{-9}$ m,

$P = 9 \times 10^{-3}$ W

Power $= \frac{\text{Energy}(E)}{\text{Time}(t)} = \frac{nhc}{\lambda t} = \frac{Nhc}{\lambda}$

[$E = \frac{hc}{\lambda}$, n = Total number of photons

N = Number of photons emitted per second $= \frac{n}{t}$]

So, $N = \frac{P \times \lambda}{hc}$

$= \frac{9 \times 10^{-3} \times 667 \times 10^{-9}}{6.6 \times 10^{-34} \times 3 \times 10^8}$

$= 3 \times 10^{16}$

06. (a) Power emitted,

$P = 2 \times 10^{-3}$ W

Energy of photon,

$E = h\nu$

$= 6.6 \times 10^{-34} \times 6 \times 10^{14}$ J

Here, h being Planck's constant.

Number of photons emitted per second is given by

$n = \frac{\text{Power }(P)}{\text{Energy }(E)}$

$= \frac{2 \times 10^{-3}}{6.6 \times 10^{-34} \times 6 \times 10^{14}} = 5 \times 10^{15}$

07. (d) Energy of photon is given by

$E = \frac{hc}{\lambda}$ ...(i)

de-Broglie wavelength is given by

$\lambda = \frac{h}{p}$ ...(ii)

p being momentum of photon.

From Eqs. (i) and (ii), we have

$E = \frac{hc}{h/p} = pc$ or $p = \frac{E}{c}$

Given,

$E = 1\text{ MeV} = 1 \times 10^6 \times 1.6 \times 10^{-19}$ J,

1 eV $= 1.6 \times 10^{19}$ J

$c = 3 \times 10^8$ m/s

Hence, after putting values, we obtain

$p = \frac{1 \times 10^6 \times 1.6 \times 10^{-19}}{3 \times 10^8}$ kg-m/s

$= 5 \times 10^{-22}$ kg-m/s

08. (a) Photoelectric effect is based on the particle nature of light.

09. (d) The energy of emitted photon is given by

$E = \frac{hc}{\lambda}$

Given, wavelength,

$\lambda = 21$ cm $= 0.21$ m

So, $\quad E = \frac{6.6 \times 10^{-34} \times 3 \times 10^8}{0.21}$

$= 10^{-24}$ J

10. (c) Velocity of photon $c = \nu\lambda$.

For constant λ, velocity of photon,

$c \propto \nu$

11. (b) In thermionic emission and other types of emission, ions emitted are atoms that has lost or gained electrons having negative or positive charge respectively. Thus, the nature of ions knocked out from hot surface are electrons.

12. (a) As a photon moves with the velocity of light

i.e. $\quad v = c$

$\therefore$ The momentum of the photon

$= mc = \frac{h\nu}{c} = \frac{h}{\lambda} \quad \left[\lambda = \frac{c}{\nu}\right]$

13. (b) Energy of photon is $E = h\nu = \frac{hc}{\lambda}$

As, $\quad \frac{hc}{\lambda} = 10^3$ eV

$\therefore \quad h = \frac{10^3 \lambda}{c}$ ...(i)

And for 2nd case as given in question

$h\nu = 10^6$ eV ...(ii)

Putting value of h in Eq. (ii),

$$\frac{10^3 \lambda}{c} \nu = 10^6$$

$$\therefore \quad \nu = \frac{10^3 c}{\lambda} = \frac{10^3 \times 3 \times 10^8}{1.24 \times 10^{-9}} \quad [\because \lambda = 1.24 \times 10^{-9} \text{m}]$$

$$= 2.4 \times 10^{20} \text{ Hz}$$

14. *(a)* The energy of a photon of a radiation of frequency ν and wavelength λ is

$$E = h\nu = \frac{hc}{\lambda} \quad \ldots \text{(i)}$$

If photon is considered to be a particle of mass m, the energy associated with it, according to Einstein mass energy relation, is given by

$$E = mc^2 \quad \ldots \text{(ii)}$$

From Eqs. (i) and (ii),

$$h\nu = mc^2 \text{ or } m = \frac{h\nu}{c^2} \Rightarrow \frac{h\nu}{c} = mc$$

As $mc = p$ (p = momentum of photon)

$$\text{So, } \nu = \frac{cp}{h} = \frac{3 \times 10^8 \times 3.3 \times 10^{-29}}{6.6 \times 10^{-34}}$$

$$= 1.5 \times 10^{13} \text{ Hz}$$

15. *(a)* Power of radio transmitter

$$= 10 \text{ kW} = 10000 \text{ W}$$

Operating frequency of transmitter

$$= 880 \text{ kHz} = 880 \times 10^3 \text{ Hz}$$

Number of photons emitted per second

$$n = \frac{P}{E} = \frac{P}{h\nu}$$

$$= \frac{10^4}{6.63 \times 10^{-34} \times 880 \times 10^3} \quad [h = 6.63 \times 10^{-34} \text{ J-s}]$$

$$= 1.72 \times 10^{31}$$

16. *(b)* According to Planck's quantum theory, a source of radiation emits energy in the form of photons, which travel in straight line.

The energy of a photon is given by

$$E = h\nu = \frac{hc}{\lambda}$$

Topic 3

01. *(d)* We know that $\lambda = \frac{h}{p} = \frac{h}{\sqrt{2mE}}$

Here, E = kinetic energy

$$\text{Thus, } \quad \lambda^2 = \frac{h^2}{2mE}$$

$$\Rightarrow \quad \frac{1}{\lambda^2} = \frac{2mE}{h^2} \propto E$$

Hence, option (d) is correct.

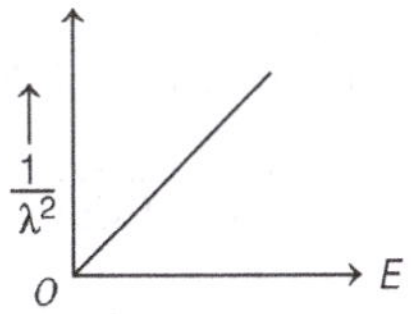

02. *(c)* de-Broglie wavelength (λ) of a moving particle is given as

$$\lambda = \frac{h}{p}$$

$$\therefore \quad \lambda \propto \frac{1}{p}$$

Hence, the graph showing the variation of de-Broglie wavelength λ of a moving particle with its momentum p is shown below.

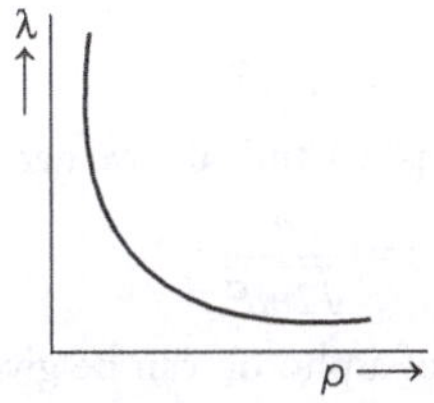

03. *(d)* Since, work function is negligible. Therefore, kinetic energy of emitted electron = Energy of incident photon

$$\text{i.e., } \frac{1}{2} mv^2 = h\nu$$

$$\Rightarrow \quad \frac{p^2}{2m} = \frac{hc}{\lambda} \Rightarrow p = \sqrt{\frac{2mhc}{\lambda}}$$

de-broglie wavelength of emitted electrons is

$$\lambda_d = \frac{h}{p} = \frac{h}{\sqrt{\frac{2mhc}{\lambda}}} = \sqrt{\frac{h\lambda}{2mc}}$$

$$\Rightarrow \quad \lambda = \left(\frac{2mc}{h}\right) \lambda_d^2$$

04. *(d)* Kinetic energy of electron,

$$K = 144 \text{ eV}$$

$$\Rightarrow \quad eV = 144 \text{ eV} \Rightarrow V = 144 \text{ V}$$

$\therefore$ de-Broglie wavelength

$$\lambda = \frac{1.227}{\sqrt{V}} \text{Å} = \frac{1.227}{\sqrt{144}} \text{Å} = \frac{1.227}{12} \text{Å}$$

$$= 0.102 \text{Å} = 1.02 \text{ nm}$$

$$= 102 \times 10^{-2} \text{ nm}$$

05. *(a)* The wave nature of electrons was experimentally verified by de-Broglie.

06. *(c)* Given, $\lambda = 1.227 \times 10^{-2}$ nm

$$= 1.227 \times 10^{-11} \text{ m}$$

Relation for de-Broglie wavelength for moving electron is

$$\lambda = \frac{12.27}{\sqrt{V}} \text{Å} \Rightarrow \sqrt{V} = \frac{12.27}{\lambda} \times 10^{-10} \text{ m}$$

$$= \frac{12.27 \times 10^{-10}}{1.227 \times 10^{-11}} = 10^2$$

$$\Rightarrow \quad V = 10^4 \text{ V}$$

07. *(a)*

key idea

You can compare de-Broglie wavelengths of different moving particles with same energy E with the help of following formula,

$$\lambda = \frac{h}{\sqrt{2mE}}$$

where, m is the mass of moving particle.

The de-Broglie wavelength associated with a charged particle is given by

$$\lambda = \frac{h}{p}$$

where, h = planck's constant and p = momentum = $\sqrt{2mKE}$ (here, KE is the kinetic energy of the charged particle)

$$\Rightarrow \quad \lambda = \frac{h}{\sqrt{2m\text{KE}}}$$

For proton and α-particle, the wavelengths are respectively given as,

$$\lambda_p = \frac{h}{\sqrt{2m_p \text{KE}_p}}$$

$$\text{and} \quad \lambda_\alpha = \frac{h}{\sqrt{2m_\alpha \text{KE}_\alpha}}$$

$$\therefore \quad \frac{\lambda_p}{\lambda_\alpha} = \frac{\sqrt{2m_\alpha \text{KE}_\alpha}}{\sqrt{2m_p \text{KE}_p}} \quad \ldots \text{(i)}$$

Here, $\text{KE}_\alpha = \text{KE}_p$ and $m_\alpha = 4m_p$

Substituting these above mentioned relations in Eq. (i), we get

$$\Rightarrow \quad \frac{\lambda_p}{\lambda_\alpha} = \sqrt{\frac{4m_p}{m_p}} = \frac{2}{1}$$

or $\lambda_p : \lambda_\alpha = 2:1$

08. *(a)*

key idea

You can calculate de-Broglie wavelength of moving charged particle accelerated through potential difference V with the help of following formula.

$$\lambda = \frac{h}{\sqrt{2mqV}}$$

where, symbols are there usual meaning.

Given, potential difference, $V = 10000$ V

If electron is accelerated through a potential of V volt, then the wavelength associated with it is given by

$$\lambda = \frac{12.27}{\sqrt{V}} \text{Å} = \frac{12.27}{\sqrt{10000}} \times 10^{-10}$$

$$= \frac{12.27 \times 10^{-10}}{100} = 12.27 \times 10^{-12} \text{ m}$$

09. *(c)* According to the question,

$$\mathbf{v} = v_0 \hat{\mathbf{i}}, \quad \mathbf{E} = -E_0 \hat{\mathbf{i}}$$

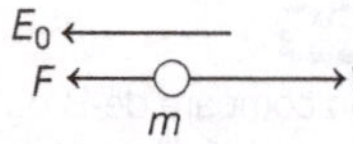

Thus, magnitude of force on the electron due to the electric field,

$$|\mathbf{F}| = q|\mathbf{E}| \Rightarrow F = eE_0$$

From Newton's second law of motion,

$$F = ma$$

$$\therefore \quad F = ma = eE_0$$

$$\Rightarrow \quad a = \frac{eE_0}{m} \quad \ldots\text{(i)}$$

or $\quad \mathbf{a} = \frac{(-e)(-E_0\hat{\mathbf{i}})}{m} = \frac{eE_0}{m}\hat{\mathbf{i}}$

From first equation of motion, $v = u + at$

Here, u (initial velocity) $= v_0$

$$\Rightarrow \quad v = v_0 + \frac{eE_0}{m}t \quad \ldots\text{(ii)}$$

(From Eq. (i))

Initial de-Broglie wavelength of the electron is given as

$$\lambda_0 = h / mv_0$$

$$\Rightarrow \quad h = \lambda_0 mv_0 \quad \ldots\text{(iii)}$$

After time t, de-Broglie wavelength is given as

$$\lambda = h / mv$$

Substituting the value of v from Eq. (ii), we get

$$\lambda = \frac{h}{m\left(v_0 + \frac{eE_0}{m}t\right)} = \frac{h}{mv_0\left[1 + \frac{eE_0}{mv_0}t\right]}$$

$$= \frac{\lambda_0 mv_0}{mv_0\left[1 + \frac{eE_0}{mv_0}t\right]} \text{ [from Eq. (iii)]}$$

$$= \frac{\lambda_0}{\left[1 + \frac{eE_0}{mv_0}t\right]} = \frac{\lambda_0}{1 + \frac{eE_0}{mv_0}t}$$

10. *(b)* de-Broglie wavelength associated with a moving particle can be given as

$$\lambda = \frac{h}{p} = \frac{h}{\sqrt{2m(\text{KE})}}$$

At thermal equilibrium, temperature of neutron and heavy water will be same. This common temperature is given as, T. Kinetic energy of the neutron is

$$\text{KE} = \frac{3}{2}kT$$

$\therefore$ de-Broglie wavelength of the neutron

$$\lambda = \frac{h}{p} = \frac{h}{\sqrt{2m(\text{KE})}}$$

$$= \frac{h}{\sqrt{2m \times \frac{3}{2}kT}} = \frac{h}{\sqrt{3mkT}}$$

11. *(d)* Since, it is given that electron has mass m. de-Broglie's wavelength for an electron will be given as

$$\lambda_e = \frac{h}{p} \quad \ldots\text{(i)}$$

As kinetic energy of electron

$$E = \frac{p^2}{2m}$$

$$\Rightarrow \quad p = \sqrt{2mE} \quad \ldots\text{(ii)}$$

From Eqs. (i) and (ii), we get

$$\lambda_e = \frac{h}{\sqrt{2mE}} \quad \ldots\text{(iii)}$$

Energy of a photon can be given as

$$E = h\nu$$

$$\Rightarrow \quad E = \frac{hc}{\lambda_p} \Rightarrow \lambda_p = \frac{hc}{E} \quad \ldots\text{(iv)}$$

Now, divide Eq. (iii) by Eq. (iv), we get

$$\frac{\lambda_e}{\lambda_p} = \frac{h}{\sqrt{2mE}} \cdot \frac{E}{hc}$$

$$\Rightarrow \quad \frac{\lambda_e}{\lambda_p} = \frac{1}{c}\sqrt{\frac{E}{2m}}$$

12. *(a)* Given, mass of electrons $= m$

de-Broglie wavelength $= \lambda$

So, kinetic energy of electron $= \frac{p^2}{2m}$

$$= \frac{\left(\frac{h}{\lambda}\right)^2}{2m} = \frac{h^2}{2m\lambda^2}$$

Now, maximum energy of photon can be given by

$$E = \frac{hc}{\lambda_0} = \frac{h^2}{2m\lambda^2}$$

$$\Rightarrow \quad \lambda_0 = \frac{hc \times 2\lambda^2 \cdot m}{h^2} = \frac{2mc\lambda^2}{h}$$

13. *(b)* The de-Broglie wavelength is given by

$$\lambda = \frac{h}{P} \Rightarrow P\lambda = h$$

This equation is in the form of $yx = c$, which is the equation of a rectangular hyperbola.

Hence, the graph given in option (b) is the correct one.

14. *(a)* According to Einstein's photoelectric equation,

$$K_{\max} = \frac{hc}{\lambda} - \phi_0$$

Given, $\lambda = 500$ nm,

$hc = 1240$ eV nm and $\phi = 2.28$ eV

$$\therefore \quad K_{\max} = \frac{1240 \text{ eV nm}}{500 \text{ nm}} - 2.28 \text{ eV}$$

$$= 2.48 \text{ eV} - 2.28 \text{ eV} = 0.2 \text{ eV}$$

The de-Broglie wavelength

$$\lambda_{e\min} = \frac{12.27}{\sqrt{\text{KE}_{\max}(\text{eV})}} = \frac{12.27}{\sqrt{0.2}}$$

$$= 27.436 \text{ Å}$$

$$= 27.436 \times 10^{-10} \text{ m}$$

Thus, minimum wavelength of the emitted electron is

$$\lambda_{\min} = 2.7436 \times 10^{-9} \text{ m}$$

$$\simeq 2.8 \times 10^{-9} \text{ m}$$

So, $\quad \lambda \geq 2.8 \times 10^{-9}$ m

15. *(b)* For de-Broglie wavelength,

$$\lambda = \frac{h}{p}$$

For 1st case, $\lambda_1 = \frac{h}{p} = \frac{h}{\sqrt{2mK}}$

For 2nd case, $\lambda_2 = \frac{h}{\sqrt{2m16K}}$

$$= \frac{h}{4\sqrt{2mK}} = \frac{\lambda_1}{4}$$

$$\lambda_2 = 25\% \text{ of } \lambda_1$$

So, 75% change in the wavelength takes place.

16. *(a)* Wavelength of electron is given by

$$\lambda_e = \frac{h}{p_e} = \frac{h}{\sqrt{2mE}}$$

$$[\because p_e = \sqrt{2mE}]$$

and for photon, $\lambda_p = \frac{hc}{E}$ or $E = \frac{hc}{\lambda_p}$

$$\therefore \quad \lambda_e^2 = \frac{h^2}{2m \cdot \frac{hc}{\lambda_p}} = \frac{h^2}{2mhc}\lambda_p$$

$$\Rightarrow \quad \lambda_e^2 \propto \lambda_p$$

17. *(d)* Radius of the circular path

$$R = \frac{mv}{Bq} \text{ or } mv = RBq$$

Given, $R = 0.83$ cm $= 0.83 \times 10^{-2}$ m,

$B = 0.25$ Wb m^{-2}

$$q = 2e = 2\times1.6\times10^{-19}\text{ C}$$

$$\therefore \quad mv = (0.83\times10^{-2})(0.25)(2\times1.6\times10^{-19})$$

de-Broglie wavelength,

$$\lambda = \frac{h}{mv}$$

$$= \frac{6.6\times10^{-34}}{0.83\times10^{-2}\times0.25\times2\times1.6\times10^{-19}}\times10^{-12}\text{m}$$

$$= 0.01\text{ Å}$$

• Concept Enhancer

When emitted photoelectrons enters into magnetic field (*B*) perpendicular to it, then these electrons move on circular path in magnetic field. Maximum radius (*r*) of circular path is calculated by,

$$r = \frac{mv_{max}}{Be}$$

where, m = mass of electron and v_{max} = maximum velocity of emitted electrons

18. *(a)* de-Broglie wavelength,

$$\lambda = \frac{h}{P}\text{ or } p = \frac{h}{\lambda}$$

$$\therefore \quad \frac{\Delta p}{p} = -\frac{\Delta\lambda}{\lambda}, \quad \frac{p}{p_{\text{initial}}} = \frac{0.5}{100}$$

$$p_{\text{initial}} = 200p$$

19. *(b)* The de-Broglie wavelength,

$$\lambda = \frac{1.227}{\sqrt{V}}\text{ nm or } \lambda \propto \frac{1}{\sqrt{V}}$$

$$\therefore \quad \frac{\lambda_1}{\lambda_2} = \sqrt{\frac{V_2}{V_1}} = \sqrt{\frac{100\times10^3}{25\times10^3}} = 2$$

$$\text{or} \quad \lambda_2 = \frac{\lambda_1}{2}$$

20. *(a)* According to de-Broglie relation, wavelength of a particle is given by

$$\lambda = \frac{h}{p}$$

where, h is Planck's constant and wavelength of an electron is given by

$$\lambda_e = \frac{h}{p_e}$$

but $\lambda = \lambda_e$, so $p = p_e$

or $m_e v_e = mv$ or $v = \dfrac{m_e v_e}{m}$

Here, $m_e = 9.1\times10^{-31}$ kg

$v_e = 3\times10^6\text{ ms}^{-1}$

and $m = 1$ mg $= 1\times10^{-6}$ kg

$$\therefore \quad v = \frac{9.1\times10^{-31}\times3\times10^6}{1\times10^{-6}}$$

$$= 2.7\times10^{-18}\text{ m/s}$$

21. *(d)* de-Broglie wavelength is given by

$$\lambda = \frac{h}{mv}$$

For same velocity, $\lambda \propto \dfrac{1}{m}$

Out of the given particles, the mass of β-particle is minimum. Thus, de-Broglie wavelength is maximum for β-particle.

22. *(b)* If energy E is expressed in (eV) and wavelength λ (in Å), then energy of photon,

$$E = \frac{hc}{\lambda} = \frac{12375}{\lambda\text{ (Å)}}\text{eV}$$

$$\therefore \quad \lambda = \frac{12375}{E\text{ (eV)}}\text{ Å} = \frac{12375}{3\text{ (eV)}}\text{ Å}$$

$$= 4125\text{ Å}$$

$$= 412.5\text{ nm}$$

• Concept Enhancer

Energy of photon is

$$E = \frac{hc}{\lambda\text{ (Å)}} = \frac{12375}{\lambda\text{ (Å)}}\text{eV}$$

Here, hc = 12375 eV-Å comes from the following procedure

hc = (Planck's constant) (velocity of light)

$$= \frac{(6.6\times10^{-34}\text{ J-s})(3\times10^8\text{ m/s})}{(1.6\times10^{-19}\text{ J/eV})}$$

$$= 12.375\times10^{-7}\text{ eV-m}$$

$$= 12375\text{ eV-Å}$$

23. *(d)* When electrons are accelerated through V volt, the gain in KE of the electron is given by

$$\frac{1}{2}mv^2 = \text{eV}$$

$$\text{or } v^2 = \frac{2\text{ eV}}{m}$$

Given, $V = 100$ V

$$\text{So,} \quad v = \sqrt{\frac{2e(100)}{m}} \qquad \ldots\text{(i)}$$

According to de-Broglie theory, wavelength

$$\lambda = \frac{h}{mv}$$

$$\therefore \quad \lambda = \frac{h}{m\sqrt{\dfrac{2e(100)}{m}}}$$

$$= \frac{h}{\sqrt{2me(100)}}$$

$$= \frac{6.6\times10^{-34}}{\sqrt{2\times9.1\times10^{-31}\times1.6\times10^{-19}\times100}}$$

$$= 1.2\times10^{-10} = 1.2\text{ Å}$$

24. *(c)* Here kinetic energy,

$E = 100$ eV

$m = 10^{-31}$ kg

Energy of an electron,

$$E = 100\times(1.6\times10^{-19})\text{ J}$$

$$\text{or } \lambda = \frac{h}{2mE}$$

$$= \frac{6.6\times10^{-34}}{\sqrt{2\times9.1\times10^{-31}\times100\times1.6\times10^{-19}}}$$

$$= 1.2\times10^{-10}\text{ m}$$

$$= 1.2\text{ Å}$$

25. *(a)* de-Broglie wavelength and it is given by

$$\lambda = \frac{h}{mv}$$

where, m and v are the mass and velocity of the particle and h is Planck's constant.

C-26

In NEET 2024, 2 questions were visible from this chapter. In past 5 years, 1 question from topic-1, 7 questions from topic-2 were asked.
For detailed analysis scan QR code

ATOMS

Topic 1 α-Particle Scattering and Rutherford Nuclear Model of Atom

01 Given below are two statements.

Statement I Atoms are electrically neutral as they contain equal number of positive and negative charges.

Statement II Atoms of each element are stable and emit their characteristic spectrum.

In the light of the above statements, choose the most appropriate answer from the options given below. ***[NCERT (New) Pg. 290, NEET 2024]***

(a) Both Statement I and Statement II are correct.
(b) Both Statement I and Statement II are incorrect.
(c) Statement I is correct but Statement II is incorrect.
(d) Statement I is incorrect but Statement II is correct.

02 When an α-particle of mass m moving with velocity v bombards on a heavy nucleus of charge Ze, its distance of closest approach from the nucleus depends on m as ***[NCERT (New) Pg. 295, NEET 2016]***

(a) $\frac{1}{\sqrt{m}}$ (b) $\frac{1}{m^2}$ (c) m (d) $\frac{1}{m}$

03 An alpha nucleus of energy $\frac{1}{2}mv^2$ bombards a heavy nuclear target of charge Ze. Then the distance of closest approach for the alpha nucleus will be proportional to ***[AIPMT 2010]***

(a) $\frac{1}{Ze}$ (b) v^2 (c) $\frac{1}{m}$ (d) $\frac{1}{v^4}$

04 In a Rutherford scattering experiment when a projectile of charge Z_1 and mass M_1 approaches a target nucleus of charge Z_2 and mass M_2, the distance of closest approach is r_0. The energy of the projectile is ***[NCERT (New) Pg. 295, AIPMT 2009]***

(a) directly proportional to $M_1 \times M_2$
(b) directly proportional to $Z_1 Z_2$
(c) inversely proportional to Z_1
(d) directly proportional to mass M_1

05 An electron is moving around the nucleus of a hydrogen atom in a circular orbit of radius r. The Coulomb force F between the two is ***[AIPMT 2003]***

(a) $k\frac{e^2}{r^2}\hat{\mathbf{r}}$ (b) $-k\frac{e^2}{r^3}\hat{\mathbf{r}}$
(c) $k\frac{e^2}{r^3}\hat{\mathbf{r}}$ (d) $-k\frac{e^2}{r^2}\hat{\mathbf{r}}$

$\left(\text{where, } k=\frac{1}{4\pi\varepsilon_0}\right)$

06 In Rutherford scattering experiment, what will be the correct angle for α-scattering for an impact parameter, $b = 0$? ***[NCERT (New) Pg. 294, AIPMT 1994]***

(a) 90° (b) 270° (c) 0° (d) 180°

Topic 2 Bohr's Model and Hydrogen Spectra

01 Match List I with List II. ***[NCERT (New) Pg. 296, NEET 2024]***

	List I (Spectral lines of Hydrogen for transitions from)		List II (Wavelengths (nm))
A.	$n_2 = 3$ to $n_1 = 2$	I.	410.2
B.	$n_2 = 4$ to $n_1 = 2$	II.	434.1
C.	$n_2 = 5$ to $n_1 = 2$	III.	656.3
D.	$n_2 = 6$ to $n_1 = 2$	IV.	486.1

Choose the correct answer from the options given below.

(a) A-II, B-I, C-IV, D-III (b) A-III, B-IV, C-II, D-I
(c) A-IV, B-III, C-I, D-II (d) A-I, B-II, C-III, D-IV

02 The radius of inner most orbit of hydrogen atom is 5.3×10^{-11} m. What is the radius of third allowed orbit of hydrogen atom? ***[NCERT (New) Pg. 296, NEET 2023]***

(a) 1.06 Å (b) 1.59 Å
(c) 4.77 Å (d) 0.53 Å

03 In hydrogen spectrum, the shortest wavelength in the Balmer series is λ. The shortest wavelength in the Brackett series is *[NCERT (New) Pg. 422, NEET 2023]*
(a) 4λ (b) 9λ (c) 16λ (d) 2λ

04 The minimum wavelength of X-rays produced by an electron accelerated through a potential difference of V volts is proportional to *[NEET 2023]*
(a) $\frac{1}{V}$ (b) $\frac{1}{\sqrt{V}}$ (c) V^2 (d) $\sqrt{V}$

05 Let T_1 and T_2 be the energy of an electron in the first and second excited states of hydrogen atom, respectively. According to the Bohr's model of an atom, the ratio of $T_1 : T_2$ is *[NEET 2022]*
(a) 4 : 1 (b) 4 : 9 (c) 9 : 4 (d) 1 : 4

06 The total energy of an electron in the nth stationary orbit of the hydrogen atom can be obtained by *[NCERT (New) Pg. 299, NEET (Oct.) 2020]*
(a) $E_n = \frac{13.6}{n^2}$ eV (b) $E_n = -\frac{13.6}{n^2}$ eV
(c) $E_n = -\frac{1.36}{n^2}$ eV (d) $E_n = -13.6 \times n^2$ eV

07 For which one of the following, Bohr model is not valid? *[NEET (Sep.) 2020]*
(a) Singly ionised helium atom (He^+)
(b) Deuteron atom
(c) Singly ionised neon atom (Ne^+)
(d) Hydrogen atom

08 The radius of the first permitted Bohr orbit for the electron, in a hydrogen atom equals 0.51 Å and its ground state energy equals – 13.6 eV. If the electron in the hydrogen atom is replaced by muon (μ^{-1}) [Charge same as electron and mass 207 m_e], the first Bohr radius and ground state energy will be *[NCERT (New) Pg. 425, NEET (Odisha) 2019]*
(a) 0.53×10^{-13} m, – 3.6 eV
(b) 25.6×10^{-13} m, – 2.8 eV
(c) 2.56×10^{-13} m, – 2.8 keV
(d) 2.56×10^{-13} m, – 13.6 eV

09 The total energy of an electron in an atom in an orbit is –3.4 eV. Its kinetic and potential energies are, respectively *[NEET (National) 2019]*
(a) –3.4 eV, –6.8 eV (b) 3.4 eV, –6.8 eV
(c) 3.4 eV, 3.4 eV (d) –3.4 eV, –3.4 eV

10 The ratio of kinetic energy to the total energy of an electron in a Bohr orbit of the hydrogen atom, is *[NCERT (New) Pg. 299, NEET 2018]*
(a) 2 : –1 (b) 1 : –1
(c) 1 : 1 (d) 1 : – 2

11 The ratio of wavelengths of the last line of Balmer series and the last line of Lyman series is *[NEET 2017]*
(a) 2 (b) 1
(c) 4 (d) 0.5

12 If an electron in a hydrogen atom jumps from the 3rd orbit to the 2nd orbit, it emits a photon of wavelength λ. When it jumps from the 4th orbit to the 3rd orbit, the corresponding wavelength of the photon will be *[NCERT (Old) Pg. 422, NEET 2016]*
(a) $\frac{16}{25}\lambda$ (b) $\frac{9}{16}\lambda$ (c) $\frac{20}{7}\lambda$ (d) $\frac{20}{13}\lambda$

13 In the spectrum of hydrogen, the ratio of the longest wavelength in the Lyman series to the longest wavelength in the Balmer series is *[AIPMT 2015]*
(a) $\frac{4}{9}$ (b) $\frac{9}{4}$ (c) $\frac{27}{5}$ (d) $\frac{5}{27}$

14 Consider 3rd orbit of He^+ (Helium), using non-relativistic approach, the speed of electron in this orbit will be (given $k = 9 \times 10^9$ constant, $Z = 2$ and h (Planck's constant) $= 6.6 \times 10^{-34}$ J-s) *[AIPMT 2015]*
(a) 2.92×10^6 m/s (b) 1.46×10^6 m/s
(c) 0.73×10^6 m/s (d) 3.0×10^8 m/s

15 Hydrogen atom in ground state is excited by a monochromatic radiation of $\lambda = 975$ Å. Number of spectral lines in the resulting spectrum emitted will be *[NCERT (Old) Pg. 428, AIPMT 2014]*
(a) 3 (b) 2 (c) 6 (d) 10

16 Ratio of longest wavelengths corresponding to Lyman and Balmer series in hydrogen spectrum is *[NEET 2013]*
(a) $\frac{5}{27}$ (b) $\frac{3}{23}$ (c) $\frac{7}{29}$ (d) $\frac{9}{31}$

17 Monochromatic radiation emitted when electron state on hydrogen atom jumps from first excited state to the ground state irradiates a photosensitive material. The stopping potential is measured to be 3.57 V. The threshold frequency of the material is *[AIPMT 2012]*
(a) 4×10^{15} Hz (b) 5×10^{15} Hz
(c) 1.6×10^{15} Hz (d) 2.5×10^{15} Hz

18 Electron in hydrogen atom first jumps from third excited state to second excited state and then from second excited to the first excited state. The ratio of the wavelengths $\lambda_1 : \lambda_2$ emitted in the two cases is *[NCERT (Old) Pg. 422, AIPMT 2012]*
(a) 7/5 (b) 27/20 (c) 27/5 (d) 20/7

19 An electron of a stationary hydrogen atom passes from the fifth energy level to the ground level. The velocity that the atom acquired as a result of photon emission will be *[AIPMT 2012]*
(a) $\frac{24hR}{25m}$ (b) $\frac{25hR}{24m}$
(c) $\frac{25m}{24hR}$ (d) $\frac{24m}{25hR}$

(m is the mass of electron, R is Rydberg constant and h is Planck's constant)

20 The wavelength of the first line of Lyman series for hydrogen atom is equal to that of the second line of Balmer series for a hydrogen like ion. The atomic number Z of hydrogen like ion is *[NCERT (Old) Pg. 422, AIPMT 2011]*
(a) 4 (b) 1
(c) 2 (d) 3

21 Out of the following which one is not a possible energy for a photon to be emitted by hydrogen atom according to Bohr's atomic model? *[AIPMT 2011]*
(a) 0.65 eV (b) 1.9 eV
(c) 11.1 eV (d) 13.6 eV

22 An electron in the hydrogen atom jumps from excited state n to the ground state. The wavelength so emitted illuminates a photosensitive material having work function 2.75 eV. If the stopping potential of the photoelectron is 10 V, then the value of n is *[NCERT (New) Pg. 299, AIPMT 2011]*
(a) 2 (b) 3
(c) 4 (d) 5

23 The energy of a hydrogen atom in the ground state is – 13.6 eV. The energy of a He^{+} ion in the first excited state will be *[AIPMT 2010]*
(a) –13.6 eV (b) –27.2 eV
(c) – 54.4 eV (d) – 6.8 eV

24 The ionisation energy of the electron in the hydrogen atom in its ground state is 13.6 eV. The atoms are excited to higher energy levels to emit radiations of 6 wavelengths. Maximum wavelength of emitted radiation corresponds to the transition between *[AIPMT 2009]*
(a) $n=3$ to $n=2$ states (b) $n=3$ to $n=1$ states
(c) $n=2$ to $n=1$ states (d) $n=4$ to $n=3$ states

25 The ground state energy of hydrogen atom is −13.6 eV. When its electron is in the first excited state, its excitation energy is *[AIPMT 2008]*
(a) 3.4 eV (b) 6.8 eV
(c) 10.2 eV (d) zero

26 The total energy of electron in the ground state of hydrogen atom is −13.6 eV. The kinetic energy of an electron in the first excited state is *[NCERT (New) Pg. 299, AIPMT 2007]*
(a) 3.4 eV (b) 6.8 eV
(c) 13.6 eV (d) 1.7 eV

27 In a discharge tube ionisation of enclosed gas is produced due to collisions between *[AIPMT 2006]*
(a) positive ions and neutral atoms/molecules
(b) negative electrons and neutral atoms/ molecules
(c) photons and neutral atoms/molecules
(d) neutral gas atoms/molecules

28 Ionisation potential of hydrogen atom is 13.6 eV. Hydrogen atoms in the ground state are excited by monochromatic radiation of photon energy 12.1 eV. According to Bohr's theory, the spectral lines emitted by hydrogen will be *[AIPMT 2006]*
(a) two (b) three
(c) four (d) one

29 The total energy of an electron in the first excited state of hydrogen is about – 3.4 eV. Its kinetic energy in this state is *[NCERT (New) Pg. 299, CBSE AIPMT 2005]*
(a) – 3.4 eV (b) – 6.8 eV
(c) 6.8 eV (d) 3.4 eV

30 Energy E of a hydrogen atom with principal quantum number n is given by $E=\frac{-13.6}{n^2}$ eV. The energy of a photon ejected when the electron jumps from $n=3$ state to $n=2$ state of hydrogen, is approximately *[AIPMT 2004]*
(a) 1.5 eV (b) 0.85 eV (c) 3.4 eV (d) 1.9 eV

31 The Bohr model of atoms *[AIPMT 2004]*
(a) assumes that the angular momentum of electrons is quantised
(b) uses Einstein's photoelectric equation
(c) predicts continuous emission spectra for atoms
(d) predicts the same emission spectra for all types of atoms

32 Which of the following transitions gives photon of maximum energy ? *[NCERT (New) Pg. 299, AIPMT 2000]*
(a) $n=1$ to $n=2$ (b) $n=2$ to $n=1$
(c) $n=2$ to $n=6$ (d) $n=6$ to $n=2$

33 When electron jumps from $n=4$ to $n=2$ orbit, we get *[AIPMT 2000]*
(a) second line of Lyman series
(b) second line of Balmer series
(c) second line of Paschen series
(d) an absorption line of Balmer series

34 In the Bohr's model of a hydrogen atom, the centripetal force is furnished by the coulomb attraction between the proton and the electron. If a_0 is the radius of the ground state orbit, m is the mass and e is the charge on the electron, ε_0 is the vacuum permittivity, the speed of the electron is *[AIPMT 1998]*
(a) zero (b) $\frac{e}{\sqrt{\varepsilon_0 a_0 m}}$
(c) $\frac{e}{\sqrt{4\pi\varepsilon_0 a_0 m}}$ (d) $\frac{\sqrt{4\pi\varepsilon_0 a_0 m}}{e}$

35 The energy of ground electronic state of hydrogen atom is – 13.6 eV. The energy of the first excited state will be *[AIPMT 1997]*
(a) – 54.4 eV (b) – 27.2 eV (c) – 6.8 eV (d) – 3.4 eV

36 When hydrogen atom is in its first excited level, its radius is *[NCERT (New) Pg. 299, AIPMT 1997]*
(a) four times, its ground state radius
(b) twice, its ground state radius
(c) same as its ground sate radius
(d) half of its ground state radius

37 When a hydrogen atom is raised from the ground state to an excited state *[AIPMT 1995]*
(a) PE decreases and KE increases
(b) PE increases and KE decreases
(c) both KE and PE decrease
(d) absorption spectrum

38 The spectrum obtained from a sodium vapour lamp is an example of *[NCERT (New) Pg. 298, AIPMT 1995]*
(a) band spectrum (b) continuous spectrum
(c) emission spectrum (d) absorption spectrum

39 An electron makes a transition from orbit $n = 4$ to the orbit $n = 2$ of a hydrogen atom. What is the wavelength of the emitted radiations ?
(R = Rydberg's constant) *[AIPMT 1995]*
(a) $\frac{16}{4R}$ (b) $\frac{16}{5R}$ (c) $\frac{16}{2R}$ (d) $\frac{16}{3R}$

40 The figure indicates the energy level diagram of an atom and the origin of six spectral lines in emission (e.g., line number 5 arises from the transition from level B to A.)

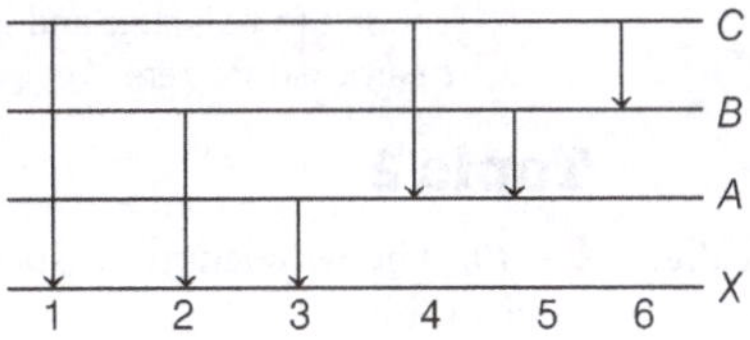

Which of the following spectral lines will occur in the absorption spectrum ? *[AIPMT 1995]*
(a) 4, 5, 6 (b) 1, 2, 3, 4, 5, 6
(c) 1, 2, 3 (d) 1, 4, 6

41 Doubly ionised helium atoms and hydrogen ions are accelerated from rest through the same potential drop. The ratio of the final velocities of the helium and the hydrogen ion is *[AIPMT 1994]*
(a) $\frac{1}{2}$ (b) 2
(c) $\frac{1}{\sqrt{2}}$ (d) $\sqrt{2}$

42 The radius of hydrogen atom in its ground state is 5.3×10^{-11} m. After collision with an electron it is found to have a radius of 21.2×10^{-11} m. What is the principal quantum number n of the final state of the atom ? *[NCERT (New) Pg. 296, AIPMT 1994]*
(a) $n = 4$ (b) $n = 2$
(c) $n = 16$ (d) $n = 3$

43 Hydrogen atoms are excited from ground state of the principal quantum number 4. Then, the number of spectral lines observed will be *[AIPMT 1993]*
(a) 3 (b) 6 (c) 5 (d) 2

44 Which source is associated with a line emission spectrum? *[AIPMT 1993]*
(a) Electric fire (b) Neon street sign
(c) Red traffic light (d) Sun

45 The ionisation energy of hydrogen atom is 13.6 eV. Following Bohr's theory, the energy corresponding to a transition between 3rd and 4th orbit is *[AIPMT 1992]*
(a) 3.40 eV (b) 1.51 eV
(c) 0.85 eV (d) 0.66 eV

46 In terms of Bohr radius a_0, the radius of the second Bohr orbit of a hydrogen atom is given by *[AIPMT 1992]*
(a) $4a_0$ (b) $8a_0$ (c) $\sqrt{2}a_0$ (d) $2a_0$

47 The ground state energy of H-atom is 13.6 eV. The energy needed to ionise H-atom from its second excited state *[NCERT (New) Pg. 297, AIPMT 1991]*
(a) 1.51 eV (b) 3.4 eV
(c) 13.6 eV (d) 12.1 eV

48 Consider an electron in the nth orbit of a hydrogen atom in the Bohr model. The circumference of the orbit can be expressed in terms of de-Broglie wavelength λ of that electron as *[AIPMT 1990]*
(a) $(0.529)n\lambda$ (b) $\sqrt{n\lambda}$
(c) $(13.6)\lambda$ (d) $n\lambda$

49 The valence electron in alkali metal is a *[AIPMT 1990]*
(a) f-electron (b) p-electron
(c) s-electron (d) d-electron

50 Energy levels A, B, C of a certain atom correspond to increasing values of energy i.e. $E_A < E_B < E_C$. If $\lambda_1, \lambda_2, \lambda_3$ are the wavelengths of radiation corresponding to the transitions C to B, B to A and C to A respectively, which of the following relation is correct? *[NCERT (New) Pg. 300, AIPMT 1990]*
(a) $\lambda_3 = \lambda_1 + \lambda_2$ (b) $\lambda_3 = \frac{\lambda_1 \lambda_2}{\lambda_1 + \lambda_2}$
(c) $\lambda_1 + \lambda_2 + \lambda_3 = 0$ (d) $\lambda_3^2 = \lambda_1^2 + \lambda_2^2$

51 To explain his theory, Bohr used *[AIPMT 1989]*
(a) conservation of linear momentum
(b) conservation of angular momentum
(c) conservation of quantum frequency
(d) conservation of energy

52 The ionisation energy of hydrogen atom is 13.6 eV, the ionisation energy of helium atom would be *[NCERT (New) Pg. 300, AIPMT 1988]*
(a) 13.6 eV (b) 27.2 eV
(c) 6.8 eV (d) 54.4 eV

• Key Index

Topic 1

1 (c)	2 (d)	3 (c)	4 (b)	5 (d)	6 (d)

Topic 2

1 (b)	2 (c)	3 (a)	4 (a)	5 (c)	6 (b)	7 (c)	8 (c)	9 (b)	10 (b)
11 (c)	12 (c)	13 (d)	14 (b)	15 (c)	16 (a)	17 (c)	18 (d)	19 (a)	20 (c)
21 (c)	22 (c)	23 (a)	24 (d)	25 (c)	26 (a)	27 (b)	28 (b)	29 (d)	30 (d)
31 (a)	32 (b)	33 (b)	34 (c)	35 (d)	36 (a)	37 (b)	38 (c)	39 (d)	40 (c)
41 (c)	42 (b)	43 (b)	44 (b)	45 (d)	46 (a)	47 (a)	48 (d)	49 (c)	50 (b)
51 (b)	52 (d)								

Detailed **Explanations**

Topic 1

01. *(c)* Atoms are electrically neutral as they contain equal number of proton and electron. Statement II is incorrect because atom of radioactive elements are not stable.
So, option (c) is correct.

02. *(d)* When an α-particle of mass m moving with velocity v bombards on a heavy nucleus of charge Ze, then there will be no loss of energy as in this case, initial kinetic energy of α-particle = potential energy of α-particle at closest approach.

$$\Rightarrow \quad \frac{1}{2}mv^2 = \frac{2Ze^2}{4\pi\varepsilon_0 r_0}$$

$$\Rightarrow \quad r_0 \propto \frac{1}{m}$$

03. *(c)* According to given situation,

$$\frac{1}{2}mv^2 = k\cdot\frac{Ze\cdot 2e}{r}$$

$$\Rightarrow \quad r = \frac{4kZe^2}{mv^2}$$

$$\Rightarrow \quad r \propto \frac{1}{m}$$

04. *(b)* For the distance of closest approach r_0,

$$\frac{1}{2}M_1u^2 = \frac{1}{4\pi\varepsilon_0}\frac{Z_1Z_2}{r_0}$$

So, the energy of the particle is directly proportional to Z_1Z_2.

05. *(d)* The charge on hydrogen nucleus $q_1 = +e$, charge on electron, $q_2 = -e$

According to Coulomb's law,

$$F = k\frac{q_1q_2}{r^2} = k\frac{(+e)(-e)}{r^2}$$

$$\text{or, } F = -\frac{ke^2}{r^3}\,\mathbf{r} = -\frac{ke^2}{r^2}\hat{\mathbf{r}}$$

06. *(d)* Rutherford calculated analytically, the relation between the impact parameter b and scattering angle θ, which is given by

$$b = \frac{1}{4\pi\varepsilon_0}\cdot\frac{Ze^2\cot\frac{\theta}{2}}{E}$$

where, $E = \frac{1}{2}mv^2$ is kinetic energy of alpha particle, when it is far away from the atom.

According to problem,

$$b = \frac{1}{4\pi\varepsilon_0}\cdot\frac{Ze^2\cot\frac{\theta}{2}}{E} = 0$$

As given that $b = 0$

so, $\cot\frac{\theta}{2} = 0$

$$\Rightarrow \quad \frac{\theta}{2} = 90^\circ$$

or $\quad \theta = 180^\circ$

• Concept Enhancer

(i) For large value of impact parameters, the repulsive forces experienced by the α-particle is weak and the α-particle is passes almost undeflected.

(ii) For small value of impact parameter, the repulsive force is large and so the α-particle is scattered large angle.

Topic 2

01. *(b)* The wavelength of spectral line is given by

$$\frac{1}{\lambda} = R\left[\frac{1}{n_1^2} - \frac{1}{n_2^2}\right]$$

A. $$\frac{1}{\lambda} = 1.09737\times10^7\left[\frac{1}{2^2} - \frac{1}{3^2}\right]$$

$$= 1.09737\times10^7\left[\frac{1}{4} - \frac{1}{9}\right]$$

$$= 1.09737\times10^7\left[\frac{5}{36}\right]$$

$$\Rightarrow \quad \lambda = \frac{36\times10^{-7}}{5\times1.09737} = 6.56114\times10^{-7}$$

$$\simeq 656.3 \text{ nm}$$

B. $$\lambda = \frac{10^{-7}}{1.09737\left[\frac{1}{2^2} - \frac{1}{4^2}\right]}$$

$$= \frac{10^{-7}\times16}{1.09737\times3}$$

$$= 4.8601\times10^{-7} \text{ m}$$

$$\simeq 486.1 \text{ nm}$$

C. $$\lambda = \frac{10^{-7}}{1.09737 \times \left[\frac{1}{2^2} - \frac{1}{5^2}\right]}$$

$$= \frac{10^{-7} \times 100}{1.09737 \times 21}$$

$$= 4.3393 \times 10^{-7} \text{ m}$$

$$\simeq 434.1 \text{ nm}$$

D. $$\lambda = \frac{10^{-7}}{1.09737 \times \left[\frac{1}{2^2} - \frac{1}{6^2}\right]}$$

$$= \frac{10^{-7} \times 144}{1.09737 \times 32} \simeq 410.2 \text{ nm}$$

Hence, A - III, B - IV, C - II, D - I

02. *(c)* Radius of innermost orbit of H-atom

$$r_0 = 5.3 \times 10^{-11} \text{ m}$$

∴ Radius of third allowed orbit of H-atom.

$$r_3 = r_0 n^2 = r_0 (3)^2$$
$$= 9r_0 = 9 \times 5.3 \times 10^{-11}$$
$$= 47.7 \times 10^{-11}$$
$$= 4.77 \times 10^{-10} \text{ m}$$
$$= 4.77 \text{ Å}$$

03. *(a)* In hydrogen spectrum,

$$\frac{1}{\lambda} = R\left(\frac{1}{n_1^2} - \frac{1}{n_2^2}\right)$$

For shortest wavelength in the Balmer series,

$$n_1 = 2 \text{ and } n_2 = \infty$$

$$\therefore \quad \frac{1}{\lambda} = R\left(\frac{1}{2^2} - \frac{1}{\infty^2}\right)$$

$$\Rightarrow \quad \frac{1}{\lambda} = \frac{R}{4}$$

$$\Rightarrow \quad R = \frac{4}{\lambda} \qquad \ldots\text{(i)}$$

For the shortest wavelength of Brackett series, $n_1 = 4$ and $n_2 = \infty$

$$\therefore \quad \frac{1}{\lambda_B} = R\left(\frac{1}{4^2} - \frac{1}{\infty^2}\right)$$

$$= \frac{R}{16} = \frac{4/\lambda}{16}$$

$$\Rightarrow \quad \frac{1}{\lambda_B} = \frac{1}{4\lambda}$$

$$\Rightarrow \quad \lambda_B = 4\lambda$$

04. *(a)* The minimum wavelength of X-rays produced by an electron accelerated through a potential difference V is given as

$$\lambda_{\text{min}} = \frac{hc}{eV} \Rightarrow \lambda_{\text{min}} \propto \frac{1}{V}$$

05. *(c)* According to Bohr's model of H-atom, energy of an electron revolving in nth orbit.

$$E = \frac{-13.6}{n^2} \text{ eV}$$

Here, for the first excited state.

$$T_1 = E_1 = \frac{-13.6}{n_1^2} = \frac{-13.6}{2^2}$$

$$[\because n_1 = 2]$$

For the second excited state,

$$T_2 = E_2 = \frac{-13.6}{n_2^2} = \frac{-13.6}{3^2} \text{ eV}$$

$$[\because n_2 = 3]$$

$$\therefore \quad \frac{T_1}{T_2} = \frac{-13.6/2^2}{-13.6/3^2} = \frac{3^2}{2^2} = \frac{9}{4}$$

$$\Rightarrow T_1 : T_2 = 9 : 4$$

06. *(b)* Total energy of an electron in the nth stationary orbit of hydrogen atom is given by

$$E_n = \frac{-Rhc}{n^2} = \frac{-13.6}{n^2} \text{ eV}$$

$$[\because Rhc = 13.6 \text{ eV}]$$

07. *(c)* Since, Bohr's model is valid for hydrogen and hydrogen like atoms He^+, deuteron, etc. So, it is not valid for singly ionised neon atom (Ne^+).

08. *(c)* Hydrogen atom can be considered to be the system of two charges, positive charged nucleus and negative charged electron. A system of this kind is equivalent to a single particle of mass m' that revolves around the position of the heavier particle. Then, the reduced mass of electron is

$$m' = \frac{mM}{m + M}$$

Its values is less than m.

Given, radius of first orbit for electron

$$r_1 = 0.51 \text{ Å},$$

ground state energy of electron,

$$E_1 = -13.6 \text{ eV},$$

mass of electron $= m_e$

mass of muon, $m_\mu = 207 m_e$

and mass of nucleus, $M = 1836 m_e$

When electron in hydrogen atom is replaced by muon, the reduced mass of muon is

$$m_\mu' = \frac{m_\mu M}{m_\mu + M} \qquad \ldots\text{(i)}$$

Substituting the given values in Eq. (i), we get

$$m_\mu' = \frac{207 m_e \times 1836 m_e}{207 m_e + 1836 m_e}$$

$$\approx 186\, m_e \qquad \ldots\text{(ii)}$$

The radius of first orbit in hydrogen atom for electron is given by,

$$r_1 = \frac{h^2 \varepsilon_0}{\pi m_e e^2} \qquad \ldots\text{(iii)}$$

The radius of first orbit for muon is

$$r_1' = \frac{h^2 \varepsilon_0}{\pi m_\mu' e^2}$$

$$[\because \text{charge of } \mu = \text{charge of } e^-]$$

$$= \frac{h^2 \varepsilon_0}{\pi \times 186 m_e e^2} \quad \text{[From Eq. (ii)]}$$

$$= \left(\frac{h^2 \varepsilon_0}{\pi m_e e^2}\right) \frac{1}{186} = \frac{r_1}{186}$$

[From Eq. (iii)]

$$= \frac{0.51}{186} \text{ Å} \qquad [\because r_1 = 0.51 \text{ Å}]$$

$$= 2.74 \times 10^{-13} \text{ m}$$

$$\simeq 2.56 \times 10^{-13} \text{ m}$$

$$[\because 1 \text{ Å} = 10^{-10} \text{ m}]$$

The total energy of electron is given by

$$E_n = \frac{-mZ^2 e^4}{8 \varepsilon_0^2 h^2} \left(\frac{1}{n^2}\right)$$

$$\Rightarrow \quad E_n \propto m$$

For electron in first orbit of hydrogen atom,

$$E_1 = k m_e \qquad \ldots\text{(iv)}$$

where, $k = \dfrac{e^4}{8 \varepsilon_0^2 h^2}$ = constant.

For muon in first orbit

$$E_1' = k m_\mu'$$
$$= k \times 186 m_e \quad \text{[from Eq. (i)]}$$
$$= 186 k m_e$$
$$= 186 E_1 \quad \text{[from Eq. (iv)]}$$
$$= 186(-13.6) \text{ eV} \quad \text{[Given]}$$
$$= -2529.6 \text{ eV}$$
$$= -2.5 \text{ keV} \simeq -2.8 \text{ keV}$$

09. *(b)* According to Bohr's model,

$$KE = \frac{Rhc}{n^2} \quad \ldots(i)$$

Similarly, potential energy is given by,

$$PE = -\frac{2Rhc}{n^2} \quad \ldots(ii)$$

∴ Total energy,

$$E = PE + KE$$

$$= -\frac{Rhc}{n^2}$$

[From Eqs. (i) and (ii)]

$$\Rightarrow \quad KE = -E \text{ and } PE = 2E$$

Given, $E = -3.4$ eV

∴ $KE = -(-3.4) = 3.4$ eV

and $PE = 2(-3.4) = -6.8$ eV

10. *(b)* Kinetic energy,

$$KE_n = \frac{Rhc}{n^2} \quad \ldots(i)$$

Total energy,

$$TE_n = \frac{-Rhc}{n^2} \quad \ldots(ii)$$

Dividing Eq. (i) by Eq. (ii), we get

$$\frac{KE_n}{TE_n} = \frac{\left(\frac{Rhc}{n^2}\right)}{-\left(\frac{Rhc}{n^2}\right)}$$

$$\Rightarrow \quad KE_n : TE_n = 1 : -1$$

11. *(c)* Wavelength of spectral lines are given by

$$\frac{1}{\lambda} = Z^2 R\left(\frac{1}{n_1^2} - \frac{1}{n_2^2}\right)$$

For last line of Balmer series,

$$n_1 = 2 \text{ and } n_2 = \infty$$

$$\Rightarrow \quad \frac{1}{\lambda_B} = Z^2 R\left(\frac{1}{2^2} - \frac{1}{\infty^2}\right)$$

$$= \frac{R}{4} \qquad [\because Z = 1]$$

Similarly, for last line of Lyman series,

$$n_1 = 1 \text{ and } n_2 = \infty$$

$$\Rightarrow \quad \frac{1}{\lambda_L} = Z^2 R\left(\frac{1}{1^2} - \frac{1}{\infty^2}\right) = R$$

$$\therefore \quad \frac{\frac{1}{\lambda_B}}{\frac{1}{\lambda_L}} = \frac{\frac{R}{4}}{R} = \frac{1}{4}$$

$$\Rightarrow \quad \frac{\lambda_L}{\lambda_B} = \frac{1}{4}$$

$$\Rightarrow \quad \frac{\lambda_B}{\lambda_L} = 4$$

12. *(c)*

key idea

Use the following data of n_1 and n_2 for solve this problem.

For last line of Balmer series, $n_1 = 2$ and $n_2 = \infty$ and for last line of Lyman series, $n_1 = 1$ and $n_2 = \infty$.

From Rydberg's formula,

$$\frac{1}{\lambda} = R\left(\frac{1}{n_f^2} - \frac{1}{n_i^2}\right)$$

$$= R\left(\frac{1}{2^2} - \frac{1}{3^2}\right) = \frac{5R}{36}$$

$$\text{and} \quad \frac{1}{\lambda'} = R\left(\frac{1}{3^2} - \frac{1}{4^2}\right) = \frac{7R}{144}$$

$$\frac{1}{\lambda} / \frac{1}{\lambda'} = \frac{5R}{36} \div \frac{7R}{144}$$

$$\Rightarrow \quad \frac{\lambda'}{\lambda} = \frac{5R}{36} \times \frac{144}{7R} = \frac{20}{7}$$

$$\Rightarrow \quad \lambda' = \frac{20}{7}\lambda$$

13. *(d)* In hydrogen atom, wavelength of characteristic spectrum

$$\frac{1}{\lambda} = RZ^2\left[\frac{1}{n_1^2} - \frac{1}{n_2^2}\right]$$

For Lyman series $n_1 = 1, n_2 = 2$

$$\frac{1}{\lambda_1} = RZ^2\left[\frac{1}{(1)^2} - \frac{1}{(2)^2}\right] \quad \ldots(i)$$

For Balmer series $n_1 = 2, n_2 = 3$

$$\frac{1}{\lambda_2} = RZ^2\left[\frac{1}{(2)^2} - \frac{1}{(3)^2}\right] \quad \ldots(ii)$$

Dividing Eq. (ii) by Eq. (i) we get

$$\frac{\lambda_1}{\lambda_2} = \frac{RZ^2\left[\frac{1}{4} - \frac{1}{9}\right]}{RZ^2\left[1 - \frac{1}{4}\right]} = \frac{\frac{5}{36}}{\frac{3}{4}}$$

$$\frac{\lambda_1}{\lambda_2} = \frac{5}{36} \times \frac{4}{3} = \frac{5}{27}$$

14. *(b)* Energy of electron in the 3rd orbit of He^+ is

$$E_3 = -13.6 \times \frac{Z^2}{n^2} \text{ eV} = -13.6 \times \frac{4}{3^2} \text{ eV}$$

$$= -13.6 \times \frac{4}{9} \times 1.6 \times 10^{-19} \text{ J}$$

From Bohr's model,

$$E_3 = -KE_3 = -\frac{1}{2} m_e v^2$$

$$\Rightarrow \quad \frac{1}{2} \times 9.1 \times 10^{-31} \times v^2$$

$$= -13.6 \times \frac{4}{9} \times 1.6 \times 10^{-19}$$

$$\Rightarrow \quad v^2 = \frac{136 \times 16 \times 4 \times 2 \times 10^{-11}}{9 \times 91}$$

$$\text{or,} \quad v = 1.46 \times 10^6 \text{ m/s}$$

15. *(c)*

key idea

You can find the amount of energy E provided to ground state electron using the following formula.

$$E = \frac{hc}{\lambda}$$

Energy provided to the ground state electron

$$= \frac{hc}{\lambda} = \frac{6.6 \times 10^{-34} \times 3 \times 10^8}{975 \times 10^{-10}}$$

$$= 0.020 \times 10^{-16} = 2 \times 10^{-18} \text{ J}$$

$$= \frac{20 \times 10^{-19}}{1.6 \times 10^{-19}} \text{ eV} = \frac{20}{1.6} \text{ eV}$$

$$= 12.5 \text{ eV}$$

It means the electron jumps to $n = 4$ from $n = 1$.

When electron will fall back, number of spectral lines emitted

$$= \frac{n(n-1)}{2} = \frac{4(4-1)}{2} = 6$$

16. *(a)* Wavelength for Lyman series

$$\lambda_L = \frac{1}{R\left(1 - \frac{1}{4}\right)} = \frac{4}{3R}$$

and wavelength for Balmer series

$$\lambda_B = \frac{1}{R\left(\frac{1}{4} - \frac{1}{9}\right)} = \frac{1}{R\left(\frac{5}{36}\right)} = \frac{36}{5R}$$

$$\therefore \quad \frac{\lambda_L}{\lambda_B} = \frac{4}{3R} \times \frac{5R}{36} = \frac{5}{27}$$

$$\Rightarrow \lambda_L : \lambda_B = 5 : 27$$

17. *(c)* When an electron in hydrogen atom jumps from first excited state ($n = 2$) to ground state ($n = 1$) energy is released and is given by

$$E = E_{(n=2)} - E_{(n=1)}$$

$$\text{where, } E_n = -\frac{13.6}{n^2} \text{ eV}$$

Energy released from emission of electron is given by

$$E = -3.4 - (-13.6)$$

$$= 10.2 \text{ eV}$$

Now, from photoelectric equation, work function,

$$\phi = E - eV = h\nu$$

$$\nu = \frac{E - eV}{h} = \frac{(10.2 - 3.57)e}{6.67 \times 10^{-34}}$$

$$\nu = \frac{6.63 \times 1.6 \times 10^{-19}}{6.67 \times 10^{-34}}$$

$$= 1.6 \times 10^{15} \text{Hz}$$

18. *(d)* According to question, for wavelength λ_1, $n_1 = 4$ and $n_2 = 3$ and for λ_2, $n_1 = 3$ and $n_2 = 2$ and we know that,

$$\frac{hc}{\lambda} = -13.6\left[\frac{1}{n_1^2} - \frac{1}{n_2^2}\right]$$

So, for λ_1

$$\Rightarrow \quad \frac{hc}{\lambda_1} = -13.6\left[\frac{1}{(4)^2} - \frac{1}{(3)^2}\right]$$

$$\frac{hc}{\lambda_1} = 13.6\left[\frac{7}{144}\right] \quad \ldots\text{(i)}$$

Similarly, for λ_2

$$\Rightarrow \quad \frac{hc}{\lambda_2} = -13.6\left[\frac{1}{(3)^2} - \frac{1}{(2)^2}\right]$$

$$\frac{hc}{\lambda_2} = 13.6\left[\frac{5}{36}\right] \quad \ldots\text{(ii)}$$

Hence, from Eqs. (i) and (ii), we get

$$\frac{\lambda_1}{\lambda_2} = \frac{20}{7}$$

19. *(a)* According to third postulate of Bohr's model, when an atom makes a transition from higher energy state to lower energy state, the difference of energy is carried away by a photon such that $h\nu = E_{n_i} - E_{n_f}$

$$\text{or} \quad \frac{hc}{\lambda} = Rhc\left[\frac{1}{n_f^2} - \frac{1}{n_i^2}\right]$$

[where, n_i = quantum number of higher energy state and n_f = quantum number of lower energy state.]

Energy difference between fifth and first orbit is $E_5 - E_1 = \dfrac{hc}{\lambda}$ and

$$Rhc - \frac{Rhc}{25} = \frac{hc}{\lambda}$$

$$\frac{24}{25}R = \frac{1}{\lambda}$$

$$\text{As,} \quad p = \frac{h}{\lambda}$$

$$\text{and} \quad v = \frac{h}{m\lambda} = \frac{24}{25}\frac{Rh}{m}$$

20. *(c)* For Lyman series for H-atom

$$\frac{hc}{\lambda} = Rhc\left(\frac{1}{1^2} - \frac{1}{2^2}\right)$$

and for H-like ion,

$$\frac{hc}{\lambda} = Z^2 Rhc\left(\frac{1}{2^2} - \frac{1}{4^2}\right)$$

$$\therefore \left(\frac{1}{1^2} - \frac{1}{2^2}\right) = Z^2\left(\frac{1}{4} - \frac{1}{16}\right)$$

$$\left(1 - \frac{1}{4}\right) = Z^2\left(\frac{1}{4} - \frac{1}{16}\right)$$

$$\Rightarrow \quad Z = 2$$

21. *(c)* We know that,

$$E_n = -\frac{13.6}{n^2}\text{ eV}$$

$$\therefore \quad E_1 = -13.6 \text{ eV} \qquad [\because n = 1]$$

$$E_2 = -\frac{13.6}{2^2} = -3.4 \text{ eV}$$

$$E_3 = -\frac{13.6}{3^2} = -1.5 \text{ eV},$$

$$E_4 = -\frac{13.6}{4^2} = -0.85 \text{ eV}$$

$$\therefore \quad E_3 - E_2 = -1.5 - (-3.4) = 1.9 \text{ eV}$$

$$E_4 - E_3 = -0.85 - (-1.5) = 0.65 \text{ eV}$$

22. *(c)* Given, stopping potential,

$$V_0 = 10 \text{ V}$$

Work function, $W = 2.75$ eV

According to Einstein's photoelectric equation.

$$eV_0 = h\nu - W$$

$$\text{or} \quad h\nu = eV_0 + W$$

$$= 10 \text{ eV} + 2.75 \text{ eV}$$

$$= 12.75 \text{ eV} \quad \ldots\text{(i)}$$

When an electron in the hydrogen atom jumps from excited state n to the ground state ($n = 1$), then the frequency ν of the emitted photon is given by

$$h\nu = E_n - E_1$$

$$\Rightarrow h\nu = -\frac{13.6}{n^2} - \left(-\frac{13.6}{1^2}\right)$$

$$\left(\because \text{For hydrogen atom, } E_n = -\frac{13.6}{n^2}\text{ eV}\right)$$

According to given problem

$$-\frac{13.6}{n^2} + 13.6 = 12.75 \quad \text{[Using Eq. (i)]}$$

$$\frac{13.6}{n^2} = 0.85$$

$$\Rightarrow \quad n^2 = \frac{13.6}{0.85} = 16$$

$$\text{or} \quad n = 4$$

23. *(a)* Energy E of an atom with principal quantum number n is given by $E = \dfrac{-13.6}{n^2}Z^2$ for first excited state $n = 2$ and for He^+, $Z = 2$

$$\text{So,} \quad E = \frac{-13.6 \times (2)^2}{(2)^2} = -13.6\text{eV}$$

24. *(d)*

key idea

You can use following formula to calculate number of spectral lines when an electron is excited to nth level from ground state using, $N = \dfrac{n(n-1)}{2}$.

Number of spectral lines

$$N = \frac{n(n-1)}{2} \Rightarrow \frac{n(n-1)}{2} = 6$$

$$\text{or} \quad n^2 - n - 12 = 0$$

$$\text{or} \ (n-4)(n+3) = 0$$

$$\text{or} \quad n = 4$$

Now as the first line of the series has the maximum wavelength, therefore electron jumps from the fourth orbit to the third orbit.

25. *(c)*

key idea

For the ground state, $n_0 = 1$ and for the first excited state, $n_1 = 2$

In the ground state, $n = 1$

$$E_1 = -\frac{13.6}{1^2} = -13.6 \text{ eV}$$

For the first excited state (i.e. for $n = 2$)

$$E_2 = \frac{-13.6}{2^2} = -3.4 \text{ eV}$$

$$\Delta E = E_2 - E_1$$

$$= -3.4 + 13.6$$

$$= 10.2 \text{ eV}$$

26. *(a)* The energy of hydrogen atom when the electron revolves in nth orbit is given by

$$E = \frac{-13.6\,Z^2}{n^2}\text{ eV} \qquad [Z = 1]$$

In the ground state; $n = 1$

$$E = \frac{-13.6}{1^2} = -13.6 \text{ eV}$$

For $n = 2$,

$$E = \frac{-13.6}{2^2} = -3.4 \text{ eV}$$

So, kinetic energy of electron in the first excited state (i.e. for $n = 2$) is

$$\text{KE} = -E = -(-3.4) = 3.4 \text{ eV}$$

27. *(b)* In a discharge tube, after being accelerated though a high potential difference the ions in the gas strike the cathode with huge kinetic energy. This collision liberates electrons from the cathode. These free electrons can further liberate ions from gas molecules through collisions.

The positive ions are attracted towards the cathode and negatively charged electrons move towards anode. Thus, ionisation of gas results.

28. *(b)* Ionisation energy corresponding to ionisation potential ($E_1 = -13.6$ eV)

Photon energy incident (ΔE) = 12.1 eV

So, the energy of electron in excited state (E_2) is given by

$$E_2 - E_1 = \Delta E$$

$$\Rightarrow \quad E_2 = \Delta E + E_1$$

$$\Rightarrow \quad E_2 = -13.6 + 12.1$$

$$\Rightarrow \quad E_2 = -1.5 \text{ eV}$$

$$\text{i.e.} \quad E_2 = -\frac{13.6}{n^2} \text{ eV}$$

$$-1.5 = \frac{-13.6}{n^2}$$

$$\Rightarrow \quad n^2 = \frac{-13.6}{-1.5} \approx 9$$

$$\therefore \quad n = 3$$

i.e. energy of electron in excited state corresponds to third orbit.

The possible spectral lines is given by

$$\frac{n(n-1)}{2}$$

$$\Rightarrow \frac{3(3-1)}{2} \Rightarrow 3$$

29. *(d)* Kinetic energy of electron

$$\text{KE} = \frac{Ze^2}{8\pi\varepsilon_0 r}$$

Potential energy of electron

$$U = -\frac{1}{4\pi\varepsilon_0}\frac{Ze^2}{r}$$

$\therefore$ Total energy

$$E = \text{KE} + U$$

$$= \frac{Ze^2}{8\pi\varepsilon_0 r} - \frac{Ze^2}{4\pi\varepsilon_0 r}$$

$$\text{or} \quad E = -\frac{Ze^2}{8\pi\varepsilon_0 r}$$

$$\text{or} \quad E = -\text{KE}$$

$$\text{or} \quad \text{KE} = -E = -(-3.4)$$

$$= 3.4 \text{ eV}$$

30. *(d)* Given, $E_n = -\frac{13.6}{n^2}$ eV

Energy of photon ejected when electron jumps from $n = 3$ to $n = 2$ state is given by

$$\Delta E = E_3 - E_2$$

Energy of third orbit

$$E_3 = -\frac{13.6}{(3)^2} \text{ eV} = -\frac{13.6}{9} \text{ eV}$$

Energy of second orbit

$$E_2 = -\frac{13.6}{(2)^2} \text{ eV} = -\frac{13.6}{4} \text{ eV}$$

$$\text{So,} \quad \Delta E = E_3 - E_2$$

$$= -\frac{13.6}{9} - \left(-\frac{13.6}{4}\right)$$

$$= 1.9 \text{ eV (approximately)}$$

31. *(a)* According to Bohr's hypothesis, electron can revolve only in those orbits in which its angular momentum is an integral multiple of $\frac{h}{2\pi}$, where h is Planck's constant. In these orbits, angular momentum of electron can have magnitude as $\frac{h}{2\pi}, \frac{2h}{2\pi}, \frac{3h}{2\pi}$ .... etc., but never as $\frac{1.5h}{2\pi}, \frac{2.5h}{2\pi}, \frac{3.5h}{2\pi}$ .... etc. This is called the quantisation of angular momentum.

32. *(b)* Energy levels of H-atom,

$$E_n = -\frac{13.6Z^2}{n^2} \text{ eV} \qquad (Z = 1)$$

$$\Rightarrow \quad E_n = -13.6/n^2 \text{ eV}$$

Photons are emitted only when electron jumps from higher energy level (higher n-value) to lower energy level (lower n-value).

So, alternative (a) and (c) are wrong.

Energy difference from $n = 2$ to $n = 1$ level is

$$\Delta E_{2\to 1} = 13.6\left(\frac{1}{1^2} - \frac{1}{2^2}\right) \text{eV}$$

$$= 13.6 \times \frac{3}{4}$$

$$= 10.2 \text{ eV}$$

Energy difference from $n = 6$ to $n = 2$ level is

$$\Delta E_{6\to 2} = 13.6\left(\frac{1}{2^2} - \frac{1}{6^2}\right)$$

$$= 13.6 \times \left(\frac{1}{4} - \frac{1}{36}\right)$$

$$= 13.6 \times \frac{2}{9} = 3.02 \text{ eV}$$

Thus, it is evident that difference is larger for $n = 2$ to $n = 1$ transition. Hence, maximum energy photon or shortest wavelength will be emitted during transition from $n = 2$ to $n = 1$

33. *(b)*

(a) Second line of Lyman series corresponds to the transition $n = 3 \to n = 1$

(b) Second line of Balmer series corresponds to the transition $n = 4 \to n = 2$

(c) Second line of Paschen series corresponds to the transition $n = 5 \to n = 3$

(d) An absorption line of Balmer series arises when electron jumps from $n = 2$ to any other higher state.

Thus, choice (b) is correct.

34. *(c)* From Coulomb's attraction between the positive proton and negative electron $= \frac{1}{4\pi\varepsilon_0}\frac{e^2}{r^2}$

[For neutral atom]

Centripetal force has magnitude

$$F = \frac{mv^2}{r}$$

So, the revolving electrons

$$\frac{mv^2}{r} = \frac{1}{4\pi\varepsilon_0}\frac{e^2}{r^2}$$

$$\Rightarrow \quad v^2 = \frac{1}{4\pi\varepsilon_0}\frac{e^2}{mr}$$

$$\text{or} \quad v = \frac{e}{\sqrt{4\pi\varepsilon_0 mr}}$$

For ground state of H-atom, $r = a_0$

$$\therefore \quad v = \frac{e}{\sqrt{4\pi\varepsilon_0 m a_0}}$$

35. *(d)* The energy of hydrogen like atom in its nth excited state is given by

$$E_n = -13.6\frac{Z^2}{n^2}.$$

For ground state (n=1), and atomic number (Z) = 1

$$E_1 = -\frac{13.6}{(1)^2} = -13.6 \text{ eV}$$

For first excited state (n=2),

$$E_2 = -\frac{13.6}{(2)^2} = -\frac{13.6}{4}$$
$$= -3.4 \text{ eV}$$

• Concept Enhancer

In ground state (n = 1) energy of atom is −13.6 eV and energy corresponding to $n = \infty$ is zero. Therefore, energy required to remove the electron from ground state is 13.6 eV.

36. *(a)* The radius of nth Bohr's orbit of hydrogen and hydrogen like atom

$$r_n = \frac{\varepsilon_0 n^2 h^2}{\pi m e^2 Z}$$

$$\therefore \quad r_n = \frac{n^2 a_0}{Z} \text{ or } r_n \propto \frac{n^2}{Z}$$

For ground state, $n = 1$

Atomic number, $Z = 1$

For first excited state, $n = 2$

$$\therefore \quad \frac{r_2}{r_1} = \left(\frac{2}{1}\right)^2 = 4$$

or $\quad r_2 = 4r_1$

37. *(b)* Kinetic energy of electron is given by

$$\text{KE} = \frac{kZe^2}{2r}$$

As atom is excited, its radius increases, thus, KE, decreases

Potential energy of electron is

$$U = -\frac{kZe^2}{r}$$

As atom is excited, its radius increases, but due to negative sign or reverse sign, its actual potential energy increases. When a hydrogen atom is raised from the ground, to an excited state the potential energy increases and kinetic energy decreases.

38. *(c)* When continuous light from a source is examined directly in a spectroscope, we observe the emission spectrum of the source. The sodium vapour spectrum, consists of a few isolated bright lines. Each bright line corresponds to a particular wavelength. It is emitted by the atoms in the gaseous state.

When continuous light from a source is made to pass through an absorbing substance and then examined in a spectroscope, we observe absorption spectrum of the substance.

A band spectrum is emitted by chemical compounds in the vapour state. It is therefore a molecule spectrum.

A continuous emission spectrum consists of a wide range of unseparated wavelengths.

39. *(d)* We know that,

$$\frac{1}{\lambda} = R\left[\frac{1}{n_1^2} - \frac{1}{n_2^2}\right] = R\left[\frac{1}{(2)^2} - \frac{1}{(4)^2}\right]$$
$$= R\left[\frac{1}{4} - \frac{1}{16}\right] = R\left[\frac{4-1}{16}\right] = \frac{3R}{16}$$
$$\Rightarrow \lambda = \frac{16}{3R}$$

40. *(c)* Absorption spectrum involves only excitation of ground energy level to higher energy level. Therefore spectral lines 1, 2, 3 will occur in the absorption spectrum.

41. *(c)* If v is the speed acquired by particle when accelerated under a potential difference V, then

KE gained by particle

$$= \frac{1}{2}mv^2 = eV \text{ or } v = \sqrt{\frac{2eV}{m}}$$

So, for two different cases of the He-atom and H-atom,

$$\frac{v_{\text{He}}}{v_{\text{H}}} = \frac{\sqrt{\dfrac{2(e)_{\text{He}}V}{m_{\text{He}}}}}{\sqrt{\dfrac{2(e)_{\text{H}}V}{m_{\text{H}}}}}$$

As $\quad m_{\text{He}} = 4m_{\text{H}}$

and $\quad (e)_{\text{He}} = 2(e)_{\text{H}}$

$$\therefore \quad \frac{v_{\text{He}}}{v_{\text{H}}} = \frac{1}{\sqrt{2}}$$

42. *(b)* Radii of Bohr's stationary orbit is given by

$$r = \frac{n^2 h^2}{4\pi^2 mke^2 Z}$$

$$\Rightarrow \quad r \propto \frac{n^2}{Z}$$

Considering two situations of electrons,

$$\Rightarrow \quad \frac{(r_f)}{(r_i)} = \frac{n_f^2}{n_i^2}$$

For ground state $n_i = 1$

$$\therefore \quad \frac{21.2 \times 10^{-11}}{5.3 \times 10^{-11}} = n_f^2 \text{ or } n_f^2 = 4$$

$$\therefore \quad n_f = 2$$

43. *(b)* Number of spectral lines observed in hydrogen spectrum is given by

$$= \frac{n(n-1)}{2}$$
$$= \frac{4(4-1)}{2} = 6$$

44. *(b)* In line emission spectrum, every line spectrum consists of a few isolated bright lines, each bright line corresponds to a particular wavelength. It is emitted by atoms in the gaseous state.

e.g. a sodium discharge lamp, a mercury vapour lamp, a neon discharge tube and a helium discharge tube all emit sharp lines of definite wavelengths.

45. *(d)* Total energy of electron for hydrogen like atom is given by

$$E_n = -\frac{13.6Z^2}{n^2}$$

$$\therefore \quad E_3 = -\frac{13.6}{3^2} \text{ eV} \quad [Z = 1, n = 3]$$
$$= -1.51 \text{ eV}$$
$$E_4 = -\frac{13.6}{4^2} = -0.85 \text{ eV}$$
$$\therefore E_4 - E_3 = 1.51 - 0.85$$
$$= 0.66 \text{ eV}$$

46. *(a)*

key idea

For solving the problem, dependence of radius of nth orbit of hydrogen like atom must be kept in mind i.e. $r_n \propto \frac{n^2}{Z}$

(where, n = nth orbit and Z = atomic number)

From Bohr's postulate, for any permitted (stationary orbit).

Angular momentum of electron revolving in an orbit is constant

i.e. $\quad mvr = \dfrac{nh}{2\pi}$

or $\quad v = \dfrac{nh}{2\pi mr} \quad \ldots(i)$

Also, $\quad \dfrac{mv^2}{r} = \dfrac{Ze^2}{4\pi\varepsilon_0 r^2} = \dfrac{kZe^2}{r^2} \quad \ldots(ii)$

(where, $k = \frac{1}{4\pi\varepsilon_0}$) Symbols have their usual meaning.

From Eqs. (i) and (ii),

$$r = \frac{n^2h^2}{4\pi^2 mkZe^2}$$

For hydrogen atom, $Z = 1$

$$\therefore \quad r = \frac{n^2h^2}{4\pi^2 mke^2}$$

$$\Rightarrow \quad r_n \propto n^2$$

$$\therefore \quad a_2 = 4a_0$$

47. *(a)* For second excited state,

$$n = 3$$

∴ Energy needed to ionise H-atom from its second excited state

$$E = \frac{2\pi^2 mke^4}{h^2}\left(\frac{1}{3^2} - \frac{1}{\infty}\right)$$

or we can say that

$$E \propto \frac{Z^2}{n^2} \quad \left(\begin{matrix} Z = \text{atomic number} \\ n = n\text{th orbit} \end{matrix}\right)$$

So, $E = \frac{13.6}{3^2}$ eV $= 1.51$ eV

48. *(d)* The circumference of an orbit in an atom in terms of wavelength of wave associated with electron is given by

$$2\pi r_n = n\lambda$$

[r_n = radius of any n orbit]

49. *(c)* The outermost electrons in an atom are called valence electrons. In alkali metals (IA group) outermost electron is present in *s*-orbital.

Alkali metals have one valence electron. e.g. Li, Na, K.

50. *(b)*

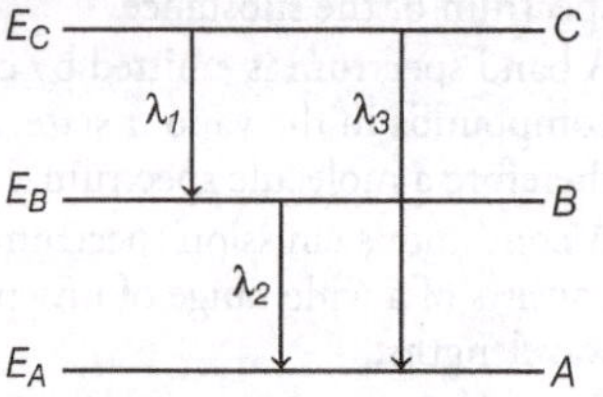

Using Bohr's postulate for radiation of spectral line, we have

Radiation of wavelength from C to B

$$E_C - E_B = \frac{hc}{\lambda_1} \quad \ldots\text{(i)}$$

Radiation of wavelength from B to A

$$E_B - E_A = \frac{hc}{\lambda_2} \quad \ldots\text{(ii)}$$

Radiation of wavelength from C to A

$$E_C - E_A = \frac{hc}{\lambda_3} \quad \ldots\text{(iii)}$$

Also,

$$(E_C - E_A) = (E_C - E_B) + (E_B - E_A)$$

$$\therefore \quad \frac{hc}{\lambda_3} = \frac{hc}{\lambda_1} + \frac{hc}{\lambda_2}$$

$$\text{or} \quad \frac{1}{\lambda_3} = \frac{1}{\lambda_1} + \frac{1}{\lambda_2}$$

$$\Rightarrow \lambda_3 = \frac{\lambda_1\lambda_2}{\lambda_1 + \lambda_2}$$

51. *(b)* According to Bohr, electron can revolve only in certain discrete non-radiating orbits, called stationary orbits, for which total angular momentum of the revolving electron is an integral multiple of $\frac{h}{2\pi}$, where h is Planck's constant.

For orbits, conservation of angular momentum is applicable.

∴ For any permitted orbit,

$$mvr = \frac{nh}{2\pi}$$

52. *(d)* Ionisation energy is defined as the energy required to knock an electron completely out of an isolated gaseous atom. When electron is raised to the orbit $n = \infty$, it will be completely out of the atom.

Ionisation energy of helium,

$$E = \frac{2\pi^2 mZ^2k^2e^4}{h^2}\left[\frac{1}{1^2} - \frac{1}{\infty}\right]$$

$$= \frac{2\pi^2 m(2)^2k^2e^4}{h^2}\left[\frac{1}{1^2} - \frac{1}{\infty}\right]$$

Ionisation energy for hydrogen atom

$$= 13.6 \text{ eV}$$

$$= \frac{2\pi^2 mk^2e^2}{h^2} \times 4 \times \left[\frac{1}{1^2} - \frac{1}{\infty^2}\right]$$

$$= 4 \times 13.6$$

$$= 54.4 \text{ eV}$$

In NEET 2024, 1 question was visible from this chapter. In past 5 years, 4 questions from topic-1 and 3 questions from topic-2 were asked.
For detailed analysis scan QR code

NUCLEI

Topic 1 Nucleus and Radioactivity

01 $^{290}_{82}X \xrightarrow{\alpha} {}^{286}_{80}Y \xrightarrow{e^+} Z \xrightarrow{\beta^-} P \xrightarrow{e^-} Q$

In the nuclear emission stated above, the mass number and atomic number of the product Q respectively are **[NCERT (New) Pg. 309, NEET 2024]**
(a) 280, 81 (b) 286, 80 (c) 288, 82 (d) 286, 81

02 In the given nuclear reaction, the element X is **[NEET 2022]**

$^{22}_{11}\text{Na} \longrightarrow X + e^+ + \nu$

(a) $^{23}_{10}\text{Ne}$ (b) $^{22}_{10}\text{Ne}$ (c) $^{22}_{12}\text{Mg}$ (d) $^{23}_{11}\text{Na}$

03 A nucleus of mass number 189 splits into two nuclei having mass number 125 and 64. The ratio of radius of two daughter nuclei, respectively is **[NEET 2022]**
(a) 4 : 5 (b) 5 : 4 (c) 25 : 16 (d) 1 : 1

04 What happens to the mass number and atomic number of an element when it emits γ-radiation ? **[NEET (Oct.) 2020]**
(a) Mass number decreases by four and atomic number decreases by two.
(b) Mass number and atomic number remain unchanged.
(c) Mass number remains unchanged, while atomic number decreases by one.
(d) Mass number increases by four and atomic number increases by two.

05 α-particle consists of **[NEET (National) 2019]**
(a) 2 electrons, 2 protons and 2 neutrons
(b) 2 electrons and 4 protons only
(c) 2 protons only
(d) 2 protons and 2 neutrons only

06 If radius of the $^{27}_{13}\text{Al}$ nucleus is taken to be R_{Al}, then the radius of $^{125}_{53}\text{Te}$ nucleus is nearly **[AIPMT 2015]**

(a) $\left(\frac{53}{13}\right)^{\frac{1}{3}} R_{\text{Al}}$ (b) $\frac{5}{3} R_{\text{Al}}$

(c) $\frac{3}{5} R_{\text{Al}}$ (d) $\left(\frac{13}{53}\right)^{\frac{1}{3}} R_{\text{Al}}$

07 If the nuclear radius of ^{27}Al is 3.6 fm, the approximate nuclear radius of ^{64}Cu in fm is **[AIPMT 2012]**
(a) 2.4 (b) 1.2
(c) 4.8 (d) 3.6

08 Two nuclei have their mass number in the ratio of 1:3. The ratio of their nuclear densities would be **[NCERT (New) Pg. 309, AIPMT 2008]**
(a) $(3)^{1/3}:1$ (b) 1:1 (c) 1:3 (d) 3:1

09 If the nucleus $^{27}_{13}\text{Al}$ has a nuclear radius of about 3.6 fm, then $^{125}_{52}\text{Te}$ would have its radius approximately as **[AIPMT 2007]**
(a) 6.0 fm (b) 9.6 fm
(c) 12.0 fm (d) 4.8 fm

10 The radius of germanium (Ge) nuclide is measured to be twice the radius of $^{9}_{4}\text{Be}$. The number of nucleons in Ge are **[NCERT (New) Pg. 309, AIPMT 2006]**
(a) 73 (b) 74 (c) 75 (d) 72

11 The mass number of a nucleus is **[AIPMT 2003]**
(a) sometimes equal to its atomic number
(b) sometimes less than and sometimes more than its atomic number
(c) always less than its atomic number
(d) always more than its atomic number

12 The volume occupied by an atom is greater than the volume of the nucleus by factor of about **[AIPMT 2003]**
(a) 10^{10} (b) 10^{15}
(c) 10^{1} (d) 10^{5}

13 In compound $X(n, \alpha) \rightarrow {}_3\text{Li}^7$, the element X is **[AIPMT 2001]**
(a) $_2\text{He}^4$ (b) $_5\text{B}^{10}$
(c) $_5\text{B}^9$ (d) $_4\text{Be}^{11}$

14 Which of the following is positively charged ? **[AIPMT 2001]**
(a) α-particle (b) β-particle
(c) γ-rays (d) X-rays

15 In one α and 2 β emissions *[AIPMT 1999]*
(a) mass number reduces by 2
(b) mass number reduces by 6
(c) atomic number reduces by 2
(d) atomic number remains unchanged

16 α-particles are *[NCERT (Old) Pg. 449, AIPMT 1999]*
(a) 2 free protons
(b) helium atoms
(c) singly ionised helium atoms
(d) doubly ionised helium atoms

17 A nucleus ${}_nX^m$ emits one α and two β-particles. The resulting nucleus is *[AIPMT 1998]*
(a) ${}_nX^{m-4}$ (b) ${}_{n-2}Y^{m-4}$
(c) ${}_{n-4}Z^{m-4}$ (d) None of these

18 The stable nucleus that has a radius half that of Fe^{56} is *[AIPMT 1997]*
(a) Li^7 (b) Na^{21} (c) S^{16} (d) Ca^{40}

19 The mass number of He is 4 and that for sulphur is 32. The radius of sulphur nuclei is larger than that of helium by *[NCERT (New) Pg. 309, AIPMT 1994]*
(a) $\sqrt{8}$ (b) 4 (c) 2 (d) 8

20 The mass density of a nucleus varies with mass number A as *[AIPMT 1992]*
(a) A^2 (b) A (c) constant (d) $\frac{1}{A}$

21 If the nuclear force between two protons, two neutrons and between proton and neutron is denoted by F_{pp}, F_{nn} and F_{pn} respectively, then *[AIPMT 1991]*
(a) $F_{pp} \approx F_{nn} \approx F_{pn}$
(b) $F_{pp} \neq F_{nn}$ and $F_{pp} = F_{nn}$
(c) $F_{pp} = F_{nn} = F_{pn}$
(d) $F_{pp} \neq F_{nn} \neq F_{pn}$

22 In the nucleus of ${}_{11}Na^{23}$, the number of protons, neutrons and electrons are *[AIPMT 1991]*
(a) 11, 12, 0 (b) 23, 12, 11
(c) 12, 11, 0 (d) 23, 11, 12

23 The constituents of atomic nuclei are believed to be *[AIPMT 1991]*
(a) neutrons and protons
(b) protons only
(c) electrons and protons
(d) electrons, protons and neutrons

24 The nucleus ${}_6C^{12}$ absorbs an energetic neutron and emits a beta particle β. The resulting nucleus is *[AIPMT 1990]*
(a) ${}_7N^{14}$ (b) ${}_7N^{13}$ (c) ${}_5B^{13}$ (d) ${}_6C^{13}$

25 The ratio of the radii of the nuclei ${}_{13}Al^{27}$ and ${}_{52}Te^{125}$ is approximately *[AIPMT 1990]*
(a) 6 : 10 (b) 13 : 52
(c) 40 : 177 (d) 14 : 73

26 Which of the following statements is true for nuclear forces? *[NCERT (New) Pg. 313, AIPMT 1990]*
(a) They obey the inverse square law of distance.
(b) They obey the inverse third power law of distance.
(c) They are short range forces.
(d) They are equal in strength to electromagnetic forces.

Topic 2 Nuclear Fission, Fusion and Binding Energy

01 A nucleus with mass number 240 breaks into two fragments each of mass number 120, the binding energy per nucleon of unfragmented nuclei is 7.6 MeV while that of fragments is 8.5 MeV. The total gain in the binding energy in the process is *[NCERT (New) Pg. 315, NEET 2021]*
(a) 0.9 MeV (b) 9.4 MeV
(c) 804 MeV (d) 216 MeV

02 The energy equivalent of 0.5 g of a substance is *[NEET (Sep.) 2020]*
(a) 4.5×10^{13} J (b) 1.5×10^{13} J
(c) 0.5×10^{13} J (d) 4.5×10^{16} J

03 When a uranium isotope ${}^{235}_{92}U$ is bombarded with a neutron, it generates ${}^{89}_{36}Kr$, three neutrons and *[NCERT (New) Pg. 315, NEET (Sep.) 2020]*
(a) ${}^{91}_{40}Zr$ (b) ${}^{101}_{36}Kr$ (c) ${}^{103}_{36}Kr$ (d) ${}^{144}_{56}Ba$

04 A nucleus of uranium decays at rest into nuclei of thorium and helium. Then, *[NCERT (New) Pg. 315, AIPMT 2015]*
(a) the helium nucleus has more kinetic energy than the thorium nucleus
(b) the helium nucleus has less momentum than the thorium nucleus
(c) the helium nucleus has more momentum than the thorium nucleus
(d) the helium nucleus has less kinetic energy than the thorium nucleus

05 The binding energy per nucleon of ${}^7_3Li$ and ${}^4_2He$ nuclei are 5.60 MeV and 7.06 MeV, respectively. In the nuclear reaction ${}^7_3Li + {}^1_1H \rightarrow {}^4_2He + {}^4_2He + Q$, the value of energy Q released is *[AIPMT 2014]*
(a) 19.6 MeV (b) – 2.4 MeV
(c) 8.4 MeV (d) 17.3 MeV

06 How does the binding energy per nucleon vary with the increase in the number of nucleons? *[NEET 2013]*
(a) Decrease continuously with mass number.
(b) First decreases and then increases with increase in mass number.
(c) First increases and then decreases with increase in mass number.
(d) Increases continuously with mass number.

07 A certain mass of hydrogen is changed to helium by the process of fusion. The mass defect in fusion reaction is 0.02866 u. The energy liberated per u is (given $1\,u = 931\,MeV$)

[NCERT (New) Pg. 311, NEET 2013]

(a) 2.67 MeV
(b) 26.7 MeV
(c) 6.675 MeV
(d) 13.35 MeV

08 Fusion reaction takes place at high temperature because ***[AIPMT 2011]***

(a) atoms get ionised at high temperature
(b) kinetic energy is high enough to overcome the coulomb repulsion between nuclei
(c) molecules break up at high temperature
(d) nuclei break up at high temperature

09 The mass of a $^7_3$Li nucleus is 0.042u less than the sum of the masses of all its nucleons. The binding energy per nucleon of $^7_3$Li nucleus is nearly

[NCERT (New) Pg. 311, AIPMT 2010]

(a) 46 MeV (b) 5.6 MeV
(c) 3.9 MeV (d) 23 MeV

10 A nucleus $^A_Z X$ has mass represented by $m(A, Z)$. If m_p and m_n denote the mass of proton and neutron respectively and BE the binding energy (in MeV), then ***[AIPMT 2007]***

(a) $BE = [m(A, Z) - Zm_p - (A - Z)m_n]\,c^2$
(b) $BE = [Zm_p + (A - Z)m_n - m(A, Z)]\,c^2$
(c) $BE = [Zm_p + Am_n - m(A, Z)]c^2$
(d) $BE = m(A, Z) - Zm_p - (A - Z)m_n$

11 The binding energy of deuteron is 2.2 MeV and that of $^4_2$He is 28 MeV. If two deuterons are fused to form one $^4_2$He, then the energy released is

[NCERT (New) Pg. 311, AIPMT 2006]

(a) 25.8 MeV (b) 23.6 MeV
(c) 19.2 MeV (d) 30.2 MeV

12 In any fission process the ratio $\dfrac{\text{mass of fission products}}{\text{mass of parent nucleus}}$ is ***[AIPMT 2005]***

(a) less than 1
(b) greater than 1
(c) equal to 1
(d) depends on the mass of parent nucleus

13 Fission of nuclei is possible because the binding energy per nucleon in them ***[AIPMT 2005]***

(a) increases with mass number at high mass numbers
(b) decreases with mass number at high mass numbers
(c) increases with mass number at low mass numbers
(d) decreases with mass number at low mass numbers

14 In the reaction $^2_1H + ^3_1H \rightarrow ^4_2He + ^1_0n$, if the binding energies of $^2_1$H, $^3_1$H and $^4_2$He are respectively *a*, *b* and *c* (in MeV), then the energy (in MeV) released in this reaction is ***[AIPMT 2005]***

(a) $c + a - b$ (b) $c - a - b$
(c) $a + b + c$ (d) $a + b - c$

15 m_p denotes the mass of a proton and m_n that of a neutron. A given nucleus of binding energy BE, contains Z protons and N neutrons. The mass $m(N, Z)$ of the nucleus is given by

[NCERT (New) Pg. 311, AIPMT 2004]

(a) $m(N, Z) = Nm_n + ZM_p - BEc^2$
(b) $m(N, Z) = Nm_n + Zm_p + BEc^2$
(c) $m(N, Z) = Nm_n + Zm_p - BE/c^2$
(d) $m(N, Z) = Nm_n + Zm_p + BE/c^2$

16 If in a nuclear fusion process, the masses of the fusing nuclei be m_1 and m_2 and the mass of the resultant nucleus be m_3, then ***[NCERT (New) Pg. 315, AIPMT 2004]***

(a) $m_3 = m_1 + m_2$ (b) $m_3 = |m_1 - m_2|$
(c) $m_3 < (m_1 + m_2)$ (d) $m_3 > (m_1 + m_2)$

17 Solar energy is mainly caused due to ***[AIPMT 2003]***

(a) fusion of protons during synthesis of heavier elements
(b) gravitational contraction
(c) burning of hydrogen in the oxygen
(d) fission of uranium present in the sun

18 The mass of proton is 1.0073 u and that of neutron is 1.0087 u (u = atomic mass unit)
The binding energy of $_2He^4$ is (mass of helium nucleus = 4.0015 u) ***[NCERT (New) Pg. 311, AIPMT 2003]***

(a) 28.4 MeV (b) 0.061 u
(c) 0.0305 J (d) 0.0305 erg

19 When a deuterium is bombarded on $_8O^{16}$ nucleus, an α-particle is emitted, then the product nucleus is ***[AIPMT 2002]***

(a) $_7N^{13}$ (b) $_5B^{10}$ (c) $_4Be^9$ (d) $_7N^{14}$

20 Which of the following are suitable for the fusion process? ***[AIPMT 2002]***

(a) Light nuclei
(b) Heavy nuclei
(c) Elements lying in the middle of periodic table
(d) Elements lying in the middle of binding energy curve

21 In nuclear fission process, energy is released because

[NCERT (New) Pg. 315, AIPMT 2001]

(a) mass of products is more than mass of nucleus
(b) total binding energy of products formed due to nuclear fission is more than the parent fissionable material
(c) total binding energy of products formed due to nuclear fission is less than parent fissionable material
(d) mass of some particles is converted into energy

22 m_p and m_n are masses of proton and neutron respectively. An element of mass m has Z protons and N neutrons, then *[AIPMT 2001]*
(a) $m > Zm_p + Nm_n$
(b) $m = Zm_p + Nm_n$
(c) $m < Zm_p + Nm_n$
(d) m may be greater than, less than or equal to $Zm_p + Nm_n$, depending on nature of element

23 Nuclear fission can be explained by *[AIPMT 2000]*
(a) proton-proton cycle
(b) liquid drop model of nucleus
(c) independent of nuclear particle model
(d) nuclear shell model

24 Complete the equation for the following fission process
$${}_{92}U^{235} + {}_0n^1 \longrightarrow {}_{38}Sr^{90} + \ldots\ldots\ldots\ldots$$
[NCERT (New) Pg. 315, AIPMT 1998]
(a) ${}_{54}Xe^{143} + 3\ {}_0n^1$ (b) ${}_{54}Xe^{145}$
(c) ${}_{57}Xe^{142}$ (d) ${}_{54}Xe^{142} + {}_0n^1$

25 In a fission reaction,
$${}^{236}_{92}U \longrightarrow {}^{117}X + {}^{117}Y + n + n$$
the binding energy per nucleon of X and Y is 8.5 MeV whereas of ${}^{236}U$ is 7.6 MeV. The total energy liberated will be about *[AIPMT 1997]*
(a) 2000 MeV
(b) 200 MeV
(c) 2 MeV
(d) 1 keV

26 Which of the following is used as a moderator in nuclear reactors ? *[NCERT (New) Pg. 315, AIPMT 1997]*
(a) Plutonium (b) Cadmium
(c) Heavy water (d) Uranium

27 Heavy water is used as a moderator in a nuclear reactor. The function of the moderator is *[AIPMT 1994]*
(a) to control energy released in the reactor
(b) to absorb neutrons and stop chain reaction
(c) to cool the reactor
(d) to slow down the neutrons to thermal energies

28 If the binding energy per nucleon in ${}_3Li^7$ and ${}_2He^4$ nuclei are respectively 5.60 MeV and 7.06 MeV, then the energy of proton in the reaction
$${}_3Li^7 + p \longrightarrow 2\ {}_2He^4 \text{ is}$$
[AIPMT 1994]
(a) 19.6 MeV (b) 2.4 MeV
(c) 8.4 MeV (d) 17.3 MeV

29 Energy released in the fission of a single ${}_{92}U^{235}$ nucleus is 200 MeV. The fission rate of a ${}_{92}U^{235}$ filled reactor operating at a power level of 5 W is *[NCERT (New) Pg. 315, AIPMT 1993]*
(a) $1.56 \times 10^{-10}\ s^{-1}$ (b) $1.56 \times 10^{11}\ s^{-1}$
(c) $1.56 \times 10^{-16}\ s^{-1}$ (d) $1.56 \times 10^{-17}\ s^{-1}$

30 The binding energy per nucleon is maximum in case of *[AIPMT 1993]*
(a) ${}_2He^4$ (b) ${}_{26}Fe^{56}$ (c) ${}_{56}Ba^{141}$ (d) ${}_{92}U^{235}$

31 The energy equivalent of one atomic mass unit is *[AIPMT 1992]*
(a) 1.6×10^{-19} J (b) 6.02×10^{23} J
(c) 931 MeV (d) 9.31 MeV

32 Solar energy is due to *[NCERT (New) Pg. 315, AIPMT 1992]*
(a) fusion reaction (b) fission reaction
(c) combustion reaction (d) chemical reaction

33 The average binding energy of a nucleon inside an atomic nucleus is about *[AIPMT 1989]*
(a) 8 MeV (b) 8 eV
(c) 8 J (d) 8 erg

• Key **Index**

Topic 1

1 (d)	2 (b)	3 (b)	4 (b)	5 (d)	6 (b)	7 (c)	8 (b)	9 (a)	10 (d)
11 (a)	12 (b)	13 (b)	14 (a)	15 (d)	16 (d)	17 (a)	18 (a)	19 (c)	20 (c)
21 (c)	22 (a)	23 (a)	24 (b)	25 (a)	26 (c)				

Topic 2

1 (d)	2 (a)	3 (d)	4 (a)	5 (d)	6 (c)	7 (c)	8 (b)	9 (b)	10 (b)
11 (b)	12 (a)	13 (b)	14 (b)	15 (c)	16 (c)	17 (a)	18 (a)	19 (d)	20 (a)
21 (b)	22 (c)	23 (b)	24 (a)	25 (b)	26 (c)	27 (d)	28 (d)	29 (b)	30 (b)
31 (c)	32 (a)	33 (a)							

Detailed Explanations

Topic 1

01. *(d)* Given,

$$^{290}_{82}X \xrightarrow{\alpha} Y \xrightarrow{e^+} Z$$
$$\xrightarrow{\beta^-} P \xrightarrow{e^-} Q$$

From $X \to Y$, α-particle is emitted thus $^{286}_{80}Y$.

Now, $Y \to Z$, e^+ is emitted, thus $^{286}_{79}Z$.

Again $Z \to P$, β^- is emitted thus $^{286}_{80}P$.

Again $P \to Q$, e^- is emitted thus $^{286}_{81}Q$.

02. *(b)* The given nuclear reaction is represented as

$$^{22}_{11}\text{Na} \longrightarrow {}^{M}_{Z}X + e^+ + \nu$$

Since atomic number and mass number are same for both side of reaction.

Hence, for atomic number,

$$11 = Z + 1 \Rightarrow Z = 10$$

For mass number,

$$22 = M \Rightarrow M = 22$$

$$\therefore \quad {}^{M}_{Z}X = {}^{22}_{10}\text{Ne}$$

03. *(b)* Given, mass number of parent nucleus, $A = 189$

Mass number of daughters nuclei,

$$A_1 = 125$$

and $A_2 = 64$

We know that, $R = R_0(A^{1/3})$

$$\therefore \quad \frac{R_1}{R_2} = \left(\frac{A_1}{A_2}\right)^{1/3} = \left(\frac{125}{64}\right)^{1/3}$$

$$= \left[\left(\frac{5}{4}\right)^3\right]^{1/3} = \frac{5}{4}$$

$$\therefore \; R_1 : R_2 = 5:4$$

04. *(b)* When an atom emits γ-radiation from its nucleus, then there is no change in its atomic number and mass number.

05. *(d)* α-particles are doubly ionised helium nucleus (He^{2+}) which are emitted in any radioactive process.

So, they have two protons, 2 neutrons in its nucleus and no electron.

06. *(b)* Radius of the nucleus is given by

$$R = R_0 A^{1/3} \Rightarrow R \propto A^{1/3}$$

$$\frac{R_{\text{Al}}}{R_{\text{Te}}} = \left(\frac{A_{\text{Al}}}{A_{\text{Te}}}\right)^{1/3} = \left(\frac{27}{125}\right)^{1/3} = \frac{3}{5}$$

$$R_{\text{Te}} = \frac{5}{3} R_{\text{Al}}$$

07. *(c)* We know that,

$$R = R_0 A^{1/3},$$

$$\frac{R_2}{R_1} = \left(\frac{A_2}{A_1}\right)^{1/3} \Rightarrow \left(\frac{64}{27}\right)^{1/3} = \frac{4}{3}$$

where, R_1 = The radius of ^{27}Al, and

A_1 = Atomic mass number of Al

R_2 = The radius of ^{64}Cu and

A_2 = Atomic mass number of Cu

$$\Rightarrow R_2 = 3.6 \times \frac{4}{3} = 4.8 \text{ fm}$$

08. *(b)*

key idea

Nuclear density is independent of mass number.

Given, $A_1 : A_2 = 1:3$

$$\therefore R_0 A_1^{1/3} : R_0 A_2^{1/3} = 1:3^{1/3}$$

$$\text{Density} = \frac{A}{\frac{4}{3}\pi R^3}$$

$$\therefore \rho_{A_1} : \rho_{A_2} = \frac{1}{\frac{4}{3}\pi R_0^3 \cdot 1^3} : \frac{3}{\frac{4}{3}\pi R_0^3 (3^{1/3})^3}$$

$$= 1:1$$

09. *(a)* If R is the radius of the nucleus, the corresponding volume $\frac{4}{3}\pi R^3$ has been found to be proportional to A.

This relationship is expressed in inverse form as $R = R_0 A^{1/3}$

The value of R_0 is 1.2×10^{-15} m, i.e. 1.2 fm

$$\text{Therefore, } \frac{R_{\text{Al}}}{R_{\text{Te}}} = \frac{R_0 \, (A_{\text{Al}})^{1/3}}{R_0 \, (A_{\text{Te}})^{1/3}}$$

$$\frac{R_{\text{Al}}}{R_{\text{Te}}} = \frac{(A_{\text{Al}})^{1/3}}{(A_{\text{Te}})^{1/3}} = \frac{(27)^{1/3}}{(125)^{1/3}} = \frac{3}{5}$$

$$\text{or } R_{\text{Te}} = \frac{5}{3} \times R_{\text{Al}} = \frac{5}{3} \times 3.6 = 6 \text{ fm}$$

10. *(d)* According to question, radius of $^{9}_{4}$Be nucleus be r, and radius of germanium (Ge) nucleus will be $2r$.

Radius of a nucleus is given by

$$R = R_0 \; A^{1/3}$$

R = Radius of atom having mass number A

$$R \propto A^{1/3}$$

$$\text{So, } \frac{R_1}{R_2} = \left(\frac{A_1}{A_2}\right)^{1/3} \Rightarrow \frac{r}{2r} = \left(\frac{9}{A_2}\right)^{1/3}$$

$$(\because A_1 = 9)$$

$$\text{or } \left(\frac{1}{2}\right)^3 = \frac{9}{A_2}$$

Hence, $A_2 = 9 \times (2)^3 = 9 \times 8 = 72$

11. *(a)* Mass number

= Number of protons + Number of neutrons

In case of hydrogen

Number of neutrons = 0

Thus, mass number = atomic number

Hence, sometimes the atomic number is equal to the mass number.

12. *(b)* Order of radius of atom $\approx 10^{-10}$ m

Order of radius of nucleus $\approx 10^{-15}$ m

Ratio of volume of atom to volume of nucleus

$$= \frac{\text{Volume of atom}}{\text{Volume of nucleus}} = \frac{\frac{4}{3}\pi r_1^3}{\frac{4}{3}\pi r_2^3}$$

$$= \left(\frac{10^{-10}}{10^{-15}}\right)^3 = 10^{15}$$

13. *(b)* The given nuclear reaction can be written as

$$_Z X^A + {}_0n^1 \longrightarrow {}_3\text{Li}^7 + {}_2\text{He}^4$$

Conservation of mass number gives,

$$A + 1 = 7 + 4 \Rightarrow A = 10$$

Conservation of charge number/atomic Number gives, $Z + 0 = 2 + 3$

$$\Rightarrow \quad Z = 5$$

14. *(a)* Out of the given choices, X-rays and γ-rays are electromagnetic waves, so they have no charge. β-particles are negatively charged particles and are fast moving electrons. Alpha (α) particles have positive charge and are a nucleus of helium.

15. *(d)* The given solution is shown by the following nuclear reaction.

$$_Z X^A \longrightarrow {}_{Z-2}Y^{A-4} + {}_2\text{He}^4$$

(α-particle)

and

$$_{Z-2}Y^{A-4} \longrightarrow {}_{Z}X^{A-4} + 2({}_{-1}\beta^0)$$

(2 β-particles)

So, by one α and two β-emissions the atomic number remains unchanged. i.e. formation of isotopes takes place.

16. *(d)* When two electrons are emitted by a helium atom, a nucleus of helium remains which has charge equal to that of two electrons.
An alpha (α) particle is a nucleus of helium.
Hence, it is also called as doubly-ionised helium atom.

17. *(a)* The reaction can be shown as

$$_{n}X^{m} \xrightarrow{\alpha(2\,He^4)} {}_{n-2}Y^{m-4}$$

$$_{n-2}Y^{m-4} \xrightarrow{2({}_{-1}\beta^0)} {}_{n}X^{m-4}$$

Thus, the resulting nucleus is the isotope of parent nucleus and is $_{n}X^{m-4}$.

18. *(a)* The relation between nuclei radius R and mass number A is given by

$$R \propto A^{1/3} \quad \text{...(i)}$$

or $A \propto R^3$

or $\dfrac{A_1}{A_2} = \left(\dfrac{R_1}{R_2}\right)^3$

Given, $R_1 = R$, $R_2 = \dfrac{R}{2}$, $A_1 = 56$

$\therefore \quad \dfrac{56}{A_2} = \left(\dfrac{R}{R/2}\right)^3 = 2^3 = 8$

or $A_2 = \dfrac{56}{8} = 7$

Thus, required stable nucleus will be Li^7.

19. *(c)* Volume of a nucleus is proportional to its mass number A. If R is the radius of the nucleus assumed to be spherical, then its volume $(V) \propto A$ (mass number)

So, $\left(\dfrac{4}{3}\pi R^3\right) \propto A$ or $R \propto A^{1/3}$

$\therefore \quad \dfrac{R_S}{R_{He}} = \left(\dfrac{A_S}{A_{He}}\right)^{1/3} = \left(\dfrac{32}{4}\right)^{1/3} = 2$

or $R_S = 2R_{He}$

20. *(c)* Nuclear density or mass density of a nucleus is independent of mass number.

21. *(c)* Nuclear forces act between a pair of neutrons, a pair of protons and also between a neutron-proton pair, with the same strength. This shows that nuclear forces are independent of charge.

22. *(a)* In $_{11}Na^{23}$, $Z = 11$ i.e. number of protons $= 11$,
Mass number, $A = 23$
Number of neutrons

$$= A - Z = 23 - 11 = 12$$

There is no electron in the nucleus.
So, number of protons, neutrons and electrons are 11, 12, 0.

23. *(a)* According to proton-neutron hypothesis, a nucleus of mass number A and atomic number Z contains Z protons and $(A-Z)$ neutrons.
Constituents of atomic nucleus are Nucleons i.e. neutron and proton.

24. *(b)* A nuclear reaction represents the transformation of one stable nucleus into another nucleus by bombarding the former with suitable high energy particles.

$$_{6}C^{12} + {}_{0}n^{1} \rightarrow {}_{6}C^{13} \rightarrow {}_{7}N^{13} + {}_{-1}\beta^{0} + Q$$

(Energy)

Resulting nucleus is of nitrogen having mass number 13 and atomic number 7

25. *(a)* Experimental measurements show that volume of a nucleus is proportional to its mass number A. If R is the radius of the nucleus assumed to be spherical, then its volume and mass no. relation is given by
Volume $(V) \propto$ mass number (A)

or $\left(\dfrac{4}{3}\pi R^3\right) \propto A$

or $R \propto A^{1/3}$

$\therefore \quad \dfrac{R_{Al}}{R_{Te}} = \dfrac{(27)^{1/3}}{(125)^{1/3}} = \dfrac{3}{5} = \dfrac{6}{10}$

26. *(c)* Nuclear forces are the short range forces of attraction which hold together the nucleons (neutrons and protons) in the tiny nucleus of an atom, inspite of strong electrostatic forces of repulsion between protons.
Nuclear forces are charge independent forces. They are the strongest forces in nature. The magnitude of nuclear forces is 100 times that of electrostatic forces and 10^{38} times that of gravitational forces between nucleons. They are operative upto distances of the order of a few fermi. They are non-central forces.

Topic 2

01. *(d)* A nucleus with mass number 240 breaks into two fragment each of mass number 120. $X^{240} \longrightarrow Y^{120} + Z^{120}$
Given, the binding energy per nucleon of unfragmented nuclei, $X = 7.6$ MeV
The binding energy per nucleon of fragmented nuclei, $Y = Z = 8.5$ MeV
Now, we shall determine the total gain in binding energy.
Gain in binding energy = Binding energy of products − Binding energy of reactants
Gain in binding energy

$$= 2 \times 120 \times 8.5 - 240 \times 7.6$$
$$= 216 \text{ MeV}$$

02. *(a)* Given,

$$m = 0.5\text{ g} = 0.5 \times 10^{-3}\text{ kg}$$

Relation for energy equivalent of mass is

$$E = mc^2$$

where, c is speed of light.

$$= 0.5 \times 10^{-3} \times (3 \times 10^8)^2 \qquad (\because c = 3 \times 10^8)$$

$$= 4.5 \times 10^{13}\text{ J}$$

03. *(d)* Here,

$$^{235}_{92}U + {}^{1}_{0}n \longrightarrow {}^{89}_{36}Kr + {}^{A}_{Z}X + 3({}^{1}_{0}n)$$

According to the law of conservation,
(Atomic number)$_{\text{Reactant}}$ = (Atomic number)$_{\text{Product}}$

$$92 + 0 = 36 + Z$$
$$\Rightarrow \quad Z = 92 - 36 = 56$$

Similarly,
(Atomic masses)$_{\text{Reactant}}$
= (Atomic masses)$_{\text{Product}}$

$$235 + 1 = 89 + A + 3 \times 1$$
$$\Rightarrow \quad A = 144$$

∴ Other element is $^{144}_{56}$Ba.

04. *(a)* $_{92}U^{238} \longrightarrow {}_{92}Th^{238} + {}_{2}He^{4}$
According to law of conservation of linear momentum, we have,

$$|p_{Th}| = |p_{He}| = p$$

⇒ As, kinetic energy of an element,

$$KE = \frac{p^2}{2m}$$

where, m is mass of an element.

Thus, $KE \propto \dfrac{1}{M}$

So, $M_{He} < M_{Th}$

$\Rightarrow \quad K_{He} > K_{Th}$

Alternate Solution

If p_{Th} and p_{He} are the momenta of thorium and helium nuclei respectively, then using the law of conservation of linear momentum

$$0 = \mathbf{p}_{Th} + \mathbf{p}_{He}$$

or $\mathbf{p}_{Th} = \mathbf{p}_{He}$

But in magnitude

$$p_{Th} = p_{He}$$

If m_{Th} and m_{He} are the masses of theorium and helium nuclei of helium nucleus is

$$K_{He} = \frac{p_{He}^2}{2m_{He}}$$

$$\frac{K_{Th}}{K_{He}} = \left(\frac{p_{Th}}{p_{He}}\right)^2 \left(\frac{m_{He}}{m_{Th}}\right)$$

But $p_{Th} = p_{He}$

and $m_{He} = m_{Th}$

$\therefore \quad K_{Th} < K_{He}$

or $\quad K_{He} > K_{Th}$

05. *(d)*

key idea

You can calculate absorbed or released energy in nuclear reaction with the help of following formula.

ΔQ = Binding energy of product – Binding energy of nuclei.

The binding energy for ${}_1H^1$ is around zero and also not given in the question so we can ignore it

$$Q = 2\,(4 \times 7.06) - (7 \times 5.60)$$
$$= (8 \times 7.06) - (7 \times 5.60)$$
$$= (56.48 - 39.2)\ \text{MeV}$$

$\therefore \quad Q = 17.28$ MeV

$\simeq 17.3$ MeV

06. *(c)* With the increase in the number of nucleons, binding energy per nucleon first increases and then decreases with increase in the mass number.

07. *(c)* Given, $\Delta m = 0.02866\,u$

$\therefore$ Energy liberated $= \Delta mc^2$

$\Rightarrow$ Energy liberated per

$$= \frac{0.02866 \times 931}{4}$$

$$= \frac{26.7}{4}\ \text{MeV}$$

$$= 6.675\ \text{MeV}$$

08. *(b)* Fusion reaction takes place at high temperature because kinetic energy is high enough to overcome the couloumb repulsion between nuclei.

09. *(b)* If $m = 1\,u$, $c = 3 \times 10^8\ \text{ms}^{-1}$, then

$$E = 931\ \text{MeV}$$

i.e. $1\,u = 931$ MeV

Binding energy

$$= 0.042 \times 931 = 39.10\ \text{MeV}$$

$\therefore$ Binding energy per nucleon

$$= \frac{39.10}{7} = 5.58 \approx 5.6\ \text{MeV}$$

10. *(b)* If the quantity of mass disappearing is Δm, then the binding energy is

$$\text{BE} = \Delta mc^2$$

We can then write.

$$\Delta m = Zm_p + Nm_n - m(A, Z)$$

where $m(A, Z)$ is the mass of the atom of mass number A and atomic number Z. Hence, the binding energy of the nucleus is

$$\text{BE} = [Zm_p + Nm_n - m(A, Z)]c^2$$

$$\text{BE} = [Zm_p + (A - Z)\,m_n - m(A, Z)]c^2$$

where, $N = A - Z$

= number of neutrons.

11. *(b)* The reaction can be written as

$${}_1H^2 + {}_1H^2 \longrightarrow {}_2He^4 + \text{energy}$$

The energy released in the reaction is the difference of binding energies of daughter and parent nuclei.

Hence, energy released

= binding energy of ${}_2He^4$

$-2 \times$ binding energy of ${}_1H^2$

$$= 28 - 2 \times 2.2$$
$$= 23.6\ \text{MeV}$$

12. *(a)* In fission process, when a parent nucleus breaks into daughter products, then some mass is lost in the form of energy.

Thus, mass of fission products < mass of parent nucleus

$$\Rightarrow \quad \frac{\text{Mass of fission products}}{\text{Mass of parent nucleus}} < 1$$

13. *(b)* The binding energy per nucleon for the middle nuclides (from A = 20 to A = 56) is maximum. Hence, these are more stable.

As the mass number increases, the binding energy per nucleon gradually decreases and ultimately binding energy per nucleon of heavy nuclides (such as uranium etc.) become comparatively low. Hence, these nuclides are relatively unstable. So, they can be fissioned easily.

14. *(b)* Energy released per nucleon binding energy of product – binding energy of reactants

$$= c - (a + b) = c - a - b$$

15. *(c)* Binding energy of a nucleus containing N neutrons and Z protons is

$$\text{BE} = [Nm_n + Zm_p - m(N, Z)]\,c^2$$

$$\Rightarrow \quad \frac{\text{BE}}{c^2} = Nm_n + Zm_p - m(N, Z)$$

$$\Rightarrow m(N, Z) = Nm_n + Zm_p - \text{BE}/c^2$$

16. *(c)* In nuclear fusion, when two light nuclei of different masses are combined to form a stable nucleus, then some mass is lost and appears in the form of energy, called the mass defect.

So, the mass of resultant nucleus is always less than the sum of masses of initial nuclei i.e.,

$$m_3 < (m_1 + m_2)$$

17. *(a)* In the sun, huge amount of energy is produced due to fusion of 4 protons (hydrogen nucleus) into a helium nucleus.

According to the reaction

$${}_1H^1 + {}_1H^1 + {}_1H^1 + {}_1H^1 \longrightarrow {}_2He^4 + 2\,{}_{+1}\beta^0 + \gamma\,(\text{energy}) + 2\nu$$

18. *(a)*

key idea

In such type of question, calculate mass defect (Δm) in terms of atomic mass unit (amu). After that, you can calculate released energy with the help of followinng formula

$$\Delta Q = \Delta m \times 931\ \text{MeV}$$

${}_2He^4$ contains 2 neutrons and 2 protons

So, mass of 2 protons

$$= 2 \times 1.0073 = 2.0146\ u$$

So, mass of 2 neutrons

$$= 2 \times 1.0087 = 2.0174\ u$$

Total mass of 2 protons and 2 neutrons

$$= (2.0146 + 2.0174)\ u = 4.032\ u$$

Mass of helium nucleus = 4.0015 u

Thus, mass defect

Δm = mass defect

$= (4.032 - 4.0015)\text{ u} = 0.0305\text{ u}$

Hence, binding energy

$\Delta E = (\Delta m) \times 931$

$= 0.0305 \times 931$

$= 28.4\text{ MeV}$

19. *(d)* Let the unknown product nucleus be $_Z X^A$.

The reaction can be written as

$$_8O^{16} + {}_1H^2 \longrightarrow {}_Z X^A + {}_2He^4$$

(Oxygen) (deuterium) (unknown nucleus) α-particle

Conservation of mass number between product and reactant of above reaction gives,

$16 + 2 = A + 4$

$\Rightarrow \quad A = 14$

Conservation of atomic number between reactant and product of above reaction gives

$8 + 1 = Z + 2$

$\Rightarrow \quad Z = 7$

Hence, product of nucleus is $_7N^{14}$.

> • Concept **Enhancer**
>
> Fusion reaction can take place at very high temperature ($\approx 10^8$K) and very high pressure which can be provided at sun or by fission of atom bomb.

20. *(a)* Binding energy for light nuclei ($A < 20$) is much smaller than the binding energy for heavier nuclei. This suggests a process that is reverse of fission. When two light nuclei combine to form a heavier nucleus, the process is called nuclear fusion. The union of two light nuclei into heavier nuclei also leads to a transfer of mass and a consequent liberation of large amount of energy.

21. *(b)* In a nuclear process, energy is released if binding energy per nucleon of the daughter products gets increased.

In nuclear fission reaction, total binding energy of products formed due to nuclear fission is more than the parent fissionable material.

22. *(c)* When a nucleus is formed, then the mass of nucleus is slightly less than the sum of masses of Z protons and N neutrons.

i.e., $\quad m < (Zm_p + Nm_n)$

23. *(b)* Neil Bohr and J.A. Wheeler explained nuclear fission on the basis of liquid drop model of the nucleus. The $_{92}U^{235}$ nucleus behaves like a liquid drop and owing to surface tension is perfectly spherical in shape. When neutron strikes the nucleus, some energy called the excitation energy is imparted to the nucleus.

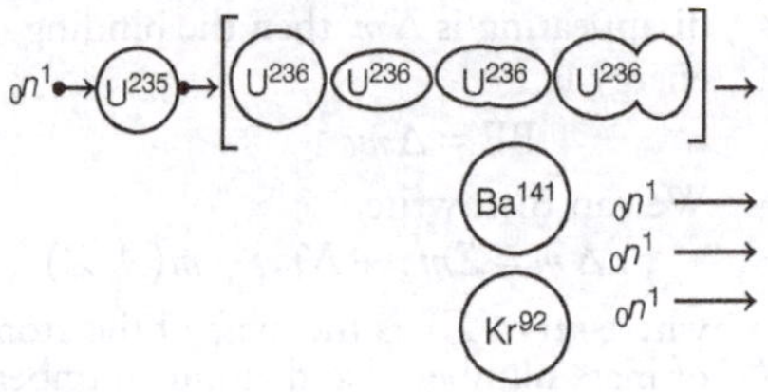

The phenomenon of surface tension tries to keep the nucleus spherical in shape, whereas the excitation energy tries to deform it. Due to the struggle between the surface tension and the excitation energy, the oscillations are set up inside the compound nucleus.

As a result, the nucleus gets deformed from spherical shape to ellipsoidal and then to a dumb bell as shown, till the Coulomb's repulsive force between protons succeeds in tearing the two bells apart.

24. *(a)* $_{92}U^{235} + {}_0n^1 \rightarrow {}_{38}Sr^{90} + {}_{54}Xe^{143} + 3\,{}_0n^1$

If total atomic number on LHS

$= 92 + 0 = 92$

Total atomic number on RHS

$= 38 + 54 + 0 = 92$

Total mass number on LHS

$= 235 + 1 = 236$

Total mass number on RHS

$= 90 + 143 + 3 \times 1 = 236$

So, option (a) is correct.

> • Concept **Enhancer**
>
> For a nuclear reaction to be completed, the mass number and charge number on both sides should be same.

25. *(b)* Binding energy of fissioned nucleus $= 236 \times 7.6$ MeV

Binding energy of products

$= 117 \times 8.5 + 117 \times 8.5$

$= 2 \times 117 \times 8.5$

Hence, net binding energy = binding energy of products – binding energy of fissioned nucleus

$= 234 \times 8.5 - 236 \times 7.6$

$= 1989 - 1793.6$

$= 195.4\text{ MeV} \approx 200\text{ MeV}$

Thus, in per fission of uranium nearly 200 MeV energy is released.

26. *(c)* Moderator in a nuclear reactor is used to slow down fast moving neutrons. Heavy water, graphite or beryllium oxide are used as moderators. Heavy water is best moderator.

> • Concept **Enhancer**
>
> In an ordinary uranium reactor, plutonium (Pu^{239}) is produced which is a better fissionable material than uranium (U^{235}). It is a heavy isotope of uranium.

27. *(d)* The function of a moderator is to slow down the fast moving secondary neutrons produced during the fission as fission reaction can only be initiated by slow moving neutrons.

The material of moderator should be light and it should not absorb neutrons. Usually, heavy water, graphite, deuterium, paraffin etc. can act as moderators. These moderators are rich in protons.

28. *(d)* Total BE of nucleons in $_3Li^7$

$= 7 \times 5.60 = 39.20$ MeV

Total BE of nucleons in 2 ($_2He^4$)

$= (4 \times 7.06) \times 2$

$= 56.48$ MeV

Therefore, energy of protons in the reaction = difference of BE's

$= 56.48 - 39.20 = 17.3$ MeV

29. *(b)* Fission rate

$$= \frac{\text{Total nuclear power}}{\text{Energy produced / Fission}}$$

Here, total nuclear power = 5 W

Energy released per fission = 200 MeV

$$\therefore \text{ Fission rate} = \frac{5}{200\text{ MeV}}$$

$$= \frac{5}{200 \times 1.6 \times 10^{-13}}$$

[∵ 1 Mev J]

$= 1.56 \times 10^{11}\ s^{-1}$

30. *(b)* The binding energy curve has a broad maximum in the range $A = 30$ to $A = 120$ corresponding to average binding energy per nucleon = 8 MeV. The peak value of the maximum is 8.8 MeV/N for ${}_{26}Fe^{56}$.

31. *(c)* According to Einstein, mass-energy equivalence is represented by $E = mc^2$.

Taking, mass, $m = 1$ amu

$= 1.66 \times 10^{-27}$ kg

and velocity of light in vacuum,

$c = 3.0 \times 10^8$ m/s

We get,

$E = (1.66 \times 10^{-27}) \times (3 \times 10^8)^2$ J

$= 1.49 \times 10^{-10}$ J

$$= \frac{1.49 \times 10^{-10}}{1.6 \times 10^{-13}} \text{ MeV}$$

$(\because 1 \text{ MeV} = 1.6 \times 10^{-13} \text{ J})$

$= 931.25$ MeV

Hence, 1 amu ≈ 931 MeV

32. *(a)* Stellar energy is the energy obtained continuously from the sun and the stars. It is estimated that the sun has been radiating 3.8×10^{26} J of energy per second for billions of years. Bethe postulated that the interior of the sun and stars provide conditions for the fusion of hydrogen nuclei to form helium nuclei with the release of large amount of energy.

Hence, solar energy is due to fusion reactions.

33. *(a)* Average binding energy per nucleon of a nucleus is the average energy we have to spend to remove a nucleon from the nucleus to infinite distance. It is given by total binding energy divided by the mass number of the nucleus.

The BE curve has a broad maximum in the range $A = 30$ to $A = 120$ corresponding to average binding energy per nucleon = 8 MeV. The peak value of the maximum is 8 MeV/N for ${}_{26}Fe^{56}$.

C-28

NEET Chapterwise Topicwise Physics

In NEET 2024, 3 questions were visible from this chapter. In past 5 years, 11 questions from topic-1 and 6 questions from topic-2 were asked.
For detailed analysis scan QR code

SEMICONDUCTOR ELECTRONICS
(MATERIAL, DEVICES AND SIMPLE CIRCUITS)

Topic 1 Semiconductor and *p-n* Junction Diode

01. Consider the following statements *A* and *B* and identify the correct answer:
[NCERT (New) Pg. 489, NEET 2024]

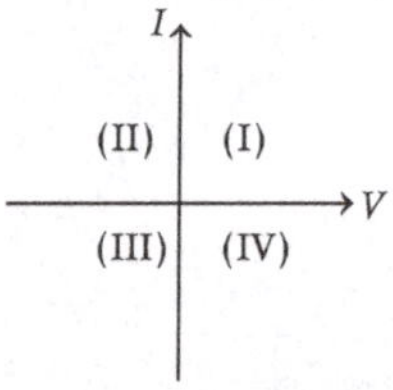

A. For a solar-cell, the *I-V* characteristics lies in the IV quadrant of the given graph.

B. In a reverse biased *p-n* junction diode, the current measured in (μA), is due to majority charge carriers.

(a) A is correct but B is incorrect
(b) A is incorrect but B is correct
(c) Both A and B are correct
(d) Both A and B are incorrect

02 A full wave rectifier circuit consists of two *p-n* junction diodes, a centre-tapped transformer, capacitor and a load resistance. Which of these components remove the AC ripple from the rectified output? ***[NCERT (New) Pg. 484, NEET 2023]***

(a) *p-n* junction diodes
(b) Capacitor
(c) Load resistance
(d) A centre-tapped transformer

03 Given below are two statements.

Statement I Photovoltaic devices can convert optical radiation into electricity.

Statement II Zener diode is designed to operate under reverse bias in breakdown region.

In the light of the above statements, choose the most appropriate answer from the options given below.
[NCERT (New) Pg. 485, NEET 2023]

(a) Both Statement I and Statement II are incorrect.
(b) Statement I is correct but Statement II is incorrect.
(c) Statement I is correct but Statement II is correct.
(d) Both Statement I and Statement II are correct.

04 In half wave rectification, if the input frequency is 60 Hz, then the output frequency would be
[NEET 2022]

(a) 30 Hz
(b) 60 Hz
(c) 120 Hz
(d) zero

05

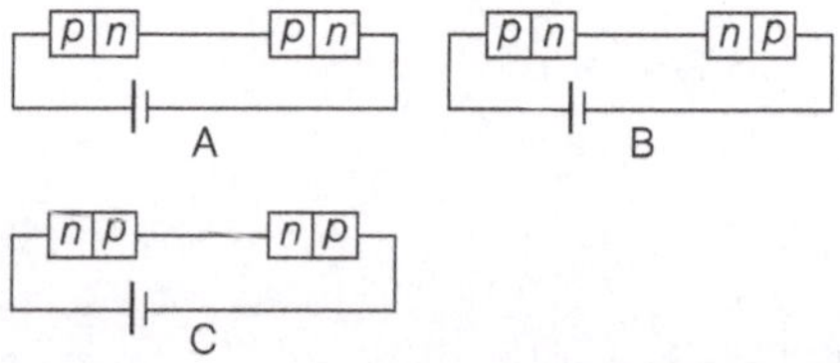

In the given circuits A, B and C the potential drop across the two *p-n* junctions are equal in
[NCERT (New) Pg. 336, NEET 2022]

(a) Circuit B only
(b) Circuit C only
(c) Both circuits A and C
(d) Circuit A only

06 The electron concentration in an *n*-type semiconductor is the same as hole concentration in a *p*-type semiconductor. An external field (electric) is applied across each of them. Compare the currents in them. ***[NCERT (New) Pg. 331, NEET 2021]***

(a) Current in *n*-type = Current in *p*-type
(b) Current in *p*-type > Current in *n*-type
(c) Current in *n*-type> Current in *p*-type
(d) No current will flow in *p*-type. current will only flow in *n*-type

07 Consider the following statements A and B and identify the correct answer.
A. A Zener diode is connected in reverse bias, when used as a voltage regulator. *[NEET 2021]*
B. The potential barrier of *p-n* junction lies between 0.1 V to 0.3 V.
(a) A and B both are correct.
(b) A and B both are incorrect.
(c) A is correct and B is incorrect.
(d) A is incorrect but B is correct.

08 Out of the following which one is a forward biased diode ? ***[NCERT (New) Pg. 335, NEET (Oct.) 2020]***

(a) 

(b) 

(c) 

(d) 

09 An intrinsic semiconductor is converted into *n*-type extrinsic semiconductor by doping it with ***[NCERT (New) Pg. 330, NEET (Oct.) 2020]***
(a) phosphorous (b) aluminium
(c) silver (d) germanium

10 The increase in the width of the depletion region in a *p-n* junction diode is due to ***[NEET (Sep.) 2020]***
(a) reverse bias only
(b) both forward bias and reverse bias
(c) increase in forward current
(d) forward bias only

11 The solids which have the negative temperature coefficient of resistance are ***[NEET (Sep.) 2020]***
(a) insulator only
(b) semiconductors only
(c) insulators and semiconductors
(d) metals

12 An LED is constructed from a *p-n* junction diode using GaAsP. The energy gap is 1.9 eV. The wavelength of the light emitted will be equal to ***[NCERT (Old) Pg. 488, NEET (Odisha) 2019]***
(a) 10.4×10^{-26} m (b) 654 nm
(c) 654 Å (d) 654×10^{-11} m

13 For a *p*-type semiconductor, which of the following statements is true ? ***[NEET (National) 2019]***
(a) Holes are the majority carriers and trivalent atoms are the dopants.
(b) Holes are the majority carriers and pentavalent atoms are the dopants.
(c) Electrons are the majority carriers and pentavalent atoms are the dopants.
(d) Electrons are the majority carriers and trivalent atoms are the dopants.

14 In a *p-n* junction diode, change in temperature due to heating ***[NEET 2018]***
(a) does not affect resistance of *p-n* junction
(b) affects only forward resistance
(c) affects only reverse resistance
(d) affects the overall *V-I* characteristics of *p-n* junction

15 Which one of the following represents forward bias diode ? ***[NCERT (New) Pg. 335, NEET 2017, AIPMT 2006]***

(a) 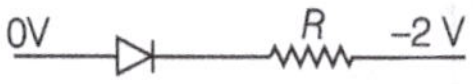

(b) 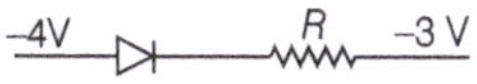

(c) 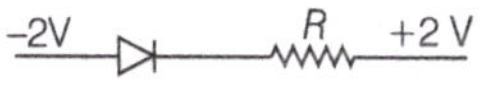

(d) 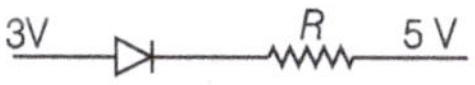

16 Consider the junction diode as ideal. The value of current flowing through *AB* is ***[NEET 2016]***

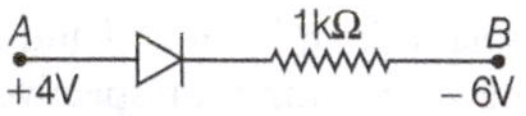

(a) 10^{-2} A (b) 10^{-1} A
(c) 10^{-3} A (d) 0 A

17 The given circuit has two ideal diodes connected as shown in the figure below. The current flowing through the resistance R_1 will be ***[NEET 2016]***

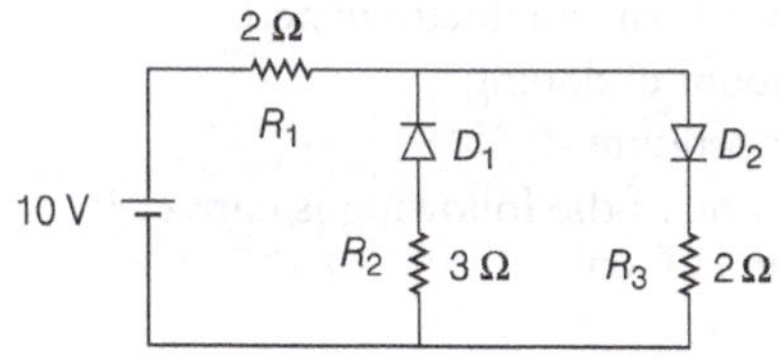

(a) 2.5 A (b) 10.0 A
(c) 1.43 A (d) 3.13 A

18 If in a *p-n* junction, a square input signal of 10 V is applied as shown, ***[NCERT (New) Pg. 338, AIPMT 2015]***

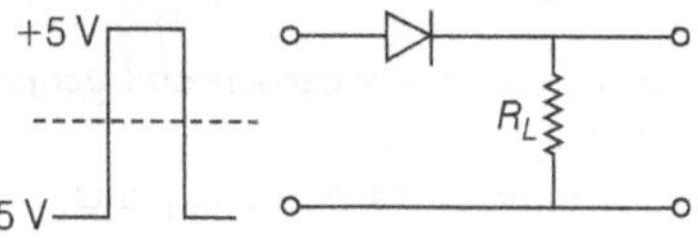

then the output across R_L will be

(a) 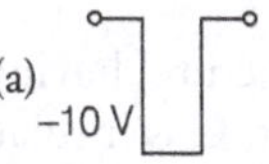

(b) 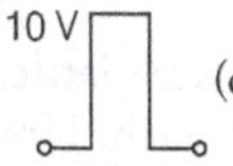

(c) 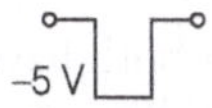

(d) 

19 In the given figure, a diode *D* is connected to an external resistance $R = 100\ \Omega$ and an emf of 3.5V. If the barrier potential developed across the diode is 0.5 V, the current in the circuit will be ***[AIPMT 2015]***

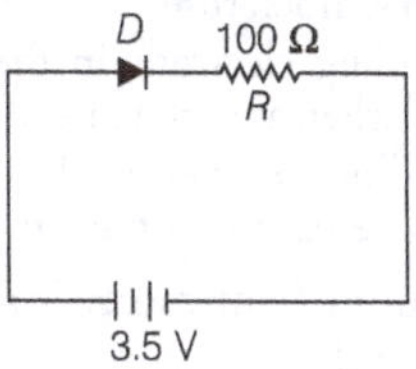

(a) 30 mA (b) 40 mA
(c) 20 mA (d) 35 mA

20 The given graph represents *V-I* characteristic for a semiconductor device. Which of the following statement is correct? *[NCERT (New) Pg. 489, AIPMT 2014]*

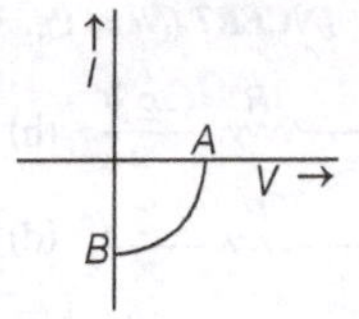

(a) It is *V-I* characteristic for solar cell where point *A* represents open circuit voltage and point *B* short circuit current.
(b) It is for a solar cell and points *A* and *B* represent open circuit voltage and current, respectively.
(c) It is for a photodiode and points *A* and *B* represent open circuit voltage and current, respectively.
(d) It is for a LED and points *A* and *B* represent open circuit voltage and short circuit current respectively.

21 The barrier potential of a *p-n* junction depends on *[NCERT (New) Pg. 330, AIPMT 2014]*
(i) type of semiconductor material
(ii) amount of doping
(iii) temperature
Which one of the following is correct ?
(a) (i) and (ii) only
(b) (ii) only
(c) (ii) and (iii) only
(d) (i), (ii) and (iii)

22 In a *n*-type semiconductor, which of the following statement is true ? *[NEET 2013]*
(a) Electrons are majority carriers and trivalent atoms are dopants
(b) Electrons are minority carriers and pentavalent atoms are dopants
(c) Holes are minority carriers and pentavalent atoms are dopants
(d) Holes are majority carriers and trivalent atoms are dopants

23 C and Si both have same lattice structure, having 4 bonding electrons in each. However, C is insulator whereas Si is intrinsic semiconductor. This is because *[NCERT (New) Pg. 329, AIPMT 2012]*
(a) in case of C, the valence bond is not completely filled at absolute zero temperature
(b) in case of C, the conduction band is partly filled even at absolute zero temperature
(c) the four bonding electrons in the case of C lie in the second orbit, whereas in the case of Si they lie in the third
(d) the four bonding electrons in the case of C lie in the third orbit, whereas for Si they lie in the fourth orbit

24 If a small amount of antimony is added to germanium crystal *[AIPMT 2011]*
(a) the antimony becomes an acceptor atom
(b) there will be more free electrons than holes in the semiconductor
(c) its resistance is increased
(d) it becomes a *p*-type semiconductor

25 In forward biasing of the *p-n* junction *[AIPMT 2011]*
(a) the positive terminal of the battery is connected to *n*-side and the depletion region becomes thin
(b) the positive terminal of the battery is connected to *n*-side and the depletion region becomes thick
(c) the positive terminal of the battery is connected to *p*-side and the deplection region become thin
(d) the positive terminal of the battery is connected to *p*-side and the depletion region becomes thick

26 Which one of the following statement is false ? *[NCERT (New) Pg. 330, AIPMT 2010]*
(a) Pure Si doped with trivalent impurities gives a *p*-type semiconductor
(b) Majority carriers in a *n*-type semiconductor are holes
(c) Minority carriers in a *p*-type semiconductor are electrons
(d) The resistance of intrinsic semiconductor decreases with increase of temperature.

27 A *p-n* photodiode is fabricated from a semiconductor with a band gap of 2.5 eV. It can detect a signal of wavelength *[NCERT (New) Pg. 487, AIPMT 2009]*
(a) 6000 Å (b) 4000 nm
(c) 6000 nm (d) 4000 Å

28 A *p-n* photodiode is made of a material with a band gap of 2.0 eV. The minimum frequency of the radiation that can be absorbed by the material is nearly *[AIPMT 2008]*
(a) 10×10^{14} Hz (b) 5×10^{14} Hz
(c) 1×10^{14} Hz (d) 20×10^{14} Hz

29 In the energy band diagram of a material shown below, the open circles and filled circles denote holes and electrons, respectively. The material is a/an *[NCERT (New) Pg. 332, AIPMT 2007]*

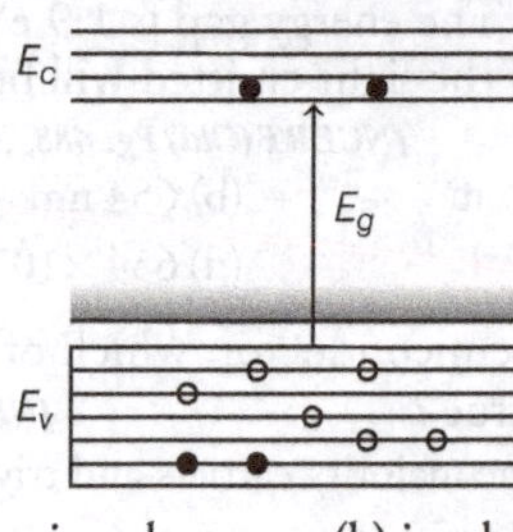

(a) *p*-type semiconductor (b) insulator
(c) metal (d) *n*-type semiconductor

30 Choose only false statement from the following. *[NCERT (New) Pg. 326, AIPMT 2005]*
(a) Substances with energy gap of the order of 10 eV are insulators.
(b) The conductivity of a semiconductor increases with increases in temperature.
(c) In conductors the valence and conduction bands may overlap.
(d) The resistivity of a semiconductor increases with increase in temperature.

31 Zener diode is used for *[AIPMT 2005]*
(a) producing oscillations in an oscillator
(b) amplification
(c) stabilisation
(d) rectification

32 Application of a forward bias to a *p-n* junction *[NCERT (New) Pg. 335, AIPMT 2005]*
(a) increases the number of donors on the *n*-side
(b) increases the electric field in the depletion zone
(c) increases the potential difference across the depletion zone
(d) widens the depletion zone

33 Of the diodes shown in the following diagrams, which one is reverse biased? *[AIPMT 2004]*

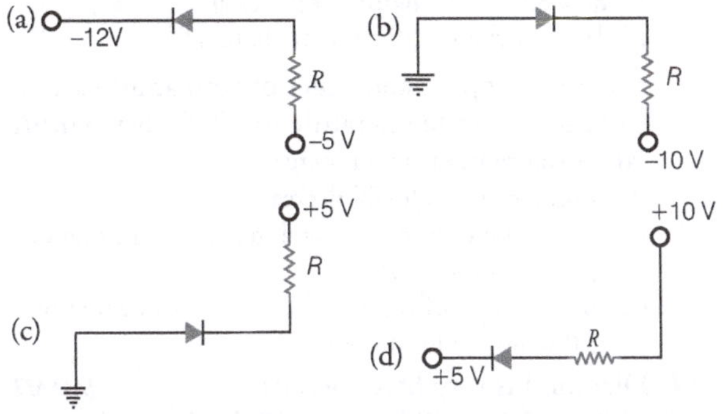

34 In a *p-n* junction photo cell, the value of the photo-electromotive force produced by monochromatic light is proportional to *[AIPMT 2004]*
(a) the barrier voltage at the *p-n* junction
(b) the intensity of the light falling on the cell
(c) the frequency of the light falling on the cell
(d) the voltage applied at the *p-n* junction

35 The peak voltage in the output of a half-wave diode rectifier fed with a sinusoidal signal without filter is 10 V. The DC component of the output voltage is *[NCERT (New) Pg. 338, AIPMT 2004]*
(a) $\frac{10}{\sqrt{2}}$ V (b) $\frac{10}{\pi}$ V (c) 10 V (d) $\frac{20}{\pi}$ V

36 In semiconductors at a room temperature *[AIPMT 2004]*
(a) the valence band is partially empty and the conduction band is partially filled
(b) the valence band is completely filled and the conduction band is partially filled
(c) the valence band is completely filled
(d) the conduction band is completely empty

37 If a full wave rectifier circuit is operating from 50 Hz mains, the fundamental frequency in the ripple will be *[NCERT (New) Pg. 339, AIPMT 2003]*
(a) 70.7 Hz (b) 100 Hz (c) 25 Hz (d) 59 Hz

38 Barrier potential of a *p-n* junction diode does not depend on *[AIPMT 2003]*
(a) forward bias (b) doping density
(c) diode design (d) temperature

39 For a given circuit of ideal *p-n* junction diode, which of the following is correct? *[AIPMT 2002]*

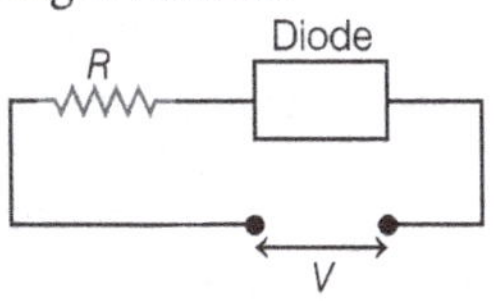

(a) In forward biasing the voltage across *R* is *V*
(b) In reverse biasing the voltage across *R* is *V*
(c) In forward biasing the voltage across *R* is 2 V
(d) In reverse biasing the voltage across *R* is 2 V

40 For conduction in a *p-n* junction, the biasing is *[NCERT (New) Pg. 335, AIPMT 2002]*
(a) high potential on *n*-side and low potential on *p*-side
(b) high potential on *p*-side and low potential on *n*-side
(c) same potential on both *p* and *n*-sides
(d) undetermined

41 If internal resistance of cell is negligible, then current flowing through the circuit is *[AIPMT 2001]*

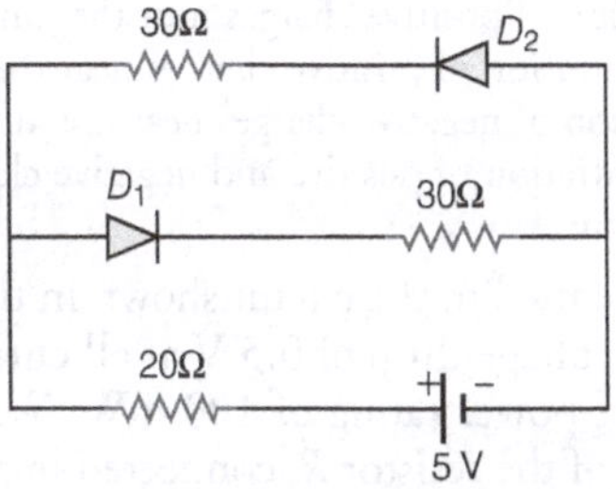

(a) $\frac{3}{50}$ A (b) $\frac{5}{50}$ A (c) $\frac{4}{50}$ A (d) $\frac{2}{50}$ A

42 Si and Cu are cooled to a temperature of 300 K, then resistivity *[AIPMT 2001]*
(a) for Si increases and for Cu decreases
(b) for Cu increases and for Si decreases
(c) decreases for both Si and Cu
(d) increases for both Si and Cu

43 In which of the following figures, junction diode is forward biased ? *[NCERT (New) Pg. 334, AIPMT 2000]*

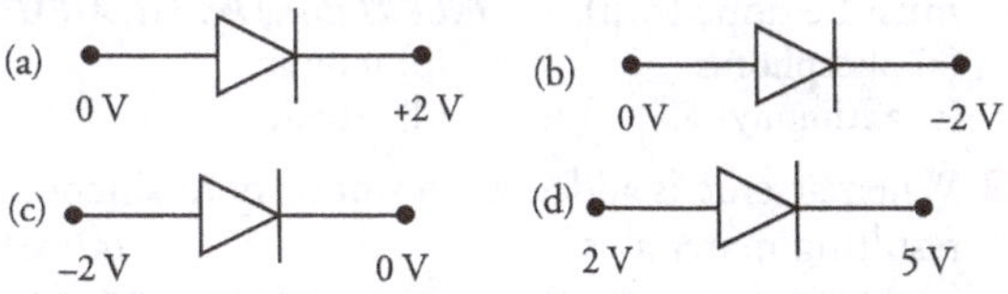

44 In *p*-type semiconductor, the majority charge carriers are *[AIPMT 1999]*
(a) holes (b) electrons (c) protons (d) neutrons

45 In forward bias the width of depletion layer in a *p-n* junction diode *[NCERT (New) Pg. 335, AIPMT 1999]*
(a) increases
(b) decreases
(c) remains constant
(d) first increases then decreases

46 Depletion layer consists of *[AIPMT 1999]*
(a) electrons (b) protons
(c) mobile charge carriers (d) immobile ions

47 In a junction diode, the holes are due to *[AIPMT 1999]*
(a) protons (b) extra electrons
(c) neutrons (d) missing electrons

48 Which of the following when added as an impurity into silicon produces *n*-type semiconductor ? *[AIPMT 1999]*
(a) P (b) Al (c) B (d) Mg

49 A semiconducting device is connected in a series in circuit with a battery and a resistance. A current is allowed to pass through the circuit. If the polarity of the battery is reversed, the current drops to almost zero. The device may be *[AIPMT 1998]*
(a) a *p-n* junction (b) an intrinsic semiconductor
(c) a *p*-type semiconductor (d) an *n*-type semiconductor

50 The cause of the potential barrier in a *p-n* diode is *[NCERT (New) Pg. 334, AIPMT 1998]*
(a) depletion of positive charges near the junction
(b) concentration of positive charges near the junction
(c) depletion of negative charges near the junction
(d) concentration of positive and negative charges near the junction

51 The diode used in the circuit shown in the figure has a constant voltage drop of 0.5 V at all currents and a maximum power rating of 100 mW. What should be the value of the resistor *R*, connected in series with the diode, for obtaining maximum current *i* ? *[AIPMT 1997]*

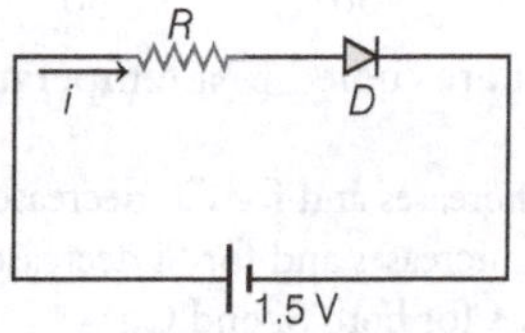

(a) 200 Ω (b) 6.67 Ω
(c) 5 Ω (d) 1.5 Ω

52 To obtain a *p*-type germanium semiconductor, it must be doped with *[NCERT (New) Pg. 331, AIPMT 1997]*
(a) phosphorus (b) indium
(c) antimony (d) arsenic

53 When arsenic is added as an impurity to silicon, the resulting material is *[AIPMT 1996]*
(a) *n*-type semiconductor (b) *p*-type semiconductor
(c) *n*-type conductor (d) insulator

54 Which of the following, when added as an impurity, into the silicon, produces *n*-type semiconductor ? *[AIPMT 1995]*
(a) Phosphorus (b) Aluminium
(c) Magnesium (d) Both (b) and (c)

55 In figure the input is across the terminals *A* and *C* and the output is across *B* and *D*. Then the output is *[AIPMT 1994]*

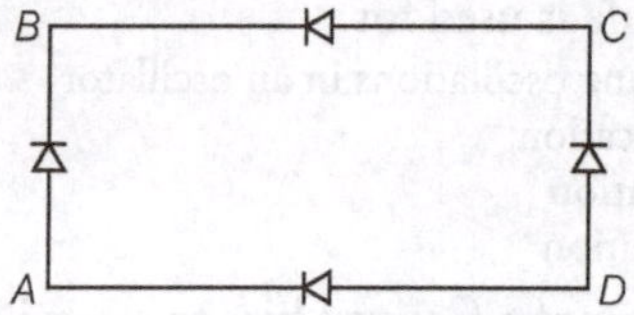

(a) zero (b) same as the input
(c) half wave rectified (d) full wave rectified

56 When a *p -n* junction diode is reverse biased the flow of current across the junction is mainly due to *[NCERT (New) Pg. 335, AIPMT 1994]*
(a) diffusion of charges
(b) drift charges
(c) depends on the nature of material
(d) Both drift and diffusion of charges

57 A piece of copper and other of germanium are cooled from the room temperature to 80 K, then *[AIPMT 1993]*
(a) resistance in each will increase
(b) resistance in each will decrease
(c) the resistance of copper will increase while that of germanium will decrease
(d) the resistance of copper will decrease while that of germanium will increase

58 Diamond is very hard, because *[AIPMT 1993]*
(a) it is covalent solid (b) it has large cohesive energy
(c) high melting point (d) insoluble in all solvents

59 Which one of the following is the weakest kind of the bonding in solids ? *[AIPMT 1992]*
(a) Ionic (b) Metallic
(c) van der Waals' (d) Covalent

60 The depletion layer in the *p-n* junction region is caused by *[NCERT (New) Pg. 333, AIPMT 1991]*
(a) drift of holes
(b) diffusion of charge carriers
(c) migration of impurity ions
(d) drift of electrons

61 When *n*-type semiconductor is heated *[AIPMT 1989]*
(a) number of electrons increases while that of holes decreases
(b) number of holes increases while that of electrons decreases
(c) number of electrons and holes remain same
(d) number of electrons and holes increases equally

62 *p-n* junction is said to be forward biased, when *[NCERT (New) Pg. 334, AIPMT 1988]*
(a) the positive pole of the battery is joined to the *p*-semiconductor and negative pole to the *n*-semiconductor
(b) the positive pole of the battery is joined to the *n*-semiconductor and negative pole to the *p*-semiconductor
(c) the positive pole of the battery is connected to *n*-semiconductor and *p*-semiconductor
(d) a mechanical force is applied in the forward direction

63 At absolute zero, Si acts as *[AIPMT 1988]*
(a) non-metal (b) metal
(c) insulator (d) None of these

Topic 2 Digital Circuits

01 A logic circuit provides the output Y as per the following truth table. *[NCERT (New) Pg. 492, NEET 2024]*

A	B	Y
0	0	1
0	1	0
1	0	1
1	1	0

The expression for the output Y is
(a) $A.B+\overline{A}$ (b) $A.\overline{B}+\overline{A}$
(c) $\overline{B}$ (d) B

02 The output Y of the given logic gate is similar to the output of an/a *[NCERT (New) Pg. 492, NEET 2024]*

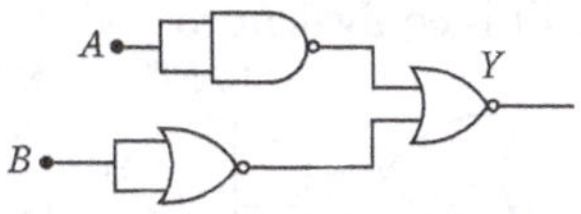

(a) NAND gate (b) NOR gate
(c) OR gate (d) AND gate

03 For the following logic circuit, the truth table is *[NCERT (Old) Pg. 505, NEET 2023]*

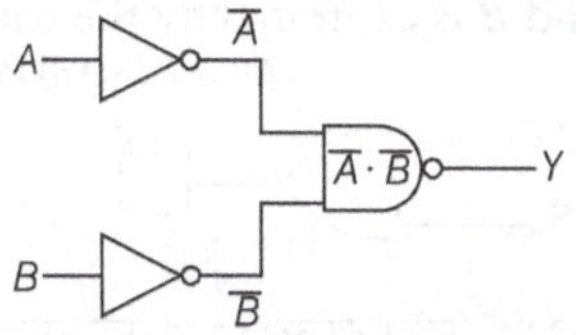

(a)

A	B	Y
0	0	0
0	1	1
1	0	1
1	1	1

(b)

A	B	Y
0	0	1
0	1	0
1	0	1
1	1	0

(c)

A	B	Y
0	0	0
0	1	0
1	0	0
1	1	1

(d)

A	B	Y
0	0	1
0	1	1
1	0	1
1	1	0

04

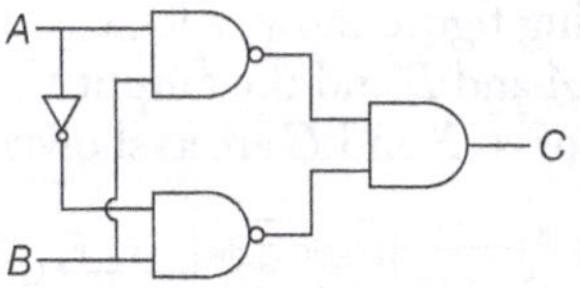

The truth table for the given logic circuit is *[NEET 2022]*

(a)

A	B	C
0	0	1
0	1	0
1	0	0
1	1	1

(b)

A	B	C
0	0	1
0	1	0
1	0	1
1	1	0

(c)

A	B	C
0	0	0
0	1	1
1	0	0
1	1	1

(d)

A	B	C
0	0	1
0	1	1
1	0	1
1	1	0

05 Which of the following gate is called universal gate? *[NCERT (Old) Pg. 505, NEET (Oct.) 2020]*
(a) OR gate (b) AND gate
(c) NAND gate (d) NOT gate

06 For the logic circuit shown, the truth table is *[NEET (Sep.) 2020]*

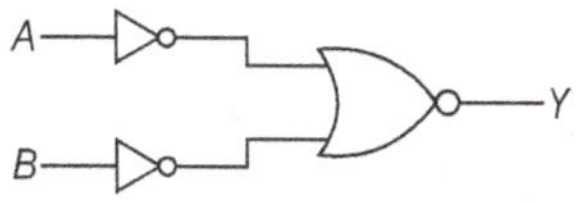

(a)

A	B	Y
0	0	0
0	1	1
1	0	1
1	1	1

(b)

A	B	Y
0	0	1
0	1	1
1	0	1
1	1	0

(c)

A	B	Y
0	0	1
0	1	0
1	0	0
1	1	0

(d)

A	B	Y
0	0	0
0	1	0
1	0	0
1	1	1

07 The circuit diagram shown here corresponds to the logic gate, is *[NCERT (Old) Pg. 502, NEET (Odisha) 2019]*

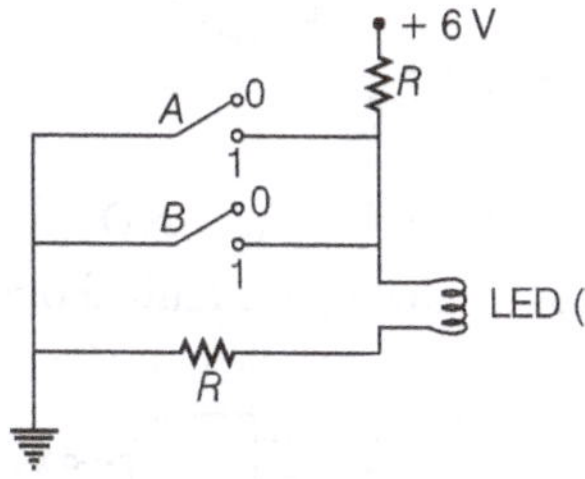

(a) NOR (b) AND
(c) OR (d) NAND

08

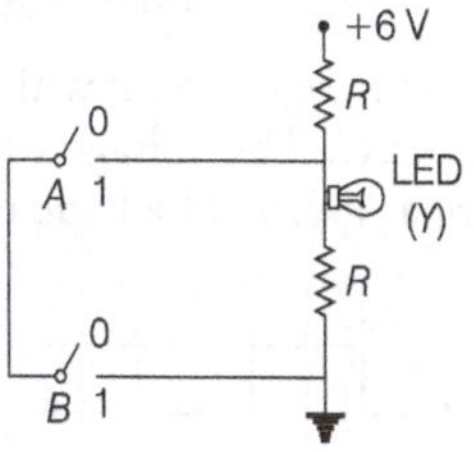

The correct Boolean operation represented by the circuit diagram drawn is *[NEET (National) 2019]*
(a) OR (b) NAND
(c) NOR (d) AND

09 In the combination of the following gates the output Y can be written in terms of inputs A and B as *[NCERT (Old) Pg. 505, NEET 2018]*

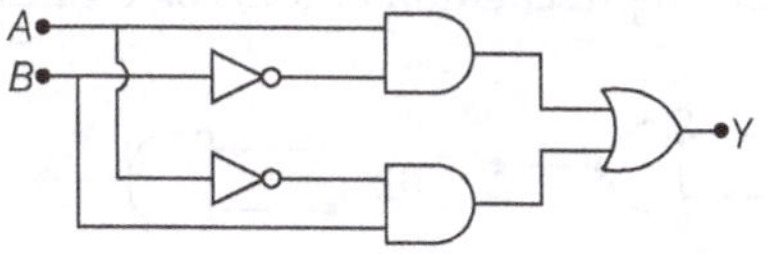

(a) $\overline{A\cdot B}+A\cdot B$ (b) $A\cdot\overline{B}+\overline{A}\cdot B$
(c) $\overline{A\cdot B}$ (d) $\overline{A+B}$

10 The given electrical network is equivalent to *[NEET 2017]*

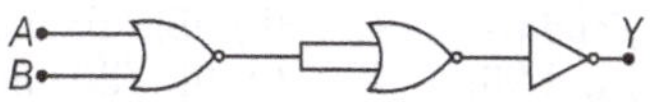

(a) AND gate (b) OR gate
(c) NOR gate (d) NOT gate

11 To get output 1 for the following circuit, the correct choice for the input is *[NCERT (Old) Pg. 505, NEET 2016]*

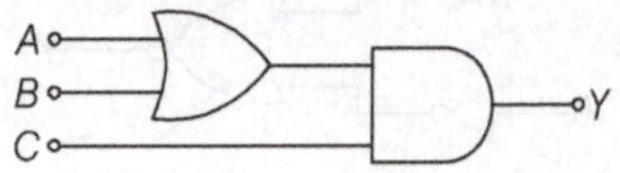

(a) $A=1, B=0, C=0$ (b) $A=1, B=1, C=0$
(c) $A=1, B=0, C=1$ (d) $A=0, B=1, C=0$

12 Which logic gate is represented by the following combination of logic gates? *[AIPMT 2015]*

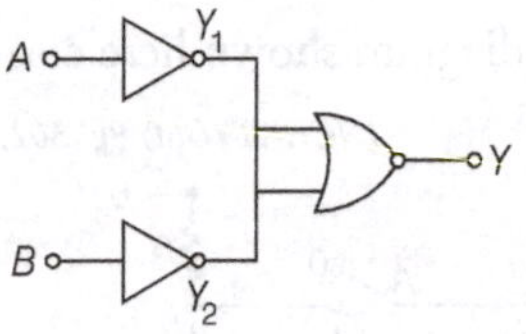

(a) OR (b) NAND (c) AND (d) NOR

13 The output X of the logic circuit shown in figure will be *[NEET 2013]*

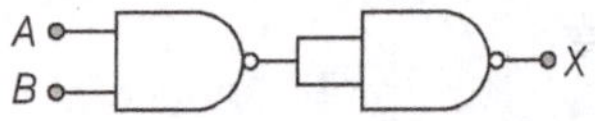

(a) $X=\bar{\bar{A}}\cdot\bar{\bar{B}}$ (b) $X=\overline{A\cdot B}$
(c) $X=A\cdot B$ (d) $X=\overline{A+B}$

14 The figure shows a logic circuit with two inputs A and B and the output C. The voltage wave forms across A, B and C are as given. The logic circuit gate is *[AIPMT 2012]*

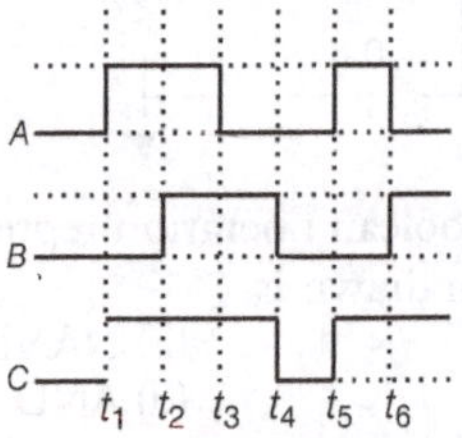

(a) OR gate (b) NOR gate
(c) AND gate (d) NAND gate

15 Symbolic representation of four logic gates are shown as *[AIPMT 2011]*

(i) 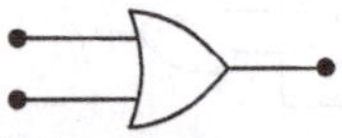 (ii) 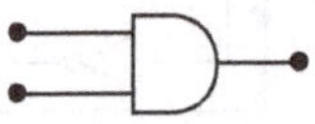

(iii) 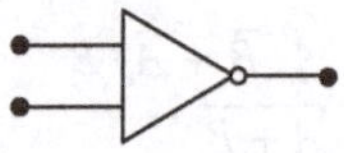 (iv) 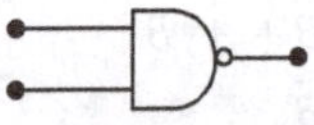

Pick out which ones are for AND, NAND and NOT gates, respectively.
(a) (iii), (ii) and (i) (b) (iii), (ii) and (iv)
(c) (ii), (iv) and (iii) (d) (ii), (iii) and (iv)

16 The device that can act as a complete electronic circuit is *[AIPMT 2010]*
(a) junction diode (b) integrated circuit
(c) junction transistor (d) zener diode

17 To get output $Y=1$ from the circuit shown below, the input must be *[AIPMT 2010]*

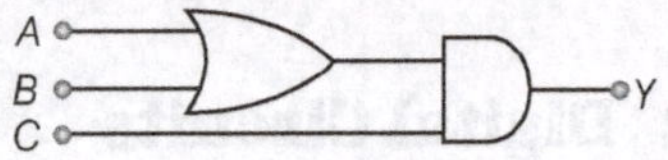

	A	B	C		A	B	C
(a)	0	1	0	(b)	0	0	1
(c)	1	0	1	(d)	1	0	0

18 The symbolic representation of four logic gates

(i) 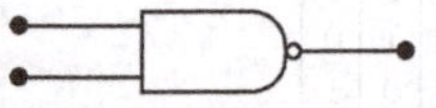 (ii) 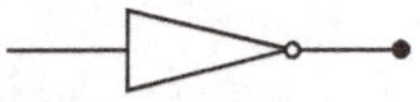

(iii)  (iv) 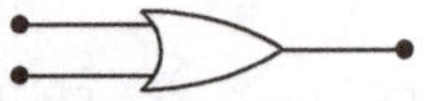

The logic symbols for OR, NOT and NAND gates are respectively *[NCERT (Old) Pg. 503, AIPMT 2009]*
(a) (iii), (iv), (ii) (b) (iv), (i), (iii)
(c) (iv), (ii), (i) (d) (i), (iii), (iv)

19 The circuit is equivalent to *[AIPMT 2008]*

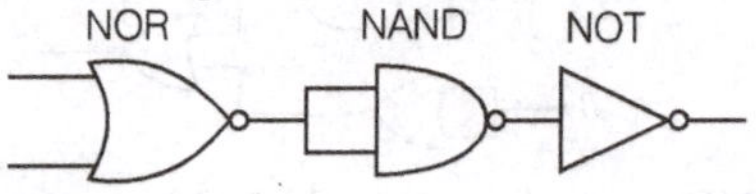

(a) AND gate (b) NAND gate
(c) NOR gate (d) OR gate

20 In the following circuit, the output Y for all possible inputs A and B is expressed by the truth table *[NCERT (Old) Pg. 503, AIPMT 2007]*

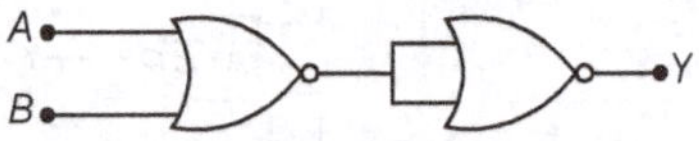

(a)

A	B	Y
0	0	0
0	1	0
1	0	0
1	1	0

(b)

A	B	Y
0	0	1
0	1	1
1	0	1
1	1	0

(c)

A	B	Y
0	0	1
0	1	0
1	0	0
1	1	0

(d)

A	B	Y
0	0	0
0	1	1
1	0	1
1	1	1

21 The following figure shows a logic gate circuit with two inputs A and B and the output C. The voltage waveforms of A, B and C are as shown below

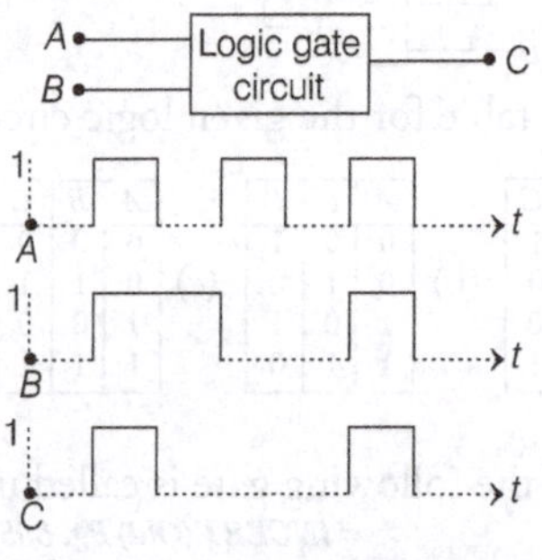

The logic circuit gate is *[NCERT (Old) Pg. 503, AIPMT 2006]*
(a) AND gate (b) NAND gate
(c) NOR gate (d) OR gate

22 The output of OR gate is 1 *[AIPMT 2004]*

(a) only if both inputs are zero
(b) if either or both inputs are 1
(c) only if both inputs are 1
(d) if either input is zero

23 Following diagram performs the logic function of *[NCERT (Old) Pg. 502, AIPMT 2003]*

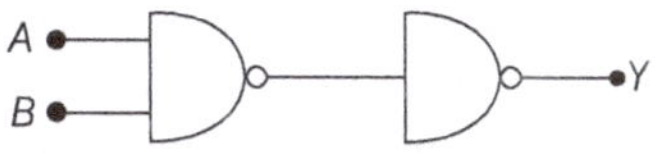

(a) OR gate (b) AND gate
(c) XOR gate (d) NAND gate

24 The truth table given below

Input		Output
A	*B*	*Y*
0	0	0
1	0	0
0	1	0
1	1	1

represents *[AIPMT 2000]*

(a) AND gate
(b) NOR gate
(c) OR gate
(d) NAND gate

25 The following circuit represents *[AIPMT 1999]*

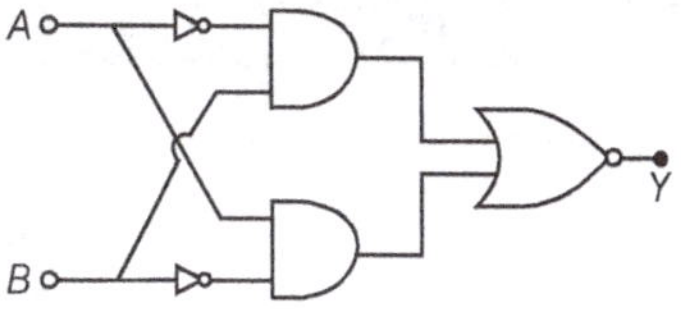

(a) OR gate (b) XOR gate
(c) AND gate (d) NAND gate

26 Which one of the following gates will have an output of 1 ? *[AIPMT 1998]*

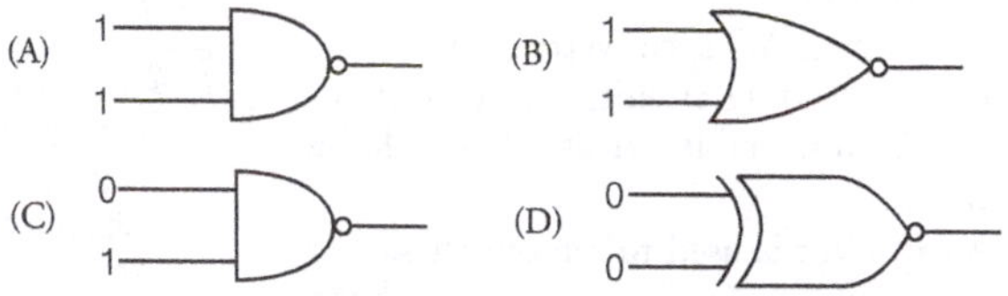

(a) *A* (b) *B* (c) *C* (d) *D*

27 The following truth table belongs to which of the following four gates ? *[NCERT (Old) Pg. 505, AIPMT 1997]*

Input		Output
A	*B*	*Y*
1	1	0
1	0	0
0	1	0
0	0	1

(a) NOR (b) XOR (c) NAND (d) OR

• Key Index

Topic 1

1 (a)	2 (b)	3 (d)	4 (b)	5 (c)	6 (c)	7 (c)	8 (d)	9 (a)	10 (a)
11 (c)	12 (b)	13 (a)	14 (d)	15 (a)	16 (a)	17 (a)	18 (d)	19 (a)	20 (a)
21 (d)	22 (c)	23 (c)	24 (b)	25 (c)	26 (b)	27 (d)	28 (b)	29 (a)	30 (d)
31 (c)	32 (a)	33 (c)	34 (b)	35 (b)	36 (a)	37 (b)	38 (c)	39 (a)	40 (b)
41 (b)	42 (a)	43 (b)	44 (a)	45 (b)	46 (d)	47 (d)	48 (a)	49 (a)	50 (d)
51 (c)	52 (b)	53 (a)	54 (a)	55 (d)	56 (b)	57 (d)	58 (b)	59 (c)	60 (b)
61 (d)	62 (a)	63 (c)							

Topic 2

1 (c)	2 (d)	3 (a)	4 (b)	5 (c)	6 (d)	7 (a)	8 (b)	9 (b)	10 (c)
11 (c)	12 (c)	13 (c)	14 (a)	15 (c)	16 (b)	17 (c)	18 (c)	19 (c)	20 (d)
21 (a)	22 (b)	23 (b)	24 (a)	25 (b)	26 (c)	27 (a)			

Detailed Explanations

Topic 1

01. (a) A is correct but B is incorrect.
In reverse biased *p-n* junction, the current is due to minority charge carriers, which is very small and hence measured in terms of μ A.

02. (b) When AC is converted into DC using a rectifier circuit, then converted DC is an unstable current that includes ripples.
A capacitor is used to remove these ripples and maintain a constant voltage across load.

03. (d) Photovoltaic devices can convert optical radiation into electricity. The basic example of such device is solar photovoltaic system which converts solar energy directly into electrical energy.
Zener diode is heavily doped *p-n* junction diode operating in reverse biased condition in breakdown region.

04. (b) In half wave rectification, input frequency,

$$f_{in} = 60 \text{ Hz}$$

Since, frequency of output voltage obtained from the half wave rectifier is same as frequency of input AC voltage.
Hence, $f_{out} = 60 \text{ Hz}$

05. (c) In the circuit diagram A and C, both the *p-n* junction diodes are in same biasing conditions.
So, both diodes offers equal resistances.
Since, both diodes are in series, therefore equal potential will drop across the junction.

06. (c) Given, the electron concentration in *n*- type semiconductor is equal to the hole's concentration in *p*-type semiconductor.
When electric field is applied across the semiconductor, the electrons and holes will move opposite to each other. The mobility of *n*-type semiconductor is greater than mobility of *p*-type semiconductor.
So, the current in the *n*-type semiconductor is greater than current in the *p*-type semiconductor.

07. (c) Zener diode is a type of special *p-n* junction diode that operates in reverse bias. Thus, it is used as a voltage regulator. So, the statement A is correct. The potential barrier of *p-n* junction for silicon is 0.6-0.7 V and for germanium is 0.2-0.35 V. So, the statement (B) is incorrect.

08. (d)

key idea
A *p-n* junction diode is in forward biased only when *p*-type is connected with more positive voltage than *n*-type. You can use this concept to solve such type of problem.

A *p-n* junction diode is in forward biased when *p*-side is connected with more positive potential than *n*-side.
Since, $0\text{V} > -3\text{V}$.
Hence in option (d), diode circuit is in forward biased.

09. (a) When a pentavalent (phosphorous) impurities is doped with intrinsic semiconductor (Ge, Si), then *n* -type semiconductor is formed.

10. (a) Under reverse bias condition, the holes of *p*-side are attracted towards the negaive terminal of the battery and electrons of the *n*-side are attracted towards the positive terminal of the battery. This increases the width of the depletion layer.

11. (c) Insulators and semiconductors are those solids, which have negative temperature coefficient of resistance. As, when temperature increases number of free electrons increases in both insulator and semiconductor.

12. (b) The energy of light of wavelength λ is given by

$$E = h\nu = \frac{hc}{\lambda} \Rightarrow \lambda = \frac{hc}{E} \quad \ldots\text{(i)}$$

Here, h = Planck's constant
$= 6.63 \times 10^{-34}$ J-s
c = speed of light $= 3 \times 10^8$ m/s
E = energy gap = 1.9 eV
$= 1.9 \times 1.6 \times 10^{-19}$ J

Substituting the given values in Eq. (i), we get

$$\Rightarrow \lambda = \frac{6.63 \times 10^{-34} \times 3 \times 10^8}{1.9 \times 1.6 \times 10^{-19}}$$

$$= 6.54 \times 10^{-7} \text{ m} \approx 654 \text{ nm}$$

Thus, the wavelength of light emitted from LED will be 654 nm.

13. (a) *p*-type semiconductors are obtained when a trivalent impurity (e.g. boron, aluminium, gallium or indium) is added to a intrinsic semiconductor. (e.g. germanium or silicon).
Thus, this addition creates deficiencies of valence electron which are most commonly known as holes. These are the majority charge carriers in this type of semiconductor.

14. (d) Due to increase in temperature because of heating, thermal collision between the electron and holes increases. Thus, net electron-hole pairs increase. This leads to increase in the current in diode and overall resistance of the diode changes.
This in turn changes both the forward biasing and the reverse biasing.
Thus, the overall *I-V* characteristics of *p-n* junction diode gets affected.

Concept Enhancer
When temperature of *p-n* junction is increased, then more number of covalent bond starts breaking. So, more number of charge carriers are produced. Due to which current increases.

15. (a) In the forward biasing of *p-n* junction, *p* side of junction diode is connected to higher potential and *n* side of junction diode is connected to lower potential. Hence, the option (a) is correct answer.

16. (a) Let us assume that current through the diode is I.
From the given condition

$$\because \quad I = \frac{V_A - V_B}{R} = \frac{4-(-6)}{1\text{ k}\Omega}$$

$$= \frac{10}{1 \times 10^3} = 10^{-2}\text{A}$$

17. (a) In the given circuit, the diode D_1 will be in reverse bias, so it will block the current and diode D_2 will be in forward bias, so it will pass the current

$$i = \frac{V}{R_1 + R_3} = \frac{10}{2+2} = 2.5 \text{ A}$$

18. *(d)* As it is forward biased, so it takes positive value. Hence, option (d) is correct.

19. *(a)* Given, external resistance $R = 100\ \Omega$ and an emf is 3.5 V.

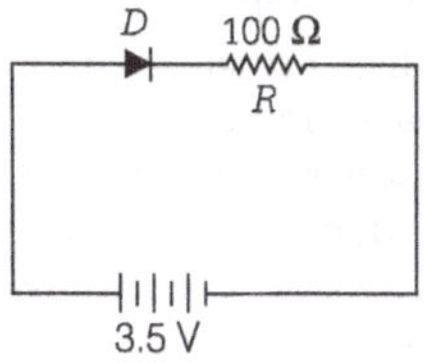

Potential barrier across the diode is 0.5 V,

Potential difference on

$$R = 3.5\text{ V} - 0.5\text{ V} = 3.0\text{ V}$$

Current in circuit,

$$I = \frac{V}{R} = \frac{3}{100}$$
$$= 0.03\text{ A} = 30\text{ mA}$$

20. *(a)*

key idea

V-I characteristics of solar cell always occurs in fourth quadrant.

V-I characteristics of a solar cell is shown. Where, A represents open circuit voltage (i.e., $I = 0, V = \text{emf}$) and *B* shows short circuit voltage (i.e., $I = I, V = 0$).

21. *(d)* Barrier potential depends on all the three options given. Barrier potential depends on the material used to make *p-n* junction diode (whether it is Si or Ge).

It also depends on amount of doping due to which the number of majority carriers will change. It also depends on temperature due to which the number of minority carriers will change.

22. *(c)* The *n*-type semi-conductor can be produced by doping an impurity atom of valency 5 i.e. pentavalent atoms (phosphorus). Holes are minority carriers in them.

> • Concept **Enhancer**
>
> In a *n*-type semiconductor electrons are majority charge carrier and in *p*-type semiconductor, holes are majority charge carrier but both type of semiconductor are electrically neutral.

23. *(c)* The four bonding electrons in the case of C lie in the second orbit, whereas in case of Si they lies in the third orbit. So loosely bounded valence electrons are present in Si as compared to C.

24. *(b)* When a small amount of antimony is added to germanium crystal, the crystal becomes *n*-type semiconductor, because antimony is a pentavalent substrate.

25. *(c)* In forward biasing of *p-n* junction, the positive terminal of the battery is connected to *p*-side and the depletion region becomes thin.

26. *(b)* In *n*-type semiconductor majority carriers are electrons. So, option (b) is false statement.

27. *(d)* Energy, $E = h\nu = h\frac{c}{\lambda}$

$$\Rightarrow \quad \lambda = \frac{hc}{E}$$

Substituting the values of *h, c* and *E* in the above equation

$$\lambda = \frac{6.6 \times 10^{-34} \times 3 \times 10^{8}}{2.5 \times 1.6 \times 10^{-19}}$$
$$= 5000\text{ Å}$$

As $\quad 4000\text{ Å} < 5000\text{ Å}$

Signal of wavelength 4000 Å can be detected by the photodiode.

28. *(b)* Let the energy of radiation falling on the *p-n* photodiode be $E = h\nu$

The minimum energy required = 2 eV

$$\because \quad 2\text{ eV} = h\nu$$

$$\therefore \quad \nu = \frac{2eV}{h} = \frac{2 \times 1.6 \times 10^{-19}}{6.6 \times 10^{-34}}$$
$$= 5 \times 10^{14}\text{ Hz}$$

29. *(a)* Since in the given diagram, we see that there are more number of holes so it is *p*-type semiconductor.

30. *(d)* In semiconductor, resistivity decreases with increase in temperature. So, choice (d) is wrong.

31. *(c)* Zener diode is particularly suitable for voltage regulating purposes or voltage stabilisation purposes.

> • Concept **Enhancer**
>
> Zener diode is also used as voltage regulator or voltage reference. It is a heavily doped *p-n* junction diode.

32. *(a)* On applying forward bias to a *p-n* junction diode, it increases number of donor on the *n*-side and decreases potential barrier. It also decreases electric field of depletion layer.

33. *(c)* The circuit shown in figure can be redrawn as

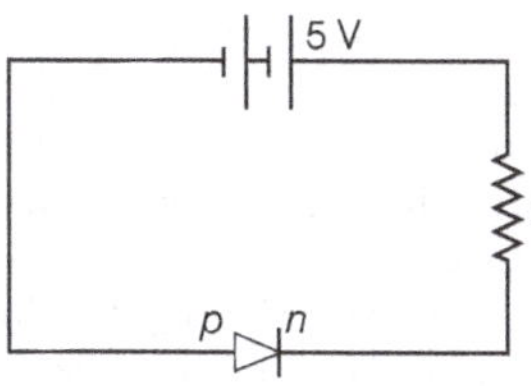

In the option (c), the *p*-end of the diode is connected to negative terminal of the battery, so the diode has been reverse biased.

34. *(b)* In a photoconductive cell, when monochromatic light is incident on the transparent metallic film, a force produced called the photo-electromotive force, stimulates the emission of an electric current where photovoltaic action creates a potential difference between two points.

The magnitude of this current depends upon the intensity of incident light. Hence, photo electromotive force produced by monochromatic light is proportional to the intensity of light falling on the cell.

35. *(b)* The output DC component of half wave rectifier is given by

$$V_{\text{output}} = \frac{\text{peak voltage}}{\pi} = \frac{10}{\pi}\text{V}$$

36. *(a)* In semiconductors, valence band and conduction band are separated by an energy gap called the forbidden energy gap. It is very small. At room temperature some electrons in valence band acquire thermal energy.

This energy is more than forbidden energy gap E_g, thus they jump into the conduction band and leave their vacancy in the valence band which act as holes.

Hence, at room temperature valence band is partially empty and conduction band is partially filled.

37. *(b)*

key idea

Frequency of ripple obtained by full wave rectifier is equal to double the frequency of input signal.

For full wave rectifier,

Ripple frequency = 2 × input frequency

$$= 2 \times 50 = 100\text{ Hz}$$

38. *(c)* Barrier potential does not depend on diode design while it depends on temperature, doping density and forward biasing.

39. (a) In forward biasing, the diode conducts. For ideal junction diode, the forward resistance is zero. Therefore, entire applied voltage occurs across resistance R.
While in reverse biasing, the diode does not conduct, so it has infinite resistance. Thus, voltage across R is zero in reverse biasing.

40. (b) For conduction in a p-n junction, it should be forward biased because it offers minimum resistance to the flow of current. For this p-side must be connected to positive terminal (higher potential) and n-side must be connected to negative terminal (lower potential). Figure below shows the p-n junction in a conducting state (forward biased condition).

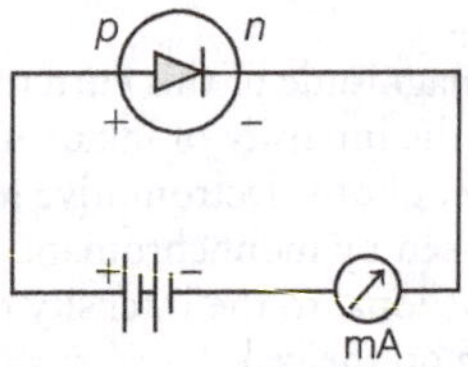

41. (b) In the circuit, diode D_1 is forward biased and diode D_2 is reverse biased. Therefore, no current flows in the arm containing D_2 and all of the current flows through arm containing D_1. Thus, current flowing through the circuit is given by

$$I = \frac{V}{R_{eq}} = \frac{5}{20+30} = \frac{5}{50}\text{ A}$$

42. (a) Here, Si is a semiconductor and Cu is a metal. So, resistivity of Si increases but that of Cu decreases.

43. (b) In option (b), p-side is at higher potential (0 V) and n-side at lower potential (–2 V). So, this diode is forward biased.

44. (a) In p-type semiconductors, holes are the majority carriers and electrons are the minority carriers.

45. (b) Since in forward biasing, negative of the battery is connected to n-type side and the positive terminal of battery is connected to p-type side, hence an electric field is created in direction opposite to the E in the potential barrier region. Thus, depletion layer of p-n junction diode decreases.

46. (d) Depletion layer consists of immobile ions.

47. (d) In a junction diode, when electron jumps to conduction band from valence band due to thermal agitation or any other circumstances, then a vacancy is created in valence band which has positive charge equal to charge of electron in magnitude. This is called a hole. Thus, holes in junction diode are due to missing electrons.

> • Concept **Enhancer**
> Hole is not like a proton. It is a empty space.

48. (a) When pentavalent impurity is added to silicon then n-type semiconductor is formed. Out of given options, only phosphorus (P) is pentavalent, so it should be doped to silicon to make it n-type semiconductor.

49. (a) We know that in forward biasing of p-n junction the current is of the order of milliampere while in reverse biasing the current is of the order of microampere (negligible). Thus, device is a p-n junction.

50. (d) In a p-n junction diode, majority carriers are holes on p-side and electrons on n-side. Holes, thus diffuse to n-side and electrons to p-side. This diffusion causes a layer of positive charge in the n-region and layer of negative charge in the p-region near the junction. This double layer of opposite charge creates an electric field which exerts a force on the electrons and holes, against their diffusion.
This electric field becomes strong enough as diffusion proceeds to stop it. In the equilibrium position, there is a barrier, for charge motion with the n-side at a higher potential than the p-side. The junction region has a very low density of either p or n-type carriers, because of inter diffusion. It is called depletion region.

51. (c) Current in circuit

$$i = \frac{P}{V_d} = \frac{100\times10^{-3}}{0.5}$$

[V_d = voltage drop across diode]

$$i = 200\times10^{-3}\text{ A}$$

Voltage across resistance R,

$$V' = 1.5 - 0.5 = 1.0\text{ V}$$

Thus, resistance $R = \frac{V'}{i} = \frac{1}{200\times10^{-3}}$

$$= 5\,\Omega$$

52. (b) As given indium is trivalent impurity so it must be doped to Ge or Si to make it p-type semiconductor.

53. (a) When a small amount of pentavalent impurity is added to a pure semiconductor, it is known as n-type semiconductor. Here, Arsenic (33) is pentavalent impurity.

54. (a) When a small amount of pentavalent impurity is added to a pure semiconductor, it is known as n-type semiconductor. Here, Phosphorus (P) is a pentavalent and silicon is a tetravalent. Therefore, when phosphorus is doped with Si, it forms a n-type semiconductor.

55. (d)

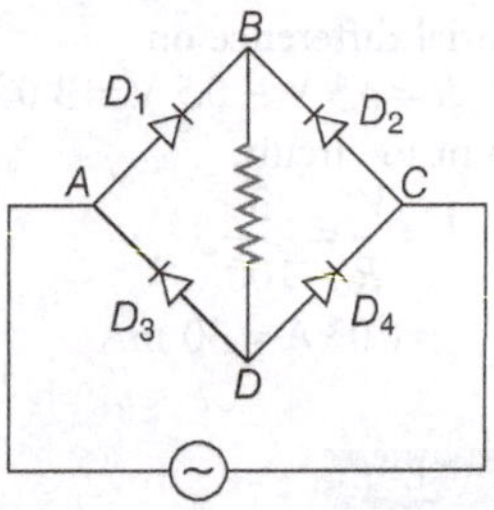

AC input is applied across A and C and output is taken across BD.

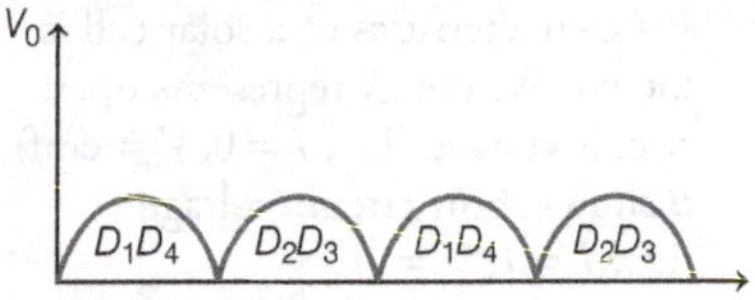

When positive cycle is fed to AC, D_1 and D_4 conduct, when negative cycle is fed to AC, D_3 and D_2 conduct in the same direction. Thus, Output across BD is full wave rectified.

56. (b) When p-n junction is reverse biased, the flow of current is due to drifting of minority charge carries across the junction.

57. (d) Semiconductors have negative temperature coefficients of resistance i.e. the resistance of a semiconductor decreases with the increase in temperature as no. of electrons increases in conduction band. Copper has positive temperature coefficient of resistance, i.e. the resistance of copper increases with the increase in temperature due to the collision of electrons. Hence, at 80 K, the resistance of copper will decrease while that of germanium will increase.

58. (b) The bond between two carbon atoms in diamond has a cohesive energy of 7.3 eV with respect to separated neutral atoms. Due to such high cohesive energy diamond is very hard.

59. *(c)* Many solids or crystals are composed of neutral atoms or molecules without any transferring, sharing or free movement of electrons. These solids remains bound by much weaker, short range attractive forces, known as 'vander Waals' forces. These forces arise as a result of fluctuations in the charge distributions of nearby molecules.

60. *(b)* The accumulation of electric charges of opposite polarities in the two regions of the junction gives rise to an electric field between these region due to the diffusion of charge carriers.

This electric field opposes further flow of electrons from the *n*-region to the *p*-region and that of holes from the *p*-region to *n*-region.

This electric field sets a potential barrier V_B at the junction which opposes further diffusion of free charge carriers into opposite regions.

In the vicinity of the junction, a region is created, which is devoid of free charge carriers and has immobile ions. This region in which no free charge carriers are available is called a depletion region. This is shown in figure.

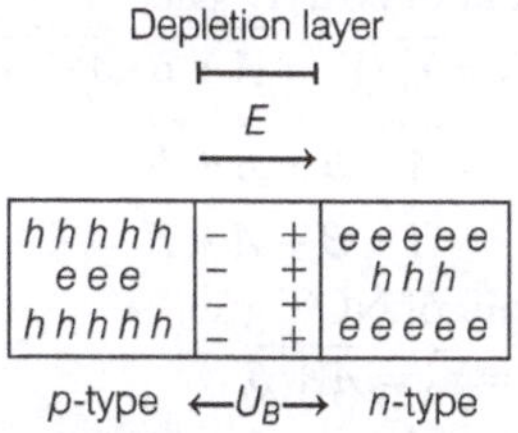

61. *(d)* When a *n*-type semiconductor is heated a few hole-electron pairs generate. When a free electron is produced then simultaneously a hole is also produced.

Thus number of elecrons and holes both increases equally.

62. *(a)* A *p-n* junction diode is said to be in forward biased when the positive pole of battery is joined to the *p*-type semiconductor and negative pole to the *n*-type semiconductor.

> • Concept **Enhancer**
>
> A *p-n* junction diode is said to be in forward biased when *p*-type semiconductor is connected with more positive voltage than *n*-type.

63. *(c)* Silicon is actually an insulator at absolute zero of temperature.

Topic 2

01. *(c)* Output from the truth table

$$Y = \overline{A}\cdot\overline{B} + A\cdot\overline{B} = \overline{B}\cdot(\overline{A}+A)$$

$$Y = \overline{B}$$

So, correct option is (c).

02. *(d)* The given combination of gates can be taken as

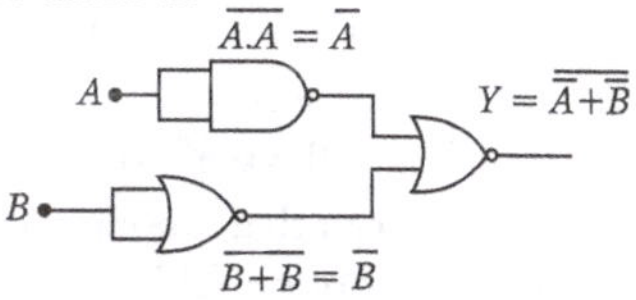

$$Y = \overline{\overline{A}+\overline{B}} = \overline{\overline{A}}\cdot\overline{\overline{B}} = A\cdot B$$

Hence, the output Y of the given logic gate is similar to AND gate.

03. *(a)* Output of the logic circuit is

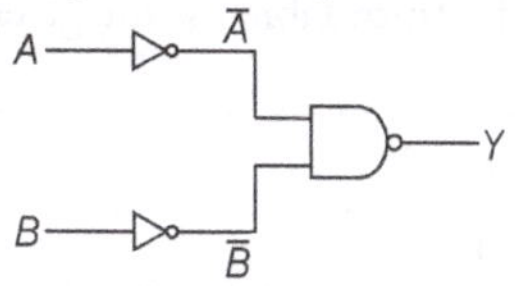

$$Y = \overline{\overline{A}\cdot\overline{B}} = \overline{\overline{A}} + \overline{\overline{B}} \; (\because \overline{xy} = \overline{x}+\overline{y})$$

$$= A + B \; (\because \overline{\overline{x}} = x)$$

= output of OR gate

Truth table is

A	B	$Y = A + B$
0	0	0
0	1	1
1	0	1
1	1	1

04. *(b)* The given logic circuit is represented as

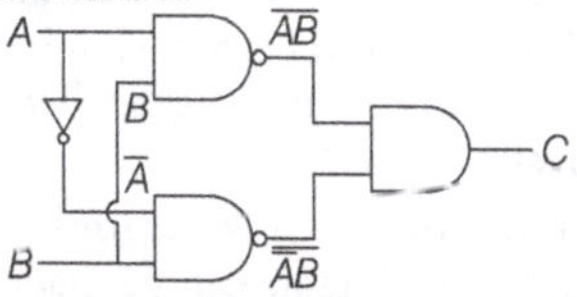

Output of logic circuit,

$$C = \overline{AB}\cdot\overline{\overline{A}B} = (\overline{A}+\overline{B})\cdot(\overline{\overline{A}}+\overline{B})$$

$$= (\overline{A}+\overline{B})\cdot(A+\overline{B})$$

$$= \overline{A}A + \overline{A}\overline{B} + \overline{B}A + \overline{B}\overline{B}$$

$$= 0 + \overline{A}\overline{B} + \overline{B}A + \overline{B}$$

$$= \overline{A}\overline{B} + \overline{B}(A+1) = \overline{A}\overline{B} + \overline{B}$$

$$= \overline{B}(\overline{A}+1) = \overline{B}$$

Truth table is given as

A	B	$C = \overline{B}$
0	0	1
0	1	0
1	0	1
1	1	0

05. *(c)* NAND and NOR gate are called universal gate because all type of logic gates and Boolean expressions can be realised with the help of NAND and NOR gate.

> • Concept **Enhancer**
>
> Universal gates can be used to design any type of logic gate.

06. *(d)* Given, logic circuit is

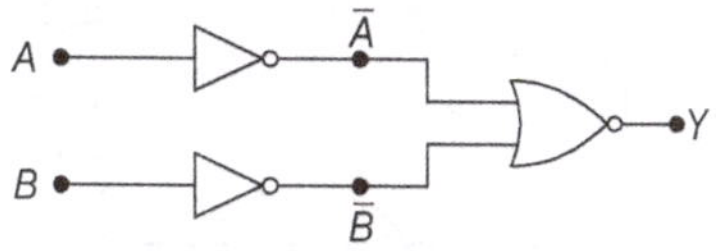

$$Y = \overline{\overline{A}+\overline{B}} = \overline{\overline{A}}\cdot\overline{\overline{B}}$$

[using de-Morgan's theorem, $\overline{x+y} = \overline{x}\cdot\overline{y}$]

$$= A\cdot B \qquad [\because \overline{\overline{x}} = x]$$

Truth table for above given logic circuit is

A	B	$\overline{A}$	$\overline{B}$	$Y = A\cdot B$
0	0	1	1	0
0	1	1	0	0
1	0	0	1	0
1	1	0	0	1

⇒

A	B	Y
0	0	0
0	1	0
1	0	0
1	1	1

07. *(a)* From the circuit diagram given below, it can be seen that the current will flow to ground if any of the switch is closed. Also, the LED will only glow when current flows through it.

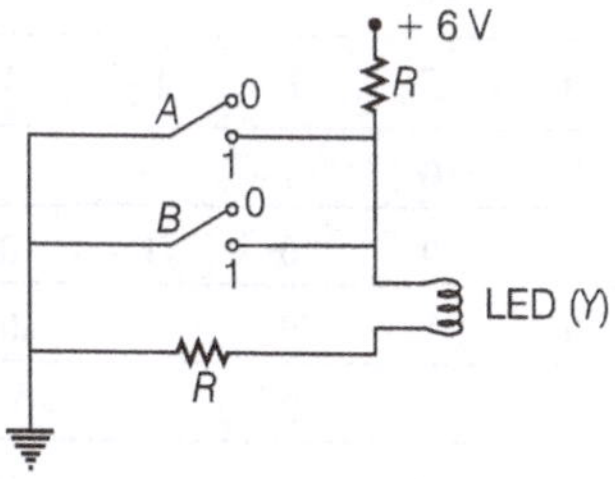

Thus, the truth table for the circuit diagram can be formed as circuit diagram in given solution.

A	B	Y
0	0	1
0	1	0
1	0	0
1	1	0

The output Y is equivalent to that of NOR gate.

08. *(b)* The LED will glow when the current flows through it, i.e. when the voltage across it is high. The truth table can be formed from this

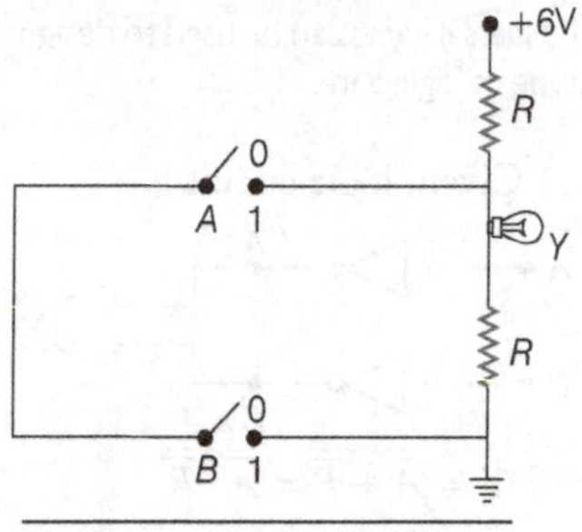

A	B	Y
0	0	1
0	1	1
1	0	1
1	1	0

The output Y is same as that come from NAND gate.

09. *(b)* According to the question, the figure of combination of gates in terms of inputs and outputs can be given as

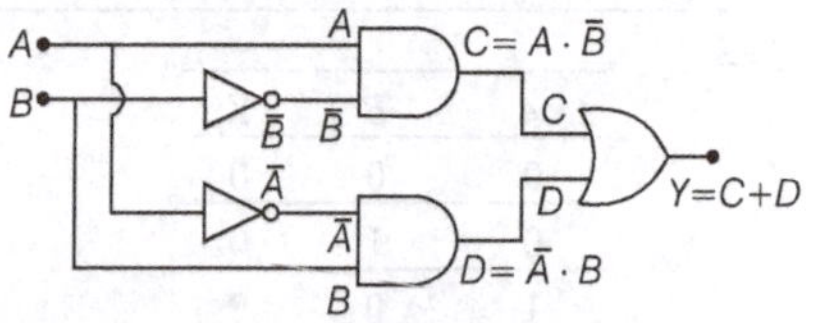

Thus,

$$Y = A\cdot\overline{B} + \overline{A}\cdot B$$

10. *(c)* Truth table for given network is

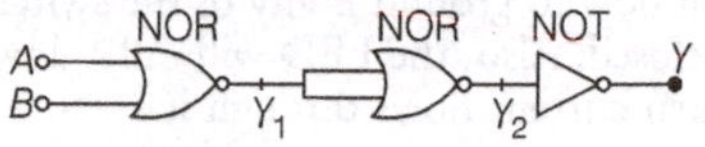

A	B	Y_1	Y_2	Y
0	0	1	0	1
1	0	0	1	0
0	1	0	1	0
1	1	0	1	0

Output Y of network matches with that of NOR gate.

11. *(c)* Consider the given figure,
The resultant boolean expression of the above logic circuit will be

$$Y = (A + B).C$$

Now, let us try with inputs A, B and C given in the options and lets see, which one of them will give output 1 at Y.

If $A = 1, B = 0, C = 0$

$\Rightarrow \quad Y = (1 + 0).0 \Rightarrow Y = 0$

If $A = 1, B = 1, C = 0$

$\Rightarrow \quad Y = (1 + 1).0$

$\Rightarrow \quad Y = 1.0 \Rightarrow Y = 0$

If $A = 1, B = 0, C = 1$

$\Rightarrow \quad Y = (1 + 0).1$

$\Rightarrow \quad Y = 1.1 \Rightarrow Y = 1$

If $\quad A = 0, B = 1, C = 0$

$\Rightarrow \quad Y = (0 + 1).0$

$\Rightarrow \quad Y = 1.0 \Rightarrow Y = 0$

So, we have seen that among the given options, only option (c) is the correct choice, i.e.

Output $Y = 1$ only when inputs $A = 1, B = 0$
and $\quad C = 1$

12. *(c)* The truth table for the given circuit is

A	B	Y_1	Y_2	$Y = \overline{Y_1 + Y_2}$
0	0	1	1	0
0	1	1	0	0
1	0	0	1	0
1	1	0	0	1

The truth table shows that both the inputs are high, then we are getting high value of output otherwise zero. Hence, the combination represents AND gate.

13. *(c)* $X = \overline{\overline{AB}} = A\cdot B$ (i.e. AND gate)

If the output of NAND gate is connected to the input of NOT gate (made from NAND gate by joining two inputs) from the given figure then we get back an AND gate.

14. *(a)* From the given waveforms, the following truth table can be made

Time	Input A	Inputs B	Output C
0 to t_1	0	0	0
t_1 to t_2	1	0	1
t_2 to t_3	1	1	1
t_3 to t_4	0	1	1
t_4 to t_5	0	0	0
t_5 to t_6	1	0	1
$1 > t_6$	0	1	1

This truth table obtained is of OR gate. So, logic circuit gate is OR gate.

15. *(c)* The symbols given in problem are
(i) OR (ii) AND
(iii) NOT (iv) NAND

16. *(b)* Integrated circuits are miniature electronic circuit produced within a single crystal of a semiconductor such as silicon. They contain a million or so transistors and resistors or capacitors. They are widely used in memory circuits, micro computers, pocket calculators and electronic watches on account of their low cost and bulk, reliability into specific regions of the semiconductor crystals.

17. *(c)* Gate I is OR gate,

$$Y' = A + B$$

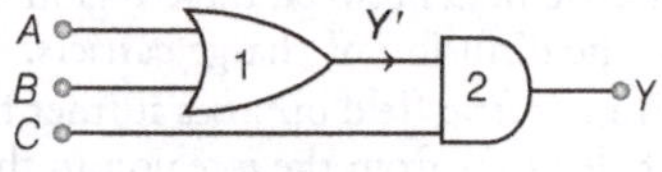

Gate II is AND gate,

$$Y = Y'\cdot C = (A + B)\cdot C$$

$\therefore \; A = 1, B = 0, C = 1$ will give $Y = 1$

18. *(c)* The symbols given in problem are
(i) NAND (ii) NOT
(iii) AND (iv) OR

19. *(c)* The gate circuit can be solved by giving two inputs A and B.

Output of NOR gate,

$$Y_1 = \overline{A + B}$$

Output of NAND gate,

$$Y_2 = \overline{Y_1 \cdot Y_1} = \overline{\overline{A + B}\cdot\overline{A + B}}$$

$$= \overline{\overline{A + B}} + \overline{\overline{A + B}}$$

$$= A + B + A + B = A + B$$

Output of NOT gate,

$$Y = \overline{Y_2} = \overline{A + B}$$

which is the output of NOR gate.

20. *(d)* We can simplify the gate circuit as

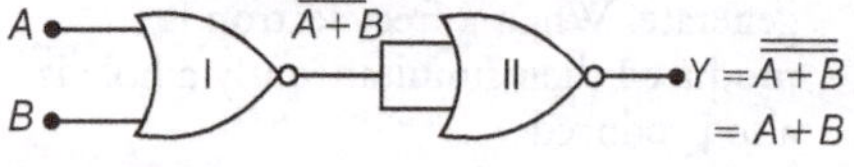

Here, gates-I and II are NOR gates. The output $(\overline{A + B})$ of gate-I will appear as input of gate-II. The final output is

$$Y = \overline{\overline{A + B}} = A + B$$

This is the Boolean expression of OR gate whose truth table is given below.

A	B	Y
0	0	0
0	1	1
1	0	1
1	1	1

21. *(a)* The Boolean expression which satisfies the output of this logic gate is $C = A \cdot B$, which is for AND gate.

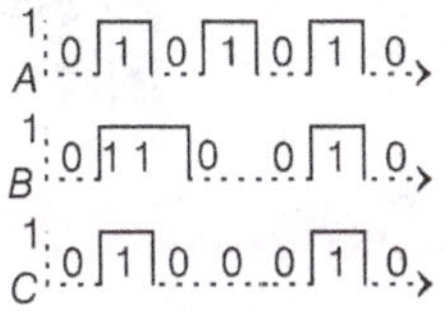

A	B	C
0	0	0
1	1	1
0	1	0
1	0	0
0	0	0
1	1	1
0	0	0

$$C = A \cdot B$$

22. *(b)* OR gate has two inputs A and B and output Y. It follows *a* logic operation represented by +. Thus, its Boolean expression is

$$A + B = Y$$

The truth table of OR gate is

A	B	Y
0	0	0
0	1	1
1	0	1
1	1	1

Thus, after observing its Boolean expression and its truth table, it is obvious that output of OR gate is 1 if either or both inputs are 1.

23. *(b)*

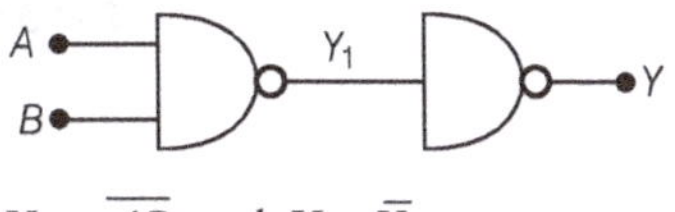

$\therefore$ $Y_1 = \overline{AB}$ and $Y = \overline{Y_1}$

$$= \overline{\overline{AB}} = AB$$

= Output of AND gate

24. *(a)* We can see from the truth table that output is 1 only when its both inputs are 1.

This is possible only for AND gate. The Boolean expression for AND gate is

$$Y = A \cdot B$$

which satisfies the truth table as below

$$0 \cdot 0 = 0$$
$$1 \cdot 0 = 0$$
$$0 \cdot 1 = 0$$
$$1 \cdot 1 = 1$$

Here symbol (·) represents AND operation.

25. *(b)* Output of upper AND gate

$$= \overline{A}B$$

Output of lower AND gate = $A\overline{B}$

Thus,

output of OR gate = $\overline{A}B + A\overline{B}$

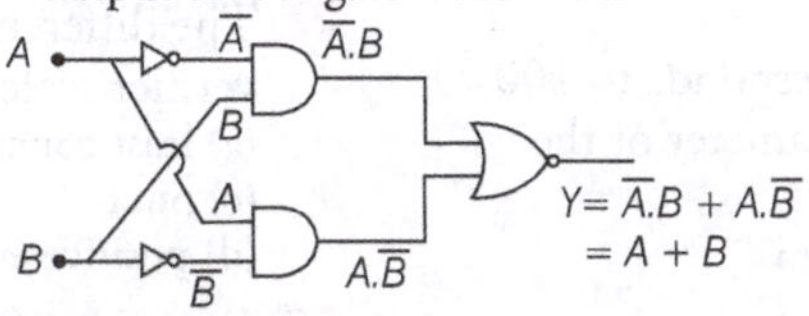

This is Boolean expression for XOR gate.

26. *(c)* (a) Gate A is NAND gate, its output will be

$$Y_A = \overline{1 \cdot 1} = \overline{1} = 0$$

(b) Gate B is NOR gate, its output will be

$$Y_B = \overline{1 + 1} = \overline{1} = 0$$

(c) Gate C is NAND gate, its output will be

$$Y_C = \overline{0 \cdot 1} = \overline{0} = 1$$

(d) Gate D is XOR gate, its output will be

$$Y_D = 0 \oplus 0$$
$$= 0 \cdot \overline{0} + \overline{0} \cdot 0 = 0$$

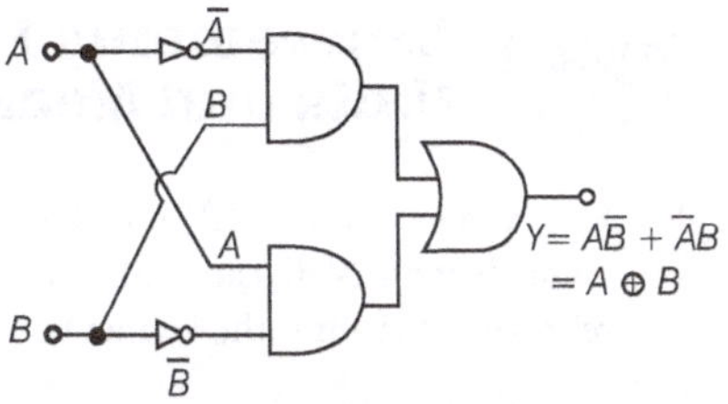

Thus, gate C will give an output 1

27. *(a)* The Boolean expression expressed by the truth table may be written as

$$Y = \overline{A + B}$$

This is the expression of NOR gate (OR gate + NOT gate)

Note The NOR gate may be shown as below.

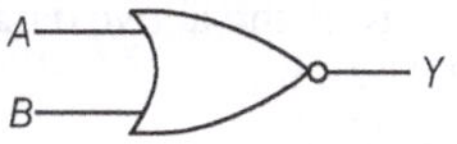

C-29

NEET Chapterwise
Topicwise Physics

In NEET 2024, 1 question was visible from this chapter.
For detailed analysis scan QR code

EXPERIMENTAL SKILLS

Topic 1 Experements Related to Units and Measurements

01 In a vernier callipers, $(N+1)$ divisions of vernier scale coincide with N divisions of main scale. If 1 MSD represents 0.1 mm, the vernier constant (in cm) is *[NEET 2024]*

(a) $\frac{1}{10N}$ (b) $\frac{1}{100(N+1)}$ (c) $100N$ (d) $10(N+1)$

02 A screw gauge gives the following readings when used to measure the diameter of a wire
Main scale reading : 0 mm
Circular scale reading : 52 divisions
Given that, 1 mm on main scale corresponds to 100 divisions on the circular scale. The diameter of the wire from the above data is

(a) 0.52 cm (b) 0.026 cm
(c) 0.26 cm (d) 0.052 cm

03 A screw gauge has least count of 0.01 mm and there are 50 divisions in its circular scale. The pitch of the screw gauge is

(a) 0.25 mm (b) 0.5 mm
(c) 1.0 mm (d) 0.01 mm

04 The main scale of a vernier calliper has n divisions/cm and n divisions of the vernier scale coincide with $(n-1)$ divisions of main scale. The least count of the vernier callipers is

(a) $\frac{1}{(n+1)(n-1)}$ cm (b) $\frac{1}{n}$ cm
(c) $\frac{1}{n^2}$ cm (d) $\frac{1}{n(n+1)}$ cm

05 A student measured the diameter of a small steel ball using a screw gauge of least count 0.001 cm. The main scale reading is 5 mm and zero of circular scale division coincides with 25 divisions above the reference level. If screw gauge has a zero error of -0.004 cm, the correct diameter of the ball is

(a) 0.053 cm (b) 0.525 cm (c) 0.521 cm (d) 0.529 cm

06 In a vernier callipers N divisions of vernier scale coincide with $N-1$ divisions of main scale (in which length of one division is 1 mm). The least count of the instrument should be

(a) N (b) $N-1$ (c) $\frac{1}{10N}$ (d) $\frac{1}{(N-1)}$

07 In which of the following measurements screw gauge can be used?

(a) measuring height of block
(b) measuring diameter of lead shot
(c) measuring weight of lead shot
(d) measuring diameter of a glass plate

08 The difference between a main scale division and a vernier scale division is known as

(a) least count (b) zero error
(c) pitch
(d) positive error/negative error

09 **Assertion** (A) If in ten complete rotations of the circular scale, the distance travelled on main scale of the screw gauge is 10 mm and there are 100 total divisions on circular scale, then least count is 0.001 cm.

Reason (R) Least count

$$= \frac{\text{Pitch}}{\text{Total divisions on circular scale}}$$

In the light of the above statements, choose the most appropriate answer from the options given below.

(a) Both A and R are correct and R is the correct explanation of A.
(b) Both A and R are correct but R is not the correct explanation of A.
(c) A is correct but R is not correct.
(d) A is not correct but R is correct.

10 The vernier scale used for measurement has a positive zero error of 0.1 mm. If while taking a measurement, it was noted that 0 on the vernier scale lies between 8.5 cm and 8.6 cm vernier coincidence is 6, then the correct value of measurement is .... cm. (least count = 0.1 mm)

(a) 8.56 cm (b) 8.36 cm (c) 8.55 cm (d) 8.58 cm

11 A student measuring the diameter of a pencil of circular cross-section with the help of a vernier scale records the following four readings; 6.50 mm, 6.55 mm, 6.45 mm and 6.65 mm. The average of these four readings is 6.5375 mm and the standard deviation of the data is 0.07395 mm. The average diameter of the pencil should be therefore recorded as
(a) (6.5375 ± 0.0739) mm (b) (6.5375 ± 0.0740) mm
(c) (6.538 ± 0.074) mm (d) (6.54 ± 0.07) mm

12 If the screw on a screw gauge is given 12 rotations, it moves by 3 mm on the main scale. If there are 50 divisions on the circular scale, the least count of the screw gauge is
(a) 0.0005 cm (b) 0.01 cm
(c) 0.02 cm (d) 0.001 cm

13 Least count of a vernier calliper is $\frac{1}{10N}$ cm. The value of one division on the main scale is 1 mm. Then, the number of divisions of main scale that coincide with N divisions of vernier scale is
(a) $\left(\frac{2N-1}{20N}\right)$ (b) $(2N-1)$
(c) $\left(\frac{2N-1}{2N}\right)$ (d) $N-1$

14 In vernier calliper, when both jaws touch each other, zero of the vernier scale shifts towards left and its 4th division coincides exactly with a certain division on main scale. If 50 vernier scale divisions equal to 48 main scale divisions and zero error in the instrument is 0.02 mm, then how many main scale divisions are there in 1 cm?
(a) 10 (b) 80 (c) 40 (d) 5

15 A screw gauge has 40 divisions on its circular scale. The circular scale is 4 units ahead of the pitch scale marking, prior to use. Upon one complete rotation of the circular scale, a displacement of 0.4 mm is noticed on the pitch scale. The nature of zero error involved and the least count of the screw gauge are, respectively
(a) negative, 2 μm (b) positive, 10 μm
(c) positive, 0.1 mm (d) positive, 0.1 μm

16 In vernier calipers, 10 divisions of vernier scale is equal to 9 divisions of main scale. When both jaws of vernier calipers touch each other, the zero of the vernier scale is shifted to the left of zero of the main scale and 4th vernier scale division exactly coincides with the main scale reading. One main scale division is equal to 2 mm. While measuring diameter of a spherical body, the body is held between two jaws. It is now observed that zero of the vernier scale lies between 31 and 32 divisions of main scale reading and 6th vernier scale division exactly coincides with the main scale reading. The diameter of the spherical body will be
(a) 3.12 cm (b) 3.26 cm (c) 3.10 cm (d) 3.30 cm

17 In a screw gauge, 5th division of the circular scale coincides with the reference line when the ratchet is closed. There are 100 divisions on the circular scale, and the main scale moves by 0.5 mm on a complete rotation. For a particular observation the reading on the main scale is 5 mm and the 20th division of the circular scale coincides with reference line. Calculate the true reading.
(a) 5.00 mm (b) 5.25 mm (c) 5.07 mm (d) 5.30 mm

18 The pitch and the number of divisions on the circular scale, for a given screw gauge are 0.4 mm and 200, respectively. When the screw gauge is fully tightened without any object, the zero of its circular scale lies 3 divisions below the mean line. The readings of the main scale and the circular scale, for a thin sheet, are 5.5 mm and 48 respectively, the thickness of this sheet is
(a) 5.680 mm (b) 5.755 mm
(c) 5.725 mm (d) 5.740 mm

19 The least count of the main scale of a vernier callipers is 1 mm. Its vernier scale is divided into 20th division and coincide with 8th division of the main scale. When jaws are touching each other, the 7th division of vernier scale coincides with a division of main scale and the zero of vernier scale is lying right side of the zero of main scale. When this vernier is used to measure length of a cylinder the zero of the vernier scale lies between 3.1 cm and 3.2 cm and 4th VSD coincides with a main scale division. The length of the cylinder is (VSD is vernier scale division)
(a) 3.2 cm (b) 2.92 cm (c) 3.07 cm (d) 3.21 cm

20 The wedge is kept below the 50 cm mark on the meter scale. Known masses of 5 kg and 10 kg are hung at the 25 cm and 35 cm mark, respectively. Where will a 15 kg mass be hung on the meter scale to balance it? (Neglect mass of meter scale)
(a) 65 cm (b) 68 cm (c) 73 cm (d) 71 cm

21 When a meter scale is balanced above a wedge, 3 kg mass is hung at 20 cm mark and a 5 kg mass is hung at 100 cm mark. To which mark on the meter scale, the fulcrum be shifted (neglect mass of meter scale) to balance the scale?
(a) 78 cm (b) 48 cm (c) 70 cm (d) 58 cm

22 In the experiment of balancing moments, suppose the fulcrum is at the 60 cm mark and a known mass of 5 kg is used on the longer arm. The greatest mass of m which can be balanced against 4 kg such that the minimum distance of either of the masses from the fulcrum is atleast 15 cm. (Neglect mass of meter scale)
(a) 16 kg (b) 18 kg (c) 20 kg (d) 12 kg

Topic 2 Experiments Related to Oscillations and Waves

01 The time period of oscillation of a simple pendulum is $T = 2\pi\sqrt{\frac{L}{g}}$. Measured value of L is 1.0 m from metre scale having a minimum division of 1 mm and time of one complete oscillation is 1.75 s measured from stopwatch of 0.01 s resolution. The percentage error in the determination of g will be
(a) 1.24% (b) 1.03% (c) 1.33% (d) 1.20%

02 In a simple pendulum, experiment for determination of acceleration due to gravity (g), time taken for 30 oscillations is measured by using a watch of 1 second least count. The mean value of time taken comes out to be 40 s. The length of pendulum is measured by using a meter scale of least count 1 mm and the value obtained 60.0 cm. The percentage error in the determination of g is close to
(a) 0.7% (b) 5.17% (c) 3.5% (d) 0.2%

03 In an experiment to find acceleration due to gravity g using simple pendulum, time period of 0.7 s is measured from time of 150 oscillations with a watch of 1 s resolution. If measured value of length is 10 cm known to 1 mm accuracy, the accuracy in the determination of g is found to be x%. The value of x is
(a) 3% (b) 2.9%
(c) 5% (d) 1%

04 Three students S_1, S_2 and S_3 perform an experiment for determining the acceleration due to gravity (g) using a simple pendulum. They use different lengths of pendulum and record time for different number of oscillations. The observations are as shown in the table.

Student no.	Length of pendulum (cm)	No. of oscillations n	Total time for n oscillations (t)	Time period (s)
1.	60	7	84	12
2.	40	8	80	10
3.	50	8	96	12

(Least count of length = 0.1 cm, least count for time = 0.1 s)
If E_1, E_2 and E_3 are the percentage errors in g for students 1, 2 and 3 respectively, then the minimum percentage error is obtained by student number is
(a) 3 (b) 2
(c) Both 1 and 2 (d) 1

05 In an experiment to determine acceleration due to gravity, the length of the pendulum is measured as 98 cm by a meter scale of least count of 1 cm. The period of swing/oscillations is measured with the help of a stop watch having a least count of 1s. The time period of 50 oscillations is found to be 98 s. Express value of g with proper error limits.
(a) $(10.1 \pm 0.5)\ \text{ms}^{-2}$
(b) $(10.1 \pm 0.2)\ \text{ms}^{-2}$
(c) $(10.1 \pm 0.3)\ \text{ms}^{-2}$
(d) 10.1ms^{-2}

06 Time period of simple pendulum inside the satellite orbiting earth is
(a) zero (b) infinite
(c) T (d) None of these

07 The graph between the length and the square of the time period of a simple pendulum is a
(a) parabola (b) circle
(c) straight line (d) hyperbola

08 In an experiment with sonometer when a mass of 200 g is attached to the string, it vibrates with fundamental frequency of 50 Hz. When a mass m is attached, the string vibrates with fundamental frequency of 80 Hz. The value of m is .... g.
(a) 500 (b) 512 (c) 450 (d) 530

09 A tuning fork of frequency 480 Hz is used in an experiment for measuring speed of sound v in air by resonance tube method. Resonance is observed to occur at two successive lengths of the air column, $l_1 = 40$ cm and $l_2 = 80$ cm. Then, v is equal to
(a) 384 m s^{-1} (b) 338 m s^{-1} (c) 379 m s^{-1} (d) 332 m s^{-1}

10 A resonance tube is old and has jagged end. It is still used in the laboratory to determine velocity of sound in air. A tuning fork of frequency 1800 Hz produces first resonance when the tube is filled with water to a mark 15 cm below a reference mark, near the open end of the tube. The experiment is repeated with another fork of frequency 600 Hz which produces first resonance when water reaches a mark 30 cm below the reference mark. The velocity of sound in air, obtained in the experiment, is close to
(a) 450 m/s (b) 400 m/s
(c) 250 m/s (d) 500 m/s

11 When you increase the loudness of the ringtone of your mobile phone, the frequency of ringtone
(a) increases (b) decreases
(c) remains same (d) can't be determined

12 When the length of a closed air column is increased, then the frequency will
(a) decrease (b) increase
(c) remain same (d) can't same

Topic 3 Experiments Related to Properties of Solids and Liquids

01 A student determined Young's modulus of elasticity using the formula $Y = \frac{MgL^3}{4bd^3\delta}$. The value of g is taken to be $9.8\ m/s^2$, without any significant error, his observation are as following.

Physical Quantity	Least count of the Equipment used for measurement	Observed Value
Mass (M)	1 g	1 kg
Length of bar (L)	1 mm	1 m
Breadth of bar (b)	0.1 mm	4 cm
Thickness of bar (d)	0.01 mm	0.4 cm
Depression (δ)	0.01 mm	5 mm

Then the fractional error in the measurement of Y is
(a) 0.155 (b) 0.0083 (c) 0.083 (d) 0.016

02 In order to determine the Young's modulus of a wire of radius 0.4 cm (measured using a scale of least count = 0.0010 cm) and length 1 m (measured using a scale of least count = 1 mm), a weight of mass 1 kg (measured using a scale of least count = 1 g) was hanged to get the elongation of 0.5 cm (measured using a scale of least count 0.001 cm). What will be the fractional error in the value of Young's modulus determined by this experiment ?
(a) 5.4 % (b) 0.14 %
(c) 9 % (d) 0.9 %

03 In an experiment, brass and steel wires of length 1 m each with areas of cross-section $1\ mm^2$ are used. The wires are connected in series and one end of the combined wire is connected to a rigid support and other end is subjected to elongation. The stress required to produce a net elongation of 0.3 mm is, [Given, the Young's modulus for steel and brass are respectively, $90 \times 10^9\ N/m^2$ and $60 \times 10^9\ N/m^2$]
(a) $1.8 \times 10^6\ N/m^2$ (b) $0.2 \times 10^6\ N/m^2$
(c) $1.2 \times 10^6\ N/m^2$ (d) $9 \times 10^6\ N/m^2$

04 A thin 2m long rod has a radius of 6 mm. A force of 108π kN is applied at one end to determine its Young's modulus. Assume that the force is exactly known. If the least count in the measurement of all lengths is 0.02 mm, which of the following statement is correct?
(a) The maximum value of Y that can be determined is $10^{14}\ N/m^2$.
(b) $\frac{\Delta Y}{Y}$ gets minimum contribution from the uncertainty in the length.
(c) $\frac{\Delta Y}{Y}$ gets its maximum contribution from the uncertainty in strain.
(d) The figure of merit is the largest for the length of its rod.

05 A solid cylindrical steel column is 8 m long and 12 cm in diameter. ($Y_{steel} = 1.96 \times 10^{11}\ N/m^2$). The decrease in length of the column, while carrying a load of 7×10^4 kg is
(a) 1.85 mm (b) 2.29 mm (c) 3.45 mm (d) 4.35 mm

06 The following observations were taken for determining surface tension T of water by capillary method
Diameter of capillary, $D = 1.50 \times 10^{-2}$ m
Rise of water, $h = 1.25 \times 10^{-2}$ m
Using $g = 9.80\ m\ s^{-2}$ and the simplified relation, $T = \frac{rhg}{2} \times 10^3\ N\ m^{-1}$, the possible error in surface tension is closest to
(a) 0.15 % (b) 1.5 % (c) 2.4 % (d) 10 %

07 A load of mass M kg is suspended from a steel wire of length 4 m and radius 1.0 mm in Searle's apparatus experiment. The increase in length produced in the wire is 4.0 mm. Now, the load is fully immersed in a liquid of relative density 2. The relative density of the material of load is 8. The new value of increase in length of the steel wire is
(a) 4.0 mm (b) zero (c) 5.0 mm (d) 3.0 mm

08 To what height can mercury be filled in a vessel without any leakage, if there is a pin hole of diameter 0.3 mm at the bottom of the vessel. (Density of mercury $= 13 \times 10^3\ kg\ m^{-3}$, surface tension of mercury $= 650 \times 10^{-3}\ N\ m^{-1}$, angle of contact with the vessel for mercury = 60°).
(a) 0.450 m (b) 0.042 m (c) 0.034 m (d) 0.240 m

09 A steel ball bearing of diameter 5 mm falls through glycerine and covers a distance of 30 cm in 15 s. The specific gravity of steel and glycerine are $9.8 \times 10^3\ kg\ m^3$ and $2.2 \times 10^3\ kg\ m^3$, respectively. The viscosity of glycerine is about
(a) 62 poise (b) 56 poise (c) 52 poise (d) 48 poise

10 In an experiment 0.30 kg aluminium sphere is heated to a temperature of 160°C. This hot sphere is then quickly immersed in 160 cc of water initially at 27°C, contained in a calorimeter with a water equivalent of 0.040 kg. The system reaches a final equilibrium temperature of 60°C. Determine the specific heat capacity of aluminium is (take 4.2 J = 1 cal)
(a) 952 J/kg°C (b) 924 J/kg°C
(c) 864 J/kg°C (d) 964 J/kg°C

11 The temperature of equal masses of three different liquids A, B and C are 12°C, 19°C and 28°C, respectively. The temperature when A and B are mixed is 16°C and when B and C are mixed is 23°C. The temperature when A and C are mixed, is
(a) 18.2°C (b) 22°C
(c) 20.2°C (d) 25.2°C

Topic 4 Experiments Related to Current Electricity

01 A variable voltage source V, two identical galvanometers G_1 and G_2, a test resistor $R_T = 10\ \Omega$ two extra resistors $R = 10\ \text{M}\Omega$, $R_2 = 0.001\Omega$ are all provided to student. The most appropriate circuit to use in an experiment to validate Ohm's law is

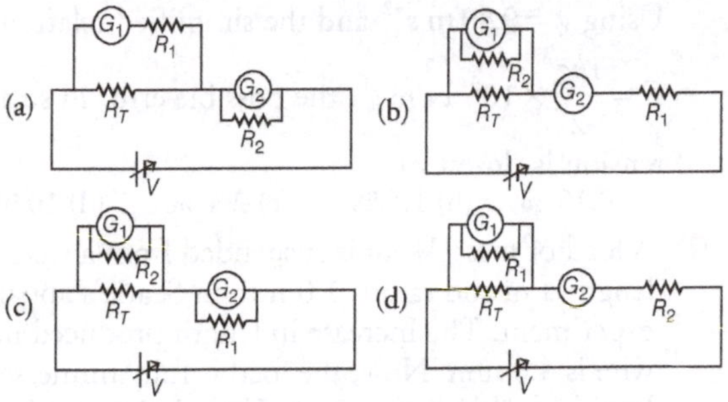

02 In the experiment of Ohm's law, a potential difference of 5.0 V is applied across the end of a conductor of length 10.0 cm and diameter of 6.00 mm. The measured current in the conductor is 4.00 A. The maximum permissible percentage error in the resistivity of the conductor is
(a) 3.3 (b) 8.4 (c) 7.5 (d) 3.0

03 In a circuit for finding the resistance of a galvanometer by half deflection method, a 5 V battery and a high resistance of 11 kΩ are used. The figure of merit of the galvanometer is 50 μA per division. In the absence of shunt resistance, the galvanometer produces a deflection of $\theta = 9$ divisions when current flows in the circuit. The value of the shunt resistance that can cause the deflection of $\theta/2$ is closest to
(a) 55 Ω (b) 110 Ω (c) 220 Ω (d) 550 Ω

04 An experiment to find galvanometer's resistance (G) was assigned to student in Physics lab. Using a galvanometer with a 1/3 deflection, students made observations. Which of the Statement is true regarding measurement of G?
(a) 1/3 deflection method cannot be used for determining the resistance of the galvanometer.
(b) 1/3 deflection method can be used and in this case, the G equals to twice the value of shunt resistance (s).
(c) 1/3 deflection method can be used and in this case, the G equals to three times the value of shunt resistance (s).
(d) 1/3 deflection method can be used and in this case, the G value equals to the shunt resistance (s).

05 In the experiment to determine the galvanometer resistance by half-deflection method, the plot of $1/\theta$ *vs* the resistance R of the resistance box is shown in the figure. The value of figure of merit of the galvanometer is equivalent to ...... (in A/division) [The source has emf 2V]

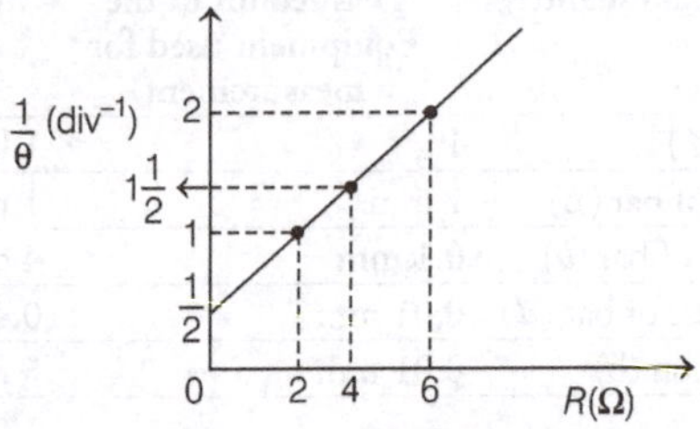

(a) 0.4 (b) 0.5
(c) 0.3 (d) 0.7

06 In a meter bridge experiment, the corresponding observation table is shown in figure.

S.No.	R(Ω)	l (cm)
1.	1000	65
2.	100	16
3.	10	1.8
4.	1	1

Which of the reading is inconsistent?
(a) 1 (b) 3
(c) 2 (d) 4

07 Teacher alloted a metre bridge experiment, S is a standard resistance and R is a resistance wire. Student found that, balancing length is $l = 15$ cm. If R is replaced by a wire of half length and half diameter that of R of same material, then find the balancing distance l'.

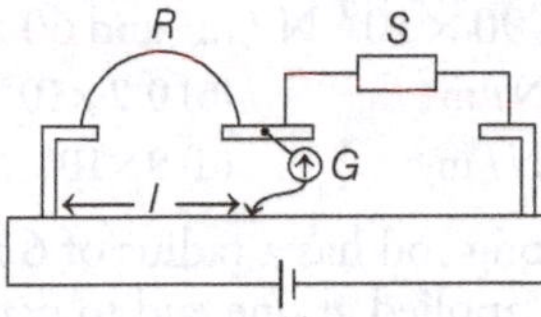

(a) 20 cm (b) 30 cm
(c) 40 cm (d) 55 cm

08 The scale of a galvanometer of resistance 100 Ω contains 50 divisions. It gives a deflection of 1 division on passing a current of 5×10^{-4} A. The resistance in ohm to be added to it, so that it may become a voltmeter of range 5 V is
(a) 50 Ω (b) 75 Ω
(c) 25 Ω (d) 100 Ω

Topic 5 Experiments Related to Optics

01 A convex lens of focal length f is placed somewhere in between an object and a screen. The distance between the object and the screen is 48 cm. If the numerical value of the magnification produced by the lens is 3, the focal length of the lens is
(a) 12 cm (b) 9 cm
(c) 4.5 cm (d) 16 cm

02 On an optical bench, an object is placed at 40 cm mark, convex lens placed at 60 cm mark produces a virtual image at 10 cm mark. What would be focal length of lens?
(a) $\frac{50}{3}$ cm (b) $\frac{100}{3}$ cm
(c) 100 cm (d) 20 cm

03 In an experiment to find the focal length of a convex lens, an object is placed at 20 cm mark and lens (focal length, $f = 12$ cm) is placed at 25.0 cm mark of the optical bench. Where will you place a screen to obtain sharp image of the object?
(a) 20.5 cm mark (b) 12.9 cm mark
(c) 16.4 cm mark (d) 30 cm mark

04 **Assertion** When a concave mirror is held under water, its focal length will increase.

Reason The focal length of a concave mirror is independent of the medium in which it is placed.

If the light of the above statements, choose the correct one.
(a) Both Assertion and Reason are correct and Reason is the correct explanation of Assertion.
(b) Both Assertion and Reason are correct but Reason is not the correct explanation of Assertion.
(c) Assertion is correct but Reason is incorrect.
(d) Assertion is incorrect but Reason is correct.

05. A student wants to choose a particular wavelength λ_0 for which the ray passes through the interface BC of combination of two prism as shown in the figure, without deviation.

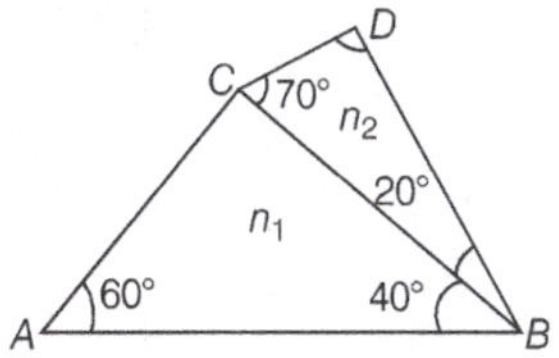

The refractive indices of prism are

$$n_1 = 1.3 + \frac{12.8 \times 10^4}{\lambda^2}$$

and $n_2 = 1.55 + \frac{3.80 \times 10^4}{\lambda^2}$, where λ is in nm.

For a light of wavelength λ_0, find the angle of incidence i on the face AC such that the deviation produced by the combination of prisms in minimum.
(a) $\cos^{-1}\frac{33}{20}$ (b) $\tan^{-1}\frac{3}{4}$
(c) $\sin^{-1}\frac{33}{20}$ (d) $\sec^{-1}\frac{3}{4}$

06 In an experiment to measure focal length 16 cm of convex lens, the least counts of the measuring scales for the position of object 20 cm and for the position of image 8 cm are 0.4 cm and 0.4 cm, respectively. The error in the measurement of the focal length of the convex lens will be
(a) 0.27 (b) 0.78
(c) 0.4 (d) 0.8

07 In an experiment a convex lens of focal length 15 cm is placed coaxially on an optical bench in front of a convex mirror at a distance of 6 cm from it. It is found that an object and its image coincide, if the object is placed at a distance of 30 cm from the lens. The focal length of the convex mirror is
(a) 7 cm (b) 10 cm
(c) 12 cm (d) 30.5 cm

08 An experiment is performed to find the refractive index of glass using a travelling microscope. In this experiment, distances are measured by
(a) a vernier scale provided on the microscope
(b) a standard laboratory scale
(c) a meter scale provided on the microscope
(d) a screw gauge provided on the microscope

09 A travelling microscope has 10 divisions per cm on the main scale while its vernier scale has total 50 divisions and 25 vernier scale divisions are equal to 24 main scale divisions, what is the least count of the travelling microscope ?
(a) 0.001 cm (b) 0.002 cm
(c) 0.004 cm (d) 0.005 cm

10 A 2 metre long scale with least count of 0.2 cm is used to measure the locations of objects on an optical bench. While measuring the focal length of a convex lens, the object pin and the convex lens are placed at 60 cm mark and 80 cm mark, respectively. The image of the object pin on the other side of lens coincides with image pin that is kept at 160 cm mark. The % error in the estimation of focal length is
(a) 0.51 (b) 1.70
(c) 0.85 (d) 1.02

11 If 10 vernier divisions are equal to 9 main scale divisions of a travelling microscope and one smallest reading of main scale is 0.6 mm, the vernier constant of travelling microscope is
(a) 0.6 cm (b) 0.06 mm
(c) 0.6 mm (d) 0.06 cm

12 In an experiment to measure the focal length (f) of a convex lens, the magnitude of object distance (x) and the image distance (y) are measured with reference to the focal point of the lens. The y - x plot is shown in figure. The focal length of the lens is .... cm.

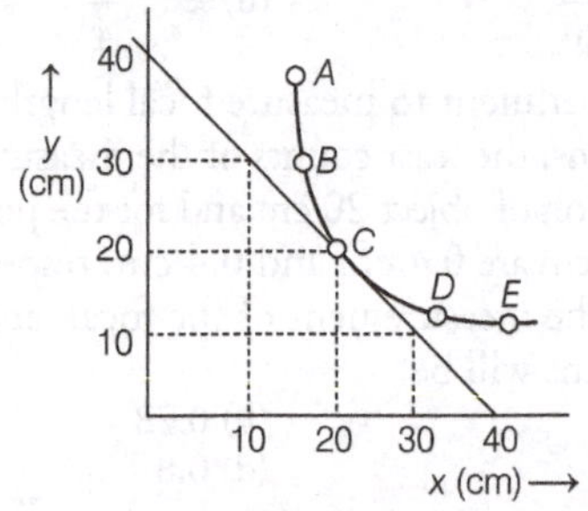

(a) 20 cm (b) 10 cm
(c) 40 cm (d) 30 cm

13 In finding out refractive index of glass slab the following observations were made through travelling microscope 50 vernier scale division = 49 MSD; 20 divisions on main scale in each cm.

For mark on paper
MSR = 8.45 cm, VC = 26
For mark on paper seen through slab
MSR = 7.12 cm, VC = 41
For powder particle on the top surface of the glass slab
MSR = 4.05 cm, VC = 1
(MSR = Main Scale Reading,
VC = Vernier Coincidence)
Refractive index of the glass slab is
(a) 1.24 (b) 1.42 (c) 1.35 (d) 1.52

Topic 6 Experiments Related to Electronic Devices

01 An experiment is performed to determine the I-V characteristics of a zener diode, which has a protective resistance of 100 Ω and a maximum power of dissipation rating of 3W. The minimum voltage range of the DC source in the circuit is

(a) 0-35 V (b) 0-28 V
(c) 0-20 V (d) 0-15 V

02 An experiment is performed to determine the I-V characteristics of a zener diode, which has a protective resistance of R = 100 Ω and a maximum power of dissipation rating of 1 Ω. The minimum voltage range of the DC source in the circuit is

(a) 0 − 5 V
(b) 0 − 24 V
(c) 0 − 12 V
(d) 0 − 8 V

03 A diode has a given characteristics.

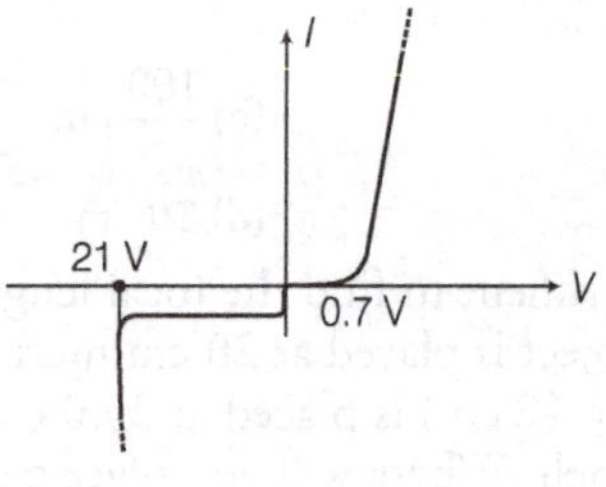

This diode is connected in a circuit as

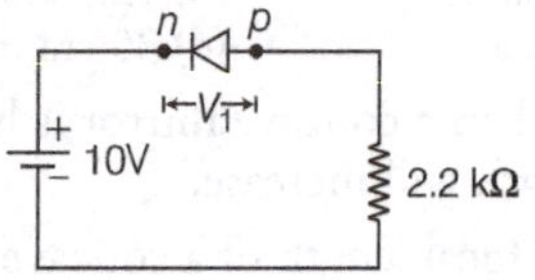

and then as

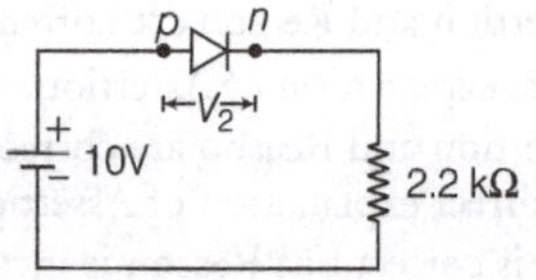

Ratio of potential drops $V_1 : V_2$ (in given circuits) will be

(a) 0 (b) $\frac{100}{70}$
(c) $\frac{100}{7}$ (d) $\frac{79}{1}$

Key Index

Topic 1

1 (b)	2 (d)	3 (b)	4 (c)	5 (d)	6 (c)	7 (b)	8 (a)	9 (a)	10 (c)
11 (d)	12 (a)	13 (d)	14 (b)	15 (b)	16 (d)	17 (c)	18 (a)	19 (b)	20 (b)
21 (c)	22 (c)								

Topic 2

1 (a)	2 (b)	3 (b)	4 (a)	5 (c)	6 (b)	7 (c)	8 (b)	9 (a)	10 (a)
11 (c)	12 (a)								

Topic 3

1 (d)	2 (d)	3 (d)	4 (a)	5 (a)	6 (b)	7 (a)	8 (c)	9 (c)	10 (b)
11 (c)									

Topic 4

1 (a)	2 (a)	3 (b)	4 (b)	5 (b)	6 (d)	7 (d)	8 (d)

Topic 5

1 (b)	2 (b)	3 (c)	4 (d)	5 (c)	6 (a)	7 (a)	8 (a)	9 (c)	10 (b)
11 (b)	12 (a)	13 (b)							

Topic 6

1 (a)	2 (b)	3 (c)

Detailed Explanations

Topic 1

01. *(b)* Given, $1\text{MSD} = 0.1$ mm

$(N+1)\text{VSD} = N\,\text{MSD}$

$\therefore\quad 1\text{ VSD} = \left(\dfrac{N}{N+1}\right)\text{MSD}$

Least count or vernier constant,

$$1\text{MSD} - 1\text{VSD} = \left[1 - \frac{N}{N+1}\right]\text{MSD}$$

$$= \left(\frac{1}{N+1}\right)\text{MSD} = \left(\frac{0.1}{N+1}\right)\text{mm}$$

$$= \frac{1}{100(N+1)}\text{ cm}$$

02. *(d)* Given, the main scale reading,

MSR = 0 mm

The circular scale reading,

CSR = 52 divisions

Now, we shall determine the least count of the screw gauge,

$$\text{LC} = \frac{p}{n}$$

Here, p is the pitch of the screw,

n is the number of circular divisions in one complete revolution.

$$\text{LC} = \frac{1}{100}\text{ mm}$$

$\Rightarrow\quad \text{LC} = 0.01$ mm

$\Rightarrow\quad \text{LC} = 0.001$ cm

Thus, the least count of the screw gauge is 0.001 cm. Therefore, diameter of the wire of screw gauge,

$$D = \text{MSR} + (\text{CSR} \times \text{LC})$$

$\Rightarrow\quad D = 0 + (52 \times 0.001)$

$\Rightarrow\quad D = 0.052$ cm

> **Concept Enhancer**
> The least count of any instrument is the minimum reading that it can measure.
> For screw gauge, least count $= \dfrac{\text{Pitch}}{\text{Number of divisions in circular scale}}$

03. *(b)* Given, least count = 0.01 mm

Number of divisions on circular scale = 50

Pitch of the screw gauge = least count × number of divisions on circular scale = $0.01 \times 50 = 0.5$ mm

04. *(c)* As it is given that n divisions of vernier scale coincide with $(n-1)$ divisions of main scale i.e.

$n(\text{VSD}) = (n-1)\text{MSD}$

$\Rightarrow\quad 1\text{VSD} = \dfrac{(n-1)}{n}\text{MSD}\quad \ldots\text{(i)}$

The least count is the difference between one main scale division (MSD) and one vernier scale division (VSD).

$\therefore$ Least Count (LC) = 1MSD − 1VSD

$$= 1\,\text{MSD} - \frac{(n-1)}{n}\text{MSD}$$

[From Eq. (i)]

$$= \left(1 - \frac{(n-1)}{n}\right)\text{MSD} = \frac{1}{n}\text{MSD}$$

Here, $1\,\text{MSD} = \frac{1}{n}$ cm

$$\Rightarrow \quad LC = \frac{1}{n} \times \frac{1}{n}\text{ cm} = \frac{1}{n^2}\text{ cm}$$

05. *(d)* Given, least count of screw gauge, LC = 0.001 cm

Main scale reading,

MSR = 5 mm = 0.5 cm

Number of coinciding divisions on the circular scale, i.e., Vernier scale reading, VSR = 25

Here, zero error = −0.004 cm

Final reading obtained from the screw gauge is given as

= MSR + VSR × LC − zero error

Final reading from the screw gauge

$= 0.5 + 25 \times 0.001 - (-0.004)$

$= 0.5 + 0.025 + 0.004$

$= 0.5 + 0.029 = 0.529$ cm

Thus, the diameter of the ball is 0.529 cm.

06. *(c)* As given, N VSD

$= (N-1)$MSD

VSD = Vernier scale division

MSD = Main scale division

$$1\,\text{VSD} = \left(\frac{N-1}{N}\right)\text{MSD}$$

LC = least count = 1 MSD − 1 VSD

$$LC = \left(1 - \frac{N-1}{N}\right)\text{MSD}$$

$$= \frac{1}{N}\text{MSD} = \frac{0.1}{N} = \frac{1}{10N}\text{ cm}$$

07. *(b)* Screw guage is U-shaped instrument used for measuring smaller dimensions with precision. So, it is used to measure diameter of lead shot.

08. *(a)* The least count of vernier callipers is also known a vernier constant. It is a difference between one main scale division and one vernier scale division.

09. *(a)* According to question,

In 10 complete rotations of circular scale, distance travelled on the main scale of screw gauge is 10 mm, so in one complete rotation of circular scale, distance travelled on the main scale of screw gauge will be $= \frac{10\text{mm}}{10} = 1$ mm

This is the required value of pitch.

$\because$ Least count

$$= \frac{\text{Pitch}}{\text{Total division on circular scale}}$$

$$\Rightarrow \text{Least count} = \frac{1}{100} = 0.01\text{ mm}$$

$= 0.001$ cm

It means, both Assertion and Reason are correct and Reason is the correct explanation of Assertion.

10. *(c)* Given, zero error,

$ze = 0.1$ mm $= 0.01$ cm

Main scale reading, MSR = 8.5 cm

Vernier scale reading, VSR = 6

Least count, LC = 0.1/10 cm = 0.01 cm

We know that,

Reading = MSR + (VSR × LC) − zero error

$= 8.5 + 6 \times 0.01 - 0.01$

$= 8.5 + 0.06 - 0.01$

$= 8.55$ cm

11. *(d)* There are three significant figures in the measured value (or readings) whereas there are 5 and 4 significant figures in average readings and standard deviation of the data, respectively. So, answer must be upto three significant figures. After rounding off the uncertain digits and considering least count of vernier scale, i.e. 0.01 mm, average diameter of pencil is recorded as (6.54 ± 0.07) mm.

> • Concept **Enhancer**
>
> If quantities have different number of significant figures, then after doing algebraic operations (Addition or subtraction), round off the result, so that it has the same number of significant figures as in least accurate quantity.

12. *(a)* Pitch of screw of a screw gauge,

$$\text{pitch} = \frac{\text{distance moved by screw}}{\text{number of rotations}}$$

$$= \frac{3\text{ mm}}{12} = 0.25\text{ mm}$$

and least count of screw gauge, least count

$$= \frac{\text{pitch}}{\text{number of circular scale divisions}}$$

$$= \frac{0.25\text{ mm}}{50} = 0.005\text{ mm}$$

$= 0.0005$ cm

13. *(d)* Given, Least count $= \frac{1}{10N}$ cm

$$= \frac{10}{10N}\text{ mm}$$

1 MSD = 1 mm

Now, Least count = 1 MSD − 1 VSD

Let x MSD = N VSD then,

$$\Rightarrow \frac{10}{10N} = 1 - \frac{x}{N} \Rightarrow \frac{1}{N} = 1 - \frac{x}{N} = \frac{N-x}{N}$$

$\Rightarrow N - x = 1$ or $N - 1 = x$

or $x = (N-1)$ divisions

14. *(b)* Let 1 MSD = x

According to question,

50 VSD matches with 48 MSD = $48x$

$$1\text{ VSD, LC} = \frac{48}{50}x$$

LC = 1 MSD − 1 VSD

$$= x - \frac{48}{50}x = \frac{2x}{50}$$

Zero error = MSR + VSR (LC)

$$0.02\text{ mm} = 0 + 4\left(\frac{2x}{50}\right)$$

$\Rightarrow \quad x = 0.125$ mm

Number of main scale division in 1 cm

$$= \frac{1\text{ cm}}{0.125\text{ mm}} = 80$$

15. *(b)* Given that number of divisions on circular scale = 40

Pitch = 0.4 mm = 4×10^{-4} m

Least count of screw gauge

$$= \frac{\text{Pitch}}{\text{Number of divisions on circular scale}}$$

$$= \frac{4 \times 10^{-4}}{40} = 1 \times 10^{-5}\text{ m}$$

$= 10\,\mu$m

Since, circular scale is 4 units ahead of the pitch scale marking which means screw gauge has positive zero error.

16. *(d)* Given, 1 MSD = 2mm

As 10 VSD = 9 MSD

or $1\text{ VSD} = \frac{9}{10}$ MSD

$\therefore$ Least Count = 1 MSD − 1 VSD

$$= 1\,\text{MSD} - \frac{9}{10}\text{MSD}$$

$= (1 - 0.9)$ MSD

$= (1 - 0.9) \times 2$mm

$= 0.2$ mm $= 0.02$ cm

Zero error $= -(10-4) \times 0.2$ mm

$= -1.2$ mm $= -0.12$ cm

Now, diameter of the spherical body

= MSR + vernier scale reading × LC – zero error

$= 3.1 + 6 \times 0.02 - (-0.12)$

$= 3.1 + 0.12 + 0.12 = 3.34 \approx 3.30$ cm

17. *(c)* Least Count of a screw gauge

$$= \frac{\text{Pitch}}{\text{Number of circular scale divisions}}$$

$\Rightarrow$ LC $= 0.5/100$ ...(i)

The actual reading (true reading)

= Main scale reading + Least count × Circular division – Zero error

$$= 5 + \left(\frac{0.5}{100}\right) \times 20 - \frac{0.5}{100} \times 5$$

[$\because$ Zero error = Least count × Coinciding division]

$$= 5 + \frac{0.5}{100}(20 - 5) = 5.075 \text{ mm}$$

18. *(a)* Given, pitch = 0.4 mm, $N = 200$

Least count,

$$\text{LC} = \frac{\text{Pitch}}{N} = \frac{0.4 \text{ mm}}{200} = 4 \times 10^{-3} \text{ mm}$$

Thickness of sheet

= MSR + CSR × LC – Zero error

$= (5.5 + 48 \times 4 \times 10^{-3} - 3 \times 4 \times 10^{-3})$ mm

$= (5.5 + 0.18)$ mm $= 5.68$ mm

19. *(b)* Given, least count of main scale

= 1 main scale division (MSD) = 1 mm

Also, 20 vernier scale divisions = 8 main scale divisions

$\Rightarrow$ 1 vernier scale division (VSD)

$$= \frac{8}{20} \text{ MSD} = 0.4 \text{ MSD}$$

$= 0.4$ mm

Vernier constant or least count of instrument is, LC = 1 MSD – 1 VSD

$$= 1\text{MSD} - \frac{8}{20}\text{MSD}$$

$$= \left(\frac{20-8}{20}\right)\text{MSD} = \frac{12}{20}\text{MSD}$$

$$= \frac{1 \text{ mm} \times 12}{20} = 0.6 \text{ mm} = 0.06 \text{ cm}$$

The zero of vernier scale lies to the right of main scale. So, error is positive.

Zero error $= 7 \times \text{LC} = 7 \times 0.06$ cm

$= 0.42$ cm

Given, main scale reading = 3.1 cm

Vernier scale reading = 4 divisions

$\therefore$ Actual reading

= MSR + VSR × LC – Zero error

$= 3.1 + 4 \times 0.06 - 0.42$

$= 2.92$ cm

20. *(b)*

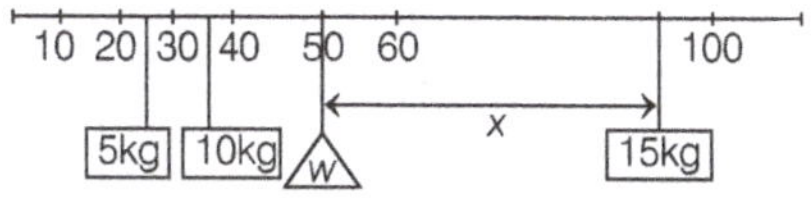

The anti-clockwise moments due to 5 kg and 10 kg are

= (5 kg wt) (50 – 25) cm + (10 kg wt) (50 – 35) cm

$= 5 \times 25 + 10 \times 15 = 275$ kg wt cm

The clockwise moment due to 5 kg

$= 15$ kg wt $\times x$ cm

$275 = 15 \times x$

$x = 18.33$ cm

So, the 15 kg mass must be hung at (50 cm + x cm)

$= 50 + 18.33$

= 68.3 cm mark to balance the scale.

21. *(c)*

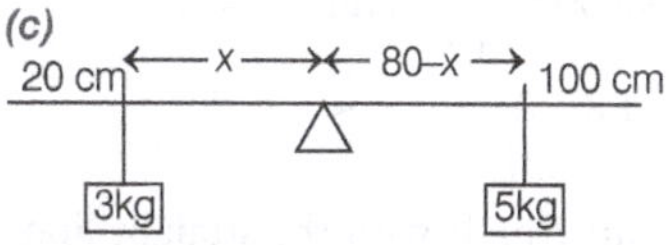

Balancing moments

$3 \times x = 5(80 - x)$

$3x = 400 - 5x$

$8x = 400$

$x = 50$ cm

So, fulcrum is at $20 + 50 = 70$ cm mark.

22. *(c)* Given, $Y_{max} = 60$ cm

$X_{min} = 15$ cm

$m = 5$ kg

Then, from $m = M\left(\frac{Y}{X}\right)$

$$m_{max} = M\left(\frac{Y_{max}}{X_{min}}\right)$$

$$m_{max} = 5 \times \left(\frac{60}{15}\right) = 20 \text{ kg}$$

Topic 2

01. *(a)* Given,

Time period, $T = 1.75$ s

Length of string, $L = 1.0$ m

Error in time period, $\Delta T = 0.01$ s $= 10^{-2}$ s

Error in length,

$\Delta L = 1$ mm $= 1 \times 10^{-3}$ m

$\because$ $T = 2\pi\sqrt{L/g}$

Thus, we have,

$$\Rightarrow \frac{\Delta g}{g} = \frac{\Delta L}{L} + \frac{2\Delta T}{T}$$

$$= \frac{10^{-3}}{1} + \frac{2 \times 10^{-2}}{1.75}$$

$= 10^{-3} + 1.142 \times 10^{-2}$

$= 10^{-3} + 11.42 \times 10^{-3} = 12.42 \times 10^{-3}$

$\because \Delta g / g \times 100 = 12.42 \times 10^{-3} \times 10^2$

$= 1.242\% \simeq 1.24\%$

02. *(b)* Relation used for finding acceleration due to gravity by using a pendulum is given by

$$g = 4\pi^2 l / T^2$$

So, percentage error in value of g will be

$$100 \times \frac{\Delta g}{g} = \left[\frac{\Delta l}{l} + \frac{2\Delta T}{T}\right] \times 100 \quad \text{...(i)}$$

Given, $\Delta l = 0.1$ cm, $l = 60.0$ cm

$\Delta T = 1$ s and T for 30 oscillations = 40 s

$$100 \times \frac{\Delta g}{g} = \left[\frac{0.1}{60} + 2 \times \frac{1}{40}\right] \times 100$$

Hence, percentage error in g will be

$$= \frac{10}{60} + \frac{20}{4} = 5.17\%$$

03. *(b)*

key idea

To find out percentage error, you can use following formula.

$$\frac{\Delta g}{g} \times 100 = \frac{\Delta L}{L} \times 100 + \frac{2\Delta T}{nT} \times 100$$

Given, time period of pendulum,

$T = 0.7$ s

Number of oscillations, $n = 150$

Resolution of watch, $\Delta T = 1$ s

Accuracy of length, $\frac{\Delta l}{l} = \frac{1 \text{ mm}}{10 \text{ cm}} = \frac{1}{100}$

Since, time period,

$T = 2\pi\sqrt{l/g}$

$\Rightarrow$ $g = 4\pi^2 l / T^2$

The accuracy in determination of g,

$$\frac{\Delta g}{g} \times 100 = \frac{2\Delta T}{nT} \times 100 + \frac{\Delta l}{l} \times 100$$

$$= \left(2 \times \frac{1}{(150 \times 0.7)} \times 100 + \frac{1}{100} \times 100\right)\%$$

$= 1.9\% + 1\%$

$= 2.9\%$

Concept Enhancer

All bodies experience the same acceleration due to gravity irrespective of its mass. The value of acceleration due to gravity depend an mass of earth but not mass of object.

04. *(a)* Time period,

$$T = 2\pi\sqrt{\frac{L}{g}}$$

where, L is pendulum length and g is the acceleration due to gravity.

Also, $T^2 = 4\pi^2 \frac{L}{g}$

$$g = 4\pi^2 \frac{L}{T^2}$$

% error in g,

$$\frac{\Delta g}{g}\times 100 = \frac{\Delta L}{L}\times 100 + \frac{2\Delta T}{T}\times 100$$

$$E_1 = \left(\frac{0.1}{60}+\frac{2\times 0.1}{84}\right)\times 100 = 0.404\%$$

$$E_2 = \left(\frac{0.1}{40}+\frac{2\times 0.1}{80}\right)\times 100 = 0.50\%$$

$$E_3 = \left(\frac{0.1}{50}+\frac{2\times 0.1}{96}\right)\times 100 = 0.2\%$$

So, E_3 is minimum.

So, minimum percentage error is obtained by student number 3.

05. *(c)* As, $T = 2\pi\sqrt{\frac{l}{g}}$ ... (i)

Now, time period of 50 oscillations is 98 s.

∴ Time period of one oscillation

$$= \frac{98}{50} = 1.96 \text{ s}$$

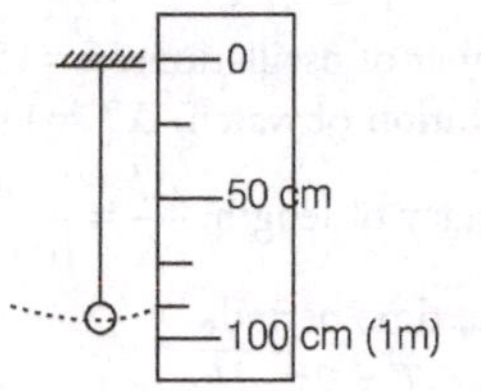

$$\Rightarrow \quad g = \frac{4\pi^2 l}{T^2} \quad \text{[from Eq. (i)]}$$

$$= 4\times(3.14)^2 \times \frac{0.98}{1.96\times 1.96}$$

$$= 10.06 \text{ m/s}^2$$

Now, % error in $g = \frac{\Delta g}{g}\times 100$

$$= \left(\frac{\Delta l}{l}+\frac{2\Delta T}{T}\right)\times 100$$

$$\Rightarrow \quad \Delta g = 10\times\left(\frac{1}{98}+\frac{2\times 1}{98}\right)$$

(∵ least count of meter scale is 1 cm and least count of stop watch is 1s)

$$\therefore \quad \Delta g = 0.3 \text{ m/s}^2$$

So, final result can be expressed as (10.1 ± 0.3) ms^{-2}

06 *(b)* As we know that

$$T \propto \frac{1}{g}$$

On an artificial satellite, orbiting the earth, net gravity is zero.

As, $g = 0$, so $T = \infty$

07 *(c)* We know that, $T = 2\pi\sqrt{\frac{l}{g}}$

Squaring both sides

$$T^2 = 4\pi^2 \frac{l}{g}$$

$$l = \frac{g}{4\pi^2}T^2 \quad ...(i)$$

Take, $m = \frac{g}{4\pi^2}$ and $T^2 = x$

So, Eq. (i) becomes

$$l = mx$$

Comparing it with the straight line equation, $y = mx$.

So, the graph between the length and the square of the time period of a simple pendulum is a straight line.

08. *(b)* $f = \frac{1}{2l}\sqrt{\frac{T}{\mu}}$

$$\therefore \quad f_1 = \frac{1}{2l}\sqrt{\frac{T_1}{\mu}} \text{ and } f_2 = \frac{1}{2l}\sqrt{\frac{T_2}{\mu}}$$

$$\text{Hence, } \frac{f_2}{f_1} = \frac{\frac{1}{2l}\sqrt{\frac{T_2}{\mu}}}{\frac{1}{2l}\sqrt{\frac{T_1}{\mu}}} \Rightarrow \frac{f_2}{f_1} = \sqrt{\frac{T_2}{T_1}}$$

$$\Rightarrow \left(\frac{80}{50}\right)^2 = \frac{mg}{200g} \Rightarrow \frac{6400}{2500} = \frac{m}{200}$$

$$\Rightarrow m = \frac{64\times 200}{25} = 512 \text{ g} \Rightarrow m = 512 \text{ g}$$

09. *(a)* Given, frequency, $f = 480$ Hz.

Resonance lengths,

$$l_1 = 40 \text{ cm and } l_2 = 80 \text{ cm}$$

Speed of sound $(v)_{\text{air}} = 2f(l_2 - l_1)$

$$= 2\times 480\times 40\times 10^{-2}$$

$$= 38400\times 10^{-2} \text{ m s}^{-1} = 384 \text{ m s}^{-1}$$

10. *(a)* Due to jagged end,

$$\frac{v}{4(15-x)\times 10^{-2}} = 1800 \quad ...(i)$$

$$\frac{v}{4(30-x)\times 10^{-2}} = 600 \quad ...(ii)$$

From Eq. (i) and (ii),

$$\frac{v}{4(15-x)\times 10^{-2}} = \frac{3v}{4(30-x)\times 10^{-2}}$$

$$3(15-x) = (30-x)$$

$$45 - 3x = 30 - x$$

$$2x = 15$$

$$x = 7.5 \text{ cm}$$

From Eq. (ii),

$$\frac{v}{4(30-7.5)\times 10^{-2}} = 500$$

$$v = 20\times 22.5$$

∴ Velocity of sound in air,

$$v = 450 \text{ m/s}$$

11. *(c)* Loudness ∝ (amplitude)^2 the loudness of sound waves does not depend on the frequency of the sound waves.

12. *(a)* Frequency $(f) = \frac{(2n-1)\cdot v}{4L}$,

where, $n = 0, 1, 2, 3, ...$

For the above formula of the frequency, the frequency is inversely proportional to the length of the air column. When the length of a closed air column is increased, then the frequency will decrease.

Topic 3

01. *(d)* $Y = \frac{MgL^3}{4bd^3\delta}$,

$$g = 9.8 \text{ m/s}^2 \quad \text{(constant)}$$

$$\Delta g = 0$$

Use error analysis, we get

$$\frac{\Delta Y}{Y} = \frac{\Delta M}{M}+\frac{3\Delta L}{L}+\frac{\Delta b}{b}+\frac{3\Delta d}{d}+\frac{\Delta\delta}{\delta}+\frac{\Delta g}{g}$$

$$= \frac{1}{1000}+\frac{3}{1000}+\frac{0.1}{40}+\frac{0.03}{4}+\frac{0.01}{5}+\frac{0}{9.8}$$

$$= 0.016$$

02. *(d)* Given,

$$r = 0.4 \text{ cm}, \Delta r = 0.001 \text{ cm}$$

$$L = 1 \text{ m}, \Delta L = 0.001 \text{ m}$$

$$M = 1 \text{ kg}$$

$$\Delta M = 1 \text{ g} = 0.001 \text{ kg}$$

$$l = 0.5 \text{ cm}, \Delta l = 0.001 \text{ cm}$$

Young's modulus is given by

$$Y = \frac{F/A}{l/L} = \frac{Mg/\pi r^2}{l/L} = \frac{MgL}{\pi r^2 l}$$

Taking log and differentiating, we get

$$\frac{\Delta Y}{Y}=\frac{\Delta M}{M}+\frac{\Delta L}{L}-\frac{2\Delta r}{r}-\frac{\Delta l}{l}$$

[g is constant]

Error in Y, $\frac{\Delta Y}{Y}=\frac{\Delta M}{M}+\frac{2\Delta r}{r}+\frac{\Delta l}{l}+\frac{\Delta L}{L}$

$$=\frac{0.001}{1}+\frac{2\times0.001}{0.4}+\frac{0.001}{0.5}+\frac{0.001}{1}$$

$=0.001+0.005+0.002+0.001=0.009$

Percentage error

$$\frac{\Delta Y}{Y}\times100=0.009\times100=0.9\ \%$$

03. *(d)* The Young's modulus of two wires connected in series is

$$Y=\frac{2Y_1Y_2}{Y_1+Y_2}=\frac{2(90\times10^9)(60\times10^9)}{180\times10^9}$$

$=60\times10^9\ \text{N/m}^{-2}$

So, the stress required $=Y\times$ strain

$$=60\times10^9\times\frac{0.3\times10^{-3}}{2}$$

$=9\times10^6\ \text{N/m}^2$

Alternate Solution

Given, Total elongation $=0.3\ \text{mm}=0.3\times10^{-3}$ m

We know that,

Total elongation $=\Delta l_{brass}+\Delta l_{steel}$

$$0.3\times10^{-3}=\frac{Fl_{brass}}{A\,Y_{brass}}+\frac{Fl_{steel}}{AY_{steel}}$$

$$\therefore\ 0.3\times10^{-3}=\frac{F}{A}\left(\frac{Y_{brass}+Y_{steel}}{Y_{brass}Y_{steel}}\right)$$

$$\frac{F}{A}=\left(\frac{Y_{brass}Y_{steel}}{Y_{brass}+Y_{steel}}\right)\times0.3\times10^{-3}$$

$$=\frac{60\times10^9\times90\times10^9}{180\times10^9}\times0.3\times10^{-3}$$

$=9\times10^6\ \text{N/m}^2$.

04. *(a)* Given, $L=2$ m

$r=6\ \text{mm}=6\times10^{-3}$ m

$F=108\ \pi\ \text{kN}=108\pi\times10^3$ N

(l) LC of all lengths $=0.02$ mm $=2\times10^{-5}$ m

$Y=?$

We know that,

Young's modulus of wire $=\frac{\text{Stress}}{\text{Strain}}$

$$Y=\frac{F\cdot L}{\pi r^2\cdot l}$$

$$Y=\frac{108\times\pi\times2\times10^3}{\pi\times(6\times10^{-3})^2\times2\times10^{-5}}$$

$$Y=\frac{108\times2\times10^3}{36\times10^{-6}\times2\times10^{-5}}$$

$Y=3\times10^{14}\ \text{N/m}^2$

So, the maximum value of Y that can be determined is $3\times10^{14}\ \text{N/m}^2$.

05. *(a)* Given,

$L=8$ m

$Y=1.96\times10^{11}\ \text{N/m}^2$

$d=12$ cm

then, $r=6\ \text{cm}=6\times10^{-2}$ m

$m=7\times10^4$ kg

$F=mg=7\times10^4\times9.8$

So, $Y=\frac{FL}{A\cdot l}$

$$l=\frac{F\cdot L}{A\cdot Y}$$

$$l=\frac{7\times10^4\times6\times7\times9.8}{22\times6\times6\times10^{-4}\times1.96\times10^{11}}$$

$l=1.85\times10^{-3}$ m

$l=1.85$ mm

06. *(b)* Surface tension is given by

$$T=\frac{rhg}{2}\times10^3=\frac{Dhg}{4}\times10^3\ \text{N m}^{-1}$$

Possible error in the surface tension is

$$\frac{\Delta T}{T}\times100=\frac{\Delta D}{D}\times100+\frac{\Delta h}{h}\times100+0$$

$$=\left(\frac{0.01\times10^{-2}}{1.50\times10^{-2}}+\frac{0.01\times10^{-2}}{1.25\times10^{-2}}\right)\times100$$

$$\frac{\Delta T}{T}\times100=\left(\frac{100}{150}+\frac{100}{125}\right)$$

$$\frac{\Delta T}{T}\times100=0.666+0.8=1.466\approx1.5\ \%$$

07. *(a)* In first case, the extension in the wire is

$x=Mg/k=V\rho g/k$ ...(i)

When the load is immersed in the liquid, then

$\Rightarrow V\sigma g+kx_1=V\rho g$

$\Rightarrow\ x_1=Vg(\rho-\sigma)/k$ ...(ii)

Using Eqs. (i) and (ii), we get

$$x_1=\frac{Vgx}{Vg\rho}(\rho-\sigma)=x\left(1-\frac{\sigma}{\rho}\right)$$

$$=4\times\left(1-\frac{4}{8}\right)=4\ \text{mm}$$

08. *(c)* Given,

$d=0.3$ mm

$\rho=13\times10^3\ \text{kg/m}^3$

$s=650\times10^{-3}$ N/m

$\theta=60°$

Mercury will start leaking when,

$$\rho gh=\frac{2s\cos\theta}{r}$$

$$h_{min}=\frac{2s\cos\theta}{\rho gr}=\frac{2s\cdot2\cdot\cos\theta}{\rho\cdot g\cdot d}[\because r=d/2]$$

$$h_{min}=\frac{4\times650\times10^{-3}\times\cos60°}{13\times10^3\times9.8\times0.3\times10^{-3}}$$

$$h_{min}=\frac{2\times650\times10^{-3}}{13\times9.8\times0.3}$$

$h_{min}=34.01\times10^{-3}\ \text{m}=0.034$ m

09. *(c)* Given,

distance $=30\ \text{cm}=30\times10^{-2}$ m,

time $=15$ s

Velocity of steel ball,

$$v_t=\frac{30\times10^{-2}}{15}=2\times10^{-2}\ \text{m/s},$$

$\rho=9.8\times10^3\ \text{kg/m}^3$,

$\sigma=2.2\times10^3\ \text{kg/m}^3$,

$d=5$ mm,

$r=2.5\times10^{-3}$ m.

The viscosity of glycerine

$$\eta=\frac{2}{9}\frac{r^2(\rho-\sigma)g}{v_t}$$

$$\eta=\frac{2}{9}\times\frac{(2.5\times10^{-3})^2\,(9.8-2.2)\times10^3\times9.8}{2\times10^{-2}}$$

$$\eta=\frac{2}{9}\times\frac{(2.5)^2\times10^{-6}\times7.6\times10^3\times9.8}{2\times10^{-2}}$$

$\eta=5.172$ SI unit

$\eta=51.72\approx52$ Poise

10. *(b)* Let S be the specific heat of aluminium

Heat capacity of water $=1$ cal/g°C

By principle of calorimetry,

$Q_{given}=Q_{used}$

$300\times s\times(160°-60°)$

$=160\times1\times(60-27)$

$+40\times1\times(60-27)$

$s\times300\times100=160\times33+40\times33$

$$s=\frac{33\times200}{300\times100}=\frac{22}{100}$$

$s=.220$ cal/g°C

$s=.220\times10^3\times4.2$ J/kg-°C

$s=924$ J/kg°C

11. *(c)* By applying calorimetry method, we get

Heat gain = Heat lost

$C_A(16-12) = C_B(19-16)$

$$\Rightarrow \frac{C_A}{C_B} = \frac{3}{4}$$

and $C_B(23-19) = C_C(28-23)$

$$\Rightarrow \frac{C_B}{C_C} = \frac{5}{4} \Rightarrow \frac{C_A}{C_C} = \frac{C_A}{C_B} \times \frac{C_B}{C_C}$$

$$= \frac{3}{4} \times \frac{5}{4} = \frac{15}{16} \quad \text{...(i)}$$

If θ is the temperature when A and C are mixed, then

$C_A(\theta - 12) = C_C(28-\theta)$

$$\Rightarrow \frac{C_A}{C_C} = \frac{28-\theta}{\theta - 12} \quad \text{...(ii)}$$

On solving Eqs. (i) and (ii), we have

$$\frac{28-\theta}{\theta-12} = \frac{15}{16}$$

$\Rightarrow 448 - 16\theta = 15\theta - 180$

$\therefore \quad \theta \approx 20.2° \text{ C}$

Topic 4

01. *(a)* To verify Ohm's law, one galvanometer is used as ammeter and other galvanometer as voltmeter. Hence, we should connect ammeter in series and voltmeter in parallel to measure current and potential difference, respectively. Also, when we use a galvanometer to create an ammeter, shunt resistance should be very small and should be in parallel. When we use as voltmeter series resistance should be large. All these criteria are satisfied in option (a).

02. *(a)* Given, $V = 5$ V

The length of the conductor, $L = 10$ cm

The measured value of the current in the conductor, $I = 4$ A

The diameter of the conductor,

$d = 6$ mm

As we know that

$R = \rho l / A$

Using Ohm's law,

$V = IR \Rightarrow R = V/I$

$$\frac{\rho l}{A} = \frac{V}{I} \Rightarrow \rho = \frac{V}{Il}\left(\frac{\pi d^2}{4}\right)$$

In error form,

$$\frac{\Delta\rho}{\rho} = \frac{\Delta V}{V} + \frac{\Delta I}{I} + \frac{\Delta l}{l} + 2\frac{\Delta d}{d}$$

Since, $V = 5.0$ V, there is one zero after decimal,

So, $\Delta V = 0.1$ V

Similarly, $\Delta I = 0.01$ A, $\Delta l = 0.1$ cm and $\Delta d = 0.01$ cm

$$\Rightarrow \frac{\Delta\rho}{\rho} = \frac{0.1}{6} + \frac{0.01}{4} + \frac{0.1}{10} + 2\frac{(0.01)}{(5)}$$

$$\Rightarrow \frac{\Delta\rho}{\rho} = 0.033 \Rightarrow \frac{\Delta\rho}{\rho} \times 100 = 3.3\%$$

03. *(b)* Initially, $I = \dfrac{\varepsilon}{R+G}$ ...(i)

Current per division = 50 μA

$\theta = 9$ division

Current = $9 \times 50\ \mu\text{A} = 450\ \mu\text{A}$

Putting in Eq. (i),

$$450\mu A = \frac{5V}{(11000+G)}$$

$$(11000+G)90 \times 10^{-6} = 1$$

$$99000 + 9G = 10^5$$

$$G = \frac{1000}{9}\ \Omega$$

$$\therefore \quad G = \frac{1}{9}\ k\Omega$$

$$\text{Finally, } \frac{I}{2} = \frac{\varepsilon}{R + \dfrac{GS}{G+S}} \times \frac{S}{S+G}$$

$$\Rightarrow \frac{I}{2} = \frac{\varepsilon S}{R(S+G)+GS}$$

$$S = \frac{RG \times \dfrac{I}{2}}{\varepsilon - \dfrac{(R+G)I}{2}}$$

$$= \frac{11 \times 10^3 \times \dfrac{1}{9} \times 10^3 \times 225 \times 10^{-6}}{5 - \left(\dfrac{5}{2}\right)}$$

$\Rightarrow S = 110\ \Omega$

04. *(b)* A galvanometer as an ammeter is shown below

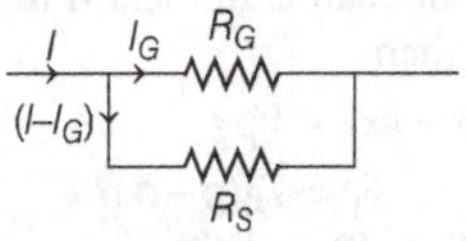

By KVL in closed loop,

$$(I - I_G)R_S = I_G \cdot R_G$$

$$\Rightarrow IR_S - I_G R_S = I_G R_G$$

$$\Rightarrow IR_S = I_G R_S + I_G R_G$$

$$\Rightarrow IR_S = I_G(R_S + R_G)$$

$$\Rightarrow \frac{I_G}{I} = \frac{R_S}{R_S + R_G}$$

According to given situation,

$$\frac{I_G}{I} = \frac{1}{3} \quad \therefore \quad \frac{1}{3} = \frac{R_S}{R_S + R_G}$$

$$\Rightarrow R_S + R_G = 3R_S \Rightarrow R_G = 2R_S$$

05. *(b)*

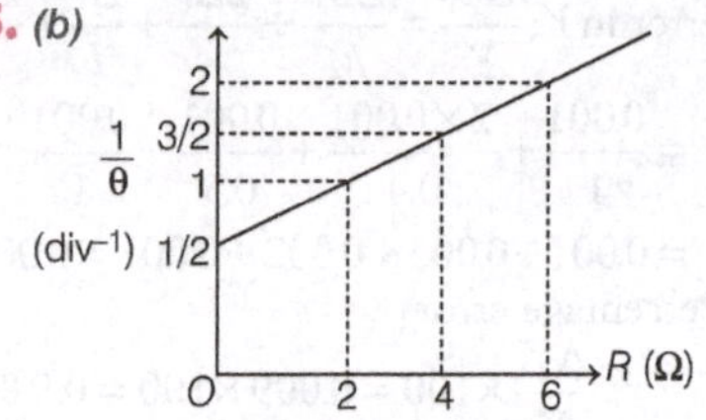

For galvanometer, $i = K\theta$

$$\frac{2}{G+R} = K\theta$$

[where i = current, V = 2 V, G = galvanometer resistance, θ = deflection]

$$\frac{1}{\theta} = \frac{(G+R)K}{2} = R\left(\frac{K}{2}\right) + \frac{KG}{2}$$

$$\frac{1}{\theta} = R\left[\frac{K}{2}\right] + \frac{KG}{2} \quad \text{...(i)}$$

This is a straight line equation with intercept on Y-axis.

$$\text{Slope} = \frac{K}{2} \quad \text{...(ii)}$$

$$\text{From graph slope} = \frac{\frac{3}{2} - 1}{4-2} = \frac{1}{4} \quad \text{...(iii)}$$

$$\frac{K}{2} = \frac{1}{4}$$

$$K = 0.5 = 5 \times 10^{-1}\ \text{A}$$

Hence, figure of merit $= 5 \times 10^{-1}$ A.

06. *(d)* $\because \dfrac{R}{X} = \dfrac{l}{100-l}$

So, $X = \dfrac{R(100-l)}{l}$

So, $x_1 = \dfrac{1000(100-65)}{65}$

$$= \frac{1000 \times 35}{65} = 538.46\ \Omega$$

$$x_2 = \frac{100(100-16)}{16}$$

$$= \frac{100 \times 84}{16} = 525\ \Omega$$

$$x_3 = \frac{10(100-1.8)}{1.8} = \frac{10 \times 98.2}{1.8}$$

$$= 545.5\ \Omega$$

$$x_4 = \frac{1(100-1)}{1}$$

$$= \frac{1 \times 99}{1} = 99\ \Omega$$

So, 99 Ω is inconsistent.

07. (*d*)

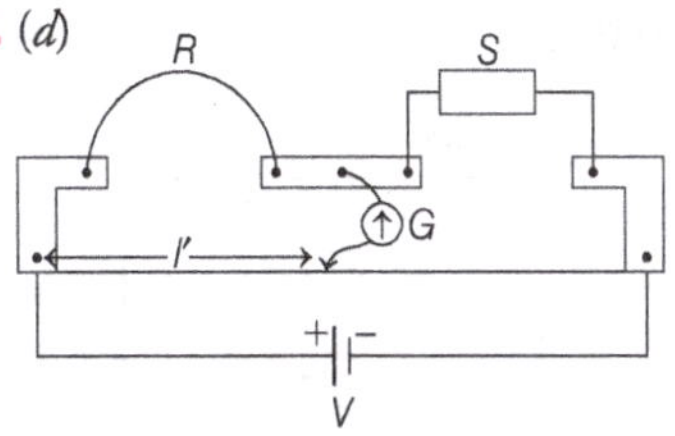

Given, balance length, $l = 15$ cm

At balance point, $\frac{R}{l} = \frac{S}{100 - l}$

$\Rightarrow \quad \frac{R}{15} = \frac{S}{85}$

$\Rightarrow \quad R = \frac{55}{85}\,\Omega \qquad \ldots(i)$

When R is replaced by some other resistance of half length and half diameter, then resistance in left gap,

$$R' = \frac{\rho \frac{l}{2}}{\frac{\pi}{4}\left(\frac{d}{2}\right)^2} = 2\left\{\frac{\rho l}{(\pi d^2)}\right\}$$

$\Rightarrow \quad R' = 2R$

Now, if balance is obtained at length l', then

$$\frac{R'}{l'} = \frac{S}{(100 - l')} \Rightarrow \frac{2R}{l'} = \frac{S}{100 - l'}$$

Substituting the value of S from Eq. (i), we get

$$\frac{2R}{l'} = \frac{\frac{85R}{15}}{100 - l'} \Rightarrow \frac{2}{l'} = \frac{\frac{17R}{3}}{(100 - l')}$$

$$l' = \frac{600}{11} = 54.5 \text{ cm}$$

$\simeq 55$ cm

08. (*d*) For full scale deflection,

$I_g = nk$

$\therefore \quad I_g = 50 \times 5 \times 10^{-4}$

$= 25 \times 10^{-3}$ A

Now, $R = \frac{V}{I_g} - G = \frac{5}{25 \times 10^{-3}} - 100$

$= \frac{1000}{5} - 100$

$= 200 - 100$

$R = 100\,\Omega$

Topic 5

01. (*a*) Let, distance between screen and object is x and magnification is m.

$x = -u + v$

$$m = \frac{f}{(f + u)} = \frac{(f - v)}{f}$$

For real image, m is negative

$\therefore \quad -m = \frac{f}{(f + u)}$

$\Rightarrow -mf - mu = f$

$\Rightarrow \quad u = \frac{-(m + 1)}{m} f$

and $\quad -m = \frac{(f - v)}{f}$

$\Rightarrow \quad -mf = f - v$

$\Rightarrow \quad v = (m + 1) f$

$\therefore \quad x = (m + 1) f + \frac{(m + 1)}{m} f$

$\Rightarrow \quad f = \frac{mx}{(m + 1)^2} = \frac{3 \times 48}{(3 + 1)^2} = 9$ cm

$[\because x = 48 \text{ cm}, m = 3]$

02 (*b*) Object distance, $u = 60 - 40$

$= 20$ cm

Image distance, $v = 60 - 10 = 50$ cm

Since, the image is virtual, it will be formed on the same side of the object.

From lens formula

$$\frac{1}{f} = \frac{1}{v} - \frac{1}{u}$$

$$\frac{1}{f} = \frac{1}{-50} - \frac{1}{-20} = \frac{3}{100}$$

$$f = \frac{100}{3} \text{ cm}$$

03. (*c*) Image distance $u = 5$ cm

Focal length, $f = 12$ cm

Using lens formula,

$$\frac{1}{f} = \frac{1}{v} - \frac{1}{u}$$

$$\frac{1}{12} = \frac{1}{v} - \frac{1}{-5}$$

(Using sign convention)

$$\frac{1}{12} = \frac{1}{v} + \frac{1}{5}$$

$$\frac{1}{v} = \frac{1}{12} - \frac{1}{5} = \frac{5 - 12}{60}$$

$v = -8.57 \approx 8.6$ cm

i.e. image formed will be virtual is at 8.6 cm away from convex lens i.e., at 16.4 cm mark.

04. (*d*) Focal length of mirror is a measure of the radius of curvature of the sphere from which the spherical mirror was obtained and it is totally independent of the medium in which the mirror is placed.

05. (*c*) Since, ray goes without deviation,

$\therefore \; n_1 = n_2$

or $\; 1.3 + \frac{12.8 \times 10^4}{\lambda^2}$

$$= 1.55 + \frac{3.80 \times 10^4}{\lambda^2}$$

$\Rightarrow \quad \lambda = 600$ nm

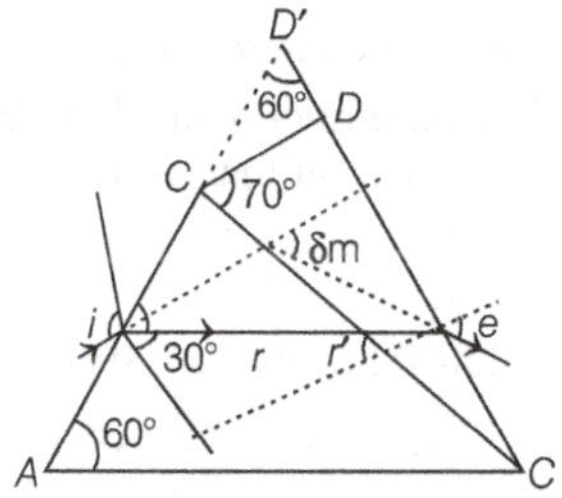

Here, $n_1 = 1.3 + \frac{12.8 \times 10^4}{600 \times 600} = 1.65$

For minimum deviation, $i = e'$, $r = r'$

But $r + r' = A = 60°$

$\therefore \quad r = 30°$

$\therefore \quad 1 \times \sin i = n_1 \sin r$

$\sin i = 1.65 \times \frac{1}{2}$

$\therefore \quad i = \sin^{-1}(0.825)$

06. (*a*) Using lens formula,

$$\frac{1}{f} = \frac{1}{v} - \frac{1}{u}$$

Taking 1st derivative

$$\frac{df}{f^2} = \frac{dv}{v^2} - \frac{du}{u^2}$$

For small change and maximum percentage error

$df \rightarrow \Delta \cdot f$

$$\frac{\Delta f}{f^2} = \frac{\Delta u}{u^2} + \frac{\Delta v}{v^2}$$

$$\Delta f = f^2\left[\frac{\Delta u}{u^2} + \frac{\Delta v}{v^2}\right]$$

$$= (16)^2\left[\frac{0.4}{(20)^2} + \frac{0.4}{(80)^2}\right]$$

$= 0.272 \approx 0.27$

07. (*a*) Here, $u = -30$ cm, $f_1 = 15$ cm

As we know,

$$\frac{1}{v} - \frac{1}{u} = \frac{1}{f} \Rightarrow \frac{1}{v} - \frac{1}{-30} = \frac{1}{15}$$

$\Rightarrow \quad \frac{1}{v} = \frac{1}{15} - \frac{1}{30} = \frac{1}{20}$

$\therefore \quad v = 20$ cm

To obtain its real image on object's place. The center of curvature of the convex mirror must be at the position of virtual image, i.e, at 20 cm

Therefore, $6 + 2f_R = 20$

$\Rightarrow 2f_R = 14 \Rightarrow f_R = 7$ cm

08. (a) If an experiment is performed to find the refractive index of glass using a travelling microscope, distance are measured by a vernier scale which is provided on the microscope.

09. (c) Travelling microscope has 10 division per cm on main scale.

$$1\,\text{MSD} = \frac{1}{10}\text{ cm}$$

$$\text{Least count} = 1\,\text{MSD} - 1\,\text{VSD}$$

$$= 1\,\text{MSD} - \frac{24}{25}\text{ MSD}$$

$$\Rightarrow \frac{1}{25}\text{ MSD} = \frac{1}{25}\times\frac{1}{10}\text{ cm}$$

$$\text{LC} = 0.004\text{ cm}$$

10. (b) Given, $u = 80 - 60 = 20$ cm

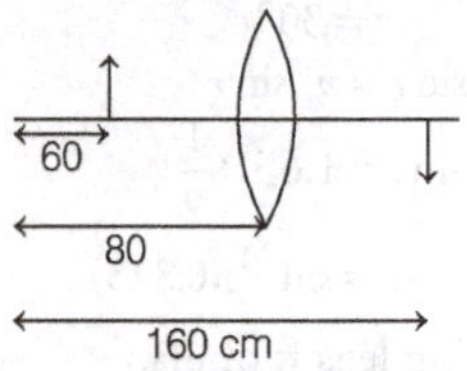

$$v = 160 - 80 = 80\text{ cm}$$

Using, $\frac{1}{f} = \frac{1}{v} + \frac{1}{u}$ or

$$f = \frac{uv}{u+v} = \frac{20\times 80}{20+80} \Rightarrow f = 16\text{ cm}$$

For error analysis, $\frac{1}{f} = \frac{1}{v} + \frac{1}{u}$

differentiate both sides

$$-\frac{df}{f^2} = -\frac{dv}{v^2} - \frac{\Delta u}{u^2}$$

to calculate Δu and Δv

$$u = (80 \pm 0.2) - (60 \pm 0.2)$$

$$= 20 \pm 0.4\text{ cm}$$

therefore $\Delta u = 0.4$ cm

$\Delta v = 0.4$ cm

$$\text{Now, } \frac{\Delta f}{f} = f\left[\frac{\Delta v}{v^2} + \frac{\Delta u}{u^2}\right]$$

$$= 16\left[\frac{0.4}{(80)^2} + \frac{0.4}{(20)^2}\right]$$

$$\frac{\Delta f}{f} = \frac{16\times 0.4}{(20)^2}\left[\frac{1}{16}+1\right]$$

$$= \frac{16\times 0.4}{(20)^2}\times\frac{17}{16} = \frac{17\times 0.4}{400}$$

Percentage error

$$= \frac{\Delta f}{f}\times 100 = \frac{17\times 0.4}{400}\times 100 = 1.70$$

Option (b) is correct.

11. (b) Given, 10 vernier scale divisions = 9 main scale divisions.

Also, 1 main scale division = 0.6 mm

$$\text{Now, 1 vernier scale division} = \frac{9}{10}\text{ MSD}$$

$$= \frac{9}{10}\times 0.6\text{ mm} = 0.54\text{ mm}$$

Least Count of instrument is

$$\text{LC} = 1\text{ MSD} - 1\text{ VSD}$$

$$= 0.6 - 0.54\text{ (mm)}$$

$$= 0.06\text{ mm}$$

$\therefore$ Vernier constant = Least count = 0.06 mm

12. (a) If we draw $y = x$ line on graph, then it cuts the curve at point (20 cm, 20 cm).

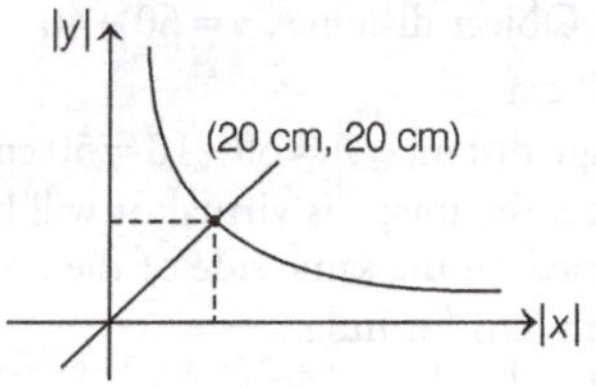

From the Newton's formula

$$xy = f^2$$

$$\Rightarrow 20\times 20 = f^2$$

$$\Rightarrow f = 20\text{ cm}$$

13. (b) $1\text{ MSD} = \frac{1\text{ cm}}{20} = 0.05$ cm

$$1\text{ VSD} = \frac{49}{50}\text{ MSD} = \frac{49}{50}\times 0.05\text{ cm}$$

$$= 0.049\text{ cm}$$

$$\text{LC} = 1\text{MSD} - 1\text{VSD} = 0.001\text{ cm}$$

For mark on paper,

$$L_1 = 8.45 + 26\times 0.001\text{ cm}$$

$$= 84.76\text{ mm}$$

For mark on paper through slab,

$$L_2 = (7.12 + 41\times 0.001)\text{ cm}$$

$$\Rightarrow L_2 = 71.61\text{ cm}$$

For the powder on the top of surface.

Zero error = 4.05 cm + 1 × 0.001 cm

= 40.51 mm

$\therefore$ Actual, $L_1 = 84.76 - 40.51$

= 44.25 mm

Actual, $L_2 = 71.61 - 40.51 = 31.10$ mm

$$\therefore L_2 = \frac{L_1}{\mu}$$

$$\Rightarrow \mu = \frac{L_1}{L_2} = \frac{44.25}{31.10} = 1.42$$

Topic 6

01. (a)

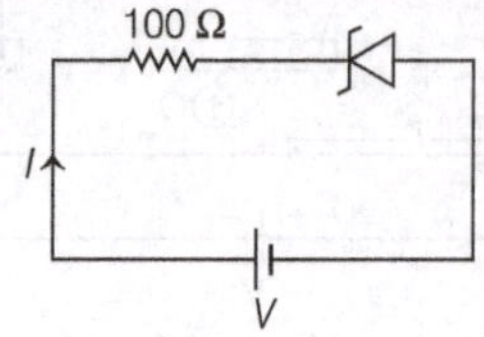

Potential drop across zener diode

$$V_Z = V - IR$$

$$V_Z = V - 100\,I$$

$$\therefore \text{Power } P = V_Z I_Z$$

$$= (V - 100I)\cdot I$$

But, $P = 3\,W$ (given)

$$\therefore (V - 100I)\cdot I = 3$$

$$100I^2 - VI + 3 = 0$$

For I to be real,

$$V^2 - 4\times 100\times 3 \geq 0$$

$$V \geq 30$$

02. (b) Given power, $P = 1$ W

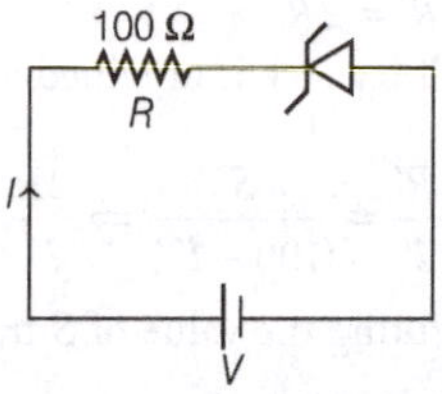

Potential drop across zener diode is,

$$V_Z = V - IR = V - 100\,I$$

Power, $P = V_Z I_Z = (V - 100I)I$

$$\therefore (V - 100I)I = 1$$

$$\text{or } 100I^2 - VI + 1 = 0$$

For I to be real,

$$V^2 - 4\times 100\times 1 \geq 0$$

or $V \geq 20$ V

03. (c) Case I Diode is in reversed bias,

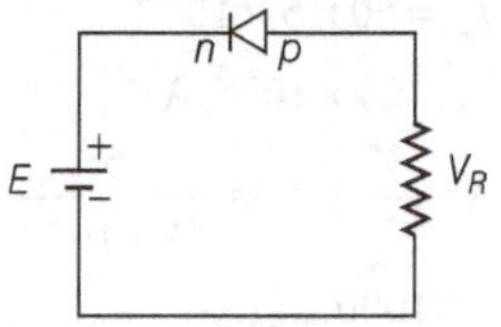

$E - V_D - V_R = 0$ (by Kirchhoff's law)

$$V_D = E - V_R$$

$$V_R = 0 \text{ or } I = 0$$

$$V_D = E = 10\text{ V}$$

Case II Diode is in forward bias, since the diode is around knee voltage = 0.7 V

$$\text{So, ratio} = \frac{10}{0.7} = \frac{100}{7}$$